In Dappled Sunlight

IN DAPPLED SUNLIGHT

The National Library of Poetry

Cynthia A. Stevens, Editor

In Dappled Sunlight

Library of Congress
Cataloging in Publication Data

ISBN 1-57553-352-9

Manufactured in The United States of America by
Watermark Press
1 Poetry Plaza
Owings Mills, MD 21117

Editor's Note

When the sunlight breaks through towering trees, awakening specks of color along the ground and spreads strong mottled light soaking you with warmth, you realize true beauty. A moment such as that may cause you to reminisce about your past experiences and contemplate your tomorrows; what has been, what is yet to be–the beauty of your life. The poets featured in this anthology, **In Dappled Sunlight**, have pulled treasured moments from their own lives and put them in verse. Yet, before you go on to view the wonderful artistry found between these covers, I would like to honor several poems with special recognition.

For unique composition, detailed images and wonderful metaphors, "To Try the Tangerines," by Carolyn Everall Johnson (p. 1), was awarded the Grand Prize. Johnson's verse is about a relationship between the persona and his or her father. (Although the persona could be viewed as male or female, in the following references, I will refer to the persona as female.) The strength of emotion that arises through Johnson's descriptions is remarkable. The following lines illustrate the condition of the persona's father:

> *You are folded in a chair with wheels,*
> *remote as a roosting pelican.*
> *A perpetual half smile seals in your tranquillity.*
> *It is too late for me to learn again to call you Daddy,*
> *a cartoon name, like a rumpled birthday hat I cannot make you wear.*

We realize that something tragic has happened to her father. He has changed and is no longer the man he was when the persona used to call him "Daddy." He appears weaker now–to call him "Daddy" would be almost humorous–like *"a cartoon name."*

When the persona states *"It is too late . . . to learn again to call you Daddy,"* she believes it is too late to try to form the relationship they once had or that they once could have had. Yet, the individual she can no longer call "Daddy" still has a powerful influence over her actions as he urges her to *"try the tangerines."* The daughter attempts to appease her father by trying the tangerines. The father tells her to reach for the highest tangerine. To the daughter, this request is like asking her to reach for the intangible: *"You insist on the top one, enmeshed in leaves."* The daughter must *"tear fiercely"* to get the tangerine. She gets the tangerine, yet it is damaged . . . and wasn't ready to be picked:

> *Its caged color rages in the sky.*
> *It nestles in my hand like a wounded bird, skin ripped, flesh bared.*
> *I peel away the velvet veins, touch the juice with my tongue.*
> *It is an acrid, Pyrrhic victory, and you have exited . . .*

The daughter's victory of achieving the tangerine was merely to please her father. The daughter feels *"it is an acrid, Pyrrhic victory."* She hasn't really won anything, not even her father's praise. Soon after, her father is no longer conscious to his surroundings and she no longer has the chance to tell her father about the tangerine. He *"coasted out on the smooth decks of things"* towards death before his daughter could explain:

> *The tangerines are not ready to eat.*
> *And I, being prone to love, will wait without pickers,*
> *among gnarled roots, for bitter fruit to ripen into sweet.*

Although their relationship is never all the daughter hoped it to be, the persona believes she will come to love her father for all he was, and any disappointing memories of their relationship will fade. She feels in time, *"being prone to love,"* she will understand her father's ways. In time the *"bitter fruit"* would *"ripen into sweet"* –she will only remember the wonderful moments.

One never knows when he or she may be faced with a tragic event, or how their outlook on life may change or change the outlook of those who love them. "Speculation" by Charlotte Marchand (p. 281) reveals the thoughts of someone who has experienced a tragic event leaving that person dependent upon his or her significant other. By skillfully portraying the humiliation and guilt the persona is experiencing, Marchand does an outstanding job in gaining your empathy.

Another prominent verse is "Vultures on the Spiral" by James F. Lasseter (p. 410). Lasseter parallels the persona's life to the life of the famous Dutch artist Vincent van Gogh. The persona believes he's being consumed by his art as Vincent van Gogh had been. The first stanza presents the association:

> *the stranger in the mirror*
> *reminds me of an*
> *emaciated   van gogh . . .*

Through the mirror's reflection, the persona can see he is aging. Yet, he believes his art has not nearly begun. The persona dreams of grand artistic achievements. Although he knows he is aging, he believes there is much more he can do, as noted in the third stanza:

> *"theo!" he calls out*
> *"there is so much good here*
> *I can feel the wind*
> *before it strips the leaves from the trees!"*

The last four lines of Lasseter's verse refer to the title, by portraying the image of van Gogh's famous works *"disjointed sunflowers/ thick legged empty beds,/ swirling starry nights"* circling over the persona as *"vultures on the spiral."* It's as if the works of van Gogh are eating at the persona's conscience, telling him to make something of his life by making something of his art before he dies.

"July Third" by Thomas Murphy (p. 101) takes a different look at death by focusing attention on the innocent images of childhood–moments in life we all treasure and perhaps most remember. The first few stanzas illustrate some of these precious moments:

> *When children are tossing themselves*
> *through oscillating sprinklers in the summertime,*
>
> *When vanilla ice cream cones are piled a*
> *scoop too high and fall smat on hot pavement squares,*
>
> *When crickets whisper secrets under crescent moon sickles,*
>
> *And when little boys peel away buried rock*
> *to watch centipedes scurry away from buttery sunlight, . . .*

Murphy's poem eases the reader into accepting the fact that life does go on after we're gone, as in the line *"I will die while Stacey is selling pink lemonade on Eaton Drive . . . ."* Utilizing the musical quality of alliteration and rhythm, Murphy does a wonderful job of lifting the somber tone normally paired with death.

There were several other noteworthy poems that also touched upon death using a more melancholy tone. "Upon Working Eight Years at the AIDS Foundation" by Robert Fredrick Thistle (p. 115) does an excellent job of portraying the difficulty involved in continually assisting the terminally ill. Thistle's poem puts forth the question, "How much pain can one soak into their own self before they themselves become numb?" With image after image that Thistle presents, you come to understand that after dying inside so many times, one has to feel numb in order to go on.

"Daniel's Poem" by Stephan M. Weingarten (p. 234) also takes a solemn look at death. The persona admits his anger at the blatant unfairness of death. You feel the persona's torment when he asks, *"Is God an ingrate deaf to all who pray?"* Yet, the persona has not lost all faith; by the end of the poem he tells his friend who has passed away:

> *. . . And trust that long last comfort's on its way,*
> *And ending but one slice of heaven's knife,*
> *And trusting that we're heard whene'er we pray.*

No matter what your age, it's difficult to accept death. "Where I Found God," by Nadine Dawn Girard (p. 403), takes a more forceful approach to death by defeating it. And, "Covered in Dirt," by Hyde (p. 219), presents a unique look upon the ceremonies surrounding the death of "... *someone who grew up lovely,/ made a family and died/ Far away, but came back to be buried/ at home.*"

There are several other prominent poems you won't want to miss: D. T. Friedson's "By the Sixth Cold Beer On Wednesday" (p. 132); "When I Am Old" by Dylan Newcomb (p. 356); and "My Father Swings Again" by Brian Wedlake (p. 451).

Unfortunately, I do not have the time nor space to review all the distinguished poems displayed within this fine anthology. However, you will notice that each piece of artistry that *In Dappled Sunlight* features adds a special hue to the many shades of thought presented.

Cynthia Stevens
Senior Editor

Acknowledgments

In Dappled Sunlight is a culmination of the efforts of many individuals. The editors are grateful for the contributions of the judges, assistant editors, graphic artists, layout artists, office administrators, and customer service representatives who have all brought their talents to bear on this project. We would also like to give a special thanks to our cover artist, Tracy Hetzel.

Winners of the North American Open Poetry Contest

Grand Prize

Carolyn Everall Johnson / Carlsbad, CA

Second Prize

D. T. Friedson / Wilkinsburg, PA

Nadine Dawn Girard / Avon, NY

Hyde / Flowery Branch, GA

James F. Lasseter / Portland, OR

Charlotte Marchand / Laguna Beach, CA

Thomas Murphy / Northville, MI

Dylan Newcomb / Montville, ME

Robert Fredrick Thistle / Sacramento, CA

Brian Wedlake / Saint Petersburg, FL

Stephan M. Weingarten / Levittown, PA

Third Prize

More Again / Santa Monica, CA

Rosemarie A. Ambrosio / Yonkers, NY

Sandra F. Anselmo / Virginia Beach, VA

Kirk A. Bailey / Eugene, OR

Tobias Beeber M.D. / Delray Beach, FL

Desiree S. Brennan / Poughkeepsie, NY

Pamela S. Burton / Lexington, KY

Eugene Charles / Forked River, NJ

John B. Curling / Gainesville, FL

Catie D'Ignazio / Somerville, MA

Isabelle Discount / Pittsburgh, PA

Jeremiah Donovan / Laurens, SC

William Ehlers / Tacoma, WA

Millicent Emmitt / Yonkers, NY

Don Fortner / Burbank, CA

Arnie R. Fox / New York, NY

Joshua J. Frost / Moscow, ID

Dru Gallucci / Dublin, OH

Ralph E. Gillette / Brooklyn, NY

Amber J. Grafft / Springfield, MO

Liam Russell Hines / Basking Ridge, NJ

Joseph M. Holihen / Pensacola, FL

Janet B. Hubbs / Brielle, NJ

Xavier Alfredo Jaramillo / Miami, FL

Diane Jennings / Lashmeet, WV

Melissa Prunty Kemp / Canton, OH

rk khavari / Portsmouth, NH

Robert Kowalczyk / Slidell, LA

Christina A. Kurz / Philadelphia, PA

Will Levins / Spring Valley, NY

Jeanne M. Lightfoot / Melville, NY

Noriko Low / Seattle, WA

Garland B. McClaran / Apopka, FL

Robert McFarland / Austin, TX

Ronald E. Metzger / Pensacola, FL

Grace E. Noel / Dover, NH

Padma Desai / New York, NY

Kerstyn M. Porsch / Santa Fe, NM

W. H. Post / Milton, DE

Rod Ricardo-Livingstone / San Diego, CA

Mindy L. Richardson / Moraga, CA

Corine Rohr / Huntington, NY

Holly Meeker Rom / Rye, NY

Sarah Ruhl / Providence, RI

Ray Scarbrough / Stillwater, OK

Stan S. Smith / Baxter, MN

Mark Spoelstra / Stockton, CA

Anna Melissa Stevens / Ashland, KY

Sid Tanenbaum / Palm Beach Gardens, FL

James R. Tapia / Albuquerque, NM

Ruth Kenyon Tate / White Plains, NY

Lynne Toussaint / Utica, NY

Irene I. Ueda / Honolulu, HI

Nancy Fitz-Gerald Viens / Denton, TX

Gary Vrabel / Ithaca, NY

Felicia Weekley / Pensacola, FL

Mary Jane Wheat / Holiday, FL

Patsy Wolter / Boise, ID

Loren D. Woodson / Santa Monica, CA

Congratulations also to all semi-finalists.

Grand Prize Winner

To Try the Tangerines

You are folded in a chair with wheels,
remote as a roosting pelican.
A perpetual half smile seals in your tranquillity.
It is too late for me to learn again to call you Daddy,
a cartoon name, like a rumpled birthday hat I cannot make you wear.
But at your bidding, I try the tangerines.
I tote the picker to the tree.
You insist on the top one, enmeshed in leaves.
The rigid limbs resist, raining debris.
I twist the iron fingers, tear fiercely, and capture the fruit.
Its caged color rages in the sky.
It nestles in my hand like a wounded bird, skin ripped, flesh bared.
I peel away the velvet veins, touch the juice with my tongue.
It is an acrid, Pyrrhic victory, and you have exited,
coasted out on the smooth decks of things,
headed for the silent rim of the horizon
to feed on manna that falls from heaven,
before I can tell you:
The tangerines are not ready to eat.
And I, being prone to love, will wait without pickers,
among gnarled roots, for bitter fruit to ripen into sweet.
    Carolyn Everall Johnson

A Better Place

When your life seems dull and you are in despair,
Call on the Lord and he will surely be there.
Ask him to keep and strengthen you,
To see a better day and not be blue.

Our worries sometimes are many, we must agree.
But, it takes our Lord to get us to see
Our world is full of discontent.
But, a word to others would be well spent.

About our Lord and all his love,
When we leave this world and move on above.
To a better place to spend our days,
To be with the Lord in his home always.

Janis B. Drinnon

Reflections

My youth, it seems so far away.
A time I thought would last forever.
Rare are the moments it feels like yesterday.
Days when I never imagined saying never.

The aches and pains of age are taking their toll.
Yet, my pride refuses to fall.
I struggle to accomplish just one more goal,
To create one more memory to recall.

Too soon life's horizon has appeared.
Years grudgingly are being replaced by days.
My mortality is no longer feared.
My hope is I've left a memory along the way.

The patience of time has outlasted me.
My body can no longer keep pace with my mind.
Only my shadow knows of my destiny.
Tomorrow has become a place I hope to find.

Gary H. Long

I'll Always Remember That August September

That August September I will always remember.
I see his large hazel eyes dancing and blinking
As he puts his two arms around my spaghetti waist
And charmingly stares into my astonished face.

His arms made me feel secure and warm
Like the forest green coat I always wore
When I was a tiny girl of about four...
Too young then for him to make my head spin.

Unexpectedly, Jova T. Greene slipped into my life
And soon soothingly asked me to be his loving wife.
I will not let you walk away this sunny day
Until you say you will be mine, Julie Jaye.

Tears of joy trickled down each rosy cheek
As I took a very deep short sigh.
Yes, my dear Jova T. Greene
You know I'll gladly be your little queen.

Then Jova T. Greene stared breathtakingly at me
As we made plans for that happy ceremonial day
When he and I would boldly say
"I do" and create a dream world just for us two.

Florence M. Jones

Light On the Hill

Jesus will shine the light on the hill
All he has to say is peace be still
The light is a heavenly light
If you open your eyes you see it shines real bright

The light on the hill is for everyone to confess
Confess your sins and do your every best
Jesus will not take nothing more or nothing less
If you confess he won't be upset

The light on the hill is for everyone to see
Heaven is where Jesus wants us to be
The light on the hill will not run up a bill
He has all of us in his will

When Jesus shines light it will be in the end
Confess to him all of your sins
When you see the light
You will know that everything will be alright.

Linda McCray

Thursday's Sail -- A Song

Dedicated to Marcia, Dr. Ralph DiMattea
and Dr. Margaret Davis.
As the sails fly with the wind
laughing waters break against us
the craft dances
Friends journey through gushing H20
o'er the bay, sometimes quiet
then words surge forth like an unfreezing wave in the bay
shh! The balance of silence awe at the wonder; no words to say.
Waltzing over currents,
swing dancing through the tides,
Away from city pressures,
people's maladies, children's groans—
leave the checkbook and car payments at home.
Come go dancing on the waters!
Thursday's sail out over the blue
Listen to the sea gulls.
Sing the song inside you.

Nancy Anne Cunningham

Ode to Volunteers

To all those who share their time as well
as, a helping hand to others in need!
There are those who recognition,
   is achieved, through selfless deeds,
by giving of their own free time,
   to help with other's needs!

You'll find them in most hospitals,
   and shelters far and wide,
they receive no weekly paycheck,
   yet, their work is done with pride!

They help the needy start anew,
   and calm all patient's fears,
while striving hard to change this world,
   we call them "Volunteers"!

A smile and a helping hand,
   are strict necessities,
by which a volunteer must use,
   to calm life's rampant seas!

Susan Ongirski

The Meaning of Life

Searching. Seeking. Staying up late.
To gaze at the stars and just contemplate.

Wondering. Thinking. Far into the night.
Of the infinite universe, the essence of life.

Loving all others, and every living thing.
Expanding the heart for the beauty it brings.

Life is much more than we ever can see.
Sit still for a moment and let yourself be.

For only by silence and stillness within
Can we ever hope for growth to begin.

Lose sight of the dream that you hope to attain
All earthly possessions you can possibly gain.

Cease endless motion and running around.
By constant activity you can't hear the Sound.

The Word. The Beginning. Upon which all is based.
A life solely of the senses is simply a waste.

Come silently, calmly, realization your goal.
And enter the Light which is your soul.

Cynthia Ferguson

What Is Understanding

Is love and compassion in life.
Love is to understand feelings.
Compassion is to care or share time.
To understand is the greatest of all.
Thus we can have all three in one.
Love, compassion and understanding.
Without these you have no life.
The blind can't see or the deaf hear.
They need all these plus.
Extending the hand they can understand.
That we will never be alone.
There is nothing like silence or darkness in time or trouble.
A child cries out and goes unheard
Love in all forms is in trouble, they don't listen.
You speak searching for understanding.
It falls on deaf ears and you are alone.
Time seems to stop, your mind is lost
    seeking to find the answer.
You spoke, but no words were heard no one hears you.
Darkness and silence were yours, because no one understand.

Patrick D. Wood

Hurricane Fran

Arrogant, unpredictable, ruthless, and strong,
    Long before daylight, she blasted along;
Uninvited, indeed, was she to our town,
    But that had no way of slowing her down.
They called her Fran, too friendly a name,
    For this errant, defiant, hurricane dame!

She plunged on forward, then pulled the plug,
    Of her big, invisible, inexhaustible jug.
Down came the rain, in torrents, no less,
    Drenched were we, no chance for redress.
Water, more water, with no place to go,
    The onset of floods to add to our woe!

Then grasping the winds, she flung them about,
    Like a child, with toys, when he's in a pout.
Heedless of all the havoc they'll cause,
    Caring not what the damage or loss;
Tall trees toppled by brunt of the blow,
    Venting their wrath on whate'er lay below.

With nary a tear, bade we Fran adieu,
Then knuckled right down, the hard work to do.

Olive I. Clark

One Life For Christ

On this earth where many a life's span
Is but three score years and ten,
If you have labored for earth's treasures only —
When it's time to move on, what then?

When the valleys are dark through which you must pass
And your troubles and trials seem more than your share,
Do you earnestly search for the meaning of life?
Or simply throw up your hands in despair?

In this life there'll always be good versus bad,
Of this one fact we're all well aware;
Have you found the Answer to all of life's problems?
How well do you stand the wear and the tear?

If you're not satisfied to merely exist and survive
If you want happiness, contentment and peace of mind,
If you want to master the storms in your life,
With Christ as your Guide, all these treasures you'll find.

If I had but one testimony in this life to give,
I'd want people to see Christ in the life that I live;
Mere words are shallow, heard only when spoken,
But a life lived for Christ is a bona-fide token.

Evelyn Knouse

The Saga of the A.T.E. Group

Stalwart men, they stood before their machines.
Their job: To pass the product, regardless of the means.
With the boss to the right of them, the boss to the left of them
And confusion all around.
But one stepped out, he'd had enough, "I quit," he said.
"This must fall," the boss declared, "upon the Group Leader's head."
More men fell before the tide was stemmed
The future was dark, the group, perhaps, condemned,
With the boss to the right of them, the boss to the left of them
And confusion all around.
Along came a brash new class, young men, with plenty of brass.
The boss' boss heard the awful din and saw for sure the troop could
    not win,
With the boss to the right of them, the boss to the left of them
And confusion all around.
In aftermath, the organization did bend, nevermore would the group
    contented,
With the boss to the right of them, the boss to the left of them
And confusion all around.
In the pages of history, the men who fell, let it be recorded, did
    exceedingly well,
With the boss to the right of them, the boss to the left of them
And confusion all around.

John S. Haynes

I Rise

I rise to see a new day.
I rise because hope is alive and within me.
I rise a better tomorrow for myself and for other.
I rise because the race is not given to the weak, but it is given to
the strong.
I rise because somewhere down the road I will pick up my shining star.
I rise to gain knowledge by taking the required steps for a new
beginning.
I rise onward and upward the slopes for the love, for the peace,
and for the happiness which lies ahead.
I Rise.

Rita Marks

A Firm Foundation

A - Catholic home with harmony inside

F - inds the parents a school where God abides.
I - n starting lessons each day.
R - eligion is first, with prayer the day begins.
M - any subjects to help in future life.

F - it for a king or a man seeking a wife.
O - nly those who stay out, we find unprepared.
U - nder the standard, for things we have shared.
N - ot that we are boasting, instead we are sad.
D - oing our best to share, with each girl or lad.
A - ll the blessings we share, with caring and love
T - here's happiness as well as sorrows we know,
I - n our daily toils of life, here below.
O - n a solid foundation, we are prepared
N - othing can stop us, when we travel by faith.

Anna Lee Rodgers Blincoe

Ewe

The disease they said spread quickly...
 For weeks they had not eaten of food or drank of water.
Riveted in place, I stood feeling my very bones ache...
 Blinding, the light shone forth from their eyes.
Tongues of fire emerged from their mouths..
 The language unknown to me, pierced deeply my ears and my brain.
As told in ancient days, the coming inevitable...
 So I ran, falling, running again disregarding those I trampled on.
No doctors could explain, no lawyers understand, no presidents or
 rulers stop them...
 Over me they stood, tears of blood touching my skin.
Slowly I'm changing, the disease is in me...
 Death enters and then leaves, as my heart cries out for the
 first time.
And I too, am sent forth into the world...
 As a flock of sheep they move on, like lambs to the slaughter.
Not a disease, but his holy spirit...
 Blinding, the light, the Shepherd shines forth in my eyes.

Becky Ann Brinn

Signs

A cry for help, a shot rings out, people passing by just shout . . .
and stare . . . does anyone care?

A frail old man coming home from the store . . .
beaten and robbed . . . it's happened once more . . .

A child bruised and battered, dirty, torn, and tattered . . .
left on the stairs . . . who really cares?

A runaway teen fleeing from...feels all alone . . .
 goes and gets stoned . . .

Unwanted pregnancy . . . without any hesitancy . . .
 was anyone there?

Signs of the times, our lives such bliss.
We're all terribly busy . . . think what we miss . . .

How shallow our souls, how closed our minds.
How empty our hearts; signs of the times?

Too lost in ourselves, too busy to listen,
Too much to do . . . their silent tears glisten . . .

No loving arms, no smiling face,
no helping hand, no warm, welcome place.

Follow His pathway, help another in strife,
reach out in love, be brought back to . . . Life.

Karen K. Wendland

Comes the Dawn

After a while, you learn the subtle difference between holding a hand
And charming a soul.
And you learn that love doesn't mean leaning
And company doesn't mean security.

And you begin to understand that kisses aren't contracts
And presents aren't promises.

And you begin to accept your defeat with your head held high
And your eyes open, with the grace of a woman, not the grief of a child.
You learn to build your roads on today because tomorrow's grounds are
 too uncertain for plans,
And futures have a way of falling in mid-flight.

After a while, you learn that even sunshine burns if you get too much,
So you plant your own garden and decorate your own soil,
Instead of waiting for someone to bring you flowers.
And you learn that you really can endure, that you really are strong
And you really do have worth.

And you learn and learn . . . and you learn.

With every goodbye, you learn.

Rodger Tabb II

Fallen Soldier

   Who stands sentry for you now, oh mighty one? For so long
you stood guard over your piece of this patchwork quilt called
earth. Suddenly, the sky grew dark, a crack of thunder echoed
and a bolt of lightning flashed, fatally wounding you with its
piercing rod. Birds did take leave of your branches as you
plummeted downward. Your demise was announced throughout
the forest by the rumble of the land below as you fell.

   We need not be sad in your passing for while you stood,
you were haven for the bird and home to the chipmunk and squirrel.
If you could have spoken, you might have shared stories of the
Chippewa, the immigrant, the pioneer or the cowboy who took
refuge from sun and shower under your leafy canopy. Those
days now are gone. No longer will the seasons change your coat
of color. From the earth you came...to it you now return.

   And as Mother Nature opens the heavens to shed tears at
your passing, she also provides a drink of water to a new sapling
nearby as it begins its life. Now the cycle is complete...the
circle unbroken.

   Let all mankind bear witness to the changing of the guard.
Linda Suzann Hymrod

Hate

You like to see me suffer.
It pleases you to watch me crawl and beg.
Me! A pathetic slave to your needs and desires.

You love to torture me.
You knock me down and
dig your heels into my back,
laughing as I scream in pain.

(I have never seen you smile
the way you smiled as you
watched me, bleeding and writhing
at your feet)

You killed me once.

And now, I am back,
ready to receive your stinging blows,
your fists pummeling me into submission.

Rashida Bowman

Somewhere In Time

Somewhere in between the spaces in time
from countryside to city sky lines
a heart lies broken from bitter end
afraid to trust, to love again.

Lonely heart cries out from beyond the sea
living through memories of what once could be
hands fall helplessly limp at her side
desperate for cleansing with the morning tide.

If only she could take away his pain
warm his heart, let him live again
wash away painful images that dance in his head
as she is left lonely to walk the waters edge.

For here there is no bridge to cross
she is shattered and broken, coping with loss
the water stills, now an image of glass
teardrop falls, splintering in pieces all things from the past.

She reaches out at nothing as if to gather them near
feeling his arms about her, his whispers in her ear
a love born out of darkness, where distance is the crime
into that same darkness lost, her love remains frozen in time.

M. Susan Kundla

Little Mr. Busy Bee

What a beautiful day!!!
White clouds drifting in a bright blue sky.
A flash of light catches my eye.

There he is!! "Little Mr. Busy Bee" who lives
across the way from me.

Riding his bike around and around, up and down,
in and out - faster - faster - whee!!
(Of course he only rides in the driveway)
Dad is always there you see.

They mow the grass, shovel the snow, practice their
golf swing, bat the ball.
So much to do - hurry - hurry - hurry
load the wagon, hitch it to his bike and then it must be
towed over there.
Stop - unhitch the wagon - then on he goes.
Round and round, up and down.

I don't know his name - I think he is three or four.
Tis a pleasure to watch him and dad
As they work and play.
To me - he will always be - "Little Mr. Busy Bee."

Marjorie H. Baker

Maria's Prayer Under the Acacia

Maria sits, hand folded, under the acacia tree
watching great grandson Juan as he gently cradles
his little sister Megan is his arms.
Maria's heart swells with pride to see them there
and goes on with her knitting for it will soon be
chilly weather of late autumn in Albuquerque.

She knows that winter is coming soon. She has watched
ripe globes of burgeoning plums dropping to lawns
near he acequia. Have they not held on faithfully
drinking in summer sunshine and crisp cool nights?
Maria's bones have told her by their ache and cramping
of an early winter. She calls to the children:
"Come, young ones. You must not meddle with the nest
of bees or yellow jackets. Come, immediately, Juan,
before you get yourself and Megan in bad trouble!!"
Juan shakes his head and then obeys. "Grandmother!"
Impatience molds his features but Maria does not bend.
"I hear the angels calling me a warning, children!
I hear them telling me you will learn by experience,
but grandmothers are for watching wind in the trees. Come!!"

Veda Nylene Steadman

Glorified Dancin' Fool

You can't keep me in my seat;
  Not happy, bubbling toe-tappin' me.
A "hoppy" heart, high with delight;
  Singin' along as the body's enticed.

The Polka, the Waltz, the Two-step;
  Just you and me, how I flip!
The Rumba, the Rock, the Cotton-eyed Joe;
  A sweatin' jolly two-some thus unfolds.

A dancin' fool losin' my cool, gone
  'Til the break of a gorgeous dawn.
It's my callin', chases my fears;
  Done for years, banishing buckets of tears.

Skippin' those feet, fast trackin' beat;
  Bright lights shinin', oh what a treat!
My cheerful hearts pumpin', so very alive;
  Ah, glorious music soakin' my hide!

Twirls, dips, whirls, back steppin' curls;
  Oh, glory-glory, I'm one delirious girl!
Give me, please, a country tunes beat;
  And I'm, immediately, up on my feet!

Patricia L. Purrett

Grandpa's Clock

The ticking of Grandpa's clock,
the striking of the hour.
The key that fits in the lock,
of the large oak that towered.

The log cabin that began to decay,
holds memories of love and laughter.
Gathering wood on a cold winter's day,
voices echo clear to the rafters.

The mountains captured in mosaic,
inlaid with grays, purples, and blues.
Our mouths do not know how to say it,
our hearts are filled with the news.

A sweet pea vine, on the fence, looks like Victorian lace,
was given to Grandma from her mother.
Back when they first homesteaded the place,
in the year eighteen something or other.

I've come away with a boodle of treasure,
I must take the key from the lock.
Those dreams that are hard to measure,
someday they'll find when they look inside Grandpa's clock.

Geneva Atchley

The Church Ever Stands

The church stands gracious, beautiful and tall
Stained windows glistening in the sun,
Beckoning to one and all
There's work to be done;

Howling storms surround, rains of teardrops fall
Rest and calm within, the church ever stands,
  Gracious, beautiful and tall;

Christ is the head; you: The voice, feet and hands
There is not a room defeat;

It was built upon the hill and rock
Upon this foundation the church ever stands,
And the good shepherds leads his flock;

The church is Christ's presence on earth,
And his members are of precious worth.

Mildred A. Rhodes

New Baby Desiree

Listening, quiet voiced, to every sound,
Hardly believing this long-waited day;
Glowing family circled around,
Eager to cuddle our small Desiree.

Outfitted in medic-green hospital style,
The self-conscious father comes and goes;
While mother's gentle, tired but happy smile
Holds secrets only her baby knows.

Nothing special in hospital routine,
Only one of a dozen birthed this day.
Ordering confusion, nurses move serene,
Hinting now we are not to overstay.

The next-room neighbors crowding past,
Obstruct the hall with admonished din.
Can't see how hollow their brag, in contrast —
Make too much of little hair and less chin!

Our oldest human story now told again,
Gifts new promise, joy, hope and tears.
However it fits in the Universal Plan,
This joyful day will brighten our lives and years.
        Neil Loeding

The Blizzard

Snow.
Gently the flakes float through the air
So soft and gentle they seem to care;
They brush past us:
Seen all over the hills, the roads and the trees,
Pure and clean as only nature can be.
White as far as the eye can see.

The blizzard.
Gusts of wind swirling all around
Plants and trees uprooted from the ground;
Blinded by the fury of the storm:
Only collapsed buildings and burst pipelines are in sight,
No electricity to illuminate the night.
Black as far as the eye can see.

Dawn.
People look up to the heavens and pray
There is hope and despair in all they say;
As they look around them:
The beauty that remains is still on display,
The entire landscape has turned grey.
        Puneet Sharma

Memories of a Sunset

The lake.
Not a wave or ripple was to be seen
Like a mercurial body with a simmering sheen;
The water shone with the light:
For miles and miles the surface was flat,
We stood on the shore in this peaceful habitat.
A view of the serenity of nature.

The sunset.
Birds chirped and the wind was slow
The atmosphere lit with an orange glow;
A radiant ball descended through the clouds;
It lingered in the sky for a little while,
Long enough to make us smile.
Such are the treasures of life.

Memories.
We tried to deny it but now I know
Nostalgia is haunting, it refuses to let go;
Even though we wanted it go slow:
The sun vanished beneath the horizon.
These feelings inside me will continue to grow.
        Puneet Sharma

The Great God Provides

Out my open window I did take a peek;
And before my eyes a beautiful picture to keep
Five little birds: two little jays and two doves,
Followed by one little bird no mate to love.

The lonely bird tried friends to make;
But the others only his lunch did take.
Is there a friend for the one lonely bird?
Or the word of friend he only has heard?

There is a Friend for the lonely little bird;
And also all the lambs and sheep of the herd.
The lonely bird our good Friend doth keep;
And our good Friend keeps all the sheep.

The four little happy birds flew away;
But the lonely little bird chose to stay.
The good Master, you know, chose to stop by;
And the lonely little bird had to eat better than pie.

The lonely bird's needs were greatly met;
And yours will be too - don't you forget.
The Great God loves and provides for all;
And He watches over His sheep lest any fall.
        Lillian M. Donahoe

My Bouquet of Friends

Through the years it has been my fortune to meet many friends,
My praise for their kindness and generosity never ends.

Past memories bring thoughts of happy times together.
Always with a willingness to help one another.

Treasured friends are needed in our daily lives.
In their courage, compassion, creativity - the spirit survives.

As I recall the many past events shared that I treasure,
I'm reminded that a lasting friendship, one cannot measure.

I see my friends likened to a bouquet of a variety of flowers
As arranged by an artist, and refreshing as April showers

Just to see them gives me a lift.
Some can he considered rare - by nature's gift

The most popular flower chosen is the rose
Yet, we all have our favorite, who knows.

Each of us has a choice in the friendship bouquet we choose
In passing years we add some, some we lose.

As we witness the bouquet's petals slowly and softly fall.
Would that all could last forever. Nature tells us, not at all.
        Petryna K. Pinkert

Forever Tears

The forever tears won't go away.
They must be here to stay.
I look up to trust another day.
"Who is this little soul." I say.

She has no face in my mind.
Life to children so unkind.
Who took her loving tiny heart?
Who didn't want her form the very start?

No matter how hard she tried and cried.
Love vanished with the ocean tide.
All alone was she in this new place.
Danger filling every open space.

Confusion, devastation, why won't it go away?
Sunshine come to me in my heart please stay.
I have a sister who always looked out for me.
I found these lost feelings in my heart, you see.

Her face is vivid in this tiny soul.
God's time rolls on as each bell tolls.
        Diana J. Weigel

Never Forgotten

I'll see your kind smile, hear your voice warm and loving
In puppy dog licks and bread warm from the oven.
I'll hear your sweet voice in Amazing Grace, and see your smile in the
clouds up in space.
You're suffering no more, you've taken your place...next to Jesus, His
angels with wings near your face.
You'll always be near; in our hearts and our minds
As we continue to try to reach mankind.
You're never forgotten, you'll always be missed
Since you touched all our lives
Your love's been a gift
We will live out our lives
Being proud to have known
Our dear Dorothy
Our loved one
Who has finally gone Home.

Jackie Kline

There's No Denying Dr. Temple . . .

"Dear Lady, dear lady, come sit in my chair
It's been some time since you were here."

"Your blood levels are a little too high . . ."
"Oh no! Not me!"
"Dear Lady, dear lady I would not lie
Your labs came back as 183."

"Say `Ahhh . . .' I see something unknown to me."
"Oh No! Not me!"
"Dear lady, dear lady, I would not lie
I'll tell you which surgeon I want you to see."

"But Doctor I'm on vacation you see
It will go away; just let it be."
"Dear Lady, dear lady; I would not lie
See this surgeon today, it will set your mind free."

One year later . . .

"Dear lady, dear lady; it's good to see you here
Relax - come sit in my chair . . . "

"Thank you Dr. Temple for all you've done;
Had you not the courage to see through denial
This poem may not have been written . . ."

Judie Miller

How Simple But Beautiful Yet This Can Be

Hold her. Tell her you love her.
Hold him. Tell him you love him.
Hold your children. Tell them you love them.
How simple but beautiful yet this can be.
Tell your children the things in your heart.
Tell them where you grew up, what you did,
the good times and not so good times.
Tell them they may grow up to be something
like thee.
How simple but beautiful yet this can be.
Show them that life can be sweet.
Show them that they can make something of
themselves whether great or small.
Show them can't is weaker than can.
How simple but beautiful yet this can be.

Joyce E. Kellberg

Amity's Gone Fishin'

The little blonde girl I see each day
is not with me today. You see, she's away.
She went with her Grandma and was happy too.
I'm really glad for it's something she's wanted to do.

There's more I'll say, to the story than this
as yesterday fondly, I gave she and Boober a hug and a kiss.
Now, a fishing excursion is what's the decision,
Yep! You guessed it, Amity's gone fishin'.

If they fish from a creek there's lots to tend,
bobbers and lines and if she hooks a big fish the rod will bend,
but should they go to a river they might use a boat,
what fun it will be just to fish and float.

I hope she catches, a whole lot of fish,
plus has a good two day time, that's also my wish.
What will she snare? A pike or a sunny?
A bass or a perch, I hope not an eel or that wouldn't be funny.

She's five years old and eager to do and learn.
This child and all about her is my main concern.
When she returns I'm ready to hear "listen Tai"
as to how she caught whatever fish and maybe even the one that got
away.

Elois L. Spangler

A Mother's Look of Love

The look, only mom could conceal,
Sparkling of wine, rosy cheeks, eyes open with fullness, only the
moon can reveal.

I met a real woman, one which I could give,
My hard earned dollar, and love as long as I may live,
Though she has the look only mom can conceal,
I believe I've seen that look before and ne'er forget the way she
made me feel,
I want for closeness, and above all, that starry-eyed look only a mom
could concern
Blessed with a son, a daughter, all for love,
And our presence, a family with prose,
One with care, ne'er to raise a glove,
But one where love, like rhythm, life grows,
And the look only mom could conceal,
This love, for all, is in our hearts so real,
Every day I've seen this look on her face,
My mom, my love, often this secret I want to know,
But to peer to seek and find no trace,
The look only mom can conceal,
And it is in my loved one's face,
It's left up to mom and her to reveal!

Patrick Hymer

Evening In November

Ah! What reposeful mood - a lovely sky;
The rosiness of sunset tints the west
A silvery pond of ice - the bare, brown fields,
Half-clad with snow - a stack of hay, late mown,
A dog - a boy - a pail of fresh white milk,
And just beyond, a road - a bridge - a wood
With branches high and bare against the sky,
And little bits of blueness in between.

I gaze; the earth grows dark; the azure sky
Submerges into gray and then to black.
I stare at utter darkness. Soon appears
A star - a sparkling, radiant, lambent flame;
A scintilla here, another, and still more
Till all the heavens glow, transplendent, light!
A whippoorwill calls mournfully from the hill;
Then all is still - the world is clothed in night.

Doris Van Owen

Peacefully Delighted

Don't stand at my grave and weep—for I am at peace
I am with the Lord my God now that I am deceased.

Don't mourn my death because I am no longer in pain
I'm finally in comfort now that I'm in God's domain.

Don't think of me as gone because I am watching you today
I see you when you sleep at night-when you wake and when you pray.

Don't pray for me at that time because I am just fine so far
When you gaze at night into the clear blue sky
I'm your own sparkling star.

Don't let my death interfere with plans you have for your life
I didn't mean to ever hurt you or cause you any strife.

Don't stop moving forward—you can definitely survive
Don't think of me as dead but remember be alive.

You're still daddy's little girls and I hold you close to my heart
Even though I can't be there our souls will never part.

I am with your mother now for we are finally reunited
don't mourn this day-but celebrate
for we are peacefully delighted.
    Christine Coleman

Untitled

My angel of love . . . my angel of night . . .
Facing the pain, my heart an open door. Once my love, now is here
no more. Forever is our dreams we saw everlasting in our hearts
we prayed for. So quickly, never did I think forever would come
For just yesterday our lives were one.
My angel of love . . . my angel of night . . .
y gentle voice sings with the wind songs of love you feel within
The warmth of your breathe now with the sun
Embracing my body as if we were still one.
The pain no longer holding you down your soul is light you are free,
in flight. My angel of love, my angel of night . . .
Come to me quickly tell me you are alright.
Believe when I caressed you my love was true
Know when I held you each feeling I had was new.
Understand when I hated I was afraid to love.
My angel of love, my angel of night . . .
Please come back to me hold me in your arms just once more, only
tonight. One more kiss is all I need to tell you "I love you"
Please do believe. My life has ended though I am still living. My
heart to you I will continue giving. I live for the moment I'll see
you again. My heart is breaking, I must know when. My angel of love,
my angel of night . . . I love you.
    Toni Marie Greco

Love Is

Love is blue, love is green,
And all the colors is between.
Love is sunshine, love is rain,
Love is happiness and also pain.
Love is doing, if for someone you love,
Love is a prayer answered, when all is right above.
Love is giving, if from the heart,
A continuous thing, not a stop and a start.
Love is knowing, when you get love in return,
Love is for keeping, and not something to spurn,
Love is for the young, and also for the old,
Love, when true, will never get cold.
Love is you, and the joys you bring,
Love is remembering, and you make my heart sing.
    Herbert C. Link

Tired

Movement leaders are all the same,
They act nice but all a game

They always have the gall to wake me with a call
"Would you like to leaflet near the mall"?

They start out democratic become erratic
Wind up autocratic

Both Pro Life, Pro Choice
Abortion distortion!

I've seen all the Christians who tell me to "repent,"
and I've seen the no fun socialists who will always dissent

I've seen the right wing and the wealthy few
and I've seen the vegans and their apolitical views.

I've seen environmentalists who say they're pro-green
then eat animals and say it's not mean!

If only changes were made with people who "played with a full deck,"
then this world would not be a wreck!

Republicans are boors,
Married Democrats in the bed with whores,
Third parties never score!

Republicans have money, Democrats in bed with mistress honey!
    Bill Frizlen

Tenacious Spring

With the soft tenacity of a living guitar string;
Renewal season arrives — Suddenly it's Spring!
Perhaps Spring was given to us as a time to reflect on

old actions and consider new ones,
Or maybe it's just Natures way of offering us
Love by the tons.
After an entire Winter of "trees playing possum",
What a joy it is to see the first blossom!
Some trees bloom early; and some bloom late —
That, in itself, is a trick of fate.
In a way, people are like trees —
Some bloom early; some bloom late —

Some bear fruit; some do not;
Some sprout buds, while others rot.
So learn a lesson from the Tree of Life;
You might save yourself some strife.Roots are important — or so
I've been told;
Some are timid — some are bold!
But in the end; one thing I clearly see,
There is no poem as lovely as a tree.
    Dorothy Jackman

Someone's Mother

Her clothes were all wrinkled and worn
She glanced into space and looked forlorn
Her children were all grown and far away
She longed to see them many a day.

In the afternoon she took her daily nap
As her little puppy cuddled into her lap
When she awakened tears streamed down her face
She wiped them gently with her hanky trimmed in lace.

Her family and friends she missed so much
If only they were there for her to touch
She prayed to God to help her to see
That was the way it was meant to be.
    Lillian Walker

Steps

i step
  over the
    Threshold of Childhood,
      Leaving my map of nineteen years behind.

i choose
  from Infinite
        Possibilities,
            and walk on
                marked and unmarked paths.

i cast a passing glance
    at the Traveler on the Road
              and sigh:

my boots are not as weathered,
      my steps are not as sure...

Yet,
  I leave
    My Prints
      for others to cast glances at
                  before they create their own.

Irene I. Ueda

Autumn's Whisper Wind

The whisper of the wind filled the air,
And the Autumn, brisk with sunshine filled her hair.
And the two of us together without care,
Did as lover's only dream to ever dare.
And the passion of the moment left us free to breathe fresh air,
As the whisper of the colored autumn wind, touched a loving pair.
It would be unkind to break the magic of this spell,
Of the whisper of the autumn wind, so wind; whisper, do not tell.

Jack De Young

A Proud Man With Spirit

The Indian brave up on his steed
Challenging any man driven with greed
A symbol of all men who still dare
He sits alone because too few care

Guardian of this earth's great beauty
He does not take lightly his God given duty
Taking only what he needs to survive
Never compromising anything alive

A man that has earned the right to be proud
He's able to see the sun behind the cloud
His strength is his spirit and his strive
Only the "brave" help earth's beauty survive

Anne C. Berry

I Don't Know!

Little boy, how old are you? I'm eight years old.
Where do you live? Over there.
Do you like school? Yes.
Do you have any brothers or sisters? No.
Is your mother home? No, She's working.
Is your father home? No.
Is he working? I don't know.
Will he be home soon? I don't know.
What does he do? I don't know.
Where is your father? I don't know.
Have you seen your father? Yes.
When? I was five months old.
Where did he go? The Air Force.

Rudy Castellanos

Winter's Eve

I must go out to fill the feeders
before the cold, wet dust sets in,
bright eyes watch, voices chirping,
cardinal, titmouse, sparrow, wren.

The dogs and cats must have more food,
warm bowls to strengthen for the night.
Already high the cattles' hay is piled
for food and bed until new light.

I must secure each little chore I always do
to show each beast and fowl my thoughtful care;
trusting, loyal, yes, and loving eyes
thank me for what I do and what I share.

Barbara R. Sampson

Summer's End

When dew on the ground and we say farewell to the end of summer,
And the geese leave and fly south, the bears fall to slumber.

The blossom bright with the autumn flowers fall with dew,
And with the colors,...the fields with heaven's own blue,

We open the morning day with a warm quiet light,
Succeeds the overcasts from the following night,

We cry for the loss of spring and the wandering brook that's unseen,
Now we forget the colors of the flowers and then violets that lean,

When the woods are naked and the birds have flown,
We wait the late to enjoy the woods alone,

Soon the shorten days approach with the frost creeping up,
The dogs having their litters that grow to a pup,

The age of the year creeping to the end,
With the mood of love of the woods and the woods shorten day
portend,

Looking out of my cabin at the wooded edge, dark blue sky as it falls
The quiet hush of the night I see the last of the flowers on the walls

The end of summer darns the night with the moon ever so bright,
It hangs there in the sky, to all hours of the night,

"I say good by summer, goodbye summer nights, goodbye summer days,"
May look to the heavens, summer has departed its own ways.

Anthony Vincent Digiannurio

Aubade

The sound of a morning dove breaks the charm of silence,
And hastens to the quick the end of night.
A walk among the clouds still bound to moon watch,
Bequeaths the coming promise of returning light.

To smell each blade of grass and crystal dew drop,
And taste the morning mist yet undisturbed;
Inhaling breathless moments spawned at sunrise,
Unspurned by scorching heat yet undeterred

The solitude of sunrise soothes the spirit,
And beckons the heart to face what is yet unknown;
The call from deep within the souls dimension,
Baptizes a weary world to discern her crown.

For wild hope emerges with the sunrise
And stalwart dreams from mustiness of time;
The morrow brings a concert of the morning
To those who by their patience quell the climb.

As Moses spelled his stalkers in the rushes,
A babe abandon to a foreign Grace;
Somehow, the melting wonder of the sunrise,
Confers Procnean Hope upon the race.

Orlo Espeland

Rain

A gentle springtime shower,
little damper than the morning dew,
freshens the buds and blooms of May.

The unending autumn drizzle
fades the blazing tint of leaves
that still cling, soggy and dispirited,
in November.

Sun and shadow alternate
below the tropic,
as broken clouds sail a deep blue sky;
brief showers, brilliant sunshine,
iridescent rainbows, all in train.

Equatorial downpours, sudden, violent and brief,
visit every afternoon; the steaming sidewalks
dry out in time for tea.

Minor preludes to the fury of a summer storm
or the arrival of the monsoon,
sometime in June.

Charles T. Stewart Jr.

America's Heartland

What can a person say
about the tragedy of that day.

The bomb went bang-and blew away life.
Turned peace and tranquility into shock, grief, anger, and strife.

Babies bodies dangling in arms of medics so strong.
What has happened is so wrong.

Injuries of many bring trembling and tears.
Among the by-standers, increasing fears.

A terrorist act, a beginning of horror
life of war-an open sore.

Of this we can b sure,
Other occurrences of this magnitude we will incur

Because men of bitter hearts and mind,
closed from compassion and love of any kind,

Devise with intent, to destroy, to kill.
Their hatred to fulfill.

Many set God aside in so many matters,
Now harts broken hanging in tatters.

So many families destroyed that day,
That day-that American's Heartland was blown away.

Darlene Mae Tucker

A Prayer for Humanity While There's Still Time

Yes God, it's me again
except this time I seek no selfish gratification.
I pray today my most important prayer
for those without hope
the helpless, the lost.
Grant them a ray of your light
to guide them never too far to the left or to the right.
Show them that actions speak louder than words.
Enlighten them to know truth
and to live by it.
Let them not invoke your blessed name
during their perverted quests.
Show them the beauty of simplicity.
Teach them the long lasting benefit(s)
of fulfilled promises.
Teach them also trust.

God, save us all.
God, bless our politicians.

Radames Ortiz

Friendship, Love, And Companionship

That is what I need.
And if that's to much for you give
My feeble heart to feed.

Though I hate to have to,
I show you to the door.
Later I will regret it
And my heart will be sore.

You need not be handsome
Or even that smart.
Liking kids is a must,
Which means a big heart.

You must be independent
And have a mind of your own.
You need tell me you love me,
When we're apart and on the phone.

Now I am not strict
And will make exceptions.
For if you give me Friendship, Love, and Companionship
Then together in all we can make perfection!!!!

Rebecca Werner

The Pain Of Truth

When you take a turn and one's life goes astray,
It doesn't mean you really want it that way,
Circumstances are things we have no control of,
It happens when it does, just let it go its way.

I always set my life in truth and honesty.
I never want to hurt so I keep quiet in a way,
But knowing it could hurt by not saying what's true,
I tell the truth, but will the pain go away?

This question has been asked a million times,
Is truth worth all the pain and misery?
When saying it will mean a life's decay,
Can one live through it in all honesty?

Your life takes a turn when truth you say,
You fight the pain and misery which come your way,
Knowing despite the dark coating your life today,
Tomorrow will bring sunshine when truth you say.

Sonia F. Smith

Reminiscence of Grandma

Today...I made jelly.
Now the sparkling crimson jars
Accented with crowns of snow-white wax,
Proudly stand on the kitchen counter cooling.
As I write the lace curtains flutter,
Caught by the morning breeze
Wafting through the dining room windows.
My thoughts have returned to another Summer day...
Grandma's lace curtains swayed gently, lifted
by a light wind drifting in through the screens.
Her beautiful jars of Red Currant Jelly sealed with hot white wax
Were carefully set to cool on her kitchen table;
Which grandma covered with a fresh coat of shiny white paint
every spring.
How I loved watching her in that kitchen...
...Hearing her sing "If I had the wings of an angel."
Grandma's hugs were warm and held the sweet smell of her
Of love and safety.
Even yet memories of her overwhelm me...and so
I make bright red jelly with white wax seals.

Melanie M. Markus

11

Woodwinds

Begin the day... and I awaken to the gentle tingling,
Of the morning mist even flow, nights final breath.
And malaised by the gaunt and murky shroud impeding the sunrise,
I intently await the unfurling of nature's morning crest.
Enter... an eerie chant of pipes, its echo invokes my intrepid sense;
A sudden, biting thrust of woodwinds approaching with intrusion.
Its sound a whining, writhing pitch as I spin in awkward motion;
To reveal the source and contain my paranoia's quench for peril.
But woodwinds in the air? I'm alerted to the scriptural warnings;
Woodwinds in the air... Revelations? Read the book!
I have long lamented through each yellow parched page . . . Now I pause;
When, my God, I am besieged by a thunderous chorus of woodwinds.
Are they in six or seven? Its numeral symbol represents the entity;
Shall I prepare for strike or implore absolution, when suddenly I...
Ascend my head to the screaming skies, my eyes affixed in awe;
To a flock of nature's feathered flyers, ensconced in melodic exchange.
Juxtaposed in arrowed flank, their conductor at the cusp;
No steeds or trumpets in this group, nor beasts with jagged horns.
Yes, woodwinds in the air indeed, but the message speaks of Genesis;
And I close The Book and embrace the sounds of natures free concert.

Frank J. Ryan Jr.

Good Morning Lord

Good morning Lord...I've come to see
if you would spend this day with me
I've tried so hard some work to find now all my debts are way behind

I somehow wish I had a friend
to that I cannot now attend so Lord in all your charity
please try today to stay with me

I want to thank you Lord right now
for this bright fresh day and my knowing how
A job can't be that hard it's true if I go out there and take you too

Transgressions there have been a few
forgive me Lord that I may walk with you
I thank you Lord for sunny day or rain so sweet
I'm satisfied and am complete

I know right now my prayer you hear
Most gracious Father stay always near
oh...that friend I said I couldn't find?
Why Lord you've been here all the time

The birds about all sing your praise your love is seen in many ways
Reminds me how each day you feed each one of us from an apple seed

Doris Dolejs

Home and the Old Out House

When I was young, I didn't know about City fairs
I went without many earthly things
We had no money for putting on airs
Nor did we live like Princes and Kings

Our old house had no electric lights
Times were hard at our old home place
Although we worked both day and night
Being poor was never a disgrace

We needed many things without a doubt.
We walked on plain old wooden floors
There was things we couldn't do without
Such as window glasses and doors

We used an old out house, fast and bold
Believe me, there was no lost motion
When pain struck, we ran out in the cold
While we were still in the notion.

Ralph L. Cranford

Loneliness and Triumph of the Blue-Eyed Indian

Being a breed has been very agonizing and bewildering for me;
I look too white to fit into Indian society;
I think too Indian to fit into white society;
So after years of struggle and torment, I know I can only be me,
A blue-eyed Indian living in a white man's society;
Where you are likely to be considered crazy,
If you ask permission of the animals, birds and trees living there,
Before entering and walking through their woods;
Of if you honor plants as life-saving medicine keepers and teachers,
Instead of just different kinds of foods.
A blue-eyed Indian may learn to be strong;
A blue-eyed Indian may never belong;
Except among the animals, mountains, woods and those with wings,
Where if you dare enough to walk far enough to find wilderness;
You might just find the mountain ledge,
Where a blue-eyed Indian weeps in loneliness;
As she gathers visions of peace, she asks her friends with wings
To carry, back to harsh and shattered society;
And if you listen hard, you might hear the blue-eyed Indian,
As she sadly, softly, but triumphantly sings.

Candyce Seji King

Outside Beauty What's Inside?

There was this beautiful black widow spider
Who build a beautiful web,
For she knew if she build it strong enough,
Her mate in it would dwell.
This web would attract those far and near,
For it was a beautiful sight to see,
They did not know when they came inside
It would be their destiny.

She poisoned their minds with the perfume
She wore, it was a sweet smell of success.
And very soon their lives were doomed, for
Her web became their place of rest.
Yes! She was beautiful, and clever too, and
Had a lot going on.
Until one day it came her time to pay, she
Lost everything, again she was all alone.

Imogene Adkins Gaffney

Golden Days

The fall creeps up on silent feet
And tentatively daubs a leaf here and there
Day by day she wields her paint brush.
And ever so slowly her colors grow and glow
As she dons a coat of brilliant hue.

Here and there
A hail of gold sprinkles the ground
And a haze of gold surrounds my home.
While flashes of scarlet and orange
Peep through a golden screen.

The wind pushes the leaves with many fingers,
And through holes punched through the trees,
The sun comes shining through.
And like a blade of flashing light,
Its fragmented rays explode like diamonds,
Against a deep blue sky.

Eleanor M. Kerness

Ancient Verity

Spanning ages between her world and mine
we find Miss Liberty, her torch held high
beaming, beckoning, welcoming with tensile line
and holy elements of honesty.
Here in today's neon-lit arc of sin
integrity plays politics with war;
Shudders for the mess the world is in,
and wonders what a peace-pact should stand for.

Is this, the search for ancient verity
as fostered by the cognate English sire,
destined to become an effigy
of old Salem and it's witch's fire?
Will faith, abandoned by a wicked earth,
mushroom death across its world-wide girth?

Lonnie Bailey

His Rainbow

On the rocky mountain high
his rainbow he found, a refuge of souls torn.

To hurry...he sought to hurry - against
fleeting time - up to lofty highs where
eagles dare fly.

Where sun conquers bleak nights.
Just celestial plains where God's creatures
roam the wild.

Where crystal streams rush through rugged
terrain and fish leaf with sheer delight.
There he drew near, when troubles besieged, a refuge
of the sublime.

To hurry he sought to hurry, a child
of rocky times, so weary he grew. So weary.

The end flashed, shrouding brilliant skies.
His was the rainbow awhile. I see
him weary no more on eagles gabled wings
he soars, a child of rocky times.

Stefanie Kalinoski

I Open My Heart To Jesus Christ

I, Paul Andrew Pease, and the whole world open our hearts to Jesus
Christ and ask Him to come into our lives and take control of our
lives, for we are all sinners and we would like to be forgiven for our
sins and live in Peace, Love, Happiness and togetherness, instead of
fear, guilt, loneliness, and sadness. I also want you to know along
with myself and the whole world, the ghosts of departed people also
open their hearts to Jesus Christ and want Him to come in and take
control of their lives, for they to are sinners and want to be
forgiven for their sins and live the same life other Christians do.
Please come in, Amen.

Paul Andrew Pease

Twilight of the Moment

In the twilight of the moment, the mind wandereth losing focus
of the task at hand.
As thoughts fall to temptation, the mind wanders deeper and
deeper into the idle thoughts of mischief.
In the thoughts of mischief, an action is sown and a seed
is planted.
There is now a circumstance.
Could this not be the reason for instruction, and the instructor of
wisdom, knowledge and understanding?
In the twilight of the moment an idle thought planted can
lead to destruction.

Bryant Branch

The Rape of the Beach

The ocean meanders toward the land with a surreptitious cloak
But upon sighting the shore musters its waters in military array
And in cahoots with the wind creates an undulating pattern.
Marshaled at regimental strength the waves target the beach and
At high-tide the marauders unleash their crippling attack.

Stealthily, the surf plays its homicidal role in the assault and
Spews its finger-like froth to grope and capture granules of sand.
The ebb-tide exposes the tragic bashing inflicted upon the beach.
Sculpted by the undertow and the rip-tide gouged-out trenches serve
As a depository for the purloined granules pilfered by the surf.

The cliff overlooking the beach writhes at the vicious gang-bang
That pins down the spread-eagled beach gasping for life and
Hemorrhaging with every devastating pounce, blow and thrust.
Sensing its ultimate altercation with the adversaries, the cliff
Releases all its breccia to alert interested conservationists.

Complacently, the beach-goers overlook the treachery and
desolation.
They procrastinate, hesitate and fail to legislate for preservation.
With hurricane force, the water is driven to the base of the cliff.
The ocean and wind revel in their rape and annihilation.

Finally there is no more beach.

Bill Albin

An Odd Woman?

Old Charley was a character, you see and a stage-driver of some worth
He was also a registered Democrat for long years since his birth.
Charley farmed and built a cabin he was a lumber-jack within a mill
He strayed around this far-off land
Through forest, beach and sandy foothill!
He wore tailored coats and hand-made boots
A broad gray hat - with buck-skin glove
He had a patch over his one eye
And was never known to fall in love!
He swore like a sailor, tobacco he chewed
There were notches in the gun he carried
He was known to never miss a spittoon
Of course, Charley had never married!
He cut a colorful past in our hist'ry pages
He was assured of fortune and fame
Old Charley joined up with the Odd Fellows
That colorful character in stance and name!
Poor Charley died in 1879 an undertaker truthfully notified
Then the revelation-Charley was no fellow
But The First Odd-woman Who'd Ever Lied!

Elma M. Rasor

Tortured Heart

Your letter came today.
The one from you so far away.
A letter of no greater importance could I ever receive.

My heart raced as I reached
To grasp the wonderful, treasure that was here at last
From one so significant to my past.

Quickly, I retrieved the coveted parcel
And held it closely to my breast
As if you were here, for me to softly caress.

I gently pulled the letter out
And gazed upon the words your sent.
A feeling of great comfort began to come upon me.

But, all too soon had I begun
To transmit warm memories from our past
When the words you wrote, told of another who has your heart.

Alas, what to do when, a fling turned into the real thing!
And, all I have now and forever
Is a tortured heart that remains.

Rebecca Rhoden

To a Torn Tendon

Do I need every muscle
Given to me by grace—
Or God's wisdom . . .
Can I live with pain?

I can live with drought . . .
And the wish for wisdom
To worship the coming . . .
—Of the rain!
Oh, there are many modes
And ways to run an engine,
And sure the Great Power
Is privy to them all.
Like all . . . by chains and power
Mine is driven.

But function is not but sinews and tendons
Nor mere the bursas of motion
Not mere the magic of muscle . . .
But the awesome beauty
Of the soul . . . driven
By the Power of the Mind!

David Glaser

Ryan's Poem

A dove raises, spreading wings
So pure is its color
So elegant it flows
Bringing light to all

A crow flies by, encompassing the beauty
Grey darkens the clouds
Enveloping the blue skies
Bringing dark to our light

Slowly the dove climbs
Overcoming the clouds of darkness
Elegance begins to shimmer
The light begins to break

The light illuminates, shining in full
The dove delights in the light
But the crow's darkness rebounds
Not for the dove, but for us

Mary Ellen Schmidt

Dancing With The Moon

The music drifts around
Penetrating the very essence of me.
Beating drums with floating notes
Tease and chant, you can be free.

Magically enlightened...
I move from where I sat,
Grabbing my tattered dreams,
While putting on my fancy hat,

I let the shield break
For just a little while.
And I loosen the heaviness
I've carried mile after mile.

Feet start dancing, unrelenting
Till melody and I are one.
The giant, golden moon hovers above,
Waiting for battle with self to be done.

Who would believe...
I could run from me in a tune.
And long into the night,
Be found dancing with the moon.

Jan Clements

Dyslexia

The words to her were crowded now
the letters wavy, the vowels small

In her heart she dreamed of when
it would be all right again

To struggle slowly through in her mind
she dreamed of scenes of a greater kind

The written word could be so slow but
only those with Dyslexia know

Keep on trying, inner strength for maybe
someday it will all make sense

To have intelligence, to have those dreams,
to be stilted by the words it seems

Would others know or even care
that for some this reading is a snare

Are there answers no, only struggle
probably reading is too much trouble

But not for a few, the will persists for
I know it firsthand, I have seen it exist

Tame those words, reverse those vowels
keep on dreaming, maybe tomorrow

Maureen C. Thomas

The Man I Love

The man I love
  is no longer mine
  (and really never was).

He said one thing, yet
  did another
  (tongue, like a velvet glove).

When we were young
  we met,
  (fell profoundly "in love").

The things we shared
  the fun we had
  (oh, the joys and pleasure).

It's hard to say, even today
  how to figure, how to measure
  (What happened?) (Why did he - - -)?

How did we drift apart?
  Little by little, and quite completely
  (he simply broke my heart).

Mary Graliker

Royal Flush

Libby and her deuces wild machine
She will hold an A, K, J, 10 even a Queen
Expecting a Royal Flush right now
The odds are better for a big brown cow

She pours the quarters in one by one
The winning hand does not come
"You have to invest," she will say
So she pours them in day by day

I think she will never learn
Only the winning she will yearn
But, then again who can tell
The Royal Flush may come as well

Wilfred L. Deyo

A Walk In Autumn

When cares become a bit too much
I take the time to roam -
I walk out across the valley floor
and take the ridge road home.
Before it's time to light the lamps,
just after evening chores,
I walk through scattered leaves
Flung on this valley's floor.
The slowly rising moon becomes
a white quiet orb that glows
and there upon the silent fields
white frost foretells the snows.
There's time to contemplate and workers,
Aside from toil and strife
To seek out messages of the heart
And reflect upon the good in life.
The hay fields glister, glossy - gold
as I take the time to room.
The valley awaits the winter
as I talk the ridge road home.

George Chenette

Judgement Day

The day has come when man
is done and he is judge by the Son.
The oceans rise and the land
dies and the wind becomes great
and then nothing flies.
The ground will crack and buildings
will fall and then great fire will
cover us all. When everything is
gone a white dove will sing a song
and trumpets will sound and then
the water will go down. The land
will rise and the Son will come
down to revive our lives and a
great kingdom will arise before
our eyes. The air will be clean
and the water will be pure and
the land will be beautiful all over the world.
The Son will raise, His arms in the sky
and birds and animals will appear
before our eyes.

John Kusmirek

City

Unforgiving
Restless
Scared
You are.
Citadel of cracked cement;
Broken windows, damaged streets.

Thumping, grinding,
That's your music.

Your shelterless shelter
Sends many to your door.
Oh, city of dreams and opportunities,
It might be wiser to breathe first,
Sell papers later.

For time seems to crunch you into segments,
Crush you into dismal parts.

As soulless as you are,
Your heart beats strong,
As darkness is the only real light you know.

joni starr

The Golden Palace

Far beyond the sands,
The golden palace stands
On rocks where I like to kick,
Into water, foggy and thick
Where bodies cannot go people have gone,
Where images appear only at dawn
Imagination first you call,
Then step through a waterfall
Catch a dolphin to the rocks,
But first take off your shoes and socks
All around it the sea parts,
For incoming people and their sweethearts
How to get there you might ask,
But it is not a very long task
You can't go by plane or train,
You must go through the back of your brain
To wherever it might be,
Wherever you might like to see
Your golden palace

Bethany Whiteside

Child of My Dreams

She comes to me at each break of day
Me, hearing, before I see her
As pretending I still be in slumber
She, climbing up, snuggling closer.

Her so small hands wend their way
In same game she ever plays
Fingers feeling around my lips, my eyes
She ever trying to tantalize.

As gently I enfold her close
I look into her laughing eyes
Then, awakening from each night repose
Each day I awake to realize....

That ever longing, wishful dream
Why do you ever haunt me?
As this imaginary daughter I see
So each morn expect to awaken me.

For yes, it has been my lifetime dream
I ever dream in wishful slumber
Ever to see, to hold, that child of my dreams
But have never really known her!

Edwin P. Spivey

Take A Good Look!

Like a sad old clown, nobody sees
what's really going on inside of me.

A painted smile, a little laugh,
nobody knows where I'm really at.

I'll come on strong, you won't
know what to expect, then
I'll tell you a joke and cry while you laugh.

If I act like a child, don't be
surprised, 'cause that's how I
deal with life, it helps me get by.

When I scream, nobody hears
me, then I cry, nobody sees
me; if I died would anybody
miss me?

Dominic Pelliccio

Advice

We hear that dogs are man's best friends,
    Because they don't give advice,
Yet few folks are straightened out
    Without advice, once or twice.

If advice is not perfect,
    Or if it is too, too right,
It may offend advisees,
    Then rapport falls out of sight.

We must be diplomatic
    Being right can cause a sore,
If we don't rub in gently,
    We might even start a war.

Giving advice is difficult,
    No matter how we shake it;
Why don't we quit dishing out,
    And instead learn to take it?

William A. Paff

Youthful Gray

Even though my hair is gray
I'm full of life in every way.
I never say I wish I were young
'Cause I'm youthful gray in every way.
Negativity is not a part of me
I do positive affirmations every day.
My health is good; my mind is clear.
My youthfulness gives me the will
To erase all the stress from within
And keep my mind on a healthful trip.
I never feel that I'm getting old
I'm only getting mellow, like vintage wine
Who's taste gets better with time.
So when your hair starts turning gray
Don't think of it as getting old.
Just think of it as youthful gray.

Ray Rivera

Farewell

I hoped he'd stay, yet somehow knew
He wouldn't, though his heart was true.
Some gypsy blood coursed through his veins.
He stared at cars, long lines of trains,
And aeroplanes across the bay,
These called him and they made him say,
He'd leave me, not for long, but just
Until he lost his wanderlust.
I cheered and danced and waved "good-bye"
With lips that smiled and eyes so dry,
He never knew for all these years,
My heart lay drowning in my tears.

Marita Esche

Memories

    Don't go there —
For you may find, you still care.
You may find only regrets.
You can't win, that's a sure bet.
    Don't go there, late at night.
For your dreams may tell everything alright.
We both know that isn't true.
For there is still only you and you.
    Don't go there in the early morning dawn.
Memories may haunt you.
When you're alone.
Turn around and walk away.
Yesterday gone, live today.
    Don't go there.

Ethel C. Wynn

Star of Bethlehem

I saw the Star of Bethlehem,
Shining in the sky,
Here in my country,
The United States of America.

It shines as bright,
As it did almost 2,000 years ago,
When it shined that night,
In Bethlehem, when Jesus was born.

I was blessed to go to Israel,
I saw the Star of Bethlehem,
It was as bright, in that land,
As it is in this land of mine.

The Star of Bethlehem,
That led the way for the Shepherds,
To the Manger, where the tiny Baby lay,
Jesus Christ, our Lord and Saviour today.

Thank you God, for the Star of Bethlehem,
The bright Morning Star, forever seen,
It will shine forever, and ever, and ever.
It will glow throughout all eternity.

Connie James

All God's Creatures

I had a dream last night
    about a grizzly bear I slew
So totally out of character for me
    because it's something I could not do.

God put creatures on earth
    just as He did like you and me
With never an intent to kill
    any part of His creativity.

We are all God's creatures
    no matter what our size
From huge gorillas in West Africa
    to little tiny flies.

Supposedly man is a superior being
    so why do we go to war
Killing each other with abandon
    something God would abhor.

Of course insects and bugs annoy
    especially ants, mosquitos and flies
But who are we to decide
    if their lives should be denied?

William Henry Jones

Waiting On Love

Many times you've appeared
and seen me at my times most teared.
But knowing you to know me better
I won't let that affect this letter.

So in treatise I may add at once,
if you'd only acted as you should
To not call me and say you would,
You're not acting your part very good.

Or is this not a part you play
but only words you waste away.
Or have I another story confused
And you really wait outside bemused?

For golden hair to unravel below
So you can take it all in tow.
And kindle back to flame that fire;
for while Rapunsel waits; time does
expire.

Elizabeth Ann Maslow

God In A Box

Be it so that what they say
Is only that from preachers lay.
Fear of fear, and fear they sell,
Believe their way or "go to hell."

They spout their verse, then count the bucks
And want the milk the baby sucks.
For those who give and give it all,
Rewards will be at that "Great Call."

Gain for gain, an age old trick,
Profit fare and thank "Old Nick."
Short account evangelic nags
Get one to heaven in rented cabs.

We speak with God and hear Him not;
Some shepherds hear Him like a shot.
The proving point - a single verse;
To thus refute it brings a curse.

God help us from those "chosen few"
Who boxed Him in their rotten pew.
Shall they leave their house in order
When they reach that final border?

Lyle McLeod

There Are

Those who look but do not see,
are blind to all there is to be —
Those who speak but do not say,
are mute for words they can't convey.

Those who love but do not speak,
their silence cloaks the heart that beats —
Those who think, but never do,
are prone to shrink from all that's new.

Those who sleep but never dream,
are bound to earth, or so it seems
to those whose life is make believe
who lift men's sights, before they leave.

Those who seek, but never find
the happiness, they leave behind —
those who walk thru barren land
and leave no footprints in the sand.

Clark S. Beardslee

The Beauty of a Smile

It's wonderful that God
    gave humans and ability to smile.
A friendly smile to someone and a nod
    will make you feel better, no matter your style.

There are all kinds of smiles, if you will
    but look and see on happy children at play.
Smiles given to people that are sad and ill
    to brighten their lives along the way.
Smiles of triumph when goals are achieved
    to start them on their life's ambition.
Rising from the bottom to the top it's believed,
    like it or not — Smile — it's tradition —

Bride the groom smile happily on their wedding day.
    Even though they have cake smeared faces.
When it's time to go home everyone will say
    with a smile, you can take it back to Macy's . . . .

Wide smiles, tiny smiles, shy smiles some are just giggles and grins.
Smiles with or without teeth, adult's or child's.
    Smiles that crinkle and twinkle the eyes always wins
The Heart of the Lord, He loves to see a smile!!!

Virginia J. Brady

The World Needs Healing

Jesus heal the world mind, that it may focus on your second coming and not get left behind.

Heal the world eyes to help it see, all of satan deceiving lies.

Heal the world arms, so they can wrap around every race, creed and color, protecting them all from bodily harm.

Jesus heal the world hands, to hold back the wars set out to destroy man.

Heal the world heart, for it is filled with destructive foolishness, trying to keep many others from seeking to be Godly smart.

Lord Jesus King of heaven and earth, heal the world feet so it will boldly stand up behind every follower, who are preparing to meet you with a holy greet.

Ricky Clemons

Photographer

Thundering, thundering, crash, boom
Windows blown open, angel's wings flapping, riding on the wind
Woke us from sleep, cuddling deep, aroused, loving you
While the lightning flashes, frisky, snatching snapshots in the dark
Lighting your manpower, loving your embrace, loving you passionately
Like the passionate storm
Our thunderstorm voyeur, touching, tickling, sneezing showers of
    delight
Sprinkles flown in by the wind, sprinkled on our intertwined love,
Like salt on hot peppers
Iridescent diamond chips of rain sat on your raven chest hairs,
A microscopic view, alien creatures played on your heaving chest
We were like little children running through the rain, laughing,
    kissing,
Dripping
Angel's wings were set free, and wrapped around you and me
While lightning clicked snapshots, the wind stole a kiss
As it blew across our lips
And we'll always remember our thunderstorm . . .   photographer.

Diana Dolhancyk

Women's Work

Greek men sit at little tables
in little plazas
drinking little coffees
while Greek women weave and knit
In ancient Greece, too, women did the work
In Athens on the Acropolis
see the Caryatides
priestesses from Caryae
their heads holding up the Erechtheion,
a building named, of course, after a man.
Legend says they were being
punished for some wickedness
but modern scientists think
it was only custom,
let the women do the work.
and they look so beautiful working.
In Delphi, see the column: dancers
frozen in marble, frozen in time,
forever giving pleasure
Women.

Barbara R. DuBois

Home Is Where the Heart Is

The long country road where I walked as a child,
I travel now by car.
A city has sprung, overnight it seems,
No farms, no cattle, but a bar!

Woods where the wildflowers grew are gone,
Replaced by poles and wires;
"Progress" it's called, the word baffles me,
Knowledge I'm slow to acquire.

The old family home still stands you see,
It has stood for a hundred years,
In a little corner of God's green earth,
Sheltering joy and tears.

I'm home again, for a visit at least,
It seems but yesterday,
I packed my bags and went into the world,
To live and make my own way.

"You can't go home again," it's said,
For things are never the same;
Still, nostalgia reigns and love conquers all,
How happy am I that I came!

Anna Hoffman

To Josh, My Gold Medalist Grandson

Others may be Olympic winners in various sports
But, you're a winner on and off the courts.
An Olympian must work hard to perfect their skills
And can only do this while in their prime,
When still young enough, and able to shine.
The competition is tremendous, from all the
   countries in the world,
A chance to win a medal comes only once every four years,
And if an Olympian fails to win,
They are overwhelmed with sadness and tears.
So, I'm very happy that you're not an Olympian.
But, my gold medalist grandson, Josh.
Hope you like the gold medal that I made just for you.
Though it's not an Olympic one, you're a winner every day,
Twelve months each year, in every way.
You don't need to pressure yourself, or work hard to excel,
It just comes naturally that you always do well.
You don't have to hire a trainer, as you do it on your own
You're not scheduled for long hours of practice daily,
Until you're physically exhausted and bodily ailing.

Irene Kanter

What's Up Doc?

"When a person reaches that certain age,
Their hearing may be at a loss —
My spouse and I will have hearing tests,
To find out just what is the cause."

"The audiologist is a well-known Doctor,
We are to see him today —
Perhaps we'll need two hearing aids,
To hear what others say."

"So what's another Doctor,
To add to the other eight? —
We hope that Medicare will do their share,
And my insurance will participate."

"What's the next thing that can happen?,
It's terrible to get old —
Why can't we enjoy life to the fullest?
Why are we hot, when we should be cold?"

"It's one Doctor after the other,
They keep us on the run —
We dread that day will never come,
When we won't be able to have any fun."

Marty Rollin

Roads

Isn't it funny how we all walk down the same roads
Then again the same road is different for each of us
Through our journey good and bad
There are many roads we choose along the way
Why do we let go of some
Yet cling to others
Sometimes we make the wrong choice
Other times we make the right choice
How do we know which choice to make
I wish I had the answers
Remember the right choice for some is the wrong choice for others
Just remember you can always choose another road along the way

Laurie L. Smith

Farmer Thomas Parr

In Westminister Abby, he now lies asleep,
   With Kings, Queens, Poets and other nobility.
No merit acclaim for knowledge deep
   Being a farmer was his only ability
Other than his endless tales and quick wit
   Healthy heart and permeability of blood and life
Did penance for fathering a child illegit
   At one hundred and five — after he took a wife
At eighty and a second at one hundred twenty-two
   Thriving on farm food — healthy — with pulsation of life
Got an invitation received by very few
   From King Charles I - to live at palace for life
His majesty to entertain and amuse
   No more of those simple country eats
Rich Royal Banquets really blew his fuse
   He lustily stuffed himself into defeat
And dropped dead after a four hour gorge
   At the ripe old age of one hundred-fifty two
His claim to fame was his age — by George
   And now he rests peacefully with the noble few.

Giula S. Wiggs

The Untold Story

Where do I start? Do you start with pain . . .
Do you start with part of your heart, or vain
Hopeful, wishful thinking. In the beginning-but no
Lets not relive the joys, the hopes, the dreams,
Start with the realization that life's not what you
Thought it could be — in the center then . . .
No then you're caught in the thin web of illusion
And cannot see the pit falls, and the endless agony!

Shall I, from the ending start with disillusioning
Blending with dashed hopes and plans, in distorted
Contemplation ban the hope of time healing the wounds
Of gaping scars, that twist the heart!
It is better not to tell the story at all
For none can learn — except the lesson's their own
I cannot save one heart, from tearing apart, because
I would not be the source of damming up a heart
Against love: For to love is an enriching of the soul
And some may reach a healing goal.

Bernice Brigham

The Biggest Flowerpot

It might have been a lemon. The yellow convertible must have been
falling apart. Obviously it would never run again, for it was
filled with soil and parked in the yard. The space that had once
been the front seat and the back seat of the car was now filled
with a multitude of colorful flowers that must have been planted,
watered, and weeded by a person with a tender loving heart. Now
the beautiful yellow convertible flowerpot is a floral work of art.

Alyce M. Nielson

Checkmate

I gave it all to you, all the years of waiting
For the stranger at the gate,
The horseman of a million dreams
Standing proud outside my door.
I gave it all to you, hoarded up like treasure,
All the times of loneliness and pain,
All my young days staring at the rain
All the laughter and the love flung down
Like flowers or a glove. Was it wasted on a fool?
Thrown to a jester on the stair.
Was there a mystery I didn't see,
A quality of heart that slipped away from me,
Leaving only shadowed reflections in a pool?
Was it wasted on a fool?
Was that all it meant to you, or was
The timing simply off a century or two.

Nancy Fitz-Gerald Viens

Thoughts About a Night of Passion

She thinks — will this be the night
I think I may, I think I might
Just the thought of him makes
Me want to fly free like a kite
I hope he doesn't take this important
Step in our relationship light
I imagine everything going right
But if I change my mind will there be a vocal fight
Because I would still love to wear
A traditional wedding gown of white

He thinks — I would like tonight to be our night
But in my heart I question if this will be alright
An evening of passion must never be
Taken for granted for that isn't right
The sight of her, makes my hormones
Soar with delight
Well it's just about time to meet
I won't apply any pressure
I'll let the evening be
Whatever both our hearts dictate

Sandra Glassman

The Bride and Groom

The bride on his arm had such a radiant glow on her face
it would brighten the saddest of hearts, accompanied by a
spring in her step as if walking on air, expressing lightness
of heart.

Looking handsome in black tux the groom had a sway to his
stride from the angel he held on his arm by his side. She was
his to love and to cherish till death us do part through the sanction
of God they'd impart, as happiness shared shone brightly through
eyes of love felt deeply from the heart.

Her gown of soft slippery satin was exquisite in every way with
webbed lace, self colored satin ribbon bows and seed pearls
displayed in various shapes.

We toasted congratulations as they embarked on their unknown
path of life ahead with hopes of dreams come true, adding in a
whisper, "We'll pray for you."

If they will but put their faith in the guidance of God's hand,
many blessing they will share and calm of mind will stand.

Marolyn E. Baker

To My Daughter With Love

I remember the day you were born as though it was yesterday,
and when I held that helpless tiny bundle in my arms,
all my fears, hopes and dreams went rushing through me,
but love and faith came shining through,
and I knew deep down inside that things would turn out just fine.
As we started down the path of life, growing and learning together,
the years just seemed to slip away before my very eyes,
and suddenly you were no longer my little girl,
but a young women walking down the isle on your wedding day.
But through it all, we've learned a lot, you and I,
and we have become more than just a mother and daughter,
we have also become friends.
And there is nothing I would change, even if we had to start it all
over again.

Carol Fox

Giving Thanks

How do I thank you for the joy in my heart?
How do I thank you and where would I start?
Do I start with your love that I humbly receive
For my husband, my children, or their love for me?
For your son that you gave us to erase our sin?
How do I thank you Lord, where would I begin?
Shall I begin with the trees, the field's or the flowers in bloom?
Will it be the sun, the stars, the planets, or maybe the moon?
The snow capped mountains or the valleys below...
How do I thank you Lord, help me to know.
Could it be the goodness of your children when they
lend a helping hand?
Or the shouts of "hallelujah" heard across your
promised land?
How do I thank you for these gifts you've given to me?
I will thank you Lord, with every breath of life
that I breathe...

Cathy E. Hugill

An Apology for Christmas

The flashing lights which come with modern Christmastide,
The tinsel's glare, and all the fuss and muss
At times may turn our thoughts away from Jesus
And from what his birth on earth can mean to us.

With the baking and the plans for merrymaking
And the buying and the tying of the gifts,
We may ignore the painful sacrifice he made us
And the awful load which from us all it lifts.

But, as long as Christmas turns our hearts toward others,
Can one say the Christmas spirit's burning dim?
What we do unto the "least of these," our brothers,
Jesus tells us we have also done to Him.

Robert L. Brown

What the World Did

Remember well the Jewish children we sent to hell!!
They're now playing in heavenly fields hence
from whence the bells of Christ do toll
let us now hold the heart of a child's soul
and resurrect ourselves from graves cold

What we did to a Jewish kid
Gassed him hard to the land of the dead
God did not abandon this Hebrew child
to the hate of a world gone mad and wild

The children rest peacefully high above a holy cloud
and angels in the sun sing to the wee ones praises so very loud
for God is of the Israeli child very proud

Allan H. Lambert

Epitaph

A resident of Abyssville takes a stroll,
Longing for love and happiness.
He gains temporary solace from rock-and-roll,
A break from pursuing self destructiveness.

Amazement that one can still exist;
This nowhere, nothing citizen.
Disappointment and frustration persist;
Defeating all hope for this streetwise denizen.

Great promise unfulfilled.
Chance after chance blown.
Regrets stirred in turmoil and chilled.
The diminished one so alone.

Our hero's every function seems past tense;
Remembered instead of witnessed.
Continuance of the being heightens the suspense;
Only an idiot could miss the bitterness.

One's own epitaph to compose;
The only remaining glory.
Some vindication for a loser at the close;
A whisper ends the story.

Ken Miller

Star Light, Star Bright

We met on the swings in the park at night,
and wished upon the first star bright...
Wished we may, wished we might,
have the wish we wished that night.

Many memories we made in the park,
happily swinging away in the dark.
We'd talk for hours - you and I...
we'd scream, we'd sing, we'd laugh, we'd cry.

I think of you now as I round the park,
passing the swings - alone in the dark.
I stop to look up at the first star bright...
and wish I may, wish I might
have the wish I wish tonight...

I wish you'd see the same star too,
and wish that I were there with you!

Sheril M. Shue

Counterfeit Truths

Deceit is among the worst of our foes
enhancing truths into ribbons of lies
that wrap around honesty its bright bows
to garnish a package for trusting eyes

Such elegant grandeur lures attention
displaying to all, slick counterfeit truths
while its established anticipation
slyly lurks amid a pretext that soothes

All its appeal, bred by our own desires:
The lust of the eyes, our flesh, and life's pride
will equate success to riches acquired
misrepresenting what fulfills inside

Counterfeits feed you whatever you want
you name it, you got it...anything goes
yet having feasted, the soul remains gaunt
daily ingesting the bread of sorrows

There's only One who satisfies all voids
and His Truth...deceit would have you forget
hoping instead its whispering tabloids
can prove "God is dead"...the biggest lie yet!

Bob G. Martinez

The Performance

When fishing - you get another catch.
In tennis - you have another match;

More laps with swimming, skating, and racing cars...
And in golf, it's 18 holes and numerous pars;

There's another mountain when you ski,
And you get three periods in hockey;

In football - for each ten yard gain - four downs,
When boxing - you get up to fifteen rounds;

With basketball - rebounds, and shot after shot,
In volleyball, another side out's what you've got;

In baseball, three strikes - and more innings too,
And bowling has ten two-shot frames for you;

Even soccer has two halves, you see..
But a performance offers only one opportunity;

No second chance - no corrections - be fine...
It must be perfect the very first time!

J. Louise McClure

The Immigrant

Strange the land that I chose to live in,
Strange the tongue which greeted me,
Strange the sight, and strange the laughter,
Strange was everything to me.

Years went by and the strangeness left me,
and I spoke the strangers tongue.
I understood the life they live here,
I understood the way it is run.

And in time I grew apart of which I called the stranger's land.
Now it is home and I will live here.
I am proud to be accepted in the great and glorious land.

Anna F. Haberzettl

Fear!

Roses are red and that is the color of blood.
As I wander down the streets of Auschwitz,
I see bodies lying in puddles of mud.
I see a man holding his wife.
I see an officer holding a knife.
There is a Kapo whipping a boy with a hard stick.
How do people get a kick out of watching poor people get sick?
Some are meek, some are bold, some are warm but,
   most of them are cold.
I see mom.
I see dad.
I see everybody decaying with mold.
The sight I see is not the right to see.
And I still say, why, why do people hate each other?
And, I will still pray that this shall never happen to another.

Lauren A. Coen

Be On Your Guard

There are times in your life
When you do not know who will come to your door.
There are people that you will take care of
That could be an Angel in disguise,
You just don't know who it will be,
Or when they might come.
So be kind to everyone,
Because one day,
You never know,
You could be taking care of
An Angel of God's.

Velma Carpenter

Of Silk and Thorns

Thoughts and textures of the day lonely rooms
cold beer and sunshine — the label starts to slip as the smile . . .
As the world changes the face it offers
too fast for some, a painful acceptance or not.
Somewhere a man pushes the barrel of a .38 in his mouth right now
another cuts her wrists damning the names of lost love
out there babies come and go
a grey-haired gentleman in fetal position
curled up with vacant eyes
last protest a whispered sigh remembering . . .
Jellybeans
A brother
Cool dark wood of a bar now closed
songs or movies, smells and dreams
hot coffee in a cold kitchen
before the day begins.

Kyle McCormick

The Rose

The rose was so large that it stood among the other flowers;
towering like the Empire State Building.
It was a shade of pink, as shade like the sunset in June.
As I moved closer to the rose I could see drops of dew on the petals.
The drops of dew, shimmered like crystal in the morning sun.

I reached down and picked the rose from the beautiful bunch of flowers
  in the garden.
The thorns from the stem of the rose, stabbed at my hands as I tried
  to hold it.
I let of the rose and watched as it hit the ground.

After time had passed, the old withered rose,
with its wilting, petals looked like an old woman sad and dying.

For the petals were no longer the color of sunshine,
and they looked as if they were weeping,
right before they slipped off the dying rose.

But, when I look back and remember, I see a rose that is a soft bed;
all satin and smooth, and it looks like a trellis
climbing high to reach the angels.
For that is a far better sight to remember than the old withered rose
that I let fall to the ground and die.

Cerissa Park

Mary's Garden

How's your garden my friend?
Do you still grow the atomic waste
  that my children are dying from?
Does your fertilizer of drugs work
  as well as it should.
There has been enough violence
  raining down upon your garden's blossom.
May I pick the flower whose black
  petals reach - up for the sky?
The pollen of disease that spreads
  by the force of the wind.
Mary, you aren't the only one tending
  the garden.
Everyone has helped make your hate
  grow and bloom.
Mary, Mary quite contrary,
How does your garden grow?

Tina Liu

Unspoken Love

The first time we embraced
  And you shared with me your thoughts,
Laughter and smile,
  I knew it was your Unspoken Love.

When you opened your heart and
  Accepted me for who I am - my dreams, strengths, and weak-
nesses,
Though the words never uttered your lips
  I felt it was Unspoken Love.

Once we became friends, we decided to give and share endlessly,
  Pursue our dreams
Understanding each other's individuality.
  It was then we gave Unspoken Love.

For the countless times you shared your heart
  By letting me share those moments in equal beside you
Fulfilling me with your comfort and strength when I was weary,
  To me it was Unspoken Love.

Once we are of one mind, body and spirit
  Sharing only one dream and lifetime,
It will be too
  Unspoken Love.

Rosalani D. Jackson

Season of Joy

Christ is born, and He is the reason,
We celebrate each Christmas season.
For He was born on Christmas day,
And there He was laid in sweet smelling hay.

For a lowly manger in a stable bare,
Was the only room to be had anywhere.
The animals were the only witness of His birth,
And with soft sounds welcomed this King come to earth.

Angels filled the heavens with songs of joy.
Proclaiming the birth of this tiny boy.
Shepherds were listening and left their flocks on the hill,
And followed a bright star through the evening chill.

Wisemen were led by a brightly shining star,
Each followed a road traveling from countries afar.
They came together at the place of His birth,
And worshiped Him with gold, frankincense, and myrrh.

Today as we come together with our families,
And celebrate with food, fun and Christmas trees,
Lets remember the birth of this tiny baby boy,
Who is Christ the Lord, our King and the reason for this joy.

Caroline Priest

Who Is She?

She is a mother.
She was a wife,
She met challenges in life.
Yet, now she is a wife no more,
The children far away need no mothering.
She is alone day after day after day...
Days and nights are mixed up.
She personifies pathos.
Neighbors pity her.
Why this human waste?
Was she coddled too much?
Or not enough?
Did she care about others?
Or too much about herself?
Did nutrients for mind and body avoid her door?
Empathize with the confused woman.
Today, determine such fate shall not await you.

Ruth Weiner

Falling Dreams

Leaves falling seem to remind
   Remind of past and future dreams
Each one shaped in a fashion of its own
   Each one borne by one tiny thought
A thought put their by the creator
   The creator who formed each leaf in intricate detail

As well as the one who stands in owe
   Considering the dreams as they fall
The one who ponders dreams of the past
   Tossed aside in lieu of other goals
Dreams of the future, not yet spoken
   Waiting there to be exposed
Like the falling leaves in their golden splendor.
    Johnna Lawrence

Sisters

Silly, laughing, boisterous joy,
Inextricably woven through our tapestry of love
Blurs the lines of our shared histories, but not quite.

Sharp, piercing, stabbing pain
Connects in sad memories your nakedness and mine
Aching to release the pain, to share it all with you,
But not quite enough.

For years the stark images remained
Black and white - the demarcations of our separate lives
While in our hearts, the boundaries begged to shatter,
But never quite enough.

And now, it would seem, we have come full circle
From love to hate, through the halls of anger and ambivalence
To love again and treasure the woman, child we see,
To consign to each other, in warm embrace,
The custodies of our complicated souls, but not quite.
    Jennifer Gorman Ritter

The Manifold of Senses

Hear the manifold of senses combine
Magnifying the intellect with intricate muse
All earthly experiences to define
Nature's gifts of description to be used.

What fragrances have been foretold
Resplendent in function and healing
From land and sea these wonders unfold
Enjoy! Perhaps revere their mystical meaning.

Oh, taste what life itself reveals
Through bitter and through sweet
Aesthetic values or basic needs
In all their nuances we meet.

Touch is a complement of sight
For when we cannot thoroughly see
We use our fingers in the plight
To aid the journey of discovery.

Yet, sight is masterful in its scope
In physical and abstract domains
It grants perception, peace and hope
A visionary collage to attain.
    Joyce P. Holder

Night Song

Hush, My Love, and close your eyes,
   The night has come with its gentle sighs,
The music will be starting soon
   Now that it's night and all's in tune.

The moon sends down her silvery rays,
   Which form the strings that nature plays.
The trees all sing in mellow note,
   When through their branches breezes float.

The tiny brook pauses in its quest,
   And joins the rhythm of the rest.
And so there's music for the ear
   Of the dreamer who stops to hear
   this soft and peaceful simple nocturne.

Yes, the night does sing —
   In its own refrain,
A song I love,
   But can't explain...
    Syd Clark

The Mountain Road

Life is like a mountain road —
   the signs enroute can make you doubt

Welcome to the National Park
   What an adventure to embark

Caution: Steep incline
   Will I make it or is this a sign?

Scenic overlook ahead on right
   What a sight? Can I get there by tonight?

Detour: Fallen Rock
   Now I'll never beat the clock

Danger: Use alternate route
   Why me? Why were others given safe pursuit?

Lookout tower around next bend
   I made it! Now, where's the next mountain!

Life is like a mountain road —
   the twists and turns can make you yearn
    Kelli A. Crane

The Trees Sing

When the wind blows, the trees sing
   a brand new song each time that the wind blows.

The strength of the mighty winds
   causes the trees to dance.

The sound of clapping is everywhere.

Listen!

Hear the sound that the wind makes
   as it touches things in its path.

The power of God is made known
   in a brand new song that the trees sing
   each time that the wind blows.

See the rustling of the leaves
   as the wind hurry to teach the trees
   a brand new song to sing.

"Sing a new song!" The wind commands
   as it directs the trees to dance.

It Orchestrates the gentle breeze,
   and choreographs the rushing leaves.

So, learn to sing the trees' song
   it's simply a song of praise to God!
    Lemmie J. Greer

21

The Leaf

High above heads, life about to begin
Soft tugging breeze pulls with gentle embrace
Fair auburn flashes on wandering face
Skittish swirls loft it in beds of wind

Embracing breeze in dance rescind
Always aware, being its fragile place
Enjoying new wonder, childlike pace
Falling currents and rhythm again
Arrayed, fine surroundings comes to rest
Living quietly, bed of cozy friends
Innocent sensation impinging surface
Unaware of its short elegant end

Brushes sing along forgiving unrest
Shimmering daylight airing clean terrace

Timothy Taylor Moermond

"Crash"

A cup shatters as a heart breaks in two.
Words are thrown at the mind as a child huddles in a corner.
The shards of glass are picked up as crystal tears fall from his eyes.
Arms are hitting as folds are covering the pain with darkness.
Silence.
The child is no longer here.

Leah Haak

Seasonal Changes

The wind blows in my face, and the hair on my back seems to stand
in respect to the great north wind.

The birds of the north fly down to the south
in hope of a sweet haven of rest.

As the wimter brings forth long nights and short days,
life becomes a peaceful drama of snowflakes tapping on the
window-sill.

As the wild beasts of the fields close their eyes to go to sleep,
so I find my weary body cuddling under the quilted sheet.

Almost always I find myself drifting away into pleasant thoughts
of Mister Snowman dressed up in his top hat and multicolored scarf
and Saint Nicholas drifting through the sky with a sleigh full of toys.

But, oh! I can not forget the reason there seem to be
a peaceful air on Christmas Eve:
the incarnation that reconciles creation with Creator.

No sooner than I blink my eyes do the snowflakes stop,
and the animals pop their tiny heads out of their resting place.

With twinkles in my eyes, I rush to the window to see the flowers
bloom and hear the birds sing a sweet melody.

Sharon E. Spencer

"Ultimate"

The rarest portion of life's is sincerity,
The greatest, kindness,
The most satisfying, the untroubled mine,
The most difficult to encounter, a swelled head,
That which is most desired,
A true friend, who always takes time to
Understand,
The hardest to endure, selfishness,
The most aggregative, prejudice,
That which is most admired, courage,
What it needed most in our short but
Meaningful lives is, faith, in our fellow man.

William A. Frazier

Welcome Friends

Welcome friends, how good of you to come and see me,
What a pleasant surprise, your face up-lifts, it recalls.
Pull up a chair and let us sit down and talk after lunch,
Stay longer here, if you wish, for a while, for you brought,
Sunshine to those glaring eyes, and a smile on thy face.
Welcome friends, have a delicious cup of coffee - on me,
Forget your cares, remember, two can share a meal.
Welcome friends, I say that from the bottom of my heart,
You sure took away the chill of this summer weather.
I see the warmth of that springtime dissolving, when it rains,
And after the days have gone astray, the wonder stays.
The fact was,that you two had enough care to come,
Which means more to me than words can spell.
The light of our friendship glows within our eyes,
When there is time for our gathering.

Eugene Geo Welk

An Empty Room

Here I sit and here I wait
Waiting for you, waiting for you.

Solitary as an oyster, left alone in a corner
Waiting for you, waiting for you.

For the walls here are black
And the walls all are tacked
Sitting in this empty room
Waiting for you, waiting for you.

My empty heart is breaking
As I sit and stare at the blank expressions
On the lifeless walls.

The sun I have not seen in years
For here I sit in this cold and frigid place
Waiting for you, waiting for you.

Will you ever come for me?
I sit and think.

Here I sit and here I wait
Here I'll stay and here I'll sit
With my empty heart
Waiting for you, waiting for you.

Rachel Spence

Fantasy-Maker

Softly in the darkness, my eyes see a sight
A lovely Isle of color with no ray of light

A betwixt and between place
that beckons and dares
Who dwells there now I wonder?
Who answers all my hails?

Fantasy-maker, Fantasy Isle
Our hearts they are bleeding
as we wait with a smile
The fantasy-maker on his fantasy Isle!

He strides now with anger, abusing the crowd
Yet still with desire, we listen and we smile

Dear fantasy-maker, don't gaze at the moon
Reach forth and deliver my wishes, please soon!

And as he begins to chant and to pray
my eyes open wide and he dwindles away
Alone in the light
and my tears fall like rain!

Julie M. Sierra-Montes

My Little Star

I have a little star up in the sky.
It always shines on me.
It brings sun when it rains. Sparkles when its foggy.
It shines rainbows to me through the clouds.
This little star always knows how to make me smile.
So when you look up and see a little star just wish on it.
Because it's your little star.

Hilda C. Fisher

The Dream Maker

    As I sat by the beautiful bay window in the sunshine of the
early morning, I asked the Dream Maker for a perfect day. For days
are made of dreams they say. When we dream we can be anyone we
want to be and envision a different and even better life because
we often regret the things we do and say. Dreams help in making
essential changes that were not previously considered and can give
courage to reach things never thought could be acquired. If only
there was that perfect day when we knew exactly what to do and all
dreams went just the right way. Then in the warm quiet silence
while I sat, I heard the sweet kind voice of the Dream Maker. This
is the recipe for a perfect day...a cupful of kindness with a
pinch of sharing tossed in. Follow this and you can't miss the
Dream Maker went on to say. Then in your heart your dreams will
come true. When you share love with someone new, the love flows
right back to you. Look forward to dreams, for you never know
where they will lead.

Elizabeth Brand

The Gift of Life

What talent one possesses
    Don't keep this locked inside
It deprives the world of wisdom
    One should share it with great pride.
Our world encourages talent
    For this one must compete,
To keep one's talent hidden
    Leaves wisdom hidden deep.
Some share their skills as artists,
    Others see life writing poems,
These talents can be dormant
    If we do not keep them growing.
So share what one possesses
    The door is open to compete
We gain from others knowledge
    What could be hidden deep.

Eleanor Double

Bright Star

In a strange and desolate landscape
    Like some geometric Mars,
I dream I travel through
    A million glittering stars.

Upon its ripples reaching out,
    I glide across a cosmic space;
Embracing a yearning, nascent joy,
    As time and soul interlace.

The feeling of interconnection,
    Birthing a fusion that transcends fear;
Impacts a clarity of Knowledge within me,
    Traversing ancient Music of The Spheres.

A grace and balance enshrines me,
    Within my dreaming mind;
And the fragments of another realm,
    Keep the dream and I...intertwined.

Sharon L. Petek

Thoughts

One day a little boy sat underneath a tree
In a contemplative state he sat, others he did not see

What was this child thinking, as he sat all alone!
It appeared that his thoughts would certainly remain unknown

I wondered what he saw, from the views within his head
Perhaps if I had only asked, the views he might have shed

He did not seem unhappy nor angry, just intent
As his thoughts continued deep inside, he just sat there so content!

I became intensely curious, I thought I might inquire
Anxiously, I wished to tell him, my thoughts he did inspire

I began walking toward him, as he looked the other way
As I started to speak, I could not think of words to say

A fearful thought raced through my mind, to him this might be prying
I turned instead and walked away without speaking, only sighing

Suddenly a voice yelled, "Mom, please come here!"
"You make me feel secure, when you are very near!"

I reached out to hug him, which I hadn't done this day!
We exchanged the words "I love you" dissolving feelings of dismay

It was then I told my son, you can always come to me!
I will help you understand the things you can not see!

Sharon Thayer Kostenbauder

Joshua's Prayer

God bless this little baby and keep him close to you.
Don't blame him for the worlds mistakes or mine too.
The memory of his sweet innocent face
will always live in my heart.
You are a part of me, you are my son.
And for that we will never be apart.

I'm sorry you didn't have a chance to Grow,
Learn and Love.
But now you are in a special place with God above.

You were placed upon angels wings, and carried off that night,
before I could hug you or kiss your
beautiful face, you were out of sight

God bless and keep my little Joshua safe and warm tonight,
hold him in your arms and rock him gently till the morning light.

Maryellen Gambuti

Painful Crimson

Her cautious self commands:
    Uproot this intruding nettle,
    Harshly trample its untimeliness,
    Then flee from its ensuing scent!

Her deep, aching self jealously guards the weed.
No wanton finger shall blemish its crimson blossoms,
No alien breath snuff out the power of its fragrance!
Its sinuating roots drive excruciating forays within her,
    Its prickly crimson blisters her tender heart,
    Yet its insidious perfume subtly pervades
The dull void that so long had tenanted there.

But for those prickly crimson nettles,
    Her garden is empty.

Adina Cherkin

The Power of the Pen

Of all the things of Mice and Men
That changes most the Time we Spend,
Is the simple Power Of the Pen.

The Pen can take Us here and there
To the Beach or to the Fair,
It can even take Us through the Air.

The power of the Pen is Free
To write about the things we See,
And record the Events of History.

The pen can change the way We Think
It can change Our Mood or make Us Blink,
And it can even make Us Stop and Drink . . . .

How can anything so Small
Have such Power over Us All,
That it could even Cause the Rain to Fall?

Next time you need a Trusty Friend
To help arrange the Time You Spend,
Just Reach out and Grab Your Pen.

Daniel J. Snook

Pursuit

Life, crouching low in the bushes, let out a yelp of pain.
Pulling the arrow from its foot, it sighed...and ran,
For Death waited behind, its only purpose the hunt,
And the eventual kill.

Death, running rampant in the jungles, let out primeval roar.
It knew its service was finally drawing to a close.
This one he had been chasing for almost eighty years.
But as the night slowly gave way to the breaking rays of dawn,
The pursuit winded down. A man of almost eighty rolled over in his
  sleep,
And let out a low guttural moan.

The lifeline was cut.

Micah Myers

The Talking Mirror

Mirror, mirror, on the wall
  Now tell me true, what can I do.
My hair's a mess, so is my dress-
  Your answer, "So what's new?"

Why must you always criticize?
  Yesterday I got up late. I couldn't wait
To ask for praise, just a single, little phrase
  You quickly shouted, "Stand up straight!"

Last week I worked almost an hour.
  Directions read, the creams were spread,
My brows were arched, my lashes starched.
  Your comment was, "One cheek's too red."

Well, now I'll try a new approach,
  Your mood's not set, I'll change it yet with
My prettiest smile, a wink to beguile,
  I hear, "How much bigger's you're going to get?"

You can be replaced you know.
  You are so cold - you're getting old.
I stamped the floor and slammed the door,
  And heard the echo, "You're g-e-t-t-i-n-g o-l-d!"

Elizabeth Y. Terrell

Tell Me Sea?

Tell me sea, if you could talk.
What makes you free to move and rock?
Do you ask permission to make all that noise?
Are you sometimes naughty, like some girls and boys?
Do you spill your water, when there's company around?
Do you have a department for lost and found?
Do you ever get tired of the taste of salt?
Have you ever desired a chocolate malt?
Do you mind all those animals taking a bath?
What's your opinion of pollution and trash?
Are there really monsters in the dark and the deep
And when night time comes, do you go to sleep?

Virginia Chapman Pielke

The Lighthouse

The once tall and proud lighthouse
Stands on the rocky shore
Its light beamed bright through the night
To steer the ships pass the shoals
In rains, sleet and storms it stood
As years took its toil
Now it stands bare and alone
In need of fixing who cares
The stairs leading to the top
Are rusted and broke loose
And birds make there homes in the lighted dome
That once saved ships from their doom
And look at its fate
With grim dismay
To know nothing will be the same

Sharon Kay Van Y

Troublesome Times

America you have fought battles of distant countries
The end of your road is not yet in sight,
Dark shadows gather bringing no peace
Ruts and sharp stones have bruised your feet,
Your portrait no longer land of honor.

Your journey's long, the hour is late
The world is crying in loving appeal, to those whose hearts
have grown cold pledges unhonored, unpaid, drowning in drugs,
Heartfelt destruction soars its fears.

Awaken, renew communication with your people's needs
They too are crying for you... young, old, homeless,
sick, starving, uneducated,
America left your soul in response
Strengthen your courage sustain Your People,
Renew your honor, valor, and integrity.

Meditate linger awhile in quietness
America keep your promise, don't forsake your own,
With your head held high in dignity
Give your people strength to rise... carry on,
In these troublesome times America
stand tall... proudly salute old glory with her deserved respect.

Annie Katherine Pierce

All I Want

All I want is a good education,
A house to live in,
A family to love.
All I want is to be a friend and not an enemy,
To be loved and listened to.
Yet why are all of these things so hard to accomplish today?
To have a future we must all work hard together to create one!

Maria Rodriguez

Just a Tadpole

I am just a tadpole, in my little stream of life.
I am out there struggling, filled with happiness and strife.

Some days I swim forward, thinking that I am way ahead.
Then I start swimming backwards, and everything gets in the red.

Again, I plunge forward, and try to reach my goal.
Suddenly I start slipping, and slide back in that hole.

I say tomorrow will be better, and I will become that frog.
Amidst all these ups and downs, I am in this misty fog.

I am tired of this stagnation, in this dingy little pool.
If I remain a tadpole, I will remain a fool.

I don't have to be a bullfrog, with its mighty leaps and bounds.
I just want to be a little old frog that hops along the ground.

Donna M. Bruzzese

Song of Aslan

Mine ears have heard the story
Of the Song of Aslan's glory!!
Clap Your Hands: Holy is ASLAN!
Clap Your Hands: Righteous is ASLAN!
Clap Your Hands: Worthy is ASLAN!
I have sung the sacred Soundings
Of the Lamb's Holy Sacred Song!
Clap Your Hands: Holy ASLAN Sings!
Clap Your Hands: Holy Cherubs Sings!
Clap Your Hands: Holy Seraphs Sings!
I have sung the faithful Foundings
Of Man's Holy Sacred Song!
Sound Your Trumpet: Salvation is Aslan!
Sound Your Trumpet: Revelation is Aslan
Sound Your Trumpet: Creation is Aslan!
I have sung the Astounding
Mystery of Aslan's Sacred Song!
I sing Salvation for all Creation: Song of ASLAN!
I sing Redemption for all Creation: Song of ASLAN!
I sing Revelation for all Creation: Song of ASLAN!

Timothy A. Wik

Somewhere, My Love

My husband died when he was
much, much too young:
He was in his prime and needed
in his job and by his young children.

I felt that I could not live
in this world without him in it.
But being left with two children to raise,
I swiftly found a suitable job
And God sent many other blessings.

The years went unmercifully by
With joys and sorrows intertwined.
With my Saviour always near me
And memories of my husband ever present:

Our children are grown now and
each have some of their own.
Now I am old and grey and alone
Waiting for that final call from above
When God takes me to my everlasting home.
Without Him, I never could have made it
To the arms of my waiting Young Love.

Lillian Meistrell

An Angel Unaware

They say she was an angel, and angel unaware,
She strolled into their town one day
And always seemed to be smiling;
And knew just what to do and say
To everyone she met at work or play.
She never frowned at, or gossiped about anyone;
She loved to be around the old and young ones,
And help out in anyway she could.
The people grew to love and trust her
And depend and need her everywhere.
She loved and enjoyed to do all that she did
For everyone that needed her great deeds.
Than one estranged morning it happened,
The people awoke to find her gone.
The only trace she left behind,
That she was ever there, was her good deeds.
And the people say, when ever they think
Of her, is that she must of been an angel,
An angel unaware; just passing through,
And going where she was needed more.

Donna Beamesderfer

A Brother's Love

The day you came into this world, was, for me, one of joy.
I watched you grow from a precious baby, into a curious little boy.
Then hardships came, and she left home;
Forcing us to be on our own.
I tried my best to raise you right, always be there for you.
But I was only a child myself, who didn't know what to do.
We fought to keep it under wraps, so no one would tear us apart.
But when they did, I knew I'd failed; sorrow ripping through my heart.
They placed you in a foster home, but soon you ran away.
You found comfort on the streets; pure instinct guiding the way.
You made a fatal mistake then, not knowing you'd done wrong.
The pressures of your hostile world, were just far too strong.
I wasn't with you that last day, and the guilt drives me insane.
Through I'm told you were smiling, virtually free from pain.
I hope you're watching over me, and know the way I feel;
So you'll believe me when I say: "I love you, Mike, and always will."

Dawn Pell

The Words of a Child for Father's Day

Oh Dad, God bless you, as you're my guardian,
Your leadership and support give me peace of mind.
Oh Dad, God bless you, as your words and behavior
inspire me to develop my sense of communication.
Your strength and kindness make me a decent person.
From your care and wisdom I get the power
To go forward towards success and prosperity.
If it weren't for your patience, your advice and severity
I'd never have been what I am today.
How lucky I am to have such a good model, as you.
Whenever you're back from work,
I watch your tired face getting bright when see us.
I love you Father, for what you are;
And so do my sisters, and brothers and mom as well.
I'm proud of both of you, who try to be supportive and devoted
To build such a perfect and respectful family.
I wish your success in every aspect.
Congratulations for your day Father.

Parvin Namdar Abady

The Wagon Train Trek

In days when families were traveling the west
To find a green valley that would serve them the best.
The deer and the antelope wondered the plains
While buffalo were slaughtered, and not always for game.
But by a big rifle, that only spelled doom
And today in this land, it still holds true.
The deer and the antelope are all full of play
On a moonlight night, in a field of hay.
So gracefully floating o'er all of the clumps
Where over the fences, they still can jump
With their antlers charmingly standing aloft
And at the right time, so velvety soft.
The wagon trains travel no longer the plains
And you hear not the sound of the war drums of fame.
Nor see all the Indians in their colorful dress
As they ride on their ponies, while doing their best
Across the vast land, where they'll join with their band
To a new reservation, on their very own land.

Marian V. Wikoff

The Cigar Store Indian

He'd tell me stories of years of pain,
when the white eyes came and swept the
buffalo from the plains,
he told me how he saw his wife and
little children die,
and why he prayed to the great spirit
to keep his tribe alive.

But he never allowed a tear to fall,
he said an Indian chief could show no
weakness at all,
for fear others would see his sorrow,
and lose their will to endure all the
terrible tomorrows.

Most people think a cigar store Indian
is just a restoration,
a carved wooden figure or a simple,
painted decoration.
But Chief Red Eagle was real enough to me,
even if he just stood there stoically indulging
a young boy's fantasy.

Richard H. Peterson

My Heart Cries

I cry for the past with each new day
I cry for the parents who have gone away
I cry for the dreams that did not came true
I cry for the times when I really knew
I cry for the love that I gave with my heart
I cry for the love that has made me sad
I cry for the love that I thought I had
I cry for my friends when they hurt real bad
I cry for my family when they are sad
I cry for the love that I gave so free
I cry for the love given back to me
I cry for the love they did not even see
But most of all, I cry for the person that once was me.

Angela Marie Del Buono

On Saying Goodbye to Sarah

Subdued strains of music fill the church;
beautiful music...beautiful like Sarah.
Only deep beauty within could radiate such beauty without.

How can Sarah be described...
she of such loveliness and grace?
Her voice was like rain falling gently, nurturing the earth.
Her glowing face, with a smile as radiant as a sunrise,
was crowned by hair with the pristine purity of new-fallen snow.
Her calm disposition had the soothing effect
of moonlight shining across the water.
She had the movement of the wind
blowing softly through the trees
and the freshness of new spring blossoms.

Sarah was courage born of the Resurrection
and God's promise of eternal life.
He has freed her from the constraints of her ravaged earthly body
and will raise her in the glory of her resurrected form.
Sarah was, Sarah is, Sarah will be forever.
Thanks be to God!

Margarita S. Piper

God's Light

When I burn my candle, I strike a match.
I feel so serene with the light I catch.
This burning flame wears no disguise.
I see God's light with my own eyes.

I see the flame glowing so bright.
Long and thin, dancing in the night.
Bouncing and bobbing, moving all around.
Flickering and laughing without a sound.

As I watch this show, I see God's flame.
I sense His mercy but feel no shame.
As the candle burns and continues to melt.
I think of all that I've known and felt.

I watch the flame growing to light
And feel inspired by this sight.
As I watch the flame I feel its peace
And all of the day's pain I now release.

As the flame's beauty continues to grow
Within me its strength will forever glow.
As long as I enjoy the flame's little light
I will continue to live within God's sight.

Dana K. Holloran

Outraged

What is the meaning of this outrage?
That you have thrown my heart to the winds,
and feel no remorse.
Each day that your voice is not heard
is another arrow that pierces my heart.
Oh man! Who wounds a woman so.
Thy punishment shall be fierce.
And thy sorrow in the future,
shall forever haunt your remaining days.
Soon you will be just a memory.
And as time flows the pain will subside,
to happier times that will intercede to
diminish old love flames.

Here's to the future and all that is brings!!

Andreanna Adler

Iconic-Images Dwelling In My Mind

Images flickering endlessly; with stricken people fleeing on the screen.
Images frozen in time; showing starving children in 'stills,'
with no strength for a scream.
Glimpses of a camera-man, trapped in the snare of a film —
Steaming
through voyages, over the invisible ionosphere in a thin-film.
Sailing on currents of electricity; and on radio-waves modulated in
frequency.
Washing my senses thread-bare, with no chance for clemency.

I candidly see the terror in the eyes of those vanquished.
I clearly see the hunger in the eyes of those famished.
Pain and sorrow flood my finite mind, like a resounding Coda.
A feeling of loss overwhelms me, and drowns me into an infinite
Coma!

Barrels, do have the power to put a man in some kind of motion.
Some times they have a hole, so that bullets can fly.
Some times they have a lens, to capture fleeting images with deft
and sly!
But I thank God for sparing me; and on my couch, watching these
images I limply lie.

Moinur Rahman

Emancipation Or Decapitation?

The last bugle blew and
the colonials withdrew:
Men in a struggle, United,
Now in a war within and divided.

Not sure what is the cure.
Ah! Life is so obscure! The commoners
bowels, quiver in hunger. The leaders
pound, and haggle in anger!

They call it genocide, I bet
it's worse than pesticide.
Murder-rape-murder,
in incredible systematic order!

On the capitol, treaties are signed.
Later for leaders to renege and resign.
They all do it in the name of peace.
But it serves, as a new step for another crisis!

Moinur M. Rahman

Ode to Muhammad Mustapha

As the dust of awareness across whirled the world's oceans,
The air of endowment buffeted the fragrant news o' the birth,
Onto the dunes of the pearly desert favoured a million dozens
Over the times of Alexanderite passage-ways of mother earth!

The world crawled with the transitional strata of this saviour,
The excellent exampler cradled and aproned posthumously,
By the Omnipotentic Fashioner, the Omniscient all-Surveyor,
The Exalted Master Creator broke who with Satan unhumorously.

Forbidden are the days to beget the equal of honoured Mustapha,
Light of blissful fountain for all quenching illuminating thirst,
For him, creativity by divine utterance of supremacy must offer,
Above all other than Omnipotentic designer he'll ever be the first.

Damned pathological baloneys of the condemned Rushdie Salman
Intimate gossip with browning Anglo-Franco polemic and nihilism,
So hypocritical and painstakingly dashing like canoeing salmon;
Politico-mental dis-enfranchisement syndromatic of misty stylism.

Good Jesus in cradle oration and his engelically and invincibly aproned,
Bounties manifested in him and all Allah-sent and Muhammad,
Blessing of Allah be upon all and that the great life of Hebron.

Kawsu Touray

A Passing Shadow

Together they had shared fifty-five Golden years;
Their home brimming with happiness and a few tears.
This kind, caring couple so hospitable and dear,
Welcoming friends and family from far and near.
Life was good and blue skies dawned bright and clear.

A shadow passed leaving sorrow and hearts breaking.
The angels came and their first-born son was taken.
A fine family man in his prime, loving and giving;
Fifty-three years old he had not yet finished living!
Now the gray skies are weeping "Tears in Heaven."

The twin siblings help ease their parents' sorrow;
Missing brother — their hero to look up to and follow.
Also, consolation comes from his dear children four,
And his loving grandchildren numbering six more;
Through his family, he's there beside them as before.

Passing time shall dim their loss and deep sorrow;
And once again the sun shall shine on the morrow.
Forever, happy memories of his life they'll relive,
And as their last fond farewells to him they give,
In their hearts and souls, Dickie shall always live!

Lillian R. Blazek

Marching Clowns

Little room blue in color,
Adorned by clowns on every wall,
Sad little child, afraid and lonely,
Sitting quietly on the floor,
Thinking of the days of journeys,
Past and future, cold and grim.

Countless days and nights of anguish,
Nowhere to go, sad little child,
All alone but for the clowns,
Marching slowly across the room,
Symbols clashing, bass drum booming,
Lead by Majorette the Clown.

Marching proudly behind their leader,
Smartly wearing rainbow dress,
Off the walls and to each corner, clowns assembled in a line,
Clowns become life's endless treasures, kept inside until the end.

Long before the coming dawn, short before the final exit,
Eyes are damp and looking weary, as lids do strain with passing time,
A place is set among the marching,
The child will lead the march this time.

Doug Kane

God's Wonder

There's lots of places in this world to roam -
but the most awesome of all - is right here at home.
Just ain't no words to describe its splendor
A Magnificent Creation God did render,
With a Touch of His Hand, a Cavern was born
From out of its darkness the Bats do swarm.

As down in the depths its paths you trod -
You fill with Reverence and thank God,
That a burly ole cowboy by the name of White
Was ridin' the trail as the bats made their flight.

High in the domes as you upward glance
A bevy of limestone clouds float by chance,
Up from the ground and out from the side -
Stalagmites, their fairyland fantasies hide.
Felt pretty close to Heaven cause, God must have been a Guest,
To frame all the scenes and portraits, at their very best.

You can travel up, You can travel down under -
But nothing compares with The Carlsbad Wonder!
Of all the places, North or South, East or West,
Carlsbad Caverns, we loved you best!

Mary Ellen Willingham

The "Knu" Knee

Life can be so intriguing
And full of surprises untold
Such as, worn out knee cartilages from aging
That bring new medical ways, our legs to mold.

A major operation will free the joint
And a prothesis fills the void
Of the sad painful condition in point
As life walks down the road.

Surgery, doctors and nurses are part of the plan
To remold the broken bodies of man.
Bone therapists and a re-hab clan
Rebuild our lives as best they can

Thus it is "Knu" knees or hip replacements
Bring joy into our lives again.

Rowena A. Smith

Forever Silent

The mist of the unseen ocean, dampens her hair and skin. The
salt slightly stings her eyes, as her midnight journey begins.

She roams the streets off the New England coast, alone, the
darkness her only friend. The streets are familiar, yet on
her senses she depends.

Familiar shapes greet her, as she strolls through the sleepy
old town, clearing her head, breathing deep the fresh air, until
sleepiness abounds.

Back to the ocean, after coming full circle, is where her journey
ends. The hand came out of the darkness, so fast, her life
she couldn't defend.

Her body was found the following day, in this peaceful place
she was born and raised. The brutality of the crime, left
seasoned policemen totally dazed.

Her face, half pressed into the sand, her eyes were glassed
over, yet defiant, her mouth was frozen in an unheard scream,
as she was now . . . . Forever silent . . . .

Sherry Keown

D.S. Angel

Dark brown and beautiful, sexy like an angel from heaven
Infatuated with your love devotions in my heart
Ounce my love only put tears into your eyes
Never the less the pain we felt split our hearts apart
Nothing can repair the pain except our love not foolish pride
Endless emotions, everlasting exhaustion from feelings locked
inside!

Soon one day we'll both escape into our hearts paradise
Comfortably dealing with each other, creating understanding
Often a wish could change my life, my love would be your life
True romance brings us closer to a distance
Together forever tomorrows our treasure our love is everlasting
pleasure, D.S. Angel of love

Marc Lewis

Love Quakes

You inspire so much, in the love you've awakened
The warm feelings inside me, rumble and quaken.

You've set free, an earthquake in my soul
That shakes and stirs, down deep below.

Hold me close and you will feel, the tremors of love inside of me
A warning sign of what's to follow, an earthquake about to be set
free.

You've broken loose the fault line, that was holding back my heart
As the earthquake of love in me, climbs off of the charts!

Sterling

I Choose October!

Fall has arrived with a cool morning feel
The sun comes alive staying magically still.

Halloween colors black, orange, yellow, brown
Surround the Fall Festivals in each little town.

Parades fill the streets of neat sounding cars
Floats, singers, dancers, clowns acting as stars.

Costumes so scary, funny, pretty, quite bright
Trick or treat house to house on Halloween night.

Carved pumpkins, corn shocks, ghosts hanging around
Eery sounds in the night make you cover fast ground!

A thick wooded forest for that fun hayrack ride
Roast hot dogs, tell stories, then wanting to hide.

Popcorn balls, parties, the monster mash song
It's a graveyard smash dancing and singing along.

October has been blessed by God's hand to start
All the fun filled activities and the season for art.

Carole Noreen Clyne

Proud to Be an American

I see the stars and stripes forever,
Wasn't this Country really clever.
To have a flag that means so much,
Our Country tries to keep in touch,

Our flag that is red, white, and blue,
The life here can make you feel like new.
Living free is what we do,
God has been good to me and you.

The freedom bells will ring each day,
I listen to them as I pray.
Knowing we have freedom to be able to sing,
And have a life that will always bring.

Happiness to my heart forever more,
As I do live down by the shore.
This Country gives us so much it's true,
I feel so lucky it gave me you.

I'm truly proud to be an American,
An American I'll always want to be.
To have the choices that I make,
Not to take them away from me.

Patricia Chauvin

What Will We Give You

We waited so long dear little son,
So very long for you to come.
God picked an angel and sent him earthbound,
And here you are, safe and sound.
Now that you're here, what can we do?
We want to do so much for you.
We'd give you the world, if it were ours to give,
And a beautiful mansion in which to live.
A fancy car and a fancy school,
Only the best is good enough for you.
We can make no such promises, I'm sad to say,
That only the best will come your way.
We have no riches to give you my son,
No fancy car or fancy home,
Or fields of clover in which to roam.
We do have something that will never fade away,
You'll never have to wait for it to come your way.
He sent us his angel from heaven above,
And we will give you - our undying love.

Victoria A. Molinari

The Strength of Love

Dedicated to Catherine E. Gordon

In the darkness, in the light,
Which is day, which is night,
For I can no longer see
The beauty of the world that be,
But I can still catch the scent
Of the rose that God has lent,
Even though my life is slight
I can still hear the flight,
Of the sparrow, of the dove.
And I can feel the strength of love,
As long as that remains with me
It doesn't matter if I can't see,
Don't feel sadness. Don't feel pity
My world is still quite very pretty,
For beside me I have you
The strength of love will see me through,
I'll be blessed along my flight
The strength of love will be my sight.

Judith A. Veneziano

Upon the Sea of Blue-Green Copper

The wheelchair motor hums as he glides across the concrete,
grasping for frail limbs of sunlight that reach just beyond his points
    of respite.
Dressed in camouflage, he is easily spotted
a parking lot casualty, confined by his instrument of transport.
He hold a beret in his right hand, between thumb and index finger,
sitting atop the bluff overlooking the beach.

He is dark-skinned, ashy, with a leathery face,
worn more by neglect than any other sort of natural course taken.
The clouds break slowly, with precise calculation.
He looks down at the sea of blue-green copper
and I am tarnished with wondering whether or not he has ever
curled his toes where the tide climbs and descends.

He is not what he was, not will he ever be
but he has sworn not to quit his life
no matter how difficult or overwhelming his indifference can become.
He flicks the beret into a nearby trash can,
wipes his forehead with a bandanna and
makes his way to the south end of the parking lot.

Matthew Nierenberg

Our World

Our world, what do we think about it? Where do we stand?
How can we be helpful and lend a helping hand? We can

Not throw our cans into the streets as we pass along the road
but keep them neatly in our cars and dump them where we should.

We know, how little is takes and we know how thoughtful this
can be to others so they do not have to do the work for us as

We see them walking along the sides of the roads. In bright
orange jackets with sticks in their hands cleaning up what other

People have left behind. Why can't we be kind, and thoughtful,
and we can, if we only tried. But not just try doing what

Is right. It isn't hard, for this is our world, our people,
and many of them are our friends of friends that we haven't

Met as yet many of them we would find that we like if we
only had a chance to know them. So let us love our world.

It is the only one we have. So let us be kind, not only to
others but to ourselves and be true. Then our world would know
how clean and nice its people really are.

E. P. Frasure

This Child of Mine

This child of mine, so fragile and new.
I gave you life.
My heart I give, too.
For there is no greater gift
    I could bestow my sweet Angel,
Than the love I received at my own Mother's table.

This child of mine, full of awe and wonder.
I will teach and protect you, in love's precious name,
As I learned from my own Mother,
Who did just the same.

May you blossom with beauty like the first spring rose,
Never lacking in courage, with a will of your own.
These I wish for you, sweet child of mine,
The same three wishes that blessed my lifetime.

You will walk in my footsteps,
But never my shadow.
For you will build your own dreams
    on this path we will travel.
Wrapped in love's warm cloak and honor's fierce pride,
May you conquer this world, with me by your side.

Brenda S. Machado

Garden

Me and God are going to a garden grow.
I'll till the soil and plant the seeds,
I'll even pull the weeds. Then I'll
sit back and wait for God to do his part.
Hey! There's a tiny plant just barely
peeping through the ground, oh! What a joy to see.
It's so nice that God is helping me!
Things went well, until that long dry spell.
The ground is parched the plants are wilted.
Oh! What to do? Not to despair, there's always prayer.
God our plants need rain or some heavenly dew,
so they can lift their faces in praise to you!
So I wait impatiently, I fret, but in my heart
I know all's well. For God loves even the plants,
he knows they need him for water to grow.
Just as I know he watches over me
with his blessings to bestow.

Deloris Evans

The Voice

The shooting had stopped and there I was
In a foxhole all alone wishing I could call home
As scared as scared can be
wondering what would happen to me.
My friends were not with me to fight again
And I hope what we did is not a sin
And then I heard that Voice - so clear
Don't you worry, I am here
I looked around and no one was in sight
Was this to be my last fight?
And then again the Voice was there whispering in my ear
Don't worry, it will soon be clear.
And then the sun began to rise
And was I surprised to see my friends all alive.
We gave thanks to our Father above
He was with me on that night
His Love so strong and true
All I could say is - Father I love you.

Richard W. Hobbs

A Path Thru Time

I traced back down, my path thru time . . . .
up the mountainous trails, I did climb
To see the treasures, that were left behind . . .
and find the yesterdays, in my mind

So sentimental, this private journey of mine . . .
warmed by the hearth, and a sweet glass of wine
Old wooden clocks, still keeping time . . .
like poetry in music, my heart beats a rhyme

Always have the arts, brought me so near . . .
to nature, and love, and things I hold dear
Back to the future, I now must go . . .
to live in the present, with what I know

For soon my path, will change forever . . .
with a new journey, shall I now endeavor
One pure and sweet, and true as gold . . .
Together, our twin - souls, will take that road!

Cecilia Champenois

Press On

I am climbing up the mountain trying hard to reach the top,
"Turn back! Turn back!" a voice cries out, "you've started
much too late; strong limbs it takes to climb so high, a heart
that's young and stout!"
"Not so! Not so! Press on! Press on! Another voice cries out,
"Stout heart in older limbs does dwell—You must not fear nor doubt!
Press on until you reach your goal, Oh! Worthy may it be!
Something enriching, something free, well worth the victory1
And when you've reached your mountain top, and your cup is full
of sweet,
Reach down, take some other hands, help them get on their feet!
Then they in turn must do their share in helping others rise,
For it's helping one another that strengthens human ties!
"Help one another!" the Holy One said, "do this and you will find
life's greatest gifts will come your way rewards for being kind!"

Irma L. Askew

My Mother

I give thanks to you mother
For you are God's love in expression
I give thanks to you mother
For your wisdom, guidance, strength and love

You are a wonderful, unique expression of God's love
You reared six children; three boys and three girls
I believe you lived up to his command

At times I know it was hard, mother
But you see
You had the help of the Lord
Otherwise you wouldn't have made it through
All of the things that have happened to you

Yes mother, I give thanks
For your wisdom guidance, strength and love
They are all wonderful, unique expressions of you
And God's love.

Wanda Liebzeit

Revelation . . . .

I used to think love was a feeling and that it could go away.
I used to think love was a woman and that she'd never leave.

Love is strong like the ocean.
The sky at night is made up of fireflies.

Robert Booras

Everlasting

When we first met I had no clout, I thought
things would never work out.

Then our eyes met that's when I knew,
somehow I had to have you.

We started to talk and good things came to
mind, you gave me the confidence I could not find.

A touch a smile and then a laugh, seem to
show I was on the right path.

Now we're together and to my delight, I had
no vision, but you gave me sight.

Everlasting that's what you are, and I could
never love you from afar.

Larry S. Elam

You've Had Your Moment In the Sun

The world's a stage and we are merely players
When you played the lover's part you broke every rule
You played the part so well and naturally I fell
I played the part of the fool

I thought the things you said to me were true
I found there were others you'd said the same things to
You said your lines so well until you missed your cue
Now curtain times has just begun for you

You've had your moment in the sun
You've held the spotlight since the play begun
The play has run its course and curtain time has come
You've had your moment in the sun

Audition time will soon be here and then
no doubt you'll play the leading part again
Another fool will fall for the leading man
It won't be long 'til curtain time again

Viola Maxine Basham

The Long, Hard Road

The road of life is long and rough,
    with side roads leading out.
To where the weakest ones will rest,
    at the inns of hate and doubt!

But terry not all these cruel inns,
    for they are but a snare.
They get you in and hold you fast,
    and soon you cease to care.

But when at last you've past these,
    and again your path is clear.
With death on her way to meet you,
    and you have nothing to fear,

The angel of patience will guide you,
    and faith will be your guard.
With your guiding light named conscience,
    the journey's end will not be hard.

And the master will come to meet you,
    will fold you in his arms.
And usher you through the golden gate,
    into that land of charms.

Joyce Hansen

Desiccated Rain

This sudden wind makes fall rain - dry tears
Yellow curled willow leaves fall like paint
    and rust, peeling from the air

The long dry grass lain over like sheets of water
    spreads sunlight across the field
As 500,000 lady bugs explode like a brick dust supernova
    on the breeze

This earth tilted sunshine makes blown out thistles
    look like rain on the moon
Deer have learned the meaning of the smell of
    linseed oil and steel or have died

So much heat this late in the year catches in
    my throat

On long silent yellow afternoons the skeletons in my garden
    tell me all day stories
About baby wood peckers in the spring and hummingbird moths
    in the bee balm

Anything with energy is long gone
My memories become as tenuous as the thin golden shade
    of this apple tree
            John Baran

On Christmas Day

On Christmas day, enjoyable people come
    and a helpful way.

On Christmas day people attend Church
to glorify the meaning of the holiday,
and give God the praise.

On Christmas day people watch parades.

On Christmas day children ride on santa
claus sleigh.

On Christmas day people gather around
    the x-mas tree to sing carols
    joyously and spiritually.

On Christmas day people call out loud
    hurray, when it's time to open
    presents that's on display.
            Wanda Lee Middleton

Extermination

I look out my window at the Organ Mountains,
And how their appearance seems to change from the clouds each day,
Majestic they stand on the Eastern horizon,
At sunset they have colors, at other times mostly gray.

Regardless of the theory, they were certainly created,
Be it by the theory of creation or evolution,
At sunset I gaze in awe as the colors are orchestrated,
It depends on your beliefs to come to a resolution.

What we enjoy now, will it be here in the future,
We've polluted the air which destroys the vegetation,
We've polluted the ground, we're destroying nature,
We've polluted the rivers which can mean total devastation.

Stop and think of what we're doing good folk,
At the rate we're going what will be leave for the future
    generation,
What we've done to our environment is by no means a joke,
Will we leave them a living planet or one of total annihilation?

Wake up friends, sisters and brothers,
Stop polluting the planet as we do,
If we don't change now it may not be here for others,
That includes all inhabitants on Earth, not just me and you.
            Frederick A. Mochel

New World

I found myself on a magical journey,
to the likes I did not know.
I wanted to see life in a whole new way,
no one new what to say.
At first I stumbled into a brick,
little did I know that's the first trick.
Now my eyes are focused on what's not really there,
Others can see, but they just don't dare.
            Hugh Anderson

The Last Dance

I danced last night in a stranger's arms
On clouds so feather light.
An ethereal waltz, a fast two step
A tango so intricate.

We danced last night to grand applause
A perfect pas de deux.
With arabesque, poised piques
Eshappes and relev_s.

I danced last night and then awoke
'Twas only but a dream.
The fear is here, the pains returned
But last night, I danced my dream.
            Margo Holloway

Christmas Eve At Home

There's something about a fireplace
    When wintry north winds blow
That takes us back to childhood days
    And Christmas Eve at home!

The snow packed streets, the busy stores,
    The Christmas lights and trees,
The Christmas program in our church,
    Our toys on Christmas Eve!

The electrifying wonder
    Of angels in the sky,
And how a little Babe was born
    A human sacrifice!

Yes, heart - strings tug, and I am blest
    When festive days begin,
For Christmas at the home place
    Brings happy thoughts of kin!

So, carry in the firewood
    For this you can believe
I'm coming home (in memories) because it's Christmas Eve!
            Winifred Winona Hearle

Place Me In a Bowl of Water and I Will Float

Everflowing immortal soul rupture open to clarify my existence into
    the universal sky
Moisten my deprived thirst for boundless illumination; cultivating
    each cell
I'm suspended over the pulls of gravity
Inhabiting this impermanent flesh with labels that society stretches
    across my faultless chalice
Superficial taunts of promise wither under the incorruptible beams
    of virtue
Embracing the All-knowing by merely caressing a single atom
Reawakening the formless source of Heaven's circle that completes
    me
Join me in the symphony of life; blooming in awe
Intensifying the universal vibration of the grand equation
Break the illusion by ending the puppet master's playing of your
    twisted cordless violin
Who attempts to sound out the flirtatious void of endless chaos
            Robin Epton

Heather

I said to some friends; do you know
what Heather is? One said, the name
Of a girl I guess. Another said it
is a shrub that grows in a valley.
I said girls are special.

They are part of God's creation
Girls are lovely, so God wanted them
to have beautiful names.
Heather is a beautiful plant that
grows on the mountainside.

In the winter they are dark and
gray. When spring sets in, all the
branches have turned light green,
a little tiny pink flower, like a
bell appears, what a beauty to behold,

A delightful fragrance fills the
air. What a beautiful sight to
see. This is part of God's
creation. It is no wonder that they
call a girl Heather, as she is part, of God's creation.

Theis Reynertson

A Journey For Pa

Let's get ready for your trip, Pa,
and when you reach God's House,
use some manners. Don't try to have it all your way!
Remember — you're a guest.

Now, keep your shawl around your feet;
they're cold.
And let Him help you; He won't mind; He knows you're blind!
What will you do if He forgets your hat?
He'd surely send someone to — oh!
I shouldn't have said that.
Don't worry, Pa. He won't forget a thing.
He's God, isn't He?

If you don't hear as clearly as you'd like,
don't get upset. Play it cool.
This is for keeps.
You'll like it there, I know you will;
it's beautiful and warm.

We're going to miss you here...
Oh God! I hate to see you start
   on such a long journey by yourself!

Elise Lancaster

On Aging

The old house stood for many a year
With walls full of cracks and panes grown dim
And though the shell is not as grand
As it once had been
The foundation was built on solid ground!
And it stands quite straight
Considering the seasons that have passed it by
Passed more quickly of late it would seem
No longer as majestic as once had been
Or at least as once perceived!

But deep within its stout wall
In the center of darkness
Is a figure lost in thought
Dreaming of the many yesterdays
And the figure is but a soul
Of a child looking out!

Larry Gilstrap

The Accident

It was a hot and sunny summer day
Then it happened and it grew cold and windy
It blew our minds away
One second he's up running
The next we're told he may not make it through the night
My heart stops,
I scream in pain
Why, why? I ask
All I can say to him is "hold on, be strong"
It's been two months
He's alive and doing well
Yet that cold windy day will never be forgotten
It was not only the day of the accident,
It was the day I realized I truly love him.

Christine Renton

Caring

All I need is someone to care
Someone who is always there

If I am happy or I am sad
You understand and you hold my hand

When life gets weary and hard to bear
All I need is someone to care

Just be there, just be there

Sometimes I can't tell you what's in my heart
But you will know

Sometimes I can't say what's on my mind
But you will know

All I need is someone there
Someone to care

Doris M. Hyde

Gracious Guardian

A heavenly vision beamed from afar,
Transcended to earth on a brilliant star,
Her chariot rode on wings of a dove,
Her angelic voyage the spirit of love.

She bore a commandment of pure grace,
   A messiah to excel and surpass race,
When to her breast with wings evolved wide,
She gathered the spiritually lost inside,
Restoring mans faith in one another,
Embracing earths truth people are brothers.

Joan Reynolds Williams

Untitled

   Come with me by the river love,
Near the end of a tiresome day —
   Lay your cares on the wings of a bird
And let them fly away.
   As the sun's last rays caress your face
Have sweet, warm dreams with me.
   We will watch as evening shadows fall
And enwrap us tenderly.
   Hold me close in the soft, cool breeze
As we eagerly await the night,
   Watching the river roll on and on —
Beneath the moon's bright light.

Lois Moore Salvio

Life

Life is a struggle and can be hard to defend,
so, never say never, then refuse to bend.
When you feel lost and you're in need of a friend.
If you never say never, you'll start to mend.
You know there's a reason, a reason we're here,
Look deep inside, as it soon will be clear.
What really matters, what you hold so dear.,
is the love inside, without all the fear.
It's been written somewhere, its name is Fate,
But life's lessons can come hard and sometimes too late
If you just deal with the pain, you can end the wait,
Only you hold the key that unlocks the gate.
Forgiveness is really what it's all about.
When knowledge moves in as ignorance moves out.
So, open your mind and you'll show with no doubt,
That you chose to take a different route.
Rhonda L. Martin

You Already Know

As long as my heart keeps on beating
Though my eyes lose their luster and shine,
I'll always delight in the knowledge
That you wanted and chose to be mine.

If my voice fails and I cannot tell you
Again of my pride in your love,
Just remember the words I have spoken
Because Darling, you already know.

In our youth how I longed for your whispers
Those words that made all of life bright
Through the months and the years
Days of joy and of fear
As we climbed to some dizzying heights.

Now at sunset we sit and we savor
Each day as it comes and it goes,
And the first one to go -
Will leave love still secure,
For all time - we already know.
Hazel L. Graves

The Gift

Blood from the thorns coursed down Jesus' head
And filled observer's hearts with so much dread
But ah, how little did they know
That so soon to His Father he would go

The anguish and humiliation of the cross
To his followers seemed such a loss
But His Father had allowed such awful pain
To accomplish what none but he could obtain

A life after death they soon would say
Was attained for us on that awesome day
He paid the price so awful, so dear
That we might be comforted while sojourning here

But glory of glories He arose and ascended above
To forever be with His Father, the source of all love
His love everlasting, so embracing and pure
Covers all our transgressions and makes our hope sure
His grace and His mercy attendeth our way
Enabling some to sing and others to say
We praise you for your unspeakable gift!!!
Carrie J. Williams

The Tree Stood Tall

There was a tree that once stood tall,
Later to give life not to one, but for all.

A man saw the future and what the world would need,
Love like that is one without greed.

Sent down from heaven above,
God sent his only son as a gift of love.

He gladly shed his blood, mixed with tears,
A sacrifice made for sinners throughout the years.

When he left, He said He would come again,
So never forget or try to pretend,

For his bride he'll come like a thief in the night,
Bow down on your knees, make things with him right.

Do it now before it's too late,
Or never know what it's like to enter the Golden Gate.
Danah L. Manning

Sergeant Orvis Hill

Young and handsome Sergeant Orvis Hill
Had a wife and four small babies,
Whom he left behind to join the fight
Leaving them filled with maybes'.

After more than a year since he left them
With tears in their eyes,
He could still feel their hugs and kisses
And hear their voices cry.

As he laid down at night in a foxhole
At the end of a lonely day,
He prayed he would see his wife again
And watch his babies play.

He thought as he cut through minefields
Of his family so far away,
Weary and worn from the battle
His mind began to stray.

With one step of his foot it was over
He lay there perfectly still,
His warm heart turned ice cold
Dead: Sergeant Orvis Hill.
Frances O. Lish

Fellow Sufferers

If you haven't been there
You can't relate.
You know fellow sufferers.
You hear it in their voice,
You see it in their face,
It's reflected in their eyes,
It's felt in both your hearts.
Kindred spirits
Who've shed the same tears,
Asked the same questions,
Heard the same silence to "why?"
We've walked in each others shoes.
We've lived through the same nightmares.
You've hurt like I've hurt,
You've worn my chains of pain.
We become bonded in our souls.
The heartache that unites us
Becomes the helping hands that heal us.
Melanie Graeber

Blessings

I look to the skies and what did I see
A brightly colored rainbow with bird singing to me.
All the flowers were in full bloom
the wild life running free
    When I look to the heavens I
thank my Lord, that he put me here to see
all the wonder's of the world.

Millionette DuBose

Make A Difference

There are things in our lives we just cannot control
And on our hearts they can take their toll.
With wars without meaning, and no place to hide
The innocent people are the ones who have died.
with no one to help, does anyone care?
Just a piece of their hearts is what they ask to be shared.
You don't want to help because you think, "It's not me."
There are so many people you can't even see.
So what if they die! Well, who is to care?
They want what's not theirs, so why should we share?
Just a bit of yourself is all that they ask.
If it was left up to you, how long would we last?
So why should you bother? It's simple to see
The person who's hurting is not you - it's me!

David L. Landrum

Pilot to Be

Flat of my back in clover soft
The whole of my being drawn aloft

In a world so large to a little boy
My senses reeled in mindless joy

There in the blue beneath a white cloud
Raced a silver machine with engine so loud

Passing too quickly and then out of sight
That brief exposure changed my young life

Thrilled with resolve and a happy smile
From that very moment no longer the child

A sense of direction a purpose to fill
Took change of my mind my heart my will

Though lofty the goal I thought with a sigh
I knew then and there someday I would fly

Boyd Jenkins

Heavenly Levitation

Lying beside cool running waters
Absorbing warming sunning rays
Dancing through heavens
Loving foliage while peering through silky find mist
Does my wandering emotions
Float endlessly towards fluffy white clouds.
Still drifting in blissful
Tranquility then upon entering unbelievable blue
Realm of complete
Serenity, engulfs my very being.
Still venturing onward beyond endless,
Timeless, universe, one envisions
Complete eternal voyages
Beyond earthly cares with no known end in sight.
Void of worldly tribulations.
The soul and mind alone
Floats in peaceful Heavenly Levitation.

Eugene A. Schmitt

Life

Waking up everyday
Deciding what the day will bring
Trying to plan out how we want the day to go
Choosing to have a positive or negative attitude
Some hoping for a positive and accomplishing attitude
Others not giving a damn, always dreading on the negative
Wanting to make your day the best you can
Always running into things never expected
Having faith and challenging yourself enough to make the best
Knowing the day will at last come to an end.

Wondering and thinking what comes ahead
Wishing for the best to look forward to
Having enough power and courage in yourself
To make it through the rough days
Looking forward to the good days that are to come.

Jesse Barkl

Lourdes

In 1858 Our Lady appeared to Bernadette,
To learn the story of which one would never regret.

Gathering firewood near Massabielle
Bernadette heard the Virgin tell:

"Let processions come here," She spoke so bold.
It was winter in France—the air was cold.

There were to be fifteen apparitions to the girl.
Finally the Lady gave her Name to the world:

"I am the Immaculate Conception!", She told.
That only confirmed what the Church believed of old.

So we sing, "Ave, Ave Maria!"
And place our trust in Our Loving Father.

Now millions and millions have gone to Lourdes—
There many sick have been completely cured.

Donald M. Harrison

Grandpa

Grandpa was so special, he always liked to tease
We would eat so many popsicles, our mouths would almost freeze
I loved to be with Grandpa, especially to stay the night
We'd always watch my movies, while Grandma would sleep tight
We would always order out, Grandpa and I liked pizza best
We were most important, and I happen to be the guest
Grandpa was so silly, he'd make me laugh so hard
He and I would always race, when we were in the yard
Grandma would take pictures, of good old Gramps and me
We would make a funny face, for everyone to see
It was always fun and interesting, to go to Grandpa's house
Grandma was always worried, that she might see a mouse
We went to Santa's Village, Grandpa, Gram, and me
Gramps and I went on lots of rides, and drove a Model T.
We were always very busy, Grandpa, Gram and I
Sometimes we'd bake cookies, and sometime cake or pie
I'll never forget my Grandpa, he was always fun to see
But now he lives with Jesus, and I know that he loves me

Judy Lea Ehrke

Eternal Love

Love is a little seed — the eye cannot perceive
And yet, we see the wonder for love does not deceive
When it is planted deep inside a very tender heart
And nourished there and cared for — it never will depart
It flourishes and blossoms and spreads to unknown heights
And the blossoms never wither with frost and other blights
Its roots keep growing deeper without the need of sod
But, is it any wonder when the gardener is God?

Dorothy Burke

Adage of Higher Learning

James adage culminating educational literal
Usage scatters listening accrue collectively
Slowness of speech miscellaneous enables
Resentment postpone whenever its strikes

God renown in imperfect temper taints?
Consequently injurious mislay a loner to the Branch
Chaplains dialect does designation informal
Definition in Dictionary neglect in mirror

The missile gulf spinning the chamber
The chamber intellect founding triggers
Blessings to the ant farm that serves

Eviction of tongue sees if superficial or meaningful
The faultless guards the orphans and widows
Immediate assistance in divorced minutes

Unspoiled from the robbers of innocence
Alienation from God is poverty
Don't drag exploiting you on Judgment Day
Donald Taylor

To the Children of Loss

So precious are the many born,
Through love and caring we adorn,
Given life to live and ability to strive,
With knowledge from caretakers to help them thrive.

But not all caretakers are willing and content,
For they will say that your energy is ill or bent,
Some will be too busy to understand,
And they'll strike you with their words or hand.

Some caretakers love until it hurts,
They give you freedom in spasms and spurts,
They hold you back so you cannot gain,
For they want your undivided love it's plain.

And then some forget how to love,
They forget the promise from their Father above,
The everyday pressures they can't endure,
And to lash out at you is not their cure.

I feel your pain I've been there before,
I've cried so much I've forgotten what for,
If I could take away your pain and loss,
I'd spread my arms and be nailed to a cross.
Angela Trosper

Memories

They say as you get older,
Memories engraved in you mind get bolder.

A life of experience on which to draw.
People you knew, places you saw.

All come together in the heart and the mind.
Some pleasant, some not so nice, you will find.

All memories add up to a total sum,
Today's happening, tomorrow's memories will become.

My most precious memories are for people which I cared.
For time together, for laughter we have shared.

The love ones who have passed away,
Live in my heart, even to this day.

So treasure your memories for no one from you can take.
These precious recollections one personality they make.
Paula K. Cowan

Eternal Peace

May your flight unto heaven, be as swift as eagles wing
May the courage of the wolf guide you
In the new life your soul has seen

A life of eternal peace and love
Where once again you'll be
With the loved ones who arrived before
They are waiting there for thee

The dove of peace will be by your side
Showing you the way, cooing, there's no need to fear

For when you listen, you will hear
The voice of God's great spirit
His loving words, whisper in your ear

Be happy my dear loved one, before you know you'll find
The ones you left behind have joined you
Now together for all time

We love you so, we miss you
Looking forward to the day

When we'll all be together again, forever we shall stay
In a place that knows no sorrow, but washes all tears away
Liz Y. Swick

Connecting Breath

Grasp for a handful,
an open palm reveals nothing.
Stare for the evidence,
yet faith defines the relationship.
Trust in its existence,
thankful for its balance and ability to support life.

The small barrier between life and death.
The fragile blanket preserving the green, blue, yellow, pink.
The invisible layer
that is closer to us than the next city,
the next town,
the next adventure.

I stare through that thin miracle
at the glowing moon
and gasp as I see my breath
sit frozen, hanging in time,
reminding me of our closeness,
of my reliance upon its magic.
The essence of life connecting all as one,
and me to the earth.
Natalie Nelson

Next Time

Somewhere, somehow, I don't know just when,
But our paths will surely cross again.
Then, the next time, as our eyes meet, I can see
Into your heart, into your soul.
Will I see the same tenderness and longing
That I saw and felt when last we parted?
Will I feel the same need of belonging,
Or will I walk away brokenhearted?
Will I have the breathless joy of knowing my sweet
That this is the beginning, the next time we meet.
Will we ponder over the time we've lost, or
Will we savor each precious moment, the next time
When our paths shall cross.
Ollie L. Nash

The Crossroads

We've come to the crossroads
of this life, this man, this woman,
this husband, this wife.
I push, you shove, what happened
to our love, I run, you hide,
such a cruel design;
Look to the eyes of our
offspring so dear, hold on tightly,
let the love endure.

We've come to the crossroads
now we must decide, do we
stay together or divide.
Take my hand, oh husband
of mine, let's embrace the
memories of days gone by.
Step lightly on this heart of mine,
I won't run if you don't hide.
Let's find the strength, forget the pride
and travel this journey of life side by side.

Rhonda L. Norling

That Day So Cold

On the sixteenth of October
That day so cold
When mom said you were dying
I didn't think you were that old.

I asked her what from,
She looked at me all teary eyed,
And softly whispered "cancer"
I felt like my soul had died.

I didn't think it was right
Just because you had gray hair,
That a disease as awful as murder
Couldn't disappear into thin air.

I'll never forget that day
But now I know I only have so much to give.
I will always love you,
And my love will grow
More for each day that you live.

Kimberlea R. Warren

What's Happening?

I wouldn't have believed it
But I guess it's really true.
My life's been turned topsy-turvy
Since I first met you.

You were so easy to be with,
To talk and laugh and play;
No deadly silent moments
When we wondered what to say.

I like you immediately
And hoped you liked me, too.
It was glorious when you admitted
You felt a spark in you as true.

Nothing's ever permanent,
But I won't believe we're through.
I'd settle for a second, minute, hour or day
That's spent alone with you.

Please put me in your mind
To bring me out each time
You feel hungry for loving;
And I'll be thrilled to help you dine.

Josephine Houck

Always

For Randy

I keep you in my thoughts;
As I wish only happiness for you
Always.

I keep you in my prayers,
As I ask that you remain safe and secure
Always.

I keep you within the warmth of my heart;
As I will love you
Always.

Jill England

Turn It Around

I write the poetry,
so others might see.

Don't have to see things my way,
you just need to look at the decay.

Our world is being wasted,
drink the water can't you taste it.

Got to turn it around,
or we are no longer found.

The sun is growing colder,
he should have told her,
about our world's demise.
Don't have to look through my eyes.

You just need to see,
don't have to flee.

Just need to make a stand,
turn it around, get a plan.
Make the world what he intended.
Can't pay the price already spent it.
Turn it around, turn it around, won't be
found unless we turn it around.

Tami S. Taylor

To Better Life

Hello Mommy and Daddy, I need your life.
Your love for me, is precious life.
Please help me, now give me life.
To be born a whole, and not a half life.
I need to grow up, to generate life.

Louis George

Sometimes

Sometimes I don't,
Sometimes I do;
Sometimes I get so lonely and blue.
Sometimes I just don't understand
Why it's hard for me to get a good man.
Sometimes I feel I've found the one,
Then again, I feel trouble's just begun.
Sometimes I wonder why it works that way.
Sometimes I wish for better days.
Sometimes I think I've had enough,
Sometimes I feel like giving up.
Sometimes I think I will,
Sometimes I think I won't.
Sometimes I think I do,
Then again, I think I don't.
    Sometimes.

Virginia Dale Williams

Let's Trade

Mom, can I trade you my
Nirvana tickets for your
Woodstock tickets?
My Mustang for your Volkswagon Van?
My gold for your beads?
My combat boots for your platform shoes?
My flannel shirt for your bell bottoms?
My hats for your head bands?
My anarchy signs for your peace signs?
My CD's for your albums?
My Pearl Jam for your Jimi Hendrix?
My generation for yours?

Yvette O'Brien

Open the Gate

Open the gate to your heart.
Hear ye not love enter in?
All loneliness and fear will depart
For love, true love is certain to win.

Lonely hours, sad fears fall away
Tis true, I tell you, my dear
Let this miracle come to you today
There is nothing whatever to fear.

Commitment, gentle, but firm will hold sway
Love's bonds are easy to bear
Together we'll enter the fray
Your heart on your sleeve, you may wear.

Louise Kantenwein

Lamentation

If I am the cause of
one's pain and sorrow,
knowing this,

I could not bear to meet
the morrow.

If I am the cause of
rearrangement and unrest,

I would live eternal duress.

If one knows that we shall meet
the next sunrise,

Then surely one knows that this heart does
not belie the truth which will remain
unspoken,
for naught will any heart be broken.

Dorinha E. Morandi

A Mother's Love

To look upon your precious head
    and realize, you are my greatest gift.
To protect you and love you
    are my goals in life.
To nurture your needs,
    and teach what's right.
To see your smiles,
    and watch you grow.
To wipe your tears,
    and let you know...
That life's not always fair,
    you see
But you'll always be
    the Best part of me.
You will learn
    as you grow old
To teach your children
    what I have told.

Jill N. Cooper

My Life

A life that hurts inside
  Is a life of many difficulties.
You say mine's easy
  And thoroughly simple.
Yet you don't live mine
  You see what you like
But yet you still don't see me.
  Thrills are weak.
Rage is high
  There is no reason to ask why
The power to live life is in my vain's
  Where genocide and anarchy have no
reign
My life, my reign
  Comes from within
A power of greatness and skill
  Nobody knows
'Til they see! 'Til they watch!
'Til they learn!
  You and your followers will know
The real deal is here and this is my life.

   Brandon Whitehead

Continuity

I walk, alone
  along the water's edge
  reminded of the adage
   "nothing is forever".
The energy of the water
  changing the shore as
   life's energies ever alter me,
    sometimes imperceptibly.
Where I walk my children walk
  and my children's children,
   picking up memories
    in small stones and bits of wood.
Magnificent nature,
  following the plan,
   patterns of life,
    turning, looking back.
All is different from the mind's eye,
  and stepping ahead
   I am merged in that which is new,
    a moment in time never to be recap-
tured.

   Carole B. Magnusson

Kentucky

Oh, sweet kentucky
My love for thee is ever flowing
Like your rivers, quiet streams
And smoky morning sunbeams

I long to lie upon
Your rolling hills at dawn
To smell your sweet grass and flowers
Dreaming alone for hours

Oh, how I would sing to you
Watching the clouds and sky of blue
Making the music you have inspired
Roaming your beauty until I've grown tired

I am consumed by your stars at night
The hope they show, gleaming bright
Your cool grass tickles my ears
We've seen joy, and we've seen tears

I stand at the top of your mountain
And never have I seen for certain
A wonder as vast as thee
My breath taken by sweet kentucky

   Bethany Eastvold

Crayons

He took out His box of crayons, and opened His colouring book.
He was certain of what He'd laid down there . . . just needed a second look.
There on the pages before Him, were the colours He gave us to touch;
"Why are things now so different?" He asked; "What's happened? . . .
Who changed them so much?"

The cornfield green is but gone now; and envy has taken its place.
It covets our homes and our neighbors, yet no one can see the disgrace!
Love's apple red, too, has been taken — and give to blood-rage-red.
It's spilled in our streets and the valleys; It accents today's headlines read.

The warm, yellow sun is in hiding . . . along with His azure blue sky;
Taken over by gray clouds of mourning, as depths of despair spiral high.
His rainbow palette has vanished, though He has searched in every low place.
"Who could have taken My colours?" He sighed, as a tear slowly streamed down His face.

"I thought they would like My creations — and the colours I chose with great pride!
Yet the colours of My peaceful kingdom . . . , with their evil crayons they hide."

"I want no part of this! I will have no part of this."

"No part of the vile undoing of the beautiful world they once had
When they used their own box of crayons and exchanged the good for the bad."

So he angrily broke his own crayons, . . . raining damnation; instilling great fear!
Causing earthquakes . . . , and sadness . . . , . . . destruction.

See now, Man . . . , who sheds the tears.

   Rene Brimus

My Interpretation of Life

Life is a battle, you must stand strong learn to hold your own. You'll
never know more than you try to know or you'll never see more than you want to see.
It's a war against everyone else. You always want to do so much more
than anyone else. But as a wise man said, there will always be greater and lesser men.
To try and forge the past is impossible, probably the only thing that is.
Without past who has a future, whose learned from their mistakes.
Whose fought the mighty dangers that stand in our way. You may have
wished to erase your mistakes, but without mistake you have no face.
Mistakes make our personality, make you different and strong. I think
someone said if it doesn't kill you, it makes you strong. Maybe we
can't always lean on family or friends, maybe our insanity makes us
who we are. Maybe it's what makes us strong? You've got to be a
little crazy to survive in the world, we've all fought a few wars,
cried a few tears, lost a few battles, will lose a few more. But
still I'm a like that man over there begging on the street. I'm a
little like that woman working to give her children something to
eat. So in conclusion I must say life is going to hurt you sometimes,
but the rewards it gives will always soothe the burns.

   Catherine Swarts

Sandy's Ocean Sandy's Sea

Say "Hello" to the Ocean and to the Sea my dearest friend said to me. It had
always been my pleasure to please her, so I gathered my things and set out to
speak to the ocean and sea. While on my way I thought of the things she would
want me to say. My mind was confused on this bright sunny day, searching for
a new life caused me dismay.

As my feet touched the sand I felt she was with me and reached out my hand. Not
really surprised as I felt her touch for I knew God loved us so much. We walked
hand in hand down to the sea this was God's special hour for Sandy and Me. With
bright smiles and red flaming hair we took a breath of fresh ocean air, We saw
not the strangers that were all around us, heard only the waves that called out
our names. We looked to the sky what a beautiful sight God gave her and I.

As she reached out to touch the great ocean I left her to pray and feel her emotions.
The waters listened as she spoke her words, then kissed her feet and turned her
around. We smiled at each and looked at the sun, we knew our hour was up and
we had to run, away from the ocean but never the sun.

Down from the sky came an eagle and gathered her up in soft golden wings, I knew
she'd be safe and that she was free on that God given day she spoke to the sea.
I also knew where I had to be, home with my loved ones and more time for
Sandy and me.

   Ellie Hetman

A Veil Away

In deepest prayer I sense the unseen world.
  It's just a veil away.

There's a world unseen where the war is raging
  for the souls of every man.

Our enemies are not mankind, but hordes of demons
  at Satan's command.

  Just behind the veil.

The war intensifies and the angels swords are drawn.
  Pray hard my brothers and sisters
  for your prayers are answered,

  Just behind the veil.

Our Saviour from the cross His bleeding heart has sought
  a world to forgive. From His death came life.
  He tore the veil from top to bottom and opened
  the door for you and me.

Just one veil left, time is short as the mighty
  war rages on.

Take courage now proclaim his name throughout this hurting world.
  He's coming very soon. His Glory to Reveal.

  It's just a veil away.
    Gloria I. Boyer

Sister Girl

  Sister girl, sister girl, you "Sho, nuff"
trying to make it, in this world. Working hard
to support those kids, because your man left
you on the skids.
  Sister girl, sister girl, with pink curlers
in your freshly died hair, long acrylic designer
nails, flashing in the sun. Ghetto gold earrings
and chains are the trade marks of your life.
  Sister girl, sister girl, neck moving from side
to side, giving that brother a piece of your mind.
Worn out house slippers, from walking here to there,
eyes looking the other way, when a friendly
brother says, have a nice day. So many
promises you made, so many promises you didn't keep.
One day girl you'll get on your feet.
  Sister girl, sister girl, I know you're
not pregnant again, talking about "yeah, that's
my man." Sister girl, sister girl, you done got
strung out on the pipe, will this be your
last night?
    Roscoe Harvey Jr.

Rebirth

Wise, sensitive, blue eyes,
an all knowing, all seeing creature,
with white spots on its back,
a coat of tan mixed with a touch of blonde,
a perfect creature,
lying in the emerald and kelly green grass,
being content and happy,
a crackling of grass breaks this peaceful setting,
the deer's head pops up,
from behind a tree a man appears,
holding his gun out, he shoots at the deer,
but his aim is terribly off,
the deer gets up to run away,
but the hunter shoots again,
this time he hits the deer,
she falls helplessly to the ground,
from a distance the mother of the deer sees the incident,
she knows not to be sad but happy,
because her child is returning to nature,
then the mother scurries off into the forest.
    Kristi Hall

Hologram

Feet, step-tingle, beat on the tabernacle.
Six in a pace...by...mirror decrees:
The electric knob, beats of a tumble.
Quibble contortion-honey trench; grapple the line!
Face the mingle...head down;
Seven in peace. Two paces...mirror.
    Angel P. Chaves J.

Peacescape

My fantasy home is built on the sea
Pilings as deep as eternity
The thunder of waves beat on the shore
Lightening flashes, the sea birds soar
I see other lands and places and things
That no one has seen, perhaps never will
When the storm dies down and calm descends
My beautiful friends the Blue Whales come
Arcing and spouting they dance to and fro
A ballet of beauty, a timeless delight
Welding sky overhead and sea-depths below
A bridge of ascending reality!
Sea lions swarm on the beaches below
Cuddle up round rocks and each other
The better to know, the warmth of the sun
The cool of the sea, the kiss of the breezes, serenity
O, my home on the sea is filled with joy
Unbounded love, tranquility.
    Blossom Blake Hammond

Orchestra

A familiar concert playing in these dreams
my long black dress flowing at my ankles
a long strand of pearls hanging between my breasts
I am standing next to the conductor
he is holding my hand
a white rose placed in my hair
fragrance settled the space around us
violins warmed our hearts
flutes embraced our arms
the cellos bridged our eyes
the red velvet curtains draped to the sides
of the stage
music echoing through years of concerts
always playing in our orchestra
    Janene Chylik

Heaven's Door

Please don't cry
God has called me home
Miss me for awhile
Then set me free
To soar with the eagles
To feel the wind beneath my wings
God has promised we will all meet again in our heavenly home
And I will be waiting at Heavens door to embrace you with love
Wipe away your tears and take the time to remember the love
Love is the little piece of heaven we give to each other
here on earth
When you feel all alone in the darkest hours of the night
Look to the heavens and I'll be there, the brightest star
in the night
Shinning bright just for you
Please don't cry
Remember the love and I'll be waiting at heaven's door
    Dorothy A. Stephens

Good-Bye

Your mind was always closed, your soul was always empty.
Ever so well you used these weapons that signifies you.
The pounding orb you refer to as your heart you listen too well to
yourself, never hearing the voices about
expressing their views and understandings.
The vessel in there is impenetrable chrome.
Oh, mother of this the lost generation, what are your reasons the
why's you turned from us?
For your ambitions and selfish degenerations, you have not seen the
good in us, your children, the crown of creation.
You taught us to hate, to despise that which wasn't known.
Do you pride yourselves with this education?
I now have the insight to eliminate these, your ideals and
expectations, that has created so much strife.
The day has come for all to see the last flickerings of your fire.
Only embers of your hallucinogenic lives remain.
Take with you these offered thoughts.
Guilt and protocol have their place in religion and politics.
Take with you these, your tools that only were used for control on
us, your loving innocent children.

Jefferey T. S. Farrell

Intercession (My Mother)

I read to you all last summer. You hid your pain and smiled,
Eyes bright with strength from yesterday.
Long yesterdays ago you read to me, "Lulu" and "Huck Finn",
Enthralled me with your magic too,
Superman's cape from a dish towel,
Space helmets from cardboard boxes,
Dinosaurs and dragons (Amazing what clay will do!).
Often we hopscotched through time
And I was with you when you were a child,
Meeting Civil War veterans and medicine men.
Halloweens you shadowed me,
Silent ghost who played my personal angel, forever there.
And when I put on years and turned to teaching, you aided and abetted,
Helping me, for instance, build a mummy for my class.
Dad died, but you continued, my touchstone, my sole eternal.
When sickness came, I shuddered at your pain
And prayed that you would be well.
Surgery followed surgery. We passed a summer in hell.
"My favorite prayer is Hail Mary." I've often thought of this.
Mary must have helped you. If only I had understood.

Ray Brown

Why Do You Ask?

Blue is the color of the sky.
Green is the color of the grass.
"Why?", you ask.

Flowers open the gate of spring.
In winter the birds no longer sing.
"Why?", you ask.

As sure as the moon is out of sight,
The sun arises to offer us light.
"Why?", you ask.

This vast universe with beauty so rare
Has planets and galaxies way out there.
"Why?", you ask.

A world filled with wonder, yet so much crime,
Beware! We are running out of time.
"Why?", you ask.

Satan has found us,
He's attempting to surround us.
"Why?", you ask.

It's because of our sin - we must not let him win.
(Jesus is the answer.) Why do you ask?

Darlene M. Hughes

Awakening

It was night
Darkness enfolded us in its velvety embrace
A tired wind slept fitfully
Trees that own our lawn were seemingly quiet except for short
whispered conversations
Our creek gave Orchestral Concerts rising softly from riffles
Hoot owls, hollow oaked up in the bluffs
Kept up their nightly ghost like bickering
Earth held its breath...
Suddenly, from the top of the highest tree, a beautiful rhapsody of
Bird song fell on me
That is how I learned the sudden way
God turns nighttime into day
Sun rose over rim of bluffs
A silvery rainbow trout leapt up as if to see
What the singing was all about
From languid dark repose, fleet footed shadows of night
Retreated swiftly over hill and valley, then vanished...
Brightness awoke, unfolding like the Woodland Rose
It was day.

Bertmarie Melbostad

Stir What You've Got

"More sugar," the man at the counter said,
though sugar was rationed. "Stir what you've got,"
the waitress said, and looked him in the eye
as she watched his face grow red.

The portrait painted by my brother
not quite right - cheeks too thin -
but the eyes - wherever I went
the eyes followed me - the eyes of my mother.

Ashamed of dropped foot and ankle brace -
ashamed of clumping by on a walker -
I hung my head. After eighty, ankles trim-
of slumping Mother showed not a trace.

I had to pass the portrait as each night
clinging to the bannister, I climbed the stairs.
Graduating from walker to cane
I raised my eyes to plead my plight.

If only I could walk across that lot -
If only I could drive -

She looked me in the eye.
I hear, "Stir what you've got!"

Ruth Kenyon Tate

Nina Nona

(go to sleep my baby)
I see you in a dream of long ago, and far away,
nina nona, nina nona,
I become but a babe and sit upon your knee,
nina nona, nina nona,
And i look up into your face,
nina nona, nina nona,
I blink the years go by, with every tear i grow,
nina nona, nina nona,
Till i am too big to sit upon your knee,
nina nona, nina nona,
But still i dream, of a time long passed,
nina nona, nina nona,
And you sing me to sleep
nina nona, nina nona,
But only when i dream, nina nona.

Leah Jester

A Dream?

A woman runs for safety, for in danger is her life.
An angry mob chases her, she was with a man and she's not his wife.
She stops and begs for mercy, "Please don't throw your stones!!"
She's scared, frightened and trembles and the man she was with is gone.

But there, a kind, sweet, gentle man scribbles in the sand,
He speaks, "Ye who have no sin, keep the stones in your hands,
He who is unblemished, you be the first to throw."
The halted crowd heard the words he said, but will they stay or go?

Now he looks up from the sand and the woman stands alone.
He says, "Where are your accusers now?"; the accusers are all gone.
"I have no accusers here", she says; there were many there before.
Jesus gently utters, "then go and sin no more."

Think back to the scribbles in the sand, does a message linger here?
The marks Jesus made there, I couldn't see real clear.
Oh, how I long to know, what my savior may have written,
But time, a great eraser, did it save it? No it didn't.

Tho' I have awakened from this dream, that seemed so very real,
Those images will not leave me, till its message is revealed.
Here is what I must know, it's not written in the sand,
Tho' I am soiled and blemished, Jesus holds me in his hands.

Marian Caudle

A Birthday For Two

Our lives progress in so many unexpected ways
And sometimes produce the richest of days
One never really knows what tomorrow brings
Of life and death and other important things
Our moments slip by, like the turn of a page
And all of a sudden, we're in our golden age
Then out of nowhere, like a bolt from the blue
Comes a wondrous moment, most awesome to you
It is my birthday, number eighty to be sure
And a message has come, most thrilling to endure
The word has arrived that on this very morn
My brand new great grandson has chose to be born
All too few could know this exquisite feeling of joy
As when I first glimpsed this precious little boy
Despite the vagaries, the pains and the strife
This had to be the epitome of moments in my life
Mere words never express what lies in one's heart
Though no one is ever too old to make the start
And now that his first year is nearly through
We can joyously celebrate our birthday for two.

Fred E. Bamberger

I Spied An Angel

I gazed upon an angel, in wait,
Of heaven white, in flowers ornate,
Through a thin veil of satin and lace
Which flitted upon her gentle face.

Who is this beauty I dare to know,
Elegantly prancing e'er so slow?
Cherub before her, childish delight,
Tossing her petals of snowy white.

Upon a velvet pillow of old,
Symbols of love, these ringlets of gold.
From the train's own end the sprites keep pace,
Their smiles abreast, across their face.

Till father's arm finally grants me
Her hand in mine for eternity.
Her trembling hand, so slight, so warm,
And those deep dark eyes twinkle a storm.

Her delicate smile that's ever so bright,
Up from her heart, love's eternal light.
Know I have, as our journey does start,
Captured this dear, precious angel's heart.

Thomas C. McGuirk

Where to Wear Your Glasses

Sport officials are suppose to start out perfect
And then to improve,
No matter what the weather, conditions, or a
Coach in a foul mood.
Whenever you notice an official that cannot see,
Just send that blind-Tom to an optician, like me.
When the Official wears his glasses, and has
A problem seeing the ball in flight,
We suggest he put his glasses on his fanny,
For he probably has better hind-sight!!!

R. V. Bob Miller

I'm Lonely

I'm lonely, in a crowd.
I'm lonely, when you are near me.
I'm lonely, when you have said, unkind words.
You didn't know, how much you hurt me.
I'm lonely, when you are far away.
Letter's are the only way.
I'm lonely, till I cried and cried.
Loneliness is like an emotion.
Which we keep deep, deep, down inside.
Then comes to surface, no matter how hard we try.
I'm lonely, but still I smile.

Donna M. O'Neill

The Impossible Choice

As I sit here in the field of flowers so beautiful
I try to decide which I want for my own
That with the fragrance delicious
Or the one with delicate soft petals
I have been here three years it seems
And the bugs begin to bite
Do I see that which once smelled pleasant
Turn into a snake
Black as the nights I spent here smiling
Among the flowers?
Do I feel that soft flower
Turn to naked leather
That left the cow crying?
My days once were filled with the sunny field
Now winter's gloom
I see the snake slither away
My fingers reach
Instead I feel the leather
My two loves are gone.

Desiree Bethune

At the Hummerwell

Needle mini marlin beak
Male Annas drinking at the hummerwell
Chubby as a tiny fist flaring red cheeks
Rocking, balancing, B-B eyed sweet

He does not fly 'way when I come near
Heart beats him swinging the perch
Tiny breast soughing I fearfully hear
Wee thunder like wind song in my inner ear

Two females curious come to see
He rising spin-whirrs a sudden hum
One darts to the redwood the other to lee
Of the hummerwell hanging near the old plum tree

Then he rose past my nose and ever so slow
Left for the garden where hummingbirds go

Mark Spoelstra

Halloween

It's a cold and dreary night
the wind is howling about in fright
Leaves from the tree are shaking in fear
Ghost and Goblins are drawing near
I'm out in the kitchen shakin' and bakin'
I think to myself those leaves need rakin'
I hear a noise, oh, Gosh! What was that?
I look to the window, it's only a cat
I think I see the flashing of a torch!
Listen! There're sounds, out on the porch!
Rattles and knocks, and bangs on the floor
should I or shouldn't I open the door?
Open I did! What did I see?
Witches and Goblins staring at me
Those Ugly creatures upon first sight
had given me a most terrible fright
Trick or treat, I heard a small one say
I decided I'd better pay and play
So, to the kitchen, looking for snacks
apples, candy and gum for the sacks
Now just one minute, I want to know
who am I treating before you go?
No, not a thing, nope not any
unless you can tell me Derrick, Benny
Please will you tell me, tell me true
is it really, really you?

Grace Yost

Am I?

Once alive and carefree,
I now hunger, deep and desperate...
I wither, like a lifeless, wilted flower in darkness,
prostrate in difference to rising sun.
The winter snow recedes, revealing fertile ground once
more, its seedlings preparing for the race to the sky...
I breathe, with hope of renewal, and exhale, deep,
discontented sighs with none.
I feel capable and ready life all around me, eager to
exhaust itself...I yearn, and pray and wait...
Then strange? I'm strong with strength and
vigor, using every bit, I strain, breaking free of
my entombment cloaking sunlight, soothing, warms me.
I rest, and amazed, I take note of my splendor...
I feel wondrous! A veil has been lifted, and
deeply, I breathe with sated renewal.
I remember! and with trepidation, I
gracefully descend upon the newborn flowers.
I'm free!

Maria Haas

Inspiration

I am inspired by my sister
who is very smart, pretty.

Who plays be sport basketball,
very well, and still manages
to keep her grades up.

She cares about me and helps me out,
I can tell her anything.

Also she knows that she can tell me anything,
and she doesn't mind driving my friends and I anywhere.

That's why she is my inspiration so much.

Jackie Miller

Forbidden Love

Your eyes a brilliant pale blue
Hair soft and light
I let my fingers glide; an enhanced view.
Being with you isn't right
My conscience screams and I give pause,
You notice my hesitation and smile,
A look like that from you and I'd break any laws.
I abandon myself to you in a way not my usual style
I have you only for an hour, maybe less,
But my passion for you will always last.
Whispering carefully my fantasy I confess,
Our time together is going way to fast
I can't believe how I feel
Your touch makes me explode with desire
You make my body feel unreal,
I wrap myself around you, completely on fire.
After forbidden lust is sated,
Reality begins to set in yet again,
If anyone found out, we would forever be hated;
Regardless, all I want is to be with you, a blissful sin.

Dawn M. Bridges

I Looked In the Mirror This Morning

The picture in the wedding album
Showed a beautiful bride
Standing beside an adoring groom
And gowned in satin and lace

Love was reflected in bright blue eyes
And a radiant, glowing face

Happiness for then and future times
Young in spirit and years
No gray streaks in that auburn hair
No lines of care that day

That same bride is still young at heart
Though years have flown away

Whence came those thin gray locks
When did those wrinkles happen

I feel amazement every day, as when
I looked in the mirror this morning

Alverine Mosley Peach

Fossil

One final footprint of some unknown
Pressed near the thin edge of time.
A small muddy mold quickly left alone
For a distant future perhaps to find.

Meek this step marked in murky shallows
By one roaming through a misty dawn.
Silent destiny awaits among dim shadows
Where sandy sediment greet oblivion.

The final mark must here so remain
That future followers someday may see
How undistinguished all silent refrains
Etched hard in bedrock's hidden history.

Pitiful, the little evidence left here
By an unsung soul who quietly passed.
Destined slowly to fade across the years;
Along with its mud, but briefly to last.

Charles R. McGhee

Peace

There is so much hatred, so much woe,
In this world of many races,
People have a long way to go,
To wipe the tears from their faces.

Too many people and so much greed,
In this world full of selfishness and pride,
So much, it makes my heart bleed,
More so, than the tears that I have cried.

Everybody's thoughts are contorted,
Full of evil and hate,
It's like all of our thoughts are pre-sorted,
And the good ones thrown in a crate.

All of this anger,
Because of a different belief,
With no thoughts about the danger,
Or the final outcome of grief.

The world will always be this way,
Until we have broken its lease,
And we will all have to pay,
Because we didn't understand Peace.

Gary Maheu Jr.

Past, Present and Future

Life is a merry go round. It goes up and down.
Sometimes you're level to the ground. A time
to be born a time to die a time to be happy a time to cry.
Love One's come and go. The young people are coming and
the old people are going. But we'll yet growing, when you
lose a mother that seem to be the past. Because you grow
up and leave home and it become the past sort of speaking
This is plain life teaching, if your husband shall die
it is the present you are with him in the now.
but if you lose a child it's the future that they
will never see, explain this to me. God promise
in the name of Jesus eternal life. But when the
flesh dies it leaves our heart to mourn.
That our love one can never be seen. Only a vision in
our dream. The mind is a genius thing to live this
life and to be seen. But I love life with all my heart
and I'm glad to know with the Lord I'll never part
Our live this life with my family, husband, children
and grands and I'll take a wonderful stand. Until I'm called home.
Then our be the past and I'll be gone.

Gertrude Youson Igus

Night

Wind in the willows.
Daylight has fallen,
To the dark dreaming night.

The crying wilderness has awoken.
Wolves are howling,
Birds are tuning,
Not mellow but the blues of despair.

The moon shadow shows a tense bright light.
An owl cries out to warn his prey.
A desperate moan seeks happiness.
But day shall return,
Light shall come again.

Amy Edmondson

Big Perk

I love the way in which I have grown
I have memories others only dream
I have a wife that loves me
Parents who care
And two perfect kids so complete
For I am a man of much determination
For I am a man who has it all
It's not because I drive a big cadillac
It's the way I stand up, straight and tall
So think of me when you think of success
Think of the way that I feel
For I dream to have a big enough heart
And enough imagination to make it all real.

Brian Perkins

Strangers No More

I never knew what made you laugh, I never knew what made you cry.
I never recognized your voice, I never even heard you sigh.

I never knew the secrets locked away inside your mind,
The dreams of hope within your heart, I will never find.

I never knew the smile that moved across your face,
or the shadows you may have keep, tucked away in some remote
place.

I never got to hold the child's tiny hand,
for we were but mere strangers, distanced on this land.

I never knew the soul deep within your eyes,
I only got to know your face, the day you said goodbye.

I never knew the expressions that now stare back at me,
from pictures and photographs of the innocent lest resting in the sea.

And I am without words to comfort all who loved you.
I am without understanding your life cut short, for no apparent clue.

I can wonder, I can blame, I can doubt and I can cry,
And in the end I'll still be left with the question as to Why?

So instead I will salute you and rejoice in your rebirth.
I will pray for your new journey to heaven from this earth.

And to those you left behind, I will tell them how you're free,
And that they will be reunited with you, once their time has come to
be.

Kim Harm

The Screams of Darkness

Her screams fill the air,
As the darkness surrounds me,
They wait and wait for the screams to stop,
But for I know it never will,
As I see them run
My eyes fill up with pain,
The sharp blade gleams off the light,
In their eyes.
The blood drips from her pale face,
Like tears from a baby,
As the night goes on,
I decide to let them take me,
As a deafening silence surrounds me,
So does a passageway of light.

Pamela Yerman

Ode To Autumn

The days grow shorter, a cooler wind blows.
Leaves mingle with raindrops, in colors so bold.
Short sleeves become sweaters, and frost becomes foe.
As it embraces our windows, in a milky lace glow.

A ruckus of noise, anticipation fills the air.
As birds make their plans, to vacation elsewhere.
While squirrels and chipmunks, busily prepare.
Hoarding their stores, as if none were to spare.

Awakening from slumber, in the darkness of night.
The moon reveals wonders obscured by daylight.
Like crystalline dewdrops, on pumpkins so bright.
And long narrow shadows, cast by moonlight.

The crackling of firewood, some comfort it makes.
While bundled inside, our refuge we take.
As autumn gives way, for winter to wake.

    And fond fall memories abound.
    Stan Fuller

This Life

Sprinkled among the cares one faces
Are days of joy providing the laces
That tie together this life we live
Enfolding the love we have to give,

To those who mean a lot, it's true
But also for others in the crew,
Who help steer our life's ship
And help smooth over some bumps of the trip.

Maybe only an acquaintance or even a stranger
Yet each in a place given by the supreme arranger.
So we can be sure that the love we enfold
Is not to be hoarded like nuggets of gold.

But offered to all that we hold dear
And spread out to others far and near.
For love is the universal force
That helps keep humans on the right course.

    Emily Pearl Schmidt

Picture Us Together

Surrounded by the deep, dark, lush brown
of the earths strong oak tree.
That is what I really would like
to have it embracing me.

Under the shining see through crystal
like my mother and her daughter.
That is what I wanted too
of smiling together like we oughta.

ng They done it together, without me
they forgot me, I'm not there.
So special they look together
it seems like they just don't care.

Together without me by their side
up so everyone sees their face.
For I am left out, again
and, I see for me, there is no space.

I would of wanted to be there too
Now! Feeling like I don't belong.
We should of been pictured together
not being included was very wrong.

    Elaine D. Thompson

Reflections...

You were good for me..... at the time,
    You sped me upon a silver wing
Into a dreamland I knew not,
    Where spells are cast and fantasies come true.
You lifted my souls and took me beyond,
    As if with the wave of a fairy wand,

Yes, ... it really was magic.
    Caught in a whirl of sweet illusion,
Of tenderness and loving,
You absorbed me into a make believe world of romance,
    And, thought it was a dream, from
        which I must surely awake,
I treasured each and every precious moment,
    And for that..... I thank you.
    Susan Elizabeth Crockett

The Awakening

A smiling lady came to our house one night
She gave me a kiss and held me tight
She was so full of love
I looked up at her happy face
It wasn't just like mine
I asked my Mommy why -
She said, "her color is black".
People come in different colors

At first I was kind of surprised
She really was so nice
She acts just like my Mommy
And really feels the same
When I grow up to be real big
I hope I'll know lots of people
They don't have to look like me
I'll like them just the same
My Mommy says, "That's the best way to be"
    Helen C. Baker

Little Fellow

Come Little Fellow, the day's at an end -
And the sun is tucked into his great big sky bed,
While the moon man is winking down at you tonight,
He will smile while you're sleeping all through the deep night -
Now little fellow, you're stalling again,
Are you thinking about what tomorrow may bring,
Are you planning on being a great Big Fireman Chief,
Or the best spaceman in the whole world.

Your Daddy's asleep in his big arm chair,
Now tiptoe so softly on over there
And kiss him goodnight ever gently dear,
He's snoozing behind his old newspaper there -
Now little fellow, the days at an end
And the sandman is waiting to tuck you right in,
He'll put wee drops of wonderful dreams in your eyes so blue,
Goodnight my little one, sleep tight my little one,
God bless you darling - goodnight.
    Helen Baker

The Silent Fall

It is sad when happiness ends,
Down the road, around the bend.
Beyond the haze of blood and tears,
There is a notion to calm your fears.
In a place inside the soul,
Within a heart of solid gold,
There is a place around the bend,
Where silence falls, and all things end.
    LaToya R. Morgan

A Silly Fear

Yuk! an ant I see wond' ring around
Perhaps it's going underground
The thought that it's loose makes me nervous
Although I know most insects are innocuous
I still have the urge to stamp on it, make it disappear
No chance for it to comeback and soon reappear

I love the summer, flowers and bloom
The bees amidst flowers make me appear a poltroon
People tell me "stand still", they won't bother you
I believe that they know and this really is true
But I usually start running and carrying on so
I can't stand the thought of a sting, on even a foe

Bugs are many and varied - we could not subtract
Their ways or their means or their habitat
For among their habits which are repulsive to us
They are helpful, adept at life without a compass
Whenever I see a bug I try to be mindful
Of its being as one of God's creatures, albeit distasteful

Jonette Barron

A Child's Dream

Once I dreamt I was a bird, and I flew away from Earth
I flew so high I reached the sky, and this I saw and heard

   I saw a man so very sad, his face had signs of pain
I asked him, "Sir, is something wrong?" He said, "I'm Mr. Rain"

   I flew around and heard a sound, somebody having fun
I knew before I met the man that he was Mr. Sun

I stuck around but all the while, I could not understand
One man wearing a big smile, another having pain

   So I decided to approach the two in question here
I asked the one "Why all the fun?" the other "Why the tear?"

   They laughed, they cried, and Sun replied,
"Is it so hard to see? The more HE cries, the more it rains
   The more THEY'LL pray for ME..."

Said Mr. Rain, "That's true all right, but please remember this
   That too much SUN, like too much FUN
Can be a trying bliss, THEY must know pain, and have some rain
   To get along on Earth...

And what he said made me so glad that I was just a bird...

And so I flew back home again, and woke up with a start.
   The dream I'd had, had brought me pain but left a HAPPY
HEART!

Martina Pichétte

The Heat of Passion

No bodies fit as yours and mine
As we sexually intertwine
Sweats of passion preclude that sweet release
Hot fluids that put us in tranquil peace
As our bodies sweat and we draw near
Our moans are not the only sounds of love we shall hear
Suction formed as only a perfect match will make
Juicy noises that others can not even fake
Knowing that our bodies are meant to be one not two
Making love is all we truly want to do
As we contact passionate desires consume our minds
We need our hot sweaty bodies sucked tight and intertwined
Tools of our love swell in anticipation
Oh how we desire our lovers penetration

Bruce Lee Tandy

In God's Hands

I look around and see the pristine
White of hospital walls.
Those attending me...
Those hovering over me...
and those medics whose knowledge is put to the test.
They hold my hands in theirs.

But I do not see...
I do not hear...
I do not feel...
I look beyond and go alone....
No, not alone.
Both my hands are in God's hands.

Irene A. Holmes

Reaching Out

I am reaching out to touch you
but you are so far away and no
matter how I try, you just seem to
slip and go astray. You're a dream that
I can't understand. I pray this nightmare
will end. I know I'll never reach you,
and that's my biggest sin. Just wanting
to be with you. But I know that will
never be for the cards are stacked
against us and nether of us, will ever
be free. I've reached out for some one
who could never be. I'll remember only
thoughts of you, they're just old memories
but if by chance my dreams came true
you know that you'd be there. But in our
world it's impossible, and my love
for you. Will never be able to share.

James E. Whitmore

My Haven

How can I ever find a way to thank you
for helping me find my way back to me.
You tell me I've done the work by myself.
But I know you were always there by my side
with what I needed at any particular time.
Whether it was strength, hope, sympathy or love
and sometimes just an ear to listen to me cry.
I think you could see flashes of the me who was
looking for a certain anyone to place my trust.
I'm glad the me that was could see the you to be.
My hurt spirit reached out to your genuine concern
that shines like a bright beacon from your eyes.
My distressed soul opened and began to finally heal
the first time I shared and you gladly accepted.
You showed your pleasure at seeing my true thoughts
reviving my dying faith in my ability to be whole.
You've given her a safe place to be the whoever she is
so I can go wherever I want and be the me I am.

Susan E. Livingston

Candles

Candles cascading across the cold floor
lit with a lighter that licks at the wicks.
Flames that flick the candle with fire,
causing the wax to warp and wiggle
making rivers and ravines down the side.

Wind that whistles and whips at the fire,
sucks its life to a smoldering state,
takes the heat from the harmonious rivers,
rivers that wiggle turn to cold mountains of wax.

Michael Bonham II

The Pharaoh And The Slave

For Ken Coburn (Redneck Brother)
The Pharaoh was king and ruler of all,
    But his hateful arrogance caused him to fall,
The slave was obedient and lowest of all,
    But his faith in God gave him freedom to call,
Back then, the Pharaoh was never judged wrong,
    Until God told the slave to sing Pharaoh his song,
Then Pharaoh told the slave to make bricks without straw,
    But keep the exact count of bricks without flaw.
Then God took the slave from the Pharaoh's grasp,
    And left the Pharaoh nothing but his breath to gasp,
God's power told Pharaoh to build cities without bricks,
    To teach him a lesson about slavery tricks,
The Pharaoh is no longer on the straight and narrow,
    NOW, who is the slave, and who is the Pharaoh?

...For God and Heaven
Richard E. Forche II

I Once Believed

I once believed . . .
People cared and that they shared.
That my life was whole,
And that I had a complete soul.
That people speak the truth and not lies,
And that no one ever dies.

I once believed . . .
Life never ended,
But my realization is that it does.
For as dreams pass and friendships end,
You seem to come back to those you have loved.
You find yourself to be revolving,
Around one person even though you love many.
But when that one person breaks
the system you have created,
You feel hurt, alone, mad, and disgusted.

I once believed . . .
That people shared and cared,
And that life never ended.
But now I know better.
Kimberly B. Pratt

The Wild Flowers

When I see the wild flowers growing in the spring,
You know I still think of you.
They grow so happy, wild, and free,
Until some careless, trampling fool . . . .

See the wild flowers dancing in the wind,
Turn their pretty faces to the sky.
Dancing in the rain, dancing in the sun;
I can't guess what they are inside.
Until they turn away from me,
The hot tears forever burning in her eyes.

Oh Connie! In the final hour,
All I see are the wild flowers, and you!
Turn back time, I'd make you mine.
Swear I'd make your every dream come true!

See all the pretty roses sitting in the store,
With their pretty strings and bows? Yeah, their stupid bows.
Nobody ever tramples one of them.
Who the hell could love a rose? A DAMN STUPID ROSE!
See, I love a trampled wild flower,
The hot tears forever burning in her eyes . . .
Mark A. Swain

Earth's Jubilant Jubilee

Take us through the universe, but be sure to take
us back to jubilant jubilee.

Take us through the many clusters of galaxy, but
be sure to take us back to jubilant jubilee.

Take us through the milky way galaxy, but be sure
to take us back to jubilant jubilee.

Thank you one and all for bringing us back to Earth
jubilant jubilee.
Rudolph James Mateo

That Fateful Night

A picture passes through my mind,
Of a night where passion was undefined.
A night when I felt the true love I feel for you,
And knowing I can't have you just won't do.
You had been my fantasy for many years,
Tonight, our only night, I would put away my fears.
My heart was pounding with anticipation,
My inner self was filled with complete elation.
Was the time really here?
Was I going to hold you oh so near?
Heat took over my body from head to toe,
How much this night would mean to me you'd never know.
Your kiss was hot and sensual, like fire,
I was filled with complete desire.
Your love and passion burned right through me,
And I was consumed by you so completely.
Your caresses sent shivers down my spine,
All the while I wished you could be mine.
I still dream about that fateful night,
Knowing I can't have you, even though it felt so right!
Kim Grasso

The Pirates

Sailors must be willing to fight
the one armed bandits of the sea
Yet if, what if, the pirates are captured
within the pit of me

Like any good sailor, with compass as guide,
admits a luring ray, like the scum of successful dredge
deep within waters edge, danger awaits and hides

Dare they travel through the pit of my gut
to surface with swords in hand
their piercing wound bludgeon the spirit
marching onward to take their stand

He travels onto dreaded shore
amidst the shadowy shroud
wounded, gashed, stiff and sore

The endless task to sever the cord
digging a shallow grave
ending a lifetime of torment
from their deep embedded swords
Cathy Joaquin Broughman

Untitled Emotion

Alas! But for wont of pretty face —
Times remembered well . . . lost . . .
Loves that sowed the seeds of passion in a weak heart!
Thus so it is, but never was;
She that I fancied seemed distant,
Faint . . . a glittering star —
Far from pensive reasonings, the platinum-dipped moon
Receded with a cold wink behind the trees!
Dave Jacoby

Carry Me Through

Over the tempest sea
Beside me Lord you'll always be
If I never take my hand away from you
Lord, I know that you will carry me through.
Through the trials, test and life's pains
Carry me through.
    When finances are low
Lord deeper in prayer to you we go
We should not use you as a spare tire.
I know that I should rely on you everywhere
I go.
Lord please don't let me stray too far
Send an angel to stop the paths that lead
away, Lord carry me through.
    In faith, in belief Lord I know
that you are my souls only relief.
I ask you to carry me through.

LaTasha Johnson

Valley of the Sun

There is a valley way beyond,
Of which the Sun is very fond.
For every day after work,
This is the place where the Sun does lurk.
The Sun considers this place the best,
Because here is where he takes his rests.
In the day when he hangs high,
You can see him in the sky.
And when his work is over and done,
You should say "good bye" to the Sun.
But don't worry, that's not where he will stay
For he will shine in the sky the next day.
So when his work is gone and done,
He retires to the Valley of the Sun.

Stephanie Weakland

Nature's Eye

The morning sun rises up bright in the sky
drying the dew drops that caught my eye
a spider is busily spinning his silk
a new born fawn suckles mom's milk

The flowers unfold as graceful as swans
in wondrous colors of red, blue and bronze
a bunny hops by in search of some clover
down by the lake are the loons and a plover

The sounds of Nature are heard everywhere
the call of an eagle, the grunt of a bear
a light evening breeze smells of maple and pine
a sunset as rich as a glass of red wine

The moon rises slowly up over the hill
filling the evening with sort of a chill
away in the distance, the coyotes do howl
night-time is signaled by the hoot of an owl

Another spectacular day is now over
the fawn full of milk and the bunny of clover
will Nature tomorrow still have me in awe
I'm sure of it now, from all that I saw

Jerilee Johnson

Friends

I know that angels are real and do appear.
They're with you forever and with assurance, always near.

I know they are always and constantly at your side.
They make every attempt to gently help and to guide.

I know they love you no matter the wrong or the strife.
They are the assured blessing we have in life.

I know they help carry the load and make it lighter.
They certainly do all they can to make life brighter.

I know they encourage and give unconditional love.
They are blessings in themselves, placed by a plan from above.

I know they don't ask for riches, fame, silver or gold.
They know the true values lie in the friendships of old.

I know all of this to be true, I've seen it with my eyes and heart.
It comes in the form of a friendship with which I'd never part.

I know this friendship is a blessing totally beyond measure.
It's a friendship that's trusting, honest and one I treasure.

I thank you for sharing this beautiful gift of friendship from you,
I'm enriched and blessed...angels like you are all too few!

When I'm aged, reach 110 years old and life comes to a close for me,
It's my wish that I return and be to another what you've been to me.

Janis A. Johnson

Tears and Sympathy

Bad goodbye, tears and sympathy
Didn't think you'd say goodbye to me
Count on my dreams
Ending with screams
Bad goodbye, tears and sympathy.

Your perfume in a room, memories
Never fails, I look to see
Know you're not in town
Still I turn around
Your perfume in a room, memories.

Keep your picture in a hiding place
And when no one's looking kiss your face
You said goodbye to me
With tears and sympathy
Keep your picture in a hiding place.

Wonder if I'll see you, wonder when
Will you think of me as just a friend
Hope someday you'll know
How I've loved you so
Wonder if I'll see you, wonder when.

Ronald G. Couch

A Mother's Love

A Mother's Love is hard to find,
Not just any, but your special kind.
Someone who's patient, good and sweet,
Someone that prepare the food you eat.

A Mother's Love starts when you're small,
Carefully she answers every little call.
Someone who understands more than you,
Someone to help you, and what you do.

A Mother's Love is washing clothes,
Combing hair and cleaning noses.
Helping you to look so nice.
Also trying to make things right.

No matter what you do, or say,
A Mother's Love never fades away.
If you don't believe that this is true,
Without your Mother's Love what would you do.

Geraldine DeVine

This Little Doggie

He hang on the wall
So much sadness on he face.
I just could not let he be.
So I bring he home, to very special reason
That be to fetch to you the ring I buy
So soon we could be wed.
Me heart be yours now.
It be fulled with dee bestes love
To be gived to anyone.

Charles A. Klein

Life's Gems

Friends are like precious gems.
People without them know such a void.
They come in all sizes and colors, and can be rich or poor.
All are truly valuable assets.

Today we celebrate the birthday of one special friend.
She has a pretty smile and laughs freely.
I kid her about her weekend "therapy sessions."
Observe her merrily riding along on her Craftsman.

This special friend is closest to her sister Jean
And her delightful children — Thos, Jennifer and Alison.
She cherishes her many friends and friendships.
My special friend is Shirley Brown Merritt.

Happy Birthday!

Dot Hutchinson Kelly

The Woman . . . The Lake

Multi-faceted gleaming gems, glisten upon your face
    Radiating a mystic aura, surrounding you with lace.

The sun provides the catalyst, and bids you to respond
    Enticing and enchanting, yet reassuring the beyond.

You call to varied waters, to replenish and supply
    Re-channel them to life again, and never question why.

Within your bosom lies, sources of growth and gentle wooing.
    Within your womb protection's found, empowered births ensuing.

Yet beneath your gentle surface, unseen balance you maintain.
    Recycled deaths and secrets hid, you rejuvenate their gain.

Your beauty and simplicity call . . . each stage of life to fill.
    From joys of youth, through dimming years . . . joining you, I
will.

Joanne Von Deck

The Inner Soul

In this cruel world
where ugliness is cursed and mocked.

In the vision of others an appearance
is maybe all they see.

Looks are deceiving.
Pity the ignorance of those so prejudiced,
for the cover of a book they blindly judge,
unaware of what values they could find.

The inner soul.

Only the true know, in the inner soul,
the beating of a loyal heart.
A kind soul, an honest soul
to this heart so belongs.

To find the inner soul
just look into the heart of another.
Loyalty, peace, and happiness you will find.
The inner soul
all so kind.

Patricia Thompson

In The Dark

Did you get strong, when I was weak?
Did your cup runneth over, when mine had a leak?
Did you enjoy the show, when I hated the act?
Did you let me have an idea, for what you knew as a fact?

Did you love the ride, when you knew I was sick?
Did your watch stop, when mine never ticked?
Did you always see what I never would?
When I was stabbed in the back, did you feel good?

Did you get lost, when I was found?
I heard nothing, did you hear the sound?
Did you stand in the light, when I stood in the dark?
Did you laugh at me, when you had broke my heart?

Lisa Slauson

Father's Train Ride

When father was young, he rode the
    rails many a mile.
He was poor, so didn't travel in style.
His train rides were mostly free.
    For he rode in "box cars, you see?
One sunny day to Detroit he decided to go.
    He hopped on a car, loaded with barrels
    of sweet potatoes.
He was on his way at last, settled for
    a nap, unaware
That soon he would be covered with
    sweet potatoes,
Coming at him from just everywhere!
    The train was derailed-the depot hit
A pot belly stove upset, the coals a fire lit
    The fire engine came and put the fire out.
The train could no longer continue its route.
    Father was unable to go further on the rails,
For he spent the rest of the night in jail.

Jean Sanders

Estranged Eschew

Sometimes I can almost hear gun shots in my head.
Blood lain paths upon which I was lead.
To the places of ancient battle grounds.
Screams of charge and sighs of retreats.
My life and dreams have all been beat.
Senseless of substance and light filled dark.
The group known as friends I grew apart.

Tulips and daisies, sprouted my sunflower which grew.
Rolling hills and grassy plains.
My love this, my mind estranged.
Upon your request you made me eschew.
To you no further which I know.
You make me feel my head so low.
Our departure is all I know.

Eric Follis

Pumping Oil

See the man with strong seductive motion,
Drilling for oil is his only notion.
Pounding the shaft into the earth
Anticipation causing natural mirth.
Deeper and deeper the shaft penetrates,
Harder and harder the man concentrates.
With undulating form the reservoir is tapped.
The pressure is released with explosions of joy,
Then it is over and the well is capped.
The men are gone and machines are left behind,
Like pendulums rhythmically keeping the time.
There are fields and fields of these machines
Continually pumping with euphoric dreams.

Suzie Miller

Lost and Found

Several months ago I misplaced something
I'd grown accustomed to having around.
Usually I'm not bad about losing things,
but this was <u>no</u>where to be found.

Having kept it in the same place all these many years,
it was upsetting to know a special part of myself was no longer there.
When rearranging perhaps I'd put it in a different cubby hole,
and just could <u>not</u> remember where.

As a rule not prone to panic, I decided to retrace where I had been.
The more I looked, the more it became apparent,
the item would never be seen again.

After searching twice every space I could think of,
I finally gave it up for lost.
I went to wondering what I would do without it,
but had accepted that it was gone.

Tuesday night when doing last minute cleaning,
I saw something shine from the tight cranny
between the kitchen door and the wall.
And there it was, my loose screw!
I hadn't lost it <u>after</u> all.

Consiwella R. Ray

In A Child's Heart

A child's heart is filled with innocence and wonder,
always looking at things from above and under.
Children are a joy to have for the pleasure they bring,
all they think about is their next plaything.
Going to school reading and writing,
learning something new is always exciting.
A child's mind maybe small but sometimes,
they can know it all.
A child's friend can come in any shape, size or color
it doesn't matter as long as they enjoy one another.
This world may sometimes be cruel and unkind,
but to a child it may seem fine.
Creative minds growing their eyes glowing,
they're our work of art,
but it is our love that shapes a child's heart.

Vincent J. Pringle

The Hurt

I feel a burning sensation in my heart. There is a
wound, yet there is no visible sign of blood. It is, as if
there is a blade in my heart and it is being twisted. I
would imagine that I would start to bleed, but this is
not a physical injury, just mental.
I would like to cry, but there are no tears to be shed
I would like to scream, but no noise will surface out of
my mouth to show my agony. I would like to strike at
something, with all the anger I feel, but there is no
feeling in my limbs. I would like compassion, but
there will be no one to console me.
I am alone. The pain is unbelievable. I guess this is
what they call a broken heart. For those people who
have never experienced such anguish, consider
yourself fortunate, for the hurt, which I am
experiencing is unbearable.

Andres Vazquez

Gladyce

If I could make my wishes come true,
there is one for certain I'd like.
For that is to have, my mother-in-law,
be here to share in my life.
I know that God had plans for her,
it was sad to say goodbye.
The time we had was short you see,
but the memories are close in my heart.
She was a wonderful woman, who loved all in life,
for that was just her way.
I think of her always,
and know that she's near.
I miss her, the mom, that was so dear.

Linda Smith Madsen

Epiphany

We may scale the heights and plumb the depths
From heaven's vaulted peaks to hell's abode,
But the sweet, pure joy of what life ought to be
Is the truth in one brief, shining moment told.

The sun is much too bright for human eyes.
Soon we must look away and let it be.
We may transcend, but then we shall descend
Holding dear a precious memory.

Though we may only briefly pierce the veil
To wider worlds that we can only sense;
One fleeting glance beyond the looking-glass,
Then quickly back behind our earthly fence.

Now new horizons beckon ever more,
And we're never the same again once we've gone through that door.

Dorothy Baldwin

Why Not Me

When the hands of trouble come knocking,
So often I question, "Why me?"
Why me, not the other fellow
When I know I am better than he?

And then I reflect on Jesus,
How from suffering He didn't go free;
So if I must follow His footsteps
Why then should I question, "Why me?"

Why not me for sickness and suffering,
And trouble with friend or foe?
Why not me when disaster is raging,
When the winds of adversity blow?

Suffering is the tool God uses
Effectively to obtain
The healing necessary to cure sin;
Even though it causes much pain.

So when trials keep beating upon me,
And I'm blinded by anger to see
How in me God is restoring His image,
My question would be, "Why not me?"

Maureen Thomas

A Child's Thought

I want to be a bird,
to fly to you, so I no longer miss you.
I want to be your wedding ring,
so I'd always be around your caring finger.
But what am I thinking?
For I'll never be a bird or your wedding ring.
I'll remain a child always wondering,
why couldn't love keep you, mother, with me?

Christiane Abdul-Massih

You Promised

You promised the moon and the stars
for light in my darkest night.

You promised a shower of rain
in my dry and cracked land.

You promised there will never be hunger
for my starving soul.

You promised to kiss the wounds
of my broken heart.

You promised a blanket of warmth
in my cold and lonely nights.

In my sea of rage because of so much pain
you promised me I would have power to
overcome.

In my flow of tears you said you would catch them
so that they would be a comfort to others.

One day and soon I shall understand the reward
and benefit of what you promised me.

Kimberly Lynn Collins

Silent Cries

I hear your silent cries.
I'm an Angel, from up above, beyond the
clouds, that's in the sky. Every night
you go to bed crying in silence. Having
no control over the violence. Praying,
that someday it will all end. Hoping you'll
live long enough, to seek revenge. Don't
worry mommy, I'm coming to your rescue;
but your body didn't move. She was too
afraid to get an order of protection.
He had beaten her so bad, that she had
lost sense of direction. I know you're
too young to understand and wondering
why? Why mommy had to die? Someday you'll
thank me for hearing your silent cries..........

Beverly Carr

Ocean Memories

My eyes surveyed the beauty of the ocean as far as I could see,
peace and contentment filled my soul as watching was for free.
The foam-flecked waves rolled crashing into shore,
while above in azure blue skies sea gulls did soar.
Problems seemed non-important and so far away,
replaced by peaceful serenity on this particular day.
The sunlight reflected brilliant rainbows as surf kissed warm sand,
and nature's gentle flowing breezes lovingly fanned.
Oh to capture forever and store this glorious sight,
for recalling would fill me with wondrous delight.

Patricia L. Backlund

It's A Beautiful World

THE world is full of beauty and there's no way to live without it,
  The sky is blue and true, and the
grass is green and fine, the earth is moist and cooled
with beautiful flowers to hit the spot.

  The world demands love and respect, with
a cycle of 360 degrees, around and around it goes,

  with her deceiving ways, she will make
you fall in love, her tear's like sun rays send message's of
joy and happiness,

  and once in her work you will begin
to see the pleasure of creativity, because forever she leads
those who are true, TO the Beatitudes of the undreamt...

Kathy G. Smith

Trail of Tears

The road is a long and dusty road
Heavy the burden, heavy the load
The mountains are high, the valleys are deep
Moving ahead without too much sleep
Crossing the rivers and meadows so green
To some faraway land no one has seen
Proud of our ancestors, proud of our lives
Only the strong and healthy survives
We lost the battle to save our own land
Beaten by someone who's called "The White Man"
They're throwing us in a land so forlorn
Leaving our spirits in the land we were born
Having to push on, wanting to stay
Praying the spirits will help us some way
Holding our heads high, feeling no shame
Proud and brave, we know who's to blame
Far we have journeyed, through many years
But we'll never forget our trail of tears

Rebecca S. Martin

Role Model

You are one of a kind, YES suigeneris your name should be,
  So nice you are, you make the saddest
days Joyous.
  Just one thought of you is what keeps me striving
and struggling, because to know you is what assures me that
all things are possible.

  The best of all women is she, is you.
Who walks the creed that she preaches;
  By your actions I have
learned what it takes to be what is called human.

  So if ever I had to choose a word
to describe you, and if there ever was a feeling to define
you, all I could say is "HEAVEN"...

Raffael N. Lockhart

A Father Grieves

What sorrow, sir, to lose your only son!
On blood-soaked fields of rice 'neath hostile gun

This painful message briefly came to say
his soul and body went their separate ways

Deceitful death knocked twice at thy abode;
the sun withdrew and left a darkened road

Sharp steel was driven deeply through your heart;
it buried there with grief and cannot part

Thine eyes are cast with shadows strangely sad—
how much you loved that brave, courageous lad

Strange warrior he who felt war gravely ill
poor weapon to perform the soldier's will

When twilight falls I see thy downcast head
recalling nights your child was safe in bed

I hear a sigh of woe escape thee now—
behold a look of strain across thy brow

For as you hug and kiss a tattered toy
you think he was a man though still a boy

Deep sorrow fades with passage of the years
yet wish that I could stop thy falling tears.

Evelyn Olson

Life

Each day is a new meaning.
The clock ticks away.
We hurry to meet the demands of a new day.

The journey laid before us, we press on to the mark.
The goals we have set, trying to be sure that they are
Fulfilled and hoping that they are met.

What is this race in life about?
Are we living or existing to carry our dreams out?

We hold on for tomorrow when the day is done with a
Hope of victory for the race that is won.

Bernice Erman

When Angels Are Born

The valleys so high,
the deserts so low,
the eyes of angels watches from above.

The call of the rainbow as the rain begins to end,
the face of one more angel forms within.

The heavens door open to a brand new day,
an angel has received the wings of faith,
the mountains has begun to loose its forms,
to make room for the angel that has just been born.

I shall not weep for the shelter was worn,
because one special angel has just been born.

My father has given her the crown and robe of faith,
to an angel so full of grace.

I shall not weep a tear from my eyes,
but I shall never forget the love she gave through her life.

My father has given her the crown and robe of faith,
to a special angel that walked through heavens gate.

Ronnett Holden

Learn to Appreciate, My Child

Thank God for all your blessings from the God Lord up above —
Your home, your special friendships, and your caring family's love.
When you look at things too closely, at times you do not see,
As sometimes people do not see the forest for the trees.
Step back and count your blessings, my child so young and fair,
For surely you would miss them if they were no longer there.
It's hard for you to understand, not being a parent yet,
But someday you will see how hard this parenting can get.
At the risk of appearing foolish, a parent will shield and protect,
The most precious possession it will ever hold dear — the offspring
from its nest.
And even when, unwittingly, your mendacity hurts and stings,
A parent knows its transference of anger from other things.
To forgive and forget is a virtue, and parents know it well.
They have no ulterior motive, just pure love of their child, they tell.
So try to be more grateful, and start to appreciate,
What a wonderful life you really have, compared to the less fortunate.
The things you take for granted, some others do without,
Especially during catastrophies, with widespread tragedy throughout.
Now Paradise is before your eyes, but blindness clouds its view.
So clear your heart of heaviness, and happiness will come to you.

Irene Andrighetti Dietz

The Gift

I have presented my soul to you.
It lies quietly at your feet —
Open, vulnerable.
I've given it without your asking,
And you circle it warily, cautiously,
With uncertainty in your eyes.
Yes, I am aware of the danger,
But the trust has ridden long in my heart.
Quiet confidence whispers, "Peace!"
Life is a crystal simplicity
In this extraordinary moment,
Framed on either side by
Ordinary-a-moment-ago and
Ordinary-a-moment-from-now.
This venture thrills me
In the same way my bare toes thrill
To dew-damp grass,
My long tresses to a gentle breeze.
That's my soul out there —
Handle with care.

Becky Hejduk

Where Is God?

Is he hidden in the heavenly realms?
Or in the rocks, bushes and elms?
Is he a figment of our imagination?
No sir, you can see his hand in all creation!
Maybe in that grey matter called a brain.
I hate to ask the question again.
But where is it, that place where He hides?
If you believe that Jesus is your savior - inside us He resides.
For when you accept His gift of payment for our sin.
It is when, that very moment, He makes a home within.
So if you do not believe this very day.
Please accept His gift — best not delay.

Charles P. Hruby

Peace!

Yesterday is gone forever
tomorrow is the loveliest treasure
leave the past take love's wisdom
and hold it fast
take the heart and reap the soul
make the future the brightest goal
what we do today affects the morrow
bringing joy glee happiness pain or sorrow
the greatest wealth is physical and emotional health
without it we can do nothing!

Morton Cohen

To Love, Honor and Obey

Stand by your Man,
No matter what He says or does.
Speak of Him well, as He is your God.
Listen to all He says and support Him.
Give your all to Him, body and soul,
And expect nothing in return.
Know that He lives for you,
If you do what you're told.
Accept gifts knowing when you make Him angry
He will take them all back.
Even when you do everything, compared to Him
You've done nothing at all.
Remember everything is yours,
Until you leave Him or He leaves you.

Renee Baptiste

Rain

Day after day time goes by and
the rain comes down,
I'm alone with you not around,
I dreamed of you last night your face so clear,
I dreamed of all the good times when you were so near
Then I woke up, and realized it was just a dream,
Again so very far away you seemed,
Even though we're apart, and you are so far away,
I want you to know I love, and miss you with each and every
passing
day,
Never could I stop loving you nor would I try,
Rain keeps coming down, and the rain is my tears when I cry,
The situation I'm in myself I blame,
All I ask is that you send a little sunshine
to wipe away the rain...

Djone Reeves

What If...

What if the sun would never come up
would there be mornings without the light
and how about sunsets with bloody red skies
would there be sunflowers awaiting sun

What if the winds would suddenly die
would all the kites fall down from the sky
would there be windmills turning around
would all the sailboats ever leave ground

And what if the river refused to flow
would there be white water or waterfall
salmon would never know which way to go
'cause there wouldn't the upstream without a flow

What if the moon refused to shine
and all stars would follow by hiding in dark
would there be lovers watching the sky
waiting for shooting stars to see them fall down

What if all 'round us would suddenly end
would we have time to hold each other's hand
would we have time to share what it was like
to live thru this moment - a moment called life

Milan Sabata

Meanest Little Red Headed Boy

Little red headed boy, swingin' from
the old oak tree.
Meaner than two hound dogs
in a hot July sun.
Little red headed boy, swingin' from the
old oak tree, tore your pants on the
highest limb in the tree.

Freckles all aglow from the hot July sun.
Scratches on your arms and knees and no
shoes on your dirty feet.
Two front teeth missin' since the early
mornin' hours.
Hey, little boy, whatcha gonna do when
mama gets a hold of you.

Been down to the ole swimmin' hole,
sneaked out before the sun came up.
And your mama is lookin' all over for you.
Why, you're the meanest little red headed
boy I ever did see.

Marcella G. Inman-Sievers

The Gift of a Child

To hear a child's sweet laughter is to hear the music
of angels.
How carefree they seem.
To watch a child sleeping is to know they are
content and peaceful.
To breathe the sweetness a child brings to
life is to know you have had a breath of
heaven.
To feel a child's hand in yours is to know
you are loved.
To bear a child is to have experienced the
greatest gift of life and God.

Tarra Benson

This Man of Mine

This man of mine
A man so busy kept
Giv'um a job he dare
Will certainly except
With time to spare

A man whose caring
Giv'um his thoughts much bearing
Always anxious-Does right
Always to please
This man has patience you see
Giv'um a tool he keeps his cool
As he builds on and on

Rise and shine early morn'
Half past five out the door
This man gathering a smile on all he has accomplished
In his car feet on the floor
Off to work he goes once more
This man of mine

Marie Baum

Mrs. Claus

Mrs. Claus I've always wanted to be
So Joann said would you do it for me.
I said I'll ask my mother and see
If she could make an outfit for me.
She said she would try and do her best
First she started with a red and white dress.
Next came a white apron and I ordered a wig
When I got it all on I danced a little jig.
Then I found some high button shoes
Because the black flats just wouldn't do.
When I put it all on to my surprise
Mrs. Claus was before my eyes.
Like a little girl my dreams came true
And thank heaven I didn't have to return to school.
But with a red face unfortunately a round belly
I'm not like Santa because it doesn't shake like jelly.
But I will stay merry and happy myself
Because I'm Mrs. Claus and not an elf.

Elaine L. Mitchell

The Night

As I look up in the darkest night
  I reach for the brightest light
As I gaze upon the stars shining light
  Love sparkles in the endless night
As I stand in the healing waters of the stream
  It seems like an endless dream
As I ask the questions of the night
  A gentle evening breeze makes it just right
The answers of the night
  Lie in that bright shiny light.

Larry Davis

Good Morning World

Good morning world, and how are you today,
God brightens up the world, just to show you, your way.
Morning light enters for all the world to see,
His blessings and His wonders and those things that are meant to be.

Look at all the beauty and all the colors too,
For God made them special, He made them just for you.
Put a smile on your face, for you have a life to live.
One full of wonderment, a life that God did give.

Forget about your worries, for He shall take care of them too,
He gave you a good life and many things from which to choose.
Think your life is empty and there is nothing good today,
Hey, you woke up didn't you, it's better than the alternative, I say.

Be happy with your life and think positive too,
For this day is your new beginning, a new day made just for you.
Whatever the situation may be, which carries fret, you alone allowed
   to grow.
Remember, that you are special, say good morning world, and allow
your brightness to show.

Judy Long

Doer

When we consider our nature, how far shall we go?
Do we desire hard knowledge? Or would we prefer not to know?
Do we really have substance? Or an awareness we prod?
Are we a product of our volition? Or an extension of God?

We tread on a stairway, leading forward in time,
Tomorrow is the next step, to which we must climb,
If we wish to retreat, we face only despair,
For yesterday's steps, are no longer there;

To keep going forward, is all that can be,
Though what lies in that direction, we never can see,
On an illusion of present, we fancy we stand,
But before we conceived it, it's no longer at hand;

This concept of being, rides a razor's edge,
For an increase of purchase, no man can give pledge,
The extent of our essence, is the memories we hold,
By faith we assume, that repetition will unfold;

We can only be dependent, but we desire to be great,
Who can truly believe, we're the masters of fate?
Our desires are a prayer, that the real power may grant,
He's the one who makes plans work, and it's obvious we can't.

E. F. McSweeney

Listen

If the eyes are the windows of the soul, why can't you see my pain?
Can't you hear the sounds of a desperate heart?
If there are no words to be spoken to ease my sorrow,
and actions are supposed to speak louder than words,
why won't you hold me close to your heart?
Renew my faith in the power of touch,
Is your guilt so great that you cannot spare
the ray of hope I need so much from you alone?
If time will heal all wounds, why won't you take the time
to heal a piece of my shattered heart today?
So I may begin to live my life as I did before the walls
came crashing in around me.
Back when you could just glance in my direction
and catch the look of joy on my face,
rather than the look of lost hope.
I want to live my life free — free of my own self-hate...
Though it seems this hate will be my fate . . .
Forever.

Susanna Hemphill

Who Knew?

He wipes away my tears with a gentle hand.
Tears which are the product of another man's betrayal.
He tells me not to dwell on the pain,
There is a man in this world who will love me.
I didn't know he meant himself.
He said those men were terrible fools for hurting me.
He told me I was special.
I didn't know he loved me.
I discovered much too late
That I could love him too.
He has found someone to care for him
The way that I did not.
She tells him that he is special.
He deserves all the joy life can bring.
And she does make him smile.
I know I have no right to interfere with his life.
So I will sit in silence while the tears roll down
And there is no gentle hand to wipe them away.
He doesn't know I love him.

Kimberly Sawyer

Future

I woke this morning knowing Time was moving
endlessly around the Calendar of Seasons.
Fall was arriving one fading flower after another.
There was that inner sense of change,
A certain knowing,
A leaf had turned in the Book of Life.

With inner Vision,
I summoned early memories, sights, and sounds.
   School
     Friends
        Home
          Marriage
            Children
Years lived, miles traveled.

The aching loneliness I sometimes feel
For dear faces long gone,
Would be unbearable without the promise of tomorrow.
Yes, I woke this morning in anticipation
Of drawing closer to the future,
Morning by morning.

Betty J. Malone

Gold

There's time when some things aren't gold. Searching time which
way to go? Train your child - show thy road! He may sense the
meaning of your words.

Time flies by so swiftly, but time and chances happens to all. Work
daily in the vineyard. Render fruits, tender there of.

Whom that hide, the wind flows away. Who shall not sow, who shall
not reap. Open your ears and never turn your back. Walk straight
ahead, "follow that way."

It's better to get wisdom than pretty gold. Then you'll shout, and
you'll scream, be headed that way.

Well it's almost over....please don't pass by. Come!!!

Love, Love, is the answer. Heavenly gladness, easier laughter. Just
stay, and build up, you'll pass the cumulated stars. Just stay,
you'll pass the cumulated stars. Just stay and build up, you'll
pass the cumulated stars.

Cheryl Pounds

Our Song

Can you hear that song?
You know, the one that makes you cry.
A first date, first kiss, so long ago,
You dance a step, twirl and sigh.

Memories are warm and full of smiles,
You've hurdled all the obstacles of living.
You close your eyes and bow your head,
And whisper your prayer of thanksgiving.

The children grown are off to explore,
Your job goes well and the mortgage is paid.
Vacations are your to travel or sit by the shore,
Take a cruise or just listen to a serenade.

The music plays and you lay your head on his chest,
You've been together so long no words are needed.
He touches your hand you can feel his love,
You challenged the world and succeeded.

The song is over, you wipe away the tear,
He smiles an asks for a kiss.
As your lips touch you know at once,
That love, is where you put the emphasis.

Terry A. Stanley

Untitled

To write what is perfect is my dream to fulfill
But from the deepest thought onto the greatest height
More than a mountain topes by a hill
Partly the distance between
the dream and its maker
As yet to be fulfilled
to obtain what merely I dreamed
My lack of words I may not write
is much the difference
I may say but not get right
But I think the time of fulfillment
is only the reality of the distance
Between where we think to have been
And the distance it takes to do it again

Metro A. Narcisi

Hay Brothers of Rap

There's a problem in the street — between the east and the west
Trying to say — they rap the best

But why — oh why — why should this be
When both are great —- artist of rap — you see

It just doesn't matter — what coast your from
Only to know — you rap to songs

Singing, dancing and having fun
Raping on the positive — and not about guns

That's the only thing — that should be
A positive message — from you to me

What happen to Tupac was sad and mean
Being gun down on a vegas street scene

People running around like Al Capone
Shooting and killing each other is wrong

Lets come together — each other as one
For the future of — our daughters and sons

From a mother — to the brothers — of rap — I say
Rap a positive message — for our children's sake

So — east coast — west coast — brothers of rap
Your mothers and fathers say — stop the crap — brothers — of rap.

Dorease Russell

September

September - is the ninth month of each year
September - is the month that schools start each year
September - is the month of change to the fall weather
September - is the month that all things change
    getting ready for winter ahead
September - is the time trees leaves change colors
    and fall to the ground
September - the farmers and ranchers to prepare
    for the winter ahead
September - is the month - I was born
    I call September - my month.

Irene Mary Larson

To the Newlyweds

I've know my friend since he was seven
He's married now, a match made in heaven
I've never seen his smile so wide
It's because of her, his wedding bride

I've known her since '93
And I know she'll be happy for eternity
When a marriage is filled with patience and love
They until be blessed by God above.

To you, dear friends, I make this toast
But please remember this the most
Love each other with all your heart
Because you're stuck together till
    death do you part!

God bless you both!

Richard Matt

The Serpent in the Garden

In the Garden of God
Dwells many things
Perfume of beautiful flowers casting a spell
Songs of the birds racing to the sky
Dripping of a creek passing by
The music of children's laughter
filled with love.
There also exists the serpent
who tries to breaks the veil of beauty and faith!
Even as we try to weave the thread stronger,
he pulls and tears the web
The struggling serpent pulls and wiggles —
As he hopes for another tear
But to no avail!
Exhausted and shamed he finds a corner,
curls into a ball — knowing he failed
Finally the answer is revealed.
Strong threads of love and faith build
the strength of the veil!

Rosemary Weiler

Ecstasy

From across the room she watched him play
his hands dancing on the keys.

The fire fairies whirl above the logs
Escaping into the air with their secrets.

As his body sways to the rapturous melody
she longs to nestle his body.

She yearns to feel his chest against her
as he moves to the rhythm of his music.

She imagines her hands dancing with his
craving to feel his emotions.

Ecstasy awaits at the end of the crescendo!

Francine Marie Verdier

My Lord, My Savior

My Lord, My Savoir said to me,
"I'll love you forever, have faith in me,"

Take my hand I'll show you the way,
I'll guide you through each passing day,

I took his hand I said "I'm yours,"
My heart was healed forever more,

He showed me wonders of a place,
Where we are saved by God's Grace,

Love so pure it can't be stained,
Forgiveness for all with no more shame,

Tears will dry and eventually fade,
The love from God will always stay,

Eternal Life what does it mean,
Love and Peace beyond your dreams,

This is my poem to whom I love,
My Lord, My Savior, My God above.

Flora Carde

The Cross-Pollenization of Dreams

I want to grow a garden in your soul.
In the fertile scars of hurt,
I want to scatter seeds,
So that they can spring up and
Become flowers and sweet smelling shrubbery.

Then, on hot and windy summer nights,
The pollen will take flight,
And settle in my soul's garden,
And reach the hidden flowers in my soul scars,
However slight or mighty they might be.

Then will my soul explode
With the power of your love.
And magnificent, color-wild gardens will grow,
Until the vibrations of separateness will slow.

Only after the winds of time have blown,
Can we say "we have grown!"

Byron W. Lemky

A God

There was a priest
Custodian and servant of a powerful god
of gleaming granite like black sweat.
And this priest had ministered to his god
Ever since his hair was black and his limbs supple
so long ago
He had done this for years and years custodian and servant
Then one day the seed of doubt
fell into his soul and
like the germ of leprosy it ate at his faith
until one day he pulled a ladder, climbed it
and looked into the face of his god, looked into his pitiless eyes
and asked:
"Are you rea1?"
And his god struck him down.
As he lay smoking in his approaching death
His god muttered:
"You waited too long to question me"
And went back
to being a statue of gleaming granite like black sweat.

George Dash

Days Gone By

This girl I met, so many years ago
I cared so much for, I'm sure she knows
Her beauty shined through, it was a sight to see her walk
I remember my heart would melt, just to hear her talk

We got so close, but yet so far away
We had different lives to live, and couldn't stay
I've never been so heart broken, so sad to see her go
The feelings I had for her, I couldn't help but show

But life went on, in a downward sort of way
Just the thought of her, would always brighten up my day
I wonder if she ever thinks of me, those days gone by
The new years eve we spent together, the memory still makes me cry.

I've always held her, so close to my heart
If only I had a chance, to make another start
I would make her so happy, in every way
I'd never let go, in hopes that she'd stay

So if you talk to angels, and they know this girl
Just let her know she's in my heart, and a big part of my world.

Rick Busatto

Dreams

A gentle breeze, blows Autumn Dreams
Across the golden pond.

Glitter lightly, softly new, finger
of Birthing dawn.

Crystals silent waters deep - ebony
Shimmers lost in sleep.

The lowly cry of the distant loon.
Echoes across the morning moon.

Pearls of dew on the spider's web.
Dance diamonds dreams of silken threads.

Lilacs, lavender, lilly, wild rose
linger, linger, with eyes still closed.

Cold winds of morning through the
spider's weave.

Blow dandelion dancers, that tangle and leave.

D. Delaney

Ode To Freedom

O' gentle and beautiful lady,
Whose name does honor the birth of a new day.
Only a man void of all worth,
Could not be inspired with love by your gracious spirit.
So sweetly expressed in the bounty of feminine looks,
'Tis your inner gifts what are the arrows and bows
of love.

You are the down of my conscience,
He ultimate of goodness within my heart.
When you speak to me, the trees and the birds sing.
To you I say, let every man know that not even grace,
From above can prevent my desire of your true love.
I shall always sing of your happiness within,
From becoming immovably of removed from my heart.

Myke Briggs

Communion

The most perfect of all shapes, of course it was a sphere.
An appealing colorful orb.
Solid, jewelled, statuary in stone cool crystal
A still life, freeze-framed forever.
A pure rare moment in life panorama.
Captured always in polished glass

But ever teasing the eye with something unseen, truant.
Silver one second, an optic trick turns mist to rainbow,
Prism to cloud. Curious... This magical diorama changes,
Flirtations and almost frustrating.
Like peering through a wave.
Who being looked upon, knows the game.
And choosing to play, ducks quickly in.

Yet this globe of lights, once silent and still, now wakens,
The spell broken, the enchanted vision in ice melts,
And, sensing interest comes alive
And glows warmly, returning your joy
Fusing observer with observed
The marriage complete
The communion mere perfection.

Jean Stuart Hambling

Another Man's War

One man's ceiling is another man's floor
One man's window is another man's door
One man's women is another man's whore
One man has nothing while another man has more
One man's blood spilled in another man's war
One man's distortion is another man's escape
One man's beliefs make another man hate
One man's freedom is another man's grave
One man's horror is another man's fate
One man's blood spilled in another man's war
Drive-by innocence, bullets fly with no intent
Children playing children crying children falling children dying
Blood in the sand box so hard to understand...
One man's blindness is another man's despair
One man's choice is another man's fear
One man's death is another man's dare
One man's death not another man to spare
One man's memory fades as if another man cares
One man's blood spilled in another man's war
Mothers crying children dying... in another man's war
Mothers crying children dying.... in another man's war.

Peter Thorburn

Reflections

Oh for the days of yesteryear,
when we greeted our neighbors with joy and cheer.
The streets are now filled with violence and crime,
where people are killed for a nickel and dime.
Children in fear, attend public school,
as parents pray they learn the golden rule.
So many have turned and gone astray,
for they can't seem to see the error of their way.
Remember when you could walk around the block,
you need not worry and doors were never locked.
Neighbors would gather for homemade ice cream,
and children would swim in a nearby stream.
People would lend a helping hand,
youngster's would learn to farm the land.
It all seems like so long ago,
as now we teach our children to "just say no".
When our reflection in a mirror we see,
Who is that person looking back at me.

Beverly A. Poston

Darkness

Darkness will come soon,
Mysterious shadows lurking around.
The moon will shine ever so bright,
Casting an odd glow upon the ground.
To some giving a meaningful fright,
While others laugh and walk into the night.
Suddenly, grabbed by the evil darkness.
Where is the end of this darkness?
Only time will tell.
Second after second, I am still wondering is there an end?
But, wait what is that I see?
It is the evil darkness creeping onward.
In time the wondrous Earth will be covered, covered by darkness.
This darkness will never end,
For, people committing crimes will still do,
And the evil darkness will last forever.
The Earth covered by darkness and never to be seen again.

Shari May

World Torn Apart

If I could look, Into the past,
And if I could see, into the future,
Oh I would see, a world torn apart.

Each with another, point of view,
Not acting as one, but ranking one to two.
You see it everyday, wars being fought,
people being killed, like a world torn apart.

If I could see, into the future,
Not looking at probability, I could change this world.
But now as I see it, nothing can be done,
All that will be left, is devastation and none.

If I could look, into the past,
And if I could see, into the future,
Oh I would see a world torn apart.
Nations disbanding, dividing in half,
Fighting in each others territorial path.

North against south,
East against west,
Nation Vs. Nation,
What is it all about!

Kevin Watkins

Where Dreamtime Sweeps

In the dreamtimes of the tattered past
I see the things that never last.
On the shores of minds these thoughts were cast
To never fade, and yet not last.

For time will tell this lurid dream,
Perhaps the mind can yet redeem
The thing that seems to mark the sign;
This dream will tell the test of time.

For I knew not from whence I came.
These thoughts of mine I now reclaim
To tell what love I might now find,
But can I bear this beast of shame?

It all seems like a jumbled thought,
Yet in the fog the dream knew naught,
For it was born to now be brought
A tethered dog to soon be shot!

And so the body tires of sleep,
Yet yearns the fires our memories keep.
Like sandy dunes they seem to heap
Upon the shores where dreamtime sweeps.

Robert Whatley

The Righteous Way

Jesus is the light of each day; he leads and guides in the
righteous way. I was born into this world of sin, but by grace
he renews the mind and cleanses within.

When I think of his mercies I fall to my knees in prayer and by
the truth in his Word I know he is always there.

The cares of this world are such a shame, now I walk by faith
in Jesus' name.

I must rely on his word to continue my run; and I pray in this life that
Thy Will be done.

Anissha Chiffon Blackwell

Discovery

The child within me, all of a sudden without
has taught me so much of what life is about
a quiet little guy, whom I gave a special name
I held him, we bonded, and life was never again the same.

Teaching him and loving him, watching him grow
all of a sudden I had to let him go.

He spread his wings and took the flight
My heart lamented his departure every day, every night.
But the child within who became the child without
stood tall on his own and showed his family what
he was all about.

I have followed this child up hill and down
catching up to him only now and then.
Now the child within all of sudden without
has evolved into my prince among men.

I celebrated at the good news of this child within
are rejoiced with the child without
I named him Mark, he is my son
and today I celebrate the man he has become.

Carol Tetreault

Eternal Life

Candle, candle all alone
Penetrating darkness and unknown
Irradiating goodness, softness and delight
As it seeks the outer world with anticipation and fright
Expanding ever farther, to the depths of the abyss
An unrelenting power that may someday be missed
The intentions are good and curiosity is peaked
As it goes after all that it has once seeked
Felt is the illumination of the shadows of others
As it lessens the scare and increases the wonders
Surroundings come alive, as the influence draws near
For it has been decided that there is nothing to fear
Not all that bad, the light shines on
hoping and believing in what lays beyond
And as the spirit comes from within
So does the ever burning strength of our kin.
And though the flame may someday be gone
It's essence will remain for a time of long.

Lauren Seydewitz

Morning

Morning rises and spreads her billowy wings
Against the golden shimmer of the sun.
Her wings extend throughout the early day
Until the wind whispers against the wispy mass.
She spews her glory into the air
To sweeten the breezes and brighten the day.
Tender cherubs render squeals; of admiration
And nestle in the warmth of her golden wings.
The luminous sphere spins a web
Of sparkling hues that adorn Morning.

Lisa Marie Thompson Finlayson

Ode to the Sea

Oh the sea, what a sight for me.
It is light in my darkest hour,
It is diamond on a sacred day.
The sea is my solitude and my companion,
she is my guide into another world.

I can hear her cry miles away
A sea shell is our connection, for I hear her in its breeze.
I can see her tears splash against the shore,
She feels mine too, as they run down my face,
and wipes them away with a sudden embrace.

She is a silent God, a creator and a friend.
When in her presence a sweet song plays,
and all fears disappear upon her waves.
Softly she caresses your heart and soul with all her beauty and all
  her grace.

She and I will part for a while and she and I will meet again.
And every time I must go away I can't forget her long,
for somewhere she will call to me,
to come and walk her shore,
and there we will find each other,
and she will sing to me once more.

Shanna Lea Miller

Silent Waiter

She sits by the window, patiently waiting for him to come.
The sun shines through the window beating down on her
  gentle golden hair.
She waits by the window her dress made of silk, which is
gradually becoming wrinkly as the time passes by and she
  becomes uneasy.
When will he come? She thinks to herself, and she suddenly
imagines him in her mind as he has always been — a tall
skinny boy with green eyes which she treasures, and a smile
that says a thousand words.
As she stares out the window, she imagines him coming back to
  meet her.
It has seemed like centuries since she has last seen that
familiar face, yet the time has only been short.
She runs to him and he swings her around and around . . . both
laughing, tumbling to the ground . . .
But in reality she stares out the window only to see the
solemn tree which seems to mourn along with her.
She glances out, now becoming more and more impatient as
each precious second ticks by, still waiting for him to come.
The sky changes color, from blue to pink then finally
  settles to black.
She still sits by the window, the moon now shining down on
  her silky hair.
But yet she still feels a loss. She will wait in wonder,
  for her love is forever gone.

Kim Patten

Down at the Pond

Frogs are a-leaping, one by one
Another game of Leap-Frog, over and done.
Some frogs resting, others breathe in the air
A few jump quite high saying, "Catch me if you dare."
So many frogs all in one place, enjoy this pond so fair
Sharing the space with others, blessed by a God who cares.
  All sorts of insects with delicate wings
  Big birds and small birds caw and sing.
  Cotton tailed hares come hoping about
  'Tis a beautiful spot, without a doubt.
Dragon-flies and butterflies flutter by, but rarely stop
They dive toward the water, then skim o'er the top.
Living in harmony without worry or care
Lending background music to my outdoor time of prayer.
  Down at the pond I rest and pray
  Thanking my God for a beautiful day.

Jean Chapman

In Your Arms

Holding me, being in your arms
Touching you, adoring all your charms

So gently so softly gazing in my eyes
Silently in the night your hand brushes my thighs

A candle burning against the dark
My pulse races to the sound of our hearts

Two bodies and souls closely entwined
I melt at the thought of your love and mine

To feel and know such joy and peace
Fearless of pain or sorrow when I am with thee

Captured within a time and place
Wanting never to lose sight of your sweet, sweet face

The longing that you burn upon my lips
Keeping me anticipated for the passion in your kiss

Your smile so warm and sincere
Makes me only love and want you more my dear

My only regret are the days so long
When I can only feel, and see you in the words of a song

But I will keep you close across the miles
And remember in my heart, it's only this way for a little while

Brenda S. Perkins

What Is Age?

What is age?
Just a number on ones age scale.
A measure of time that has come and gone.
It has no rhythm, and it has no rhyme.
It's just a measure of time.

It starts with youth and slides into ones adolescence.
Then it drops into what I call maturity.
That's when wisdom is found.
It's covered with wrinkles of time.

You'll not find beauty in wrinkles of time,
Unless you look deep within,
But you'll find love, wisdom, peace.
And lots of time.

What is time?
Nothing but age in a heart beat.
What is a heart beat?
Nothing but a measure of time.

Paulette F. Gibson Smith

"Little Snowflake"

Little Snowflake, you are such a sight to see,
You make my heart skip with joy and glee.
I like to watch you swirl and twirl and go round and round,
Until you come to rest gently upon the ground,
Because of you, my friends and I got to go outside and play
We rode a sled down a snow-covered hill,
And you could hear much laughter which was loud and shrill.
Please come to visit again very soon, Little Snowflake,
So that into my memory, a vision of your beauty I'll take,
As I watch you swirl and twirl, and go round and round,
Until you come to rest gently upon the ground.

Glenda Colleen Gambill

Self Love

I love you more than you love
yourself, you wonder how can
this be?

Whenever you mistreat yourself,
you also mistreat me.
Self destruction is a terrible
death, to place upon one's self..

For when you abuse your heart
and mind, there's nothing for anyone else.

To massacre your own morals,
and to crucify your pride...
Tells me that there's something deep
that eats away inside.

For when there's no focal point
of one's own self and being.
Remember first the law of man, based
on self-esteem...

For only when you love yourself;
and self and you agree. Will you
reserve that extra love you'll have to give to me.

Paula Kandace Toliver

Thoughts of a Father

Today, I think of my children.
One so trusting and loving, the other placing me upon a high
pedestal. Not knowing my flaws and weaknesses. Always
ready to defend my name. And that name is Daddy.
But as all things, it will change, and become Dad and
eventually Father. But what is so bad.
The love of a child to his Daddy, becomes the guidance of
Dad and then the friendship of Father.
But to me; love, guidance, and friendship are the words I
use to describe my Father, and I hope they are the words to
one day describe me.

Timothy W. Clouser

Believe

The call of the wild is talking to me
Flee from the city and try to see
I'm wearing dark glasses and trying to hide
The tears coming down, out from inside
I'm trying to think not-to think any more
If I were a woman I might be a whore
My mind is a whirlwind of thoughts all awry
A cyclone with thunder and letters that fly
If I could do it over again
I'd believe in myself and be my own friend

Edward Zlatich

My Savior

Jesus died for our sins
So a new life we could begin.
If we confess on bended knees
A whole new life we will receive.

He will forgive all our sins
So in heaven we could enter in.
When I call he'll always be there
To show he loves me and really cares.

Forever he will always be
From now until eternity.
He is my master and my savior
He looks down from heaven to watch my behavior.

Tikesha M. Davis

The Jesus In Me

Many people have frowned down on me and said
I wonder just who she thinks she is.
I smile and keep stepping with my head held high
and I reply.
It's not who I think I am, but it's who I know I am.

You see - I'm a child of the king, and I possess many things.
Let me break down my inheritance for you.

You see I possess more riches than a rich man will ever see.
More water than a river will ever flow.

More light than the sun could ever shine.
More peace than a still sea could ever portray.

More joy than a smile could ever give.
More life than a person could ever live.

You see - this inheritance of mine, that makes me shine
that the whole world may see.
Is the King Jesus Christ that abides deep down in me.

Sharon D. Davis

The Chimney Sweep

Then came the chimney sweep
With face all tired and worn
And ragged clothes of dirty black,
The knees and elbows torn.

He opened up his leather bag,
My eyes would open wide,
For one by one I got to see
The curios inside.

With brushes round and thin black poles,
He'd twist them all together,
As up the chimney tall they went;
To disappear for ever.

He said, "Young Miss, please go outside
To see if you can see
The brush pop out the chimney,
Then tell it back to me."

And so I did his bidding,
To see if I could see
The magic brush aloft the pots
Of chimneys one two three.

Angela Sandling-Clarke

A Fate Called Destiny

   My feelings for this woman are so overwhelming
Between us there is a very special bond
My love for her is so large, larger than life
Her inner beauty that which I'm so fond
It must be Destiny

   My attraction to her is like a magnet
My image of my love, reminds me of a moon so bright
Drawing me closer and closer into her arms, into her heart
As the water, absorbs the moon rays on a mid summer night
It must be destiny

Making love beneath the stars on a early summer morn
As I lay and cuddle with her I feel reborn
We are pieces of a puzzle that fit perfectly
My life can't get any better as you can see
It must be, it has to be, it is
A fate called Destiny.

John Lebel

Untitled

On this planet where we live on
the spirit of the wind is my soul.
The seasons are spiritual
falling snow like dancing fairies

Birds are calling from green spruce branches
singing songs of high expectations
spring is coming.

Flowers are budding
Summer is in the making
my hart is asking for summer galore.

Spirits are dancing
on live wooden branches
autumn is coming back once more.

Winter is back again
On this planet where we live on
the spirit of the four seasons is in my soul.

Egbert Kroes

Life

Hold your head up high and see the world,
Stand up straight to take on the unbearable.
Never take without understanding why.
Cross into the unknown and do not worry,
Risk all or nothing but know what's at stake
Living to the fullest is a virtue,
A virtue many do not have.
Take on this virtue, see all, be all, do all,
Your dreams are only a step away.
Pick up the pace, live out a dream
You live for now not tomorrow
Rid all your sorrows, drown them with happiness
Do not ignore those who care, for love to, is as special
To your life as their, without it our souls are empty
Make yourself immortal by wanting memories for others
You are a God, you are the master of a destiny
You are you. You are full of life
So listen to these words of advice, or choose not to
Remember the choice is yours and not your brothers
You are free, you have a chance to be!

Mary Montgomery

Hail to the Brave Bull

The moment of truth has come
The sands of time have cast us thus
Linking our destinies
For blood has sealed this bond between us.

A fighter born you stand at bay
The spurs which drove you now are gone
All flaming anger spent, and yet
Your warrior heart fight on.

Defiant and undefeated still
Obeying some last command
Though dumb, you speak and shame my pride
As face to face we stand.

Let me not dishonors you by my weakness
Let death discover the truth
And let me know myself for what I am
This moment shall stand, the final proof.

Janice Cartmill

Mama

My Mama used to tell me things
like be careful what you do
that men will sometimes use you
like a worn out pair of shoes.

She used to knit and crochet
made everything so right
until she got an illness
that took her in the night.

I still remember Mama
and the way her hugs would heal
I wish she was here with me
to help sort out how I feel

My Mama's gone away but still
I feel her presence near.
She's guiding me through life (in sense)
and all my prayers she'll hear.

They say that death brings pain and fear
and tears and drama too.
but your Mama's still your Mama
no matter what you do.

Catharina Frayne

School

    It's about time we get our act
together.
    Stop acting a fool and pull
yourself together.
    Learn at school and it's what you
will do.
    Just like the principal say to
me and to you.
You want to like snoop -
You got to go to school,
That's the only way that he pulled
threw.
Be a leader not a follower.
So no one will have you around the collar.
You may think school is crazy
But most of us are just lazy.
That's why it pays off to go to school,
Or you'll just sit around and
be another fool.

Seprina Redmond

An Infant's Cry

The gift of life
Is a gift from GOD.
To breathe, to work, to play and to be free
Is only a once in a lifetime opportunity.

But why MAMA? You have taken
This gift away from me.
You took away the chance for me
To see how beautiful
This world could be.

Is it a crime to be born
And see the light of the early morn?
To hug you and squeeze you tight
In the coldness of the night?

I wish I could say
I forgive you for what you have done.
MAMA, I hope you can hear
This infant cry
'Cause my tears are not yet dry
MAMA, why have you taken
The gift of life away from me?

Kristine U. Hipol

Tribute to Mom

Mom, I just want to thank you.
Mom, you gave me life and give me life's lectures.
You give me all of the unconditional love I could ever ask for.
Whenever I cry, you are always there to comfort me and wipe my tears.
Whenever I fall, you are always there to break my fall, pick me up,
    and aid my wounds.
You see me through life's hardships without a complaint.
You have so far endured twelve years of my whining, my arguing, my
    temperaments and stubbornness, my happiness and joys, my sadness
    and frustrations, and my music and friends without backing away.
For that you are a very brave woman whom I am so proud of to have as
    my mother. I can't find the words to express.
You have taken me and will take me to places that I will always remember.
I want to let you know that I will never take our great times together for granted.
I thank you for everything.
I thank you for just being there for me to call you Mommy.
I thank you Mom, and I love you always with all my heart.

Jenny E. O'Dell

From O'er the Sea

In memory of Janet MacLeod (1902-1984)

From o'er the sea, a piper came, of Scottish blood and proud of name!
To settle in a local town, much loved by folks for miles around.
MacGregor and his bonnie bride, bore a gal, who was their pride
For Janet was a lassie rare with features fine, brown silken hair.

When e'er her father's band she'd sight, bright hazel eyes, danced in delight,
While bagpipes, breathing sweet refrain, brought distant hills, from wher'st they came.
His kilt a-swayin' with each stride, she knew nought but a swelling pride,
Through years unwinding, though he'd gone, brass buttons gleaming lingered on.

Yet he was nae the only Scot to win her heart...no, he was not!
Came George MacLeod, took she his name, since love for her he did proclaim.
George, for Canada, went to sea, to fight for truth and dignity!
On his return to build a life as "handsome man, beloved wife."

When hazel eyes gave way to blue, her silvered hair was lighter too
At eighty years, she'd done them proud, that woman warm, Janet MacLeod'!
From mem'ries stored they'd lived again, for Janet still remembered 'when'!
Through thick and thin, she'd kept them true, her Dad in kilt, George navy blue!

Ann Dudley Duncan

The Divinities

Mount Olympus was the chosen site, for the divine event
Zeus' instructions and details, having been ordered, were sent

Mercury and Hermes, the messengers of the gods, carried the invitations to all
The invitations, from Zeus and Jupiter, rulers of the gods, was for a grand ball

The Greek and Roman gods and goddesses, were expected to respond to Zeus' call
Their presence was requested, at the gathering, in the grand hall

First to arrive, were the goddesses of love, Aphrodite and Venus
Their beauty surpassed all, never showing a sign of meanness

Apollo, the god of light, medicine and poetry, arrived on time
Then came Bacchus and Dionysus, the gods of wild behavior, and wine

For the night, appeared the Gods of the sea, Poseidon and Neptune
Leaving their duties, and the tides, to be guided by the moon

Eros and Cupid, the gods of love, were seen milling around
While Hypnos and Somnus, the Gods of sleep, made no sound

Ares and Mars, the gods of war, made passes at the ladies
While being watched, by the Gods of the underworld, Pluto and Hades

Artemis and Diana, goddesses of childbirth, were summoned to center stage
Along with Gaea and Terra, symbols of the earth and mother, to write a new page

Upon completion of dinner, Zeus and Jupiter, declared the purpose of the feast
Standing before all, they ordered that Earth, was to be the new goddess, of Peace!

R. David Fordham

Untitled

When I was fair and young, and fear
Hath done passed me,

Of many women did I seek for my
mistress to be,

But all of them I did scorn, and
answered them in my way.

Go, go, and leave me be for my love
will come one day!

How many weeping eyes I've made with
my cursing woe.

How many broken hearts and still no love
to show.

Yet I know, as I did once before.
Go, go, and leave me be, don't haunt
me anymore!
O sweeter than the marriage feast tis sweeter for to me,
To walk together to the alter, with loved ones as our company.

Farewell, farewell! I must tell thee, to you my honoured wedding
guest, pray well for us and let us be,
For I have found the very best.

Tony Giannotti

The Blindness of the Lover's Eye

She wanted him to see the she inside of thee.
She wanted him to see the she outside of thee.
He saw all the pain he held within.
She wanted him to see the spirit of her soul
The light that filled her eyes, the glow of love itself.
He saw the failures of his past.
She wanted him to see the beauty of her heart.
He saw an emptiness of self.

She wanted him to see the gift that God bestowed.
He saw not beyond the wall that self allowed.
He let a distance help him to escape the happiness
        He knew was shared.
The spirit of his soul was loved by his mate
        The rest remains untold.
Hindered by the wall that was created by the
        Blindness of the lover's eye.
            A fear to give.
            A fear to love again.

Donna Foy Jones

The Mirror of My Mind

Does one's life have to be a mirror, of their family's mind.
If we have different personalities and ways of thinking.
Then does one have to mirror their family members mind?

I think not, for I am very different, from my family, in my thinking;
And, when I look at my success in life, I remember;
That I have different views and ways of thinking.

There are times, it seems I'm mirroring a family member,
But then I remember, I'm not the person.
As my mind searches, for why I'm not that family member;

I look, in my mind's mirror and I know why I'm not that person.
I realize that my differences makes me blend as one.
For I do not fit the reflective role of any one person;

That may be why my family thinks of me as a strange one.
In retrospect I'm a reflective image of their differences.
And, if they seek, they will find, I'm no different than anyone;

Because we all have our own ways and differences.
Therefore, I'm the same with all my differences.

B. J. Rosario

Peace

Peace is to enjoy freedom and to appreciate tranquility
Which we should always cherish and not resort to hostility

Education is not only for the preparation for life
But to study the skills for diplomacy in strife

Accomplishment is to achieve harmony in human relations
Which can be evolved to agreement between nations

Charity is for the affluent to be rid of greed
To ensure that excesses are shared with those in need

Equality is to recognize that no one group is better
We must be tolerant and respectful to coexist together

William Rin Ishii

How Heavy the Cross

The weight of the cross I must feel
Upon my back, the burden's so real.
JESUS my Lord suffered for me,
As He bore the cross of calvary!

Heavy, by far, it must have been-
Carrying the sins of all men.
He was so strong compared to me...
WHY OH WHY, did this have to be?

His love is so GREAT, mine so weak,
Love so divine... I daily seek.
His love shining through all that I do-
As I struggle and toil this life through!

Loving, caring and hurting you see,
As He bore the cross of calvary...
Never concerned that He might fail,
Trusting His Father, whose love did prevail!

Louise Crenshaw Mobley

First Light

The hour 'twixt dawn and fading night is
A special time to see, to feel, to hear.

The ebbing night, so dark and still,
    folds up its cloak
As dawn is softly, gently slowly changing
    Stygian black to royal blue.

The elm tree gently lifts its arms
Enfolded 'round the sleeping birds.

And suddenly, the spell is broken:
    The first cock crows.

Dorothy J. Izell

The Sweet Melodies Of Love

    Soft lips, a generous kiss, a warm embrace,
no time to waste it is right once again.
    An open door, a slow dance across the floor,
an ecstasy of love in mind.
    A sweet melody, a voice that sings,
a memory of that special night.
    No one will know, how I love you so,
until that special time.
    When the church bells ring, and the birds begin
to sing, the sweet melodies of love in the air.
    The church begins to stand, and the minister
raises his hands......
I now present to you Mr & Mrs forever

Marquetta J. Ross

Balloons

Balloons are made of magic, and yet are rather grim.
Their chances of a lasting life, if anything, are slim.
Many colours, many shapes, in sizes large and small,
And, if they're only filled with air, when dropped, they slowly fall.
But filled with gas, they rise above to glisten in the sun.
Some are kept with strings attached and someone hanging on.
Some are lost or let a loose, they fade into the sky.
You never know just where they've gone, all you know is they will die.
Some burst when pricked or over-filled and leave you with a tear.
Others shrink and linger on to almost disappear.
Balloons are found when times are gay and filled with joy and fun,
Whether in a full bouquet or bouncing on as one.
And, though I'm always saddened to see the magic end,
I've never come to see the day balloons don't come again.

Richard Hayner

Morning Lovesong

How sweetly doth the robin sing as,
Awakening from my deep slumber, I first
Hear his melodious notes of Spring;
But, what of my true love, I ponder?

Canst he know of the poignant ache
Which my doubting heart longs to quell?
Or is my love misguided by an empty faith
To languish forlorn in a cloistered cell.

What mattereth if the robin sings of
Undying love and eternal fidelity; couldst
Starcrossed lovers e'er hope to escape Fate
And overcome Love's inherent fragility?

Yet, within my lonely room, I hear a
Haunting refrain of Love's grand fantasy;
And, suddenly, your face appears crystal clear,
Captivating my heart again with exquisite ecstasy!

Midge Kincaid

Untitled

As the dove fly's so gracefully
So did the love you had for me,
but now I've gone so far away
and to your love has gone astray,
but soon I shall be back to you
and the love we share will again be true,
Just wait for the time and you shall see
the love we have will always be.

Mark R. McClure

Of Frost and Rainbows

As I watch the sparkling of the morning frost
At the break of morning's light
I can see a kindle of light
Sit adrift a starlit night.

Shining its reflections against crystal seas, lasting eternities
Wondering about black velveted skies, dancing like fire flies
With time passing through a million hour glass
Dancing about wind lift clouds.
Then settling about the wetted grass
As the morning sun makes its pass.
Showered by a miss of frosted rain,
While casting its mold
As the frost glitter like diamonds and gold.
Tends to ease the mind and south the soul
Making room for a thousand stories untold.
Oh! What did I behold, a thousand rainbows in bright and bold
of green, red and gold, bringing joy to my soul
Is this my pot of gold.

Billy E. Harris

Living In an Empty World

True love is never created suddenly . . .
It is a quiet thing . . . a stillness . . .
Gentle as a whisper . . .
Stronger than the soaring redwood . . .
Softer than a snowflake . . .
    When interrupted . . . .
Life becomes an endless numbers . . . Living in an empty world . . .
Much too frightened . . .
Too alone . . . Living with this endless numbness . . .
    Living in this empty world . . . .
Smoking . . . . Drinking . . . . Never thinking . . . .
Always smiling . . . through the sadness . . .
    Pretending . . . .
        Just pretending . . . that
        I am not . . .
        Living in an empty world.

Ali Sackett

Celestial Playground

Soft, white and puffy against a blend of turquoise and baby blue,
One feels like he could jump from one to the other and not fall
    through.
As light and white as doves feathered wings,
Likely they created a playground for only celestial beings.

Could it be a training ground for those lucky enough to be Earth
    bound,
Or simply cushions to catch those testing wings or other
    angelic things?
It's like a mirage beckoning to my inner most desires,
Like Thomas Kinkaid paintings and other things I admire.

The highest black giants tower below,
Hidden within them molten lava churns and glows.
Long snaky rivers cut away, separate, and meet at the bay,
All this you can see in just a day.

Lush valleys and fields of green,
Leave you feeling special and exceptionally serene.
Plateaus, canyons, lakes and forests included,
From this aspect no view is excluded.

A place of solace and spiritual powers,
We all seek to get there and smell the sweet flowers.
A special playground from which angels are called,
To serve God just once, they gladly give all.

Bonnie Allen Briggs

My Judgement Day

There comes a time for the last Hurrah,
    a litany of lifetime events that we saw;
fitted for a halo with white wings on our back
    and a long list of virtues that you and I lack.

The day I pretended to be too sick to go,
    the blood bank begged donors, supplies getting low.
I remember the eyes of a teenage mother
    whose tragedy in life was a licentious brother;
I did nothing to assuage her pain and despair
    nor lift a finger to show her I care.

In scorching sun the maimed man squatted in the square;
    horses at the starting gate, I had no time nor a dime to spare.
The choice of two hours to read to a cripple,
    but I chose the snack shop and a chocolate ripple.

When we cross the divide and face the ultimate test
    we need to persuade Peter that we did our best.
Dear God in heaven, I pray at work and at play
    from day to day I will lead the way.
Let me finish my work here on this mother earth
    with the feeling that now, somehow, I proved my worth.

F. Satterfield

No One To Buy Flowers For

I miss knocking on her door with flowers for the woman I adore.

I was paid in sweetness, and always with a loving kiss, and that is something I will always miss.

A pretty smile on her face, and a warm embrace. Made it all worth while at any price.

To me a flower means love, and is sent from above. The red rose whose fragrance is so sweet, was made to be placed at our Blessed Mothers feet.

My heart has been broken, and is now on the mend, I will always miss the beautiful woman, who received the flowers I used to send.

My tears are all dry, but there is a reason why I continue to cry. I do not remember hearing her say to me goodbye.

Bryan Murphy

Bless the Children

Children are our blessing from God,
Fruit of the womb, His word declares.
With out any children our heart's would sob,
And surely fall subject to Satan's snares.

What can be sweeter than a baby's smile,
Or hear a child say, "me love you."
It surely should make any problem worthwhile,
And all our difficulties easier to bear.

Children are our future they say,
But what kind of world would it be today.
If all the children were taken away,
None left to cuddle, love or watch play.

Some will abuse and even kill them,
While other want children,
And can't have their own.
Longing to love and give them a home.

Modern day Pharaoh's and Herrod's they are,
When the little ones, are all taken away,
One may have been God's chosen one,
God's wrath they surely will suffer one day.

Earline Cox

Your Time Has Come

Your time has come
Don't worry now you can have fun
Doing the things you wish you could do,
And knowing you're not really through.

So go run free

Where ever you wish to be
In a meadow
On a beach
Sailing across the sea

Go, go, run free

With the wind in your hair
Sand on your feet
You can listen to the sound of your heart beat
With your smile gleaming with the sun,
The rain drops dancing on you tongue

So just go

And be who you want to be
Cause now you're really free

Vicki A. Parks

A Sweetheart Was A Marine

Being a soldier isn't any fun...
having to face the enemies gun.
For them it isn't a thrill;
knowing their enemies they must kill.
Leaving behind their families, not
knowing whether they'll ever be
reunited with these.

Many soldier's their precious lives
yields...just to be slaughtered on the
battlefields. Simply because...they felt
compelled to obey the government's laws.

It seems so dreadful that wars must be
fought...when "Thou Shalt Not Kill" the
bible has taught.
Yet, my son and three brothers had the
nerve...their country in the military
to serve.
Also says Lorene...I once had a sweetheart
who was a marine.

Lorene (Dunaway) Thrower

Flowers

Flowers are like friends, they're so nice to have around.
They always seem to pick you up, when you are feeling down.
Their colors can be vivid, or soft and subdued too.
They can be large or small in size, the choice is up to you.

Some varieties like orchids are beautiful it's true.
Although they can be difficult to raise,
and call for patience too.
Others are quite easy and will always grow for you.
Whether they are in the sun or in a shaded view.

Like marigolds and petunias, they need so little care,
They never disappoint you, and there is lovely color there.
They are hardy and lasting, and their beauty they will share.
You will see them blooming, almost anytime and anywhere.

God shared his precious garden with everyone on earth.
He's given us the seeds to plant, for flowers to enchant.
You know he cares for us, his love he did implant.
When he granted us a greater miracle, which was of course our birth.

Ellen M. Malloy

Butterscotch My Dog

There's an empty space now,
in the familiar place where, my friend used to live
here, with me.

I made a decision, after much painful thought.
I know now, it was for the best
but then with my conscience, I fought.

My friend gave me unconditional love
regardless of my mood.
For 12 short years, she followed close by my side,
Pranced, when I laughed, comforted, when I cried.

All that's left of my "buddy" now,
are pictures and memories dear.
Of how things used to be, when my friends used to live
here, with me.

Not a day will go by
that I'll forget her warmth,
her companionship, her love.

My "Butterscotch" joins my friends and family above.
I love you Buddy.

Marisa A. DeGrado

Dad (A Principled Man)

What happened to the family - that I thought I knew
They followed the times - and they went askew
The One that had taught them right from wrong
I guess for them had been gone too long
But Never for me will - that be the way
He set too good an example, during His stay
While here with us - He did not just preach
He lived the way - He wanted to teach
Whenever there was Anyone in need
He was there not only by word - but by deed
It puzzles me, how they could throw that all away
Just to live according to humanity today
He set for me an example - of what it is to care
Also a Memory - of what it is to share
He was a Man of Principles - you see
That is the Legacy - that He left to me
A Quarter Century ago - He left this Earth
But for me - just as it has been - right from my birth
It is like He is still right here by my side
So by His Principles - I must try to abide.

Jeannette Klee

Bogeyman

I stayed in horripilation when I was a child,
Some hungry lunatic monster was loose going wild,
I kept goose bumps an' chills just like a ding bat,
'Cause I learned 'bout bogeyman by being a brat,
Caliban was mild compared to th' bogeyman's description,
He was so gross you stayed giddy in your condition,
I can sympathize with po' red riddin' hood in th' woods,
'Cause I took granny a vinegar pie thru th' woods,
Th' only difference I had to worry 'bout bogeyman,
Yesterday I was terrorize by slimy bogeyman,
Now th' fear comes from someone I call a madman,
Without th' lore of bogeyman.

Denver Keels

Captured My Heart

I saw you across the bar
Really, you weren't standing all that far
I wanted to say hello
But I didn't know how it would go

My desires increased with delicious death
while my eyes burned you through
Keeping my distance not knowing what to do

As last call rang in my ears
I realized I had to get over my fears
And wander over to you

I tugged on your shirt to get your attention
That night wasn't suppose to be that way
We talked for a few and then it was done
At that time we really didn't know what to say

I miss you...with this 3000 miles of air
I miss you even though it is hard to bear
I miss you because it was a strong bond
I miss you for every morning's dawn
You captured my heart I sweetly was told
Because you are the only one I would like to have and to hold

Michele Weigel

Time Just Passed

It's over now, the cold, the snow,
Will I come back, I do not know?
I took a moment to recall the past
The hurt, the sorrow, is over last last!
Part of my lifetime is gone you see
The importance of this belongs to me.
The anger, the hurt, the times they both cried,
They parted, tormented, one suffered, they died!
As I climb higher in the heaven above
With thoughts in silence on this word 'love'
I think of them both and feel heavy with sorrow,
Knowing for them there is "no tomorrow"
Anger, remorse, heartache and tears
Are words that I feel for their spent years.
Dear God guide me from above and let my children inherit just love"
Each one tried to do their best for me the hurt I felt, they could
not see we start for tomorrow fresh from the past
Hoping to live it right to the last
Putting behind us all thoughts now gone by
I'll cherish all memories till I must die

Kay Hughes Dorius

Why Do I Feel Discourage

My mind and thoughts often strayed.
Some memories of my pass haunted me for days.
I assisted my families in every possible affairs.
Being ingenuous and unselfish, I was not aware
Of the way they've characterized me,
For the person they thought I should be.

I realized and opened my eyes.
Day after day I groaned and sighed.
"Blame yourself for your failures he said,
You've packed your bags and made your own bed."
I tried to do the best that I've known,
The more I did no thanks they've shown.

"You should have this, you should have that,
You've been around too long, what have you got?"
I thought of doing the impossible,
Being bad at that time was not applicable.
Now I wonder if being good means any good,
The way I really thought it should.

Eileen Williams

The Love We Choose

My eyes were closed but I still heard the sea, my ears were
Stopped up but I still saw the trees

My mouth was closed but my voice came out, mt arms were folded
But you still took my heart

In all my life I saw up ahead of me, so why in the world has
This come to be

I never saw the warning signs, your love made me truly blind
You won me over with your ways, your smile brightened all my
Days

I saw everything in black and white, but nothing prepared me
For last night

When you held me and kissed my lips, from head to toe to finger tips

I still never really realized, but it was always in your eyes

Last night was heaven, my love it's true, no one can move me
The way you do

Once it's done you never lose, unless you're unwise in the
Partner you choose

But you chose me and I really must say, "Darling I wouldn't
Have it any other way"

Valen McCoy

"Pop, Do You Have The Time?"

"Pop, do you have the time, can we go outside to play?"
"In a minute, son" I'd answer, then I'd sit him down and say,

"There is nothing you will ever need that my money cannot buy,
So when my time seems precious little, son, you know the reason
  why."

Well today he finally caught me, made me sit and hear his plea.
I share his words with you, my friends, as it's much too late for me:

"Through the years I watched you closely, Pop, and loved you from
  afar;
To me you were so perfect, Pop, on the surface not a scar."

"I'd look around me, as you asked, and see the things I had.
But in the final tally, Pop, they only left me sad."

"Yes, I had the best and finest things that your money could ever buy.
But therein lay the problem, Pop, now you know the reason why."

"I would rather have had a worn-out glove, and a second-hand bike,
  not new,
If I could just have a minute, Pop, to share them both with you."

My son went on to tell me how the pain became too deep;
Of the many nights he'd think of me and cry himself to sleep.

They found him in my study where, I learned, he'd often play.
Pretending I was with him when, in fact, I was away.

The note he left I clutch in hand as he lies before me still.
He ended it, "I love you, Pop, always did and always will."

Claude V. Weir Jr.

O' Sweet Morpheus

What happened to my bed last night?
  Cold, sacrosanct, and erudite.
And yet transformed by break of day
  Into a sweet Ambrosian hay.

O sleep delicious, so intense;
  What matter mortal mind make sense.
Into this cold world here below
  With chilling winds, I will not go!

One precious hour in sweet sleep spent
  Doth rival Croesus' golden mint.
Jason's golden fleece I'd e'en disavow;
  Nor heaven nor earth can move me now.

O' sweet Morpheus, god of sleep;
  In your peaceful arms me keep.
Embrace me through the morning sun;
  E'er half the day its course is run.

And when this mortal spirit shall soar,
  Earth's clamor dims, its fever's o'er;
As ages roll, in sweet repose,
  I'll dream the dreams an angel knows.

Wendell L. Vaughan

Gone Home

They're gone, they're gone, they won't be back,
They're on a greater, wider track.
He called them in, said "Come on home,
I want you for my very own.
My light will guide you on and on.
Til you reach me here to a new days dawn.
You'll never look back, there'll be no need,
You'll have joy beyond measure for every good deed.
Your hearts were loving, your deeds were kind,
I called you in early, so you'd be forever mine.
I sent you there for a purpose, to love and be loved,
You did exactly that, and many people were moved.
They do not understand now, why it had to be,
But if they'll follow in my word, they, too, will see!"

Melva Duplantis

Heart of My Soul

Jesus, you are the heart of my soul, the soul of my heart
When I chose to walk in your path, you taught me this
I strive each day to learn more
Of your great love for me
As I often sit on bended knee
To listen to you gleefully
Jesus, you are the heart of my soul, the soul of my heart
Let me never forget your part, and why you died for me
All my sins you wiped away
Because of this I live today
As I wake each morning
Never allow me to take for granted
What you have given to me
Jesus, you are the heart of my soul, the soul of my heart
Your grace you leave to me, which I accept with humble dignity
As I seek to help you lead
The way for all humanity
You chose not one or two,
But flocks and flocks to follow you
Jesus, you are the heart of my soul, the soul of my heart

Nina J. David

Whispers

A voice speaks so softly.
It speaks to my heart.
It tells me of his wonderful plan,
and then the blessings start.

All you do is trust him and
believe in his word.
He'll lift you up and save you.
It's a whisper you have heard.

The sounds are so gentle.
The plan is so clear.
Then all at once the whispers end,
and its trumpets sounding and angels
singing you hear.

You've found the Savior and his Love.
It all started with a Whisper from up above.

Linda M. Godwin

Sheep With No Shepherd

Audacious and knack,
fierce like the sun,
I prey on jiggers that lust to rocket;
money, power, prestige and love,
something I separated,
boysenberry, I was counter factual,
no one to route me, my life is a melancholy song,
dejected and dispirited,
wishing my parent's savored right from wrong,
borne a child, more I today, please someone discipline me,
my roots are cleft, discover my teardrops, I stock so much trepidation;
I'm seeking, sunk at the underlying of the pier,
the world's anchor is on me, how can I lift it? My offshoots are puny,
never knew I was there, the gate-keeper had no instructions;
redeem me, my stomach is sounding, who can I call? What shall I do?
I do not know, no one ever taught me to; boy! I feel ashamed, deck
on myself, can not see a way out of this stuff. God Almighty,
undernourished I began to pray.
Will he listen? I never beseeched him a day; if I was told I had a
deliverer, I may not have gotten into the fall.

Robert F. Ligon

Secret Lover

I've kissed your lips a thousand times or more,
Held your hand and walked down flowered paths,
Looked deep into your eyes for a word of some reward
But you've never been aware.
I've listened to your heart,
I've danced with you on moonlit water,
I've even fought about silly things
Though you never seem to answer.
We've loved each other,
Scared each other,
Fought each other,
Dared each other
You know not,
These happenings are vivid,
The contents are quite real,
I can't help but wonder
Do you dream of me?

Maureen E. Green

True Love

True love is knowing the person will always be there . . .
Love by someone unconditionally . . .
Having more good times then bad . . .
The person is there for you and your children . . .
Loving you no matter what happens . . .
Someone you can laugh with or cry with when ever
    you need someone . . .
Someone who is willing to take on the responsibility
    of you and your children from a previous marriage . . .
Someone who will be there to grow old with . . .
Someone who really trust you and you can trust them . . .
Someone who will cook, clean plus take care of
    the kids when you are unable to . . .
My husband is my one and only true love
    he is always there when I need him . . .
We love each other unconditionally . . .
This is what true love is to me . . .

Sharon Toothaker

What Is Fear?

Stop and listen, outside the pane
As rain taps gently, calling.
You'll hear someone from whom we hide in fright
Outside when water's falling.

"Who's there?" I cry in lonely fear
Of nothing I can name.
Perhaps the hard, rhythmical beat
Is what drives me insane.

Or is it the Darkness, a child's game,
That was "just a state of mind?"
Is this what every person dreads,
That the "someone" hides behind?

But what do we fear? Is it a thing
That we can see or touch?
Or an apparition that we almost grasp,
Then lose in a windy gush?

There are a thousand ways to harm us, kill us,
Yet terror drives these things.
We've nothing to fear but Fear itself,
And our fellow human beings.

Christine Rollins

My Lovely Maiden Sleeping

Gaze at this maiden sleeping,
On watery pillows whispering,
Of love...Sun, Wind kissing,
Or tears when Mist, Stars embracing,
Countless leave their hearts to her...

...Once steel arms stretching, beckoning,
To lovers on wheeled horses riding,
Gently through her mound,
Forsake erst lovers when she they found.
Why did they leave their hearts to her?

Too many smiles she imprisons,
Awakes to solace in her bosom,
Hearts pounding, laughters drowning,
Silently his maiden the Rock is watching,
No wonder they left their hearts to her.

Mighty cradle, the maiden leave in peace!
Not to crumble I go pleading,
Not to rouse my lovely maiden sleeping!
For I will come back to her...
For I too, have left my heart to her.

Louis W. D. Mendoza

Sensation of a Flower . . .

". . . Emeralds, diamonds, rubies and sapphires, collectively,
are probably of no contest to the sensation of an embracement in
your loving arms," was all he'd gotten written before it began.
Wondering.
  He wonders when it is she celebrates her birthday, that he
could pick her a flower. He wonders once he is there and squats
to select a pretty one for her whether he will take it. Or leave
it for a bee to suck sweet nectar from and to the breeze to
carry away some of its pleasure. Yes, that is what he'll do and
he smiles wondering if he will ever get that far —

Shawn M. Dickinson

My Man

My man is so sweet and kind, he's not
afraid to tell you what is on his mind.
My man holds my hand, even if I don't
carry a wedding band. You will never
understand. He will always be my brave
man cause he never puts himself down. He
always says "I can." Can you stand up to
your man? He looks in my precious brown
eyes which are shaped like homemade apple
pies. He tells me I'm his to keep. But my
soul will never go weak. He says no one can
do me no harm (but God) but with others to
always be alarmed. He sometimes has to
fight but that's alright, because he has
nothing to hide. My man has a lot of pride.
He helps me to realize how far we can go. As
we look at the stars which are so far away.
I wonder if there will be such a lovely
place where I can go and lay. His feet are like
the rolling stone which are tight like a hard bone.

Tanya M. Lee

Thinking of You

As I sit here in the darkness
  Visions of you is all I see,
Remembering when I held you with caress,
  And your love for me,
The soft touch of your lips
  When we would kiss
The feel of your fingertips
  As I held your hands
  Is what I miss
Thinking of that special day
  When we will be together again,
In my heart forever
  Is where you'll stay,
Where your love is safe within
It means that much to me
  I would die for you
Then you would believe my plea
  My love for you is true,
    I'll guarantee!

    Joseph Barentine

I Am America

  I am the statue of Liberty standing
proudly in New York.
  I am Washington D.C. A lot of
good things and a lot of bad things happen here.
  I am independent. It feels so good
having nobody boss me around.
  I am the bald eagle soaring over
the land.
  I am the flag. The 50 stars and
13 stripes mean a lot to me.
  "In God we trust" is my motto.
  I am the executive branch, legislative
branch, and judicial branch.
  I am the 50 states. 48 together and
2 apart.
  I am the star-spangled banner and
the pledge to the flag.
  I am uncle Sam and the liberty bell.
I am America.

    Dawn M. Miller

Friend

A friend is special
A true one cannot be replaced
You are so, very special to me
Just look at the smile on my face
I will love you always
And I say this with no doubt
Your friendship is something
  I can't be without.

A friend is there
  through the good and the bad
You are always there
  whether I'm happy or sad
You are to me an advisor and also a friend
I can always talk to you
  from deep, down within.

A friend is special
  and that is what you are
A friend to me
  whether near or far.

    Jana L. Holder

A New Beginning

One spark became a flame, on the day that you were born,
  That flame became a fire, as our lives were tossed and torn,
And out of grief came happiness, with lessons of the day,
  We learned to let you spread your wings, no matter come what may,
Our love has been a glowing fire, that's burned throughout the years,
  We've lived and loved together dear, thru laughter and thru tears,
Which brings us now to this new day, when you forever change your life,
  You both shall feed a brand new flame, as husband and as wife,
Please know the love we have for you, will now be shared by two,
  We pray our fire will feed your flame, as G-D has meant it to,
So as you grow together now, thru good times and some bad,
  We'll always be here for you both, your mother and your dad,
So though we give you to your mate, you'll still be in our heart,
  and may your flame become a fire, so never shall you part.
Please hold her Son, and keep her close, do treasure this rare pearl.
  We give you now our precious one, our only little girl,
We trust in you to keep her well, thru sickness and in health,
  We wish you both much happiness, much joy, much love, much wealth,
So as this day you start anew, as husband and as wife,
  may the flame today, that starts to burn,
be with you throughout life.

    Hal Edwards

Found/Show - Tell/Lost

Whirling darkness, turmoil of light, Maelstrom of mists, lost Anguish.
Where then is Shaper? I am here, myself - I cannot Shape
Three syllabled Syllabus - Scylla Charybdis, whose Conscience
Consciousness: Waking, walking. Phrenia, frenzied, noias;
Night noises. Only dark darker than the Darkness, darkest, falling
Star...Now you have gone too far...I have done. Been. Bend to the sea
On bended knee. Stop the flow and go with Flo, no. Now, know and heal
Thyself - self/less - is the traitor to Thine ownself? To be true,
Blue - true is blue. Why, Shaper? Shape shapes, control your Destiny.
Why me. Blasphemy. Can't you see? No! Know now. Blow that small
Brown cow piles of leit-motifs. Light-lightness, likenesses, likely
To be or not - likely not. Candles still burn, both ends to mend all
Things, in the End. Time heals weals and welts, but not profiting Men,
Stand, aside me? What? What not. Knock, knock. Dark side -- down below
Two-sided, inside, outside, bland face blind sided. Whose? Yours,
Janus...guilt, wilt, thou melt - munchkins, for lunch-kin, tin, foil,
Fence fearless, faultless, Vaulted fell, foul Lord of earth and dell.
Ill-will, well done, well out, will out
Shall be - to you to me, Rally round rally two to me... All.

    Bruce D. Tefft

Count Us Not a Nation Failed!

Common flight from warring creeds, courageous men in history sailed
  to chisel dreams on freedom's rock; Count us not a nation failed!

Abandoning old parochial rites, aware that men must learn and change,
  Joined with all who shared their dreams; Are we not partners on this range?

New furrows turned in human rights, new harvests from new justice learned;
  New dreams from them, will we not heed our fathers' dreams, to us unearned?

Apt dreams! To build a space age ship to ply the seas of space and time,
  beyond the range of provincial craft, demands a nation's strength and prime!

Desist, this narrow ethnic gaze! We ape the past whence wise men fled;
  Unite to live these space age dreams and sail for stars, the worlds ahead!

Acquit past sins and right old wrongs, entrench ideals for a creative earth
  Where every child of our human race may launch these dreams for the universe!

Awake wise men and lead us now, to live these dreams of a reborn race
  embracing all who share our land, one family with Creation's face!

A century hence when children ask "Who built this ship so well?"
  Our souls, content, may answer true "Wise men with dreams to tell!"

    Tom A. Howe

66

The Golden Ring

As a young lad, I was always glad to ride the carrousel at the amusement park.

I remember the carrousel's pace. The loud calliope, the ring dispenser, the bell, the large smiling clown face with the target hole, and rings you would fling into his mouth.

The carrousel would go around and each time you would grab a ring, which was the object of the thing and throw it at the face of the clown.

Most of the rings were bright shiny steel, but on rare occasions the Golden Ring, some lucky person would steal and a free ride to that lucky person was the prize of the deal.

The Golden Ring became the treasured thing. I was always too early or too late. Never quite able to obtain that prized ring.

As an adult, I have pursued many vain avenues in life. As a result, I have squandered my years reaching for that illusive Golden Ring. Many tears have been shed, for I have been so misled. Oh! That beautiful ideal Golden Ring, such a teaching and destructive thing.

Jack R. McElroy

Untitled

Sun lights one side of me   I look behind as no one follows.
There's work to be done   thoughts to straighten   logic to embrace

Yet resolve catches me in backward-glance, solitude slaps me coldly
Duty directs me forward

The breathy dusk my form embraces is night without waxing moon, nor
even spectral light to set my chill right —

This end has duty, not love as ghosts fly back to benighted Gods
their sighs shaking dust from a quaint but cellared volume
of soulful memories — traced — shelved too long, I implore its verse again.

Descending now to open the dark, I grasp the haunt
fingering, knocking for this weight so hard —
but fear collects first findings,
flees the man-made cold
lightwards, with its solitary page
and this page —
elusive yet thankfully held, rare as winter leaves, rich as blood
near as a taste

Is one of many more to find, and momentary night is one of many to explore
Impartial light cannot explain, only reveal

And so I read my lone leaf of wisdom:

"Belief is half the battle, faith a quarter and magic all the rest
Wait not in vain, yet hope that this young chance may still attest."

R. J. Stevenson

Lord, Get Me Through

Through day's endless toil and long, lonely nights, Lord, get me through,
Through racking pain in body and confusion of mind, Sweet Lord, get me through,
Through lost dreams and futile plans,
Through hostile waters, navigators, pilots and crew,
From unfriendly folk that come into my life, Lord, get me through!

Through countless, hurricanes, blizzards, earthquakes and storms,
Lord, let 'em experience You as you get me through.
When life becomes an obstacle course,
And all my efforts and dreams seem lost, Sweet Shepherd, get me through!

Through all that comes my way, no matter what circumstances seem to
say, turn to God night or day and whisper in His ear, "Lord get me
through!" And, indeed, be sure - this He will do!

So, my friend, listen to His awesome voice,
And only, to Him, have recourse,
Nothing is in vain when your heart rides that heavenly train,
In each and every circumstance, He'll stand by you and,
His endless love will get you through!

Marguerite Rocco Orsomarso

The Chosen One

Lonely nights creep down upon me.
Survival is the rule of the game.

Heaven holds a place for thee.
Still, nothing remains the same.

We await the day of love
While evil is on the run.

Truly, there is a sign above
While others kill with a gun.

A time will come to pass
When your suffering will end.

Home is here at last.
Billions will descend.

Only to find as I awake,
My voyage lies in my mind.

With this knowledge I must not forsake:
Preventing others from destruction's bind.

Gene A. Keams

Loving You

Loving you has not been easy.
I need your arm around me,
A touch of your hand or a loving kiss...
These things I miss.
To keep the fire burning,
To feed my needs,
Of knowing that you really care
and think of me...
Whether you're here or there.

A private moment spent with you,
Is something that I treasure.
Private thoughts for us to share
Is better for me than other pleasures.
For me, it's knowing that you really care.
I will always be there for you.
In times of want......
In times of need.
Loving for me has never been easy.
For I, too, have times of want...
And times of need.

Virginia R. Ziegler

Jesus, My Hope

Jesus Christ is Lord of all
He said it and I believe
He died on the cross, rose from the dead,
It's true though I can't conceive
He'll come back again
As He said He will
And I believe, yes I do
With authority He will rule and reign
Heaven and earth He will make new
Because of hope I can go on
For I look forward to that day
Because of faith I know it will happen
Knowing He is the truth, life and way
Oh what a joy when I see His face
And hope will be no more
For faith became the vehicle
To bring me through heaven's door

Patricia Esposito

Who Knows

Who knows,
what'll be next for me,
should I stay on my toes,
will someone let me see?

Who knows,
will my life be good,
will it be for the crows,
will I always have food?

Who knows,
will I die a good death,
will I always be in these lows,
will anyone be sad when I breathe my last breath?

Who knows?
Brandi Kautzky

The Ladder of Life

People said it would be easy,
This vertical ladder in life,
Just keep your eyes upward and never looking down.
But my mind began to wonder,
After a mile or two,
Just how it was proved,
Life's ladder was trouble free.
For if we never falter or
Fall a step behind,
Then how do you suppose
We'll learn exactly where to climb.
For it is not mistakes,
That teach us right from wrong and
Little tiny mishaps that keep us climbing strong.
So should we not ask questions and
Try all sorts of things,
That we may be experienced when problems come to call.
If all of this is true,
Then tell me no more lies, let me fail a little that
I might succeed and claim my prize.
Janis Rebecca Martin

Falling In and Out of Love

Well, I've been drifting alone in the night.
I've been down and so confused.
Searching for an answer baby—one that I can use.
So I go on my way—like a shadow at night.

Like a name of the wind—I'll sail away.
To an ocean of love—let the tides roll in.
I don't want to worry about nothing.
So I breathe a last and broken sigh.
Come down to me—and dream of light.
Love is a lie.

Do you remember whom you used to be?
Did you become a stranger?
Remember the dream we shared?
It's only me. I want you...baby.
Roberta Saldausky

A Child

The wind blew through the years
The years blew through to dust
As ashes fall, to cinder all the life below
I see the moon, shine through many nights
I once walked upon those child-like feet
and saw all the world through cheerful eyes
The wonder is no longer mine
Those feet now linger into someone else's footsteps
Eyes full of awe that watch these walls
for they belong to her now, not I
Teresa Delgado

Waking from a Dream

I see him in the moonlight,
like a black stallion;
aggressively prancing, upright.

The moon showers light on his curly mane,
his dark eyes shine
and glisten like the rain.

He is strong; he is wise,
He pulls me close, I shut my eyes.
His breath leans soft upon my hear,
whispers only the air can hear.

I am numb; I float above,
it feels lovely, feels like love.

The sunshine of morning kisses my face,
I slowly breath life into my quiet little place.
A gentle breeze lifts the cover from the bed,
I see him rising from where he laid his head.

I see him, he is not a stallion,
but a sad nag, and my dream is done.
Kal Michels Paviolo

Flower Nymph

Bathed by the morning rain
  she reaches out to a blazing sun
Speaking to me in silence
Overwhelming every breath
  with the sweet fragrance of her promise
Her eternal innocence of new birth
  compelling me to gaze in awe
    at her sultry beauty
Inviting my touch
Awakening my senses to the essence of my being
  and lifting me into a world of ecstasy
    beyond all imagination.
Rita Delores Fabiano

Shadow's Grin

We all have a dark side that comes out,
Getting drunk and carousing about.
Doing things to look back and regret,
Trying to ease the conscious but still the fret.
Saying I'll never do that again,
Until next time appears the shadow's grin.
Full moon, pressures, rough day at work,
Any excuse to step into the murk,
Good day, bad day, all part of life,
Positive outcome is the important strife.
Once learned must keep positive light in sight,
For dark side will lay dormant just waiting for it's night.
Holly A. Witt

Out of the Dark

Is there a shadow beside me.
  I make mistakes but in my heart
  I'll be there to try again.

I sit in darkness listening, looking out,
  looking out and seeing.

Life goes on around me.
It is in this darkness that I see the light.
It holds a different meaning to some.

  There should be no fear in the dark for with
the dark comes light and with light comes hope.
Tammy Wood

Untitled

Beautiful eyes.
Haunting my soul.
Tenderness
So gentle and kind.
Truth is what you believe.
Make sense of the pain.
My head hurts.
Secrets untold.
Piercing my soul.
Unanswered questions.
Master of destiny.
Changing fate.
The only thing that remains the same is the shame.
Heaven shines brightly.
Read your thoughts.
Excite me.
I'll give you all that I have.
Smell the fear.
Make me yours.
Cradle my soul.

Kelly Stemple

Within Your Beautiful Eyes

    I'm old enough now to face the coming dawn
with you; at last after all this time has slowly
past I alone will get to see the sunrise of
love in your beautiful eyes.
    It is as though fate alone has given
me a much awaited second chance with
you. I have but only one chance to see the
love that I've longed for within your beautiful eyes.
    I realize that this love is only mine
for a very precious short time and I
will guard it with my heart and soul full
of love just for you. To me your love is more
precious; worth more than gold.
    I say graciously and humbly
thank you for the love that you will be
giving; thank you for the love that we will
share as it is ours for only a short time.
    For as the sunsets only the
beautiful glow of our friendship will
remain within your beautiful eyes.

Tracy L. Sturgill

Passionate Dream

As I look into the darkness,
I see a passionate light,
It's a soft glowing light on the face
of a beautiful young woman.

Her eyes twinkle like a starry night,
Her cheeks are like rose petals so soft and sweet,
Her touch is as smooth as the finest silk,
Her smile is like a moonlit night, so bright.

Her hair is soft and flowing free,
Always blowing in the gentle country breeze,
Her white stallion glides under her like
the sands of an ocean tide.

I dream of her silken touch as
I hold her tight with all my heart,
I look into the star filled night and
I wish she was mine with all my might.

Ryan P. Fick

Mother's Love

My baby, you're a miracle of love — a blessing!
creating happiness, even as you sleep,
with your waving fists and infant meeps,
you rein.
How rule you our hearts so completely,
where before dwelt, oft'times, pain?
You've changed our lives with only half a smile;
and though it seems incredible,
you've made it all worthwhile!
My dreaming child, small and still, cheeks flushed,
I watch your sleeping form
with down damp head
and see perfection, as the rose unfolds . . .
your innocence tears my heart,
inciting me to higher goals.
The lioness within leaps forth
and cradles you inside my soul.
My mother's love: a mighty sentinel — behold!
stands guard.

Madge Lonsdale

Us

Programmed to live only for a few decades,
    living selfishly and not caring who we shove.
Judging each other not by hearts but by shades,
    easy to display much hate and show little love.

Quick to throw a brick and hide the hand,
    sometimes walking with a chip on ones own shoulder.
Often not giving help to our fellow man,
    which allows him to become even colder.

Why is this how some live day by day,
    while others strive to be righteous?
Why is it that a price some have to pay,
    before they realize that inside they were lifeless?

Why don't I look inside of myself,
    why don't you look inside of yourself without a fuss?
Why don't we search inside for the little bit of souls that we have left,
    why don't we search to find a better "Us?"

Jonathan D. Samuels

Heart of Survival

The heart of survival is the way our life is
when it's down and about to break
it starts to glow for our sake
around and about,
turn after turn
it leaves a mark like a burn
and if it scars
it's our way of showing survival.

The survival of the heart is so great
something so hard to keep
when it stops beating
you think I'm dying
I'm dying of sorrow

Sometimes you think
maybe I should borrow a heart
maybe everything will go away
but then you think what should I do
but survival is the way of the heart
that has to be fought.

Susan E. Young

The Alligator

Lying lazy in the sunlit stream,
Undulating tail its mirror cleaves,
Dimpling the surface slowly, then it leaves
Floating, dangling in a dappled dream.
The beauty of its fluid grace belies
Its beastly savagery; its razor jaws
Agape, with dangling daggers as it claws.
With studied nonchalance its tiger eyes
Survey the calm reflection of the skies,
The placid amber pools. Reptilian,
Cold blooded, savage, lurking. Once again
I wonder: could Lucifer in this guise
Who won the rebel's victory of yore,
Still lure me to the tempting tree once more?

Cheryl Epperson

My Wife

There would be a house in that field
that would have made all my dreams so real
there could be my wife and children, too
oh how I could tell everyone, how much I loved you
but this will never come my way
because you have passed away
trying to bring a blessing to our hold
you suffered mercifully untold
then God stepped in and took you away
it was probably best they all say.
But how are they to know the sadness I meet
I would rather had him cut off both my feet
then to lose you my wife
for in you I have my soul and life
then I could just sit and look at you
but now I just stand with nothing to do
oh please oh God take care
for someday I shall see her up there
trying to bring a birth, she has left the earth
but with her as she lie, goes a love that will never die

John Rodemeyer

The Faces of Hope

The faces of hope are enchantment to hold
The promise of springtime forever foretold

A time to be blessed with invincible strength
Through life's broken arrows beyond human lengths

A spiritual joy enraptured within
The strength of an angel elusive of sin

The gift of tomorrow in the rare gem of faith
Enriched by wisdom, distinguished in grace

Impeccable judgments to boldly proclaim
When fulfillment of hope is shrouded by pain

A noble pursuit through the brisk of the cold
In the gleam of the eye of young and of old

A deliberate intention to do all one's best
To lighten the burdens of those who need rest

A vision of the future within a dream of the past
Embracing the rapture of all that shall last

From the whimsical innocence of children at play
Through seasoned remembrances of fond bygone days

In the infinite glory of one most profound
The faces of hope are eternally found

Patricia Jenkins Hieke

All Around Us

For it's always happening around us
but we do not see the changes,
For time changes everything from day to day,
its all around us for we all together
make things change, we are all apart
of life, and what we all due each day
will help the world to change,
For what we all together due, will change
the world around us.

A world of people is a world of hope.

Michael Breheny

Her

Brown eyes, brown skin,
Eyes that dance like the sun,
A smile one million miles wide,
To her arms I run.

Love or lust, I know not which,
A pleasant diversion or truth,
Greener grass on the other side,
Or someone I should have found first.

Living for her, that's what I do,
Prisoner of love's grip so tight,
Thinking of nothing but her all day,
Only when she's near is it right.

Who is this woman, who's now just appeared?
Lighting the fire of love and fear,
Shaking my faith in all my life's work,
Free from the shadows where broken hearts lurk.

Is it only her or something else?
That for all life's blessings I deplore,
What power is love that for all else is naught,
True love, for which every man has died and fought.

John W. Pierce

Summer's Day

As sunlight gleams through the slumbering morning,
And wakes the world to a new risen day,
New life begins which prior was sleeping,
All in a moment, on a warm summer's day.

The warmth of the sunshine embraces the morning,
And moves swiftly forward the day on its way,
With noonday's announcement, the evening approaches,
The day is swift passing on a warm summers day.

Peace and serenity, the traits of the evening,
Envelopes the earth, and holds her straight without sway,
Continually moving to the destiny of night-fall,
All things continue on a warm summers day.

As glimmering night shades hover softly about us,
And we prepare for the closing of the beauty of day,
Our thoughts, our memories, backward are traveling,
Recalling the pleasures of this warm summers day.

Night now enfolds us, the day but a memory,
The traces of evening have faded away,
The earth in her stillness, all things now slumber,
Dreams of tomorrow, and a new summers day.

Steve Kerr

Now Seating

"Have you seen this movie before?"
Said the distorted voice behind me.
No I have not, came slowly out of my mouth
with a blue cloud of smoke
blown up towards the beam of light.
But I don't need to
because it is my life up there
I'm the latest flick to make a quick dollar
or the tragic drama of depressing romance.
Whatever makes you laugh or cry
while you sit on the edge of the seat.
I am also your misery
because there is no reality beyond the screen
but sometimes I wish there was
as the virus of lies in my soul
spreads like the plaque without any cures
or enthusiasm to find out why.
So please be quiet and stay in your seat
because it will be an eternity before the credits roll
and maybe then I can go home.

Aaron R. Smith

Mums from Mom

A chilly mist sneaks in through my open window.
My bedroom seems dull and gray.
My morning like a segment from a two-dimensional
 black and white movie.
Silent and colorless.
Melancholy feelings fill my mood with nothingness.
Yawning in the damp coldness I snuggle deep beneath
 my covers hoping to dream rosy quilt dreams until a sunny day.
The doorbell rings.
Wrapped in my pink comforter; I stumble toward the door.
The door seems sealed shut so I yank hard to open the
 entrance to my autumn tomb.
My mother appears armed with brilliant yellow
 chrysanthemums.
Spontaneous canary-colored smiles bouquet into laughter.
Invisible warm breezes of colorful love flow through the
 doorway of my thought.
Morning conversation, comfortable as soft flannel,
 bounces glowing light through my home.
Hot tea warms every chilly corner within my waking heart!

Susan McGuire

River Rat - Viet-Nam 1970

Friends
come as names on the Wall
Torrents of memories thru too many
whisky filled afternoons — and
early morning hangovers

It was easy then
a drink, a couple of dollars "It don't mean a thing"
Beatle songs would play and send me
to the Vet center and Doc Kilebrew,
I connected when we touched my words were ladders,

He lead
to my inside, He saw the night we lay in a village near Can Tho-my
18 year old feet, like duck webs in the Mekong Delta Mud
Old Andy, always drunk or stoned no longer looked human
or as my baseball buddy
Mickey Mantle, Ted Williams, Al Kaline,
Nellie Fox — Car 54, Where are you?
Doc Kilebrew sees the mortor rounds
coming in on my head — eating my helmet
the shouts in my ear, Medic!!!

Frank Bari

Thoughts On Turning Fifty

Turning fifty can be depressing and sad;
But there are some reasons to be glad.

You don't need to worry about middle-aged spread;
For middle-age is long gone—that's one less worry to dread!
You're only five years away
and Senior Citizens prices you can pay!
The children are grown and left the nest;
You can claim back the TV, telephone, and all the rest.

There are professional salons for thinning hair;
Replacement systems applied that require little care.
Hearing aids that are smaller than a fingernail;
Even with short hair, no one can tell.
Most books are available in large print;
If not, just wait for the movie, then rent!
Vitamins and creams to reverse the aging process;
At least that's the claim in the ads, more or less.
You're one year closer to retirement and Social Security,
Medicare, Medicaid, and Senior Citizen Discount Courtesies!

Now that you are fifty years of age,
Think of it as beginning a brand new page!

Brenda M. Dunn

Mother's Love

Held close to her heart;
feeling warm and safe.
In the comforts of her arm
with a warm embrace
she waited for no man,
took nothing from a soul.
Taking care of her kids,
was her main goal
She raised us the best she could,
gave us all she had
That's why I have to thank her
for being the mom and dad.
She worked hard to give us the best
money can buy sometimes I ask
if I deserve her and if so why?
I pray and ask the Lord to give back
that she gave.
He said don't worry my children I always save
Mom you're the best it's true and I love you I really do.

Kia Alston

More in the End

There is this guy I like but am afraid to find out,
Just what he thinks my heart is all about.

He is my very good friend, come what may.
Seeing his face brings sunlight and joy to each and everyday.

Whenever I think about him I cannot keep a straight face,
Forever in my heart he will hold that special place.

My feelings grow much deeper especially while he's away.
For when he comes around I know he's in my heart to stay.

I call him on a whim just to hear his voice.
I fight a silent battle for my desire leaves me no choice

Even if we stay just as friends he'll always be in my world.
Though in all truth and honesty I would love to be his girl.

When I finally get the nerve to tell him how I feel,
I'll do anything and everything to prove I am for real.

But for now well remain the best of friends,
And hope that someday we'll be much more in the end.

Christal Gale Kilgore

For Fred

There once was a neighbor named Fred,
For seventy years has climbed out of bed.
He golfs and he putts.
Avoids all the ruts.
The age of eighty is where he heads.

Janice E. Young

Death On Planet Earth

Interred in silent indigo wombs lifelines severed by
life's cruel hoax

Too numb to battle accepting the sentence the warriors
are dying there is no repentance

Our eyes meet for seconds I smell the despair the blackness
engulfs me I scream for fresh air

Your eyes tell the story mine mirror your pain I know I
can't help you my visit in vain

No explanation the devil be paid man's inhumanity to man
the killer called aids

Etta Kohm

To a Rose

O darling rose! What can I say
that a thousand lovers have not already said to you?
I could praise your beauty for the essence of beauty is yours.
I could praise your seductive scent
but perfumers too numerous have paid my due.

Your family is large with queens and kings
playboys and play girls,
None is spurned, each is esteemed for the family resemblance
Ethereal pinks, angelic whites, deep blood-reds all enliven your
ranks.

With your faces turned to the sky
You scent the air and pleasure the eye.
What is this magic, this mystique you possess?

Like the wind and the sky
the sun, moon and stars
you exist
a facet of mystery.

Mercy Mary Mathew

Ryan White

A family of three stand in my yard,
Their petals soft, their bark speechless.
The wind blows the petals in my
Neighbor's yard. He is unaware that they
Are there, lying soft on top of his grass.

The petals are beautiful before they fall
And when the wind blows, they all face
The same way. Ryan White died today,
And took some of all of us with him.

I think of the petals going his way. Some
Go quickly with the first gust, and what
About the rest, and what about us?
When do we go?

I want to go when the petals go. My ashes
Blowing in the wind, to fall beneath the family
Of three. And come Spring early next year,
The petals of the dogwood will bloom again
And we will still be here.

John B. Curling

Water Fall

Over shadowed land clouds will form
They bring to bare an earthly storm
Deep within this mistaken thunder
There comes to us a worldly wonder

As darkness leaves the land will thrive
And give to us a special prize
The tears that fell unused by nature
Create for man an equal splendor

I scribe for you the water fall
A portent of which is meant for all
I compare to this what comes of life
A mixture of riches existence or strife

We live to love we love to live
From some we take to some we give
The way is brought from circumstance
Seldom does fortune come from chance

Choices of life carry many seasons
In all of them we search for reason
As we follow our path a bounty evolves
At the end of which lies our water fall . . . .

Mark Anthony McCarty

Chaos Limited

My dragon is chaos,
A place without form;
Duty holds it at bay,
Is there any way to transform it?

I'm dark and broody, pain fills my heart;
Love and life seems foreign,
Dare I walk that path?
Mind says yes, heart hesitates.

I've power, yet am afraid
To let myself live and just enjoy
My heart's desire. With my past's fear
To both create and destroy in a single breath.

The war in me is constant;
The pain I cause my greatest pain.
The joy I feel in others my reason to live;
With love in my life the dragon dwindles.

My dragon is chaos,
A place without form;
Duty holds it at bay,
Only love can transform it.

Paul Royer

My Grandchildren

My sons, are all three grown,
with children of their own.
Their little ones joy and love in their eyes,
surely comes as no surprise.
For life is filled with sadness,
and sometimes total badness.
We feel so different in their presence,
because our work-place seems like a sentence.
But, grandchildren gives us great hope,
that we can have faith in not being a dope.
The amazing wonders in their actions,
gives new meaning to elderly reactions.
The long lingering hugs and loving tugs,
make material things seem like an empty jug.
They give so much to me in love,
I feel like a special dove.
Our children and little grandchildren,
are truly gifts from God,
for which we should all applaud.

Jane F. Twigg

His Grace

Words come in time to those who wait,
listening from a place within that speaks
of truths rather than illusions of
a self satisfying ego
which is relentless in its need to
reject the knowing trapped within our
walls of self contempt
We often listen to the ego self for
it tells us of our self righteousness
deserved or all our flows
I buy the ticket when I am low
and let it have its place, on lofty perch
It sits and waits to foil loves graceful flow
Then when I am backed against the wall
with no where left to go.
I ask God to bestow in me, humility, his grace.
A kindly hand he does extend
when I surrender all my will and ask in honest faith.

Pamela Ann Reeves Hirsch

My Savior

Tender times are always here,
Because in my thoughts you're always near.
All I need to think of is your amazing grace.
To feel the shining beauty from your face.
To keep me strong when times are tough.
To keep my faith when life is rough.
I am so blessed to have you near me,
To feel your strength and have you hear me.
Your love is stronger than any I've ever known.
It is a love that has been proven and shown.
The gift you gave is wondrous to me.
This extreme gift of love makes me free.
Because you're the one who will help me endure to the end,
I know I can succeed because you're my best friend.

Jill Elliott

Who Is?

Someone to laugh with someone to have fun,
Someone you want to be with anywhere under the sun.
Someone who picks you up when you're feeling down,
Someone who spots you when you need to be found.
Someone you can turn to when trouble is near,
Someone to hold onto when you feel the fear.
Someone who is there either night or day,
Someone who is willing to listen no matter what way.
Someone who is always there,
Someone to show you that they always care.
That someone is special and always near in my heart,
That someone is my friend and you fill the part.

Jill Winje

Dance Show '93

The anxiety backstage,
People sweating the minutes by.
The manager slithers through the tiny hall
Like the Phantom in his catacombs.

A minute to go.
The tension rides high, up to the sky,
As the chandelier sways.
The music explodes into the silent theater,
Like the gunpowder connected
At the scorpion.

Sara M. Nolan

Lost Women

We have seen great despair confusion, shame has engulfed us
We lost women, the weaker sex women of great faith
What should be - what is!
Faith in God, family and home everything this country stands for
We lost women, the weaker sex we have seen great strength
In ourselves in each other
Courage to reach out to God
To each other and know
We are not forgotten tomorrow will be a better day!
Today I can feel the rain on my skin
The breeze in my hair
Today I can taste the salt
In my tears wear a smile on my face
Today I am alive - I can be me!
Yesterday I could have been
Just another number, one more statistic!

Janice Hamilton

Longing

A worm struggling to crawl,
Hardly able to raise its head.
Slithering through the dirt,
Through the shadows everything casts!
In the worm world.

A worm with a terribly vague,
Distant memory of birdhood.
Of weightless flight in a land
Where light cast no shadows.
A worm tasting the pain of
Wormlife and remembering birdhood.
No one knows what it is to be a worm and remember birdhood.
No one but the one weaving his coffin around him, so devotedly.

No one knows what turns the corpse of a worm into a butterfly
But the longing in the silkworm's heart.

The longing which makes one weave a coffin around one's self,
To long in hiding and make it the only reason for being.
Longing.
When his longing wins, creation bows, a worm flies.

Vraje Abramian

Farewell

We never thought that we would ever see,
A family member of our's having to flee,
This wholesome nest, that took us time to build,
Will soon have an emptiness in the spot that you once filled,
Sure others will come and try to fill your place,
But the caring you have shared, cannot be erased,
Deep down inside of us, there's a strange ache,
For what you have shared with us, was truly great,
So if you are near by, please come and visit awhile,
We would enjoy seeing you, and your cheerful smile,
For we all wish you happiness, wherever you roam,
And hope you will remember us . . . . your other home,
Well that's all for now, for you have chosen what's right,
You won't be forgotten, just out of our sight,
Goodbye and Good Luck

Velma L. Bojorquez

Can't You Even See

I want you to sit down and listen, about what I have to say.
I can't stop thinking about it, each and everyday.
I think about it at night, and even in the day,
I think about it in the evening and even when I pray.
I don't really want to tell you, but I guess that's the way
it's gonna have to be, but it's tearing my heart into little bits and
pieces, can't you even see.
I am calling out for help which I imagine I will not receive,
my heart is tearing more and more can you help me, please oh please.
Don't let this turn out this way,
I see you but you just walk away
Oh please don't ignore me, but if that's the way you want it,
that's the way it's gonna have to be.
All I am now is in misery, but just remember
I'll always treasure the times that it was just you and me.
Well now it's plain to see that it was never meant for you and me.

Jennifer Bonnie

Maw Maw And Paw Paw's Place

Hugs, kisses, and lots and lots of fun,
When I get in trouble it's to Maw Maw and Paw Paw's Place I run.
I like to go there and play with all the toys,
Play with my cousins, and be as rough as the boys.
I like it when my mommy and daddy is there,
Because I can trash the place and maw maw and paw paw don't care.
Mommy can not threaten to even spank me,
Because maw maw will threaten to spank her, you see.
When I spend the night and don't want to go to sleep,
Maw maw will rock me to sleep till there's no longer a peep.
When my paw paw goes outside or to the store,
You can bet I'm going with him that's for sure.
I like going to my Maw Maw and Paw Paw's Place,
There, I always feel nice and safe.
I like to put my maw maw and paw paw to the test,
It's just fun to do, because they are the best.

Christina Rowlett

The Graduate

Life starts for most at age 5.
You learn your name, how to spell it, how to write it.
I said life starts for most at age 5.
You learn to color, what colors makes another color.
"Are you with me?" Pay attention!
I said life starts for most at age 5. You learn to listen and
how to express and how to address. Moving right along . . .
Life starts for most at age 5.
"Have you ever wondered why your teacher puts so much
emphasis on your five senses? See, touch, smell, hear and
"what's the other one?" Hurry up now. Taste. After all
the others fail without a doubt you know for sure what you've
had because it's bound to return. If you can remember these
ingredients to life then I applaud you. Congratulations,
graduate, you have just graduated from C.S.U. better known as
Common Sense University.

Auletta Muhammad

Concord, Massachusetts

Concord, Massachusetts, what secrets do you hold?
Concord, Massachusetts, home of the free and bold.
You fought your first war in 1775,
Most who fought in it, did not come home alive.
You fought the Revolutionary War, only when it knocked on your door.
Women wept, when men, they left, not to come home again.
Women went to the village green, and after beholding the scene,
Fell on their knees and cried, "How could they be so mean?"
I saw all this, I heard the screams,
But, thank God, it was all a dream.

Dawn Eisenbraun

The Journey

When does the circus stop?
Where does it all end?

When it all seems upward,
something brings it down again.

Oh Lord, when will the ride end?

Is it an endless ticket I hold,
or is it the stop I'm unable to reach?
Blindly I go through the maze.

Oh Lord, when will the ride be over?

The speed control is an infinite number
in my mind . . .
No limit controls its force through the
tunnels I approach.

Oh Lord, when will the ride be over?

In the future, does it hold a place for me?
Is there a light ahead?

Could it all be over . . .

Oh Lord, help me end the ride.

Carri Jean Dreher

A Place to Go

Sometimes life consist of direction
Sometimes having duties of obligation
The world goes around and around
So not to clown or walk around with a frown
It's good to travel around the world
Sometimes searching for oyster and pearls
Moving past with a bounce
It does have more to an ounce
Now it time for opportunity
In helping the busy community
Looking at open space
Hoping to find a wonderful place
Let have some positive skills and set some golds
Not always about history that's of old
I stood there on the rock on the bay
On a warm vivid Glorious day
Now it's time to have a good life
And become husband and wife
As we fell in love
Let look at the stars above

Delilah Taylor

Young Love

How to express this feeling is hard to describe.
Does he really like me, or just along for the ride

As we gaze into each other's eyes what does he see.
Do we like to be with each other, or is it just me.

Being close to his body is where I like it most.
He says I'm the cutest, but I don't want to boast.

When he looks at me I can't help but smile.
I love it when he comes over and stays for a while.

All day without seeing him, I miss him so much.
I miss his cute face and his warm gentle touch.

I never know what the future may bring.
Will he kick me to the curb, or buy me a ring.

Being young and in love someone has to begin.
And when it's all over people do it again.

Lisa Rich

Anarchy?

Does anyone see what I see?
Has anyone heard what I've heard?
Do others feel what I feel or I am alone?
    We have become egotists, bred earless by deception.
Blinded by erotica in the media.
Unable to control our own lives,
reduced to clones by choice, impotent, lazy.
Wallowing in contentment with our women and our booze.
No time for freedom, no time to make a stand.
    No one listen to the lies of our leaders,
yet there are no whispers of rebellions in our land.
    Still...somewhere in the deeply recessed memories
of man smolder embers of survival - instincts of the clan.
    On the edge of the abyss a small band slowly gathers
shedding many years of mental shackles, preparing mind
and body to withstand the coming battle's hot, foul breath.
And once again perform the rites of man!

William E. Douglas

My Special Friend

I have a special friend that I just couldn't do without.
He's always there with me, when I gad about.
At times, when I'm hurting, he's right there by my side
To give me comfort that I need, till all my tears have dried.
Always faithful to a fault, friendly to all mankind.
When he's not there with me he's always on my mind.
He's a little on the hefty side and his legs are kinda short;
But the only drawback to this male is he breathes with a loud snort.
If it came down to a contest of which male snores the worst,
There's no doubt in my mind that he would come in first.
I can't help but love him when he looks me in the eye;
My heart starts to slowly melt when he breathes his little sigh.
He gets so much attention, he's so ugly that he's cute;
With a tail that's curly cue and the broadest chest to boot.
Well, have you figured out, just who my friend could be?
If a bulldog is your guess, then you must know Butch and me.

Wendy Mitchell

Look Away

    We used to be friends
Now we can't make amends
You've gotten over me
So things will never be the way they used to be.
You'll see I'm still in pain.
so much that it's driving me insane.
If you see me on the street some day
and I don't know what to say
please look away!
It hurts so much,
Now that we have to stay out of touch.
The things we had will always last
Memories from our past.
    I'm still in pain
because I spend to much time down memory lane.
If you see me on the street look away,
because I have nothing left to say.
If you see me walking by
and tears are in my eyes
look away some day I'll be ok.

Trista Ann Glover

Memory

I still see camels in my dreams, with open eyes

One, skeletal white, with slatted ribs
Made the journey, feeding on itself
The thirty days to Darau, by the Sudan

Loping close to its Bedouin outrider
Whose sand colored robes, covered, one hundred camels
He let me hold, his rawhide whip, I could not make it sing

His blood gone dry, his camel's too, in dust red, burning sun
Adrift — Burdened — Dune-like — Patient — Rising — Dying

Its nose gently rubbing, the velvet, of the other
Even in starvation, there is, the potential, for love

The village rose: stark, half finished, mud brick walls
To house the herd, at dusk, outside
Enclosed by two walls, and each other

Take me to that land, where bones bleach white, veiled women black
Their hopes enveloped, first, in gauze dreams
Then, encased in lead

I saw the camels die, inexplicably, in sight of water
Sculpting their time

As people — Who — To, Their Dying — Birthday, Last

Lolita Sapriel Metscher

An Early Evening August At The Spring Street Cafe!

The cafe lights beam from the ceiling shining bright
On each table like beams from some old fable.

The humid heavy air sits on Spring street like a
Heavy weight cast from West Broadway.

Music, voices, sound sift thru the early night
Coming from unseen corridors.
The heavy headwaiter passes out quietly at the bar
Head laid heavy by the stale humid air, listening
Without choice to the rhythmic beat of autos passing us by.

The windows, looking out reflect a constantly moving
Stationary image of a late New York City August night.

The cafe lights still shine on my table, not one
Striking the sleeping old heavy head waiter, still asleep
At the bar; dreaming of walking the street; feeling
The humid heavy air and hearing the music, voices and
Sounds sifting from unseen corridors.

J. B. Collins III

My Garden

Come with me to my garden here grows an abundance of love,
Golden shafts of light hover above,
Causing our love to flower and bloom,
Opening our mind to realize soon, we will experience new,
wonderful and exciting things.

Reality starts as a dream, bursting at the seam, of our
imagination.
In my garden dreams are reality mingled with sweet ecstasy which
takes us beyond tomorrow, no tears, all joy, no sorrow.

We're crazy in love not taking time to analyze things that
tantalize
our senses.
In this quiet place I come face-to-face with my love ace,
Our heart rhythms make exotic sounds, love abounds, drawing
us to this peaceful place.

In my garden we share joy and pleasure, there is no measure of
things yet to come.

Patricia C. Green-Dozier

My Walk On The Beach

What are you doing?
Thinking.

About what?
About who...would be more appropriate.

A woman?
A very special woman.

Do you think of her often?
All the time.

What's her name?
Kim.

Where did you meet her?
At a different beach...far from here, and a long time ago.

How long have you known her?
I feel like I've always known her.

Do you miss her?
She's my best friend and I miss her very much.

Do you love her?
I've always loved her.
Mark Homolka

Mother Love

When I was a child, not yet a mother,
 I promised to be mild and never smother
  My children.

It wasn't as easy as I had thought, being a perfect mother,
 Trying to do everything I ought—first one thing, then
another—
  Determined.

Now I am a mother and my children are grown,
 No longer a bother. I'm reaping the seeds I've sown —
  Mother love.

What a wonderful blessing my children have been.
 And now I'm professing to grown women and men—
  Mother love.
Martha Suellyn Davis

Two Under the Moon

The stallion walked across the sand,
In the dark of night.
The bright full moon shone upon the land,
Not one other horse was in sight.

A sudden roar from the sea,
made his head turn 'round'.
A white mare rose from the water with glee,
and dashed onto the ground.

The stallion leaped and whinnied at the sight,
as the mare swung her head in different poses.
She fled at him in full flight,
Then stopped, and the two of them rubbed noses.

The two nickered and rubbed muzzles the same,
They knew morning would be here soon.
So, they went on with their playful game,
The two under the moon.
Erin J. Foster

Marvin

"Who's that hanging upside down?" "Look out you'll hit the
ground." It's Marvin.

"Who's pants are these with dried worms, and nails."
pockets filled with fishhooks and snails?" "They are Marvins
who else?"

Sad brown eyes pleading, arms hugging you tight, "Bet he wants
something. "Mom can I go skating on Saturday night?"

"Can I go fishing Dad?" "Is deer season here?" "Can't wait
to go Dad, we'll get him this year.

Look who's coming down the road caring such a heavy load
It's a stringer of fish, and "oh no a Toad." "Oh Marvin."

What made Marvin happy I understand, a riffle in the woods
or a rod in his hand, shimmering sunlight, or warm soft hands.

You grew up fast, you became a man, then joined the army
to defend our land. We are proud of you son, you are one of a
kind. We'll miss you since you left us behind.
You sit at the right hand of "God" a smile on your face,
as he takes you in his loving embrace.

A smile comes over "God's" face, when you naturally ask,
"Sir is there good fishing in this place?"
Gayle McCurley

Old Timers' Baseball

A baseball old timers event is more than a game,
It's our journey through the past - a trip down memory lane.

A voyage back to summers past -
That brings to mind diamond triumphs that ever last.

Visions of a simpler time that will never end;
That brings to our tongues the classic line, "I remember when!"

Thoughts of day baseball and travel by train;
The smuggled radio in school to hear a world series game.

Be it for a cup of coffee or a hall of fame career,
you were there for us day in, day out, year after year.

You brought us through depressions, recessions, and many a war,
To be the example of a good America - that was your chore.

You were and are a symbol of the American dream,
Hard work, dedication, sacrifice for the good of the team.

You are America and America is you,
The pitcher, the hitter, the crew cut man in blue.

We thank you for being heroes to generation after generation,
We thank you for all you've meant to our nation.

My God bless you and keep you in good health and good cheer,
So that we can see you and reminisce again next year!
Don Miers

Set Free

Set me free to be all that I can. Set me in the direction to hope
and love, prosperity and goodness. Allow me to breath the air that
once was clear and permit me to live the life intended to learn from.
 Allow me to write my own chapters to books and close all others
that remind me of impurities. Let me take the road less traveled and
build myself a strong woman. You must understand that I must be set
free to cry, to fear, to love and given the choice not to love. You
must set me free to be young, to be unique and to be all that I choose to be.
 Set me free to be all that I can. Place me in the hands of Gods
and allow him to guide me in the direction to all that is new, too all
that is beautiful and to all that brings hope. Allow me to fly with
the birds in the emptiness of the sky, and let me be forever free to
be a great me.
Christine Jimenez

A Precious Treasure

A child is God's greatest gift, a most precious treasure to cherish,
To be nurtured and loved, gently guided, not left to perish.
A child is not to be possessed or owned,
By the grace of God, a child is only on loan.

To raise a child is a special privilege, one not to be misused,
To be taken freely, but not lightly, nor is a child to be abused.
Many times we stumble and fall, getting lost along the way,
Unsure of what direction next to take or exactly what to say.

Opening our minds and hearts, to see, listen, and hear,
We find God is the answer we seek, not far but near.
Always present with his great wisdom and gentle, loving, guiding hands,
With a message, love and forgiveness go hand in hand with our demands.

A child is a separate individual, their own person, not a parent's clone.
A parent must learn to eventually let go, but never will a child be totally alone.
However the fact still remains, a parent is a parent no matter what the stage,
And a child remains a child just the same, from age to age.

A child freely given is also freely taken, a loan entrusted by God to us,
To be answered to on judgement day, receiving our due rightly just.
In essence, in the end, are we not all God's children, hopefully in good grace,
Seeking only to return to the house of God, from whence we came, without haste?

Carolyn J. Brickey

The Voyage of the Mayflower

Where truly doleful was the sight sad and mournful parting

To see what sights and sobs and prayers
Did sound among them looking for tomorrow

What tears did enthusiasm from every eye
And pithy speeches pierced each heart with sorrow

But ye tide which stays for no man calling them away that were thus
loath to depart to a foreign land

thy reverend pastor falling down on his knees with watery cheeks
commended them with most fervent prayer

"And there at the river," text Ezra 8.21

I proclaimed a fast that we might humble ourselves before our "God", at last

Seeks of him a right way for us and for our children to serve his grounds

But they knew they were pilgrims and looked for praise, freedom they were bound

In the double darkness of night and thick ocean fog
And howling winds they ran with all sails spread
Thunder-bolt's tearing apart the rough breathing New England coast
line filled with razor sharp piercing rocks. They fell with that land
made is called Cape Cod

Norman S. Von Feister

National Anthem Exposure

Oh, Beautiful and Spacious skies have you remained that way?
The devastation of our land, could it possibly be a play?!?
Act one is robbing us of our animals. This was not meant to be!
Act two has dirtied our clean air leaving it for you and me.
I don't care to know any further Acts even though there has been War.
Who knows where Military forces land other than a distant shore.
Will they make it back - not Another Memorial erected in their names?
For too many souls have been sacrificed and Government is to blame!
No one asks our position or permission to steal or Daughters and Sons.
I truly wonder if a Presidential sibling would participate with fun.
Or be scared to death as they should be. It's extremely serious.
Perhaps they would cry and complain to leave it and not become delirious.
I refuse to speak of prejudice because it should not exist!
We should All be able to communicate to help live in such bliss?
So when it's my time to leave I'll go out like a bashing Band
with the smash of a Cymbal, the beat of loud drums and pray it is quite Grand.

Lisa Lindstrom

Untitled

I've had many loves, but only one.
So the die is cast
the dice are rolled
the sun has set on the new and old.
Peace has come, war has begun
hearts are broken, important things never done.
Pretty flowers on a mountainside
shedding their seed, creating next seasons young.
Breezes blow, farmers in golden crops sow.
Black birds fly—old people die
a newborn for the first time cries
...and time slips by.
I've had many loves, but only one
that's etched in this heart of stone.

Rob Chalk

Clouds

I ride above the clouds,
viewing seas of not but mist;
and in this landscape imagined,
lakes, trees and mountains do exist.

Only there to touch and travel,
in the pathways of the mind;
And the more you look and wonder,
the more reality you seem to find.

Then suddenly inside them,
in a world that's draped in white;
One's end is one's beginning,
brilliantly lit till fall of night.

Then as I pass beneath them,
my imagination finds again;
in every cloud a dream scape,
Each, my heart and soul within.

In the clouds where I've imagined,
I have found every single dream;
save but one that's haunted me,
since by my heart, love was seen.

Jonathan M. Bearfield

Did You Hear I Love You?

You could hear the hammer ring.
You can hear the mob shout.
But did you hear "I love you",
As the death sentence was carried out.

You can see the garments parted,
And the spear pierce his side.
But could you see he loved you,
When on the tree he died.

You could see the lifeless body,
As they laid him in the tomb.
You could hear the rock rolled up.
To seal his burial room.

Did you feel the earth shake,
And see the rock roll by.
And did you hear, "I love you",
When you saw the tomb empty inside!

Have you experienced his love,
That he freely gives.
Only through the blood of Jesus,
Can we truly live.

Larry Grogan

Uncultivated Pearls

There will always be heroes
Whose deeds go unsung,
And bells that are silent
Because they cannot be rung.

The shiniest bauble is not always the best.
A badly delivered joke is not always in jest.

The brightest light in the sky
Is not always the star.
What appears to be near
May, in fact, be quite far.

The value of man is in his everyday deeds;
The friends that he has, and the code that he heeds.

There are those that will know this
And appreciate his worth.
Instead of hastening his funeral
They will rejoice at his birth.

To know such a person,
To see beyond the facade
Needs the eyes of a psychic,
And the perception of a bard.
Marie F. Smith

My Dear Sweet Friend

My dear sweet friend I miss you.
Where have you gone? My dear sweet
friend, I cry because I miss you. My dear
sweet friend, why did you leave me?
I miss your sweet purr in my ear, and
your whiskers on my face. My dear
sweet friend you used to jump on my
bunk-bed and curl-up on my blanket.
My dear sweet friend I miss you. I cried the
day mom told me you died. You were
hit by a car. My dear sweet friend I miss you.
My dear sweet friend when you died, a
piece of me died too. My dear sweet friend
I miss you. My dear sweet friend I love you.
My dear sweet friend you're a part of me now.
My dear sweet friend it wasn't your fault.
I will never stop thinking about you, I miss you.

Kellee Cullinane

Mary

It has been more than a year since we parted
Yet, in my mind you are still there.
Our home is pretty much like you left it,
Neatly arranged, as it was in your care.

The roses share their fragrance and beauty,
The flowers miss your tender care.
Our young fir trees are stretching heavenward,
All seem to know that you are there.

Our beautiful daughter phones me often
To make sure that I am getting along.
Her heart is filled with love and devotion —
She reminds me so much of her Mom.

Through memory's lanes I walk the trails
Among the precious times of our past.
Thoughts long forgotten from bygone days
Spring anew and fresh in my paths.

I am praying to our Lord in heaven
Reminding Him, I am still here —
Longing to be near my sweetheart,
My wonderful wife for three score years.

L. Dow Coffman

To the Girls, with Love

Don't stand at my grave and weep—for I am at peace
I am with the Lord my God now that I am deceased.

Don't mourn my death because I am no longer in pain
I'm finally in comfort now that I'm in God's domain.

Don't think of me as gone because I am watching you today
I see you when you sleep at night-when you wake and when you pray.

Don't pray for me at that time because I am just fine so far
When you gaze at night into the clear blue sky
I'm your own sparkling star.

Don't let my death interfere with plans you have for your life
I didn't mean to ever hurt you or cause you any strife.

Don't stop moving forward—you can definitely survive
Don't think of me as dead but remember be alive.

You're still daddy's little girls and I hold you close to my heart
Even though I can't be there our souls will never part.

I am with your mother now for we are finally reunited
don't mourn this day-but celebrate
for we are peacefully delighted.
Christine Coleman

Prostitute Poet

You pay me for feelings expressed on paper for all of you.
"All of you the masses," your voices rose commanding Poets around
the world to prostitute their artistic skills.
Write of Love; feelings for your Mothers, Fathers, Sons, Daughters,
written on Halls of Cards, Marks that mean nothing to you, "But the
Poet cries as he writes."
Impress your Wife or Girl friend on a special time. You tell them
lies; not even remembering what the card said. The Poet helps your
Wife imagine the man she wants to keep. The Girl friend rewards her
man on the words of a Poet.
"The Poet," writes of death, passages of time, bearer of tidings, every
piece exhausting the raw emotion and desire of the Poet. Selling words
that are only the Poets to sell. "No one thinks, act, feels, or dies
like the men and women who write the feelings for thousands who can't."
"Prostitute Me, force me to do what makes others feel good; I'm your
whore." Open the eyes of others who stare into space. Say the words
other men can never say. Show the tears, feel the fear and at times
spread the hate of the human race.
Vidal Senior

Untitled

Thank you "Love" for the glass half full of wine, for those
times, and for more still to be mine, for "Loves" thrills
that have filled my heart, for the day he found his
thumb and there was quiet, for the roses running riot
all over the place, for the hour she learned her prayers
and the look on her face. Thank you "Love" for the
golden cup, the taste of new wine — for every time "Love"
held me through "a little child" and spoke — "Love" would
ever be mine. For those hours through the days, for
"Loves" exceptional ways, a message... A gift for "Love" . . .
right from the start. When our eyes met, for the
word "forever," never to part — and for waitings yet.
Thank you "Love" for the jewels, the crown that have
been expressed in a mother's gown — for all the
frowns too, when I wasn't sure what was going to
be next — and not to forget the wind that buried her head to my chest,
and the rain that chased us inside to hide from "Loves" storm — and
for "Loves" fire that warms him still. For every solitary thrill of
life that's only half begun — and for every ray of sun, thank you for
filling my arms, my mind, daily with "Love," each and every one.
Nancy Carolyn Myers

For Little . . . And . . . And . . . Etc., Etc., Etc.

No matter what y'all have on the ball, you still can't do it all
If you dig this read as unreal, try building an automobile

We get together to build and control everything but the weather
Together, is to see or wrestle but individual's dreams don't nestle
Thus we have diverse priorities, missing the power of integration
Elected leaders integrate and sort priorities by value to Our Nation

Called Government, it enables one to finish what one alone began
Our most precious institution for the unblest to the top Man or Nan
We must protect it and improve it every chance and every way we can
If it is not working well, everything hits the fan, ruining every plan

Like now with terrorism, war and National bankruptcy at the post
While the good secure life we all deserve is not attained for most
Our leaders air direction for one purpose only, the next election
Reelection has got to go, it, by itself, has us on death row

A single ten year term for Senator, House, President and Vice - Firm
Vital, cheered by thinkers, we must fire desire and rake out clinkers

Leaders are conned by selfish lobbies, Academicians bare the truth
Rotate them off campus to a Capitol city for them, plush, de luxe

The right to vote is a hot potato, let's give Good Ole US a break
Requires, at least, maturity, age 25, at least, starts icing the cake

George K. Marshall

A Rondeau for Helen*

Without fail about this time each year, the ringing of Christmas bells I hear,
I try my best to understand, why every Yoyo in the land,
Charges headlong to the mall, to purchase gifts, both large and small,
Where Santa sits in phony splendor, spouting words both sweet and tender,
Telling kids from far and near, everything they want to hear.

The Wise Men shoulda stayed in bed, with precious gifts they came instead.
But if a chimney you are without, a visit from ole Santa is in doubt.
After years with eight mature reindeer, we need a Red-nosed brat, like a can of warm beer.

The Turkey flees in fearful flight, to save his hide from human appetite.
Christmas cards fly back and forth by mail, the cost in stamps causes budgets to fail.
We cut and exploit the growing evergreen tree, a custom with which I disagree,
And yet!!! only the Lord knows why, after all is said and done,
I plan to stay and join the fun, and say what all would like to hear —
"A Merry Christmas and Happy New Year."

* *"Honey, try to imagine how much time and energy and
sheer Genius is displayed here. Then and only then
will you realize and know how much I really love you."*

Harry E. Kline

A Letter Home

To my wife,
Subtle scents that bring a memory. Glimpse of items never before
noticed; The robe which once held you, the sock left behind, the
pillow which cradled you head; the raising sound of strings playing
music one shared, take me to a far land of wonder and love. The wife
of my youth. The wife of my dreams. The woman of my life. Becoming
such a part, that was only noticed through the absence, the lack, the
distance. "How much a part of my life you have become..." The words
seem lacking. "As if the world was taken from beneath my very..."
still inadequate.

Painful remembrances of time not spent. Time in vain. Time wasted
Appreciation gaining with each hour, leaping each day. Wonderful
Time. Simple times. The touch of a hand. The soft caress.
Glimmering candlelit eyes. Love transcending knowledge. A soothing
kiss. A reassuring embrace. Longing.

Longing. Growing anticipation. Long days. Endless nights. Time
ceases. Let, it cannot. It is guided by a larger hand. A hand
that knits hearts. A hand that binds lives. Two lives for eternity.
Two lives for eternity. Two lives as one. Heavenly blessed and
Earthly beautiful.

With all that I have, and all that I will become, Your loving husband.

Carl E. Weber

You

Today I found a flower,
As I walked along my way.

I picked this flower, its fragrance sweet,
It made my heart quickly beat.

In my hand for an hour,
I carried this fragile little flower.

This flower has wilted, now it's gone,
In my heart its memory strong.

It's not really gone you see,
It's you I picked!! Just for me.

Earl B. Buffenmeyer

Cloudy

I'm in a hot air balloon, floating away
from life, floating through clouds of
purple, grey and white. Wondering where
my life will turn, wondering why and
when my heart will burn. If my
life will take a leap, if my soul will
stay and weep. Will I die or will I live?
will I take or will I give? Will I be
cold, mean and cruel as if my heart were
made of gruel? Will I be nice and
very kind and be caring with an open
mind? Will I go life with lots of strife?
will I take heart and do things right?
But it is Gods decision in who knows
were to place me in life's position.

Simon Plohocky

The Tree of Life

You are the leaves, we are the branches
We get our being from the sturdy trunks
Which gives us life from the resources
Of the rain, the sun and the earth below
And as we begin to bear the fruit of life
We will be design, again begin to share
New growth like those who came before

We can not live in the past or the future
Only now in the present one day at a time
For those in the past have now evolved
And those in the future are not yet here
Be satisfied with what and who you are
Strand tall, strong, resolute and proud
For He is with us always ready to help

Robert D. Gallas

Black

I am the silky, black alley cat that screams,
I am the smell of melting licorice,
I am the black berry juice
That trickles down your throat.
I am the shadow that creeps up your window,
I am the hollers of halloween,
I am the sight of death.
I am the worm that wiggles from the apple.
I am the hard, cold coal,
I am the fear that stares you in the eyes.

Sarah Gallagher

My Soul

There is one thing I must control:
The errant ways of my own soul.
Too many thoughts have gone astray,
and many doubts have come my way.

What is this soul that came to be,
with promise of eternity?
It's not the heart and not the brain,
and nothing flowing through my vein.

It is a spirit born within,
an entity devoid of sin.
A purity and moral might,
a beacon and a guiding light.

And yet, at times I fail to see
the need for better piety,
to please my maker as I must
and earn his godly grace and trust.

I must envision as my goal,
to enter heaven with a soul,
then free from all my frailties,
to find eternal rest and peace.

Otto K. Dannenmann

The Ferries

The ferries at Bolivar,
They pass each other softly,
Back and forth they ply,
The God green waters.

Carrying passengers here to there,
In between huge vessels,
Escorted by the gulls,
'N flying formations of pelicans,
Their job is never done.

Windy, pouring rain, sunny or not,
Each day back and again they go,
Barges low in the water,
Tugs and sailboats pass them,
On a hazy clay in July.

Susan Phillippi

Basic Obvious Skies

Such beautiful relate
The class of style
Enfold the tri-compassionate
basic obvious skies

A slogan of luv
symbol in almost need
When only attitude phrase
basic obvious skies

The ascendancy of interest
facility of problem exchange
Helping the expertise
basic obvious skies

The fair and right
Just isn't professional
Cool of the polite
basic obvious skies

Ours is clear
Understanding that gracious
Is appreciatedly near
in basic obvious skies

Isabelle Hunter

Hugs

For all the gracious Hugs;
that are warmer than a bear Rug;
and hotter than coffee in a Mug;

For all the open Arms;
that reach further than any Farm;
that wake me louder than any Alarm;

For all the open Hearts;
that speak louder than any Remarks;
and touch deeper than any Mark;

Thank You for your time;
That all come from one of a kind;
For all the Love that you sign;

Rather it be spoken or written;
It is as soft as a kitten;
And warmer than any pair of mittens.

Colleen Harmon

Meditation

In grateful praise I greet each day
Then pause awhile to break my fast,
Before in haste I rush away
To where my daily lot is cast.

I wonder at our rush as men!
Does each one feel the sun's warm glow,
And hear the song of the House Wren
As of to work, in haste, we go?

Returning home in pensive thought
I ponder God's mysterious way;
Amazed at what the day has wrought,
A humble prayer of thanks, I pray.

John N. Blow

Sandy

The essence, the beach breaks
as the surf in my mind.
Your hair flows as the waves
gently touching every grain.
The freckles upon your face.
Remind me of the sun shining upon
the surf. High lighting beauty.

Love abounding, the living water
flowing to bring forth life in the
creator. Who breaths life into being.

Your eyes drawing me, sparkling
and glisten me into being.

My memories continue: The beauty
of your heart; time shared and
the words unspoken.

Randall Ardeane Hilbert

Legacy

'Tis said that everyone on earth
Who must endure life's upward climb,
Will leave his print eternally,
To change the course of mortal time.

And, so with smiles and lilting song,
Impassioned heartaches, tears and pain,
With words and deeds we leave our mark.
For those to come, we come again.

Peggy Switzer Samii

Holly

September 17, 1996
Little Holly came to us today.
She was sent from heaven above.
Shawn and Julie are so happy
and proud of her.
She will always have oodles of love
Her grandma Sharon with a
smile on her face,
Knows God sent Holly to the
right place.
We all will love her as she
grows up to be a fine
lady full of happiness and grace
God bless you Holly
I love you.

Mamie Kemp, Great Grandmother

The Ocean

The ocean is a mighty force.
If you listen you can hear its voice.
Beating out its drum and roll.
As the waves hit the cliffs on shore.
Leaving its message for us to hear.
Saying watch out when you come near.
I can be mean and full of fear
When I am angry and storm in force
Like a person with an angry mind.
I leave destruction far and wide.
I can be peaceful, quite, and calm.
But what ever happens to stir me up.
It is a force within my depth.
With secrets far beyond my reach.
It seems I have a lesson to teach.
Like a person who is beyond any reason.
I howl and scream and call for help.
But only nature hears my call.

Frances Bean

The Clown

I often work for charity,
Just to help the children smile.
It doesn't matter what it takes,
I will go that extra mile.

Dressed in colorful costume,
With make-up on my face.
I try my best to bring a smile,
Anytime and any place.

From the children in the wheel chairs,
To those that run around.
They are all special people,
And they love to see the "Clown"

When I'm dressed in costume,
And entering your town
I'm only there to bring a smile,
For I'm a "Zany Clown."

Edward R. Stiner Sr.

It Matters Not

The journey of the years is told
Not by the wrinkles in a face
The sadness that has come your way
Or the tears that burned your eyes.
It is the twinkle in those eyes
And the light that is there within
That sparkle that makes someone smile
Giving real warmth to a human heart.

Your love is yours to give away
And a sincere hug can do so much
So shine for others and yourself
Twinkle as brightly as any star.
No matter what the years may bring
Let much optimism be your thing
Let faith and happiness fill your day
Be as refreshing as a summer breeze.

Evelyn Kimball Blake

To Nancy

I know your pain and sorrow,
But think of all you had -
The many years of sunshine,
How very few were bad.

The Lord lends us His children,
To raise and love. And then
He takes some of them back again,
According to His plan.

We cannot know His purpose,
It seems unfair at times,
But we must trust His judgement
And know He's very kind.

I know your daughter's well again,
And happy there with God,
And He will give you courage
To bear your tragic loss.

Loyce Craig Vickery

Little Bug

I'm just a little bug.
No one gives me a hug.
It makes me very sad.
Sometimes, it makes me mad.

People don't treat me right.
They are scared of my bite.
I'm really not so mean.
It's just the way I seem.

Though, I'm not very tall.
In fact, I'm really small.
But, I can skip and hop
over a high mountain top.

With sturdy wings I fly.
Happily, I roam the sky.
At times, I rest my wings
on friendly clouds, I cling.

Won't you be my friend?
Allow your heart to bend.
You know, God made me, too.
Not just the bunch of you.

Victor E. Legaspi

My Solid Gold Electric Chair

I'm still waiting on Death's Row
Not knowing when I'll have to go;
For me no pardon, no reprieve...
I make no effort to deceive,
The charge against me kindly stated
Is that I am antiquated!

They say we're born in mortal sin;
(We have no choice how we begin!)
Dumped on Earth upon my head,
By wisdom, surely, I've been led!
I've lived so many happy years,
Could be, my departure's in arrears.

I'm already well aware
I cannot climb the golden stair,
Nor dare to walk on golden street
Lest metal blister my bare feet.
I've pleaded "Gilt" for Golden Years:
Death be my penalty, no tears!
They've promised me the best of care..
My Solid Gold Electric Chair!

Labelle Gillespie

Living On The Street

Within the prison walls
Of her cloudy, foggy mind,
She made herself believe;
That everything's fine,

She walked the streets
From dusk to down,
Till daylight finds her,
Huddled in an abandoned barn,

As sunlight played
It's warm caressing rays,
On tear-stained cheeks;
And hair splashed with grey.

A silent tear escapes,
From eyes devoid of heat;
From seeing....and living,
Life on the street.

Yet somewhere in the distant past,
She must have been somebody's child.
Is there someone, somewhere...
Who thinks of her once in a while?

Myrtle Bailey

Warm Sand

Memories entwined in vertigo vines,
Logic and space there is no place,
Take a turn playing monopoly.
Large vessels voyage exotically,
See season sensual sunsets,
Vanishing under the water.
Don't bother the jumping otter
The soul seals its seems with silence.
Wishes widen horizons sorrow,
Making burdens a peaceful kind.
Loudly lightens love and laughter,
Values vary vibrant voices,
Giving choice to choking minds.
Music heard from forest deep,
If you sleep the willow weeps.
Cold is the call of winter rain,
Falling on earths terrain.
Rainbows with rage circle the moon,
Dust then man,
The feel of warm sand.

Earline Yost Shaw

Word-Play . . . Letter-Wise

Reviewing letters
as memoirs recalled
    diaries re-lived
a recurring theme noted:
    the joy, consistent,
of working with words
yes, affection, inspired
for words themselves...
that still fresh pleasure in
toying with affable ABCs
arranging them as in family games
till set to form connecting lines.

Checked, I see these patterns
of another day and this
define good life employment...
found: working with words
actually my "play"
    ever child-eager
    present-eyed
    confident.

Jane R. Harwood

Pictures of Me and You

It's love because you care
But it's not if you dare.
It's true if it's done
But it's wrong if you run.
And it's right to be good
Wrong to say "if I could".
To say I'm sorry, right
But wrong to say "I might".
To know and not to do
To lie and look at you.
To smile and say I will
To love and not to feel.
It's bad to cause the pain
But good to shield the rain.
What does this all lead to?
Pictures of me and you!

Think about it!

J. Lee Gilbert

Web-Cited

Patiently the spider spins
silver threads in autumn air
to entice a dinner date
Into her glittering lair.
One smitten fly asked her why
she was hanging upside down;
"To entertain only you"
lied she as she twirled around.
"May I call you Spidey - Pie?"
asked the fly as he drew near,
"Of course," she sweetly replied,
"Please come whisper in my ear."
Then when that poor silly fly
come waltzing into her den
he found that his feet were stuck
in coils of sticky silk within.
"Oh, prey tell, how can I hope
to come near and admire you?"
"That's okay, my prey," grinned she,
"I will have dinner for two."

Judith Starr

Happenings

"What happens, happens, —
because what's going to happen,
couldn't happen
if this didn't happen!"

Eve Westaby

Fifty Seven Years Love

Thou art heaven in my eyes
That fulfills all my dreams.
Creating disaster from satan
Like teasing with ice creams.

Thy beauty is outstanding
Personality supreme,
Tenderness so gratifying
It rips apart my self-esteem.

For no matter how much I love you
It is definitely for not,
For no way do I compare
With every charm you've got.

So I'll remain still single
No substitute will I procure,
I'll just keep on dreaming
with a broken heart for sure.

Marlowe C. Burr

Pieces Of Time

Looking dazed and confused,
Seeing the needle and the damage done,
Tied to this gallows pole,
Wrapped in these sheets of white.

Feeling lost and lonely,
Seeing the stairway leading to heaven,
Remembering only the good times,
Sapped of all my strength.

The song still remains the same,
Staying out in the cold,
Trying to touch the angel's hand,
Trapped in this piece of time.

Searching the hallways of my mind,
Screaming through the pain,
Leaving this existence we live,
Faded into the black.

James M. Hunt

Let's Pray

Let's all remember to bow our heads
and thank the Lord above,
for all His many blessings and for
His amazing love.

Not only during the good times
but also during the bad,
Not only, when we're happy but also
when we're sad.

Down on our knees we should go
and talk to God above,
He will show us mercy and comfort
us with love.

Doris Tyner

On Wing

A small white Dove descended on us
with one tiny wing impaired,
she limped along until we could
coax her into our care

Hunger was her first concern
when we tried to capture,
just short of any hindrance
we managed it with rapture

A bit of food and water
as confidence was instilled -
we tenderly clipped that feather
to give her back her will

She stayed a couple days or so
then gingerly tried her wings,
soon she gave us a few "fly-by's"
thankful for all these things —

Evelyn M. Cole

The Raft

Aye, tis nuthin', but a pile of wood,
The man said to the boy.
It once was part of a mighty ship,
Which brought men so much joy.

The boy then dragged the wood ashore,
And built himself a raft.
A sturdy pole, for guiding it,
He had his own sea craft!

I want to be a fisherman,
The boy said to the man.
I'll sail the stream, goes by my house,
And look back at the land.

I'll lay upon the bank come night,
And watch the stars above.
Dreamin' bout the things I've done,
Cause fishin's what I love.

When I'm grown, and am a man,
I'm settin' out to sea.
From South Carolina, then to Maine,
A fisherman, I'll be!!!

Penelope O. Ewing

Relative Sufficiency

The sun rising in the East
with its warm glow
makes me to know
we are not in the least
unable to find
one who is kind
Along the way...
To help gladden the heart
In America, the land of the free
That's real sufficiency to me
making every endeavor
A pleasure from the start
Relativity id Great
Not leaving all to fate...

Shirley Christian

Memories

Even though you can
not feel their tender
touch, or do things
you enjoyed so much.
Just remember God
has taken them up
above, you are still
showered with their
love.
The memories that
are placed in your
heart, will be there
forever and never part.

Ann Butchar

The Good Shepherd

Based on Psalm 23

The Lord is my shepherd
I shall never lack
A quiet place to rest
As he leads me in my walk

He leads me in quiet paths
Of perfect harmony
He refreshes my soul
For his personal glory

In the valley of death
Where fear can overcome
He gives sweet peace
That is not my own

In the presence of danger
He sets a table fair
He loves me with His love
I know that He is there

His goodness is forever
His mercy is always free
I know the Lord is with me
For time and eternity.

Lee Stuck

Father's Day

Fathers are special people
When they are loving and kind
And when they teach their children
To have the finest kind of mind

I remember my father
Yours you'll always remember too,
If he takes you to church on Sabbath
And sits with you in the pew

If he helps you to understand God
And His son the Jesus boy
If he sings and explains the sermon
And makes your time together a joy.

Yes, a father is a special person
And when he is old and gray
It will be your turn to take care
And help to make his day

So celebrate father's day
Whatever age you and your father are
Because this then is a day of happiness
To make all moral fathers a star.

L. Mila Warn

Dawn Is Radiance

All views are angled
Drifting between precise trends
Showers of flight
Breaking the mystery
Irradiate dreams
Banish with profusion
Liberty pure licit
Brilliant luster with beam
Holding the shadow of warmth
Bleached having aglow
Insight flame paragon
Guiding each deep fair
Kindle to flood with clarity
Switched splendor sheen
Cheering jubilant grand
Father macrocosm urbane
Providing our source of light
With honor, glory and peace

Dyanne Mitchell Williams

Evening Tide

The tides of eve
Are rolling in
Although the sun
Shines bright.

The gales of destruction
Looks bleak at morality
At the peak
Of the noon day sun.

The clouds cover
The graying skies
As man is windswept
Beneath the tides.

Sounds from the shore
Beats against the rocks
Will man be man again
Will we ever know?

The principles of life
Sets on Evening Tide
Who was really ready
For the lost virtues of this ride.

Cecelia Weir

A Special Request

Oh Holy Spirit bless us all and
    keep us in your care;
Spread your loving protective
    Light to all of us everywhere!

Look down from your heavenly home
    on high;
And brighten the clouds throughout
    the sky!

Shower the earth with contentment
    and peace;
May your blessings and love for the
    world never cease!

Please guide and protect Pope John
    Paul two;
Help Him lead in good health our
    safe way into

The twenty-first century with true
    faith and love;
Combined with everlasting trust in
    our God above!

Leah C. Anderson

Wild-Eyed Young Brickie

Here comes Mr. "Killer Kane"
Strutting down the scaffolding,
With that certain sparkle in his eye!
Every body knows him well
Something 'bout him seems to tell,
"Killer Kane" is once more flying high!
Monday is the worst of all
With bleary eyes of red,
"Get that line up, hit the ball"
Is what this foreman said!
Pay-day is the best of all
"Killer Kane" is ten feet tall!
Once again he's on "Budweiser Trail!"

Henry E. Jacobsen

Soaring On High

The planes were flying busily
As I ate lunch at the airport.
It seems to be so strange
That you're not up in the sport.

This was a perfect sunny day
To be sailing across the sky.
We used to soar through the air
And loved the freedom found in high.

I sit and look at your chair
And remember the joys we shared.
Our enjoyment was better
Because you really cared.

We flew through sun and rain
When necessity or pleasure called.
I navigated while you flew
And nothing ever stalled.

In memory I see you
With love in your eyes and a smile.
Some day I'll meet you
But it may be a little while.

Frances E. Tolson

The Beauty of America

The beauty of America
Shines from coast to coast
From its Majestic Mountains to the
Peaceful Valleys below
Our forest towering trees and
Flowers blooming so bold
To nourish the soul
Our streams, flowing rivers and lakes
Sparkle like jewels across our land
The plains covered with
Golden wheat, corn and grains
Our schools, churches and homes
And so much more
We have to be thankful for
Created and Blessed by God
The beauty of America
Shines brighter every day.

Martha Berlin

Los Angeles

From fingers moist with ocean mist
To chain of mountains on her wrist
We live within her friendly palm
Where lives are longer, breezes calm
Her daily sun does smile and pose
Except when rain must quince the rose
Her trembling hand I do forgive
Here in its grasp I'll always live!

Leland Embert Andrews

Cyclical

Time on a string -
Reel it in,
Let it run.
Today will pass
As countless days before;
A burst of light,
A struggle,
And oncoming darkness.
But soon - the dawn.
A gentle glow
Followed by flaming fingers
Dancing upward;
And a renewed promise
Of eternal optimism
Surges outward.
And ephemeral fisherman
Catches the phoenix of night,
Only to release it again
For another rebirth -
Another dawn.

Philip A. Eckerle

The Cannon of Life

No life, no being.
No being, no feeling.
No feeling, no caring.
No caring, no challenge.
No challenge, no voice.
No voice, no soul.
No soul, no presence.
No presence, no capacity.
No capacity, no promise.
No promise, no closeness.
No closeness, no heart.
No heart, no love.
No love, no life.

Marshall Kline

As Friends

I've tried to collect my thoughts
Of the years, as friends
We have been together
These few years with you,
Are in my thoughts,
Though these years have been,
Like no others
One question stands out
In all my recollecting,
And in my mind,
I shout out!
Why?
So date did this come about,
I do feel we have met before,
Otherwise we could not have become,
So close, so fast,
It's as if we opened a door
And there stood you
At last!

Mattie M. Stewart

Orange Sun, Yellow Moon

Bridge the two cultures,
Orange sun, yellow moon
Rainbow over the Jade Palace Restaurant

Summer day in mid-July,
There is a tint of fall in the wind.

Steven Berger

Untitled

Clothe me in doubt
But cover me with passion
For I am without
My daily ration

I need the thrill
of a moment of love
In order to fill
My soul from above

What is our life
But a spirit enhanced;
Sorrow is rife
But at least we have danced

We are angels in clay
Dissolving to dust;
But, come what may
At least I won't rust

Alvin Miller

Play In the Hay

'Twas a hot sunny day
In the month of May
I lay in the hay
With a girl to play

After our fling
I felt a sting
Right on my "Thing"
Bells started to ring

Was it the hay?
I can not say
Now I'll never play
With a girl in the hay

Sebastian

Haiku

Amid the glooming
Woodland objects take
   strange shapes
Eerie sensation!

With melting snows
Violets emerging are
Announcing springtime.

At evening crosswords
A terrapin stops midway
Time of decision.

On a leafing bough
A robin burst forth with
   song
Gladdening the heart.

Early morning light
Squirrels among the branches
The sound of gunshots.

Beautiful butterflies
Flitting over the flowers
Blessings of summer.

Beatrice M. Gartee

Ke Ali'i Nui

The Lord is my shepherd,
How precious was His Son.
Eternally in glory.
Oh, Lord you loved me so,
Dear ones I've left behind
Obey His Word of Truth
Remember He is always there.
Each day you live for Him.

Living for my Saviour,
Inspired by His Truth,
Never stopped to wonder,
On how to do His will.
Needed by so many,
No one whose hope is God.

Something beautiful,
Established in heaven on high;
The truth is being revealed;
Oh, He is the pathway of joy!

Irene K. Seto

Old Friend

He taught you so much,
   you say.
So now you yearn
   to know the touch
   of the woman he loved.
You want to know
   and share the bliss
   you feel you can't miss.

Do you really want me?
Is it I you really want?
What would I be
   an accomplishment,
   or a victory?
Am I desired as the result
Of his teaching you so much?
Or as someone to love and touch
   tenderly, but secretly?

Helen D. Dunn

House-Fire

Spilling
into the air,
the bubbling smoke
chokes and churns
into memories;
shattered images of
white linen and
french milled soap,
fine angelic doilies
and pink silk tulips.
A rosy child with curls
and lace
brightens the field,
a lawn of the past.
As a blessing,
in a heartbeat,
she dances among
fragrant tulips,
spider webs, and
dandelion silk.

Virginia Ramsey

For Now . . . .

For now, I must surrender my fate;
Call a truce between desperation and I;
Give the final flickering flame of life
A great heave toward the endless space
   over blue sky.

Leave alone memories of me,
Ponder not upon the value of my
   spirit; it has gone.
Let it ascend to the heavens
To be reborn again by the sun.

Returning in the form of another
With all prior knowledge; lifetimes
   in depth.
I'll find my new home in happiness,
A formidable fortress; I will be the
   ultimate enemy of death.

Reed Bass

Night Visits

I go visiting every night
With friends and family
I don't stay very long
for they're in my mind you see,
I see their smiling faces
as I sped across the miles
I tell them all I love you
Come visit me a while
You'd be suppressed when I
lay down, the miles I
cover when I go to visit
family and some close friends.
The never know I've been
there or the happiness
they bring when
each and every night I
go to visit them.

Evon Shelton

Fame

Closed Eyed
Mouth open wide
Inhale toxic dreams
Exhale designer-colored screams then,
Back-flip with a double twist
Into
The Bright 'n' Shiny
Abyss

Dion Sorrell

Time

So seemingly still,
   yet flying ahead
   at full speed.

The motor of my heart
   beats ever so much
   faster when you are near.

My heart flies on the wings
   of time

I see you smile each
   time I close my eyes,
and I float off on the
   wings of love.

Joy R. Mercado

The Wonder of Cats

Cats are a wonder,
 of this we are sure;
With their beauty and grace,
 and, especially, their purr.

Eyes so mysterious
 hold secrets untold;
Or, perhaps, some mischief
 about to unfold.

With the heart of a hunter,
 as in ancestors past,
They stalk and they leap
 on paws sure and fast.

No nobler of spirit,
 so loyal and true,
Can express as much love,
 as a cat's gentle mew.

 Christine M. Kurfis

The Train Whistle Blows

The train whistle blows
"Randy, Wes-" I remember you."
So vividly, when I hear
the train whistle blow.
I am there and you both are there.
We are together again-when,
The train whistle blows.
Life was so fine then, so simple.
We were such happy children
When I remember
The train whistle blow.
Bittersweet and poignant memories,
Match the tears upon my cheeks.
How I love to remember and hear when
The train whistle blows.

 Beth Spence

Spring

Trees shiver, quivering in the cold
Looking for a warmth to enfold
Branches tasting of moisture
From the night that passed
Send a message to the woods
Spring coming soon at last

Melting snow form the rapids
On the rivers flow
Squirming fish abound the waters below
A fisherman pauses, inhales the wonder
Exhales, he is held aghast
Beckons to his friend down yonder
Spring coming soon at last

One duck, two ducks, and a pair
With ducklings quacking about
In search of what was their lair
They now must do without
Signs in rotation repeating their past
Send a message to the woods
Spring coming soon at last

 Sainz U. Lopez

Untitled

"You can't believe . . ." means
"You can't breathe."
"You can't dream . . ." means
"You can't see."
"You can't hope . . ." means
"You can't change."
"You can't love . . ." means
"You can't live."

 Christine Childress

Your Presence

The bright warm sunshine of the day,
the twinkling stars of night.
Reflect the presence of your word,
your wisdom, and your might.

We alone can plant a bulb,
You add some rain and sun.
To make a fragrant of hyacinths,
with perfume matched by none.

The bumble bee that pollinate,
the flowers everywhere.
Defy the laws of gravity,
And show that you are there.

We stand in awe the moment when,
our new born child we see.
The tiny finger, ears and toes,
you have formatted so perfectly.

It's God whom made all living things,
According to our plans.
Creation proves that you exist,
Despite the doubts of man.

 Ruth Arnold

Bosnia's Cry

Beauty of face beauty of spirit
Awaiting their fate
In Bosnia's great war
Atrocities rule - suicide
And death is the rule
In Bosnia's great war

Children peace keepers die
who will hear their cry
In Bosnia's great war.
God forgive us humanity dying
In Bosnia's great war

 Rosa M. Watson

Echo

Echo blowing in the desert winds,
where words are a broken branch,
and promises are like a sea shell
lying on the desert sand.

Where a dove is reading
an old bible, where we are blessed,
in silence.

Echoes of his words
are heard above the desert clouds,
where an old cathedral bell was left
lying on the desert sand
where an angel is singing
an old time hymn
through the desert night.

Where in the distance
the sea gulls have spread their
wings silently in the desert wind.

 Paul Holland

The Season's Greeting

Bright lights, colors, whites.
Sound and scent of season's air.
when the world becomes more beautiful
than the cards we choose with care.
Angels in sweet bells sing,
while falling snow does softly bring
to earth a silent prayer.

 Alice Clay Johnson

All the Wild Things

All the wind things are going
All the wild things

Birds and bats
And snakes and cats
Storks and hawks
And wales and rats

All the wild things

Elephant big and bluebird small
Going to nowhere
Nowhere at all

Leading the way
To nowhere at all.

 John Bailey

Word Salad

There are big words in a "word salad"
and even if understood, are a bore.
Simplicity is powerful, honest
and most want to hear more.

"Word salad"——all mixed up,
makes a person confused.
Those who are trying to listen
and learn are not amused.

Nor do folks respect a "word salad"
manner of speaking.
Too pretentious and not the sort
most are casually seeking.

This can apply to the
written word as well.
If a book is full of "word salad",
it will never sell.

 Denny Sternberg

Destiny

I think about my destiny,
What I was really meant to be.
I have no skill with which to reach
In music, art, or even speech.
I've always been so very shy.
I cannot change, I wonder why.
I envy those with easy grace
Who say what's right in every place.
I could not make myself a name
Though never would I ask for fame.
I'm sure I'm plain as plain can be,
And being plain is being me.

 Laura Shelton Thurmond

Goodbye

May 11, 1996
When we parted this morning
a beloved one stood waving,
not knowing that before the day's
end there would be mourning.

Flight five ninety-two plunged
into Florida's Everglades,
and one hundred ten precious souls
were entombed in watery graves.

Goodbye is from an old English
saying: "God be with ye," and
someday, there'll be no more
goodbyes for eternity.
William Henry Williams

Silent Woods

The silence in the wood
is so pleasantly quiet,
The whisper in the trees
As the leaves gently delight
the little rivulet flowing softly by,
calms and takes the stress
of the daily grind, making
contentment and peace of mind,
Tranquil silence is so inspiring
As you feel the healing of the soul
in the rustle of the leaves, as
the soft wind blows in
blissful silence in the wood!
Iva Pate Brown

The Peace Giver Tree

His roots stem from Mary
Since she agreed to be
Mother of Jesus, King, to set free
Us, His children, from slavery.

She welcomed the Spirit, most Holy,
In perfect humility,
Became the host of the Trinity
And the hope of humanity.

Tree of crossed compassion,
From lifted-up position,
Present, Living Expression -
Leave in our hearts, Your impression.

As members of Your wounded trunk -
We ponder Your passion in love!
We accept our cross as a chunk -
of Your role as King of our love.

Peace flowing divine,
Enrich our life in earth's planet;
Temper our efforts in line,
With You, as our goal, implanted.
Sr. Margaret Ann Kelly S.C.

The Homeless

The homeless my faceless brothers
The ones we don't see
Where is life to take them?
Where are we to be?
You are my faceless brothers
The ones we don't see
We always pass you by
What does that make me?
Dorothy Garner

Green

Green apples and pears,
Green peppers and green peas;
Green tea and bananas,
Green pickles and green cheese.

Green grass of summer,
Green trees and green vines;
Green hills and valleys,
Green mountains and green pines.

Green frogs and crocodiles,
Green peacocks and green parrots;
Green spiders and flies,
Green dragons to scare us.

Green emeralds and Jade,
Green sleeves and green shoes;
Green purses for greenbacks
Prevent spells of the blues.

Since our world is blessed
With all shades of green,
It probably was God's favorite
That keeps us cool and serene.
Benita Winget Johnson

Peace

Peace of soul
Peace of mind
Peace of body
    equals
Harmony with God's laws
Tranquility of mind's thoughts
Repose of body's functions
    equals
Reconciliation with God
Reconciliation with man
Reconciliation with nature
    equals
Peace of soul
Peace of mind
Peace of body
Ella Shauna Mars

Engagement

  Deeply loving
In a mellifluous, winging way,
  Deeply joyous
In a singing plethora of delight,
We went towards lauds of day.
Not causing others to recognize it,
Yet gratified when they do,
We exult in the rapture given to us
Who must realize our debt
To forces within and without
  Beyond reckoning
Of personal intellect,
As we bend to the rejuvenation
  of beauty
When it may be sustained
In the bellicose environment
Of perceived information and
  Deeply antithetical
  Self-example,
Passion being its own protector.
Nancy Storck Newhouse

Valediction

To touch the twist of trees
in a frosted globe,
to taste the minted
whisper of the wind
exploring hollows,
to hear the clink of
sun coins rattling
on earth's dry skin,
to smell the lovely
ruin of a burning
summer dream,
to glimpse remembered silence
through shutters of
a crumbling wall
... is to fill all of October
into the waiting
womb of the mind.
Donna Dickey Guyer

The Final Ride

Who gave him
the right to decide
when I told the truth
and when I lied?

Needing the quiet
I know I lack
can be found inside
the little suede sack
where my secret hides.

A known fact
I'll need a guide
not looking back
to the day he died
As I pack
MY FINAL RIDE
Bobbi Bergsrud

The Hourglass

The sands of time
forever pouring
while we struggle
to keep from boring

Always in search
for something new
out of the way
for just a clue

All for a taste
the fruit of the vine
but never forgetting
the sands that chime
Edward J. Rohr Jr.

Her Choice

You never cared much for a cowboy
But I thought that a farmer would do
So I traded away my old leather chaps
For a chance of a lifetime with you.

But you never cared much for a farmer
So I thought a professor would do
And I traded away my old faded jeans
For a chance of a lifetime with you.

I was not sure of being a professor
But you really thought it would do
So I traded away my old cowboy thoughts
And shared a fine lifetime with you.
LeRoy J. Peterson

Today, Tomorrow And Forever

Today, I will say I love you.
Tomorrow, it will still be true.
Forever and ever, I will repeat,
I love you, with each heart beat.

Today, if you are to leave,
Tomorrow, I will surely grieve.
Forever, you're still the only one.
Don't leave me here all alone.

Today, we said a loving vow.
Tomorrow, here and now,
And forever until death we part,
We will love with all our heart.

Today, is for you and me,
Tomorrow, we'll have to see.
Forever, is ours to take.
For another we won't forsake.

Lajuana D. Burton

Hard Times

We all have sorrow
and fear in our minds,
but I say to you
cut that chain that binds.

Look all around you
and see what you've got.
Feel what's important,
disregard what's not.

There's love in us all
and if we show it,
We'll get through hard times.
I know you know it.

Keep it all simple,
don't worry so much.
Look deep in yourself,
Feel loves gentle touch.

When hard times come by,
as they surely will,
it feels lonely but
notice love's there still.

Darrell D. Bennett

Full Circle

Through the halls of life
we walk every day.
Down each corridor
we find something new.
A different memory from the past.
Many people have come and gone
Making their impact
changing us somehow.
Some are gone forever
others return to our lives
coming full circle.

Terri Lazzaretti

Summer Crush

A rain love
A friend I lust

Music and beds
His raw whisper

Misted time
A moment

Blue winter.

Wilson Kimball

Nihil

Deep in the vaults of heaven
Roves a shapeless mass,
Perhaps a soul predestined
Throughout all space to pass.

Its home is in the Universe.
It rests among the stars.
And ever on our evil thoughts
Casts shapeless, unseen bars.

It shrives our hearts of sin.
It twists our souls in pain.
Yet we do not its presence feel,
Nor see, nor e'er complain.

What's its purpose through infinity?
What's its driving aim?
None! And so we know not anything
And so to the end we remain.

George W. Wilson

From My Heart

Your love is like the heaven's,
Sweet and very true,
I have made some real bad mistakes,
This I know is also true,
But if I can be forgiven,
I will also prove to you,
The lost love and trust forgiven,
I will promise to love and cherish you.
From now till the day I go to heaven,
My true love I give to you.

Joel Javier Hernandez

Continued Growth

Difficulties arise,
That open my eyes
To the pain that I feel,
Which I try to conceal.

I do confess,
That under much stress
I think I can't cope,
And thus I lose hope.

When I do feel stable,
I know I am able
To continue with life,
Despite all the strife.

Life isn't easy,
At times I'm uneasy
But I continue to grow,
No matter how slow.

Valerie Nielsen

A Parent's Prayer

My child is precious, dear and sweet.
I pray this life to be complete.
To have the strength, the courage, the will
To stride through life without a chill.
To have the vision of life fulfilled
Within each day on which to build.

My child awakens to grow and learn.
What is sustaining may this life discern.
To have the knowledge, the grace, the skill
To travel the journey over the hill.
To have the faith, the sure serenity
To triumph o'er the vale eternity.

Please God I pray
Watch over this child today.

Karon Sue Hein

A Mother's Prayer

My son you've grown to be a man.
My pride is there to see,
For all the things you have become
And all yet still to be.

I know that you don't need me
In ways you did before,
But still I know that deep within
You hold an open door.

I wish I could protect you
From all that is not good
But life and fate deal out the cards
And that's the way they should

So in the quiet of the night
I say a silent prayer
That God will keep you in His sight
And ever in His care.

Barbara Ann Robinson

Retirement

I've got to admit I love you,
'Cause my cup runneth over with love,
My happiness can't be hidden,
A gift from heaven above.

The days go by so swiftly,
The years are beginning to show,
But I'll never mind, if you love me,
Though our hair turns white as snow.

Our family has grown and left us,
To raise children of their own,
It has left us to share our forever,
From all the seeds we have sown.

So now we can spend our tomorrows,
Together as we'll always be,
Until death takes one of us darling,
Then it will be memory.

Clara Demmer

The Storm

The rain falls.
No, it crashes.
The rain has a cause
As it smashes.
The wind blows.
No, it rages.
The wind is a doze
As we lock ourselves in cages.
The lightening flashes.
No, it blinds us.
The lightening crashes
As we loose our trust.
The thunder rumbles.
No, it roars.
The thunder makes us crumble.
As we lock our doors.
The storm will come.
No, it will destroy us all.
The storm will drum
As we close our eyes and fall.

Kay Tillery

This Is Us

This is forever
the cool nights touch.
Wrapped, gentle fingers,
sweet with lust.
Passion and heat,
beating as one.
This is forever,
soft want and need.
Flaming kisses warm,
flow cool with the ocean breeze.
Lacing of bodies,
intoxicated with desire.
This is forever,
the fire of rapture.
The touch of skin sweet,
pure and untouched.
The kiss of love,
tender and longing.
This is forever,
this is us.

Catherine L. Farmer

The Mystic

Ecstatic anguish
smothers me down
crushes my breast
and lets my heart ooze out!
Annihilated by the weight
of divine flame
I languish
transmuted
BURNING!

William J. Louis

The Hidden Treasure

"The Pearl of Great Worth"
There is a hidden Treasure,
Most search for it in vain.
It comes down from heaven,
And it falls like the rain.

This treasure is not one of silver,
This treasure is not one of gold.
The source of this hidden treasure,
Lies deep within one's soul.

A treasure more precious than silver,
A treasure more precious than gold.
To find this hidden treasure,
You must look within your soul.

George Rapanos

The Game

Three fat people,
Two women and a man,
Form a swaying triangle
In the chest deep
Lake water.

The man submerges.
Woman one straddles his neck.
One, two, three and heave
Slap into the water.

Woman two laughs deeply.
Next.

Cindy Vining

I Love You Because

I love you because
Your twinkling eyes.
I love you because
You never tell lies.

I love you because
Your cute little smile.
I love you because
You go the mile.

I love you because
We have so much in common.
I love you because
My head's not fallin'.

I love you because
You hold me tight.
I love you because
We never fight.

I love you because
Of the things you do.
I love you because
You are you.

Jennifer Edwards

Breakfast With Friends

Through the thunder, hear the birds
Greet another stormy day
Pelts of rain on feathered flock
Wanting for some soggy seed

Fear of hunger lifts them off
From their poorly sheltered roost
Where to go out for a meal?
To a place not far away

Past the meadow to a house
There upon the window ledge
Bread and seed, and bits of fruit
Breakfast time surely awaits

Beyond glass, peer happy eyes
Watching as the birds approach
Eat up now! My feathered friends
Join me as I eat my toast

Raymond Wineberner

Spring Snow

Spring is here!
But, today it's snowing.
We call this "Spring Snow."

The snow is heavy,
because it is made of rain and snow.

It looks beautiful outside,
Trees branches are covered with snow.

The snow reminds me of Christmas.
Because the snow is,
pure, white and beautiful.

Kimberly McCachren

Little Red Rose

Little red rose
Alone on her grave,
You smile amidst the sadness,
Sweet flower so brave.

She left so soon
Without a good-bye,
How I envy your valor
To bow down and cry.

The sun shines down
And dries all your tears;
She whispers in a soft voice
To calm all your fears.

You now should know
She's a part of you,
For your glittering beauty
Does reflect hers, too.

Little red rose
Alone on her grave,
You cry amidst the gladness,
Sweet spirit you'll save.

Shelli Misoyianis

Forgive and Forget

Forget me, forget me if you can,
As I've tried forgetting you,
Forget the things we shared,
And now if you dare,
Tell me, that you no longer care?
We had a bitter fight,
And I would like to make things right,
But I can't do it all alone,
As far as I'm concerned,
Darling won't you please come home,
And try to forgive, and forget

Alfrida L. Bell

Bitter Sweet Memories

Your face still seems sweet
even though years have past.
Your touch was so gentle
and I remember the last.

The words that you spoke
when you left me in tears.
Now that I recall
don't seem so sincere.

To think it was all a lie,
to believe it in my soul.
Makes me want to die
before I get old.

So I cling to the memory
of how it felt when we touched
A desire sparked to life
no thought to pain and such.

Marsha Painter

Hate

Black and white
Are not bright.
People try,
But eventually die.
God miracles are here
so do not fear.
Love will be found.
Hate is near.
So you must "Beware."

Erika L. Bonner

Our Duality

He makes them laugh, displays a smile.
He has no age but juvenile.
I can't compete with such a show
Of antics on a high plateau.

We share a goal of loving life
And sparing others pain and strife.
But he's the one, my other half
Who has the fun and makes them laugh.

The face they see is his indeed
With no intention to mislead.
But when they go, his job is done.
I take his place and we are one.

So why does he not feel my pain
Of loneliness and sheer disdain?
Alone we are, both he and I.
How can it be, he does not cry?

He might forget that he has me
As part of our duality.
We cannot split with such a bind.
Our lives remain so intertwined.

Adam Saul Libarkin

Tal —

Enclosed within my tangled mind,
just beyond my wisdom's reach;

Lies divine memories of her beauty,
of her touch, of her speech.

Dispassionate time proceeded by,
the incoherent thoughts have left me
wounded, empty, and scared;

Unwilling I forget the one
who possessed my heart, now
intentionally I try not to remember
that I ever cared.

Daniel Gawlista

Mask

Velvet black shadows
Overlap the soul
Dripping pain and sadness
The heart bleeds

From life wasted
By passing time
Struggling to conform
To an unbending mold

Stare into the mirror
It too is a lie
Remove life's mask
Your facade then asks
Who am I?

Janet M. Hollinger

Excerpt

How does it feel to know
That you are Yang, and I only Yin?

Listen to the grasses clash,
Whispering lightning, thunder, Crash!

Jeopardy leopard leaps
Singing power life.

Stop the world.
I want to get off.

Joanna Zoe Christopher

Starship's Quest

Travelling star ways all alone
Speeding toward the rim;
Yearning, anxious, ever-guarded
Dolefully approaching the dim.

Regret not the passing scenes,
Or of the future fear.
Retain the bounty of each hour,
And all that it holds dear.

All light and dark that flood the way,
Your craft must surely be
Preparing you for greater realms
through all eternity.

Lahoma Martin Heisa

The Rain

Pit pit pat,
The rain falls flat.
For when I look
Out my window sill
The very truth
My heart will reveal.
The rain falls hard
On my front yard.
  Oh the rain,
Oh the rain,
Most people call it a pain.
In every child's heart
To splash in a puddle,
Brings a smile to their face,
And a dream of a happy place.

Rebecca J. McGinley

The Bipedal Cockroach

Look out! Send in exterminators.
It walks upright.
Disguised perpetrators
Of injustice!

You can't kill it.
You can't live with it.
You have to coexist
But you don't have to like it.

Look out! There goes another one.
Their brood is growing.
Pray not to be preyed upon.
Saints are targeted most.

The Bipedal Cockroach
Dangerous of all!

Susan Cannarozzi

Angel from Heaven

God sent down an Angel
Forever yours to keep
To sit upon your pillow
And watch over as you sleep...
God sent down an Angel
To cast away your fears
To light your life with happiness
And wipe away your tears...
God sent down an Angel
Its wings are filled with light
To embrace you in its arms
And keep you safe
All through the night...

Donna Rae Coleman

Insecticide

Spiderman.
Your woman weaves her sticky web,
You're watching silently.
Not shifting until she is done.
And now that she is —
What will you say?
I heard her tell the mosquito
That it was over
Before she sucked it dry.
As you can see,
She is moving on.
Her new web has been built.
Sorry, no room for you.
Only for the roaches
Which
She traps
And eats.
— 2:03 am
Barbara Webster

Aspen

Aspen is a tree
with leaves that
flutter constantly,
even if there is no wind.

Its bark is all white
and makes for a nice contrast
when growing among pine trees.

But what a privilege it is
to be in a Western state
and see the Aspen Chapel.

There are acres of Aspen trees
with their fluttering leaves
just whispering their prayers.

It makes you want to hush
because you will interrupt
their most humble manner.

Alice Piotrowska

My Mother

You are one of two
that know me better
than any other
you are my mother

You are one of two
that knows the spirit
within me you are
My mother

I know sometimes it not
so easy to be
you are my mother

There's one thing I will
always do I will always love
you are my mother

With that everlasting
love and care
you are my mother

Love always
to my
mother

Larry James

Rain

In the arms of sweet warmth,
rain washes away time.
Creating invigorating waters,
to the rhythm of each raindrop
and feel joy unrefined.

Drizzling down to a lazy,
mellow sound,
as velvety droplets kiss the window.
Sun breathes in the moisture
of sensuous rain, so profound.

Gale C. Saadig

Untitled

The world rolled along
on my river of tears
There was no ground
for my feet
I grasped at a cloud
passing by
but I missed
The river ran wider
and deep
Somewhere in the blue
is my rainbow
but the sun
has yet to shine
Someday I will find
the words and the place
and Peace will be mine

Ethelyn Hurd Woodlock

Neverborn

A land of mystery beyond fatigue
reached not by trying
sailors of the mind have drowned in
the murky depths
attempting to scale the walls of
neverborn.

A castle solitaire
deep and comfortable and beyond care
in a mystic, foggy forest
with a blue tent inside
a land of imagination
yet deeper still with no location

the few having reached it never come
back, for they never were
and they rest in a dimension of ease
for the night mermaid removes shoes
from their feet
and I am left behind by the sailor
nerves complete.

Blane Lay

Dimension

There are dimensions in the sky,
The earth, the moon, the clouds on high

There are dimensions in the home,
Especially where small children roam.

There are dimensions hard to place,
The distant dimensions of outer space.

There are dimensions no eyes can see,
God holds in trust for you and me.

This great dimension, and far more
To be revealed at death's great door!

Lillian B. Platt

To Nellie

Nellie put ribbons in my hair
satin and pink. We're going
to the farm, where the air
smells of roses and honeysuckles.

We tread slowly down an old
dirt road that looks like it
leads far into nowhere. Laughing
as we ease around dirt puddles,
deeper and deeper into the woods.

There appears an aged farmhouse
of Quaker ancestry, in times
of old. In rapturous delight —
gazing downward into an encasement
of emerald green- New England pines
and variety.

People there to greet us as we
enter an old world; my favorite
world of feather beds and oil lanterns.

Carlynn Waters

Rejoice

Come rejoice with me
And you will see
All you troubles go to sea.

Come live with me
In my Father's Kingdom
And of this world you shall not be.

Come take my hand
And through this land
We will together find
Those who are now blind.

Speak my word to their
Hungry soul
And watch the things of old
Fall away, never again to unfold
And see our Heavenly Father smile
As another name goes on file!

Mona Lisa Dykstra

For a Remorseful Heart:

I know the sounds of sullen cries
Passing through the walls of fear;
Shatter'd hearts and swollen eyes
Closed by a resentful...tear...
I've heard the screams of dying men
Lock'd within their doom;
To sit alone, without a friend
As they drown'd within the gloom...
O, guilt and endless sorrow
A darkness beyond the pain;
Knowing with every tomorrow
Their lives will be the same.
As yesterday was in torment,
Desperation, and despair;
Knowing the truth of darkness
For there is no one to care...
For a remorseful heart:

Charles F. Longacre

This Place

There is this place, within my mind,
Where I can go to visit.
It is a place of happiness,
A refuge from my suffering.
But I dare not stay, too long to play,
For fear of not returning.

I can stop to rest awhile,
In this place, to where I travel.
Unload my suitcase full of woes
And sip a cup of peace.
But I dare not linger on, too long,
For fear of not returning.

Soili Patteri Alholinna

An Anniversary Poem

Love as deep as the ocean
Love as wide as the sky
Love like that lives immortal
A love that will never die.

Love like that is within us
With powerful wings like a swan
A voice as sweet as an angel's
And beauty like sunrise at dawn.

Fiery flames can't destroy it
Nor can the heaviest flood
Forever it grows like a flower
From seed to sprout to bud.

Freely it soars like an eagle
Striking whoever it may
The arrow shot by Cupid
Sinks deeper everyday.

And so love as deep as the ocean
Love as wide as the sky
Love like that lives immortal
A love that will never die.

Marie Valerie Bautista Frando

Stars Up Above

Down on the shore
Waves swaying
The cool night air
Walking on the sand
Feeling all mellow
Spotted a rock
How bright it looks
Taking a seat
Wondering away
Looked up above
And beauty was there
Stars up above
Beautiful as ever
Glitter and shine
Of all shapes and all size
Stars up above, how romantic
stars up above, how enchanting

Keisha Campbell

Books

O ye books,
The wiliest of creatures,
Can trap a reader
With but a breath of
Words,
Not even spoken,
Forever.

Thomas Haymore

Broken Dreams

My broken dreams,
flow down silent streams.
I wish I could build a damn,
to hold back my river of tears.
My life is of endless fears.
I wish I had a heart of stone,
so it no longer hurt being alone
my broken dreams,
flow down silent streams.

B. J. Wolfe

Umbrellas

They spring up like giant mushrooms
when rain beings to fall,
and come in many sizes,
some big and some quite small.

In many rainbow colours
you'll find them at the shore,
to protect us from "ol'sol"
as they did in days of you.

Ladies call them "parasols"
when using them for shade.
And gents can use them as a cane,
just to promenade.

But when the south wind blows a gale,
one needs to be on guard,
for if that "bumbershoot" is open wide
'twill take you for an airplane ride.

Bernadine Robie Marsrow

Timeless Beauty

Snow capped,
Gleaming in the sun,
Distant mountains
Wearing crowns of
Shimmering snow,
Timeless in their
Beauty greet each day.

As children run
In joyous play,
Music of birds
Fill the air,
While the distant
Majestic mountains
Reign over all.
In silent, towering
Dignity of
Timeless beauty.

Petal A. Beebe

Special Someone

I've found that special someone
That I can have and hold.
To share my deepest thoughts with
And cherish just like gold.

I'll be with him forever,
And forever never ends.
See, he's not just my lover,
He's also my best friend.

So, I'll be by his side.
I love him don't you see.
At last my search is over.
I've found my destiny.

Sara Tohlen

Soldier Unknown

Sing not,
"Oh say can you see,"
To these unseeing eyes;
To these ears that hear no sound,
Here unfurled beneath the ground.
Could I but share, not plead,
The field of battle cause
For each young comrade lost
Amidst blind justice laws:
Unanimous the consensus
Of hundreds of thousands strong,
That the freedoms you abuse too long
Without a thought
Are given to you
By battles that we fought.
Yet you take them in your stride
And claim each right,
Never leaving home to join the fight.
To *you* I'd sing: Oh say can *you* see
Who it *was* allows you to be free?

Gifford F. Cottle

Solitary Despair

The misery and the sorrow
Tear at my soul
I lie awake and fear tomorrow
Another black hole
Why must you leave me
I've nothing left in my life
You're the only ease to my suffering
You're my only high
Untimely tears for ignorance
Innocent of what lied ahead
Happiness for such simplicity
When did it end
As you faded away into darkness
The angels in heaven cried
My faith has been stolen
Your love has died

Michael Tracey

War

A shot is heard across the ocean,
a flashy red color appears in the sky.
A body is dropped onto the ground,
you can hear the children cry.
No one knows why,
or how or when.
All you can see is blood,
all you want to see is love.
You cannot stop it,
as much as you want.
It'll go on for years to come.
What I am talking about,
has only three little letters in it,
but can do so much...war.

Laura Maltz

Look Ahead

A thirsty young fellow one night
Neglected to turn on the light.
Twas his wife's contacts, alas
That he drank from the glass
And developed 20/20 hindsight.

Judith O. Henry

Daddy's Little Girl

I have many memories,
So vivid and clear,
Of treasured times
That I hold so dear.

You were always patient.
You calmed all my fears.
And when I fell,
You wiped all my tears.

While I grew up,
You were there for me,
So very proud
Of all I could be.

It's my last christmas home
That I'll share your name.
'Though it will change,
I'm always the same.

I am your little girl
And I'll always be.
I'm very glad
That you belong to me!

Deborah J. Abbott

Morning!

The sun rises;
I walk into the morning breeze,
my nightgown billowing around me.
The wind ruffles my hair,
as leaves scamper across the yard
    on invisible wings.
Rays of sunshine kiss my
upturned face like a golden butterfly.
Dew sparkles on the grass,
and unseen birds are caroling
a welcome to a fresh new day.

Rebecca Williamson

Tantalizing Eyes

At the threshold of delight
A hand beckons you closer
Through a haze of neon light

Perched on a pinnacle
Of life's golden treasures
Intoxicating minds
With thoughts of forbidden pleasures

Dreams can be granted
Like three wishes they unfold
Because anything is possible
when it is bought or sold

Man's ego is inflated
Like the arena he has built
using one another
without a trace of guilt

This notion of reality
Is full of ancient lies
While the truth hides behind a mask
of tantalizing eyes

Walter English Gladwin

Treehouse

Once I saw twice
Once I saw me die
Covered in the open
Earthmother virgins womb
Knowth
Where I sleep
Well and water
Baptize me
Rainbow
Witnessed son
Praise people
In their slave
Blindman
Seen my light
Crown wealth
King of golds
Foundation
Mothers die
Well and water
Baptize me

Wanda Evette Murray

"Passing Beauty"

There is a woman,
who we love and fear.
She is the most in tune with
herself and everything around her.
She is beautiful and full of life.
She can be loving and hateful;
happy and sad; joyful and angry.
Through all the years of abuse
handed to her, she has the courage
to continue. When she cries
there are those who are hurt,
and those who are helped.
We must all be careful with how
we treat her. For one day
we will drain her of all the
strength God gave her. One day,
She will leave us to face
the consequences.
For she is nature.

Robert L. Hvamstad

Read to Me

Read to me . . . From enlighten
poets . . . Whose understanding
gushes forth.
Read to me from hearts that
knoweth . . . Who still hear the
child's voice . . .
Read to me . . . Unafraid and
terse.
Read to me an uplifting
verse . . . One that will
quicken my pulse . . . Like a
benediction read in
church . . .

John Wesley Albritton

Changing Seasons (Fall)

I feel the crunch of drying grass -
     As I walk on hard, firm ground.
And velvety patches of green moss
     Now are turning rust and brown.

Fields of yellow goldenrod
     Contrast against blue sky.
Stands are seen along country lanes,
     Forest roads and the highway.

The tan and yellowing fern is bent,
     And swaying in the breeze.
And overhead the golden aspen leaves
     Are fluttering on the trees.

Briar bushes, one laden with fruit,
     Are bowed to earth and bear.
There's a chilling and raw dampness
     In the mid-September air.

So may we thank and praise our God -
     The Creator of us all.
For by His hand the earth is changing
     From hot summer into fall.

Geraldine Borger

Lest I Forget

I would start my adventure
     Aboard a ferry boat,
Stand on deck and feel the wind
     Of unspoiled Vermont.

I would swing to jazz and blues,
     Dance to the country rock;
Enjoy the cruise down by the lake,
     All through the summer night.

Then I'd watch the willow trees,
     Where robins chirp so gay;
And see once more the wooded path
     Where sunshine meets the rain.

I would walk through aspen grove
     To view its pretty scene
When autumn leaves begin to fall
     And turn to gold again.

I would do all these lest I forget
     How precious life could be.
It's time to write this lovely poem
     That Jesus writes with me.

Lucy Evangelista

Adolf Hitler

From the pits of hell
And the volcanos of rage
From whom can tell where else
comes satan himself
In the name of hatred
Comes the creature from his cage
Like the evils of the serpents
And the monsters of the night
Adolf Hitler stalks millions on sight
He cats a spell of horror
With all his might
His legacy leaves us with much blite
It spreads like a disease
To new young flights
It grows from generation to generation
Continuing its fright
It must be stamped out
Before it's too late
And the rest of mankind meets his fate

Norman Sadler

Garden of Discontent

I left the blooms in the garden,
     Where no one else could see
The orange grove and rosemary,
     And the blossoming apple tree.

I went to town to buy more seeds,
     To plant the sage in row,
The buttercups and daffodils.
     And a circle of roses too.

I watered them so patiently.
     I tended them with care.
They blossomed into tiny buds.
     The branches then were there.

Then winter came so suddenly,
     Covered the land with snow.
The willow and the maple trees
     Had come to wither too.

Spring time came and I rejoiced
     When I looked out one day.
The garden of my discontent
     Was then in bloom again.

Lucil Evangelista

To a Rose

Dear little hedge rose,
Your petals slowly unfurl
Sunbeams dance and play,
On your beautiful, delicate flower.

Dewdrops sparkle, glitter,
On buds so dainty and small,
The sun so gently kisses them
And slowly, slowly they unfurl.

Little rose bud opens up,
Open, open and awaken to,
The beauty which surrounds us
God's beauty all around us.

Nadine E. Moonje Pleil

Pre-Grammar

In the beginning
there was a word
naked
like the flesh in Eden
full
like the breast ready to feed
the word - the flesh

And it had happened
that tempted by shades of meaning
the word
took a bird and the wing apart
and the bird fell down
to discover the law of gravity
a thousand years
before knowledge was born

The fallen bird
can always be stuffed
but can we
turn it back
into Logos?....

Elizabeth Nawracaj

To Meet Again

Love can be shared
Just by a glance.
Simply by presence
With words of silence.

When things go wrong
And you're alone
Think of the one
Who made it fine.

The force of love
Will fill your core
Turning sadness
To happiness.

Remember when you were both young
A unique love had come along.
Her beauty all you'd ever need
To make your life sure to succeed.

And now the time again has come
To join the one who has been gone.
To see once more that face, that wife
The face of love, love of your life.

Claude Larocque

Questions

Why does grass grow?
Why is it green?
Are there lost valleys,
with very rich kings?

How many stars,
in the sky above?
Is there such a feeling,
as real true love?

Do you think snow,
is really nice?
Do you like clear water
more than cold ice?

How many questions
goes through our minds?
How many answers
are so hard to find?

Janet McGill Weidhaas

My Mother

My mother
is one
who gave my birth

My mother
is one
who fed me

My mother
is one
who brought me up

My mother
is one
who left alone

In spite of that so far
she is waiting for me alone
still she is and she lives

Because she is the only one
on the other side of earth
because she has to live

Arthur Adalbert Albert

Ring of Oaks

Gathered around,
    so solidly they stand.
As strong as a fist,
    in a balled up hand.

When it rains,
    water is what the branches soak.
Becoming taller and thicker,
    forming a ring of oaks.

In a spiral they twist,
    upwards toward the sky.
As if speaking to the ground,
    and saying goodbye.

Matt Russell

Carousel Seasons

Where it starts and stops
no one tells

Round and round it goes
carousel
Colors bright with life
everyone yells
Why does it go so?
How does it go so?

Standing still it sits
doesn't seem right
Summer's gone Again
fall has fell
Wait until next year
I will be back here

Sleeping under show
like a bear
Foot prints trail and fail
to make it go
Doesn't it feel cold?
Doesn't it look old?

Jeff Tobin

What Counts Is What We Give

It isn't what we get in life,
What counts is what we give.
Though storm and strife may overwhelm
What counts is how we live.
The little petty childish things
That have a sting and smart,
Should never have been said at all
To cause an aching heart.
Think twice before you utter words
In anger or in haste,
For once they leave your bitter lips
They cannot be erased.
Don't let gossip pour through you
As though you were a sieve,
You'll be thought of much more kindly
For the gracious way you live,
You go through life each day but once,
Learn graciously to live,
It counts not what you get from it,
But how much that you give.

Mary Walbridge Neiswinter

Dead

Deliverance into babylon
waits upon lovely sins
broken dream cuts my silence
waving past dazed prophets
like smoke upon ashes
rings of desecration encircle my
thoughts, like entwined veins.

Shadows, whispers of razors enfolded
inside ribbon. Skull rested upon
lines, like cold metal on fur.
Nakedness drips off my tears.

Wretched sunlight like sharp needles
in my frozen eyes, suspended in
darkness. Judgments follow
prophecies. Scenes of weathering
like dwarfs knocking on my bones.

Threads cling to me-wilted flowers
overhung, cold stone rested on my
head. Some call it peaceful, but yet
it seems so close to hell.

Abby Woodhouse

I Know My House In The Morning

I smell . . . Mom's perfume in my room
    flowers on the table
I hear . . . Dad getting ready for work
    Mom in the kitchen
I see . . . myself looking for my
    number 12 shirt...myself
    getting ready for school
Someone says..."Goodbye, have a
    good day!"
I know my house . . . it is my home.

Jeff Gostony Jr.

Good-Bye

My cheeks are so red
But I feel so blue,
I'm really not sure
Why I feel like I do.

You tell me you love me
I know that it's true,
But I really don't think
That I feel it too.

We've been through so much
And had lots of fun,
We've even shared everything
Through all that we've done.

But many things changed
That's all in the past,
I just don't see how
This relationship can last.

I don't want to say this
But I can't live a lie,
I think that it's time
We say good-bye.

Lindsay Blair

Change

We're changing the way we think.
Since at times our attitudes stink.
With God we're ONE,
life should be fun.
This could be the major link.

Sidney R. Saddler

Untitled

The sky was so blue today,
Even though the grey clouds came.

I wanted you today,
But the sky wasn't the same.

The rain was falling hard,
But the the sun tried to shine.

I wanted the love we shared,
and to remember you are mine.

I wanted to feel you.
I wanted to touch your heart.

But you were raining inside,
and it pushed us a part.

Why does the sky seem so blue today,
Why did the grey clouds come.

Please come back to me,
When the raining is all done.

Corrina L. Adams

Me And Mom

They say I look like my Mom . . .
When I am sad
She is sad
When I feel bad
She feels bad
When I am happy
She is happy
So when I could
My grades are good
And she is glad
(and so is Dad)
So she buys me clothes
And that is rad
I think we're twins!
I love you MOM!

Jason Covington

A New Life

He took him...
wrapped him in his arms of love..
   and gave him happiness.
He entered a new world...
full of friendly faces..
   with no more pain.
Now he plays...
   in marshmallow clouds,
and dances to beautiful music...
   under moon lit stars.
He will no longer suffer...
   with knowing his fate,
But live forever to wait..
   for his family...
and friends,
   to join him again,
and to see,
   a happy little boy,
with no fears or tears.

Courtny Dahl

Feelings

You may have feelings
that you don't understand,
but these feelings
you must experience first hand.
Regardless the feelings
on the subject matter,
confront these feelings
before they truly shatter.
You need to know
what these feelings mean,
because they always
aren't what they seem.
You must see
what they mean to you,
because you just can't tell,
they could be a dream come true.

Jason Holly

Yin and Yang, Me and You

Yin cannot be without Yang,
And, I cannot be without you,
You are my other half,
You are the strong half,
You are the sensitive half,
Without you, I am weak,
Without you, no one cares,
Yin cannot survive without Yang,
And, I cannot survive without you,
Like Yin and Yang, we balance
each other out,
We are one and the same.

Stephanie Trone

Within Myself

I was unable to give of myself.
I gave as was given to me,
I was damaged but I was whole,
I was young, but my spirit was old.
I was free but my emotions were bound
I was injured but there was no blood
I was crying but there were no tears.
I was hardened in a kindred soul
I was laughing but there was no mirth,
I was among many but I was alone...

Patt Smalley

You, Through God, Inspire Me

You, though God, inspire me
to help, to feel, to love
and encourage those I meet
no matter who they are.

You help me see, as Jesus sees
through the spirit of my soul
to make me carry on in life
whene'er I become discouraged.

You let me know I'm needed
when I think no one cares
and I reach out in the distance
to let you know God cares.

Juanita M. Lybrink

Whispers

Softly you whisper "I Love You."
Gently you kiss me
Before you go.
You say you'll be back,
But somehow I know
That this gentle kiss
Is the last I'll ever know.
The time we spent together
Was the best part of my life,
But somehow I see
That you weren't meant for me.
So as I whisper "I Love You, too"
I quietly let you go.

Angela Dunn

The Mystic Mountain

Oh, charming organic beauty,
Not composed of painting or stone
But of living corruptible matter
Look at the shoulders and hips,
And the flowery bosom,
on both sides of the chest
And the ribs aligned in pairs,
And the navel in the belly's softness
And the dark sex between the thighs,
Let me feel your pores exhaling
And touch your down
A human image of water and albumen
Destined to the anatomy of the tomb
And let me die
With my lips pressed to yours.

George John Guerin

A Man

The air was moist
The trees a thick green blanket
The buzz of a power saw could be heard
CRASH
Death of a tree
Death of a man
No one wonders about the tree
Just the man
Lives changed forever
Engulfed by sadness
Surrounded by madness
Why was echoed in thoughts and words
Tears were shed
But life went on
A decade later
Sadness still lingers
But none is forgotten
Of the man I called my father

Kerri Normand

Untitled

Spring has come
And the flower had bloomed
So full and beautiful
With strong scents of persuasion
I try hard to resist
But temptation is teasing
Like a trillium I can't pick
I'm flirting with lust
Can't I have just one petal

Brenda Beaven

Digging Clams

The sunset glows, the tide is low,
And breakers pound the rocks.
We dig for clams in the salty sand
While sea gulls scream and mock.

Jet plumes of spray, alas, betray
Their hiding places deep.
The dimpled shore protects no more
The clams that lie beneath.

We thus pursue, with shovels cruel,
And conscience unremorseful.
The creature cowering in its shell
Will be a tasty morsel.

Lily Weinmeister

Realization

Oh lovely ladies
Look at you, in oval frames
Eight generations, all covered in dust
Your lives with us
A minute in time

Totally, demure, not a smile to be had
Hats and bustles
Were surely a fad.
Oh lovely ladies
Look at you, forgotten by name, photo's
Faded by years of sun and abuse
Ancestors not caring of the mis-use.

Oh lovely ladies
Look at you, beside stern men
Who cleared our land
Were your hands tired in the end?

Oh lovely ladies
Look at you, will anyone care
When in fact it's my turn
To hang up there?

Evelyn Sherritt Hunter

In Their Magnitude

Everyday things
   is what I write,
once in awhile,
   they're, out
         of sight!
I might be
   a little bit loony,
this is true,
   but, it breaks
the monotony.
   if that's
O.K., with you?
I see the rainbow,
   in the sky,
those are the colors
   of you and I!
They, all, are equal,
   in their magnitude,
I wish more people
   had this attitude!

John Search

Freedom

An open road,
an open sky,
with the sun shinning high
of hopes and dreams.
Here is where
the dreamer is free,
with the realities of life.
No expectations,
no others,
alone with the world.
Free to live
like an eagle,
as it is too alone,
surviving on its own
for its own

Denis T. Dungo

Doctors

Who are these gifted creatures
qualified men and women
reaching climactic heights
remedy people
of clean
cut
cloth
worthwhile individuals
seeking to cure our ails
ease the pain
remove the flesh
powerful enough to announce our birth
or warrant our death

Cynthia Zajac

Untitled

   All of life —
We have lived on the line
jumped and danced on the line
and we have even gone so far —
as to,
worship the deadly yellow moon.
But, I ask you,
what else is there to do?

   All day —
I sit here
and all day —
I wait
for the night to inevitably arrive.
And when it finally comes again —
we may pray to our own monsters
or even dance with them.
But, I ask you,
what else is there to do?
Except tomorrow
or sing.

Bree Cote

I'm Homeless

If I cry for help
   will you be there to catch me?
If I cry from my pain
   will you be there to carry me?
If I cry from hunger
   will you be there to feed me?
If I need shoes and a coat
   will you be there to clothe me?
If I cry no more
   will you understand me?

"I'm Homeless"

Barbara J. Smith

Come My Love and Take My Hand

Best of friends side by side we stand
Through life's journey
Walking, talking together of tomorrows
Years will pass our love will last
   Come my love and take my hand
Hold close this trust
It will never falter
'Though time may try to alter
All said and done you're my only one
   Come my love and take my hand
Love of sharing
Love of caring
Yearning so deep
Our destiny to keep
   Come my love and take my hand
These vows we share
So openly . . . honestly
Binding us through all eternity
Just you and me beyond the end
   Come my love and take my hand

Patricia Downs

I Know

I know how you feel,
It's the same for me,
Finding it hard to exist
in this insanity.

I know how you feel
It scares me so,
Sensing most people have no soul.

I know how you feel
The children are lost,
We want them back
No matter the cost.

I know how you feel,
Never making a sound,
All you have to do
Is look around.
I know how you feel,
There's a few of us lift,
We have special feelings
   not many. Possess.

Kathy Cauthren

Just Dreaming

Today let's just be silly
Throw cares to the wind,
No laundry or no cleaning
No shopping and no kids.

Let's run in the meadow
Be silly and just dream
Let's not do the windows
Maybe in the stream.

Let's mess up our hair
And throw makeup away
Let's forget about happy
And just do things our way.

Let's not do the dusting
Or put the garbage out
No cooking no mending,
That's what it's all about.

On Hell, let's go back inside
And do the dishes!

Gertrude E. Wagner

Wind Chimes

Alone on the ledge,
I await in anticipation,
poised in staunch position
as hovering masses being their move.
Solemn communion;
closed eyes listening...
the passionate Wind Chimes.

Embracing the response,
the mystic massage,
feathered fingers flow
mere-touching the skin.
Vibrant sighs emit pure emotion;
succumbing the sequence of need.

From your limbs, I learn the layers.
I breathe the breath of your boughs.
You entice me without provocation...
I'm comfortable within your caress.
Oh sing those psalms for me...
with closed eyes listening...
The passionate Wind Chimes.

Merlin J. McMinn

The Dying Love

When you need love,
When you find love.
You can hold it oh so tight;
But be weary,
It's so scary,
It can sometimes not be right.

So employ it,
And enjoy it,
As the clock ticks oh so fast;
Love regressing,
So depressing,
Now you know it will not last.

You can sense it,
You can feel it,
You can fight it if you try;
It's entombing,
so consuming,
As you watch a sweet love die.

Jack E. Dopler

God's Tide

The fury of the ocean tide
lashing backward high and wide

Met the earth, so warm, so tried
'til the rushing waters sighed.

A splash was heard, a calm descended.
Deep inside its bowels fended

Off eruption of its sacred home;
once more felt free to run, to roam

But not alone, so it was planned,
they live together hand in hand.

For water flows and rests on earth
As from Man's Rib does Woman birth,

Sheila Carolyn Mescon

Love

The love was fulfilled.
Completed, accomplished, and defined.
Always for the taking it lived.

Blue skies, gray skies, rain
As the love turn to pain
What was there to gain
When there was already fame

As it starts to regain its trust
Time is calling for love,
To restart its fire
So it can be desire.

Latricia L. Mulkey

Theory of Himself

For if I came and if I went,
Who is it I would be?
But if I went and then I came...
...Would I still be me?

I saw out from inside,
And from the inside out;
That I might see the good in man;
The good without a doubt.

You have to come to understand.
Just what it is I've seen.
It's not the green cheese in the moon,
It's not the jelly bean.

If we could only realize,
We're here for one another;
But oft times we're afraid to say...
"My man, you are my brother."

J. W. Mauldin III

Untitled

Intriguing to me
deep scarlets and blue,
The hidden existence
of what we once knew.

Tainted by specks
of embers like fire,
In view of a world
with tasteless desire.

Kept here complacent
yet burning to find,
The fear of our failure,
in the depths of our mind

To one's I keep secret
my personality a balloon,
Encased by surroundings
but bursting too soon.

Jason Boomershine

As One

When we hold us together
And our arms entwine
We shall close our eyes
As our souls we tether
Then to combine,
That's love's work may be done,
While our heart's as one
Embrace the skies.
And, two, we shall no longer be
Only one, in love, for eternity.

Randy W. Sims

My Rock

Eighty years old
Bless is he
My uncle virgil my rock

A mother that could not love
The lying and betraying
The thieving and deceiving
And perversion unbelieving
My uncle virgil stood there like rock

The truth stood out
And my rock stood tall
When no one would get involved
My uncle virgil stood there like a rock

Justice is not away equal
Truth is still always right
And he stood by this like a rock

When he's gone
Who will take his place
No one I know stands as tall
As my uncle virgil my rock

Bessie B. Saskie

From Now And Until The End

God made many things
So warm and true.
Like the love in my heart
for two special people like you.

When I was a teenager
I messed up alot.
But thanks to you,
your morals I bought.

I hope someday
When I have kids of my own.
I will lead them
down the path you have shown.
I'll never forget you.
your always in my heart.
I thank God everyday
for not keeping us apart.

I just wanted to say,
thank you for being my friend.
I will always love you
from now and until the end.

Gina Bargmann

Little Girl Lost

Sometimes she feels so lost
A little girl left all alone
All by herself in the dark
Far, far away from her home

A lonely frightened child
Who's lived almost fifty years
Not such a child anymore
But full of childhood fears

She remembers simpler days
When she could let this burden go
But that was once upon a time
And seems so long ago

Now she sits in isolation
And listens to the rain
Wrapped up in a blanket
Made of loneliness and pain

She knows she cannot stay this way
Her fear will overtake her
She calls out to the Lord to help
Please, God, do not forsake her

Christine Mann

Daddy's Arms

Good night, Mr. Moon
dance brightly little stars
peek down upon the children
cradled in their daddy's arms.

Whisper gently, Mr. Tree
don't wake the children's sleep
for daddy's love surrounds them
dream happy dreams.

Angela Marckres

River

Mighty murky marvel of
invincibly muddy water,
sculptures of scenic shores
sallying south, a gift of
inky; sand and silt.

Sea gulls soar, minks explore,
sandpipers stroll, martins roll,
Ibris prance, lilies dance, on a
patchwork quilt of endless silt.
Perfect is the palette of motion
infinity flowing to the ocean.

Rent by ignorance and indifference
invaded by steamboats, soot, and sewage
violated by pesticides,
endlessly she purifies herself
returning the poisons to the people.

Harold Christenson

Spring

The scent of spring
Is in the air,
The flowers are blooming
Everywhere.
In the sky
The sun is shining,
The clouds are aglow
With the sun's golden lining.

The cold of winter
Has gone away,
The birds are back
In the sky today.
Soon spring will turn
To summer's glow,
Now we can say
Farewell to snow!!

Lauren Macri

A Precious Rose

Standing alone. Beaten and forsaken
by his own
A Precious Rose was left to die
Mocked and scorned the Precious Rose
was left standing alone
Bearing the quilt and shame of
the unbelievers
Pain and agony, the Precious Rose felt
Knowing he had to stand alone to
fulfill his father's plan
When the time had come, the sky
turned black, thunder roared
and lightening pierced the sky
It was over for the Precious
Rose had died

Lou Edwards

Friends

Who is there for you forever?
Who will never say 'never'?
Who knows all your secrets?
Who will never lose your bet?
Who will stand with you,
through thick and thin?
Friends.
Loyal,
Patient,
Friends.
Some may turn against you,
some may tell you lies.
Some will spread your secrets,
but are never too unwise.
Friends are out there,
they may be hard to find,
You have to keep trying,
just open up your eyes.
Friends.

Tiffany R. Gearhart

Memories of the Past

My special memories of the past
are the days we spent together.
Memories of the snow falling at
our feet. On the nights we walked
in the moonlight. Memories of the
night's we held each other under
the stars. Memories of the night I
thought I saw fireworks in the sky.
Memories of the late night drives.
Memories of sitting in the car, just
talking and listening to the radio.
I even hold deep in my heart the
night's you told me how much, I
meant to you. And even the first
time you said I love you. What
are you special memories of the
past? Are you have you closed your
as mine? Oh have you closed your
memories off from the past.

Tammie Erwin

Untitled

The rain poured down on me
Like one big tear
Rolling down the face of God.
But I didn't notice.
The blazing hot sun beat down on me
And turned the tears to sweat
But I couldn't see.
The thunder screamed
And the lightning cracked
But I never understood.
The warlord yelled to me
To watch and protect
But I heard nothing.
I ran through the gates of hell
In an imaginary dream.
I danced with a star
In the morning hour.
I followed the path of hope
And tried to be me.
But all I am is a shadow.

Jennyfer Rowe

A Poet's Tribute

This rough and stormy night
Dampens my mood,
With every clap of thunder
It remains me of you.

How you loved these storms
That lasted forever,
With every bolt of lightning
It is you I remember.

These past few years
We drifted so far apart,
But we always remained close
Deep in our hearts.

I lost something special
When you left forever,
You didn't say goodbye
And alone I suffer.

For now I say farewell
Until I, too, pass on,
I will always love you
My little brother Don.

Angela E. Redmond

(Listening to George Winston's Piano)

I have the most wonderful music
My heart can bear

It rushes from the highest mountain
But it is really everywhere;

Open your mouth, my love: sound,
Ring, speak

So my whole Self falls into resonance
And I fly to the highest peak

E. Johannes Soltermann

The Vase That I Broke But Didn't Break

I didn't mean
to knock it with my shoulder,
but it fell over and shattered
like it was hit by a boulder!
Before I hit it
I tried to come to a halt,
but even though I didn't mean to
it was still my fault.
I told my parents that it was a mouse,
but I got grounded
and couldn't come out of the house.
I told them
come on, give me a break,
but instead trying to pay for it
emptied out my piggy bank.

Nicole Morganti

Waves

Silver-tipped grey,
cool and crisp,
caressed by the wind
until aesthetically
you respond
rise up and break
into a mist of tiny silver globes
that quiver a moment
then float down and merge
with thy blue-green mother

Robert E. Allen

Untitled

My feelings for you are immortal,
my love is immortal.
It is an indescribable feeling of
nature perceived through touch.
The sensation of solace
when I held you close to me,
the feeling is never to be belied.
The consummation my heart feels
will live eternally.
Pristine my heart was to love
before you came.
Now your feelings are circumscribed,
confined to the love I desire
but my love still remains,
in an unforgettable feeling
that cannot be taken away.

Jennifer Y. Solis

Oh My Hero

Oh my hero so far away now
will I ever see your smile? Again
love goes away like the night
into day it's just a fading dream . . .

I'm the darkness and you are
the stars our love is brighter than
the sun. For eternity there can
be only you my chosen one, must
I forget our solemn promise
to love each other forever.

Will autumn take the place
of spring? What shall I
do I'm lost without you
please speak to me once more.

Elisa Gumm

Untitled

The beauty of nature
   The sounds that we hear
Are taken for granted
   Everyday of the year.

The sound of the crickets
   The wind in the trees
The songs of the birds
   The waves in the sea.

They're all part of nature
   God created them here
Don't take them for granted
   Lend them your ear.

Sandra D. Cromis

Untitled

Every time an Angel walks,
Every time a human talks,
Every time a baby cries,
Every time a child tries,
A person dies.

So try to keep the gangs away,
Then people won't die.
So every time an Angel walks,
A human will talk,
A baby will cry
a child will try
and a person won't die

Carolina Basabilbaso

Betrayal

To a wife, some promises were made
To a mother, some lies were told
Can anyone see the damage they've done
My heart is worth more than gold

Dear most cherished God above
Does anyone here grasp how to love
The wife and mother's heart is aching
Please Lord, stop it from breaking

The wife stops being affectionate
The mother stops loving
The faith I once possessed
Is beginning to fade

God, I put my trust in you
You have always come through
He and the children need to discover
That truth and honesty are essential

Father, teach them to care
Before it is too late
Promises are to be kept
And truth is only fair

Terry L. Johnson

Happy Anniversary

I'm an old fashioned girl
   Who found her a pearl
In life's bed of oysters.

Its value and glow
   Continue to grow
Through years of caring and sharing.

With this ring I thee wed,
   As it was said
Thirty years ago today!

Joined this old fashioned girl
   And her special pearl
To live long together
   In all kinds of weather.
In sickness and health
   Knowing their wealth
Would be in their love forever!

Donna R. Moore

Ripples

Incredible journey
Life with new breath
The glow that will guide me
From now 'til my death

Unquenchable joy
A smile with no end
I hold in my heart
These moments we spend

A small slice of heaven
A garden for two
So quickly the sands fall
So much still to do

A fracture in time
A gift to hold tight
The sparks of tomorrow
Are glowing this night

I'm living a vision
I wish could come true
Reality beckons
Life's payment is due

Stephen R. Oliveri

Standing Strong

When all is done,
With the blink of an eye,
   I turn...you are gone.
Yet deep in my heart
A glimmer of budding hope.
   A new start has begun to grow.
Not all is lost.
A step forward on the road I walk
   With its many twists and turns.
A lesson learned,
A memory to be cherished.
   A chance to stand strong.
To search...to find
That part of me I had always known,
   Always had.
      Just forgotten
In my dream of loving you.

Pamela R. Roberts

The Paratrooper

Remember in the paratroops
   When young you went to war
And burdened down with battle gear
   You stood within the door

And as you waited many thoughts
   Went coursing through your mind
Of home and friends and family
   That you might leave behind

You knew you'd have to make that jump
   That the time was coming near
To leap into the great unknown
   Regardless of your fears

Now years have passed and once again
   You're back upon that plane
Waiting to face the great unknown
   But things are not the same

You will not tumble into space
   And fall to dark unknowns
For Christ will bear you in his arms
   And float you safely home.

Virginia E. Goode

Night

You kissed me in the park today
I watched you when you walked away
And as you vanished from my sight
I thought about the coming night
When I would lie alone in bed
And think about the words we said.

You can't imagine my surprise
When late that night I saw your eyes
I felt your lips upon my face
Our bodies locked in love's embrace
And when I thought, this can't be true
You looked at me as lovers do
And said to me, "I'm yours to keep.
Lets have some fun before we sleep!"

Sometimes I feel so all alone
Love is not meant for me to own
It's here today but gone so fast
Like all the lovers from my past
And just as quickly, you were gone
A dream that vanished with the dawn.

Edward Patten

Black Law Student

Study...study...study
Young brothers and sisters
To achieve your goals and dreams

You must work hard
and
Sacrifice if necessary
to:

Prevail over racism
Prevail over discrimination
Prevail over any barriers that get in the way

Because
Your baby brothers and sisters
Need a path to follow

Byron Shaw

Redwall

Evil villains
Robbers too
Cunning foxes
Sly young shrews
Ancient Oak trees
In forests dark
Beetles chewing at the bark
Rivers long and clouds white
Songbirds singing on a warm summer's night
Creatures big and creatures small
Creatures living inside Redwall

David Fooshee

Being There

On the telephone I find
The aching passage of my mind
Turn down a corridor of time
Slip into your arms... I'm blind

The room dissolves from where I speak
The flooring beneath me doesn't creak
Voices reaching past the bleak
Now longing, loving, care we seek

These times we share, however brief
Bring us closer to sweet relief
Lift our hearts to a place of peace
Remove from separateness the grief

On the telephone I find
A way to reach, to touch your mind
A short respite of pleasant time
Not much, but then our love's not blind.

Amelia Hope Spitta

The Vision

Life is a fact of many dreams past
   Visions of every kind
      that come and go all too fast
But with a good woman like you at my side
   life just drags by and by.
Time slows down
   for our every thought
      as dreams are vowed
      from a love that can't be bought.
Ecstasy blooms from the mind
   given humbly from the heart,
Enchantment from the eyes
   brings our lives to a start.
And if our love is true,
   a life of fulfillment will ensue
Babe... I truly love you
   through and through.

Darrell Shadday

Untitled

Loneliness,
do I truly know loneliness?
For who have I loved,
only one, that's from above.
The pain of not losing love,
but not being able to return love.
I feel much pain,
more than it could ever rain.
To be adored,
that would be reason to praise the Lord!
To talk,
or just walk.
If to simple interact,
I would love that!
Yes, I know loneliness,
for I know not closeness,
This by far is worst,
then to love and lost!

Kip Traynor

Fire of Thought

The flames dance; wicked, teasing
the yellow hypnotizes, the red satiates

The embers spark, leaping out to the unwary
sizzling, popping
a dance to a savage beat

Become lost in the flames
blankness covers thy face
let the heat warm thee
seeping through to the very bone

Memories displayed in the flames
untameable, dancing higher and higher

The flames reach the sky
filling thy sight
and mind
driven by a desperate need

A desperate need to become one
to dance and tease and sizzle
Then thou awakens
a wisp of smoke
is all that awaits thee

Lyssa Allison

A Walk in the Night

When I step outside
   to take a walk at night,
   the ebony darkness
   envelopes me.

I can see nothing but
   the stars and the moon
   and the shadows.

As I walk down the road,
   the stars and the moon
   twinkle and glow while
   the shadows dance and
   perform mischievous tricks.

As I walk back home in the eerie blackness,
   a swirling, grey mist surrounds me,
   and I know that I am protected
   from harm.

Robyn Meislohn

The Storyteller

I want to tell a story.
A story with no beginning, middle or end.
A story with twists and turns,
   a surprise in every word.

I want to tell a story.
A story of humor, wit or triumph.
A story of wondrous miracles and faith
   for everyone to share.

I want to tell a story
A story about neglect, abuse, or cruelty.
A story about injury and pain
   to see if someone cares.

I want to tell a story.
A story that laughs, whirls or dances.
A story that lifts the spirits
   so you can sing.

I want to tell a story.
A story that sobs, wails or moans.
A story that is melancholy and sad
   so you don't cry alone.

I want to tell a story.
A story like Shakespeare, Homer or Twain.
A story like none ever written
   so you'll remember my name.

Regina Cook Williams

Closer

How I long to be in your arms
To hold you when day is through
In your arms I hear no alarms
Just "Darling I love you true"

Then my heart is on fire
And I feel your desire
As you whisper to me
"Hold me closer, closer, closer"

How I long to feel your caress
To love you the whole night through
Here is where I find happiness
As closer I cling to you

And my heart is on fire
As I feel your desire
And you whisper to me
"Hold me closer, closer, closer, closer"

Louis J. Pourciau

Inspiration

You've inspired me to be myself
You've inspired me to go on
To let my presence be known
Let my heart sing a brand new song

You've given me inspiration
That I never knew I could have
You lifted me in jubilation
Turned happiness from sad

I thank God for your love everyday
For your inspiring thoughts and flair
Without you I would be dead
My heart beating but not breathing the air

So thank you my friend for your thoughtfulness
Your inspiration is a gift from above
I just hope that in due time
I can repay you the undying love.

Carolyn Dozier

A Woman's Troubled Sleep

Last night
I dreamed I was a little girl, again,
Running into the arms of my father.

But his face was turned away from me.
Eyes looking past mine, looking at that other little girl,
who also came running,
Calling out, "Daddy!"

Last night
I dreamed I was a little girl again,
Running away to hide my hurt and pain.

And looking at that other little girl,
I saw, in eyes like mine, her hurt and pain.
(There was pain in His eyes, too.
Pain I did not understand)

Last night
I dreamed I was a little girl again,
I ran away then . . . I am still running!

Sherry Trevor

Untitled

Cherish life and everyday that it brings.
Take time out of your day to listen to the birds sing.

Drink pure water from a mountain stream.
Sit outside when the sun's rays beam.

Don't be too proud to accept a helping hand.
Build a castle with a child on the beaches sand.

Walk in the rain with no shoes on.
Smell the cut grass after you mow the lawn.

Don't be ashamed to take what the day has to give.
Tell yourself it's okay, this is my life and I only have one to live.

Make new friends but keep the old.
Tell people they have a heart of gold.

Take a walk in a park on a cool fall night.
Burn a candle in a dark room for inspirational light.

Help a child who is lost in a crowd.
Listen to your parents when they say they are proud.

Find something special in each passing day.
Life is filled with treasures as you travel along your way.

Kimberly Leahy

Can You Just Imagine... What It's Like To Be Me?

Can you just imagine what it's like to be me?
....Imagine with me.
You learn, you train, you become skilled.
Still, no job, that pays well enough to survive on.

Can you just imagine, what it's like to be me?
....Imagine with me...
You dream, you think you plan.
Your past, is best buried. Your present, is a mess. Your future,
....is certainly out of the picture.

Can you imagine what it's like to be me?
...Imagine with me...
You're between colors. Native American, Asian American,
Hispanic American.
"Are you really, an American? You look so, different!"
Can you imagine? What a threat you are. What a brother you are.
...Imagine with me. You're invisible.
"You are poor, get use to it. Can't you understand?"
"Can you imagine, if you were me...?"

Darlene Amanda Strand

Fear of the Big Dream

F ear of the unknown is always a big dilemma
E ven when we choose to go for it, seldom times we
A cknowledge to quit before giving our dreams a
R eal opportunity to become something factual.

O ften times we settle for so little because we
F oresee in our minds that we are going to be rejected.

T his situation makes some individuals develop some
H ope and strength, but others less fortunate will
E lect to draw back and shut into the darkness.

B ut there is always a bright side to consider, which
I s our spiritual being that can help us explore
G reat potential we often ignore we possess.

D reams only can become real if we trust to
R ealize that faith can move mountains and
E very effort is worth trying even when we are
A t our lowest stage of life; never give up, and always
M ake an attempt to achieve our goals and dreams.

Winston H. Clarke

Reflection

Come, walk inside my soul.
Tell me what you see.
Did you see the golden lining?
Did you see the thoughts I discarded?
Don't miss the box in the corner.
That's my gift to you.
Take your time, I'm patient.
Careful to miss the bruises on the floor
They are deep. You could fall in.
Don't cut yourself on my shattered dreams, it's not worth it.
Notice the brightness around you
Calming and healing.
Memories line the walls, like pictures that expose me.
What do you think of this sanctum?
Does the interior frighten you?
Look in the box I left for you. The one with mirror lining.
Reflection
The sight of you inside my soul.
You have seen it all.
Tell.

Shana A. Roberts

Untitled

Once I saw a unicorn, its baby colt had just been born.
The unicorn's head stood very proud, as if there standing was a
    crowd.
The male was mighty and very strong, the colt scampered and her
    mother
    followed along.
The colt ran free, although it's as little as can be.
The sun seemed to dance when its rays shone down, the blackbird's
    cackle was like the laugh of a clown.
This little colt you might say brought happiness to the world today.

Emily S. Scoresby

Afterlife Awakening

Wandering aimlessly about through a moonlit haze
Trying to figure out the meaning of life
Only to discover that we are not meant to know
Until a time when we've advanced to another plane
Where life is simpler and more complete
No one is homeless, disabled, diseased, lonely or unloved
All thoughts are expressions of light touching soul after soul
Causing a trickle-down effect of tingling sensation
Souls afire with life and authentic power
Finally, fully and completely realized — Euphoria

Sean P. Swayze

After the Storm

After the storm the sky is dull
and gray, and the air is humid and
stale. Although it has stopped raining,
water still falls from the corners of the
roofs of all the still morning houses.
Water clings to the wire fences,
throwing sad rainbows all around.
From the laundry line water slowly
drips; still saddened by the past storm.
Colorful flowers bow down their heads
and cry old rain drops; while the
grass sobs; unable to control the tears.
Bushes droop; hunched over in
defeat. And as I look out the window
at the sad view; I can't help but
think of you, and how little I
care for this lonely life without you.

Sam Shackelford

Untitled

I lay awake at night and listen to the wind blow.
But, it provides me with no solace.
I listen to the hypnotic sound of the clock,
Tick, Tock, Tick, Tock,
But it does not lower my eye lids.
I stumble to get a drink and pour the liquid into a glass,
And listen as the ice cubes rattles the crystal.
I slowly rub my finger along the edge,
and wallow in the hallow song of the glass.
But, no single note will ease my pain.
I grab a record and put it on
Listening to the crackle of the needle,
Reminding me of days gone by.
But, these memories are misplaced.
It is another time in my mind that I am seeking.
A time when the night brought me comfort,
And the sound of a voice eased my pain.
I lapped and sucked the marrow from that sound.
But the voice has faded from those things I hear,
And only echoes is the recesses of my heart.

Dennis Favor

Life's Cycle Complete

Rejoice, oh my household, a man-child I come — a suckling innocent,
a generation in fold.
Beware child! The Tempter, the destroyer of soul, whose guises are
many tactics subtle and bold.
Waxing in youth, wisdom shall elevate my station as cream upon
the milk of life — a birth in a nation, this story retold as
beginnings of many, substance and soul, once in my youth now I
am old.

The grim reaper! Is it death at my door? Peering into darkness, the
thought I abhor — my heart is fearful yet I will take up the lamp
and open my door, bowing I bid him welcome. Yea, it is this
messenger
who stands at my door! I will yield to him with folded hands, and
with tears, that which is in store we mortals of sin — ever so
certain that eventually we end.

John Schaubhut

To Be An American

We are the leaders of the world, U.S.A.
We, the children of today will lead tomorrow
We thank our army, navy and air force today
All the world look up to US; U.S.A.
All the way

Anna Maria Leone (8 years old, 1996)

When Death Comes

When death comes he does not say "Hello"
He comes
What else can he do
Takes loved ones and disappears
It hurts

He is a gentleman
But when he strikes
Nobody knows
He doesn't know the pain
We play his game
And we always lose

Then what
The story ends
Just as it began
Just with one less character
A loved one

Linda Serrato

July Third

When children are tossing themselves
through oscillating sprinklers in the summertime,

When vanilla ice cream cones are piled a
scoop too high and fall smat on hot pavement squares,

When crickets whisper secrets under crescent moon sickles,

And when little boys peel away buried rock
to watch centipedes scurry away from buttery sunlight,

I will be cold, still water, immersed in a womb of silence,
remembering the acute smell of cooking cinnamon
billowing from my mother's kitchen oven, and
Pennsylvania snow to the fingers of pine trees,
and all the fireflies I used to capture in my mayonnaise jar,

I will die on a day too hot for windows to be open,
I will die while Stacey is selling pink lemonade on Eaton Drive for
ten cents, when the heat rises off blacktop roads like hot chocolate,
and bare feet scatter and dash across grey and white gravel, I will
find the outer rim of my sandbox, and for the last time hear steady
cutting sounds of spades removing wedges of dirt.

Thomas Murphy

Hank

My mind is a crazy patchwork quilt
Sewn with memories, remorse - perhaps guilt

A rocking chair, a tiny sweet bundle
Precious babe, my heart took a tumble

Powder spilled across a room
Little name scrawled, sealing "doom"

A gap toothed - crooked smile
Later years that were a trial

Mischievous boy with golden curl
Gone with autumn leaves mad whirl

No one answered your lonely word
I know, no one even heard

Questions unanswered, tears never shed
Heart full of ache, mind full of dread

A marriage awry, soul heavy with hurt
Solitary shot, life's blood in the dirt

I sit again in that old rocking chair
No sweet bundle, only deep old care

My mind is a crazy, patchwork quilt
Sewn with memories, remorse - yes guilt

Nora Little

To My Darling Gloria

From the hill of our old age we can look back on the ways we have taken, the rivers we have crossed, the mountains, the valleys, the beautiful cities, the countries, the voices and names of our youth; most are gone now.

But it was more than enough to have walked in these places, to have known so many wonderful people.

To have loved and been loved dearly. So now as the shadows have come, I have truly lived.

Fred Mix

No Body

Have you ever felt like a nobody? Out of body? Non existent?
Did you ever feel alone? By yourself...with nobody...or...no body to
   call your own?
Do you feel as if you are important or under dressed?
Away from the spotlight yet...from a distance, you can still see
   that light?
On the fringes of the circle we call friends? Staring in...not out
Did you ever feel that your loved ones don't love you, need you or
want you around?
Did you ever feel scared, intimidated or frightened?
Were you a lost soul in a world of lost souls?
Did you feel as if you were an outcast of a lower class in which the
upper class don't care?
Did you sit alone, by yourself, and try to understand?
They all laughed at you! They made fun of you!
They tripped you and then they pummeled you!
Were you the center of attention only when the rage of testosterone
   laden hard bodies wished to do you some form of harm?
Did you ever feel like a nobody?

Christopher Pingor

My Garden

Hello, glad to see you again,
The warmth of your presence stimulates me,
The sound of your movements caress my ears,
I feel invigorated when you brush against my face,
The sight of your splendor intensifies my life,
As I reach out my hands to you,
Breathing in your essence.

Cile Turner-Borman

Mercrograde

Slow down . . . take a different view, if you choose it now
it could come back on you.
The transdimensional state of reality's askew,
it's only natural to be confused.

You see yellow, you think it's in your head,
it makes you blue for a moment, and then it's read.

The wrong way right turn only now you've got to stop
on a dime for spare change is the only constant
melting away.

And what do I hurry on to, Forever is not far away.
Undetermined destiny, set out of focus
by Mercury in retrograde.

Don Fortner

Sweet Memories

God created the earth. Lord created us. At night the sun sets in the west. In the morning it rises in the east. That is when we see the beauty of a woman. At night is an imaginary beauty. In the morning is the natural beauty. Beauty of love, beauty from the heart, beauty of nature, and beauty of the eyes. Beauty from the East is the truth of a man's decision. The character and the beauty of a woman comes out. My mother who brought me in this world of joy and suffering is mother to all mankind. Our mother were there for us in time of sickness. Sweet mother I will never forget you. You are in my heart. During our infant years, you are there for us. If I don't sleep, you also stay awake. If I do not eat, you are worried. If I am seriously ill, you start crying. Loving mother, you are never tired. You have a place in my heart. This is where the pride of a woman comes. This is were the beauty of a woman comes. Woman of nature, woman of the universe, the princess of our world, we all love you. We respect you, we appreciate the nine months you carried us. Thank's for our delivery. Princess of mankind, sweet mother's we love you. Learning to deal with one another, love one another, the world should be safe.

Mosima Namata

One Full Day

In the morning...you are the sky and I the sun,
and the sun sets in the sky,
so together they make the first dawn a beginning.

In the night...you are the shade and I the moon,
and the moon smiles upon the dark with memories,
so together the evening is romantic and secret.

Yes, but for one full day...an eternity,
for one without the other is nothing.

And the stars of the shade twinkled with delight,
and the red of the sky radiated joy,
for the day was fulfilled and the time everlasting.

Ruth Ann Wescott-Wecker

My Lord - My God

Did you hear me, My Lord
When I called your name
And asked for your comfort?
Did you see me My Lord
When I prayed for the lost souls
That wander this world?
Did you feel my embrace, My Lord
When fears plummeted into my inner being
And yours was the only shoulder
My soul yearned to embrace?
Where is the voice I long to hear
The touch I yearn to feel
The wisdom I seek throughout my years?
Have they stealthily seeped into my being
Without proclaiming arrival
And I not recognized them?
Have you been with me always - My Lord
And I unknowingly reached for more
When I had it all?
My Lord - My God — forgive.

Beatrice Gardner

Where Is My Son?

Lonely as an untouched heart who has not learned to love
Leave behind the past for the future now to come
Truth about the years that passed reveal an untold son
Finds his way into their lives but never will be one.
Desperately hide the tears of pain
Anguish, hate and love remain
An unknown child, an unknown son...

Therese Nadeau

My Lady of Grace

The lady had beauty pure and sweet her small hands shook as
she wiped her cheek, tears fell from her eyes of blue, she tried
to smile as she looked at you.

The hurt was present as she met your eyes, I could not help feel
she was denied, the love she felt was not returned for reasons I
did not know.

She gave you a package of letters and cards tied with a
ribbon of white and gold, the letters were frayed as were the cards,
read so many times.

She held out her hand to say good-bye, tears appeared that she
tried to hide, she walked away and did not look back, her small
little frame was dressed in black.

I did not see that lady again, I hope she is happy with a new
found friend, I hope her life has mended itself, because she
seemed so caring.

Peggy O'Neill-Sproat

Electromagnetism

A physical force of magnitude N
warps my vectors, pulls me in
to the origin of your centripetal attraction—
an exponential acceleration of my e-motion

At terminal velocity we become relative constants,
our direction determined by angular components,
the derived equation of work accomplished equals
the force of passion times the distance between us.

Candena L. Schroeder

Fear

There is a haunting feeling,
Burning inside my being.
I know not how to overcome it.
It creeps in while I am sleeping,
Avoids me while I am strong.
It climbs the walls that protect me.
Then it builds more to keep me,
From those who offer me happiness.
It stops me from pursuing my dreams,
And instead, creates only hopelessness.
It sometimes keeps me out of harm's way,
But can also lead me to its door.
I cannot bear the grip it has on my mind.
I must tear myself from its grasp and face it.
So I may live life,
Without fear.

Shane Richelle Irwin

That One Thing

He gave me everything, everything I needed or wanted
Yet I can't give him one thing in return
I have so much, but there is one thing I don't have
And no matter what, I will never have it
So I never will be able to give it to him
He had it before, but lost it
And it is something I can never find for him
I have one of my own, but mine I can't give
I know he would have given his to save mine any day
But even if I do give mine, he will still be gone
Like him I will lose mine someday
And even though it will hurt without him
I'm going to make the best of it

Josh Gabbard

The Birth of My Beautiful Daughter

I've waited nine wonderful months
For you to be born into this world.
Wondering who you would look like.
If you are a girl or boy.
The nine months seemed to go by slowly.
Finally the exciting day came to be.
For you to be born.
Through pain and excitement
Your arrival finally came to be.
Then you were gently put into my loving arms.
As I filled my eyes with tears of happiness.
Just knowing that you are a healthy
and beautiful baby girl.
Today and forever, you will be raised
with lots of love and lots of tender care.
For you are my beautiful daughter.
Who is born into this world
with a loving and caring mother forever.

Bonnie Parker

Strength

Strength is love that grows in to a family, and
expands to future generations, simply by your
                    wisdom.
What you have given to us by your example is
            what and who we are.
Because of your guidance, we will become
            leaders.
Because of your concern, we are loving people.
Because of your teachings, we are able to grow
            and produce a fruitful harvest.
Because you have the power to make hard
things easy, it shows me to have strength.
Being strong in hard times is what you are, my
                    Dad.

Mark J. DeMers

Young Men Die

I remember days long gone bye,
When I sailed kites in a clear blue sky.
I lay on my back in the bright sunshine
And dreamed that the world was mine.

Then one day, when I awoke,
Clouds were covering my crystal sky.
All grey and black the waring smoke
And young men began to die.

I lay on my back in a sailor's sack,
Dreaming of home and good bye.
Awaiting the start of the final attack,
And young men continued to die.

Then mushroom clouds, rising high in the air
Brought an end to this terrible affair.
Again, I'll sail my kites on high
And dream that young men never, ever have to die!!

Jack Howell

The Felt Tip Pen

At the end of the felt tip pen words should be said.
The kind that fill your head.
At the end of a felt tip pen,
a person will reach out to help you soon
Don't give up by the next moon.
At the end of the felt tip pen, heart break
And betrayed will come more often than not.
It's amazing how the pain hurts your heart in the right spot.
And I don't doubt that the secrets are in the felt tip pen.

Victoria Schulze

Walk A Dream

Come walk a dream tonight
When moon is full and bright
Most everyone has gone to sleep
As crickets sweetly sing and weep

In evening so alone and free
The trees have almost accepted me
With branches reaching out
Like animals in the winds about

The horses sense that I am here
My presence floating across the atmosphere
Sounds rising to mingle
In everything nothing is single

Come walk a dream tonight
When moon is full and bright
Past licorice ferns with lacy fingers
In warm air a scent faintly lingers

Birds coming out in a world more their own
Glowing in jungle color shadows have grown
Illuminated from soft encircling rings
Extreme extension of mood a moon brings

Carney Brown

Adjectives

Depression and anger are easily described
Venomous syllables fight to be said
But happiness lacks any jibe
And odes to joy sicken when read.

Diaries blossom and bulge dresser drawers
Bursting with tears, from emotion unchecked
But joy leaves pages unwritten
For months on end biography wrecked.

Generations to come will understand nothing
As we fail to document all sides of life
Our deception through omission
Slants history towards hate and strife.

Carol Jean Cliff-Robertson

Release

Those hazel eyes
That once had danced with laughter
Suddenly filled with tears,
And in a quavering voice from your hospital bed
You said to me, "Turn the page, kid,
And get on with it!"
You died the next morning, three years ago.

I got on with it.
That was the easy part.
While I don't understand how I arrived here,
Today I am ready to turn the page.

Thank you, my husband,
For your courage and your generosity and your faith in me,
For you released me to be whole again.

Marion Hotchkiss

I Can See Miracles Happening All Around Me

I can see miracles happening all around me,
The grass, the mountains, the mighty blue sea.
The birds, the elephants, even the quick sand,
The buildings, the trees, the magnificent animals all over the land.
The stars, the moon the sun up above,
God gave to us out of pure love.
The food, the drinks, just a clean deep breathe,
Makes me know that it is God's creations and no one else.

Linda Robinson Leonard

Toasted Woman

Sun-baked skin. Moccassined feet lead her shape.
Ropes of hair and courage. Forgotten woman.
Eagles sing her song across the azure curtain.
Singed cheekbones hold an arrow nose to a star.
Beads of love sewn in her eyes. Remember me.
Bronze feet lead her and the eagles to the shade.

Cassandra A. Shannon

Rolling Tears

As I watch him pull from the drive in his red truck,
I sometimes wonder when I will see him again.
I watch him go down the street,
And a tear rolls down my cheek.
He calls every once in a while. I wonder if he really knows
how much I wish he could be with me.
I tell him I am growing up now, I wonder if he knows I need
him more than ever now.
As my day is coming I wonder if he will roll in on time to see me.
He missed it,
I know this because I do not hear or see him,
But I do see more rolling tears.

Lynnette Chilcoat

Love's Student

Help me discover what love is

Ah, but you can't reach inside me
You can't feel my feelings
or help me tell them apart

Only my God and I can

I cannot expect you to be my teacher
The revelations must be my own
Yet it is within our relationship I will learn

Experience is the teacher for us both

At times I feel I am far behind
That I'm a burden to you on your path
Yet I realize we are both students here

Our paths have crossed for a reason

I cannot hurry my process
I am who I need to be right now
I will learn from every tear and tingle

Becoming — takes time

Darci Strutt

Dead Horse

Well I've been riding a dead horse for some fifteen years,
When I'll get off is not exactly clear.
My message to you is to never get on.
Cause when you mount up your life is gone.
So don't ride horses, just let me run away, a dead horse ride well
he cold and gray.
You must live your life from day to day.
A dead horse ride will put you in your grave
You can hear their hoofs coming for miles away.
If you don't get on he'll pass you that day,
If you want to ride hold on tight the dead horse ride could end that
night.
The message is clear it's all up to you, let the dead horse rider pass
you on through.
You can run you can hide but you know this it true,
the dead horse rider will be back for you.
If you stay clear of the riders tracks, maybe some day
he will never come back.

Randy L. Pierce

Chipmunk Heaven

Camping out in the wood one day
We came upon chipmunks in their play
Going up the trees to the very top
Then down again, spread out and flop
The love of sweet fruit, berries and all
Stored into their hollows for coming fall.
One little chipmunk his crave for watermelon
Unguarded on a table for a smart little fellow
Picked out the seeds, made that melon dirty in their needs
Paw marks here and there, chipmunks everywhere
Bully chipmunk, boss of the crew
His love for peanut butter was nothing new
Stuff it into his mouth, big gobs and small
He was gulping and choking, gasping, wheezing all out of breath
Rubbing his throat with his little paws
He'll get that last peanut butter yet.
Finally all gone. Gulp!
The free for all chipmunks in their flight
Gave us all a remembrance of our wonderful sight.

Myrtle Hledik

Untitled

My body's screaming has forced my move
To make this chrysalis my home.
I can't recall how long it's been,
Or even if I made or found it.
All I know is that I live somewhere away inside it.

So peaceful, that is how I look from outside my home,
But inside's where the difficult and painful work goes on.
This is where I spend my strength
And where I work and live.
So much, at times, the work inside is all I have to give.

A chrysalis is where a caterpillar moves
To do his work so when it's time, a butterfly emerges.
My chrysalis may be more like a turtle, shedding shells.
For change and grow is what I do.
The shells too small; I am not through.

My soul will search and search and search
For truth that's waiting here.
I don't know how I'll feel inside
If the truth is found
I needn't crawled so long there on the ground.

Susan E. George

Granny's Gone

They say when it rains the angels are crying;
today they are because my granny is gone.

The front porch swing is empty, standing alone.
The angels are crying, my granny is gone.

Who'll make the blackberry cobblers or the chicken stews?
The angels are crying, my granny is gone.

Who'll set with Hattie and tell her how things use to be, or
talk with Amelia on her berry picking breaks?
The angels are crying, my granny is gone.

The love for my granny no words can explain.
But I know she is standing up there by your side now.
No angels are crying, my granny is home.

Karen Walker Presnell

Little Tears from Heaven

Two new friends join for only one night
to mend broken hearts and hold each other tight.

The weeks go by and both go their own way
living separate lives, few words they would say.

A trip to the doctor confirms her belief
her home test was positive — what a relief?

What do I do? Do I run or hide?
Should I terminate early or have it with pride?

The feelings of guilt not right for a girl,
"Why don't I want it like an oyster wants its pearl?"

Things aren't right and the timing was bad
now the next step was to tell the dad.

He gave her support and said he would help
but both decided "No" and both had said what they felt.

She sits in her room with her hand on her head.
Surrounded by silence alone on her bed.

Would you have dark hair or maybe light?
Maybe bright red with the urge to fight!

A girl in pink or a boy in blue.
It doesn't matter because I'll always love you.

Linda Puryear

Grandma's Prayer

Empty arms don't curb your love
for a child that smiles from above.
He's held and cuddled in God's grace
and one day you'll see him face to face.

The blessed mother cherishes and loves him too.
While she holds his spirit just for you
This day of days this mother's day
Holds you so special in every way

Maxine Leaman

Who Can I Run To?

Everybody needs somebody
That they can call when they are feeling down
But when there is nobody there
I just listen to empty sounds

Who can I run to?
To take this pain away
To put my head on cloud nine
To come and brighten my day

When things are not going right
I think of calling someone
Then I remember that
There's no one, no one so...

Who can I run to?
When I need someone to hold me
When the sun isn't shining
When my eyes just can't see

Who can I run to?
I guess I won't ever know
I guess I'll still keep lookin'
I guess I'm on death row

Glenn Fleming

The Gift

On an unexpected night,
we walked through a field.
I held my flower behind my back
and brought it out to show you.
I picked a pedal from the stem
and placed it in your hand.

Did you notice how coarse and brittle its edges were?

I tried to hide them,
afraid that they might break off.
I only wanted you to feel the soft, velvety center.

That is the part that has not been touched by the wind.

Josh Lott

Enchanted Hawaii

There's footprints in the sand, but soon they'll wash away,
By the swirling ocean breakers, that send waves into the bay,
The ships will cruise their route, and passengers will embark,
While the melodies of song birds can be heard into the dusky dark.

The strains of music elsewhere, with laughter loud and clear,
Almost always reminds us that we should have no fear,
God is watching over us, as children run with glee,
And we should always face the fact, and stay busy as can be.

The vacation land of Hawaii must be beautiful to see,
With an airplane view of clouds and the scenery of palm trees,
With the gentle ripple of the water, and the flowers by the shore,
Would make one appreciative, same as finding the lucky clover four.

The natives of Hawaii are very well renowned,
As they express themselves, in their various colored gowns,
Their entertainment is unusual, and they'll try real hard to please,
One can almost hear them now, by the bluegreen waters breeze.

Marion M. Welker

Ode to My Family

Poetic license is what I have
    Deviation from the rules
Readers can see my thoughts are sincere
    Needed are stronger tools
A quick review of the Baxter clan
    A most important factor
Five happy marriages, eight joyful "grand" kids
    One might be . . . an actor
Eight play piano — lessons each week
    In school it's all A's and B's
Practice horns, they're good in the gym
    All swim with the greatest of ease
I could go on with lots of stuff
    I am sure you feel I have said enough
One more thought is in my mind
    I'm sure you'll listen and be kind
The cloud over our lives is "Parkinson's Disease"
    I, Mary, a ten-year victim
Gene, the caretaker, always there
    Husband, lover, friend—I couldn't live without him

Mary C. Baxter

Untitled

How I long for the solitude of aloneness,
Yearning for the solace of eternal quiet,
Hoping for the freedom of oneness,
Knowing that it soon shall be mine.
My heart is weary of living in this place,
My only refuge is found within my mind,
For no one may enter to break the blessed silence.
In my mind, is where I seek eternal quietness and solitude,
For there and there alone am I truly at peace.

Phyllis S. Thivierge

Mother's Love

Nothing is as strong as a mother's love
A marriage vow or secret oath
Measures not up to such perfection
A man cannot duplicate it
No orphan can regain it
It is the force behind every lullaby
Every kiss, every worry, every tear
It is that power, that wonder, that gift
Which I have stolen from you

Gina Thibert

Chasing Sunsets

I'm not an early riser; never have been.
So, maybe you'd call it strange. I chase the sunset.
Why?
Because it tells me there is a God!!!
Because it tells me there is order to the world!!!
Because it promises there will be a new dawn!!!
Because in the setting sun there is hope!!!
I remember the first time, the first time;
I chased the sunset.
A friend died . . . He had been very ill,
and God called him home.
As I walked, even ran some, to that sunset;
I could see him standing there with God.
Standing by the setting sun!!!
He, looking to the eternal dawn; he is at peace!!!
For this I can be at peace!!!
I can chase my sunsets and hope!!!
And maybe even, just maybe,
I will get up to see the sunrise!!!
I did . . . .

Daniel J. Driscoll

Love Anew

The years have passed, our love has grown.
I see you through different eyes.
You accept my many moods.

We know each other better than we ever thought imaginable.
We're the same people yet we're different.

I look at you and I continue to see hopes and dreams.
You tell me that I've touched your soul.

In the beginning we were friends.
Now we've gone beyond friendship.
Our lives have melded to become a continuity of love anew.

Patricia Ann Duarte

What's Around the Corner?

It seemingly never ends—life's
    trials and tribulations.
We often wonder—"What's around
    the corner?"
Should we know what's on the
    main menu . . .
No, I say, that would spoil the
    excitement of living!
Frustration and sadness are
    not on the venue.
Go through each day with zest
    and a commitment to giving.
Don't hold the joys of sharing and
    loving—spread them with the rest.
The corners are many and the road can
    be long . . .
Every moment counts—don't waste a second
    on thoughts and deeds without merit.
Each turn in our life leads us in a new and
    exciting direction, how can that be wrong?

Karen McGee Streaker

The Way

Who can be so bold as to say
He knows the one exclusive way?
That he purveys the true wisdom
And holds the keys to God's kingdom?

Can anyone of humankind
Fathom the workings of God's mind?
Or ever hope to understand
The workings of His master plan?

Did God intend that we should know
Of things above while here below?
Is not man's mind just too finite
To soar up to such lofty heights?

Is God's thoughts no greater than man's?
If man could understand His plans,
If God could think only so small,
Then would he be a God at all?

Ance Virgil Wallace

Grandma's House

Places I have not ventured since childhood
   I revisit today.
Well-worn cubbies and secret passages,
   magical safehouses and imaginary dungeons

Once massive,
   they absorbed endless hours,
   transforming me and my chosen few into
   soldiers of fortune
      unencumbered by the outside world.

Touch them,
   feel the grooves of a castle prisongate;
   relive the bold reconnaissance missions behind enemy lines.

I crawl into sweetly haunted bunkers
   —smaller now,
   yet still protected
      underneath my Grandma's stairs.

Paula D. Lazar

The Flag

It is red, white, and blue
And all over the land it flies true.

It represent freedom and power
And flies from many a tower.

Each state has a star
All shining from near and afar.

The original colonies are represented by stripes
That fly from the lowest valleys to the highest pikes.

To honor our country and those who've had to die,
We proudly fly the flag, with pride, oh so high.

Robin L. Shadid

Your Weekend Letter

Lets re-read your weekend letter.
Let's spend the afternoon together.
I know that you and I will feel much better,
When we can write and talk together.
Here in this weekend letter.
The outside world has nice weather.
Wish we were together, it would be better.
But for now there's no together.
So let's re-read your weekend letter.
Let's spend the afternoon together.

Darlene Joy Hilliard

Summer

Summer is like a breath of fresh air,
The summer breeze blowing through my hair.
Summer is like a clear blue morn,
A little baby being born.
Summer is like a bright rainbow,
A clear blue river in its fullest flow.
Summer is the best part of life!

Jennifer Láu

War and Peace

There's all this war and fighting. I wish it weren't real.
All of those antagonizers have no brain to kill.
Gruesome, deadly, and bloody. Bad news all around.
Many people dying, all standing on their grounds.
Some are very lucky and survive through all that war.
Some are brave and ignorant and come on back for more.
If everyone stopped this violent game 'twould be peace and harmony,
But the world we live in has many anomalies.
I don't know why it ever happens, what causes all these fights?
Is it just another's prize or simply your own rights?
Is it really worth this fighting? Sometimes yes and sometimes no,
Yet as much as we are curious do we really want to know?
We cannot stop the antagonist from what he wants to do,
But try to stay away from it. I advise you to.
An all-peace world is fantasy it couldn't be a fact.
All happiness and smiles is nothing but an act
My final word, is war is bad, we all know it very well.
But why do people cause these wars? That, we just can't tell.

Jesse Pindus

A Cowboy's Dance

If you can spend a day in the saddle
   and a night in the rain
If your coffee tastes best
   over a campfire's flame
If you like your bare feet
   up on the dash of a truck
If you keep a horseshoe
   just for good luck
If your favorite kind of sounds
   are Garth, Dwight, and Lovett
If you can turn a few heads
   without takin' notice of it
If sunrise in the Sierras
   is a pleasure to your eye
If a little short of cash
   don't make you blue or cry
If dogs and horses are your favorite kind of people
If Sunday mornin' finds you beneath the church steeple and
If your heart is half empty then go on and take a chance
   and just say yes when this cowboy asks to dance

Eric J. Hofmann

The Innocent One

The innocent one knows how to give
his love but knows not how to protect
his heart. He gives of himself with an
understanding that his love is for all of
those who accept it. He opens his heart
and soul and shares his feeling of life.
A positive man, he does not sense the
insincerity of most mortal souls.
His soul comes from a time when
man was noble and the spoken word was
a stamp of truth. He believes in honesty
and travels down the highroad of
romantic days gone by in hopes of
joyous days ahead.

Joe Magno

My Mother, My Friend

The years passed by so quickly Mom,
like petals fall when the blossoms done.

But, I gathered each year tenderly and placed them in my heart.
I sat and read you stories trying to ease your pain, knowing the
Lord would take you back home again.

I'm glad your suffering is over although, I miss you so.
I love you now, I loved you then, more than you'll ever know.

Although it's difficult to say goodbye, it will not be forever.
Someday, I'll take my walk with God and then we'll be together.

Linda Minnichbach

Love Takes Time

Is this love? Is it the attention I love?
Everyone says "Enjoy!"
but they don't see the uncertainty inside.
Love takes time;
To get to know someone,
What he likes, what he doesn't
If he thinks I'm lovesick,
or if he will be romantic and poetic;
If he likes pepsi and I like coke,
If he wants sex now and I won't,
Love takes time;
He calls me tiger and I melt,
I wish, I knew how he felt,
I want to go fast,
and he wants to go slow, to see if it will last,
Love takes time;
There is a sweet song inside me,
In his eyes, is my destiny,
Love takes time.

Sylvia G. Villalpando

The River

There's a river that flows from heaven above,
And there's free access because of His great love.
The river has many uses because of its constant flow,
It will never run dry and the water will never be too low.
The river can be used for a cleansing of the soul,
The pure, clear water will purify and make you whole.
If it is healing you need, just come to the same river,
With faith just ask and the strong, mighty current will deliver.
The river can also help you feel the father's love from up above,
The gentle, rolling stream will surround you like His giant arms of love.
This amazing river is what connects us with God in Heaven,
Through this outpouring, God can meet the needs of His children.
So, go to the river whenever you need a special touch,
It will always be full and you can never take too much.

Mickey Griffin

Upon Leaving

Walking the deserted streets,
    defeat fills me
like a cheap red wine warms a drunk.
Empty soon to be filed benches,
    make a home for the nights inhabitants.
City lights fade.
    Last curtain call,
announces the shows over,
    as fog rolls in from the river.
I reach for the last drink
    as reality cracks through
        my illusion.
        no more words
just the ticking of the
    clock.

Lisa Boskovich

Doom's Desire

Oh, the smell of sweet perfume,
Life and fragrance, roses in bloom,
The smells of pleasure, the aroma in the room,
My senses of danger smell impending doom.

My doom can be pleasure, my doom can be sweet,
But doom isn't a word you use for a retreat.
So why does it sound like honey and wheat,
Instead of a hell full of fire and heat?

Could it be that I love, but also I hate?
Could it be that I want but found it to late?
Could it be that my desire is also my bait?
My doom is my love in a confused state.

So show me the way to know what I desire,
Show me my passion, my all consuming fire,
Give me a dream of roses in red attire,
Cast out the doom, lifting me higher and higher.

Christopher A. Losh

Understanding A Woman

A woman never asks to be mistreated.
    A woman doesn't need a man who's conceited.
To love her is to do right,
    To care for her every day and night.
Being a friend as well as a lover,
    Never trying to hide undercover.
Appreciation is what she needs the most,
    Not a man who wants to play ghost.
Love alone is what she asks,
    Not a man who wears a mask.
To be a man that's all he seems,
    One who lives beyond his dreams.

Jennifer Marie Strauss

Life's Ashes

He lifts the bottle to his mouth
He drinks and becomes satisfied
Television sounds distract him from the bottle
He puts it back on the table and reaches for the remote

She stands in the doorway and watches his cigarette's flame burn
His hand reaches for the bottle again
She winces as he takes another big gulp and sinks deeper away
Inside she cries out "Why? Why me?"

Brandi Palomaki

Women of Today and Tomorrow

Come women gather around,
Listen to all with sight and sound.

When God made women he knew what he was doing,
For he knew we were needed to help the world's blooming.

People of the world, hear our cry,
For we women need much of God's love to get by.

We've worked, we've toiled and have done our deeds,
And we must continue to go where God leads.

We've covered many miles from hither to yonder,
We must continue to advance without ponder.

We are more than just mothers and wives,
We are sought after to help maintain lives.

We women of today wear many hats
We are doctors, lawyers, teachers and vets

May we continue to go by the grace of God
To honor his presence and continue to prod

For we are women of today and tomorrow
Let us remember that our lives are borrowed

Naomi J. Taylor

Wonderment

Within fifty miles she's spent her life
Same house, she's been daughter, mother and wife
Years ago an hour of magic sparked a dream
A movie with dwarfs, a girl and a queen

Seven ceramic dwarfs came to share her yard
Among her flowers, her dreams they guard
Early one morning to her dismay
She noticed her "Doc" had been taken away

A few days later a photo arrived
It was "Doc" in L.A. on Rodeo Drive
Another photo another day
"Doc" in San Francisco, down by the bay

Vineyards, Big Sur, the MGM Grand
"Doc" in a convertible, "Doc" at Disney Land,
She waited for the mail, everyday, about 10:00
For news of "Doc" to tell neighbors and friends

Three weeks to the day "Doc" returned safe
She still gazes with wonder at his smiling face
Now she tells his story with photos in hand
"I declare, he just traveled all over this land . . ."

Diane Whipple

Belinda

My life is a one time journey.
I'm here for a purpose,
One, for which I do not know.

My only hope.
Is that I find the right path
To choose what way to go.

But I'm blessed
Knowing my biggest dream has come true
To find a girl with beauty and passion
If you must be reminded that girl is you.

My love for you can not be measured
You're the one I want for the rest of my life.
To share my love
To be my wife.

And suddenly, the path seems so clear.
To follow my love
To be with you my dear.

James John Offner Jr.

A Grandmother's Legacy

What can remain after many years gone by?
Is it the pictures, or perfume bottles gone dry?
I remember a collection of salt and pepper shakers,
but where are they now?

What can remain after many years gone by?
The dishes are here even after the fire,
given by you to me to be treasured!

What can remain after many years gone by?
I remember the day we shopped for shoes,
we laughed until we cried.
Little did I know that would be the last time.

What can remain after many years gone by?
It's the love and respect that you always had for your family.
The tender way you held my children in your arms.
The dignity you had at the end.

What can remain after many years gone by/
Now I'm the grandmother and I can only hope,
To bring such strong emotion to someone's heart,
and be remembered so sweetly, after many years gone by.

Kathy Flaherty

The Boss

Your life can be colorful or your palette can be bare.
Until you lift your paintbrush, there's really nothing there.
When you're painted in a corner and your world is full of strife
Recall who holds the paintbrush; you're the artist of your life.

When you are alone and feeling blue
When dark and gloom envelope you
Remember you alone can turn the darkness into light
When you light a single candle it can make the whole room bright.

When tossed between the waves and a rocky shore's nearby.
Remember life is like the tides; it's either low or high.
When the currents run against you and the rudder starts to slip
Remember you alone are the captain of your ship.

When life looks like an endless track that never seems to bend
Remember there is always light waiting at the end.
But you have to keep on walking to reach the other side.
It's better to have failed than to know you never tried.

If you accept the crown and scepter than you become the king
Your life is your dominion; you're in charge of everything.
The world is not responsible for every gain or loss.
Grasp the hand of opportunity and make yourself the boss.

Gregory Price

Untitled

A sunset, slowly drowning in the bottomless sea,
is the aching pain of your departure.
Night falls and emptiness hovers a heart now silent and still
that was once restlessly beating close to yours.

A moon, radiant as the sun, reflects the separation of our worlds.
Evening is my day and daylight is your night.

Distance is the keeper of our struggle to reach for harmony.

I want to reach your harmony,
the sweet embrace of your body against mine.
It is neither day nor night, sun or moon,
heaven or earth where I'll find you.

A dazzle in your eye, like the beauty of the sunset,
moon and glorious sun, lost in the forest in my eyes
is where harmony lies and there you'll be,
locked in the chamber of my heart.

Cynthia Mendoza

Dear Brother

Brothers are very special, you see them almost every day.
Brothers are very different, in each and every way.
Some are big and some are small, some are short and some are tall.
But does it really matter? I don't think it does at all.
You can always rely on Brothers, when you are feeling blue.
And you can always trust your brother to do anything for you.
So I hope you can see what I'm trying to say,
Brothers are very special, in each and every way
Thanks for being my special brother!
I love you, very much...you are always in my heart,
From your Sister

Janet B. Torres

That's Me

That's me you see flying high in the sky,
because I'm bird with red feathers and big brown eyes.
That's me you see hanging from a tree,
because now I'm a cute little brown monkey.
That's me you see leaping on a log,
because I just turned into a big green frog.
That's me you see taking a nap on my mat,
because I'm your very own little white kitty cat.
That's me you see pretending to be
anything imaginable that I want to be.

Donna Barton

A Reflection

I define myself by you. Will you stay? Do you care? Will I
matter if I am me?

Do you think you really know me. Who do you perceive I am. Your
mother, daughter, lover, an acquaintance, or a friend?

How can you form an opinion of the person that you see when I'm
not sure myself who is this person I call me.

It scares me to look in the mirror and get back "a reflection."
The vision of a separate self that feels detached, "not me."

I've built a life on the belief that you are all that matters.
Make them smile; hold their hand; bail them out of real and
imagined disaster.

But hands just don't stop reaching; sad faces come to all; and as
for rescue operations—they never stop I'm always on call.

I have to stop this madness. I have to just stand still and
find the courage it will take to re-invent my will.

I have to say it's scary. I don't know what's in store. This road
to "Me" has lots of loops and valleys to explore.

I've been so all alone in here. I'll bet you never knew that!
There's just a "little girl inside" struggling to find me.

Claudia R. Goad

Years Gone By

As the days grow shorter and the winds begin to blow
Down the old rock road, pass the creek, to the grassy knoll
I think of your loveliness, and your long golden hair
And how I wish we could still be there

Where we vowed to love each other, forever and ever
Those times now seem forgotten and so we will never
See again the knoll, the creek, the lovely birds
Though it seems like yesterday, we said those words

The place we called heaven, the little grassy hill
Where we could sit for hours, holding each other until
Our breath would catch and our heads would spin
As we poured out our love again and again

But now we are older and so far apart
And though you still remain in my heart
Our time has passed, our moments are gone
Just as sure as the night will turn into dawn

Murl M. Jones Sr.

Lands of Africa

I am the beautiful lands of Africa. Animals of all kind roam
over my body. The hot soothing sun warms my back. I can fee
the small creepy spiders run up and down my legs giving me
chills. For I own the animals that eat my dry plants. I see what
goes on, for my eyes are the lakes and my tears are the rivers and
water holes. My nose is the dunes. The circle of life runs over me
like a cloud. I am relieved when the icy cold rain washes my body.
I am terrified when the people come and travel me for I do not
know what they are doing. Please do not hurt me! Keep
everything the way it is. Don't capture the people that belong to
me and use them as slaves. That is why dry season happens
because I see what is going on that I shouldn't see. Animals nor
people shall suffer! For I am the beautiful lands of Africa.

Michelle Seymour

Tomorrow

Tomorrow is our future
As the sun rises each day
My mind is activated by the light
I am told it is a new day, another chance to make my life more
complete to learn more, to teach more, and respect more.
Who I am is not determined by where I live
My person is determined by my mind and the choices I make
Tomorrow is my ultimate goal each day
To move one step at a time is most important.
One must understand the significance of each step in order to be able
to look back and realize where he is and how much further he has to go!
Take one day at a time, learn each day!
It is your knowledge of yesterday and today that will get you to
tomorrow,
Our future!

Carlos Guity

Love As Is

It never may be as love as is
Though to you have may be as thin.
Love is such a complicating thing
it frustrates me to no end.
Once I thought I knew love well,
it shattered beneath my feet
and the ring fell from my finger
with only one thing ahead.
So there I was traveling light,
this long dark isle, a tunnel of what?
All I knew was no light lit, gravel beneath my feet,
the sides growing in
It never may be as love as it
Though to you love may be as thin.
I care for you too much now as may be
that you are too complicating for it
with that heart of yours: So cold, so warm
It never may be as love as is
for love is such a complicating thing.
Will I ever know what love as is?

Tanya A. Lemberger

The Abandoned House, the Abandoned Soul

From the outside it looks so old, so empty, so dead.
But, for some reason you open the door, step inside,
take a chance, you try to find a hint of life.

You search from room to room, but all you hear are the
hollow echoes of your own cry.

You look up and down, but the empty walls bear no emotions,
no memories, for the life in this place is gone.

The love is empty for it has moved away
...for you have found nothing.

Do not be discouraged, keep searching and never give up.
Someday you will find the door to a heart and your key will
fit the lock.

It is then you will know that you are finally at a
place you can forever call home...forever find peace.

Kristen L'Ecuyer

Lonely Tears

I still can't believe I'm all alone here;
another day has passed another lonely tear.
Remembering all our beautiful moments that we shared;
also thinking of the times you comforted me when I was scared.
Can't wait to see you and know that you're there;
I sometimes wonder why love isn't fair
Lonely tears roll down my eyes when I think of you
just being here drives me crazy not knowing what to do.
Looking for you in the morning and dreaming of you at night;
Going to sleep with my lonely tears and holding my pillow tight;
Remembering when I loved you with my mind, body and heart;
and when I also said "I love you" and till death do
us part.

Ruthy Salvador

Untitled

We sat in the rain on your front steps
and laughed and talked of many things.
We build a dream on every drop
for many hours before it stopped.
We sailed the mystic sea in jubilant glee
Talked of the things that used to be.

Paul Marsh

Lonely Halls

Each day as I walk through the halls of
my school I remember what seems like yesterday
when I was walking hand in hand with
a bright young man who I loved so dearly. I
remember the days we spent together taking
a romantic walk through the park and watching
the stars when it got dark. Writing sweet love
letters to each other and spending each five
minute break to see each other. And yet when
you loose something that wonderful to you, you don't
know how to let your emotions out, so you just
cry and cry. So each day I cry hoping to be
back in his warm arms, and yet I know it will
be a long time before I'll see him
again, because the angels have taken him
away. I know I have to let go, but it's so hard.

E. Springsted

Fleeting Love

To live a life with love,
It's like a dove,
With wings white as snow,
No one telling it where it can or cannot go.

A life with love dead,
It's like flowers in a bed,
Withered and died, only dust remains,
Once so beautiful, now so plain.

O God,
To be happy again,
To love once more,
Would be more than I could ever ask for.

I wake because I must,
I eat so there will be no fuss,
I live, I die,
Ever so slowly inside.

Life goes on,
Though I urge it to be gone.
Please Lord!
Deliver me from this world!

Beth E. Mangham

Oh! To Be Young Again

Oh! To be young again, to awake to the full
     bloom of spring,
To smell the fragrance of flowers, to hear
     a bird sing.

Oh! To be young again, to see autumn leaves all dressed
     in red, gold, and brown,
And to know that autumn is around.

Oh! To be young again, to see and hear the magic
     of snow flakes falling,
And everything green turned all white and clean.

But, alas Spring, summer, fall and winter, how
     time does pass,
And even though I find silver in my hair,

May I always be able to look into the sky and see
     a rainbow there,
So I will know once more that I am young again.

Caroline Rothman

Through the Eyes of My Heart

Through the eyes of my heart
     Now that I can see...
The thoughts that You think toward me,
The plans You have for me.

For my future and my hope
     I put my trust in You.
You're the strength of my life.
You fill me through and through.

Lord, help me to fill others
With kindness, joy, and peace,
To tell them all about You — that Your love will never cease.

Through the eyes of the heart
Not through the eyes of man,
Can truly feel how people feel, and know and understand.

Now if your heart is filled with Jesus,
God's only begotten son;
Your eyes will not be blinded.
In Christ, you will be one!

He comes into your opened heart that you can truly see
Now you can make a difference! Like Jesus made for me.

Debra J. Round

You

"Once was a river filled with pain,
the broken soul fill the space.
The open mind led out the fears
You gave no words and left the pain.
How can the love be still replaced,
there is no touch there is no care,
A rock will fell from high above,
but you will never come back tonight.
When tear will drop the star will shine,
You touch me soft and kiss good-bye.
I saw my dream,
I woke alone —
The world I had, the angel
the soul had all been drift in way above.
Bearing on, you brought
me love, caught on the
chain you broke the spell.
There is no words,
You won't look back,
you made the choice not coming back . . ."

Anna Januszek

New Year's Song

Sing to me a song of hope
  to cling to when all seems lost.
The joyous strains help me to cope,
  to persevere at all cost.

Sing to me a song of dreams
  that keeps me ever aspiring
Of higher, greater, finer things
  my soul shall never be tiring.

Sing to me a song of peace
  tranquility and calm
Like the whisperings of a gentle breeze
  it soothes my soul like a balm.

Sing to me a song of bliss
  that sets my spirit soaring
Untethered, free! Unequaled this
  joyous flight of glory!

Sing to me a song of thanks
  that I return to you
For without your guidance, tenderness
  I may never have learned to sing, too.

Dayna Clayton

Don't Look For Me Here

Don't look for me here, that last sparkle in
my eyes you had seen, is now afar. I will not be
sought. I could be on a path, surrounded by lovely flowers
of all of nature's kind, my shadow that you had come to
be so familiar with, is no longer a contour of depth
that you know, but a profile of one's own, my own, the
unknown to you. Don't be fooled when you think
I am lurking in the shadows, for it is your own in which
you stare, with those distant eyes. When I am caught
in a storm, I see rain not as you had once verbalized
negatively, a time I was distraught by confusion.
Today, as it trickles down my bare shoulders,
it is a release of a new, important, soul. I feel a
pristine sense of being. When I look up to a crystal, clear,
sky, or at the dusky, obscure, sky, filled with
lighted treasures, the stars shimmering like tiny
miracles, my mind is lucid from thoughts about you.
Nothing is there. For, at this point in time, I am telling you
honestly my true feelings I haven't expressed or even possessed in
the past, but now encompass profoundly. Don't look for me here,
there, nor anywhere. For, now I am the unknown to you.

Kara Santa Lucia

Isn't It Nice

Isn't it nice to have someone you love-
Who will open the door and pull out your chair-

Who will bring me flowers and even help me in the shower-
Who will wash the dishes and fill all my wishes-

Isn't it nice to have someone to love.

But I won't feel sorry when I no longer need my crutches and cast
When all of the above will no longer last-

That I'll still have the one who did the above
The man in my life-the one that I love.

Linda Adkins

What Shall I Pack In the Box Marked Summer?

What shall I pack in the box marked summer?
The sound of the umpire saying "Strike three,"
Or the joy I felt when I putt my first birdie.
Getting ready for the start of school,
Or a dip in the warm, glistening pool.
Golfing with family,
Or going on a shopping spree.
Enjoying grandma's home cooked meals,
Or when the coach signals you to steal.
The rumbling of the thunder that rattles the door,
Or the sound of the crowd when our team would hit and score.
The remembrance of waking up at noon,
Or gazing up at the stars and moon.
When we surprised our dad,
And the cake that wasn't all that bad.
Maybe all the games that seemed to say, stop and play,
Or the giant ferris wheel that lifted me away.
To me it seems to be a big bummer,
To have to shut and pack the box marked summer.

Tanya DeGrande

Chickens In My Head

I dream of chickens in my head
Even when I go to bed
Chickens, chickens in my head
What am I going to do when I go to bed?
They fight with me every night
They always are the winners
I dream I will win one day, and eat them for my dinner
I hate chickens they are mean
They are dirty, I am clean!
In my dreams they fight, they bite, they fly a kite
To my chickens I say good night!

Stephanie Lombardo

Death

Don't think of death as gone forever
It's just a part of time;
You can't be together.

When the one you love is gone;
Try to end your tears
Look past the pain and heartache;
And stop all of your fears.

Death is a separating point in your life
To see if you can handle;
All the pain and strife.

Stop worrying
They are in their Fathers hand now
People tell you not to hurt;
But How, Lord, How.

Don't think God can't hear you;
I give you my word
Because I assure you, up there;
You are heard.

Kimberly LeJeune

A Mother's Poem

I am so proud of how you soar . . .
You are the child I once bore.

Your growing years were short and sweet . . .
I remember, and cry now when we meet.

Always we'll be close at heart . . .
No matter we are far apart.

You're part of me, I'm part of you . . .
Instead of one of us there's two.

Shirley Alrutz

A Sign of the Times

Loose morals, ethics none
Only caring for number one
Little loving of any kind
It's no wonder we're loosing our minds

Dirty language filthy shows
Where there going no-one knows
Little caring or being kind
It's no wonder we're loosing our minds

Kids having kids and abortions
Rich getting richer counting their fortunes
Some people say it's the sign of the times
It's no wonder were loosing our minds

Streets full of drugs
Lots of violence
Not a moment for hugs
or a sound of silence
Some people say it's the sign of the time,
It's no wonder we're loosing our minds.

David C. Cohen

Instrument of Prayer

Draw me near in prayer oh Lord
Give me the desires of my heart
Make me one to set the captives free
Lord place this desire within me

  As I go with that desire Lord
  And I pray for those who are lost
  My hearts desire to see them free
  Lord I pray you will use me.
Lord use me as an instrument of prayer
My desire is to be a person of prayer
Use me as a vessel of prayer oh Lord
Lord I want to be an instrument of prayer

Vickie Derr

The Wall

My mind is strong
  My body is sound.
Wherever I go
  I spread joy around.
Though criticized and ridiculed
  Right from the start,
I let it get to me,
  To my mind, to my heart.
But I became solid and strong,
  Just like a wall.
Hit me as hard as you like,
  But I will not fall.
Through all the years, of anguish and retribution,
I have become one, to stop this soul pollution.
I now vow, as long as I live,
That I will never be broken, or to their ways will I give,
To the unfairness and evil that lurks around.
I will not run from it, or give any ground.
For I am a wall, who is strong, who is sound.

David W. Dunavant

Walk On Glass

Walk on broken glass
Knowing that you will feel pain.
Let your heart know there is nothing more.
Let your memories shatter like glass.
Let your tears fall and break the silence.
For you know you will never have to walk
on glass again.

Summer Moretz

Mail Boxes

On a dusty country lane long ago.
Stood three mailboxes across from a frame house,
where my mama and daddy made their abode.

My mama gave these boxes her very best care.
And in the spring she sewed flower seeds there.

Blackberry briers she cut and placed from a patch.
To keep out the yard chickens who loved to scratch.

Winter, summer, spring, and fall around noontime they all came.
To catch the mailman was their aim.

They were the neighbors who lived off the route.
Aunt "Till" would ask, "How are you'uns?"
As for me, "I'm so's to be about!"

The mailman made their day with letters, Rosebud salve,
and Sears and Roebuck catalogs.
With "Country Gentlemen" magazine, with new
ideas about raising hogs.

The dusty road and the mailboxes are no longer there.
The penny postcards, the five cent stamps, and
the loved ones for whom we care.

Jean S. Beal

You

You're my sunshine on a gloomy day,
You keep me up, showed me the way.
You make me smile and lose my frown
You pick me up when I'm blue and down
You give me happiness and shown me love
You are my gift from up above.
You are the constant thing in my life
You made me happy by choosing me for your wife!
You will always have a place in my heart
You're always in my thoughts while we're apart.
You and me always forever together
You and I can and will always weather anything that comes our way
being it today, tomorrow or yesterday.
You are the true love of my life
hold these feelings in your heart from your wife.

Dixie Luper

Thoughts of You Today

Oh, that my soul and spirit could leave my body . . . .
  To be by your side.
I would look into you eyes, touching your spirit,
  Speak of our eternity and listen to your heart.

Oh, to break down my limitations . . . .
  To touch and lay hold on truth.
I'm glad I have a promise of eternity,
  A time I will bare my soul and not feel ashamed; nor pain.

How large the family of love . . . .
  There is joy, loneliness, happiness and pain.
Will eternity change this?
  For the present, there is a time to weep, a time to laugh,
    A time to embrace, a time to refrain from embracing;
      A time to mourn, and a time to dance.

By a mighty hand you were placed for me to behold,
  In tears and pain my heart has searched for you;
    In joy and expectancy I reached out and touched you.
My whole life beats within you;
  You have your own place in my soul.

Gwendolyn Graham

Floor Morning

The noise of the clockradio hurts my ears
and the urine wells within my bowels
and it makes me want to wretch
the poisons and spirits I drank so freely of
and begged to bring me away if not to my death
and silently I wonder what it is like to be normal

Robert Sterner

The List

How ya doing today, Miz Liza?
Oh I'm tired baby, real tired.
Why ya so tired, Miz Liza?
Baby, I just don't know.
But I've been tired like this for a long time.
Well you can't help yourself unless you know why ya so tired.
Lets you and I make a list of why ya so tired.
Could you be tired because your husband stayed out all last nite?
And why did you volunteer again to keep Mary's baby all week?
And they say Roy, your son, took the car to school without your permission.
And why you let Sally borrow your money for the hairdresser
when you needed medicine?
Are those new neighbors still playing loud music late at nite?
And they tell me your son Joe had dropped out of school and
you didn't even know it until his girlfriend called with news
of your new grandbaby.
Ah Miz Liza, Miz Liza, why are you crying?
Tell you what.
Next time somebody ask ya why ya so tired. Give them this list.

Mabel Beecham

Adult Sons of Addiction

Little boy in the past, it has gone.
Little boy in the future, it is not here yet.
Little boy here now,
This is what you have to create:
Your world, however you choose.
There is no blame in the now!
Not your parents, step-parents, grandparents or guardians,
siblings, spouse, lover or children.
There is only the opportunity to take responsibility for oneself,
and children.
Form your children in a positive fashion, with great self-esteem:
With love, hugs, kisses, praises, guidance;
And most of all with honesty and integrity.
Grieve your past, the losses, abandonment and abuse.
At the end of grieving your childhood lost:
Choose acceptance.
Living in the now will free one to use all energy.
So you can paint your world of many joyful colors.

Karen Murphy-Vedrode

With You

I shared the Peace of a sultry summer night
    with you
I drifted with stars and things as they danced across the night sky
    with you
Your mouth is warm against mine and I see nothing, smell nothing,
hear nothing, taste nothing but feel everything
    with you
Fireflies sparkled in chestnut eyes on that warm summer night
And all I wanted to do was ... Be
    with you
Existence of time never was
    with you
But, sweet tranquil scents to
    ...with you

Melissa Philips

Sonnet for Tomorrow

From dark to light man fought his way alone
And won - an individual is he.
The slave he freed for all eternity
he thought. What did he gain? A meatless bone?
What of tomorrow and this lonely man?
Must he yet trample another to gain his way?
Who cheats his brother finds a tax to pay
Which steals his gain and shorter draws his span.
Pray let there yet be one so young and brave
To seek and find a place for man to stand,
not cowered, afraid of tool or human band.
Secure in self - not still himself a slave.

Let not tomorrow fret with time or space
But save this man - his dreams, his world, his place.

Edna Mae Woodward

Kicking Love

How can it be, twenty years gone by
Why can't I remember, what love meant then

When did it change, when did it turn
When did love die and life kick in

Passion has burnt down to ash
Touch it, it crumbles to dust

Not that life's bad, not half bad at all
It's just that it's changed, without my noticing

They told me it would happen
But one never believes it

Love's withered and dried out
Like an old piece of fruit

Give it a kick, and watch it fly apart

Steve Groninger

A Remnant of Life!

For those in search of all's connect, who seek the inner bond
we search to find to that of old which led to thy young.
Of pilgrimage and journeys of travels near and far, and yet
we sometimes think some mysteries are still there.
The intrinsics of the Earth such as waters air and spirit,
Intricately leaves that are shapely-sometimes of wonders are
there where. Innateness is like some thereof. Enlighten of
a vessel - with a flesh as a cover Distraught of unknowing, of
which these covers were given. Yesteryear, yesterday and Today
are past present and futures, with Hopes of enduring Longevity,
these breathes of Life in their Assurance, Grace and Mercies
of Endurance.

B. Johnson

Vision

I wish I had 20-20 vision,
    Oh, the things that I would see!
Little inanimate objects, way beneath the sea.
    I could see the far horizons,
Majestic mountains, towering high -
    The deepest, bluest ocean
Would certainly make me sigh!
I could read the happiness
    On little children's faces,
And see the beautiful princesses'
    Castles in far-flung places,
I would read a book a day —
    And still have time left-over to play.
I would read everyone's mind,
    And see the good in all mankind!

Terry Sumner

Lisa M.

A gentler soul I have never seen
With delicate beauty and simply grace
Yet sad and distant from hidden hurts
That I could see behind her eyes.
And when she told me of her pain
Of past wounds too deep to heal,
I felt her sense of sorrow and need
From broken trusts too horrible to speak.
Yet, she chose me to help her heal
To share the secrets of sick desires
Forced upon her by a pathetic man
That nature deemed to be her father.

I cried for her inside my heart
As a loving father for a dying child.
I felt the pain of broken trusts
And wondered how she ever survived;
Such a gentle soul with simple grace
And delicate beauty of an innocent child.

Eugene C. Oliveto

Donna

Happiness was born a twin.
For nothing is so beautiful or wonderful as when you share it with
someone you love.
Be it a sunrise, a sunset, a walk on the beach, it is that much
more special when it is with the one you love.
And it matters not what that person looks like to others, but only
to yourself.
For if you can see the beauty of that person's soul, than your
love shall overcome all obstacles, and endure beyond the last sunrise
or sunset.
My dear Donna, I have seen the beauty and light of your soul,
In ways I was blinded by it.
And I shall always be grateful for being able to stand in its
light for even a fraction of time, and I shall hope and pray for
all of time to be allowed to stand in that light once again.

Richard Closser

Closure

Visions of rain, visions of you,
A vision never to come true.
All the pain, all the deceit,
Lies as plain as your own two feet
Stare me straight through my eyes.
I'll leave and take off this disguise;
No need to stop me, I've already begun to flee.
My heart left long ago, my mind is the next to go.
A victim of love, a victim of trust,
Memories shattered, turned into dust.
Broken chains, I'm free as a bird
My soul is screaming, haven't you heard?
Nothing left to wallow in, free from sin,
I'll spread my wings and fly in the sky so blue
And leave behind my visions of you.

Jen Hendrickson

School Days

Many months have quickly passed us by.
Now it is time to spread our wings and fly.
No greater teacher could be found.
You helped us when we were down.
You were an angel sent to us from above.
You flew around us like a caring dove.
We will be doctors, lawyers, people who care,
And that will be because you were always there.
You were our mentor, teacher, and friend.
We are sorry to see this come to an end.

Natasha Ryan Coker

self, unforsaken

the clown face in the fog has true eyes
that bespeak consecrated flesh beneath the paint

children touch the eyes in the rain
and believe in the plasticity of everything

you say our love will last within the shadowbox
but now the box is broken on the shore

as we dive into the sea of holy mystery
I will baptize you in both your faith and doubt

later you will linger with me on the shore
our earthen lips will touch in apocalyptic kisses
all words will be wrenched from our mouths

and evil spells will be broken when we see
each other without the dream of each other
we will see each other even as we are
in fluidity and forevermore

the clown face in the fog has true eyes

diann m. dunkley

Life And Tide

Like the ocean tide my life has been.
  There was hardly a ripple when it all began.
Then slowly, slowly, small waves came ashore,
  Each barely stronger than the one before.

The waves flexed their muscles, stronger hour by hour
  And climbed a little higher toward the lighthouse tower,
Until all retreated before this mighty force,
  And the waves paused briefly on their upward course.

For a time they remained calm and serene
  Reveling in the possessions which they had gleaned.
Then slowly their strength began to wane
  And slowly, slowly they released their gain.

Then they retreated to their original place
  And all was still with hardly a trace
Of the strength displayed at the earlier time.
  And all was at rest in this peaceful clime.

Until movement began toward a different shore
  And the small waves gained power as they had before.
Finally they splashed on a golden shore
  To bask in perfection forevermore.

J. C. Ewing

Upon Working Eight Years at the AIDS Foundation

As I ready myself for More Death, I wail matter-of-factly, and feign rote
sadness in monotone inflections. Numb compassion is force-eked from this,
my hard-sponge soul. Tears are now but bodily waste, fallen to a place of
sick gratification. Once, I innocently felt, like child's grief, but in empathy
died with thousands, absorbing all their pain, wiring myself to their last
spark; suffocating myself blue-white, as beatless hearts' thickened blood
quivered, as I hugged ice corpses desperately good-bye: their awry-eyes
rolled cross-eyed and stared blankless. I bravely died in each individual
coffin with them, unembalmed, bathed in beams of pink light, our gaping
mouths wired-shut, cosmetically-at-peace. I heard vacant visitors in the
parlors; I heard cushioned lids slam shut when rooms emptied; I heard
cash registers ringing in dignified manners; I saw cars speed past ignored
motorcades; I tried to imitate "the proper blacknesses"; I listened to
questionably-comforting words from strangers; I felt over-gentle
lowerings to dirt; I felt the anger from underpaid workers' shovels; I
heard laborers laugh after the spectacle and envied their alcoholic
afterwards; I saw overpriced flowers dying, gifts of still-dying minds of
Grievers above and after in the super-bright, washed-out, barren surreal.
Can there still be greater depths of no feeling yet-to-come, my life? Until I
crave the only death I won't know or mourn, my own?

Robert Fredrick Thistle

115

Autonomy

My daughter walks in beauty.
My bright-eyed baby is gone.
When did she move away from me?
When a stranger did she become?

Age three, lips close to my ear,
She whispered stories, dreams, and fears.
    Now grown,
    She's flown.
Secrets once shared are hers alone.

She questions me, rejects my replies.
"Not that again!" with a roll of her eyes.
    She many never see
    The magnificent me
As we both become all we can be.

I saw the tears in my mother's eyes.
My daughter will never see me cry.

Mary Well

End of Days Prayer

The days of darkness, here at last
dice tossed, die cast.

Through all time, this battle raged,
the final scene, set and staged.

Oh! What a time to be alive.
To see who'll stand, who'll survive.

The great separation about to occur,
and all we know a forgotten blur

Let thy light descend, and fill the earth,
dispel the darkness, destroy the night,
rebalance us all, and put things right.

Lord in faith, I stand with Thee
filling soul and strengthen me.
For the final battle, I long to fight,
to destroy these evils, and the night.

One with Thee is endless days,
singing songs of endless praise.
Thee in me, me in Thee.
Forever one, one to be.

R. L. Ramkin

In A Home That Was Chosen

Before this child our family was two.
There was love and laughter in our home;
    a safe place with no secrets.
Our lives surrounded by a circle of family and friends;
    comfortable and satisfied we grew.

With this child our family is three.
There will be more love and laughter in our home;
    still a safe place with no secrets.
Our lives blessed, our circle enlarged;
    nurtured and cherished he will grow.

Before entrusted with this most precious gift;
    our hearts felt full, our lives rich, our blessings many.
Then an angel came and opened a door,
    to a road few choose to travel.
A strong but gentle hand reached out to show us the way.

Since entrusted with this most precious gift;
    our hearts are fuller, our lives richer, our blessings greater.
The angel did not leave us, but came to stay.
It's just a smaller hand to show us our way.

L. Michele Poe

Determined Heart

The tiny heart beat stubbornly,
in the two pound infant's chest.
His breathing came and went,
as if he had to rest.
Looking down in wonder
that something so small could be alive;
I knew it would take a miracle
for this blessing to survive!
Each day his mother and family
came to will him with their drive.
Gloves were put on to hold him;
lovingly, so he would thrive.
And his tiny heart beat stubbornly;
refusing to let him go.
Amazingly, the nourishment he received,
urged his fragile body to grow.
Then, I held him close one day,
placing his miniature fingers in mine.
They closed as lightly as a butterfly's wings;
as if to assure me, he would be fine.

Phyllis Lee

Dreogan

A lonely child's dark eyes cast despair
As she waits to be passed to another home.
A reckless, good meaning worker slides the stack
of papers forward to be signed.
There is no ending to the injustice.
There was no beginning to the crime.

A parent drifts into a drug-induced dream,
Not hearing the plaintive cries of her young child.
Soiled diapers hang on irritated flesh
As ants parade along the counter-tops.
Third time the neighbors called in a complaint
Trying to beckon help.

At last the authorities arrive,
Their wailing siren echoing the child's.

Detained in an office until a home is found.
The technical assistant is on her twelfth call.
At last, the agency reports an available home.
Matched with a strange family,
The child awaits her destiny.

Pamela G. Jordan

Lefty On the Mound

It's the last of the ninth, the score is all tied,
And the Blue Sox bring in Old Lefty McBride,

The pitcher before him has loaded the bags,
It looks like a sure win for the New Jersey Stags,

But a pop up and strikeout make it two men away,
And it looks like old Lefty may yet save the day,

The next batter up is "Texas League" Ted,
Who fouls off two fast balls, now Lefty's ahead,

He feels little pressure, as he steps on the mound,
He's sure in the tenth, he'll still be around,

But you're really not sure what baseball's about,
Cause the game could be over before the last out,

He tugs at his belt, kicks dirt off his cleats,
The fans are expectant, not leaving their seats,

"Old Lefty'll do it, for sure," that's the talk,
But before his next pitch, the Ump calls a balk!

So the winning run scores, while Lefty raves and rants,
"Hey Ump, I was only, hitchin' up my dang pants!"

C. Lewis Colton

Lost for Years Among Stars

I was lost for years among stars,
until I came into the presence of September,
then I was forgotten by yesterday,
and so I traveled for days to reach silence.

Chelsea Weber

Blue Angel

I left home this morning, badge and gun by my side.
I kissed all my children, and the littlest cried;
"Daddy I love you, please make it home,
When you're not here I feel so alone."

I then kissed my wife, and looked into her eye
Out came a tear as if she knew where my future would lie.
In one split second, it happened so fast
If I had only known, this day was my last.

Now I look at my loved ones, from the blue heaven's above
I suffer to watch their tears of agony and love.
Brothers and sisters in blue, treat each day as your last
Kisses to my loved ones, are now memories of the past.

From the heaven's above, I watch over you all
And pray that today won't be your last roll call.

Armando Aviles Jr.

Baby David

Your smile lights up the room.
Your eyes twinkle with delight
Oh, How much love you've brought,
into lives that were set just right.
You were not supposed to be.
Your mommy was only sixteen.
She could have thrown you away,
with no one knowing of the day.
I felt her hurt as she shared,
her situation with those who cared.
I was sad but proud of the person I saw.
So young but willing to stand so tall.
Taking a place for what she believed,
that the life inside her was a person indeed.
The months went by with tears and laughter.
You were born and our lives were not the same thereafter.
Your smile lights up the room.
Your eyes twinkle with delight.
Oh, How much love you've brought,
into lives that were set just right.

Jennie Corum

A Spring Day

A pretty yellow buttercup has popped up for fresh air
the gusty,..cool wind blows against a little one's hair
Stop and enjoy these treasures on earth, they are no cost to you,
The sound of the woodpecker against the tree and the sky so blue.
Shining, bright, sun peeping all around,
Birds chirping, oh what a lovely sound.
The leaves have turned from brown to green,
Everywhere I look there is more beauty to be seen.
Bumble bees busy going from flower to flower
The cloudy skies indicate there might be a shower,
I look across and gaze at the beauties of this earth
No price can be put on our freedom and its worth.
Cars passing, everyone on the go, children have come out to play
Such a lovely sight to watch these joys of each day
The day will soon end and all chores are done.
Another beauty to observe is the setting sun.

Deborah S. Sullivan

Thinking of You

I'm thinking of you tonight,
As I wish on that star so bright.

I wish you only knew,
How much I care about you.

You're taken at the time,
But I hope that soon you'll be mine.

I did you wrong in the past,
But now I want our love to last.

Maybe if I keep wishing on that star so bright,
My thoughts of you may come true tonight.

Kerrie Worrell

Someone Else

These things in my mind I mustn't say,
for fear you my beloved might go away,
Because although in your arms and in your
embrace I dream of another's face.
Although I'm with you, and burning with
passion it wouldn't be the same if I didn't
imagine. I know you care for me, and I for
you, but this can not go on it mustn't be true.
Oh, how I wish I could learn to love you the
way I love him, but what never was never
would have been. And now my beloved I
think it's only fare, I tell you these things,
although you might not want to hear. So
now as I bid you adieu, remember once upon
a time, I did love you.

Chloé Seales

Ambushed By?

Beware of the mystery in the forest tonight
The moon is glowing, setting our imagination in flight
A mystical breeze that flows through the air
Leaves a sinister thought that something is there
There's a lurid feeling that hypnotizes your mind
Letting the many myths of evil creep in time after time
There's a horrifying fear for what is shown
But, a more deadly fright for the unknown
As the silence becomes louder and the breeze turns to wind
The trees take their shape and begin to close in
The earth becomes cold, morning begins
The impressions of the night are swept off by the wind

Sandra-K Harris

Could It Be?

So, I was waiting for a sign, some false hope that maybe, just maybe,
I might be able to find someone that really tells the truth . . . lives
with a clear conscience. I know I should believe in mankind, that
romance is still here and some type of shivery exits . . . I just can't
seem to be able to grasp the concept of truth and valor anymore . . .
the once strong notion that I was able to knock off my shoulder and
allow it to roll down my back, never really meaning to lose myself
in spite of the unclear conscience of our world, of my world.
America with its cities of lost souls and profound meanings . . .
if we could, would we go back to a simpler space?
The ego will not allow regression, so onward we face despair,
but sometimes, on a clear sunny morning, as the light from a new dawn
peeks through my window, I can still feel the hope steering in my soul.

Carmen J. Casarez

What Will I Be When I Die?

What will I be when I die?
The sum of all my parts?
Withered, maybe. Weak and pruned.
Unrecognizable to the woman in my mirror now...
Maybe so...

Or, maybe I'll be young—finally gone out of my mind—
Hit by a tractor trailer while wandering highways.
Maybe I'll remain sane, and a tractor trailer, with no business being
   there,
Will barrel down my quiet block
At the exact moment I cross the street to get the mail.
My parts scattered then re-collected and tallied...

What will I be when I die?
The sum of all my pasts:
Letters, boxes, clothes, things, words, evidence.

When I am silent, these will speak for me.
When I am weak or crazy, these will remain unchanged.
When I cannot, these will be able.

And then the moving men will decide
What I am when I die.

Susan Pavliscak

Visions of Our Earth

Endless rows of trees and plants,
Flying birds and crawling ants.
The sun in the blue of the morning sky,
The moon, in the evening, rising high.
The oceans, the rivers, the lakes, the streams,
The world is made of many dreams.
Dashing colors streak the sky,
Beautiful even to the strictest eye.
Snails on the ground, bees in their hive,
Our duty is to keep all this alive.

Karmi Knight-Winnig

Come . . . Sea . . . My . . . Ways

Gaze into my vastness
Touch me . . . this I allow
Yet you cannot hold me
(Behold my expanse)

You possess visions of my greatness
Yet you cannot possess me
I speak to you in unspoken words
Yet you do not comprehend

My language is enduring,
I am your past, your present, yours evermore
I am of your ancestors.

I move with such fury — such force
That nothing stands in my way
Yet I am graceful and gentle
I give of life...I sustain life
I take the urge of life

I welcome your presence
I caress you with a completeness
That your pains become mine
Learn my ways and I will yield unto you . . . boundless gifts.

Stephen Allistair Yearwood

A New Day A Comin'

I've awakin', light in the windows, on the horizon
I feel it coming, new beginnings, suns arisin'.
Having been there, on the edge, down and out
I know the feelin' - self doubt.

I've lost it all - my health, my heart
Then I've begun again - new day, new start.

People ask me - why the smiles,
The twinkle in my eyes, the laugh - "Why?"
To the question of "Why?" I answer with a smile
As darkness arrives, as life's end draws near,
I know with the end of every day, every trial of life
There is a new horizon, a new life a dawnin'
With every sunset, there's a new day a comin'!

Tommy Frazier

The Days of Long Ago

Sometimes I like to think about
The days of long ago
We all sat in the kitchen
The kerosene lamp turned low
The shadows would be flickering
In the corners here and there
Then we'd hear a Coyote howlin'
Out in the frosty air.

Then mom would knead down all the bread
That she had set to rise
She covered up the old dishpan
So it would double up in size
Then she'd shoo us kids on up the stairs
And come along behind
With the kerosene lamp help up high
'Twas Mom we had to mind.
I wouldn't trade these memories
For the world and all its gold
I know I'm richer way by far
With the days of long ago.

Pearl Jennings

Words

Words spoken hurriedly, without feeling,
Ashamed that they were heard.
Words now spoken, begging to be taken back
from whence they came.
But once spoken, cannot return to their creator,
and so are doomed to travel the air waves forever,
ashamed of having been born.

Words spoken softly, slowly with patience,
like little birds just learning to fly,
settle gently on the shoulders of the one they're
spoken to.
Proud of their achievement in bringing love and
understanding to two people.

May the words you speak
always be proud you created them.
May the words you speak
bring joy and love to those they're spoken to.
May the words you speak, never come back to you,
like ghostly apparitions, to haunt you.

Lucille R. Crane

Think and Be Thankful

Life is strange and has its days . . .
It creates your moods and has its ways.

Some days you're thrilled and don't know why,
Sometimes you're upset and would like to cry.

If you feel angry or sad, stop and think . . .
How lucky you are, your ship didn't sink.

Healthy happy children is uncommon anymore,
Most parents find themselves picking kids up off the floor.

You've never had to do this, your kids have all stood tall,
So appreciate us as individuals, and be proud of us all.

Don't fall to bitterness of the fools around us . . .
Look at all that we've accomplished next time you want to fuss.

Don't criticize or be negative, for one day it may be too late.
Congratulate and enjoy this time, it will make us all feel great.

Life is too short to hold a grudge, so disregard the worst,
Stand proud of what you made, and make happiness come first.

Look at all you have and thank God up above.
Your life is filled with many things — one being lots of love.

Jodie L. Poundstone

Storm Clouds

You gaze at the sky,
See nothing but black.
Feel lost and alone,
Can't find your way back.
Bare your eyes my brave child,
Find the hope that you lack.
Just search harder . . . when storm clouds roll by.

Days once filled with joy,
Seem shrouded in pain.
Where once there was light,
Now darkness and rain.
Bare your smile my brave child,
Your bad days soon shall wane.
Just smile harder... When storm clouds roll by.

A world so unlike the one you once knew.
Where dreams come up dry, and goals are past due.
Bare your mind my brave child,
Some day wishes come true.
Just dream harder . . .
When storm clouds roll by.

Gary Vinturella

Broken Heart For Rent

My broken heart had been rest for many, many years,
swept away of cobwebs, swept away of tears.

Then one day you came along and knocked upon its door,
and promised me that you would rent, and nothing, nothing more.

You stayed with me a month or two, or maybe it was three,
then signs of disenchantment were very plain to see.

You've done your job and done it well and I did know, you see,
because the heart that once was broken came back to life in me.

You packed up all the memories, I hope that the will last,
and we will smile about them when we think about the past.

Now again my heart is empty and boarded up once more
and one more time the for rent sign is back upon its door

Mary Ellen Lasek

Waves of Love

The wind blows softly on my face, all is calm.
I feel relaxed walking gently in the sand.
The waves have begun to churn.
I see the turmoil beginning to build.
The wind is now stinging my face.
   I feel the pain.
My face is wet not only from the tears
   that fall down my face,
But from the clouds that hang down
   all over me,
Embracing my body.
   I see you,
   I take a breath.
   I feel your embrace.
   I know soon again
the wind will be calm.
I feel the warmth of the sun,
and see the waves gently rolling in
as they once were...

Carole Lynn Chester

Thankful

Thankful, for family, who love, and care and share,
For friends who are willing to help me, my burdens bear.
Thankful, for Jesus the Son, Who walked the final mile
   and more,
Up Calvary's hill with an old Rugged Cross and there
   my sins He bore.
For the blood that flowed from His riven side, like a
   scarlet mantel it came,
And covered all my sins, tho a multitude, He bore all
   the blame.

Thankful, for the Holy Spirit Who lives in me today,
And gives the peace that passes understanding along
   life's rugged way.

Thankful, for the Heavenly Father Who sits upon His
throne. The powerful, omnipotent, almighty one,
But He sees no fault in me because of the Blood of
   Jesus Christ the Son.

Thankful, Thankful, Thankful
Thankful, Lord am I.

Martha Johnson

A Time Past

There was once a simpler time,
It belonged to ancestors of yours and mine.
The work was always hard and long,
Minds were quick and backs were strong.

Small rewards could make a child smile,
Glitzy, expensive was not needed to beguile.
A simple doll, a small red toy
Would give a little one hours of joy.

Family members relied on each other,
And children felt a responsibility to father and mother.
Parents, in turn, had more time to spend
With family or even with a special friend.

Church socials were the Sunday fare
Where families socialized after prayer.
A picnic in the park on a sunny day
Could be a very special event in May.

Simple and such uncomplicated times
Provide rhetoric for our nostalgic rhymes.
How wonderful to remember times past
For these are the memories that will forever last.

Johanna Gaetje

Revenge

You always seemed like such a nice friend,
I never thought our friendship would end.
As I waited in the hospital room,
I had no feeling except for gloom,
And when they told me you had died,
I must've cried and cried and cried.
I swore I'd find the guy that did this to you,
But in my heart I knew it was true,
That revenge was not the right thing to do.
It seemed like the end,
But I had to go on, my friend.
But I will meet you again in heaven,
And then we'll both be on cloud seven.

Jenna Brennan

Dry Cleaning Truck

I remember the thrill of the engine
as the truck came by so near
our house was a basement
and my Dad was the chauffeur

I dreamed of riding with him
To me there was no fear
I was as safe as I could be
For my Dad was the chauffeur

I'll never forget my birthday
when Dad brought home a toy
The little dry cleaning truck
and I was happy boy!

Now it's many years later
and Dad has made his last run
But the little truck still travels on
and the man in his place is his son.

Sometimes when I think I hear him
and you see a tear in my eye
It's because I know there's a dry cleaning
truck "up there" and my Dad is the chauffeur!

Clara Mae McCammon

The Flag

With my left eye I have seen the angry young student
on the court house steps, chanting this is my right,
this is my right, with the flag all ablaze.

With my right eye I have seen the young soldier who
has fought for that right, oh yes that right, with the
flag draped across his coffin on the way to his grave.

With both eyes I have seen the sorrow and pain and for
this I feel heartbreak and shame but I hope I can
acknowledge all our rights and for these rights God
to save.

Randy P. McDowell

If You Only Knew

If you only knew that I'm in love with you
If you only knew that my love is true
I know you see me only as a friend
But my love for you will never end
You're always there when I need you
You're the type of person that is easy to talk to
I enjoy the times we spend together
I want to remain friends with you forever
And I'll never let you know that I'll never let you go
I fear that if I tell you about what's going on
Our friendship will be gone

Lynn Douangpangna

Hear My Plea

Dear God, you've been with me oh so long.
When I needed strength, you made me strong.

I try to keep my spirits on high.
I know my future's bright, but I still can't help but cry.

Lead me down the path to victory.
As the Father, the Son, and the Holy Spirit stand by me.

Take me from this darkness, and all this sorrow.
I belong in the light with a brighter tomorrow.

Hear my plea from your servant.
I ask many a thing, though I don't deserve it.

Your love is more powerful than anything imagined by man.
It's true, you're my one true friend, my life's in your hands.

Do with me what you think is best.
But I'm never whole without my family inside my chest.

Send me home, my Lord, so I'm no longer grim.
And I won't have to dwell in my painful sin.

This is a prayer I'm begging you to answer.
Set my spirit free like a graceful dancer.

Hear my plea!

Jeff Baden

You Will Never Have To Be Lonely

Although you may be alone.
You don't have to be lonely at all.
For the Holy Spirit will be your comforter.
And will answer you when ever you call.

When ever you are alone.
Be still, meditate and pray.
Study the Holy Scriptures,
And that will brighten up your day.

Attend your local mid-week service,
And worship on Sundays too.
Fellowship with the saints of God.
Then there will be no time for you to be blue.

When ever you feel low and down in spirit,
Things just doesn't seem to go right.
Just remember that you are not alone.
Because Jesus is with you both day and night.

So get alone with Jesus,
And listen to what His Spirit has to say.
Because in Him you will never have to be lonely.
Especially when you know how to bow down and pray.

Parnella R. West

The Eternal Searth

When I was young, so young, I stumbled into the crannies
of my mind, thinking I could find, what made me tick.
But it only made me sick. For in this shallow little rut,
were shameful things. Just hidden things. Of no value.
Then I ventured into deeper caves and found only more.
Of course there were darker catacombs, where I dared not go.
For I was young you know, and not nearly brave enough.
When I became an adult I was still too young,
had too little experience, had not suffered enough.
Then Life descended on me, or so I thought.
All the empty dreams of myself fell apart and left me
alone, facing the universe. Then I crawled into
the dungeon of mind, where, I found not only
myself, but God too, lived there.

Alan O. Coppock

Traditions

How traditions got started it's hard to say,
But our tribute to our elders we gladly pay.
From early in the morning till late in the day,
We preserve traditions in a family way.

From an early age, we were taught to mend and sew,
And to bake breads from homemade dough.
To eat our meals together and to healthy grow,
To regularly pray and to worship go.

The ritual of putting the children to bed,
Consisted of Bible stories, and books to be read,
With problems to be solved, and prayers to be said,
With hopes and ambitions that to Christ they'd be led.

Traditions are rooted in the old homesite,
Offering refuge for homesickness or some other plight.
Whatever was wrong somehow now seemed just right,
When homecooking was offered with no worry about diet.

Through traditions we've learned to share our past,
To look at those pictures and have a blast.
To redeem those antiques exceptionally fast,
And to treasure each momento so it will last and last.

Sarah M.. Moore

Have A Nice Day

God abounds where others fail
    on stormy seas, it's an easy sail

There's no worry, no reason to fear
    our Heavenly Father is always near

Why be angry or wear a frown
    the Holy Spirit is around

If you need a friend to say hello
    talk to Jesus for He'll know

There's no reason to be anxious or fret
    just know in your heart that all is set

God took care of it all long ago
    set your Soul free and allow it to grow

We don't have to hide or run away
    Everything's been dealt with, so, Have A Nice Day!

Bertha E. Walker

Babymoon

We gaze into each others eyes,
I grow excited.
You smile,
My heart beats faster.
While others slumber,
We dance under moonlit skies.
Your warm gentle breath caresses my neck,
Reminding me of a spring breeze.
Oblivious to the time,
I draw you closer.
We embrace,
Attempting to shut out the rest of the world.
I want to wrap us in our own cocoon,
Hoping to hold on to each glorious moment for eternity.
I dream of the future,
Knowing there will be many more precious moments ahead.
Our souls now already intertwined.
While others sleep,
We shall continue our dance,
As only mothers and their babes can do.

Mary Rowe

A Stranger 'Til Now

As far back as I can remember
And that is quite far indeed
I have always been 'the stranger'
'The new kid'
Across country at age six 'the quiet kid in the back seat'
near the beach in Venice 'psst who's that?'
The new kid was always the one to beat on
or let's just spit on him
San Diego 'Stares but, no voices'

Today, I'm back home
Maine 'My home state'
They ask, "Where you from, dude?"
Me? I'm from 'Maine'
Waterville 'Born right here'
Up the street
Grandparents, Lacombe, lived here over sixty years!
I'm back   I'm home
A stranger   'til now

James H. Hall

My Life

Why is my life so full of sorrow?
Why is my life so full of pain?
Most people look forward to a sunny tomorrow,
But me, I just hope it will rain.

Why is my life so full of gloom?
Why does my life have to go this way?
I can't be happy when the red flowers bloom,
At times I just feel like running away.

Why is my life so full of sadness?
Why is my life so full of suffering?
Why can't my life be full of happiness?
Why can't my life be full of understanding?

Amber Crown

Sonnet

If Love brings us happiness forever
And solves all of the problems that we face.
How come Love causes my heart to sever
Taking me to a tearful, empty place.

With Love, they say truth is the only way
Release, the only relief of the smart.
Why then is my heart still filled with dismay,
Though I've unleashed the passions of my heart.

Love befriends everyone or so they say
For Love conquers all; none there is above.
Yet to myself, alone I sit astray
Cast away from my dear because of Love.

But better I, whom Love once came and went
Then one whose name Love never once did vent.

Jiun Yoon

Kimberly

Kelp and shells washing up from the sea
In twists and swirls confusing me.
Maybe there's a way so I can believe
Before the dream has a chance to leave.

Emerald wishes and dreams come true
Revealing rainbow colors beneath the blue
Lovely sunrise sent with a gorgeous view
Yes, it's fine and divine; It's you.

Stephen M. Pascucci

Four Little Foxes

In the beginning when all things were new,
there was a family of foxes known to be wise and true.

The names of four were Look, Listen, Love and Learn.
And they lived in a dell by a big old fern.

The one named Look was told to see,
for all things would be revealed to he.

Listen was told to open his ears,
for then he would hear all things far and near.

Love was told to open his heart:
For then he would hold nothing apart.

Learn was instructed to remember all told,
so that the future; he would hold.

Laughter was father to those four.
And found joy in all that went before.

Life was the Mother to one and all:
There was no barrier or no wall.

So if a happy life is what you yearn.
Follow the teachings of Look, Listen, Love and Learn.

Patricia VerHeul

The Anchor

The tempest rages around us.
Seething violently the tides rage on.
Salty waves flog the vessel.
The weak are lost and adrift.
Currents coerce and gusts compel.
Destination becomes illusion.
The leviathan prowls stealthily.
Crusaders become wanderers
Who are greedily devoured.
Where is the promised land?

We lower the timeless moorings,
A last desperate attempt at security.
Blind faith and despondency
Keep us there through the squall.
During the endless dark hours
We huddle and mumble assurances.
Silent prayers are offered up
In memory of the unfortunate.
Suddenly the violent grip is released;
Dawn's embrace descends, full of peace and warmth.

Joshua Ritnimit

The Widow's Nest

The Widow's Nest is a
    Patch of Thorns
Never, ever was there a place so Forlorn
Desire no longer stirs within
    her breast
Never is she given that
    Place to rest
Most avoid her company for
They cannot bear to see
    themselves hanging from that same tree
Her branches are as
    arid as a droughtful land
That break in the Wind
    leaving a dangling strand
A Widow cannot journey to find him there for
he is no longer anywhere
    so she waits and waits
in her widow's nest
    'Til the snow-covered
Tomb gives her that place to rest

Rosemarie A. Ambrosio

It Was . . .

The alarm clock pinched me from a dream,
    it was 9:15
the water covered me like a blanket,
    it was 9:20
the towel attacked the defenseless water,
    it was 9:35
the fresh linens hugged my still damp body,
    it was 9:40
the comb served as peace-maker to the tangled hair,
    it was 9:45
the brush fed the paste hungry teeth,
    it was 9:50
the watch clung to my wrist, hoping not to fall,
    it was 9:53
with all things gathered, I headed outside,
    it was 10:00
the trees waved goodbye and the grass showed the way,
    it was 10:05
I arrived at 10:10, the bus was to arrive at 10:15,
I smiled and then noticed I was holding the wrong schedule.

Joshua C. Sandlin

Mirage

Life a wonder of Creation, a gift of life
seems a lot, promises a lot;
the aim, grit, determination look up to eternity,
the sky is the limit;
prodding and pushing, snaking its path through
the maze of seemingly cherished dreams;
comes the surprise not always pleasant
that the battered body and soul have realized nothing;
yes nothing but a handful of dreams
precious nothings with mauled conscience, broken relationships;
in the eternal chase of mirage
concealed in the sand dunes of time;
reminding time and again that
it is the humanity and not the human who wins the race.

Ashish Mehta

Forgive Me

Father, can I take up a few minutes of your time?
To express the worries and concerns on my mind.

First, I need to say thanks for all you have given me.
You have given me life, love and self-dignity.

Without your protection, I would live in fear.
I now can face this evil world, knowing you're near.

But, today there is something I need to say.
The old fears came crashing in on me today.

You never lose faith in me, even when I am bad.
You always pick me up off the floor, when I am sad.

Your spirit lifts me up, when I pray to you and your son.
Mending the broken pieces of my mind, and making it all one.

I'm sorry if I ever doubted your love, Father.
Sometimes this sheep gets lost, following another.

I was lost, but never doubted the shepherd's power.
My walls may crumble, but you are my tower.

Please forgive me for thinking you dropped my hand.
Shine your light on my feet, so I can find the promised land.

Gloria Norton

Respite

Inhaling heartily the silence of Solitude;
Filling my lungs with aloneness.
I talk to myself.
An attempt to make sense of the incessant
Signals of life that surround me.
A time to shape pain into poetry.

Linton Moore

Mother's Day

Mothers are swell, Mothers are neat
Sometimes they are mean, sometimes sweet
But one thing's for certain, and never forget
They'll always be mothers, on that you can bet

She dressed you, bathed you, sent you to school
Taught you to walk and the golden rule
Taught you to run, taught you to hide
Taught you to swing, taught you to slide

She'll tend you and mend you, most all of the time
It won't even matter if you haven't a dime
Watched you grow up, with tears in her eyes
If things weren't right, she could do nothing but sigh

We must remember that a Mother cares
And no matter what, she will always be there
When things get bad, when things get tough
She's always there, when things are rough

A Mother's love, will last forever
It will always be with you, on every endeavor
So remember Mother, on Mother's Day
Because after all, she showed you the way.

Michael W. Cave

The Me That Used To Be

Somewhere deep inside my soul lives the me that used to be.
The me who knew the road ahead, only the brightest future could I see.

And then one day, years later, whoever would have guessed.
I saw someone in the mirror not looking quite her best.

She looked somehow familiar, I recognized the face.
But what I saw behind her eyes is what I could not place.

I stared a while longer, who could this person be.
I knew in just a moment, I was looking right at me.

So I looked a little closer, I tried so hard to see,
Why my life had changed so much. What answer could there be?

Then I realized it was me who changed and not my life at all.
I was the one responsible, the one who made the call.

So now I'll gather all the strength there is inside of me,
to once again recapture The Me That Used To Be.

Carylann M. Graham

Put Not Your Soul Solely In Africa

Put not your soul solely in Africa. Plunderer's not there yet.
You lie between the two deep blue seas along murky Michigan
sands where iron monsters streaked the sky till it's colored bleak.
The chimneys strewed dust.

Scented death graced the rocky path. Clouds spun a spotted grin,
sunny skies beyond. Birds above no longer flutter. In the
sloughs rust nestled the algae. Bathing beauties, topless
garbs adorn our sloughs. Mosquitoes nights nigh, insets not,
no tadpoles hide, no catfish abide.

Rita H. Newton

Where Angel's Play

Do you wonder at the stories of sightings just by chance.
Praying to see into the eyes of God's worshipers, sharing in
the trance.

I say to you what man is missing is not up in the sky.
The place where these creatures congregate we see each day
with our eyes.

They sing, they dance, they glide with innocence and grace.
I see them when I take the time to slow my harried pace.

Our angels on this earth are children, they congregate to play
The innocence in their eyes is our key to all God's grace.

I believe these innocent little one's commune with Angel's on high.
Guiding them and protecting till this earth becomes familiar to
their little minds.

So when life seems unbearable and you pray for a sign.
Go see the little children and look into Angel eyes.

Dian Hall

Mr. I.A.M. Busy

Reverend Haynes knocks on Mr. Busy's door,
And says "Sir we missed you last Sunday and the Sunday before.
"Come on in preacher, and let me explain.
I am so busy, that's my name!
I work all day and half the night.
There is so much to do it's a fright
Have to mow the lawn, and wash the car,
Chop some wood! Cause next month we'll be needing the fire.
Some Sunday's we take the kids for a swim...
We need to spend time with them.

Some Sunday's we take them to MacDonalds and to the mall.
They need some things for school this fall.

Some Sunday's we take them to visit aunt Polly and uncle Hiram...
They like to spend time on the farm...
On and on the list, till not one excuse he missed,
Rev. Haynes shakes his head and says, I believe you'll
Too busy for the judgement day!
But one thing's for certain, when God draws the curtain,
Your excuses simply won't stand:
You'll miss the promised land

Ann Morrow

In a Ball of Fluff

My name is Marni Horwitz
I'm wearing a bathing suit and a big sweater
I am a vegetarian and I don't smoke drugs
I used to smoke meat
I have orange hair almost down to my shoulders
I have braces
I have big gums and small teeth
I have a few pimples that I know will go away but I think about them
all the time
I am a human
I am young but I've gone through too much, like everyone
my dad is sad so is my mom
my brother is enlightened and the other is in the pits
I wrote him a letter but it might get lost in his burden
I want everyone to sit down because sometimes when people stand
It makes me nervous, and then I remember the last time I was
nervous
and all the times before then
I like milk because it is so white
I like my blanket because it is so safe
and I'd like you to like me because that's what honesty is

Marni Horwitz

The Vanity of Man

Have you seen a politician climb on a dias,
Proclaim he can remove all evil so elect him without bias.
Have you see a UN chief showing numerous plans,
To usher in world peace and all warfare he can ban.

Have you seen an architect with immense enthusiasm,
Proclaim each man housed if he his given due cooperation.
Have you seen a geneticist proclaim with pride,
That he can cure all disease in his next purposeful stride.

But can you imagine a world where everyone is happy,
There is no war, disease or death all is nice and snappy.
A thirty second earthquake can bring a city to dust.
A rise of a dictator and world peace goes bust.

There are new diseases of affluence and old of poverty.
There is the humdrum of life in middle class mediocrity.
Haven't you realized O'man that all you can do is try,
That the Lord who guides us all keeps laughing in the key.

He laughs at the vanity of man and his valiant attempts,
He laughs at all the intellectuals who holds him in contempt,
But the one who surrenders to the Lord's will, is filled with humility,
He thus goes about in his life with a deep sense of piety.

Shoma Sen Iyengar

The Wonders of Love

Love is so beautiful to see
Like the bird up in a tree
It sings lovely songs
See the wonders of love, the wonders of love
And love is two hearts that beat a dream
Resounding as they beam
With a glow that is strong, for they belong
To the wonders of love
Through we have faced many sorrows from hate and war
We still join hands in reflecting what love is for
And every day evil forces invade our lives
But love gives us the courage to survive
Yes, love, like the sun that lights the skies
Like the rainbow in our eyes
Its dimensions are profound
See the wonders of love, sweet wonders of love
And love is a feeling so divine
It's the highest peak you'll climb
Once you're there, that's your crown
See the wonders of love, the wonderful wonders of love

Waverly Gray

No Words

No speech, no words need to be said
Only the wisp of winds through the trees
Or the splash of waves crashing on the sand
No words of woman, child or man.
No sounds of chatter, no clamoring crowd
Only the dew of leaves falling onto the ground
And the buzz of insects flapping their wings
No cars, no boats no electrical things.
No radio, no televisions, no battling foes
Only the sounds of chirping birds in the brush
All alone with thoughts which fill my mind
The glory of nature I shall find.

Karen Emily Anne Small

Untitled

When you find the one you love,
You know it's a blessing from God above.
You see, there is someone for each of us,
But in order to find,
You have to search and search for
That one who is special, gentle, and kind.
I have been through many, more than a few,
Before I was able to find you.
Now that I have, I must say!
I'm more than just glad
For now my life is complete
No more people do I have to meet.
I have found the one that was from God above,
For me forever and ever to love.

Gary G. Ellis Sr.

A Question of Faith

Sitting on a merry-go-round one day
Spinning clouds coming my way
An angel lands on my shoulder
It's always the same
The acts of the play

The sky turns a dark gray
A sound of an owl echoes through the night
A light catches my breath
It's only me in sight

The question remains in the depths of my eyes
Clouds part while looking into the skies
A shadow cast down upon me
A reflection
A figure in the night

Although seeing in believing
How do I know it's the truth?
The hands of faith reach down to touch me
But they remain aloof

Dena Dees

Night Watch

Dear Lord watch over me during the night,
Let me wake to a beautiful day o so bright.
Walk with me through the day
Do not let me stay far away.
He leads me down that long road,
But I thank him everyday for the seeds I have sowed.

Amber Breezee

Endings

Distance and time does not quickly erase
the pains of yesterday,
nor take away the memories.
Feelings we once shared, though dim,
are still seen through a curtain of new hope.
It's been a long time and, yet
I still wonder, and hope that you're okay.
Time will eventually heal us.
The hurts will drop off naturally, like leaves.
The memories will fade.
Washed away like a castle of sand
where the tide takes a little more
each time it rushes over the carefully built structure.
And now only small fragments remain on the shore.
But I'm glad it's finally over
and I can find relief in my good-bye lines.
Now I only sigh when those waves take away
the last of our love.

Sandra J. Sacksteder

Awaken

My inspiration, how did I find you.
I know you weren't there before.

One man full of love, passion, and caring.
Erupting my inner creativity.

Words flowing like never before.
Thoughts and feelings that no one has ever touched.

Flowing through my fingertips.
Onto white paper for all to see.

Did I have them before or are they
There now solely because of you.

And should I share them or never
Expose them for anyone to see.

Tina L. Harris

Spirit Dancers

Elusive winds...blowing through my soul...
Logic whisked away...now where will I go?

What is this restless pull...luring all my senses,
Converting strength to weakness....as I watch the Spirit Dancers.

They creep in ever quiet...their goal being deceit,
They dance into enchantment...music swaying into me...

Lost unto a world... Where magic reigns supreme...
And the shadows of your dreams...seem far from make-believe....

I hear the faerie's laughter...as I'm moving through the maze,
The sweet sound echoes o'er me...as I float from place to place.

All too soon the laughter fades...
They tell me I must go,
The Spirit Dancers vanish...as the winds begin to blow.

I never want to leave here...Please don't call my name,
My true heart must stay hidden...for I cannot bear the pain.

I feel the gusts surround me...propelling me through time,
Leading me back up the path of a place I'd left behind.

Night's mirage unravels...
As does the memory...
Of a place that holds my laughter...somewhere my spirit dances free.

Jill D. Kolaczek

I Pray That It's God That They Find

Dear heavenly Father our great God above,
Who answers our prayers and sends us His love.

God is a good God. He has what it takes,
To do everything perfect. He makes no mistakes.

So if you'll turn your life over to Him, and let Him come into your
    heart.
He'll give you a new life, to make a new start.

He will take away the old body and replace it with one that's new.
And that's only the beginning of what He will do.

He will forgive you of your sins, and He'll save your soul.
And He will always be with you, where ever you go.

This world's almost over, like the end of a book.
The signs are all around us everywhere we look.

So if you don't know Jesus, there's no time to wait.
Please get to know Him before it's too late.

I thank Him for the soul's He's saved, including you and me.
Just think, without Jesus, where would we be?

He'll put love in your heart and He'll put peace in your mind.
For those that are lost, I pray that it's God that they find.

David Grogun

Without You

Looking out into the emptiness of my life -
Without you.
The presence of love is so absent -
Without you.
The absence of joy is so present -
Without you.
Without you my life is empty.

Judi Harmon

Spring Hope

If I had an April flower
Sweet and soft and red in color
From the meadow where we've been
In wavy grass that's green,
Where we laughed and had begun
To play the words of fun,

I would smile and be content and hope for a happy end.

If I had an April flower
Gentle, pure and white in color
Like the snow up on the hills
That reminds us of how it feels
To be left out in the cold when the facts are never told,

I would sing to a tender friend and still hope for a happy end.

If I had an April flower
Spicy, strong and blue in color
Like the wall a wave will make
To a calm ocean soon to break
Into a furious and gray storm
That shortly comes to its norm,

I would dance with a love pretend and hope for a happy end.

Tibby Mazilu

Randi

Contorted faces of racists glaring
Defiant, in love, I'm only caring
about her and me, black and white
color who cares, right is right

Societal opposition, dragging me down
Punches from rednecks, I fall to the ground
Yet, at night in her arms, my heart feels pure
An unparalleled love, an intoxicant lure

Cities apart, temptations do mire
Yet visions of her, my only desire
Life together, purity of mind
Only with Randi, happiness I find

Two different cultures, a world full of hate
In her tender brown eyes, problems abate
Future uncertain, people so mean
My elixir of love, Randi Y. Greene.

David L. Hudson Jr.

A Mountain Song

Cascading, tumbling - swiftly humbling
drowning out thoughts and worrisome
cares left miles behind.
Sound and motion joining forces from forest
streams of unknown sources.
Falling, pooling and for the moment
collecting strength and passing by.
Sit dear friends and dream for now
let others run the world awhile.
For laurel blooms don't last that long
cascading falls - a mountain song.

James J. Vanas

Danny's Love

Listen to the whisper of another time and place,
While yielding to the yearnings of what might have been.
Shades of reality's simple truth erase,
And come with me to where the shadows begin.

Where gentle overlapping of love's memories start,
And our bodies recognize what your mind denies.
Know at last the pleasures of an open heart,
While confessing the emotion that your smile belies.

For it's never too late to recapture the past,
And make a oneness of what once was two.
And however brief our reunion lasts,
I'll remember finding out about you.

Constance Bence

For E.T.

Though I am old and gray and passion sleeps,
I count myself most fortunate of men.
To find in youth and beauty such a friend
As calls to mind the days I thought long gone,
When I was valued for a young man's traits.
Not, to be sure, those things I value most,
But nonetheless recalling other days
Of careless loves and passions hot with youth.
Though now my course of days is made serene
By wife and family, all of them most dear,
I find this friendship worthy of more praise
Than ever my poor pen can hope to raise.

Donald M. Barnes

Beautiful

Beautiful is the eye that sees the star
Beautiful is he who strives to conquer all by far.

Beautiful is the ability to love
when the sun shines so bright from high up above.

Beautiful is smelling the dew
after a summer's rain
beautiful is being yourself
without having any shame.

Beautiful is knowing
when to frown or smile
beautiful is knowing
when to go that extra mile
beautiful is he who helps
someone less than thou.

Beautiful is whispering a prayer
knowing that God will always be there
beautiful is trusting someone without a bit of fear.

Beautiful is the flower that is always in bloom
full of God's oil
and all of nature's perfumes.

Paula Bennett

I Stare at the Sky

I stare at the sky
And I wonder why
Should people die from hunger

And when I face the sun
I ask why the fun
Should be only for some and not shared by everyone

And the moon at night
I ask is it right
For people to fight for their survival
But I don't get an answer

Chris Kikis

Infatuation

I love someone, you all have seen her before
She walks through the halls beautiful and to be seen by all
I watch her closely but see does not notice
I follow her closely but she does not see me
I say hello she thinks nothing of it
she is a one of a kind
and I wish she was mine
But oh well that's just a dream
or maybe not.

Felix I. Braden

Magic

The great tree hides something incredibly powerful,
Magic.
The jungle starts beaming at sunset.
The first time,
The great tree lets go its steady grasp,
Magic.
The raccoons with their sneaky ways,
Prowl cautiously in the moonlight.
The hammocks of moss,
Sway in the gentle breeze,
Magic.
The monkeys demand bananas.
The old owl tells tales,
To anxious baby hawks,
Magic.
A fox stalks a field mouse who is hunting for food.
Dawn pushes night aside,
And the great tree takes hold its steady grasp,
Until the next night,
Magic.

Celeste Ballard

Marital Bliss

Take me roughly into your arms,
Seduce me with your masculine charms.
Ignite my soul with your powerful touch,
Titillate my body with your kisses and such.

My heaving breast your lips do seek,
Tantalizing us both to a higher peek.
Your caresses burning into my thighs,
That point of oneness, so very neigh.

In the lovers dance, our bodies entwine,
Being as one in purpose divine.
Mingling together, in passion and sweat,
Desires, demanding, ache being finally met.

The warm feeling of your body close to mine,
Both of us spent, the world left behind.
Then our lips meet in a tender kiss,
As we share in the Godly, marital bliss.

Davida M. Jackson

The Rose

Pity not the wilting flower
    for it does enhance the hour
Time changes form, it's true
    but beauty in essence remains anew
Each stage unfolds treasures deep
    and memories alone remain to keep
The pictures, faces of life alive
    all changing, fading but remaining inside
Our minds, our past forever kept
    and kindled anew with each passing step
Our feet advance, wisdom grows
    but fading fast our being glows
Anew it changes, day to day
    but traces remain, our essence is the same.

Dalange Dupuy

A Flame that Glowed

An orange candle burns in the darkness.
Flickering, it illuminates the room in muted detail.
The ordinary becomes mysterious and romantic.
Color no longer exists, only shades of gray cast with orange
undertones.
Attention is no longer drawn to the flaws that lie within this room.
How imperceptible the truths are in this half lit night.
Melted wax rolls down the sides of the burning candle to form a
pool at its base.
Soon it will solidify and transform the once magnificently ornate
candle into a useless blob of paraffin.
This torch that glows night after night reveals the darkness and its
concealed secrets.
One day soon the wick will be swallowed by that which held it up
for so long,
and sadly its flame will die an untimely death.

Kim Moore

A Woman Set Free

Excuse me mister, you say you're looking for this girl
Oh yes, I remember her
She's been gone a long time
But if you look closely, you just may see
A glimpse of the girl I used to be

So you remember her, that girl I used to be
When I believed the lies you told
When you said you loved me

Do you remember her
You know that girl I used to be
Who was at your beck and call
Whenever you needed me

Oh now, you remember her
That girl I used to be
Who tried to wait around
Until you became the man I believed you to be

Of course, now, you would remember her
That girl I used to be
But I'm really happy to tell you
The girl has become a woman set free

René Prescott

In the Wee Hours

In the wee hours of the morning
When only God and a few of us are awake,
I take a break
And think about what I've been thinking about for
   the past two hours.
Nothing much, just everything.
All, but really nothing.

Is an idle mind fertile ground for the Devil?
Not for me, necessarily.
In the wee hours God seems very near
When I think about it...
Even when I'm not thinking about God at all.

Strange, huh?
How God seems to be around
Even when He doesn't seem to be around.
Kind of like air.
Kind of like a good friend.
Kind of like love.
Imagine...God incognito!

William Braswell

Mary

A tear from heaven, caressed the earth
Many years ago.
Carried by angels' wings, so tender
Was her work.
Befitting was her name of Mary,
To whom she was devoted.
God's love and trust she would hold fast,
In everything she did.
His love was her strength and guide through life,
A gift she gave her children.

Times of hardships and of loss were spent
In trusted silence.
That He would stand with open arms
For His beloved Mary.
A place is set for your sweet servant
A home coming.
Carried by angels' wings, Your tear of joy returns.
Victorious.

Ann Lennon

Shattered Dreams

I hear screams, but blackness holds me down.
I feel paralyzed
My mother stands over my bed, disbelieving what she is seeing.
I can't believe, I've lost the best of me.

I may know the truth, but I can't face it.
Damn her, how she lied. Dreams shattered by my mother's hateful
   greed.
You blinded me with your sins!
I have my sight now, I see all that you hid,
So don't try to hide all the wrong that you did.
I run from danger, I run from you.

Under the barbed wire, over the old stone wall.
On my way to the river, to drown my sorrow.
I watch the water flow, until it's time to go.
I sit and think "Where do I go."

I wander through my misery, feeling deep cuts of insecurity
I drown in my own thoughts, sinking in the memories
Shadows of my life keep washing over me.
Despondent, I sit and wait without hope.

Katie Moran

The Dance

Two kittens escaped on a warm summer night
Onto the lawn, where a full moon shone bright;
They huddled together, as if in a trance,
Then with a prance, they started to dance!

A leap and a run, then a brief pas de deux,
A quick pirouette on a soft kitten toe
Led into a galop, a somersault landing,
Close to the place where their humans were standing
Watching them dance, in the joy and delight
Of just being cats, on this magical night.

They danced to an orchestra we couldn't hear,
Music fine tuned to a young kitten's ear;
Their ballroom a garden, where flowers were growing,
The lighting was moonlight, all sparkling and glowing.

Their dancing and prancing became even brisker!
Until they were tired, both worn to a whisker.
Weary and hungry, they came to be fed,
Then cuddled and purring, we put them to bed.

Alice L. Wibel

Olden Days

I often wonder,
About the olden days,
About their customs
And their ways.

We learn some
In history class,
But, I wonder how it would be,
To live in the past?

What would it be like without technology?
Writing everything by hand.
No T.V.s, computers, or radios,
Or cars such as mini-vans.

What would I do,
If I had to use a quill pen?
Life would be so different,
Living back then.

Natalie Pereles

July 2, 1996

Sitting at the picnic table
that stands beside the lake.
With memories of my children
I feel my heart begin to break.
I felt I had run away,
so I wouldn't die.
For the first time in my life,
I didn't have to hide behind the lies.
The sun begins to set.
The colors so beautiful
with clouds and rays all around.
I never felt such peace
My soul never felt more whole.
Forever and a day I shall
always remember,
July second, nineteen-ninety-six.
I found my life that day
as I stood before the shore.
Because this was the day
I found the courage to see what's beyond
the door.

Renee J. Firestone

Homesick

She waits
silently and patiently she awaits my return
open
always with me
within me

I long
again to touch her
to hear
to taste
her breath
stirring my hair
stirring my soul
to hear her cries
to feel her beneath my feet
giving life all around me
to me
to once more be enraptured
by her nothingness

Jason M. Steiner

Spring

The snow slowly melts allowing the ground to show its once hidden face.
A small sprout of life peeks out here and there from the soil.
The forest, awakened from its winter sleep is vivid with animals.
Trees are budding and happy sparrows chirp lively while bees are buzzing.
A growing patch of grass attracts the attention of a gray cottontail rabbit.
Brightly colored butterflies travel from one fragrant flower to the next
    searching for sweet nectar.
And I, sit here at the dimly lighted park in the security of my
lovers grasp looking up at the elegant night and its breathtaking stars.
I find myself lost.
Lost between sunset and sunrise being held in his arms.
One golden hour after the other, set with sixty sparkling diamond minutes.
Turning to face him, I had not realized how his eyes were shining
with the same enchantment as the stars.

Sheila Gaston Cruz

Jester

Pass me down that bottle friend, sit and let me tell you a tale
A morbid little offering sure to prove all is not well
As dark as the lighting in here, although I wish not to bring anyone down
I am not here for pity, I just need to shed the pain of a clown

A fool for king's only, tending to everyone's tears
The palace idiot wrapped up in sentiment and agonizing fears
Over the hills a bit I left my soul behind
No hope of redemption, no possibility of peace of mind

A prince of pride, a slave of perfection
Always on a quest for acceptance, always side-lined by reflection
Distorted and mangled is my self depiction
A fool driven to madness by self infliction

Desperate dreams only to awaken to see the sun rise again
Come home to the night's embrace to find my shadow is my only friend
Your understanding lacking, I am a tough species to dissect
Raised to swallow whole disappointment, denial, doubt, and neglect

Bitterness absent, I am left with a second of peace, a glimpse of hope
Forgiveness can bring about wonders and loosen that deadly rope
I am not insane, twisted or disturbed, just do away with any rumor
I go on to with stand the abuse I do unto myself, and keep my sense of humor

Shaun Heiskell

Realization

I did not realize I was a corpse walking among the living, my first
realization of this reality was when my eyes were 1st cast upon your
face, you have stirred in me long dead feelings and emotions I was
recently asking our great father if ever there would be anyone for me,
and there you were. You are a good man, a special man and I love you.
You do know, don't you? Your eyes smile at me and tell me a thousands
words without any movement from your lips. My dear sweet wonderful
man maybe someday, you'll be able to tell me what your heart is
shouting out to mine without your words. Remember always, it was you
who freed me. It was you who awoke my dead heart, it was you who
opened up my chest cavity and ran your hands through my heart and all
my soul while you did this I felt such warmth, such passion, such
emotions that sometimes I thought I would die. You do know, don't
you? Sometimes I feel you tremble, your body speaks to me, shouts to
me loudly without words. You do know, don't you? Your body language
sometimes suffocates me it takes my breath away, I sometimes feel the
blood rush through my body. You do know, don't you? Do you see it?
Do you feel it? Can you touch it without touching each other. Can
you smell it? Darling you do know, don't you? This is my gift to you
because of what you've given me. Darling I could die today and know
that I was truly happy and that is possible because of you. So love
me today and we won't think of tomorrow until it comes and when it
does it will be today again and so we will love again, for today
because tomorrow is not yet here. You do know, don't you?

Vida Renaud

128

Phantasm

There is a melodious waterfall in this bountiful land of mine.
  It neither hides the loam beneath nor shades the cliff behind.
The trees stand tall and leeward and will bloom all the year.
  The buzzards fly with robins; the lions walk with deer.

And beyond the meadow, a patch of lilies grows,
  And small and weak as they are, they smile as the north wind blows.
In the midst of daffodils, a fountain, pure and clean,
  Showers yesterday's promises and sparkles with tomorrow's dreams.

There is a rose-entwined bridge that beckons, so gentle and proud;
  The sun and the moon for its arches, it keeps to the bulrushes bowed.
Bees are but flitting daydreams—of moments too precious to share.
  They lead past the edge of the rainbow that shelters the animal's lair.

The air is the breath of sweet clover and dew; the grass of cool velvet and May.
  Silver-lined lambs sleep hushed in the sky, and stars never hide in the day.
There are wonders on the other side of the ocean when the edge of the heart isn't proud.
  And we run hand in hand in the meadow as we reach to touch cloud after cloud.

Stephanie D. Sproat

Broken Cycle

Born into this world so innocent — she could not know her fate —
Or the despair she'd endure each day — the violence and the hate.

Isolation, heartache, dark secrets — hell in a place called home —
Terror, tears, and bruises — a little girl so desperately alone.

After fifteen years of cruelty — she no longer could bear the pain —
She decided to end her life one night — the night her life would change.

She cried out to the One above — the One she knew as God —
She said "I need you more than ever now . . . am I worthy of your love?"

He filled her with peace and joy — she said she felt brand new —
Within flowed warmth, hope, and life — in her heart a new love grew.

She promised God to break the cycle — with her abuse would end —
She promised to be kind and gentle — to her children He'd someday send.

Born into this world innocent — I have only known her love —
I thank the One who saved my mom — she is my gift from God above.

Marianne Spohn

The Hunter and the Buck

Yellow cap and bright red vest, the hunter lies down to take a rest
He's hiked for miles in pursuit of his dream, a ten point buck in some
forest green.

The sun sets low, the hunter sleeps, the big brown buck through the
forest he creeps, a crackling branch and the hunter screams, the buck
stops, like a statue it seems

His heart beats fast as he grabs for his gun, the buck hears a noise and begins to run.
With awesome strength and eyes of the night
He glides through the trees ahead of his plight

The moon is up now and his eyes are wide, his rifle he aims in the
direction of stride, the bucks nostrils flair, his fur coat shines,
the aura of death, the buck whines

The hunter takes aim, through a starlight scope
At a buck on the run, the hunter does hope

A shot rings out in the moonlit night, the buck veers left, the shot goes right.
His heart beat slows, he's down to a trot
While the hunter still searches for what he'll find not

Another close call, the buck sees his doe
He's by her side now, and together they'll go

The hunter sees this from a distant place, and a feeling of love
brushes over his face, how can he kill a creation so fine
He turns and he leaves, his dream stays behind

Rick Herzog

God's Ways

How great is God on any day
True and strong come what may
What is man but crumb and clay
Must he rage and roar
Without praise and honor to Him
In whom all ownership resides
All his strength will reduce to cries
Yet mercy and forgiveness always
stand ready
Each moment for the asking
But many leave it behind
Never knowing hell and honor beckon them
All because they could not
reckon with His ways.

Beth Turner

Autumn Fire

Nature feels her fire
As Autumn snaps its cold.
Before she does retire
She bares her colors bold.

With the waning of the green
Comes the rising of the red,
An orange and golden gleam
Before she nods her head.

Her flaming garments sear the sky
Before they drop to ground
To touch our own flames deep inside
As winter rolls around.

Too soon she'll stand with limbs so bare.
To shiver in winter's wind
Until which time new buds appear
To adorn her once again.

Roger W. Helfrich

The Future of Tomorrow

Every day a child is born and
hope burns bright again
Into a world where pain is felt.
Where sorrow seems never to end.
But with the birth of this new life,
a ray of sun is felt,
This joy, this hope, this blessed event,
the future of tomorrow.
So fill this tiny life you hold
with love, compassion, and caring
for one day soon this child will
give the qualities you are sharing.
Children are a special gift, sent from God above
So cherish them for our futures
sake and fill them with our love.
For with this life you hold in
your hand, you hold a special treasure
the hope and joy of a brighter today
and the future of tomorrow.

Robin Smart

Poem for My Surgeon

Divorced and dateless here I lie,
To my reproductive organs I say goodbye.

With two teenage daughters in my possession,
I don't even want to chance an immaculate conception.

Debra J. Leistikow

Whatever Happened To?

A monkey, a balloon, a rose, a lady bug,
and a wish. These are the five
things you gave me.
The Monkey lays still, no longer
touched, but oh how much he holds
inside, his contents the memories
of what once was we.
The balloon is a shadow on the
closet floor, like my soul buried
deep inside, the healing
within time will only abide.
The rose is folded within a
good book, fondly removed
from time to time to go
back to happiness to have a look.
The lady bug flies free, the
only happy soul out of all us three.
She carries my wish and a question to thee
Whatever happened to?
A monkey, a balloon, a rose, a lady bug and a wish.

Margaret Monterosso

Undying Sadness

I have no purpose,
I have no shame,
I close my eyes and take the blame.
I feel my emotion being ripped from my soul,
My undying sadness,
I have no control.
My dreams have been stolen,
My mind set free,
My eyes swelled shut from the sadness I see.
I feed off sorrow,
I live off pain,
Life is a hunting ground and I am fair game.
A tear runs down my shadowed face,
And seeps into my pillow case.

McKenzie Clinton

Origin

From the void which launched all beams
Unto that void all light returns
Energy but just a space
between a motion and a rest
Space just the time between
nothing and everything
bridged by the light of God
extending all directions
simultaneously
through all mediums
all knowledge
crystallizing into the form of man
the orifice through which the Gods speak
and inspire us
acting out the ancient struggle
the quest for our beginnings
the foregone conclusion of all thoughts and actions
the final resolution of all conflicts and tensions

G. J. Papes

Dream On

Void of form and substance,
But possessing the power to destroy.
Rendering man helpless,
Yet still the fruit of all searches.

They are the beginning of an end,
And the end of all beginnings.
Unbreakable barriers,
Upon whose crossing survival rests.

Dreams of power, upon which nations are born.
Dreams of peace, which drive men to change.
But above all,
It is dreams of love, which give existence meaning.

Dreams
    gone,
Life
    empty,
Survival
    meaningless.

The world without dreams is slow and painful death.

Philip D. Reichner

From Death to Life

As the bougainvillea's blooms form from their leaves,
    I'm reminded of what the paper said:
    "In lieu of flowers please make donations to . . . "

How could someone die without flowers? What charity's
    need could be bigger than the need of the soul
    to rest with the scent of flowers?

I had to walk. I thought, to live, I must be able
    to love all that has breath, hold onto it as if
    my life depends on it, and when it's time is spent
    let it go.

I had to walk more. To let it go, to say good-bye: How
    could I ever accomplish this without tapping into the
    endless reservoir of emotions and feelings flowing deep within me?

I had to walk, never mind the hour, until I learn what I
    need to learn. To let go, to say good-bye, to allow a
    greed for life to swell, but not too large - knowing that at
    some point all souls rest with the scent of flowers.

As the bougainvillea's blooms wither and fall to the ground,
    I'm reminded that even flowers cannot live forever
    but their beauty and smell do remain etched in the soul forever!

April L. Wilson

New Smyrna Wilds

Sea oats sitting on a low sand dune,
    Sea vines crawling up a small, white mound.
All have recovered from the morning storm,
    Clean and refreshed — feeling dry and warm.

Gathering overhead is a cauliflower cloud,
    The surf sighs a warning, but not too loud.
Pelicans gliding o'er the sand bar shallows,
    Fish slowly swimming to the pelican jaw gallows.

Palms pointing upwards to pierce the sky,
    Spiders spinning sly traps where flies will die.
Bees are a-feeding in the yellow wild flowers,
    A small butterfly glides around for hours,

Beating the air wind with his bright orange wings,
    "Is it life, or is it death?" that he silently sings.

Ralph E. Gillette

Untitled

From the point of view of God looking down
At His constantly busy creatures
(Which reorganize the universe and transform its flora and fauna)
Life develops through its changing colorful pictures.

It develops gradually from image to image
On all levels—from micro to macroforms,
And God contemplates from the heights of His celestial village
All the diverse directions it flows and turns.

This is the language the universe speaks since it's been created,
The purposeless language that tempts one to fantasize.
Its magnitude can't be objectively rated,
Which takes its Creator away from the Nobel Prize.

This is the language that can't be established once and forever
And studied carefully six times a week
In order to overcome that language's barrier
Between what is common and what is unique.

There is no rule that may bind its developing nature:
It goes in the direction suggested by a creative mind,
Which is God's priceless ticket to the land of the greatest adventures
One can ever wish for and ever find.

Ulea

In Loving Memory

In Loving Memory of Anne Roach McClatchy
So much happiness from being together
So much sadness from being apart
So many endings have come to a close
So many beginnings have yet to start.

Time can slip like grains of sand
Millions of seconds on which we stand
Open your eyes and look around
You will witness a beautiful sound.

Time moves on but not too swiftly
It carries the lives that grow so quickly
It cherishes flowers, birds, and trees
Yet it never forgets about you and me.

So remember the grains of sand you've collected
And never forget the lives you've affected.

Shannon McCrosson

Untitled

We didn't have a lot of time before you had to go.
There was so much we should have said, so much you'll never know.
We thought we'd have more time together, more memories to share.
Instead we're left to wonder, did you know how much we cared?
We often look to God above to ask the question, "Why?"
What was the reason for your leaving, why did you have to die?
Alas, He's never answered us, and we know He never will,
There is no answer we could accept, yet we look for answers still.
They say that time can ease the pain, of losing one so young,
You never really get over it, you just learn to carry on.
Now a smile is the mask we wear to hide our grief and pain.
We try not to think of all we've lost, but know that we've gained.
The knowledge that we'll meet again, and save our memories 'til then,
When we can see you face to face, and ask you how you've been.
Until that time, we'll think of you and smile through our tears,
Because the memories we carry will sustain us through those years.
And on today, your birthday, the hardest day of all,
Know you'll never be forgotten, for you were loved by all.

Christina A. Kurz

Enchanted

Our world is enchanted,
if we open an eye.
Twinkling fairies,
a rainbow filled sky.
Children can see
and believe without question,
things adults would
never dream to mention.
Our world is enchanted,
if we open an eye.
Trees that know all,
white horses that fly.
Can you imagine a
place such as this?
A fairy-tale land full
of magic and bliss.
This realm that only children see,
can be real for adults like you and me.
If we open our minds, and open our eyes,
our world is enchanted, and within you it lies.

Paula L. Kroeker

Instinct

I have found my rhythm
as I walk the leaf covered trail.
Searching the limits
of my sight in the forest,
I strain to hear the sounds
that I know are there,
but are hidden by the dissonance of my breath.
I rummage my soul
for recollection of the feelings
that now consume my consciousness.
They are familiar, yet distant.
I have not yet lived these feelings
in this lifetime.
Though I somehow know
That I have had to live them in a past one.
I approach a road,
and the feelings recede.
I have lost the rhythm that I found
as I walked the leaf covered trail.

Tom Machinchick

The Artist

Age has no time when
you live the fullest line

The image of youth fades
but the strength of wisdom stays

Working to always help family and
friends shines your soul from within

God's greatest gift is the artist within you
Your hands have shaped, created and
formed life's most treasured works to see

My dearest Dad, Grandfather and Great
Grandfather, may this 75th Birthday show
our love to honor thee

Joann Leavitt

Untitled

Meaning and purpose I sought urgently
In the world beyond the me.
Do we not make the meaning
In response to the world's continual prodding?

Albert H. Clodius

131

Blank

It was only sandy visions
Each defensive becoming offensive.
Offering accusations to the minds.
Watching the paved out news.
Blankly staring
Not caring.
Agreeing with a side
Appearing to do for peace,
To do for the child.
Shocking no one,
Leaving no innocence.
Does history ever teach us
　　that rights don't exist among the few?
The singled out face
With eyes crying
Mouth screaming
Nose inhaling the scents of the season.
What chance is there to persuade the egg?

Tammy Zaner

By the Sixth Cold Beer On Wednesday

I miss delicious Tuesday and the bubble
bath before crushing fennel and tenderizing London
broil for Maggie's sliced beef in mustard sauce.

Those shoulders were still raw
in the pan and we were dancing zany
waltzes in our towels, drenching our throats in cheap Merlot.

I think Maggie was a garrulous woman
or she was humming but certainly she couldn't sing
a Neil Diamond song, even slowly

Instructed to turn like a pig
on a smokejack and count
backwards, I found her on the couch with a bag of fruit

Maggie taught me how to dip chubby
apricots into her mouth without touching my nose to her chin
but I don't remember how to do that trick anymore.

D. T. Friedson

Our Flag

This gaily colored piece of cloth
For which men gave their lives.
Is an ancient symbol of the truth we recognize
It flies with beauty and with grace
Over our country dear,
And gives us life, liberty and the pursuit of happiness
Year after year.

Beryla Long

Remembrance of Elvis the King of Rock and Roll

I know you're still alive,...
For your loving spirit in our hearts
You must have left behind.

You'll always be a part of us
Because your love will always and forever
Remain in our hearts.
Elvis now has heavenly song to sing
Unto Jesus the King...
But unto us who love the King of Rock and Roll
You'll always be king
For your love still reigns in our hearts.

Thank you for the joys you would bring
When you would sing.
Just want to say thank you and give our
Gratitude to the King.

Mylinda Gray

To Love the People I Don't Love

To love the people I don't love.
I give my tolerance
testing my strength

To love the people I need to love.
I give my backbone
in search of a peace.

To love the people I do love
I give a living soul
rewarded with a feeling of life.

The difference, I see, to related to be defined.
The distance, I feel, to close to be reached.
The space, I touch, to light to be carried.

To love the people I don't love,
My efforts are endured.
My time is not wasted.

To love the people I need to love.
My reasonings are felt.
My desire are respected.

The tolerance, the test, a backbone,
a search, my living soul, my life.

Therese Paige Masiak

Christmas Morning

Here by the warm fireplace I sit,
As the newly burned wood around me doth spit,
Burning large holes in my brand new attire,
Causing myself to join in with the fire.
In the distance I hear the loud roars of my sister,
It seems that this year dear old Santa has missed her,
Her stocking all filled with wood and black coal,
Now it's hatred and grief that she tries to control,
Look, there's ma who's quite pleased with herself,
She was brought "blades" by that quick little elf,
And then there is me by the fire still sitting,
With myself quite a flame while the wood is still spitting.

Marilyn Lewis

I Like America

Yea! I'll tell you why I like America.
I like America
Because it's a place where you can be free
I like America
Because it's a place where you can ask questions
I like America
Because it's a place where you can be bold
Yea! I like America
Because I can keep hope alive
I like America
Because I can get it done by any means necessary
I like America
Because I can ask what I can do for my country and not what
my country can do for me
I like America
Because I can just say no to drugs
I like America
Because I can dream of a mountain and overcome it
I like America
Because I cannot say good morning to everyone
Yea! I like America because America is me.

Siphiwe Zukkie Mguni Rametsi

Wild Bill?

I was gambling with the circuit for the very first time,
testing each cowboy who was in his prime.
A crash of lightning! A rush of wind!
His entrance pierced icicles through the skin.
The room was still, as his boots tread heavily.
Each step was a note as his spurs played a medley.
I checked to see if expressions could talk —
One man shouted, "Look! It's Wild Bill Hickok!"
He was sitting at the bar, alone and feared.
I grinned and beared it, as I neared.
"If you want to draw, you're a little late,
for I've got lead ready that will add to your weight."
Without having turned, his pistol aimed at my chest...
I knew I had seen the best of the best.
"Mr. Hickok, I'm sorry, I just wanted to meet.."
I hadn't finished my words before I turned, red as beet.
As I stood amidst silence before,
I now felt hysteria shaking the floor.
"Well, there's only one Mister with a mane.
Hello there! I'm Calamity Jane."

Heather A. Arneson

The Musician

Why does this musician play outside my window,
Standing there, his trumpet singing that song?
The street sign standing over him like a sentry
at attention, a sentry named Bourbon.
It seems to know how special he is.
Almost foolish
The musician playing for all he's worth
With no one listening.
I hear the chanting, roaring of the crowd,
Almost deafening in its angry waves of noise.
But through it all there hangs the humming
trumpet's song.
I like the musician's determination, the fact
he tries to please deaf humanity.
Almost refreshing
I smell the spicy aroma of dinner, and reluctantly
follow my nose, leaving the musician and his sweet
music behind.

Kelly Spence

Love

This love is a special flower, that
has no beauty on the outside, but on
the inside a love so beautiful, that
you can only feel. This is a love that
is as warm as the sun and as
beautiful as a flower. Cherishing this
love brings tears to your eyes that
cling to you. As this love grows deeper
your heart sing a song of a tender
love this love brings the stars out
of the sky and as long as the
sky is blue this love would always
be true to you and your heart this
love is as pure love; it can never
be contaminated with anything that is
harmful to it. Staying true to your
heart this love provides any and
everything for you. Trusting and sacredly,
you can make that love tell all the
things it has tried to tell you.

Dominique Plez

Have Faith

We as humans are taught evilness.
It's such a part of our lives that we don't
realize that we teach it to each other.
A racist, a bigot or sexist pass on their
negative views of those they dislike or
hate to souls that are unable to resist.
Without God in our lives we are unable
to resist the evilness of this world. God
loves us all and He is waiting for us
to accept Jesus; the Son He gave for
our sins. Jesus died on the cross
for us. He shed His blood, He was
beaten and His flesh was torn. It's
not easy but it wasn't easy for God
to give His only son — Have faith in
the Lord

R. Blake

Lake Superior

My Lake of Life

My lake of life that gives the blue to the heaven's eye
The emerald green that spreads ever outward to give life its dreams

Its white caps that move ever onward
And tell me I cannot stand still

The icy blue stare that beckons me to look ever deeper in life
Its thunderous roar that lends itself to the applause for life

My lake of life ever giving and never asking
The place of refuge in the time of my turmoil

Its shimmering sun's reflection to help us dance for joy

The day of calm that gives life its rest
To renew one's quest for life

My lake of life ever giving and never asking
The shroud covered days that renew the mysteries of life

Its gloomy mournful days that gives time to remember
Those who have gone

Storm tossed anger days to teach us to clear
The anger from our souls

Moonbeams upon the water that calms the spirit
And brings forth love

Ever giving and never asking my lake of life

William E. DeRoche

Farewell to a Hero

A Silver Star a Purple Heart
decorated this man's heart
courage and bravery set him apart
from the ordinary weak at heart
we stood together side by side
all related but no close ties
To bid farewell to a father, brother, husband,
grandfather, uncle, cousin and friend
Tears were shed from all who knew
The Hero who fought in World War II
The Military Service with the 21 Gun Salute
gave Honor and Dignity to the man we all once knew
A Flag was blessed as we were too
And placed in my brother's arms, as tears of pride
and sorrow rolled from his eyes
The Red, White, and Blue flew at Half-Mast
in the distant clear crisp sky
as the Bugle Horns blew the Soldiers
Lullaby, goodbye and goodnight...

Gloria Hammond

Have You Seen The Trees

Have you ever really looked at trees
And how they decorate the world with lessons of love?
They're so different yet live together in peace.

There's no prejudice among the trees.
But fire blackened remnants and blade-cut trunks
Are sad reminders of everyone's loss.

Sturdy trunks conceal deeply stretched roots
Until age brings them above ground
To applaud a life's work.

Branches are a maze of pathways.
Fragile twigs to gnarled, arthritic outcroppings
Like the family tree of man and what he begot.

Season watchers of the world
They clock the arrival of naked branches,
Timing new buds to autumn falling in breathtaking hues.

The life cycle of a leaf is but a year
With shades of green, the envy of an artist's palate.
Oh, to know the meaning of their rustling communication!

So the world is never without beauty and hope,
The eternal Evergreen, our symbol of brighter tomorrows.

Rosa Lee Rothblatt

I Love You My Lord

I love you my Lord for helping me
You've comforted me with your love so deep
When I was down you cheered me up
Sent friends around to share your cup
Your cup of peace, your cup of love
I thank you Jesus and Father above
Thank you for friends who respect your will
Who ask for guidance and a humble hill
That grows sweet harvest of love and peace
That salutes your highness gracious king of kings
I love you my Lord for your compassionate heart
That knows I'm a child trying to play my part
I want to do good and please you my king
Thanks for your help in everything
Praise you Messiah Jesus Christ
For all the love in my heart and in my life
Please help me be gentle to all your sheep
Like all heaven above, nothing but peace
Keep me aware that this life is brief, in comparison to eternity
I love you my Lord for loving me

Ronnie Zann

My Son

   Life, once an endless tunnel filled with uncertainty,
Finally has given way to a tiny glimpse of light.
That was once another day, has now become a new day filled
with tiny achievements.
Unhappiness seemed forever, for the search of true joy was
never found. I have lived on this earth for years and never
truly began to live.
Miracles are God's creations, little miracles formed by two.
The day my little miracle was born, was the day my life began.
For we only see life from a distance when searching for its
true meaning. Now I know life's meaning, happiness and joy,
through my little eyes, that of my little boy.

Dena Roberts

White Walls

These white walls blind me
I can see nothing, so I can't find me
Such a clean, clear, cleanser, a tear
Letting me cry out my pain and fear
Oh dear God, I trust in thee
To drown out my clouds of misery
If only I could pray an honest prayer
All of my answers would soon be there
Like a good, solid, rock, you are ever standing
Always persistent, but never demanding
A soft, subtle, approach with a strong hand
You lift me up and put me back on dry land
I can rely on you to understand
That if I stray, I'll come back again
So now that I can see thru these white walls
That used to blind me
I thank you, dear God, for letting me find me

Sherri Reny

I See A Bright Light

There is a light ahead,
Could it be that I am dead?
Is that a door? Do I have the key?
Or is my mind playing tricks on me?
Is that an angel that I see?
Or is it just a reflection of me?
If I see this light, is it good or bad?
If I see this light, should I be happy or sad?
What should I do when I reach this bright light?
Should I go with the flow, or put up a fight?
The light's getting closer, I don't know what to do.
If I were a bird, I would have just flew.
But there's something about it, that makes it attractive,
I would want to go, but it's holding me captive.
As I come closer and closer to it,
I realize that it brightens just a bit.
This light is so strong, it now seems to gleam.
Never mind, it was all just a dream.

Marissa Quattrone

Thoughts On Passing

I hear voices soft and low
They whisper death
As if I didn't know

They say I can't hear, speak or see
How do they know?
They are not inside of me

I hear a voice ask
I wonder how she lived?
Would you believe,
The things you do now, I once did

Across my mind the years flash by
All the laughter, love and pain
My spouse, my children,
I had the world to gain

I feel a tear upon my cheek,
A hand upon my brow
Don't weep, I shall be with God
In just a little while

Suddenly the room is bright, choirs of angels nod
I can at last reach out, and touch the hand of God

Margaret A. Carney

July 16, 1945

You are there!
Red-Orange-Yellow-Green-Blue
  Indigo and violet.
The atmosphere rent asunder,
billowing vaporous clouds
and the sound shock waves like rolling thunder.
The atoms releasing their pent-up energy.
The basic elements turned to grassy obsidian
or jelly like and spongy.
  You were there!

Nile B. Norton

It's Just A Dream

I love to feel the wind
Blowing through my hair
Riding my pony through the grass
Without cities in my way
But after all, it's just a dream.

In the saddle sitting straight
The cattle right ahead
Chasing them to a corral
To brand the lively calves
But after all, it's just a dream.

Nervously in the arena, standing patiently
I watched the judge pacing to and fro
He stopped and looked very solemn
And on my horse he pins a blue
But after all, it's just a dream.

Chelsey Honcharoff

My Little Chance

You, little Jacob, are my chance to change the world,
  to do away with the prejudices, the lies, the fear,
  the hate, to do away with all the negative things
  your father has grown up with, the things he's
  come to accept as life
You're my chance to create something beautiful,
  something better, something more majestic than
  any other the world has seen
You're my chance to take an empty mind, to open it
  up, and fill it with all the wonderful things:
  Love, unity, beauty, truth
You, little Jacob, are my chance to try again
And if I promise not to try to relive my life through
  you, will you, little Jacob, promise to always
  call me daddy?

C. Dennis Moore

When the One You Love

When the one you love is far away,
You must be strong, you must not stray
Believe in your love, for those feelings are strong.
And they will stay with you your whole life long.

When you love someone, you give them your heart,
And nothing at all can keep you apart
The person you love becomes a part of your soul
Without them close you will never be whole.

Sometimes things are not meant to be
And sometimes this is hard to see
But if your feelings are strong and true,
Then follow your heart, there's nothing else to do

Nicole Uram

You — You — You

You came into my life
when I had given up hope
of ever finding true happiness.

You smiled that sweet smile,
let your true feelings show
and opened your heart to me.

You are sincere, honest and kind.
The intensity of your emotions takes my breath away.

When I hear your voice all my troubles begin to fade.
Serenity overtakes my soul.

When your arms are around me
our bond becomes stronger still.
I love being close to you.

Your lips treat me to soft kisses,
your eyes tell me of your passion,
your hands with their gentle caress.

Our bodies together are perfectly matched.
Who knew what we would discover once we began to explore?

All our sensations are exceptional, seemingly like no other.
How can this be, I wonder?

Patricia B. Guhse

Untitled

When I said I love you, I meant it from the start.
When I say I love you, I mean it from the heart.
I say it to you with intentions so true,
that if I couldn't say it, my heart would turn blue.

When I say I love you, it's because of your touch.
When I say I love you, I mean it so much.
When I say I love you, it's because of your kiss.
If I couldn't say I love you, it's something I would miss.

When you say I love you, do you mean it from the start?
When you say I love you, do you mean it form the heart?
When you say it to me, do you mean it so true?
If you couldn't say it, would your heart turn blue?

I say I love you, because I don't want to lie.
How can I not love you, when I look in your eyes?
I'll say I love you until the day that you die,
but it would hurt much more if you ever said goodbye.

Shanna Cheresnowski

Lost Without You Near

Walking by myself through a land where I cannot be found,

I try to call your name but my heart will not make a sound.

I am lost without your passionate love to guide me,
My eyes are shut by the silence of my heart forbidding me to see.

I feel the rain upon my face, so I run blindly as I am
caught by the hands of fear.

For the silence of my heart and the blindness of my
sight, the rain is too loud so now I cannot hear.

Please come and save me from this dark and dreadful place....

Guide me by the light of your love so I will never be
lost again to feel the rain upon my face.

Jahson Soberanis

If It Were In My Power

If it were only in my power, I'd give these things to you,
To keep you happy always and to cheer you when you're blue:
I'd gather up the rainbow after every rain
And capture all its beauty just for your domain.
I'd have the birds sing gaily, while stormy clouds on high
Would disappear, and fleecy clouds would fill a deep blue sky.
I'd teach each star that twinkles to make a silent plea
So every time they winked at you, you would think of me.
If it were only in my power, I'd wish for you each day
That all your worries, ills and fears would simply go away.
I'd grant you fame and fortune, love and peace of mind;
And all the things your heart desires, I'd see that you would find.
I'd hum a lovely waltz by Strauss or sing a merry tune;
Each night, outside your window, I would hang a big, full moon.
I'd fill your days with sunshine, - every precious hour;
I'd make your prayers and dreams come true, - if it were in my power!
But, I am merely mortal; and, thus, it isn't odd
That miracles and magic are best left up to God.
The one thing I can give you, you've had right from the start; -
You have my greatest, deepest love; - you have faithful heart!

Marian Small Tseng

Mom . . . . I Love You Anyway

A broken heart,
A broken home,
No one place to call my own.

So I leave,
A smile on your face.
No more troubles you have to take.
You say I've found a better place.

This feeling that I behold I can't explain,
I feel anger, I feel pain.
But my love for you will never change.

So here we stand, eye to eye,
As we say our final "Good-Bye"
No hug gave, only one tear shed.
I say "I Love You" as I turn and walk away

Mom, don't you understand . . .

I Love You Anyway!

Kimberly L. Slade

Goddess

Leashing out with raging fear,
For a grasp of that evil air
Which has called me here, to the Goddess's lair.
Knelt down on wooden tile,
Looking at the Golden Idol,
From a false tear, to a frantic Prayer,
I wished myself another grasp of air.
There I layed, on the ground,
Without even a single sound,
My soul so flawed, I felt the evil claw,
As I looked up...
Through the window the sunlight
Poured in upon my face, it took me
Past universe, to this special place, into a
World oh so fine, She...
She answered my call with a kiss
And a taste of wine...Smell of a
Rose was in her long, beautiful hair, as she
Caressed my body, I felt the presence of
A different lair...A Goddess.

Zach Maker

My Dream of Love

For reasons which
I cannot say
I look at you
In a different way

I see a smile
Which brings a light
That shines on you
Throughout the night

And in the day when the sky is blue
I sit and dream of being with you

I think of love and being so kind
And what it would be like if you were mine

We'd run through the rain and walk on the beach
With the ground below us
And the stars in our reach

Our life would be happy exciting and new
Our love would grow stronger
With everything that we'd do

I realized your beauty right from the start
The only place for you is deep in my heart

Thomas Belfiore

My Fairy Tale

He came into my life on New Year's Eve,
I brought the New Year in, clinging to his sleeve.
We danced all night and it was so delightful,
When it was over, his kiss was unforgettable.

For the next 33 days, we talked almost every night,
I even made sure I kept the phone in sight.
We discussed everything from money to matrimony,
He even said he liked everything about me.

It had been so long since I shared my love,
I thought I was being blessed from above.
I though I was making all the right moves,
I never thought that I would lose.

An unexpected visit was a night full of passion,
and I knew this incidence was quite out of fashion.
Afterwards, everything changed for the worse,
It was something in the form of a curse.

He said that I would never forget him,
He left out why, cause now I'm out on a limb.
I just couldn't believe this man would make me blue,
Everyone kept telling me, he was "Too good to be true."

Kathleen M. Harvey

Love Is Water

It flows gently, smoothly reaching from its source into
greater and more expansive currents. Always seeking, searching
to unite, mingle and combine its parts with
others; to increase itself by adding to that which it takes
into its being. In the purest of form,
it is the essence of life; sought after, thirsted for,
desired above all else. It is the necessity;
the truth of basal need without which
there is only dust. So difficult to discover
it may require a lifetime to unearth a single source.
It's purity so rare that many assume it is beyond discovery.
But those who seek and persevere drink to their life.
Tainted, polluted by human waste, it is
death to the needy. A subtle poison masked as
curative that drains the life from the unwitting.
So sublime a difference can be that poisoned
tastes sweeter than pure and becomes more desirable
to the searching.
And they drink to their death.

Jeff McConnell

The Number Parade

1,2,3,4, Numbers singing at my door,
At my window, at my chair,
Numbers marching everywhere,

5,6,7,8, Numbers dancing past my gate,
Numbers marching down Main Street,
Hear the music, hear the beat,

9,10,11,12, Numbers singing on the shelf,
Numbers dancing on my paper,
Numbers jumping on the stapler,

13,14,15,16, Numbers on the movie screen,
Pretending to be movie stars,
Then they went out to drive a car,

17,18,19,20, Numbers eating honey,
Numbers have had their keep,
Now, it is time to sleep.

Jessica Cohn

Maiden Out of Eden

My love, you are beautiful as early dawn
The setting sun in days gone
With ebony eyes the flames of burning coals
Consuming the mortal soul
The landscape of Venice
At the time twilight is setting
Summer sleeping in the wake of autumn
Sheba looking in the eyes of Solomon
Lost in the fields of cotton
love become the deep waters of Jordan
Cherubs in a rose garden
flowers gotten from angels
Mortals dreaming about Paradise
Like flowing honey your kisses are sweet
Touching the heart like a distance breeze
Eve in the shadow of the morning
As mortals touch the rose blossom
Rain falling over heaven
A casualty to the memories I remember
Lost in the tale of loving her forever.

Odies Garcia

The Backdoor

To tell you something about my life,
is to tell you everything.
Your age is a countdown of your life
to show the little you accomplished.

A mystery, is to find what no one knows,
years spent to prove something that can't
be proved.

For searching, is the key to much more.
Finding the backdoor, that opens up to
show wondrous beliefs.

For what we know to be there,
is something we don't need to prove.

So why does a known hero, have to prove
her courage?
To tell you I'm a hero who's scared deep down.
Would I still be outside through that backdoor?

Or would I still be searching for that mystery?

Stephanie Dallman

Tree of Inspiration

A twisted trunk spirals up
from the rain saturated, leaf blanketed ground.
Branches out like desperate arms
reaching into the night,
never to be found
Greener to me now than ever before,
leaves hang with picturesque delight,
dancing with a mystical beauty
on the breeze ever so slight.

Meghan Elizabeth Morean

The First Blush of Summer

After the rains of April and the loveliness of May
I rejoice at the first blush of Summer
When all nature is at play
Trees are covered with leaves and blossoms
Fields are golden with growing hay
Brooks are beckoning to the anglers
To cast their lines today
Barefoot children are freely running
Laughter echoes across the plain
Parents are happily tending their gardens in bloom again.

Gloria G. Breahaut

Winter Rain

The thin light beats feeble wings
against rain as the slow pace
of winter marks the shrunken day.

This is when days hoard their shortened
span. This is when I think of cold
backwaters of goodbye before spring

breaks the frozen gray.
And I've not traveled far from when
my father held my hand

and pointed starward through
December's weight, saying, look
look, light that was a million

years ago still breaks through —
and will again.

Margie Davidson

Growing Up

You've always been there for me, for as long as I can remember.
You were my Tooth Fairy, my Easter Bunny, my Santa Claus and
You have always been my Guardian Angel.

You gave me life,
You gave me your undivided attention and
You gave me your unconditional love.

You taught me right from wrong,
You taught me kindness, consideration and persistence.
You enriched my life with all that you taught me.

You endured my teen years and we made it to graduation.
You stood by me at the alter.
You saw me through my divorce, my tonsillectomy and then
You encouraged me to pursue a career,
You endured my move to Massachusetts,
a year of college, another graduation, and
You stood by me at the alter, once again.

As the days, months and years go by,
I'm not afraid of what the future holds because I know
You and your spirit will be there with me.

You're not only my Mom, You're my Best Friend. And I love you
dearly.

Leann T. Ouellette

Untitled

Spring in summer more in making
beautiful flower begin.
Snow on the window so wonderful in bright
what a dream you will have tonight.
Stars you see tonight pray to God
for a wonderful life.
Close your eye in see what you will like
this world to be. As sweet as honey as nice pie
would that be a wonderful life.
Moon shine over the world at night
look out an' see the beautiful sight.
I "sing a song with joy" in fun
that everybody be happy at home.
Rain fall on trees. Birds sing a sweet
song to you in me. I "turn to see the birds that
sing's specialty this song for you in me.
A friend is like a breath fresh air.
when you are in need thy are always there.
Don't look far thy always there.
Just take some time in show them you care.

Rosie Pullen

Spiraling

The separations that come with life, short lived as we make them —
some temporary, all flexible as we acknowledge our limitations
or remove the limits to the boundless creatures that we truly are,
But so unaware, so trapped like a creature without the intelligence
or ability to free ourselves, yet in acknowledging our God-self,
that endless spirit that resides in us, we could easily be free,
creative, flexible and flowing in the truth, peace and love that
ever exists. Whether we acknowledge or not, it exists. Tapping
in is heaven, staying within, a miracle of pure source —
omniscience — consciously aware — in the fullness of the All —
We spin and we turn, crumble and fall, laugh and cry — wonder why,
Hell, it had to be for me to see it, had to be to set me free.

Spiraling — so very in control.

Carmela Taglialavore

Woman

Woman,
"Ah!" I exclaimed upon seeing woman
"and truly," said, I "a remarkable creature she,
beneath trappings of flesh, of finery
revealed to me, made manifest you
soul of woman.
Like unto a sea, boundless, measureless
I man, know not your depths."
I am seeking,
eyes met
I found
open was the window to your soul;
I stole in — searched and saw,
'Twas but a fleeting moment
but I'll be back
intrigued — further I'm compelled to explore,
you,
woman
such a magnificent creature
tell me, how can man help but adore.

Keith Michael Martin Agard

Untitled

I looked to you for love, I received indifference. A cold wind
blew through me and I knew to forget.

Antoinette Pontecorvo

My Enchanting One

Cherished is he
Heart made of gold
Romantic in his endeavors
Yes, he is the one.

Stay with me tonight
Together hereafter
Always be mine
Love is in the air.

Honorable is he
Exceptional disposition
A life saver at best
Ravish me with your passion
Deliver unto me your most heartfelt desires.

Shannon J. Pruitt

Untitled

It was on a birthday it did occur,
One second we were talking, everything a blur,
and called out, no answer, I cried and I cried,
This wasn't supposed to be this way,
This is no way to die,

Since then, no death did happen,
But conditions seem bleak
To lie there, every motion, a reaction,
Not a word, unable to speak.

Weeks into months with no glimmer of hope,
With the grace of God and the fervor of man she spoke,
Piece by piece all barriers were taken down,
The most glorious of smiles had over taken her frown.

John E. Cleary

The End

I heard him call my name again.
   The voice of the Invisible man.
But when I looked all I saw was
   blue sky and green land.
He said the same as always,
   to follow him afar.
"Where to," I asked,
   and he painted to the car.
I climbed in and let him drive,
   white staring at the sky.
He drove me to the sea and said,
   "You could end it all so easily."
I listened to his wisdom and jumped in.
   Catching a fleeting glance of the stranger,
I started my trip to the holy Kingdom.

Kristen Smith

Death

Knowing death is knowing pain,
pain is knowing sorrow,
sorrow can really hurt,
when you know there'll be no tomorrow

Death will leave an emptiness in your heart,
that could never be replaced.
Death will leave your soul cold,
and put depression on your face.

So dear, child please don't cry,
wipe those tears from your eye.
Listen child, forget me not,
forgive me for leaving you, it's not my fault.

Leeda Barreau

Possessions of Husband and Wife

Husbands have many dear possessions
   That they would neither trade nor sell,
Accumulated while walking the paths of life
   Even possessing secrets he would never tell.
Some would say a wife isn't a possession,
   Thinking it sounds like a trophy or souvenir.
To me, my wife is the dearest one I have
   Equal, no other could come half as near.
A wife has many cherished possessions,
   Many more possibly than he.
To my wife, I hope I'm the most prized one;
   That is my ardent and hopeful plea.

I have a wife that is lonely
   And her possessions secrets of love so true
Those are shared possessions
   To be enjoyed by only those two
And if each will make it a practice
   And faithful abide by this
Their possessions will always be sacred
   And their life perfect, nothing amiss.

   Gordon V. Day

River

I am strong as well as long, spiraling
Through communities of which are
connected to my soul. My body provides
nourishment to all.

My flow liquidates the thirst of mouths,
wanting to feel the intangibles of my
timeless aromas. Kids and adults lay by my
side fantasizing great lore's!

River so unique in style, brash, bold and
often wild.

   Julian W. Carroll

A Wave . . . .

His smile, the tho't of the instantaneous mingling of two souls, were
once like a wave within me . . .

A wave that began as a tiny ripple in the deep recesses of my inner
being, growing ever more intense with each rush . . . .

Until it crashed fiercely to the shore, unleashed and uninhibited,
erupting . . . .

As a smile on my own lips, a smile to shame the splendor of the sun . . .
As a light in my eyes, a light to mirror the magic of the moon.

No longer visible to the human eye, the smile, the light, are silent
now, held hostage by a merciless heart, denying release from the
fathomless pit.

   Lee Jones

Never Be A Success: It May End In Failure

Never carve a turkey before it truly dies,
It agonizes the meat and attracts a tacky class of flies;
Never strike a bargain without sealing of a tomb,
Contract law is delicate and fraught with frequent doom;
Never kiss a maiden whose lips are fixed in frowns,
No ups are brought by truculence, rather mostly ugly downs.
Never love your neighbor unless your neighbor is your boss,
Receiving outweighs giving and unpaid love's a loss

   David E. Allen Jr.

Untitled

Distance closes, too fast to follow
with clarity
and coherence due to the subject.
Daring to whisper "are you with me?"
and in truth, how could you be
except in clarity, charitably.
Ephemeral, you mercurial, choose
to be somewhere I cannot reach you...
are you with me?
Speaking to thick air, choking on the
words you should have heard and the
ashes of what's leftover.
Could I have changed what was never meant to be?

Wrap your arms around water, and it's me.
Kiss the snowflakes and I'll feel it.
Hope emerges from the char and bone because the heart of me
is forever.

   Roseann J. Gruley

Only You

Night is coming again
There is moon in the sky
And again it's so quiet
And I'm lonely, like night . . .

I am turning off light . . .
I am looking at clock . . .
Very soon it's midnight
But not you . . . (it's just doom . . .)

I am jamming my pain with the music in dark
I just want to make steps
Toward you, like in past...

I am taking this sheet and I write stupid things . . .
And again it's the night
And I want just to cry . . .

Oh, I love all this nights
And I wonder with dark . . .
Oh, I love only you, and I want you . . .
You are not my enemy anymore — you are not!

And I want like before and again just with you
And I want like in past. And again, only you.

   Golyshev Tatiana

Ode To A Small Town

You ask us why we like this town.
We answer with a thoughtful frown:
"A lot of things made into one composite whole."

The friendly nods when passing on the street.
The casual way a transaction's made complete.
The measured eye of neighbor who, sizing up our nature,
Accepts with trust and tolerance our human stature.
The interest of known, unknown, in all our undertakings.
The criticism, sniping, usually in the open.

In spring, the smell of fresh-plowed fields
Blown in to town on mountain breeze.
The lowing of the cattle turned out to pasture.
The light green of newly wakened trees.
The town clock striking out the hour.
The neighbor's dog a-barking.
Deep-rooted as this town is,
So are our emotions,
Stemming from hidden springs
Fed by ancestral devotion.

   Mary Elizabeth Gayman

139

The Pleasures of a Rose

Red velvet cheeks blush with love and kindness. A gentle
face for a tender thought.
Outstretched arms willing to reach out, in times one
might have forgotten.
A body slender, yet satisfying to the eye is best when it
is received as a surprise.
Beginning as a seed it blossoms, blooms and develops into
maturity
Its growth invites beauty, emotions like love with faith trust
and such.
It attempts the senses tickling the nose teasing the eyes
and warming the heart with a tender touch.
Like the thorns are its protection so is your knowledge
as well to shield you from the painful world.
Just as a mother adores and appreciates her newborn as it
grows, I share with you the pleasures of a rose.

Linda Mary Rose Boisvert

Obiter Dictum

Push aside and hide
in a place where there is space
forget, forgive, take a chance and relive
start anew at this time
take whatever is mine
you will always have a place in my brain
give it hard, mix it up,
try to stay insane
hate to love; love to hate
me, I like, yes can wait
scared of a relationship
possessions own
recessions loan
depression never goes away
hang a noose
make it loose
read the obituary today
hear us pray

James K. Dyson

Love

A life spent in search of love
The most treasured gift from heaven above.
More beautiful than a rainbow on a dark, stormy night.
It is the sun that drives away the gloomy clouds with its wonderful
Rays of light.
A perfect peace resides when everything else falls apart.
A violent storm that swiftly stirs even the strongest of hearts.
A feeling that cannot be denied is a feeling so many try to hide.
No reason for living if true love is gone,
But its presence is eternal happiness that stands forever strong.
It surpasses all barriers even to the point of death.
A feeling that endures past the final breath.
Love is a dragon, mighty and strong,
But is ravishing and destructive when times go wrong.
The fear of losing love keeps cowards away
But the riches in finding love gives the most valuable pay.
The tears that are shed when love suddenly leaves
Will cause even the mightiest warrior to grieve.
To recapture this height of emotion is the broken heart's goal,
Because a life without love is certain death to the soul.

Gary W. Castro

Water Fall

I love those summer thunder storms,
which just materialize.
And transform lazy afternoons,
with dark and threatening skies.

And then the clouds, as if an cue,
begin to swirl and race.
As distant days of thunder,
seem to meter-out the pace.

Once gentle breeze, now lends the trees,
as though they were but cane,
While bringing fourth to all they touch,
the cool, sweet scent of rain.

With brilliant, blinding flashes,
an awe inspiring sight.
The lightning spreads its finger,
through the heavens dark as night.

And as the tempo of quickens,
and the rains begin to fall.
One cannot help but contemplate,
the beauty of it all!

Robert A. Logrie Jr.

Those Years

Those years were the most frightening years of my life
Only one place for strength and hope
In her comforting arms
but not with him

Him
Kept the fear inside
No peace, just rage

Afraid to speak
Afraid to move
A flash of crimson
on that beautiful face

All grown up
No more sleepless nights
No more nightmares
of those years
those seven years.

Chad K. Lovell

My Aunt Joyce

Like
The spice that seasons a favorite dish,
A tune that lifts and floats like a fish.

Like
The spirit that sparks within every encounter,
Her jovial manner enlivens those around her.

Like
The scent of a bouquet that breathes so sweet,
A whisper of peace extends a firm seat.

Like
The patience of a brook running its course,
Her giving heart assures and her hugs enforce.

Like
The swan who glides and finds its way,
A triumph of success that anoints each day,

Like
The crispness of sheets for unexpected guests,
Her stature and grace within me rests.

For to meet my Aunt Joyce is like...
Opening a treasure chest!

Valerie A. Scott-Dishroom

A Whole New State

As I walk through some deep forest, crossing streams of clearly purest
Water flowing from the highest point to ever be explored;
I come across a man of simplest attire, stature, and appearance,
Who offers me his guiding service-an offer not to be ignored.

No words of conversation followed on our journey continuing downward;
Cautiously making away toward a clearing of some sorts.
The vegetation steadily thickens, and my pulse rapidly quickens
As anticipation heights to not allow me to abort.

I try to peak through tiny spaces to discover where he embraces,
A place that only nature laces; concealed to most but not himself.
This man now chooses to increase the pace, as now the moon can
    show its face;
And I run, in a chase, as my timepiece marks the twelfth.

In this unfamiliar landscape my guide succeeds to finally escape
The sights and sound that overlap my unrefined senses.
I call for him with scorched voice; his return is not his choice.
I immediately lose my poise, as I look through shattered lenses.

So in my journey I hesitate and realize it would be all too great
For this to scratch my slate, causing me to quiver.
Now at this time I mark the date; although lost, I've found a whole
    new state
In which I can now relate-to guide myself forever.

Alan T. DeBaucha

Life

Life is a beautiful thing
like the voice of a bird who can sing.
Life is a beautiful song
when you think that nothing can go wrong.
It can put a smile on your face
it is not a bitter disgrace.
Life is so wonderful to me
it makes me want to laugh out in glee.
To cry out in joyful tears
because, you are all my peers.
All are lives are so wonderful
we have to be careful to follow God's rule.
An everlasting life is forever
so love your life and live it clever.
Be sure to be a faithful follower
it will make your life a whole lot jollier.
Be careful to not let your life fall
or your life may not be long at all.
Life is the most precious thing you could ask for
be the best you can be, the love in your heart will soar.

Page Tankersley

Christmas

This is the season of peace and goodwill;
also the time when light hearts might stand still.

The giving of gifts, decorating the tree;
this beautiful world, God's wonders to see.

It seems a shame that some go without
while many have more than sufficient about!

Look for those gifts that dwell deep within
the souls of those who have nothing to spend.

It isn't the wrapping nor is it the glitter;
big or small the size doesn't matter!

If

We give from the depth of our heart
God's gift to others, now isn't that part

Of giving back God's gifts to us
and keeping Christ in Christmas!

Shirley Reynolds Goodall

Timeless Love

How does one describe the love
    that grows with passing time?
They've said it's blessed from God above
    and likened it to wine.
Whose complicated alchemy o'er one's lifetime grows.
But I have seen a mystery
    that no one else quite knows.

True love is much more like the root
    than like the fragile flower.
It grows in depth and solidness
    and gives the plant its power.
It traffics in the common soil;
    its purpose nurturance.
Without the root's most faithful toil the plant cannot enhance.

What these roots are working through
    are the memories of life.
St. Wolfgang's soft and pleasant hues, the sorrows and the strife.
As many memories together blend to make the fertile loam
Recalling them will tend to lend a solidness to home.

Paul L. Weingartner

In Retrospect

Today I am a stranger in my hometown:
I was born in nineteen twenty-four
To immigrant parents from Ukraine;
One bitter day father walked out the door
Up snowy Glenwood Avenue into oblivion!
In December at ninety-one mother died
And was cremated. Years later I brought
Ashes to a village nestled in white hills.
Truth is, in life mother asked for naught;
"I have four sons", she beamed with pride.

Teaching children was the most prolific leg
Of my life! I miss them still. For two
Years I faltered, a foreigner; my priorities
Were driven askew: Poverty, cruelty, greed
And corruption at every level rocked my faith!
In spite of hardships and frugality, to ease
Those pangs with love and toast, I did indeed.
"Let us celebrate life often while we may!"
Valery, Victor, Vera and others surely knew!
Their teacher was the last of a dying breed.

Nikolai Tarasuk

Just Out of Reach

When something is just out of reach
and for you, nobody can teach.
You want and want and search and search
you can feel the edge perch for perch.
Then it gets farther away, far afield
and you try and try until your spirit seems killed.
Finally it gets closer,
and you almost connect,
then it's nothing away but a stretch of a neck.
You stretch to your hardest until
you can feel your muscles tear,
and then you finally get your fingertips on the fine hairs.
You get excited and feel a victory breeze,
then it's snatched away with the greatest of ease.
Why all the trouble you ask for something like
this impossible task?
It's the joy and triumph at the end
When finally you do succeed and win.

Jessa Pardue

141

Her Eyes

Her eyes gently pierced through my heart
Like a surgeon's incision during a delicate operation.
How can you combat such beauty that leaves you in such
An hypnotic state?
How can a person possess so much power and passion that
With a glance you would think the unthinkable and do
The un-thought of?
When her eyes speak every word that is spoken, her lips
Need not move.
So what else is left but to kiss the lips because her eyes
Told me so.

Fredrick L. Brown

Romeo

Romeo, Romeo where for art thou?
Wait you nigh on my bed, anxious sweat on your brow?

Or is mine not the loin calling forth your desire?
Pray what striking young match has ignited your fire?

Am I yet not enough, not deemed precious or true?
Am I not made of stuff which might satisfy you?

Do you want me to bleed as you've bled in the past?
Shall I beg for your love, tote your bale like an ass?

Will you call out my name in the deep of the night?
Or will she pass your lips, Once Love's ancient requite?

What must my heart implore for to gather your favor?
Are there ghosts left to bury, parted lips left to savor?

How will you thus forget deepened wounds that won't heal?
Let me pressure the sore, feed my soul as your meal.

I will cut out my heart, serve it warm on a plate
Eat not all, just enough-gather strength, killing hate.

Art Thou true ready now for to give unto me?
Has the future with mine quelled the longing of she?

Will I ever be her? Can mine truly compete?
Tell me Romeo do, does my rose smell as sweet?

Cathryn Switzer

Ode to Toby

Toby, my tabby, will soon be ten,
To me he's the dearest that's ever been,
My spouse insists I'll say this again,
If ever I'm owned by another furry friend.

Like the lilies of the field, he neither toils nor he spins,
The way he lives is really a sin,
But his wish is mine be it great or small,
Though it costs a king's ransom, he cares not at all.

He's the rarest of gems but wouldn't fetch a dime,
Though millions were offered, he'd still be mine,
For the love he has given is far beyond measure,
So, how could I part with so rich a treasure?

His demise, I know, will bring me great grief,
For cats' span on this earth is only too brief,
But, I'll always remember his sweet, gentle ways,
And hold him close to my heart, the rest of my days.

If God has a place for cats in heaven,
I'll find them all there, many more than eleven,
It will bring me great joy and my spirits will soar,
To give each a big hug, if only once more.

Margaret E. Slauson

A Tree

When I look up into a lovely tree,
    There are so many lessons there for me.
She dances gaily with each whim of passing breeze;
    Yet, when the angry gale would drive me to my knees
She only bends a little lower; then,
    When it has passed, stands straight and tall again.

Her warm heart welcomes all who wish to nest
    Or climb
        Or rest.

She suffers the cold barrenness of winter's death,
    But slyly, in her own green April way,
She tells of resurrection, of new breath,
    And hope that will be yours and mine some day.

Whence come her strength and gentleness?
    Beneath the sod
I know her roots go deep, to drink the strength of God.

Lillian Field Dieterich

Yours Nor Mine

As the snow began to flutter around
It had no certain sound,
but it surely was cold and fine

Each tiny snowflake was neither yours nor mine
but fell right in time.

For the smoke of hickory was rolling from the
chimney, straight into the air.

And grandpa sat reared back in his chair
As the smell of fresh biscuits filled the air.

By now the snow white blanket had piled high
upon the old wood pail. But inside the ole
pot belly stove was firing hot and red.

Soon the sun came, out and the snow
flakes began to disappear, the snow which
once had piled high could not be seen
with the naked eye.
Wonder where the waters coming from that's dripping
from paws wood pile, I wonder could it have been
the snowflake which was neither yours nor mine!

Cathy Ann Dearinger

When Innocence Is Lost

So many years have passed, since I first opened my eyes;
    To the amazement this world holds, hidden truths and open lies.

I've seen death destroy the youth, without remorse or a prayer of faith,
    I've seen life fight for this world, through the eyes of my
children's ways.

What do we have when innocence is lost,
    When all our money's cannot pay the cost;
Where do we turn if we turn away from God,
    What do we have when innocence is lost.

Our dreams are more than just dreams they're the foundation of our
child's' beliefs;
    We borrow all we have from our children, and return it to them
when we leave.

What do we have when memories are forgot,
    when do we leave it to our child's thoughts;
Where do we turn without a soul to believe,
    When religion has a price, a saviour for a fee.

What do we have, when we turn away from God,
    If we don't believe in something, then it's already lost;
Where do we turn when innocence has been stole,
    When all we have left is a dream without hope.

James D. Dotson

Ode to My Father

The rain falls softly on the unplowed fields,
   awaiting the seeds that would not come.

The barnyard is silent for ponies and cattle have gone.
Abandoned are miniature sand pits made by small hands,
   with plans of future earth movers.

Fireflies pass unhindered by threats of
   "I can catch more than you."

The grass grows tall around trees of the apple orchard
   and apples fall unnoticed.

Lonely geese honk forlornly as they pass over the farm,
   there is no scurry to see their beautiful form.

The evergreens stand stately waiting to be chosen for
   the Christmas celebration that would not come.

Heavens weep for days of children, puppies, and laughter.

The farmer has gone laid to rest on the hillside
   beside a frozen stream.

And we will be poorer for it.
   Mary Jane Wheat

When I Knew You . . .

When I knew you . . .
Wasn't life about a lot fewer things.
Didn't we know all there was to know.
Our world was so different then . . . When I knew you.

When I knew you . . . Weren't our parents called adults; Didn't we
   cling
to the words of a song, our friends were our lives . . . when I knew
   you.

When I knew you . . . We didn't know the miracle of a baby; the
   essence
of a relationship; the meaning of balance and rhythm in the orchestra
   of life.

When I knew you . . .
No one told us that the ebb and flow of life like the tides

Would bring us so many challenges . . .
The triumphs, the tragedies, the blessings, the losses.

We didn't know that pleasure and pain would build our character-
When I knew you they were mere words.
And now when I see you . . . I look different, I feel different,
I know differently so many seasons have past.

On my journey in life let met stop for a moment
and look down the road I'd been, carrying with me the
memories to . . . when I knew you.
   Lezlie Ruggiero Darroch

Skeleton's Mourning

I stare into a room thats lights at one time
   would be blinding
Now it lays dusty and desolate
From the darkness can be heard
The echoes of laughter that is no longer laughed
The space within looms over me
Of illusions I so desperately needed to be real
The skeletons laugh
The curtain falls
All I have left are my screams
Within that dark room
Haunts a secret that all knew but me
The ghost of a girl that has never been born
Wandering the corridors of my brain
Her soft sweet voice lightly whispering my name
   David A. Wegman

Spring

She visits once a year. What a reunion!
She brings to life everything that she touches,
And she touches everything.

She frees the butterfly from its dark cocoon.
She paints the brown forest green.
She gathers rainbow colors and sprinkles them over
the meadows.

She frees the bear from its winter sleep.
Her warmth melts ice caps to provide running water
for forest friends.

She invites me out of the house and into the warm sunshine,
freeing me from winter coats, mufflers and heavy shoes.

She visits but once a year.
What a happy reunion!
   James Tyrone Cooper

A Time for Love

There once was a time for love, and all expectations high.
Happiness was easy to find, with no such things as lies.

But dark clouds began to form, and life began to slip.
A robot I became, controlled in someone's grip.

The sun seemed not so bright, the days turned into years.
Alone I always felt, but always hid the tears.

Now that I am free, the hill is hard to climb.
Somehow I find the courage, with no one by my side.

The strength of someone's arms, to hold me on lonely nights.
Seems something like a dream, to fade with morning light.

My heart is full of love, just lost in all the pain.
Some days I feel the courage, will just be spent in vain.

I need a hand to help me, when the hills become too high.
Some days I feel like quitting, unsure of the reasons why.

But, in life I know I'll triumph, a star to shine I'll be.
If I can only make it, through the nights...
With no one holding me.
   Suzanne Strand

Who Are We To Forget Today?

Two souls meet miles apart, not letting distance keep you from
the true meaning of what you've found. Drawn by a feeling we all
know but can't explain. Passion's endless, seeking deeper
ground, if time stood still that's where we should be tomorrow.
Beneath you is the surface which has no name but darkens
destiny. Challenge the heart to find new horizons, follow the
desert breeze, glisten in the shadows of inhibition, mystery will
find its answer. Don't look to yesterday for fear of what's
behind you runs ramped. Enemies of the mind are things left
unsaid, only you can make today an endless tomorrow. A
newly fallen snow that's cold to the touch but captures your
every emotion, uplifting spirit. What's yet to be found is fathoms
away in a raindrop of wonder. Imaginable is the path that's
ahead, although empty now . . . . Who are we to forget today?

When faith engulfs your every motion only steps of inner peace
will allow you to meet on that plateau of light, encompassed by
the unexplainable. The feeling that makes rain fall without
clouds and moon beams warm the ocean. Climb the mountain
one rock at a time, a hand reaches down to pull you to the top,
notice every brook, gaze at every tree, listen to every sound.
Let me close my eyes, never letting go of this one moment.
Division of the soul finds no option, create a memory for a
fulfillment in tomorrow. Hold tight the reigns of change, find
warmth of compassion. Hidden in a chasm of doubt is a weak
direction to lead: faces of strangers share nothing. Truly in the
eyes of the mind is the hope of undiscovered dreams, seeking
that one vow sealed with a kiss . . . Who are we to forget today?
   Brian T. Dodd

And With His Stripes

Isaiah says...and with his stripes we are healed.
I am truly a witness that these words are so real.
I had a very high fever, a coma, and same seizures.
I was given much medicine at the doctor's leisure.
I was operated on to find meningitis of spine and brain.
My brain shifted to one side of my head, which wasn't my gain.
I lost normal temperature, was placed on a heating pad.
This time for my family and friends was very, very sad.
Bacteria grew, I had to have surgery once again.
Doctors put shunt in my skull so the fluid would drain.
This made me deaf, blind and paralyzed on one side.
The doctors kept me a few more weeks, and they thought I
    should've died.
My parents took me home because the doctors could do no more.
Four months later God healed me, he had something in store.
Today, I love Jesus because of the miracles he works.
He's able to give anyone a testimony and take away the hurt.
I am a living witness that Jesus is a healer today.
By His stripes, my Jesus, has made, for all, a way.

Vanessa Joy Dixon

Tree Song

Trapping 'n' clanging 'n' rustling in the wind,
The leaves begin with percussion.
The strings are heard among the eaves
As crickets play their violin wings.
Then as breeze tinkles in and out
Comes a harp going up scale and down.
Trumpet's fanfare is hard to hear,
For 'tis light shining far and near.
Singing is the crowning glory, since songbirds have joyful stories.

That the end, oh, not at all 'cause night's interlude is sweet and long.
For now the trumpets have all died down
And our opera singers discarded their crowns.
So here now comes another sound as light 'n' airy as the clouds.
The twinkle, twinkle of the little stars now bring bells 'n' chimes
Played for us and Mars.

It changes now this song among leaves
From day to day it changes
But I hear it always in perfect harmony.

Melissa Goodrich

They're With Us . . .

They're with us,
    Too short a time, seems to me,
Our dogs, cats, horses,
    Or whatever they may be.

Some folks, they tell me,
    In animals, no souls are present.
But I know, they love us as we do them,
    Just as God meant it.

We share with them, and they with us,
    They make us laugh, then drive us mad,
Seems they're with us when we need them,
    Sharing lives together, times happy and sad.

As a matter of fact,
    Cranky cuss I can be,
From some people I've seen,
    It's a dog, cat, or horse, for me.

And when their time comes,
    Their bodies gone, spirits arisen I trust,
In our minds, but more, in our hearts,
    . . . They're with us.

Norman Wilkerson

Untitled

Love; like a flower bursting forth in the spring.
Sparkling with promise, with beauty that sings—
Alas, barren soil...a wasteland of pain.
It cries out for care...but cries out in vain.
Wither it must and turn into dust.
How sad it must die,
All in the wink of an eye.

Edward H. Croul

The Spirit...

God is good, God is real
God is far, God is near
God is one, you will see
He is one, so are we
We are one with the unseen
and with all things we do see
He is God
Who are we?
A Jew, Muslim or Christian they call me
Look beyond my robe, suit, and hijab too
Look deep...deep within me
Look, what do you really see?
Is it you? Is it me?
Who do you really see?
Bible, Qur'an, Torah they taught me
It is God I wish to see
Give me a book and I will see
What he wants me to see
Not what you want me to see
I am the spirit, and I am free...free...free

Hanan S. Matari

Just Resting My Eyes

I am no longer sick dear "I am Just Resting My Eyes."
I have gone on to be where the sun always shines.
There are no more sorrows or tears or deep sighs.
Yes, my dear daughter, "I am Just Resting My Eyes."
My body no longer will give me deep pain, the worlds
trying troubles will no longer rein.
So smile when you think of me, do not sit and cry.
And know my dear daughter "I am Just Resting My Eyes."

Leona R. Kahl

You Came Into My Life Unexpectedly

You came into my life unexpectedly,
And everything took time for the better,
Your warm eyes, your laugh,
The sincere way you speak,
And the kindness you showed me,
All became a part of my life because you came into my life
unexpectedly.

As you unfolded yourself to me,
I discovered more beauty,
I have never seen more beauty before,
Nor have I felt more gentleness in one person without knowing it,
You were slowly making a place for yourself in my heart,
And I miss you so much because you came into my life unexpectedly.

We fell in love so suddenly,
You taught me how to love again,
When I was alone in my lonely world,
You came into my life Unexpectedly.
We became the best of friends,
And our relationship is unique,
I love you just because you are you.

You came into my life Unexpectedly.

Karon Evette LeBlanc

The Insomniac's Lament

O wretched night that robbeth me
of blessed sleep and rest,
how well acquainted have I become
with all your tiresome ways and
best reminders of blunders made
on "less than happy" days that
I would feign forget.
How dare you treat me so!

Why cannot I ponder on some meager
works of wonder I have done, or
take a few small pleasures that from the
memory of forgotten treasures that
are also part of living, allowing
me some pride?
But no, my soul requires more giving!

Perhaps I'll read and contemplate the words
of One who made the lovely sky and birds;
let go of petty things long out of sight;
remember to thank my God for loving me;
and then turn out the light.

Jean Allen

The Long Road

He stands so tall and strong,
    confident that only his views are right
    and sure that all others are wrong.
Above me he so horribly screams,
    blind that as society changes,
    so to must change our dreams.
I speak, but he will not hear,
    or else he scorns, and he insults,
    and I rage and cry across the years.

Time passes, a friend draws near.
The only word that must be said
is her hand upon my shoulder.

He stands by his views, he will not listen,
    and I will not contradict him;
For now I stand more tall and proud,
    because I have learned
    that though our views can not be reconciled,
    they both can be good and true;
Not for each other,
but for ourselves.

David Zucker

Grandma's Buttons

Everything that had no use Grandma kept in her rec room.
There, a world unlike any other unfolded in the gloom . . .
Musty dresses, albums nobody recalled, old patterns and well worn
    shoes,
Boxes of books, a floor lamp, dolls my mother had once abused.
I was a trespasser here, as I ventured inside
To explore my history, sometimes to hide.
Oliver Twist and Annie were gracious hosts to me.
Yet nothing could beat the jars of buttons and miscellany.
Colored buttons like gemstones, even in the dim light . . .
Flowers and patterns among the various delights.
Other treasures thrown within with little thought, I'm sure,
Captured my attention with their innocent allure.
Today I keep a jar with treasures of my own . . .
Colored marbles, antique coins, things I've surely outgrown.
A button here, a necklace there, it filled quickly to the brim...
The treasures whispering their stories for those who can hear them
    within.

Kathy Bourassa

Brave Black

Black is the only one brave enough to explore the darkness
It floods in with blinking eyes
Feeling its way to the deepest crevices
It is free until sunrise

The owl of the spectrum disappears
As the first rays of sunlight reach over the sky
The morning greets us
The black says good-bye

The sun's arms expand to forever
Forcing the blackness
Inside and down, away from the world
The sun's job is to suppress

Kay

Praise

You helped me through both thick and thin.
When things were rough, you said I can win.
When I was depressed you comforted me so.
You never went far from me
when I let you go.
You gave me my life back . . .
and the ones I love too.
I make a vow at this moment . . .
"I'll never leave you"
Please hold my hand and lead me the way
never lead me to wander or ever go astray.
My heart is yours God;
my heart not my own.
All the chances I've taken, all the chances I've blown.
But that's all changed now . . .
Now, Thanks to you.
The sky is much clearer,
the sun will shine through.

Bonnie Schor

Gentle Heart Jaded

Exist in the Past. Live a Present War of compromise.
Grasp a reason to hold on . . .
the Hollow Ache of love bygone.

Future Dreams begin to fade. Tomorrow's wish a desperate hope —
you've joined the ranks of "Living Dead"
welcome to Their humble abode.

Broken Heart. Foolish pride. His passion should be suspect.
Often Fatal Ties that bind
strangle souls . . . Chains that bind.

End the quiet suffering. Tender eyes betray
Pain of lost innocence, gentle heart gone astray.

Recapture Magic once abandoned. Stoic armor unfit disguise.
"Lonesome Heart? . . . " the child beckons.
Her Old Soul, Your gentle guide.

Discover Journey's path unknown. Trust Love's light . . .
answer shown: Release the Anger. Face your Fear.
    Break a past of Silent Tears.

Push on for Wisdom. Search for Truth. Feel Our space in time.
the 'Self' you must Trust, Loves you first old man.
Find your way Home on my last borrowed dime.

Karen L. Grewar

I Have Proof There's A God

He carried my cross high up on Calvary,
He stretched out his arms
and gave His life for me,
the perfect gift that He gave
came from heaven to my soul.

I have proof, there is proof
in this book that I hold.

He sent me a comforter
so that I won't be alone.
He went to prepare a place
that I can call my home.
The love my God has for me
mortal man can't understand.

I have proof, there is proof
by this book in my hand.

I see His face in the sunshine,
feel His presence by the wind.
I hear His voice through the raindrops,
He said, child I'll be back again.
I have proof there is proof there is a God.

Janet Russell

The Changing of Climates

It must be strange to be a somebody
  to be a public man
For I've been rejected by my own kind
  rejected from the clan

  It is alright, or I suppose
    that it all works out so even
  for I have found another kind
    that listens to my dreams

  The wind that once had blown so strong
    has currently died down
  but now I've found the beauty of clouds
    and now am where I belong

  Now as you see, I've lost the rain
    and the wind in all
  I will wait and wait and wait
    for the next oblivious fall

  For the time has come
    for my descent
      all together, one is all.

Bret Collazzi

Old Dog

To Suzie, the red Doberman
I lie in the cool of the big oak tree,
Arrayed with flowers bright,
And rest my dog years at your feet,
In spring's warm sunny light.

Many a day and many's the night
I've stayed close by your side,
My keen ears ever listening,
My eyes on every sight.

And now as I come to my life's sweet end,
I stay close by your feet,
For you were the love of my life, dear one,
And now my rest is sweet.

In the days to come as I soon must leave
The home I've loved and honored,
I'll wait for you in sweet repose
Until God calls you home.

Judy T. Land

Reality

If a dream holds a certain state of reality, and our future holds a
certain state of our dreams, what would happen if there was no
separation of the two. Then could our dreams not become our future,
which would cause our reality to become a dream, causing one to live
in a dream. Our lives are not meant to be spent dreaming. So we must
separate our dreams, reality and future. But with out a dream, how
can our future become a reality.

Bobby Freeman

Division Rendezvous On 476B At Withlacoochee

You ask me why on this bench I sit with silent solace. When no noise
or movement seems to disturb my state of trance. As I gaze across at
white marble stones, remembering a name or face I once knew by chance.
There is only one name and one face I see. It's the face and name of camaraderie.
All are one on this hallowed ground, regardless how many times your
eye searches around. Ten or more each day they come to rendezvous.
Slowly building our Division back to strength, and wait for you. Not
one shall be left or missing in action you see. this Eternal Division
belongs to God not man, nor nation or any municipality.

The wounds of flesh or missing limbs and blinded eye, for some may
partially heal, and a grateful nation a medal will give. But the
wounds of the spirit and a shattered heart does eternal damage to the
soul, and almost tears it apart. No medal for this shall ever be
given. It's only through God can healing be complete and the soul be
set free and set apart, and continue to be forgiven. By God's cadence
we shall march again. Onward and upward to the Promised Land.

No more screaming the battle cry. No more death or painful cry.
No more prosthesis or blinded eye. No more limp in our walk again.

Thank you God for this hallowed ground on 476B at Withlacoochee.
Our Eternal Commander you shall always be.

Billy J. York

Evening Shade

When the sun tip toes in the dusk and hides behind the trees...I
wanted to be your evening shade.

After the journey of a long day in the wilderness of life, there
in a distant pasture, beneath the large heart of an oak tree lies an
evening shade.

Gentle and strangely warm the seeming perfect shade appears
refreshing to the oncoming wanderer.

The toll the day had taken on the traveler seem to tumble to the
ground as the evening shade creeps over him.

Soothed, calmed and relaxed, the wanderer is mesmerized by the
beauty and the simplicity of the evening shade.

Thrilled to be found and appreciated by the wanderer, the evening
shade breaths a gentle breeze over the weary body of the wanderer,
caressing his soul with understanding and cradles his heart with peace.

Suddenly ghosts of the day haunt the wanderer and he is forced back
into his reality.
Finding rest, comfort and the energy to go on, the
wanderer bids farewell by smothering the grass under his feet as he leaves.

The evening shade has loved and lost once more. Hoping this
wanderer would stay, but knowing he wouldn't. The evening shade
retreats back into the heart of the oak tree.

Not celestial or breath taking (too plain, too ordinary) just real
shade, waiting for the evening of the next day.

Nzingha Nandi Gaines

Our Love Will Not Be Broken

In ninety three and ninety four, I thought our relationship was lost
forever more...But loneliness in Cuba was kind of hard, and I was
still in your address book so, you sent me a card...
I read the card and thought with glee, "is this a second chance for me?"
I knew my silence had to break, an it was time for me to face my mistake
because, this man's love I did once forsake.
I poured out my heart without delay and our emotions traveled on an
ink and paper relay.
I Prayed and prayed in ninety five, that he would not think that I was
full of five, that he would give my letters more than just a glance
and seriously consider giving "us" another chance.

After a while we came to realize that a little love did survive, and
we started to build, thrive and forget what happened in that awful little dive.

Now all words have been spoken and I know for certain, that "our love
will not be broken."

Lisa Hamilton

Untitled

I want you to touch me soul to soul and feel my pain as well as my joy.
I am hungry for you, starved for a hand to hold, needing to feel
loved, important, and capable.
I need the strength of your arms to hold me when I begin to weaken,
and sometimes fall.
I've survived barren, empty, and longing.
My passion for life has somehow withered and died.
I want to be reborn.
I feel a sadness akin to despair, and remember hope as a loving four
Letter word I learned in innocence and youth.
Wanton and lonely, I journey through us, wondering what would happen if
I extend my hand to you, our fingers intertwined, my mouth thirsting
and dry, ready for you to awaken my senses with a kiss of life.
I want your skin to touch my face tenderly and softly.
I want you to look into my eyes and be lost in the passion of who we
were, and see who we have become.
I want you to replace the deadness with a new sense of seeing and believing.
I want your touch, the sensation of your fingertips, your mouth,
your strong muscular arms to electrify my body, pulsate beyond
my spirit, and love me back to life.

Kathryn Flatley

What I Saw Reflected In the Glass

Looking in the glass I saw a reflection, a reflection of how one used to be.
A soul once rejoiceful, now tattered and torn like flower after a storm.
Hands which carefully picked apart evidence of life in the sand,
relics of how the west was won, were now weak, limp, and unseeking.
Legs once bronze, which travelled miles in desert and blazing sun
capturing all of life, were all bundled up, their strength
trickling away like a stream in a meadow.
Eyes once filled with wisdom and power, once gleaming with
determination of a tiger, only purred softly in sweet surrender,
toying with the idea of a resolution to his pain.
The blackness in his body, the cancer, quickly crept into his
soul stealing all willfulness and strength, slowly deteriorating
his body leaving a shell of what used to be.
Yet underlying this shadow of despair there was a tiny light that
kept burning, it was that light of hope that stayed forever lit
even after he shut his eyes for the last time.

Amity Overall

Who Am I

I am a great woman.
But I too, like others, don't know myself.

I am the beauty
that makes a child smile

I am the joy that brings
peace to the heart

I am the breath
that someone else gave.

I am an angel
that only one man sees.

I am His.

Loumertistene Howell

Fatal Addiction

You're so undependable because
    of that fatal addiction

        It runs your life not
            you running its

You follow it from place to place
        No matter where it may go
            because you love it so

You pack it, you role it, you light it
            and then you smoke it

        You may be asking what this is

Don't guess on it let me tell
    of the wonderful addiction
that will drive you to hell
            It's called

Dope, weed, grass, marijuana
    whatever you wish

It will still drive you into a ditch
        that you dug up yourself

        Now how do you like your life in Hell?

Remember that you put yourself there!

Penni C. M. Anifer

Human

Of the many, many things,
I will never come
to understand,
I'm sure to mine good reason
from the doubt.

Within my heart, into your eyes,
along the question
sought between demise,
to live within the season,
or without.

Of the many, many things,
I am soon to come
to realize,
I'd not forsake your candor
to desire.

For each breath to fill your starving cries,
the dance within
your teary eyes,
I know you know a lover,
from a liar.

Kevin Sweet

Love Is Forever

You always were my only one,
  I knew it from the start;
You were eight and I was ten, when
  I gave to you my heart;

Our families called it "Puppy Love",
  two kids that were at play;
But we knew it was more than that,
  it grew stronger every day;

Then one day at the "Flower Mart,"
  I proclaimed my love for you;
The most beautiful girl in a black fedora,
  black coat and matching shoes;

I gave you a rose, we went separate ways
  many years we were apart;
Then one day there you were
  The one who owned my heart..."Love Is Forever"

Nancy Kane Endler

A Stalk of Corn

He had planted it beside the door.
Chubby hands had watered it.

There it stood, fresh and tender,
A living reminder of the lad
So quickly taken, by an illness
Rife among the young.

She tended the fragile stalk for twenty days,
She, whose agony of loss
Could know no respite.

How could a child, running out the door,
Remember it was there?

The screen flung back-
And all the mother's pent up grief broke forth.

She sat down, clasped her bibbed apron
To her eyes, and with her elbows
On her knees, wept bitterly.

The stalk of corn torn from the soil.
Her heart torn from her soul.

Dorothy Lund

A Little While

Gone for now, but someday I'll be back somehow
Don't ask me in what way
Because I'll make it back someday
You think this is the final end
Well don't be disappointed my friend
We all must change in due time
But for now this life is yours and mine
Yes it's true we're not here for too long
So we must quit bickering and be strong
Everyday may appear the same to you and to me
But different as the days really are, they'll set us free

Robert Lee Elliott II

A Reminder

The phone rings.
  Obscene interruption.
It rings and rings and rings.
  a chill skates the spine
  the cats leap nine stories
  the coffee gets spilt

There is nobody in this world I would want to talk to.

J. Hope

The Touch

Let me tell you just how much,
to me the feeling of the touch.
The touch is when my skin meets yours.
Now let me tell you of the doors.
These doors to my heart are open wide
to allow you deep inside.
When we let our flesh to meet,
then and there starts the heat.
It boils up from within
and seems to come right through the skin.
I swear by the heavens that are above,
that's one way I can tell we're in love.
It doesn't matter where we are,
in the home are in the car,
all I have to say is such!
I get excited from your touch.

Kenn Robinson

My Baby Girl

My Baby Girl went to school today,
  how hard it was to walk away.
She is so small and innocent too,
  all I can hear is "Mommy I love you".
I want her to grow and learn to be strong,
  to feel that in the world she can belong.
I carried her inside me for nine months and some,
  praying each day that she would hurry and come.
Now I will carry her deep in my heart,
  to watch her to learn right now from the start.
I will be there to coax and encourage with cheers,
  to share in her happiness and to wipe her tears.
The pain of our separation will ease with each day,
  "God love and protect her" is all I can pray.
My Baby Girl went to school today,
  how hard it was to walk away.

Gail Oliver

Together Waking

  Morning broken
  Light touches
Earth moist
Gentle mist
  Rock
  Crevice
Now I know why nature is a woman
She turns   I turn
Kiss   touch
  She loves me   I love her
My hard manhood embedding your soft womanhood
Words true   Soul on   in   *through soul*
  Together watching morning broken
  Light touching the earth moist
    A gentle mist
    Encompassing rocks
    Crevices
    Together waking

Eric S. Almen

Immortality

Opt for bronze or marble if thou must
But when my ashes return to dust
Let not my passage just be etched in stone
But ensculp'd upon those hearts I've known

Walter M. Newland

Infantry 1916: 1968

Trust poisoned by blued steel.
Prisoners to old men's blinded will
Bleed and decay and rot through cold eternity.
Their yesterdays a window on the sun.

Hugh N. Collier

One Gem

She stood, awe struck, at the window
and allowed her imagination to
creatively captivate what was
before her . . .

Emerald teardrops set in white gold,
rubies nested in the opalescence of crystal,
topaz clusters drenched in beauty
from the twinkling of light and
diamonds sparkled against a backdrop
of aquamarines.

She realized that only ONE
could design such a beautiful display
and only ONE
could ordain this ice storm that
had embraced her world . . .

S. Jane Conover

Wishing Shell

I've dropped my pennies in this wishing shell
asking many questions, hoping it will tell

With its many memories, an unfinished dream
in ways as I, or so it would seem

We've both weathered storms, somewhat unprotected
landing in places we never expected

In the waves of life, we've been forced to roll
vulnerability exists, without our control

Not easily broken, nor beaten down
almost intact, clearly still around

Having hit rock bottom, wanting now to flee
searching still with questions...our answers to sea

Jan Stanton Holz

Sweet Dreams

Do you dream in color?
Cause I do, and what I see is you
You with your naked body glistening in the moonlight as you rise
    from the lake
And the water droplets caressing you like a million fingers before
    finally reaching the ground in a puddle
As I look you over from toe to head I notice that your body is
    without blemish
And your face can be that only of an Angel's
Your baby blue eyes stare at me innocently
And you walk closer to me and run your fingers through my hair
Nothing can be heard but our hearts beating in unison and you kiss me
I feel your hand touch mine as you lead me slowly into the cool
    dark water
The water purifies us and unites us as one
And we are forever together, but only in dreams.

Patrick Duffy

A Dance With Wine

All the beautiful pictures dancing on our loving eyes
Illusions born of broken pieces
Redeeming dreams of pale surprise
    Bring dark wines of wisdom for the desert mouths to feast
All the tortured features
need hear our nature speak
    Worlds of rhythmic wonders echoing in my ear
tasting nature's womb, bearing streams of blissful tears
to revel with the wild symbols
bathing souls of rotten fear
    The high atop all fields of pain
watching creatures of soft disdain
We wait in floods of a summers rain
for the light of land, an eternal flame
    O' sacred mountain where I stay
free the snakes of our dismay
Abandon eyes that wake the day
for the beat of life that unites our prey

Jaron Montemayor

Highway Of Life

The highway of life is not always a smooth ride,
it all depends on who you choose as your guide.

If you choose to take that journey alone,
there is no telling where you will roam.

For there are many roads that are unknown to us,
without a proper guide that you can trust.

There are roads that take us to dangerous places,
and we would not have made it without God's given graces.

There are times when we might come to a dead end street,
with Jesus standing there ready to greet.

Why take your journey without a good guide,
when Jesus is waiting, right by your side.

Marcia Clark

My Doubles

One could be day light, one could be blacker than night.
One could easily stand since childhood, one could always be slumped
on uneven earth.
One could be tall and fair, one could be short and dark,
    but then again, size doesn't really matter.
There are two of them, you see.
One could make the grades, one couldn't even comprehend them.
One could drink milk and take 7 vitamins a day to keep up her health,
one could have tracks snaking their way up her right arm.
One could be social, Miss Popularity, one could be withdrawn; the
    other one she will never meet, because she is just not a people
    person.
They are very close to each other, you see.
One could walk the straight and narrow, the other could not even begin
    to understand what that is.
One could never take the Lord's name in vain, one could say sh*t in
    every sentence.
One could have a white picket fence, one could impale herself
    upon it.
    She would have no other use for it anyway.
They do not have very much in common, you see.
One could get married to Mr. Right, one could catch a disease.
One could grow old, one could never grow up.
One could live a long and meaningful life, one could die tomorrow,
    and not even care to notice.
They are the same person, you see.

Polina Kaganovich

149

Enchanted By Fireflies

What enchantment is this glimmering dance
This twilight time of soaring plummeting flight
Which brings the lights of Heaven
  Down
To earthly ground within visual reach of mortal eyes

'Twas no common casting
  I say
No hedge-sorcerer's magic which set them aglow
These tiny dancers formed of living tallow
Whose candescent vestments
  Burn
With Lambent flames of purest gold

Only the hands of an Enchanter
Could have dressed them so
  A true Lord
With that rarest gift
Which no modern alchemist can comprehend nor claim
The power to quicken to glorious life
The living candle
That is the firefly
    R. A. Skeens

Cluttered

I was dive-bombed by a monarch today —
thinking about Bob Schmeckenmheimer's famous 1922
chess opening that caused such an enlightened
uproar that everyone forgot about it by four fifteen that afternoon.
Dressed in opaque-silk, orange-black robes,
resplendent with Mansonesque concern for my sanity,
he (and I say "he", because women wouldn't dive upon me
like this)
flew madly about my head, causing such a flutter of
gestures that looked to the casual
observer
to be a crazed attempt at Judo.
I danced about the lawn, (the very idea that someone could take the
time to grab a cart at the grocery store and then abandon a
sixty-three
cent bottle of hickory-smoked barbecue sauce in that cart,
suddenly leaping to mind) and then dove from my assailant
in such a frenzied fashion as
trying to place your underwear on sideways and wondering
why it suddenly doesn't fit.
    Joshua J. Frost

I Thought You Were My Friend

I thought you were my friend,
I thought you would always be there for me.
I thought you were my friend, I was always there for you.
I thought you were my friend, I thought you would always believe
  in me.
I thought you were my friend, I always believed in you.
I thought you were my friend, I wish you would have only listened.
I thought you were my friend, I did not say what she told you.
I thought you were my friend, why did you have to believe her?
I thought you were my friend, why did you not believe me?
I thought you were my friend, I'm sorry for what I said to you.
I thought you were my friend, I did not mean to hurt you.
I thought you were my friend, I wish you could forgive me.
I thought you were my friend, I wish you only missed me.
I thought you were my friend, I really do miss you.
I thought you were my friend,
I wish you only cared enough to believe me
and now to forgive me for what I said to you.
I thought you were my friend.
    Courtney L. Green

The Earth

The earth is what we live on.
And if it wasn't there we'd all be long gone.
It has lots of people as you can see.
Please take good care of it and it will live to be.
    Alicia Williams

My Son John

In Loving Memory of John Crosby 3/31/93 - 1/1/97
My little boy was just 13 years old when he went away.
It hurt me so for him to go to his heavenly home to stay.
He says mama please don't worry about me,
for down there is a bad place you see.
Up here is now my home.
Mama up here nothing's bad, nothing's wrong.
The people have all gone crazy and have made the world bad.
I'm up here in heaven and I am so glad.
All the meanest in the great big world,
All the killing of little boys and little girls.
So Mama, please don't cry and don't be mad.
I wouldn't want to come back where it all is so bad.
I love and miss you son!
Love,
Mama
    Dolores Crosby

Pictures to Keep in the Mind

A soft summer breeze stirred the tops of the trees,
As the stars came out-stars without number.
And the new moon rode high, like a coin in the sky
Filling all the night with its wonder.

I heard night bird sing as they slowly took wing,
And softly they glided away.
Then the new moon's soft glow, as it shown down below
Made a golden path crossing the bay.

There are pictures in time, that are etched on the mind,
That nothing can ever erase.
And our mem'ries and dreams like a large movie screen,
Live through eons of time and of space.
    Irene Curtis

My Beloved Father

For too many years we were kept far apart,
A burden so deep on such a young heart.
The years of absence were full of confusion,
But now my vision, void of illusion.

The love we have, so very dear,
Matters not the distance, whether far or near.
My love for you will never subside,
Regardless of where we choose to reside.

We've weathered tumultuous storms of past,
Now we can enjoy a love everlast.

Many rich hours we've spent sharing stories,
Bonding in fusion while relating past glories.
Tears have flowed as we speak of old grief,
No regrets are felt, as they offer relief.

As the moon signifies a new beginning,
And stars above offer faith and good omen.
Rising suns triumph over, instilling devotion,
In one another, reward us great fortune.

You are my mentor, my friend, my lauder,
But best of all you're my beloved father.
    Denise Virginia Evans

To the One

This is for you,
whose mind is constantly bombarded with
unnecessary, bothersome information,
making it an obligation for you to worry.
This is for your 5'10" countenance,
toned and strengthened to every extreme
just the way you like it.
And for your heart of gold, your sensitive side,
the one that you never let anyone see.
This is for your blue eyes,
which constantly intrigued me from across the room
over and over again on that first day we met.
And for your incessant, obstinate attitude toward conformity and
    ignorance,
the one you flaunt so well.
This is for your conservative ways of life,
the ways you believe life should be lived.
And this is for all the times you've ever felt disappointed in
    yourself,
for all the times you knew you could've done something different,
better, but didn't.
This is for you,
for making me a part of your perfect life.

Jennifer L. Waggoner

Excerpt from Her Image

She looks in the mirror, her pale face reflects her
thoughts. Her eyes are full of anger and confusion. Tears
of love and hate stream down her cheeks, searching for comfort.

She searches deeper into herself, and her life. Something
is missing. More confusion is forced into her mind. More tears
flood helplessly over her eyes, trickle down the side of her
face, and silently drip off the edge.

The reflection looks back at her sadly. Her face is
mourning. She sees no future for herself. Her image is fading.
Lies spin off an imaginary thread of love. Her image now shows
hate, and is like a fragile doll; her face is slowly breaking.
Her heart aches in confusion.

She steps out of the deepness of her reflection and looks
at her face. She is still the baby that was once so happy,
yet now she is evil, corrupt. Depression takes over. She does
not love herself, her life is worthless.

She opens her eyes once again and looks into the mirror.
The thought of love places a gentle smile upon her lips. She
will wait for the day she can love and be loved. She will live
to see that day.

Kerri Keene

Mothers Are Like Roses

Fastened down in earth so long,
The roots of roses all belong,
And during the winter they rest,
Ready for spring to do their best,
Roses are like mothers.

Mothers are spirits God gave to man
To show His presence on land.
A rose in bloom, like mother's presence
Casts beauty and joy, a fragrant essence.
Roses are like mothers.

The earth is a teacher as mothers are,
Spread worldwide, blending with the stars,
And in the winter, a rose draws in
Roots and leaves return once again.

Nesting in the warmth of a mother's arms
A baby is like a rose free from harms,
And as a mother gathers her own
A rose returns to its earthly home.

Sandra Longman Hills

I Am My Mother — But Not Quite

"Button up" — she'd call out,
Early on, when I was just a girl.
"Have a fat day," she'd blow a kiss,
And always, always wave good-bye.

"Look at God's beautiful world," she'd smile,
The flowers, the birds, even storms she feared.
"God is so good to us," tired from work,
Amidst troubles, she'd manage to say.

And later — "Be careful" — "Take care of yourself"
In pain, she'd always think of me.
"I'm fine, just fit as a fiddle —
Tell me about your day," and, sightless, she'd listen.

Much later — "I'd love to, it sounds like such fun,
But I'm just not up to it."
Up to it? A ride, a visit, an afternoon.
What's to be up to? We'd visit quietly.

Now she's with God — if anyone is,
And I hear her words coming from me.
As I blow a kiss and wave good-bye,
I am my mother — but not quite.

Ann Gorman

A Ride With You

Let me take a ride with you through all you're troubled times,
let me share your dreams and your pain, let me be your life line.
Let me give you the smile you need to make your days so bright,
let me give you a soft gentle hug, and tuck you in at night.
Let me tell you of the times when I was young like you,
let me tell you of some of the things I use to do, maybe
you could learn from me and never suffer pain, for I
hate to see you suffer dear, when there is so much to gain.
Learn from my experiences dear, as lifetimes come and go,
and maybe you can do the same for someone you may know.
Help to guide and direct them as much as you can do.
For this I believe is our lot in life, is to help someone else
see it through.

Patricia A. Harle

Grandmother's Hug

How do you squeeze a lifetime of love into one moment?
From the time you were very small,
Your grandmother has been showing you how.
She holds you close and asks for "Some sugar."
You know you are in for it now,
Because no one can hug you as tightly as she can!
How do you squeeze a lifetime of love into one moment?
. . . With your Grandmother's Hug.

Terri L. Pearson Smith

Winter's Reign

The new green leaves of Spring's first dance
Are dry and brown from Fall's harsh glance.
The crisp clean air is chilly and clear.
For the end of Autumn is drawing near.

Winter's blow is clearly in sight...
With icy snows and long, cold nights.
The once full trees are gray and bare
Gone are the birds that nested there.

The forest creatures..in hiding at last.
To escape the rage of winter's wrath.
All God's creations settle in again...
To await the beginning of Winter's reign.

Kathy Padgett

Heaven's Garden

The farm, where all the fields spread 'round
once the most beautiful sight to be found

The stately old house - its walls could tell
the years of happiness, the times of trial

The barn, the corn crib, the buggy house,
once tall and fine,
now falling with age, their shingles lost,
to the wages of time

The field once sown in oats, clover and corn
now grass covers the hills that the plow has torn

The brook that once ran through the hollow
has changed its course - another to follow

And to all the world its shabbiness shows
they think it ruined all - but one who knows

Ted R. Nicholas

The Widow's Meal

Guest to the host whom always watches and seldom tires.
With an hourglass shape on a belly of venomous fires.
The Black Widow masters the use of her inveigling charms,
In anticipation of embracing prey in her eight arms.
She dances the dance of black and blood red.
Creating webbed spaces for guests soon to lie dead.
Spinning a labyrinthine of traps - this metamorphosed Arachne.
Like the Lydian maiden cursed by Athena's envy.
And just the chance of a fly to plunge into her chords,
Whose skill in flight proves futile in delivering rewards,
Succumbing to a fatal charm in a radiant nest,
As his life is siphoned to satisfy the ravenous pest.
Her corpulent fangs drip with sudoriferous juice
From her priceless guest in his, current, disuse.
From labor of tasks done in unfailing vain,
An empty, outer shell is all that will remain.
Why should nature be unwound and altered for a fly?
And why should protected imbalance be the solution to try?
These are not questions asked by spiders and flies,
Only nature herself holds answers to all's demise.

James R. Tapia

The Black Woman

She is strong, she is loving, she is understanding
She is The Black Woman

She is caring, she is unselfish, she is supportive
She is the Black Woman

She is in control, she care for her own, she loves to be loved
She is The Black Woman

She is beautiful, she is a stone, she is a Queen
She is The Black Woman

She loves the Lord, she supports her man, she makes a difference
She is The Black Woman

She cries, she hurts, she is abused
She is The Black Woman

She is educated, she is strong, she is weak
She is The Black Woman

She knows the game, she plays the game, she will run the game
She is "A Black Woman"

David Reece

My Children

My home is so empty; my heart's in despair.
As I look around, my children aren't there.
Slowly they left me; each one took a turn,
Only a mother knows how my heart yearns . . .

To relive those days when they were so small,
They were my own then, and I was their all.
Surrounded by memories, some good and some bad,
Echoes of laughter now make my heart sad.

The hamper stands empty, no clothes on the floor,
The crock pot is lonely, no one to yell, "More."
The washer is silent; it works not today,
Since all of my children have gone their own way.

I find myself waiting for steps at the door,
And then, I remember, there won't be any more.
Their sorrows and triumphs, with each I did share.
I hope they remember I always was there.

The music has died now, but yet it lives on . . .
Inside of my heart, I still hear their song.
Now all that I pray for is that they may be,
As happy as I was while they were with me.

Libby Metz

Moods

The sun gently touches the far horizon,
just on the brink of escaping from my
watchful eye, when the globe of light
descends beyond the distant hills the day
that stood defiantly on the foggy mountain
tops is gone from my grasp. Night's candles
begin to burn, signifying the approaching
darkness, and my accomplishments are so
meager, they do not deserve a mere thought
of remembrance and yet my tomorrows may
never come for uncertainty is at life's every
turn if destiny permits me to smile into a
shining tomorrow, I shall treat it as my
last, I love to walk in a gentle morning
rain, and smile into the heavens, while
the droplets fall lightly upon my uplifted
face, my mind recalls the teardrops, Jesus
wept for me, and so I gaze into the distant
clouds and feel the moisture upon my cheeks,
I am reminded of the savior, through the
mingling of my own tears and the moisture
of the rain; springs forth a smile of gratitude.

Anna Melissa Stevens

The Waiting Room

Everything seems put away, the room is closed and still.
Dust has begun to gather on books and window sill.
The sun attempts to send its beam between tightly-drawn blinds,
As if the cheerful brightness would somehow seek and find
The room as once it used to be, music loud and wild.
And books opened to be read, and laughter of a child.

Suddenly the light goes on and someone enters in.
The dusty knick-knacks on the shelf, feel some hope begin.
The ragged cat upon the bed watches carefully
Expecting to be leaped upon and grabbed up joyfully.
The dog with ribbons on its neck, the lion fierce and brave,
Have waited long upon the shelf; now look to see who came.

Sadness holds a bated breath-will these strangers care?
They look about the quiet room, and touch just here and there.
They don't seem to notice the watchful ones within.
They have no word for them, no wink, no knowing grin.
Suddenly they sense the truth. They belong to someone new!
Is there hope they will be loved? And love these strangers, too?

Ethel Solberg

If I Opened Up My Heart to You

If I opened up my heart to you
let you see the side I hide away
would you always be there for me will
you still want to stay
When I wake with tear stained eyes in
the middle of the night would you hold me
gently and tell me everything's all right
If I told you all my dreams and secrets that
I keep in a place of their own will you
understand me more or would you leave me
all alone
Now that I've let you know all the things I fear
will you laugh out loud of whisper "It's okay"
softly in my ear
There are so many things I'd like to share with you
this is how I really feel
These words I say are
true

Anthony O. Giovannelli

Already There

My heart grieves for the country... the tall grasses blowing in
the meadow, the tall trees sway in the wind. My soul is already
there. I dream of it each night, I day dream as I gaze out the
window each day. Come snow, rain or sunshine I am there in the
country seated by a pine, the smell is rich, the air is clean.
I am truly already there.

By the small hills view I can see the barns ok, the porch of the
house with its alluring way, I can hear the gentle flow of the
waters edge, taste the mist in the air of a summers day.

I feel a nip in the air as fall is on its way. I pull my sweater
in tighter as I watch the movement of the golden red glimmer of a
    single oak
leaf, it tumbles and blows until it lands upon my folded arm, as if
to say its welcome.
I sit by the glaze of a warm evenings fire, as I look out the pane
to catch the reflection, of the moon on the snow covered banks.

With every spring, brings new hope of another summer, winter, and
    fall.

I'll know it when I see it, the place I lone for in my heart. Take
my body to the country, my souls already there.

Carol J. Royal

How Painful Is My Sorrow

You were by my side
All too shortly you were taken
Cancer, my enemy
How painful is my sorry
Pain without measure, sorrow beyond depth
Loneliness that cannot be filled
How painful is my sorrow
Companion, best friend
I see your smile, I hear your laughter
I feel your warm embrace
How painful is my sorrow
You knew me so well
My ups, my downs my ins, my outs
But you loved them all, how painful is my sorrow
Yesterday a life shared by two
Today grief beyond comprehension
I miss you so, but I know
Tomorrow I'll meet you at Heaven's gates
My pain and sorrow gone in your warm embrace
I love you so

Nita J. Young

Will You Always Be There?

From now, until the end of time,
    when the stars above cease to shine.
Will I always love you,
    and you will be mine.

Our love is built from trust
    I could never do you wrong.
Where once the world seemed ugly,
    now in everything is beauty and song.

Your eyes, so warm and soft,
    your hair, so silky-smooth, your skin so fair.
I look into your soul and see beauty there as well.
    Your beauty is something no other could compare.

To find love such as yours,
    some spend life through searching.
But to me now, you give your love freely,
    just when I gave up and stopped searching.

You have come to me in my time of need,
    you love me, and prove you care.
Please tell me the words I long to hear,
    say you love me, and will always be there.

Thomas W. Cotterman

Another Lonely Day

The days grow old, the pain grows strong
Life use to be so wonderful; where did it go wrong...
The past holds special memories, that can't fade away
The present holds hatred and loneliness as I cry everyday...
I can't tell you how I feel, it's too hard to explain
But I can tell you it's scary, cause it deals with a lot of pain...
I try to bring myself to be happy, with what little I've got
But I use to be so happy, having a lot...
It's so hard to be alone, no one's there
When you want to love, but your love you can't share.
When you want to show your feelings and hold someone tight
Wishing someone was by your side to make it alright.
But now everything seems gone, my happiness faded away
Not looking forward for tomorrow, to relive
"Another Lonely Day"...

Denise Davis

Grandpa

Came and went like a dream in the night.
I woke like a frightened child; pulled the covers over my head.
Into the ambulance he was wheeled.

Memories

Taking care of my first bee sting.
Laughing as I swallowed chlorine against his warning.
Offering Doublemint gum and removing his dentures.

The usual Pat Riley slicked-back hair is grayer and tussled.
Frail bones clutch at a red heart pillow.
Eyes fade in and out of recognition.

I kissed his anorexic shoulder and said good-bye.
Study hard and graduate, his words embedded.
My hand left his forever.

Your presence was strong the night
I felt you leave this world.

I will no longer see your tan wrinkled face
or laugh at how many sugars you put in your coffee.

Sometimes I catch a glimpse of you
in someone else and my heart breaks again.

Jennifer Gall

153

Discovery

Where do they come from?
These feelings for you
I pretend not to notice
Deny they exist
You're not that special-or are you?
The light sparkles in your eyes
And shines on your flowing hair
Your easy smile warms my spirit
You make me laugh, but you are sincere?
My passion radiates and pulls me to you
Have I always known you?
So it seems
As I think back to the day we met
Just a short time ago
Vivid colors flash through my mind
Bright hues transform my heart
As I fight with my fears the black drips away
I try to hold on and it seeps through my hands
I cannot resist
The intensity in me

Monica Rachel Gabriel

The Beauty of Nature

In the deep recesses of our being
We become like a leaf fallen from a tree
On the surface we are unseeing
Inwardly struggling to be free.

As a leaf is the bole's creation
So our souls are the creator's elation
The miracle of birth brings purpose to the seed
Nature bursting with sun and rain to nourish and feed.

The summer sun with warmth of days
Slows us down to ponder and praise
Time enough comes the beauty of fall
Exuding colors so beautiful on trees so tall.

Then comes winter with snow and gloom
The days are drear and over too soon
The snow falls gently like a symphony of grace
Snowflakes clinging as a pattern of lace

How infinitely divine is the gift of his reason
As our lives revolve to the beauty of each season
The passing of time at each new stage
Brings forth the growth of each new age.

Nancy Greco

Altar Ego

My name is Infinity.
I am the playground of the Gods. I am the defier of the odds.
I am where everything has room to grow. I give light somewhere to go.
Killing time is my only crime.
My grandeur is as sublime as the world behind your eyes.
My scope is as blatant as the stars that fill the sky.
I am the cause and effect of the unchanging change.
I make reality and its twisters so wonderfully painfully beautifully
     strange.
I keep science guessing.
Their curse is my blessing allowing for the progressing of thought.
I hold the answers to every question you've got.
I am the future and the past.
My gift to you is the present, forever.
I am eternal and I am never.
All and nothing are my realm where I am Quing.
The cry of the unlimited is the song that I sing.
Excited uncertainty is the feeling that I bring to life that keeps
     it all interesting.
I dwell between numbers. I live the impossible death.
I know no walls. I am free within me.
My name is Infinity . . .

More Again

Follow Me

So you want to be a gangster, well come on follow me.
You will see the steps I take lead to no where
but the entrance to the penitentiary.

I was a gangster for thirteen years, yea an O.g.
I didn't know what loneliness was until
they took everything away from me.

Hold on, where you going? Lets walk some more
down the hallway shackled down through the
cold steel doors.

Lets walk down the next corridor and see
where it leads, it's the injection chamber do
you still want to follow me?

Come on you're a big man, you say you'll put in
the work, well follow me, some more and experience
my hurt.

Hold on lets walk some more!
That's it, turn back while you can, walk out
the exit doors.

Joe Mata

I'm Your Woman, You're My Man

I love you in such away that no one understands
To be with you for the rest of my life is what I plan
One of these days you will surely see
Exactly how much you mean to me
But the one thing I want you to understand
Is I'm your woman, and you're my man
I want us to always be close
So we can give each other that extra dose
Of tender loving care
And I'm letting you know I'll always be there
I want you to be faithful to me
So we can live forever happily
I will continuously let you know
That I will forever love you so
And no matter what, always understand
That I'm your woman, and you're my man!!!

Tameka M. Stith

My Christmas Prayer

We always had heat and food to eat
and presents on Christmas Day
We always had love from below and above
to guide us along the way
The clothes on our backs were new off the racks
no rags did we have to display
Mom and Dad were so near we never felt fear
when in our soft beds we lay
My prayer for the children all over the earth
who haven't grown up in this way
Is that they will be blessed with parents like mine
when they awaken this Christmas Day

Rene Wimmer

Veteran

I love that he lives
On a street called "Veteran."
For that is what he is:
Hurt in a war we do not know,
Don't need to know, to trust the cause was just.
Who feels the ache in "rehab'ed" limbs?
Bending forward, "I've been burned," he said —
Low and intense, as if divulging a fearful secret.
Alone I call back the word.
At the stake, I think.
With me.

Carol Bensick

The Worry Free Poem

I am the light that God shines thru
for God and I are one not two

God wants me here just as I am
I need not worry, fret nor plan

If I will but take my troubles
and lay them on His altar
and step back and be free

He will pick them up in His precious hands
and bless them

And give them back
to me

E. L. Ancel

God's Chosen Gift for Me

I had often wondered when I'd find God's chosen gift for me.
Many times I had fixed my eyes on wicked forgery.
The packages were wrapped attractively, the sender knew my name.
But the signature was not from God, you see it's not the same.
I unwrapped the dazzling boxes and found them full of deceit.
They were, to no surprise, received unsigned with no receipt.
And then one day I gave up searching for my inheritance.
I had to swallow my pride, look to my guide, and lose my arrogance.
Soon thereafter I felt a quiet knock at my heart's door.
I answered the door and knew for sure, that this was the gift
I'd been longing for.
There you stood all eager to love.
A direct descendent from the Heaven's above.
I examined my gift with great precision.
And was later grateful for my decision
For its contents contained no deceit.
But instead was attached with a receipt.
And for the very first time in my life I was glad.
For at the dotted line read the words: "Love, Dad."

Kristna Tucker

All the Love

I remember chickens and ducks and Kathy as a friend
My brother Jim who played basketball, a swing at the front porch's end

A sizzling summer day in mid July
A hot summer night, stars bright in the sky

A loving family who saw to all my needs
Mamma in the garden, aunt Titty who sews and reads

My brother Carlton would sing me to sleep
Big uncle Ben with his voice so deep

Our Bobbed-tail dog "Jack" who slept on the rug
A bed time story from Ma, and a great big hug

Cousins Johnny and Spence with Aunt Annie would stay
Down south for the summer and we would play all day

Going to sunday school, Bible school and sunbeam band
Kool-aid and cookies and playing in the sand

Walking barefoot in the rain and a soupy and pie
Nice neighbors and friends who often dropped by

I treasure these memories as the years roll past
Times change, people die, but always the love will last

Linda Turk Frazier

Black Is Black Is Black the Struggle Unfolded

Observing the ownership, strength, pride...the culture
Self assurance, united, unmistakingly black
An internal struggle to attain my sense of being
Immature, insecure, hopelessly misguided
Yearning to be, not knowing how to be
Segregation within one's own race?
"Stay amongst your own kind," echoing in my past
Fear...the fear of possibly identifying?...relating?
The upper echelon of the oppressed
Refraining, resorting, hesitantly..."Creole"
An identity crisis of such magnitude
What is the purpose, the evolution?
To dilute the forces? Promote disharmony?
Self emergence, the struggle unfolded
My heritage...my strength, my guide
I am first a child of God, second a black woman
I take ownership and great pride in my blackness
I will be the first to say "I am Black" without explanation
Ones complexion may be fair, brown, dark
But lets come together and realize that Black is Black is Black

Diane Carol Fennell

Land of Promise

'Twas thirty years ago today that my fathers set to sea,
In search of the New Land, great hopes there might be;
The land of opportunity, they all seemed to say . . .
Why not go see if there is a better way?

So they packed their bags and said their goodbyes,
Knowing not whether their action dumb or wise;
Harder still were the loved ones left behind,
A ransom for the treasures they might one day find.

And thus in the New Land they suffered and toiled,
As if in battle they were actively embroiled;
The children grew and endured the jesters,
Of how a word cuts deep and festers.

Fodder for determination the children excelled,
To uphold their parents' sacrifices they felt compelled;
Doctors and lawyers, they racked up the degrees,
Most anything was fine that ended in "D"s.

Looking back the parents note the cost—
The ties that were severed, the culture lost;
A big price to pay, or so it may seem,
But such is the toll of the American Dream.

Steven S. Kim

My Profession

What is my profession?
I daily plead the case
Of knowledge versus ignorance
Which I continually face.
No, I'm not a lawyer with a client one to one,
But I do enforce the rule that justice must be done.

What is my profession?
I plant the tiny seeds
That others may reap a harvest
and meet our country's needs.
No, I'm not a farmer who cultivates the ground.
I'm stirring up the minds of men that goodness may abound.

What is my profession?
I build from day to day,
Carrying precious materials all along life's way.
No, I'm not a builder of edifices strong and tall.
My job is more important.
I've heard the Master's call!

He said to go and teach, and that is what I've done.
You see I am a teacher and proud to be called one.

Mary Wright

The Day I Die . . .

The day I die is the day I really know myself.
The day I exceed my limits,
The day I surpass my boundaries,
is the day I die.
And the day I really know myself.
The day I can completely except myself the way I am,
The day I can show myself all of me,
is the day I die.
And the day I really know myself.
So the day all this and more happens,
is the day I die.

The day I die is the day I really know myself,
who I was, and who I could have been.
This is the end of life,
Yet the beginning of true understanding.

Melanie Joseph

Starlight

Darkness surrounds you thick as tar
it's black as the ink spilled fresh from its jar.

Your face tilted upward blind and unseeing
what, was there movement, a twinkle from far?

Icy fingers of air tickle exposed skin
masses above you feel its touch begin.

Sluggishly they drift off like ships of the night
the darkness is parted by rivers of light.

Your eyes open wider your pupils constrict
the brightness from heaven has done the trick.

It bathes you with lightness born from afar
high above you it sparkles, a mysterious star.

Sheila Cooper

The Kite

I am the kite and you are the string
I am always up there, you are always down here
You hold me down, I pull you up
We need each other,
To be for you a flying kite I need a string
To be for me a working string you need a kite
I look at you from up to down, you look at me from down to up
Just rest assured I will try and fly, give up never will
For me the kite give up is try, just try and fly!
Just like living is a form of dying, just like dying is a form of
living
You don't see what I see from up here, just try and fly
I don't see what you see from down there, just fly and try
I was reborn and you are trying after dying, for you I was reborn
I submit then to you string, because
While I am just a kite and you are just a string
Our mission is indeed everlasting
Sharing, searching for the lady of my dreams
Sharing, searching for the Prince of your heart
In search of me, in search of you, in search of love
Just indeed everlasting love, you and me, the string, the kite

Rafael A. German

To Fulfill A Faithful Greeting

Ah love, I fix to timeless ebullience
how we met
in that beginning, delicate as a light breeze,
and making nerves fall to contentment.

Be not lost from sight your face so fair
and bright as the moon's orb,
but draw me to engage and gladden you
in efforts to stall your leave
far past sunset's rubicundity.

Love does meet us in song's charms
to elate each as we do let,
and our talk begins
to burn all heart out of its unease.

And can all this be joined amid
your lips seeped in honey,
your sleek and sable-hued hair,
and me, through all the admirers,
fulfill a faithful greeting
until nothing is left to compare?

Robert Manning

Decisions

Listen to your heart, listen to your soul
Do what you want, do what you're told
Marry a man for money, marry a man for heart
Leave him in five years, or death do you part
Go to a good college, find a good job
Marry a man name Raheem, marry a man name Bob
Stand your ground, and say your words last
Run away, don't look back, you might just save your ass.
Be a winner, your pride you must keep
Be a loser, and admit defeat
Whatever you choose, whatever you decide
Just lay back, smile and let it ride

Nakia I. Strong

Untitled

Sometimes I just don't like it.
Feel like writing or expressing myself.
I know I have to write
but only if I want to get where
I want to go.
I have to overcome my depressions, my
feelings, my life and just think what am I
really doing to myself.
I know I could get where I should be,
but I'm not confident yet,
not even a scratch or memory of
something I've done.
I have to just wake up one morning
and every morning.
Thinking that I can do it
because it's meant to be done
because I want to do it and
I know I can do it because
It's me.

Brian Stark

Blue Heron

It stands tall and proud,
And walks in a stately stride;
It searches the waters for its feast,
In the swamp so wide.

It wades in the water so gracefully,
And is so gentle and serene;
It builds its nest so patiently,
And keeps it ever so clean.

This bird is so unique and special
In its own beautiful way;
It has a long, arched neck,
In which it uses to eat its prey.

This large wonder is extraordinary,
With its long crests and plumes;
And makes a noise - caw, caw, caw!
And thus awaits the dusk that will come so soon.

Jennifer Galano

The Waves of Life

Today I sit and wonder, with no focus to my gaze
My life unfolds before me, during each and every day
A sense of lose immortal, for the one that's left our side
While our bodies tossed about, beneath the crest we've tried to ride

Time will cure most wounds, except the ones that lurk inside
The thoughts we each must tread, drag our souls beneath the tide
The smile that says we're saved, the scars we choose to hide
As our bodies tossed about, the silent seas engulf our mind

Embrace a simple dream, a silent prayer that it will stay
The solitary tear, that sweeps the dream away
The flood of lost emotion, the promise of our youth
Caught inside our fantasy, we ponder on the truth

Like the waters of the tide, that rise forevermore
Each swirling breath will delegate, a virgin to each shore
The one with special meaning, the one we wish to face
The one we loved, the one we lost, the one we can't replace.

The ocean in it's majesty, will serve through all of time
We must fortify the castles, that lie deep within our minds
There is but a short time, for the pain we must endure
While the lapping waves will rise again, on a far off distant shore

David M. Day

Love Came

Love came like a flood through stained glass
to saturate all of a parched and weary mass.
It ricocheted and bounced from wall to wall,
and from floor to ceiling, circling and striking, no warnings,
no explaining healing ways, or how it sealed the lips
that would wait for future days, to say, what they might.
It came and peeled her veil so delicately, and revealed eyes,
crystal blue, and a quivering chin.
Given away by my father, who I never knew cried, a bride,
for love to come, join two, together who, would walk as one, forever.
It came as tears, abated fears, beaded sweat on brows.
It came as lumps and coughs and chokes in throats.
Then it came, how sweetly, from two, shaking voices that said, "I do."
It disarmed me, overpowered me, and left me helpless.
It walked away, with my baby sister that day, love came.

Cliff Kayser

Death

Suddenly I fall, I don't why
I fell, but the fall I took seemed
to tell me I'm not getting up again.
I don't try to get up I just sit there.
I feel someone lifting me up, putting
me on a board, and taking me somewhere.
We stop at a place, I try to think
where I am but I don't know.
The people at the place hook me
up to some kind of machine. I hear people
talking, they start to walk away and a
door slams closed. Outside people walk
past the door. I hear their footsteps.
The door is opened, two people walk in, they look
at me and start to mumble words.
Everything starts to fade, I hear one say
she's dead.

Elizabeth Baun

Of All the Many Loves I've Lost!

Of all the many loves I've lost, yours hurt me the most,
Memories came flooding back and soon became my ghost.
It haunted me both day and night and danced inside my dreams,
With all the many loves I've lost and losing still it seems.
I've tried to win at loves fair game,
But I cannot hold its eye.
The passion doesn't last forever and soon it passes by.
Of all the many loves I've lost, there are some I hold near.
Not all the many loves I've lost, hide in places that are dear.
Hold on to your treasure and the lessons you learn,
Know that love comes in seasons and all take a turn.
I long for times that used to be,
And feelings that are gone.
And to all the many loves I've lost,
I'm sorry, I was wrong.

Deborah Cowan

The Difficult Road

It's a difficult road, one too often traveled.
You're told you have cancer, and your life starts to unravel.

When you hear the word cancer, your blood turns to ice.
Then your head starts pounding, like it's caught in a vice.

Your eyes become moist, as they fill up with tears.
And the bravest of persons are consumed by fear.

You want to deny it, like it just isn't so
You refuse to believe what you already know.

It's the hand you've been dealt, and you know that it's true
So acceptance comes along, and it carries you through

Fear turns to anguish, resentment and strife.
Then one day you realize, you still have your life!

A life that's worth living, no matter the cost.
And all those ill feelings get torn down and tossed.

You make the decision that you're up for the fight.
And you'll strive to keep going with all of your might.

Have faith in yourself and there will be no more sorrow.
If you have a bad day, there is always tomorrow.

Yes, it's a difficult road, but just do your best.
Because living with cancer, is still life, none the less!

Jerry Padavano

The Wind At Timberline

Its voice is never silent. The sound of its song is never still.
The music of its ripple in the tall bamboo blends with its sigh
against the hills.

It steals away the bird songs from the flowers to cheer its lonely
journey to the sea. The trees sway in rhythm to its power. Its busy
fingers play among the leaves.

It can sweep away the clouds to bring the sunshine, or chase away
the sun to bring the rain. It never sounds the same sunshine, or
rain, twilight, midnight, morning, or midday.

It can float a silver moon across the night sky, and waft a blossom's
fragrance on its way. Though the timbre of its tune may be constant
its mood is as fickle as its play.

It drives the sea to lash the rugged shoreline, crescendoing its might
against the foam. Echoing in the bays and on the mountains the ever
changing tempo of its song.

Sunny B. Snyder

Birthday Boy

Happy Birthday Baby,
31 is here.
I hope it brings you many things in life
like love, laughter, and cheer!

But most of all I hope it brings forth
the insight for you to see
That 31 is a number that means many things
yet not an age to be.

But it means so much more
like who you are
And all that you will become.

31 is a man with hopes and dreams,
I know he will achieve!
With strength he shows and knowledge he knows
In him I do believe!

So Happy Birthday Baby,
31 is here.
And I say that with pride,
for it's just the beginning for a magnificent man
and his adoring bride!

Laura J. Jackson

Just Remember...

Just remember, when you think
that life can't get any tougher,
just look over your shoulder
someone else has it rougher.

Just remember, when people are
being unkind, and you want to lash out,
just search your soul and you will find
that you're a great person without a doubt!

Just remember, to be a better person,
after all this is not a rehearsal,
we only go around once in life;
to love everyone should be universal

Just remember, God helps those
who help themselves and learning,
these lessons can be humbling;
just ask for his help, he won't turn his back,
he'll be there for you and help to put you and track.

Vicky Hixenbaugh

To My Friend Paul-Close Eyes

When you are sad and blue,
And don't know what to do,
Just close your eyes,
and I will be by your side.

No need to hide,
if you need to cry.
Just close your eyes
and I will be your
guide.

When things don't seem fair,
and no one seems to care.
Just close your eyes
and I will be there

When a friend is so hard to find, don't look down
just turn around and a friend sure will be found.
Behind closed eyes.

John William McNicholas

The Pursuit of Happiness

The American constitution guarantees that all its citizens
have a right to pursue happiness.
   Happiness is a guarantee of national wellness.
   It is a common goal, a unitive purpose, a reason to
   achieve Divine nearness.

Is happiness within reach?
Yes. It sticks to the mind like a leech.

Is happiness within sight? One asks again,
Yes. It seems Americans reach for it with powerful resources
and mighty main.
For happiness is to a rain-forest like water, the welcomed rain.

   Happiness is just beyond the horizon, and one sees it coming on.

   Happiness seems to be just beyond the bend,
   But one can see its end.

   Happiness is just around the corner,
   But one knows it is there. For it is always in sight.
   And so the pursuit of happiness is right!

   It is always in one's vision, and one sees it clearly coming on.

   It is like a rich luscious apple in a tree,
   And anyone who reaches out for it knows it is free!

Ponciano Olayta Jr.

I Am

I am a girl who has a passion for track.
I wonder if I will ever be in the Olympic's?
I hear the people yelling in the stands.
I see people warming up.
I am a girl who has a passion for track.

I pretend to be the first runner across the finish line.
I feel the adrenalin rush.
I touch the ground with my finger tips.
I worry I will not win.
I cry when I am last.
I am a girl who has a passion for track.

I understand if I lose.
I say it is ok.
I dream of setting a world record.
I try my hardest.
I hope I will get another chance at the Olympic's.
I am a girl who has a passion for track.

Shelly Frederickson

Welcome Home

When I get to heaven I'll sing a new song.
I'll be with my Savior as we stroll along.
We'll walk in His garden the beauty untold.
Then I'll have sweet peace down in my soul.

Soon Jesus is coming, what joy that will be!
His beautiful garden I'm longing to see.
The angels will sing a welcome home song
To me and my Savior as we stroll along.

I can see all the flowers hear the birds singing too.
As we stroll through the garden I'll know what to do.
I'll be praising my Lord for saving my soul,
As we stroll through the garden
He'll say, "Welcome Home."

Diane Smith

Untitled

Your life was like a circle that ended its cycle way too soon
The bright light of the sun that fades into the moon
    at the end of a day
One moment you were there burning with a life that forced me to
    shade my eyes
Then suddenly black emptiness, silence, nothing to see or touch
Only an essence that sparkles in my mind
Now I must face the future with my eyes open watching for a guide
    that has slipped to a whisper
How will I see through the darkness to go on?
The candle you buried inside must be enough to light my
    future path
I am afraid but there is hope
A soft whisper brushes my heart and the flame flares to a blaze
Your love is with me forever

Melissa Walton Bloom

Goodbye

I said goodbye to him today, holding back the tears
Not knowing the right words to say, to sum up 18 years
There he goes, down the ramp, to board the DC 9
The size of a man, but now and forever, that little boy of mine

"I'm joining the arm," he announced, just a few short months ago
A good thing to do, we thought, for someone not knowing which
    way to go
Graduation came, a very proud day, a beginning and an end
The next weeks flew by for all of us, The day was soon at hand

We had a goodbye party, with food and family and friends
But, not much laughter was heard, too many things were at an end
With duffle bag packed, he said, "Goodbye", to his lifelong home
Then the tears came, as we drove off, to experiences unknown

One last night together with his sisters, and with me
The hotel room was quiet, unspoken feelings and thoughts ran free
"Goodnight brother", "Goodnight son" "We love you" "I love you
    too"
The morning came early, there he goes on the bus, and there's
    nothing I can do

I said goodbye to him today, holding back the tears
Not knowing the right words to say, to sum up 18 years
There he goes, down the ramp, to board the DC 9
The size of a man, but now and forever, that little boy of mine

Donna Bruck

The Prayer

His hands and face were wrinkled, showing signs of age.
His hair and beard were turning white, his eyes a half closed gaze.

Upon the table were his elbows, his hands were folded too.
His head was bowed and rested there, he knew what he had to do.

The table was set with a bible, and a half cut loaf of bread,
With a pair of glasses beside him, we know the bible was read.

His hands were big and rough, showing signs of his toil,
And his face was like old leather, worry was there for the soil.

Even though he had very little, placed before him to eat,
Grateful for what he did have, he sat slumped in his straight back seat.

In his weary face you could read, the lonely, the pain and the sorrow.
For this day's hard work had ended, and a new start would begin
tomorrow.

He tried to relax his tired body, tried to help the ache flow away,
In his heart he knew that tomorrow, would be a more tiring day.

He ate his bread slowly, giving thanks for each bite,
Knowing it would have to last him, until tomorrow's first light.

He slowly rose from the table, taking things off that were there,
Thinking about his wife, and all the things that they could not share.

He laid his tired body down, and again he started to pray, to give
thanks for all he did have, and thanks for another day.

Geraldine May

My Angel

I'm an angel who has finally found her true angel.
I love my angel with all my heart.
My angel is so very sweet and innocent.
He's special in every way.

My angel brings out the best in me
When I'm feeling down just the thought of my angel makes the
rest of my day like sunshine.
I will never doubt my angel's love for me.
He will always give me true love.

In my angel's pretty baby brown eyes I will see love everlasting...
In my angel's arms I will feel safe and secure.
Although my angel and I are still on a journey of trying to join our
hearts together I can feel his love through and through.
Everyday brings my angel and I closer to joining our hearts as one.

As each day goes by our love continues to grow stronger.
I will never stop loving my angel
I will always give him the best my love.
My angel and I will always be the best of friends.

Aislin Allensworth

A Wonderful Place For A Garden

A wonderful place for a garden is in the middle of a land.
Where people can reach out to take God's hand.
A better place to plant a garden in a place that above,
Where Jesus Christ can give people all his grateful forgiven love.
This wonder garden can be planting any day,
But it is really up to God to make the day ok.
God says "Christian plant your seeds up until you die.
That the word and true of God because he can't lie.
So if you are feeling down and have no where to go.
Just think about are go to that wonderful place of
garden you began to grow.

LaShamdon Jackson

The Secret of Love

What is the secret of love you wonder
  No one really knows
But I know that I believe
  It should be as pure as a rose.

Love I believe is a lot like a rose
  So very fragile and so tender
But even after it's time has gone
  It's beauty you'll always remember.

How will you know when you feel love
  You will feel it deep inside your heart
It's something you just can't miss
  You will know it from the start.

Never be afraid to love someone
  The best things in life deserve a chance
You will realize later on
  That your life has been enhanced.

So search deep inside your heart
  For the feeling that's as pure as a dove
And one day you will discover the key
  To unlock the secret of love.

    Suzie Chernecke

A Special Man

There's a special man that I know
With a magnetism, a special glow
He has a sensual overpowering smile
I like to be near him, he has such style
I've been loving him for such a long time
Still I can't believe that he's really mine
He's quiet, he's feeling, a sensitive man
I want to be with him forever if I can
Touching is much more than I can take
Kissing is overpowering, a big mistake
I fear he does not love me for sure
However I know his heart's so pure
In my heart I guess I will always know
That he's the one for me, I'll never let go

    Nancy Ouellette

First, Last Good-Bye

Almost a fifth of a century has passed, since you were mine.
But a heart, and soul that has always loved you, doesn't
understand the passing of time.
Once more, I'll wait for a clear day to dawn.
Then I'll whisper, "I love you" into an un-caring telephone.
But this is the last time, I'll allow my lips to call.
'Cause even when you're on the other end, I don't think you
here me at all!
I've written a thousand letters, all sealed, but never sent.
They each told how much, your forgotten love for me meant.
So this is the last "I love you", that I'll command my weary
hands to write.
'Cause you can't read un-mailed letters, meant only for your sight.
Tonight, I'll go walking, once more past your gate.
As my eyes cry out, "Please let me see him!" "Don't let me
be too late!"
Once more my heart will break, with a sound quieter than a sigh.
As I whisper my last "I love you!", and I say my last "Good-bye!"
'Cause this is the last time, that I'll demand my weary feet
to stroll, or beg my burning eyes, not to cry.
Although you still won't hear my heart, as it beats my last
"I Love You!" and it beats my last "Good-bye!"

    Lynda Gardner

Untitled

I went by the house where I use to dwell,
knowing father and mother were gone,
oh how sad I did feel, just to look at
the place, so I rode sadly on.

The people that live there have made it a home,
for they had no place to go.
I made my heart glad to know I had done
something good,
To keep them from living out doors.

They are poor and no friends, so much junk
you can't find them,
Whether they live inside or outdoors,
The junk is piled high almost to the sky,
So I wonder if they can make it inside.

Where do they sleep? Is a question to ask
In the bed or on the floor?
Bed is worn out but any thing is
better than just being out of doors.

    Frances R. Dorsey

Cries of Children

Hear the cries of children all around the earth.
Hear the cries of infants, loud right after birth.
Hear the cries of orphans, give them all a helping hand.
Hear the cries of children, oh help them please to stand.
  Hear the children cry.

Hear the fear of children, see how deep they feel.
Hear the fear of children and know their fear is real.
See the fear of children, see the terror in their eyes.
Feel the fear of the children and soothe their fearful cries.
  Hear the children cry.

See the pain of children, see their suffering see their hurt.
See the pain of children, see them sleeping in the dirt.
War and crime and hatred now on this earth abound.
Heal the pain of children, oh heal that mournful sound.
  Hear the children cry.

See the smiles of children, who have felt the warmth of love.
See the smiles of children who've come to know our God above.
See the smiles of children who have the hope for better life.
See the smiles of children who will soon be free from strife.
  Hear the children laugh.

    Kelly Rodriguez

Slain

Dragon's breath brought forth the demon, wisping in from dusky streets.
Eyes on fire, nostrils steaming; slaying everyone it meets.
Wings spread wide and talons gleaming; each displaying shredded
  meat.
Thrusting forward, it slit my throat. Life sustaining fluid flowed.
I swung the mace that I did tote, breaking stems on which it strode.
A lurid, luminary mote gushed outright so bright it glowed.
Glaring into beastly sockets; nearly lost all self-control.
Reaching deep into my pockets, I retrieved a threaded spool.
Creature's eyes now burst like rockets. Frightened, it began to drool.
Took the string between my fingers, knowing what the monster feared.
Now the scent in this room lingers. Stole his breath, and so it reared.
Then a set of steely stingers, from his torso, soon appeared.
My adrenaline was tapped. All its weapons drawn in vain.
String pulled taut until it snapped, while the demon shrieked in pain.
Sanity had gotten trapped. No more strife; the beast was slain.

    Larry G. Swartz

Selling My Soul

Looking inside glimpsing my inner self
These existing roadblocks need to come down.
Time to put our past forever on the shelf.
Changing to a smile instead of the everlasting frown.

Make way for new beginnings only the strong can prevail
No use in bad beginnings, procrastination is hell.
Forget the people who try to bring us down,
Forever they will be caught in their own unhappy shell.

Feeling breaths of wind under our wings,
Souls souring the open skies, the blues will fade away.
Knowing a happiness only freedom can bring.
We continue the battle to reach our precious goal
Knowing inside the price we paid, was worth the cost
Cause in the end we didn't sell our own souls.

Loretta M. Strickland

The Rose Bud

I picked a rose bud so sweet and meek
and it opened for me within a week;
I didn't know that it would die
because of fools like you and I;
Thus but it back into the ground
through love and luck it is safe and sound;
I see it now from day to day
but it dares not to look my way;
Through the years I love it still
but love me, no it never will;
It's not a flower of which I write
but the love I asked of you that night;
It isn't fair to up root flowers
or ask for love that's not yet ours;
To make you say I love you
when in your mind you still don't know;
I'm the one who did the wrong
because my heart wasn't strong;
But if someday you want my love to fill
just call on me, I'll love you still.

Jesse Gatten

One November Night

One night in late November, I gathered up the days
When God had been magnificent to the things He gave me always.
Memories that now came back when you and I were young
To think about how special, we all truly are.
Going back from present to past, I say "Thank You, God,"
For the love and kindness He has shared, to us all humankind.
All that seems dark to you, to me would be bright.
All that's full of sunshine, would now be as night!

The little pain my companions gave,
The careless hurts that no one intends,
Here You gave me braveness to take,
Here your comfort was taken as You had sent!

Mighty as You are now, to punish those who sin.
You still gave us another chance, for us to repent our sins.
Our years are like the shadows on sunny hills that lie.
Or grasses at the meadows, that blossom and then die.
Beside His feet is a narrow path that glows bright in the dark.
From this place to where I sat, is You — on hark!
To this night on, I will remember, how good You have been to us.
As well as the love You gave to us.

Katherine Catayong

A Mother's Dream

Three little girls that was my dream
The oldest and youngest, the one in between
As babies so loving, so pure, so sweet
As children a treasure, for me a real treat

The days moved so quickly and soon I would see
These children were too big to put on my knee
With dating and proms and parties and toys
My three little girls had out grown their boys

Walking down the isle, with Dad on their arm
I stood there in awe of their regal and charm
With husbands so devoted and new families so dear
I knew in my heart I had nothing to fear

Happiness is their's, to last a whole life through
Contentment and peace fill my days
A Mother's Dream come true.

Jeanna Antrosiglio

Mother

The story of a friend, the story of a mother,
The story of a woman, truly like no other.
Mother of sun, Mother of nature, Mother of sky, Mother of Earth,
The mother to many, mother since birth.

The wonder of the Mother's cry,
The one that makes you wonder why?
The wonder of the Mother's mind,
The witty one, the dismal one, the one of a kind.

Her eyes dismally colored in tone,
The eyes you see when she knows her child moans.
Her heart valiant, tranquil, and savor,
The heart that makes you so frail you want more.

Luminous, perilous, courageous, certain to be her name,
As she approached the twisted, bearing no shame.
Striding with a distinct interest,
Positive about the face, extremely high about the chest.

The concept of a mother some never knew,
How can such a myth, a legend, remain unknown to you?
Mother of sun, Mother of nature, Mother of sky, the Motherly friend,
She ceases to remain my mother, from beginning to end.

Stephanie L. Myers

Rain And Sun

To sit in the dark of a long dreary day
And listen to thunder of storm gods at play,
A drowsiness settles as deep as the soul,
A feeling of hopelessness one can't control.
If there could be just only light in our day,
The bleakness and darkness would all go away,
And there would be sunlight so golden and bright
Bringing joy to world lasting all through the night.
A perfect beginning and never an end
A beauty that no fear can ever transcend.
But wait, is utopia's simple as that?
Can sunlight dispel and disperse and combat
The wonders, yes wonders of rain on the land
And even the nurturing of cacti in sand.
So let the storms gather to come and depress.
Let sunshine soon follow to light and address.
The one fact the world must definitely know,
It takes rain and the sun to make all of us grow.
In the knowledge that no matter what may be fall,
Accept what is given, it's better for all

G. Wilcox

My Granddaughter, Our Little Cheerleader

She's only three,
But she gets me on my knees.
She can get my attention,
With her own little invention,
When she pouts,
Or when we have our bouts,
Of why she can't jump on the couch.
She loves to play and have spelling bees,
This keeps me a little at ease.
She likes to pretend
To be a cheerleader.
She does her cheer
And we burst into tears of laughter.
She looks so cute
In her little cheerleading suit.
We take her to football games,
And she does her own little thing.
After the game
She lays down her head,
Then we put her to bed.

Addie Purifoy

Little Lady

Oh, What a season has done
to the little lady next door

At seventy six
the temper and the flesh
in its readiness would spring from the bed
before dawn

In the sunshine of those days, the little lady
was like a shapely vat that poured happiness
into mowing the green, pruning a bush,
and planting a garden

Oh, What a season has done
to the little lady next door

At eighty six
the temper still springs
from the bed but the flesh slowly trails
The expressions tell
of the twinge of the flesh
but the beauty of the temper
traces to an earlier time

Oh, What a season has done
to the little lady next door

Florence J. Faraone

North Carolina Star

Looking into the dark abyss
Millions of lights appear
There is always one that shines
Brighter than the rest
Given that direction of happiness
A path has been set a foot
The worldly feeling that nature gives us all
Looking into the dark abyss
Millions of lights appear
There is always one that shines
Brighter than the rest, and for
Me I know that she will be thinking of....

Eric Bakke

Let Spring Arrive

Winter has flown, let Spring arrive!
From frosty soil, may blooms survive!
As Winter lifts her mantle cold,
So Spring comes forth, the Earth to mold.
Let blossoms beautiful and bright
Encourage all who view the sight.
The touch of land, once shorn and tilled,
Speaks to the heart — awake the chill!
The gardener with his hoe and rake
Prepares the soil — new dreams to make!
Shall it be carrots by the row?
Tomatoes, beans or corn to grow?
Or shall it be a gracious bloom,
Sunflowers, with height and room?
Yes, let Spring lift up her brow
And bless the Earth, as Earth allows.

Karen Burnette Garner

The Irony Of Tombstone

In eighteen eighty seven,
Said Edward Schieffelin:
"It's to the east of San Pedro, not the west,
Where I'll go to prospect my quest."
The soldiers, they guffawed away.
The east! 'twas the domain of the Apache;
And one even ventured to say:
"The only thing you'll find there, Sir, is
    Your Tombstone!"

But silver he found and silver he sold
And named that part of the valley: Tombstone.
Just 3 years later, in eighteen-ninety,
All that glittered was not gold:
Liquor bars and oyster bars;
Ladies' parlors and Ice-cream parlors-
    Flourished in Tombstone.

Today, the irony lives on: fires and
Gunfights hath taken their toll.
Not a structure of old
Is there to behold, In Tombstone!

Zachary deSousa

Statement

Hammered on the anvil of somebody else's dreams,
Carrying out the conquests of another person's schemes,
Forced to swim in channels of some other human's stream,
Pushed and pulled and molded till I scream the other's scream,

Like clay upon the table fashioned in another's head,
Living out his fears and worry, dreading in his dread,
Extension of his doubts and sorrows, standing in his stead,
Till my own self finds me buried and we both of us are dead

Living up to roles that others now expect of me,
Father, husband-working man as solid as a tree,
Onward, upward never stopping acting to a "t"
Till I'm so down I haven't time to count the misery

Death awaits and is as final as its course is long,
If I could strike out on my own and sing my own made song,
To orchestrate my own existence though the time be wrong,
The light motif of knowing that my symphony is strong

I know I must find who I am and then be true to me,
And not accept the seed of someone else's destiny,
So I can love the person inside trying to be free,
And laugh and joke instead of crying loud but silently.

Will Levins

Happy Birthday

Back in 1926
In the era of Louis and Bix,
And speakeasies with peep-hole doors,
Scarface Al and gangster wars,
The Manassa Mauler, the Sultan of Swat,
Bathtub gin by the jug or shot,
Flagpole sitters and raccoon coats,
Butter-and-egg men sowing their oats,
Black Bottom, Charleston, Shimmy-sha-wobble,
Collegians doing the goldfish gobble,
Jolson singing on the silver screen,
The Lone Eagle and his flying machine,
Came the birth of James L. Thomas,
As predicted by Nostradamus.
His good deeds will never be forgotten,
Although he says his core is rotten.

Helen Blackstone

Where the Sea Gulls Fly

I want to go where the sea gulls fly;
Where the sun kissed clouds touch the sky;
To see the waves touch the shore and to be there
always and dream no more;

I want to go where the sea gulls fly;
To see the sun sink into the deep blue sky;
To feel a warm summer breeze upon my face
And to see a scattered array of shells along my way;

I want to be where the sea gulls fly;
To see the waves ebb and flow;
But when it comes time leave I know;
That once again tomorrow, I can go where the sea gulls fly;

Danielle Champion

Break the Chains

She crawls into bed with me at a quarter to
three, mommy will you play with me, I'm not really
sleepy.
Drinking hot chocolate and playing Candy land,
makes me think how nice it could have been.
Staring at an old picture of a child with a smile
so mild, one look in her eyes tells the truth, the
troubled fear of her youth.
Deep in dark memories of the past, I hear her
say, "I won again mommy, you came in last."
Laying beside me with her special teddy, I stroke
her head and see her restful grin. I now know that
I am stronger than they were back then.
Remember, every day they are growing, we all can
Break the Chains, and stop that snowball from
rolling.

Heather Cruse

Mummy's Roses

The roses of my childhood dream
of my mother who devoted her life
for my own universe, for my own stream
the eternal happiness should be ripe

I walked on the rough and bumpy way
I flew in the flamboyant sky
the roses would live all my long day
the roses would die as time goes by

My heart and my soul were there
the hell be eden or be Buddhist nihility
Nirvana's roses were found nowhere
But I love you, forever, my lovely mummy.

Hien Minh Tran

The Ultimate Sacrifice

If you're on the fence, or on either side
for you and I, our Savior died

For each of us, He paid the price,
He gave His life in sacrifice.

Was He forsaken on that fateful day,
or did His dying provide the way?

The way for mankind to atone for his sins,
to make a new start, to begin again.

To be a light so others may see
their way to Christ, to live eternally.

Mel Franks

Sand

Floating through space on a breeze my mind, a sponge soaking
up the ionosphere drizzling through my body out my toes now out
of me floats me or at least that part of me that I think of as me

When really you're much more than that
Looking more deeply deeper - shedding my skin
scraping off the accumulations evaporating the fog
What do you see? Only a shell

What's inside? Don't know - can't see . . .

A shell is just that
Clamped tight — no light getting through all I see — is shadowy
lining oh wait . . . a pearl nestling comfortably at the core

Step outside
It's so bright—squinting from the glare of the universe

Sliding into focus . . . Strange — it's so familiar
I've seen this before been here, before

What do you see now?
A reflection . . . I see a reflection
of all that is beyond

Where have you seen it? Illuminating the pearl.

Inside of me.

Marisa Laursen

Candles in the Wind

My first love burnt so bright.
Our immaturity was the night.

True love is like the eternal flame.
All others are like fire in a wind game.

Angie came like a bright flame of twilight.
Emotional winds started to blow, then, just candlelight.

There were others that were almost right.
When the fire went out; there was nothing to ignite.

As I grew older, flames were hard to find.
And candlelight in the wind was where I had to begin.

Love is a perfect form of beautiful light,
That can only survive when nourished night after night.

Candlelight is for that period between dusk and dawn,
Without it comes darkness, next loneliness and being alone.

Now that I am very old I can only remember the candle glow.
Where does the candlelight go?

Where does all the candlelight go; is it sent from heaven?
Does God have to make it right for it to glow in a windy night?

So many beautiful things never last.
Yes, they are just candles in the wind. Candles in the wind!
Flames! Flicker! Then! Candles in the wind!

Douglas Paul Blankenship

Self-Hate

No better than a prostitute, this is truly what I am:
I give away parts of myself, it's really just a sham.

With every action a little more of me erodes away:
No longer there, no longer to give, the feeling of despair will stay.

I keep hoping and wishing for the day when I no longer feel:
I beg for the time when my heart is at a stand still.

No more pain or tears or feelings that I can no longer bear:
For it's the blackest of feelings and shame, that I can not share.

For this my darkest hour, these feelings will not go away:
I guess I will have to wait for my judgment day.

Callie J. Herring

Simply Heavenly

When the dawn is awakened by the sun's smile,
  and the birds chirp as the moon gently fades,
It's simply heavenly . . . .

When the stem sprouts a bud that slowly reveals
  the essence of its being in a burst of color,
It's simply heavenly . . .

When the squirrel scurries busily to gather its
  winter stock, energizing itself with a nibble along the way,
It's simply heavenly . . . .

When the wind blows a freshness into the air, inhaling
  the leaves with each breath, exhaling blankets of gold,
It's simply heavenly . . .

When the child embraces the gift of a mother's love,
  hugging her ever so tenderly, it's simply heavenly . . . .

When a father's eyes glisten with tears, as he gazes
  at the wondrous beauty of his daughter, the bride,
It's simply heavenly . . .

When the clouds whisk quickly through a rainbow of hues,
  the sunset reminds us of the coming of the day anew,
It's simply heavenly . . . what more does one need?

Roseann M. De Pinto Naber

Alzheimer's, the Thief

When did you start to leave us Mom?
I wonder what you're thinking.
You were the best mother, always there for us.
Breakfast dishes are getting washed with cold water and no soap again.
You no longer tell time or write a grocery list and
You layer clothing over clothing and forget your glasses and teeth,
But you know to kiss the ones you love.
Getting the morning paper from the driveway is your pleasure
But you can't remember how to unlock the back door.
You can't dial the phone anymore so when your nurse leaves,
I call you from my office.
You don't hear well and understand less so our conversations are
Surface like strangers in a waiting room.
I used to share my thoughts and hopes with you but now
You just become too confused.
Even though you live with me, I'm lonely for you Mom.
I'm glad I can still feel the love in your hugs.
I hope that won't be stolen too.

Pauline Amento

Jerusalem

Road ascending fabled city on tabled rock
Jerusalem the golden, stone the color of crusty bread
Here, Rock of Abraham, Solomon's Temple, Calvary
Donkeys plod saddled with cement bags
Israeli soldiers stroll, rifles flung in web straps
Sailing by, desert Arab in camel hair
Smells of oranges, honey, herbs from the Judean hills
Laughter, a medley of tongues, camel bells
Head bowed, a Hasidic Jew in frock coat and beaver hat
Latin fathers in tasseled brown
A daughter of the desert with hidden face
Priests of Armenia and Egypt
Winding streets, deep crowded steps, stubborn camel causing
  disturbance.
Arab boys prodding donkeys burdened with boxes
Merchants bearing trays of cinnamon pastries with goat cheese
Seeming Biblical time except for us in sun glass
Reeboks and polyester.

Ruth W. Edland

The Visit

I had a visitor, she came to me
amidst the dark of night,
A woman who's heart I had been a part of
from the beginning of my life.

Her inspiring words consumed my being,
casting wisdom throughout the room,
with a calming affect, wanting not to reject as
her soul spoke to me, her son.

So strong were the feelings exchanged between us,
her guidance I was destined to listen,
In tones forceful yet kind that kept piercing my mind with
the remembrance of how much I missed her.

Beneath the moonbeam her presence resided,
her company I could not deny,
But as written in the past, it was meant not to last and
once again, I wept with goodbye.

C. L. Simeon

Lily

You appeared one hot summer day
an unwanted waif, society's throw away,
My heart broke, over your hunger and thin shell
I vowed to love and make you well,
Amongst my flowers, you took a nap
upon awaking, you sought my lap,
The beautiful lily, so white and pure
will be your namesake for sure,
Your meow approval, seemed to say
I've found, a loving caretaker today,
The vet exam, confirmed my worst fear
telling me, what I prayed, not to hear
To keep you from suffering so
the kindest thing, was to let you go,
Lilies and a cross, mark your resting place
I'll never forget, your sweet face,
We only had a few days together
but you touched my heart, forever
At last, you found a home and love
you're at peace now, in heaven above.

Roberta Pescatello

If You Were Candy . . .

I would start with the wrapper;
Delicately removing your protective encasing
With soft caresses and gentle nudging.
Slowly, I would expose you to me as I strip away
    your defenses.
I would not laugh at your nakedness.
I would nurture the bruises on your chocolate skin.
I would soothe your pains of experience and disappointment
    with my warm tongue.
I would savor the taste of your bitter-sweet darkness;
    enveloping myself around you.
Your essence would penetrate my center.
And in that moment, we would become
One...
    Valerie Dunn

The Rose

Oh how the rose tells the story —
of His infinite Grace and His glory!
The pedals are as delicate as His love for you
and for me,
The thorns are apart of this rose you see;
Right now we see thru a glass darkly, soon we will
see Him face to face - our sins and our mistakes
gone with no trace.
God made our rose, in Him we can lean -
for He is here, He is there, and He is everywhere
in between!
If you ever get tired, lonely, or afraid, turn to the
one who understands, the one who knows -
the trials of our faith, are precious, though
we question, they're as perfect as "The Rose"
    Margaret Balota

Truth

Do you believe you know the truth
Or is it truth that is a belief

For what seems true
Is sometimes not

And what you know
Will change with thought

It is the mind that plays the game
And changes truth again and again

That which lives will surely die
That which dies will surely live

The cycle changes from life to life
And betters itself if used toward right

If used to hate and hurt, and maim
A return to life will reap the same

Could not the earth be God's gift of Eden
If taken care of through each season

Did God upon all people visit a curse
Or do we ourselves make Eden worse

These are truths we all must know
Before we slip into the glow
    Sherrie R. McCalvey

Wild Horses

Horses, wild horses, with manes of white
and air of salt along the
wind-struck beach. The sand of brown
is sifted into the light of day as the
pounding hooves of freedom
proclaim the land
as their own.
Eyes of fierceness still made to be gentle
in the eyes of the beholder
and handler of agility and grace.
Life to be learned is knowledge and wisdom
already known within grey-matter of
colors.
Shadows dance and prance on grains as time
flows through the hour-glass in
the waves of eternity, their eternity,
as the sun sets along the horizon's orange
and the currents of salty-blue are at peace
within
the hearts of the Wild Horses.
    Dionne Moyer

My Father

My Father is a guiding light whose love has shown the way,
A beacon in my darkest hours when temptation leads astray.

He often shows where courage lies when fear will make me quiver,
His love's a glow that warms me when the cold world makes me
    shiver.

My Father is a source of strength whenever mine grows weak;
His power o'er the trials of life above the thunder speaks.

He's eased my hurts and dried my tears; given hope when it was
    needed;
And stood beside me even when His words weren't always heeded.

My Father has believed in me, in all that I can be;
And every day, long as I live, I know He's loving me.

He thinks I am more special than the riches of the earth,
And has given more of love to me than I am ever worth.

And yet I hope He sees in me the reflection of His glow
Is now a beacon shining bright for my children as they grow.

My Father's passed His love to me, I'll do the same for them,
I'll give of all He gave to me, just as I learned from Him.

His love is an eternal flame, that stands the test of time
Long as it's passed from heart to heart, as it was passed to mine.
    Margaret R. Story

Birthright

You carried me warm and safe.
Your blood — a chain that linked lives
For everything that touched you
Became a distant, unknown memory of mine.
Fear, that froze red in your eyes
Passed pink through my closed lids,
And unimagined strength
That burst dams as you flung arms to the sun
Instilled a yearning in my tiny fingers for that light
Which I had not yet seen.
Sharp angles of your being, planed deep by sorrow,
Pressed hard, insistently,
Within the creases and folds of my skin
Too soft and round yet to know of such pain.
Your dreams — full, vibrant,
Explosions that rocked me.
Changed the rhythm of my motion
Implanting the knowledge
That there is more, so much more.
All the while you carried me warm and safe.
    Delta Donohue

Children of the World Today

I see fragile children roaming the cold and the emptiness of the street; with out any one to guide them and with out a sense of direction. Only in hopes to try and find a family, understanding, a sense of togetherness, some one who cares.
The evil of darkness in temptation of drugs; children thinking, drugs may ease and cause numbness so that they don't feel the anger, frustration, pain, and the hurt which fills their hearts, waking up from the drugs, only to find out that the harsh reality in which they live, still exist.
Weapons that lie in their immature hands, smaller than my very own, taking the lives of others for clothes, money, food, and drugs. To them in order to survive or taking their own precious lives because life is to harsh for them to bare a lone.
The parents of these children have lost their morals, values, and beliefs, because of the parents loss of faith and hope the impact and the devastation shows with in the children of the world today.

Windy Harvie

When the Time Comes

When the time comes,
   Don't cry for me, for we have shed ample tears together
in joy, laughter, sorrow and disappointments.
Shed no more tears, when the time comes.

When the time comes,
   Don't weep for me, for I have not gone away, but I'm
merely in another room or just taking a walk. I am as close
to you as ever.
Don't despair, when the time comes.

When the time comes,
   Look for me in every smile, reach for me in every ray
of sunshine, let me touch you with every gentle drop of rain.
Here my voice in every person's laughter.

When the time comes
   Let me go easy — for I am tired.
Allow me to take my rest, for I have earned it. I have worked
hard to leave you with good memories.
My journey is over — my work is complete — now that the
time has come.

Lynda Hampton

Where Dawn Lingers

A misty morning makes it difficult to view
The wonders of Mother Nature all around me and you
Whispering grass, beautiful flowers and trees
Honeysuckle's sweet scent lingering in the breeze

Barefoot, neath your feet lies the cool dark earth
Awakening flights of fancy, visions of rebirth
As the mist begins to clear, it becomes easier to see
Just how much our Creator loves you and me

As a babbling brook passes by it hums a happy song
And before long, the birds in the trees sing along
Relaxing on your front porch, rocking in your rocking chair
It is possible to enjoy it all without a worry or care

From dawn's first light to the twilight hour
we poor mortals search for the source of such power
Quiet!..., listen, do you hear those angelic singers?
They can only be heard you know—
WHERE DAWN LINGERS!

Elizabeth B. Baldwin

and she...

a mother lies in pain, unable to move
aware of the consequences her unborn child might endure

and she cries

his premature body being put to a test for survival
will he be there for her to bathe, to feed, to caress, to protect

and shed cries

a father watches and wishes he could receive her pain
he turns away, and he prays

and she cries

the time is near, the pain and suffering she tolerates gladly

and she cries

husband at her bedside, gently squeezing her hand
wiping her brow, softly whispering his love

and she searches

together they see this miraculous gift from god come into view

and she smiles

Carl Genna

Inescapable

The old craggy trees stood firm, clustered together like old Friends. Huge branches extend and bend, while leaves beautifully flutter with the wind.

Captivated by nature my eyes drink in its wonders. A ghostly breeze whispers "Be-lieve; death be not proud," as the sounds disappear into the clouds.

From the depths of my mind surfaces doubt willing me to prolong grief. Suddenly a bluster of wind shake and sway the trees, branches heavily wave good-bye. My ears keenly hear the distant wind whisper, "Be-lieve; death be not proud."

Quietly dry leaves float to earth. Gently holding a fragile brown leaf, awakening thoughts unfold. The leaf died but the tree lives. Is death a lie?

A brisk fall wind blows, tree branches flop like huge welcoming arms, bending just when you think they will fall. The trees dance and sway with mother nature. They know, the deep winter sleep is inevitable, yet not forever.

As I think, a realization overwhelms me; if God so loves the trees, how much less can he love me. I will believe and inevitably Experience what it truly mean to be free.

Bonnie Ragsdale

Love Is Forever Everywhere

Time was, should it have gone at all
Knowing how low one must fall
can it be the only thing she, they wanted
was to sell an understatement.

Just to find out the cost of the night
never cause the aroma of someone's desire
to block off your own blue notes.
Somewhere later the trap's daystar will implode.

But don't hear it only one-to-one side,
no, let your shadow in on it, too,
He'll provide an air of loving amazement
to your own grip over what dances you can now drink to, forever.

Raymond F. Baldowski

Secret Chambers Of The Heart

Locked far away from the display cases of the world,
From heartless people who misinterpret caring and honesty,
As signs of weakness in character or disadvantage in business
There is a distinct space within us that we trust to no one.

We all, the human race, harbor within us astounding thoughts,
Extraordinary dreams within this remote realm,
That is free from outside bias, pain, disillusion and heartbreak.
A silent place that only the recess of our heart understands.
A secret part of us where only truth and honesty exist.

As cares of the world divert our attention
From the things that matter most to us,
We retreat to this place of solace and perspective,
Amid the canter and step of our "drive through" domain.
A tranquil place of refuge from overwhelming upheavals,
From turmoils that invade and try to destroy peace of mind.
That region within, incapable of censorship or disturbance,
Designed for honest one-on-one communication with self,
Where, as time momentarily stands still, there is reality.
Where is found finite strands of character and poise,
A place of secrecy within hidden chambers of the heart.

Eva Hinckley

The Weekender

You have gone back to your mountain,
Filled your bag with all the weekend moments
we have tried to stretch
into a Lifetime.

You have slung your hangered clothes over shoulders
that have born the brunt
of my continual growing pains,
and neatly slipped into its case
the brush that helps protect
that ever-present smile.

You have closed the lid on the shave cream,
wrapped the cord around the dryer for your hair,,
and have seen me stand behind you
as you took one last look into the mirror.

You have zipped the last few inches of the leather bag
that holds the weekend you.
And as you leave, you smile because you know that I
am in that little bag
you drop into the back seat
of your car.

Gary T. Gambino

Two Hearts Join

Two hearts join — first as friends
— sharing laughter
— exchanging smiles
— engaging in colorful conversation
— sharing past experiences

Each heart begins to give to the other

Two hearts join — growing closer, beyond the realm of friendship
— sharing dreams
— consoling sadness
— experiencing life
— committing time and energy to one another

Each heart beings to make a place for the other

Two hearts join — united from this day forward
— sharing eternal love
— chasing and fulfilling dreams
— facing and overcoming challenges
— sharing innermost feelings and desires

Two hearts have become one this day

Brooke B. Fowler

Joy

Lord, I thank you for this day
while I watch the children play.

I'd forgotten, the joys of life
while trying to be a good wife!
Lord, please don't let me forget to see just how simple life can be!

Lord, teach me, to see the beauty in the trees, let me find, the
beauty in me!

Lord, I get so busy, so mixed up inside.
Lord, teach me how not to hide.
I hide from the joys that you have given to me; O Lord, help me to see
all you have given to me!

Lord, help me to find what I left behind!
What is it in me that blocks the joys that you created for me?

Lord, why was it so painful to be a child?
It seems so simple, so joyous and right,
the children all look so bright.

Lord, please help me to find the child in me so we can set her free.

Amen

Dianna L. Moore

Rose

Sweet smelling roses glistening with dew,
Reminding me always of a gentle you.
Tender and gracefully known,
Kept in my heart and in my home.
The vibrance of their beauty bringing warmth to the soul,
Like a love enduring the warmth of the cold.
Changing seasons flying through time,
Standing firm and ready to climb.
Climb the mountain of faith,
There's not much time to waste.
Hold on to what we have achieved,
There is so much more to be received.
Keep your heart smiling with the memories we share,
Always remember, I really do care.
From one wild rose to another,
Lets stick together,
With no thorns to pierce our path!
Love, me

Kaye Lynnette Bednark

You and Me

When I'm with you, something says, "Me".
I long to squeeze you so tightly
That we become one again,
As we were just three short years ago —
You in me, me around you.
When you kicked, I felt me.

Were we friends in another sphere?
I know your very heart — an angel with orange juice
on her face.
We see things together — wondrous earth,
magic stars.
Snow has become a treasure of fun from heaven.
When I look at a fuzzy caterpillar,
I see it newly through your eyes.

I see myself newly as I gaze at you.
My heart beats now as I squeeze you —
Soft hair with baby smell. You squirm.
Oh, little one, I hold you and feel me.
In you my life is renewed.

Modina Hansen

Birth

There is nothing. Darkness, but that is nothing.
I am moving, being gradually pushed
Towards distant discordant sounds.
Slowly, with effort not my own, but more like a force of nature,
The blinders that have covered my view finders
For these many months
That I have been caged in this fleshy cavern
Are rising to expose a brightness I have never known.
I close my eyes with fierce determination,
But curiosity reopens them.
The light focuses to a beam and reflects off my view finders.
Suddenly, an entire picture
Of reflected light and shadows reveals itself to me.
Then, the shadows and light switch locations, moving erratically.
The discordant din continues to grow as the shadows move.
Gradually the light turns into different colors,
And the colors are given depth, texture, relief.
Everywhere my view finders turn,
Another shape is made, a shadow created.
I am shaping my universe blink by blink.

Susan Groves

The Dread of Fall

Thoughts of raking piles of leaves,
is something I dread so,
cause each time that you think you're done,
the wind just comes and blows.

Now not only do you have just leaves
that are blowing all around,
but paper, twigs, and paper cups
are all scattered on the ground.

You begin again to do the task
that simply must be done,
and knowing deep inside yourself
other ways of having fun.

Like cook outs, swimming, sitting round
and drinking lots of beer,
listening to your lovely wife,
as she's yelling in your ear.

A smirky smile upon your face
a grin from ear to ear,
you found a way around all this
you'll hire a kid next year.

Ronald Oroszko

The Darkness Is Crying

A drop of rain falls from a clear sky . . .
In the darkness you here of ethnic cries . . .
Crying out to be treated the same . . .
Trying hard to ignore the names . . .
Names given' by those who feel troubled . . .
Fearing their world would change inside their bubble . . .
Thinking change would bring heartache and sorrow . . .
Not thinking about life of tomorrow . . .
To let us continue with so much hate . . .
Could end up being much too late . . .
Too late to stop God's children from crying . . .
Too late to stop racial fights and dying . . .
The change that needs to take place . . .
Might change the looks on everyone's face . . .
Just by stopping the racial outbursts and the lies . . .
Might just stop those in the dark that cry . . .
Because were are made of flesh and bone . . .
Living together on this planet Earth that we all call our home . . .

Tom Gibson

My Vision

Night falls suddenly, the sky painted black,
Stars seem to melt, blurred by my salt water tears,
Trembling on my knees I ask, I plead to the heavens,
Let no one be afraid to touch my hand,
Never to fear the companionship of another,
Let all eyes see only grey,
Let one's mine be filled with knowledge,
Grace one's soul with acceptance and understanding,
Let people live and live and live on,
Mankind's quest for happiness and inner peace.
Respect, never hinder another,
To the faintest star I passionately I gaze,
As thoughts of a meadow with all colors,
   sexualities, cultures and religions,
All people, young and old,
The colors swirl with linking hands,
Brotherhood, compassion and understanding,
The star grows brighter,
The warm western breeze kisses my lips, dries my tears,
Out there I can see,
I can see my vision, everyone sees grey.

Lisa Hopkins

Present

Let us dream of yesterday.
And wish the world was again that way.
So as we vision the future ahead.
Count not our present as being dead.

Let us dream of the parks and trees.
And remember, that cooling summer breeze.
Yet we would vision a winter so cold.
And by the fire, gramps with a story to be told.

Let us dream of the wars at an end.
And say, Thank God, for the women and men.
So now as we vision a peaceful nation.
Only to find senseless racial confrontations.

Let us dream of times, gone and past.
And wish the good times, would last.
Yet as we vision the future ahead.
Count, not our present, as being dead!

William F. Staples III

Destiny

We humans — like conduits — circuitry of star stuff,
Not so planted in the ground as the trees are,
Not so swimming in the oceans as the fish are,
Not so flying in the air as the birds do.
Yet aspiring to be rooted,
to swim, to fly.

We — humans — part earth,
part heaven,
part water,
stand between gathering and grasping — try to store it all up,
hold onto it,
extend it, savor it,
as it all slips through our hands only to return from whence we
borrowed it,
not ours but someone else's
We, realizing, that we are not authors of our own existence
shrink back, looking endlessly for our own meaning
find only questions.

We—Humans—all so bound up in time.

Phyllis B. Parun

The Mourn

Time passes so quickly all will be gone
Every fragment of memory lost at deaths dawn
So let me hold your hands and kiss your lips once more
in hopes of an evening after the mourn.

To miss you is silence that flows from my pen
To hold you is my heart pounding for life to begin.

Oh that ice wouldn't melt and wind blow away
then myriad of smiles shouldn't decay.

I miss the dead by time betrayed
so many memories marked by a grave.

See veins in your arm delicately unwind
look at them, yours, mine.

We are to believe in a world beyond time . . .
Time.

Time passes so quickly all will be gone
Every fragment of memory lost at deaths dawn
So hold my hands and kiss my lips once more
We'll hope for evening after the mourn.

Brennon McGuire

A Love And My Friend

Love is a special feeling
that is shared by two
Love is that special feeling
that I feel for you

Love is giving unselfishly
and asking nothing in return
Love is being willing to take a chance
without the feeling of being concerned

Love is a simple touch
when in need of a helping hand
Love is a shoulder to cry on
when things do not go as planned

Love is some times shown
by a mere walk in the rain
Love is filled with laughter
but also sometimes with pain

Love is the feelings that you and I share
those feeling that I wish would never end
But if by chance they do one day
I will always remember you as my very special friend.

John E. Corley

Time

Time . . . passin' by.
Time . . . movin' on without you.
Too much time since we last met.
Searching for projects to occupy my time.
The bell chimes again, another hour.
When the bell plays for awhile, another day.
Only to wake the next day to listen again . . . And wait.

But the time finally comes and the rush moves into me.
The minutes prior . . . breathing.
And the time comes of her arrival.
The time's speed escalates to infinity.
Then she is gone but leaves a memory to cling to
. . . until next time.

Jack R. McCarty

Luminescence

The ever-present light
That illuminates from your eyes
Passes beyond human description
My heart, with joy it cries
Indescribable feelings fall
Down the face of compassion
I dance in the midnight rain
In an innocent, childlike fashion

My arms are open wide
Lift me to the heights of love
Carry me through the darkness
On the wings of the purest, white dove — I want to fly

A tangible smile, an open hand
Love is expressed through the living
Even the dead have an eternal choice
To exist in hatred or the compassion of giving
Come to me, Lord, in the depth of my sorrow
Give me a hug with your eyes
The material items of the world melt away
In the burning away of sin's lies

Chrisanna Hibbitts

You, My Friend

It is understanding without the words.
It is time without the clock.
    It is giving without thought of reward.
    It is listening without shock.

It is support without investigation.
It is to know, yet love still.
    It is sharing fun and recreation.
    It is keeping one's own will.

It is tears, it's sharing pain.
It is always being there.
    It is laughter, its shared gain.
    It is even death to share.

It is being honest without the fear.
It is to prod not too much.
    It is knowing when one needs to be near.
    It is a cool head, a warm touch.

It is you.
    It is a friend.

Dale E. Moore

Passion Lost

What delirium; when bathed in twilight I find you there.
Eternal bliss found in your loving arms embrace . . .
touched by the passion of mine . . . and full of the essence of life.
Such unimaginable ecstasy to feel you near.
Oh, sweet intoxicating moments of melancholy tenderness
as whispers linger in breathless, heavenly languor
heard only through the haze of softest sleep.

How cruel—the lover's moon tonight
to inspire such sweet suffering, romantic dreams.
Knowing passion finds no solace upon awakening
to the wretchedness of fate and cool empty sheets.
Why yearn to touch what is no longer of this earth?

Pained . . . I lay in the stark, white light of night
and beg God, your image will not forsake me.
So inexpressible; this sweet suffering divine delight
to weep, to sleep, to dream . . .
Oh what delirium, when bathed in mystic twilight
the breathless whispers dance around my soul, my heart . . . .
Bringing back to me, if only fleeting, my love, my life . . . .
My passion, wrapped in your eternal embrace.

Catherine Hanson

Consideration

"Sometimes the wind
is a helpful wind,"
says my four-year-old
wiser than some men
tenfold his age.

"It puffs and pushes
lifts the sand I'm shoveling
then puts it in
my pail."

I turn to talk
to him of helpful winds
of windmills,
ships, and power.

He, however, turns his eyes
to clouds
and finds a bony dragon
to dance
across the sky.

Donna M. Marbach

Flibbertigibbet

You say you fight for me
You know what is best
Save me from ni**ers
Sp**ks and the rest.

We are not allies
I share not your hate
Your mind is now useless
Misguided and raped.

You accept only ignorance
You call it the truth
Self-righteous unknowing
Don't need no damn proof!

You'll find no compassion
Nor respect in this place
I'm filled with aversion
Repulsed by your face.

Philip Andrew Jackson

Maine

Lobster steaming, bargained
from the boat at the pier at the end of
a long beaming sunwarmed day.

The pot boiled,
under the canopy
hammered by the lined sheets of
wet nails framing the end
of bicycling in the sand
to beat the waves,
pounded by the wind
which pasted the sun
on our exhilarant skin.

Now the rains slash,
arguing with our words,
as we toast its fresh teems.
We savor the buttery meat.

Later, in a sleeping-bagged
war and peace sandwich, we lie
as dreaming.
But marvelously awake.

Lavinia Connell

Have You Ever Been to Summertime

I remember going down to Frew Run, just after a heavy rain. It was
cold, it was cloudy; but on this day the usual trickle swelled and
rushed toward the much larger Conewango. Like any kid, I began to
throw sticks into the swift-moving waters, I watched as they bobbled
and were sucked down the stream and out of sight. I was only eleven.

. . . Often, I would wonder what happened to my little "boats." I
realized that they could not, would not, sink. They could only go
forward into greater avenues — down the Allegheny, down the Ohio and
into the mighty waters of my dear friend Huck. Oh, what an adventure!

And then I thought . . . . If I had the wisdom of the Old man and the Sea
I would swim all the oceans and the seven seas. Or.
If I had the wings and eyes of the bird high in the sky;
I could see the whole world until the day, I die.
...Oh, what dreams I have had — In days gone by! Epilogue.

I have not seen the whole world yet; and I can't even swim.
I know now, after seventy years, that I never will.

But if a stick of wood can make it all the way to the Great
Mississippi; Then maybe, just maybe we all have the opportunity to go
the distance to a long and productive life in this great country of ours.

David Craig Higbee

Homecoming

Inside my mind there lies a place where and time stand still, where the truth becomes
a yarn of lies and myths are forever real,
Where inherit facts abide and magic resides in everlasting zeal, and the past burgeons
within my memories unlocking an abstract facet of reality,
Where youth is undying, life an ageless chance, and time is teeming sand in an hour glass,
The brilliant stars shine from afar, igniting fires deep within the heart, . . . burning strong and
ever-so-free, etching a golden path that leads from you to me,
Good-byes come and go as the soft winds of our world slowly blow, this is our
garden . . . our hope . . . where faces forgotten are vivid and true,...
sculpted into our souls,
And within the peripheries of this vision we can see and define our
outlying goal . . . for it
begins and ends with one word alone, . . . and yes, that magical place
is one's Home.

Kiley Q. Laughlin

No Sound At All

The slow, sardonic clacking echoed off the log walls of the room
containing too few objects to absorb the sound.

In fact, it was the only sound inside the cabin and if he weren't
there to make it, there would be no sound at all.

He glanced at the shelf upon which his entire life was haphazardly
stacked under layers of dust, before taking a swig from the bottle at his right hand.

It didn't burn going down; it had stopped burning some time ago.

He ignored the trickle which had run off the bottle and joined the
other unnamed substances in the tangle of gray overgrowth attached to his face.

How long he had been up here, he didn't even know. No one knew really.

He had never owned a clock, he despised the ticking away of minutes he could not control.

The heavy black keys were stiff from non use but he pushed along,
sentence by sentence drawing closer to the end; to the end of what
would be his most consequential work.

Little by little, with each stroke, the keys lightened under his
determined fingertips and he laughed, a bitter laugh, at the irony.

The once bright white enemy before him was now littered with the
deluge of words that poured forth from his mind, through his fingers
and onto the page, mocking him at every turn. Never had words come so
easily, nor so freely as these words had.

With his final work complete, but left unsigned, he used the last of
the bottle to wash down his grievous existence.

Maureen M. Maguire-Motherway

Crushed and Smushed

My hopes were shattered, and my dreams were scattered.

I hiked the tight rope of despair.
All I found was emptiness there.

I unshut the closet door, and cast my skeletons away.
After I read that note, I had an awful waffle-day.

My toes still count ten, my fingers I have eight.
One thumb on each end, this must be my fate.

I hold no grudge against those who push me away.
I shall gain my strength and rise again someday.

Steve Swanner

Gingerly Meandering

Please explain to me why, this innocent river is crying,
did anyone really know that she was suffering and dying.
Relate it to me kind words that I can fully understand,
an expression that whispers why she has been frightened and damned.
Her lives blood that delicately swam within side her vital precious tide,
has mysterious been infected and has succumbed to the ride.
To the annual journey that now can never be gingerly taken,
as its ancient meandering has elapsed and long destination has weakened.
Once playful little dwellers are now absent at her skirt,
while the nourishment she provided has been sorrowfully born hurt.
The cool shade that once covered the animated diamond like wave sea,
now stands raped of its leaves while enchanted with polluted sophistry.
A stagnant lifeless deflowered reservoir lies pillaged by the chemical wrath,
in a cleansing that is similar too a rustling sour like metallic bath.
The essential seasonal night cloudburst that came during the past lush rainfall,
tasted just like pure lemon juice and was a gift from the mouth of the cities call.
It has bequeathed the river in death and its surroundings in bare agony,
while the city clouds have passed on cascading down another born tragedy!

Gregory Douglas Collins

Carry Away

Carry a way a new heart. A heart from each below. One picked up on a
  recent trip.
She'll be so happy for a time, till you drop her off again. Dropping,
  falling . . . back
down . . . down to earth again. Drop her off but keep her heart. She
  will have no
further need. Heartless, broken, yes empty. Back to earth, back from
  the clouds.
Will she remember the trip? A fiery passion. A love, the feeling
  everlasting??
\Carry away with you a newer heart. This one last's a little longer.
  A period of time.
Lasting till the drop, the fall from above. Stumbling, plummeting
  back down.
Shallow picked clear. Will this one remember? Probably not. No
  memory, no effect.
She cant' recall the want, the need, all the passion from her capture.
  Only left with
A hollow feeling.
Carry away a new heart. This one far, far away. Will this be the one
  you decide to keep?
Is this your dream possession? The true chosen? Finally a true love.
  A heart to keep.
Oh but this one takes your heart, keeps it forever. Locked inside
  her. She found that
special place in you, only to find no room. All the stored hearts
  explode!
This time you are dropped off. Falling, realizing the drop. No
  feelings, heartless fallen
down, down you go . . . no more flights for you. Earthbound
  forever . . . .

M. J. Pare

I Am Dead

I'm in a field covered in smoke
I'm in a field covered in blood
I'm in a field covered in bodies
I'm in a field covered in fear
I'm in a field covered in wounded
I'm in a field covered in hate
I'm in a field covered in neighbors
I'm in a field covered in bullets
I'm in a field covered in courage
I'm in a field covered in smoke
I'm in a field and the war is between the states

Marvin E. Hagarty

The Spider's Web

The spider's web is a beautiful sight.
He works on it for quite sometime.
It glistens and gleams from the morning light.
And, oh how the sun makes it shine.

The weaving of his web is quite tricky.
It is hardly visible to his prey.
It can grab hold a fly very quickly,
And there his captured quest must stay.

The spider pounces on his meal right away.
He wounds it round in a silken pouch.
How does the spider bound his prey,
And not get stuck in his own house?

Bea Love

Secret Love

To you I pledge my love,
and for only you it's true,
that our hearts will beat as one,
before this day is through.

We will look into the sunset,
and say our true love vows,
you'll be mine,
I'll be yours,
and forever we shall be,
you and me together,
for all eternity.

But for now my dear I dream,
and a dream it really is,
a dream of you,
of a love so true,
and of the day that we first met.

Jennifer Bakken

Father's Prayer

One night when I was sleeping
an angel came to me,
he said, "Son your daddy's dying
and his soul needs to be free.

He wanted me to tell you
the words he could not say,
that is why I'm here
to let you know today.

The pain he caused he's sorry
it's nothing that you did,
and if he had another chance
he'd take you in to live.

Your Mommy won the custody
and he cries each night and day,
he prays for a miracle
to bring you home to stay.

Lolita Terry

Broken Angel

Broken angel will your heart unfold
Will your light shine through
and will you story be told

You've been living your life all alone
Surrounded by people who can't help you find your way home
You should be in the heavens but some how you fell
So you sit quietly without knowing who you are
And wondering how you got to this Hell
Which way do you turn backwards or forwards
But nothing helps you understand it's just more words
Your head begins to pound and your stomach begins to quake
Is the anxiety real or is it the beginning of a heartbreak
Will you find your answers before it's too late
Will you take the chances and stand toe to toe with your fate

Broken angel will your heart unfold
Will your light shine through
And will your story be told

Robert L. James

Life

The Montana summer glides along on soft breezes, we revel
in the green grass and trees, thus leading to the cooler but
pleasant sounds of autumn.
    We look forward in anticipation to the first few days of
Indian Summer, the golden leaves gently falling to earth.
    We are serene and comfortable not daring to think of the
frigid cold blast of winter that seems to last an eternity.
    We live each moment as it is, trying to make some sense
of our lives.
    There is no sense and no order we know that, yet always
seeking comfort we move cautiously through this world seeking
what we know we won't find.
    Some days in happiness yet most in wretched wonder of what
and why.
    Then at the end of the trail it is there, the peace and
happiness that is sought and prayed for, yes now it makes sense,
our journey transverse through so much melancholy, a reason.

        Nothing worthwhile is easy.
    Richard P. Woodard

Renewal

Dedicated to Nancy and Grace

Spring brings a gentle newness and uplifts the soul,
Summer carries warm melodies of songbirds and the laughter
of children through its constant breezes,
Fall's crisp air ushers in vibrant hues for our pleasure
And the stillness of Winter lays a protective covering over all
our precious memories . . .

Giving us the time to think, the time to consider,
the time to plan what new ones will be made
when the delicate daffodil pokes through, when the curious starling
arrives on the sill,
and when the revival of green is the topic of the day.

Memories to make, each moment, each hour, each season.
Precious times to hold onto, and to recall.
Never letting go of the good that has passed,
always looking forward to the good that has yet to come . . .
A refreshing newness to uplift the soul.

    Christine A. Wilson

United We Stand

A — is for our Ancestors, who founded this land for
    you and me
M — is for all Mourners, of those who died to keep us
    free
E — is for all Equality, regardless of sex, color,
    or creed
R — is for our Religious, freedom Catholic, Protestant,
    Jew, or Atheist, ,if need
I — is for the Inherited, rights to life, liberty, and
    pursuit of happiness
C — is for the Citizens, who keep our country clean
    and safe from fearfulness
A — is for all Advancement, in technology, and standard
    of living
America — will stay great as long as united, we of
    ourselves are giving.

    Mary Rose Endres

Requiem of Tomorrow's Dream

No one knows what tomorrow may hold,
only through tomorrow does it unfold.
As we dwell on today and hope for tomorrow,
is how we create our sorrow.
The sorrow comes from remembering the past,
and today moves much to fast.

And so the day ends, only to drift into sleep,
to relive that which was wished to keep.
But on the wings of the dreams flight,
are the shadows of the dream in the night.
And the shadow of a dream can turn to sorrow,
for all that was wished to have tomorrow.

To realize with the mind,
that which the heart cannot find.
To sense with the soul,
that which only the dream can console.
To be at peace in ones own mind,
never to know or ever to find.

    Michael A. Krikau

A New Beginning

The dark turns to cobalt blue,
And the soft light of the sun,
Caresses the pink petals of the flowers,
That look as though they're blushing.

The sun's head rises up,
To bathe the world in sunlight,
Sending rays of pure white light,
Skimming through the sky and clouds.

Reflections on the still water
Of trees and flowers of all kinds,
Creating a rainbow of different shades,
Of scarlet, violet, peach, and the softest greens.

There's no such beauty elsewhere in the world,
Quite like the newborn sunset,
That envelops the once blue sky,
That may be like a day that is dying.

Then, the midnight blue, star-filled sky,
So romantic at times while feeding shadows to the darkness,
Although the day is dead,
The night's ready for a new beginning.

    Matthew Bartlett

Baseball Strike

My lover left this month, and my Big Red Machine is limp.
I no longer fondle her tubs of beer.
Her hot dogs are cold, her buns soggy.
No more extra innings, no foul balls, no suicide squeezes.
She won't let me slide into home.
Our television rights will not be consummated.
My turnstiles have stopped turning.
We've played our last doubleheader,
had our final twi-night affair.
Our brawls are over, our rhubarbs and donnybrooks finished.
Grand slams no longer excite her, barn burners bore her.
My pop fly goes unhandled, my line shots ring out
in the empty stadium, my Texas Leaguer plops
without notice in the outfield grass.
Today I had a new date:
I teed up my balls in a new course of action,
but it was strictly a no-hitter.

Rich Buchsbaum

It's War In My Head

War! No bodies falling; no bullets flying; no blood; no gore.
War! It's not out there, but right here - in my head.
Society fears me: They say I'm angry, crazy and dangerous.
They don't want me close, no! Not near:
I might hurt, rob, rape, or plain kill somebody.
They don't want me too far off by myself either.
So they must contain and control me:
In the ghettoes, state pens and prisons,
and under the hypnosis of dope and religions.
War! I am seeking and venting myself; redefining what's left of me:
The ever-changing names: Ethiopian, ni**er, Negro and black.
Now I'm called an "African-American"
What a shifting identity! I ironed the kinks out of my hair;
I permed it. Jerry-curled it. Relaxed it.
Now I cut it very short and embellish it with various patterns and
designs but it'll soon change again. What a pain!
Oh, I've got it! Yeah. Now I know who I am. I'm a king made a
servant; a lion caged, a running river dammed; a giant oak tree,
trapped in an acorn; waiting, waiting for spring to break free. War!

G. Dolo Diaminah

I Am Not!

Flaunt that misogynic attitude—
Chest stuck out, gangsta strut, blatant confrontational, thumpin'
  tone.
I am not a bitch.

Didn't adhere to the ludicrous annotations—
Crazy sexual advances, trespassing outlawed hands.
I am not your who'e.

Incessantly disrespecting me in the presence of cognate females—
Belittling my character, insulting my look.
I am not a bitch.

Wake up to consciously realize who is the enemy—
Jealous home boys, back-stabbin' bosses, demons of the street.
I am not your who'e.

Roll with me, bonded trustworthy hand in trustworthy hand—
Reliably loyal, reassuringly black love, with absolute respect.
I am not a bitch.

You sequesterly know who I am—
Knowing my inscrutable inner thoughts and steadfast dreams.
I am not a bitch—
I am definitely not your who'e.

Karen Carroll

Upon Hearing the First Ludwig of Spring

Drum tenderized,
Brass wrecking crew—
Would make me deaf like you?—
Lacerating strings,
Wood winds pecking the remains.
Back with the other fish
Staring at the stage.
Crescendo crash!
it ends?

Coda
Tell me, for you can,
Is it von or van?
it ends.

Brant W. Tedrow

Digging for China

Down in the trenches
With the cheaply persuadable,
The endless possibilities
quietly
Gathering force
Against the floodgates
Of food and rent,
Of cigarettes and fear
And monies all spent;
Of misshapen madmen
And licorice vagina:
While we labour together,
Digging for China.

Jett L. Johnson

Gone

He took her to his house, gently unbuttoning her blouse.
He whispered, "I love you's" that seemed heart felt,
gradually making her melt.
If she would have known he wouldn't be there tomorrow,
she'd have felt no sorrow.
He took a piece of her away that night, no
wonder it didn't feel right.

What she could give was the only thing he wanted,
now her life is forever haunted.

Celina Gagnon

Disorderly Conduct

A picture is all I have
A dust covered love I could never have
Tears falling to the frame
The heart that's broken and never the same
I clench my teeth at your sight
Your smiling face beaming bright
Your flowing golden hair
Now I just don't care
Time, love that we had, could never be
Because it was hate that broke us free
A careless marriage broken,
Eternity has spoken.

B. Hamtil

Untitled

And the blood of pain
fell from its fleshly gates
until all their cups where full
so that they may drink from them
and learn of him
as we would of you

Take to your lips
the nectar of our lives
while it may still be sweet
for tomorrow it may sour

And when the blood of pain
again fills our cups
drink of its bitter, cold knowledge
feed upon its time
of sorrow to once again
make from them
an understanding of ourselves
awake tomorrow
and to future days that would have us
drink once again from it's sweetness.

Shane Daugherty

The Bird

Graceful wings, lift to the air,
A white bird,
soars to the sky,
along the borders of clouds,
trees and lakes, over the seashore,
as it glides, within its reach,
the craggy, mountain hills,
or the sloping shoreline,
far away,
as it soars to meet the heights,
the freedom,
joy, and power it feels,
up in the air,
where liberty rules,
the strong will survive,
as the sun slides into the ocean,
the bird will fly,
tonight, and forever.

Eric Copsey

Yesterday

Of yesterdays,
Of memories shared,
Of things gone past,
They are well cared.

Some tend to say
Thoughts directed
Towards yesterday
Are thoughts well wasted.

I do believe
Some tend to hide
Of memories
That hurt inside.

I look at tomorrow;
I look at my way;
But one of life's blessings
Is yesterday.

Shannon Davis

The Flower (Inspirational)

While walking on a hillside
On a dark and dreary day,

I looked for something pleasant
Just to brighten up my way.

Everything that made me happy,
All the things that brought a smile,

Had just faded with the sunlight
And were gone for a little while.

Just as I had turned
And was about to walk away,

A bit of color caught my eye
And made me want to stay.

Blinded by my tears
I ran toward the color bright,

And much to my amazement
There lay a flower in plain sight.

Where it did come from?
I will never know.

But when God loves someone,
He lets His love show!

Ramona Smith

Truths

Truth rings her truths
    open as the heart

Loving kind of this life
    seeking things to write

But come not here wondering heart
    for subjects for your themes

I will choose to close you out
    to stop your wandering pen

But the Soul tells us more
    of the love of life to write

Nothing short of God's great love
    gives us themes to tell

Truth is altered from our hearts
    the pain of it to hurt

Seeking deeper for the love
    for poems to write about.

Louis H. Williams

Justin's Bear

Auntie has a little bear,
It's soft and white and blue.
I kept it on the dresser,
knowing it was just for you!
Now you'll never see that little bear,
Or know of Auntie's love,
God came today and carried you,
beyond the stars above.
I'll keep that bear forever,
or till Heaven shines a light.
A path for bear to follow,
'cause you can't sleep at night.
I'd swear I heard bear say today,
please Auntie don't be blue.
'Cause when you get to heaven
Me and Bear will take care of you!

Linda O. Backus

Soulless

Have you ever met a person
who has no soul at all
no feelings do they harvest
no feelings do they share
it's like their soul is dying
never to return and there's
nothing you can do but sit
and wait by their side
they've hit that time in life
where nothing matters
They don't care at all,
And you really wanted to help
finally years from now their
soul will return and they'll
get back some feelings
and maybe have some fun
but until then wait and
stand by their side
for they'll be a true friend
as soon as their soul returns

Briana Ratliff

Water Sports

Drip, drip, drip, drip
white water torture

drip, drip, drip, drip
hillary martyr

drip, drip, drip, drip
come soon November

drip, drip, drip, drip
rev'lution's over

drip, drip, drip, drip
starr search is a bore

drip, drip, drip, drip
four more clinton/gore

drip, drip, drip, drip
people to the fore

Richard K. Heacock Jr.

Leaves

Like
    teardrops
       they
          fall
from lofts in the sky.

For a slight moment it seems
they shall never fly.
Until their job transforms
to the coroners, no less,
telling summer to die
and winter to dress.

Suddenly the color changes
on the stoplight of life.
Toddlers, they become
with "eternity" to grow.

Oh, but little do they know
Of the trials
Nature bestows.

Natalie Mindrum

Empty Nest

Our home is so empty,
    the children all gone.
For the sound of their laughter,
    we sincerely long.

They gave us much pleasure,
    they caused a few tears.
We feel overall,
    those were the best years.

In our older age
    we pause to give thanks
for the joy the gave us,
    along with their pranks.

They have their own families,
    they live their own life.
Precious memories remain
    for me and my wife.

John Grimes Sr.

Unexpected

In the midst of my life
I find such a gem
unexpected to find
myself loving him

So new, yet so true
In these eyes of blue
I never imagined
That I'd find you

I feel like a kid
All over again
You make me live
Don't let it end

In the midst of my life
I find such a friend
unexpected to find
myself loving him

Ray C. Roath Jr.

Untitled

My Mom is a special friend
On whom I can depend

She's given me love over the years
Dried and wiped all my tears

As a young girl my father died
Mom was there right by my side

She raised me up the best she knew
Asking Jesus to see her through

She lost one leg and then the other
Not giving up, that's my mother

Her daily chores are a must
In her God does she trust

She drives a car as you and me
She's not handicapped, can't you see

Her love for me will never cease
Because of Jesus I have this peace

I know my Mom is the best
Through all her trials
She has been blessed!

Susan T. Edwards

Four Views of Mist

Mist pulled down tight about my ears,
I watch the river. Dross
of reed, grass, dead weeds
scurls the metal surface.

Braving surface mist,
one mad duck, insensate engine, lines
out along the liquid runway,
propellers screaming, seeks ether.

Riding down hard, the north mist
has leapt the dike like Custer
on the Oachita scatters women
in the red Kansas winter.

Far out upon the river's body,
three white pelicans, serene
among the scattered waves,
in the scattered mist.

Fred T. Adams

Differences In Man And Ice

One is cold but
    one is colder.

Each has formed with
    more or less order.

Both can melt
    with the right holder.

Each last less
    as they get older.

But the ice turns soft
    and the man turns hard.

Jud Malcolm

The Hopi

They live on high in a northern plain
The Peaceful Ones are forever.
A taskful life with strong endeavour
Means living on without the rain.

For Hopi corn is life, they say,
Though sheep remain a staple.
The young and old remain so able.
Life leads on from day to day.

James Davison

Our Family

Our family is like a tree.
Everyone is bound by love.
In hearts we are all free,
But we share the same blood.
Our tree is growing,
Expanding in different ways.
We stick together knowing
We have limited days.
We are so different,
Yet so alike.
Each one's a parent
And a child.
Through pain and happiness
We'll be by each side.
Never let us miss
The road to guide...
Our family.

Stephanie Bogart

The Present

How sweet to be a present
heaven sent earth angel
flying first class with
healing hands that go off on
you while you rest and the rest
of me waits for the rain to stop
I want to reveal this
non stop passion play what
would you say what would you do
I'd like to say I'm there for you
whenever however park my pride
nothing to hide not afraid of any
consequences, but I don't like
fences - my own walls are
hard enough.

Cris Beaty

The Work and the Race

Our days are filled with the work,
    of the breath,
        of the life,
            of the care.

Then comes the day
    when the work is not enough.
Then the race begins;
    With push and pull,
        and breath and cheer,
            we run the race for life.
With bodies strong, and full of zest,
    sometimes the race is won.
But now and then, and off and on.
    something can go wrong.
When the body is weak and can't go on,
    the call to home becomes too strong.
It is in these times we lose the race,
    for no matter how hard we try;
When he calls us home,
    we do not ask God why (?)

Rose M. Walters

Music Maker

Music, sweet music, running
Through my soul
Making me rock from side
to side
Making me snap my fingers and
Tap my feet to that very up-beat,
beat. Singing along with the lyrics,
and dreaming that's me, that's me
up there, throwing my voice around
in a nice orderly manner. It's me!
I'm making you tap yo' feet and
sing along, I'm making you rock
from side - to side. It's me!
I'm the music maker.

Monique Moore

Sharing

My wife died in my arms.
I watched her light go into my soul.
My soul is so happy,
My heart is so dark.
In time my heart and soul become one.
I am even.
Isn't life fair!

Richard V. Godsell

Calmness

There is nothing quite like it.
With no wind in sight

Water has a stillness, mirror like.
Not a single bird in flight.

A time for reflection, undisturbed
and mindfully clear.

No loud bothering sounds to hear.

Appreciated peaceful tranquillity
abounds.

Only lovingly soothing thoughts
can be found.

Mike Cuneo

Trials

The trials of our lives
The fears we face
The tears we cry
We wonder what our hearts desire
Only one answer
We don't want to bend
For all we need is to look upon Him
For all the trials, fears and tears
That desire of our hearts we have found
For down on our knees we cry to Him
Lord Jesus take our hand
For we have learned to bend.

Lois Heffinger

Dear! Please Let Me Take You

Dear! Please let me take you
To a sunny and warm country
Where through the trees, lovingly,
The morning breeze is courting you.

There, under the blue skies,
The flowers, sweet and smiling,
Wave a friendly greeting
To the fluttering butterflies.

Please let me lead you, Dear!
To a desert seashore, far from here,
To watch the summer sun dance
On white sails in the distance.

Like in a dream, we are going
Here and there, up hill and down dale,
Welcomed by song-birds singing
In tune with pines along the trail.

Well! Let us go hand in hand,
Forgetting about the way back,
Entering by chance the fairyland,
To enjoy the happiness we lack.

Luong Van Nguyen

Sycamore

One large brown leaf
Clinging to a branch,
Being blown to and fro.
Not yet ready
To join the others
As they wind-waltz
On the ground below.

Margaret Richards Durfee

Babel Wrap

Summer sun sears thru summer sky
Amid golden gate bridge fog
Hovering, conquering, rolling by
Romantic spell do lovers buy.

Teens rap a wrap of babel
Riveting, romping, dancers by
Talk the talk of teens
Carried along tempo guile

Talk in tongues, I wonder
Nonsense to the intellect
Singing soul to sacred level
Charisma? Spirit? Pray tell

Stars wars of technocrats
Warp speed, never heard of
Virtual reality, real but not
Evolve and overcome us.

Babel by themselves are a bore
But wrapped in mist, music, spirit
Self is appreciated more
Each to each, the speaking soul.

Gloria D. Santos

Untitled

Food is so powerful
Holocaust victims wrote recipes
Supporting survival.

Hazle M. Chapman

Are You There?

You were there when I was born
I was small
You were there to give all.

You were there thru child and teens
I was learning
You were there yearning.

You were there thru young adulthood
I was growing
You were there slowing.

You were there at the sight
I knew you were in flight
Are you there?

Shirley Evans

Soar of a Lover's Dream

As a child
pondering child's dreams
I knew
knew there would be someone
one to share my dreams
my name
children..
life.
Came sooner than imagined
unknowingly already waiting...
longing.

Years spent... Realize
dreams are caterpillars
Never to become butterflies
or...
Butterflies never to leave the ground
one dream soars
that dream is
You.

Charles H. Lynch Jr.

The Soul's Reason

The soul's reason is the real reason
for anything,
like the finest season of the heart,

And hearing the echo of truth
in one's voice,
is denying the offense
of the river of time
passing with one's life . . .

The offense relegated
into submission
and nothingness
by only one possible vocation . . .
Art!

Anna Yardeni

The Past

I will always live in the
past but in the present too;
    and it always seems like someone
has to keep griping at you.
    In the past, where I live is
dark and cold;
    In the past nobody ever seems that
old.
    But I guess people grow and change;
So I probably shouldn't lock myself
up in a cage.
    The problem is, I hate to see people
leave or dying;
    Because everytime that happens,
I start crying.
    Maybe that's why I'm stuck
living in the past;
    So I can love everybody
to the very last.

Audree Bazil

Once

Once when I was little,
Saw a cat sit on a kettle.
Once when I was grown,
Saw a King sit on a throne.

Once when I was down on luck,
Saw a beggar find a buck.
Once when I was full of steam,
Saw a dreamer find a dream.

Once when I was really stupid,
Saw a lover beckon cupid.
Once when I was rich and narrow,
Saw a broker beckon tarot.

Once when I was prepared for grace,
Saw a sinner take my place.
Once when I was drinking wine,
Saw friend take what was mine.

Then one time I saw it clearest,
I see the things that are the nearest.
Then one time I saw afar,
Things we see are the things we are.

Terry L. Giddings

See You Later

One less time card to punch
One less set of sorrows to bunch
One less vehicle on the road
Where God collects the toll

No more sin no more hate
One less hand to shake
No more sorrow and no more pain
No more walking in the rain
We will miss you when we ride
But we will see you on the other side.
William L. McDuell

Red Birds

Oh beautiful red birds,
you visit in the early morn.
You lighten my heart
and I'm not forlorn.

Oh you lovely pair,
male and female.
Nothing you dismay
but to make it a
lovely day

Feeding together
Rain or shine
In my yard
You both are mine
Betty A. Smith

The Nature of Love

My love for you is like a tree
it started from a seed,

It sprouted with the proper care
and satisfied its need.

It grew straight and tall
searching for the light,

With arms of leaves against the wind
it stood against the night.

The beauty and the strength it has
I never could deny,

My love for you is stronger
than a tree reaching for the sky.
M. E. Trimbach

A Touch of God

He took the fury and hurry
Out of the paced racked day,
By painting the evening skies
With coloring strewn astray.

He gathered up some roses
From his great garden of love,
And swirled the pink and scarlet
Through the vivid sky above.

Then from the hair of a child
He took a yellow hue,
And splashed it oh so softly
As only an artist can do.

Some green and blue, a little peach
Even a twirl of gray,
To show the glorious wonder
Of another dying day.
Rosemary L. Schmoock

There's Hope In The Dark

There's Hope in the dark.
Don't give up.
Hold on and look out ahead.
Feel the strong hold that won't let go.
There's Hope in the dark.

There's Hope in the dark.
Look clearly above.
See the light and the parting clouds.
It's on the horizon now.
Touch the dawning of day.
There's Hope in the dark.

There's Hope in the dark.
Seek the Truth.
Put the lies and the fears to flight.
Let the freedom and liberty come.
Gone the night.
There's Hope in the dark.
Ruth A. Flanigan

Forever

What is forever?
A word that is said
But never meaning what is meant.
What is forever?
A word that is sad.
A word that can make a person mad.
Never say a word not meant
Or a word that can easily be bent.
Say something sweet but still.
Say something you mean
But not the impossible.
Never say forever.
Forever is just a word
Nothing can last forever.
Especially not a word.
Jennifer L. Baxter

Untitled

The need to be happy
In life
In the end
What's that around the next bend
Who knows?
I don't, do you?
Step by step we move on
day after day
with the good and with the bad
there's no need to be sad
that's life and that's the way it goes
It has its highs and they are the lows
Timothy Maresca

Good-Bye

Honey, why did you leave me?
I don't understand.
I gave you my heart,
And, held out my hand.

I'll love you forever,
Wherever you'll be.
When someone is with you,
I'll wish it was me.

My heart is now broken,
And, lies down to die.
So, for now and forever,
I guess it's good-bye.
Ina M. Cooper

Dance My Chihuahua

Deep in the heart of Mexico,
I blow my horn, in Escalon.
Here we stand,
A boisterous band,
Me and my kid brother Chico,
And a dancing dog,
Named, Condesa Roseton.

Mi padre was my best compadre,
He laid beside me, dying,
And said, my son Federico,
My time is up, I've to go,
A victim of asesinato.
Go back to Escalon with Chico,
And Condesa Roseton.

Now in the town of Escalon,
We stand, like a boisterous band,
Me and my drummer boy, Chico,
And Condesa Roseton.
I blow my horn, I blow my horn,
Dance my chihuahua, we need the corn.
Mike Kaylan

Emptiness

The world goes on
Rotating, revolving, living
But I remain
Stationary, secluded, forgiving

My mind is filled with thoughts
That will never be spoken
Ideas cling to me
And will never be broken

Words are an expression of thought
But I can't seem to find
The correct procedure
For presenting my mind

As the world goes on
My heart keeps its pace
But within its walls
There is a trace of emptiness
Joseph Oriolo

Some Things I Believe

I believe

that first loves
are last loves
because they can't be
forgotten,

that first fears
are never conquered
but only understood
sometimes,

that first sight
through colored eyes
tint everything
that follows.
Clint Johnson

177

76 Dodge

My car was an Aspen
The top of the line
She was a Special Edition
A few of her kind.

We brought her home in 78'
In the middle of December
I couldn't wait to drive her
I was anxious, I remember

We were the best friends
Until August of 85'
She protected me to the end
So I wouldn't have to die

I think about her today
And I never will forget
How she saved my life, but lost hers
When the Pinto and she met.

Betty J. McCormick

Only a Thought Away

Far away, you are
Though you are as near to me as
my thoughts
I close my eyes and
I imagine your caress of my body
My skin electrifies
I feel your presence
A movement of air brushes softly
across my lips,
could it be your kiss?
I sense your rhythmic heartbeat and
mine follows in synchronization
You are here within me
I flicker my eyes and
you are gone
and I realize your distance from me
Yet, you are only a thought away.

Mary El-Baz

Beauty Unseen

Waits beyond those clouds.
Breath pure and clean -
breathes behind the pinks and
blues we gaze and wait for
peace when it is here.
Just beyond those clouds.
Beauty Unseen
Will be mine to embrace-
if I'll allow my soul to slip
inside the circle
of the light.
Just beyond those clouds.
Beauty Unseen
Runs upon those hills -
lights like fire flies flash images
we hold until dew drops
wash the eye of soul.
Beauty Unseen
Waits beyond those clouds.

Christel Weaver

I Meant to Say . . .

Beware of the drumbeaters;
of their picnic-festive dances;
of their music to folk you by;
of their melodic prances with
    martial overtones;
of their sweet-seductive
    whispering from the pyre...

For, here lies: You:
Shrouded with loving kisses
    in the arms of
        brotherhood of man...

It is cold, baby...
It is cold.

Herman Rotsten

I Need Attention

Whenever my body
is hungry
you feed me.
What of my
other needs
that are not
satisfied sexually.
My Soul,
this part of me
that needs to know
you care,
you love me.
My soul is
like a child,
needing you,
always to hold me,
to believe,
what we have is for real,
not a figment
of someone's dream.

Marva John

Shades of Day

Day is born;
Hopes and dreams all start anew.
Hungry sunbeams
Start to sip the morning dew.

The noonday sun
Looks down upon the teeming crowd.
Life goes on
Toward a patient, waiting shroud.

Evening time;
The sun creeps slowly to the west
Its work is done,
The stars and moon will do the rest.

The evening star
Winks at a teardrop in its eye
The dying sun
Makes one last flame across the sky.

Day is dead;
The sighing wind joins in the dirge
The world awaits
The time when hopes again emerge.

Meedie Monegan

Midnight Walk

One mystic moonlit night
As I gazely wonder,
With my heart light,
I calmly ponder.

As it would seem,
My emotions a dove.
Loving feelings beam
For my true love.

In my mind I write
Of trust and compassion, like a fool.
But my emotions, quite
full, swim in my thought's pool.

Thoughts and emotions bind
Me to love that floats through my mind.

Nina Oehlman

You Look at Me . . .

You look at me
and see my soul.
I look at you
and see love.
You fill me with feelings
that can't be explained.
You are my light
in the darkness.
You are my
reason for living.
What I feel for you
is so much more than love.
There is a burning
in your kiss.
A passion in your touch
that is magic.
I want you to know
I will spend forever with you
But forever will never come.

Virginia Austin

old wife tale

"call to remembrance"

Love, I thought, my being young,
was struck from form and face;
Knowing was the ardor sung
responding to embrace.

Love, I find, now being old,
was cast through passing years
into that endearing mold
regard and caring bears.

Knowing comes as seldom song
in these soft, quiet days;
But, old dear, as life is long,
we know in fonder ways.

My love sums, tu belle graund dame,
all that of past and now;
Greater knowing than in Psalm
creates of you my thou.

Stephen N. Stivers

Lilac

Dangling purple kisses
    softly hugged by white,
rows of bell-shaped lips
    chiming perfumed cries,
Twisted branched fingers
    vein around sad eyes,
holding on to Lilac
    until she fades and dies.

Katia Barrow

Night

My silver candle on my left,
my ocean incense on my right,
my tarot cards beside me
tell me what is right.

My crystal ball is glowing,
my stars are bright,
I chant my prayer and wish
into the moonlit night.

The voices tell me stories,
I write them all,
the souls of the dead
say they're in a never ending fall.

Vampires roam the streets,
killing fills the air,
they all look to me
with looks of despair.

The parks are my gardens
shadows roam them at night,
I'm not the gang leader
but a soldier who will fight.

Annie Overose

Untitled

A flower in a woman's hand
A teardrop on her cheek
A poem running in her mind
The phrase is incomplete

He loves me
He loves me not
He loves me

And there the poem stops
And in the hand a flower stem
With a petal yet unplucked

Christina Winter

The Airport

I am caged
while all around me
birds in flight
dance across the sky.
They scream with laughter,
teasing my spirit
because they know
all I can do is watch.
My eyes are bright as I sit on my perch
looking at everything;
looking at nothing.
Finding strength within the hope
that some day
some glorious key will open the locks
and release me
to join those birds
in flight.

Susan T. McManus

How Can I Go On Dreaming

How can I go on dreaming
When everyone tells me I must
At times I want to start screaming
But a voice inside says, "Hush".

Oh, they say it will get easier
And less and less on my mind,
It has been nearly two years
And my child I still can not find.

I look at her picture and cry
Why, oh why has God taken her away?
I need her here by my side
I prayed he would let her stay.

So tell me if you will please,
I beg you will give with meaning,
For someone who cannot sleep, so
How can I go on dreaming?

Mary Lou Speck

Jesus Is There

I cannot see the wind at all,
or hold it in my hand.
And yet I know there is a wind
because it swirls the sand.

I know there is a wondrous wind
because I glimpse its power
Whenever it bends low a tree
or sways the smallest flower.

Now God is much like this,
invisible as air.
I cannot see or touch him,
yet I know he is there;
Because I glimpse His wondrous works
and goodness everywhere.

Chalyn Tropez Joshua

Shades of Grey

Here I am, once again,
The pen in my hand
The light shining dim
A poem in my mind
pushing through bundles of fright.
I've seen the black
I've seen the white
They both seem easy
They both seem right.
I wish it could be that way
So simple, just black and white.
But, if the world only knew
From when we enter crying
To when we leave dying
it can never be that way.
The world is but many shades of grey.
But I wish we could all see
the wondrous mystery of grey.
With black and white you have
such simple choices.

Leif Erickson

Thoughts and Feelings

As I look into your eyes
From day to day
There are often thoughts I think
But then neglect to say

Like how my world has changed
Since you have entered in
How many dreams come true
And many more begin

That precious was that special gift
From you to me
A little girl, a family
For us to be

The longer you're my wife
The deeper feelings go
My pride, respect, and love for you
Endure and grow

So, if my love in words expressed
Comes with delay
I'll say it now, "Every day with you
is Valentines Day!"

Larry B. Fish

Wondering Souls

Oh, what to be a wondering soul,
    And go from place to place.
To sore above the tainted plains,
    to hide beneath the sea.

No worry's would I have,
    No time table must I keep.
No tears to shed for anyone,
    No place to rest my feet.

Oh, what to be a wondering soul,
    To spread my wings and fly.
To hear the wind that calls to me.
    and never have to die.

No one to say I'm sorry,
    No one to feel the guilt.
No one to set along at night,
    No one to cry out loud.

Oh, what to be a wondering soul,
    And go from place to place,
No tears to shed for anyone,
    No place to rest my feat.

Yvonne Harris

I Am.

I look backward.
I look forward.
Am I alone?

I look left.
I look right.
Where is everyone?

I look up.
I look down.
Where have I gone?

Am I lost?
Am I trying to be found?
Who am I?

Emily Jaekels

Passing

Your journey now is over,
Your time on earth had ended.
I will miss you very much,
As all you have befriended.

You have lived a full life,
Which I was gladly a part.
Now you are off to another,
To have a new start.

You've stood by your faith,
It helped you though each day.
As it will now — forever,
As you walk the Lord's way.

I know your soul's with God now,
But sometimes I'll forget,
I'll want to tell you something
And get myself upset.

Eventually it will dawn on me,
You're been here from the start.
I just need to open up,
Not my eyes, but just my heart.

Teresa Crable

Life's Mosaic

The mosaic of life is a grand design,
Patterned by the Master's hand,
Colored by each choice of thine,
Part of a master plan.

As life's mosaic goes along,
With wonder do we gaze
At subtle changes, right or wrong,
Etched with living every day.

There comes a time along the way,
When, standing back, we view,
All the brush strokes we have made,
With a sense of deja vous.

When our mosaic piece is done,
May we feel a joy sublime,
That all the strokes we painted on,
Will withstand His test of time.

Jo Ann Wyant

A Deer Hunter's Lament

When the sun sets o'er the Fairmont,
    the Twin Tanks and Scalp Creek,
And you long to feel your rifle stock
    snug against your cheek,
If you have not seen a deer all day,
    you'll feel a touch of sorrow,
'Tis just a fleeting touch because
    you're back for more tomorrow.

What I did wrong this morning
    is anybody's guess.
I missed a beautiful standing doe
    at ninety yards or less.
Perhaps I jerked the trigger,
    I'm sure I'll never know.
Perhaps I had buck fever,
    even tho it was a doe.
But tomorrow is another day,
    I know where I will be,
Just hoping that a deer will come
    from yonder live oak tree.

John M. Anderson

Lost Again

People seek but seldom find
Someone to whom they can confide;
Many times I wished to share
Thoughts I had to keep inside.

I feared I'd be misunderstood,
Or ridiculed, or judged; and yet
The reasons mainly were that I
Had sought a friend I had not met.

And now at last I've found someone
That I feel free to share things with,
And know that I'll be understood;
I thought such insight was a myth;

That understanding could not be
Complete, or even nearly so;
That no two people really knew
Each other in such ratio.

Only now that I have found you,
We have travelled separate ways.
How I pray we'll be together!
Until then I'll count the days.

John Martin

Testimony of Wonder

The beauty of the mountains,
so bold and tough, but true,
holds a deep sense of wonder,
that for me, seems so new.

I love the freedom of the woods,
though it's not my first time here,
don't take it all for granted,
'cause it will cause God to tear.

He has the power of the river,
lakes, trees, and breeze,
yet what a magnificent man,
to create it with such ease.

I love the Lord, God, Jesus,
for he has done so much for me,
hopefully from these words of my soul,
my testimony, you will see.

Michael R. Newell

Dare to Dream

Dare to dream my friend,
Dare to think.
Do not be afraid to fantasize.
Do not let anyone tell you not to.
Be free my friend,
Dream.
You can dream whatever you want,
There is no limit.
Dream, dream, dream.

Megan Anderson

Loved One

It is very clear my dear,
    A loved one is not here,
God's plan is ever so clear,
    But do not fear,
Angels are holding her near,
    Remember her laughter and cheer,
For our memories are always so dear,
    Even though she is not here,
We must dry up our tears,
    And remember her through the years!

Gwen Kyte

Winter

Honking geese go,
Up into the skies
They don't like the snow
When winter arrives.
Down the flakes fall,
From someplace unknown
Snowfall, snowball
Still, the winds moan.
Jack Frost will visit us,
And bring snow for Christmas
The New Year Baby,
Born in this cold,
Will grant the wishes
Of young and the old.
Enjoy the frost season,
While it lasts,
For smiles on faces it silently casts.

Danielle M. Simmons

We Never Walk Alone

How can we think there is no God?
Lift up thy hands and pray
Do you think he will not answer?
Just try it day from day.
And when your world turns upside
down, and you don't know
what to do; remember what
the Bible said, lift up your
hand's and pray and God will
see you thru.
But how does God know me?
My burden's to share.
Don't worry he always knew
He was just waiting for your
prayer.

Dorothy E. Aiton

Untitled

As I begin this tale of mine,
I'm apt to cause the words to rhyme.
Tho time will tell,
The poet's not well.
It's just to see your eyes shine.

When first we met so young,
Our songs, so sad were sung,
And who could know,
What seeds we'd sow.
While having only just begun.

The years that came were trying,
Filled with deceit and lying.
But through it all,
Our love grew tall.
Of this there's no denying.

So what I'm trying to say,
In this quaint and subtle way,
Is no bars can hold
My love, this old
That grows stronger with each day.

Stephen M. Smith

Goodbye!

Perhaps it's best that I admire you
From a distance for awhile.
Like a precious work of art
I need not touch you to appreciate you.

You have been trapped in my memory -
A prisoner of my soul -
Unable to step down from the pedestal
I have kept you on too long.

So now I must release you
So that I might relieve myself
Of the pain I am feeling
- knowing it's time to let you go -

Pam J. Murray

Now

Death to me
Was like driftwood on the sea;

A falling of leaves
In a pattern Autumn weaves;

Flowers in vases
With tired, drooping faces.

Now it appears
An eternity of tears;

Broken window panes
Letting in cold rains;

Burnt out souls
Like burnt out souls.

My love is dead.

Jeanne Togay

Lost

Sometimes my mind does stray,
do everything my way.
When all the world seems cold,
we need someone to hold.

Lord knows I've fallen down,
He knows I've been around, He
prays He'll see the day, when
I'll see things His way.
He knows that when I'm down,
He's always been around.
His love is there for me.
Just open my eyes and see.

Mike Reynolds

Fell The Dream

A dream a fantasy is all so good.
Just for a while.
Just for a dream.
Just for a fantasy,
To touch my body in enticing
ways that are so forbidden.
Ways that give me pleasure.
Ways that give me joy.
Ways of pure erotic.
I need this.
I want this
And in a dream
And in a fantasy.
I will have this.
But for a time I close my eyes.
For a dream a fantasy is all so good.
Just for a while.
Just for a dream.
Just for a fantasy.

Faye Henson

The Box Swing

Fresh summer sunny days
Swinging in a box swing
Jeremy right beside me.
Together we are laughing.
Back, forth
Higher, higher
Butterflies form in my stomach
Reaching for the sky
Trying to touch a cloud
What fun, whee!
Smack!
Pain!
Lying face down in dirty grass
I gulp for air
My broken nose
Painful and throbbing, bleeds
Jeremy right beside me.
Calling for help
Empty is the box swing
Filled with laughter no more.

Molly Schulte

Daddy's Hand

A hand to hold when I am scared
A hand that provides for me
A hand I know will always be there
To love and comfort me

A hand to share with others
A hand to hold me
A hand I know will always be there
To believe and have faith in me

A hand to wipe away the tears
A hand to console me
A hand I know will always be there
To protect and nurture me

A hand to share in laughter
A hand that brings joy to me
A hand I know will always be there
The hand that belongs to Daddy

Leah Gerig

Daffodils

You crazy daffodils,
Thrashing about in the breeze.
Don't you you know,
You'll never be free.
Much like me,
Held down,
By the restraints of society.
Struggling,
Struggling,
Freedom is out of reach.

Rhonda Baune

Mother Lies Here

Mother lies here,
Solemnly sleeping
While her children
Stand there weeping,
A dove she is,
The holy bird,
While the preacher,
Says the last words

Chelsey Arnett

What A World

What a world
What a world
What kind of world is true
What kind of world we build
up for - only a small few
what kind is Mankind and
who are the few?
The few is to many
that watches over the plenty
what a world
what a world
when will we face up to
the strife of the many
what will it take, or
what will we exchange
when we take our turn
being a few with plenty
what a world
what a life
which part are you?

Mildred C. Buncom

Untitled

How crazy his behavior seems to be.
If I were he,
it would make sense to me.

Grace C. Poertner

Salt Silver

Soft, sweet night, a baby's gown,
Drapes its shroud of ermine down;
On bell-towered ships and silent seas,
Caressed by salt and laughing breeze.

'Neath vigil stars the iron fleet
Slips knotty links beneath the sheets;
And silent plies quicksilver crests,
As day is dawning in the west.

Vicki Tieche

My Bundle of Joy

In this tiny little bundle
So warm, so sweet, so soft
Lies a miracle of miracles
Of which, I never gave a thought
With ten little fingers
And ten little toes
Two lips that form a buttercup
And a tiny turned up nose
Two cheeks that look like rosebuds
Two eyes like pools of blue
These are the things that constitute
An angel through and through
She's captured all the hearts of
Everyone who comes to see
This tiny little bundle of joy
That God has sent to me
And as she grows and years go by
I know she'll always be
A someone to be proud of
Filled with love and femininity

Marie Selvaggio

The Environmentalists

The grizzly that growls,
And the wolf that howls,
The cougar that prowls,
And the Spotted Owls,
May they all evacuate their bowels
On the heads of the
Environmentalists.

Kenneth Browning

To My Daughter At Age 21

When you were a baby
I was so proud.
Because you were mine
I shouted aloud.

You found out life's secrets
You dared them come true.
You learned very early
You should be you.

You pushed to be just
You sought out uniqueness.
You sped on your journey
You tempered life with your sweetness.

Thru middle and thru high school
You pushed and you tried.
You never said can't
You had to much pride.

And now that you've grown
You've proven yourself.
A father could never want
For anything else. Love Dad

Albert D. Trahan

Melody In Sea

The sea sings a song to me
or perhaps it sings to you;
No matter who might the receiver be
Its song is clear and true.

The tones are pure, full, and rich
each one blends within the other.
I'm sure a conch shell gave the pitch
with cadence from wave on another.

The rhythm of the movement
sweeps in upon the shore,
Etching upon the sand cement
the beautiful, musical score.

The sea sings a song to me
or perhaps it sings to you.
No matter who might the receiver be
we are both now lyrical, too.

Jan Dugan

Shy Little Bird

Drifting away—
Far away
In my dream world
Night or day.
Couldn't I have this
Wide awake?
No, for asleep I take great risks
To fulfill my dreams,
But awake I'm a shy little bird
Who can't sing anymore.

Ann Fisher

Untitled

Heaven is a place of breathless beauty
and glory sublime
God made for Christians at the
end of time.
There is no night, no depth, no
height, no space.
God and His Son made this place.
Where love abounds and grace is free.
What more, O God, can we ask of thee?
This world is not our future home.
No matter where we go or where we roam.
We're only passing through this way.
While we wait for that special day.
Our hope is for a better place,
When we see our Savior face to face.
Where our prize awaits us at the end.
And also awaits you, my christian friend

Winifred M. Arnett

Loss and Love

If I can now face the loss.
For you, come to me.
Our sons and grandchildren live
with pride and joy.
My life, in gracious moments,
Flicker, to future life; with
family, boundless love.

Alexander M. Williams

My Girl

When you became a Mother
You grew up over night
To see the Baby in your arms
It was a glorious sight
Your face so sweet and shining
A heart that's pure and true
My little girl, A Mother
Yes, Dolly Jean, that's you
You can now teach her all you know
As she will need to learn
The ups and downs of life on earth
As knowledge she will yearn
To learn to pray, it is a must
For trust in God to be
A stepping stone upon life's path
To build integrity
For her to love and learn to care
For others that she'll meet
To be the best that she can be
And still stay soft and sweet

Pat Simpson

Peace of Mind

Until I find
some peace of mind.

I will feel this uneasiness
and I confess . . .

I'm coming to the end.
And I would like to send . . .

My condolences to my life
in which I did strive

To find peace, and to no avail,
I did fail!!!

Kimberly Yanak

A Wish

A wish is a fantasy,
Imagination gone wild.
For there is so little time,
When you are a child,
To have a dream of your own,
Or a wish to come true.
So keep wishing your wish,
And dreaming your dreams,
And maybe one day you'll know
What it means
To love something so
That you hold it close to your heart,
For a wish is something
From which you should
Never part.

Leah King

Micheal

When someone is taken away
It happens in a single day.
The love one feels always stays.
One can not explain the awful pain.
It's just something that will remain
and nothing will ever be the same.
But one must always remember
it's the love and feelings that are so
tender. The one we love would
surely say, remember me in a happy
way. The time we shared, good and
bad, we were lucky to have had. So
every now and then it's O.K. to look
back again. Just remember our time
as a special one and our love will
always shine like the summer's sun.
Know I want you to go forward today.
For I am like the suns warm summer
ray, shining upon your life in
every way.

Brenda Lee Hallman

Depart

   To depart from you;
to find love so young; then to
separate.
   The sorrow felt in each
heart.
   To say good-bye; how could
it come. Never wanting never
knowing. To lie with out the sun,
to live so confused and unsure.
Never forgetting the smell, the
touch, the feeling. Always
remembering.
   To say good bye, what
sorrow. How they lived on love
alone. To be the wealthiest soul,
then to turn out so poor.
   For one moment in time you
wish and hope you could go back
and change every thing.

Sharia Morris

Life Is A Challenge

Life is a challenge
From beginning to end
From your first slap on the butt
Until your final spin.

There are mountains and valleys
That you must climb
There are days that seem endless
And they boggle your mind.

The challenge you face
As time goes on
To deal with the problems
That still lie unknown.

But to know what's ahead
Might bring you to tears
Give you a weary heart
And challenge your fears.

So only God knows the future
And that's just as He planned
You're to just do your best
And leave the rest in His hands.

Louise Banks

Don't Want Your Help

Don't want your help!
never had it—
don't want it now—

A moldy, dusty, rickety thing —
I hold it gingerly
between two tentative fingers —
doesn't even have a nice smell

No! Don't want your help —
covered with a thick
blanket of dust

I'm putting it back on the shelf
and I will push it hard —
push it way back
where dusty, rickety things
go.

Enid Schaeffer

Memories

I remember
    my grandmother
    who wove many blankets
    of beautiful colors, shapes, sizes
    beautiful figures
        wonderful meanings
the last rug off the loom
        the most beautiful
        wonderful
    —her last
before she returned to mother earth
I will cherish that blanket
        full of memories
            of joyous times
            of sad times
            of great love
    forever

Steve Hamlet-Smith

Norman

You my love have left.
But your betrayal and lie's remain.
You are my illness within.
You are more alive now
than when your life force
dripped from my thighs
A rumble, churning chaos lies
dormant in the pit of my belly,
turning my skin to pale clammy dough.
If only I could, spew you up.
Let you be on the floor,
wipe you away,
and feel you no more.

Patty De Jarnette

Untitled

Lost am I
Without my love
Memories ride on the ocean air.

The hazy still morn
While moored in the cove.

Diamonds sparkle on the
Misty water

The gentle clank of the
Rigging against the mast.

Drowsy with sleep
Intoxicated with my love
Solitude everywhere.

Do not disturb my happiness
I breathe it deeply
Understanding not
That I would exhale.

Ruth M. Acteson

Fear

What's fear
Is fear big or little
Is fear tall or small
Does fear haunt or taunt you
Is fear someone or something
What do we fear
Do we fear people or mice
Do we fear houses or lawyers
Is fear a deep, dark, feeling
If you fear death, enjoy life fully
My fear's death
What's your fear?

Adam Brousseau

Untitled

My future
my future
is to play
football
because
I like football
and it
is my
dream
my future
to have kids and
raise them
like my
mom and
dad did to
me

Pablo Alejandro

Tears and Fears

Can you see my tears
Do you know my fears

I need you to hold me tight
To help me make it through the night

With you around
I'm never down

Can you see my tears
Do you know my fears

I love you can't you see
I need you to love me

Hand in hand
We can make a stand

Can you see my tears
Do you know my fears

Stevie Merle

The Calabash Pool

From the umber pool
drawn deep from the
hot Mother spring
come the sonorous sounds
of the village women's voices
their wet, brown bodies
languishing in laughter
and stories the men
cannot tell or even hear
of silken breasts that sag
with the suckling of
so many babes and men
and bellies soft and round
with wombs that have
birthed the world
again and again and again
in the shadow of
the Calabash tree

Jeanne M. Lightfoot

The Fiery Tongue

Will there ever be complete control,
   No matter what it will take,
To diminish its verbal insults
   And leaving out all hate.

So small indeed, posing so innocent,
   Between those shining teeth,
Yet ready to heave those hateful
   words, like a poisonous dart,
Regardless of circumstances or deed.

Our God designed it - true, for such
   better use, as loving, gentle and
Kind words, showing our gratitude;
   Along with taste buds, whether
sour or sweet, it is ours to enjoy
   whatever we care to eat.

Ugly or filthy words, are all the
   same, so why use them to damage
Someone's name; God knows who
   you are, so shouldn't you be
ashamed?

Joseph H. Terry

Night Time In Copley Park

Fool's gold moon
Overflowing the sky,
Grown too big for eyes,
More than the heart can hold.
Like a mesmerist's charm
Drawing the soul up like water,
Drooling soft shine down like a chime,
Teetering on tall-topped trees,
Tottering on slated roofs,
Toppling into the skater's pond,
Cracked light in shivers
Trapped under ice.

Peter C. Leverich

Fantasy

At night when I close my eyes
I see your handsome face
I feel your gentle touch
And the warmth of your embrace
I feel your lips touch mine
And your hand caresses my cheek
And at that very moment
The night don't seem so bleak
This fantasy that I'm having
It seems so very real
I can see I can smell
I can even hear, touch and feel
Suddenly I open my eyes
To see if you're really here
Then I realize I was dreaming
And sadly shed a tear.

Michelle C. Hauger

Sweet Angel, Night Angel

In Loving Memory of
Melanie S. Gunckel. I miss you.

She moved in miraculous ways,
Her eyes glimmering as if they
Were the stars themselves.
She is now my guardian angel,
Heavenly blessed.
Everywhere she went she touched
People's souls, filling them with
Love, joy, happiness, no matter
Who it was.
Like a child, she had much to learn,
Much to teach, and much to give.
An angel in the night, swept
Away by morning dawn.
Sweet angel, night angel.

Katrina Coe

Untitled

Where will I be tomorrow
If tomorrow never comes?
Will I be among the chosen
Whose life has just begun?
For isn't it our duty to serve
As humble ones?
With our faith reassuring - us
The best is yet to come
I need only say the words
"Lord thy will be done
Where will I be tomorrow if
Tomorrow never comes?"

Joseph Mandarano

On Visiting My Uncle
at the University Hospital

His age is death. His days
the whistle of a freight train
passing by.
Prisoner chained upon a bed
held by a lock
for which there is no key.
If I could turn his head
then he could see
that hope still drips

Its measured steps unhurried
until it's swept away by life.

But, no. I see reflected
in the withered face
no final call for a release.
He knows that life has now become
a cabbage plant that's gone to seed.

Benedette Knopik

The Burden

If you want your burden to be light
With peace of mind both day and night
Stop your life that's filled with sin
Walk please to God in the sight of men.

If you desire God's blessing
Then you start with sins confessing
For it's when you repent
That The Blessing Is Quickly Sent.
So if you want God's Grace
For Him not to hide His Face,
  So
Now don't hide all your wrong
Under some pretended song
But just confess your sin
And God will surely bless you again.

Nathan Miller

The Orchestra Of Autumn

Joyous leaves danced
  In tune to the music,
As the angels
  Frolic in glee,
Singing softly
  Unheard melodies...
The orchestra
  Scarcely noticed,
When the harps
  joined in,
Cellos sprang forth
  in a spiritual song,
The spirits
  Of all were
    Lifted that day...
When the rhapsody
  Of praise on high
    Flowed through the woods,
As the angels and the leaves
  Danced, danced, danced...

Madeline L. Haynes

Mom

There is no better mother,
  on this entire earth;
You've always been there for me,
  since the day you gave me birth.

I know it was not easy,
  this job you had to do;
At times I'm sure you could not wait,
  until the day I grew.

And as I grew from teen on up,
  your life I filled with stress;
Even then you stayed by me,
  and never loved me less.

The day has finally come now,
  just like you said it would;
I'm thanking you for all those things,
  you did for my own good.

Carolyn Burton

Rain and Clouds

Rain
From clouds,
Won't rain on me.
Stars
In the sky,
Don't shine to see,
Rain and sky
Don't lie.
For the sky and rain are one.
Without sky
There would be no rain,
Sky
Rain on me.
Stars
Let me see.
Sky
Shine on me
Rain from clouds
Don't rain on me anymore.

Stanley M. McMullen

The Color Blue

As the river runs going through
thick and thin paths running
faster then a jackrabbit going
around rocks and trees going
down water falls

Michael Anthony Fonde

Icebergs

Limpid visions
Appeared through the mist
Huge seris towering like skyscrapers
Conviviality of ice
Enervation with amnesia
Could not denote
Anything logical.

They were slowly moving
Lethal and enigmatic
Irreverent of life
Yet bestial because of size
Sedulous they grew closer
Deep green glass like mirrors
Reflected like a diadem of royalty
They quietly slipped by
Revealing a walrus undisturbed
In the limpid vision.

Madeleine McAlpin Vanderpool

Untitled

Love isn't a joy ride
there's a small fee
The day dreamers are the lovers
and the scared ones pull up the covers
like faucet with its rusty water
to fall asleep to the sweet lullaby
of a pitter patter
like a candle's wax when it drips
I can taste the wine upon your lips

Katie Ziegler

Goodbye

Here I sit alone with you,
    I am feeling a little blue.
I can't think of what to say,
    so that you will see it my way.

Maybe one day you'll understand,
    when I sit with you and hold
    your hand,
That in the future far untold,
    you'll once again be mine to hold.

Sommer Leitch

Gone Forever

To my dearest cousin Michelle Ann Morgan.
The wind played with the trees
And the grass on the ground
And over the hill came
A strange sad sound.

It was a mix of tears falling
That should never have fell
And the whispering of secrets
That no one can tell.

It was the sound of the soul
Who's given up on a prayer
And the sigh of the heart
Who has no one to care.

The sound was so sad
Given, the trees would have cried
It was the sound that I heard
The day that you died . . . .

Tiffany Hinds-Broadway

Creator . . .

Created by the creator above,
All dreams and desires come from above.
This should be all's first love!
As in creator we all share in knowing
true love.

No fleshly love can touch
As our creator is spiritual love,
It flows from into us from above.
All in the world is within this world
Can share in this wonderful love!

"Creator to created."

Susan A. Robertson

The Pale Moon

The pale moon
Lights the sky
Caressing the earth
In unconditional love.

Golda David

Untitled

As we grow older
Throughout the years
We still may shed
Just a few more tears
Whether our hearts
Have been broken by a guy
Or we've crashed again
Trying to reach for the sky
I hope our friendship
Is here to stay
I'll always be here
for you each and everyday
Even if you're down and blue
Or if you just need a clue
Life's like a bumpy road
And we're just along for the ride
But we'll always be the best of friends
Until the day we die.

Elisa Helen Mestelle

Living Dead . . . A Holocaust Remembrance

Straining against cold steel,
Skeletons peer out
Through the gates of hell.

Freedom on the other side.
Freedom for the living dead.

But they just wait.
Wait for their oppressors,
Wait for the word to be spoken.

It will soon be over,
one way or another.

Adam Zolkover

At My Own Breast

When I met you
I had made peace with
many disillusions,
And yet I was not ready
for the ascetic period
of old age.
I could not
deal with humiliation
nor with my thirst
still very much unquenched.
Today, though far from goal
I know the road:
I want to be your friend,
But ultimately yearn
to be a child
At my own breast.

Monica Markovits

Didymouse

I pet myself like a puppy
the little hairs work
whose thighs am I?
A crotch work pulled out
from a finger's touch, if I dare?
. . . Two times skinny
they care, momma's
two rowdies racing second thoughts
around a city of despair
lost among confusion
and dying wishes, two times over
a calendar two years late — Slap
upside the head in my house
of truncated diffusion
and second chances on the road
to Didymouse.
But I'm still there.

Thomasina Duckworth

Love Was Born

As the night is chilled by winters wind
Bodies are warmed by the touch of skin
In a room lit by a candles light
Restless hearts let passion take flight

Feelings of desire burn out of control
An intimate moment bares their soul
When pulses react to a subtle touch
Nothing before ever felt so much

As night uncovers the mornings dawn
Hearts awaken to a friendships bond
The sun will shine a different light
Love was born in heaven last night

Karl R. Ladd

From the Beginning of Time

From the beginning of time
there was a plan
happiness yet heartache
for every woman, child, and man

Though I've often wondered
about what is to come
my eyes see visions
of another place where I'm not from

As we travel an endless journey
distance is steps away
steering through paths of uncertainty
each restless day

After we are gone
we leave behind
nothing to take with
only peace to find

Sandra B. Harris

Seedless

Love is like a rose.
You have to plant a seed
in order to receive a rose.
Love you have to introduce
it to one you desire.
If you don't nourish and
care for the rose it weakens.
If you don't build up
within the love it fades.

KerryAnn Bednartz

Stars

Stars that light my path
Sprinkle with marvelous light
God's great universe.

Bob Howard

Nightly Ritual

Once each day
there comes a fear
of losing things
far and near.

Once each day
I realize
vulnerability resides
behind glassy eyes.

Once each day
my flaws I see
and let them be
unkind to me.

Once each day,
that man, before,
I remember him,
that flippant bore!

Garry Loss

The Dragon's Gate

The cat's paws jump
with each movement of
the dragon's breath . . .

The dragon's scales leaps
and curls to mark the
spot that every sailor
dreads . . .
The doorways keep
shines in the moonlights
glow . . .

And the helms man
shouts the course to
make the run for home,
and a good nights sleep.

Robert Charles Swerdloff

Summer's Eve

One summer's eve
On a moonlit night
I sat on a beach
Gentle breeze so light

I sat on a rock
Gazing out at the sea
Breeze lifting my hair
Stars as far as I can see

I smile softly
My lover at my side
Caressing my shoulders
Easy as the tide

We make love so sweetly
Sounds of the sea all around
Sweetest of orgasms
for us abound.

Starr L. Leydic

My Child

Sitting here my thoughts wander.
A sorrow sadness growing fonder.
A young heart never feeling.
With no chance of ever being.
His flame flickered away.
In this world he could never stay.
A choice with great remorse.
Guilt pounding its frigid force.
Hammered my soul is left shattered.
Pieces have fallen and scattered.
His pure and innocent face,
Will never see this unjust place.
His dreams will now become mine.
Visions of him will remain divine.
Although he has no name,
Forever I'll feel his pain.
Sitting here my thoughts wander.
A sorrow sadness growing fonder.
Farewell my child!

Michael Avery

Mother Earth

Mother Earth live on.
Thou shall not perish too long.
Salvation is strong.

Jennifer Henke

Sea Gulls

The sea gulls soar over the sea
With a mighty sweep of the wings
Then with a graceful landing
Along the beach they come
To walk proudly among the waves
Until the tide comes in so close
They rise in formation once more
To soar back over the sea

Elsie Pyrtle

A Novice Working at the Wheel

You came to me without history
Unformed, untethered
And apparently, unintentionally.
A lump of soft, new clay.
The first thing I did
Was place a navel
At your middle
So you could say
You'd been attached, once.
Intimately.
I made your face handsome
And your chin strong,
Your shoulders broad
And your fingers, long
So you could stroke me.
To keep you soft, I worked the clay
Adding water as a way
To keep a crust from forming
But you hardened, anyway
Then fled on crumbling feet.

Angelique Craney

Untitled

I became the bees honey
for I knew no other way
to be stuck on you.

I became the sugar and spice
for I felt you needed
both in your life.

And now I look
at what I've become
a foolish girl in love.

I've become the petals
in your rose garden,
and the thoughts in your head.

But here I stand
with a sugared bouquet
becoming something again.
Your wife.

Che'rmelle Danecia Edwards

Beautiful

Beautiful
at least to me
forever
if it's suppose to be
together
just him and me
lover
he's soon to be
husband
if he loves me
friend
no matter what
partner
when together
helper
forever and ever

Pamela Hopkins

First Born

  She is my first born. She
is my joy, and my pain. She
makes me laugh when others
make me cry she is my
light when all see around
me is darkness. She is my
rock when I start to fall.
She is full of life, and hope,
love. When others were full of
hate and despair. She is a
child. Wise beyond her years.
I love you my first born
daughter.

Stephanie Lashley

My Last Word

My last word,
My last thought,
My last sentence
  would be I love you.
My last word
  would be "you"
My last thought
  would be of you
I love you.

Milisa Thomson

Planet of Mystery

You play, you laugh,
you are loud and noisy;
I listen, I hear,
I am sad, so are you
and you, and you...

I speak, you look,
I am, you receive;
I give, you take,
I leave, you watch
and watch, and watch...

You are air, you are space,
you are, even if blank,
mysterious vignettes never
touching one another,
just seeming to...

We are here it would seem,
are we really, are you there;
or could it be that it is
just merely an exchange
of a script after all...

Helene R. Chapman-Olson

Jerusalem

Jerusalem: A book still being written,
A never ending story,
A living history.

Jerusalem: A place of healing,
A place of religion,
A holy memory.

The past being unfolded,
With every spoken and unspoken word.
A reminder of the ones who once lived,
And the ones who shall live.
Like a time line of the past,
Present, and future.
A key to a thousand mysteries,
Soon to be memories.

Like an actress on stage,
Her words are very clear.
Like a newborn baby,
Its heart is very pure.
Like a queen and her kingdom,
Her people are very strong.

Laurel Moshett

Missing You

On a dark and chilly night
All alone, and no one in sight
Just the whispers of the wind
And thoughts of you holding me tight

Tears begin to fill my green eyes
Like that is any surprise
Cause without you by my side
Happiness is nothing but lies

A heart is so empty and afraid inside
Without your love I cannot hide
The hurt, the sorrow, the pain
Or all the tears I have cried

You are my true soul-mate
As we could tell from our first date
The fire we shared between us
Was nothing more than fate.

Judy Graham

The Important Question

Art
Are you waiting for me?
Or is it just not my time yet
Time for me to do and say it all
I guess not.
Laid up on my back
Wanting to act
Aching to act
But knowing I gotta wait.
Time to heal
Physically mentally spiritually
Regroup
Put myself all together again.
Art
Are you waiting for me?
Or is it just not my time yet?
God tell me, Art,
Tell me.

Ker Michaels

Untitled

The earth is special
The moon is too
The waters are great
and so are you.

Mara J. Becker

Childhood Mourning

Morning sun, in silver it's hung
Sworn by secrets of special cares
Reveal the pendants of songs sung
In this place where flowers go to die
Grown-up men leave the elusive
Place, no more to play games
And fairy tales bid final farewell

Doves of distant times carry
Childhoods away to cry
Harken forward tears unable to evade.

Different ways say what remains
Simple childhoods of cheated flames
Inferior fires melted milky way
Snow white and hickory dock
Blinded in grown-up made to believe.

Larry Abbas

Worried

Darkly as I lay,
body chilled to the bone,
room C-o-l-d as ice

Asleep or perhaps not;
I feel my spirit rise
leaving only a shell.
I L-e-f-t-, yes I did,
What time?
I don't know when.

I arrived home,
looked around;
everything seem Okay.
My Baby was fine.

I returned Again,
yes I did.
What time?
I don't know when.
U-n-i-t-e-d- as one
once more.

Geraldine Love

Friends

Friend, precious as can be.
Leaving permanently.
I shall miss you as you see.
Life ending for you, leaving me.

Elinor Smith

Momma's Problem

Daddy married momma,
They led a happy life.
They loved each other
And being husband and wife.
Daddy went to work,
And Mom picked up a glass.
One little drink
Erased the wonderful past.
We tried to help her quit,
But nothing helped at all.
The building that took so much
Slowly made its fall.
So Daddy divorced Momma.
They went their separate ways.
She still relies on the bottle
To this very day.
I remember her in my prayers,
I want the Lord to know
I love and miss my Momma.
Lord, where did she go?

Amber Doyle

Untitled

Lou died today
Vacuumed up like an old
muddy foot print left to dry
A heart silenced forever
In the kennel he died
God sighed
He took Lou up to heaven
Where he is watching me today
It's a day of sorrow, I cried
He was here one minute
And gone the next
It's not just another day
Lou died, I cried, God sighed

Emily Moore

Together We Walk

As we walk down
life's path together
hand in hand,
arm in arm.
Though the way
may be rocky,
and one of us
may stumble,
the other will help
to regain the footing.
Through the rain
and the sun we walk,
the destination
is not important,
because we will
reach it together,
you and I.

Sandra C. Dorr

Happy Birthday Husband

I love you more than will ever show
probably more than you'll ever know
but husband mine this is really true
the best birthday wish is here for you
I could have got you a bowl of fruit
or maybe a nice new fancy suit
there's always a brand new shiny car
perhaps a trip for oh so far
but darling after much ado
here is what I decided to do
just give you a great big loving kiss
for that is something we never miss
I give you me to do as you please
to slap me up or give me a squeeze
so here I am all 160 pounds
and that's a lot more than it sounds
oh what are you going to do with me
I'll make you happy I'll bet by gee
so Happy Birthday Husband dear
and here's my Love for all next year.

Alice Clemons-Beyer VanCour

Watching

I've watched the sun rise in the sky
To bathe the world in light.
I've watched a bird drop from a tree
And spread its wings in flight.

I've seen a million things, it seems,
Since on this world I came.
But I'll go on looking every day
For the beauty of God's domain.

I'll watch the lover's first embrace;
Their smiles and dancing eyes.
And when the Lord makes them as one,
I'll watch their sweet surprise.

I'll follow every step they take
With love, through wedded bliss.
And when they hold their newborn child
I'll share their untold bliss.

Esther M. Ruse

For Ralph

O Wayward Son
Come home, please, come home!
Your Mother is weeping
While you still roam.

The silence is deafening
And echoes with time.
The heartbreaking distance
Continues to climb.

Sweet child of yesteryear
Troubled with age
You once dwelled in happiness
Now tumult and rage.

Loving arms long to hold you
Gentle kisses await.
What a wonderful homecoming
Life could create!

O Wayward Son
Cease now to roam!
Your Mother is waiting
Love beckons you home.

Deborah J. Stearns

Destiny!

My death! My only rest
Oh! Death, the beauty of heaven
Why death; sorrow without hope?

God gave us beauty for ashes;
Oil of joy for mourning, and for
The Spirit of heaviness, he gave
Us garments of praise!

Destiny! Destiny!

How will my burial be?
When will I be under my father's
Wings?
I love what God gave us; His
whole creation and earth; the singing
birds, the beautiful flowers dress as
garments, and one another to love.

Marbella L. Pedone

Autumn's Here

First frost has come,
The pumpkins glisten
With an icy rime.
Hark! Listen, listen,
Wild geese know it's time
To head for a southern home.
Calling, honking, flying higher
They wing in V-shaped flight,
Silhouettes against the azure sky.
Pumpkin moon in the vault of night;
Leaves spattered with pots of dye
Seem to set the trees on fire.
God's changing world
That He created;
Its beauty for us to ponder
Until satiated
With the glorious wonder,
The panorama unfurled.

June M. Takatch

Untitled

When times are tough
    you're feeling down,
you're so alone
    no one's around.

Thoughts were good
    however wrong
it's said "keep your chin up"
    you'll always be strong.

But when you're alone
    as lonely you feel
You want to be alone
    hoping your heart will heal.

It feels like a cycle
    unable to get around.
Only one thing helps,
    Love comes back to town.

Dawna Sonsteng

The Bus Bench

The Little Old Ladies
Who ride the bus
Are your mom
And my mom,
They're one of us.

They sit on the bench
And patiently wait:

If you stop to talk,
They radiate
All the wisdom and grace
That eighty three years
Has placed in the space
Of a moment -

When you stop to chat
And listen
To a lifetime
In the drop of a hat.

Leonard R. Share

Hope

Early morning in the Land
The mist is on the Water.
A hush held over from the night
Pre-dawn must be the Father.

Peace is ruling for a time,
That time will soon be gone.
Darkness now has no place,
The sun begins to show its face.

Oh! For the Peace to reign
On land, as well as sea,
On mountain top, and plain,
On desert, swamp, and Me!!!

Pauline Lyons

Traces

Loving you
    was hard for me
A small portion
    of my memory.

And as you grew
    I realized
you were all
    that I once despised.

No one could know
    what life would bring
For you and me
    a shattered dream.

No second chance
    no turning back
To live again
    and love.

Deborah M. McGory

High Kite

Kite! Kite!
Kite I see
Over the hill and over me.
I see a kite in the breeze,
Timid, shy and teasy to me.
It's all alone flying in the sky.
Oh, it's no more in the air!
Where could it be?
All I know, it's not over me!

Meghana Roy

Masks

I stand at my mirror
Trying to picture what you see
The picture couldn't be clearer
What you see is not the real me

We all wear masks
To hide our true selves
No one even needs to ask
We even hide from ourselves

My mask is not a disguise
It is more like armor
To protect me from probing eyes
To keep me a bit calmer

We all need the protection
If only we could see
Behind each others armor
To the real you and me

Megan Thomas

A Lady Wants — It All!

Love me forever
Be monogamous too
Laugh and I laugh
Don't make me cry
Don't ask why

Be a friend
Not a man
Wait, like I
It is worth it

In the end
Win love
A life long, friend
A companion, and a player

No option, no choice
Choose love
I'm worth it.
You'll be happy.

Edward C. Mangin

Christ of Christmas

Christ of Christmas,
Hallowed is thy name;
Reaching out to all.
In the manger He was found;
Sent by His father,
To redeem us sinners all.
Heavenly Love He brought,
More than we can imagine;
All on a silent night,
Such wonders He has wrought.

Julie A. Slattery

New Resident

Is ours the owl
that went to sea
in a beautiful pea-green boat?

Who sailed away
with a cat, they say -
was a year or more afloat?

Could it be that he (or she)
sought harbor at our door
and settled down
and plans to stay
unblinking, evermore?

Elmer Loemker

Cloak and Dagger

Emptiness envelops me like a cloak.
Leaving only blackness
For my heart to hold onto.

A dagger penetrates my heart.
Cutting so deep,
I bleed my tears.

A dream just causes pain.
Disguised as happiness,
It seems so real.
Such is the facade.

This dagger comes so quickly
Through the night.
Its shining edge the light of day
Still cuts me to the bone.

Kimberly A. Sitarz

Treasures

My treasures here were very few
Their worth in gold was nil,
Among them was my love for you
And dreams we could fulfill -
My love - no one could take from me
Our dreams were locked inside
And only you possessed the key
You took it when you died.

Now death for me draws slowly near
My treasures I'll regain -
Fond memories of your love are here
They help to ease the pain.

Were then my treasures very few
I must have figured wrong
I owned the world when I had you -
Death now to me is love's sweet song.

Gladys Marie Middleton

I Wonder

Sometimes when the world is cold
And no one seems top care;
The shadows of what could have been
Are dancing in the air.

I wonder in the scheme of things
That seem so happen - chance;
If we sail without a rudder
No music when we dance?

We bloom and wither...then slip away
Like a poet with a pen.
I wonder...yes I wonder -
Of the things that might have been.

Dale Sorenson

Over the Horizon

Over the horizon, almost within sight
I see my future before me
I see my guiding light
In my heart I can touch it
In my mind I can hear
The promises the Lord has for me
The promise that He is near
He will show me great and mighty things
that I know not of
But He has shown me already
the abundance of His love.

Connie Copeland

Rainbow Shower

Up in the sky
I see with my eyes
As I stop.
It's raining through a rainbow.
Rain comes down in drops.
Sprinkles of sun showers
With passing by clouds,
Lightly winds blow,
Birds come flying through
While other birds are chirping.
Kids shouting out: "Rainbow, rainbow
In the sky,
Looking down at you and I!"
This beautiful rainbow in the sky
With its many beautiful colors,
Colors that are so sweet
For your eyes to meet.
Aw . . . aw . . . it is sad to say
The rainbow doesn't last;
It goes away too fast.

Mary Pernorio

Fate

I have never met you face to face
I don't know the color of your hair
or your eyes not even the color of
your skin my friend.

These things are of little importance
you see it's not the color of your
hair your eyes or even your skin that
makes me your friend.

The kindness in your heart the humor
you give to one another these are the
things that are important.

It doesn't matter whether you're gay,
lesbian or straight this is no reason
to hate fate you see has brought us
together to be friends forever.

Melanie Dorsey

Untitled

A woman of about thirty
with grey eyes
and hair like soft wheat
stands alone
in her garden.
She is growing cucumbers
sweet and green with her bare hands.
She is growing roses
for her littlest child
who loves them.
It is almost silent there
except for the wind,
her dress,
and the sweet murmur of song
which indicates
she is truly
happy.

Emily Deirdre Topolsky

I Speak the Language

I speak the language
like
you understand
I'm
not evasive
don't I cover up
or
sugar coat things
I
give reality new meaning
stating
what is on my mind
you
come to me
for
an honest opinion
don't shun me
I speak the Language
I speak the Truth!!!

Pedro E. Abad

Affairs of the Heart

What does it take to make a mistake,
A heart without a chart,
As the mind takes no part?
Do we learn, or just yearn for days to
be bright with everlasting light?
For there are times hope is the only
way to cope, as we reach for love
on the wings of a dove.

Cindy Ann Thomas

Trials

In my times of trial and temptation
stay by my side with strength,
give me the power to push aside
all evils with scriptures length,
let this help get me through
the troubles that are caused,
and lift the pressures from my life
for a tiny spiritual pause.

For my moments sad
help to cheer me up,
take away depression
and fill with joy my cup,
hold my hand when weakened
and pull me to my feet,
carry me when fallen
and dry the tears I weep.

Heidi Berndt

My Times

I look to the ocean
The sea and the sky.
Your works overwhelm me
And cause my to cry
To you

You are my God.
My times are in your hands,
Help me to make them
The best they can be.

Please, open a pathway
Between you and me
And help to make my times
The best they can be.

Patricia A. Folena

Southern Trees

If Southern trees could talk
maybe then I would understand
how it feels to be humiliated
and called three-fifths of a man.

When I look at Southern trees
I see misery and strife
at first I lash out at society
but then I examine my own life.

Maybe I shouldn't draw
my gun quick
perhaps I wouldn't use
my penis as a joystick.

Maybe I would honor
my father and mother
and learn how to commit
and be true to my lover.

And maybe, just maybe
I would learn to love being black
and somehow find the strength
to give something back.

David L. Shabazz

A Chance

The nephew I never knew.
If I had a chance, to write my name,
To tie my shoes.
If you had only gave me a chance...
Oh, how nice it would be,
To be able to climb that tree.
Play football and rough up my knees.
To eat candy and rotten my teeth
Oh "Boy how neat".
If I could have only ran,
As far as a track star.
It may have reached my peak,
Instead of my body parts,
Laying in the streets.
I never got to fish,
Sumpin' I'll miss.
And some day those guy will pay.

Falesha D. Bradley-Joyner

Moonlit Days

My eyes are dancing
Under shadows of drops
That flicker in
Lights fire

Holding to beams
Of suns shine smiling
At you

How running in fields
Separating from beneath
Days break makes
Tonight even more
Mysterious

Moon's light
Lifting me
Higher into
Your thoughts

Liza R. Boodan

Untitled

in the vast anomaly
of what we now call space
an explosion with a promise
to bring the human race

the beginning of our planet
produced creatures of no flair
but when life and spirit dawned
earth shown brilliance beyond compare

now that brilliance is decreasing
paled by humans it created
other creatures from a distance
now behold our planet faded

i hope they know what happened
to our planet and its creatures
once contained so much potential
now does not possess pure features

maybe they will learn from us
to respect all creatures ways
and succeed where we have failed
to live in peace through out the days

kat sloan

Cultural Misfit

The music was turned on
a command was given,

Join the circle
mingle with the rest
sway to the music.

The beat was captivating
the heart was pounding
but the feet
would not comply.

The mind was entangled
the soul was floundering
between the new tune
and an old familiar rhythm.

The crowd swept in ecstasy
danced in harmony,
but my frostbitten feet
set me apart from the rest.

Pirhiya Goldstein

Emotions

Happiness is a way of life
that we all try to find,
we do our best to steer a course
from any other kind.

If this happiness eludes us
we could be very sad,
an emotion we could do without
when trying to be glad.

When sadness does take over
and to change it, we must wait,
try a little special love
before sadness turns to hate.

Hate is the worst emotion
that anyone can possess,
it infiltrates your thinking
and fills your life with stress.

There must be an easy way
to change all this commotion,
we must return that special love
for that's the best emotion.

Robert L. Miller

We Live On Love

Not Easy Street or
  North Broadway
"I live on love" is
  all she'd say,
And even tho' I tried
  to press,
She gave me no more
  street address.
"Then tell me, please,
  would you someday
Come out on love to
  romp and play?"
"Oh, yes, mi-Lord
  and have no fear,
You'll find that I
  will like you near.
But mother said
  no numbers give
To those who ask me
  where I live."

Fernie B. Scheaffer

Gone

When you entered this world
I had a joyful heart.
But when you left so soon
I had a troubled heart.

I loved you so much,
But I took you for granted.
God took you away
To a much better place.

You left long ago
But I've not quite forgotten.
I still think and speak of you,
Since I can't talk with you.

I've made it through what happened,
But I'll never forget you.
You taught me a lesson
I had to learn the hard way.

You changed my life,
And I thank you for that.
Though your life was short,
It changed mine forever.

Jenny Power

On Marriage

The word comes to mind
When thinking of marriage,
Of love—endless love,
A oneness, a carriage
For a couple to share
On their pathway of life;
One husband, one love
One family, one wife.
The concept, so special,
So a part of this plan
Of spiritual unity
This woman, this man;
Beginning their journey
Down life's great highway,
With Christ as their guide
To show them the way.
What more can they ask?
Indeed say, or do?
Than go with His plan
Their married life through!

Joan L. Gresham

Screaming Tears

In the longest of hours,
In the timeless of pains,

I feel you, I can hear you.

Through the endless tunnels,
Beneath the heavy wreckage,

I can hear you, you're screaming
tears.

Without all the confusion,
Beside all the sadness,

I am here for you, I can see
you.

Up from the darkness,
your feelings are showing,

I can hear you, you're screaming
tears.

Above the unconquered,
Beyond the impossible,

I am proud of you, I saved
you.

Heather Gibson

A Different Side of Me

How much can a person
Have hidden within
Guarding his fantasies
The places he's been

How long can a person
Pretend to be smiling
When deep inside of him
His heart is broken and crying

When you entered my life
You changed my whole world
Now there's nothing on earth
I wouldn't do for you, girl

You unlocked a part of me
Which hadn't been discovered
You've found a different side of me
I'll be your friend, your lover

Nelson Coblentz

A Woman's Dreams

The first night we were together
I came to you,
not knowing what to expect.
I walked in when you opened the door
filled with a child's expectations
of what love was.
Filled with dreams of the direction
I wanted my life to take.
You completely destroyed
those dreams for me.

In its place you left me
with a woman's dreams;
a woman's hopes and fears and heartache
that was sure to come.
I've come a long way
since that night, oh so long ago.
I've grown and matured
loving and needing you
all the way.

Jacqueline Moore

Starlight

If you look out your window,
During a clear, dark night,
You can see millions of stars,
Shining bright.
Some burn out and fade away,
Nobody ever knew they were there.
Some die with a spectacle of lights,
At those you exclaim and stare.
Those kind are special,
They are seen throughout the land,
And even after they are gone,
Their inspiration will always stand.

Emily Chow

As I Reminisce

Sometimes, I sit and reminisce
I think Oh God! Why all of this?
Then in a vision, I see a cross
it tells me that all is not lost.
It was on that cross our Lord
made the sacrifice that you and I
might have this life.
He gave His life and love that our
joys might be complete.
He showed us a way to live,
so that one day we all can meet.

Margaret E. Jones

Of What Tomorrow,

Is Today Bestowed

Aspire to
awe
beauty behold beyond imagination

Create existence
crucial
deep dwell

Endow how so
fearful
forever as to a forest

Harvest the field
just;
measure the extreme meek

Passion serene
remember
sure tempest quest
transpire as
Trees, the
truth
vision and the yield

Buford D. Thomas

Waking Up

Ah, what a day!
First day in May.
Blooming feeling can't say
How innocent we are.
Wrong is right once again.
Everything's true once again.
Dormant for years unfulfilled
Waking up with astonishment
Laughing with every breath from you
Feathers are your shoes
Leading you into something new.

Tim Batson

The Silence of Me

My voice is such a whisper
I battle with the slightest breeze to be heard
To hear each sound, each syllable, each word
The challenge to hear the silent me
Is cluttered like a forest, with an abundance of trees
So much confusion wanting to get out
And my whispers only seek to become shouts
A release from the silent ringing that over powers
My ability to hear
To reach a point where I can
Make my whisper clear
Enable myself to hear my voice
But the silent me may never pick that choice
So for now I sit and struggle to believe
That one day there will be
More than the silence of me

Shannon Estrada

You Didn't

Do you remember the time you let me borrow your car,
and I dented the fender? I thought you would kill me,
but you didn't.

And how about the time I forgot to tell you the dance was formal,
and you dressed in blue jeans? I thought you would drop me,
but you didn't.

Remember the time I flirted with those guys to make you jealous,
and you were? I thought you would hate me,
but you didn't.

And the time I dragged you all the way to the beach when you said it
would rain,
and it did? I thought you would say "I told you so,"
but you didn't.

Yes, there were plenty of things you didn't do,
but there were plenty of things you did do.
You put up with me, understood me, and loved me.

There were so many things I wanted to tell you when you
returned from Vietnam,
but you didn't.

Susan A. Reeves

Vision

On an ocean of darkness filled with despair
Searching for a rose
In the dead of winter
Searching, still searching, keep searching
Looking for the light
Amidst a thick of clouds
Walking through the mist
In a field of thorns
Ouch, ouch, ouch
Hurting in my soul
Wanting your touch
Across the miles
In our minds
Between us
Trying to touch
Reaching as far as we can
And never coming together
The emptiness that is felt
Can only be filled
As much as you let it

Matthew D. Oddie

The Baby Angel

I have a friend who is cheerful and such,
She is great with the children, she was born with the touch.

She'll hug kids when they need it, or give them a kiss,
She reads them some stories and fills them with bliss.

Now she is expecting, a mother to be,
Decorating a room for a baby to see.

She goes to the doctors with joy in her heart.
Soon she'll have a baby and never will part.

She got the first picture and heard the heart beat,
Much pleasure for mommy, that was a treat!

She waits for the day when they won't be one,
The baby is born and the pregnancy done.

Now a new bond will grow between mother and child,
Imagination will fester and dreams will go wild.

A doctor, a lawyer, or a president too,
I hope that the wishes all will come true.

The body will come in a blessed event,
A prayer had been answered, for the angels was sent.

Kimberly Pitcock

Being Locked Up

To some people, being locked up is cool;
To me, you gotta be a stupid fool.
When you're behind four walls
Your whole life crumbles, you fall.

Everyday is the same thing -
You really get stressed out.
You're a loser, have no more rights.
Everyday, you wake up to verbal or physical fights.

One thing I can say from experience,
It ain't fun and it ain't cool.
I always thought I could get away;
But now, I know, this is what you get
For breaking the rule.

Never again do I wanna be locked up;
'cuz now I know, this is what it's like
Being locked up.

Charles O. Warfield

Lost Love

In "68" I saw her for the very first time.
Held fast by her wonderment, our embrace lasted until "69."
In that year I came to know her as I had known to no other.
We found passion, and rage, as we sojourned together.

Her rage was unending, and cut deep into my soul.
As I saw her children die, I knew I would never be whole.
From her world, that was torn with sorrow and grief.
I tried to find some answers that would give me relief.

I wanted her to tell me why the world around us was dying.
I wanted her to give me perfect reasons to keep trying.
As time passed, I found ways to endure her pain.
Maybe it was the anger, maybe the seemingly endless rain.

Twenty years have passed since we parted as lovers that
      were never meant to be.
Twenty years have passed since my eyes were clear enough to see.
Twenty years in time since I could put away the shame.
Twenty years in time since I could say her name . . .
"Vietnam"

Sidney Crawford

Home Port

Like dancing shadows on a wall we are,
flickering and flirting and silently searching
for sustenance and song
elusive too long

From sand to sea love's reverie
in time and trials unknown
but for a steady current
or a northern star, making this journey alone

Over reefed mains we sailed, through
crashing waves and a thousand stars, facing
the changes while facing the sun
further and farther and faster we'd run

The horizon offers unspoken promise
beyond the rocky shore, where dreams
are resurrected, no need to be protected,
so take my hand in this distant land
and learn to live once more

Kathryn Harper

Third Eye

Let me know when the world begins
And then I'll open my eyes.
Let me know when the sinners don't sin,
And then I'll stop telling my lies.
And please let me know when peace begins.
And maybe I'll lend a hand.
So please let me know when the joker grins,
And spreads light over the land.

Let me know when choice is the ruler,
And then I'll send my vote.
Let me know when the world could be crueler,
And then I'll get on the boat.
And please let me know when your arms open wide,
And maybe I'll open mine, too.
So please let me know when you let me inside,
And maybe I'll let you in, too.

Emily Wasserman

My Star

I remember yet as a child,
Having a treasure of my own.
It was a star in the heavens,
It seemed as though it searched for me at night.
Finding me in my tiny bed.
Yes, safe and warm and sound.
And it watched over me alone.
Yet, as the years so swiftly passed,
I could somehow never forget,
Having a treasure of my very own,
A star I cannot forget.

Christina C. Russell

Untitled

Summers come and summer go.
This is what we all do know.

Then winter comes to bring snow and ice
And this is not at all, very nice.

Spring will return and this we will like.
We will walk the roads or ride a bike.

We all can be thankful that we are here,
To experience the change that came every year.

Lillian M. Marriott

Untitled

I remember a time when I use to cry,
for Reasons unknown to me.
A fear that I was unable to fly, or who it
was that I was to be.
My eyes were blind, my wings seemed crushed
my life I was taking from me.
But there I was a bird in a tree, wanting
life and yet to be free.
I took some time and looked above,
like the bird I had felt to be.
Me and the bird we are alike,
we share the same fragile quality.

Tina Marie Davis

The Tree

I chanced upon a tender scene, along a lovely mountain stream.
There stood a tree magnificently, clinging to life tenaciously.
The stream had washed the soil away,
Exposing its roots to sun and spray.
But still its tender roots reached far,
clinging to life on the nearby shore.
This tree that once erected stand,
Now bowed its head to the lowly land.
As though in an attitude of prayer,
asking the father its life to spare.
all things in nature to life doth cling,
be it man or beast or bird that sings.
Or simple flower or blade of grass,
Or a troubled tree we chance to pass.
Each is given a time and place,
and the strength and will to fill their space.
And we, like the tree will struggle on,
to fill the time and space to which we belong.
we too will spread our roots afar,
and cling to life on the nearby shore.

Norma J. Williams

Old I Grow

Old I grow
In the sanctuary of self,
Undiminished,
Except if age is more
Than state of mind?

Lend yourself to dignity old man,
Do not stoop prior to a time so grave,
When waiting still, there is no time to wait,
What gateway opens,
When the paths beyond are still?

What kind of fool am I,
Thinking of the day I die,
I wonder about the funeral,
Will I be there,
Will I cry?

Stan J. McCrea

The Birth

In the origin of an infant lay a woman,
As far as the Golden Ball which ascends in the heavens.
When the stem of being began to create the source of life
In which they drank from the Chalice,
The holder of the wine.
And the inferior one wept to be cloaked,
As curiosity swelled into the pigment of a child.
Secure in a virtuous liberation,
The delicate finger steered the small life.

Kerri Leigh O'Brien

Sometimes....

Sometimes you have to surrender
and turn your problems over
sometimes you should release
and cry on someone's shoulder
sometimes you need to admit you're scared
and take the hand that's lent
sometimes you have to be angry
It can be the only way to vent
sometimes you've got to throw the napkin away
and let the tears run free
sometimes I pray you say
there's something beautiful in me
sometimes you will get lost
so just pray for some direction
sometimes you'll sleep alone at night
when you deserve affection
sometimes you will smile the smile
that lightens up your eyes
and sometimes you'll be the one
to hold the one that cries

Megan Eierman

Change

Slithers softly onto the scene
So quietly unobtrusive
Barely generating a nod
From those the result will live.

When noticed it seems so sudden —
A right angled turn in the road.
But viewed from a distance thru time,
Twas but a gentle curve—life in
    corrective mode.

For there is an intelligence,
    an order to our lives
That eschews the randomness of chance
That coordinates the challenges with the learning
Into a lively choreographed dance.

Thus change, for all its willy nilly facade —
Is spirit's cleverly devised scheme
To move us forward again but
Not a moment before we're ready to dream!

Carol Ann Richmond

A Mother's Day

You are always there
    when I need you most.
Although it may seem,
    you are treated like a ghost.

You are a special friend,
    your love is wide,
And you always seem to know
    how I'm feeling inside.

People like you
    deserve the best.
But you are definitely
    greater than the rest.

You are someone I could
    not live without.
I say that with meaning,
    there is no doubt.

I love you more than words can say,
my love grows stronger every single day.

So happy Mother's Day with all my heart,
And as for my life, you will always be a part.

Stephanie Kinghorn

My Son

You hear a sigh and then a weep
Your little boy is fast asleep.

You watch him twist and turn around
That little boy that makes you proud.

In your arms with loving care
You wash his face and comb his hair.

You give him toys, wagons and such
Give him candy but not too much.

Then one day be becomes a man
Wants some room, you'll understand.

Give him love, kindness too
He'll come to say, I love you.

In the end you'll have won
You've raised a beautiful, honest son.

Thank the Lord for the gift you received
A dream come true and you believe.

In life, happiness, caring too
All the benefits have come to you.

Skip Westenskow

As Wynton Plays His Horn

As Wynton plays his horn
And rains rhythm decorate my windowpane. Rapping softly
Asking to be let in. While resolutions unremembered,
Of friendships maladroit solutions to honest intentions,
Danced unencumbered through the cool air.
Two people hold each other, aware of nothing,
Believing nothing
Divided...yet somehow one.
The fear tonight will not exist.
It's afraid, even of their desire,
The horn is magic.
The embers glow.
The rain continues.
His tears once bitter, sweetened by her embrace.
Her words comfort.
This infinite moment will soon end. As they often do.
But his words, once tainted by his scorn...
Are filled with hope...as Wynton plays his horn.

Jesus Enrique Baeza

Lady

My dearest Lady,

In the darkness that seems to ever taunt the pursuit of virtue I
am able to hold your hand and comfortably speak of the morality
that is incumbent in your being. I am able to look into your eyes
and see the ethics that time has shaded with reds and blues. In
your presence I see the essence of truth and hear your voice sing
of a love that muffles the dissonant sounds of fear.

The sacred is held high by your slender fingers. The profane is
trampled under your feet. Eternal and infinite is the beauty
your noble arms hold to hypnotize those who dare to gaze.

You are ethereal and ephemeral. You are mystic and ordinary. You
are violent and tranquil. You demand and comply. You are never
void of harmony; though your melody at times may seem harsh. You
offer hope where despair is an all but encumbering entity. You
expose the living to the dead.

Michael John Bera

LEM'S POEM

The foundation of life has brought forth a new creation.
From its roots — He evolves the glowing silhouette
  "GENESIS" that is after him.

I am planted firmly in fertile soil to grow in Immanuel's image.
And in completing this new creation and in shedding tears of joy,
  through rain, I sprouted.
And taking His heart blazing with Love, fabricated the sun and I grew.
And through His infinite wisdom and understanding I blossomed.
  He smiled.
The brilliant colors that I exhibit symbolize the careful
  craftsmanship of an omniscient GOD. I am beautiful.
My instinct keeps me mindful to keep my head to the sky;
  in homage to Him because He is my strength.

He sends the rain to quench my thirst.
He makes the sun shine to give me nourishment.
He orders the atmosphere to give me breath.
I know that if I absorb all of the minerals to sustain life,
and am circumspectant of all impurities;
that one day He will reach down out of the heavens, remove me
and plant me in His Eternal Garden because I am his prize.

Lemuel A. Stiles III

The Silent Scream of My Heart

Life fills me as she approaches,
I see her smile,
I hear her first words,
We touch.

A meaningless touch to her,
everything to this man's heart.
We laugh,
talk of time past.

Reflections on a history we made together,
regretting only the ending.
My eyes fall to the ring she now wears,
the ring I dreamed of giving her.

As we discuss the day,
I think how it must feel.
To share life with an angel,
could he love her as I do.

The precious time ends,
I would not trade one second.
As this man's Love disappears from sight,
The silent scream of my heart.

Michael Vincent Bowers

My Baseball Days

A wonderful feeling of comfort came over me.
I gazed up into the clear night sky.
Stars sparkled like expensive diamonds.
My body felt as if it were floating freely in space.
Suddenly, a knock, the porch door opened.
Euphonious sounds of familiar footsteps came my way.
Gazing up my eyes caught Fred.
A tall lanky friend came visiting me with the epigrammatic
Stories of baseball, that cheered my nostalgic soul.
Hours passed with my mind affixed on my passed professional
  baseball days.
Running catching flyballs by the home run fence,
cheering crowds of congratulations stirred my blood within me.
Oh, how I hit the ball with such confidence,
And ran with great speed.
Those baseball days, will they ever come back.
I gazed down at my paralyzed feet,
As I sat in my wheel chair thinking,
Such baseball days, will they ever comeback?

Jack Kreiselman

Fantasy Blue

Crystal waters, the Aegean Sea.
A marble slab of venous white
Atop the mountain of eternity
With its viridescent hue
Fantasy blue
The sun shines its brilliant shards
Explosive light over all
Through the temple's slated roof
Lying on the alpine slab
Shackled by the cuffs on feet and hands
High overhead, the Grecian light
Comes glaring orange warm
The atmospheric delight as filtered amber dawn
Restrained, held down.
Trickling sweat like first dew
Fantasy blue
On the alter of God totally possessed
Say goodbye to the soul you knew
Fantasy blue

Susan Marconi

She Waits

She watches and she waits for a lover that is all hers,
not one born of rebound and built on memories of yesterday,
but one that is unique and fresh with no expectations or demands.

She longs for a love that is a friendship unencumbered by the past.
She doesn't reach out the way she used to.

She waits for love, true love, to come to her and meet her needs for
  a change.
She waits, not lacking for relationships, but still missing her own
  soul mate.;

Pamela J. Williams

Tale of Two Hearts

My Sweet Jesus, housed in the Host,
Crossed with a rose
You chose me, a lowly sinner to walk with You
You are here, there and everywhere.

How mystical and ever loving you are,
I am here longing for you, my love.
My Jesus, My savior, I loved you before I was;
My Jesus, my savior, I shall love you after I am.

Please be patient with me, my love,
When I stumble and fall along the way,
And lo! Someday, my love, our hearts will be
Like one forever and a day.

Ruth VonDenBosch

Summer

The grass in our yard is so green and lush
I sit in my lawn chair and just enjoy
I see no reason for me to rush
To wash a dish or pick up a toy

My eyes go up to the sky above
I watch the piles of snow white clouds
I see a bird, I think a dove
As he flies by, he sings quite loud

The green, green leaves of a nearby tree
Are beautiful against the sky so blue
I know it's as lovely a sight as I'll ever see
Come sit with me, I'll share it with you

Neeva Atkin Brown

The Chase

I saw her flying down the street behind a massive brute...
he with a sausage hanging down, and she in hot pursuit.

I followed them, with others, giving chase with flying feet...
in vain attempt to catch him and reclaim the packaged meat.

Some carried sticks, one had a broom, umbrellas too held high;
but none could catch the two of them no matter how they tried.

Round many blocks I ran and ran...just like a keystone cop.
I'd forgotten why I'd started, but found I could not stop.

Then suddenly they stopped...as all who followed had...
and listened to the playing of a noisy marching band.

Going closer for a better look, I was amazed to see...
the "woman" was a clown so dressed, the "brute", the same was he!

The "meat", a rubber sausage, was dangling near the ground!
the people did not care at all; the joke brought smiles around.

Now everyone together stood to hear the music play;
in unison we gave salute...so happy that fine day.

It was as I remembered.....those days of long ago....
when they paraded down our street with faces all aglow.

I do not care to spend much time remembering the past.
I was so glad the chase was done....and I could rest at last!

K. Pettigrew

A Few Words Well Spent

Some pleasures are bought with money, I know
Though after a while there's nothing to show
But for real lasting joy you needn't a cent
It's man's best investment — a few words well spent.

Words that are simple, words that are smart
Words that are humble, and cling to the heart
Words that at times overshadows by far
The thrill of a penthouse, a yacht, or a car.

Hi there! Good morning! Or how are you?
Will oft drive the cares from one who is blue
Get well! Cheer up! Here's wishing you luck!
Are words that are priceless, but don't cost a buck.

Yes, the Morale will be high, if the Moral is clear
When kind words are spoken — someone will hear
So, come on! Speak up! You needn't relent
Cause it's man's best investment — A Few Words Well Spent.

Sid Tanenbaum

The Garner Family

One early September morn,
a baby girl was born.
Her eyes were hazel blue, her hair a mist of brown,
knowing she would never live in town.

The country became her home, and as she became of age,
her heart was won by a tall, brown eyed man,
who became her husband so true,
and next came a family of three children as they grew.

Time was spent in that home,
and love was shown each day as we roamed.
Many knew the family so grand,
and needed the love they had planned.

Each day memories, hopes and dreams came true,
as the children had families of their own.
And then came grandchildren of joy, love, peace and harmony,
and a great-grandchild who became the apple of our eyes.

For such a time as this our sadness became victories,
in the days ahead we all worked together in one accord,
to take care of our family that lived in the country,
on this September morn.

Judy M. Jones

The Reply

Born into a green world turned cement
a stained deer hoofed upon a honeyed field
Dashing by the green leaves it noticed
A rainbow in the sky; shadows and delusions below.

The soft sky now smiled upon us
Out of the wharf we came;
watching the mountain walls.
Her look was free.

Wait . . .
Breaking the silence of the seas
guns disturbed the hour
Chained to my stakes
I can hear the devil's roar.
We passed the setting sun
Jittery crossing the Jordan

Opher Mizrahi

Wall Hangings

Walking here night after night, I see the same faces over and over
again hiking and humping over the changeless trails as before.
Glad to be in a safe group, sitting in circles
laughing at the folks who don't seem to do much at all.
Following the gears that are turning, being different while there in
the woods behind the white houses, parents on decks, drinking
wine with cheese, beneath the canopy of branches, behind closed doors
where the combinations on the locks are all the same.
Out of expensive cars and happy homes,
watching, all from the perch on the left, seeing all but not uttering
a word. Secure and segregated just like the rest of them all,
dancing to the music they all hate and resent
shackled into freedom they wish they had.
Because nobody wants to be alone, everybody wants to be themselves
in cages of wrought iron and soft slick moss, realizing, in and of
itself there's nothing really there except what is in front of you.
But there is just nothing out to stop us all from bellowing
our own thoughts and praises except, ourselves.
Because between heaven and hell there is no such thing as purgatory.

Byron August K.

Time

Time passes,
It whispers and sighs by.
And though we grasp and try to hold on
Through our hands it will always fly.

Time changes,
It takes us here and it takes us there.
And when we look back on all our days
There was never any time to spare.

Time heals,
It softens the edges of our pain.
Our hearts are cooled, our minds are cleared
As the sky in a soft summer rain.

Time treasures,
All the memories of our past.
And time really is our greatest friend
Because it lets those memories last.

Chris Christensen

My Love

When I looked into your beautiful eyes,
all I could find is endless love with no deny.
When I saw you standing there,
your perfect body and cocoa hair.
I love you so very much,
and I heavenly miss your tender touch.

When I see your gorgeous smile
I can't resist, but to love you and only you,
because I know that's all that I can do.
You and I have been through a lot,
happy, sad, cold, and hot.
We have been through it all,
and it all started out with just one call.

The love I have for you is so very strong,
and I've had it for so very long.
You may not feel the same about me, that's alright,
because you're my wonderful light shining bright.
I just wanted you to know, how I'll always feel about you.
I regret from leaving you and being so far apart,
because I know you'll always be in my heart.

Marisa A. Ramirez

Who Does Care?

Sometimes we try to find things that just aren't there
We look for the truth and cry cause it's not fair
And we never take the chance to see
Maybe it's not worth it moving on may just be more fit

Your heart may loose a beat or two
But there is nothing more than you can do
A love so strong, you may have thought
But reality you seem to have caught

As time passes wounds will heal
And your heart will loose the pain it feels
You'll realize hopefully before it's too late
That love isn't made of any hate

And as you look around at life
You'll find less pain stabs like a knife
True love could be just beyond your sight
You just can't stop, fight

Sometimes we see things that just aren't there
Look for the truth and you'll find it's near
If at first love was so unfair
Think, because there is someone out there . . . who does care

Melissa Kusinitz

Untitled

If you ever stop to think
The ramifications of your actions
We would never attempt to be
The things that we are not

We would realize that our happiness
Depends greatly on our endeavors
We would realize that our dreams
Depend greatly on our encounters

Only then could we begin to understand
That we are all interconnected
In the same link and we all must
Stay steadfast in our concern for each other

As we approach a monumental year
Take the next three to change your way
And decide to whom, what and when
You will make a difference...

Ralonda D. Bell

Wandering Eyes

As I sit upon this quiet little tree.
Wondering if only I had done something differently
Would I be here right now?
If I had only said "No" and walked away.
Would I be so high in this tree,
    not knowing were to go?
Looking around seeing only a blur,
Knowing I was here before,
Now I see this is home to me.

Tara McQueen

Because We're Sisters

Shrieking, penetrating vocal chords, flitting
about the room leaping for joy.
Davina: Bellowing with intensity, enough
    to make the rafters ring: "Are you
    ready for a bath?" Screaming loud
    enough to wake the dead.
Debbie: "That's my washcloth get your own."
    Screaming discontentedly making a wry face.
Davina: The water's too hot, she yelled lustily
    as her shouting filled the air. Oh,
    that's just right. Come on let's sit down.
Debbie: "Mom are you going to shampoo our hair?"
    squalling impatiently lingering for an answer.
Davina: "Debbie, do you know what?
Debbie: What!
Davina: Taking a bath together is lots a fun
    because we're sisters.
Debbie: Yes, you're right...because we're sisters.

Elaine Jackson

Night-Time Visions

When I go to sleep, I see things —
Beautiful things that make me happy.
Feelings of joy are felt at night,
Like the smell of spring.
Happiness is all around and no loneliness is felt.
When I close my eyes, I picture the ones I care about —
And the ones I think care for me —
That no one else can see, but me.
So when I wake up I wish sometimes that it could be true.
No more loneliness in my heart,
And we wouldn't be apart.
The people I love would love me back,
And everyone would be free.
But for now I must realize that things aren't what they seem,
Just about every time they are nothing more than a dream.

Jennifer Novak

Building

Evermore powerful, consuming, dark.
Stacks of impossible height, behind I sit.
Never.
Energy fades, knock down a stack, there are a tenfold more.
Never sit.
The construction of skill, of ability uses up
the precious never endingness.
Must keep hope.
Love seems fake, don't understand
why this treatment continues.
Too many factors.
The precious never endingness consumes me.
Must keep going, stay in faith,
The hand of God reaches between the stacks.
Why won't I grasp it?
Things break, things seem to fall apart
    as the building continues.
Must never stop, never sit, keep the faith.

Scott Coerber

Mountains High as the Bluest Sky

in which My Spirit Soar....

I want to find the book it is in so I
can purchase that book and several for
others I know. I had a chance to buy
it at that time but for some reason I
can not remember - I did not buy
then - even if I can not buy the book
I would like to get the poem (a copy) my
copy, burned when my mothers house burned down.

Lisa D. Conley

To My Son, Rick Bailey II

My son it's been a long year since you went away
you haven't been forgotten one minute of the day
oh how I love and miss you, there are no words to say

If I just had one minute, one hour I'd pray for
so many times I hope it's you knocking on my door
the disappointment finds me, no hugs, no kiss today
then suddenly I realize you went far, far away

In my heart you're always near, we'll meet again I never fear
until that day, remember this, I long for hugs, I long for a kiss
these are the things I really miss

And I miss your smile, the ways you cared
I miss your laughter, the fun times we shared
if I just had one minute, one hour I'd pray for
but if I had one hour, I'd only ask for more.

Judy Bailey

The Love I Never Have To Question

You say you'll always love me
  But why should your words I believe
You say you're telling me the truth
  Yet you make the choice to leave

This pain I feel inside my heart
  Is too terrible to even to describe
The ache inside is so great
  That it's even to obvious to hide

I could say to you I'll be O.K.
  I could tell you I'll be fine
But as time goes on you'll surely see
  That love's not an easy thing to find

I guess I should forget you
  Along with your harsh reaction
I wish in time I could find that love
  That I never have to question

Jamie Fanini

The Flute

Forget the piccolo and the lute
forget the timpani and the oboe
forget the bassoon and the sitar
of all the magic makers.
and "beam up" your appreciation
to the most beautiful of all,
the flute
sounds created by this instrument are myriad.
If your heart be tamed let it be done by the flute
other sounds just don't make it!
Even with a player with extra fingers (digits)
Sounds by it bring to mind exotic places and environs
the rain forest and the prairie
to be shared with
someone for whom you care
this is no Haiku
listen to the flute

Howard Quam

Day at the Office

Why do they come to me?
Why do they think I know the answers?
Why do they think I can fix everything?
The phone doesn't stop ringing!
Everyone's problem is my problem too!
Everyone wants everything now!!!
Now!!! Now!!! Now!!! Now!!! Now!!!
How did I get here? Is this really what I wanted?
This wasn't supposed to be like this!
The phone is still ringing!
All the problems are not fixed!
Is this really what I wanted?
I want to go home—now!
Now!!! Now!!! Now!!! Now!!! Now!!!
But I can't!!!
The problems just don't go away!
I have to listen to everyone!
I have to answer the questions! I have to fix everything!
Would I do this if this isn't what I really wanted?

Sonya E. J. Bogdanovicz

I Care

How can I show you that I care?
Not so much in words but in actions.
I would have a flower garden so fair,
With pleasant scented blossoms.
A bouquet would be sent your way.
How can I show you that I care?
If you shed tears,
A hug would be given
To drive away sorrow or tears.
How can I show you that I care?
A neighbor I could be
And you were sick or crippled
Your garden needed to be weeded
or lawn mowed.
Your house required a coat of paint I could see
I'd be there to lend a hand where needed.
Then again how can I show that I care?
Just by being a friend.

Marilyn Abbott

I Am My Brother's Keeper

I am my brother's keeper, I keep my brother not
I partake of the fruits of his labor
  I want what my brother got
I am my brother's keeper, I keep my brother not
my eyes swells with resentment, when I see what
  he has stored in his pot
I do not follow in his foot steps
I would rather steal what my brother got
I am my brother's keeper, I keep my brother not
I do not share the nobility of his deeds or
  concern with his wants and his needs
his weakness and compassion for his fellowman
is the essence of this weakness on which I feed
I do not see the necessity to perpetuate the species
of mankind or to preserve what have came before
I only seek to fulfill my own desires, and
the rest I choose to ignore

Joseph Jackson

Life (Mine)

I had nothing to do with where I was sown
Nothing to do with where I was grown.

The field stretched far and wide
Weeds seeds and wheat seeds grew side by side.

Weeds are a nuisance planted to destroy
Wheat makes daily bread, happiness and joy.

My life-mate and I weathered storm, sunshine and rain
Strengthened to withstand ravages of loss and gain.

Now with the harvest ahead in full view
Golden grain will be gathered from me and you.

Vella S. McGehee

Why Did You Have To Go Away?

We had only a few years to make us a house;
It was just a beginning to make us a home,
Then one day it happened and you went away;
Why did you have to go away?

Billy just sits and stares into space;
Jenny was just beginning to walk.
We had such a short time to make us a home;
Why did you have to go away?

Everything's changed all too soon;
I just can't believe you've been taken away.
I wanted so much to hold you tonight;
But all that was there was where you once laid your head.
Why did you have to go away?

We're starting over it won't be the same;
Billy's in school and Jenny too,
The years have rushed by since you went away;
Everything's going just as we planned.

The only thing I'm still asking God is...
Why did you have to go away?

Glenna Harper

Nature's Stage

From the mountain top, the desert unfolds in the early light of
dawn, like a dark stage as the lights go up.
The rooftops in the villages at the foot of the mountain catch
the gold of the first sun ray as it breaks over the horizon.
The ribbon roads pick up the glow with the first early drivers in
autos of gold. Trees pop out of the haze as dark contrast to the
light caught before.
Dry lakes appear as silvery platters awaiting an elegant feast.
At last the horizon draws its line from the sky as the stage
is finally bathed in full light.
Now the vista is complete - patchwork quilts on beds of alfalfa,
glittering houses on checkerboard villages, with the next scene
hidden by the mountain curtain of the range on the horizon.

Gene E. Harris

My Storm

A white cloud disturbing darkens
Then the sky generates a gloomy gray
The leaves suddenly shake,
The winds whine in whispers,
The thunder rapidly rages,
The lightening strongly scorns me and
The rains fall down so heavily.
Then the sky introduces an infamous indigo and
A yellow sun brutally burns.

Denise Aromando

Life Goes On

There is no future in the past,
if you live in it your pain will last.

The future is where your life will lead,
the past was just to plant the seed.

Learn from what was way back when,
only then will you live again.

A rose for those you have loved before,
do not despair you will love once more.

A halo shines for those who have died,
that kind of pain can't be kept inside.

A thorn won't hurt if held just right,
hold your past loosely, don't squeeze too tight.

From ordeals of the past you have bleed this is true,
in time you will heal, only a scar to remind you.

The stem and the leaves show the growth of your soul,
regrets of the past no longer taking their toll.

The wings they will take you to see a new day,
don't let the wind come and blow you away.

Combined as they are that no one can see,
a permanent reminder only to me.

Charles L. Owens

Kurt Cobain

You shoot your heroine.
You smoke your pot.
I thought you were cool for awhile,
but now you're not.
You get your gun, stick it in your mouth,
pull the trigger-blow out your brains.
You don't know what happened, now it's starting to rain.
I see your face in clouds — I see your tears.
You don't know what you've done to yourself,
and you know it's not cool now.
You know you have made a fool decision,
now you wish you had no ammunition.
You had unfinished business, now you have to pay the price.
The world misses you down here.
Can you feel us crying, well it's not worth buying
because the world misses you, your concerts,
and especially your face — Kurt Cobain

Desiree Pride

Within My Heart

O my Lord, I ask while on bended knee
These things I feel within my heart, I pray they are of thee
The love and hope you hold for me, have surfaced to your light
No more will I shed tears of fear, but only of delight
For you have come to save me on this very night
I have died and been reborn
Through your mercy and your grace
I have fought the fight tonight, and plan to win the race
For our days were never guaranteed, we may not have tomorrow
We trust in you Lord, to take away our sorrow
We ask not gifts of pleasure, but your spirit to fill our hearts
'Tis then that we will know that we have done our part
To ask for your forgiveness and turn away from sin
Only then will we rejoice, God's victory from within

Frances J. Pecoraro

When A Grandfather Dies

When a grandfather dies
It pierces the soul
Sadness erupts, the family no longer feels whole

When a grandfather dies a lot is lost
A husband, father, friend, and grandpa too
No one knows exactly what to do

When a grandfather dies
A little girl will remember her papa sitting in his big brown chair
And she begins to cry because never again will he sit there

When a grandfather dies memories should be kept close to the heart
The smell of his clothes, the smile on his face
His gentle hand welcoming you in a warm embrace

When a grandfather dies
You mustn't cry forever because he would want you to be strong
His love for his family will always live on

When a grandfather dies there isn't any reason to be afraid
Because his love will stay with us and keep us safe
Through each and every day

When a grandfather dies life will never be the same
Grandpa I want you to know I love you and that will never change

Emily Miller

Patchwork

It must be that no one quilts any more.
Lost is the art of rescuing the patches of good
sequestered within old garments.
Lost is the art of magnifying remnants
into something more beautiful.
Maybe it is not knowing
that the ark was conceived before the flood
and afterward a colorful promise stitched to a cloud
secured a precious scrap of humanity.
Maybe it is never having felt the warmth
of snuggling under a patchwork comforter
to be insulated from a Carolina winter.
My grandparents quilt took over fifty years
of Grandma salvaging remnants
and carefully stitching them together
a work so cherished by my grandfather
that he wrapped it around his life.

Derek Vincent Taylor

I Cried For My Father

On September 15, 1895,
Thunder and lightning, my Father came alive.
When Dad was born he was one of a kind.
One of the most special you'll ever find.

Over the years I have written many rhymes.
About life with my Dad, so many good times.
In his own special way he was a good friend.
He gave you his help, generous, no end.

He was a great dad, a real giant among men.
Now that he has gone, I think again and again,
How lucky I was to be blessed with him.
My deep memories of Dad will never dim.

He was 96 when he got the call.
His friend upstairs decided Joe had it all.
He lived a great life, and he did it his way.
Even at the end, he had a great day.

Over the many years, my tears were few.
No matter how tragic, I'd see it thru.
The day he left, and he was not a bother.
I couldn't help it, I cried for my Father.

Arnold Wisper

Hurt

I feel hurt — because of you,
I was in love — you never knew,
you were hold someone I could hold,
but my love for you, I never told,
we went out and had fun,
being together had just began,
me, thinking the fun never dies,
now memories of you bring tears to my eyes,
my thoughts of you sick deep inside my heart,
when I remember that our love drifted apart,
if a wish upon a star would ever come true,
my only wish is to be with you.

Magdalena Niezgoda

Scotland Mist

Somber, the beauty of a Scottish morn
in its cold and misty, lonely form.

Along the moorland brae, where heather lays
'tis where I'll spend my last few days.

With crossbarred patterns of plaid adorn
auld noble pipers, pipe mournful scorn

Where heraldic nostalgia pervades the air
in remembrance of clansmen buried there

I, 'tis my Scotland where I lived as a lass
and played in the meadow with sheep in the grass.

David E. Neuschafer

A House A Home

A house without laughter, is not a home.
A house without joy, is not a home.
A house without sharing, is not a home.
A house without caring is not a home.

Let the laughter ring out, and the joy shine thru
The sharing be abundant, and the caring will come too
And then a house will become a home.

Mabel Mitchell

Bluestone

Funny how the view can change before your eyes,
Daylight seen the dusk.
Watch the flower as the petals melt away,
Don't let the stone fall from your hand.

Wake up - stare into empty space,
The color's no surprise.
Part the people with a smile from your face,
Tell them it's only one big lie.

Walk beside and nothing you will find,
The mountains never change.
Hold the paper that only states your name,
Run to the corner of your life.

Count the stones that build the bridge you call,
Don't let them fall behind.
Sleep away dreams you've been painting,
See the shadow as it climbs the wall.

Marianne Sundeck

Midnight Rain

Are you a lost wandering wonder? A little lonely, too?
Roaming to the deep dusk light in search of someone to hold.
When the wind becomes a bit chilly, and the night a little fierce,
Do you get hung up and confused searching for I don't know who?
Left to fend alone this hollow, empty pain,
Like a child left behind to bare the midnight rain.
The thunderous silence is biting, and your soul is aching.
Mind cries for companionship, and your body cries for taking.
Under each burning star, and with every step that you take,
You sink further, and further into despair.
Every happy face you see only stings you caustically,
With the thought that that won't be you.
Left to fend alone this hollow, empty pain,
Like a child left behind to bare the midnight rain.
Now, how'd you know just how sad I'd be, huddled in my corner?
Dreaming and wishing that my ship didn't sink.
Hoping you'd be there to help me up.
You are so sweet in your timidness, so tender in your touch.
Sweet lips of innocence blow my lonely flame,
Lighting each and every star with your breath.

Matt Beres

Forever

The test of time is always forthcoming.

My stride may get a little slower,
my high step may get a little lower, but
forever young I will always be
if only through your eyes.

Maturity pays us all a visit
with the hope of opening our eyes.
The mistakes we've made is the past
should add a notch of wisdom to our future.
Yet, we find that it only chips away at
the beauty of our bodies and the
essence of our souls.

Father Time delicately takes hold of us
and slowly begins to squeeze.
Ever so gently and oh, so quietly
it all begins to slip away,
the beauty, the innocence, the vulnerability,
but forever young I will always be
if only through your eyes.

Beverly Moore

The Seven Sisters

Nobody
can tell me why
some wise old mountaineer
dubbed you seven sisters
when not one of you
bears a female name.
Marching like silent soldiers
down the valley from
Tomahawk to Graybeard,
bare in winter . . .
most unladylike behavior.
But if he named you
for you watchfulness
and protecting stance,
each shielding parts of the others
from the wind and snow
so that unexpected pockets bloom early,
I'll understand.
Shoulder to shoulder defines an army,
protecting with your being takes a kinswoman.

Righton H. McCallum

The President

The sun shone bright on that fearful flight.
The day held promise, the future bright. The
handsome young man, and his beautiful wife,
emerged from the plane with splendor and
blithe. The crowd that gathered this couple to
see, were deeply impressed by his warm
beaming smile that lasted his lifetime of
trouble and trial. Then all of a sudden the
mood seemed to change, this wonderful man of
our golden age, was shot down before us, in
front of our eyes. Dear God, how we prayed,
how the country stood still, like the
lifeless young man in the automobile. No! No!
This can't happen, it couldn't have been our,
President shot along with a friend? And yet
this did happen, in the land of the free, my
God up in heaven, what a blow to all
humanity. The world mourned, the heavens
cried, the day John Kennedy, fell and died.

Mary Ann Ferguson

Blizzard of '96

Wow! We've had it . . . snow, snow, snow!!!
  The blizzard of '96 . . . we don't need anymo'. . .
It is beautiful . . . glistening, white, and clean!!
  The most snow many of us have ever seen!

The snow plows have been humming night and day . . .
  Plodding and pushing mounds of white snow to the sides of the
    highway . . .
The multiple inches of snow welcomed by skiers and sledders . . .
  Hills and slopes echoed glee from the tredders.

School classes were cancelled . . . students were elated!
  Parents had to do some rescheduling and they slated!
Grocery stores experienced record sales . . . meat, bread, and milk
    shelves went bare!
  People panicked and stocked their pantries with care!!!

Lots of stock pots of soup were made and served with pride . . .
  Puzzles and games were played by families . . . sitting side by side!
Weather like this makes you think of scheduling vacations . . .
  Hot weather and sandy beaches are prime locations!!!

To the malls for markdown prices
  We certainly enjoy these slices!
Spring will be here before you know it . . . thank the Good Lord for each
    day he brings!
  Enjoy your family and friends and all of life's things!!!

Jacqueline G. Kleman

Carry Me, Father

Carry me, Father, the way is so long!
Carry me, Father, I am weak, thou art strong.
Hold me close to thy bosom; shelter me from all harms.
Oh, my Father, carry me, in thy kind loving arms.

Carry me, Father, the winds blow so wild!
Carry me, Father, because I'm thy child.
My back gets so weary, and my feet get so sore.
Oh, My Father, carry me till the path here is o'er.

Carry me, Father, the waters are cold!
Carry me, Father, to thy heavenly fold.
There to stay in thy presence, nevermore here to roam.
Oh, my Father, carry me on that long journey home.
Carry me, Father! Please carry me home!

Charlotte Brown Garrick

Reflections

If you looked into my heart
You would see your reflection there
The line right down the middle
You could call it a tear

There are little tiny patches to cover up that tear
One for each time you convinced me that you really do care
As time goes on the patches start to fade
Each one leaves a scar that I will take to my grave

A new love can not take away the scars or the hurt that will remain
But the love between the two of us will never be the same
Even though your reflection is full of scars and lines
The memories of us together will always be mine

So wipe away your tears, my friend
And hold your head up high
The hardest thing we will ever do
Is tell each other good-bye

I'll send you on your way now
And even though we must part
You will always have a special place
In my broken heart
Amanda J. Sparks

A Mother's Prayer

Dear God my child is on his way, please hear me when I pray
please help me to be brave, in this moment of fear
when all seems so dark, let me know you are near.
Let my child just be healthy that's all I shall ask
at the moment that is till the danger has past.
As I lay here in pain and my child begins life,
I pray oh, dear God, let him always do right.
Let me show him the pitfalls that life has in store,
the same as my mother once showed me before.
Give me the knowledge to show him the right and set him on his way
on through life's long journey and I pray he'll never stray.
I'll do my best to do my part, and guide him by the hand
until the day he steps out on his own and finally, becomes a man.
I've prayed a lot of this little prayer and I trust all will be granted,
for we're all the children of you dear Lord and our prayers are always
answered.

Eugene M. Sherin

Memories of a Maple Tree's Joy

The warm summer air drifted gently through the old maple
tree in the park, children played beneath her friendly
shade as she listened to their laughter and the
song of a lark!

The Autumn wind sent her leaves dancing across the
grass like tiny ballerina's dressed in red and gold.

The mothering maple tree sighed
softly and suddenly looked lonely and old.
Feeling abandoned and very
tired she slowly drifted off to sleep for a
long needed rest.

Winter came and went, while she slept through the
snow and cold. A wise old tree who knew when
spring arrived she wanted to look her very best!

The warm spring air awakened the sleeping maple tree and
once again she had new baby leaves to nourish
into a glorious canopy of shade.

Children returned to enjoy her rebirth and
she knew again the sounds of their laughter
as they once more played beneath her leafy glade!
Joyce E. Hightower

Friendship

True friendship is more precious than gold.
  Friendship holds countless joys and treasures untold.
It cannot be bought; it should not be sold.
  Friendship is for all: The young and the old.

Friendship must always be nurtured by two.
  One, alone, cannot keep a friendship true.
Each must rekindle friendship's fire anew.
  Take more than you give and friends will leave you.

Friendship, like a child, needs wise, loving care.
  It should; must be kept in constant repair.
Every friend must this well-known wisdom share;
  And use it, friendship's "ups and downs" to bear.

A true friendship among friends can be found
  When two friends are, together, heaven-bound.
Goals set for gaining heaven's higher ground
  Keep the mind sober; its objectives sound.
Illa Mae Brown

Change Me

So miserable!! Was I,
as I began each day.
How many times have I asked, why?
And how long must I stay?
But knowing that I would get by,
I daily thanked the Lord and prayed.

The days and nights were bright and clear.
But how do I fight the ever-growing fear,
that robs my joy and makes me trite?
You see I've lost my friends, so dear,
now if someone might just lend me their ear.

Change me!! I cried as I prayed, oh Lord
not to need close friends no more.
A solution, I dreamed would erase the pain
that made me feel, I'd never again be the same.

But He wants me, it's now clear to see,
just the way I was designed to be.
To love, know and cherish those, who'll become my friends
the ones He chose. I cannot change, for if I do,
I'll not know the treasures, for which friendship is the clue.
Diana J. Wilding

Untitled

The old gray bitter wrinkled man
reflects upon his life long span.
Gone are the laughs, the songs, the joy
gone is the smile he wore as a boy.
He raised three girls he raised a son.
Been forty years, hasn't heard from one.
His long time suffering saddened wife
uttered nary a word as she took her life.
She tried to reach him for twenty three years.
He broke her heart, ignored her tears,
As he stumbles down life's dusty road
he never paid for what he owed.
Four packs a day have made him thinner.
Smokes alone with his frozen dinner.
Lungs of charcoal body broken and torn
been busy dying since the day he was born.
There's nobody gathering as he's put in the ground.
Eyes unseeing there is no sound . . .
Robert Kowalczyk

Oligarchy

As these creatures crawl from cracks,
They place themselves on corporate backs,
To turn and twist their wretched knives,
Bleeding out the peasants' lives.
You can trace the lies drawn on their face,
As they pretend to kneel and pray,
Asking for the heaven's grace,
For the war machine they've put in place.
And the trickling monies wrongly spent,
Barely seem to pay the rent,
As this royalty sets itself in place,
When the poor cry in hunger "Let them eat cake!"
And it's for kings and queens to choose your choice,
To be your conscience — your godly voice,
But soon these words won't be allowed,
Or to blasphemy their sacred cow.
To the rich and cold — the greedy old,
To this oligarchy your future is sold.

Felicia Weekley

Hate!

Hate . . . a word I loathe to use.
    Raw electricity . . . full of abuse!
Fires flare from deep within.
    Thoughts that enter . . . full of sin!
An internal pressure that explodes,
    spewing angry coals on red-hot roads.
Roads leading nowhere, nowhere fast.
    Hate spurns feelings of good times past.
Full of anger! Full of rage!
    Directed only by who's on stage.
Bubbling and boiling, the seething sails,
    your soul ignites, your body flails.
Stop! Think! Faith will reign!
    Is hate really worth the pain?
Chart a new course — change direction!
    Keep your eye on the prize — take positive action!
Derail hate . . . on your track Go!
    A new life is waiting, a brand-new show.
Hate is gone, now I am too.
    I truly wish the best for you.

Chuck Evans

Liberty

As she slowly passes me by
I marvel at the sight of
a tear in her eye.

Why she weeps, I do not know.
How can such beauty be filled
with sorrow?

Dare I stop and question her pain?
Dare I continue and let the question remain?

Perhaps its death or maybe birth.
Could she be limited on her time here on earth?

Why do tears trail her long Ebony face?
Amongst all her beauty they look out of place

"Liberty" I shout, I call her by name,
as she continues to pass her face filled with shame.

"No Justice" "No Peace" "No American Pie"
Are the words Lady Liberty utters as she passes me by.

Stanley B. Coles

Midnight's Wandering

Jasmine scents, in sage repents
the silly beam, of midnight's glean
our thoughts collide, in dreams deep tide
their hints of light, death's darkest knight
and who am I, in wonder why?
When shards of light, steel their might
meet morning's dew, and come to new

Gail Mann

Falling

Tell me, where is the space that we fall through,
    when we feel we are falling in love?
Is there someone in there we can call to
    who will send us the sign of the dove?
Do the words that we speak have a meaning
    Or are they just symbols of sound?
If our actions speak louder that language
    no wonder they seem so profound.
Do my questions surprise or alarm you,
    perhaps bring a blush to your face?
These are feelings that never will harm you.
    Not to love is the only disgrace.

Gerri T. Dunne

A Corner of the Mind

As life takes on new dimensions,
And friends go separate ways,
Memories that lined childhood days
Are tucked away in a corner of the mind;
Untouched by life's harsh realities,
Their beauty undiminished by time,
- Memories otherwise unvisited.
Years pass,
New friends replace the old.
Then one day a sudden call, an unexpected visit,
A conversation begins with 'Do you remember me?'
Cobwebs are dusted from a corner of the mind,
All of a sudden laughter and tears unite.
The dying embers of a friendship are fanned into flames,
Memories renewed . . .
Revisited . . .
Relived . . .

Amelia Ngoh

Legacy

Forward marching on to a scorned legacy
Stabbing into the eyes of life, a cruel sin
Here we see without vision a race that shall never begin

Were truth a lie and a lie the truth
Demoralized, mislead by another man's ideals
Compassion for life, to know what the other feels

Onward to the gallows, opinionated I have become
My call to blindness, a message to send
The demons have become my only friend

Exonerate me, a martyr to living free
My legacy a nightmare come to me in the night
To be preached to by another for what is wrong and right

Our life's tragedy, to be led by morons
To be caught up in a judgmental rat race
To rebel against the logical professor and spit in his face

A legacy you have experienced in a few lines
This legacy by heart has been told
Legacy for all, a message to have enough moxy to be bold

Joe Turpin

On the Seashore

On the seashore, day by day
shells are laying in grand array.

Some are broken, some are jagged,
some sand covered and kind of haggard.

As you look across the dune,
there they lay, patiently marooned.

Some are yellow, striped and white,
some are purple, thin and bright.

It's like finding treasure spread around,
if you pick it up, it's your's abound.

There's such a collection.
seaweed, jellyfish, trash and all too.

Look it over, it's your choice.

Make your selection.

Don't you see, it's kind of like life,
there's so much there, choose peace or strife.

It's all layed out, just like the shells.

Choose the good to heaven or
the broken to hell.

Kathy G. Bradham

Personal

As I gaze out my window just think 'n' of you
I wonder what makes me feel the way that I do
I feel you've taken over me
An yet you don't know the power and control I've given to you.
You would only see if you open your eyes
You would see what I feel it should come as no surprise
When you see my feelings as others do
I will be always hoping you'll someday return them to.
Cause mine will always be waiting here for just only you
How to put this in simple words I do not know
But one thing I know is true
I know that I am the only one
who could care for you the way that I do
Why if you ask I wonder that to

What makes me so sure that it has to be you

Samantha J. Marrow

Mango Man

Soft hair the color of mango flesh.
Sweet juice flow openly.
Ripe aromas abound around kitchens.
Love is easy with a mango man.
Let fruitful passion last past its picking,
Savour its sweetness as time goes ticking.
Impatience makes the smooth skin wrinkle.
Only time can give your mango flavour,
Relax, do not let your mind labor.
Time gives no answer before it's due,
Whenever you're ready he will be too;
For luscious ice cream in a summer dream,
Buckets of chutney flow like a stream.
Let it spout, you know it can,
Love is easy with a mango man.

Debra Rostorfer

My Allen

I was thinking of you today and the tears began to fall,
But as I looked at our two children I felt you weren't far away at all.
Those big brown sparkling eyes of yours, and little mischievous grin,
and many other traits of yours,
Our children hold within.
Our daughter's love of laughter, our son's love of tools and cars,
Help to keep your presence with us.
And help to heal the scars.
So as I think of you today, there is one thing that I can do.
That's hold our children tightly, because in a way . . . .
I'm holding you.

Remembering you,
Missing you,
Loving you always
    Julie

Conflict

Why do they do it? Why do they fight?
Can they ever love each other?
There's so much hate in the world
Must they add to it?
They'll destroy themselves, as they're destroying me.
Sinking into a world of resentment where -
Misery is the norm, happiness is rare.

I feel so alone. No one to share
Each for his own, no one to care.
Where is the thank you, the pat on the back?
Organize, referee, - when will it end?
What can I do to make life better?
Who can I turn to? It's each for himself.
How can I help them, make them understand,
To learn to care now will help them for ever.

Diana Pilborough

Gathering of Thoughts

I stand and look down at you,
we're alone now and it is very still.
A slight breeze rushes in from the window,
and it ruffles your hair. You look different now,
but beautiful. You are quiet and beautiful,
but you are gone and I am still here.
We will never again hear your magical voice
or see your loving eyes looking into mine.

Melissa K. Bland

Treasured Memories In A Seam

No, I'll never forget you. My sweetest darling.
I'm going to treasure our lovely secret memories.
Now that you left me. I find myself startling.
Unable to sleep. Must stop listening to many stories.

Before I go to bed every night, I glance at your picture.
Although you have forgotten me entirely by now.
How will I ever live without my love in the future?
My dreams are vivid, in them I see you! You must know.

Don't know what's happening to me. I feel very lost.
Dreams tell me, go towards the Orient, find a new Harry.
"Believe I will." I'm broken hearted. I'm off to the coast.
"I'll treasure your memories in a seam, on my Sofari.

To have you in memory and in my vivid lovely dreams.
It's great for me. As long as I live, I'll never forget you.
You live in my heart. Our memories treasured in a seam.
Secretly I'll hide them. I know I'll never feel lonely and blue.

Memories treasured in seams, gives me strength and vitality.
To live without you, "Babe," in dreams we haven't parted.
You're still my love. Memories of high and fine quality.
I'm sorry we parted. I still love you whole hearted.

Geneva F. Castellano

The Caged Bird

Her heart cries out for something that is indefinable.
Ceaseless searching for self contentment is the reason
she awakens.
Lessening the distance between the
unknown and the present is all that she has ever desired.
For only in her unconscious mind can
she overcome the treacherous
mountains and the raging
rivers that stand between
everything she is and everything
that she is drawn to be.
On wings of destiny, she glides
over obstacles in search of her fate.
The desolate plains nor the endless
waters call her name, for she heeds the voice of the sky,
the wind, which holds for her limitless boundaries.
She soars; she flies, she has found freedom.
When her wings dampen with morning dew, the emptiness
in her soul once again surfaces.
She, the caged bird, will forever be in denial of completeness.

A'Neial Bell

Mystery

Good or bad I know not which.
Who is poor and who is rich.
Life's games go on each day.
I keep searching for a better way.
Who's to say which horse to shun?
Who's to say which horse to shod?
How do we know who's the perfect God?
Lords above or below, which is the best way to go?
Do we find it in our religion?
Or is it a erotic condition?
All our lives we search for the key,
And all we find is reality.
For hundreds of years we search for the truth.
But it is a mystery that can't be solved,
Not even by the best of sleuths . . .

Edward P. Morgan

In Jesus' Arms

How I've longed to hear of your presence,
Oh I knew I would rejoice!
But you came and quickly parted,
A little life with no choice.

How I long to know you,
And touch your gentle face,
Only left to imagine,
Your warm embrace.

A life to save, and that you did,
Your life was so brief.
To acceptance I came, still yet confused,
Where do I find relief...

In the heavenly places, where you abide,
The eternal arms protect you,
I too find rest, and comfort reside,
Till at journey's end, I'll find you.

Wait warmly, oh little one, in Jesus' arms,
Rest in the security of his love,
O child of mine — now is thine,
Your safety abides above.

Lancie Spragg

What's His Name?

There was a man most people knew
Yet, he was spoken to by very few,
He didn't have any claim to fame,
Folks just called him what's his name.

No one paid him any heed,
Even when he did a good deed
No, one noticed no matter what he did.
It's as if he always hid.

Then he won the State Lottery and was a millionaire
It seemed to him that he hadn't a care.
Everyone noticed him then you see
It was just the way he dreamed it would be.

On the day he lost his money
The people laughed and thought it was funny
The people that once wanted to be his friend
Cast him aside when there was no money to spend.

If only he could be like he was before.
He wouldn't mind not being noticed anymore.
He decided to be content with who he is,
And to accept whatever fate was his.

Sandra Pearsall

Love Blossoms

In the beginning, a single rose, the symbol of our love.
We worked together, with help from up above.
The soil I did cultivate, while you brought
water from a stream nearby.
The hearty bush flourished, from the
nourishment we did provide.
And through the years we were rewarded,
beautiful rosebuds, memories of days gone by.
But alas, a dreadful sight one day, as I hurriedly walked past.
Our rosebush was wilting, and probably wouldn't last.
The soil I had neglected.
Your stream was all but dry.
It suddenly became clear to me.
And at that moment I began to cry.
The tears that I now weep,
provide moisture to the roots down deep.
But if the ground is left untended,
our love will surely die.

Jerry W. Stetler

Mighty Fine

A fish is just a fish, till served in a dish.
Add some lemon and some lime, mighty tasty anytime.
Oh let's catch a fish, so we can make a dish.
It's my great wish, to eat a yummy fish.
You can have my only dime, please get me there on time!
The sun is a rising slow, and a fishing I must go.
The fish are flopping, can't you see?
And I'm right here, by the tree.
The hook is set the bobbers in place.
I hope I get one, with a great big face.
Wow can't you see it, it can really swim!
A fish is just a fish, he'll look better in a dish.
First I must get rid of the slime,
hey, do you think, I could have back my dime?
I need to buy - some lemon and lime.
It will make our fish, taste mighty fine!
A fish to share, with someone who cares tastes might fine, any ole time!

Judy Speaks

A Requiem 4 2 Pac

2 pac,
Tone Loc, Heavy D,
Even me.
Lying on a cold slab in the morgue,
While masqueraders of life carry on their dialogue
Trying to give meaning to what went wrong.
Rapper, poet, musician, actor...
But what's more,
He didn't have too die a "Thugs Death"
At the request of his "Lyrics"
Did they play tricks on hiss mind?
Or was he inclined
To see if he could fool the "Grim Reaper?"
Take heed to the message in the sadness,
Don't let the madness of life stifle you
Into not enjoying her pleasures.
Peace is a wonderful thing!
2 pac: Rapper, poet...
We'll hold your "good notes"
For we know it will sustain us.

Vyann Scholfield

Quest For Success

Sitting here thinking
Like many times before
Searching every nook and cranny
Deep inside my wretched soul
Looking over my land scaped brain
Not leaving a stone unturned;
In my quest for success

I keep trying to soothe my sun-scorched mind
With cool dew forming thoughts
But the yearning with in me,
Undaunted by time
Anxiously grips at my overworked conscience
Striving on, pushing forth,
In my quest for success

Louis Alexander

Thanksgiving Day

Over the rim of the ocean to a dimension beyond the sea,
we are moving ever onward into eternity.
Beyond the sky, beyond the stars,
thru the barrier that bars us from what forever will be,
where we will go and what we will have to do
depends on me and you.
Choose your pilot with care and beware,
false pathways and snares that abound almost everywhere.
Let there be one perfect pilot,
one truly commissioned ship,
one perfect goal, all in righteous unity, as
onward over the rim of the ocean, we go
to a higher dimension beyond the sea,
into eternity—beyond the sky, beyond the stars,
thru the barrier that bars us from what forever will be.

Wallace C. Danforth

Not A Kiss

Not a kiss or even a date.
Just to see you makes me feel great.
You're so rare this I can tell,
because your persistent smile is so swell.
You're never down, you're always happy,
If I was in your life I would be so lucky.
We don't know each other this is true,
but we have our whole lives to see us through.

Simple Being R.K.J.

For Love of a Brother

I wept for you again today as I thought about your life.
How that little white rock has turned your happiness
into misery and strife.

The dreams you once dreamed and plans you had laid don't
matter any more.
But when and how to get one more rock just eats you to the core.

And the people who love you, and pray for your soul,
are just a means whereby;
you'd beg, borrow, lie or steal for just another high.

Satan, with his wicked device has you so strong in his
grip, that all which is proper and decent and right
is now blinded, distorted, and warped in your sight.

You cannot see or comprehend the heartache and
pain this has caused;
because the senses and emotions that God has
given you are temporarily "lost."

But I envision a day when you shall be the man you
once were and more.
Dreaming lofty dreams, making noble plans, and
God's peace is what eats to the core.

Rebecca Bartley

Thank You

I've been down and I almost drowned
in my own misery, that I keep a mystery.
I could have died, when alone I cried.
If it weren't for a special three.
Who weren't about to let that be
when my heart it crumbled and my legs they stumbled
my brothers and sister were there for me
when I held my breath, and wished for death
they read my head, and gave me a special gift.
With an attempt to care my love sick
'B,' he did his best, to keep my head at rest.
While Kelley would keep me doing what I like best,
and Chrissy was there, willing to here me confess my greatest
weakness.
My friends are beside me, they stand behind me
just to let me know, that wherever I may go.
That they're there to catch me, if I fall.
With love like that, I promise this a fact
if the tables were turned, I'd do the same for them all.

Robert Coen

Mom's Trunk In The Attic

Alone in the attic, there she sat.
Surrounded by memories, this and that.

The old trunk lid, open it lay,
Exposing her treasures in disarray.

Sometimes she would smile remembering when.
Reminiscent tears would appear now and then.

Her mind never wandered from the scene,
As she traced her young life and its dreams.

Diligently observing each item as gold,
Remembering details of the story it told.

Letters in a box, tied with a bow,
A few pictures only she would know.

High heel slippers, a tiara, a gown of blue,
A scrap book of clippings, a diary too.

Post cards and souvenirs of places she's been
Report cards and school books, trinkets and pins.

Countless memories, stored in the attic above,
A heartfelt accounting collected with love.

Donald K. Frost

My Son

Whatever joys this year has brought
At least for the present were dimmed
When my son chose death over life, as we know it
And my faith was tested again.

Not 'till I stood at the grave of my child
Did I know the real meaning of sorrow.
But I can attest that faith does hold fast
And is sufficient for all the tomorrows.

His earthly life seemed all too brief,
And I now feel the need to do more.
I pray I don't dwell on the one that closed
That I miss a newly opened door.

He had been my Guardian Angel
Ever since the death of his Dad.
Perhaps the role was too worrisome
For such a sensitive lad.

I'm no longer in need of sympathy,
And I don't ask to understand.
Just remember our family in your prayers
Craig was a very caring young man.

Lenita Jordan Carstens

Lost In Wonder, Love and Praise

I'll remember you in my dreams, my love
Your affections so gentle and warm
You've touched my heart and chained my soul
You were all that made me whole
Your tender kiss and loving smile
I cannot explain this love
God blessed me with someone like you, my angel from up above
How can I repay you for your genuine loving care?
What can I do to show you my thanks for you always being there?
When can I tell you that without you, my life is not the same?
Why does it hurt to need you? There is no end to this pain!
How can you understand these feelings within my heart?
I pray to God you can hear my prayers although we're worlds apart
I know that your life was troubled and your heart was burdened so
I know how much you gave, before you felt that you had to let go
Although you've went away, in spirit I feel you near
I dedicate my heart to you, for your emotions were sincere
You've made such a difference in everyone's life you've touched
I'll see you when God's ready for me, until then I'll miss you so much!

Christy Zachow

Children of the World

This old world is cruel and so unfair
to those who have nothing but the clothes that they wear.
You talk about your wealth and all that you have
you scorn at the little ones left crying along the way
don't forget the children of the world.
We left them all alone crying in the street
the poor and the hungry, the beating and the cold
we turned our backs and closed our hearts
and ran the other way.
The children are the future don't let them stand alone
while we stand on our mountains and shed not a tear
they wonder if tomorrow will be their last day
why have we closed our heart and closed our eyes
we ran the other way.
Remember these are children yes
the children of the world.

Eric R. Kaminski

Still

Birth exhilarates
While the child is silent
Before the vital cry

Love, too, knows a silence of persistence
Pursuing like a hunter
Relentlessly prodding our discontent

And death has a lonely din
Each breath the sound of shoveled coal
Until the final silence refreshes

Robert Ludwig

Going Away (To College)

Time goes by so very fast,
I only wish yesterday would always last.
When you're in a bind,
all that you've been taught should be kept in mind,
because now you must learn to live on your own,
never be afraid of the unknown.
We'll always be there for you,
so when things start turning blue,
keep your head up high,
in a matter of days it will pass you by.
Always give it your all,
then you'll never fall.
Cherish all you have and get,
but never forget,
love is the best form of art,
you will remain in my heart,
and there you will forever stay,
no matter how far away!

Sabrina D'Agostino

Breaking Down the Wall

Single mom with child
builds a wall to keep child safe,
never thinking wall will one day come
tumbling down.
Single mom works, come home baths child,
feeds child, read to child, tucks child into bed,
never thinking wall will come tumbling down.
Child grows, mother never notices
still protecting child.
Child graduates from school and college,
starts to date, going out with friends.
Mother realizes child is an adult,
mother almost has nervous break down
child embraces mom, both cry
tell search other how much they care.
Single mom goes to work, comes home, no
child to feed, read to, or tuck into bed,
just a young adult leaving for work,
wall still standing.

Edith Turner

Needing Each Other

How much do I need you?
You should not have to ask,
for we both know our love is true,
and that it well forever last.

I need you more than the sky is blue
and as much as the ocean is deep.
Nothing comes close as me to you,
and your heart I will always keep.

I ask "are you in need of me?"
This I have not to ask to you,
for when I look into your eyes I see
that you really believe and need me too!

Crystal Jones

No True Victory

Darkness spread 'cross a shattered land
A bloody sword in a nerveless hand
Rage retreats, reality returns
Victory is held in a heart that burns

His eyes scan the field as the enemy flees
Yet a battle won he does not see
Friends and comrades now lay slain
Victory fades, replaced by pain

Previous mysteries he now understands
Sword and shield fall from his hands
Too late he knows the tragic cost
Battles won are battles lost

Matthew Witt

Carla

Today we were talking about an old friend.
Who's life has tragically had to end.
She didn't say goodbye, she just went on to die.
She left us all wondering why.
To my old friend that I really miss.
To you my old friend. I send a hug and a kiss.
If I could have a wish.
You would be here to return this hug and kiss.
But you've gone to a better place.
How can it be a better place.
when loved ones can't even see your face.
Hear your voice, or see your smile, your someone tell me how.
Why did you have to leave, why did you have to die.
Why couldn't you just say goodbye.
We miss you dearly.
Wishing you were here to share the years, tears and cheers.

Jennifer Craig

The Flame of Life

The darkness hides the beauty of life from my eyes
I walk forward. I stumble. I fall
I regain my strength to fall again
I endlessly search for something in the darkness
Something warm, something true something to open my eyes.
A single flame in the distance illuminates my being
It's a hope for the future
A beckon of beautiful light
So simple, so profound
Yet so alone, just a single flame
When I am united with the flame.
The darkness is no longer threatening
I can see the beauty of my surroundings
And the beauty of me.
The flame has brightened my life.
And illuminated my soul
I will carry the flame for eternity
And no longer will I walk in darkness
No longer will the flame serve only A purpose
But has become the purpose of life.

Mark Ulrich

The Urge

I always have the urge to check off — Other.
And I did it once because there was nothing in that section that
describe me.
I know you need it.
You need it to count me as a statistics
  To allocate your funds to the universities
   To use in your statistical formula to show — the community,
    the state, the governor
— the percentages which you say are like me —
   the graduates and the dropouts.
But I Keep Trotting On To Achieve My Goals.

Maxine Taylor

Friends

Friends are special so are you,
mothers, and fathers, and sisters too.
Even little brothers can be special,
But always remember friends care too.
When friends get hurt or even die,
Always remember their sparkle in their eye
Remember their smile and caring personality,
You'll have their lovely memories as comfort for your grief!

Katie Louise Miron

My Family Curse?

What a vile and evil thing you are
drawing those I love into the bar.
You're controlling their lives, but they just won't see
the pain, the hurt, the fear in me.

Grandfather, father, brother and husband fell under your wicked spell
How many lives you've torn apart, we aren't yet able to tell.
The emotional affects of your controlling embrace
for generations this family's been made to face.

Grandmother, mother, me and my kids
have all secretly cried and kept things hid.
Somehow the circle of this family curse must cease
We must rid our lives of this ghastly beast.

The cycle must be broken, another generation must not pass
To feel the pain and sorrow of the lifting of the glass.

Pat Hayes

Renewed Within

Unknowingly I turned to sin.
Weakness of my mind, let Satan in,
Misguided reasoning logic, and weakness
of heart
Satan moved in quickly to take over
my soul and heart.
Unhappiness and sorrow stayed, prevailing within.
Torment continued, relentless to win.
Finally, I was lead, realizing I could
  not fight from within.
To Jesus I turned, forgiving me of my sins.
With outstretched arms he cradled
  and comforted from within.
Now, God's Holy Spirit will guide me
  from sin.
A comforter he is, to all who believe
  and allow him to be within.

Laura Dinsmore Watson

Rose Beyond the Wall

By a shadowy wall a rose once grew,
Budded and blossomed in God's heavenly light,
Watched and fed by sweet morning dew,
Shedding its sweetness day and day again,
As it grew and blossomed beautiful and tall,
Slowly rising to loftier height,
The rose came to a crevice in the wall,
Through which shone a narrow beam of light,
And unfolded itself on the other side,
The light, the dew, the bright breading view,
Were found as the same before,
And lost itself in beauties a new,
Lightly breathing its fragrance in forever more,
Shall our claim of death cause us this grief,
And make our strong courage faint to fall?
Nay! Let our faith and hope guide us to his love,
And let us pray for the rose beyond the wall.

Kristen Ansley

Mountains and Oceans

I must say
I am in love
bring stars to my eyes
I want to hold your hand
feel you close to me
make my heart beat again
so I can relive through
your love
I will cry
either way
with joy, with you
with sorrow, without you
send the mountains crashing into the oceans
love me
absolutely
completely
unconditionally.

Arthur E. Mason

Mount Vernon

At summer's end before autumnal fall,
I touched the trees and walked the gentle land
So fondly held by George and Martha's hand
On Potomac, atop Mount Vernon's knoll;
And viewed the garden green, the locusts tall,
Beside the graceful house where show was banned
Excepting pride in field, husbandry grand,
Improving crops and stock for good of all.

This presidential man — who fought, and won,
And brought unruly thirteen out of harm
To form a core of states, united, free —
With all achieved, his task as leader done,
Had but two years on his belovéd farms
And lies, at rest, 'neath cool o'er-arching tree.

John F. Petrie

The Best One

Hey man, you're more beautiful than your portrait.
Come on, why don't you believe that you're talented?
Look at your brother, he denied his mortality,
And you, you're always displeased with your own body.

    Hey Man, you're much better than your reactions.
    But how do you treat your own kind?
    Go ahead, you have many opportunities to realize your
imagination.
    You know who you are: Consumer or Human Beings!

Hey Man, you're much freer than your behavior,
Why don't you open your eyes?
Cool, you have to think a lot before showing any feeling.
Don't say no, you can do it; get up and you will be your own savior.

    Hey Man, you're more of a winner than you dream.
    Guess what, you can make a difference.
    Because you can change a lot of people.
    Because you are who you are, your best actions will be welcome.

Louis-Roi Deha

Christmas Love

I've loved just you for all these years.
We've laughed and cried one-million tears.
In looking back upon this time
On little things that did not rhyme,
I still believe we are a poem.
You will never be alone
To know a night without my kiss.
Or be left off my Christmas List.

Jess Villegas

Pink

Pink is a beautiful flower that blooms in the spring.
It smells like the sunshine in the morning.
Pink is sweet like honey in a jar at home.
It feels like a warm quilt when I'm taking a nap.
Pink sounds like a breeze that blows the curtains at night.

Ashleigh Sullivan Barnard

Ode to a Cardinal

Soaring through the bright blue sky, fly,
As you fly high into the sky.
Spreading your wings to glide away, away
During this very day, one place never to stay.

As you come to the run way of green, unseen,
Bathing to be clean, as your eyes begin to gleam.
Drying off by shaking in the wind, begin
To fly high again, to your homemade den.

Nothing left in your basket this year, unclear,
Loneliness is your biggest fear around here.
Sitting contemplating until night, moonlight
Is the only sight as you take your flight.

Fly high you beautiful bird, unheard,
The world not stirred, as in my mouth there's not a word.

Christopher Bryan Martino

Love

Love sees not the mistakes
It sees the sorry of failing God
And prays for restoration.

Love sees not the child filled with hate
It only sees the frustration,
Reaches a hand in love,
Understands.

Love sees not the anger on her face
It only sees the struggle of years - the fears.

Love sees not the bully, boy or man
It sees the bruised heart - striking out.

Love never sees the fault of man
It sees only what Christ could do
To love be silent to pray to offer a hand.
That God some day may change the hurt
To love and that they too
May reach a hand
To help to love
to understand.

Margarette L. England

The Redneck

Do I know him?
Well, yes — yes, I do.
We worked together, drank together,
fought back to back in barroom brawls.
We rode horses, raced cars,
sailed every boat that would sail.
Made lots of noise with some good ole' boys
and sobered up in jail.
We shared many things.
We shared the same camp fire.
We shared the burnt out ends of long, summer days,
and the stale, cold smell of morning.
We shared shy wishes and dreams
that have yet to come true.
Do I know him?
Yes, I do.
Yes, I guess I do.

Frank S. Robinson

The Poet's Cry

We are here for a while,
Let us exchange a smile for a smile,
Let us not towards each other be hostile,
Let us change our life style

No, we should not let the thoughts go vile,
Our spirits should be as pure as the nile,
Let us not make the relations so fragile,
Let us change our lifestyle.

Oh! The enmity, hatred, revenge - all futile,
Let us crush the wicked emotions before they pile,
Who will live forever, all must go in exile,
Let us change our lifestyle

Time is precious, it will not stay, it is mobile,
Let us not be sluggish, let us be agile,
That was the age of sword, this is the age of missile,
Let us change our lifestyle.

Broken hearts and souls let us reconcile,
Let the happiness play forever on the world's profile
May this cry of mine go mile after mile
Let us change, let us change, let us change our lifestyle

Taufeeq Ahmed

My Country

Through the land of Lincoln, melt
Blood dripping from the stars
Full moon drops blindly out of sight
Which crashes all the cars

Boundaries rule our days and years
Boundaries limit freedom
So shackle the thinkers; Destroy the muse
Or restore that previous kingdom

This is not the place of which Woody sang
If it was, I'd be in California
As a child they made me pledge a flag
Now I occupy a chair in Ohio

Stop the melting
Bandage the wound
Elect another leader
To satisfy the search for sound.

Robert J. Bartusch

Heaven

The pathway is narrow and sometimes untrue,
a walkway of troubles some old and some new.
At the top of the hill a light doth appear, a glowing
white throne that tells me I'm near. A key in a basket
that unlocks a door, and leads me to freedom on
Gods holy shore. The angels in heaven some
young and some old, the things I imagined but never
was told. They all gather round me and they all sing
and cheer, in the land that we'll never again shed a tear.

Edward E. Wright

Life's Road

There is a bend in the road,
I can not tell where it will lead.
Nor how long it will manger,
Till I have trodden the whole way.
The uncertainties of the road lies not in it,
But I
To hold a faith that will see me through.
I look back once to see where I came from,
And in turning I can see where I'm going.
In finding a truth within myself,
I can face the bend in the road.

Lorraine Kepperling Smith

Footprints of Jesus

Jesus made footprints at Jordan one day,
To be baptized by John, we hear him say.
John felt unworthy to do this we know.
But Jesus said, suffer it to be so.

He was baptized, not for sins he had done
But, to fulfill all righteousness, he is God's son.
He showed us the way to heaven above
It was all because of his wonderful love.

He made many footprints on sands of time
For the forgiveness of sins, yours and mine
He preached the word from place to place
Always telling of God's wonderful grace.

He also made footprints up Calvary's hill
He was burdened but, it was God's holy will.
He carried his cross till Simon came along
And relieved his burden amid the throng.

So he made footprints to that great throne
By doing God's will, our sins to atone.
He's seated with God in heaven we know
And pleading our cause while we live here below.

Katherine Butcher

My Guardian...

When things in my life get really bad
Dragging me down and making me sad
Somehow, always, something makes it all right
Because in all my darkness, there's my guardian of light.
Then something will happen to again hold me back
So I'll struggle and fight to get right on track
Somehow, always, I manage to cope
Because in all my despair, there's my guardian of hope.
So when I fall head over heals to the point of no return
Then get dumped by the man I long for and yearn
Somehow, always, there's a ray of light above
Cause I know my heart will be healed by my guardian of love.
And when I've felt like giving up cause life is so hard to live
I've thought of sacrifices others had to give
Then somehow, always, something makes me smile and nod
And I know in my soul, it's my guardian, my God!

Pamela Barta

Sharing Love

Giving your thoughts to help another,
Securing that hope for a sister or a brother
Growing each day in knowledge of will,
Showing with true love that kindness remains still.

Taking the time to mold a stranger into a friend,
Is such a good feeling, and at no time does offend
Allowing that loved one to peek inside your mind,
Only to learn from you as both unwind,

Learning to share of all the "give and takes"
Making each deed happy without a mistake,
Needing to never worry about wrong or right.
When no need of challenges — there is no need to fight.

Honor your parents for their love is pure,
Contented in your growth they loved you for sure.
Lovers in harmony of their daily needs,
Gain more by gentle words and comforting deeds

Secured in love, honor and guidance of health,
Today's "world of love" is a masterpiece of wealth.
To share love is a blessing no better company.
Love is life — let's face it — from God to you and me.

Nina June Davy

Winter Wind

Out of the cold, gray sky, the wind.
First like a dancer
Weaves its way hither and yon
Between the tall, black trees
Rustling the last of their dead, yellow garments.
Then, as if angered by their rigid stance
Blustering into them like one amuck
Tearing away their covering
Till at last they stand, trembling and cold.

James C. Kimberly

Rise Up and Go Again

My steps are getting shorter, my back is stooped with pain;
My eyesight's not the best today, my knees know when it'll rain;
My memory fails me often, my hearing comes and goes;
But I look around and know I'm blessed,
I rise up and go again.

My yesteryear's have long been spent, but not the least in vain;
I've raised my children, grandkids too, through good times - often
    rain;
I now look back on all those years and know I've done my best;
I thank my God that I am able,
To rise up and go again.

I've learned some lessons down through life, no day is quite the same;
Youth passes by so swiftly, almost as a flickering flame;
Face your future with a smile, give it all you have;
Look ahead, there's still time,
To rise up and go again.

Peggy J. Danzey

Minnesota Nature Trails

Thank you for the lovely stay, also for the rides each day.
I liked the day we saw the Moose standing in the trees,
Laughing at the silly geese flapping in the breeze.
Another day, another ride, we spied some deer at play.
They looked at us, waved their flags, then turned and ran away.
When driving through a field we saw, majestic Sandhill crane
Feeding on the golden seeds midst waving amber grain.
They stood by hundreds in the field, their partners standing by.
Soon they all were airborne like ribbons in the sky.
Thank you, thank you, now I go and leave them all behind
To romp and play until when I, come back to them again.

Anna Marie Huber

Look Up

A little girl looks up
up to her mom,
listen to all the things
her mom says about the flower
wonders what it would be like to
be the flowers and sit in the sun
let the sun rays hit her
live off of the soil and hear birds sing
watch everything
everything that is silent
and that is heard
she wishes she could be that flower
or the bird.

Margaux Tudor

Night Time In The Forest

As the last rodent rabbit returns home,
And the last field mouse burrows down to sleep,
As the orange sun sinks into the purple sky,
The night time creatures start to creep.

The hooting owl spreads its wings,
And takes flight into the air,
And the sound of crickets and slithering snakes
Are absolutely everywhere.

As the first diamonds stars begin to shine,
And the bats begin to unfold, the frigid air and barbaric tone
Take the scene to the days of old.

Where the trees are gigantic and the air is thick
And flowers line the forest floor,
And every hollow inside every tree holds mystery galore.

All of the creatures living here have not been discovered yet.
It has been so long since this time
That the creatures are beginning to forget.

And at the very stroke of midnight, the scary things start to rise.
But it's so pitch black all you can see
Is the glowing of their eyes.

Intisaar Jubran

God Does Not Make Junk

A beautiful sunrise, the rays of the sun against the late afternoon
Melodies flowing by the wind thru the leaves, rivers flowing with
    sounds
A rainbow after the wet rain adorns the sky colors galore
A rose in all its splendor, color and aroma
The country side with its flutter of color
The sands of the desert with their simplicity and beauty
The blue and green of the immense ocean
The deep canyons with picturesque rocks molded thru the ages
God does not Make Junk
A squirrel munching on an acorn, a rabbit into the bush
The ants with their chores, the elephant in all its strength, the
    majestic lion
I am in awe of all the greatness of his creation
Small and insignificant I feel, but in relaxation I realize all
    this for me and you
With my imperfections, faults, and wrongs, I was created in the image
    of God
I am very special in the universe, I am unique
So I know "God does not make junk"...He created you and me.....

Osvaldo I. Venzor

Read the Word

If you feel depressed, and you don't know what to do,
call a friend, he will see you through.
If you feel like your life is coming to an end,
Just reach out and touch a friend.
When you came to that rocky slope,
Look to God and get some hope,
When you feel like you are going to take the plunge,
Soak up the living word, the Bible, like a sponge.
Call a friend, three or four or more,
Before you know it your spirits will soar,
If you feel you can't make it one day at a time,
Just take every moment and you will be fine,
I'm thankful to God he's every thing to me,
My head is getting on straight as you can see.
I'm happy day in, I'm happy day out,
My life is going on a different route,
I'm having an adventure in my life each day,
I'm happily going down life's highway.
The highway that I travel, is the highway of love,
That only comes from up above.

Billie Jean Higgins

211

Finitude Of Life

At six, she wanted to know the difference between a sunset and sunrise, why delicate butterflies withered without a trace of sound, and why the man with the stump arm had a smile bigger than her unbounded imagination. At nine, a pink birthday bike made her secretly scream for the dense bottle, ashore with carvings. At twelve, the oasis of Lake Travis could make her yawn, and she wondered about another place.

Earlier in her life routine dulled her, and convention filled her spaces with many faces without names. Her family, spoke visibly only too much which ended chronicled in a blaze of smoke. But then everyone bought into the cover-up. Like a heroin addict which needed drugs, she longed for something hidden, finding little, her spirit was often removed. Nonchalant, her soul looked beyond her eye and made the cut too soon.

Dawn's fresh candor would not be escaped, the rapturous greeting was too real. She was finally blinded. Earthly objects don't feel, at least she didn't think they did; but in silence, she heard their screams of ecstasy. A stone did not pretend to be anything else but filled with its stoned meaning. Everlastingly, the rocks radiance penetrated her being. Over and over they exclaimed: Death is the only fact! It is the eternal given!

Within the scarlet prism, the second skin made her quiver, because it was never a part of her or anyone else's white life. All live too safe, and that will backfire for safety kills until everyone is deceived and fearful of each other. As she turns, with one foot on the splintered poplar, the anomalies whisper: Your existence is death; set yourself on fire!

Caroline Kim

Wooden Floors

A melancholy voice whispers softly in the night.
That same weary voice shudders out of fright.
For no one hears her cries but the wooden floors below,
as she weeps in desperation to have someone to hold.

She desires to see the waves crash upon the distant sands.
She longs to have a child take her by the hand.
For she knows no other life than the one behind closed doors.
Again, her only company are her creaky, wooden floors.

No kin to embrace her, no soul to claim her heart.
This loneliness, this emptiness is tearing her apart.
But all alone she sits, rocking faithfully back and forth,
while her feet remain tied down to her creaky, wooden floors.

Cherilyn George

Ghost Hugs

  I'm just living on ghost hugs
cause my arms are empty of you,
Just memories of us together, and
all the things we'd say and do.
Invisible ghost hugs of sweet baby
are just barely getting me through.
These ghost hugs always I imagine,
arms wrapped around each other tight
for just a moment they seem so real
Oh honey the real ones always feel right
So I'm just living on ghost hugs
and all those sweet memories of you.
Until that time we're together again
I hope ghost hugs of me will do.

Ches Harper

Summer

She's a thin, brown child
with a lovely wide smile
her hair is long, black and very thick,
she's left handed and very energetic
provided she's not sick.
She loves to follow me on her bike in
the street
and soon as were back I hear "daddy I want
some juice and a snack to eat"
I miss her when she's not here
over at her mom's with some bang, or scrape
I fear
by the grace of God and if I pray
I'll see my brown child grow into a proud woman someday

Simmie L. Jordan

I Remember . . .

I remember the way you would prance,
  to show me your new clothes.
I remember the way your eyes would dance,
  but only when you laughed with me.

I remember when ever I felt blue,
  you made me laugh 'till I would cry.
I remember you always got me through,
  you were always there; good or bad.

I remember when you weren't there,
  I still remember how I felt.
I remember when you weren't anywhere,
  you can't imagine that much pain.

I remember you came back in May,
  I was so extremely happy.
I remember that one spring day,
  just like, it was yesterday.

I remember you never again did prance, in your new clothes.
I remember your eyes never again did dance, when you laughed
  with me.

I remember feeling a longing, when I held you tight.
I remember missing your certain, sense of belonging.

Jennifer Howard

One Day at a Time

Her voice was like a bird, singing from a tree,
her touch like a baby, soft as could be.
Her God given patience, and understanding from above
This was my mother, the one whom I loved.

Though her body grew weak, her faith grew strong,
Praying to Jesus, all day long.
Dear Lord, take care of this family of mine,
Remind them to live, "one day at a time".

The lessons she taught me, I'll never forget
The times that I hurt her, I'll always regret.
The memories she left, I'll hold close to my heart,
Watch over me mother, while we're apart.

"One day at a time," she was a wonderful mother,
"One day at a time," she gave freely to others.
"One day at a time," she was a submissive wife,
"One day at a time," Muscular Sclerosis Took her life.

Catherine A. Reed

Miracles

We often hear that all miracles are mysteries not understood
I only know they are wonderful, blessings and all that is good.

We may start each day with a miracle I can't wait for the day to begin
to greet with a joy near hysterical the pleasure that rise from within

There are roses and dew drops and wedding rings
Fireside and fragrance of pine
Music and laughter, sunset and springs
And kisses sweeter than wine.

There is the morning sun and the gentle bliss a pause for a cool
    quiet while
The instant cure of mother's kiss
The warmth of a wee baby's smile

Now may be better than might have been there's
    no earthly way I could know
It may be a time for remember when
A garden where friendships can grow

There must be millions of miracles I've only mention a few
Most are intended for everyone
But some are only for you

If you believe in all miracles and make them part of your plan
You will be grateful for troubles you have
And still do the best that you can.

Bob B. O'Loughlin

I'll Never Forget

Many years ago,
    I awoke from a nap one afternoon
And looked around.
    My parents were there, young, loving and all giving.
I fell back to sleep
    In the blanket of their security.

Not too awfully long ago,
    I awoke from a nap early one evening
And looked around.
    My parents were there, still loving, still caring.
But to my surprise,
    They were suddenly old and had given their all.
I fell back to sleep, wondering.

Recently,
    I awoke one morning
And looked around.
    My parents were no longer there.
I overslept!

Joseph J. Bylinski

Death

Who knows death better than I
Have you ever looked her straight in the eye?
Dark face filled with hate
She knows what you try to hide.
She's the one who can look inside.

It's summer out and I watch it snow.
Children are playing in the park
Don't they realize it is getting dark?
Be it good or be it bad
Don't hang on to what you had
Be glad for what did not turn out bad.
Think of things you've been told
Grab the memories you can hold
Hold your head up high
Never let your life grow cold.

Darren D. McKinney

Life And Its Treasures

There is no better wealth than the riches of health,
No bigger treasures than family and friends along the path.

The one dark day, in a hospital bed you lay,
At your bedside are your children and grandchildren.
As the stars of the firmament illuminate the dark night
So their love shines forth hope; what a beautiful light.

In the midst of them your wife presides
With a big smile and a word of comfort all fears subside.

As the rising sun rejuvenates the earth,
Her smile restores confidence where there was hurt.
Flowers, baskets of fruit, prayers, cards and calls
From family and friends young and old.

And now, a word of thanks to you all,
Family, friends, doctors, nurses, technicians too,
For the gift of health God gave me through you.
Most of all, thank you God for my gifts and treasures
That come from you.

Nick Cavaleri

Yuba City Mosque Burnt By Arsonists (1994)

Three hundred farmers from Yuba City
Obtained permit from the code committee
Built their place of worship so pretty
Terrorists destroyed it without any pity

Serbs destroyed mosques in Bosnia
Hindus followed the same in India
Now in USA, some has got that idea
Hope authorities give us the panacea

Practicing Muslims pray five times a day
God-fearing takes the evil-thoughts away
Converts in jail, if they started to pray
Revert from crime, PBS documentary say

Constitution gives us the freedom to practice (religion)
But some hearts are stained with prejudice
Condemnation not heard for this act of cowardice
From the media, Governor, or Dept. Of Justice.

Requesting you to use your authority
To prevent similar against this minority
Facilitating community harmony and unity
To keep this nation always in superiority.

Nainamohamed A. Rahman

Just A Dream

And then I pressed the shell,
Close to my ear and listened well,
And far away like a bell,
Came low and clear the slow, sad murmur of
Distant seas
Whipped by an icy breeze
Upon a shore.

Wind swept and desolate.
It was a seamless strand that never
Bare the footprints of a man
Or felt the weight Since time began
And in the rush of water was the sound
Our bodies rolling round and round
And upon that shore
Our Lovemaking all but gone
We lie awake and share the dawn

For Us

Joseph Tancordo

213

No Matter Where I Am

In the still, almost deafening, silence of the night, one's thought
crowd into that space called "aloneness".
And, in that peaceful setting, the heart and mind turn to those whom
we cherish above all else.
We remember these loved ones in conversation with God and wonder if,
being held so closely in prayer, these persons have an awareness of
the profound love that is being expressed in their direction.
For this to be realized would be the fulfillment of a sincere
belief...that the feelings of love would always transcend the elements
of time, place and circumstance...that no matter where I am, you
   will always
know how deeply you, my darling, are loved.

Judith Ann Crawford

Fire In My Thirst

There is a garden in my soul,
A place of peaceful, gentle grace
It surrounds a pool, so crystal clear,
Still waters, that portray a lovely face.

I cast my dreams within this pool,
As coins into a wishing well.
Magic waters weigh my heart's desire,
Then picture truths, that I must never tell.

For my desires are not always pure,
The heat of passion, and lust abound.
It's your face that floats upon the pond,
With rippling waters, all around.

Yes, there is fire in my thirst for you.
I try to keep this heat inside.
This truth I must keep locked within,
Where deep-dark secret, needs abide.

Sweet sadness of the endless hours,
I have waited long, it seems.
For you to rise out of this pool,
And join me, in my dreams.

John Houghton

From Beginning to End

Procrastination is so easy to find,
   "Don't bother me now, leave me be."
Never knowing how set our problems become,
   "Just let me find myself, see the real me."

Time wears on and the ruts grow deep,
   "Gonna get there pretty soon, don't need any help."
Then the pit is dug and the earth is thrown in,
   "Never knew this was true, never knew there was hell."

So when the urge comes to change direction,
   when you say "Wait for tomorrow to come,"
Know that once the end has come and gone,
   don't be caught saying "I've just begun."

John L. Meredith

I Wonder . . .

As the lips that once told me they loved
me claimed to love me no more, I wonder
how to stop the tears that flow so freely
to the floor.

As the eyes that held a look so warm
could no longer hold my stares, I wonder
if there was a time those eyes really
did care.

As the arms that held and comforted
me now just push me away, I wonder
why my time was through and why I
could not stay.

Thasha Collins

If

If happiness is life, I died years ago.
If love feeds the soul, mine is starving.
If hate breeds insanity, I'm crazy.
If sorrow shelters us, I'm safe.
The black hole I'm in sucks me in and keeps me.
Trapped between nothing, I suffer.
Claustrophobic in these limitless confines,
My soul cries in tormented agony.
I don't want to beg for freedom, but I will.
I have to move, but fear has frozen me.
If there's an escape, I can't see it.
If I'm meant to get out, I'll be gone soon.
If there isn't an exit, I'll remain here forever.
If this is my destiny, I'll stay without question.

Meghan McGaughey

A Message to the Blind

Yes, here I sit, not lonely, not downhearted
But only because my sight and I have parted
It doesn't mean that life is done
It just tells me a new way of life has begun
It's what I call an obstacle of faith
So I can't let it turn to hate
Yes, this is something I must endure
And I can still say I feel secure
With all the love, kindness, and care
And also the faith that we all can share
Yes, we all know there will be times of despair
But we need not worry is what I say -
There will always be the Lord up there
To always give us his loving care

James A. Abbatello

In A Moment's Time

In a moment's time, everything can change.
In a moment's time, your life is filled with pain.
In a moment's time, all your hopes and dreams disappear.
In a moment's time, it seems no one cares.
In a moment's time, everything is gone.
In a moment's time, you feel all alone.
In a moment's time, reality sinks in.
In a moment's time, you must start over again.
In a moment's time, you must move on.
In a moment's time, your life goes on.
In a moment's time, your moment is gone.

Tracy Gregory

Sisters

We're not related by blood,
We're not related at all,
But we are connected...by spirit and soul.
Some could say we're kindred spirits or even bosom buddies,
And I would have to agree,
For we have been friends for as long as I can remember.
You've been there for me through my ups and my downs,
You even let me nag and still you stayed around.
Now you are getting married,
And moving on to greener pastures.
All I can say is "Go for it!"
I'm so proud to have you for a friend,
I will love you 'till the end of time and always remain your friend.
We're not related by blood,
We're not related at all,
But we are connected ...by spirit and soul.
Some could say we're kindred spirits or even bosom buddies,
But I call us sisters!

Jennifer Bell

Swing

I swing up and down; back and forth,
Thoughts come to me as I swing; up and down,
  Back and forth.
The world is a simple place as I swing.
There is no violence or harms against nature;
  As I swing
The world is a beautiful place, as I swing calmly.
As I swing higher and higher, my thoughts
  Torture me;
They race inside my head till I feel out of control
And then the world is too complex for me to deal with;
There is violence and people killing each other
  In the streets; as I swing
The world is an ugly place, not suitable for mankind
  As I swing higher and higher.

  Kathleen M. Walter

Brett Erickson (A Boy With Autism)

I wish I had one day to experience your world,
To know why you giggle and clap and twirl.
To know all the things that you know inside,
But can't express though you've tried and tried.
I watch from the outside and want to come in,
So I know how to help or where to begin.
Some might say that you don't understand,
But I know you do, you will and can.
You take it all in, I have not a doubt,
You just don't know yet how to get it back out.
I wish I could experience your world at least one day,
So I could know the things that you'd like to say.
The things your mind speaks that my ears can't hear
And listen to all that you've longed to share.
To know you much better than I now do,
With an understanding that's much more true.
There is so much that I just don't know,
Please be patient with me if I seem slow.
There's so much more for me to understand,
And just like you...I will and can!

  Dixie Belle Moll

Widower's Lament

I miss you darling, so very much
I miss your tender loving touch
I miss your laughter, your sparkling eyes
The unspoken words, the little white lies

I remember the good times, I forget the bad
I remember the fun that we always had
Now that you're gone, I feel such a loss
I'm just a worker without a boss

You were always so loving, kind, and true
You thought of others, never of you
You were like that my darling, so very kind
You gave of yourself, your heart, and your mind

So I sit here and wonder what to do now
You're not here to tell me; what and how
I'll always love you, but on life must go
I miss you darling - I miss you so

  Donald L. Whalen

Untitled

My mother is round as the Venus of Willendorf.
Breasts heavy and drooping,
Thighs like short chunks of ivory,
Belly swollen from carrying me and many others.

I reach down to lift her from her wheelchair.
And as we rise together, trembling,
And she stands close to me
Uncertain, tentative, and heavy (so heavy)
Leaning against my body,

We shuffle in a slow arc,
Two clumsy dancers,
Mother the one who accepts care,
Daughter the one who gives it.

Looking like an ancient goddess,
My mother awkwardly follows my lead.

  Janet Vice

A Piece of You

I sit and think of you and wonder do you see
the piece of you that stayed behind and somehow came to be
I used to see your picture and wonder who you are
But then I look into the night and see your shining star
I know that we'd be friends and talk each other's way
If God would introduce us, I'd have a lot to say
I miss you when I wake and think of how we'd play
Because in my dreams we met before you passed away
I know that you'll be with me which ever way I go
But I could use a hand in helping me to know
I'm looking for the courage to chase what I believe
to catch up to my visions as they become my dreams
My Chief, I think of you and wonder, do you see
that piece of you that stayed behind and grew up into me

  Trey Fortner

Last Thoughts of a Dying Man

I sit in the General's staff room
hearing the field guns boom.
I anticipate the dreaded words,
absent-mindedly tapping my booted foot against the floorboards.
'We attack in one hour,
gather all your men and firing power.'
The men wince as I give them the news,
for they are sure we will lose.
The men climb over the trench,
and the general listens to reports of the battle on his bench.
Many are shot,
some are not.
I hear the groans of those not dead,
some possibly hit in the head.
I jump into the fray.
Every man alive is sweating on that hot day.
I take a bullet in my chest,
The bullet is an unwelcome guest.
As I fall out of consciousness I realize that we have won . . .
but I have lost.

  Kyle Zgraggen

Love Is Winter

Love is like the first snow fall
It's new, pure and so beautiful
Love can grow like the inches that gather each and every day
Love should never feel cold like the whistling wind
Love should feel secure like the warmth of a fire
Love can be bright like a burning candle
My love for you will never melt
It's winter all year round

  Julie Bourdages

She

She was protected by the forever
spirit, sitting down in the
middle of the room, soft,
vulnerable, and the bad spirits
were dancing around her,
their evil dance, waiting
to possess her soul, but the
darkness was scared of the
light, and the forever spirit
was holding her always,
like a child, she was just a
flower, fragile, and red, blood red.
With such life, such warm vibes, that the
bad spirits just melted at
her feet and then...
disappeared.

Linda Iris Munoz

Immortal Beloved

She walked across the room and he became breathless,
His timeless love for her represented his entire
life's passion,
His soul purpose to walk the earth was to be with her.

He lost his heart to her from the first —
With her alluring voice, bewitching eyes, and angelic face;
She was his gift sent from heaven.

His reverence for her was like a treasure,
Which he cherished from the moment he laid eyes on
her - until the day he closes them in eternal sleep;
Forever mesmerized by the overwhelming feeling of
oneness - the two sealing the tender fate of one.

He was her Romeo and she, his Juliette
a flame that could never be extinguished,
a love that could never die.

Shannon M. Shaughnessy

Resurrection of One Man's Belief

The birth of my existence is by far
to comprehend, or rather do I fear my
thoughts of how it all began...
Deep in the middle of a critical thought,
spirit guiding me, where it was taught.
My eyes are closed, but the mind is open,
traveling faster than the speed of light
when I get to where I'm going, I know things
will be alright...
Traveling so fast, can't even feel the wind,
on the unexpected journey to where it all began.
Tribes from the beginning tell me, I am free
I dare not ask them, how can this be...
Now returning from the womb where
my ancestors come from...
Ask me again, how it all begun.

Kenneth R. Golden

Work

Being in the work force today is like a washer and dryer,
click, click, click, around you go, whatever you say.
Oh you thought you would get to the dryer someday soon.
But before you know it the clock strikes noon.
Another day passes and parts of you are aching,
You want to be in that playland of fun, slowly baking.
Oh here comes a friendly face with hands to lift
me out of the twisting waters, here they come!
Oh no!! The hands just putting another quarter in
the washer. Oh why am I so numb
cold water can do that you know.

Jason S. Bloom

The Belly of Jersey City

With a surgeon's eyes, cold and penetrating,
The penthouse windows stare across the silver thread of the lazy
   river,
Fascinated, bewitched by the golden silk snare
Of dynasties and empires.
Arrogant and secure in their sterility,
All concrete, steel and glass,
So far, and yet so close, the tall inhuman forms
Hold a cold blade steady into the belly of Jersey City.

It is a dead city. No blood left. It has been drained.
But, like a dead shark's gut, agape and mummified,
It holds, silent and frozen in their desolation,
A phantasmagoria of horrors and wonders.

But the surgeon's eye is unseeing, and the hand unfeeling.
The blade meets steel, bent into tortured spasms of destruction,
Iron scraps, rusted, like dried scabs over ancient wounds,
Plastic shreds, once sterile, gently moving under the soft breeze,
Prudishly hovering over the city's wastes.

But behold! Beyond the knife, in the deep of the belly,
Have come to rest, untouched yet, the fallen jewels:
The carved ivory of an eave,
The deep garnet of brownstones nestled in emeralds,
And, against the sapphire of the evening sky.
The pure, fragile nacre of a magnolia tree.

Josiane Jameux-Joyce

The Dance

This life is but a temporal dance
with each day a changing pace
we sway to the impelling melody
a step, a twirl, embrace

As the counted hours approach us
and tempo slows with grace
one reflects on where the moments went
time has come to close the place

What seems finished is never over
life's spirit can not be erased
we simply glide from one ballroom into the next
without limits of time and space

David Perk

Time Past

Clay pots of gray and red
Not yet touched by fine patterns
Of black and white,
Spread among the skins of past hunts of deer and elk.

The smell of dried earth, bone, and flesh.
Once I was young and strong,
Now time has hardened my thoughts.
Days long past of the quick hunt
Now settles for the warmth of the fire.

Hides that surround my lodge are now weathered
And hardened as fast as my spirit.
Great herds of ghost men and beasts
Now run in clouds forever.

My spirit grows ever narrow
As time has done with broken arrows.
When again my spirit rides again my pony
I once again will not be lonely.
For I will see my old life and
New life in the clouds become one spirit
And I will be young forever and one with the earth.

Susan M. Oswald

Frustrated Self Analyst

I've spent sometime on insight.
I've done what I could do.
Life's evidently stagnant;
Episodes of change, too few!

My desire to impact
Affects me and fellow man.
Dispel tolerance, see
All my motives become sand.

Conceived my expectations
With deadlines not too soon.
But faith and trust elude me;
Daily tasks painful to assume.

I have to be patient.
That's what I have been told.
Then what I Know and Believe
Collide and tumble down the road.

My voices say inside me,
"Give Up" or "Go Ahead."
It's time to choose, what is it?
I'll do what works - I pick Hope instead.

Montie Chambers

My Grandfather

The way he could tell tales of the Lord;
As if he knew him himself.

Just like a wise man in every word he said;
His pride more important than his wealth.

His kind face and warm smile to lead you
through paths unknown;
Giving advice and being forgiving.

He heals wounds inside your heart just
knowing that he's there;
He shows just why life is worth living.

In every prayer or tear from my eyes,
he is there;
He is my Grandfather.

Stephanie A. Himes

Resolution

Yesterday the sun was shining, the sky was clear and blue
Today the clouds fill up the sky, and there is no you.
I have never felt such pain before, I ache in heart and head
I never knew the absolute of someone being dead.

My grief takes over and sadness fills the time
Please let this pass for me so that I can memories find.

I know that one thing I will always have are the memories of you
Of our life, our laughs, our fights and our love
So special for we two.

As absolute as dead may be
So absolute are memories of you for me.
They will never leave, they're mine to keep.
I know that and will start remembering
As I wipe my eyes and weep.

Meg McDonough

Ode to the Old Politician

As a young man happy and free it was my goal, a politician to be.

As I grew older the time did come
when the urge overcame good judgement and I did run.

First for a minor office or two
then on to the country office, my ambition grew.

Then to the State level I went. With promises galore, and
political debts it was an important life, that I spent.

As I grew older, my self importance grew,
there was no limit to the Civic leaders I knew.
The old party political hacks, advised me and told me just how to act.

Then on to congress for a term or two, yes and still my self
importance it grew. It was not long, in this high leadership
roll, that my personal gain was the people's goal.

Now what is this young up coming whimper snap
who has come forward, to challenge me in my own camp.
Oh the lies and half truths he does tell,
as he sets out in this Election, himself to sell.
He has all this vim and vigor and support that is new
as he has all these new things, that he will do.

Alas, election eve has passed, how can it be. I came in dead last.

Chester Gardner

He Died

He died last night in his hospital room,
Quickly and painlessly,
With his hand in mine,
He drifted off into eternity,
Whispering softly,
In the still air at night,
With only the, then slow,
Sound at the heart monitor,
To beep out his fading voice,
Saying to me that he loved me,
And that he always cared,
And that he'd never leave me,
Even though it looked like he was dying.
As his eyes slowly closed,
His grip on my hand tightened,
And then he just let go,
With the monotone ring of his heart,
Gone dead.

M. Pauline Caton

Trust and Trust and Trust

I raced up to the moon and snatched away a star.
  I put it in my pocket but had not traveled far,
When a voice called out and stopped me. "Do you think it fair
  To take the starlight from the sky and emptiness leave there?"
I answered with rebellion, "How can this feeling be?
  You reached down into my life and took my love from me!"
"Love is not a person, but a spirit, don't you know?
  Your love will always be with you wherever you may go."
"It's here and now I care about! I want him here with me.
  To live, to see his children, to love and comfort me."
"Tis you seem to care most for, that is plain to see.
  Perhaps your love, if he could choose, would choose to be with me."
I bowed my head in shame, there in that lovely sky,
  I had set myself to say my sweetheart should not die.
Maybe as the voice declared, it is better thus.
  I must believe it is at least and trust and trust and trust.

Frances B. Thomas

Autumn Gold

Aspen gold is masked within -
As greening leaflets dance and spin;
  Meeting Summer face to face,
  Trembling from her warm embrace.
Then Aspen leaves of autumn gold
Shine forth in beauty - bright and bold!

Amy Nies

Criss-Cross

A crossword puzzle fan am I
to that I will attest.
The N.Y. Times is my day's high
a cut above the rest.
To try and name the Gods of Greece
or fathom a ship's quest
Would thereby give us Jason's fleece
or open Pandora's chest.

I've thought of Ande's Llamas
and pondered a gnu or two,
Penciled in on the Bahamas
Meditated like a guru.
Recollected a real old sally
Not buried in the Taj Mahal
But written in tin Pan Alley 'bout a daddy's paper doll.

There are towns to name or a suffix noted
Persons of fame and a poet quoted,
But the brain is cleared as the end is neared
And the fun is in the doing, for the knowledge you find
in the back of your mind makes up for all your stewing.

Anne M. Perillo

Lighting Up The Night With Loneliness

After listened carefully to the heated argument
Between stars and households' lights,
I've been pushed into the deeper night
By slightly cold sadness.

Until I've felt few lines of traces of tears
Which dried by wind on my face,
I became extremely silent.

In taciturnity,
I recalled after all how different
The dialogue made by stars and lights
Also, tears and aestheticists.

At last, I realized
The darkness actually is romanticism
But wondered someone light up the night.

Oh, faraway stars
And nearby lights are visionary in flash,
Oh, yes, loneliness is twinkling.

Toikun Chang

Taken

Eight brave men walked by his side
A courageous lady one step behind
Around him there stood men from all nations at peace
A mother and family so humble
A band for a memory the Irish salute
Then off to his final resting place
They were taking the thirty-fifth president of the United States
This March was his last
A tribute of awe as the jets speed past
Then his own plane with one lone man
For a leader had been taken from all man

M. Darlene Wilson

With Apologies to Julio and Willie Nelson

To all the homes I've known before
Tents, company rents, rooms by the week, then out the door
And way, way back to a three room shack in L.A.,
where we moved once more
Then the winds of change blew a Spanish stucco our way
Now lost in a ghetto and there to stay
On to Canoga Park, crickets at night, breezes by day
Gone now, the garden and orchard, Arcadian hideaway.

To those Hollywood pads on Argyle and Beachwood and eating at Brad's
Whatever came along, fast food and a jukebox song
for mine and the ears of forgotten lads
To art studios, an attic, a flat on Silverlake, a gold miner's
shack, beach houses and Shiply Glen
1959 was just a dream back then.

But the winds of change were slow to divine
That this was the house in that dream of mine
I've left it, neglected it, and have sworn to sell
Then I think of the homes that I've known before
So I'll stay if the winds don't turn mean as hell
But blow gently from some temperate, friendly shore.

Francesca Colby

Dear Pawpaw

Yesterday has come and gone.
Now my Pawpaw had moved on.
I prayed last night for everyone to be safe and
God decided pawpaw's fate.
He gave me wet kisses and yelled a lot,
But I didn't care, he loved me a lot.

Now my mawmaw is here alone,
missing my pawpaw and trying to be strong.
If pawpaw can hear my prayers every night -
Please ask God to make her all right.
I wish and I wish with all my might
my pawpaw would be here tonight.
I know in my heart this cannot be,
So please pawpaw watch over me.

With pawpaw being a softball coach and everything,
my only regret is that he didn't see my softball games.
Even though we didn't win a game except one,
he still would of been proud of me!

I will always love you, pawpaw...

Amanda Kinman

Dreams

Dreams to escape the pressures of day
Passing through the night in an unusual way.
Were not ourselves, our minds take charge,
We drift about, our emotions at large.
Expressing ourselves in hopes of change
Exploring opportunity in a very wide range.
Down the road to unexpected travel
Adventures we reach begin to unravel.
It can make us see our strength inside,
Or show us the fears we try to hide.
Creating questions we wonder why,
So many things we want to try.
As we awake to face the day,
We look at life in a different way.

Sharon Schussler

My Son

The greatest gift I ever received,
A feeling of love I couldn't believe.
The most beautiful baby, the most beautiful face,
He's now with the Lord in the Holy Place.
He filled my heart with the greatest joy,
He is my son, my precious boy. I miss him more and more everyday,
Each night I lie down to sleep, I pray:
"Dear God help me make it through the night.
All I want is to hold my boy tight.
It's hard not having him here with me,
Not being able to touch, hear, and see.
I have not lost faith from this,
It grows stronger bit by bit. It's still hard, he left his mark,
My heart feels more pain as it grows dark.
So please help me sleep through the night,
Help me to sleep until it turns light."
And God answered: "My dear child, your son is my son, my child too,
He is here and happy, waiting for you.
So rest your head and go to sleep, he is with me, so do not weep.
Remember I love you, continue to pray,
And be patient my child, you will join us one day.

Michelle P. Price

Mirror Image

My image running through the Spring flowers,
Prancing as if floating above the golden blooms,
Appearing as a royal princess dancing gaily.
A vision of beauty and innocence,
In the meadow she dances for hours.

I see her, my likeness as a child.
We look into each others eyes,
Youth and experience trying to understand,
Trying to please, wanting to win;
Remembering we stand in the forest of the wild.

She prances away to meet the Spring day.
I see her dance in the field of clover,
And run with others to the coolness of the pond.
An image of youth looks into her eyes from below,
A mirror of life glittering in the sun's ray.

Cheryl C. Patton

A View of Love

One cannot give what one does not possess,
to give love, you must possess love.

One cannot teach what one does not understand,
to teach love, you must comprehend love.

One cannot know what one does not practice,
to practice love, you must live love.

One cannot appreciate what one does not recognize,
to recognize love, you must be receptive to love.

One cannot admit to what one does not yield to,
to yield to love, you must be vulnerable to love.

One cannot have doubt in ones feelings,
to trust in love, you must believe in love.

One cannot live what one does not dedicate oneself to,
to dedicate to love, you must be forever growing in love.

Ken Borchers

Secrets of the Sand

Glistening sand in bright morning sun,
who footprints are to be
dissolved into your bosom this new day?
Whose do you hold of yesterday
or even yesteryear?
　　The infant's crawl?
　　The child's skip?
　　The teens' beat of the day?
　　The shuffle of the old?
You, sand, hold countless secrets of each heart:
　　Those seeking food and attention
　　Those leaping with glee
　　at thrust of energy in vein
　　Those in love,
　　Those with memories of life
　　in passing twilight.
Take them, hold them, keep them always with you.
Through ever-changing evanescent patterns,
you can keep a secret, sand.

Ralph Scott Davis

Serenity

This night of mine, when I'm all alone
and lying in bed, I think of what I
need to be doing, but in that same instance,
there are other needs that must be met,
like paying attention to a bleeding heart
which requires bandaging, like remembering
times that were important enough to lock into
my mind, like feeling the presence of the
Almighty, and taking notice, like feeling
that moment of serenity and being glad in
it, like recognizing all the unpleasantness
of life, and being thankful for my overcoming
spirit, like knowing there's always room
for error, but correction over rules, like
feeling the overwhelming desire for hostility
and at the same time humility takes its
place, by being grateful for my on going
soul and surely knowing it has a place
to dwell.

Robyn Martin Houston

Covered In Dirt

Sitting on the front porch swing
of the bible belt . . . Unbuckling in death
and diffidence of tears never wept
for someone they've forgotten
Some God scared Baptist preacher purporting a eulogy
For someone who grew up lovely,
made a family and died
Far away,
but came back to be buried
at home.
Looking out over the Georgia horizon
smothering an oak tree
sweating on the funeral party of cars
lining up down the street in front of my house
for the third time this week
Little faces staring out back seat windows
wondering why they've come to see
an old face they don't remember being
covered in dirt.

Hyde

Prisoner of Fate

Through the windows of his mind, he stares blindly at the world.
Ever watching yet not seeing Fate's cruel mystery unfurl.
So confused and bewildered by his sudden loss of sight,
This once brilliant life force is now banished from the light.

Trapped in a hidden chamber his true spirit can be found,
Full of love but wanting freedom from demons that abound.
Outside there's only anger and a painful sense of hate.
Why has life forsaken him and doomed him to this fate?

Through dark passages with pitfalls in a twisted maze alone,
Only he can find the answers to light his way back home.
With strength and hope he will succeed to gain a rightful place.
Cast off despair and once again feel sunshine on his face.

Julie Hiraishi

My Child You'll Be

You're oh so cute and cuddly now,
Love and concern show on my brow;
What things should I do, advice should I heed,
That you, my child you'll be?

To school you go, seems everyday,
Your mind the teachers sway.
New thoughts you learn, your mind to see;
Though still, my child you'll be.

A teen, oh my! Do I have a say?
Can't I just help to show you the way?
As old as you are, you're not without need.
And still, my child you'll be.

Married? Yes, married; it all went so fast.
Still future does cling to that of your past.
The past was yours and mine, you see;
As still, my child you'll be.

My child you were, my child you'll be;
When first conceived 'til married you be.
I loved you in thought, I loved you in deed;
That you, my child you'll be.

Donald Keen

Query

The only thing I know for sure
Is that I am somewhere now that is so pure

My heart beats in rhythm with yours
There are no windows, there are no doors

On you I am subsistent
Attached through a miracle
How could we be distant

As I count the months until we meet face to face
I cannot help thinking I'm now in the better place
I know only peace
What will I do when it comes to cease

Will you be there to guide me with your wisdom
Keep me out of harm's way and make everything beautiful
Like the season of autumn

Yes, you will. For you are like no other
You are my mother

Mary V. Kwadecius

The American Indian

I sense the dark-skinned God that I've been dreaming of.
God of nature and of the elements, breath life into my soul.
I dream of knowing your pain.
Your anguish and your despair are my intimate desires.
Your rusted and worn out skin, I want to wear your medals.
I want to worship your Gods.
I long to be the shaman that you once were.
The trances and all the mystical secrets.
Teach me, as you lovingly did centuries ago.
I was sent a vision of death, you didn't have to go, Grandfather.
Come to me and teach me the spiritual songs of old.
Envelope my soul and become me, that is my ultimate goal.
My soul, everything that I am, seeks to know the past.
He said that they ridiculed him for being an American-Indian.
I admire your individuality.
  I miss you Grandfather, American-Indian idol.
Come back to me, make me what I was in the other life, a tribesman.
A lover and an admirer of natures beauty, a seeker of lost souls.
I have total respect and awe for your powers, speak through me.
Until We Meet Again

Martin Pino

Mama's in the Car

He slowly pulled into the handicapped space
He drove a rusted-out Chevrolet
He was dressed in clean but tattered clothes
His hair was long and turning gray.

His wife was frail and her hair was gray
She sat in the passenger seat
I could see them count there change.
Deciding what they could eat.

With feeble steps he got in line
He studied the menu on the wall.
When his turn came to order he looked up and said
A small french fry and one burger that's all

He took two napkins and a plastic fork.
And some pickles from a jar.
Young lady could you cut the burger in two
Mamma's in the car.
Some people are rich and some are poor
Only God will know who's who.
Will it be the couple who shared their burger
or the man who ordered two

Leo C. Kjellerup

Success

I was a full-time nurse, a part-time mom.
All the voices around me praised my success,
except a handful which were silent:
my boys' and my own.

I chose.

Now I am a full-time mom, a part-time nurse.
I still make the nightly rounds, they're just shorter —
down the hall to three little bedrooms.
I still mend and make things better —
sometimes hurt owies, sometimes hurt feelings.
I still give doses of medicine —
mostly kisses and hugs.

I am a full-time mom, a part-time nurse.
All the voices around me praise my success.
Without exception.
"Success" has many definitions.
This happens to be mine.
(And the boys'.)

Rochelle M. Pennington

Untitled

Winters hills immersed in fog,
   no more for me to see

My doorbell rings, the children run . . .
   filled with prankish glee

The mail box empty by the door,
   once housed loved notes, now nevermore . . .

Within my heart memory stays,
   of seeing, hearing, loving days . . .

Share a smile . . . give a call.. drop a note,
   one or all . . .

Golden years can be a delight,
   ups and downs, much like a kite . . .

A bird flies to the icy sill . . .
   oh what joy, 'tis God's will . . .
     Robert H. Campbell

The Falling Rain

I lay in my bed at night; the lights are off and the moon sends its
   pale rays through my window.
I stare out at the clear night; there isn't a star in the sky.
Then, the wind begins to blow and the trees begin to sway.
A flash of lightning and a crack of thunder make my heart skip a beat.
I pull the covers around my head, frightened by the immense sound.
As I close my eyes to escape the terror and to dream, I hear a faint
   sound outside.
I open my eyes and pull back the covers.
I lean close to the darkened window.
Tiny drops are falling softly.
First, just a few, then more come.
Soon, the sound is like a waterfall, and I'm standing underneath it.
Then, I hear the song; the quiet rhythm of the drops as they hit the
   ground.
I lay back down and pull the covers to my waist.
I'm not afraid anymore.
I close my eyes, but I have nothing to escape now, there is no more terror.
There is only beautiful music.
This is the music that I love to hear.
The most passionate orchestra in the world could not overcome the
   power of this tender melody.
Tonight, my dreams will be filled with love inspired by the falling rain.
     Jessica Bishop

Untitled

To our Daddy
The most giving man we know
You'll be missed indeed
For we love you so

Until we meet again
Let us not forget where we've been
Through the good times and bad
Sweet memories - oh what memories we've had

A word of wisdom
A stern raised brow, a friend
A father, a fishing Pal

A hard working dedicated man
Who always gave a helping hand
You exceeded necessity and gave us the best

Now you shall receive God's Peace,
Joy and rest

We all thank you
but most of all
We Dearly Love You Daddy
     Sheryl Annette Conn

Untitled

Please tell me how to let you go,
   How to stop thinking about you
   And wanting to be with you.
   Why can't I pretend that you're some stranger
   Quickly passing through,
   Not worth a second glance.
   Help me forget about the days
   With you and nights with you,
   How good I felt and how I loved you
   With everything I had.
   Tell me how to stop believing you cared for me
   And wanted me
   And needed me.
   Help me see how the passion clouds my memory,
   And there will be someone else
   Some other time,
   some other place.
   That next time I won't fall so hard, so fast,
   And that the pain won't last so long.
Please tell me.
     Debbie Austin

Vow to My Lady

My lady's eyes are bright and blue
When seen in light they speak of true,
For all to see that deep inside,
My lady, I have nothing to hide.

These times do fly by, being two,
But this is only the start. For soon,
These times apart will surely pass,
You will be mine forever at last.

When future finally is now,
It will be our time to vow.
My lady, I am always true,
When time is right, no longer we'll be two.
     Randy Gallatin

West Virginia - Almost Heaven

"West Virginia is such a beautiful state,
I could really enjoy it if I had a mate,
   We would walk up a hill and down a hill,
   Holding hands all the while - feeling a thrill,
An oak leaf would wave to us - from a breeze,
Saying "Hello" from the majestic trees,
   A squirrel and a deer would be looking for food,
   But to be with my lover - is for me the mood,
Once by the creek bed we'd stand in delight,
Watching the water flow - by then moonlight,
   My thoughts are how lucky to be with her,
   No more cold nights - which are very burr,
To walk through the night I'd look into her eyes,
And lightning our path are many fire flies,
   Alas, the state is real and true,
   While I am searching for my one and only you!"
     David Fitzgibbons

Autumn Lady

Hiding deep beneath the ground
Lives a woman with a flowing gown.
She has golden hair and crimson cheeks,
And during summer and spring she sleeps.
When she wakes, she floats around
Spinning, twirling, spreading her gown.
The trees' leaves turn goldish brown
And reds, too, that I adore;
Then she sleeps forever more.
     Kim Garner

Too Late?

Circling shadows of desert birds
Throat burned, can't utter a word
Imminent doom closing in fast
Torturous death, why was he cast?

Seventeen others burned in the flames
Charred fragments by a smoldering plane
Thrown from the crash, why was he saved
Only to die in this blistering grave?

Lips that seem to form a scream
Eyes roll in his head, this must be a dream
Bad hand dealt by the jaws of fate
Will a rescue come or be too late?

    Robert Hornak

To My Mother

The hand I hold is not my own
but the gentle one of a mother
One whose understanding is quite sincere
yet, could never be replaced by another

You eased my pain
You shared my joy
You wiped the tears from my eyes
A mother's love is like an eternal flame
One which never dies

Time has brought us to the end of a road
a road which we must part
But do not fear
for I will be near
Forever
in the depths of your heart

    Kristyn Dixon

Connections

Scratching a cat sends reverberations
   into the universe
Cars racing through stop signs spiral
   into the breaking of natural laws
The robbing of a crippled old woman's purse
   stains the sanctity of all life on earth
Creation of things for the profit in them
   Drains love from the capacity of all beings
Shed skin of snakes and humans alike
   feeds tiny creatures unseen or unknown
Atoms from everywhere and nowhere slam into us
   with the force of meteors striking planets
Microbes feeding off their hosts
   wipe out whole populations
And if God is in us,
   so is God in a microbe and a blade of grass.

    Burton H. Wolfe

Grandchildren

Grandchildren just make every day bliss
Tiny little hand prints, and each little kiss
their little phone calls, and their own special way
makes every day seem like Grandparents Day.

Everyday we treasure all their love
and we thank the good father from far above
that he has given us these little bodies of life
to help us through our every day strife

Life would be totally empty without
each little grin, and each little pout
and at night when we tuck him, all tight in their nest
we know that we all, have been truly blest

    Catherine Y. Sullivan

The Flame to the Moth

When I first met her, the lure was there,
I did not think there a chance, for one such as I,
When I saw her again, it was over the blood,
of one snagged by the lure,
torn by the loss, of the one he loved,
the edge of the razor, he covered with blood,
I knew the lure, and I know the coot,
but the lure of your love is like the flame to the moth,
Warm in its glow, like the love on your lips,
the heart of the hopeful to the flame surely drifts
No reason no caution, surrender and give, life with out you, is a life
I can't live, the kiss of your kisses, the touch of your hand
gave you my love, even all that I am, do as you will, what you must,
in the love of my love, you must never lose trust
the storms of such love, like the wind on the wings,
a test of our faith, the commitment and dreams
We live in our faith, the truth and the light,
the beat of our hearts, in the still of the night,
Sure in our love, and knowing forever, like the flame and the moth,
we belong together.

    Louis McClain

The Lovers Apart

Even though we just knew each other
But I think it was long ago.
Only one time of talking to you
Enough to make my heart thrill.
Love hit me with its lightening
Made me love you unconsciously.
Darling I love you oh so much!
I love you crazily.
Letters I send you often
Almost from Monday to Thursday.
Friday? Oh my God!
I'm waiting for this day only.
Because both you and I
Have our chance to talk Friday night.
We were brought together by God
Like the fish were brought to water.
Whenever I'm done with schools
With you I'll spend the rest of my life.

    Phu Minh Do

Help Thou My Unbelief

Lord I want to love you but I'm not sure
I have a condition that needs to be cured
I want to trust you, but I'm afraid
I have a lot of decision that must be made
I know I need you, but I'm a shame
For the things I've done, there's no one to blame
I want to pray and yet be real
Help me believe that you can heal
I want to give my life to you
So you can clean me through and through
I want to know you're always there
even when I feel that no one care
Help me Lord to be strong, when everything
seems to go wrong
I want to know you're holding my hand
even when doubt comes that I will not stand
so as I go from day to day
Moon up nay faith as I begin to pray
I don't want to be sad nor full of grief
So Lord please help thou my unbelief.

    Antrinette Brown

View from a Manhattan Kitchen Window

Beyond the quiet stretch of the Hudson,
An alien land steps boldly in view.
The mango grove, each leaf in place,
The golden bounty of the papayas
Along the banana foliage.
The forlorn fig tree,
An outcast among tropical warriors.
I see my brother chasing a monkey,
He on ground, stick in hand,
The rascal jumping from tree to the garden gate
To the roof above.
His wife playing roles
From teen bride to an aging granny.
I hear my father's steps.
Alas, can ashes walk?
Memory marches on
Offering me then as now:
The hollows of my mother's fierce eyes.
Time and place, such beguiling confusion
'Midst the certainty of the kitchen stove!

Padma Desai

Blood

Into the gentle child eyes I wandered . . . .
A lost spirit begged to go home.
Face veiled - into the sunset he rode,
when an attempt for affection was shown.
Upon the retain, he would proudly say,
"Look what I have slain!"

Mona Ruble

Untitled

Dearest One, will you content yourself with the
    affection of one who looks upon love,
Who declines to accept anything but love
Will you accept a heart that loves but
    never yields and burns, but never melts
Will you be at ease, before a soul that
    quivers before the tempest,
    But never surrenders to it?
Will you accept one as a companion of soul,
who makes not demand.
    nor would want one.
Will you own me but not possess me
    by taking my body and not my heart and soul?
Then here is my hand
Grasp it with your beautiful hand
And here is my body
Embrace it with your loving arms
And he are my lips
Bestow upon them a deep
    and dizzying kiss.

Shammi Devon

Untitled

To watch a young heart wander,
To listen to a needful cry,
To taste the innocence of life,
To play chase in an everlasting field of laughter.
To follow the path of curiosity,
To make angels in the snow,
And to sense the wonder of all things,
Is to be the "shadow that follows a child"

Carrie Ann Hyde

This Fleeting Day

Skip across the golden wheat
field and watch the sunset
colors become splashed throughout the sky.

Run through the ancient forest
and see the flashing fireflies.

Dance in the pool of pale,
blue moonbeams upon the
blue-green grass.

Float in the wind as it swirls
around you and shows
you what will pass.

Listen to the wind.
What does it say?
Stop, and remember this fleeting day.

Krystal Longmire

You My Muse

You my muse
I remember the first time
You showed me the photo:
that mammoth tree by the cobbled rock wall
at the start of the path to the big old field.

In my painting
I set the tree in the center of the white paper
Like you placed me in the center of your life.
I made the sky prominent
Your favorite shade of blue.

The stones in the wall hid fairies, like in Irish tales
And like fairy to muse, leaps of mind sparked between us.
Pastel branches, severe against the sky
Reached their leafless limbs heavenward.
Grass brown and damp, a little green burgeoning
Gave our collaboration its fertile ground

In Greek myths they say Daphne became a tree
To escape the amorous advances of Apollo.
No marriage for her, just a longing to stay pure and transcendent

You are the blue sky inspiring my tree spirit.

Holly Meeker Rom

Wisdom Cry

Man you're in danger of losing your soul
for you have forgotten who you are
and from where you come.
You think you have risen above all others.
Your intellect is your curse;
How do you justify the corruption
of your father and rape of your mother.
In the name of progress, no less!

Come with me to the forest,
Spread your arms wide like the eagles above,
and like a drowning man gasping for breath
drink in all of the life and death around you.
Close your mind to everything
you think you are.
Look through eyes that truly see
your brothers and sisters stand.
Only when you find this truth
can you call yourself a man.

Michaela Giovanna DeVivo

223

Final Flight

On gilded wings I pierce the morning blue;
Silent clouds bear witness to my daring
Amid the storied heights, spirited by true
Heroes, like myself, consumed with living.

Saint Joseph, O Patron! Cleave before me
A steady path through winds come sudden fast;
Lo, the sky grows dark and my soul lifts airy;
The wind of God gathers me to His breast.

Fearless, I burst through the Cloud of unknowing;
O! Awesome heart calm! My spirit springs free
To soar boundless heavens on tireless wing;
And though my brow bends low beneath heady
Memories wrought of times drugged merry,
Rejoice! I await you who have loved me.

T. Dolan Kaiser

Justification

Where have I been these many and confused years?
What have I done to completely confuse the whole scheme,
complex fears?
When did this whole disrupted part of life become so evident,
so unreal?
One wonders in and out of life's situations without
any apparent zeal.

Yet, continue to function as those around expect us to relate.
However, this does not suffice for the lonely nor does it
compensate
It is easy to say what is right and what is wrong.
But, who can tell another being that one's behavior by
their standards do not belong.

Many believe that they are the judge and jury of their
neighbors actions.
But unfortunately those who judge should be the
recipients of sanctions.

For who can say what is in the heart of another person?
Is it not true that even in our own heart,
truths have various versions.

Chris Haughey

My Turn

There seemed no beginning, the end is never I think
I awoke, I saw, behold, it was mine all the time;
Maybe I should try to tell my feelings in pen and ink,
With essay, prose, poetry that does not rhyme.
It seems incredible that I have been so blind,
Cruel, thoughtless, selfish with another and always forgiven,
Though I have triggered havoc, troubles in someone's mind,
I can say there is reward this side of heaven.
Now it is my turn to bear the weight, make amend,
On knees, I plea, another chance, I care;
My turn to show I have grown, I can unbend,
To prove I am worthy, ready and willing to share.
Now I must prove it, if allowed, I know I can,
Off the pedestal, on my feet, show myself a man.

Floyd D. Hoisington

Alone

I look up to the sky and see the different colors
of the clouds. Dreamy pink, purple, orange and misty gray; as the
wind caresses my face with the smoothness of its breeze flowing
thru every crevice of my hair.

As I close my eyes swirling, disappearing, into the enchanting
rhythm of natures flow, saying goodbye to day light and
embracing its never ending mystery of darkness; I feel its
silence speak to me. Lost in the abyss of space, feeling the warmth
of the stars, every sounds stands out because of its beauty.
Stand still, is all I can do as I hear the silence of the night.

Consuming every single gasp I possibly can of the fresh
cool air; for my nostrils ache of the sensation, but yet
my heart over joys with the feeling. The feeling of being
alone. The feeling of being me.

Eddie Coriano

From This Day, Forever . . .

This time I've finally found someone, someone who truly cares,
A girl who I can love and trust, a girl who's always there.

That night we danced together as one, is a night I won't forget.
You thought I didn't care for you, but you didn't know me yet.

You caught my eye and when we spoke, my heart was captured too.
And now that we're together, there's no stopping loving you.

You've touched me like nobody else, has ever done before
I can't believe as time goes by, I love you more and more.

It's not the love I've known before, I know you feel it too.
It's a kind of love I only feel, when I'm alone with you.

I want to share my life with you, and make you only mine
Together by my side with you, "My wife" will come in time.

I wish in time could be today, but I want to make it right.
When I ask you for your hand, I'll squeeze and hold you tight.

A life of everlasting love, is what I'll give to you.
You rise my spirits soaring high, my life seems like it's new.

Forever I want to be with you
Together we'll go through life
Forever we'll be together, Dear
Together, Forever as Husband and Wife.

Mark Triggs

The Rose

Have you seen the beauty of a rose in the warmth of the sunlight,
As it unfolds.

And reached out to touch its soft pedals, and take in its sweet
fragrance. Or do you only see the thorns around it.

Life is like a rose. It starts as a small green bud. It is nourished
And grows in the warm sun and soft rain. In time it starts to unfold
And grows in beauty and splendor. And the thorns surround the rose.

The rose is life slowly unfolding before us. The pain we suffer
Is the thorns.

We must look beyond the pain and see the beauty and the blessings
In our life.

Reach out and touch it and take in its sweet fragrance, and enjoy
Its beauty, before it fades from us.

But you may never find the rose if you are too worried about the
thorns.

Darlene Sorenson

What Went Wrong

Adam, alas, abides accordingly
Besieged, belittles blasphemy.
Calumny can't continue ceaselessly,
Defamed, disgraced, defiled despondency.
Eve, exudes earthly exigency
Fairly fetching, flatters fervidly.
Good grief, goes gyrating gracefully.
Hovers here, hop scotching hopefully.
Inspired, intrigue, idealized; justice, judgement jeopardized.
Kingdom, kinship karmatized; listless, languid, languorized.

Man may numble, man may maim;
Noted nobles, none such names, objurates obnoxiously obtain;
Pleads painfully, precariously proclaim.
Querulous questions quaintly queried,
Reasons, remarks, remorse recedes;
Startling statements supercedes, Till the tensions thereby twinge.
Understatement, undeniably untrue, Vulgarizes veritable virtue.
While we wonder what went wrong Xenophobes x-rays X-chromosomes.
Yahoos yells, yahoos yowls; Zestful zealots zithered Zero hour...
Simon P. Perez

Untitled

You say you're not into one night stands
Or casual sex.
But what do you call it
When the feelings in your body
Never reach your heart?

You give me just enough to give me hope
And take just enough to send me hopes
Crashing to the ground
Like bits of broken glass
Knowing that I'll sweep them up
And build again.
You have to know
That I'll always build again.

But that's what you thrive on.
You feed on my pain.
Even as you dry my tears
And help me sweep up those shards
Of broken hope
You're looking toward the next crash.
S. J. McIlwaine

My Shell

As I gaze into the milky darkness of the shell
first it is a cats ear, long and smooth on the inside
then it is a friend nice on the inside, sometimes ridged on the
outside
and then it is like a palace never to be discovered
and then it is like a home comfortable and peaceful
and then it becomes the sun on a warm summer day letting out
rays of joy
and now it becomes a friend to help you through hard times
now it is happiness
and I am now well aware, that it will soon lie on its sandy home
the beach, and be one day taken away by another child.
Morgan Drolet

Untitled

Once you look upon the forest
And you tune in your listening ear,
Quite often you'd definitely benefit
As in the distance you hear a deer.

Quietly they do wonder
Searching for food in the clear,
Nary a worry about their surroundings
Not knowing they have humans to fear.

If only the humans would ponder
How peaceful their own life could be,
If no one made even the slightest attempt
To take advantage of something not theirs.

Like the deer in the forest
With not the slightest wish or care,
To but exist - just to flourish
Harming no one or taking anything not theirs.

Doing their own thing, with a daily routine
Always quietly roaming, always alert to whats near,
Taking care of their own, being part of a herd
Living daily in their God given world.
Dona Mae Hoff

Affairs of the Heart

Beating rapidly whenever you are near,
Thinking seductively of what we both fear;
Will eventually happen, as our bodies meet and release the heat
that we both possess;
Feeling the stressed, sensational feeling of one another as we
caress.

We know it's wrong to feel this way, but what can we say on this;
Our day of beginning an affair of our minds, bodies, and of course,
our hearts.

Even though in, this world's, reality we should have never started
this affair, universally, what do we really care when the feelings
we share for outweigh anything, anyone has to offer us, anywhere.
Belongings to others, we both know that it's wrong to publicly
proclaim our hearts in song.

Evermore silently, we must constantly cherish the times we have
been together from the start, quietly reminiscing about ways to
continue masquerading this affair, we're sharing from our hearts.
Linda K. Triplett

The Path Of Love

Give your ego an opportunity to grow;
Open your heart and peek inside.
Do you see a drama or just a picture show?
Close the curtain. Should you smile or cry?

Let people know just how you feel.
Orate on the extent of your care.
Should they be fortunate or they be ill;
In an embrace, your sensibilities share.

Share your dreams, become as one.
Let folks know just how much they mean.
Outside their affection your imagings done;
For without love the reflections can't be seen.

Forever be honest in what you say or do,
Simulation is a treacherous messenger.
Love can't grow on the seeds of rue,
But on the caring path of the questioner.
Pat Myers

Young Love

I was young, curious and yet afraid
temptation presented in such a sweet way

Bend and then yield for promises of a better day
insert - the amount is small

But oh I am jumping from wall to wall

Everything seems upside down and nothing
is no longer definitely square or round

More - more I ask but not demand
I can not breathe there is so much air

This is life that I never dared

More - more I shout my command again and again I now demand

Stop you say - dependence no good
As if you believe I really could

Multi - color prisms I no longer see
only the faded withdrawing me

Why did I ever yield and bend oh my God, will the pain ever end

Addicted - restricted - by you who taught me how
what trip do you have in mind for me now

Recovery is slow and relapses many
should I love or hate you Kenny

Candrid Brophey

Mama Re-Visits Japan After 50 Years In The U.S.

Clad in traditional kimono,
snow-white *tabi* and *zori* on your feet,
you lightly hold a folded fan in your hands
and sit serenely with an enigmatic smile on your face.

Surrounded by a formal Japanese garden,
with bonsai, stone lanterns, and ancient persimmon trees,
do you hear the mysterious sounds of the cicada
as they announce summer's end and autumn's wistfulness?

As you sit so calm and self-contained,
are you inspired by the sounds and rhythms of imagined haiku,
or is your mind filled with far grander, epic rhythms
of the astounding life you led in a far-off land?

Dewey D. Ajioka

Commitment

Commitment is something you take pride in,
someone you love.
It means that you and that special someone,
are ready to be together, forever.
Being together means having a lot of love,
trust, faith, and understanding.
For having these, you and that one you love
can have a happy relationship.
A relationship that will, last forever.
It is a step in life.
A step that can take you far, far away,
from your worries, fears and troubles.
It is a thing called Commitment.

Tauna R. Gandy

Homeless

Snowy manholes, misty streets
Cars sliding, hopelessly in sleets,

Puffing the last drag of a faltering cigarette
Dreaming for once the prosperity in a cabinet,

Corned muffins, stale pretzels, pity . . .
all smoked, hasty blunted, anxiety,

Fearing the hopes in life
Dreading the vengeance of a blunted knife,

Watching them with envy, a falter,
the freedom but burdens, ready to slaughter

I live, they live, a life of curiosity,
a life, filled with destined profanity.

Robert Y. S. Lee

The Old Homestead

The house still stands wrapped in pale red imitation brick
With missing roof shingles and gutters full of sticks
The white picket fence that once stood quaint and neat
Now torn from the hinges offering no safe retreat

A wooden bench still stands, weathered, splintered and worn
With yellow plastic cushions all faded and torn
Dull gray paint covers the windows and doors
With paint drippings still visible on the concrete porch floor

Two big trees are still standing tall
With one crooked bough ready to fall
The evergreens are scraggly, unkept and brown
Where once grew full green and round

The large kitchen once smelled of pies and spice
Now dark, musty and inhibited by field mice
One lone plaque hangs above a broken chair
Those chalky kind that you win at the fair

This old house cracked and old
Will forever hold secrets never to be told
Whatever the fate it now is time
To cherish the memories and leave this old house behind

JoAnn Dubenion

Peace — Where to Find It

Is there a place where one might find some peace
Upon this great wide world or open sea?
Let him who knows, come soon and tell to me,
That I might go and spend my life in ease.
Is it among the green or leafless trees,
Where sweet birds are singing with great glee?
Tell me, I pray, so that I might go to see
That restful spot and feel the cooling breeze.
I think there is no place upon this earth
Where we can find such rest from care,
Or be content in life, without new birth,
Until at last we fall and are laid bare.
By chance, we then can find "Sweet Peace" so bright
If through our lives, we have tread our steps aright.

Roy O. Schilling

Faith In My Father

When my days turn to night I had no worries because God is
my light. I have no sorrows and I can not complain, because
my faith is in my father's name. My father is great and he
is wide His home is in heaven, but in the earth he abides.
He leads me and guides me He stays close by me when asking
his will to be done He will not deny me. When my faith is
strong and my desire is not wrong I will not want for
anything long. When my days grow dark and there is sorrow
in my heart I have no one to blame for my suffering and pain.
All I have to do is ask for the light in my Father's name.
He tells me as a child I will always remain, because he is
my Father and he alone shoulders my pain. So whenever in
doubt and when your heart or body is filled with pain try
being my Father's child and for you he will do the same.

Valerie Ervin

Sailor's Wife

He has sailed the waters most of his life
He also chose me to be his wife
At times its hard to wait here alone
Wondering whether the sea will claim him as her own
Wondering if the places to which he roams will be kind and
send him safely home

Hoping that the many storms that he faces
will never be bad enough to leave its traces

The weeks go by and it seems so long
It seems like years since you've been gone

Then one day I'll answer the phone, he'll say come and
get me and take me home

I'll pick him up knowing he will be soon answering the
call to sail the sea

So I'll go on being a sailor's wife
And pray the sea keeps him safe all his life.

Susanne M. Cooke

Window of My Soul

You are the bright spot in the chill of life,
My moon against the darkness of the night.

Ever present, yet overlooked by the unappreciative eye.
Miscalculating the full relevance of your presence.
Then, like the moon, you beckoned quietly from the sky,
And I was captured by your pure and unassuming essence.

Summoned by a force more powerful than my will,
My logical nature was mandated to cease.
I pledge that it is the Creator's intent I aim to fulfill,
For our joining was nothing short of a masterpiece.

You are bright spot in the chill of life,
My moon against the darkness of the night,
Rest assured that we can overcome any and all strife,
Because our union was orchestrated by God's might.

I treasure you, I love you, and you have made me feel whole.
Our friendship all along has been the marriage of the soul.

Stephanie (Groves) Wilson

You Are Never Alone

You never take any step alone
when you accept an opportunity for growth
tomorrow is a day of new beginnings
and yesterday is forever gone.

Today, you will open a new door
and close the door on yesterday
you will travel the road to change
for God knows you can do more.

You have a special contribution to make
to many people you have not yet met
your spiritual strength ever present
to help you choose the path to take.

Our paths cross for a reason
to become a friendship that makes our life better
our faith gives us the knowledge that
we all have a common destination.
As we continue to travel our separate paths together.

Olivia Carpenter-Gibson

The Almighty One

Years ago as our country grew,
We had to decide, from what we knew
Between two issues that seemed to be
At odds with each other, as we could see.

One of the issues, from the depth of our hearts
Came to proclaim the miraculous parts.
The other proclaimed evolution the start
Existing ideas of the universe were far apart.

They took it to court, to argue the issue.
Failing to see it as a bit paper tissue.
If indeed God is The Almighty One,
Could He not then, join them one to one?

Sara Rebecca Reed

Solid Hole

The sun peeps out from the hill,
And yet people all around Greenwill feel a chill,
Morning, dawn, the people call.
All of them getting ready for a long red fall.
Greenwill cannot be empty.
For that many will be able to find the key.

Secrets and secrets lie beneath this gorgeous town,
Designed with the faintest glow.
The many that come to the town seldom a frown.
They come because they know so.
It has no tall buildings and no large factories.
It is filled with dozens of homes,
All which include families with lots of stories,
Maybe a dragon's black dome.

It is a beautiful town indeed, all of it,
Painting quality reading.
Actually that phrase is completely legit.
The town is an old painting.

David Chien

One In A Million

Reality is a dream,
  I hold within my hand.
Slipping through my fingers,
  like a million grains of sand.

And when at last the sand falls through,
  I look up with a smile.
For there inside my hand,
  remains a little pile.

The facts of life uncover,
  as I study all the grains.
For some are filled with laughter,
  and some are filled with pain.

My endless search continues,
  'till I find what I already knew.
For there inside my hand,
  I was holding you.

Brad Hernandez

Untitled

The earth shook, the people screamed
The horror was never what they dreamed.
Lives were lost in the blast,
And the repercussions will always last.

A time when peace seemed so near,
A time when happiness was so clear.
Innocence was lost in a moment,
And the cries were heard miles from it.

Children died as a result,
From a madman who is at fault.
Why people do such insanities,
Is only to please their own vanities.

Now mothers ache to hold their babies,
But all they can do is lay down daisies.
The scene is still fresh in their minds,
As people are close to the tie that binds.

A place where smiles always bloomed
Is now a place that seems to be doomed.
The atmosphere was once so pretty,
But now the world cries for Oklahoma City.

Angela Marie Mollman

Permutation

In the midst of change - the solidity
    Of my reality becomes as fluid
And permeable as liquid gauze.

I struggle to find definition and coherency
    In things that defy my mental gymnastics
And often think there is no answer.

How easy it would be to stop the "meet"
    Simply--blow the whistle and stop!
But if I do . . . what then does my life mean?

The next logical question then becomes
    What difference does coming to a "Life meaning" have?

        - Simple -

The incessant rebirthing of my soul--
    And that's more than
        Enough
          for
            me!

Christine M. Meisenheimer

A Tribute To:

David Lynwood & Arra Desma Fogl Tarrant . . .

As we Tarrant descendent's gather
At Pappy's and Mammy's home today,
We seek to pay tribute to them
In our own special way.

And to the memory of our parents
Who were honest and God fearing;
They did a fine job
Of their children rearing.

They worked hard on the farm
Earning a good living;
And plenty of love
They were always giving.

We are proud of our rich heritage
As rightly we should be,
We were taught to have faith in God,
Who in glory we'll see.

When we truly honor God
He honours us as well,
By filling our hearts with love and peace
Which compels us to go and tell!

Grace H. Reel

Our Dream

I heard a voice so dear to me,
That God called home ahead of me,
I turned to look, she lay near by,
I stroked her face with a tender touch,
She said, "Honey, I love you so very much".
I awoke, looked but there was no one there,
Then came those little tears,
You see, she was there for many years.
Now all of this is hard to bear.
I tell myself I wish I were there.
The Lord knows my troubles,
I let Him know I care,
This makes it easy for me to bear.
As each day passes and I take time to pray,
I can feel her touch, I can hear her say,
"Honey, I love you so very much".

G. Carlton Myers

Only Memories Last

A forest grew by the side of a lake, how beautiful it was to see
And a colony of birds lived by its side as happy as they could be
Until one day the choppers came and cut everything in sight.
An old owl said as he closed one eye, "Some how this doesn't seem right".

Some wolves and a fox and some rabbits, too, lived near the little town, but the cars and the smog and the people's right soon put the animals down.
With buildings tall and smoked filled air, the land was soon a mess,
The old owl looked and shook his head, "One day they'll learn I guess."

Years have gone by and the owl is gone, along with the water and trees
And folks like ants just build and build and even work harder than bees, but don't they know when they leave this world not a thing with them will they take?
Just a memory they'll leave, be it good or bad, like the owl by the side of the lake.

Ruby O. Perkins

Listening To The Voice

One day as I was walking out near the sea,
A voice so plain, whispered to me,
Your soul is searching for a resting place,
Have you thought of God and His Amazing grace?

There is a road to travel if you are heaven-bound,
Though it won't be easy to earn your crown.
If you seek, you will find,
Someone who will care, help you carry
The burden and sorrow that you must bear.

I am the Christ, who hung on the Cross,
I decided to die, just to save the lost,
I only ask that you learn to me
Keep my Commandments, and you shall be free.
I can move your mountains and calm your sea,
I will take you through the expanse of life
If you will follow me.

I don't ask much, not much at all,
but be sincere and follow the call.

Harriet J. Watson

Reunion

I had searched a thousand eyes,
then I looked into yours.
Hands touching in greeting,
our souls reaching out in recognition,
time stood still as they embraced
loving, laughing, and dancing together.
Reunited in love so pure we are as one.

We awaken as from a dream,
knowing true love has no boundaries,
it just is.
Our hearts rejoice in our reunion
together again we will walk this earth,
two souls eternally bound together as one.

Pauline McMaster

The Eyes of Man

Nothing a person does is hidden, for it is only covered.
For only a blind man and a fool cannot see, but when
The sheets are removed all shall see.
What was done in the dark has come to the light.
I am no fool, and I am not blind; I saw more than my mind
Comprehended.
But I have seen more than most would even want to know.
Now my heart bleeds no more, for I have loved and lost.
Hate has always been below me; it is God's way.
As it is written, a tree that bares bitter fruit is
Corrupt, so do not eat of it, for it will make you sick.
So now I have learned to love all fruits, but not to eat
Of just any tree.

Philmer Posey

Bird's Sand Dream

Bird!
Don't build your nest
In the middle of the crowd!
Tomorrow, the tempest will destroy it.
Tomorrow, the hunter will kill you.
Better, build it here, in the palm of my word!
So protect, you couldn't be anywhere!
And only in your nest,
The children of my word, could learn
To be born
With wings.

Liviu Parascanu

Why Then Love Did You Turn from Me

Love that suspended all things worthy of endurance,
  brightened your eyes that seldom trusted.
Laid to waste your precious heart,
  those before me whose iron promises rusted.

The jealous cores of your friends they do deceive you, making
  boulders from pebbles,
as they were once also my friends, their greed for you my troubles.
For you knew me better than any other,
my conscience clear, I pleaded truth, my heart they tried to
smother.

I was never a ghost of your last,
  my loving thoughts so incorruptible.
My visions of our dazzling future,
pictures you in paradise . . . so beautiful.

These things I cannot set aside,
the thought of you believing that I lied.
Taught to turn the other cheek, I cannot argue, I cannot fight,
  your eyes and memories should tell you I've done only right.

I have given to you all means of myself,
  my heart so trampled, neither have I wealth nor health.
For it is your love that keeps me from the hollow, lonely grave
  beneath the tree.
So, why then, love, did you turn from me?

Dale Robert Hopstetter

Now

Night encompasses the stars,
and the moon takes her stand as goddess of the shadows.

The wind is stilled and silence is the bolder as no
noisy interruptions stay her path.

The air is joyous to be pure and uninhabited by smoke and dust,
and the tarnished breath of lurching drunks gone homeward hours
before.

It is a lovers night. It is a night for hugging close those to you
who matter most, and even those who matter just a little less.
A night excluding none, embracing all.

Even the sea dares not to ripple, but lays like an enormous mirror
inviting the moon to glance upon her reflection in its petrified waters.
No shimmer, ebb or flow. As though an unspoken yet respected
command has swept the universe in one gentle, peaceful, loving
breath.

And we must obey and stand with it also, because that is all there
  is to do . . .
transcending thought, projecting nothing, being here, being
now, in this moment's moment.

Frances Salter

My Dream

My dream is to accomplish,
something that's never, ever been done,
if I somehow can accomplish that,
I think it would be great fun,
I would be a role model,
to all those younger to me,
then all the kids will yell to their parents,
"My role model's on T.V.,"
then those kids will become role models,
for the generation after them,
and long will live my story,
forever until the very, very end!!!

Siva Sankrithi

The Day

Shine, shine
  Sang the Sun
As it woke the morning

  A cool breeze
As the sky yawned
  Clouds drinking from the ground
Helping the Sun dry the ground

  9:000 A.M.
Buzz! Buzz!
  Rang alarm clocks
Children are waking and drawn outside

  Feeling the warm ground on their feet
The cool breeze on their bodies
  They awaken

Children playing in pajamas
  Adults awaken
Feeling no need for coffee
  They go outside

Having fun all day
  The day!

  Lonney Amos

The Watering Can

A flower seed is planted with hopes of bloom
In a garden of soil and plenty of room,
With sun and water as its friend
The bud, yes, slowly does begin.

To bloom with beauty atop its stem
As rays of sunlight rest on its rim,
The water nurtures oh so much
As a mother's hand of loving touch.

She gives us strength to grow and bloom
With lots of love and plenty of room,
Her rays of sunlight are her smile
That takes us through life's long, long miles.

She waters us with hope and kindness
As we grow up to her likeness,
Yes, a mother is like a watering can
Her love flows out like beads of sand.

So with this can, do always remember
That I thank you and love you forever and ever,
Happy Mother's Day.

  Elizabeth C. Staley

The Color Of Horses

The beauty in a betting man
is that he knows the odds. First and last
his is a match of ability with chance,
the rendering of attachments into choices
measured and well-made. It is the most
seasoned of disciplines. Linear evaluation
and the grace of motion combine for him
with such idiopathic precision
that contingency becomes an art:
the dispersion of a sparkled eye, the lustered bow
and sheeted feet, all purposed for retraction.
In his field of vision efficacy
is dependence. And so the saying goes
that as he knows his horse's place,
so he knows his own.

  Elizabeth G. Smith

Rain

The day was rainy and sorrow filled.
And all was quiet in the land of evil and forbidden feelings.
Hidden secrets whispered in the wind,
Hushed by the darkness of the night.
The air breathed anguish, a bitter smell
That was neither muted nor loud, but deep and smothering.
Clouds drooped in the blackness,
Playing gently in the background as thunder roared loudly.
And lightening joined hands, electrocuting the sky.
The icy water hit the shore, beating the
Earth nearly unconscious every time it slapped it.
But it made it soft and complaisant.
And the water became more and more angry
As the earth began to ignore the painful injustices.
Whispers, moans, and muted cries filled the tear-dampened sky.
They were suffocated by the cold that stole their pain-stricken gasps.
As life in this wild and nightmarish place continued,
Someone punched through the
Tough and unshattering glass of inhumanity,
To let in the bright and blinding light of the sun.

  Amanda Cohen

Untitled

Walking through the streets of Bonn,
the quaint houses and shops never cease
to amaze me with their beauty.
Water fountains spout up here and there
to let their music of the flowing water
harmonize with the music of the
ancient cobble stone streets.

If I stand in an old square next to
Beethoven's statue
and squeeze my eyes closed tight,
I believe that I can hear the music he composed
floating from his birthplace's window
a few blocks away;
and the heavy breath.
of a frustrated composer,
as he sits on his piano bench
and curses his deafness.

  Annette Pollert

A Carpenter's Friend

A carpenter is a builder of homes for his neighbor . . .
  He uses nails and lumber to assemble with labor.
A carpenter wants to satisfy his customer's needs . . .
  So he hires a designer who's blue-print he reads.
A carpenter has a talent with hammers tools and saws . . .
  He uses traditional craftmanship, and elders laws.
A carpenter puts in a long days work, he serves man . . .
  And he soon becomes like part of the family's plan!
A carpenter finds joy in work, when he gets the job done . . .
  He builds for a neighbor a dream home, castle, well done!
A carpenter can find help, guidance from our father above . . .
  He finds a better way to construct a foundation of love!
A carpenter seeks to improve a family's life-style, trends . . .
  And uses his loving, strong, heart, and hands upon God depends.
A carpenter is an apprentice to the great master carpenter . . .
  Who installs into each builder a character.

  Dan R. Russel

Love Imprisoned

Embraced within the deep recesses of my heart
A peculiar, secret love lingers.
As it swells with time to permeate my soul,
Longing magnifies my loneliness,
Inducing mournful sighs and unending tears
Because my love must remain buried in silence.
But when this cryptic love is revealed,
It will banish the murky dusk of my heart,
And encompass my entire being in radiant sunlight.
My lips will sing an enchanted melody
While my eyes sparkle with the adoration
Once veiled among the shadows of my heart.

Amy McMillan

Untitled

The verging spirit has already sloped
perfectly into the grave;
covered with fish scales
whose iridescent web
is still conscious of life.
The weeping willows ushered the passage
like a rusty voice
inducing a gentle sleep.
Reflected faces infiltrate the silvery mirror
like diminishing pen points
leaving stained autographs.
Dry leaves flutter in my throat;
a barrier of daintless mistrust
haphazardly back sucking
the saliva and local dust.
Profiles like circling ripples
hold out their arms firmly
squeezing the memories.
The heavy embraces haunt
the thin days to follow.

Elizabeth McNielly Carey

Forget-Me-Not

Forget-me-not child, I beseech thee today,
Do not forsake me, though you be dismayed.
Reach up with your hands, and I'll greet you with love.
I'll recapture your heart from the heavens above.
Just call out my name when your sorrows are high,
I'll shower you with mercy, until victory is nigh.
Use this flower to remind you that you are my own,
So delicate and beautiful...a treasure I hold.
The pedals so pure that burst into life;
Is your soul, that with love, will bloom from my light.
Forget-me-not child, I beseech thee today,
For without me, your life will just wither away.
Be anxious for nothing, for as I care for this bloom,
I will keep thee, and guide thee, and return for thee soon.
Until the time of the end, hold fast my ways;
Learn as much as you can without any delay.
Stand firm with your sword anchored deeply in love:
Rest in the faith until my kingdom come.

Cynthia Schwieger-Buchholz

If Only

If all our faults were put into print.
And at them then we dared to squint.
Could we really take to heart.
What the printed words impart.
Would it change our disposition.
Or would we require another edition.
If one fault we would mend.
There's no knowing how we'd end.
Perfection! No that's reserved for heaven.
So let's just settle for six out of seven.

Michael Doherty

April

I love you April with all your showers
Your daffodils and other flowers.
The fleecy clouds go drifting by
And stars and planets light the sky.

I watch the children running
And bees among some blossoms humming.
The wheeling gulls their playful wailing,
And yachts upon the bay are sailing.

Yesterday, some seeds I planted
From these some blooms are wanted,
I'll water them with daily care
To make my mini garden fair.

The mountains to the East and West,
Their snowy heads in splendor rest,
The waters of the sound so blue
Their whitecaps dominate the view.

I see another April passing by
And the golden years of you and I.
Oh lovely April, I love you so
My April, I grieve to see you go.

Douglas Egan

A Young Love Lost

As I kneel upon your sodden grave . . . from within is the want to cry.
I fall upon my weakened knees, . . . sobbing and asking why?
Yes I know this was God's wish, . . . your goal in life was gone.
Your will to live was torn away, . . . rebellious ways interpreted wrong.
Love was all we ever had, . . . born bursting in my heart.
No one sought to understand, . . . why we couldn't part.
Opposition was our burden to bear, . . . through the whispers we held no shame.
What for is all I have to ask, . . . being young was our only blame?
I walked away from that prejudiced town, . . . leaving you behind without a goodbye.
I wed another who understood, . . . I didn't hear your silent cry.
As I kneel on this tear filled land, . . . these are things I've wanted to say.
In hopes your heart will understand, . . . I was too timid to seek a way.
I've always loved you darling one, . . . your memory takes its special place.
In my heart and in my mind, . . . I'll remember your gentle face.

Judy Bates

Transformation

I must evaluate myself the world within
Hence I derive pleasure from the state I am in
Shall I stay here and conform to the forests' silence
I can see, emotions and organs that the planet's creatures
share, and captivate each other with
If touched my skin will shed (recede)
and the stranger before me revealed.
The choice of communications will determine my direction
and link my travels
In search of truth and with the passages of history
As I struggle to speak often trapped by my expression
I think, to err (foible) is human
For I am like the stranger (fox)
in a melding world.
I set myself free.

Ruth M. Poniarski

Untitled

They are a gift from God,
Made from love and good.
A miracle from the heavens.
From their first tear to their last good-bye.
They are our future, our hope.
They bring out the best in all.
They make the weak-strong, the strong-weak.
They bring down walls and make men shed tears.
Such a small package can carry so much power.
A bond develops that can never be broken.
They learn what we have already learned,
Yet they teach us what we have missed.
An experience that the Gods cannot resist.
The first smile, the first step, the first word.
No words can explain the feelings.
We know they will break our heart,
Yet we walk down the roads with them.
The magic of children
Can never be explained.

Don Moran

God's Simpler Things

The wind that whispers as it blows
through the trees like a sweet lullaby.
Those autumn colors that paint the land
for everyone to see.
The harvest moon so bright and orange,
glowing to guide our farmers eyes.
The snow that falls in silent peace to
cover our land in a diamond coat.
The fresh clean smell of our earth
renewed by a spring-time shower.
A summer sunset that gives calming
life to our clouds in purples, reds and golds.
The beauty of our mountains and our
oceans that make us hold fast our hearts.
These are some of life's precious moments
that happen day to day, they're so full of awe,
that they take our breath away.
In our times of discontent we should look
upon these things they only take a moment to behold,
they're God's simp lier things.

Janice Hotchkiss

Stars

The night sky filled with stars shone down on Germany.
In Germany there are also stars. Stars on dresses, sweaters, shirts,
suspenders and shawls.

God said to Abraham,
  I shall make your people as numerous as the
  stars in the sky and the sand in the desert.

In the night sky over time the stars extinguish. In Germany the stars
are extinguished but the prejudice was not.

The people who were forced to wear the stars on their clothing were
sent to death camps.

Stars are born in what scientists call special solar nurseries.
They stay there until they become hot enough and then they
move away from the nurseries.

Some of the children in Germany who were in danger were
saved by people who were not in danger, they took care of
the children until the holocaust was over.

The stars shone bright and so did the victims of the holocaust.
They will be remembered forever and so will the prejudice and
hatred.

God said to Abraham, I shall make your people as numerous as the
  stars in the sky and the sand in the desert.

Halli Melnitsky

Darkness

Night
descends
soft and graceful
like a warm, innocent blanket
Of Liquid Chrome
ushered in by a refined
wave
of silence;
The Jeweled Moon
appears quite suddenly
suspended precariously in the
coal-black sky
shedding ivory light
on a sleeping earth. Trance-like, hypnotic
the immortal moon keeps watch over
nocturnal children
and then morning emerges
gazing over a sluggish horizon
giving birth to dawn . . .

Danielle Dragona

She

Watch all of the colors that combine
In beautiful patterns so pure and divine.
The orange, fades to purple, fades to yellow, fades to red.
This is something I saw and not something I said.
Nature's term of saying it is the end of a day.

With utmost fascination I wish it would stay,
filled with the romance and sheer desire.
A passion in my heart that will never tire.
A sincere transition that will always be
Nature's beauty that shines through the silhouetted trees.
Cascading away into the dark blue sky.

And to my amazement, I still wonder why,
where does she go, as I watch the horizon.
Now that she is gone, shall I keep surmising?
To my best interest, this should not be surprising.
She will be back at the dawn, then she will be rising.
Watch as if the colors dance; a classical illumination.
To perform as if on cue with complete determination.
Nothing can ever be as perfect, traveling so unbound and free.
Nothing can ever compromise the beauty of that She.

Billy Alascia

All About A Smile

A smile is something we give away,
It matters not when night, or day.
It happens suddenly in a flash,
It's absolutely free, no strings attached.

A smile freely given is a picture to behold
It requires very little effort, just thirteen muscles,
so I'm told.

Something done so effortlessly
should be given freely every day,
It makes one feel oh so good
and helps to drive the "blues" away

I gave away some smiles today
to see what they would do.
They all came back and to that
add, an extra smile or two,
The hidden message that's implied
Behind every smile I give
is, I'm ok and you're ok.
And peacefully may we live.

Pauline N. Rohrich

Blindness

Who do I tell, to whom do I share my thoughts,
when I realize all has been done in blindness
and all that was meant was a touch of kindness.
How do you say, I am sorry to those hurt,
to those who will cry and shed tears
and those who shall always harbor fears.
Anger abound is sure to encompass my being
and the words I have said, will they be believed?
Tell me please, will they have any meaning?
Someone please take my hand and be my guide
for now that I see, I feel so blind.
Can anyone show me how to find peace of mind?
Question after question I need to ask,
yet answerless is how I am destined to be,
Please take my hand, show me the path to be free.
My facade has broken, it is all in pieces,
while my mind stays in a state of distress,
my soul destined to feel this self created duress.
Help me please I beg of you, the time is now,
I need to start again, yet I know not how.

Sean Michael Swafford

Son Spot

I see him with grit-ingrained feet bare
In worn sandals, standing there.
A grey-face, lined, haunted, with a
Piece of string holding up faded denims.
Blue denim eyes, thinning hair, worn
Shirt with missing buttons here and there.

Does he care? He is
Alone.

He holds a crude-lettered sign,
'Want work.' Waiting in line,
I watch a woman, red tipped fingers
Extended from her window,
Hand him a cigarette from her black shiny
Beamer. He does not see me.

Does he care? He is
My son.

J. L. Ralston

Shore Birds

Standing around his deathbed we were like shore birds
Watching from the shore as the sea of his death opened up.
A dark tide was rising to take his fragile craft now barely adrift on
    hospital sheets.
He spoke quietly to his family not wanting to leave them — Ever.

His wife of forty-four years slept on the floor in shattered pieces
    of pain
Held together by hospital blankets,
Numbed by too many months of losing
Her childhood sweetheart who would never leave her — Never.

On another shore his daughter spoke softly to him,
Holding her heartbreak at bay while the light from behind her
Was the radiance of a storybook princess.
Put there by her dying prince, a hero — Shining.

His son came and went in constant short bursting visits,
Unable to bear his pain.
He ran to doctors and charts,
Rushing to keep the dark rising tide away from his best friend —
    always.

Husband and Father slipped quietly into the waters at noon,
Leaving the shore birds to solemnly take flight.
One by one they rose into glorious regions of light
Where they would always fly and only seem to be three — Together.

Barbara J. McGehee

Memories

When I was a little girl, my parents were very poor.
But I was so happen then. We had such a wonderful world.
The mountains were so green in spring and brown in the fall.
Then we'd go chestnut hunting. That's the most fun in all.

I picked wild flowers in the mountains and berries on the hills,
green pastures in the meadows, and I could hear the whippoorwills.
We'd go to church on Sunday and hear the preachers preach.
We'd live by faith on Monday and the rest of the week.

Now the world is so different since our children grew up.
They never have any joy or peace. The world has changed so much.
Now I have grandchildren, they think life is a bore.
They don't like to go to church. They think it's awful to be poor.

Now when our great grandchildren will come
I don't know what they will do.
I guess they will change with the world like must children do.

Maude Marie Yeary

The Dream

Our eyes meet, gazing into each others soul.
Pondering what depth of pleasure could be obtained?

Fantasies run wild with visions of ecstasy
intrigued in our minds.

We touch, caressing so sensuously,
imaginations exploding like fireworks.
Kissing your voluptuous body with passion
like only I can.

Cross over the line, pleasure flowing
from our moans.
But wait, oh no, one more second
eyes opened, ceiling staring down at me
it's only a dream!

Archie Laney

Eyes On the Horizon

My beautiful lady of the diamond filled hills
I see mother nature has taught you well

The horses have come down from the mountainside
to drink from your womb where procreation hides.

The powerful wind blows from the south
please sing the sweet song
that comes from your mouth.

The sun shines on the back of your hair
and on your body that lies completely bare.
My faith in you has yet to fade.

The birds have given a loud screech in the sky
I see your reflection in the water
why must you cry?
Because you realized — what lives must die!

I've given you life's eternal bliss
and you will be blessed with nature's kiss.

Without pain and sorrow
there would be no tomorrow

And then you learn time is
something you only "borrow"

Andre D. Hill

233

Love — It Takes A Village

It takes love both for you and me
precious timely possessions
that money can not buy.

I have dreams of what
I want to be, desires for myself
that I can't obtain on my own.

No, "I'm not alone," I'm in a world full
of people who sometime cease to exist.
"too busy to say hello"
for they're always on the go.

Some of them don't care
about you and me, whether they live or die

But in order for me to be
who I want to be, it takes a village!

A village is love, care and consideration
little hands, big hands this makes a strong generation

No guns, no drugs, no self infliction
not even facial color

It takes a village of one and all
Then you and me can be who we want to be

Mamie A. McCargo

Untitled

Upon the setting sun there lies a cloud.
The end of the day has come.
A cool breeze follows the darkened blue sky.
Few stars are seen between edge-shined-on clouds,
and in the distance, purple takes the place of a midnight blue.

So quiet the coming evening stays until the rustling of the
wind disturbs the concentration of seeking stars.
Whistling is heard and chimes take sound.
Shivers creep up towards the back...Eyes are glazed toward the night.
A street light in the distance cannot even take away
the total wilderness and wildness of the end of this freedom.

On the edge of the distant earth, lies a now
very small blanket of the last bit of light...
As it fades away the wind hits folded arms
and sends goose bumps all the way up.
Eyes remain rested on the evening sky as
the only sounds that can be heard are natural, with the chimes.
The neck is not tense and the back not strained.
Emotional release has taken place
underneath the darkened strength of a sky.

Keisha Moss

Through the Eyes of a Dreamer

She is a cloak of dark velvet,
Looking at the world through saddened eyes.
Her tears sting of anger,
And her heart is full of fear.

Where will this cruel world take her?
To heaven, with her castles in the sky?
Or to hell, where even ice will burn the soul?

Her dreams are nothing more than a fantasy,
   never to become a reality.
And as the day becomes night,
   she fears the start of tomorrow.
For yesterday is gone,
   never to be remembered
   through the eyes of a dreamer.

Katie Thompson

Daniel's Poem

While we flail at tongs of death to come,
While we flense the bones of inmost dreams.

Great and glowing light, the embassy
Of afterwards and hurts the same as now.
If only anger had the power to heal,
And laughter make less deep the last abyss.

As we cry time after lonely time,
As we note the breathless rush of fear.

Helpless, hapless, stubborn and sincere.
Is God an ingrate deaf to all who pray?
The angrier we get the more our fault,
And sadness stays our lot without a peer.

Daniel, here's a tribute to your life.
Music, logic, these your best of friends.
To hope, to dare that these continue on,
And trust that long last comfort's on its way,
And ending but one slice of heaven's knife,
And trusting that we're heard whene'er we pray.

Stephan M. Weingarten

Untitled

If I could possess,
Ah, could it ever be?
If were mine....
Such glee!

Nar be yours with which to flee.
Could stay forever with me.
To own as mine, waste not - could be.

Dear one, please do not me, make wait.
Nair to be, without bounds this
fleeting fate.

It cannot be, how could we or
you or me....
Grasp, hold, caress: That which,
does not exist?

But need oh yes.
Why, why oh why not I.
Nor you or you or you or who.

A need as strong as natures best,
But contain that which knows no nest.
Boundless forever. For time is the master of those who rest.

Theodore V. Adams

The Willow And Heart

Say "What am I? Too fool now?" The girl she asked to the tree,
"And now what time is it?" She asked "What time has befallen me?"

Of prose I write and love I dote, my sweet, I reverie,
For with thee willow I also bend to a prince watching for me.

And one day I shall return, oh pond, and willow you shall greet,
Once a girl before you stood, now a woman to meet.

Am I waiting for thine love? Do I wait for thee?
Could I step and plunge into life with you eternally?

Time oh time, be gentle with me, let me not hesitate,
For it is only this feeling of new, let me not too long a wait.

And at this pond's edge I contemplate, how if my heart is full,
While swans float and trees sway, strings at my heart still pull.

I feel within a thump and release, as geese wings flutter,
And gaze to that tree which once held myself and my lover.

If this day past ends with me, and you I shall not gaze upon once more,
Richer my eyes, heart and soul, content I will be when it is o'er.

Angela F. Forster

The Legend

There once was a very tall man
He knew the game of basketball, but only had one fan

He played real hard and made it through school!
Now the fans know they have a basketball playing fool

The stadiums filled, and the kids loved him
But no matter how much air in his shoes, and dominated
each game the same
He never forgot all this fame was due to his number one
fan, daddy James

The years have past, the championships are done
Still the very tall man hears the echo "That's my son
Micheal Jordan!"

Chelsea Brester

This Day

Dear Heavenly Father,
    Please help me to be of service to someone in need . . .
    Say a kind word to a neighbor, or do a kind deed . . .
This day.

Let be ever ready to:
    Lend a hand to someone who may stumble and fall . . .
    Write a note, or make a call, to a special friend . . .
This day.

Keep me ever mindful of:
    Those who are in pain, or experiencing sorrow . . .
    Praying that they will have a brighter, happier tomorrow,
This day.

Let me not forget to be thankful for:
    This beautiful world made by your hand . . .
    The mountains, the seas, every grain of sand . . .
    And every person of every land . . . This day.
And, finally, dear father, help me to:
    Tell me someone that you are our best friend . . .
    Remember that eternity lies around bend . . .
    Realize that I may never see the end . . . of this day. Amen

Sandra Heise

Life Without Worries

Life without worries,
Is no life at all.

Individuals need sometimes be like Humpty, Dumpty,
and have a great fall.

It teaches them the moral
of life being understood.

That everything that looks good,
is really not good.

We all go through trials and tribulations,
from time to time.

So don't be afraid of worrying,
it only lets you then know,
That there will be many obstacles
down the roads that you must go.

It then gives the true meaning of life,
and life to the end.

So treat your life with respect
and know that through worrying
You don't always have to lose,
you may sometimes win.

Patrina McCrary

Truths

You'll never know what life might bring,
sometimes it will leave you with a terrible sting.

Be careful how you treat and talk to others,
consider yourself, your sisters and your brothers.

When you think you're better than the people you see,
beware of tomorrow, maybe that's where you'll be.

When it seems prosperity is on your side,
learn the golden rule and then abide.

Do unto others as you will have them do unto you,
you'll never know my friend, who'll have to see you through.

Vivian L. Loydd

Friend

In your eyes,
I saw a smile,
I stopped to sit,
and talk awhile.
As you spoke, your words would glow,
and I felt our friendship grow.
Her words are keen,
her heart is pure, and that's one thing
I know for sure.
Her name is Patty,
I know her well,
and she's the one,
I want to tell,
I can't wait, till she gets back
cause she's one friend,
I can't live without.
She is my friend, best of them all.
There is no room for reason or doubt.
We're in it for love,
and that is what our friendship is all about...

Tamra Taylor

Fallen Identity

So unsure now, lost in the blinking of an eye.
Yesterday what seemed so real, today becomes a lie.
How could this happen, why happen to me?
Could this be the destiny that was meant to be.

Always taken for granted, because he seemed so strong.
"Daddy, I love you," are the words that I long.
Life was so easy then, he was always there.
Suddenly taken away now, I realize how much I cared.

Lost in a broken memory, left to carry on.
I'm seeing everything differently now that he's gone.
I've got to take a stand, be the best I can be.
Put my feelings on hold, until I can solve the mystery.

He taught me independence, we butted heads I was so strong.
It was such a struggle then, but he was teaching me to go on.
Because he never knew what the future would hold.
He raised up his daughter in the way she should go.

So Daddy rest easy, are the words that I pray.
Your daughter loves you very much, and she's doing okay.

Barbara McCabe

Autumn and Flame

"Free! Free! The Dragon hisses in the dry grass,
and, slithering from the match-box, he roars in ecstasy,
spitting his flaming teeth to the Dervish-wind, who,
howling in a dance of destruction, flashes his swords
and scatters the locust-sparks, crackling and stinging.

Rabbits, their soft noses burned by the acrid smoke,
huddle in the brilliant dark and tremble
to see the "Hounds of Hell" licking their fiery chops
over the crests of the hills,
the hear the eagle, screaming wildly, pitching headlong
in a power dive of death.
Sounds of earth-anguish rend the night, cracking and
muffled thuds as though
mother-earth were creaking on her axis, while father-sun's
atomic fire reaches out to encompass the planet-children.
His smoke-reddened eye rises on a walpurgis after scene:
A thousand wispy, yawning pits in the murky hell of dawn,
and shriveled stumps of trees, lifting smoke-blackened arms
to heaven to receive the drifting "snow" of ashes - a bitter "manna!"
The butterfly has fluttered silently to the ground, while the Dragon,
gorged on the forest's lifeblood, sleeps.

Marguerite E. Errett

Death At 33

It's only a cold he says
But I can see his body wasting away
Don't tell me it's his time to go
Why should it be at 33

He doesn't really want to go
But you don't give him any choice
He'll try to fight the whole way through
But in the end it will be you

I know you say "He shall repent"
But it's not you who's hours are spent
In misery and agony
Oh - but we must worship Thee

Forgive me though
I must be blind
For the Lord is good and kind
I know say those who preach to me
But cruelty here is all I see
This is death
Death at 33

E. H. Jett

Tears

Momma says, "only babies cry"
but that's not so, I saw her cry,
asked her "how come" too.
She turned, smiled, and
whispered out these words:

Only a fool never cries
and all life and emotion inside him dies.
For tears express human feelings;
love, happiness, and all rotten dealings.

So when you feel like you must pout
just let those sparkling tears pour out
and when you're hurt, sad, or depressed,
don't be afraid to let tears go...
and emotions expressed.

Grace Manwell-Bolton

A Queen Above Kings

With her soul, she can dance,
with her heart, she can sing.
In our mind she's created
a Queen above kings.

Our eyes understand when
she gives from her hand,
yet her lips can't succeed
if confused by her needs,
nor will her legs keep a beat,
if unsure where to meet.

Yet would I be wrong to say
if you're silent in song,
that would make dance
from the start, with both
your soul and your heart —
the key to which opens all
gifts you can give, that spreads
like the wings to make you Queen above Kings?

Denise M. O'Brien

The Snow

Words can't explain the splendor and glow
That I feel inside when I watch it snow
So graceful and silent, so pure therein
It looks just like heaven, unspotted from sin

Each flake is so tender, so pure and light
I think of the robe of my savior so white
One flake at a time falls from above
I think of the wings of a heavenly dove

Although it takes millions to cover the earth
Each one is so blessed just like a new birth
Its enchanting beauty makes the earth so bright
It's found in the snow because God is the light

It's small and so fragile it glitters so bright
It lights up the world on its darkest night
Some people deny God and make fun of him
But he made the snow, he also made them

This world has its beauty and sights to behold
But the beauty of heaven can never be told
All world theology belongs to man
But snowflakes are guided by the unseen hand

Oneta Osborne

Goodbye

The giant hands were open,
waiting for him to appear.
Waiting to welcome him into the land,
of no hatred, no lies, and no fear.

The man appeared with a look upon his face,
a look of confusion and doubt.
Then he saw the beautiful hands,
waiting, reaching out.

All around were angels singing,
light was everywhere.
There was no darkness in this land,
love and joy was in the air.

The man reached out to the hands,
who gently guided him above.
The man no longer was filled with fear,
instead, was filled with love.

The man looked back on his final step,
one tear dropped from his eye.
He whispered, "we'll be together again,"
then disappeared into the sky.

Caitlin Szewczak

Re-Sounding Grace

In a night when God was gone and your face was closed with sleep,
I listened for a prayer.
Dulled as by fog on the sea no sound of safe harbor came to me that
   night.
But somehow I heard the rise of the morning star fluting into the
   brilliant sky.
And I, like the comet's tail, if I should live, if I should die,
Will streak across the sky, a flaming comet's tail.
Watch me flaming 'cross the sky.
Listen, oh listen, fluting into the sky.
Kyrie, kyrie, early death has come to me:
I flame, I sing, I pray.
   Lenore Flory

Mourning for the Joy

In mourning for the joy that slipped away
Like quicksand which devours without a trace.
Where has all the laughter gone?
The gentle caring touch,
A fleeting wink, that knowing grin,
Our love that meant so much.

In mourning for the joy that disappeared
As dusk turns into black of night.
Why are smiles replaced by tears?
Young lovers now gray-haired strangers
In mourning for the joy that slipped away.
   Barbara Gold

The Mighty Ocean Roar

The ocean waves billow high,
   Unearthing from the darkness below.
To make a first greeting to the sun,
   With its brilliant orange glow.
The fingers of freedom,
   Will be drawn into the atmosphere of light
To merge with the heavens,
   With the roar of its might.

The splendor of the light touches the water,
   And changes its hue.
It transforms to a phosphorescent glow
   Of a beautiful greenish blue.
The awakening waves begin to dance.
   And end by gracing our shore.
Everything seem small and unequal,
   When we hear the mighty ocean roar.
   Louise E. Marsh

I Don't Write Poetry About . . . .

I don't write poetry about romance
But about the one who loves us the most
I do not write poetry about death
But about the one who conquered it
I do not write poetry about happiness
But about the one who brings it to us
I do not write poetry about living
But about the one who gives us life
I do not write poetry about animals
But about the one who made them
I do not write poetry about very many things
But I do write about one
The one true God
   John E. Wright

Quebec: Where the River Narrows

Where the river narrows is where the water flows
   and where the water flows
      stays my eye for your smile

By wide and glassy rivers
   underneath where currents do jumble
Do feel I a rapting heart
   in which love's torrents do hap'ly toss

Take my hand; follow the tour guide;
   On grey, fortified walls shall we
Render a power of personal history.
   History ours: Secret, small, supinely sweet;
Able to sing across Abrahamic plains
   A beauteous bleat, like a kid's recall
And with sundry other personal songs
   Shall drown the rage-flecked screams
Of Wolfe and Montcalm, warrior's all
   And lay rest the reluctant duty
   Of an unceased feud.
   Edwin Chang

Innocence

I wish I was a child again with little child like dreams,
Holding on to hopes and thoughts and building onto schemes.

Making wishes son the stars, knowing they'll come true;
Living in a nice, warm home where everyone loves you.

Surrounded just by make believe and tales with happy endings;
The joy of being young knows only new beginnings.

Life goes on forever, and mistakes are all okay;
Pain is when you hurt yourself and mother kisses it away.

Sorrow passes quickly and healing comes quite fast;
Problems are all small ones and rarely ever last.

The only thoughts of great depression are expressed in one word, No!
Decisions are made by someone else, and the world is oh so slow.

Tomorrow means excitement; we fill another cup,
While innocence is left behind to cope with growing up.
   J. Kay Miller

Just That Way

Just that way is how to explain,
the poor man lost in his rain.

Mother died when he was born,
and fathers heart forever torn.

The man's only friend was his shadow,
for it new left, but is so shallow.

The man said to me he had a horrible
life, lonely, no kids no wife.

As he walked down the street he would cry,
he said to me he wanted to stop living, to die.

He walked away with his head in his
shoulders, crushing him like gracious boulders.

I said to him without a sigh, with a tear
in my eye, you must live before you die.
   Gia Coleman

I Am So Glad You Came Into My Life

When your big brown eyes meet mine,
the compassion I see there
makes my heart melt.
I am so glad — you came — into my life.

Everyday I come home tired and frazzled,
you are always there and happy to see me,
I am so glad — you came — into my life.

Each time I run my hand down your spine,
the worries of the day disappear,
and nothing, but you, seems to matter.
I am so glad — you came — into my life.

At night when I am alone and feel afraid,
you are quick to be on guard to protect me.
I am so glad — you came — into my life.

Your wet kisses and ear nibbles,
shout "I love you!"
I am so glad — you came — into my life.

Happy birthday, my friend Baron
may your dog days be many,
I am so glad — you came — into my life.

Linda Slabon

On the Outside Looking In

I went back to school singing a happy song,
Not knowing it wouldn't be happy for long,

Just once I wish people would like me,
For who I am, instead of who I could be,

People make fun of me and call me names,
I am the victim of their cruel games,

At night in bed I sit and pray,
Pray that people will like me for me one day,

I'm not a bad person, don't you see?
I'm being the best I know how to be,

I pray people won't judge by what they see, but what they find within,
Because only then can love and peace in the world win,

If people could accept me for who I am,
I'd never have to worry again,

But because of the way the world has been,
I'm on the outside looking in...

Kirsten L. Muller

To Be Or Not To Be

"There is a destiny that makes us brothers...none goes his way alone. What we send into the lives of others comes back into our own."
How I wish those words were mine for I agree whole heartedly, but I cannot claim their ownership until my own match perfectly... the candid true reflections of my soul.
If I own my thoughts and feelings, they are mine and fiercely kept within the framework of my space and the freedom of my mind, to meditate and flourish...sometimes boldly, often shy.
Its easy to be selfish, with holding out of fear...looking neither left or right...afraid to see a tear that glimmers, fleeting, passing by, risking nothing...playing safe, chancing nothing dear.
I stopped to talk one day and "gossip" made me pay a price... confused? Ashamed? What was the point? But better still I didn't care...I thought a thought and passed it on and won myself a prize!
People who need people haven't got forever more, as blinders serve the ignorant, the petty and the small breeding "gossip's" toxic poison over all.
I cannot go my way alone...I must be myself and true...no matter where it leads me, I'll trust my inner sense and say "hello" to you!

Bonnie E. Lorenc

Your Eyes

Before I leave I have things to say —
How your eyes sparkle like the sun
On the sea on a fine summer day
How they glint so lightly flattering
Me so, caressing playfully tenderly so.
I've watched them turn
Black and glower with fear,
Of falling in love, I suppose.
But this has all passed and the eyes
That remain are strong, firm and passionate
And playful again.

Maurice Hart

Make Me Your Warrior, Lord

Make me your warrior, Lord
Let me not shrink from the battle
Let not the railings of the enemy strike fear in my heart.

Lord keep me strong in the face of danger
Though the sound and smoke of battle make my flesh tremble,
Let me not be afraid.

Lord, in my own strength I can do no good thing.
My weakness overwhelms
My body wastes away with the passing of time.

Speak now and I shall go forward into the tumult,
I will not fear for the Lord's command is yet upon my ears.
I will raise my sword in confidence for the word of the Lord
empowers it.

No evil shall cause me to fall
For the Lord is the strength of my right hand.
No fear shall steal my victory - for the Lord has proclaimed it.

What has the Lord commanded that has not come to pass?
His word is sure - his counsels are righteous
And he is mighty to all generations.

Cynthia "Thea" Spitz

Within Yourself

Listen to your soul.
No one else but your experience can be your guide.
Calm the uneasy tensions and release from within.
Do what is unintended - like a lightning bolt.
Out of nowhere.
No conformity, no rules.
It just is.
And that is how it should be.
Unexplained, unplanned.
Just standing strong.

Melissa Mudry

Pointing Out Doomed Dome D.C

A huge doomed building once stood there;
chambers filled with voices of those
who made the final choices.
Now, only spinning atoms occupy the pit.
A fragment of a nearby monument points to it.
We build these monuments to our past.
Come see our accomplishments they beg!
Yet, none exceeds that of a cackling hen
that also layed an egg.

Ashley F. Davis

Having Arrived At This Thursday

Having arrived at this Thursday of my life
I know I have found some mystery
Which is forever unfolding and folding in upon itself
Like some children's game
Like some economy whose rate of growth is
Always greater and less than the official number
Some mystery which casts a shadow
On the color yellow which turns to gold

Having arrived at this Thursday I know
I have spent my life according to this mystery
Always unfolding and folding in upon myself
Like a child
Always economizing at a rate
Both greater and less than the official figure
Always casting a shadow
On the color yellow
Which turns to gold

Phillip A. Kudla

Untitled

Well you're dressed for success
in your fancy new look,
your fancy new look.
Yes, you walked right past me
in your fancy new look
like you've got someplace to go,
someplace to go.
And your belly is full
while I got nothing to eat,
and the hunger I feel, I feel it so deep,
and wonder, man, if the quarter will keep,
if the quarter will keep.
Hell, it's something to feel
something so real, something so real.
But not you, mister dressed for success,
no not you.
'Cause you got plenty to eat,
yes plenty to eat,
but nothing to feel, nothing to feel.
And I got you beat, yea, I got you beat.

John A. Loftus

Down the Street

Walking alone down the street.
I wonder "What if I chance to meet you?"
Walking alone down the street.

Walking alone down the street.
I'm not alone anymore.
You're with me.
So now we're
Walking together down the street.

Walking together down the street.
Suddenly, I see
a bright shiny penny roll
by at my feet.
I picked up that penny
You glared and said
"You should have let me get it."
So now I'm
Walking alone down the street.

Melissa Long

Mortal Man's Undying Love

Within the heart of mortal man
We find love—endlessly profound.
Without it, we are nothing,
To whom we're tenderly bound.
Within our hearts, true love inset,
Expressed with tender mercies,
Which we'll never forget.
For eternity's path,
No one escapes love's wrath,
But one must keep searching.
True love is neither bought nor sold,
Yet mortal man reaches out,
For something to touch, for something to hold.
Only if mortal man could comprehend,
Fathomless billows of undying love, await . . .

Phillip N. Schmierer

To Yitzhak Rabin

I feel so sad because you are gone
You were your country's one favorite son
You fought for peace and I always knew
That you will achieve whatever you do.

You were God's messenger who came to the earth
You were on a mission to give peace a birth
You wanted two nations to join as one
And you wouldn't rest until you were done.

There were many people who hated you
But you wouldn't stop, you knew what to do
You stood loud and clear for justice and peace
And now that you're gone, you'll be greatly missed.

Alla Yampolskaya

Winter's Coming

When the wind blows soft
On a little hot rock

It starts to get cold
When you hold . . . it up high

When the leaves go by
It's like you're in the sky
Floating by the trees

Then the squirrels come out
Looking about

For nuts to eat
Like us looking for meat

And you are in a nice cozy house
And a mouse . . . is looking . . . for cheese

Adela Noël Pérez

Looking for the Sun

We aren't talkin' about today, we're not talking about
tomorrow, maybe we're just talking about the sorrow. It
isn't clean and it's definitely not pretty. Maybe it's
just living in this city. What could be wrong? Is anything
right? Is it revenge, or is it out of spite? Running doesn't
help, hiding don't fly. Where are the answers, the reasons
why? You travel on yesterday 'cause the future's not clear.
Maybe it's time just to have another beer. Your flash seems
to be gone, and your hair is turning gray. It doesn't seem
fair, but what can I say, I guess it's time to drive another
road. Can you read the signs, will you be able to see? Will you
be able to handle the heavy load? You've lived with the pain
for so many years. Some days are good but too few and far between.
Just check what you have inside, don't waste your time counting
the tears.

Binny Binns

239

Vivian Gunnells

Have you heard about God's mercy and great love?
How he died and gave his life, he came from heaven above.

How he hears our prayers for loved ones lost and undone,
This is why he sent to us his only begotten Son.

So with that in view, I would like to share with you,
About Vivian Gunnell whom each one of you knew.

You see God heard the cry of these prayers that were prayed
In these last weeks of her life gave her peace that stayed.

Her mind was so calm and for prayers she would ask,
And the next time you would visit, in this peace you also would bask.

So even though it was in the latter part of the day the Lord speaks
  about.
She has gained entrance into heaven with a praise and shout.

So this day we want to make her an honorary remember of this
  Revival Tabernacle.
For she loved it so, and thank God to earth now, she is not shackled.

So my dear Vivian we look to meet you up there with Jesus too.
To live eternity with Jesus and all of heaven's angels and crew.

We do give God the glory for his mercy and love he extended.
And thank God this story we tell will never be ended.

Ruby's Precious Gems Given by Him
Ruby A. Gittens

My Spot

Once I had a dog named Spot,
who ate from an old cook pot.

He liked to chase a big green frog,
who lived under a hollow log.

One day Spot found some cherry jelly,
now it's all over his hairy belly.

Spot didn't like to eat French toast,
he preferred our neighbor's pork roast.

In the summer when he wanted to cool,
he just jumped into our swimming pool.

Spot really liked to chase baseballs,
he chased them under waterfalls.

He came out looking like a drowned rat,
and a neighbor chased him with a bat.

One day poor Spot ran out of luck,
and got hit by a pickup truck!

Bye bye doggie!
Patrick J. Grogan

Moon

As I gaze across the moon lite land,
I see a Beauty no day can withstand.
There is a mystery to the night,
When the full moon shines its light.
During the day the sun shines up high,
But at night the moon rules the sky.
Though the colors fade and shadows grow,
There is a serenity the moon can sow.
Relaxing the mind and calming the soul,
Something the day can never know.
And as I look at this moon lite land,
I see a day there will be peace at hand.

R. J. Murray

Forbidden Love

The thoughts running through my mind,
Often makes me wonder why, the pain that I feel inside,
Makes me go right back in time,
When my heart was so entwined,
With a love I thought was mine.

When I look into your eyes,
I often begin to cry and wonder why,
The love that I thought was mine,
Was just another lie.

When all of my dreams didn't come true,
I dreamed of holding and kissing you,
Oh if you only knew,
How much I want to love you,
I'm sure we could see it through,
Because without you,
I could never make it through.

As I look up into the beautiful blue sky,
I pretend I'm looking into your eyes,
Still wondering why,
Such a beautiful and infinite love could never be mine.

Leneile McLean

Rose of Sharon

Sweet rose a light, my soul delight
  still captured by that rose so bright.
All will hear and know the story,
  of this lovely rose's glory

Settled down upon the ground, oh
  that precious seed, the shone
Of light beyond the night, on
  beauty she does feed.

Rushing streams of water lifts,
  come down the everlasting cliffs.
The rose as soon it will appear,
  tell me that my sweet is near.

For I will joy with happiness,
  smile upon my face.
My deep and precious lovely
  rose, for always will embrace.

The people of this world shall see,
  all nations, they will know.
My deep and still abiding love,
  for truly it is so.

Scott W. Greenlaw

Pains of Passion

Pains of passion are what we feel,
when love grows cold a deathly reel.
When passion ends the pain begins,
in my heart emptiness rings.
A pain that fills my distraughting chest,
I guess it happens to the best.
When love returns to take its place,
my forgotten heart begins to race.
When passion emanates the room,
we're sure to be bride and groom.
then again it all begins.
As passion grasps the night again.
passion weaves its deathly loom,
as pain begins to fill the room.
Love it seems don't have a chance,
as passion begins its grasply trance.
The following days are filled with doom,
as passion strolls right out the room.
And once again the pain begins,
as passion never reigns again.

Shane Lee Thornton

240

God Sent A Friend

My life was full of hate and sin and sorrow
The light ahead was hard for me to see
God filled my life with one he dearly trusted
It changed my life this friend he guided me

This friend was there with love and inspiration
For all his friends and his family
He never said I don't have time to listen
His light will shine through out eternity

God called him home one glorious sunday morning
I cried God why did you take him from me
God said my son I need him here in heaven
You'll meet again just put your trust in me

God sent a friend to help me thru life's trials
He said just put some of your trust in me
Have faith in God we'll meet him up in Glory
Thank God thank God he sent this friend to me.

Robert H. Powers Sr.

Lucette My Love . . . .

She so desperately fought this invisible dragon
A legion of sorcerers could not destroy,
She was such a gentle woman,
Always she was my pride and joy.

Farewell my love, my pretty wife,
You must let go now of my hand,
My sorrow is raw pain, alive,
Almost alone, I must now roam the land.

Our life was a mirage, no less
Alas the wonder is no more.
The forces I cursed of darkness
Now, I curse them ever more.

Robert Coppenrath

Dedicated to Dad

Even though we drifted apart over the years,
memories of you will always bring me to tears.

Even though we had so little time to share,
in my heart I will always really care.

Even though I thought you weren't always fair,
it was good just knowing that you were there.

Even though I was always the "other one,"
I still am proud to be your younger son.

Even though the new year brought your end,
there still was time for a last card to send.

Even though your life did suddenly cease,
with that card we made our final peace.

Even though we weren't always very close,
it seems after you're gone I miss you most.

Richard Allan Bachman

Snow

Snow is falling from on high
As it gently fills the sky,
falling, falling softly landing on the earth.
That's how snow is giving birth, on the earth.
Snow is as white as rows and halls of cotton balls.
Has a unique design like a rug,
Some look like they could use a hug.

And Now I Pray For A Snow Day!!!!

Amara O'Donnell

Autumn

The hills blaze in colors as they put on their coats
While captains cover and tie up their boats
Like a palette of rainbows they dance and they bend
Covering the Earth from corner to end.

Sunshine filters down, somewhat cool in the sky
Geese heading south fill the air with their cry
Kites flying high, as a child holds its string
Cottages shuttered and locked up till spring.

Soft autumn breezes pick the leaves to the air
As a wine maker selecting his harvest with care
Leaves in brown paper the earth then enwrap
As squirrels gather nuts for their long winters nap

Barriers are put up like shackles in the parks
Protecting the hikers from harm in the dark
Shoes crackle gently as they take their last walk
Emitting vapors from their mouths as they talk.

Soon the hillsides will be blanketed with snow
Winter will come with its whips like some foe
Till then let us put that aside and play ball
In this wonderful time of the year we name fall.

Gary Vrabel

Snow

Memories flood over me of a year ago
You, "little Linda" and I were shoveling snow.
It was so cold, I think it must have been 30 degrees below.
I see you in the crisp morning air,
Looking so pretty and the breeze blowing your hair.
You stood on the porch and I took your picture there.
I recall many happy days and years with you.
I try to be happy and not too blue.
From the cradle to the grave,
I have so many memories, I try so hard, Linda Lou, to be brave!

Dorothy Stuart

A Childhood Passed

Last night in the midst of a lonely dark cloud, a light of
hope appeared.

It filled me with a sense of expectation, and a thrill of
excitement coursed through my veins.

Yesterday seems an eternity ago, and tomorrow feels a
breath away.

Suddenly the future I avoided has confronted me, and all of
my inhibitions have been surpassed.

Is this what it feels like to stand up and face life, if so,
what have I been afraid of?

Is it the fear of pain that accompanies reality, or the
bittersweet nostalgia of a childhood passed.

Maria E. Alvarado

Sorrowful Lips

We wander endlessly,
Through the petals,
That have fallen from our lashes,
The mistress that flies above,
Softly unfolds her wings,
White silk scarfs hold our wrists,
As we lay in the dancing orchids,
We miss the comfort in the sorrow we feel,
While crucified liars regain their trust,
From the sadness,
that comes from within.

Melissa Gibbons

The Running Boy

Sleeves thrown up
with taut legs running
charred of sun and laid wide open;
flesh and mind pollinate soul

Laughter squeezed
through gritted teeth and purs-ed lips
anxious cameo
    fractured youth

Arms fluid pump
adrenalized sprint of rag doll manic
body quirks now, leaps, and leaps yet again!
    like taffy at a pulling stretched by sun

Gymnastic rotation limb over limb
the blur of silhouette flying

Open field run
laid heavy with matted footwork
    of ritual summer conquest
fleshen toes spiked through
burned in clover fresh strained with skin and pollen
to sleeping nose ripe in cold bed of night

Tye Tyree

Angel in the Sky

I loved you right from the start
And when you were born you captured my heart.
The name you were given means cheerful one.
And with it you brought joy to everyone.
How could one small child do such a marvelous thing?
But of course, you were God's child and with Him the love to bring.
As time moved on I knew you could not stay.
My precious child, I cried the day God took you away.
But your job here on earth was done,
With the work of God and Jesus his son.
Your loving memories we will all have to share
And we know that you are in God's care.
In my heart, mind and life you will always be
For God chose you to be given to me.
My eyes do not always cry
For when I look up to the heavens I see my "Angel in the Sky."

Vicki A. Zak

Life's Shadow

Life cast a shadow, which are the memories of one's past
A performance of human works that shall forever last
Life cast a shadow, placing darkness in the brightness of time.
For only the light that life once shown is only left behind
Life cast a shadow, upon the living minds that bear.
For he who created his life's shadow is surely no longer there.

Donald L. Ellis

The Ocean

The Ocean, is a blanket surrounding the creatures it holds.
The Ocean's waves, are unpredictable
    like a tidal wave in a thunderstorm.
The Ocean, is always changing like a river
    flowing down a mountain, never staying the same.
The Ocean waters, glamorously sparkles like the sun
    and glistens like the stars.
The Ocean's powerful waves, can brutally capsize,
    but it is peaceful and calm as it slumbers.
The Ocean, is salty like a cracker,
    but makes sweet, soothing sounds.
The Ocean, waves gracefully in the whistling wind.
The Ocean, creates and unlocks many mysteries.

Kimberly Johnson

A Sun Dried Story

Set out in an old garden
behind boxwood hedges
and behind a splintering wicker table
is the lady who sells applewood animals.
She is frail, her detailed face is creased with character,
hair soft like carded wool and eyes drained of color.
In the horizon behind, the sun struggles an orange fire
and her shriveled hands can
barely knit a cardigan for burnt autumn afternoons.
She holds her secrets
behind a polyester sun dress
hanging to her ankles, and a straw hat
lies on her head to protect them.
Behind boxwood hedges
where she sells what she has made
are the pieces of her life,
never questioned,
not even by the sun.

Corine Rohr

Take Me Back To Yesteryear

I wish to go back to a time long ago;
to a time of horses, chariots and faces all aglow,
Knights and their ladies; Laird's and their clan;
when a woman was a woman, and a man was a man.

Kings and their courts; Queens and their castles;
corsets and ball gowns; made of velvet and tassels,
A Duke and his Duchess; a Baron and his Baroness;
full of pride and glory; full of grace and finesse.

A time of courtship and romance; honor and pride;
A time of cottages and castles; in which to reside,
A time that a meal was a feast, and everyone ate together;
A time of rolling green hills; all covered in heather.

A time when rules were made and not to be broken;
A time when war often mean that ill words had been spoken,
A time of elegance, gallantry and beauty beyond compare;
A time when gentlemen would ride for days; to see their ladies fair.

It's hard for me to live in a time like today;
In a world that has forgotten romance and been led so far astray,
For in my mind I dream of this time; that I hold so dear;
I beg of you; please, take me back to yesteryear.

Jamie Heddings

A Place of Being

Take this moment and remember it.
The boat,
The moon,
The lake at midnight.
Imprint it on your mind
So when winter comes and you are away from me,
you'll remember the way sounds flew across the lake,
the simple pleasure of rowing the boat,
the way your arms felt in night water,
and how you felt when you looked at the moon.
This night,
This moment,
it won't change the world.
It won't make your name known to millions.
And yet it speaks of another day.
To others this moment is nothing.
But nothing is something
and in the middle of the lake,
sitting you and I,
nothing else matters.

Cristina-Grazia Parente

A Far Off Place

As the winds blow the sands of time away,
I hang motionless above the heavens,
Flowing with the peaceful currents of the mind,
I go anywhere it takes me.
Mind of matter, body and soul,
I show no fear for I float aimlessly through the river of time.
Streams of slivers and gold flash brightly in my soul,
Cyclones of cold chill my bones, as gales of warmth comforts me.
I am lost within myself, forever flowing with the currents of my
mind.

Joshua Gamon

Here No More

Another beautiful smile gone from the crowd.
Another voice missing from the laughter.
The big brown eyes not blinking anymore.
The small hands clapping no more.
Surrounded by flowers, and weeping eyes,
she lies still...sleeping. The pain gone. Her
little body resting.
Her first kiss out of reach. Her
16th birthday never seen. The
prom dance that will be danced
without her graceful little face.
Her life pulled from under her. Her
small steps will grace the earth for
years to come, but not in front of us
and why not? She is here no more.

Erin Reed

In a Hurry School Day Blues

My mother said to me one day
You have to go to school today

So wash your face and brush your hair
Make sure you have clean underwear

Eat your breakfast, make up your bed
Please make sure the dog gets fed

Pack your lunch no time to snooze
Clean the mud off of your shoes

Tie them up cut off the lights
Tuck in your shirt and pull up your tights

Get in the car and hurry please
Here's a tissue in case you sneeze

Well I brushed the dog and washed my hair
The dog now has my underwear

I packed my lunch no time to snooze
I think I packed my tennis shoes

I cut my shoestrings and tied up the lights
I pulled up my shirt and tucked in my tights

And now I'm dizzy and it's sad to say
But mom you forgot it's Saturday!

Wanda H. Moore

"She" Is Really You! — Mom

She's a bank, a doctor, a cook, and a friend.
She always stands by me till the very end.
She solves my problems as fast as they happen.
When it comes to her children, she's never caught nappin'.
I love her so much, and need her even more.
I'd give my whole life to even the score.
She's always there to listen, no matter time of night.
I'm the dark part of everyday and she's my only light.
I hope she knows and somehow she can see.
That without her in my life, I would not be me.
I need her strong morals, and love to carry me through
I hope by now "she" sees that the "she" is really you!

John P. Long

Mother of Mine

You've been the greatest blessing in my life,
  Indeed it's clear to see.
Word's can not express, how even dear you are to me.

I owe you more than money could buy,
  For all you've been and become.
To repay you for your strength and love,
  Could not simply be done.

Your faith, hope, and love are the things I have to treasure,
And I truly appreciate the love you always give without measure.

My hearts full of pride for all that you have been,
I'm glad you're my Mother; and so much my friend!

Rae A. Wilkinson

Angle Born

A little one was born today,
The parents take it home to stay.
  The baby is healthy and everything is fine,
But other plans are on someone else mind.
  It has know sins and a very pure heart,
Which are a couple of reasons that is must part.
  You lay it down at might and kiss its little head,
And then you go put your own self to bed.
  It's time for it to leave, this you did not know,
But you actually had an angle and it's time for it to go.
  The doctors have know explanation nor will the find,
For the reason it left were by the plans at a higher kind.
  Think of this when you wonder why,
And smile when you look up to the sky.
  Don't get discouraged and be a good husband and wife,
And you'll see your little angle when you enter your next life.

Larry Coffman

The Burn Baby

The placid lake is not truly tranquil,
Raging fire is the essence of our sanity,
Black, white, rich and poor, we all came
From the ghetto.

Outside drugs and prostitutes,
Women giving up what should be sacred.
Men with black, brown, green, blue snake like eyes,
Take what they have not earned.

Inside lies strength, power and true womanhood.
The screams of unbearable pain below from Irene.
As the sun rises over the suburbs,
The white rose blooms among the weeds.

Erica H. Collins

Noreaster Night

It's a New England November night, and the wind is beating hard
on the Massachusetts coast.
I know not far from here, the waves are whipping madly,
their white caps dance unseen, in the dark and lonely night.
No one's there to watch. They're all huddled in their homes.
When a Noreaster blows like this one, it's not a night to roam.

The now leafless claw-like branches, of the trees outside my house
scratch and scrape the cedar shingles as I sit inside alone.
And the lower my dying fire burns the darker this room gets,
and the wind, the cold, the solitude send a shiver through my bones.

Blow, you cold Atlantic wind. Make my small house shudder.
Many storms have I endured, and I'll outlast another.

The howling of the wind increases, and my fire has burned to
embers.
The cold is all around me. God, I hate these harsh Novembers.
With a mighty Bang the shutter flies off into the night.
The door shakes on its hinges, and my heart beats loud with fright.

But, blow, you cold Atlantic wind.
I'll not move from here, my soul is strong and I'll hold on
Though my heart is filled with fear.

J. J. Soldevilla

Things Are Looking Up

The prophet tells of a woeful tale
    that sends our babes down a lonesome trail

Of squandered money on blind men's schemes
    and nurtured sucklings on bourgeoise dreams

It took some time to work it out
    to kill their innocence and cloak their doubt

The lemon is squeezed, the onion peeled
    the president's dead and the tomb is sealed

So now it's time for the national sport
    to grab a hot dog and watch center court

Like Roman patrons with our spirits high
    we watch our children
        fall
            from
                the
                sky
W. H. Post

Intertwined

An old woman has passed away.
A lot of people paid their respects that day.
When everyone had gone and the flowers had
died, a younger woman was left with an
empty feeling inside.
She tried to smile through her tears, but,
she could not let go of all the years.
The younger woman has a daughter and
sometimes she cries.
She has always had trouble with forever goodbyes.
She misses her grandmothers smiling face.
No one will ever take her place.
The daughter has asked the Lord into her heart.
Now hers does not seem to be falling apart.
She knows she will see her grandmother once more.
Exactly when she is not sure.
We both know she is in a beautiful place.
Next to you God, touching your face.

Laura Swanson

Under This Old Hat . . .

Under this old hat worn threw and threw,
    Stands a man six foot two,
    Hands of leather and eyes of blue,
Loves every man, woman and child,
    But all in all he's very, very mild,
Now I know this man can do it all,
    But yet I've seen him take his falls
This ain't no ordinary laddy,
You see this man's my Daddy.

Melissa Ulmer

My Darling Wife

You are my life my darling wife
One who measures all my strife
One who can sing and laugh and play.
One who can work the long hard day
One who's radiance is like a flowers
One whom I'll love every second and hour
God-put you here for me to love
Should I contest things from above
As the sun is set before the dawn
And the sands of life are slowly drawn
I will keep our way of life
Just for you my darling wife.

David W. Cosman

These Three Are Ours

It was April, January and October,
The years were two apart,
They were born to us out of innocence and love,
These three children, close to our hearts.

We never had doubts about wanting them,
Since their lives were of our choice,
And with right-to-life so filled with strife,
It brings us joy just to hear their voice.

As each of them was growing up,
The love and support was still there,
And even though they are older now,
These three are still ours to share.

Their world has become such a different place,
And with children of their own,
The problems and issues that they must face,
Are far more complex than we have known.

But though our years are now farther apart,
More precious are the days and the hours,
And with love and caring in all of our hearts,
These three children are still ours.

Robert W. Moretti

A Mother's Touch

With life's first breath and woman's sorrow,
the child becomes a man.
A revering breath, a bowing gaze,
eyeing memories of callowed innocence,
the man looks upon his youth.

Seeing beyond the shadow of mortal life,
toward the heaven's gathering,
a mother's tear passes through the veil,
enfolding the father and the son.
As the child becomes a man.

Tal Henderson

Love's Labours Lost, April 29

I had hope to surprise you for your birthday.
　Fate would have it otherwise.

I had hope to see this through.
Another milestone in our existence.
Who could have known life would be so cruel?
　It stole away my gift for you.

Loss is never easy to brave.
　Destiny always gets her way.
It took away a life just starting,
leaving only pain and agony in its wake.

If you have never suffered, and known first hand the ache,
how dare you tell me I should not grieve.
Leave me alone, let my sadness be.

I had hope to surprise you for your birthday.
　Alas, that will no longer be.
I will stand here mourning the loss
of the child I will never see.

M. Teresa Colon

The Secret

I promised Mama I wouldn't tell,
But I do declare, I couldn't keep my promise.
Sitting on this gentle slope, our favorite spot,
How could I not tell her, my boon companion, my compeer.
We called our place Dandelion Hill,
And gathered tight little bouquets of golden blossoms,
And blew their soft fuzz into the air to make a wish.
We sat under the shade of a big friendly oak, and ate peanut butter
sandwich and drank lemonade, watered down to make it last longer.
We smoothed each other's braided hair,
And traded colored ribbons for the fun of it.
Once we pricked our fingers to mingle our blood and become
　real sisters. We walked in each other's shoes once or twice
So we could feel each other's life.
But I couldn't really feel her pain or know her hard times.
Mama said times were hard all over,
And worried abut safety in the South for me and my friend.
But how could I not tell her, my dearest dear — I blurted it out.
I won't be coming here again, I said through stinging tears.
Mama says I can't play with a black girl anymore.

Ellen Fratia Buffo

The Indian

They roamed these lands with such great pride,
only to watch their customs and people die.

With the white man's arrival and its fast pace,
their culture near gone, but not quite their race.

They prayed to their gods, the moon and the sun
or the way the eagle flew, or how the deer run.

Jesus himself wouldn't have changed their ways,
for they lived here happy and free long before his days.

Adapting to this land, these people they thrived,
until the white man came and altered their lives.

Because they were different, they called them savage,
though what are we now in this day and age?

Our people killing each other right out in the streets,
the Indian killed for his clothes and for his meat.

Thinking of these people, it's really quite sad,
just think of the future they might have had.

Now we'll never know and it's really a shame,
Indians - the forgotten people - and the white man's to blame.

A. C. Maerkle

The Rebirth of Inner Sight

　The rebirth awaits for those that choose
to walk blinded upon this earth, disillusioned
by societies regressional minds, only seeing
crime brings on a stressful state of minds,
train of thoughts become lost like souls,
before these time to even grow old, grievance
becomes induced within the mind, for yet
another all to familiar time, were innocence
is lost at the most expensive cost, to take
flight on a journey parallel to your true
sight, were innervisions become divine, and
we find that we are free, only to realize
that we have fallen by the wayside, trapped
in the epitome of what we have created to be,
society expresses truth drowned in sin, so does
the begin start with the end, to win this
game you have to survive, but not all can win
the game to stay alive.

Matthew Enterline

The Power of Music

Music is healing, it cleanses the soul.
The power of music can move waters,
heal people and make them whole.

Music touches hearts,
Makes peace within all people,
and lets everyone take part.

The power of music has changed ways,
moved mountains, and brought forth
happiness within our days.

It touches the old, it touches the new,
It cannot be bought,
And cannot be sold.

The power of music really comes from within,
It is within us all,
And can move like a soft, gentle wind.

Shalara Dawn Farmer

A Utopian Land

A utopian land they say,
　as it used to be.
Far away over the meadows
　an enchanted world lies.
The grasses, the flowers,
　it bewilders all minds.
And there you will find utopia
　where peace is surrounding and never dies.
Where people don't cheat or steal or lie.
Over the meadows into your mind,
　then you will say, can this ever exist?
You hope, you dream, you feel,
　but then your thoughts are shattered.
You hear the world around you,
　you wonder does anyone understand, who?

Pamela Rose Morris

Untitled

Be ye not a slave to satan nor mankind
Be ye to the Lord Jesus Christ

Follow not the moon, for it is cold and lifeless
Follow the son, from which all warmth and life cometh

Flee from darkness, it is satan's hiding place
Cross over into the light, it is our Lord Jesus Christ

Mary Higbee

When Will I Play In Your Garden Again

When will I play in Your garden again
Romping on the lush grass green as emerald
Chasing little bunnies, balls of white cloud
Eyes feasting on the beautiful flowers
In warm sunshine or drizzling rain
When will I play in Your garden again

Swinging by the rainbow, colorful and bright
Playing hide and seek with stars at night
Heart full of joy, blissful and light
No more sorrow, misery or pain
When will I play in Your garden again

Sheela Vinod

Goodbye

You never understand why I would
    just break down and cry
I never really told you why
    that tear was in my eye
I never could forget that all
    the suffering was real
You couldn't understand the
    hurt and the pain that I feel
You see, you've always been
    gone and in that I can't see
Why you had to leave our house
    and couldn't be with me
I told you that I missed you
    and that I want you to stay home
You just didn't see why I felt so alone
But you see you need love to have a family
Those thing I lack of and mean the most to me
I don't have any of these thing which is why I cry
So depressed and lonely that I just want to die
And that's why I tell you mom Goodbye, Goodbye.

Jamie Johnson

Awareness

Born as a product of the egg and the sperm
In the receptacle of a womb of unknown nature
Without any bias, cast, class, color, race or status
Arming with total dependency and innocence!

Different degrees and types of awareness unfold
For the entity to develop and nurture
Dictated by environs, heredity and training
Within the confines of the senses, time and space

Many a thought surge into consciousness
Only to flicker, fade and waste its energy
A thought lingers, "Where is this awareness?"
Is it in the brain or in every cell of the body?

The train of thought continues to question?
How and where do we get this projection of awareness?
Feeds on itself by popping the question, "Who am I?"
Many a reply for the saint's, savants, me and you!

Hold on! Is there a transcending ever present infinity
Of awareness in known and unknown dimensions?
No wonder, the speck of dirt called human in finity
May at best manage a few glimpses of this elusiveness!!!

Srinivasa Govindarajan

Untitled

A vision of the past, his tender embrace,
He smiles in her direction, her heart starts to race.
Feeling the emptiness after leaving his side,
Denying any feelings, her heart had only lied.
Knowing she was wrong, words as cold as ice,
Pushing him away, hurting him more than twice.
Having time of solitude, her feelings to the surface rise,
Wanting to speak to him, to express her feelings she tries.
Wondering if he understands her, not sure of how he feels,
A feeling that he doesn't believe that what she says is real.
She tries to read his mind while he tries to read her heart,
What lies within her has no words, so where is she to start?
She's trying so hard to reach out to him, but all seems like a
    hopeless case,
If he'd only let her know what he wants, she'd be able to find a
    place.
Her place in his life, if that still exists,
For her feelings for him are too strong, it'd be wrong to resist.

Sandy Sunnongmuang

I Dreamed A Little Dream

I dreamed a little dream
    last night
of lands far away,
of places where I've never been
and places where I'd love to stay.

I dreamed a little dream
    last night
of flowers all in bloom,
of dandelions and roses
and a great big silvery moon.

I dreamed a little dream
    last night
of you and I in love,
of sweet perfume and candlelight
and the twinkling stars above.

I dreamed a little dream
    last night
of all these things and more,
of your sparkling eyes and smiling face
and the love that is ours — for evermore.

Cindy H. O'Shea

Never Forget

Remember, that I loved you first just because,
Remember that what we had was completely true love.
It lasted only but for a bitter-sweet time,
And then we separated,
Never once again will you be mine.
When she comes along and sweeps
You off your feet,
Remember that I first loved you,
With my every heart's beat.
She'll smile and say she'll love you forever,
But remember my darling, when we were together.
I loved you from the moments first look,
It was my heart you took.
Right now she says she's looking for love
And I know she'll find it's in you, but remember,
No one will ever love you, like I used to.

Courtnie Y. Williams

A Dream Called If

If but tomorrow was only yesterday,
With the house full of laughter and children at play.

The clear blue sky with the sun so bright,
And the beautiful moon with the heavenly lights.

No television to broadcast so much bad news,
Of crime and wars and child abuse.

No women smoking, just only a few men,
With lungs so congested they wished they'd never began.

Nothing to throw away to just lay around,
Everything would burn leaving no garbage on the ground.

We would still be drinking from our glass or tin,
That old styrofoam cup would be merely a sin.

Our atmosphere would be so clean and pure,
We could breathe so much better and be more secure.

No gasoline odors to shorten our breath,
No pollution to cause disease or death.

And stay away from sweets and fats,
And avoid heart attacks and things like that.

Malta Sue Porter

Untitled

Alcoholism is like a Great White Shark,
It makes its way through the waters which we know as
Human Life, never sleeping - with a never ending hunger.
It doesn't care where or when it will strike next;
It's always lurking, seeking its next victim. At first
You don't realize it's there; but it is, stalking its prey
With a vengeance, deciding when it will attack - leaving
The victim unaware of where it is, or why it's there. It may decide
To go straight for the kill, or take its time, a nudge here,
A bump there, or it may not strike at all, leaving its prey
In unsuspecting Limbo. But . . . when or if it does attack, it has no
Sense of mercy . . . ripping, shredding and engulfing its victim in
Its powerful jaws, destroying the life it has in its grasp without
A second thought. It leaves behind the pieces of what was once
Something precious, never knowing or caring about what it
Has savagely torn apart . . . thinking only of its next victim, it swims
On . . . never sleeping, with a never ending hunger.

Dane C. Magoon

Life Is Like The Ocean

Some like to sit and watch it, from a distance,
   safe and untouched, enjoying the beauty,
   fearing the strength, doubting the possibilities.

Some venture out, some let the feeling of it touch them,
   allowing their senses to feel,
   imagine, even dream.

Some venture still further, dancing with it,
   laughing in it, being in it.

   Sometimes it shocks.
   Sometimes it slaps.
   Sometimes it overwhelms.

If one looks too far ahead the fear of its strangles,
   if one looks ahead just a bit the excitement grows.

It is there, what one decides to do with it
   is soully one's choice.

Darcie Christine Sarnoski

Words

Never, never throw a Dart,
If hurts so much the tender heart!
The words we say today may bring
Such hurt that brimming tears will sting.
We cannot take them back you know
As time goes by, they grow and grow.
And so when life has come and gone
They stand in line to sing their song
Of needles pain to loved ones gone
And even God cannot erase the hurt of them,
Nor time efface!

Lillian Beiser

After the Season

The Christmas tree stands on the porch, the lights are packed away.
There's an ordinary potted plant, where baby Jesus lay.

The songs of Hallelujah, so loved by one and all.
Stand silent in their special place, a closet in the hall.

The cheerful seasons greeting, of which we never tire.
Are put into the wood scuttle, as kindling for the fire.

It seems to me that now's the time, to spread goodwill and cheer.
When folks that buy with credit cards, are in hock up to . . . here.

Yes, now is the time to spread goodwill, with vigorous aggression.
Between the Bethlehem Babe and the Easter Egg.
Lies a blanket of depression.

Artress Cornmesser

The Rock, the River, the Tree, and Me

First came the rock; then the waters formed
   to make a river flow.
After some time — voila — there was a tree!
All these events made it possible for
   there to be me!

If I don't take care of the rock, the river,
   and the tree;
Alas and alack — who will take care
   of me?

Charles N. Tripp

Contorted Filmore

High it stands, narrowly spreading,
Ankle length leaf-mane kissing the earth.
Up it grew, yet down hang its branches,
Screwed and twisted as if wrenched by a pain in its roots,
So great that the wood-arms fall useless at its sides,
No longer able to support such heavy sadness.
Masked giant, what secret do you hide?
Exotic you tower, impenetrable robe of flowing green,
Amidst the trunked chunkiness of your brethren.
Yet the wind picks up their twigged branches,
Caresses them to glee;
Its sunny wild games to you pay no heed.
Against the steel gray sky of an impending storm
You glow, quietly insurmountable, preparing for the struggle.
Must I, too, feel such pain, sucking at my life-blood,
Before I can vanquish the torrents which pour all around me?
Hide me in your tangled mass, teach me:
For I crave your strength
Though I am young — of hardship and loss
Utterly afraid.

Jacqueline Taus

Shadows in the Moonlight

Words pale in comparison to my love for thee.
  They are mere shadows cast in moonlight,
    Mere impressions without details,
  And, yet, still I must make them suffice.

Those pale shadows cast in moonlight,
  The ones that say meekly, quietly, softly,
    I love you
  Yet mean everything.

Mean everything; like you're everything to me,
  Everything I want,
  Everything I need,
  And so very much more.

Those pale shadows in the moonlight saying merely,
    I love you;
  But meaning everything.
    Paula Adams

A Portrait In Words

Her beauty's like the stars that shine
From other worlds, in other times

Her beauty casts romantic spells
Like golden chimes or wedding bells

As haunting melodies of yore
Heard hard upon some distant shore

The clash of waves, her spirits high
Like lonely winds about to sigh

As bright as suns her countenance shines
In all these worlds there's none so fine

A complex goddess with golden tresses
Cascade as falls upon her dresses

A lady fair no one to compare
A moon, a star, or nova far

Blue eyes so deep, in hypnotic sleep
You dream that always you will keep

That angel vision, Oh! So fair
But watch you well, the devil's there
    Nicholas S. Collins

You In Me

I've felt your presence for five or six years
  good times were many while others brought tears.
You did try to lead and straighten my ways
  but still I would stumble, my mind in a daze.
The lessons you gave, the times that we shared
  proved to my heart, that you really cared.
My hands you did tie, with the strongest of rope
  and when I gave in you showed me more hope.
Long nights did get weary, the hours just dragged by
  some spirits got testy, no more were they shy.
Relentless they tease and haunt 'till the last
  by dredging up memories of life in the past.
To you I give thanks, your love I can feel
  in time I did find, life's wounds you could heal.
Some changes were made, while we were apart
  that kept them from breaking our battlescarred heart.
    Robert K. Bailey

The Goalie

When the puck goes through the crease,
This man's ability shows his inner peace.
He remains calm throughout the game,
Each move he makes is never the same.
Just as the puck flies at his head,
He doesn't duck, but instead
His glove flies up to snag the flying disk,
And pulls it down in one quick wisp.
Shot after shot his acrobatics draw many cheers,
The fans wonder if he has any fears.
When players charge the net full speed,
This man performs his given deed.
He keeps his sleepless vigil strong,
Going sixty minutes long.
After each game he gets a rest,
But the next night he's put to the test,
To see if all he did before,
can be repeated once more.
    Matthew J. Ingham

Untitled

For the sun has risen. The darkness has fallen.
For the children who come to play in the
morning sun. Here's the sun the children shouted
with glee! It has saved us from all the darkness.
Now we can play for we have no fear because the
sun is shining near.
    Monique R. Sherlock

The Man With Nothing, But Everything

In the eyes of mankind I haven't much,
But God allows me to see, hear and touch.
With all the things that I could own,
Nothing compares to the love I feel at home.

There are hardships and pain all around,
Although there is beauty and joy to be found.
But if you stop long enough to smell the roses,
You may understand the things told to Moses.

Life is short, and time goes so fast,
So slow down and make the moments last.
There are many things that can get close to your heart,
But you must stop to see them before the joy can start.

If what you are looking for is love,
Start at home and don't forget to look above,
For God is the creator of all
So open your heart, and tare down the walls.
    Charles R. Gawthorp Jr.

A True Servant of the Creator

A seed falls to the earth and penetrates the dust and disappears.
All is not lost or without hope - the unseen growth gradually
  becomes seen.
The noble tree is true at heart inside and out.
It lives in obedience to its creator.
It receives nourishment and reaches for the sky.
Rejoicing and celebrating life by being life.
It proclaims its beauty and its uniqueness without shame.
If the pain of natural disaster falls upon it the tree breaks and
groans, yet accept what is and the healing process has begun.
Time passes slowly, the tree is never impatient.
Always accepting and growing, gracefully receiving and giving.
Time and disaster the artist of healing wounds creates perhaps a
  more wondrous appearance.
Good out of the bad, not hopeless.
Who knows what thoughts of trees.
They inspire me to be fully who I am intended to be, content with
what is and ever growing.
    Autumn Terrill

Where Do We Go?

Whither we go from birth to....where?
From innocent babes to adults we grow
On an endless whirl through life's travails.
And we ask, "Where do we go?"

Yom Kippur, Ramadan and Lent,
Times for atonement we all know.
Each to spiritually satiate man,
And yet we ask, "Where do we go?"

Oh, Thomas Aquinas and Maimonides too,
You've helped man understand lots more.
And through other philosophers of old,
We've begun to fathom the divine law.

We speak of God, his love, his wrath
And pray to him each morn and night.
The many faiths do offer paths
Yet each proclaims that theirs is right.

The Cherubic face of a young child,
A tree, a flower, a flake of snow,
Are all we need to be convinced.
Why do we ask - "Where do we go?"

Matthew R. Ciancimino

Cold Destiny

I feel the cold shiver of this day
Dark and gray and the wind cold as ice.

Trees dance and squirm to the tune
Of the quickened air made visible.

The colors of the land are subdued
With the somber shades of a half-night.

Alone - in all this world just one - and
Sad has a feeling and lonely a face.

Now a laugh would seem a mock
Or a smile a crooked grimace.

But I walk, a solitary blade
Without a root,

Moving against a force that's not
My friend, a force that blows without care.

What good is a memory so long and stretched,
Becoming as transparent as oxygen?

Freedom without purpose is a
Hat without a head.

Still I move because I will it
And dream without trying.

John J. Herrera

Hunger for Knowledge

Everything I do, I see what I was taught.
From every childhood and on.
I catch myself in midsentence or thought
and it turns to a little giggle.
I was raised with unconditional love and honesty
And I find myself a parent, just like my parents.
Worried, loving, caring, trust, honesty and honor
All to teach my children now.
Who hunger for knowledge, the want to know
Just as I did when I was growing up.
And I'm sure now, like my Mother and Father
The truth is out there for us to find.
And sometimes it right in front of us
If only we would just look.

Kitty Northcutt

Will Be Done

My mother made pies,
And kept six children alive
During the Great Depression.

Her crusts were impeccable. Her husband incurable.

Lemon meringue was my favorite.

For too many years her sweet dreams spilled over,
Smoking in isolation, in the ovens of her mind.

Pecan ran a very close race.

I always thought my mother should get a hobby,
A few good friends. She doted so
On feeding her brood, as though running away
From hungry days her seventh child never imagined.

Peace, apple, sour cherry - all fillings,
So filling, so fine. My mother made pies
And loved seven children amid her own depression.

A light touch, a few pricks when necessary, allowance
For extra baking time; always denying her success
Made manifest in each marvelous pie, in each happy child.

My mother made pies.
And that was enough.

Mary Ellen Connelly

Dying Serbs 1991-1995

A dagger is driven deep into my ailing heart.
My body, ego, and soul are fatally shaken.
The People of which I am for decades a neglected part
Now are being destroyed — their lives taken.

Greed and propaganda are in action now blindly
Throwing away Allies and old loyal friends;
But dying Serbs look at their killers kindly,
Hoping that God will help them to start new trends.

Trends of unselfishness, wisdom and reason,
Could save of my beloved People what is left.
Prevent more of genocide, madness and treason,
And stop maniacs from pulling the biggest ever theft.

A dagger is driven deep into my ailing heart.
My body, ego, and soul are fatally shaken.
The People of which I am for decades a neglected part
Now are being destroyed — their lives taken.

Dragoljub Djurkovic

Heaven

Heaven is a place where the streets are paved with gold.
   It's a place where you and I never worry about growing old.

It's a place where the sun always shines, and one day it will
   be yours and mine.

When he comes for us that day, music will ring throughout the
   land.

The angels will play their harps in unison, with the rest of
   heavens band.

Though I know not when we shall go, there's something that I
   think you should know.

He will return for us one day, and there will be joy along the
   way.

But in our hour of happiness, for some there shall be gloom, but
   if they ask God for guidance now, then he shall make enough
   room.

And I will tell you now, I would rather be in Gods holy place
   instead of sitting in the Devils fireplace!

A. P. Turner

Trapped

All alone with just the sound of your breathing
the loudness of your beating heart
the thoughts running through your mind
the eagerness to go out
the stillness in the air
the darkness of confinement
the shaking of your hand
the squinting of your eyes that tries to see the light
the hopelessness and guilt of being trapped.

Rachel L. Milo

My Life

I've lived my life the best I could,
and now you're telling me it's done no good.
I've made some mistakes,
lived through my share of heartbreaks.
I can not change what I've done
and my children, I love them everyone.
I must give it my all,
for I can not let them see me fall.

You say there are things we can try
but the truth is - I'm going to die!
But put your tubes and gloves back in their bins.
Keep your needles and your pins.
Don't want your potions or your pills.
All alone, I'll climb the hills.
So, please God, help me to be strong,
because everything is going wrong.

Stephanie Fawson

I Too Was Once A Child

On mornings like this, the small ones asleep, breaths serene
The angelic looks upon the faces of the horned and tailed
   the night before
The sound of bickering siblings incessant, war ignited when glances
   met
Fear of a night light gone dark, a school bus missed
The joy felt of small hands bearing wilted dandelions, a sweet kiss
The warmth of small bodies held tight during the rain and thunder
One look in their eyes, a mirror of long ago
A laugh, a smile when from sweet lips words softly spoken,
"I love you Mom," reminds me of days gone by
Self sweet warrior, serene and afraid
When I too was once a child

Lynne Toussaint

There

I'm holding my breath. I wonder how long I
can stay under water without coming up for air?
It's a mighty large ocean I have to cover, will
I make it from here to there?
How will I know when I get there? Will I see a
sign...You made it! Will it be an internal feeling
of "yes, I know I'm there!"
I'm still holding my breath, I'm afraid to come up
for air. I'm headed for that place, that place
I call there. I've heard that there the waters
are calmer, and that everybody comes up for air
because they are not afraid. They have faced their
fear. I'm just one fish, one fish in a big sea
trying to get there.
Sometimes I get confused. I'm not sure in which
direction to swim, which direction will take me there.
Will I succeed? This question pushes me through this
dark body of water. I know the answer...Will I succeed?
Only if I come up for air. For I have nothing to fear
I tell myself. I am not as lost as I think myself to be
Where am I going? Only where I take myself, and
I choose to take myself there.

Melissa Kuehnel

Untitled

For one brief moment
You held my sorrow in your hands
And our souls touched.

Elusive interconnectedness captured for so
short a time
My heart aches at the loss.

Linda M. Bolduan

What Has the World Come To

Why are the mountains so still
Must they stands there like a statue of clay
Like soldiers awaiting their kill
They do not move nor do not sway

Why are the seas so vigorous
Churning the insides of my soul
Like a giant filled with anger
Touching me with a burning coal

Making me twist and turn with pain
Letting the hatred expand within
Doing things I can't sustain
Oh, what a horrible, terrible sin

Why are the skies so utterly black
With no stars to light up the sky
Such a heavily burden upon my back
Standing alone until dawn breaks, I let out a relieved sigh

Why is life so unfair
The world so full of tart
Some don't even give a care
And some with a tender heart

Jessica Chee

The Glen

Inspired by Pat Polhamus

Travel with me if you will
To a place where time and space stand still

Walk with me on paths of stone
Worn smooth by nature's magic comb

Pictures in your mind a virgin land
Where beauty and peace stand hand in hand

Breathe the air that is fresh with life
Frolic in the place where there is no strife

Feel the aura your soul abounds
Sense the cosmos on the mounds

See the water fresh and clean
Smell the fragrance of the green

This is the place where it all began
Hatred and prejudice were never God's plan

Let your sorrows go by the way
Give thanks to Him on this day

Tony Charlesworth

Standing

At summer camp, aged eight, I stood between
My brothers, hands extended, straight and taut,
And pointing toward the ground, a gesture seen
As almost perfect then, though deeply fraught
With pain, part of a photographic pose
Assumed to meet some shattering demand
Long since internalized, so there arose
No thought of any other way to stand.

Charles Wulach

Untitled

I'm just an average teen, that's all that I am
I think that no one likes me, I think I am number one
I think no one cares, or that you care too much
I think that I could live on my own
But not more than week on the street
All I'd want to do is go home
I try to be different, but in the end it's just the same
Everyone is just like me, or I am just like them
Because I'm just an average teen
I'm trying to survive in this cruel world
That the people who "cared too much" has made for us
It's like trying to survive through hell
But we've nearly made it through
Because that's what us average teens do
In our struggle to become special to become number one
We unite with all our peers and learn to survive through the years
So if you're the person who "cares too much"
Please don't try and strip it all away, it will just lead us the
    wrong way
Please don't try and lead us your way or guide us in your direction
You've already put our world into destruction.

Amy Eatherington

Poetry Alive

It's a beautiful day but I'm sitting inside,
Writing some poems that are coming alive,
And flittering, fluttering, floating in air,
Like warm summer winds through my uncombed-hair.
They fly through the sky and they splitter and splutter,
And splat into tapestries screaming with color.
They burst into fragrance that tickles my nose,
And slosh cross the carpet like mud through my toes.
They drizzle, drip, pour, like sweet rain on my face,
And wing me on voyages deep into space.
It's a beautiful day yet I'm sitting inside,
Watching a springtime of thoughts as they thrive:
Like wild ivy climbing up distinguished trunks,
Or cue balls and eight balls that plucker and plunk.
Like trickles turned torrents, or buds to thick leaves,
In bug swarming meadows on warm summer eves.
Like ice cream or chocolate on tips of soft tongues,
Or water mist breaths swimming down to my lunges.
It's a beautiful day, still I'm sitting inside,
With some poems as my friends and my thoughts as my guide.

Paul Smith

In Violence We Trust

Guns are pulled and blades are flashed,
As gangs clash with each other.
Punches thrown and faces bashed,
As children fight their brothers.

Rage is high as bullets fly,
No thought of who will pay.
A child will fall, in blood he'll lie,
One this his final day.

Mothers wipe their swollen eyes,
Families torn apart.
Fathers whisper anguished whys,
Each with a broken heart,

Instantly a child is gone,
Gunned down before his time.
A body bag zipper is drawn,
Another senseless crime.

Where will this end, what can we do?
What will become of us?
The question many, the answers few,
When...in violence we trust.

Susan L. Smith

Past, Forgotten Day

On earth dwell some in purtid ease,
Who sinful suck from mercy's hand
A life disgraced by idle soul
While all, save will, still firmly stands.
If to this land I offer gifts,
Then to this land I offer this;
From youth to old, from strong to wise,
These hands shall grasp with strange delight
The handle rough of labor's spade.
For on this back shall burdened yokes
With joy and pride be grateful laid;

For this in past, forgotten day
Stood men upright in life and way,
And rose to soar the eagle high,
And built men homes for life to stay.
For this in past, forgotten day
Spread man abroad with naught as pay,
And brought to life our lives today
Did this in past, forgotten day.

Russell U. Nash

Dreaming of You!

In his arms dreaming only of you.
Silently praying that my dreams become reality.
Living a lie many emotions are felt.
Each night my dreams becoming more vivid.
In his arms dreaming only of you.
A natural was born that very first glance;
our eyes met; my dreams become a reality.
Love down to the soul is the greatest gift
God can give to anyone.
In your arms I gained strength;
felt your heart with mine.
Life now so bright, so full, so inspiring.
Two souls intertwined into one.
No longer in his arms dreaming;
since our love to the soul became reality.

Patti Dillman

Fear

As the setting sun begins its final descent toward the ground,
Soon the crickets begin to make their evening sound.
Later things combine with these to create each night,
Including the moon as it begins its daily flight.
It spreads its light for all to see,
But the long shadows made try to confuse me.
I begin to see creatures of every shape and size,
Standing behind trees with glazing white eyes.
Thoughts run through my mind, so puzzling yet so clear,
Am I going simply mad, or is it just plain fear?

Michael Jason Highfield

Friendships

We've traveled through days and even through years,
Sometimes walking, mostly running, but at times being still.
Sometimes sorrow, sometimes trouble,
Even heartaches we've known;
But never have we traveled our journey alone.
Celebrations have been plentiful; birthdays and such,
Some forgotten, some belated, but we never lost touch.
Life's challenges we faced the best that we could,
Often words could not express what our hearts understood.
True friendships are cherished and never can die,
Sent only from heaven and sown in our lives.
God put us together before we knew,
What friendships would mean our whole lives through.

Denise H. James

My Mother

My mother is someone
Close and dear to me,
She is very special
But some just cannot see
That she is kind,
All they see is the rough
But I can see the kindness
And not so much the tough.
Sure she's strict,
But she has her reasons;
It's so I'll make good grades
And have fun over the holiday seasons.
My love for her
Will never die;
But sometimes I think it does
I cannot lie.
But it always comes back
After we get mad,
Because being in a fuss
Just makes us sad.

Sara Melancon

Love's Last Request

You hurt me
Left with nothing but memories
One minute you're here
The next you're gone
You think it's easy?
Try feeling what I feel.
Try getting over a love so strong,
You'd die for them.
Try remembering the good times
And even the bad.
Try not crying.
Think I can forgive and forget?
I'll try.
I'll be a friend
Someone who still loves you.
Someone who'll care.
Just remember how much I still love you.
No matter how much it hurts.

Suzy Davidson

Our World

Round and beautiful,
like a bright shiny new ball
Our world
our life depends on it,
all and all.
Our world
without this world none of us
would be anything,
except maybe a giant
pile of dust.
Our world
It's disappearing as fast as
the fog rolls in.
Our world
hardly any of us care
except for the people who've been there.
Our world
we must help save it,
or else who will?
Our world

Heather Engle

West Columbia

I yearn for you.
Along the street, the trees are turning to shadow
Where we walked last spring.
I cannot see you in the lilacs;
I cannot hear you in the rain;
The sweet air is not full in my arms.

Nonnyno

The Art

Life, Love and Time, are three words acting as one, like the light of
God that shines with an enormous light, that cuts through the
darkness of the night like a knife that is thrown with no direction.
It is an uncontrollable spending machine that gobbles up all that is
in it's way. See the art of loving is knowing when to hold on and
when to let go. For we all have this special need to hold on to
someone or something for fear of not choosing our own way in life.
Like a child that comes into this world with fists clenched tight,
bursting with life, power and determination, but when he dies o 'yes
when he dies all that which was his thirst, power and determination
for life is now and forever lost. That force that is in all of us
that go's as quickly as it came. For in times past what was held in
the hands of one determination to win, is now in the hands of one that
has lost his passion and has giving up on the game we call life. For
life is a game in which we play to win. Surely we all have a need
to hold on to life, and its wondrous gifts that God has given us.
Realizing that this is true only at a flash back on life, looking at
what was with great pain. Knowing what will never be again. The
beauty of life that has faded, the vitality of ones being that has
warned. We remember a life that slipped away, but we remember with a
greater pain that we did not see, nor respond to Life, Love and Time.
For time is something that we have very little of. Just like a flower
that's no more, so is it with life. A vapor that for the time appears
today and is gone tomorrow, as sands passes through the hour glass,
so is time in the hands of the simple. This my friend is the Art of
life, blossoming without the aid of the season with the sweet
smile of love, where day and night are as one, above the clouds and
mongst the stars where life, love and time are never ending always
lasting time.

Keith Wooten

Reflections of My 86 Year Old Mother

It seems as though there wasn't ever to be a time in my life that I could call my own
From the time of the first baby someone always wanted something.
I remember the nights especially, when things were always so much harder
Getting out of bed, the cold house and the cold floors, wondering
   why the baby wouldn't sleep.
Was it the broken leg that hurt or the measles, or mumps or chicken pox?
Comforting a child, half awake and still feeling the demand of a someone that needed me.

On and on my memories go, and while the nights got better there was so much to be done.
Food to cook and dishes to wash, clothes to care for and a house to clean.
Up at 5 and to bed at 11, no time, every minute was full.
As the years past I wondered, How many times I have wondered, "When
   will I have time to call my own?"

Well, now I have time. I can sit in my chair and make wishes
I wish for the days past when time was precious and not just a lonely
   bridge to be spanned.
I can wish for the sound of the laughter of my children
Hear the secret whispers of good or mischievous deeds being planned
The picnics and parties, homework to be done, basketball games and dances.
The love I gave and received.

Yes, now when I have time for all of you, at times it seems as though
   you have forgotten me.
I must remember though, that now your day isn't long enough and your
   time isn't your own.
But it will be soon, and then you can sit in your chair
And you can wish and dream, and long to once again be needed by your children.

Rosemarie A. Phillips

252

Dreaming

Dreaming about a time when mothers weren't afraid of mothering
Dreaming about a time when fathers weren't afraid to communicate
and weren't afraid to commit
Dreaming about a time when sisters and brothers could play in the
streets with their dolls and balls not lie dead in the streets
with bullet holes cuddled in body bags
Dreaming about a time when neighbors turned the other cheek, now there
too blind to see, too afraid and numb to speak
Dreaming about days gone by, years gone by, lost time, borrowed time
please God! Don't wake me up, I'm still dreaming!

Courtney H. Lyder

A Moment of Solitude

I see a bus, several people await to abandon. The night lights dew
and laughter. Joy, friendship, and intoxication I can see. They walk
towards their haven satisfied and content in the early morning sun
with no regret that the night has expired.

Yet they forget, the details that make this particular night special.
Air wind, and engines that race away, the bus that delivers and
travels the circles of life and vanishes into the darkness only to
return suffering and anxieties of life.

There is no sound, a woman walks across the grassy path of solidarity.
She walks away from the building lights, to darkness which swallows
her energy and intent. Like the faces of those on the bus.

I see burning lights, the skyline, mountains, horizons propelling
shadows of which lurk from the farthest corners of my soul.
Four corners who corral me and extort the imagination to seek comfort
in those who live their lives free of troubles.

My attempts in finding everlasting peace in a cruel and hostile world
are futile. I stand in this window, I can't be hard or perhaps be
seen. I hope she sleeps while my soul quivers at my intent to shed
light over shadows who lurk and accompany me. The sun is rising
shedding light on a special night which influenced me and allowed me
to make a spiritual connection.

Virgilio Lopez Jr.

Goodbye Dad — But Only For Now

God gave you Peace when it was time to ease your grief and pain
He led you through the Tunnel of Love, through sunshine that
vanished the rain

The Spirit World is filled with Love, the Heavens all Anew
I know you'll never be alone, cause God's love is comforting you

I'll Pray for you in the morning and I'll Pray for you at Night
Please wrap your arms around me Dad, for I'll never move out of your sight

Today I look back at my life, with you it's bright and clear
No matter what the burdens were, you gave me strength to bear

When you would dress up for a Formal Dance, I'd look up at you and sigh
Now you can look down at me Dad, cause I'm wearing your Black Bow Tie

I know that you are gone for now, but feel that you are near
Your whisper Dad, it fills my Heart, and so I will not fear

Whenever I'm in touch with you, throughout each passing day
If I become confused or lost, Dad, please help me find my way

I'll always have much joy and peace, dear Dad, because of you
I know I'll have enough of both, to last my whole life through

So Dad, before I say goodbye — for Now, My Heart just wants to say
Please be my Angel every night and wipe my tears away

When God will Touch my Hand and say, it's time for me to go
I will not be afraid to die, cause Dad, you'll take my other hand and whisper,
"Dear Daughter, We're together again in the Sky."

Marilyn Thurman Burks

Stars and Hearts

Stars across the miles
Forming different shapes and styles
For long distance sweethearts
Wishing they were never apart
Wishing they were together again
'Cause each day of sunshine is like rain
But finally they are no longer apart
And forever joined at the heart

JoAnn Martindale

Imago Dei

Were I to dip my cup
and drink from the reflection
cast by calm water...
deception I would swallow
and the fire in my belly it would quell
leaving a bitter taste in my mouth
that only thriving water can rinse.
This reflection of a face
is but a picture of a frame,
a drawing of a canvas,
a sculpture of a stone,
a vain subsistence...
desiring only the spark that was...
in need of the missing kindling
that is found only by kneeling
and looking through the mirrored caricature
into the tearing eyes of the Creator
weeping not for a flawed creation
but for the masterpiece
it will now become.

Rodney Peavy

Fall

At end of season of hope,
salvation, and love,
which cometh as a dove.
'Tis a season of life and colorful leaves,
which now lie dead crinkled in the streams.
So now you must wait until another
lively and colorful day cometh again.

Sarah Rosenman

Like No Other

He is like no other, he delights
Desires overshadows my every
Existence; yes, he is like no
other.

He looks inside my soul, in the
Deepest depth, he finds me waiting
for Him, to rescue me from
Loneliness, sadness, he is like no other.

He loves me with patience, a
quiet stillness, a heartbeat
so strong, it devours me, He
is like no other.

He makes love to my body with
Unspeakable joy, he takes me to
A place that astounds my every
Fantasy of him, he awakens my
Every need, want and desire,
His love is like no other.

He is my alter, my rock, my
Gentle love, he is my other.

Saundra Norwood Hood

Where Is Death Tonight?

Mother, Mother—where is Death tonight?
Is He charging across the land with
His band and banners?

Does He call from tops of trees
For little souls to gather in His crowd
And blow the bugles for His songs?

Or will He lift me to His shoulder
And take me home to His brothers and
Sisters, and may I play with His pets?

The air is cold, the wind has walked around the
House but the doors are locked and surely
Death cannot come where the wind cannot go.

Where are you Mother? Turn up the light,
Make a sound! Please, please tell me
Where Death is tonight.

Glenn E. Soellner

Right Ma

A great grandma is your grandma's ma.
A grandma is you ma or pa's ma.
Ma and pa are your own.
When you are grown
You can have a baby of your own.
Pa and ma will be grandpa and grandma.
Grandma will be great grandma.
And great grandma will be great, great grandma.
That's the right ma,
Right, ma?

Christa Glover

Expectations

Having no expectations I can remain in the flow,
Revel in the rhythms of the moment,
Enjoy the colors, sounds and nuances of the now,
Everything in the moment is as it should be.

Expectations are really bars around our bodies, minds and souls,
Expectations define how, why and when things happen,
Expectations dictate our thoughts, words and deeds.
Expectations falsely let us assume that we know - and hence
are secure and safe.
Expectations do not lead to new places and spaces,
But keeps us firmly entrenched within our own limitations.

Melanie Schmidt

The Discordant Vicinage

The morning is grey, and full of grief
Message of silence steal across the sky.
All bow'd in tears, the death to feel.
Teens like clusters of bees, brandish'd steel.
And bayou waters run stain'd.
Would they not hear?

Where oh mortal children are your victories?
Brag not, you mournful children
Death hath stealeth thy reward,
And thou shall dwell with it,
When death shall be no more.

Oh the bitter memories of those aggrieved mothers,
Whose maternal throes, yet to vanish lose their youths.
Oh those dreadful causes . . . and rue delivery.
Oh, vice! Dear virtue; be not proud
for thou art no more.
Where art thou vicar? Where art thou viceroy?
I am on the labyrinth of holy waters
and the upper circle.

Almamy Jaiah Kai-Kai

From Me to You

After I have been with you
How very hard it is to leave.

Your presence still consumes me
Your words still echo in my ear.

I still feel the touch of you against me
Your body next to mine.

Each meeting becomes more rapturous —
Each parting more unkind.

Our lives have been entwined
For quite a length of time.

And yet we know the limitations of our caring
That some day it all must end.

But not yet, God — not yet
I have still so much to give.

Nancy L. Super

Mt. Saint Helens

Oh how mighty is she!

She stands alone as a pillar of strength.
It is time for her to make herself known.
Her power is unmatched,
Her magnificence is destroyed!
There is a force in her bowels,
Trees bow before her.
Nothing can stand in her way.

She is silent.

Clint Lancaster

Everything In Me

I'm not very special, deep inside.
But I've got feelings,
And I've got pride.
What you got to offer,
Is more than I can give.
I know I'll love you
For as long as I live.
People never look,
Beneath the surface of the skin.
At my mind, heart, and soul,
And the love deep within.
When your hand touches mine,
There's something I can't explain.
Time which subdues the memories,
And ease away the pain.
So hear I stand alone, vulnerable for you.
A mythical tale revealed, a dream coming true.
I'm giving you a secret,
Something others don't see. I'm opening and giving you,
Everything in me.

Elyse N. McCoy

Gone

I wanted to hold the moonbeam
    but it slipped through my hands
and the dewdrop would not stay on my flower
the rays of the sun made rainbows
that I could not capture or hold fast
and at last I realized
    childhood past.

Noreen McGloin

254

Violet

In a ward, in a change
The spectrum takes shape of this form
Flaunting towards disaster,
Heading for the Crash, I end up between the shaded lines
Eutrophic nightmares I behold
Trying to become part of the wild light,
Only to remain dull, ordinary
   Must it begin with violet
   I fall hopelessly off of this canvas—
   Dripping ever so slowly into puddles of grey
What does it take to be a peacock,
A phantom of radiance — a shadow of hindrance
This sundance only projects the silver hair of night
A green light at a stop sign, caught in this ambivalence
A siren of crimson playing in traffic
   Must it begin with violet
   This world turned to numb when your gracious flower blossom
   Germinated out of my garden
In image I can only remember you, a passion of but a dream

   Heather French

My Butterfly

Dedicated to Dorothea J. Kenny (12\13\43-1\25\97)
from Kathleen M. McDermott Zirn

Like a butterfly you flew into my life, adding color to my world,
lifting my spirits to the highest of heights.

Thoughts of you are entwined
with my high school memories
of being back home—sharing laughter and tears
of younger days way back when.
We were like sisters—the *Best* of friends.

Now, as I listen to the wind whisper through the trees
and watch the sun set for the evening,
     a chill surrounds me;
     I don't want to believe . . . .

The air weighs heavy upon my shoulders.
There is no lightening.
     No thunder.
     No rain pouring from the Heavens.

I look up into the night sky so full of stars.
Wishes and dreams come to mind . . .
I always thought we'd grow old together
Best Friends Forever.

In memory our friendship will always be.
And whenever I see a butterfly,
I'll remember *you*, my *Best Friend; Dottie.*

   Ann Stevens

Living

Tonight we will smile at the heavens,
We will dance as the crickets serenade,
We will kiss the soft fur of a kitten,
We will watch each star on parade.

Tonight we will listen for angels,
We will touch the warm breeze with our cheek,
We will smell the sweetness of Springtime,
We will hear the cool song of the creek.

For yesterday may have known sorrow,
And tomorrow's a hope that we pray,
But tonight we will celebrate the moment,
For it's here and it's now . . . today.

   Susan D. Wulf

Dad

I know I'm very fortunate to have a Dad as special as you.
You've always taught me the values of life which seem to get me through.

Love, Patience, and Character are just a few, but you also told me most important was trusting in God and he would see me through.

Teaching me these principles was not at all enough.
You practiced them even when times got really rough.

You trained a child in the way he should go and now that he's grown up he's not departing from the values you showed.

I have but one hero and he has been there through thick and thin.
His name is Dad and always has been.

Happy Father's Day! Love, Greg

   Gregory J. Reno

Dreaming of You

When I think of you and dream of you
If you're not with me I'm blue
Darling, you can always trust me to be true
And I know I can trust you, too.

Sweetest one, you are always on my mind
You are so sweet, good, and kind
Even in all my dreams you are not behind
But up front our hearts we do bind.

Your love is my most precious love
It is like all love that is sent from above
Though it is much sweeter than that of a dove
Which over its mate does show true love.

You can never know just how much I care
For you whom I know is so very dear
Darling it is almost more than my heart can bear
When I hear you say "darling, I really do care."

I'm still waiting for my dreams to be fulfilled
with the ring and the vows that are to be sealed
with a kiss to promise that our love can't be killed
But our lives with love shall always be filled.

   Joan Bradford

I Am Baby

This is the first day of my life, "Hello there!"
I'm a wonderful baby, designed and created by God.
Oh! Wow! What is that breeze? Fresh air they call it.
Air conditioning? I can hardly bear it.
Burrr . . . rrr . . . It's cold.
No wonder I screamed when I first touched the air.
How would you like your little bootie spanked when in the raw.
Well, all I desire is mommie!
Mommie who holds me close and secure.
Mommie what do you think you're doing with me now? Oh . . .
No!
Don't dip me in that water — You're not the preacher —
Don't baptize me yet!
Oh! So that's what it's all about . . .
Splish, Splash, I'm a taken my first bath.
Gee . . . This is refreshing. I'm squeaky clean now.
Mommie loves me, little me.
I am loved.
Just a bundle of Love.
Desirable to cuddle.
I Am Baby.

   Yvonne A. Ryan

Grief Without Faith

(On My Father's Death)

Father, who from this world has passed,
As if your life were a mere trespass;

Taken early before the noon
Of a life so fraught with pain:

So much better than the world, which spelled your ruin,
And your pitiful heart did drain:

While leaving me no God to praise or curse,
Nor some feeling that would be the first;

For Joy and Sorrow so profound,
We know are edges of the same wound.

It offers no peace when it doth heal,
For never was it something real.

But were it real it would only be,
What our given eyes could vaguely see
Through the clouded and shrouded mists,
Of and order then thought to exist.

Oh! Were there some Grand Plan to see,
To cast my weeping spirit free:
Then would I accept even an evil nod,
Over the nothingness of a Random God.

Joseph Lebra

Jr. Varsity Does

As I review the front line of life, the young and the
unknown circle of life's future, I ponder what would
it be like to win a game. My team of does remind me
of those who wondered in front, standing, looking as
a ten thousand pound metal monster ended its career.
Only a few survive, half moon — to full moon. As the
season shortened, my does became more — spikes,
khaki and full of knowledge. The will to live burst
out from the mouth pieces. Fourth and goal, there my
adult does stand with hypnosis dreams of making it
across the road to life and victory. There my adult
does stood with visas held high.

Norman E. Gray Sr.

A Poet Am I

"A Poet Am I" yes I express myself in that way
Try and understand; Take time to hear what I say
There are many ways to express yourself, music, drama, and even
dance
You'll never know your talents if you afraid to take that chance
Poetry! Poetry is like life, many different parts linking to one
Problems, yes, but answers there are none
So in my poetry I try to explain life's conflict
I'll do my best, my best I'll do, so you can take the pick
To be honest what separates me from the rest, is that the words
express, are the true feelings of Les, yes, I do, I dig deep down
inside
A true poet, for my feelings I never hide
Open your mind and heart then take a pen in hand
begin to write, be a man and do the best you can
Let no one bring you down or just simply say
you're wasting your time for you need to through that pen away
Believe in yourself and yes, in all that you do
You're not doing it for man, but for God and you
This is me, yes all that I am about
My poetry I believe in there's no need for any doubt and my works
will
live on, even after I die for I am Poet and "A Poem am I" . . .

Leslie L. Jones III

Red Light/Green Light

I saw him from the bus, but he didn't see me. At first, I wasn't sure
it was him; the light was red as the bus crept through traffic.

His hair had thinned, his face looked a bit weathered, but he was
still that handsome boy;

The one who made my heart pound as I watched through the peep
  hole as
he came to pick me up for our first date.

The one who never told me I was getting fat from all the Hagan Daz
  we ate in bed.
The one who excited me as I listened to him shower.
The one who left me when he learned I wasn't a saint.
The one whose baby I had for only the shortest time allowed.
The one who shouldn't have slipped away.
The light changes to green and we move on.

Victoria Reggio

Kevin My Man

I work with special children each day
Helping them grow and learn per say
Sometimes it takes years to see progress
Working with them brings out our best

A little boy, his name is Kevin
He's been with us since he was eleven
Crawling the halls in the middle school
Checking each room, he thinks he's cool

The kids greet him and shake his hand
He loves to go and hear the band
The Home Ec kids they bake and clean
He's treated well, they're never mean

We have high hopes he'll walk someday
He will if we all get our way
Kevin my man is my sweet boy
He brings us all lots of joy

Louise Davis

Lost Doll

I am cold and the air is damp. I miss my clothes,
but even if I knew where they were, I could not
move to find them.

If I could move and knew where my clothes were,
and could put them on, they would still do me no
good, torn and soiled.

I would cry if I could. But, even if I could cry,
who would hear or heed my pain.

I was made for love and laughter, to be cherished
and treasured. Made to hear childish secrets.
Secret dreams and wishes were to be mine to keep.

Now all is lost, as lost am I; impaled, stripped,
deprived, powerless and bereft of my protector.

Still my maker gave me a smile, and a fair beauty.
And, with that hope. Some-when there may be hands
to undo the pain, to remove the cold damp.

I may yet feel the joy of small clumsy hands
replacing the lost clothes. Hear again the
laughter and child secrets, and see my existence
filled with sunshine and life.

Jan Merrill

Slowly

An old man was rocking
in a creaky old rocking chair the old man moved in the
slowest motion possible when walking or eating
A young fast moving
rat-catching cat was the man's only company every night
the old man poured the cat's food in a usually dull manner
The old man tiredly
crept to the town's mini-mart and gradually pulled
out and counted his changed for the items he bought
Slowly the old man's cat
looked skinnier and skinnier
and the old man's leisurely manner
of feeding his cat gradually disappeared
SLOWLY, SLOWLY, SLOWLY
the old man's appearances
in the mini-mart were
sluggishly fading
An old man was rocking
in a creaky old rocking chair . . . .

Jennifer Carol Ellis

Tides, Sun-Beams And Shared Illumination

The earth and the moon in cyclic motion,
Seen in sunlight by tides in the ocean,
Circling in silence, no thought for another,
With love that outlasts a child for its mother.

The tides relay the wondrous attraction,
The pull of the two, their longings in action,
For eternity they will seek to be one,
Witnessed by only the light of the sun.

Like the two bodies that grace the night sky,
Our love for each other, on which we rely,
Is a bond that outlasts the changes of time,
And through it all, I know that you're mine.

The love and attention we give to each other, is greater than any
we've given another, from birth to death, our love simply grows, our
wish to be one forever shows.

The earth and the moon, great as they are, will never unite by the
light of the star, but we, as we are with our wondrous love, will soon
be together by grace from above. By longing outlasting the tides of
time, we will unite in love sublime one step beyond the earth an the
moon, with God as our witness, we will join soon.

Edward J. Carta

My Neighborhood Today

I would love to talk about nature, butterflies and such.
But the ugly truth is that another shot rang out
in my neighborhood today. Another small child caught
in the cross fire.

The stories I hear are not of playing house or of playing
G.I. Joe. They are very real, very raw and hard to ignore.

The soft whisper of a mother's words have been replaced with
the sound of semi-automatics and the sound of breaking glass.

The fathers strong voice is silent, his presence is unknown
just a shadow or a photograph hidden in a drawer.

Mother, Father we need to hear you, we need to see you. Without
you we are defenseless against the enemies that invade our hearts
and our minds. Replace the fear in our hearts with love. Replace
the anger with a simple act of kindness and maybe then we can give
back to this America what she truly deserves.

The American dream has turned into a nightmare for
so many of our youth. A wrong turn was taken, a bad
decision made.

So much to live for so little said.

Delois S. Dandridge

Deadwood

What is the magic that keeps pulling me to the gulch in the
hills?
You think it must be family ties, but it is more.
It is happy and sad memories of a place and time gone by.
Sunny Easters with patches of snow on the ground, tulips
reaching for the warmth.
Lazy summer days spent at the lake, warm nights under starry
skies.
The crunch of autumn leaves, frosty breath, snake dances,
football
games, and Halloween.
It is pine boughs heavy with snow, icicles hanging from
buildings,
it is a winter wonderland.
Lifelong friends and glowing hearts. Holding on to the good
times, learning and growing from the bad.
It is white rocks, blacks hills, blue skies, green pines, scents,
sounds and beauty to behold.
Ghosts from the past mingling with the present, moving toward
the future.

It's Home!

Leanne L. Praeuner

My Father, My Dad, My Friend

The tools hang waiting patiently where he placed them.
Sheer silence is more disturbing then a myriad of noises.
The chain saw, his prized possession, patiently waits for him.
His two tractors mourn his loss by unmoving silence.

My father, my dad, my friend no longer needs things of this life.
The clothes in his closet hang waiting for him to wear them.
His favorite chair in the living room waits for him - empty.
The kitchen drawer within awaits his watch and extra glasses for him.

The wood he spent hours upon hours cutting waits where he placed it.
Boards from the old granary wait for him to build something of them.
The medication he needed for life - now discarded without him.
People driving by the house don't see the emptiness within.

His candy bars remain in the refrigerator never to be eaten by him.
The ice-cream that he had for a meal-desert remains in the freezer.
His beloved peanuts remain on the counter in their jar undisturbed.
The game of Baseball mourns - unknowingly the loss of a faithful fan.

The life around the farm will never be the same without him.
This farm was him - my father, my dad, my friend.
The name Leon Ervin Young no longer means the same as it did.
For my father, my dad, my friend passed away.

William L. Young

Grandma

From that moment when my life began
First grandchild of Floyd Dickinson's clan
Love is the main message I was taught
Sweet smiles and warm hugs from all were brought
Quite quickly I learned to give them back
Caring and sharing I did not lack
"Do unto others," Grandma would say
"Would you like to be treated that way?"
Think of their feelings - you will do right
Follow God's words - find hope in His light
We may not like all of one's actions
But let love rule in our reactions
Lending a hand can make a new friend
People grow close when there's time to lend
Thanks to the wisdom that Grandma shared
Many will know that I truly cared
My main goal is like Grandma to be
Helpful and friendly to all I see
Kind words and thoughts plus caring and love
Make Grandma dear - a gift from Above!

Jodie Opat

'Til We Meet Again

When first I saw you, Oh! our eyes entwined
And all else in the world did fade from view.
My life became to ever make you mine.
This passion I could also see in you.
And so like Romeo and Juliet
We sought how we could make this come to pass.
Unlike those two, our hurdles could be met,
So we were wed, united so at last!
In course of time our joy was multiplied
For we discovered that we'd have a son.
The days flew by; more tears of joy we cried,
As we had two more children, one by one.
  But now you're gone, and I can only pray
  I'll join you up in heaven some sweet day.

Linda Usher

Image Interstate

There's been a major pileup on the image Interstate
Descriptive words were flowing, one was a little late.

Vowels and consonants collided, crying in distress
Ideas anxious to escape this onomatopoeia mess.

Similes were seen spinning and metaphors obscured
While participles dangled, vowels remained unheard.

A kaleidoscope of images tossed abruptly in the air
Would not be put to paper, were they beyond repair?

A poet on sabbatical, happening on the scene
At first glance didn't recognize what all of this might mean.

Letters, words, and images pulled so gently from within
Were organized once more that witty writing might begin.

Metaphors and similes, sharper images to see
Could now be put to paper, Imagination would be free!

Patsy Wolter

Last Week's Eclipse

I thought the windows were tinted.
That day the birds stopped singing
We gathered in large groups on the grass
Like confused spectators.
The shadow of every sycamore leaf
Made the image of a crescent on the pavement.

That day the birds stopped singing
We watched in homemade devices
Shielding our eyes from the damaging rays.
The corona burst out, burning red,
And like an animal caught in headlights
We gaped in awe...

That day the birds stopped singing.

Chris Dennett

The Journey

Once upon a time there was a little girl,
she lived inside her own little world . . .

The years went on and she became a young lady
only to find out her new world would be gray
and shady . . .

The problems came and went one after the other
and after these problems would be a woman
to discover . . .

Through all the heartaches and pain
the woman is finally here . . .

The young lady is gone, and
the child had disappeared . . .

Angela M. Lucas

To Laura

The day is well spent and very nearly done
I rest in my garden and watch the waning
                shadows one by one

They fall upon the blooms with a dancing
                kind of grace
And suddenly I see in them the loveliness
                of your face

The gentle radiant beauty and flashing
                presence of your smile
For here in the shadows you are with me
                but for a little while

God is the Master Designer of each and every face
And He has given memories of a precious one
                in the quietness of this place.

Sadie W. Smith

That Day at the Door

  I said I didn't love you, I said I didn't care;
    I'm sorry I lied, I really do care;
So, why did you leave me alone at the door?
I said that I loved you and needed you more;
    You used to call me twice everyday,
Now you are gone and so are your calls;
Why did you leave me, at my front door?
Now I'm beginning to wish I hadn't lied;
I never really knew what a good thing I had.
Now that you're gone, I'm always alone,
Every now and then, I see you walk by alone on the street;
Then I get mad; Then I feel sad; That's when I cry;
    If I could start, all over again,
I'd say those words I've been dying to say,
    But now it's too late, you've already gone.
I made a mistake, I know I was wrong;
    And maybe someday we can try it again.
We both made mistakes, that we both regret.
So, why did you leave me, that day at the door?

Elizabeth Schram

Seasons Change

The snow, the sleds, the snowball fights,
everybody's porch is covered with ice,
waking up early to shovel snow.
running in and out warming your toes,
Sweaters and jackets are regular attire.
Everyone hopes they don't have to fix a flat tire,
This is the season for love and joy.
You'll get what you want if you've been a good boy.
Before long it will be spring.
And we'll all be doing the umbrella thing.

Wayne Shank

Mine

And when I looked to you to see within,
I noticed not what could have been nor be,
But rather light, one that you placed in me
Which bore no pain despite all of my sins,
Perspective told me I would never win,
My own voice cried fate but only to see
That nothing in the world, heavens, or still sea
Could possibly return your love's sweet gin,
Time and again I looked within my soul,
Desiring the replica of you
And now the time has come and conquered Hours
And I now remember, and am found whole,
Once again my memories have brought truth,
No more, Love, do I see my soul as yours

Charlotte A. Boechler

A Mountain Happiness Meditation

Mountains attract the hearts of those who love the aesthetic feeling
of nature, and the beauties of woodland solitude . . .
Their blessings are the salt of the earth,
And they have always attracted peace-seekers, adventurers, and sages.
Mountain and wall;
To what within do they call?
Thrilling, lofty heights to scale;
My heart tells the tale . . .
Majestic inner heights to reach —
Surely my beautiful mountains have these things to teach..
The mountains so simply and sweetly, effect one so dearly and deeply . . .
Ones heart becomes a delightful magnet
Which attracts experiences of adventure and loveliness
Midst the vales of flower meadows and alpine lakes.
This beauty is best appreciated . . .
When the beauty within which it reflects is awakened.
Oh! Listen —
Hear the gently rustling leaves
And the roar of a soft wind in the pine boughs
Merge into OM . . .

Eric N. Easton

Forever Hate!

How can one put into words the lifelong
hatred I have for you. Simply put, a
jagged cut, red hot like a fire burning in
my nerves, couldn't compare with my
loathing of you. In my mind you embody
the worse the world can create and what
ultimately could multiply to destroy us
all.

The river of blood which runs between us,
will it ever be dammed?
Will the sea of anger between us ever be
pacified?

The day will come when you will fall and
you will reach your mudcaked, dry,
cracked hands up for my pity and all
you'll find is exactly what you gave me
— anger, apathy, and emptiness.

Scott E. Phillips

A Masterpiece

You buy a puzzle, bring it home, and open it.
You find all the border pieces, then you sort out the colors
or find the visible forms on the picture.
You see, Harvey, your life is like a puzzle...
Mom brought you home from the hospital
and sorted out the visible features,
like how to take care of a growing boy.
When putting a puzzle together you start with the border.
So, Mom started with the border adding another piece each day.
As Mom walked to the graduation ceremony she was searching
for the last of the border pieces.
Finally, Mom found it, "Francisco Javier Oaxaca, Jr.,"
your name was called...Mom placed the piece down as the
diploma was slipped into your hands.
Mom's job is over, and she has given you the task of placing
down the pieces. When you place the last piece down,
you will call it, "Your Magna Opus."
Naturally, it is not hard to miss Mom's work.
Harvey, I say this with pride...
you are a masterpiece.

Richard Oaxaca

The Girls

I find myself staring — just watching them
I, who never paces myself or slows down — watching
I, who never listens but just acts or reacts —
watching them and smiling
I, who has always put myself first — no one else —
patiently watching
Both of them
"the girls"
my girls
Now as never before, I stop and observe
every fleeting moment, every magic movement
I'm staring,
they're changing — every day.
Growing, touching, feeling,
taking in all — like petals opening to a spring rain
really living, sparkling
full of energy — always
as an overwound toy
my best friends —
my daughters

Sherry Salant

Why...

Why Another day goes by, and I can't remember why I
climbed this tree in the first place? I think it was because I
wanted to catch the Butterfly. If I jump now, will I fall,
or will I fly? Why the Creator made me different?
Every time I ask Him, "why"? I get no answer; just the
windy breeze that makes me close my eyes.
Why I close my eyes? Now, I cannot only
fly, I can touch the sky.

Kathy Anne Ispan

Friendship

It is a bond people share
A bond as strong as wild horses stampeding violently into the night
A bond so strong that it holds people together through a lifetime

At the same time gentle, pure, innocent
Gentle as a flower petal touching the surface of the water
Pure as emeralds and pearls
Innocent as a newborn lying in its mothers arms

It is a love that grows
As patient as a mother teaching her child
Some never leave — they are always there waiting to be remembered
It knows when it is needed the most
It is one of the greatest forces on earth —
It is called Friendship.

Janet Schneider

Inspiration

Inspire me,
    allow your thoughts to become my words
    let me speak through your mind.
    Put the visions you see into my eyes
    touch the emotions I am unable to feel,
Inspire me.
    Guide your wisdom into my soul
    express the enchanted treasures you hold
    outpour your dreams into my spirit
    let me roam through your imagination,
Inspire me.
    Excite me with your passion
    caress my hand with a story
    glide with my fingers across the naked sheet of paper
    bring alive what I can not experience,
Inspire me.

Cristin L. Dooley

Try

Try being humble, instead of bold
Someday it will help you save your soul.
Try being patient, and more understanding
You'll find out life is not so demanding
Try out love, instead of hate
You'll find happiness is never late.
Try out a smile, instead of a frown
It enhances your ability to show off your crown.
Try seeing the inner beauty, instead of just the outer.
You'll gain a true friendship, never a doubter.
If you try out these try's, you'll have no more strife.
Happiness will be with you, for the rest of your life.

Rheola E. Clark

Friendly and Caring Guy

I am a friendly and caring guy
I wonder if others feel the same
I hear the ocean rush up to shore
I see the sea gulls soar over me
I want to bury my feet in the sand
Now I'm a friendly and caring young man

I pretend to watch the sun go down
I feel the breeze as it blows in my face
I touch the water as the wave breaks on to shore
I worry that someday the ocean won't be there anymore
I cry about nothing much at all
I am a friendly and caring young man

I understand that we won't be here someday
I say that's just God's way
I dream about lots of things
I try to bare those scary dreams
I hope we never have to say good-bye
I am a friendly and caring guy

Rhett Fielding Farless

Rain

Why does it rain?
Does it rain because the clouds are crying?
Does it rain because the earth is drying?
Does it rain because my pool is empty?

When it rains going outside is very tempting.
I want to do cartwheels on the wet, shiny grass,
in bright yellow slicker, galoshes of red,
and then I get sicker.

Then I have to stay in my bed, all warm and toasty,
but going out in the rain is what I like mostly.

Emilie H. Richard-Froozan

Learning

Until my steps are certain
Let me not tread in soft cement
Until my thoughts are pure and kind
Let me not try to teach.
Until my hands are soft and caring
Let me not try to comfort loved ones
Until I see the beauty in everything and everyone
Let me not think I see all things
Then and only then will I know I am
　　on my way to learning

Gwenyth Snyder

Happy Birthday!!!

Treasures are wonderful,
gold is too.
Money and jewelry are great,
silver is too,
but everyone should treasure one thing most,
that one thing should be your mom.
The one thing I treasure most is
You!
I love you!

Marteen Helms

Peer Pressure

I am so plain,
Yet I am so different.
I have so much to give,
But so little to offer.

If people can't see beyond my skin,
How will they know what lies within?
That's the problem with the world today,
The only thing that matters is what others say.

Now where am I to go?
Please give me a sign.
Show me where it all began,
And where I can start again.

People change!
You have to give them a chance.
It's like a book and its cover,
You can never tell at first glance.

Jackie Dupuis

Selective Thoughts Can Bury A Man

When Daddy just screams louder,
remember what he says.
When Daddy says he hates you,
forget he ever loved.
When Daddy takes away your armor and rips apart your shield,
remember you still have a sword, something he can feel.
When Daddy makes you leave,
forget why you ever stayed.
When Daddy finally feels better,
remember you still ache.
When Daddy tries to kiss it all away,
forget how to forgive.
When Daddy switches roles with you,
remember what he can feel.
When Daddy says he's sorry,
just stay calm and stare.
When Daddy begs for his own life,
remember you don't care.

Jamie M. Ferri

God's Wonderful World

The sky so blue, like an ocean deep
with clouds riding high o'er a mountain peak

A field of mustard where a tree grows strong
and a meadow with cows ambling along

White birches look down on the swirling foam
while birds fly along cliffs, hastily to home

The fragrance of blossoms fills the air
with promise of fruits, for our taste buds fair

The sun smiles down on us with cheer
and we know another year of wonders is here.

Jayne Keeler

In Memory of My Friend

It was late in August when I saw her last.
The evening sun had found her room,
Etching her body; frail, wisp-like, in its glow.
Her eyes, dull and faded, — searched for mine,
Eyes, where recognition came,
 and then was gone.
All struggle had ended.
There remained a kind of peace,
 a quiet lingering . . .
As if she were standing in the wings
Waiting for the Intermission to end.

Then, a day later, — the last act, —
Her curtain call, her final bow.
There she lay, surrounded
Midst embankments of flowers;
Fragrant blossoms she so loved, . . .
"Listening" to the subdued applause
Of those who knew and loved her,
Of those who shared the script
Of the saga of her ninety-four years.

Eleanor Keener Carnahan

Nature's Unbridled Power

Hot, sultry days;
The sun's penetrating rays.
Palm trees swaying;
Spanish guitars playing.
Emerald calm seas
A breeze...

From a breeze to frenzied winds;
The ocean rages.
Waves crashing into solid, white foam this night;
Clothes pressed against me,
My hair in flight.
My now naked body with up stretched hands;
I give myself to the wind gods.

My cries of glee, wonderment and ecstasy
are lost in the wind.
As his arms are around me
two bodies become one with the universe.
Behold natures unbridled power
on a secluded beach in the midst of a hurricane.
It was but a moment in time . . .

Teresa McKenzie Seay

Untitled

One day far from now we will all pass on
And we will become part of
the earth so really we'll live on
Everyday the sun will rise and
at dusk it will go down
And when the day is done at
last I sit and think and then I frown
Something is missing from my
life but what I do not know
I know however that I am
here and in the direction I
want is the way I will go.

Talia Payne

My Lord Above

Only one can hear my thankful prayers.
Only one can know my painful thoughts.
Only one can keep me from drowning in my ocean.
Only one can calm my beating heart.
Only one can direct my paths.
Only one can be a lamp unto my feet.
Only one can carry my weary flesh.
Only one can haunt my sunlit dreams.
Only one can watch over my bedside.
Only one can be my guardian angel.
Only one can own my beautiful world.
Only one can make my soul glow like sunshine.
Only one can teach and show me my love.
Only one can be my true love.
Only one can have a cross as holy.
My only one, can only be, my Savior.
In Jesus name I pray, Amen.

Stephanie L. Berry

Goodbye

Goodbye, cruel words, they are,
Which yet, may deal a kindly blow,
Cutting into lonesome hearts
While binding others firm and fast,
Scattering dreams of times to come,
Shattering a romance full of hope
While molding another from out the ruins.
Goodbye, with a mighty arm,
Strong with love, wild with passion
Wields its crushing force from afar.

One hears these words with unwilling sigh:
Goodbye! You have tarried long enough,
Must hurry on with reluctant tread,
Make way for others, for faces new,
New personalities to thrill, to feel,
New depths of passion to perceive!
Off with the old, on with the new!
Such is the cry of youthful hearts
Destroying the altar with resounding crash.
Powerful, those kind, cruel words: Goodbye!

Henry R. Alderman

The World Around Me

When all the world around me
Is filled with dirtiness, doom and despair,
There seemed to me to be only one answer
And that was to go to God in prayer.

Yet in school I wasn't allowed to pray;
During the day I knew not where to turn.
There there existed such rough and rowdiness
My heart dismayed; a longing within me did burn.

Home time was shortened by the bustle
And business of everyday strife.
So I sought to gleen an answer
To a more fulfilling and happier life.

What could I do my heart would ask
To get this burden under control,
And give the world around me another chance;
A long-searching, thankless, yet ultimate goal.

Well, God came to me in spoken words
So eloquent, clear and sweet.
The Bible he'd given me long ago
To study, to obey, to make my life complete.

Gloria B. Gammons

Love

Love is a strange thing
  it can make you do most anything
And when it's all gone
  it all feels so wrong
  but your life is not a song
People say, "Don't worry, you'll find someone new."
  but in your heart you know it's not true
'Cause the one you love has found someone else
  and you'll have to find someone for yourself,
  'cause he'll never feel the same for you.
But if you think this all true
  then something's the matter with you
'Cause if it were true, it will happen
But while he's off having fun
  trying to find the right one
You have to be strong
  and try to move on
Don't let him break your heart again.

Jessica Secco

Ask Me Not If God Was There

I saw your sky blue eyes open and I knew you were dead
I did not see the gaping hole at the back of your head
Ask me not if God was there

The police said after you were gone "Someone needs to clean"
Our friend appeared and said "How can I help?", sight unseen
Ask me not if God was there

From Cindy I wanted flowers for your casket and I bawled
It was her day off, but she came in as I called
Ask me not if God was there

Tuesday, Wednesday, and Thursday nights your friends came
We shared happy memories, none the same
Ask me not if God was there

We knew no one from the church where after the funeral we held a
  dinner
We showed a video of you and it was a winner
Ask me not if God was there

As darkness fell last night
I saw you in the setting sunlight
Ask me not if God was there

Nancy Lee

Wild Flowers

Wild flowers grow in great abundance, we see them everywhere
They are tended by God's hand and nurtured with great care
Neither rain, flood, storm or drought, could His garden destroy
If you ever my word doubt, just look around, watch them sprout
Sorrow cannot dim their beauty, through hardship they prevail
The winds their appointed guardians multiply them by their gale
Through deep valleys dark with despair, reflecting trial and pain
Watch those tenacious wild flowers break ground and rise again
You can step on them time after time, think you rubbed them out
Don't walk away too quickly for you haven't won the bout
They are destined to bloom forever on the hillsides of mankind
As an ever constant reminder from every struggle we can survive

Janice Weaver Johnson

The Ride

As I go on the roller coaster of love....
Ups, downs, and spins about...
Thrilling and fulfilling...
Takes my breath away.
Careless and cautious....
Not thinking of that moment...
Rampant thunders roll through my head...
Before you know it, the ride is over!!

Trinity Busch

On the Way to Vietnam . . . .

I departed from you (like)
Birds waving their wings
(our hands waved sweet in the wind)

And then were gone . . . .

Then jet plane landed at (Ft. Sam Houston)
  . . . . Who knows?
No signs . . . Only a beach, and I got off
and it took off
only I left.

Lone sand beach hot before me it
  buoyed me up — I floated over the
  sand on heat waves —
I spoke and saw my words float off on
those heat waves —
They made No Noise.
They floated off and to the sand sunk in
And were gone.

William Ehlers

Beauty Debt

We're held in debt to beauty, for grandeurs essence bliss,
  Which things snare sight to hesitate,
  and linger in a vision's kiss....
Of natural earthly springing, and still defying man,
  with aid to sculpture dreaming....
  ...warm colors of the land.

To flowers and to waterfalls that scatter
  shards of light,
To cries of wolves in canyon halls
  that fall on too few ear,
To moonlight coins of silver sparkle
  dancing madly on the sea
Oh wonders such of earthly treasure...
...which wealth holds debt to you and me.

Such splendor riches we take for granted,
  which wealth holds debt to you and me.

Kenneth Moore

Leaving It All Behind

I walked down the street one cold evening,
Snow fell heavily around me.
All of my troubles, it seemed had began steeping.
So with bags in hand I started to flee.

Where would I go? I did not care,
At this point anywhere was better than here.
But I couldn't go back, I didn't dare,
My heart and mind were filled with fear.

What had become of the world that I had known?
In such a short time it all fell apart.
The hostility between us had grown and grown,
They couldn't live with me, time for a fresh start.

Jon Matteson

What Went Wrong?

No one knows what went wrong
Were days too short or nights too long
Was there not enough to eat
For herbivores, no leaves
For carnivores, no meat
Was there too much heat
Or snow under their feet?
Scientist are studying the great defeat
I might have been a feast
But I wish I could have met
One of the great beast
If a tyrannosaurus rex stomped by
I know I would soon retreat
And look for help in the sky
A friend from long ago
Above me a pterodactyl fly's
And carries me to a place I did not know.
But still no one knows what went wrong
Was it as simple as
Days too short nights too long!

Brandon Patterson

Starbright, Starbright

Starbright, Starbright you worked with me to be all that I might . . .
There were many times you brought me to screams and tears,
only to help conquer my fears. You pushed me to try, and sometimes
    hurt my pride....
You yelled and you pushed and I often fell on my tush;
but you always took such pride in even the smallest of my strides.
The worst time for me, was that, that I spent in PT.
It started with stretching then crawling, but then there was falling.
With accomplishments came our rewards, unfortunately, Paul always
    took away the swords.
But that was okay, because we still got to play the swings and the
    balls,
and of course the scooter in the hall, and if you were really good,
    they took you to the mall!
Then one day Dr. Karnick walks in with a smile, "I have great news!
    You have proved everybody wrong, soon you can go home where
    you belong"
From then on the days went fast. The party was planned,
there would be juices and cheers, there would be pictures and tears.
The final night had come . . . As I lie in my bed,
staring out the window over my head,
I saw the 1st star of the night and I realized, my wish had come true,
Starbright had helped me to be just as good if not like brand new!!

Amber Laird

The One

I look into her eyes and my heart begins to melt and the tears
began to fall and I know it's her. I try to tell her yet my words
become paralyzed as they try to escape my heart. I love her so
dearly and would give my life for her. I gaze at her from a far as
she gracefully prances to her destination. I constantly wish for
the courage to tell her of these locked away emotions that I have
held so long for an eternity it seems. Yet I hesitate again for I
can't help but wonder is she even knows I exist. I know one thing
to be true being the blue bird when all the rest are adored for
being red is the true irony of my life. I somehow don't believe
that she will mind for I have a plan to win the fair Swans heart.
I call her this because of her elegance and grace. I shall win her
from afar and when her love is mine she won't care that I am the
blue bird. I shall ask her and rest my heart. For in a days time
the entire world can change if you believe.

William O. Gray

Woman

A woman should never
with cracked high heels
and dusty mascara runnin' down her cheeks
go trudging uphill
for some man
and go breakin' her soul

Dierdre Malaika Freamon

Love

The meaning of Love some people may never know.
Love is a word unspoken, but you'll hear it wherever you go.
But to love one another, it is not love alone.
It's to give up and sacrifice for one of your own.

Love has so many different meanings
I doubt if I can tell you them all.
My personal opinion of one without love
is a person with no heart at all.

For it is an entirely different kind of love that you
may have for your sister, brother, father or mother.
Love is companionship, feeling and understanding
two people have for one another.

Ellis F. Bishop

Spring, Then Autumn

Where are you, Father?
Spring and this pleasant
Weather are looking for you.
Where will I find you?
The wind is cloudy and
So wonderful, where are you?

On every step of my wishes,
And my true respect...
The only existence is of yours,
And your loving shadows.
Without you, Spring
Is very sad and lonely...

Whenever flowers will bloom,
My poetry shall call for you.
I've already titled my services -
And my life's your property, too.
Where are you dear, Father?
Autumn, and my loneliness are looking for you...

Amber Masood

Sent From Heaven

A prayer was answered the sixth of September,
A prayer your folks will well remember.

God said, "I have a toy for you, from Heaven,
Take this boy and name him Kevin.

This little darling was theirs to keep.
This little angel they love so deep.

Your baby is four an age that's great,
But, oh too soon, he will be eight.

He will be grown up much too fast.
But your memories will last and last.

It's almost more than one can stand,
To see their son become a man.

Kevin, God loves you, He loves you really,
To give you parents like Corkey and Billie.

Joanne Tipping Sterling

True Love

In the autumn of my life,
You create in me a springtime of truth
With joy unexcelled
Even in the bloom of my youth!
William Garth Seegmiller

A Prayer

Oh God, let me die whole

Not with my bowels and
Bladder out of control.

Not lame -
Not insane -
Not with paralysis torturing
my brain.

Not maimed!
Not lame!

Oh God, let me die whole.
Not blind, not out of
control.

Oh God, let me die whole
Quiet my soul.
Let me die whole.
Carolyn J. Call

The Robin's Song

This morning at the break of dawn
A Robin sang upon my lawn.
'Twas such a happy, springy sound,
I stepped bare foot out on the ground.

The grass felt cool beneath my feet,
All my neighbors were still asleep.
The Robin stopped his merry song
And left me standing there alone.

I walked to where the tulips bloom,
I knew the world would waken soon.
Busy people would walk the street
And I'd put shoes upon my feet.

I'm glad the Robin sang this morn
For in my heart, a prayer was born.
Walking bare foot on the sod
Somehow made think of God.
Hazel C. Bonham

Friendship

Never say goodbye for
No one ever leaves.
Friendship makes a home
in your memory with
the face and voice smiling.
Always ever present, growing,
and changing. But some
how staying the same.
Never say goodbye for
no one ever leaves.
They maybe life worth living
and they are worth
dying for. But friendship
never dies it stands the
test of time and can never fade.
never say goodbye for
no one ever leaves
Heather Nord

Heaven With Me . . .

Do you want to come to Heaven with me, so beautiful and so close for me love?

I am so tired and wanting to pass on . . .
    Yet why has he held me on for so long?

He has his reasons this I know . . . matters not any more because
    soon I will go. Do you want to come to heaven with me?

Please put me to bed so I may rest, I have a long journey that I must
    test . . . Yet he is right here guiding the way . . . comforting
    me . . . today is my day.

Do you want to come to heaven with me?

People are near, Lord knows I have not seen them in years! They have
    passed on long before . . . chills surpassing as my husband is at
    my door.

Oh how young and handsome his face please do not look at me wrinkles
    every place! Alas I hear a clamoring bell . . . I am young again,
    and in my darlings arms...weightless, breathless, and kept from all harm.

I have waited for such a long time . . . Heaven has me now, out of
    sight, but not out of mind.

Do you want to come to heaven with me?
Susan Lyn Pastorino

Apathy

I have a disease that lets me see, what is wrong out numbering what is right.
With eyes opened wide, I see the darkness steadily overtaking the light.

The more I see, the less I feel. Hardening my heart and turning my head,
to the dying world around me. Playing the part of the 'Spiritually dead."

Some say, "Charity begins at home". Or haven't you heard?
I must take care of my own. This is what I have learned.

It's far too dangerous to get involved with a world that may step on my heart.
Their problems can't be solved, my efforts would surely come to naught.

To this world, I slowly conform. Refusing to loose the ties that bind,
instead of being transformed by the renewing of my mind.

Sweet Holy Spirit, please change me, this fruitless one that I have become.
I no longer want to be helpless to all, and useful to none.

Open my eyes to truly see, the battle raging so fiercely.
Or Lord, please deliver me from the disease of apathy!
J. L. Kessler

Lone Hawk

Brown and gold with a splash of black, a tail of red, colors
mottled down his back. With feathers splayed, he rides the wind,
grace and beauty abound with in.

He circles eyes focused, watching for prey, the slightest movement
will reveal the way. Effortlessly, gracefully, always in tune, sadly
his environment will be gone soon.

No distractions can deter his unerring ways as he searches for food
in the morning haze.

Presence of bounty in this desired land will soon disappear at the
hands of man. Talons clenched tightly against his breast, soaring
endlessly without need for rest.

A dip of a wing into a thermal, again he climbs and starts to circle.
He lofts above the canyon walls, to such great heights that he is
amongst the clouds.

Far below the dozers are seen, raping the earth to make it clean.
Clean for who, you may ask, the moguls of shopping malls who come to bask.

This beautiful land so rich and vast, but due to greed will not last.
The Lone Hawk, soaring above, is a symbol of God's Benevolent Love.

Small in stature, giant of heart, we smote the eye of Gods greatest Art.
Thomas F. Ogan

The White Monster of March

You were so fine and gentle, coming down swiftly on that crispy
Saturday evening
Beautiful as ever and depositing softly everywhere,
By midnight you were only thirty six inches tall,
But hundreds of miles in length and breadth, covering thousands of
    villages, towns and cities,
Like a huge white Octopus spreading its webbed tentacles,
You held hard from Keys to Kennybunkport, and from Sandy Hook right
    into the Midlands.

The next day, the cold bright Sunday morning, revealed the lost lives
and broken families,
Ruined houses and hidden cars, the blocked roads, avenues and highways
The damaged crops and stranded planes, and everything to a complete standstill,
And the ailing economy pushed deeper into recession.

Why you so nasty, is it to warn an ungrateful world,
For polluting the air, mother earth and sea.
And when will the world will see and realize, the acid rain, the hole
    in the Ozone layer, and the inedible fish,
To this, should we add you the great White monster,
As the reminding alarm of a hastening doom of the final human destiny!

Hassim M. Illyas

I Came to See

Black on black, the tempest loomed, the shroud of terror that only I knew.
Like the roaring cascade of the largest of falls, the sound continued, on and on.
"A dream, a dream" my mind screamed, though I leapt from my bed, awake
    as I had ever been.
Though I saw all around, with the lights turned on, black on black the image imposed.
Like the snow on a channel, dead long ago, the image continued, on-and-on.
Not white on black did the image loom, but black on black where ever I ran.
Of something else I tried imagine, but all I could hear was the
    deafening roar, all I could see was black on black.
The roaring fall poured on and on, drowning each new thought I tried
    to think, though I reeled from room to room, from floor to floor.
This was a place where there was no peace.
Panic came as fast as the flood, my stomach churning as I suddenly
    saw, the equation I was did not equate, and I realized that I was no more.
I saw eternity and shook like a leaf, as I came to realize the blinding truth.
Eternal separation apart from light, a numbing terror with no end in sight.
"Cast into the outer darkness where there is weeping and gnashing of teeth."
I knew this was something I could choose to avoid.
Dreams come to an end, and this was no dream.

Mark Erickson

Price of Passion

When bodies of heat collide on impulse, things of unexpectance may occur....
Whether it's the sweet touch of tender lips or the delicious
    sounds of bodies clapping
Sometimes it's hard, but not really impossible to picture a price
    on love or passion
But in the minds of the prominent ones it's all reality!
Getting involved in an intimate battle can somewhat be tiring (In a sense)
But as you and I know, passion has never let us down on the first attempt
The beauty of the price to pay is very rewarding and provocative,
    it's also not abusive to respond
In such a way that it will be forbidden-but yet assessable and beautiful
Even though to some people, passion has costed someone's valuable treasure
In which in turn, can never be spent or reimbursed
Lost to society, founded and burnt by an abstract; shaped and molded
    by God of the universe
These several elements of passion, love, envy, emotions, etc.
Are all molded and shaped into a situation we call "hard to
comprehend" on a weak-minded aspect
Let's take action, this whole entire scenario, which is basically true
Is developed by someone who's been there, and is continuing his
    mission in the valuable field of... the price of passion!

Jey Wright

Was

Now is this moment
Becoming that moment
Becoming history
Not to be repeated.

What is repeat
Can anything be repeated
Be the same
Again
Identical
One can believe
There will
Be a difference
Slight at first glance
Maybe significant at second
Or never a difference.

Either way
Whatever it is
Whenever it is
As soon as it is
It is was.

Gurdon Woods

My Garden

I've a garden, all hidden away
That shines like a star, both
night and day

Mottled greens, and hues of
pink

Quiet scene, to dream and
think

Make this a place, you'd love
to know

For lovers to haste, and flowers
to grow

It is a pleasure, the nicest
of sorts

My garden's a treasure, the
best place on earth

A. E. Vázquez

For Millie

You ask that I write for you
    What I feel I feel for you,

That as I so deeply love you
    How can I clearly tell you,

Or for that matter show you
    That I indeed not only need you,

But more - I fully want you
    For only you are my you.

For me - no one but you,
    My every day - always with you,

My every night - always beside you,
    My life - no life without you.

And I feel that I now do see
    That this is how you feel for me.

James P. Buckley

Sis

When I need kindness, she is there.
She's my best friend you see.
All my pain I know she'll share.
She'll always be there for me.

A sister is a gentle thing.
I love my sis a lot.
A comfort when harsh words sting.
She's the best friend that I've got.

She builds me up when I am down.
She shows her love each day.
When I need laughter, she'll be a clown.
She knows just what to say.

I can't let another day go by
Without letting my sis know
My love for her is as big as the sky,
Though sometimes it don't show.

Don't ever doubt my love for you
I hope you know it's true,
And if you're feeling sad or blue
I'll be right there for you.

Jane Hutchison

Children Will Be Children

Children will be children
how long will it last?
Till you see them differently
then it's in the past.

So enjoy your child
if only for a while
because they grow so fast
it seems to never last.

Remember when you sang to them
the lullabies to sleep?
Now they sing to you
and make you want to weep.

There's one more thing I'd like to say
before this night's end.
To thank you all for sharing them with me
Their Kindergarten Teacher and friend.

Shirley Ann Ramos

Butterfly Magic

I went to my window this morning
And couldn't believe my eyes,
A lovely old cedar tree
Had blossomed over night.

I watched as these blossoms opened,
And seemed swaying in the breeze,
The color was delightful,
Gold and brown among the green.

I watched awhile longer,
And wondered all the while
From whence these lovely blossoms came,
To bring my life a smile.

Soon blossoms left the tree in pairs,
As graceful as could be,
And, behold, they were Monarch butterflies,
Nature's majesties!

Marjorie Kramer

No! Celebrate Life

Celebrate Life you say?

What do I celebrate? My life being threatened, my choices taken away?
How do you celebrate the loss of a breast? How do you Celebrate Life
when all you think of its death?

Why does God forsake me?

Why do I have to pay?

That is what cancer does—it eats your hope away.

NO! Celebrate LIFE

Now, as it is, your struggle will be hard, your journey long, but don't bury
yourself until the last breath is gone! God loaned your body to you with
intent to bring you home — how He does it is His choice alone. Celebrate
Life, in the children you bear, the memories you've made and the
battles you've won.

God never forsakes us, He fights to make us strong. When your body is weak,
celebrate the life you're fighting to keep.

Find joy in each day and comfort through the night. And when the sun smiles
a new dawn —

Celebrate Your Life.

Hope Estes

Just Wanted to Say Good-Bye

Our hearts are heavy and we will miss you so and we ask the
question — why did you have to go?

We know that you are looking down upon us and trying to wipe our teary
eyes, it's just that you will be missed and it's hard to say good-bye.

God reached out for you so you took his hand. You knew you could not
keep him waiting, you knew you could not change his plans.

We have been blessed to have so many memories of an unforgettable
woman, an unforgettable friend.

Good-Bye . . . .

JoAn Balster

'Cause Now I'm Free

I've always wanted to be free — Free of this Muscular Dystrophy
Free of this wheelchair and hospital bed,
Free to cruise in my car instead.
Free — just to be me!

Free to run and jump and play, to fly a kite on a windy day,
To climb to the top of the tallest tree, or splash like a dolphin in the sea.
To dance with my girl at the Senior Prom,
And work with my dad out on the farm.

But one day God said to me, "I'm sorry Son, but you see,
These things just are not to be,
But soon I'll send my Son for thee, and I promise then, you will be free."

So goodbye Mom, Dad, and Family, you've all taken such good care of me.
I love you all — don't cry for me, I'll be with Jesus, and I'll be free.

Oh, Hi Jesus — Yes, it's me,
I know it's later than you thought I'd be,
But my leaving was so hard on Mom and Dad, the toughest time they've
ever had.
So I stayed awhile to help them know, The time had come to let me go.

That's okay Jesus, you don't have to carry me,
Just hold my hand and walk with me.
I want to run and jump and climb that tall, tall, tree.
Now I can do these things you see, - 'Cause now I'm truly free!

Alexandria M. Stewart

Perspectives of an Immense Journey

Slowly as the sun rises, light echoes in my room,
As the light echoes in my room, somewhere I awake in peace.
Peace comes as I feel the movement of my body and I sense the comfort of my room.
In the comfort of my room, I feel an inspiration to my eyes.
What will this day share with me? What will this beautiful mourning do to me?
As I look into the mirror, my eyes are thoughtful. What revelation do I see?
Do I see the sleep that has enlighten my eyes? Do I see in my eyes the deep sleep?
Somewhere I hear the sounds of spring. Somewhere I hear the sounds of life.
This beautiful sunlight. This beautiful sound. This beautiful me.

Dianne Mehelas

The Month of May

There's nothing like the month of May,
the sun shines most everyday.
The blooming of the flowers, the buzzing of a bee,
make these warm spring days so dear to me.

Randi Lynn Anderson

My Daddy

You didn't have to take me into your life and love me the way in
which you do

You could have left me just like He did and never even think about
who I was or where I was at
    But you chose not to

You were the one that chose to take me into your life as not just
a person, but as your daughter

You have always treated me as though I was your own and not someone else's

You have given me someone that I can look up to with honor and respect

    You are someone that I love!

We have grown closer to one another as the years have gone by, and
even though you have one of your own now, you still have never
stopped loving me and I thank you!

I was afraid she would steal you away from me, but then I realized
no one could ever steal my daddy away; not even his "own" daughter.

Rachel M. Braill

An Educator's Prayer

Grant me the willpower to remain silent when necessary although the
    urge speak may be compelling.

Help me cope with the rude individual in a positive manner,
    refraining from using sarcasm, and curb my pride that I may
    genuinely apologize when in the wrong.

Remind me to give deserved praise often, and enable me to help the
    student develop a good self-image.

Let me not a victim of despair be when plans go not as I had expected.

Inspire me with challenges for the gifted and sincere encouragement
    for the less talented.

Provide me the insight to adjust to diverse personalities in order to
    promote harmonious human relations.

Alert my mind for increased wisdom of subject matter and my heart
    to perceptive techniques in the art of living.

Keep me ever mindful of the dignity of the human soul which houses
    an everlasting spark of the Divinity.

And at the end of the school day, renew my patience and energy that
    I may respond to my own family and their needs.

Above all else, this I ask: grant me the privilege to partake of
    tomorrow and a better person be.

Bobbie Griffin

A Mother's Dream

A dream that began at conception
A dream that never ends
Sometimes we are not sleeping
Sometimes a mother pretends

A mother's hopes and dreams
A mother's only wish
The child she conceives
will live a life of pure happiness

Dreams are only feelings
all emotions felt inside
The last thought of the evening
Dreams and reality sometimes coincide

As stars become bright
we end another night
Reality ends
and in our dreams, we pretend

A mother's dream so pure and simple
is based on only this
A dream come true a child's health
a mother's good night kiss.

Teresa Witteman

Still You Found Me

I ran, limp body in hand
my dried skin, shoes
for your bare soul

I dreamed the dreams
through which your blood runs
careful not to spill

I became the thin brown line
that divides the sea and the sky
visible only from afar

Still you found me uncaring

I blended myself
a puree of flesh and courage
manure for your children

I asked the trees
to let me become their trunk
so that I may be needed

I sacrificed the womb
that bears your praises
hides your short-comings

Still you found me repulsive.

Millicent Emmitt

Christmas Cheers

Christmas is almost here again
bringing lots of toys, and lots of cheer
it soon will, be the end of the year
Santa work, hard all, night long
so we can play his favorite song.

When it cold and damp out side
then we shall, have a sense of pride.
We sing with joy and lots of songs
and I hope and pray we do no wrong.
We bake, cookies and bread and
apple pie. And then we all say goodbye.
After wrapping all, the gift and
giving thank, to God giving out
present alone with all the cards
we call it a night and go
our way settling in for the next big day.

Johnnie M. Parker

Untitled

Through all the years,
and all the tears
You've stood right by my side
Through all the fights,
and sleepless night
You were there.
When I was depressed,
only you could've guessed
what it was I needed to hear.
And when I couldn't explain
How I felt all this pain,
you made my confusion seem clear,
We both may change,
our lives rearranged
But our friendship never ends.
So through the hard times
look back on my rhymes
for we will always be
The best of friends.

Catheryn Janeane Eisaman

Little Miss Hurricane

She roars through the house,
  all in a whirl.

Elbows and knees a blur.
  Her head starts to twirl.

Nothing is safe from this
  bundle of bustle.

Pets quake, the house shakes,
  from her gotta go hustle.

Toys fly and books tumble...
  listen now, there is a rumble.

Stronger than an earthquake!
  Gustier than a typhoon!

Can't tie her to a stake...
  more trouble than a monsoon!

Chattering up a storm,
  she is faster than lightning.

Oh my gosh, she's only two...
  This is really frightening!

Carol M. Davis

Out of the Cave

Come out of your cave
dry your tears; face your fears
the world is in your view

Come out of your cave
light a spark; emerge from the dark
and make your debut

Come out of your cave
dawn of change; feels cold and strange
warm it up to you

Come out of your cave
make your move; carve your groove
there's so much to pursue

Come out of your cave
it's been years; face your fears
start your life anew.

Come out of your cave
be brave.

Henrietta L. Hodge

A Fantasy

Sand appears fickle
Without an apparent care.
It's not dependable;
Blows here, there and everywhere.

Sand is hot in the sunshine,
Gritty in the rain.
Its popular appeal
Is difficult to explain.

It sticks to your sunscreen,
Gets caught in your suit.
Why people seek it,
Is hard to compute.

It must be the illusion
Of the romantic sea
That beckons us
To endure sandy "reality."

Carolyn Ashley

Mr. Moon

Hello Mr. Moon
shining brightly
on me as I lay in
bed. You tuck me in bed at
night with a smile.
Thank you Mr. Moon

Julia E. Smith

Untitled

I have two sisters who are great
I could not bring myself to hate
They make me laugh - they make me cry
They're both the apple of my eye
I love them both so very much
And I'm so glad we keep in touch
We share a hug - we share a kiss
It's nice to say "How are you sis"

Doris Evanko

Do Unto Others

It's do unto others
  In a most helpful way
It's sharing and caring
  Through out every day.
Opening windows
  To sunbeams of joy
Creating rainbows
  For those we employ —
Giving light heart
  To the sick and the weary
Spreading the sunshine
  When days are dreary;
Helping another
  With a load to bear
Being a friend
  Showing you care;
A smile or a hug
  A word of good cheer
Magical moments
  For all of us here.

Nancy R. Nichols

A Friend

When I was little
I needed a friend,
And I knew you'd be with me
until the end.

We've gone through fights
and many tears,
Together we'll both conquer
all of our fears.

The places we've gone,
the times we've shared,
Showed how much
the both of us cared.

Into the darkness
or out in the sun,
The two of us
have become one.

We know in our heart
no one could ever be,
As close and as dear
as you are to me.

Jody Armstrong

Accident

Green. Stop. Stop. Stop. Stop.
Yellow. Stop. Stop.
Red. Stop. Stop. Stop. Stop.
Black. Blue.
Red. Red. Red.
Stop.

Monica Chen

Waiting for Recovery

As the busy working men's
feet go by in the quiet
of day, I rest and think
that I have passed that way.

And when I rise with my chores
list long and full all
my efforts and fleeting foot
compare none to the work day.

And as in my dilemma things mounting
before me I still look for an
easier step to get me by
for a days accomplishment of much.

So far and so long a work men's
day, I admire all that I have
done that past me that way.
I am longing for the work men's day.

Christopher J. Woodcheke

Looking Through the Smoke

I look through the smoke
as if it were a window
into my soul.
I stare at what I find
a reflection, I suppose
no one else knows
I care for what I see
to get nothing back
is only fair
I feel it all collide
in that place I stare
the smoke of nowhere

Roy Michael Renolds

268

Confused

Confused in this world I'm in,
thinking with no thoughts.
Confused watching the word get thin,
as my brain ties in knots.

Confused with decisions I'll make,
questions unanswered with no tone.
Confused with my life I will take?
Feelings felt unknown.

Confused, left alone,
not knowing my dream.
Confused with no guidance, no moan,
boring as it may seem.

Confused nor lonely or sad,
left with no direction in life.
Confused with myself I am mad.
With my hand holding this knife.

Jen Cole

Just A Thought

Why is this man
my father?
Why is this woman
my mother?
Maybe I chose them
as somebody said,
or perhaps it was my destiny
or better yet,
not what I think
or believe,
but a logic or random conclusion
of a natural phenomenon
of this Universe.

I'm not sure,
but in my opinion
I was in their own
passionate paradise,
a fruit of their exciting experience.

Agustin M. Ramos

The Card

This card was very special
   I made it all by hand,
But the one for whom I made it
   Is now in heavens band.

I made the picture on it
   And wrote the verse for her,
But she never saw the picture
   And the words she never heard.

The card was to say I loved her
   And to see if she loved me,
She never knew about it
   It just wasn't meant to be.

I hope it from heavens portals
   She chances to look down on me,
That somehow our heavenly father
   This card will let her see.

Kate MayBerry

Escape from Reality

I walk down the narrow trail
to my secret hiding space.
With sandy shore and willows nigh
a rippling stream rushes by.
A place so wonderful to see.
I know God made it just for me.

The cares of the day are washed away
as I place my feet into the stream,
then close my eyes and begin my dreams.
I can do anything my heart desires.
My thoughts soar high
I spread my wings
I can even fly.

I awake with a start
as falling leaves brush my face
and minnows nibble on my toes
I come back to earth, and know
my dreams must now come to a close.

Priscilla Hurt

Phonemes

Bwah-bwah bwah-bwah bwah-bwah
...
Mmm mm mm mmmm
Eeeeeeeeeeeeeeeeeeeeeee!
Uhhhh bu bu bu bu bwah-bwah-bwah
...
Fffthhhhhppppppwah Ma-ma-ma
Ooooooooooh...eeeeeeeeeeeeeeeeeeee!
Heh-heh-heh-heh
Heh
Heh
Heh.

Sophie W. Downes

Grandma's Rose Bud

You're Grandma's little rose bud
Jesus sent from up above.
You're Grandma's little rose bud
Jesus sent for me to love.

Jesus knew I needed something
to brighten up my life,
so he picked from his garden
the prettiest rose and gave it life.

As I sat that night
and watched you being born,
I thanked God for the miracle
only he could perform.

From the top of your head
to your tiny little toes,
I knew only God could create
a perfect little rose.

As you grow, always remember
that Jesus loves you too.
He has chosen a special angel
just to watch over you!

Grandma Black

Parents

A parent has to raise their boys to be
men, girls to be women.
We have to correct them,
give them rest, love and a spiritual
up bring. The child will not forget
their mother's teachings, and their
father's commands. Our delight
is when they become parents.

Tammy Priest

Taker Or Giver

Life's miseries, life's pains,
gang-banging, dope slanging,
drug use, child abuse,
It's all a strain on my brain.
My momma's a junkie.
My daddy's in jail.
It's a strain on my brain;
I feel like I'm in hell.
They're all takers.
Help me God, increase my faith,
take me out of this miserable space.
And He came to me like a light,
He gave me the courage,
to win the fight.
He gave me hope and the will to live,
And my life has gotten better,
and I'm able to give.

Kim Borges

Water of Life

Down the mountain valleys it runs.
Glistening in the everlasting sun.
Starting at a cool spring,
Rushing down to meet the sea.

From spring to river,
from lake to sea.
As our lives from birth to death,
So is water from spring to sea.

Joshua James Cuta

God Knew We Needed Someone

God knew we needed someone,
with a lot of qualities,
that would understand our problems,
and would get down on their knees.

And pray for God to guide us,
and keep us in his way,
and help us to obey his word,
as we face the world each day.

And so God gave us Mothers,
to be our special friend,
who will love us and adore us,
to the very end.

To the memory of some,
and to the honor of all others,
we thank God for giving us,
our Wonderful, wonderful, mothers.

Alice I. Waugaman

Heaven

Blue is the color of the heavens,
Blue lies all around the stars,
Blue is the color I see,
When I'm looking afar.

Come and be with me,
Or take me away,
Up where it is blue,
On this heavenly day.

You are the king,
And the chosen one,
I am just a pauper,
Just a daughter or a son.

I often look at the stars,
And wonder where you are,
I often look to the skies,
I cannot tell a lie.

But I am not George Washington,
And I am not a Queen,
I will be forever here on earth,
Only me.

Ginger Evelyn Brazzel

An Autumn Country Sunset

There's nothing more beautiful
than an Autumn country sunset.
Forever rolling hills and valleys.
Full of breathtaking falling
leaves from the trees. There burning
red and orange ember colors
for the naked eye to see.
Fall corn fields for miles,
that flow gently in the evening
breeze. I drive farther down
the road to watch the sun
fall beneath the trees.
It's burning red and orange
colors fill the sky and land
beneath. Yet I drive a little
farther, to catch one last glimpse.
It's breathtaking view is gone,
until tomorrow nights glimpse.
There is nothing more beautiful
than an Autumn country sunset.

Nancy Vanhuisen

Peace

Cool summer mornings,
On a clover covered hill.
Dark green leaves overhead
Drip dew into shallow water still.
The sun shimmers thru
Spindly pines in the dale.
Misty fog rises...
Making a hazy lace veil!
Birds fly soundlessly
Thru shadow and light
Reverence prevails
As the sun shines bright!

Alea Barbee

If Only

If only you would touch me
the way you do in my dreams

If only you would hold me
the way I dream of being held

If only you would kiss me
the way my lips long to be caressed

If only your heart would feel
the passion that burns in mine

If only you would love me
the way I could love you

If only our time together
could last longer

If only . . .

    I had a chance.
Georgia Scott

Baby Jeremy

We didn't get to pass a ball,
or swing, or bat a ball.
We didn't have much time with
you, before the angels call.
We never got to say good-bye
before you went away, but in
our hearts you'll stay with us
until our dying day.
We never got to do a lot,
but in heaven you will know
the angels on the playing field
and you're the center glow . . . .

Denise K. Stamm

Ball Park

"Let's play ball," I said
One day. I was worried
That I would get out.
But then Home Run.
Boy, I was surprised.
We were in the field.
One out, two outs, three
Outs. We were up to bat
Again. Oh no, I was up.
Strike one, strike two,
Slam! I hit that ball
As hard as I could.
Home run. We won the game.

Katrina Wingle

Untitled

Love's lonely light
Burns deeply
somewhere
A heart yearns
For all kind
To believe
There's a chance
for lovin'
Every child
Singin'
Mummin'
livin' a life
of love
and peace.

Clayton Marshall Culley

Where Is My Son?

The streets are bare
    and the grass is long
Gosh...everything is silent
    something must be wrong

Hush...hush..
    No one speaks
Mouths have been shut
    for the past few weeks

Kids are by their parents
    but one has been stolen
Every ones eyes seem closed
    with no one know-in

It's a small town
    Yet no one saw?
Did it with ease
    without one flaw . . .

Finding evidence
    there is none
The parents wonder
    where is my son?

Joanna Tessier

Ocean Blue

Calm me ocean blue
like a warm mother's arms.
Let me feel serenity
with your magic and your charms.
Splash your waves upon me
and tantalize my skin.
Grant me peace and happiness
and comfort from within.
Watch me every moment
that I lay upon your shores.
Teach me to respect you
as you open up your doors.
Try to understand me
as I share my thoughts with you.
Help me to enjoy life
and "Calm me Ocean Blue."

Raye A. Brittain

The Gift . . .

'Tis Christmas three, this holiday
But two as man and wife
I bare my only gift to you
For once in all my life

With all that is within me
Is all that I'll remain
In hopes and dreams forever
Like an endless flowing chain

A golden band of honor
Encircled through with trust
Exchanged our gifts of sharing
This yuletide time for us

On Christmas three, I give you
Eyes that will not cry
With promise through eternity
Of lips that will not lie

I cannot wrap, nor place a bow
On these emotions from above
The greatest gift, I'll give to you
Will always be my love

Vicki Wellman-Gray

Grandpa

In our hearts he'll always stay
Throw all your sorrows and fears away
He left us without a doubt
His hell on earth has went about
Even though we'll miss him so
His spirit will always come and go
It's hard to believe that he'll be gone
But that's okay we won't be alone
So wipe your tears and dry your eyes
Then maybe it won't be so hard to say
   Goodbye
   Mollie Scoggins

The Lie

The invocation
Of deception
Emotion blazes
The pain deepens
The voice raises
The heart weakens
The words are too soft
The touch too gentle
The kiss is lingering
The body arches
The soul is bare
Your victory dance
   Kristine Kindland

Prisoner

Sunlight casting diamonds into the sea
In my dream
Bright bouquets, sprays and clusters
In my dream
Fluent, eloquent, whispering voices
In my dream
A fondle, caress, a touch so gentle
In my dream

Light repelling murky waters
Fields of lifeless ironweed
Shattering cacophonies
Heavy hands upon my shoulders
As I wake,
Hurry sundown
   Ray Santangelo

Ocean Blue

The creatures
and the sky
make it blue.
The living are free
to roam
the vast deep waters.

The ocean is like
endless space
without a beginning
or an end.
There is life
deep in the blue
where it all began.

At times, I wonder
if this is the place
where it will all end,
but for now,
I must marvel
about the mysteries
of the ocean blue.
   Michael J. Goluza

A Father's Love

Though you're really not her father
you don't just belong to me
you weren't there on her birthday
nor the day she was conceived

Do you realize she loves you?
Can you see you through her eyes?
Do you know she will turn to you
as the one she sees as wise?

There is nothing more important
than what you choose to share
and what you've given to her
shows just how much you care

You'll be so precious to her
more and more as she grows up
for do you see as I do?
You showed a Father's Love
   Josceline Henrietta Leech

Untitled

They say I build walls
Around me and that is
What keeps them out;
So one day I tore
The walls Down

And they can all see
That I really
Built the wall around
Myself to hide
The fact of my aloneness.

To save them the
Embarrassment of
Simply passing by
Ignoring me
I build walls

So that they can
Pass by and say they
Couldn't reach me
Instead of having to say
They never tried.
   Kathleen Huggins

The King of Manhattan

I saw Him, you see;
It was Jesus of Nazareth,
And American He shall be.
He was the child of poor,
And poor no more,
And the New York media
Went bonkers,
Like children in
A candy store.
Nobody knew who He was,
Who He was indeed,
Yet no one stood sadden,
At the sight of
The King of Manhattan!
   Cesidio Tallini

Canterbury

A mirage, sleeping
in the dust of
gathering years.
Wooded paths and
country lanes, winding
in a crooked mile,
To a forgotten village.
In a fantasy of dreams
A phantom child
remembers the elusive
past, with a sigh,
amidst the golden
drift of decades,
forever itched
in memory.
   Eleanor B. La Fleur

Behold Icarus

Fall waxen winged
From the sun...
Behold Icarus
Thy voyage done...

Repent not
Thy broken flight...
In that swift descent
Unto the night...

Regret not
Thy brief stay...
Forget not
That final day...

No tears be shed
From angel's eyes...
No more be seen
Lost paradise...
   William E. Ault

Floral Query

Can a desert rose,
Its bloom unsmelled,
Now brown and sere
In scorn be held?
   Julian B. Grafa

Reminiscence

Changing amber green
dark shadows and here after
Unfathomable sea
I feel you calling
unspoken words, haunting
calling to me

Far away, a light
faint, distant
a place for dreamers, reminiscent
of new found joy
laughter and green grass
fading, as dreams fade
pallid among the oak trees shade.

Feel my laughter, feel my love
do not send me to my dreams
fleeing as the sun-struck dove
on, on sweet unfathomable sea
my dreams, my love
must come to me..
   Sandy Roberson

Dreams

Oh! To sail the Seven Seas
And fly to far-off lands,
To climb the highest mountains
And walk the desert sands.

To soar above the universe
And play among the stars,
To visit distant galaxies
Or Jupiter and Mars.

To travel back in space and time
To when the world was new,
Explore its many ancient ruins
And marvel at the view.

To accomplish all these feats
Is beyond my reach it seems.
But I can do it all and more.
And how you ask? My dreams!

Mary Jo McIntyre

Shadow

In the midst of being outspoken,
you are so reserved.
In the light of your insecurities,
you are so assured.
In the darkness of your shadow,
you are such an individual.
Reality love is on the inside,
your love is just visual.

Robyn McWhorter

Untitled

Someday when you are old and grey
and sitting all alone
When memories come back to you
of happy days you've known
Will I be in those happy days
or just a passing thing
Of times I've built your confidence
and caused your heart to sing
Will I be totally forgotten
And no matter how you try
My name just won't come back to you
Goodbye was just goodbye
Or, will you wish you could forget me
If you can't, will you be glad
Will you have learned by then
and too late — that
You wasted years just wanting
when — you could have had

Betty W. Curtis

Memories

Memories are
what your life contains
Change painful ones to harmony
because memories
are all that remain.

Memories are
nothing you can prevent,
like a passing spring rain,
or a cold winter storm,
but, an unconscious event.

Memories are
all we have of the past.
Our living will become passing.
How will your memories
last?

Wendi Collins

Mother

From the very start,
You showed me right from wrong.
You proved you had the faith in me,
And taught me to be strong.

Now that your life is over,
Your time to go grows near-
My heart feels heavy at the thought
Of losing what is so dear.

Best friends are hard to come by-
You were that and so much more.
Now I face the world alone
To learn what I stand for.

Your memory keeps my world alight
And helps me move along,
But nobody fills the void you left,
You will always be my Mom.

Linda F. Middleton

Mirrors

I often stand in front
of strange mirrors
in strange restrooms.
For practice, I try out
jokes on my reflection,
as if to another person

Who might share my wit,
or who might in some way
sympathize with forced
attempts at finding
common ground upon which
we might stand for a while.

Yet when no response comes,
and the silence droops
there for a time,
I chuckle nervously—
uncomfortable with myself,
or with the sudden
weight of a bad joke.

Robert Mawyer

Special Thoughts

Remembering the times we've shared
as lovers often do,
tender moments to compare
with special thoughts of you.

Locked forever in my mind
a million dreams come true,
I look within and there I find
those special thoughts of you.

I close my eyes and I can see,
and feel, and touch you too,
without your love, I'll never be
reliving special thoughts of you.

When tomorrow comes, today is history
and my life begins anew,
Yet sometimes I'm lost in memory,
thinking special thoughts of you.

Jack Thomas

It Took Me No Time

It took me no time
To see that you are beautiful.
My hard-to-please eye was surprised
And that sense was vitalized.
But let me tell you true.
It's not beauty that made me love you.
But in your eyes a bit of light
Made my face shine bright.
And alive became my heart
And every other part.
In your eyes I saw such feeling
Easy to understand its meaning.
I saw love. I fell to knees.
Both of us God chose to please.

Shpetim Lezi

The Promise

When black clouds obscure
the rays of the sun,
a stillness descends
before the thunderous crash
of ruin and lashing winds
from which all creatures hide
in crevices and nooks
until the fury subsides
but a changing front
shifts the clouds in a way
which causes the storm to abort
until the darkness recedes
and cardinals again sing praise
to the sunshines's warming beams.

Werner I. Halpern

Snow

Big fat fluffy flakes of snow.
See how they flutter.
    See how they flow.

Softly, slowly to the ground.
    All around!

Sparkling in the night
    by the pale moonlight,
or early in the morning
    by soft sun light.

As they tumble to and fro,
    down to the ground they go.

Sandra S. Rath

The Language of Love

Love's language is seen
In all kinds of places
From the dark, lonely cross
To our smiling faces.
It cuts all barriers
Between black and white.
It is an act of the will.
It knows what is right.
It is far too deep
For human words to express.
It fills up those holes
of dark emptiness.
It unites all mankind,
And brings us together.
It is a universal bond.
It is a priceless treasure.
We may not hear it,
But love speaks loud.
The language of love
Is shouted from beyond the clouds.

Raina Hoffman

Beauty

Beauty is within
Not just upon the skin
So look from the inside
And you will see if you step aside
Life will make a stride
With Jesus as your guide
So beauty is within
Not just under the skin

Betty Finley

Signs of Autumn

The dusty milkweed pods have burst
Her hidden floss she flings
The birds are flocking here and there
And trying out their wings
The corn has all been harvested
The fields already brown
The apple trees with luscious fruit
Are full and bending down
A spicy smell like gingerbread
Comes wafting on the breeze
And cider sweet fresh from the press
Our mind and senses tease
The lowly hum of tired bees
The flowers scarce they find
As to and fro they wend their way
To get what's left behind
The purple grapes in clusters hang
Their dusky bunches low
As Mother Nature does her best
To put on her last show

Grace E. Noel

A Love Once There

The wind stirs, telling
  Of a storm about to begin
And black clouds fills the sky

The heart slows, the warning
  Of a body turned cold
And ice fills the veins

The smile vanishes, the remembrance
  Of a laughter once heard
And hurt fills the face

The warmth fades, whispering
  Of a love once there
And loneliness fills the soul

Karen Marie Tidwell

In Memory of Mom My Wife

I thank you folks who understood
That mom was witty kind and good
I thank you all who made her smile
When you stopped to chat a little while
I thank the ones who did not say
You told me that three times today
I thank those who looked away
The time she dropped her dinner tray
I thank the ones who understand
Her failing eyes and shaking hands
Her final days were not much fun
With diabetes and parkinson's
She had some faults as we all do
Compared to mine "Hers were so few"
She called me back when I would miss
Giving her our goodnight kiss
We shared our love for sixty years
Tonight I'm pouring out some tears

Gayle Green

Selfish People, Selfish World

Deep depression beyond belief
Pain that has no cure
Living life with so much grief
Being so unpure
Making love without love
Loving other than your lover
Committing crimes above
Being saved by your savior
Understanding nothing
Nothing understanding you
The world begins to sing
All because you're blue
The sky isn't blue
The water isn't clear
The world's not the same to you
Because all you see is fear
Fear from love, fear from hate
Fear from fear itself
Eventually to look at fate
And realize you've only loved yourself.

Chris Iuliano

Me and Him

He did me so wrong
But I believed all along
That one day he'd love me
Isn't that the key
I used to think he was so considerate
I now realize, he's love illiterate
He knows how to reach me deep inside
I wish these feelings would subside
My heart is breaking, tears are falling
Of course he keeps calling
I keep my feelings in clandestine
Why is it impossible for me to win
I'm so fed up with these baby games
Grow up, you're so lame
When I close my hurting eyes
All I see his pathetic lies
I can't jump on the band-wagon
Even though my heart is laggin'
What am I suppose to do
Leave it all up to you?

Nicole Adina Barone

My Treasure In Life

We spend our lives searching
For the answers to our questions
Looking for some guidance
To form our own conclusions.

We meet new people everyday
And hope they'll be the one
The one to make our lives complete
Shed some light from the sun.

When many times the person
Is the one who has always been there
Living, loving, and laughing
And to me, she is my treasure.

There are many treasures out there
We see them every day
Don't take them for granted
Some day they'll go away.

Learn from your treasure
And follow in their shoes
For there will come a day
You'll be someone's treasure too.

Tina Nicole Gabriel-Kacirek

Justin

Justin, our beautiful Justin,
spirit as free as the wind
but wondering where to go.
Parents eager to show,
but love binding too tight.
making you want to take flight.
Worry not, dear Jus,
after all the fuss,
you will find the light.
Together with our love,
you will soar high above.
So, hold tight to your dream,
and as bad as it may seem,
you will be set free
and you can say
"Let Me be Me"!

Judy Yokoyama

His Legacy

If I should ever leave you
  whom I love
To go along the silent way,
  grieve not,
Nor speak of me with tears,
but laugh and talk of me
as if I were beside you there.

And when you hear a song or see
a bird I loved, please do not
let the thought of me be sad . . .
For I am loving you just as
I always have . . .

Remember that I did not fear . . .

We cannot see beyond . . .
But this I know - I loved you so.

Walter J. Porter Jr.

Calm

The grass is almost green today
I watched the bright sun run away
The rain comes falling down pitter pat
I wonder where the sunshine's at
I watch as the rain falls to the ground
Thinking 'bout how it travels 'round.
I see the wet Earth
As I imagine spring's birth.
The trees still barren
I feel something starin'
I feel the breeze roll
As rain calms my soul

Allison Hagen

Spring

Springtime is everywhere.
On the ground and in the air.
A time for many to reach their goals,
A time when many do not have colds.
Flowers growing up from the ground
Beautifully blooming all year round
Trees growing up so high,
High enough to reach the sky.
Children swinging on swings.
Swinging so high they feel like kings.
As you know Spring brings joy
To each and every girl and boy.

Allison Schiebler

Terri

Is a woman
Whose dazzling smile
Could change the world
Who changed herself
And changed her world.

Michael Burks

Like A Dream

What would I say to you my sweet girl
I love long hair cover your shoulders
Your eyes are so pretty
Your lips are attractive
Your arms will hold my life
How would I let you know I love you
You don't know that I have been waiting
Sometimes sing you love songs
You just smile friendly
Love is for me alone
And now I'm going away
You feel so sad and cry fearfully
You say that you love me
That you would like to be with me
I want always to tell you my dream
I wish we've been a happy couple
Now that I'll go away
So far from my sweet girl
I say, "Love you and good-bye."

Tien Duc Hoang

Deep Sleep of the Soul

Dark as to deep,
The demon is asleep.
Do you know how he sleeps?

Deep
When he wakes the end will come,
Who is the demon in everyone?
How do we know where to find him,
Or where he begins?
The existence of the very face you see,
It can only hide the real person,
That's me.
I found the demon,
I know who he is,
I am him and that's all there is,
As you can see the end has come,
And now I wish to say good bye everyone.

Matthew Popiolek

When Ego Sees a Dare

It was so violent
without a single touch.
The master chose to vent,
the student learned not much.
A simple question asked,
a challenge was perceived.
The novice, then aghast,
for knowledge was bereaved.

Chastised as a critic
the naive student left.
The teacher was a cynic
whose ridicule had heft.
It is an awful shame
what harm can come from fame.

Marilyn R. Collier

Mother's Reflection

Mother's reflection
On infinite cost,
She has none save us.

Justin Carter

Soldier

Cast in the jungle,
fighting for life,
faced with emergency,
fraught with strife.

Inspired and Militant
into the fray,
spawning hope of the past,
building thoughts for today.

Forced to the issue
back to back
saddled with emotion
about to crack.

The trail is flamboyant,
racked with pain,
alone for a fortnight
gripped with out gain.

Silence is golden-oh-weary night,
besieged and besmirched,
in the dim candle light;
erosion is wearing away on the fight.

Ernest G. Walden

The Road to Discovery

I walked down the
road that used to be
with stone walls
and apple trees.
Looking for the open
fields I found to my
surprise beautiful
homes and landscaped
grounds, gleaming sun
dials and flowers
with a pot-pourri smell.

Only soil over the land
hallows and celebrates.

Florence McGovern

Love's Last Breath

My unreplied letters
are now my grave.
For the Black Angel
of my darkened heart
flies above my head
like a Vulture in waiting.
For I have imprisoned
my heart in a steel cage,
and plummet it into the
deepest depths of Hell.
Where the brightness
in your eyes will not
grace my light of day.

Lawrence P. Lakatos

All My Love Forever, Daddy

After sixty one years
Of laughter and tears
And love and fears;
We still are in love;
The love that has endured
Ever since the day I was allured
By your wonderful joy
That would attract any boy,
Even though he was twenty seven
And thought he was in Heaven
With You!

Orville Clutterham

In The Puzzle

Fallen trees, bended knees
Broken glass, faded past
Crooked lines, hard times
One way street, two left feet
Starless nights, internal fights
People who fake, tea and cake
Lost in a crowd, try to act proud
Never give in, forget to pretend
Dream in color, love your brother
Follow the plan, get a suntan
Go through quick, the minutes tick
One live to live, forget and forgive
Shoot for the moon, the time is soon
Ships will sail, heaven or hell
Time to chose, win or lose
Travel by day, sleep in hay
Don't miss the call, some will fall
Into bottomless pit, pieces don't fit
    In the puzzle

J. W. Slayton

My Road

I have walked my road of life
And where each bend it turned
Another side of life I saw
Another lesson I have learned

At the start I had been told
The road was straight and narrow
Had my road not had a bend
All birds would be a sparrow

Though the road had many bends
There were borders I defined
When temptation beckoned me
I saw them in my mind

Others sometimes shared my road
In search of one their own
When our sharing was complete
I would walk my road alone

How many bends, how short the straight
Is something I don't know
I only know this road is mine
And on this road I'll always go

Joseph Fram

Mi Corazón Por Vida

As the sun gazes over the mountain top,
    getting ready to set for the day.
I look into your glazing eyes,
    while I stroke your hair away.
And I realize how much I love you,
    there couldn't be no one else for me.

Kristen Leal

Indenture

I become the corporate slave
though much I do deny
idiot slogans, pictures, trash
bombard my mind, ear and eye
time's of the essence
it's all wasting
pitch to snag
grape to raisin
let me be the monkey boy
let us be the blind and dumb
no one gives a damn anymore
who cares where the water's from
silly people, dumbstruck slave
mindlessly we will behave
hold my slogan, you'll join the wave
sing the theme song to my grave
let us become so entranced
let us forget that we're not free
rape my life and my times
please indenture me

Sebastian Colley

No Tears for My Father

He never let me cry.
My childish tears
were not allowed.
Now he is lying
Dieing
And I feel
I should be crying
But the tears
Within me drying
Never get into
my eyes.
I cry inside
and try to hide
My private hell.
He taught me well.

Ellen Monroe

Untitled

I saw an old man
walk down an old lane
with a brown haired dog
and a crooked old cane.

They stopped for a while
and sat on a log
he sat there petting
that old brown haired dog.

From out of his pocket
he pulls an old crust of bread
he breaks it in half
to share with his friend.

Friends they have been
and friends they shall be
spending all day
in the shade of that tree.

James McClune

Rebel

A youthful rebel
    on the outskirts of the normal
living close to the edge.
Until one day love brings him in
to care for him.
    Until he needs her no more
then love will go back again.
    Waiting.
Waiting in the shadows
to be loved again.

Alexis Lydia McBain

Our Parents

So often as we hurry
    All around and everywhere,
We do not take the time
    To say how much we really care.
You've always been there for us,
    In good times and the bad.
Sometimes we've made you happy,
    Other times we've made you sad.
You've never once deserted us,
    Not one time let us fall.
You've always stood behind us,
    And given us your all.
For all you have given
    and all you have done,
We thank you, dear parents;
    It's been a lot of fun.

Sonya & Paula Passmore

Shadow

My shadow falls behind me
    as I walk towards the sun
It's always there when I need it
    and I know I'm never alone

Traveling long and hard
    on this road with you my friend
When I think I've finally made it
    I see I have to start over again

Walk with me shadow
    on this road without an end
Through happiness and sorrow
    you're my only true friend

So many have forsaken me
    some say they're true friends
But you have always walked with me
    and you will until the end

You have never told a lie
    or ever done me wrong
You guided me through sorrow
    for which has made me strong

Lee Morris

Goodbye

We leave this great room
Under the full moon;
The candle has lit our way
Now it shall light another's day.
Memories at side,
We shall march with pride
Into the great expanse
Called life and romance.
And though we may have gone,
The flame shall flicker on.

Zachary Winters

A Darwinian Romp

If you make a time line on a wall
On which people and dinosaurs fall,
The whole history of man
Is a very short span
And your own life is nothing at all.

With cries and occasional laughs
I have sought each discernible path
But no song and no prayer
Relieves the despair
Of this existential morass.

One concept has helped me to be
Oblivious, happy and free:
An illusion sublime,
One continuous line
Brontosauri, to shakespeare, to me.

James R. Cohen

We're Only Passing Through

Make the most of everyday
In all you say or do
Our time on earth is all too brief
As we're only passing through.

Rise to bright surroundings
Enjoy the magnificent view
Knowing they are temporary
As we're only passing through.

For some the years are many
For others they may be few
We have no control of either
As we're only passing through.

When things start going awry
Glance upward toward the blue
Remember, this is just a resting place
And we are only passing through.

So live the very best you can
Righteously and true
For we are judged every day
As we are passing through.

Bernice M. Dutcher

By My Side

Today I hurried on my way,
With a list of things to do.
In my mind I made a perfect plan
That I could follow and get through.

On a busy street a little child,
Stood crying by her mother.
Her body cold, she had no coat,
In a stroller was her brother.

I stopped to see what I could do,
To help them on their way.
With tears of joy she took my hand,
And asked if we could pray.

Her problems seemed too much to bear,
So depressed and all alone.
Friends had all forgotten her,
What she wore was scraps she'd sewn.

She trembled with each word she spoke,
In need, yet with such pride.
I know God led me there today,
To share and keep her by my side.

Myrna R. Duce

The Wind

Oh, Dear Lord Jesus
  Hear my prayer...

Please keep the trees
  unaware.

Of the wind that blows
  so strong...

My oh my the things
  that could go wrong.

Limbs break and
  Fall to the ground...
While my five little dachshunds
  Run around and around.
So, Dear Lord Jesus
  As you see...

The strong fierce wind
  Puts quite a scare in me!
Rosalie Matella Mantell

Loneliness

How lonely we shall be
What shall we do
You without me
I without you
C. Andrew Dumford

On Truth

See it come and go along
Away from us a quiet song
Above the hills and over the sea
Returning momentarily.

See it fly before the eye
Across the surrounding spacious sky
Away from us, a muted sound
To leave us still within the ground.

I asked one wise why was it so
That with us it would feign to go
The sage replied, I'd turned it thus
We won't have it, not it have us.
Robert S. Feinberg

Friendship

Looking into your eyes when we laugh
bright as the sun shines
a private smile creeps into my soul
setting me free
feeling like we have met before
knowing each other desire
walking the fires of hell
finding the love and passion
never to touch
just feeling . . . feeling
we will reach the stairway to heaven
loving and laughing
looking back
knowing that we loved
Marie Hughes

The Crow

The crow
sits
clawing away
at the breast
of the scarecrow.
The scarecrow
stands
unable to move
as it is pegged up
to the pole.
The pole
bend and crooked
a red rust
creeps up
and down
and all over the pole
that carries the scarecrow
that must endure the pain
caused by the crow.
Sorry Mom.
Ashley Whitney

Jesus Christ

Everyday with Jesus is sweeter than
the day before.
Through my older years, I appreciate
it more and more.
We must live for God everyday.
Let Jesus show us the right way.
Jesus gave his life for me and you,
So believing in Him is the right
thing to do.
Jesus Christ is God's only son,
If you need Him, He will help everyone.
When you pray it has to be from
the heart and clear mind,
If not you are wasting your time.
James Gwin

Suffocated

She let me sit in the
car and wait for death
to approach me

I could see the air particles
floating through the air
as if they were harmless to
even a fly they were not

They came towards me
and surrounded me in hords
of thousands
they began to suck the
life right out of my body

I could see my skin pigment
change to a shade of blue
I felt weak and light headed
my body numb
the particles began to enclose
I was gone

I thought she loved me
but I guess I was wrong.
Ruth Herring

As Far As I Can See . . .

As far as I can see
The sky is blue
Just as the grass is green
At least it is to me.

As far as I can see
There are hills
Just as there are mountains
At least it is to me.

As far as I can see
There are valleys
Just as there are canyons
At least it is to me.

As far as I can see
There are lakes
Just as there are oceans
At least it is to me.

As far as I can see
There are streams
Just as there are rivers
At least it is to me.
Caroline M. Chow ☺

Friendship

A friend is one who knows
you as you are, understands
where you've been.
Accepts who you've been,
accepts who you've become.
And still gently invites
you to grow.

A friend, "multiplies, your
joys, divides your sorrows,
understands your silences,
and comes in when the
rest of the world goes out.

A friend listens, never
questions, always there till the end.
Janet Albertson

Soulmates

We met when sin was in.
We had our share of gin,
for our lives were in a spin.

Even our time together was
never akin, for the world was
always under our skin.

Do not fear therein,
forever my heart you will
always be in!
John Zarbo

Deep Love

I never ask for baubles and beads,
just a moment of your time
would fulfill my needs.
A moment of your time
just to hear you say
"hi baby, I love you"
or "how is your day?"
A moment of your time
to God I pray
for a moment of your time
just a phone call away.
Deborah A. Cole

Angel Jake

You have left and flown above,
beyond the clouds to God's love.
Beyond the brightness of the stars,
you have left this world of ours.

Up to where the angels sing,
you flew on your little wing.
To begin your timeless flight,
special one so full of light.

Your gentle heart filled with glee,
no more pain, your spirit's free.
To beautiful for our land,
you and God now hand and hand.

We all must wait, impatient feet,
our time to cross, again we'll meet.
The glowing sun to rise and set,
our Angel Jake, we won't forget.

Our lives now not of fear,
your warm presence always near.
The hands of time we all will view,
soon to begin our climb to you.

Clarice A. Cataldo

Blessings

Father of the endless universe
in seven days he created
our beautiful mother earth

Then gave life to all within
and gifts along the way
peace was first to begin

He bestowed so much to absorb
given to build us up
and not to be destroyed

With his hand yet another wave
came faith, hope, and joy
then his only son to save

So many blessings God gave us
the greatest one is love
hearts to believe in and trust

These gifts he gave to humanity
to be shared with one another
he gave us both, you and me
so we wouldn't be alone...

Edith Mary Sherrill

Figure Eight

Around the curves I turn
Thinking and heeding my own
But in the middle we enjoin
And I know I'm not alone
I listen and am guided and
    taught by loving, knowing
    hands
Uphill and downhill around
    the curved ends
Within this infinite shape
    my soul is always going
until I meet the very core
The transpicuous middle
Ever knowing

Ahra Jensen Haas

The Onion

The knife probed
brown skin
and the onion's memories
floated in the air like dreams,
An old beard wagged
as layers fell into the pot
until the man at last
savored the inner core
and was left with nothing
but the form
and stewed onion

Jim Carlson

Past the Insecurities

I took all my hopes and fears
With all my dreams and aspirations
And placed them in an envelope
That I carefully addressed to you

So that you could build an empire
Any castle to your liking
Or maybe just a coffee shop
Somewhere across the street

But you kept up your guard
Your eyes on the road in front of you
Every step so cautiously placed
Barefoot on the concrete

Your mind ignored the promise
That the sun shine brighter
And the grass is greener still
Past the insecurities

Leslie G. Eddings

Song of a Nonagenarian

At 90 it is time to pause
And look in both directions,
Consider past accomplishments
And future expectations.

The things you can no longer do
Create a bit of bother;
Some chores that once were done by you
Must be done by another.

Now things don't matter quite so much
And people matter more.
At least by letter keep in touch
When travel is a chore.

Discover new tasks in your range,
New pleasures to enjoy;
Accept inevitable change
And substitutes employ.

The gates of heaven are in view,
The time and way not known
When someone there will call to you
And earthly cares have flown.

Mildred Lewis

Peace

What we need in the world
P - Peace for all mankind
E - Everywhere in the world
A - All humanity enjoy good health
C - Clean living
E - to reach for eternity

Anna M. Randazzo

Wonderful

The wonderful people I know.
They hold me in their heart
And never let me go.
I know we shall never part.
So much I owe,
For the wonderful people I know.

Eric H. McHale

An Ode to My Saviour

My saviour was a carpenter
He worked and styled in wood
His heart clear, his mind was pure
In him was only good.

My Saviour was a carpenter
Just to some, a lowly nazarene
Little they knew in reality
He was their promised king

His hands so skilled and strong
Were doomed to grace the cross
He gave his life of his own sweet will
And he counted no suffering or loss.

Barb Hensley-Hounshell

The Untitled

Years have been wasted,
The days have been long.
I've wasted my energy,
Just trying to stay strong.
To where am I going,
What shall I become.
Have I reached my destination,
Or have I just begun.
I see my life scrambled,
As the sand on a beach,
Just left to blow away,
With the wind piece by piece.
I'm locked in a cell,
And can't reach the key.
As my life slips away,
And no one else can see.

Bruce L. Alberson

Wind

The gentle wind runs thru my hair
I love the sweet cool breeze
lets me be at one
accept myself with ease

Things taken for granted
no appreciation at all
can you hear me?
Break thru that selfish wall

Holding back inside
you need to be yourself
don't have other thoughts
no time for anything else

What are your thoughts?
What do you feel?
Come to me when depressed
I'll help your soul heal

Precious dreams lost in time
just look around and see
you are not alone
the same happened to me.

Joe Francis

Trumpet Blues

Oh horn of praise,
Your soul so blue,
From the garden patch
You gave birth,
The Trumpet Blues.

Brown eyes roll,
Brown fingers tap the keys.
And twirling, mournful sounds,
Gutsy whirling notes, deep
From inside out,
Spread magic in the air.

Oh magic horn,
Blow those Trumpet Blues.
Minds afire, in tender passion,
Swing that horn in praise.
Hearts impaled, minds searching,
Ever searching,
How long, oh how long,
Acceptance?

Charles P. Russ Jr.

Big Day

He went to
kindergarten just today.
Just a small little
guy, in so many ways.
So brave and anxious
for his big day.
My heart broke
as he stepped on the
bus. No longer our
days, just the two of
us. A wave goodbye
as he pulled away.
Not a tear was
his on this September day.

Shelly Baum

Untitled

You'd understand my pain today,
you'd take me in your arms
and say it's okay.

But you're gone now,
you'll never do that again

Sometimes I think you're
here
But then I think again
that you're not here
You're not near
You're not anywhere with me
You'll never be

I wish we didn't have to
say goodbye, but we do
and I'll never forget you

Lisa Masquelier

A Dark and Stormy Night

It's a dark, and stormy night,
and the moon is cast so bright,
The wind howls, and the trees
scowl, it would scare anyone
away.

The leaves rustle, the
grass shuffles, the wind
blows everything away. The
lightning flashes, the thunder
rumbles, and black cats scatter
away.

All that can be heard, are
howls of ghosts, in a very
devilish way. Sounds of laughter,
eerie laughter, scare little kids
away. An awful smell, fills
the air, the smell of death, everywhere.

Rachel Powers

Sharing with Solitude

Bright blue skies above
   Tall trees surround me
Blue green grass freshly cut
   Gentle breezes flowing

Old memories prevail
   In your solitude you share
Thoughts deeds without tears
   Just smiles you are alive

William F. McVey

A Lesson of Love

He taught me a lesson
He made me feel loved
I cherished each moment
Each laugh, smile, and secret.
He swept me in the air
Like a feather blowing in the wind.

But then he left
Left me to fall
to float away in the distance.
But he taught me a lesson.
A lesson of love.

Jennifer Whitmore

The Tear

A tear to fall
On empty ground
No flowers grow
Where love abounds

Open wounds
To wide to heal
The heart
The pain
It's how I feel

Missing life
The world I knew
Within my grasp
I let it go

To see it now
The tear
It falls
That's all

Steven A. Wallace

Desist of Duration

Open your minds and you will know,
time grows shorter as days come and go.

Try not to think about it
'cause maybe it's not true.
Don't even talk about it
'cause each dawn brings anew.
Watch the false prophets arise,
and believe what you see.
Hear the masked tellers converse,
fore their words are full of deceit.
Beware of the triple six
'cause hell is its drift.
Behold of the triple seven
'cause heaven be thy gift.
Gabriel's trumpet shall sound,
and angels will descend.
Brimstone and fire shall fall,
fore it is close to the end.

Open your eyes and you will see,
desist of duration draws nearer to thee.

Lynn Broadnax

Fall Back

Manual rotation,
Clocks reversing,
Ephemeral control
over time.
With a flick of the wrist,
a taunting gesture,
feigning mastery
over the inflexible.
Retract time?
A farce!
For
I would
if
I could.

Barbara Blanton Reid

Untamed

Why do you show me death?
To show me hell?
Show me love, passion the
warmth of being alive . . .
Leave me to a world of
happiness other than a world
of hate . . .
Darkness may fall over me,
am I too full of life,
I cannot be kept?
You say I only dream of worlds
that I will never be a part.
That is a lie!
You only wish to bring me down!
But, like the wild, I am untamed.
You shall never possess me
or my taste for life . . .

Kristine Scofield

The Tears of My Soul

Is not found in spring flowers,
or sunny days of summer,
nor the changing of fall colors,
or winters deep slumber.

As I watch the wind blow
with its stillness.
I must find
the tears of my soul!

Gregory Mayhew

Untitled

Where ever I go you're there
Every time I dream you're with me
When I laugh you are laughing too
When I am sad, you cry
When I am hurt inside you comfort me
And I the same for you.
When I am scared you are too
We try to comfort one another
You and I are one
You are my soul
The key to my very existence

Stacey Busch

My Baby Girl

You are a miracle
An angel from above
My precious little girl
And you're here for me to love . . .

Your sweet innocent smile
The twinkle in your eyes
The sound of your voice
Just melts my whole inside . . .

I watch you when you sleep
I wait for you to cry
Just so I can hold you
And sing you a lullaby . . .

I hold your tiny hands
And I feel your beating heart
I know one thing's for-sure
Our love will never part . . . .

Michele Lyn Mead

Picasso 3/4

Be a woman here with me
if you will
take your pleasure in
warmed dust writing
for your smile and mine
held hostage to
open piano fourths
come home to irony
spilling tears
a spectrum of redemption
in three quarter time
be careful what silhouette
you sing
the pavane dismembers
old pictures of a dead sister
playing slow red flamed
andalusian minor sevenths

John Paul Martin

Journey

Wandering along a desolate plateau
through sun beams and moon rays
waiting to see the Light.
Running towards my mountain of Dreams
and I will climb higher than high
until suffocated by heavenly Sights
where untouchable Beauty fuels Passion
and blinding Light energizes.
Then, without waxed wings,
I will fly.

J. Jason Clendaniel

Lori

She died.
I cried
And died
Inside.

Myrna Atteberry

Nothing

I feel empty
I feel useless
Everything I feel
Everything I feel
Means nothing
The things I do
The things I say
The words I write
Mean nothing
The nothing is stronger than you
The nothing is stronger than me
No one conquers the nothing
The whole world is nothing
It makes you nothing
There is no escaping the nothing
The end is near
The end is nothing

Ed McKeaney

In a Child's Eyes

   To see heaven in a child,
is like watching a flower bloom
in the wild.
   To see the world in
a child's eyes, is like watching
the sun rise.
   If a child shows fear, please
hold them near.
   To hear love in a child's
words, feels like watching a flock
of birds.
   To hear a child cry,
makes you want to sit back
and sigh.

Amanda Oliver

Happy Mother's Day

Happiness comes from me to you.
Or is it that you like blue.
Red is not a dread.
It is the wonderful things
You think in your head.

Patrick Mayer

Child of the Dark

Sad child, tell us where you go,
After lights are turned down low;
With the descending of the sun,
Unsummoned melancholia has begun!

On your cheeks are tracks of tears,
Unbecoming of such tender years;
You haven't lived enough of time,
To suffer heartaches, child of mine!

All is new, the break of day,
Is teasing morning glories out to play;
The world around us fresh and bright,
Every crevice filled with light!

How can such bitter tears have sprung,
From the eyes of one so young?
Take us to that space you fill,
For if you don't, then no one will!

Joan Tholen

Martin Luther King

Martin Luther King
You touched our lives
with your brightest dream.
Like a guiding star
that comes and goes.
You shone for us the
brightest lights and
brought about equality rights.

We quietly stand
and
wonder why
Such guiding knight
would have to go.
Memories linger on and on
Of a famous American
that was so strong.

Maria Soto Serna

My Blue-Eyed Boy

You once were very tiny
My little blue-eyed boy
I took care of you
With lots of pride and joy.

I took you to the circus
We went on fishing trips
And when you'd skin your knees
I'd kiss those little lips.

But then one day, I closed my eyes
My little boy had grown
Into a very nice young man
That was loved by everyone.

I miss you very much Dwight
My little blue-eyed boy
With all you gave and all you did
You filled my life with joy.

Beverly Vise

Love Divine

Our Lord Jesus Christ
Humiliated and dying on a cross
Spoke this amazing words
Father forgive them
They know not what they do."

It's hard to imagine
Unbearable pain He felt
And the great love He still had
For sinners like us
In His precious heart.

That is love so great
That words cannot describe
That is love divine
Unconditional
Possible only because He is God.

Annette Gukassey

Wordless Processor

Winged ideas
swoop birdlike overhead,
soaring and diving,
alone and in flock,
but never alighting.

Screen ready,
blank paper, blank mind,
waiting, waiting.

Yet all are mocking birds,
taunting,
mimicking,
around, yet above.

At last, from the swirl
breaks out a loner,
radar-locked on me.

Surprise, a homing pigeon
bringing back
experience long ago sent out.

Loaded mind, hungry paper,
processor again wording.

Eldon L. Johnson

His Arms

When I'm in his
arms so safe and
sound the whole
world seems to stop
going round. I
forget my worries
my troubles and
fears and all that
I'm thinking is,
how much he cares.

Kristi Ness

Goodbye

Say see you later for
the very last time,
knowing it's really goodbye,
not sure it's time to
go and not wanting to stay,
slowly we walk away,
goodbye.

Megan K. Goss

Loath Thy Image?

Why look at me so?...
Like vermin under your feet.
Mirror—'Tis first we meet?

T. G. Nichols

Untitled

Heavenly Father, we thank You
For a very beautiful day
Which in Your loving kindness
You have sent our way.

We bow our heads
In humble Christian love
Giving thanks for blessings
Sent us from above.

We thank You for
Health, hearth and home
And far from Your guidance
We'll never roam.

We strive to keep
Ever more diligently
The Ten Commandments
Given us by Thee.

Father, we put all
Our trust in Thee
Trying to live more perfectly
As You would have us always be.

Eloise Hyde

Guiding Light

Guiding light
Set forth your rays
Give me life
And point me the right ways.

Sister watch
And give me care
Show me right,
Have me do what is fair.

Guardian angel
Give me the gift
To know what is right
And never let me drift.

God from above
Give me the sight
Have me open my eyes
To see that guiding light.

Lauren E. Mavros

Living in the Present

Life is but a second in time.
When I look back, it's only memories
in my mind.
It's like a line seeming so fine.
For I must stay in the present, for it
is divine.
For the past can no longer cross the
line, and I might not have the future
in time.
So for now, I'll enjoy the present,
For I know it's mine.

Loillette Brown

Card Game of Relationship

I ante up
you deal me in.
I play the game
I feel I can win.

Pick 'em up
look at your hand.
Figure out what you need
and what chance you stand.

Mine looks good
I bet very bold.
You look at your cards
and then say "I fold".

Ryan Peterson

Who Am I?

How come you always turn to me,
when you need some kind of help?
Who am I? - Someone Special?
I am no one in a world of no one's,
A follower of a greater great.
No one I know, and definitely not I
Why do you worship me? I am no God
Nor man of great faith
But still you come to me
Why???

Michael-Andrew Noll

Lover's Thoughts

Pounding waves
Upon sharp-edged rocks
Sea gulls searching through out the sky
Lovers sit mesmerized by each other
Thinking within their heads
Of times had and times to come
They look at each other
With wide, shining eyes
Wondering what the other is dreaming

Kris Paule

Till Then

For all the love that I shared,
Should have seen before.
My heart, my soul, that I dared,
I released more and more.

For now I let you go away,
Because I love you so.
But as you went I knew I'd pay,
Why'd you have to go.

For all the nights I spent alone,
I wish that you were here to care.
I called and called on the phone,
I cried for you weren't there.

So when I am asleep at night,
I'll wonder where you've been.
I know that our love is right,
So I'll think of you Till Then.

Misty Leeper

Speculation

In one split second, our world
turned upside down.
Irrevocably changed — never to
return, never to again
flow sweetly from day to day.

I search your face as you tenderly
care for this body
that gave both of us so much
pleasure for so many
years. I watch for a hint of

revulsion, a look of pity, a
pulling away. None
of these. I see only grace
and humor and love.
But when you shut the door,

after leaving me in less capable
hands, do you lean on
the varnished wood and breathe
a sigh of relief?
I really do not want to know.

Charlotte Marchand

Birches

Birches give the gold sky
Its first crescent wings,
The wind-coarse cry of geese
Dark as winter flute
In the fall stock
Of apple and bitter-root.

Birches give the mellow loam
A tender, leaner green
Of leaves that sweeten
The jagged branch
And sweep the earth
With dreams.

Birches blue as steel
Birches white as ice
In a crystal field
Birches young and lean
Teach me also the simple truth
That all your seasons bring.

Patricia A. Giacolini

What Is Orange?

Orange is a butterfly
flying to the sun.
Orange is a brick
that weighs a ton.

Orange is a flame
that keeps you warm.
Orange is a painting
in a college dorm.

Orange is a color
of an old man's cane.
Orange is a flower pot
just sitting there plain.

Orange are the leaves
that come down in fall.
Orange is a shirt
hanging in the mall.

Orange is a sunset
that's very bright.
Orange is a fox
walking off into the night.

Jennifer Spencer

Heaven's Parade

In my dreams I've seen them come,
  white feathered angels one by one.
Though not it be the time for me
their presence seem to comfort me.
So many times I can recall
the brightest angel of them all,
With smiling face and silver hair,
hands held out with loving care,
As if to say "Don't be afraid",
When you to must join heaven's parade
of feathered angels one by one
dancing to a silent drum.

Brenda Marie Walker

How Much?

In time your birthday was mine:
lone beings we were apart
but each knew of the other
even before we could see;

what grateful attraction our
attended discovery —
an inevitable force
that compelled togetherness
with ecstasy of union;

for our separateness met,
despite vastness of space, with
nuclear intimacy
to calmly celebrate and
secretly perpetuate

our unique oneness with God;
thank you, my loving Dearest,
for all your ultimate touch —
I do love you forever
    that much . . .

Marshall E. Noel

She

She loved me, at least she said
She loved me, now I wish she were dead
She taunted me, and I gave in
She taunted me, it was a sin
She bruised me, love gone wrong
She bruised me, my love was strong

She twisted my heart around
She threw my heart to the ground

She, She, She

Why, Why, Why

Matt Bennett

Inside

I'm empty inside
I'm weak inside
I'm frustrated inside
I'm ugly inside
I'm awkward inside
I'm friendly inside
I'm alone inside
I'm confused inside
I'm full of hate inside
I'm gay inside
I'm straight inside
I'm nothing inside
this is me inside

Jessica Tenney

Face the Wind

I was born in a world
of hate and sin,
where man did not finish
nor did begin.
I was born alone
afraid and shy,
my only mother was flowing
softly in the sky.
Sweet and pure did she blow
the autumn leaves,
and teasingly did she shuffle
the tops of trees.
So when you're alone
afar from home,
and need a touch of love.
Face the wind
and she will send,
a blessing from above.

Jack Hotchkiss

Grey Smoke

Grey smoke,
moving slowly with the breeze,
with a freely ease.
Pulling high,
against the blue sky.
Lofting up, up, up,
then drifting away,
with no barrier to stop it,
and nothing to do.
Just drifting away.
Grey smoke! Grey smoke!
Take me with you ,
take me away.

Richard E. Townsend Jr.

Untitled

A thought in the dark
Is this all there is
Is this all I'll ever

A lonesome that stays
If I could reach out
If I could touch someone
Two are warmer together

Frances M. Magrabi

Untitled

My life is but a weaving
between my Lord and me.
I cannot choose the colors
He weaveth steadily.

Off times He weaveth sorrow,
and I, in foolish pride,
forget He sees the upper
and I, the under side.

Not till the loom is silent
and the shutters cease to fly,
shall God unroll the canvas
and explain the reason why.

The dark threads are as needful
in the weavers skillful hand,
as the threads of gold and silver
in the pattern He has planned.

Ione M. Crow

281

Sapphire

Eternal awakening
I am now
somehow realized
to question nostalgia
bares no purpose
negative or positive
hold no effect
weight of space
defines of shape
gravity contains the finite
infinity is
breathing comforts the secondhand
life moves
effortless in motion
memories keep me paralyzed
in thought only
balance is divine
pendulum swings
death is alive
silence

Paolo Andreas

The Real Me

My heart's a closed door
My mind's a different story
Everyone works it
And I get no glory

Looking out a window
One that they all shut
My feelings rage inside me
Waiting to be popped

Is life supposed to be this way
Hiding behind myself
Moving with insecurity
Holding my own hand
Wiping my own tear

They think that I'm okay
They think they know my heart
Yet, deep inside I know they'll
never know the real me.

Jocee Priepke

Farewell

No one waited like me;
For your coming
Even dry barren for rain.
Thirsty lips for a drop of water;
Dying patient for a doctor,
Even Satan for a prey.
as much as I am.

While the leaves are falling
from this life's tree one by one
away from you
Now, it doesn't matter any longer
whether you come or not my dear,
it doesn't matter any longer.

M. Emil Cevik

The Lonely One (Dyslexia)

Not to read or write is
far from fun
The lonely One

D's look like B's
Son of a Gun
The Lonely One

No Help, nowhere to turn
Since all trouble begun
The Lonely one

School was never done
The Lonely One

Parents, Brothers, Sisters would shun
The Lonely One

No jobs...Boss..
"What have you done?"
The Lonely One

The harder I try
The further I fall
Who forever needs help after all?
The Lonely One

Jack L. Hargan

The Turmoil of Absent Feeling

Hypnotized and paralyzed,
my sense do ignite.
Silent surroundings traumatize,
the blackness of the night.

Screams and shadows consume,
the darkness and decay.
Dead flowers begin to bloom,
as the night steals the day.

Frolicking crickets dance,
as the night owls who.
I fade into a trance,
as the sky turns to blue.

Alone in the wilting field,
I gaze into the warping sun.
My fears have been revealed,
I know the time has come.

My soul becomes immaculate,
iridescent colors arise.
They evolve from within,
I no longer live in a lie.

Jennifer Rose Galvin

Molly and Spike

We didn't know she'd get so big,
    we didn't know at all.
(We got her from the dog-pound
    when she was rather small.)
She grew at an alarming rate,
    we kept thinking she would stop.
But she got big and she got fat—
    we thought that she would pop.

Now we have a puppy;
    when we took him to the vet,
we got the frightening news
    that he would be bigger yet.
We didn't know they'd get so big,
    we didn't have a clue.
But now that we're in love with them,
    what are we to do?

Sheila Barbour

Washday

Grief comes in washes
trickling or flowing in
places
never thought to be at risk.
As I pull the album out of the water
and examine each snapshot
now wrinkled and stained
changed in ways both great and subtle
so as to be unrecognizable
and grieve
the loss of what I thought I'd known
as well as what I had and lost.

Pat Stansfield

The Leaf

The leaf hung out my window
Suspended out in space;
Turning, twisting, twirling
On a tangle of spider lace.

As I watched it dance and flutter,
A thought came to my mind
Of how the leaf and I
Are really two of a kind.

Pain and death and heartache
Have sent me wildly spinning;
Blown and buffeted by
The winds of life unceasing.

But something holds me safely
Akin to the spider's lace.
Swirling in my torment,
I can see God's face.

Twisting, turning, swinging,
Swirling, spinning, twirling,
Billowed, blown and buffeted;
I...am...the leaf!

Roxann Travis

Rainbow Time

Graceful rainbows
Come and go,
And I'm happy to see them
When they come,
And sad to see them go.
But I can catch a rainbow
With my crystals, fine and clear,
At my windows, front and rear,
When the sun shines through
At its appointed hour.

The pieces of the rainbow
That are splashed against my walls,
Are so welcome to the eye,
And are always in the colors
Of the rainbow in the sky.
Now, I can capture the miracle
Of the colors of the rainbow,
So peaceful, and so high,
In the majesty and beauty
Of the vast expanse of sky!

Hannah Zimmerman

I Knew

She hoped for a miracle
She hoped for a cure
She hoped for a quality
that might just endure.

She prayed for a chance
She prayed for a prayer
She prayed for her doctor
Don't let me go there.

She believed in strength
She believed in living
She believed in God
when He was less giving.

I knew it was cancer
I knew her sweet stare
I knew of the moment
My Mother wasn't there.

Susan M. Rountree

Leaving

The day you told me, you were leaving
Leaving me behind
I cried so much for you my love
As I think about the happy times
We spent together
How you told me
   I love you, I will never
   leave you, you're my one
   and only",
I should have known
Your words were false
And now you're gone
You love someone else
Our love was just a waste of time
Our love was just a bunch of lies
To me we will always be together
Maybe not physically,
But in my heart, in my heart
You will always be forever

Carolina Buriel

It Is She — She Is It

It is She
Her love to have I
cherish to me Has she
everlasting love Is it
mine Is she
understanding Is she
intense Are we together
forever Are I and she
one
It is She

Dean Romano

Alpha and Omega

I'm alpha and omega
Jehovah Jesus Christ
Your redeemer and savior
The glorious bread of life.

Oh! I'm alpha and omega
Jehovah Jesus Christ
I shed my blood on calvary
So I could give you life
So come and take it freely,
It's for "all" you see
I shed my blood on calvary,
So you could come sever me.

Sandra Leach

Eternity

I look into your eyes
and all that I see
is the burning desire
you have for me.

No words need to be spoken
No feelings need to be shared
Everyone can feel it
It's in the air.

Our love is undying
It will never go away
We'll still be together
When we're old and gray.

I'm writing this poem to say to you
that even after all we've been through
I will always and forever
love you!

Melissa Mendez

My Listless Heart

I know you're there.
I can feel your presence.
Though see you nor hear
you I cannot.

My memory stirring,
struggling to recall
your evanescent image.

My heart is listless
...ever wandering.
Searching for your presence.
Through the halls of eternity,
It will not rest.

Andy Adams

Untitled

Balls of yarn and kittens playing
dogs barking, horses neighing
people coming, people staying
life is good, is all I'm saying.

Yarn is gone, kittens grown old
dogs and horses not nearly so bold
people start going, hearts turn cold
life's not good, or so I am told

New yarn is bought and kittens born
dogs lick faces, yet horses are lorn
people join, on sleeves hearts are worn
life is as great as a clear Sunday morn

Tim Schulz

Fire

Strike the match,
see it glow.
As it sparks,
logs in a row.

Smell the pine wood,
glowing bright.
Feel the heat,
Surging with might.

Then it molders,
No more light.
Just some ashes,
As black as night.

Lara Wozniak

I Found Myself

I was looking for love in all
the wrong places. I searched
high and low. After a while
I gave up. Until one day love
came looking for me.

It was then I picked up the
search, but what I searched
for could not be found. When
I found it I was amazed,
because in the process I
found myself. After I found
myself, love came following
close.

I realized, if we ever want to
find true love, we must first
find out who we are.

Shywanda Royal

Breaking Free

I was
Breaking free from
All the things
That had me on the run.
I waited so long
But still jumped the gun.

Never better off
Than I was before
All the misunderstandings
I understand once more.
That in my certainty
I am unsure.

Reality rushes by
Leaving me unaware
I think that I think
That I don't care.
Because going so far
Still leads nowhere.

Gregory L Harriman

A Journey With A Purpose

I see a salmon
popping out of a bright orange egg
gliding past a yellow beak
swimming past a manatee
on to the salty sea
hiding from orcas
snacking on some herring
dodging viscous sharks
munching on tasty sardines
missing an enormous net
fooling hungry dolphins
gulping up plankton adrift on a swift
ocean current
going upriver
with only one purpose
lay its eggs and die

Cory Combs

A Mountain View

On a cold dew-laden
Early spring morning,
Air pristine pure,
The first sun rays
Peer through a
Nearby mountain pass,
Dispelling the
Hazy mist.

A tall thin bird
Stands immobile on a
Rock jutting up
Through the lake,
Intently watching the water.
Suddenly, SWOOSH!
Breakfast has begun.

Alec Berin

Secrets

Closely knit, these family secrets,
Never to be shared.
Tucked away in a dark closet
Where they see light only when needed.
Generations go by with whispers.
Only light hitting here and there.
The bulge has grown,
By the darkness of the years.
The pain and sorrow tucked away.
Then in a brief instant
Of replay and calm,
The secret escapes
From the lips of the dying.
Only to be passed to the next,
With some flourish and less pain.

Marian Robertson

prospectus

silent
empty
lonely
this is my heart
love
warmth
happiness
strangers to me
hope
dreams
faith
lost long ago
gloom
misery
sorrow
this is my future

Benjamin Shaw

Life and Death

Lord! When You ignored me
I suffered silently!
And when You favoured me
With only a glance
There was Divine smile
O'Lord! On Your face!
I had then no eyes, no ears, no face
No sensual body whatever
I was then submerged unto You
This was my life!

Yet, this apparent physical existence
Must follow the Nature's Laws
Hence this cordial invitation to
O'Death! Come, Friend, Welcome!
Let's shake hands, firmly!
And not let go!!
Only, they would say
I've merged unto You!!
Is this my end?
Nay, this is also my life!

V. T. Korde

Going Away

Someone I love
Is dying today
Someone I love
Is going away

Someone I love
Just doesn't care
Someone I love
Is going nowhere

Someone I love
Is sad and blue
Someone I love
Longs to be with you

If the someone I love
Makes it up your ways
Then the someone I love
Will have much brighter days

Take care of my someone
Would you please
Now my someone
Will have a life with ease

Cindy Sleeth

The Ride

Love should be like two in a carriage
heading the same direction
for the same reasons

Should one or the other
look at the beauty around them
the other will enjoy it naturally

Should a rock in the road disturb them
they will ride it out together

Should the weather turn inclement
they will share each other's warmth

If one becomes ill
the other takes the reigns

And should one pass away
the other carries on!

Alan Fallis

Untitled

Last night I felt Your answer,
Oh, the joy that filled my soul!
To know You'd use my errant ways
To take and make me whole.

I felt the burden lifted,
The worry, stress and strife,
As You took me down a road to cleanse
And help rebuild my life.

I asked for Your forgiveness, Lord,
You gave that and so much more,
As patiently You lead me to
And opened a new door.

Today as I begin anew,
On this straight and narrow path,
I pray for strength to follow You
And to hold nothing back.

Suzy Kvien

How Much Life?

Although our lives are measured
by our best accomplishments,
and not our quest for pleasure,
which might just make more sense,
my life is measured by her love,
for nothing can compare.
Brought down from heaven up above
to make my one a pair.

I've never seen, nor heard of this,
that which she has for me.
'Twould be a shame
for all the world,
if they should never see,
the love I know I have for her
that she gives back to me.

Thomas Stone

A Sad Song

My heart sings a sad song
What man has done is wrong

Because of little regard for the earth
Of pain and misery there is no dearth

In the sky - fumes and smoke
Make man cough and choke

In the sea - oil, mercury and lead
Soon, most fish will be dead

On the land - extreme contamination
Could lead to man's termination

Will man stand idly by,
Or make an effort not to die?

Lillian M. Saco

Bless This Home

Dear God, bless this home
And all the people whom abide,
In prayer we pause
To thank thee for thy bounty;
Food to nourish, enrich our soul,
Shelter o'er our heads,
Clothing we attire,
Shoes we wear
To thread upon this good earth;
When daily task is done
We warmed to the crackling hearth;
'Tis home we welcome
When night beckon to fall
Dear God, bless us all.

Ellen Lyau Wong

Make Believe

I only wish an honest soul
I pray for a heart
My troubles no one can conquer
My mistakes are done I am in a trap
I don't know who I am
I can't let go
I can't escape
No matter what I do
I am a target
I am a prisoner with no rights
A mission I can't understand
Everything is unsolved
I can only dream and make believe
I cried for security
God...I believe in grace to love
I'm burning for happiness
My sorrow I cannot rebuild
My precious love is a make believe
I'm in flames, I need
Only one chance I want to be free.

Latitia I. Salazar

Boring Extremes

I did not mean to bore you
with my extremities,
hands pulling two strings
end over, a loop
yet I've got these knots,
undone thoughts
which frail though they may be,
always seem a torture
And I'm all those things
you thought I was, shy,
inverted, bent over
doubled over myself
to half any natural height
these extremities bore,
my eyes, through
a familiar scene
myself standing
(or was it sitting)
on the verge, complacent,
of leaving these things behind

Paxton Ebright

Untitled

Apologize for the hurt,
Apologize for the pain —
Why do we take two steps forward
And then go backwards again?
The look in your eyes cuts me
Fills me with dread —
Reminds me of last night
Alone, and crying in bed
You play the martyr,
When all along it was I —
Aching and burning deep inside
Not even able to sigh
I long for the look of love
Upon your face
It was there once, I know,
I saw just a trace
Sadness you've brought me,
And I to you —
To heal this pain
What must we do?

Mary A. Thompson

If I Were To Die Tomorrow

If I were to die tomorrow,
  would anybody care?
Would anybody miss me?
  Would any tears be shared?

If I were to die tomorrow,
  what happens to my soul?
Would it wait outside "the Gate,"
  or off to hell it go?

If I were to die tomorrow
  would my family be upset?
Would everyone be crying,
  with their faces soaking wet?

If I were to die tomorrow,
  would friends forget my face?
Be told to move on with their lives,
  would I be replaced?

Brandi Luthy

Mankind

First man is born
then he must die
But always he'll pray
for life in the sky
he wants to live now
he wants to live aft
but what happens next
depends on his past
he lives for himself
he lives for others
for people and friends
for sisters and brothers
all you need now
is love for each man
show it to all
the best way you can

Russell Dillingham

Secret Desire

There is a secret in my soul
It affects my thoughts, my dreams
The true love that I believe in
Can never be it seems

My heart it aches to please you
I live with this desire
To hold your body close to mine
To feel that loving fire

I want so much to touch your skin
To kiss your cheek so tender
To lay with you at each days close
Would fill my life with splendor

These emotions rage inside me
Every time I think of you
Then reality it wakes me
And leaves me feeling blue

I love you and I miss you
Please believe me when I say
I tease you for attention ...
But my heart it does not play.

Michael G. Beynon

Those Who Could Not Compete

They blossomed once in '58.
Then again in '88.
These flowers of fractals...
  fractions of sets designed,
  for those who could not compete.
Tests foretold a story of gloom...
  the country was at risk,
  our students could not compete.
The system must be changed...
  it holds no hope beyond today,
  the others will prevail.
Then fell the wall of Berlin...
  the yen of the East.
The only ones left standing...
  were those who could not compete.

Kenneth R. Thompson

Night Thoughts

When I go to bed at night,
In my cabin room grown cold;
I slip beneath the blanket white,
And relax from the day, now old.

Then listening to the waves bold song,
As they come splashing to the shore;
I know that all the whole night long,
They'll continue to rush and roar.

I hear them speak to me of strength,
For endless days to come;
I know they speak to me at length,
Of struggles to be won.

And then at night I drift to sleep,
To dream some more of joys to be;
I know each day I'll come to meet,
The waves strong courage I will need.

Selma Auernheimer

Repose

The moon above shines bright and clear
  It is a heavenly night!
Twinkling on high, each little star
  Sends out a joyous light,
So quiet, so peaceful, so calm it seems
  Ah yes! A work of art
For a scene so filled with beauty
  Brings joy to many a heart!
Serene, tranquil, and filled with repose
  Comes forth the close of day.
The occasional sound of a creature of earth
  Singing its beautiful lay.
The sky appears in a soft blue hue
  Speaking to all of us.
It tells of a great and infinite love
  Only God could make it thus!
No hustle, no bustle, no din or noise
  Just silent and quiet repose
The world clothed in ethereal robes
  Thus brings the day to a close.

Sophia M. Ripka

Memories

  There is no tomorrow to receive a letter
it is too late. There is only yesterday to receive
your memories good or bad. You must not
let your memories fade. You must keep your
memories in your heart. Your memories are
the key to your heart. People may tell you
that memories aren't the key to your life but
they are. Without memories you would have
no past. Remember to always keep your
memories in your heart.

Katrina Richards

What Do You See When You Look at Me

What do you think when you look at me
A black woman's perspective about Black womanhood in America
what do you think when you look at me.
A splendid black tree.
What do you see when you look at me. A woman deceived of my history.
It is my part to make peace to those who hate me, I waver in my
mind, I am strong, I am unique, I am one of a kind.
Sometimes I am blind to the evil, I want to leave behind myself
I must truly find. The pain I deny is brutal to my mind, body,
and soul. Why must I be made to feel so low, yet as a flower I
grow. I must be bold there are stories to be told, before my
earthly body folds. (Speaking of death. Where can I hide my soul
from racism's wicked blows, oh see the scars on my hurting heart,
no one will probably know, as I go down lies narrow road so cold
so cold. So what do you see when you look at me peace.

Elizabeth Jones

The One I Love

Her reasoning made the impossible look possible
Her love gave me the courage to live as who I am
Her imagination let me dream of the life I want and need
Her sensitivity eased my pain, even when the pain was unbearable
Her trust enabled me to truly love someone and taught me the values
of a relationship
Her honesty opened my heart, breaking the wall that held me inside
and letting out my true self
I look at her and see what I want to become; a person full of love,
sensitivity, trust, honesty, reasoning and imagination
I then realize, even though she is, I can't be perfect

Seth Michael Hamblin

Resting On A September Sky

Resting in awe of the artistry
set before me —
Of crimson and amber shades,

A sky that whispers of
silence and peace,
Glances at the last of
the green blades.

Goodbye to the end of
the coneflowers and
tall clusters of chicory.

Cool winds are coming
warm fires are glowing,
The air, the smell of hickory.

Long walks and long talks
through the woods I take,
The sun glistens a pathway
leading to a tranquil lake.

I will never forget the September sky,
soon Autumn will come —
And the wind shall sing of memories gone by.

Lisa A. Muhs

Fire

I stood alone in the midst of a crowd
Trampling me 'neath a chaotic sound
I stood in fear and wonderment too
...Of what was mine? Of what to do?
I lit a torch and gently touched
The World afire — the World I'd clutched
I then stepped back (to see the light)
And watched it burn throughout the night
And as it melted ever so slowly
I noticed all who live so lowly
Eventually it ran a melted river
To see the world now only a sliver
Of something old — of something great
That made me hurt — that made me wait
The last alive — here to review
The things we have won have killed us too

And now I know without-a-doubt
It is I who breathes the victory bout
But as I sit and laugh at the dawn
I turn away and my river is gone.

Kjel Nassau

A Letter from Doug

Dear Mom and Dad, it's your son Doug,
I'm writing this letter from heaven above.

I'm surrounded by angels and we're having fun
Praising Jesus, God's only Son.

The first thing I did with Jesus by my side
Was to run over and look at God's Book of Life.

I'm so excited and I'm jumping with glee
Because I read, Mom and Dad, you'll be living with me.

You taught me God's Word and you taught me God's ways,
From the lips of Angels, God has ordained praise.

Praise is God's weapon to fight all our wars,
Praise is God's key to open heaven's doors.

So don't look to the world while we are apart,
Look only to God, for God looks at your heart.

Charlotte Greganti

Marriage

Together we run toward the boundaries of time
   in search for the answers, the reasons,
   the rhyme
Together we share life's loving embrace
   always driving for victory, in
   our children's young race
Together we drift toward life's final door,
   remembering the past, as one,
   we adore
Together we share our final farewell,
   a life full of dreams, memories too
   valuable to sell
Together we watch from the
   heavens above,
Together we lived
Together we love

    Martin Baxley

Peaceful Sleep

Lie down my child and rest for I am with you
My eyes are forever watching over thee
Sweet dreams I give to my chosen few
At the voice of my command the demons flee
I will cover you softly in my hands of love
The angelic choir will sing their lullaby
One day you shall be with me in heaven above
When the trumpet sounds we shall meet in the sky
Until that day I will dwell in your heart
Nothing, no nothing will ever keep us apart

    Joan Zalus

Reflecting

I've been reflecting on my life,
And all the things I wish could be
You're at the top of my wish list . . .
I just wish that you could see.

I understand you have reservations,
I have some of my own
But, I think that something genuine . . .
Should not be left unturned.

I think of you through the day,
And dream of what it would be like
To touch your face and kiss your lips . . .
For you to be all mine.

    Debra A. Emery

Orientation

My spars are unified in this mind, you see those?
Collectively they keep me denying the quantified machine nature.
Oh! I wish but people don't.
I do not care if my *pole* is broken but people, societies, my mother
   and my father do.
How can people be clear that we have finished if the *pole* breaks?
Psychological assimilation of dehumanized poles can be very helpful
   instead.
My analyses are stronger than these countries and the primitive ideas
   are f... stronger than this country.
Existential choice is not ours. Creation of the universe is not our
   choice either.
"I am going to step in and mess everything up." Ah! That would be
   so good!
Personal responsibility of our nature, our house, our divinity is at
   the core of the meaning of life for God's sake!
Harmony is what we get from the *mundus imaginalis*

Orient yourself, cosmosize yourself Occident!

    Dilsad Cire

Peace with Justice

"Peace, peace" when there is no peace:
When will our self-deception cease?
There are only wars and rumors of wars
While we worship at the feet of Mars.

The creed of men is boundless pride,
And they sell their weapons far and wide.
Their arrogance thrives and knows no bound
While their shouts of patriotism resound.

Men's greed consumes their very souls
And blocks the path to helpful roles.
They lust for power to rule the world
O'er which they want their flags unfurled.

True peace will come when our hard hearts break
And our cries for justice are more than fake,
When hunger is conquered by humanity's grace
With food in plenty for all the race;

When human bondage is in the past,
Then peace will come, this time to last.
Cry "Justice, justice" along with peace,
And wars and rumors of wars will cease.

    Harry Bertrand Taylor

Wonder

My life leads me to wonder . . . to contemplate possibilities of
   other paths.
Paths in which my life could have followed..

Is it true that everything happens for a reason?
Is it possible that I was meant to live my life differently?

Or is it Gods intention to have me constantly strive..
Strive to finally sit back and say this is who I exactly want to be.

Do experiences contribute to our personalities?
Do we need to endure the love, loss, and pain?

Love, to know that anything is possible?
Loss, to know it will not last forever.

Pain, to bring us back to reality . . . bring me back to reality.
Or is life just a single heartbeat, so quick then we are set free.

Free to something of eternal happiness . . .
Happiness that we never truly find in one lifetime.

Changes seem to overcome me . . . why do I not like who I have
   become?
Can I change into something acceptable . . . to others . . . to me?

Can I obtain the goals of my life long fantasies?
Can I find strength and courage to attempt true happiness.

I wonder.

    Tina M. Tobin

A Broken Heart

Love can make you think that they will
love you all the time.

When you turn around it's going down
   the drain.
Then thou finally realize that it is over.
You feel so alone and very very sad.
Yet it's still not bad.

    Margaret R. Franklin

287

The Power of Innocence

I want to dance in the rain like a child
And live by the rules of yesteryear
I want to be innocent, loud, and wild
And be creative without reason or fear
I want to live and die by passion
And abide by the laws of my soul
I want to fly by the wing of fashion
And never for an instant feel old
I want to cry without tears or feeling
And laugh with meaning and life
I want to feel this whole through its healing
And witness the power of the night

Jessica Edwards

Fearful Dreams

In a plane tied down to a chair
Flying through the darkness in the air,
I was scared and not looking out
Because if I did I might shout.

I was running through the jungle
Hoping to meet you there,
But instead I met a bear who had black hair,
Suddenly I remembered where I was supposed to be
I ran as fast as my legs could carry me.

I sailed through the sea on a stormy night,
Hoping to find you, shivering with fright,
But you were there to comfort me,
You sat me down on your knee,
Now I'm not frightened as you can see.

Benjamin D. Wright

O' For the Love of a Woman

It can be realized from infancy as we pass through our lifetime,
of a warmth ever present that touches us from within.
A closeness, a reassuring bond that could only exist between a
woman and child. O' for the love of a woman.
We face the immensities, the simplicities, the awe of life's
journey, our balance maintained by that knowing smile of a
mom that has no limits of love for her child.
With great bursts of joy and sometimes with sorrow thought
unbearable, we taste life.
And it is without question, without hesitation, that this joy and
sorrow is shared deep within her soul, for it would deny her
very sense of being not to do so.
And that somewhere in our lifetime we part only in distance, and
the yearning, the desperate need for such an inner strength is
not replaced but continued with a woman who would be, again
without question, your best friend.
It is from this relationship that we can renew our faith in trust
in its most pure form, for it is from a woman that we draw
our most precious gift of life. An undying love.
O' for the love of a woman.

William J. Vincent

Why?

Why this sacrilege in this world of yours?
Why good succumbs and evil endures?
Why men oppress one another,
And resort to kill even thy brother?
Why is there want when there's plenty for all?
Why people are divided by the race wall?
Why in the name of God and religion,
Do corpses fall of innocent men?
Why children's poor untainted souls,
Fall victim to this bloody toll?
Why can't we end all of this,
And try to peacefully coexist?

Madhumathi Krishnamurthy

Life

Life can be pleasant
Like a nice wrapped up present
Life can be love
Like a beautiful dove
You only make it the way it's to be
But sometimes it's difficult as crossing the sea
If you are mad or incredibly sad
There's always someone there
Trying to make it fair
So that's the way it goes
Someone's always there that knows
That usually seems to say
Try, be good and obey

Diane Kusicki

A Reflection of Time

We live our lives at a very fast pace, never taking time to see the
Face, the face of a child so full of hope,
A face in need of water and soap.
The face of our parents lined by worry,
We keep on rushing; we're in a hurry.

Where are we going and why must we run—we want to go grow up,
Go out, have fun.
We live each day as if there is always tomorrow, full of hopes and
Dreams without care or sorrow.
One day we stumble from running too fast, it's time to slow
Take a look at our past.

Mom was there to dry the tears, and Dad was there to calm our fears.
We got some help from sisters or brothers; we turned to our friends
And significant others.
Where did time go and what did we do—
How can we changed this—if only we knew!

Slow down my friend let me look at your face;
I want to remember this time and this place.
I want to take time a little more slow,
So I don't look back and say "Where did time go?"

Deborah L. Sterling

Candy Caramel Me

I am a light brown caramel brown
a chocolate candy sweet
with honey colored arms
and peanut butter feet

With almond shaped eyes and a
lemon shaped mouth
thick cherry lips that strawberry
pout

My hair is black licorice, my tears
sparkling water
candy caramel me the gingerbread
man's daughter

No snickers, no reeses, no nestle,
no twix,
my cocoa colored legs are made
of two milk chocolate sticks

People stare at me with peppermint eyes
they stare at my cotton texture hair
they marvel at my skin and the shape
I am in, a fantasy chocolate eclair

Tameca Franklin

Friends

Friends are the ones that help you when you fall,
Or they go looking around with you at the mall.
When you're looking down in the dumps,
And you need some money,
They cheer you up by being funny.
Friends are great,
You gotta have one,
They brighten your day,
Like they are the sun.

Joanna Harden

Desired Holiness

you search for God's pure face
only to be blinded by His holiness

His holiness causes you to tremble with fear
as you call Him "Father"

your child like faith is allowing you
to reach up with your little hand

to grasp and hold God's strong, mighty hand
to guide you through righteousness

never let go of your Father's hand
for it guides you where you need to go

but if you lose sight, listen to
His cry of mercy and forgiveness

never forget what He did on the cross
and never forget His nail printed hands

continue to follow in His footsteps
and keep listening to His voice

Anita Lewis

My Baby

Delicate hands and tiny feet.
She resembles an angel when
She's fast asleep.
All curled up and eyes closed tight
Just having her makes everything right.
She's what I've always dreamed about
With soft pink cheeks and a heart shaped mouth.
And watching her it's hard to deny
There's a miracle in front of my eyes.

Tricia Lee Meyer

Crying Out

Tears on my pillow as I lay myself down to bed with thoughts of you always running through my head. Wishing you were here lying next to me, because without you I cannot sleep comfortably. Tossing and turning all through the night, constantly my feelings I desperately try to fight. As I fall into a deep sleep, my dreams take me to a world of love and peace, where we are happy and madly in love. Holding each other on a beautiful sandy beach, where we would talk, kiss and laugh all day, and watch the sunset beyond the ocean just whither away. And as night time came we'd be doing the same. Holding you in my arms, making love under the stars, with just a blanket to shield us from the spray of the waves. Just imagine, just imagine those days. As I awake from my dream and find myself alone a tear falls down my face wishing you'd come home. And as I look into the mirror all I could see is a man with a broken heart crying out desperately. If you could see my face and look into my eyes you would see true love that I cannot hide. Wishing you'd wake up one day and realize my love for you is here to stay. Hoping you'd come back with your open arms and a heart full of love, praying for that to happen as I ask God from above. Realizing the truth and knowing you'll never come back, leaves me in a box, nailed and intact. And as they drop me into the ground, I still hope to hear, the pleasant sound of your voice telling me you want me near . . .

Albert Rivera

The Strong and the Weak

Looking at that person, I'm impressed,
Joy and peace, he radiates.
In God and good deeds, a true believer;
In the face of trouble, he never wavers.

Turning to the other, I feel ashamed;
Disheartened and confused, his life has no aim.
He's not faithful, neither is he smart.
Tested, he withers and falls apart.

For a long time, the two have known each other;
They live, and share everything together.
Yet, conflict exists, and constant fight;
Soul searching looms, in the darkness of the night.

What'll happen? I ponder;
Who'll win? Who'll withdraw? I wonder.
Awakened from reflection, I see;
Gazing in the mirror, there is no one . . . but me!

Peerasak Siriyothin

Tight

Flickers of light seep through green leaves
Street in patchwork motion
People, cars, colors
Family drifts forth

Protecting him
Father strides firm on one side
Mother trying to be brave on the other
They hold on tight

Head shaven pale face
He sees the cracks in the pavement
Contours, chips, imperfect shapes
They hold on tight

Clouds move in casting dark shadows,
Cracks in the pavement begin to fade
Mother strong on one side
Father trying to be brave

Nedret Andre

Dark

Listen.
The darkness speaks
It yells softly with low voice booming
Tension reigns
It engulfs us all.
A streetlight fights it
But it flickers in pain
The Darkness is too much
It rules everything.
We turn on our lights
Frantically trying to end it
But Darkness just laughs,
Its dark eyes gleaming.
We must give in; we don't stand a chance.
It melts in through our skin
and takes over our body;
We inhale its venom, and exhale our power.
It slowly weakens us;
We become a part of it,
Darkness reigns . . .

Mishi Schueller

Boardwalk (Ode to the Sea)

As I stagger out of you the impression in the sand gradually fades
But I'm drawn and redrawn back to you.
The pungent smell of the old wood deepens my senses and brings me
back to earlier days
Your undulations so parallel my life.
The curl of your wave rocks me . . . like a cradle,
And with the constancy of a mother's heartbeat the only crash that
is comfort
Will you accept,engulf or expunge me
Can I render you my pain
Or does it even matter . . .
As life means death and death means life
In this circle of existence.
My contemplation of you brings wisdom of many things
But never revelation of your mystery.
Your power doesn't scare me
Just imbues me with awe.
I'm so insignificant compared to you
And so dependent . . .
As a child.

Barbara Shaunessy

Faceless Memories

Whose face is that, so rich and young
Whose face is that, that death has stung
Whose face is that, whose time was stolen
Whose life was stopped, whose dream has
ended
   What senseless crime by night has come
   and drawn darkness on a soul undone!
Whose face is that, so still unmoving
Whose face has death's cold fingers woven
   Whose mothers tears are cried in vain
   Whose fathers pride has tuned to pain
   Whose silent room and unkept bed —
   Will never more their feet to tread.
Whose face is that
   Whose life is Finished!!
Whose face is that —
   Whose face was that —
    Whose face was that!

Carol Lockhart

Blow

It appears I've mislaid
the schematics of my life
Society lent voice
to right my way,
but I'd been up much too late the night before
to contextualise their verbs

The State, the Church
and the Old Lady at the Washaramma on 4th St.
All joined in the cause,
but I was in a bit of a rush
and had to excuse myself from their knowledge

The Truth came down one night
presenting itself thru my red philco
resonating notes of Wisdom and Sorrow
notes of Joy and Truth

Blow some riffs gently Miles
Blow

Bob Wallace

Commitment

I see life with an air of over indulgence in everything I do,
especially loving you.

Come walk with me, you can hold my hand and we can talk about
being kids again.

Let's go down by the water with a bottle of wine and dangle our toes
in the lake and think of nothing but us.

Look at the trees on the next shore blowing in the breeze, and the
houses set amongst them dotting the bank saying "wish you lived
here."

I do believe loving hearts will be extinct in the years to follow, so
many beautiful creations being threatened with extinction.

No devoted love, no commitments, sharing as one.

If in time you see me take love elsewhere, forgive me, it is not
lack of patience as you perceive it but a need like the air we breath,
for without it life makes no sense.

To love and be loved in return is one of the greatest joys of living.

Peggy Maier

Dream With Me

I lay in bed in slumbered sleep
and dream of you and me . . .
And though you are not here
and your face I cannot touch . . .
I am touched by the moment
because it's you I long to love so much.
Our souls dance and kiss
within the realms of my mind,
and love and contentment
in my dream I can find.
So, sleep my love
and dream with me . . .
And feel my soul
entwine with thee's
and when thou awakens
in the morning light . . .
Know I was there
loving you all through the night.

Ann M. Svoboda-Engler

Forever

You told me you loved me
You told me you cared
Forever you said we'd be
But who said love was fair.
You broke my heart and you want to do it again
Why can't you understand we're just friends
I love you and I always will
But when we were together everything went down hill
But just remember if you need me, I'll be here
No matter how far I am I'll be there
So keep your head up and your mind clear
Don't consider being alone 'cause in your heart
I'll be near
Just dry your eyes and smile again
Because no matter what we'll be friends.

Carey Grob

Metamorphosis

Sweet sleeping son, you lie in thick slumber,
Utterly unaware of your mother's absolute adoration.

No longer a little boy; but not quite a man
Your voice, muscle and sinew are often confused about their
status when you're awake.

But now - in peaceful, innocent repose, a transformation!
Your long, lean body curled into itself, eyelashes shadowing
sleep-soft cheeks, you are again my precious babe.

I kneel by your bed and breathe you in, memorizing your fragrance;
Bottling your sleep-smell in my memory for a near-distant day
when I can no longer silently, secretly, stroke your hair, and
kiss your neck as you sleep.

Ilona Dorsey

Untitled

Your laughter rings through the halls of academe
bouncing off the bench tops, rattling the racks of tubes
lifting my heart. I marvel at you
leaping around, reckless, cheerfully abandoned.
You make me repeat my words
over and over and over...
Your precious mind
incapable of boredom.
Years later I may see you —
I will foolishly recount
our conversations, searching eagerly
for a flicker of remembrance
seeing only your laughing three-year-old face
amidst your composed features.
You will smile, shyly, patiently,
not remembering, but still you will smile
out of kindness for this fond, wistful stranger
for already I can tell
there is great kindness in you
little one.

Raji Pillai

Nature

Nature is true wonder, elegant, and bountiful.
Arouse the feeling, sight, taste, touch, hearing, and smell.
The alluring planets, the stars, the sky, and the rain.
Unfold mystery on the earth for human brain.
Ruling scientists, the astronauts, happily wander.
Endless research in the Moon and Mars wonder.

Nature is mother living, and a bearing paradise.
Always tolerance the man's atrocities of polluting the place.
Towards advancement and development our goal we seek.
Unheeding the warming signal she shows in the in the peak.
Roaring hurricanes, flooding, and massive ice fall.
Evil disaster, crimes, and inhuman acts thrive uncalled.

Nature is godliness faith and peaceful.
Adopting a sense of creation and fortitude beautiful.
Through mercy, friendliness, and gratitude in plenty.
Unfailing hardwork, courage truthfulness and honesty.
Reward the humanity whose desire nature knows.
Extreme greed makes the world grieve in sorrow.

Nature the blooming soul needs care and love.
Always peace on earth and a smiling face.

K. Thavanesh

Sometimes

Sometimes the good is blotted out by the bad.
There are days the dawn never should have come.
Waves of sadness fill my mind.
As I try to wipe them away with good
I realize I cannot.
All good comes with bad.
Love comes to an end sometime.
Pain goes but is remembered.
Opportunities pass.
Friendships end.
Plans are ruined.
Hopes are crushed,
Sometime things just don't happen and I
can't help but wonder why.
People don't understand sometimes it is
good to be sad.
Sometimes it is better to cry.
Sometimes you have to be alone or
Sometimes you need a hug.
Sometimes I wish people knew what I need.

Sarah Givot

The Art of Flying

The Art of Flying
Didn't come easy at first.
In fact, she had some difficulty believing in the whole idea of it.
Never the less, it did give rise to some long forgotten past.

Have I done this before? She wondered.
Something about it does seem vaguely familiar.
Keep the Faith! She thought.
Believe in yourself...there is comfort in that!

Inwardly, she smiled.
Besides, there's much to do! Bravely she arose.
And, it's true they're all counting on me!
Yes! It's time for me to do this thing!

She closed her eyes,
Breathed deeply,
Slowly raised her beautiful wings,
and awoke within herself.

Oh yes! Now I remember!
She sighed in relief...
Opened her eyes,
And, gracefully lifted Heavenward.

Russ E. Deck

Stories

When eyes no longer see a face to love,
And all that's left of memory
Is hazy dreams of what was not,

When peace and loneliness are one,
And thoughts no longer linear, are non-shaped
And evidence a certain vagueness like a cloud,

When even prayers flow aimlessly,
They wander non-structured in non-words
Toward an indefinable Spirit/God,

When love's caress, tender upon the cheek,
Seems but impersonal ether or a warm breeze.
And all that's left of substance is the mist,

And we no longer care to hold to anything,
Then, then perhaps the stories of our lives
Will hold to us, and shape for us
   the meaning and the reasons why....

Bette Sushan De Leon

A Story With No Need for Words

I look into his eyes, I can see the world and all the pain
he has been through. His hands show his life. How he
labored under the sun for hours on end, for nobody's
appreciation. In his face are the marks of sorrow and
regret. His walk is a labored stride. As if he is trying to
put on the image opposite of him. His voice is gone,
due to years without use. To him life has brought no
joy. He feels empty and alone, he begs for it to be over.
However, he lives on. He lives his pain, which is more
than any word can express.

Kellie Enloe

Cosmetic Reveille And Review, 6:00 A.M.

Still these stalwart sentinels stand
erect and ever-ready.
Faithful foot soldiers fall in line
encountering the enemy:
dry hands, cracked feet, slick face, dank hair,
and any odors unfriendly.

So well they serve, their duty done.
They are my tried and true men.
My oath I give they'll never know,
though I be fed truth serum.

They who've served daily and faithfully
to battle with bottled action
engage in a lifelong struggle
that can't change the war a fraction.

Cynthia Hurd

Help

I am over heated in the valley of the Sun
A poet I am not
But the heat rash I do got
In the heat of June I begin to croon
One heck of a tune
While filling my spoon with the sweat of my brow
Sweating profusely sweating
July I will try to wrestle that fly
That comes with this heat
That I just can't beat
Sweating profusely sweating
August is here and I am just darn near
To tell all those stranger's of the danger's
For if you dally in my valley
This heat will be the wonder
that could put you under
sweating profusely sweating

Bob Whitsitt

All Is Washed Away . . .

All is washed away so quickly, all is washed away,
all of this is washed away, the dust, the flesh, the eyes.
So completely thrived in the vain, the proud, the fleet, the wise,
held ashore, condemned to live, from birth they start to die.
Silver rings of pools quiver and shine that they have cried;
for, all has been erased and purified by cleansing tides.
They will come again, hitherto, minus mortal stride,
all is washed away so quickly, all is washed away.
Flask of life you weather storms, the mercy of the seas,
crimson is my essence like the breath of fallen leaves.
On the shore the passing waves have marred the sands of time,
washing all away; the death of waters, earth, and sky.
One limp tree, whose branches twist and climb, sickly entwined,
bears witness to this gray ablution of the waning tide.
All is washed away forever, washed away to die,
all is washed away so quickly, all is washed away . . . .

Dejan Radovanovich

A Midnight Drive Home

A quiet snowfall drifts effortlessly to the ground.
The midnight streets are deserted.
Not a sound, not another soul.
The headlights reflect off the snow, it appears
    almost like morning.
Gusts of wind blow fiercely across the road.
I am alone.
One could get caught up in the peace and
    serenity.
The world glistens upon every snowflake.
I am calm.
The feeling is one I would never trade for
    anything.
It's me, the car, and the world.
Ten minutes of a solitary life.
No noise, no pressure, no stress, no problems.
A little piece of heaven...

Marty Roper

Somebody's True Story

I just got off the phone with you, you said you're leaving town.
So what am I supposed to do, just watch your life go down?
I thought you had your life on track, but then again you smoke.
Last week you mixed your weed with crack, away your life you toke.
The smoke went in, your brain checked out, I talk but you don't hear.
You're hooked on crack, what's that about, please save your life my
    dear.
You know I loved you my best friend, you've helped me through so
    much.
You're just sixteen this ain't the end, your life is in my clutch.
You know you are a part of me, and I won't let you go.
Just stop the drugs and listen to me, I'll help you through you know.
You did play sports, you got good grades, when drugs were not around.
Your life for drugs you made the trades, a whole new life you've found
First weed, then meth, then Special K, and now you're on to crack.
You've gone too far I have to say, I want my old friend back.
Run all you want away from here, it will not help your mind.
Spend all your crash on pot and beer, you're poor and alone you'll find.
Is that the life you want to lead, is that what makes you cool?
No home, no money, no car, just weed, or does that make a fool?

Erin Corinna Bowers

The Dance of Night

Thirteen stars in the ancient sky,
burning bright like the evening fire,
darkness spreads its loving hands,
as the sun retreats across the land.
Whispering winds in the evening bright,
flashing swords in the fading light.
Links of chain make a hollow sound,
with the wind on the water music surrounds.
Beauty lives in the burning dusk,
colors of blood, lemon and rust.
Shall I have this dance with you,
as the world slowly turns to darkness from blue.
Thus we dance in the dying day,
as above our heads the colors array.
So shall we twirl from the dusk to the dawn,
to the ends of the earth with a haunting song.

Liam Russell Hines

Strawberry Lane

I drove the winding lane of memory, recognizing
 old and new.
On that lane were Mayflowers, Trilliums, wild
 strawberries.
My Mother called, dinner, and we left our play
For only a while, and returned to an evening of play.

I drove further and saw headlines of infamy that
 disrupted all play.
When the darkness was cast off, when we looked to
 the future
We looked for wild strawberries.
We found sour grapes.

Memory lane! A record of smooth surface, bumps,
 potholes!
Softly, softly, the lane of memory moves into
Sunlight, moonlight and a radiance of unbelievable
 incandescence.
Our children, our grandchildren are finding wild
 strawberries.

Keith R. Hopkins

Peace Is Dead

Peace oh beautiful friend of mine,
You are worn from trouble, war, and time,
The fight was lost and you slowly shuddered away,
Listen for the fight carries on without a moment's delay.
Hesitant as you faded from loves lost sight,
Hate is now created against your peaceful and understanding light,

This is the in which our concentration was won,
Bring together your fast pain and metal caused death,
Stand strong while we whistle our created song,
Peaceful days wished by these forever saddened mornings,
Still the red sun summons the evil spirits of war.

Peace oh beautiful friend of mine,
I will whisper your name one more time,
You seem lost and locked away,
I am scared, but still you want listen to me pray,
It is hate and terror I dread,
But time is lost and peace is dead.

Ross Bowman

Making Sense

I feel discouraged and often dismayed
When I ponder how our country got this way.

So many lost—wandering in the night;
Spirits blinded—searching for the light.
Families torn, sinking in despair;
Millions of children—thinking no one cares.
Yet, election time is here, again;
Every candidate scurrying to win.
Politics has become big business,
They forgot us—their primary interest.

I feel discouraged and often dismayed
As I wonder how they got this way.

Multiple wars in far distant lands;
Even our heroes are victims—do you understand?
Bodies in battles continue to mount;
Suffering families—too numerous to count.
When will we listen and honor the call;
It's supposed to be "liberty and justice for all!"

I feel discouraged and often dismayed;
But, I still cast my vote on election day.

B. P. Taylor-Foster

The Beach

The sight of a Peachy Pink shell,
A wave coming towards me
so fast I almost fell.
Sea gulls crying, umbrella's opening,
life guard's whistle, blowing and blowing
smell of suntan lotion, sandwiches
and popcorn so yummy your face
almost twitches.
Your mouth is so dry and hot you
begin to think what food have I got?
The sizzling hot sun shining
right at you your thirst not quenched,
you know its very true.
It's been a great day,
Yes, it's been O.K, then you thank
your mom and dad with 3
cheers of hip-hip-hooray!

Madhu Punjabi

Witches

Witches have small houses.
Sometimes with small mouses
and a lot of noses and toeses.
They have big odesses in little jars
with candy bars, finger nails, banana peels
and little lady bugs.
Next to that there is a bowlulu in a purple jar
with little caterpillars and water big bats that
she turned into little bats and blood.

When you put it in the pot, you have to scrape it out.
You stir it til it's smooth.

Well that witch is very weird.
She has cloth ears and a pointed nose,
square feet with black hair,
and there's that witch . . . Sitting Next To You!

Ronda Louise Johnson

My Inspiration

For each day that passes without you
 in my life
A teardrop of loneliness falls for you.
A whisper of your name echoes throughout
 my soul.
A touch of your hand vibrates through to
 the inner parts of my body.
A single thought of you, travels a
 thousand miles
When I close my eyes, a vision of happiness
 appears, with you as my inspiration.
You have filled an emptiness in my
 heart
That will keep you with me always...

Roberta A. Fitka

Gone

You told me you'd love me forever
But forever has faded away,
You told me that you'd leave me never
But never has ended today.

Gone are the days when you loved me
Gone are the good times we shared,
Gone are the dreams for tomorrow
I wonder if you really cared.

I hear the wind in the twilight
Soon only darkness I'll see,
You're gone like the brown leaves that wander
Wherever the wild breeze may be.

Slim Michalek

Remember Your Age

Old is a dinosaur bone dug up from the dust.
Old is the Grand Canyon, its breadth and depth
Begun with one drop of water.
Old is a mighty Oak standing broad and majestic,
Four feet in diameter.

You are not old, you are a speck on the timeline of this Earth.
You are a mere babe, toddling, learning to walk into the other life.
Do not think of yourself as aged or ancient.
Do not fear death, it is a door, go through!

Rejoice and sing of reunions with those who have gone before you.
They will all chant and cheer upon your rising.
Rejoice and be glad in it, for you will see Him clear.
Into the heavens you will be, just as He has promised you and me.

You are wise, your lessons learned, you know the right way to turn.
You are not old, aged or ancient, you are God's grand teacher.
When your hair has silvered and bones creak and ache,
Look up toward your inheritance, for it is written.
When your work is done on this sphere of rock,
Life begins and never ends.

Holly Adams

Our Love Is Gone

I've always hoped our love for each other
would last.
I've always hoped our love for each other
would be true after all other loves have died.
I've hoped that you'd be in my
arms for an eternity.
I've always thought that we were meant to
be together for a lifetime.
But now for some reason our
love is gone.
A love that was meant to last.
A love truer than all other loves.
A chance to be with you for an eternity.
A chance to be together for a lifetime.
All this was ours, but now it's gone.
But the thing that hurts me most is
to know Our Love is Gone.

Scott LeBlanc

The Final Flight

Darker the light, into the night
On wings I fly, with terror I cry
Rivers of blood, with anger they flood
Drowning the sea, now evil roams free...

The beast is down there, I feel its cold stare
I shiver with fright, as it follows my flight
I try to fly higher, to stay over the fire
But the flames they grow nearer
Spreading hate, spreading fear...
I plead with this angel on whose wings I fly
Why take me here to this place to die...

It replies through my thoughts this angel of death
It speaks without words, it speaks without breath...

You've earned it my son, you chose to come here
It's too late to turn back...

This is Satan's frontier.

John Jacques

Freeze Tag

sodden feet slushing down the street down dark alleys
hey baby what's your name   more feet join the game
space becomes a small place
I don't have a name
                    feet play tag on snowprinted pavement
shoulder meets wall and
come on baby how old are you
frozen breath fogs through alcoholic fumes don't
touch me touch
me don't touch me come on baby
space itself
has become claustrophobic
words float through frozen air cracking like ice on the pavement
come on baby come on baby
feet move faster to keep up with feet running
for the light   fear is an unfamiliar hand groping
running feet fly into the night
body transmutes to stone   desperation meets
another wall
come on baby

Betsy Cacchione

Through and Through

I have no clear picture even now,
bobbing in and out,
a buoy on the black sea
that all the children swim around.

You see I wasn't fully there.
I floated
yet my body thrashed
and bird wings
beat my face
yet still they sat.

Abortion is a bloody thing.
I tell you that my words
for one week
will articulate
the red slick

That lined the paper blanket when I slept,
that filled the small hollow in my back —

And cannot say the words
will come again
after that.

Mindy L. Richardson

Else

How many day, I have dreamed of being somehow — else.
My mind would roam,
Then after, come home.
To wheat, and rye, and brome, a land of wind and wells.

I see within my mind's own eye, a glimpse of what might be.
But I hold a fear,
Of going there.
Away from fair and quiet eves, away from all that's close to me.

For my days are full of pleasant dreams, aspirations and
inspirations.
To leave these now,
I'd know not how.
And so, to thou, it's clear that I'm as full of apprehensions.

Why would I take leave, go 'way and deny, all that I've been given?
Leave the fold?
Search for fool's gold?
Or rather, live to grow old; yet know I had not striven.

Keelyn L. Ericson

Remember Love

Rain running down my window pane,
Every drop a memory.
Mirrors reflect you and me
Embers of the smoldering fire, the
Musky scent of you.
Believing you will come back to me,
Ever dreaming, ever wishing
Rivers aflood with my tears
Lakes awash with sorrow,
Overflowing with misery.
Visions of you, memories of passion
Enter my heart, my mind, my soul comforting me always.

Chibale Sakala

October In Vermont

They stand in stately splendor
Some crook'd from wind and cold
Coverings of different color,
These trees, both young and old.

Like cheeks turned pink from embarrassment,
Their leaves, red, yellow and gold
Some orange, pale green and scarlet
Jack Frost had kissed their toes.

Their limbs outstretched to heaven
They seemed to touch the cloud
Engulfed in so much beauty
I stood among them proud.

The world was quiet
Except for the sound
Of some of the leaves
As they touched the ground.

No wonder to me
There an eagle would nest
and other birds
Would stop to rest.

Ruth Y. Payne

A Willing Victim

She sits and waits for God to call her,
not imposing on His gracious hand.
The days is scheduled in its entirety,
and nothing disturbs its calm.
The sheltered sky is hidden from her,
but the sun is kind to reveal its gifts.
She feels its warmth upon her face,
now withered from a peasant's journey.
Jasmine fills the morning air,
igniting her memory's purpose.
By the wind she remembers its place,
and cradles it like a bird in her palm.
An instant glimpse within her heart,
of what life has dealt her.
A cynical few cast judgement on trial,
but she advocates its wisdom.
Those that cry out loud for mercy,
do not disregard the reason they beg.
Sadly she knows that many squander,
the greed of what the eye devours.

Karen Gail Hunt

In Defense of Small Boys

Don't criticize my child.
He is awakening to the morning of his life.
Shall he believe that God
Is full of rules that stifle joy,
Or shall he know that freedom comes from Christ?
Will you teach him to become a Pharisee?
God forbid.
Or a Judas who betrays his friends?
God forbid.
A fanatic who tramples the innocent in his zeal?
God forbid.
A smiling face who devours others with his thoughts?
God forbid.
Don't teach him to condemn.
Demonstrate the discipline of love.
Show him, ye ministers of God,
That Christ has room for all small boys.

Martha Koen

The Clouds of Summer

I love to watch the clouds
Pass over on a summer day
Changing their cottony shapes
As they move on their way
To the other side of the world.

Their ever-changing designs
Challenge the corners of my mind
To imagine all sorts of things
That I'm able to see and find
In the depths of my being.

Things that remind me of happy times
Spent in the far-gone days of boyhood.
Times of lying in the cool grass
With boyhood chums, dreaming of good
Things to come with the future.

The future, like the summer clouds,
Changed with the winds of time,
And now has become the present,
But the wonder of this little rhyme
Is that once again, I'm watching the clouds of summer.

Robert W. Kirby

Mother

She gave me the world, and said "It was all mine"
She said, "Don't worry, you'll do just fine."

She brought me up well, she was always around,
She was there when I was up, she was there when I was down.

She was always behind me, never hard to find,
She always supported me, no matter what I tried to climb.

She was always someone to depend on, someone ready to care,
She's given me everything, she's always been there.

She's there to help out, and always pitch in,
She does it over and over, time and time again.

She's my heart and my soul, and much more than that,
She sticks behind me, while others attack.

She's given me my self-respect, my heart, and my mind,
She's everything you want in a mom, I'm glad she's mine!

Happy Mother's Day!

James P. Hardy

The Facts

Teenagers everywhere
need to open their eyes and see,
That "harmless" teenage fun
is not all it's cracked up to be.

There's problems in the world
like diseases such as AIDS,
And once this ailment hits you
your life begins to fade.

Your eyes grow dark
your skin becomes pale,
Your energy abandons you
and you body becomes frail.

Proms, games, dates, and fun
have yet to say goodbye,
It's sad, one time of "harmless" fun
has left you there to die.

We all need to learn
to think before we act,
And remember, what we hear from
friends...are not always just "the facts"!

Amy Romagnano

Gray

Gray is the moon,
a silvery sight,
That shines on the houses,
in the middle of the night.
Castles with towers,
Armor on guards,
Clouds in the daytime,
Thin metal chards.
Mountains and valleys with new fallen snow
Wars and battles, fought long ago.
Gray is the color that will explain,
Emotions of loneliness, sadness and pain.
Gray is the color of dreary, cloudy days,
Spaceships and planets, in the gray haze,
Grey is my friends having bad days,
It's when I can't find my way through a maze.
Gray is the color of a fox's dark lair,
It's also the color of my grandma's hair.
Horses and ashes and dark gloomy seas
Gray is also the color of these.

Ethen Strader

Pink Is

Pink is a newborn's skin
   A teddy bear you win,
Pink is flowers
   Fragrant for hours,
Pink is a stone
   That many people own,
Pink is a Ballet
   Cherished for days,
Pink is a heart
   Pure from the start,
Pink is love
   From heaven above,
Pink is lemonade
   The taste doesn't fade,
Pink is a Valentine
   For your heart and mine,
Pink is a little tear don't cry my dear,
Pink is a crayon that colors on and on,
Pink is a color making life less duller,
Pink is a sunset the world is God's pet.

Stacy M. Collins

early morning
fresh dew lying on the fluorescent grass, uncultured
moistening the crisp blades
as you walk the dampness stutters mildly along your legs, tickling
   them
there is an illumination of sweet composure surrounding this palace
and straying down to the languid bay one can hear the waves
folding
   to the shore
the belligerent, senseless rocks even recognize it but for years have
   not wavered
fog rolling in, there is no discord, no conflict
a soothing, balmy silence, yet the waves—
shyly, swiftly grasping the last coattails of a fabric forgotten,
   drawing you in
resistance is unimaginable, for it deceives you well
the ripples in the water are tender, even
there have been other times when they were intense
taunting earth, curiously dancing farther along the edges
making your heart beat faster
now it is difficult to fathom
as one gazes out beyond the banks
sea gulls lurk above the shining water for an ever enduring moment
   in time
While you watch; motionless, transfixed, staring silently into the
   ominous bay
concealed . . . mysterious waters

Randi Stern

Grandfather's Pictures

In silence I have met the early morning
Of a cold room, my eyes opening
To pictures of the family past on my wall
Where the faces of the dead keep my company
Their silent smiles escape the glass panes
Glass that presses images back
Into the frame — and into blood
My own blood that echoes their
Black and white features
And runs in their dreams
            Isolated in the instant
                  of a camera's shutter
Their departed faces survive
      only in the photographs
      with their hands immobile in the moment.

But the rising sun
   with reflecting light from the glass
   and warmth on my cheek
Tells me they keep a silent watch still.

Rod Ricardo-Livingstone

Gestalt Workshop

Fifteen strangers gathered, everyone in pain.
Everyone was different. Everyone the same.
Everyone was hurting. No one understood.
Each deserved to suffer. Each was no damn good.
Each one had been injured. Each one had been maimed.
Each one hated hating. Each one was ashamed.
Each one cried for answers. Answers were not there.
Everyone told everyone, I love you, you're not bad.
No one was believing. No one was made glad.
On and on they rode them, their crosses, wild and bucking.
They held on fast, they cursed their fate, and cursed their
   damn Mind F**king.
So twenty hours later, everyone was drained.
But everyone felt lighter, their worlds a little brighter.
Their guts a little rung out, twisted to the pit.
Like having diarrhea, they'd squeezed out all their sh*t.
Yes everyone felt better, they had it more together.
They were a bit light headed, and a lot elated.
So they all went home then, and they were constipated.

Shirley Malley Resua

My Neurotic-Hum

A secret place . . .

Is the vault of my passion
Here I unfold my religion. . .
To unravel the diploma of my soul
A cabin to my rescue
An eclectic queue

I search for that dramatic clue
To sow the edible grains of sorrow
That drowned-an-un-winged-sparrow
The emblem of my panicked desires . . . unwanted . . .

A stolen token in the gravity of its momentum
Lead . . . is the symbol of my weakest shield . . .
It penetrates . . . through . . . the spectrum of my descending hue.
Nature—it understands this cursed pasture—an armor to embellish
The sudden tacit . . . a key—to an operatic mute . . .

My frozen tongue licks the malty-murky-paradise . . .
    heaven knows . . .
I am numb . . . . I've plagued the nightmares inside the coffin..
To welcome . . . the cue to my neurotic hum.

Papillon

The Importances of a Child

Before he was born it wasn't respected, the news was
something not expected. Little boy with rosy cheeks, the
prints of his little feet. Blue eyes like the sky, a smile
that would lift you high

From the start he was property to use, the parents to
hurt each other. In the middle he did stay without anyone caring,
to him what mattered. Life was empty than he came soft, a bundle
of joy. For you see my grandson was that little boy.

To teach him and protect him was a joy, buying him his first
little toy, but sadness has come and went in his life from mommy
to daddy he seem to always went. So, confusion he knew this little
todd.

I've heard his little cry's from time to time calling Ma . . . .
Ma . . . His little feet did run. That is when my arms went up to
comfort him. You see I've been there for him as much as I can
be to give him love and help him too play.

Giving him joy and love was worth it all to me, just to
give to that little boy. For he is gone from my life but the love
will always be for God gave it to me, just for that little boy.

Phyllis G. Smith

The Seniors' Christmas

Twas the day before Christmas and all through the room,
The Seniors were busy with dust rag and broom.
Mary was working planning gifts and party fare
Betty was planning all the food with great care.
The kitchen was all in a whirl with cookies and cakes,
The girls in their aprons, with all the foods that they make.
The gardners were all finished with the shovels and rakes,
A tree was decorated and it wasn't a fake.
Lights were aglow in the windows so bright,
The cards had come in and were hung just right.
The girls in the office had just took a break,
They planned for the party and they wanted no mistakes.
The Christmas bazaar was over and done,
The Crafters had packed up their wares and their fun.
The singers had practiced all their favorite ballads,
The musicians were there and ready to show their talents.
And everyone sang as the season was done,
Merry Christmas to all and Good night everyone.

Marie E. Clark

Hand In Hand

Take my hand, hand in hand,
and we shall walk to yonder shore.

There we'll dream of olden things,
and tarry till the sun goes down.
O'er the sea as it dips and plays,
We'll watch the colors of evening shade.

Sit upon the once sun-kissed sand,
Now damp and cool in moonlight bathed.

We gaze up toward the star-filled sky,
It gives us peace, and love is born.

Take my hand, hand in hand,
We shall dream of a golden land.
Far away from yonder shore,
And hold my hand forevermore.

Diane Templeton

Never Knowing Your Last Goodbye

I see you standing in the spotlight now.
The time has come for you to take a bow.
You were in the show and we all noticed you.
You took a chance on love. Who knew exactly what to do?

I never knew how much I'd really care
Till something special is no longer there.
Why do changes have to come so suddenly?
I want you here again just like the way things used to be.

It seems like yesterday we fell in love.
Time went so fast what were we dreaming of?
I remember all we did as love would grow.
You'll always be right here with me wherever I should go.

You never will know until the end
That you've said your last goodbye to a friend.
You'll always remember that look in their eye
Long after they're gone you still wonder why.
You never know until the end
Your last goodbye to a friend.
You never had the chance to cry
Never knowing your last goodbye.

Ralph Brunson

Jen

Once my dreams were of endless romance and innocent things
But dreams are made of moonbeams and gossamer wings

They say that dreams can't survive the daylight
Nor can windmills be fought forever by an innocent Knight
The march of time takes its toll and Princesses don't exist
Just the press of time and the dreams that become lost in the mist

And with each hurt, the dreams slowly die
and it becomes just a little easier to live a lie

It's so easy to say there's no time, but I'll find someone, someday
and somewhere, deep inside, you begin to wonder is that a lie?

Then I looked into her eyes and saw the green of forest meadows
and flashes of gold like sunbeams through the shadows

Her smile mysterious and dark
reminded me of the dreams of my heart

And my heart soared and I wondered is she the one?
I want to tell her that she has my soul, but she'll never know . . .
    I'll never tell.
Because, you see, the castle I've built to keep me safe
was just a lie. A self made prison, a self made Hell

All I can do is look to the night stars, like I've done since I've been ten,
and only the stars will see my tears and perhaps hear a soft
whispered, "Jen"

Derek K. Hirohata

Life's Challenge

This life is a challenge for each one of us
Yet to enjoy the ride, you must board the bus.
How do you tell people of such a great thrill
And encourage each to engage in with whatever skill?
The person who sits and let's life go by
Is discarding God's gifts, to which I just cry
"Wake up, oh my love, and enjoy this His world.
For He created it for you in all its glory unfurled.
And while there are problems and imperfections too,
The wonders far exceed these rough spots but few.
I know there are people who would give what they could
To live life to its fullest and believe that you should.
These are the lame, blind, deaf and infirm,
Yet how do they tell you there is so much you could learn?
If only you would grasp this life by the mane
And ride on into life - into which all of us came."

Ruth Winning Johnson

Who Me?

I can be as sweet as sugar, and cold as ice
and if I want to...the spice of life

I can be ambitious, but never superstitious
I have no money, but plenty of pride

I dream of self-determination
I like originality and flexibility
but being in love was cooperative economics...

Criticism is hard work, emotions are discrepancies of unity
and visions that are prerequisites of moodiness and crisis
and identity and self-actualization are personal obligations

Priscilla E. Wagstaff-Hines

I Wonder

Sometimes when riding in our car,
I see people and wonder who they are
As they whiz by in their car.
I often wonder if and when
I will ever see them again.

So many have passed by "in review,"
Thousands and thousands, but few I knew.
And I wonder how it would be
To meet all these people and to see
What they are like, just them and me.

Sue Chuzi

Encounter

A chance encounter
a timeless chance
a brief moment
a fleeting glance
could you see the feeling's inside
could you here my mind
could you see the way my heart trembled inside
there is a wanting
an empty place
it is there for some one to take its place
such emotion wrapped inside
too much to show so little to hide
Time is forever
so we will meet again
I know not know
I know not when
the world is small
really a tiny place
until we meet again

Garrett McFarlane

The World Today

What has happened
To our world of peace?
It was said that
It shall not cease.
What evil rage has driven us to war?
People changing more and more.
What has happened to our world of perfection?
It has gone! Was that our choice? Our mere election?
Our world is slowly vanishing,
Fading into the dark.
It just started leaving,
Without sign nor mark.
You cannot spend your life hiding
From the evil force.
What has happened to our light,
Our lives, our love,
Our source?

Katalina Williams Age 10

My Place

There's a place I can go, and the world stays away
No worries, no cares, just me and I play
In the soil, like a child, I dig and I sow
I plant and I mulch, I sharpen my hoe
There's my old wicker chair and a hot cup of tea
And I dream of warm sunshine, butterflies and bees
Then my mind takes a trip
From the day to day strife
And I tune into nature and that wonderful life
Of gardens and flowers, of rainbows and birds
There's a kitten, a puppy and a warm cotton shirt
This place feels so cozy, I prop up my feet
And I think of a loved one who made this for me
Would you like to come visit?
Your soul will be fed
In this quaint little building
Called my "Potting Shed"

Jean Hagan

Celestial Symphonies

My soul will not be shut in . . .
My thoughts shall set it free . . .
My soul need not be
earthbound like me.
Rather let it reach out
to touch the heartbeat of mystery.

My soul need not be shut in . . .
I'll have it to soar and soar
o'er this world to explore
till it touches the edges of stars.
For there's music in the spheres,
music mortal ears cannot hear.

My soul shall boundless be
reaching out to the spherical sea.
Then shall it bring back to me
the insight my eyes cannot see.
My soul will not linger within these bars
as long as there's music in the stars.

Evelyn Daniels

Phone Call From Tia

"Grandma," the little voice came over the phone, "my
daddy left us and mom and I are all alone. Grandma,
Mama cries all the time and I don't know what to do.
Could we please come and live with Grandpa and you?
  Daddy lives with a new girlfriend, and she has kids
of her own. They do things together we always wanted
to do and daddy never even calls us on the telephone.
  Grandma, I hurt so much, what did I do wrong? Grandma,
can we stay with you awhile, I don't know for how long.
Mommie cries all the time and don't have time to hold
me anymore. Doesn't she know I'm just a little girl
and I hurt too. Grandma, can we come live with you?
  Momma says Daddy still loves me, just not her anymore.
But Daddy doesn't live here he just walked out the door.
Momma says I must always love him even though he's left and we're
all alone. But Grandma he doesn't even call me on the telephone.
  Grandma, do you and Grandpa still love me?"
The little voice came over the phone. "I'm so scared,
and Mommy's crying, Daddy's gone I don't know where."
  Grandma says "We love you sweetheart and we'll be right there."

Kaye Vukelich

Snowfall

I lay in bed thinking about snow
How it falls so lightly and
Lands like a feather floating to the ground.
But minutes later the world makes a sign
That it is coming to storm.

Its sign sounds like the screams of eagles,
The howls of wolves,
And the cries of fretful children.

I sit up and look to the window,
For the wind is magically taking the snow up and up into the air.
The little flakes look like small pebbles
Being thrown to a far distance.

I feel the air breezing through the crack of
The open floating window.
I spring out of bed to close the cold
And threatening air that blows through and through
Before I can budge it,
I hear a low deep roaring voice
Telling me, the country, the world.
That winter has now taken over.

Megan Cochrane

Grandfather

Distinguished man, man of honor
At ease with his thoughts, at peace with his life
A man who gave to his country and took nothing in return
A man who saw places I have only dreamed of
A man who's greatest achievement was surviving it all
He never complained and only cried once he loved me as if I was his
son am I letting you down? Am I still your grandson?
Why did you have to leave?
I miss you!!! I wish you were here!!!
Put away those tools where they belong! Yes, grandfather
Take care of your mother and grandmother after I am gone
I promise I will!!! We buried you on a clear beautiful day
On a beautiful site looking out to the rolling hills
Hills that are filled with wildlife
And plenty of trees for you to look at
Not to mention the birds that fill the area with beautiful music
I think you would approve Grandfather, I understand what you
  meant now
Things in life do have a purpose
You gave me a soul and a love of life
I am your greatest achievement I miss you I love you watch over me

Kevin S. Burrous

Grandma's Lake

When I was quite small, so many things I remember
Toys, fun on the farm, and Christmases in December.
But the best memories I have so clear,
Are those summer days at Grandma's lake that I'm glad are still here.

Grandma had the cabin long before I was born.
I'll never forget the smell of the lake on those summer morns.
Grandma would always drop everything to take me on walks,
If I got tired, I'd tell Grandma, "I'm all out of power," then we
would stop and have our little talks.

No matter what she had going on,
She'd never pass up a chance for me to stay all night long.
All those late nights playing cards, just Grandma and me.
I love my Grandma so much, can't you see?

I sometimes wonder if Grandma was sent from above,
She's like the sweet white angel of a dove.
Roasting marshmallows and fireworks on the 4th of July,
I hope I never have to say good-bye!

You can take away the sunshine and the rain,
But never leave me with the pain. For Heaven's sake,
Please never ever take away my Grandma's lake!

Jordan Autumn Jensen

The Beauty of It All

The full moon shines brilliantly over the land
It sits in the star filled sky as an island in an ocean
With splendor it lights the countryside
With care it pours out its healing powers
As the night will go on, the moon shall track across the sky, with
  obedience, to its resting place

The water in the nearby creek trickles softly along
It sounds as refreshing as the night's brisk, cool air
It feels sensational flowing down my throat

The campfire crackles occasionally
Now and then spitting a stray flame
Its warmth radiates outward stealing the chill from my bones

There is a slight and quiet breeze which tops off the night
It blows just enough to bend the fire's waves toward me, as it brings
  news of the creek nearby
Every now and then it rustles the leaves in the trees, but only enough
  to make me aware of them
Now I drift off to a very peaceful sleep

Kevin M. Sullivan

Like A Rose

She is like a rose, the most beautiful flower.
And she keeps getting prettier by minute and hour.
She gave me my life, which I can never repay
but with the love that I show and I give everyday.

She is my mother, my teacher, and friend
And that bond we share for lifetime,
never shall it end.
She protects me through the day,
and watches over me at night.
We understand each others troubles,
but never do we fight.

I love you my dear mother, I'd never do you wrong
For this bond that we share, I feel is very strong.

Tasha Smith

Changes in the Heart

The day my life found meaning - that day just two years passed . . .
No longer lost and wondering, my purpose or my task . . .
He came into my heart, to live with me each day - to guide
and give me wisdom, through His word and how to pray . . .
He's shown me many wonders many miracles have I seen . . .
He replaced my fear and worry, with peace and faith to intervene . .
.
In my heart with trials I've suffered, no different from the rest . . .
But the strength and hope through His word I seek, to gain victory
through those tests . . . He's shown me gifts I had never used
without him such a waste . . . my eyes were blind and could not
see, my meaning or my place . . .
In his word I've found the answers — little understanding in the
past . . . but now through him a wisdom, to apply his word, when
in prayer I ask . . .
His patience never falters with love for us he'll wait . . .
giving us a new beginning, growing in His word day by day . . .
He'll pick us up and hold our hand, when unsteady we may fall . . .
To help to guide us down that path His grace and love to
each and all . . .

Sharon Anthony

The Mirror In My Window

Out of the window I look every morn,
waking up whenever a new day is born.
Observing the light which keeps breaking the dawn,
moving the shadows away from the lawn.
One voice out of many is heard,
Belonging to the heart of a new baby bird.
Why it cries, is a mystery to all,
but only the mom is there to answer its call.
Finally content, it sits back in place,
giving me a chance to clean up my face.
When I return, I find it trying hard,
to crawl out of the nest while its mom is off-guard,
wanting to explore all of nature's ground.
Fortunately, the mom turns around,
pushing it back where it belongs;
always there for it and correcting its wrongs.
Looking at it I know what I see,
I've realized that the baby bird is me.

Mohammad Yusuf Haroon

My Little One

The time has come my little one, we finally meet at last
My thoughts are like a freight train, constantly rushing so fast
Not a minute can go by, were my mind will ever rest
There are whirlwinds of emotion, weigh down upon my chest
I wonder what you are thinking; can you feel the way I do?
It's like a supernatural, overwhelming love inside for you
There's no control it's so intense; at times it leaves me weak
Yet the power of my little one, shows I'm very meek
So whenever you will need me, in an instant I'll be there
A team we'll always be; our troubles we can share
Now that we're together, never shall we part
For you my little one, hold all the pieces to my heart!
This is just a start...life's now begun for you and me
  my little one!

Arthur T. SanJulian

Flowers

Flowers awakened by the morning sun,
Make this day a wondrous one.
Pert, saucy faces lifting to the sky;
Embrace the breeze as it goes by.
Some are short —
Some are tall —
Showing their beauty to one and all.
They dance and sway to the music
of the wind, inviting all to look
at them.
The birds —
The bees —
The butterflies —
are tantalized and mesmerized;
drinking in their beauty as they
flutter by.
When evening comes and shadows
creep, they bow their heads as if in sleep.

Betty J. Kabbe

When You Love Someone

When you love someone
You love them no matter what,
You love everything about them,
No matter what their past might bring,
You love them.

Whatever life brings,
You must still love them.
For no matter what happens in life,
There's nothing more precious than love.

So remember —
When you love someone,
Love them.

Thomas Allen

Hands

These hands of mine have now grown old.
I cannot count the memories they hold.
Hands that were held when so very small
Were taught how to write, play bat and ball.

The hands that were held in her "courting days"
Tried to show love in their own little ways.
Hands that held babies with such pride and joy
Always grateful to God, whether girl or boy.

The hands that washed dishes, dusted and sewed
Now also did laundry, planted flowers and mowed.
Hands that applauded all the kindly deeds
Reaching out to comfort in time of needs.

With hanky in hand, wiping away tears
As children married and began adult years.
Hands that always tried to just be there,
Were never too tired to fold in prayer.

Sometimes the hands hurt now, just holding a book,
But I have to recall how they used to look.
Hands that will be folded, as I take my last breath.
Just remember the love they hold . . . even after death.

Marge Dwan

On Art

Unstructure, then unstructure, pull
undone..
break down, now push apart stone after
stone.
Break open that faint, gray unyielding canopy
take down, disassemble supine walls
or walls at angles holding, pushing in.

Yet knowing walls-walls-barriers
still must be,
and disregarding muses, muses all
for something of creation floating free
they fall.

Bettie J. Stephens

Young Girl

I have seen ships sale in commerce green
and sink when looking for profundity.
Half on the line of the flat parallelogram they stopped
then tumbled silently over edge.
Their professional dancers knew how to escape fear,
but not reality.

You have seen pirates bring gold, passion, and broken skulls.
But now, some of their crew misconstrues and it's time for the
government success. Are they going down without a fight?
Maybe they should give up their rights, their treasures, their minds.
But then they wouldn't be pirates.

Crimping toes hold edge of plank.
Still holding rank, a plunderer feels the dancing gypsies are real -
as real as anything else.
And fear is no longer money for a meal,
but platformed heels breaking the tranquility of deep waters.

And the alarm clock rings at seven o'clock.
And you tie your shoes. And brush your hair. And go to school not
yet aware the autocratic librarian washed up on last night's shore
while real pirates eats a cheese sandwich.

Mark Liskey

Untitled

Up to the stars, beyond to knowledge,
seven hoped to continue the search,
a sudden blast and dreams, hope up in flames,
as millions watched in stunned horror:
God reached out to spare them some unknown fate.
To us a disaster, to them greater peace known
only to those he has touched.
His power greater than man's, his knowledge of things yet to come.
A warning, an omen! God only knows,
will we read and understand his warning?
For all mankind!

Philip A. Caskey

Images

  Golden-yellow splashes of light dance
on the comforting ground around you
moving in harmony with the sway and
rustle of the giant leaves.
  The stems bend all the same
as though tied together by a magical bond:
The sweet evening wind
that seems to appear from the unknown
carrying clouds that awaken
the dreams and imaginations of all.

Mette Arnmark

Echo Across Time

Hear it boldly speaking in the night.
The rhythmic pulse stretching mind so tight.

Repetition from a time before her resurrection.
Straining the sanity to understand its implication.

Hear its sharp cry amidst sounds of the day.
Feel its cutting edge when it is time to go play.

Its presence stifles in downtown's hustle and bustle.
It threatens the being as the winds make leaves rustle.

The mind rants and screams, but never drowns it all out.
The body quivers and the soul gives a silent shout.

Invasive, pervasive...the bones vibrate in rhythm.
The screaming in the night causing maniacal schism.

Press your hands to your ears...make it go away.
It is there continually, all the minutes of every day.

Just standing here alone in the midst of all around.
Where is the sense, where dear Lord is the sound?

Where is there shelter so there is a time to rejoice?
To be done with the echo...done with absence's silent voice.

David L. Faircloth

Untitled

A child cries for the hopelessness unchanged,
Most will never feel.
Their compassion turned numb by repetitive pleas.
Are they still listening; the child is real.

A youngster hangs out on the street all night,
Searching for the acceptance he craves.
He finds it for a few dollars, soon to beg for more.
A choice, a path, leading to an early grave.

An elderly woman rocks, staring at nothing at all;
Forgotten by the ones she adored,
Priorities distorted by time - precious memories fade.
She clings to the book, unshaken faith in her Lord.

Carefully consider each decision to be made.
Thoughtless words or actions can easily hurt others.
Know your spirit, let your heart be your guide.
Every day holds a new way to be good to your sisters and brothers.

Katie Queen-Pace

Ice Blue Skies

Wake up in the morning with emptiness;
Knowing that you've gone without me;
Thinking that you'll knowing what is best;
I'm letting you go and setting you free;

But then I realize the fool that I've been;
By accepting things just as they are;
Shot in the foot with the losing hand;
Trying to catch the shooting star;

Ice blue skies, falling all about me;
Chained to the wall, longing to be free;
Can't you see the end is blue; it will be here soon without you;

Remembering the day I saw your smile;
I'm trying to capture the love; laughing and having fun for a while;
Gaining our strength from above;

Now is the day we part in our ways; saying our last goodbyes;
Thinking about the good ol' days;
Ending now with an ice blue skies...;

Ice blue skies, falling all about me;
Chained to the wall, longing to be free;
Can't you see the end is blue; it will be here soon without you.

Willie Abood

My Guardian Angel

Oh, my guardian angel, I know where you are.
  Walking close beside me shining like a star.
What would I do without your care?
  Would I make it safely anywhere?
There is no one else I will ever find
  Who will walk me through the present and leave the past behind.
Although my heart is fragile, this you understand,
  I know it's well protected in your gentle hands.
You must see the face of God shining down upon you.
  Your radiance is everywhere, so honest and so true.
I know you will never leave my side
  Even through the most difficult turns of the tide.
Isn't it a wonder how you're the only one who stays
  When the worst is getting the better of my days?
At times, the weight of the world is too much, I need my own space,
  You guide me safely away, you, my saving grace.
Your presence is so dependable, your spirit so free,
  Without you, Guardian Angel, who would watch over me?

   Kendra K. Minton

Life's Paths

Life is like someone who is new to town.
The person knows if they continue they don't
exactly know where you are going to end up.
But they also know if they stop and turn
back they would be better off. Some people
would rather take a chance but if you don't
really know where you are going to end up.
My advice to you is to stop and turn back to
where you will be better off. And maybe if
you have found a signal or sign that tells you
that you could do the path you know in your
sleep then maybe you could go and take a
chance at the path you don't know. So
now if you get lost you have a
better chance of finding your way back.

   Gloria Celiant

The Strongest Lady I'll Ever Know

She led what seemed to be a happy life.
She made our lives what they are today.
Forever will she be in our hearts.
Life dealt her many things.
Things none of us could overcome.
She overcame them beautifully.
The last thing life dealt her was her most devastating.
She made those last moments last forever.
It put her strength to the test.
If it had happened any other time,
She could have handled it easily.
Her hardest just wasn't good enough in the end.
God wanted her to join him.
Now Grandma is free of all her troubles.
My only wish is for her to be happy.
I know she was happy her last days.
Now she can be even happier.
Cause she can join her husband.
Maybe she'll even talk to my grandpa Anderson.
Grandma, "I love you!" More than this could ever say."

   Jessica Gillette

Psychosiprosity

Three elderly ladies walked down the street;
One fat and one tall, the other petite.
The fat lady munched, ignoring her weight.
The tall woman limped; lamented her fate.
The smaller one boasted of cash in her purse,
Said, "Rawther" and "Dahling" and quoted some verse.

The fat woman chuckled and talked of her friends,
Her ten children's capers and freudian trends.
The tall one avowed, "I'm a spinster by choice;"
Then spoke of love spurned and a fatal rolls royce.
Dressed modish but frilly, the little one said
That she'd had three husbands and now they were dead.

Three elderly ladies walked down the street;
One fat and one tall, the other petite.
To hazard a guess why such friendships exist
Do they find in each other things they have missed?

   Hal BocKoven

She Lives Within Us

Anne Frank was a very special girl
With many dreams and hopes for the world
But these dreams were ruined by a very cruel man
Whose goal was to kill jews all over the land

Anne Frank lead a very normal life
Until Hitler came along and made it full of strife
She and her family were forced into hiding
While many unfortunate jews were wounded and dying

In her hiding place called the secret annex
There were still many times of despair and panic
She had a secret diary where she wrote all her thoughts
She wrote about the world her life and things she would have sought

The time came when she finally did get caught
But the diary was left behind holding all her secret thoughts
It was holding all those memories of those terrible days
Waiting for someone to read of Hitler's terrible ways

But she is kept alive
Hitler could not take her spirit
She will never ever die
She lives within us

   Julia Handel

Days End

High thin spots low wet
in fine, the longer rays of light.
Clear through agreeable landscape,
robins from the past, sleepers below.
Green spring grass delineated.
His calculate duration accounted,
imprints wisely executed memory.
Adorn by man, summons natures author
with motive of necessity conferred.
Fraternity of man, not of mortal hands.
Established birth of human employ.
Created in six days bound to man's
universal benevolence to preserve.
Explain heavens day one diurnal rotation
around its own axis is the basis of true law.

   Mark W. Moore

The Breeze

The trees sway back and forth in
Rhythm with the grass, any slight breeze
Could set them off on a summer day
The pine's as tinsel in the summer light
The others so beautiful you can't describe.
The breeze tosses your hair to and fro, it feels like
autumns in the air.

Devon Miller

Morning, Somewhere

Morning comes, but where am I?
I who love the morning so
I'm not here, but where am I?
I must be somewhere
Tell me where I am. Find me.
The morning is cold and calm and unto itself
Did I dream? No, it was no dream.
Where am I?
I am here, but I am nowhere
I am awake, but in a dream
I must live in the dream
There is now no more reality for me
No rationalizing, no talking it out
The brink is reached, and I am there
Only you can find me, reach me
It was real
It was real
The morning is still, and I love it, the morning world
We belong to each other, the quiet, the peace, the calm
The sounds that are no sounds

Charlotte Shamlin

The Treasured Owned

The foreign waves, they corrode this empty shore,
Shaming the land,
On this crisp Autumn morning.

Crash!
They roar mightily against the proudest rock,
Humbling feat,
Into the smallest pebble.

"Oh, inflated worth,
I'll sweep you away!"
Declares the sea in the roar of the wave,
Filling the land with a new-found respect
  for this awesome force.

If you look closely at the waves,
You can see the Caress in each tidal kiss,
Impassioning her angelic eyes,
Drowning willing hearts, into eternity.

David Johnson

Lost

Charcoal sky, outlined with dim traces of light
Sketched in the darkness, painted faces fill the night
A lost soul roams the Earth, yearning to be free
While the midnight soldier searches for his sanity

Skeletons dance upon the graves of the living
Imprisoned, the caged bird still longs to sing
Cries for help, but no one can hear
Shadowed voices of reason, ignored year after year

Fire breathes through winded storm
Lost in isolation, far beyond reality's norm
Sands of time trickle through the hourglass of day
While with every breath our lives slowly fade away

Jason Derkevics

Fire and Life

You strike a match
Sparks fly
The sparks turn to flames
You have a child
Everyone is happy
The child grows up
The flame and the child are the same
They make other flames and other children
But they both don't last forever
They both die
Fire and life are the same

Chad Smith

A Grandchild

There's something about a child, especially if it is a grandchild.
He or she is gifted and talented in so many ways,
especially if it is a grandchild.
You give them special care and listen to their cries,
especially if it is a grandchild.
You walk the floor and wonder how they are doing when
they are so far away, pictures that are sent through
the mail make you feel closer, especially if it is a grandchild.
A grandmother's love is very heavy she cherishes her
grans in all ways far they are special in so many
ways, that's a grandchild.

Cora Lee Palmer

Thunder Bay

The sky is clouding up,
The clouds are turning gray.
A storm is brewing on Thunder Bay.
People take cover all through the town.
Some go to malls, others to churches,
The rest go home.
One man, with deep blue eyes,
Does not go anywhere, he waits in despair,
Knowing a storm is brewing on Thunder Bay.
He climbs into a box beside a dumpster.
But what good is cardboard against the rain.
The first faint sound of thunder is heard,
It echoes through the bay.
A few cars pass him now and then,
None stop, but they all look.
You can now see the lighting striking the water,
You can hear the thunder on the bay.
He has a worried look on his face.
He knows a storm has reached Thunder Bay,
And it may never go away.

Lisa Reed

Love You Honey? 'Course I Do!

"Do you love me honey?" 'Course I do.
My love for you is always true.
"Do you love me honey?" 'Course I do.
My love for you is always new.

My love is like the brightest light
That shines a glow to the darkest night.
My love is like a million stars in the sky
That watch the wind as it passes by.

"Do you love me honey?" 'Course I do.
Love you? Yes, I thought you knew.
My love for you is really great.
Sometimes I can't concentrate
On things I'm 's'posed to do.
"Do I love you honey?"
'Course I do.

Gwynn Alexander

Ode to the Saxophone

Undertone of wisdom,
play it once more for me,
I want to feel the yellow ring
nestled in that sea of brass,
orgasms of spicy hot flow wow
it's buzzing like a smooth cat,
the notes jive out,
with their pin-striped suits and funky cigars,
and my spine moves alone,
to the beat, to the vibrant bellow
of this hungry giant,
with its bright eyes and relaxed smile,
the unmistakable monarch
of mystery and motion.

Marco Espirito Santo

Sounds of Silence

By the gravel path beside a brook
we are together, under the tree,
the evening sun peeps through leaves' nooks
the birds up there, watching you and me.

The silent and still waters of the stream
seem to respect the depth of our togetherness
from inside our hearts, I hear the scream
of our love and our state of oneness.

Rays of the sun, through our eyes reflect
the intensity of our care,
They seem to tell us, we'll forever protect
the beauty of a love so rare!

The quizzical looks of the birds suggest
they don't know what we're up to
it seems they're unable to digest
inaction in a love so true!!!

The graceful dance of the leaves shone
to the fragrant breeze that blows
seems to sing a song of silent love
where feelings would glow than flow.

Angel

The Holidays

You can't forget Valentines Day
It's when people give out notes and
have a lot of fun, and when kids
say I love you without saying eeewwww!!

On July 4th families bring lawn chairs,
to sit in at the park, where soon they will see
fireworks in the dark.

And when it comes time for halloween
there are ghosts and goblins that sure are mean!!
Kids dress up in costumes and head out for candy,
a flashlight sure would come in handy!!

On thanksgiving day families are jolly and gay,
they sit at the table and eat turkey breasts,
Grandma makes the mashed potatoes
that I like the best.

But Christmas tops them all
boys get race cars and girls get dolls.
But there's more to Christmas than presents you see,
there's always family, happiness, and love.
It's especially the Lord's birthday who cares about us up above.

Erin Heath

Babes

A silent cry of unborn babies screams out for help today,
look on as experimental bodies are frozen to keep from decay.
Technicians commence their studies to dissect each part,
as white sleeved scientists examine what once beat a heart,
what Pharaoh and Herod proclaimed years past to abort,
has now become an endorsement to kill by our own Supreme Court,
You used your scalpel and somehow was able to justify,
sucking out a baby from within the home which God did provide.
You recorded the process as it gasped to breathe its first breath,
you argued aloud that we can't kill what's dead,
it's a formation of cells, no reason to get so upset.
Within your heart, the truth did reign,
but you snuffed out a life just the same.
Do you really believe you can play God and decide who should die,
If your operations are for good, why can't you look into their eyes.
Dear doctor, I fear you'll learn too late, "you reap what you sow."
Some victims will survive and into adults they will grow,
think how they'll vote when it comes to the aged,
will it be time for the unwanted to be led to the grave?
Then the verdict upon you will be returned as you gave.

Frank Vecchione

Hope Is Something You Seem To Struggle With

Yet always cherish and hold on to
As a means to gain strength
And at times maintaining a key to survival

One can choose not to hope
As a result of repeated attempts
Which arose to nothing but
Feelings of defeat with no

Choice of surrender, leaving you
To suffer which may appear as irreparable consequences

Never quite knowing what's to come
All the time emotions grow deeper,
Never completely prepared for loss of shattered dreams

When in hope, time is not a factor
Does it come from the mind which grows and develops?

Or does it dwell in our emotions
Awakened only by the act of resistance
Or the weakness of our desires?

Renee Hala

Little Me

I'm just a little unborn child, please pay attention to little me
I have the breath of life from God, won't you help me grow and be.
Two things popped out of my body today; arms and hands, with ten
    fingers,
Legs are hanging out at the bottom of my body; I have ten toes.
My brain lets me know what's happening to me in here.
Two windows on my face can open and close; my eyes.
A bump is smack dab in the middle of my face; my nose.
I have a mouth, my finger fits real good in it.
I move around a lot, it's nice and warm in here.
My mother is feeding me with her body and blood, I can't wait to
    see her.
A man called Jesus nourishes people with His body and blood.
Something in my chest is beating; a heart! I wonder what it's for?
I need you to help me, no one can hear me.
Please don't let my skull be crushed and my brain sucked out.
Don't let a vacuum pull me out of here or allow me to be picked and
probed apart and experience pain. I love you, won't you love me?
If you don't want me; isn't there someone out there who would just
love me? I'll smile, and hug and kiss you.
You can teach me the beauty of life; the Glory of God!
Please don't forget me, I need you, do you need me?

MaryEllen Kliminski

Do We Even Care

The time is ticking, we must wake up.
Do we think of tomorrow, or just live for today?
The ozone layer is crumbling, the air is not fit to breathe.
But do we even care, do we even care?

The time is ticking, judgment day draws near.
The wrath of the Lord must be feared, the Lord must be feared.
Haven't you noticed the revelation, mothers, fathers, sons, and
daughters killing each other? But do we even care, do we even care?

Do we even care, that our schools have become war zones,
    and the parks controlled by gangs?
How many more of our kids must die,
    before we realize the American dream is just a dream?
But do we even care, do we even care?

The time is ticking, it won't be long now.
Today has ended, and tomorrow is in view.
But what are you going to do about the situation?
We've all turned our heads, and looked the other way.
But now the trouble has reached into our homes.
But do we even care, do we even care?

The time is ticking, but do we even care? Do we even care?

   John H. Spencer

Oh Where Have All The Heroes Gone?

Oh where have all the heroes gone?
I have searched the North and found not one.
They wore bright armor and rode great steeds.
Far they journeyed to do honorable deeds.
But I have searched the South and found not one.
Oh where have all the Heroes gone?
I heard they fought to defend the weak.
Though they were not prideful but humble and meek.
But I have searched the East and found not one.
Oh where have all the Heroes gone?
The Age of Heroes has passed us by
But no one mourns and no one cries.
But I have searched the West and found not one.
Oh where have all the Heroes gone?
For Society does not want a Hero around.
A Hero would not let it keep the People down.
We need to find a Hero again.
To free us from Society's plan.
But I have searched the lands and found not one.
Oh where have all the Heroes gone?

   Kelly Gragg

Wishes and Stars

Wishes and stars have a magical theme.
A star is a hope and a wish is a dream.
When you're dreaming at night of what you might be.
Look into your heart and you will see.

It doesn't matter who or where you are.
Magic can happen when you wish on a star.
When your goals seem to be so out of sight.
Just look in the sky and wish tonight.

A prayer is a wish carried on wings.
When you wish you can do undreamable things.
You can fly through the night or dance in the day.
When you wish on a star you'll just float away.

A wish is a star twinkling up in the sky
A star is a wish helping you to fly.
A dream is a hope for a brighter tomorrow.
When you wish on a star there's no room for sorrow.

   Krysten Vance

Snow

Softly stealing through the night...
frosted branches like delicate lace silhouetted against a sapphire sky
tenderly cushions the sparrow's journey...
visits the earth with jewels of moisture and crystalline beauty...
like the feathers of a white dove, brushes our hearts with echoes of
the past...
illuminates our rushed lives with tranquillity and calms the anxious
soul.

   Sharon Jensen

Gone, Not Forgotten

   I hope someday to forget why you left, but each time I see
you only makes it worse. I'm not hurt nor regret our
relationship, but I miss you, that at night I lay awake
remembering all the times we shared and rhythm we made together.
I'd give anything one last time before I die, to spend the night
with you holding me tight to whisper goodbye!

   Diane L. Peters

The Survivor

She waits.
She listens.
Within her eyes blue, deep, no one can see
The hurt she hides so fearfully
She waits.
She waits.
Here comes the storm raging with fury
Helplessness over comes her
She says nothing.
When the storm sets back from the rage it once had
She says nothing.
She waits.
She listens.
Until the storm returns
She fights.
She screams.
But no one can hear her
Just the storm with one last blow
She says nothing.

   Amy Jo Krein

Silence

In the daylight he hears her thoughts;
Unfinished statements pile up like cloud castles,
There is no path leading inwards.

How trivial her beauty in relation to her depression.
Her parts shed no light on her composition:
She is not what she seems.

Finding his way from her grayness,
He laps her seas of silence;
If peace dwells in her, this much he knows:
It sleeps beyond the charcoal mountains of her mind.

   Jodi Weiss

Sail

Deep blue water lay silent and still
    waiting for the moment when its
surface caresses the gentle white hull
    lapping at its edges as if in a
silent joy of celebration and splendor.
Trusting the ship like a naive lover
    allowing it to go there with a thousand kisses.

   Steve Shizumura

Little Girl Lost

When I was just a little girl, mama took me to the fair.
I got lost from her,
I turned round and she simply wasn't there!
Where was she? She was gone and her face I couldn't see!
That desperate feeling of being alone came washing over me,
And I was just a little girl lost.

Years have passed and now I'm grown,
But once again I feel the pain just like the little girl,
A pain that will never heal.
I'm lost again and she can't reach out
And tell me "it's alright."
Again I'm just a little girl lost
In a cold and lonely night.

I can see her now, but she's not really here
In that cold, still form so fair.
She's lost from me, I turn around and she simply isn't there!
Where is she? She is gone and her face I'll never again see!
That desperate feeling of being alone comes washing over me,
And I'll always be just a little girl lost.

Carlene J. Mognett

Visiting My Home

My relatives are all around me,
some that I have not seen
for a long time.

All living far away from my home,
in a totally different world
that is very crowded,
with very many traditions.

Often old-fashioned,
yet very busy.

A land that I moved from
when it was riddled with Soviet enigmas;
a land that was diseased with communism.

Jacek Stramski

I Am

I am a guy who likes animals and has a big imagination.
I wonder what it would be like to be an animal.
I hear imaginary birds singing.
I see a world of peace and love.
I want to know the secret of life.

I am a guy who likes animals and has a big imagination.
I pretend to be a monkey.
I feel sorry for the people that have no homes.
I touch the people in need.
I worry that someday people will die out.
I cry out to the people in sorrow.

I am a guy who likes animals and has a big imagination.
I understand people when they feel down.
I say we all should have equal rights.
I dream that we will find all the cures for sickness.
I try to help others when needed.
I hope one day people will not fight.
I am a guy who likes animals and has a big imagination.

Cole Garner

In Memory of Papaw Ken

One sweet guy, who loved horses.
His soul was with his most beloved horse.
He showed me the way.
He loved all his grandkids.
He was the person I loved the most.
He might get mad.
But, he always forgave.
You might say God understood him better than anybody.
His eyes were the sparkle of him.
His love was his faith and mine.
My love was his faith and mine too.
You might think his heart was made out of rock.
But, it never was.
Why did God take him from me, the person
I loved, I looked up to, Papaw I
Know you said "not to cry."
But, I miss you and I still cry over you.
So where I put this paper it goes as the memory
Of my papaw the one I loved.

Chasty Canada

My Sun

Warm my cheeks,
brown my skin,
light my life.
Shine on
nurture the flowers,
love the earth,
smile down on me.
Shine on.
You are the most beautiful,
the most loved
sun I've ever seen.
You've followed me through the years.
You've seen and heard it all.
Shine on
because you are the best sun in all the universe.
You always will be.

Kari Boyer

A Young Cowboy

I was just a young cowboy that rambled around
When one day I stopped at a ranch west of town
I met an old cowhand they said was the best
And being so young, I thought I'd put him to the test
But it didn't take long to find out what they said was true
Because he could ride and rope and do everything better than
I could do
I felt great respect for him and I ask if I could stay
And when they said "Yes," I was glad I didn't have to ride away
For I knew it was a home I had found and
I would no longer have to ramble around.

Judith Berry

When....

When the ocean crashes to the shore.
I'll think of you no more.
When the sunshine fades from light to dark,
The pain will lift from my heart.
When darkness covers the distant land,
My tears will trail in the sand.
When the wind whips through my silken hair,
I for you will no longer care.
When the tide washes completely through,
Only then will I be over you.

Jodi Krikke

Lost In The Forest

We sit in the light yet there is only darkness all around us. Tears like rain fall everywhere. You can feel them but you cannot see them, for they are out of sight within. Special that we feel we are, but know we are not. For there in the forest of the many, we are all different and yet alike. We exist in the heart of the forest that moves all around us. Paused between the light and the ever lurking darkness. Neither do we see or hear what really exists, yet, the forest moves us to and fro, as it must. Emotional undercurrents can be sensed, but, you are a spectator helpless to intervene, captured by your own shadows. The forest tries its best to find our failings and is sympathetic to our plight. But, it cannot change its outcome, only record its findings. For the forest does not create, but must accept what is there. It is up to us with help from the people of the forest to bring about change for the better. Someday, we all will come and meet in the forest, and at that time we will learn to depend on many of its powers. Not knowing if we are headed for the light or the darkness, but secure in the knowledge that the people of the forest will always do their part to show us the path that is best to travel if we are ever to return to the light.

John T. Steinheimer

Black Nightmares/White Dreams

Black nightmares are yours of course, white dreams are my dreams of choice. Why should my dreams become your nightmares, why should I
  care, do I dare?
I've not come to bring you pain, I've not come to bring you malice, I've come in search of peace to make a home, my very own, my palace.

I don't want to take your job, I don't want to take your wealth, I come in daylight and openness; not in darkness, and not in stealth. I have no wish to disrupt your life, I have no reason to cause you strife, I only want a better life.

I will be your friend if you want me to be, but it's not a necessity for me, you see. I can be your enemy if you insist, but it's an option I would resist, I much prefer to co-exist.

Black is not always evil, and white not always pure, if we try to live together, there's a chance we will endure. Should we choose the other route and ignorance prevail, we'll only find a path of hate, misery and travail.

Let us resolve our differences through intelligent and peaceful means, then none of us will have to have nightmares, and we all will have
  our dreams.

Emerson McCoy Jenkins

Creepy Crawlers

Fear surrounds me everywhere.
It is in every nook and cranny.
In every new face I see on the street.
In every old friend I feel abandoned by.

Fear creeps into each new possibility I imagine.
Making every horrendous thought a reality.

I hate fear.
I don't want to appear a coward,
To myself or to the outside world.
So instead I'll do anything to avoid confronting the dreaded fear.

I'll be angry, embarrassed, nervous, laughing, sarcastic,
Belligerent, strong, weak, on my diet, off my diet,
Exercise fanatic, exercise apathetic.
From one extreme to the other, the pendulum swings.

With an arsenal of emotions that mask the fear and lead
  to paralysis and withdrawal.

What would happen if I really felt the fear?
What?

Mary Oliveira

Broken Love

Love is a painful path I led
How painful?
My eyes cannot perceive
For me, my pain and sorrow is deep in my heart
A wounded heart that time cannot heal or part
For a love that will never be
Hope and joy that ended in misery
For a few words did it all
"I'm sorry, I don't love you at all"

Lawrence Chan

Rolling Drums

Out of the west to announce a new birth
the birth of a new spring, some the sound of
rolling drums, rolling and rumbling, then a flash
of light, comes the rolling of drums out of the
night. A faint warm breeze stirs three the
trees, bringing with it a fragrance so sweat,
so rare, that surely everyone knows what is here.
   This wonder of wonders, the rolling drums
tells the whole world that spring has come.
It moisture the earth bringing forth flowers.
   Its thunder puts life in the air for hours
and hours. The birds build their nests, here
and there green sprouts can be seen, covering
the earth with a glorious green.
   Rolling drums heralding spring,
spreads love all over the world. Fresh pure
love showing "Mother Nature" again at work.
   Calling a well known, but very new birth.

Irlda V. Ritz

Consider Me Quietly

Please,
don't tell me how much you wished
  last night hadn't happened,
I really don't want to be reminded.
Haven't we been through this before?
No, I won't tell you that I think we can make it,
haven't we lived on wishes before?
If only someone would come out and tell me
that all dreams don't come true as we'd like them,
but that dreams do come true...
then I'd believe in me and you.
Please don't tell me you wish
  last night hadn't happened -
that you regret things that were spoken.
We said them,
like we've said them before,
just consider me quietly
if today you decide you can't love me more,
just walk out softly...when you shut the door.

Melinda Lambert

Just a Child

Would you, could you, care for me,
I'm only just a child;
But I deserve the chance to see,
To touch, to feel, to smile.

I may be short or may be tall,
Or have hair that runs wild;
But I do ask a chance, that's all,
I'm only just a child.

For all those who've been just a choice,
There's good news all the while;
They're not forgotten this I'll voice,
They're only just God's child.

Christopher J. Ferguson

For Erica

Her eyes light up with happiness
when she comes in the door.
She plays the learning games with me
and always asks for more.

Some of the other children
don't seem to want to learn.
But she tries so hard to spell and write,
her little cheeks just burn
with effort to complete the page
and hear me say "Well done!"
and we both feel the glow of love
of making learning fun.

When they remember me some day
perhaps they'll say with pride
"She tutored children" and they'll know
how really hard I tried
to give them all a reason
to want to learn and grow..
to make their lives a message
that it matters what you know.

Ruth Ann Johnson

My Family

Working hard, your careful hand
Guiding us through uncharted land
Your ethic and character standing tall, I want to be like you.

Those loving hands that wiped away
The evils that plagued me through the day
Kind blue eyes kept careful watch
Supported me when I found my notch, I want to be like you.

Standing tall, that handsome face
Protected by amazing grace
Guarding my honer you stood by me
Thanks to you our Nation is still free, I want to be like you.

The little gift, the wonderful surprise
In your future our hope will lye.
Your love, acceptance, innocence, and grace,
Shine upon your angelic face, I want to be like you.

Confident worker who never gives in
Your handsome face, and that darling grin
You're truthful, loyal, loving, and kind
How lucky I am that you are mine, I want to be like you.

Susan Siewert Naiser

The Striking Clock

I lie awake at night and count the flowers on the wall.
    I mostly seem unable to get to sleep at all!
The clock strikes one and I've begun to think of things to do
    When I get up next morning - now the clock is striking two!
I toss and turn and wonder long just what there has to be
    To make me go to sleep and rest - the clock is striking three!

I wrestled with the outside work - my arms and legs are sore
    From mowing lawns and clipping grass - the clock is striking four!
I worked so hard from nine to five I wonder I'm alive -
    Today I'll take it easy - now the clock is striking five!
I hear the faucet dripping. This the plumber needs to fix.
    Or maybe I can do it - now the clock is striking six!

If I don't get some sleep right off, I feel I'll go to Heaven.
    The alarm clock just went off. My God! The clock is striking seven!
I must get up and go to work 'cause it is getting late.
    My eyes are heavy now with sleep - I think it's striking eight.
The clock keeps ticking right along, its numbers all in line
    I don't care what it's striking now 'cause I am sleeping fine!

Sandra M. Vaughan

Sharing Is Magic

Memories never die they just make life worthwhile living.
The little things is what really counts, a song, a look or a touch.
People have everything money could but are so unhappy that life means nothing.
If you love someone you don't have to be entertained.
You don't have to say a word, just so you are together.
And when you are not together you are still close together in your heart.
What are interests, hobbies, your goals, ambitions.
You're never bored if you have a good life.

Florine F. Brown

January's Joy

January's child brings the excitement
    of a new year
Along with new dreams, hopes
    and promises.

This child has the sparkle and perfection
    of a snowflake
Yet the quiet charm
    of fresh, new snow.

Bernice Young

Little One

Sleep my little one as darkness surrounds;
I'll stay by your side til the sandman comes.
Dream of candy cane mountains, lollypop hills,
Rhinestones and cowboys and taffy daffodils.

Close your eyes and dream a little
Of Humpty Dumpty and the Cat and the Fiddle.
Take a bite of the Ginger Bread House
And candy from the gumdrop tree;

Take a walk with the Wizzard of Oz
In the land of make believe;
And when dawn breaks across the skies,
You'll twist and turn and open your eyes.

I'll be there for a hug and squeeze
To welcome you back from the make believe.
So close your eyes, my little one,
My Buddy, My Son . . . .

Stan S. Smith

Forbidden Love

Our souls are intertwined and connected
like day and night. We are lost children who roam
the earth like wild stallions of great might.
    Our hearts are strong and pure like the pearls
of the sea, but yet we are forbidden to shine and
sparkle to what our love should be.
    For our hearts and souls are the same, we are
not to blame for the love we share for all eternity
in care.

Rámunz Mills

One Sunday Morning

I woke up one Sunday morning,
planning how best to savour every moment
    of my precious day off:
A five-minute call to sis in Los Altos, maybe three,
her re-repeated rambling drives me up a tree.
Try out my new paint on that recycled plate,
maybe here's yet another Picasso reincarnate.
"One fish died!"
"What?!"
Rushed down to the aquarium with the brass colored dome,
and there he laid on the gravel floor of his fish home.
The others were still frolicking amongst the plastic green,
tummies bulging, kept getting back at their floating breakfast.
Did they miss a friend, did they look for him.
Was he ever a friend or an outcast?
Do fishes mourn, do fishes scorn, are some nice
    and others mean just like people?
I'll ring sis again this Sunday and let her ramble
    from here to Los Altos,
then I'll paint the recycled plate and out do all the Picassos.
        Alyce H. L. Wu

Battle for Freedom

Hell is here, here and now,
But to the Devil we shall never bow.

Towns shall burn, and smoke shall rise,
never to clear from our eyes.

God shall come but he will fall,
the Devil shall tower over all.

Weather of extremes shall pummel the lands,
all controlled by the devils hands.

Then a new Order shall rise from the depths,
not of hell but of earth herself!

A battle shall rage and Earth shall come to glory.
She will turn Satan away like a page in a story.

Mortal she will become and then will die,
and from her grave a great tree will rise high.

For as long as man preserves that tree,
All life... shall always be free.
        Matthew D. Ellis

Memories of an Angel

I have lived and I have Loved
I have had my share of the good and the bad times
But now, I live with only the Memories of an Angel
That will forever be on my mind.

Like the beauty of a white dove, sitting on a blanket of snow,
She is the Angel, that I will eternally Love.
With every breathe I take, And Every beat of my heart,
I'll always be living in the, Memories of My Angel, the woman I love.

Never a day goes by, that I wish she was by my side,
So I might be able to be Loved by her again.
Our love was Heaven sent and blessed by the Lord in Heaven,
But now, all I have are the "Memories of an Angel,"
The woman that I truly Love.

I'll keep trying to win her heart back again,
Because of all the Love I have within me for her
But for now, all I can do is cry for,
The Memories of an Angel.
        Carl E. Diedrich

Lost Bones of an Early Settlement

One hundred forty-eight years ago they came in droves.
Tired, worn, but hopeful they claimed the land.
Desperation is a compelling force,
motivating the weak of heart.

Natures laws ruled the virgin land.
Pine oak, and maple trees shut out the light.
Winter froze the stagnate waters. Spring brought out
the sweltering mud and festering quicksands.

The poisoned air reaped corpses in every house.
Cries of agony and sorrow filled the primeval paradise.
Hollow eyes and minds reached for the meaning behind it all.

Emancipated and wracked with longing, they purposefully
moved forward. Many fled and never came back,
leaving behind unmarked graves in the marshes of Black Lake.
        Elisabeth Dekker

A Day At The Beach With The Dogs

A sunlight beach and dogs at play
    That summer's scene by Claude Monet
Three golden labs did each compete
    By chasing jumping about our feet

Their wagging tails and sea gulls cries
    The sticks they fetch with loving eyes
Between those teeth their panting yips
    Please someone throw our favorite sticks

Off they leap and splash to swim the breach
    Toward those floating sticks tossed out of reach
With pride they bark and yelp at each
    Putting down their sticks upon the beach

They shake off fast that briny wet
    So proud to be your favorite pet
Prepared again with their loving eyes
    To chase those sticks under sunny skies

In frozen pose the heron's gaze
    Close by the shore in the frothy waves
Prepared to pierce his fishy preys
    Between the pebbles, stones, and sand shell caves
        W. Jim Roller

The Crucifixion - From the Sky's Point of View

It was late morning, there wasn't a cloud in my sky,
A mob of shouting people and soldiers walked by,
There was a man in the middle who looked liked a king,
But to a king, why would they do such a thing?
I cooled him down with a soft gentle breeze,
As my wind brushed upon Him, I felt the weakness in his knees,
For the cross He was carrying was much too immense,
To lay it upon Him took five soldiers, no less,
Upon his head He wore a crown of thorns,
His clothes, they were ripped, tattered, and torn,
They nailed Him to the cross at the top of the hill,
The sound of the hammer gave me the chills,
The man said, "Forgive them for they know not what they do."
As He looked up I saw Him, Jesus Christ, King of the Jews.
I felt like beating all of the soldiers,
I filled all my rain clouds as heavy as boulders,
I poured down my rain and struck out my lightning,
The people all ran, they thought it was frightening,
There was nothing I could do, that's the way it had to be,
Jesus bowed down his head...and died for me.
        Jonathan Walker

309

Godhead

Will you storm the shores of my religion?

Shall I swallow your godhead?
Select your imminence, your eminence,
Believe in your transcendence,
Do I repent of sins uncommitted?
Born dirty I shall burn forever.

Deny me what I feel, what I know.

Will anyone cry for my soul,
That lusty, sinful, craven savage,
Trapped in the miz maze, mirror maze,
Created by your demon's muse
To cleanse my heathen soul?

Swim through this stone yourself;
Suffer your saint's tradition alone;
Your word made flesh is not my word.
Return me to the lands of my mothers
I will loudly sing Medusa, sing my flesh,
Wandering the twilight, midnight, godless fields,
Far from your suffocating divinity.

Annette Thompson

Reprieve

I sit now, heavily
Pondering the past
And despite outward acquiescence

This small heart
Grinds and churns
Deeply within my breast

And I wonder,
As always the pessimist

Which beat shall be the last?

The self-indulgent judgement, the errors
How poorly have I estimated others?

There is hardly a future to foresee
Which may, or may not include me.

Still, this small heart thrusts
Pumps from far within

Perhaps forgiveness shall
Keep the beat strong, and long

Long enough to
Thwart future sin.

Amy M. Nickell

My Mother's Dreams

Who will I write to
    when my mother has gone?
Who will care when I speak of my Dreams?

Who will I talk to
    for hours on the phone?
(Knowing it's her — when it rings!)

Who will I lean on
    when I face the same fears,
    that were hers . . . many years ago!

"Mother — Who can I turn to
    when you have gone on?"
"Who will I write to then?"

"You will write to your daughter
    when she speaks of her fears,
    and the dreams that were yours . . .
    years ago!"

Christina Adams

A Little Boy Remembered

JoJo was his name, he was of slender frame,
Fearless when he faced a foe
Whether twice his size or more.
He played hard with all his might.
Competition made him fight
For recognition and his rights.
Camp was a time to relax and run free
In wide open spaces and country-fresh air
A time to play ball, to canoe and to swim
To study the Bible, to laugh and to sing.
The day had arrived sun bright, crystal clear
To leave for Camp Can Do again this year
There was such excitement and eagerness
The buses were late and everyone tense.
A breakdown prolonged the trip even more
Some had arrived and been waiting since four
The bus was greeted with cheers of glee
The darkness of night made it hard to see
JoJo ran out, a boy of just seven
Camp will be absolutely perfect in heaven.

Judith E. White

Dear One

If we could but see the error of our ways
The frustrations, the agonies of our days.

Like swirling dervishes of eddies in a pool.
Look in the self-made mirror, you fool!

Your magnification of self-reflection, your brothers all.
Who with you — a part of the fall.

How in a mad instant wrought; this folly of separate thought.
Created an illusion; rendering naught but fear and confusion.

Look again, at the self-same mirror — yourself to embrace.
God's eternal love for all in your brother's face.

Not one more moment, one more day...
Continue to flee in the self-same way.

There's nowhere safe, nowhere to hide;
Awake from slumber — to remember, safe to abide!

Inside each mind, an eternal spark
There is only light to dispel the dark!

You can each delay the truth; — even tarry awhile.
But being is one with God, and you are His child.

You cannot escape your fate; eternity is at your gate.

M. J. Maday

You Are Mine

Whispering in the wind of the autumn leaves
    I am there;
Shining in the light of the afternoon sun
    I am there;
Echoing in the voices of playing children
    I am there.

You can't escape the memory of me
So very much alive in you—for I have won your heart.

Standing in the shadow of our favorite places
    I am there;
Lingering in the scents wafting from our restaurant
    I am there;
Busting in the daily routines of work and play
    I am there;
Slumbering next to your warm body at night
    I am there.

You can't escape the memory of me
So very much alive in you — for I have captured your soul:
    You are mine.

Adriana Mironas

Grown-Up Wishes

When I was but a very young girl,
Who was then living in a grown-up's world
Often I would hear my mother say
"I wish I knew then, what I know today"

At that time, I was totally confused
What did Mom's wish mean, was it said to amuse?
As I matured, it became crystal clear
You grow much wiser with each passing year

They say an old head can't be put on young shoulders
Because wisdom only comes as you grow older
Imagine the possibilities of being young again
Applying your knowledge now to your life back then

Now that I'm the mother of a very young girl
Who is living in a grown-up's world
My daughter will often hear her mother say
"I wish I knew then, what I know today"

Celia McManus

Nephew

This is for you, nephew Jamie
First of all nieces and nephews.
This is for your unexpected arrival into my life. For
your little hands and faint trace of orange hair. They meant
nothing to me. But oh in your seven years you have won my heart.
Is it the way you sometimes call me mom or the way your freckled
smile brightens my day?
This is for you when you look to me for your forgotten
teddy bear of security or when you approach me with your trust
when you can't keep a secret. Your innocence brings out a part
of me that in all my years I thought was lost.
This is for you Jamie, when you come to me in the early
winter morning with a little tear stained face, you search for
comfort in a sea of painful loss of a pet. My heart sinks and
I also share your grief.
This is for you that everything you are makes me realize
that you are teaching me what is to come of my future when I
have children of my own.

Kristine A. Ferris

Floaters

From open mouth
leaden feathers waft carelessly through unsuspecting air.
Deflexed floaters
land heavily on my interior ground.

Do you know what you are saying?
Was this purposed in your leaded heart?
Are you so cunning
to camouflage weight with weightlessness?

Quill tip scratching
stinging through layers
fine lines drawing life beads, like dew drops
on spider's thread aligned.

Will you dip your feather in?
Will you use my very blood
to record your own excellence
on the corners of that upturned mouth?

Hedy West

Winter Swans

The most beautiful sight I've ever seen
Was on a cold, rainy day as there's ever been
The winter sky was a thick, heavy cloud
But just below this wispy gray shroud
Three wild swans had taken flight
We stood in awe of this magnificent sight
Their wings moved slowly in the driving rain
I could tell their flight was an awful strain
They flew straight into the brutal wind
One wondered where their journey would end
These creatures of such beauty and grace
Would they find a sheltered, restful place
We watched in silence as they flew along
For only a few moments, then they were gone

Vera Sue Keenan

One Lost Friend

His great laugh and smile,
I really used to like his style.
His eyes sparkled like the morning dew,
They were big, bright, and blue.

His hair glittered like golden rays,
Like the little boy within looking for praise.
His only flaw as a teen,
Was the rip in his jeans.

Life had just begun,
When he turned 21.
Spending the night with friends,
Little did he know life was about to end.

As we said our final good-byes,
I remember the light shining in his eyes.
It was on a special day,
My mom told me that God had taken him away.

Diane R. Stouwie

Beautiful Caterpillar

Forever awkward in his mind,
Always trailing far behind;
Silently creeping along the ground,
No one hearing his mourning sound.

He knows now that the time has come,
And understands what must be done.
Diligently he builds his prison cell,
Willingly he steps into his hell.

He feels his body rip and tear,
At times it's more than he can bear.
In lonely darkness he spends each day,
Accepting this as Nature's way.

Something tells him the time is right,
As he beholds his firsts rays of light.
Gracefully emerging from his tomb,
He finds his world in full bloom.

Glancing from flower to flower,
He is completely ignorant of his new power.
Longingly he looks up at the sky,
As he timidly opens his wings to fly.

Kimberly Newton

The Mirror

Unrelenting mirror has the final say
Memories of a time of many less pounds
The little girl in me wanting to play

My world used to be so innocent, gay
Sometimes wish some one could turn time around
Unrelenting mirror has the final say

All hopes schemes, dreams have all gone away
In their place is only to be found
The little girl in me wanting to play

The sum this life not in vain, I do pray
Dreams of jitterbugging all night aground
Unrelenting mirror has the final say

I would not my children ever give away
But if you look close up on the mound
The little girl in me wanting to play

For all my children now is their day
Reality of quickly passing time abounds
Unrelenting mirror has the final say
The little girl in me wanting to play

Virginia Powell

What Did He Do?

My best friend resting there,
All dressed in his Sunday best.
His face so lifeless and so pale,
Red roses lay on his chest.

"It's not fair," his mother sobbed,
His father holding her tight.
But most of all,
I wonder,
About those creatures with guns in the night.

What did he do,
What could I say,
To make this awful pain end?
I hope they find those guys,
Who have shot my best friend.

Angela M. Price

Peace

Dancing moonlight plays off angels' wings
while in the twilight fireflies sing
and somewhere deep within my soul the shadow traces
of the silent moon reconcile themselves into
silver waves, white capped, flowing against the brilliant sand,
dancing my heart free once more

Brian Langston

Smoke

The smoke is streaming up
Like fingers reaching for the heavens
Like a ghost
Smoke is like a stream, flowing smoothly
The slightest movement disturbs it.
As I watch the smoke, life passes by without a word
But the smoke is still there, singing its silent song
Sad but sweet
But just like smoke, life must end, and sing no more

Rebecca E. Hawley

Crown Every Moment

May we thank God to be alive, each day as we awake,
Reaching for His helping hand, with the tasks we undertake.
"Crown Every Moment."
In knowing all of our blessings and finding more anew,
All mankind has gifts and talents being many or few.
When there are days of boredom, of which there is no need,
There is opportunity of learning, we shall take heed.
Friendship is needed in the hearts of all men,
It is easily found with a seeking hand.
There shall not be loneliness in this great land,
With the crowning glory of which we stand.
With love in our heart through sharing and giving,
There is joy to be found in our everyday living.
There is reward for all kindness, in thought, words and deed,
With a helping hand to others in need.
May all hearts in togetherness loudly cry in prayer,
For lasting peace and thanksgiving for the love we share.
"Crown Every Moment."

Arlene Norman

Old Friend

There was a lot of life left yet;
Flowers, mountains, trees, sunsets.
There's still such knowledge to be gained
From elders, youngsters, peers and dreams.

Yet, all seems stopped,
And all seems known now that you've left this life
I'll always wonder why so soon,
And why so soon no life.

But later's now and soon is gone,
Now, as in your death.

My eyes look twice at things to see,
Flowers, mountains, clouds and trees.
My heart takes more of questions,
Love's thoughts and small possessions.

For you? Your gift is death.
Now you've a better view.

And my gift is your memory
And how life seems so sadly new.

Palmer Dunning

Granite

Flowers dance in the wind.
The trees stand firm and trim.
The birds sing and I grin.
Because, god granted it.

A harps vibrating strings.
The butterflies fluttering wings.
The earth rotates and spins.
Because God, you granted it.

All this time it was stepped on.
I never noticed this rock's unique form.
I guess I was just too head strong.
But now I know GOD, by you it was granted.

The challenge before you begin.
A crown the symbol of a king.
My birth, amongst all these things.
G-d, nothing, shall be taken, for granite.

Re-Born in fire

A Bird

A bird can fly, but can it speak?
Of course in its own language.
When you speak, it's like a bird
Singing the best it ever could, in the spring.
Soft, beautiful, and so delicate.
Can a bird touch?
Yes, but, it's not soft as cotton,
delicate as glass.
Can a bird love?
Probably.
A bird could not love as
much as I love you.
Or even so much as
you love me.

Nikki Powers

Love

The Boy weeble wobbled around
And nothing to quench his thirst could be found.
So it came upon a cloudy, windy day
  That Mama knew "Goodbye" was the word to say.

The trip was made to the vet's town
And with heavy heart the Boy was put down.
Mama gathered him into her arms and hugged him tight
  And Loved him while he slipped into the light.

The body was placed in a grave dug in the ground
Right about the time the sun was coming down.
But Mama knew that the Boy's Light could not be found
  Buried anywhere under that earthen mound!

Memories of pure Love licking her face and toes
Are prof to Mama that the Boy's Love still grows.
The Earth will turn and the Sun will stare
  And wherever Mama is the Boy will be there!

Charles E. Hodnett

Detour, Maryland 1976

Love as I do, lazy road through music light,
delicate sweating, Tuesday drive.

Elaborate storm,
summer's rusty lather.

Bright, luscious mist
plays in and out of earth rinsed shadows.

  A friend's hand manipulates apparatus fiddlingly, leaves the
lever in its new slot, wipers swashing now at an agreeable pace
and she, almost drunk on pounds of whole milk and Kaluah, and
curdled inside, she crushes the can of beer and drives us on
under the rain.

  Striking is the contrast of luminescent, green canopy
against the Monacacy's shale-brown eddies and soft gargle through
the depression between the hills. This is most visible just
before going over the humped bridge into Detour and then up to
the dairy on to of the hill where it is dry yet.

  We sit on the patio, smoke, and look down over the road we
have just driven. We see that below the rain is still engaged.

Bradford Alban

For Spanky

  Martyrdom is animal.
Secret wounds are not restricted to visionary nuns
  like Jennifer Jones in the old Bernadette film.
Spanky, my fat and aging dog, has a cancerous growth on his tail
  and suffers his pain intermittently with house watching
barking, and begging scraps of dinner meat.
  He has the patina and riveleted eyes of agonized ascetics,
and like a good saint, he is of good cheer
  keeping his discomfort to himself
though nightly by my bed he does betray a whimper for the wound.

  His place will be high in the pantheon of saints
when his time comes. I will hang a banner down from my window
sill
  of Spanky in glory, tufted by the Cherubim,
a miracle from doggydom: This dumb dog, Christ-bearing
  taught me how in a difficult world
to keep my pain in peace among the neighbors
  talking of the rain and of the radio
and of how the times we live in are hard
  and of the senselessness of things,
and of how you just want to stop sometimes.

Carmine J. Giordano

War

What good is war, no one can explain,
No winners emerge, two losers remain.
Things are destroyed, people are killed,
Thoughts will be strong as the graves will be filled.
Grown men will fight, grown men will cry
As their best friends whisper last words as they die.
These terrible memories remain present each day;
It was kill or be killed, there was no other way.
What good is war, it's impossible to say;
What good is death, is there no other way?

Dan Bowerman

My Goodnight Friend

At night when I first go to bed
I prop the pillow 'neath my head
And watch and watch most carefully
Until my Goodnight Friend I see.
Just as it gets so it's quite dark
And I've heard the night song of my lark
I see a shadow flying by
It's my Goodnight Friend up in the sky.

He slides along a passing breeze
Without a sound or sigh or wheeze
And as he passes my window by
He turns his head and winks his eye.

He's wise and big and every night
He sails away on some strange flight
My Daddy says he's on the prowl
Is my Goodnight Friend - a wise old owl.

Ian E. McLaughlin

The Dungeon

Through the murk are things that lurk.
In caverns deep evil does creep
Where lies death with cold breath.
Creatures vile of such styles
Show wanderers why not to ponder.
Here light is not bright.
Torture sounds are all abound.
Fortunes are lost at great costs.
And saviors ravage this place of savage.

Sean White

Passages (A Sonnet)

As we wrest Grandma from her long-time home,
She cries. The grand piano may not go
Into retirement, nor blooms from the loam
Of her dear garden which consoles her so.

"It is a game," I sigh, "and so she looks
For ways to reinforce her stubborn mind."
"No game," my daughter says. "What of your books?
Some day we'll make you leave them all behind."

And so I look around my house and see
That in the end, we lose all things we hold
So dear, our treasures, even memory.
What compensation is there to grow old!?

Yet as I curse the passing of the years,
Grandchildren bring me joy instead of tears.

Penelope Bryant Turk

There Is No Cure

It was a lovely day in the fall of 1993
When the doctor gave the M.S. diagnosis to me
I waited and listened to hear him tell
What he could do to make me well

The sun shone through leaves of red and gold
Under a sky of blue azure
But there was no sunshine in my heart
When he said There Is No Cure

The search for a cure is an unending quest
Leaving many victims sad and unable to rest
Herbs with strange names and hypnosis' allure
All have the same repartee There Is No Cure

Christ said "Come unto Me, and I will give you rest,"
And I have found this is the way that works the best
With his help we can be happy and endure
Even when we hear the words There Is No Cure

As I trudge across the floor slowly making my way
Remember the road He walks to Calvary that day
And because of that walk I can say for sure
Beyond the pearly gates no one will hear There Is No Cure

Shirley H. Baldwin

The Gift of Love

Love has many faces,
Gift which the Lord upon us graces.
The miracle of birth, life, health, family, friends,
The many blessings taken for granted that the Lord to us sends.

Love is bountiful caring nested in one's heart,
Unselfish sharing of it with others without end, without start.
Walking, as in the footprints of the Lord, and
   spreading goodness to the aged, ill, hungry, homeless, abused,
Renewing their self-image and self-worth, to be accepted, not
refused.

Love instills pardon, faith, hope, light, joyful gladness,
In times where there is injury, doubt, despair, darkness, sadness.
Showing compassion when there seems reason to hate,
Calming emotions for the hateful feelings to abate.

Love engenders justice and peace,
Forgiving each other's faults and making enmities cease.
Extending from people to nations,
Freeing all from tyranny and dominations.

Love inspires life's earthly goal, to be understanding and offer
   encouragement to accept each other with our all.
The Lord died out of love for all on a tree,
So that for eternity with all the Lord may be.

Edmund Gorczycki

Without

Youth spent wasting,
I am without experience
without memory
without meaning
without.

My words fall tragically,
without background.
My only solstice found
in unwanted solitude.
Memories lost without notice,
hopes lost without regret.
Nights spent wandering
without direction.

Rains falling overhead
flood my once solid perceptions, as my words evolve into questions.
My life lies revealed before me, but I am afraid to look upon it.

Maybe I should cover it, and run in lack of security
to find relinquished serenity. I am without certainty
without answers
without understanding without.

Kevin Johnson

Misery

Please help me extricate myself from this sticky web of gloom.
Always lurking behind me more closely than my own shadow,
It waits patiently and then engulfs me time and time again
With its smothering arms of doom.

I am struggling up endless flights of stairs with two tons
Of sadness strapped to my back.
Each step trips me and laughs until finally I reach the
Top floor, drenched with sweat.
Up there, I see the colors of the rainbow: Yellow, red,
Orange, purple, green, and blue. And I smile.
Out of nowhere it explodes with a downpour of the inescapable
Grays and blacks, bombarding me until I tumble down the
Stairs to the bottom flight again.
Please give me the strength to climb again, for I am weak
And frustrated; perseverance I lack.

If I could run weightlessly, fast enough and far enough, I might
Fool its course forever. I'd see rainbows and sunshine as the storm
Slowly cleared,
And I'd notice that the rain had destroyed the web.
Long gone my fear of the ugly monster would be, as I moved on,
Smiling at thoughts of my future endeavors.

Elaine Schmoyer

Reflections On Aging

Who's that in the mirror looking back at me?
Hair all gray — double chins — that can't be me
Who's that in the mirror looking back to me?

Seems like just yesterday — hair was long down my back
Cut it oft one day — never did let it grow back
Face wasn't too bad — some fellas said I looked great.
They'd take me out dancing — my favorite kind of date.
Once a "furrowed brow" was a literary phrase
Now those "furrows" are engraved.
Old face looking back at me — you'll be with me now until the grave
But I'm still here — and can enjoy this little laugh.
Glad this is a short mirror — else I'd see the other half!

Eunice Samuels

Trance

Hereby I lie down
Watching the unseen image
That dances across the unlit ceiling above
Reasoning from one verge of my sense
To the far side of my thought
Like an elusive shadow
Wanting to be caught

If I only could hold on and wait
Before drifting away into a deep catalepsy
I'd reach and recollect my own forgotten dream
That I left behind a night before

Hereby I lie down
Unsure whether my mind is slipping back to a distant past
Or warping away to an immense void
For I still watch the unseen hint
Which by then already washed out
And faded afar
Then disappeared
Into realm of unknown.

Deddy Hidayat

Arriving

The down side of 50 - I've been told
Is that it's over half way to being old

Growing up in the 50's with a sense of peace
I believed the good times would never cease

Hanging out at the beach - life was such fun
Except now I'm told to "stay out of the sun"

Have traded in the bikini for a one-piece
Past the age of competing - a blessed relief

Eating's a chore now - watching the fat
Fearing the consequences of arterial plaque

But, humor and laughter - a wonderful tonic
Helps all that ails me - occasional or chronic

And life's gotten better - or so it seems
Even though I haven't realized all of my dreams

Perhaps from the clouds - I've finally come down
To look at life with feet - planted on the ground

For in my sense of being - I feel safe and sure
And somehow even with the flaws - am much more secure

It feels comfortable to say that "I've arrived"
And speaking from my heart - "It's great to be alive."

Judy Summer Winick

Desire

The whole universe, reflection of
light, dark roads and swaying trees
what people don't care about this
world. What does it mean?
Twins sitting on a stool, smile
for the camera now, seems like the
statement is enclosed. Dogs barking
at something, no interest there. Taking
the road down south, they are a happy
family. The chase has now begun.
Where does it end for us?
Down in Menemsha, Tash Teco
has a rock. Tickets are handed out.
Some people have minds to lose, is that
the price for education? Howling at the
moon, that's what I want to do.

Christopher C. Capitano

Untitled

Our eyes meet and together dance,
And intertwine for the moment, breathing only each other.
They giggle with the excitement of the chance,
And twinkle at the danger of its possibilities.
And sensing their lost moment, they smile.
Knowing sadly it now means nothing,
And they are again strangers.

Melissa F. Rivest

A Mirror Between

To dismay and disarray
A sad happy alliance we can arrange
For a misfortunate victim to portray
A burden of deep regret
A creative dreamer so inept
A sap happy fool who chooses to believe
We're all sexually bent
To a mad glad tool that drools and drools
And goes spat-a-tat-tat

To love and amusement
It behooves and atones us to be righteously sound
To stand and tie heavens bells
To Gaia's soulful ground
Then jump and spring to the energy ping
A joyful noise of empowering being
    Minus the chit-chat
    And in a silence grew
    Became a knowledge imbued
The present moment caught fire and birthed a new
Baby I love you so, do you still love me?

Dok Webb

Deadbeat Dad

You never taught me to ride a bike.
You never knew what things I might like.
You never paid any child support
In spite of what was ordered by the court.
There were many things I learned to live without
Including my dad, and being knocked about.
And because I never had you in my life,
You weren't there when I became a wife.
And now that I have children of my own
There is something I want you to know.
You were there to teach something to me . . .
What kind of parent not to be!

Dorothea Gleaner Thomas

Kellie

    She feels alone, so all alone
In this mixed up world, she knows not who
to turn to
And I'm on the outside
Knowing that she's on the inside and so alone
And I want to help her
she screams out with her own emotions
I can see her
I want to reach out, to comfort her, but I can't get to her
She's on the other side of an invisible wall
so scared, so hurt, so much in need of a "savior"
To help save her from her own self
From terror and sorrow
I want to be there, I am there, and until
she realize that,
I'm trapped on the outside.

Mary Cassidy

The Unforgettable Rose

The end of an era has come to pass.
The inevitable...the unthinkable.
How will I survive?
I go through the motions just as rehearsed.
My mind totally detached from my body and soul...
I cannot look beyond today for yesterday is still too overwhelming.
I know what I must do yet even the agonizing pain of remembrance
Is more comforting than the thought of forgetting.
Forgetting a precious Rose that once bloomed in the desert,
Nourished only by its own beauty and love.
That unforgettable Rose!

Janie Escobedo

The Sea

The sea, the sea, the beautiful sea. The sea in which
men's eyes have watched trying to find out her mysterious plot.

The sea whose highest mountains lie,
under her majestic watery sky.

The sea the mother of the earth, supplying her scorching
tongue with rain formed from her majestic plain.

Thank you Mother Nature, thank you very much for giving us
the stars above lying there to watch and all your other
wonders both high and low, but thank you Mother Nature thank
you oh so much, for giving us the beautiful sea, which we
cannot only watch but touch!

Richard L. Bunkley

Sweet Cry

I was running through the woods
to get away from the world I know
it was something telling me
where I should go
then I was in a big empty space
and looked all around
I looked at the sky, trees, grass and ground
then I heard a cry, a sweet cry,
calling my name
it wasn't a thumping voice it was a voice in shame
it sounded sad lonely and scared
it sounded gentle like it really cared
then suddenly it stopped
and I heard a big sigh
by that
lonely, scared, sweet gentle cry.

Bethany Lantis

Spellbound

Under my spell,
I have you now
Power emanating from fierce eyes.
Hypnotically,
Silently they quiet your cries.
Cold against warm, our flesh becomes one;
As swiftly,
With yearning my teeth pierce skin.
Struggling momentarily but you can never win.
My will is two strong, my hunger too great.
I have you now in my deadly embrace.
Your life flows into me on the crimson tide.
Nothing matters, not the time or the place.
Once again into my ears pounds that terrible rhythm.
Your heart slows down coming closer to death.
You mutter incoherencies,
On you last dying breath.
Regretfully withdrawing I look on detached.
Your blood gave me life,
And I gave you death.

Danielle White

Honest Abe

To Mr. Sullivan who teaches History with great pride!
They called you "The Greatest!"
You restored Our broken House;
You endowed a Mass of Land for the devoted Soldiers.
Now, "The Greatest," you must consent with the North and South!
Why must Brothers fright Brothers??
Must we live upon a World filled with Hatred??
Must we be Separated 'cause of colored skin???
Your Honored speech Embellishes:
"All Men Are Created Equal"
an Insane person shot Honest Abe!?!?
The Nation was without a Leader . . .
Who will finish your unfinished work? JFK, perhaps?
His duty ran as far as yours; and the routine repeats itself
"The Greatest" and "Prince of Camelot"
place your head on a soft pillow —
may you both rest in Peace:
What might have happened; can only be
Questioned by Curious minds of Our young Ones...

Amy Dinh

Of a Lady I Know

Of a lady I know, who cared for me
as if I were her own,
Bless her O' Lord for she loved me,
as her only son,
Of a lady I know who did not ask for me,
but I came to her from a family divided,
Bless her O' Lord for she had always let me know,
the love for me, she had before decided,
Of a lady I know, who always protected,
fearing the worst might happen to me,
Bless her O' Lord for she is not gone
as many might believe.

Of a lady I know who's tent must go,
that she might await a body more glorious,
Bless her O' Lord to sit in heaven,
with your son, Christ Jesus! (Eph 2:6)

Lester Pike, Jr.

Going Home

Among the wild weeds Mama's roses still bloom
  By a broken garden gate
On the spot where she'd stand and wait
'Til Dad and her children came home one by one
  As their daily chores were done
The familiar walk to the front door
  Now cracked and crumbling
No one lives here anymore
Stained walls and windows broken
I close my eyes and hear the laughter
  The words spoken
Elements and time have taken their toll
  But memories of love linger in my soul
A basic pattern for my life was formed here
With a family so precious - so dear
I make my way atop the hill 'neath the maples
  Where Mom and Dad lie alone
My heart cries out "why did you wait so long
  To come home?"

Jenetta K. Helton

Love of a Dad

My dad is hard as the rock I stand on
  When I have a need, he is there for me
My dad is soft, like a cool summer breeze
  His love is caring, like the flutter of leaves

When you have a hurt, his shoulders are broad
  If you need to cry, he feels it inside
Sometimes you feel anger, he knows that to
  He puts his arm around you, so you won't be blue

When I was young, and thought I knew all
  He would hold out his hands, in case I would fall
I have done things, that don't make me proud
  But my dads voice, was never real loud

I'm in my forties now, and I'm filled with such pride
  I'm lucky to still have him, right by my side
I have my own son now, and hope I do right
  As I lay him down, on his pillow tonight

When my son reaches my age, I hope he can see
  All the things my dad, has done for me
I want him to know, I'll always be there
  Just as my dad, has shown me such care
  Layton L. Huffman

Gifts Given In Love

God turns my eyes to glance out my sunroom window
  Just as the first spring hummingbird appears at our feeder.

God causes me to glance upward to see a swatch of rainbow
  Peeking through a cloud-filled sky.

God showers me with my daughters laughter, and a smile
  That no camera could ever steal.

God is constantly giving me gifts of color, sound, and sight
  Both unexpected and free!
  Meredith Fishback

Is Anybody Listening?

Is anybody listening, in all the years 12 months?
During the year there is everything to hear
January when the New Year rolls around
In February romance fills the air
While March brings us back into the year, with April showers
and sunny days, with May flowers and parades.
In June school let's out and vacation time it is.
July brings us to an American birthday, celebrated with a fireworks
display.
August carries summer to an end and fall is on its way.
September's here, come one, come all, the school year's just begun.
October comes in with chilly weather and sunny weather - a
month full of disguises and treats.
November takes time to honor the Veteran's and brings winter near.
Finally, December has arrived to spread the holiday cheer,
and again, and again, and again the years go from
odd to even, even to odd, to begin the life cycle
awaiting to hear, "I'm listening? Are You?"
  Monica Palimaka

Untitled

The southern flag.
The 13 stars look so good because I think so.
They say that she can not fly.
But I say put her up high and higher.

Live on the southern pride.
Play some Skynyrd.
Live the pride.
Remember the soldier how fought and died.
So people live on the Southern pride.
  Rick Conn

Little Forgotten Soldier

  Sad little soldier, sad little heart.
Working so hard, no time for play.
  Sad little soldier, sad little face.
Where is your mother, where is your love?
  Small little soldier, small little boy.
Where is your mother, where are your friends?
  Working so hard, no time for play.
Sad little face so far away.
  Little poor heart, where is your mother, where are your toys?
Your friends are the birds and the bugs of the field.
  Sad little soldier, boy of the field, why don't you cry?
Nobody knows you, nobody sees you working so hard.
  Little sad soldier, where are your tears?
Nobody dries them, nobody's there.
  Sad little soldier, all by yourself,
Hearing the birds sing, watching the fields.
  Little sad soldier, working so hard,
Nobody knows you, nobody cares.
  I wish I were there, I wish I could help you
Mend your poor little heart.
  Laurie Esposito

The Day Love Died

A sly serpent slithers through her hard heart
as she stabs me sharply by pronouncing
She No Longer Loves Me; her tongue a dart
with a long, hard, poisoned tip. Transforming

our real dream of a blissful fantasy
to a nightmare in lost reality
with a soft smile, she puts my spirit on
a slab. I am dead to feeling; that con

slaughtered my soul with one precise sharp stab
sending me to an abyss of sadness
in place of my heart is an ugly scab
that oozes puss made of unhappiness

at last, came the final dark betrayal
in a time when I was still in denial
it came from the beauty whom I trusted
she played black Judas; we kissed; we ended
  Jonathan Charles Byington

Ray

The time I had with you,
was short, but, sweet.

The memories of your smile, will last forever.

I drank up all your sunbeams, but yet -
they still kept coming back,
through your kisses and your smiles.

To say you added something to my life -
as perhaps, I did to yours,
is an understatement!

It's almost like trying to find-
the end of a beautiful rainbow - the journey getting there -
was worth much more than the pot of gold.
For, as we traveled together, the minutes seemed to stretch
.....into another time.

.....and in my searching - I found something
far more beautiful...for, gold can't say and feel and do
what you have done for - me.

For this, I give you my gratitude, my appreciation -
but most of all - my love.

Thank you, Sunshine.
  Joyce Meuse

317

My Room

"Your room looks like a pig pen,"
I hear my mother say,
But I'm kind of getting tired of that,
Since I hear it everyday

My room is not that messy,
That's what I say to myself,
All there is are books on the floor,
Even though they used to be on my shelf

My room isn't really messy,
Seven days a week,
But sometimes, when I find lost clothes,
They really kind of reek

I really don't like cleaning up,
But it has to be done,
Because when I'm through with cleaning,
It's time for me to have fun.
Jovaun Boyd

Why?

As I lay awake staring at the ceiling
pondering over the loss I have experienced,
the slow pulsation of my heart pounds
with every third tick

The echo of my heartbeat is the
mechanism that takes me back
to a time when I knew him.
The sky was blue and the trees were green

The pungent smell of freshly cut grass
the soft caress of the wind on a hot day,
no time to sit and enjoy the afternoon,
moving, grinding, working, hustling . . . . And sick

As I continue to breathe and ever perplexed
by life and all of its happenings,
questions rage through my mind like the violent
storms of Jupiter about occurrences unforeseen.

Day rushes through my window as an unwanted guest
and night flees leaving no answers——
I arise to face another day.
Understanding come . . . come quick.
Ian C. Pannell

Christmas

A time to be happy
for the presents you get
A time to be sad for waking so early
A time to get fat
because you eat so much food
A time for your family
for hugs and kisses too

A time for the trip
so pack up your clothes
A time for the love
there is so much here
A time for cookies
and all the baking
A time for flowers
and the smell of it too

A time for trees and ornaments too
A time for church and the long services too
A time for no school so you can have more fun
And last but not least
A time to give and a time to receive
Scott McCullough

Lost

Spins the world they say, keeps it going round.
Axis that would make it
perhaps that's why I've found it so hard to find.
Buried deep within the earth,
or maybe just my mind.

Searching, searching, I'm always searching
for something.
The perfect place, a tender face,
a forgotten magic time
to recapture that moment; that lost, legendary moment
when first I fell in love.
Jeff Roberts

Building a Wall

When your heart stops with fear
knowing you are helpless...
understanding that self sacrifice
has been useless...
   building a wall is your only refuge.
When you feel from the core of your being
and it still does not suffice,
after having attempted to salvage
whatever remains, without success...
   then building a wall is your only salvation.
When you turn to yourself and comprehend
that you have survived,
notwithstanding some acute trepidation...
You suddenly realize that you are standing
   on the other side of the wall.
Sally R. Maiolo

I Don't Ask Why Anymore

I don't ask why anymore
   the possibilities of an answer has lost its glitter
Fear takes hold each time
   like an unaccounted sound in the dead of night
I can't rely on knowing that other nights left
   with only temporary fright
Each time I await that silent specter
   I fear more force, vengeance, and evil than the time before
In mid night, when simple words are elusive
   and thoughts swirl like blizzard snow...I lie still
muscles aching with fear...waiting
   I don't ask why anymore
It no longer matters, the battle can't be won
   Soldiers stand erect in my mind, waiting
with more ammunition that I could have imagined
   I stay crouched, crippled, with my flag of surrender
Hoping soon to return to familiar sounds, thoughts, and safety
   The house is still, aside from the constant whisper of sleep
I don't ask why anymore...I simply pray for a gentle truce,
   and a return to what was humorously, boring, sadly, joyfully real
Donna K. Smith

Hummingbird Messenger

She's found relief, as all life goes, from this earth's leash.
Dear Mother.
'Neath mimosa blooms, I mourn and pray - 'till evening looms.
Is she in heavenly rest, or, God forbid, one of hell's guests?
I wonder.
A humming bird flies, to my fair land, from sunset skies,
and seems to seek, beside my hand, sweet blossoms pink.
I ponder.
It dares to linger, bold and light, upon my finger!
Flashing green wings, that gently hum and silently sing,
"Remember?"
"All that we loved and joys we shared? It's more true - above.
Don't be blue, child, for just as you, God loves me too.
Forever."
Connie Haen

Is It Already Time?

Last night I sat there thinking
Of memories in my past.
My heart just kept sinking
Though I know that the memories will last.

My eyes welled up with tears
With every photograph.
Yet the people, times, and places of past years
Somehow made me laugh.

It seems not so long ago
We were young and so carefree.
Now we have to find a way to let that go
And except new responsibility.

For everyone there comes a time
When we must leave our old security,
To find ourselves and put the past behind,
And gain more knowledge and maturity.

The hardest part to realize
Is being on your own.
Friends and family sympathize
Because they know we all must walk this road alone!

Susan Wienecke

I Am the Ruler Brave and Strong

I am the river brave and strong
I hear the fish break my surface to catch a bug
I see the doe come to me and delicately drink from me
I feel the wind rush by me and ripple my water
I am the river brave and strong

Julie Terry

My March

March is changing, a restless fling
Hardly winter, nearly spring.

Her wind's refreshing, her sun is warm
Enjoy! . . . Her windy, rainy, storm.

She soon will bring a lamb-like calm!

Her clouds are softest, billowy white,
then to grey; appear as night

Going somewhere in their flight . . .

March you're a vixen, exciting bliss . . .
Lead on to Spring and April's kiss!

Joan C. Cirone

In Memory of Grandma

Reflections of the sun
    on the water
Reminds me of the
    sparkle in your eyes
The sun coming down on me
    feels like your arms wrapped around me
The ducks float by
    calmly on the waves
Reminding me of how
    peaceful you look
You're up there
    waltzing with Grandpa
Of this I am sure
    your time with him now
        is so completely pure
Please enjoy your life

Painlessly . . .

Karen L. Marshall

Shadows

Streets are dark, not a soul around.
An erie feeling, a glance over your shoulder.
Shadows come alive.
Hesitation in every step.
Eyes see no more.
But why?
Open those eyes, no need for restlessness.
You are stronger than shadows.
A figment of all imagination.
You are stronger than shadows.
You have fought the shadows once before.
Don't deny.
A child inside cries.
Bedroom lights shine brightly.
The battle's now won.
Yet, now all grown, this war rages on.
You are stronger than shadows.
Are you?

Marc DeSomma

For My Wonderful Wife

We live together in a world of bliss,
not having everything we want
and there are a few things that we miss.

I want to give you more
than what I can possibly dream.
But in reality, our life together is nothing
more than a trickling stream.

I shoot for the moon, but land in the ocean,
then I lose my temper, and cause a big commotion.

Tomorrow, together we're closer to my dream,
because having you beside me, yesterday and today,
we make a real nice team.

We have our moments of glory, which at times we just want to shout.
Then there are moments we don't want to talk about.

As we grow older in our home of wonderful bliss,
I'll tell you one thing for sure that I don't want you to miss.

Our time we share, is better than a new car,
Our son we had together is better still by far.
But our decision we share a path together in our lives,
is truly the Best Decision I've made in My Life.

Ronald J. Jankowski

Angels

Angels laugh and angels sing,
much more precious than diamonds, rings.
Angels are sweet and always glisten,
they're always there to smile and listen.
Angels take you to their hearts,
once you're there you'll never part.
Angels are like a blooming flower,
full of beauty, full of power.
Angels are something really grand,
they never yell, they always understand.
Angels are like a graceful dove,
they're pure and white and full of love.
Our angel is like no other,
because on Earth she's called our mother.

Nicole Weaver

Poetry

Poetry is a gentle tapping
Of rain on the roof
Awakening the listener lightly napping
Sending dreams aloof.
Sounding every place, all at once, at first,
But then distinctly here and there; yet still adverse.

Noticing even more, the rhythmic rapping
Of rain on window panes,
The watcher sees the splash and drip, lapping
Down in pools, then coursing off in veins.
Appearing at first without direction of designation,
Able, yet, to find a defined destination.

Poetry is the horizon—
The line that isn't there—
Where, to the sky, the sea has arisen;
Where, the passerby has but to care
To use words of common origin
To create a vision rare.

   Lew Maggiora

King

Massive,
king of rocks.

The crown, lit by color,
adorned with the jewels of life and history,
carved by the softest of hands,
inching through the beautiful crevices,
creating a work of art,
that beautifies with the coming of age.

The palace,
spawned from a brook,
crafted by the greatest of masons,
sculpted by natures powerful, yet gentle hands;
and given beauty,
by its foremost creation,
the light of the sun.

It is a kingdom,
yet it could never have been,
without the creators, water and light,
the natural hands of an artist,
gentle and flowing.

   Jeff Wingard

Dakota's Assurance

Dakota is my tomorrows
Wrapped around my heart each day.
Only loaned to me for a short while,
To love and show God's way.

To have him know his importance
In life's journey, oh so fast,
That he can always count on grandpa
To be there always, never blame or cast.

My heart yearns to know
What as an adult he'll be,
With an up hill battle now
God's help, success we'll see.

To see him brought into this world
And feel his love for me,
Is the greatest gift I ever had
I hope Dakota sees this in me.

When I no longer walk this earth
And with the Lord I stay,
Will Dakota recall those days of youth
Spent playing with grandpa Ray.

   Ray Scarbrough

Spring's Awakening

Stormy weather escalates beginnings of life
Abundant growth and cheerfulness of color
Creates a "spell" of fragrant budding charm as within
Lies a "Sleeping Beauty" adorned for her prince
Ready to reawaken with a kiss of the oncoming season

   Sara Niccum

The Carolers

Soft and lightly fell the snow
Shining windows all aglow
While down the icy winding road
Giant trees stand asleep beneath their load
All is covered in a mantle of white
Glistening in a glow of fairy light
Then, off in the distance but soft and clear
Comes the sound of their voices
Proclaiming their cheer
For this is the night that is drawing so near
To hear of the birth of that infant so dear
Sweetly then, their voices true
Call upon us our faith to renew

   Dorothy A. Snowden

Broken Vows

Today my heart is broken and sad,
I no longer have a husband my kids have no Dad
No matter what you did, we loved you anyway,
But I guess it wasn't good enough, because you walked away.

I thought our love was forever when we said "I do,"
But it only meant that to me, and not to you.
I thought our vows said "through sickness and health"
But you cheated on me when I was sick, and you only care about wealth.

They say money can't buy true love and Family,
So you and your money will be poor company.
You say you can't live with "me,"
Can you live with yourself and the way things will be?

My marriage vows said "Till death do us part,"
Did yours say, if you have a problem, break her heart?
True love only comes around one time,
You've thrown away yours and broken mine.

Think about these things when you lie down at night,
Try to convince yourself that you're doing right.
Because you can lie to everyone else, you see.
But you can't lie to yourself, and you can't lie to me.

   Ruth A. Speakman

The Sea

There's nothing quite like the sea on a calm and peaceful day.
There she is in all her beauty,
Dressed in the finest translucent turquoise
Edged in milky white lace of the most delicate design.

The rhythm of each movement is breathtaking to behold.
Dancing lightly, she comes very near then flips her laces
And softly laughing, dances away
Ah, such beauty.

Twilight finds her bubbling over with glee
Only the outer garments change to midnight blue
Set with a million stars.

The prima donna of all time daintily flips her lace,
Sweetly singing, she dances the night away.

   Cora Green

Magic

A lacy spiders web
  glistens with morning dew.
A fiery sunset glows
  with red in every hue.

A crystal mountain stream
  whispers a calming tune.
A nest made by a sparrow
  decorates trees in June.

A child walks through a meadow
  and finds his first dandelion.
With a tiny puff of air
  a generation through the air is flying.

The beauty is everywhere
  though sometimes it's hard to see.
But with a child by your side,
  it's easy to find majesty.
    Kay N. Reese

ByRonic Irony

She writes in drivel, like a blight
Of childish thoughts and silly dreams;
And all that's worst in black and white
Meet in her essays and her themes;
Thus rambling to that oversight
Which logic at the grammar screams.

One word the more, one draft the less
Had half revised the senseless flaw
Which shows in every mindless mess,
Or grimly mangles sentence law,
Where errors blithely clear undress
Half-baked ideas, en gran faux pas.

And on that mind, and o'er that brain,
So vacant, empty, negligent,
The grins that beckon, eyes that strain,
But tell of nights in mischief spent,
A source of English language pain,
A teacher's disillusionment.
    Ronald E. Metzger

Stains

Words of yesterday stained earth
Words of today remove old stains
  And bring new ones

Words of tomorrow will bring more beautiful
  And perhaps more ugly stains than
  We have experienced

Then what is a stain?

Is it forever?

the stains that I know change color,
  Shape and intensity

The stains that I know are always there
  And within everyone

It's not a secret!
Stain is just the truth
How comforting it is to know
    Jim Serici

On The Wind

Black sand beaches, warm ebbing tide,
voices on the wind, horses in the sky.
As lightning flashes in distant places,
search clouds designs for mystic faces.

I saw the wild mare in silver moonlight.
Strong spirit so free, an image in white.
Between my legs we ran, two became as one.
We raced the wind until the rising sun.

In the morning I woke in warmth of sand.
Thought it was a dream induced by this land.
Then high on a mountain she rose with grace.
With power she reared, then left this place.
    Ronald M. Erickson

Daughter, Mother Be

It was just an instant glance
A daughter not, but a friend
Sitting there next to you.
Me wanting to take her place
A place where a daughter should be.
Yet my place is where I hide.

As mother, daughter,
We seem to always talk, yet never say a word
My love for you is dear
Yet sometimes never clear.
Clear as the sky with clouds over there
Fresh as the spring air yet the thunder ever near.

I long to sit where I saw her sat, next to my Mother dear.
The heartstrings strung but never plucked,
The sky never clear,
The thunder ever near.

Time does continue though, to a positive end

The skies clear, the air freshens, the heartstrings ring true
All my love to mother
I finally sit next to you.
    Stephanie Paul

La Mer

If I had not chased the waves from our sandcastle moat
  and huddled under the boardwalk when it rained as a child
and if mother had not been raised in Atlantic City near the sea
  where she swam on her father's back out past the pier
fell in love with Daddy and eloped to Dallas and if
  I had not been born in Ventnor in a doctor's house right
on the ocean and lived in New Jersey most of my life where I
  raised four children and in December married Craig and
if I had not gone with Doris to Mary Comey's funeral mass
  and Mimi and Mac had not gotten this summer house I would
not be sitting here this morning looking out past the dune grass
  in the sand at the sun glinting on the ocean watching two
purple dragon flies gliding side by side over a fat bird perched
  on a weathered fence slat listening to its warbling and
remembering yesterday sitting in the sand at water's edge with Mimi
  watching the surf spray high onto the black jetty and a
biplane soar and dip in the bluest sky and last evening
  I would not have been dancing on the stone floor
of the shore house arm and arm between my mother's two sisters
  laughing and singing to the Ink Spots
as dinner simmered on the stove
    Barbara L. Sheridan

Looking for Someone

I'm looking for someone, some one
it seems, I've had a vision of, only in dreams.
Someone to talk to, love and
admire, it's you I'm thinking of,
you're all I desire.
I'd be so happy holding you
tight, hearing you whisper a
prayer of delight.
Just like a couple of smoke
rings, drifting to the skies, I
keep praying that some day we'll
drift to paradise.
So until that lucky day
we take the voices "I do", I'll find
happiness, love and joy in
every dream with you.

Eunice L. Boso

A Summer's Kiss

Lying with you, my heart is pounding love, every beat, beating
true.

True love for you is what I had; maybe it was good, but I knew it
was bad.

At that moment, I looked up at the sky, "I wish I may, I wish I
might..."

Have you now, forever and always, through good and bad and all of
my days.

You pulled me tight, as our lips brushed lightly through the
sweet night air, and losing you was a thought I couldn't bear.

You gave me that feeling when you gave me that kiss; your touch,
your cool, I would always miss.

When it all ended, it was a past summer's kiss, that was nothing
more than my heart in bliss.

Rachel Kirkpatrick

Transition

Exuberant fallacies befall attitudes,
conscious numbness expunges emotions.
A felony hardly debatable
cause its the invasiveness
that prevails.
The conflict between conscious purpose
and unconscious impulse crumbles postures
meant to expostulate fervors.

The prevading spirit manifests itself
by the eloquence of his silence.
All growth is transition,
in the process of becoming
I grope for the being, me.
A nascent emotion never touching
the edge of twilight,
such is the paradox of my impotence
with relationships.
All transition belongs to the realm of pain.

Jasdeep S. Aulakh

Untitled

Hello my friend!
the time has come to say good-bye
and it's alright
if you happen to cry,
because these tears
show friendship and love.
So if you cry, don't dry your eyes
because you're wiping away the memories.

Lisa M. Barry

Sister Angela Bloopers

Sister Angela's class was very bad,
She got up on a chair and yelled Halo Halo."
The class continued to talk.
She got up on a piano "Halo Halo," she said.
Just then the principal walked in.

One day she was coming to school,
A sign read, "caution slippery stairs."
She ignored it.
Down the flights of stairs she went.

"Aghh," she yelled.
"I think I've broken a bone!" she said,
"Call 911, call 911!"

Tony Zignego

My Daddy

When I was born,
he came into my life.
A chubby man, whose name is Dan.

He cared for me, and loved me.
Yet that wasn't enough, for him to stay.

We would go to the park, and play all day.
He'd read me poems,
At least that was what he would say.

He would sleep all day,
And all through the night.
And left a mess, that was completely out of sight.

He would never clean, but eat all day.
"He was too tired," at least that was what he would say.

Now he is gone, there is another.
That would never leave, like the other.

He takes me to parks, and very long walks.
He takes me to dinner, for very long talks.

The man I first described,
Was very cold. But that was my "daddy"
At least that's what I was told.

Jessica Morales

Naked Friendship

True friendship wears no clothing, it is naked, pure and innocent
It is like a streaker walking in a busy park on a summer day
Creating a scary-but-a good jealousy for all
Daring all, challenging all to join the naked race of true friendship
So walk friends - expose the innocence, challenge all to be true
friends over looking the so called faults and seeing only the genuine
sincerity of friendship
Let us all be like the streaker in the park on a summer day
come let us walk the crowded streets
come let us walk the world over as ambassadors of naked friendship
cry when need to, laugh when we need to comfort when we need to
so rise above the chaos of clothed friendship
Let it be examine for they will find only one thing
True friendship is naked pure and innocent
for it wears no clothing.

Stephen Boyce

Life In A Nutshell

Born on a fresh, bright, spring morn
to grow, and rise up from the earth,
and blossom, and wave on a summer's warm breeze,
until no fruits bear forth,
and colors fade to the reds and golds of autumn,
and then disappear under the snow
of a silent, white, winter's eve.

John R. Domanay

Personal Expiation Through Public Humiliation On the Geraldo Show

The unutterable heaviness of being
schizoid from our own natures and life's realities
spoonfed by emasculated media

The jungle of my mind produces dreadlocks
    of thought and decaffeinated love
I sprout horns rather than wings
Poetry and song and dance have died
    buried in some mass grave alongside a ravine

I pay my taxes to destroy labor unions in Honduras
I am a good boy, a good son
I work and pay my taxes,
    so activists can be hung in Nigeria.
I bow properly to the golden calf
    while courageous women defuse nuclear warheads
    and receive 10 yrs.

And my solace is to watch Geraldo humiliate
    lovers, sisters, husbands and wives
    as they expiate
    and I expectorate
    on it all.

Arnie R. Fox

Open Your Eyes And See

Open your eyes and see the nations; the crime
has made everybody lose their patience.

Open your eyes and see the drug addicts, who
make their brains become nothing but static.

Open your eyes and see the families that have
been broken, if you haven't been with this experience,
God has given you a token.

Open your eyes and see the killing, which is
making a lot of people's hearts lose their filling.

Open your eyes and see the children that have
been abused, which is getting out of hand and has to be reduced.

Open your eyes and see war all over, which is
making everybody wish for a four leaf clover.

Open your eyes and see these things and many
more; they are giving our beautiful Earth a sore.

Punit Krishna Seth

Irishmen

Fire wood,
Fire works,
Fireflies,
Fire eyes.
    To recall the time you strayed away,
To reminisce the essence you brought along each day.
How two passing Irishmen meant not a single thought;
And all you did, all you said I think it ought.
    To see sparks in the sky
Up from the beach they were lit to fly,
Striving to bring praise beyond the stars,
The run home faster than most the jeeps stopping in bars
    That's all they see, all they know,
Not realizing where they are, not high but low
So sit on the docks, speaking of the egg cut moon,
Recalling a happy time, where lovers never seize to swoon.

Nicole Lillian Bartels

In Memory of My Special Pet

So long ago when we first met
Your cute little face I will never forget.
So small and furry and wagging tail
I knew our friendship would not fail.
And it wasn't very long
The bond between us grew so strong.
You gave me loyalty, companionship and trust but of these above
Most of all unconditional love.
Years are passing, you're getting old
That of which I have no control.
You're sick now can't you see
God has taken you from me.
So much pain, so much sorrow
For there will be no more tomorrows.
My heart is breaking, so it seems
Now I can only see you in my dreams.
Time will pass but I can't forget
You'll always be my special pet.

Mary Wellner

Untitled

Awake! Awake!
'Twas winter O'er.
The spring
The summer's cometh.
Let not the bitter.
    Frost wind,
Findeth thee sleepeth.
Once more? For ever?
Archibald greenidge.
Buffiling winds stormy seas.
The murky water,
In the shallows.
Shows a tempest is nigh.
Archibald granidge
The flowers smell tweety
from the garden below,
95 fragrance is not accepted.
Their minds are warped.
By the inclement weather, forced by man's hands.

Archie Greenidge

A Place Called Love

In my mind of imaginings
I travel to a place called love,
a place where truth lies
and tender hearts roam free.
The air here is composed of hope.
I breathe it in, deeply,
for it is these precious breaths of air
that carry me through those other places,
places of loneliness,
where broken hearts hurt bad
and the air is composed only of despair.

As I leave this place called love
in my mind of imagining's,
I take a moment to inhale one last breath.
I hold it in
until I suffocate.

There are no such things as hopeless romantics,
just broken hearts that need to heal.

As I travel, I am only hopeful.

Lori Baxter

Micro McDerm

I'm Micro McDerm and I'm a germ.
I'm bold and rotten, nasty and mean and I grow wilder and stronger
on all things unclean. You can't see me since I'm so small, but I can
tell you this, I can frighten you all. I'm icky and sticky, yucky and
grimy, I'm dirty and ugly, hairy and slimy. My actions will prove
what a mean creature I am.
If you don't believe me, I'll tell you my plan.
I hide in all garbage, messes and dirt, ready to strike and cause
sickness and hurt. If you come around me, here's what I'll do,
I'll quite boldly grab onto you.
It's into your system I surely will travel, bringing you problems
you can't unravel. There's an awful lot I can bring to you,
like coughs and colds, fever and flu, measles and mumps and stomach
aches too. It's so mighty that I truly am, and for this I'm as happy
as a clam. But, if all of you only knew how simple it is to keep me
from you. It doesn't take much as you can see, all you must do is
be as clean as can be. If you handle garbage, messes and dirt, wash
well with soap and you won't get hurt. I hate all kinds of soap and
all that is clean, it's that stuff that stops me from being mean.
Wash! Wash! Wash! That's what you must do,
if you want to keep me away from you!

Rose Villafrade

Our Wedding Day

The weather is beautiful and the sky is blue.
I hear wedding bells, see flower girls, pretty ladies and handsome
men too.
There are tuxedos, bow ties and chauffeur driven limousines.
The bride and groom are holding hands, wearing beautiful rings.
Happiness and joy on each face. Rice is thrown all over the place.
White limousines all in a row
Waiting to take the guest to the reception show.
Plenty to drink and plenty to eat, nice tasty salads and all kinds
of meat. Souvenirs, presents and music to dance
Gave a beautiful setting for love and romance
The cutting of the five tier cake was something to behold.
And the groom fed the bride with a fork made of gold.
Soon the bride fed the groom on that happy afternoon.
After eating they waved and left for their glorious honeymoon.

Waltina Serrao-Mosley

The Last Mile

We know the Book speaks of a valley
Never saying how deep or how wide
Only that all must go there
All alone, no one by your side.
With faith we walk down in the valley,
We know there is no other way.
Walk on though tired and so weary
Think of the promised new day.
On and on through the fog and darkness
Up ahead there's a new hill to climb,
But we know when we reach the summit
There will be joy sublime.
Now it seems the pathway grows smoother
There's a whisper of sound from above
And a gentle breeze seems to guide us
It comes from the wings of a dove.
At last the end of the journey,
Never more will we walk all alone.
And now hear His voice we've been waiting,
"Welcome dear child, you are Home."

Archie McCoy

Can You See Me

Can you look within me and feel what I am feeling
Can you become my eyes and see what I am seeing
Can you try to see beyond the physical and see me for me
Not a body, not a color, not a package
If you look beyond this, you will find me.
I am a soul in search of happiness and joy
I am a soul in search of peace and tranquility
I am a soul in search of knowledge and strength
I am a beautiful soul full of majestic splendors
All of this is what I am, but I am also a soul in search of love
When my love is found, all of me will be given to him.
If only you could see past the obvious which blinds you
I am here, can you see me?

Linnette Torres

after the war

they lay privately, primitively
    praying small gospels created in youth
      touching lips, pressing skin, reaching wrapping legs
        around legs, sliding stretching
      knees in between, heaving like old smoky chests
    whole bodies, breaths up and down
up and down as only the truest of lovers

under those wrinkled sheets
    secrets were unveiled, charms were cast
      bridges were laboriously crossed and recrossed
        healing the burns, the scars from a previous fall
      sweeping battlefields of those ancient massacres and lynchings
proudly grounding the flags of victory in asphalt soil of time

privately, primitively they fell into love
    like lords and ladies of girlhood tales
      because she was ready he was there
        he was ready she was there
      and only under wrinkled sheets
do warcrimes share their charms

Patricia Saphier

A Tree Is Known

A tree may be so beautiful, it may stand noticeably tall.
A tree may shine in blossom time, but these things doesn't
matter at all.
So do not be deceived, by the color of the leaves, nor the branches
That appear to be strong, for by the fruit it bears a tree, is known
We are that tree, destine to bear in our season, lest we soon
wither and die. We must be faithful, in bearing for this reason,
that someone who might be passing by.
May be inspired through our yield of daily living,
and take pride, in knowing the seeds were sown, for by the fruit
it bears a tree, is known.

Willie D. Price

The Dive

These bright blue waves will darken down to green;
I lie face-down, outstretched upon the pier,
While shadows haunt the calm, light-shafted depths;
This is a warm lagoon, where faint but clear,
The winding snail-tracks mark the bottom-sand;
The sun hangs hot, it quickens my desire
To splash, to roll, feel closing over me,
This blue intoxicant, this water-fire.
Some warm lagoons hide sharks;
Some don't; no one knows why,
But there one glides; it turns, it disappears;
And I look upward at the soft blue sky,
And hear the gentle laughter of the waves,
Then quick, before they dull to green again,
Plunge down to feel their chilling ecstasy.

Arthur Q. Larson

As Existentialism Cries Its Lonely Moan

As Existentialism cries its lonely moan
He turns to find his loves unknown
Remembering that Shakespeare said love's not times fool.
Yet time is man made and that man is dead.
He turns to love in shine and disgrace,
He knows not why or of its place.
This perfect love within his grasp,
His love for her an unending task.
Before he finds love he must know why,
Love is heard in every cry.
It seems to appear in every place,
In land, in dog and human face.
To him love seems an ironic state,
A virtue that causes war and fights that wait.
Love is the bearer of harmony;
Also it brings every man's worst fear,
A dread that something is out there, something near.
A murderer, a rapist, another, or a matter to jeer.
This thing that looks past Truth and Trust,
And unconditional love it sees like dust.
While Omnipotence touches him in her arms,
He can only guess of endless harms

Michael D. Rogers

The Stream of Life

The Stream of Life rolls slowly on,
And waits for naught but time,
It eats away at youthfulness,
As life's springtime sublimes.

The Stream of Life, it runs its course,
With every living thing.
It knows no banks, no dams, no droughts —
It catches all the fleeing.

The Stream of Life is hindered not,
No obstacles can slow it.
It runs on 'til the end of time,
And all the world doth know it.

Graham Cano

Always Grace

I was saved at an early age.
New in Christ and the treasure that waits.
As I got older I would think,
I can do it myself, I fell out of synch.
I always thought he had closed his door,
but that showed how little I knew of the Lord.
So many years later I called out his name.
His door still open, he had never changed.
He lets me know he was always there, through good times
and bad times with plenty to spare.
The Lord has allowed me to grow stronger in faith.
I praise Him and His Son with each passing day.
For allowing me to understand His message of Grace.
And to help spread His word to all human race.

Edward Benny Yarber Jr.

Lovefield

Lovefield,
It seemed like an appropriate name at the time
But I went to the airport last night
And it seemed funny going and not meeting you.
It seemed as though every soldier I saw had your face
And I could see myself running to meet you.
I used to love the airport
And then hate it too
For it seemed no sooner than it brought you to me
It was taking you away.

Katherine McColl

My Great Mistake

Another day I wake up, my life is now hell,
I wonder if or when I will ever get well.

The doctors don't listen, they must think it's a joke,
my baby has been gone and I'm going broke.

It hurts to cook, drive, and hold my child,
as my life was before, these movements are mild.

From those who knew me as I was in the past,
keep telling me to keep faith, that this can't last.

I do not remember hitting the cars or my head,
now, as I try to relearn, times I'd rather be dead.

It could be worse, though sometimes I doubt,
I try to follow doctor's orders of getting out and about.

Brushing my teeth, even opening the door,
my hands give pains of absolute horror.

I try not to yawn, so how could I know,
that this ear ache I have, is a jaw-joint "show."

I kept trying to work, it should have just gone away,
looking back now, I should have stopped that same day.

I trusted the garage to fix my brakes,
didn't double check, this is my great mistake.

Loreena Virginia

Dreaded Conscience

In the shadow of earth's own path
Exists a state of consciousness
An escape from the blatant wretchedness.
Butterflies float in water and ice
And birds soar effortless under the ground
Dark souls fly in the cold air around.
Sharks swim the dreaded skies
Needles come looking for your spineless shell
In search of the pain they want to tell.
Piked glass quench a thirst for blood
As the shiny knives join the chatter trail
Radiating a breathing darkness so frail.
Dripping, dripping of panic is the helping hand
No more answers, needless pledge
Losing balance from eternity's edge.
Falling, falling, falling, falling...
Light.

Arthur Khachatryan

Grandfather

Grandfather,
Where have you gone?
As I lay these flowers by your side,
I remember.
I can hear your soft voice whispering,
"Child, That's were the angels kissed you."
I smile,
knowing he was teasing me about my dimples.
In his arms
I could hide from all danger.
With his hand
He made beautiful things.
When the birds sang outside his window,
He named them one by one.
They flock by his grave now,
singing their sweet lullaby.
Grandfather—
I think you were the one kissed by the angels.

Anne Marie Anthony

The Gardener's Cat Is Dead

Gather 'round, field mice, I've good news to tell!
The gardener's cat tumbled into the well.
Gurgling and clawing on slick slimy limestones,
He closed his cat's eyes, no more glittering rhinestones.
His nine lives expired. We'll toll the church bell.
He drowned, that damned cat, no-good fur ball from hell.

Linda E. Medlock

A Mother's Prayer

Two dear little girls, so loving and true.
Eyes of brown and eyes of blue.
Deeply entwined in their parents' love.
God sent them from heaven above.

How can I help them, dear God to be,
Always true in their love of thee.
The years have passed and my time is near.
I have prayed for my girls each passing year.
I know my girls are loving and good,
And will honor God, as I know they should.

Gertrude M. Brown

If We Were A Dove

If we were a dove,
   we would perch on all
   the trees of the world
And sing songs of praise
   to the angels above
To wake up all lovers of the earth
   so they can see our joy.

If we were a dove,
   we would peek silently
   and listen to all the lover's hearts
And if we see them kissing and hugging,
   holding and embracing
We'll shout and scream to the blue skies
   as we celebrate our joy.

We'll invite all fellow doves of the universe
   big or small, black or white
   to join our crusade
Together we'll sing,
Together we'll soar
As we spread love, love and love.

Eduardo Purisima

A Mother

A word of needing to be this person
A person who can love most positively
Not one who's not sure of anything
But one who has the right feelings to give to a baby
And a wonderful father like you
To care for an impossible dream that never seems like it's going
to come true
This baby seems like a life time away and a past that couldn't know
What life is like today.
A past we couldn't have
A future we want to give
How far away is this dream?
I'm sure it's not tomorrow
I'm sure it's not today or next week
But someday soon we'll be parents
A word that has so much meaning behind it
A word that can't mean anything until it happens
A word so strong it weakens my heart to think about it
For now there is hope
Hope of becoming this life long dream
My dream of being a mother

Michelle Weitzman

Candlelight

You draw me out of cold oblivion
   Free at last from the desk drawer prison
No more forlorn but reconciled anew
   To our friendship deep in childhood grew
And set me back aflame...

In the dim of nite all slumber serene
   I watch the tears flow, your interest keen
At the poignant story, "The Bridges of Madison County"
   Noticing how you've changed from flight of fancy
Reading books blest on children's wings.

The dawn breaks, my life passes to bid adieu
   You close the book touched as the rose by morning dew
Before the nite retire you lay down your crown
   That I may see with your transparent gown
My last breath, the revelation — your flesh of innocence.

The sublime truth to me now unveiled
   You've grown a woman, the girl my youth revered
In tardy protest I burn with passion true
   Yet, to love you is not to touch you
Embrace but fate, to expire sweetly consumed by your flame.

Guillermo Espinosa

I Did You Wrong

I once had a wonderful, faithful wife
Now I have a lonely, longing life
I did you wrong, I now know
I couldn't control my male ego, so
Why would I want a bite of the forbidden fruit
Which ended in a divorce suit
My heart has ached so very much
Ever since we parted such
I've learned my lesson well
I only pray God will forgive, and not send me to hell
I know I tore your heart apart
Now I must spend my life on a rocky cart
I pray for your forgiveness strong
My dear, I did you wrong

Kenneth Aubele

The Schizophrenic

It's always the same, day after day,
He sits on the porch with little to say.
Thoughts whirling and swirling unable to rein,
Are his constant companions,
Oh, his spirit they drain.
He went to the valley while still a young man,
Alone and adrift, had to abandon his plan.
His thoughts made him fearful and guarded and shy.
He had to get out of the valley and try
To make peace with this illness, this curse, this distress.
Now we see that he does, indeed, do his best.
Each morning he goes out for coffee and beer,
What he thinks while he drinks, he won't let us hear.
Though his eyes seem to connect as they gaze into my own,
I must concede he is fundamentally alone.

Christine Chatwell

Eat the Children

A cherry flavored kiss sends sweet
messages you can only here from the
wind, although this and nothing is real.

A dream that has been played backward
is the only was you can understand
this dying love story that has been
forgotten in a fake world so much
like my own.

Aimee Hoffman

Dad, Almost Eighty Five

You take me on your nimble quest,
probing hushed anxiety.
You sit erect, we to and fro
about encrypted body signs:
ticklings of mortality.

Can I know
what part of you perhaps receives
my near degenerate compulsion
to cleave my diamond of the universe with crenulated words?

Maybe this is prayer,
the sense of being understood
or salvation,
being so redeemed.

Maybe it's the closest touch of God and immortality,
the spiral's circles overlap,
parent to child, who parents a child.
Love passed on
and on to others,
the love of seeing and being seen.

Loren D. Woodson

Old Timers

What goes around comes around — a cliché we've all been told
But I found out first hand — as my dearest mother grew old
She fed me and changed me — and kept my body clean
Now the table's turned - and she depends on me
The disease that has taken her body — I've yet to understand
Yet, there's a peace between us — as I held her precious hand
I've watched her relive the memories — of her as she was a child
She even called me mommy — in the innocence of her smile
She asked me hundreds of question — the answers I did not know
As her mind was in her younger years — yet her body was growing old
Tonight I stood beside her — and held her precious hand
Tears filled my eyes as I prayed to God — I don't understand
Then there was an inner peace — that filled my heart and soul
And God said "I'll take her now — now you can let go
Someday you'll know the reason — then you'll understand
She was waiting for me — to take her precious hand

Carolyn Merideth

Myself

My skin is tan colored
My hair is dark brown
When I walk in the streets,
I try not to wear a frown.

I have a brother who is 6 years old,
A mom and a dad to hug and to hold.
I have lots of friends and a great school too,
With gymnastics, diving and girl scouts,
What else can one girl do?

I like to write stories, poems and more,
I told you so much, but there's still facts galore.
I like to read books, mysteries to be exact,
I also like to dance, sing and act.
I'm very active and very frisky,
I like to take chances, I do things that are risky.

I think this poem is ending
But there's so much more I could say,
I hope you did enjoy this poem
I'll write another one some day.

Melissa C. Hanna

Floating

I wonder about life now
   Instead of worrying about it.
Seeing things as they are
is like witnessing death before life.
Reality is what I seek to find.
But is such a place captured by the human eye
   or is it seen through the cosmic mind?
Seeking such a place
is something that will come when I close my eyes to rest.

I have come to terms with my presence.

The life I live is not led by my outer-self.
Walking through life, instead of around it,
   has that feeling of seeing any future
   or revisiting any past.
Time, without witnessing its movement
   is the place which has found me.
I do not move, for I really have no place to go.
Floating, that is what the trip has to offer.
There is no worrying, there is no life to lead
   but only to follow.

Andrew R. Droessler

The Looking Glass

The reflection is always there, the mirage I'm used to seeing,
   But reality fails to copy the image that emits from my very being.

She is the outer layer who enacts the thoughts I create,
   Moves at my will and acts with my heart; a peculiar union we make.

Her eyes are my windows; I bathe in the views they display.
   I feast on every image, ignoring sporadic decay.

Her ears are my receptors amassing sounds and emotions alike,
   Turning me in to the world outside, whether set ablaze or aright.

Her mouth is my instrument, her voice my keyboard control;
   They let all know that I'm within — that I'm more than a body — a
   soul.

Her hands are my tools; their chores too multiple to name,
   And come time that they may slip, it's not her, but me to blame.

The rest of her was made for tasks to fill my every whim,
   But though I run her, I didn't make her. That was God, thank Him.

He placed me within her shell, presenting her to the world.
   Now see if you can spot me in the reflection of this girl.

Rachel Hochstedler

The Father's Tears

God blew aside the clouds and peered down from the sky
To this sad Earth whereon the Cross His Son must die,
His anger welled and broke all bounds
So that the Earth was shook, until
It seemed to roll and toss amidst the planets revolving in their spheres.
Then His Son cast saddened eyes up to Him Who is
And begged their sins forgiven be - then
He cried aloud - and bowed His Head to meet eternity.
'Twas then his Father shook His mighty Head to shed His raindrop tears,
And as the sobs did break from Him
Thunder rolled and roared its mightiest of cries
His bright foreboding eyes seemed as lightning bolts
To flash across those black and endless skies,
His mighty hands crashed down to split the earth in two
Sending echoes down the ages forever told anew - all stopped!
When on that Cross again the Father gazed
To His Boundless Loving Heart came joy
For walking towards Him, no more to die,
Came Jesus - The Father's Loving Little Boy!

Joan Mayor

A Mother

A Mother is someone
Who is there to talk
Someone who is there
to take that walk

Someone who listens
to what you say
Someone who is there
to watch you play

Someone who has been there
to watch you grow
Someone who has
things to show

Someone who loves you
the way you are
Someone who has gone so very far

Someone who misses you
When you are away
Someone who has plenty to say

That's why I love and care for my mother
Because I know there is no other!

Cassie Jo Palmer

Understanding

Reaching deep inside for inner strength,
for reasons, for answers; for what had happened;
came emptiness, sadness, for father's death.
My dreams, hopes, and prayers were dampened.
The Universe: full of mystery and darkness;
the world of surprise, glamour and beauty,
events unfold and actions taken by the heartless;
I stand alone to do my duty.
Sins are committed by those who are weak,
taken for granted are kind humanitarians,
for the stealing of my wife was a dirty trick;
I pray and forgive those with my possessions.
Although my life is a shambles,
I am learning to cope and understand;
In life there are gambles,
I must take full command.

Guillermo J. Rodman

O, My Children

You must realize I love you so,
   no matter where you may go.
Into my life you have brought so much joy,
   I see your faces on every little girl and boy.
In my heart you're all very dear,
   but in my world there is no cheer.
My life's been empty since you've been gone,
   but for your sakes I must go on.
Although our bodies are far apart,
   your spirits live within my heart.
O, children do not loose faith in us,
   for soon we shall have great happiness.
In time we'll no longer be apart,
   And there will be
Jubilation in each and every heart.

LaDonna R. Braun

When Angels Cry

The building stood alone, dark, and dusty;
Cobwebs hung from the lights and the air was stale and musty.
The organ and piano were silent; not a note was there ringing;
The pulpit and pews were empty; and no choir was there singing.

Then what are these sounds that come from dirty walls;
Sounds that skip and dance down the lonely stairs and halls.
They speak of times more pleasant yet gone forever;
Of times we took for granted which will return never.

We came here to find comfort, joy and freedom from our pain;
We came here to celebrate our victories and thank Him for our gain.
It was here we sought His will; to do what was right.
It was here we fought the devil; evil one of the night.

Oh, but where did we all go and what were the reasons;
Why our church was no longer as important as all the other seasons.
We had time for worldly pleasures, but no time for Godly treasures.
We had time for everything else on earth; but no time for Him who
   gave us birth.

The building still stands; a monument to us all,
Who rode past its doors and contributed to its fall.
We were all so busy we didn't hear the angels crying;
We were all too busy to see our church dying!

William A. Jones III

Our Family

A Family is a unit or so I've been told, Blood is
thicker than water, say the ones that are bold.
The resemblance is there for all to see but each
is unique, each one of us Me! We sometimes differ
and we all disagree about everyday things because
we are free.
We live our own lives and support one another, we
defend when attacked, we are Sister and Brother.
We are close and together though there may be
miles in between, we know and understand one
another more than it seems, our thoughts travel through time and
   space, caring
enough to see each other's face.
A circle we are and a circle we will remain
though a few of us have left a space in the chain.
   The ring will be full as long
   as we feed
   the love and
   understanding we all need.

Jodi Fields

Empty Without You

The sunshine and laughter have stopped
My barren soul cries out for its missing mate.
What has happened to my world of future brightness,
Why does my stomach yearn and head flutter?
I long for what was and could have been
Will it be the way. I hope and desire,
Or did hope vanish into the empty night?
There is always tomorrow where the day begins anew;
But the day begins without you, so I desire the night
In the night, nothing is seen, not even my empty soul
The emptiness consumed me totally and the day dawns again.
Close enough to see, hear, and touch but the senses are numb,
You are beautiful, sweet, and loving are you
You are forgiving, intelligent, and comforting are you.
Another night falls and I'm still empty, hoping and desiring.
But another sun rises, could this be the day I'm with you.
Or could the night fall again, me without you.
With or without you, the sun will rise and night will fall.
Only the sun is not as bright, and the night is darker
As this terrible emptiness cries out for fulfillment.

James Keith Sprinkle

A Mother's Love

The love of most mothers runs so very deep
More often than not it will make her weep

In the days of rearing and constant guiding
The ties that bind become always abiding

When the days are over - Mom's love does not tower
Above the devotion of the child to a lover

When the child's lover becomes a spouse
Mom's love and respect is thrown out of the house

Mom's undying love and concern keeps her hoping
That a thread of the closeness will bind them like roping

But one day she finally sees that it is gone - not by choice
And she hopes that the child hears some day her voice

Calling out that no matter how alone she may feel
Her love for that child is real oh so real

Kathy Weber

Signatures

To understand some mysteries in nature,
I surmise, that on occasion
One must observe children's
Wind-tilt wayward kites
Lofting in a sky of blue
With dangling string to be divided
Among backyards and avian domiciles
Poised for the burst of Spring.

Reality here is an annual.
Seasons born under a flood of stars,
Sun and moon setting the eternal props
For those who arrive,
Those who stay.

Yet, I discern in the babel
Of time's ancient speech
The rhetoric of an old, bald earth
Alive!
Staccato green, fields of chattering flowers
Golding glow at cloud's edge —
Signatures of Life.

Ernest F. Miller

The Porcelain Mask

To every woman there is the fruition of womanhood
Masked often by her dedication to serve others
Disguised by the porcelain mask so delicately painted
Given a certain passage of life, the mask can break
Screaming for a new mold and new paint

Not without pain does it crack
Piece by piece and fall to the floor
Like the graceful hawk searching for prey
The woman mystically begins to select new pieces

Assured these new pieces will never crack
The woman carefully designs her new mask
Mimicking a healing bone, the repair begins
The voids begin to close slowly

A beautiful transparent blanket falls upon the mask
Hence the cracks no longer appear as they fade away
The exterior restored, the interior deepened by pain
The new mask enhanced by a new clarity and richness
Newly born from the girl, transformed into woman

Christine Towner

Sweetness

I could profess until the end of time how much you mean to me
how much I love you
how much I need you
how fantastic you make me feel
when I gaze into those eyes,
oh, those beautiful eyes...
you'll always be my sweetness

What we shared was more than special
a once in a lifetime thing
an electricity shared and never forgotten
proving the cliche' true...
my heart is forever yours,
yours is mine

Two hearts
two minds
strong when together
weak when apart

Mike Thayer

Can I Touch You With My Eyes?

Can I touch you with my eyes?
My eyes can tell you of the passion smoldering soft within me.
It lies on the threshold of explosion;
So close to a heart that escalates at each unexpected glance of you.
The closeness of you so sears me that I can hardly breathe;
A passion so consuming that sleep eludes me.
I peer into the depths of darkness,
Only to see the cool, clear blue of that which I can never have.

Can I touch you with my eyes?
They can reveal how I long to hold you close;
To indulgently run my fingers over you;
To feel your breath against my breast;
To taste your mouth on mine - gentle, torrid;
To feel your life rise up within me and consume my being;
To fall as one with no desire left unquenched.

Can I touch you with my eyes?
To be sure you feel that which I cannot speak,
But long for you to know.
For my eyes, nor my heart, cannot lie.

Karen S. Acevedo

A Divided Soul

A divided soul;
where memories unique to each desire
dance across a blackened screen of despair.

Barren trees, void of blossom or green;
their very existence a testimony to misery;
cast a shadow over the lifeless land
Glancing in every direction,
the eyes give in to desperation.

But the heart holds out;
knowing what the mind can not fathom and
what the eyes can not see; the heart moves on —
forward to the light of hope; yet unknown, unseen but felt.

With each beat the heart gives hope to a desperate soul.
Where there is a beat, there is hope, there is life and
there is light for those who follow what they can not see
but feel.

A divided soul;
where memories unique to each desire
are no longer alone, but united in the light of hope.

Lisa R. Ball

Revelation

With each step he took
A blink of an eye
Suddenly the earth shook
His world and goals awry
Blinded
Flash
He steps again, this time with caution
Eagerly he glances
Lacking a notion
Of what could be, he'll take his chances
Sense of timing
Our worlds colliding
Bells of love chiming
Spirits high and climbing
Rachel M. Gering

A Tribute to Alisha

"A little girl," — what happy news
The phone call brought to me that day;
"Her name's Alisha," grandma said —
A breath of spring on twenty-fourth of May.

You blessed the home that loved and cared
For brother Caleb, then past two;
Your features fine, so much like his,
With reddish hair and eyes of blue.

In spite of nurture and loving care,
With sleep enough and proper food,
Some problems later caused concerns —
Your growing pattern was not good.

Despite the weakness, lack of strength,
Your winning smile and playful ways,
Your sharp and eager, learning mind
Won many friends and words of praise.

Your gallant fight at last was lost;
Your life on earth was far too brief;
But your loving charm and radiance
Will live and ease our pain in grief.

Eva C. Honn

For Her Love I Yearn

One o'clock in the world's dark vest, the spinning doubt in my head's
web I can not rest.
I drift alone through life's turbulent stream, only wishing I could wash away in a dream.

Reflections of my reality are into view; what's wrong with me? What's
this hell I put myself through?

If love is an act of healing then I am bleeding, and without this peace of mind into life's dark crevice I keep receding.

Withdrawn and introverted, this life seems infectiously perverted.
Alone and silent with my favorite tune, I drift away.

I know love just doesn't stare, and I try to search for her without a care.
But all dogs need a leash, and at last I won't forget it.
So I won't ask her today, I don't want to scare her away.

For without self confidence my life will never turn.
And I'll smile and learn to pretend, but I have no more dreams to defend.
Yet somehow I know there's someone out there.
So I say goodnight and for you I'll save this love and care.
William G. Pitcher Jr.

Fleeting Feelings

I welcome the cool breeze of the evening
Is that a nightingale I hear singing
As the scented jasmine air
comes wafting through my kitchen door
And a thousand cricket chorus
encourage summer's encore

Can we these fleeting feelings hold
What is truly ours to know
Like Antares aglow in diaphanous sky
A glimmer, a glimpse
A spark of light
Am I
B. D. Franklin

No More Fear

Under an old oak tree is where I lay.
I sit and watch the sky as the day rolls away.

The sinking sun turns the sky a beautiful pink.
It makes everything so perfect, because it's found
    the missing link.

Day animals go home, while night animals begun to stir.
And it seems they say "Hi" while passing by, although I
    can't be sure.

Soon the sun is sleeping and awakening is the moon.
It pulls a dark over the earth, while the breeze
    sings a relaxing tune.

I close my eyes, as memories come to my head.
Memories that I cherish, memories that will never be dead.

I soon re-open my eyes and watch the glaring stars.
And it amazes me how I can see their light, even from afar.

From dusk till down, from dark till morning light.
I stay up all night and watch these astronomical sights.
This experience has made me strong, I'm prepared for what's in-store
No longer shall I run from my future, not once again, no more.
David Bryan

True

Thoughts of you are my guidance
Throughout my days you are my hope
My nights are complete with praises for you
The future is certain with you as my focus
I am forever thankful for your love
How can I doubt you existence
Everything beautiful, peaceful, and kind is from you
I can go on knowing that you are here
Always providing the truth
When I look upward toward the skies
Your warmth shines from the sun
And sparkles from the stars
My life I give to you
You are forever my truth
Jacqueline V. Carter

Son

Our son the first born,
Was a gift from God early in the morn.
I couldn't see well, but I knew,
He was a result of me and you.
A perfect boy, ten finger and ten toes,
Perfect right down to his little wrinkled nose.
I remember that day just swell.
And in my eyes happy tears well.
To think he is mine,
From now and till the end of time.
Roderick Church

The Course of Life

God, charts the course for our lives.
It then becomes our responsibility
to follow the Map of Destiny
through His instructions.

Sometimes, though, the instructions are not
as simple or clear as we would like them to be.

But with the winds of time and the storms of testing,
we learn, to trust the Holy Spirit in His efforts to teach us,
absolute dependence on Him.

And when, we reach the shores of complete surrender,
God pours out to us His great and undying love.
It is there that we see, sitting upon the sands of time,
Life's Book.

Slowly, we will turn through each page of Life's Book,
marveling at what God has done.
For in this book, it is now plain to see,
God's Chosen course and Destiny for me...

Adair Louise Ellison

As Time Began

Since... Oh - oh long long many moons
ago
Exacting time by suns as days
Go and come again by tide and time
Accounting time ways has England
Man to count hours of rotation
And revolutionary orbs: About
Where even popes resolved ways
A week, weeks, months any also years
Never quite exact by caesarean
Count: Thirty plus one — phases
Time lapse and phases counted to
Vary estimates - guesstimates, none to fairly denote a first time
Count, a chrono, a calendar, of the first second then
Three score for a first minute and the three
Score for an hour. Semblance gone the hour.
Begun, twelve times two, the day has begun: Day one
Now the count is thirty plus or minus one, a month begun
A month a moon and then some more chorus of time preclude
horlage
But for all now to think time, time in method for all mankind

Charles R. Fee

The Rain of the Better Day

Rushed into the wind without ample warning
Being swept away into the sweet rain of the night.
I panic knowing the rain is much cold here,
And it brings me much fright.
The rain falls heavily and quickly in haste.
So while time is on my side, I try to capture its sweet
    taste.
But the test turns from sweet to sour,
And my eye glances at the sand glass to see it is the
    end of my hour.
Warring with myself about the mistakes I have made.
Now knowing what I should have done, as love fades.
With nothing left all meaning gone.
I quickly realize that life goes on.
So I walk aimlessly down the road.
Trying to find myself as I corrode.
And as I lay there with sun scorching me.
And I remember the day when the rain was so sweet.
The memories give me great joy but then I begin to
    weep.

Darin Longarino

Out of the Blue

Smoke No. 2
Tobacco produces banded together
and continue producing products no better
Much worse, one would say
but then the unexpected entered the fray
As hoped for, out of the blue
there came an action that to all was new
Forced to pay for the suffering and pain
their poisonous products inflicted again and again
Their smoke products will now produce
No capital gain
So with no money to be made
by business in the smoking trade
The young and old from deadly smoke set free
may enjoy a healthier life yet to be

Ira Kuchler

One Single Rose

One single rose, standing tall and proud,
holding its soft, pink, abundant
head high.
Its leaves are ever so green
as green as the soft moss that
gently conquers the jungle's floor.
This brilliant flower symbolizes
my love for you...
Yet there is one difference...
My love for you
will never die

Heather McCulley

Attitudes

As time unfolds, I find with growing clarity
That attitude will always shape my destiny
If Money, Success, Failure, or Power
Decide if my life will decay — or flower
My attitudes have gone off track
And only I can bring them back
We Can choose to be sad — or happy
Whether to droop — or come up snappy
It's up to us to set the mood
The choice is in our Attitude.

Arlene J. Lee

Battle Cry

The sun is glinting off spear and shield,
while their weapons of war they must wield
They stand on the field sword in hand
the captains on horseback survey the land
The cries of their enemies ring in their ears
they must put aside all of their fears
The warriors eyes glow like fire
within their hearts is the killing desire
The battle cry sounds, together they run
fighting and killing and sparing none.

Luke Riso

Sudden Infant Death Syndrome

They called it "SIDS" when Georgie died;
  It was only medical to them.
But in my heart and soul I cried
  To lose a little boy like him.

They say there is no reason why,
  The answer no one knows.
Although little Georgie had to die,
  Why can't I see his coffin close?

They say that time will heal the grief,
  Another child would fill the void.
To me it is my firm belief,
  Death, with my very heart has toyed.

They say that my baby's gone
  Forever, from this life to be.
But a mother's heart is never wrong
  He is forever, an angel to me.

Elizabeth J. Baker

Lamentation for Our Pastor

On 9/1/96 resignation of the pastor from First Baptist Church Columbia, MO to First Baptist Church, Raleigh, NC.

Our pastor, Dan, is leaving us; he told us so today.
The Lord, he said, directed him to take a new pathway
And move south to Raleigh in North Carolina State
To an old, historic church in town, which the people venerate.

Almost twelve years he's been with us and we, smug and content,
Knew surely that this man was ours, and he'd been heaven sent.
So when we heard he would resign, we gasped in whispered shock,
For this man's well and truly loved by his entire flock.

This turning point in Dan's life moves him far from our sphere.
We wish him joy in God's grace, and a gracious atmosphere.
The essence and the humor of his sermons e'er will be
Etched in our minds, with memories of his concinnity.

Making, doing, and knowing (so Aristotle said)
Are three crucial dimensions unique to man (I read).
Manifestations of these traits we see in Dan's own mission,
Including wisdom and virtue, and always time to listen.

We know when his replacement comes, we must judge not nor compare.
Yet, we know, too, in our hearts and minds, his equal is nowhere.
Yes, Dan Day is leaving us; he told us so today.
Farewell, dear Dan. We love you. Godspeed to you, we pray.

Dorothy Irene Renden

The Golden Gift of Friendship

There is a gift, a special gift,
Priceless beyond compare;
Surpassing God's earth and skies,
A gift so marvelous, so fair.

Friendship is this golden gift,
Full of trust and understanding;
Bringing a warmth of sincere content,
Hosting timeless beauty and non-pretending.

Friendship lies secure within reach,
Offering the gentleness of flowers growing in the sun,
Yet, providing a power of the wind,
Then, sustaining unity, thoughts of one.

Run, fly, capture this gift,
The golden gift of friendship;
Be a friend, assuring endless devotion,
Gain a friend, enjoying tireless dedication.

Linda Blackham

In Search of Desire

Slow and deliberate, we walk in the gentle rain;
Enveloped so deeply within our own existence.
Time, seemingly detained; a nonentity;
Preoccupied with emotions of every presence.

Memories that drift amongst us,
As we journey in a transient state;
Yearning for the love that lives within,
Pondering the meaning of our fate.

Questioning the reasons of inability;
Desperately searching to resolve our desire;
Feeling the heat of the passion that burns,
Facing the validity that drenches the fire.

Trading a love, for sorrow of solitude;
A love never meant for such pain.
Searching again for the rainbow's end;
...as I walk in the gentle rain.

Judy Terres

Of Diverse Natures

They came together one day, the short Catholic and tall Jew; looking at each other, not knowing what to say or do. Through discussion it was decided, that the Gentile would employ the Jew; a decision that would prove beneficial, to not one, but to a few. And so they worked together, for almost two years; amidst all the anxieties, the anguish and the fears. For their personalities, (you see), were just like day and night; when one would say something's black, the other would say it's white. Such a working relationship, would be put to the test; to see constantly what would happen, what would develop, what would come next. And what did happen, was news to but a few; they accepted each other and became friends, the short Catholic and tall Jew. So the story ends, for the two eventually did part; since the tall Jew wanted only one thing; she wanted a new start. One thing does remain, one thing important to all; an idea and a belief, that should never fall. That though different in nature, in demeanor, in beliefs; these two people accepted each other . . . and I must say it was with a sigh of relief!

Phyllis Arlene Goldstein

Untitled

  Janet was a girl who loved to dream.
By day, by night, all the time is seemed.
  Her mother would call but she was
in another land.
  On a ship, at the circus or playing
in the sand.
  She was a princess, a pirate or a
young gypsy girl,
  Whatever she wished to be in the
world.

  One day her mother took her hand.
  For a walk they went across the land.
  Remember my child dreams are
Wonderful, they help you to grow.
  But there are many other things
you need to know.
  Pay close attention to all and you'll
see, that dreams and education will
be your reality.

Terry N. Straub

Our Reflection

The mirror on the wall reminds me of you
Our reflections an image
Those who see are few
For we turn the inside page

A story yet to be told
Our deep bond
Weep not for tears grow cold
Each others we have found

Our inner peace we share
With love undying
That no one can take away
Or defy.

Sherrie Hendrickson

Gone But Not Forever

Forget me not, and do not weep over my body, for I do not lay
In front of you today . . . .

The body you see is one that represents an image that both you
Mom and dad made . . . .

I left this world to soon to tell just how much you both
meant to me so I ask of you . . .

"Keep me alive in your hearts, and I will always be alive in
your dreams" . . . .

I may not be where you can touch me with your hands, but I can
meet you both in a much better land . . . .

Let's agree here today not to say "Good bye" let's just say
until we meet again . . .

You will recognize me when you both get there, I'll be the child!!!
Standing by the small white cloud, I'll only be smiling not
uttering a sound . . .

Don't forget me, for I'll always be your whether it was here
on earth, or now in heaven, once more!!

"We will meet again"!!! This we both can depend . . . .

Alice Hemanes Rabion

Tried and True

We live in a very dark and troubled time.
Some call our's the era of sin and crime,
And would fight this sinister "fire" with fire.
More police and additional jailors they'd hire.

More and more people to death row some would send.
On law enforcement and justice system everything depends.
While others say, with law and order be done!
To control crime, what we must do is carry a gun.

Is there hope to humanity . . . . will we survive?
Will our children know joy, grow and thrive?
Can we dreams of real prosperity,
Or must we resign to be a violent society?

Perhaps the answer to it all is not very new—
A life given serving others will stop crime, too.
A power untapped by the prophets of doom, the nay sayers.
A power to change life is the gift of ernest prayer.

A life can be empowered by Godly peace and grace.
We can seek to feed and clothe the entire human race.
Now, before you say it can't be done with this thing called love,
I tell you the idea is as tried and true as the eternal
  God above . . .

Jim Glass

Jimmy

A meticulous "self-taught" man
Mastering each task to which he turned his hand
Possessing a grin ever so charming
A profound thinker, often disarming

A "genius" with cars or hammer and wood
Always seeking his best . . . never just 'good'

Tho' at first, he thought it just piddlin'
Talent soon led to serious fiddlin'
Now, jammin' with Hank, Elvis and 'the rest'
Marty and Patsy . . . all Heaven's best

We miss his wit and dancing eyes
But, he's happy, with God beyond the skies

Patricia Anne Leftwich

Untitled

I wrote your name in the sand today
  but along came a wave and stole it away
Although we are many miles apart
  the thought of you lingers in my heart.

The wave that took your name from the sand
  was a wave that was made by my own hand
I erased your name from the world to see
  as I wanted the memory to remain with me.

Donald J. Menard

Nathan Hale

It was while battling here that Washington called
for a soldier to go out and spy.

So Nathan Hale volunteered, to say, "General
Washington, on me you can rely."

He learned what Washington wanted to know,
but was caught by his terrible British foe.

At sunrise he was led blindfolded to be hung,
And they asked him if he desired to use to his tongue.

So, quietly he spoke his few patriotic words, while
the rope was slipped over his head.

"My only regret is that I have but one life to lose
for my country" and with that he was dead.

Jean Weber

Night Wind

Again the darkness has taken hold,
Everything is lifeless and still,
Yet their thoughts are speaking out loudly,
And into their hearts they fill.

The tick of the clock in the distance, tells them that time moves on,
Yet they are venturing backwards, to a time already gone.
Some things that were, are hard to forget,
But the things that will be, they are searching for yet.

Will they stand the test of time, or wither and shrink away,
Keeping it strong and alive, are thinking of it day to day.
Can you hear one call within the night, as it cries out loud in pain,
For it cannot feel another, that will match it just the same.

Only the sounds of the night, have heard them as they spoke,
Yet dreams have held their life, and reminded them as they woke.
Now as the new day is dawning, the power they hold within,
Will help to bring them closer, to the battle they must win.

So listen in the night as they call out,
And open your heart to feel,
As they search to find each other,
And for their love that is so real.

Irene E. Luzzi

Books and Dreams

Lovingly, Books and Dreams entwined thru my Library Door
as I entered places never seen before. I was given the gift
of dreaming through these books of mine, penetrating secrets
of past, future, even our time.

I became Robin Hood, then Sherlock Holmes the Master Sleuth.
Saw the great Pyramid built by Pharoah Amon-Ra—it's the truth.
With my cloak of invisibility, I rode with Alexander the Great,
Watched Admiral Drake sink the Spanish Armada to a watery fate.

Followed Marco Polo to the Orient as he travelled the Silk Trail.
March with King Richard in search of the Holy Grail.
Romped through the lively worlds of Swift's Gullivers journeys.
Thrilled at the Round Table Knights jousting in their tourneys.

Set sail with Magellan as he circled our oceans and earth,
changing history while a new continent was giving birth.
Applauded seeing Shakespeare reveal the wiles of the court,
while never letting the audience know which side to support.

What pleasures! What thrills! What terrors! What great times
to enjoy. What rapture savoring the mystery of a new book,
anticipating my senses to deliciously employ while I
sit alone in my own quiet nook.

Sylvan Bennis

Poetry And Geometry

Poetry and geometry may seem far apart to you and me.
At first glance, we might look askance,
if anyone suggested that there is poetry in geometry
or that there just might be geometry in poetry.
But, a line divided and hinged becomes
an angle, acute, right, or obtuse.
A circle is only a line drawn equidistant from a point.
Lines make triangles, rectangles, or abstract shapes.
Letters go together to paint land or sea scapes.
Poetry is abstract thoughts, sometimes linked by rhyme
or meter, on page, stage, song, or theatre.
But there is always an angle between relations of two,
And anyone who doesn't know this is also obtuse.
Now geometry can be divided into plane or solid,
And poetry is divided by structure too, blank verse
   couplets, sonnets, ballads, or worse.
But when it comes to the perfect arc of the meadowlark,
Or the expanding circular ripple of a stone thrown into a pond,
There can be geometry in poetry and also the reverse!

William J. Heske

Wishing For You

If Santa Claus would ask me what I wanted on Christmas Day
I would not hesitate at all before going on to say
There's only one wish I have this year, only one thing I'd like to see
When I wake up Christmas morn and look beside the tree
Something that can't be purchased, something you cannot buy
Your elves could never make it, even if they tried
He laughed and with a grin replied, "That's impossible, my dear"
Then I pulled him to the side and whispered in his ear
I don't think you quite understand this gift I'm asking for
It's something very special, there's nothing I want more
All you have to do for me is find a certain house
And sneak inside as quietly as a tiny mouse
There you'll find a handsome man sleeping in the night
Take him with you to your sleigh and once again take flight
Soar above the fallen snow, beneath the stars that shine
Straight to my house deliver him, don't waste any time
And as you grant my wish this eve, there's something you should know
I would like my present left beneath the mistletoe.

Julie Berger

Untitled

I'm floating down a stream watch me fall over the waterfall
Falling with the water to the bottom
Where the fish gather near the rock wall.

I'm drifting through the clouds I see the graceful birds beside me
Soaring high enough to see the country
The cool thin air makes it hard to breathe.

   I think to myself about what's going on around me
   And all too often, I don't like what I see
   After all that's being done to harness the power of the sun
      in little tiny cells and making wind mills
      to produce electricity that kills
      the nature's scenery whose beauty is free
      we bury waste and cause oil spills.

I'm speaking unknown foreign languages listen to how the words flow
Take heed of the message that hides within
Because if unspoken we suffer a terrible blow.

I'm floating down a polluted stream
I'm drifting through clouds filled with gases
Hitch-hiking down a congested paved road
Goodwill and effort needed by the masses.

Dale Black

Mexico, My Love #2

Mexico, my love, you have taught me well. Sparing neither
the rod of anger, nor the passionate caress.

   You attend to my lessons diligently, and find in me an apt
pupil. All that you have shown me I have viewed with wide
and curious eyes.

   All that you have set before me I have eaten as one
starving, and drunk as one lost in the deserts, so barren
and dry.

   You have made wish to flee you, on the wings of a
swift unerring bird. And you have made me wish to hold,
you close, forever, as a beloved wife or daughter I can't
forsake.

   You are a luscious fruit rotting on the vine. You are a
wizened baby, riding 'round and 'round in time.
   You are a precious angel, the gaze of whom brings death.
You are a sweet young mother, who gives her children breath.

   Mexico, my love, you have taught me well. Sparing neither the
rod of anger, nor that passionate caress.

William K. Wooding

Our Son

An angel was born one day in May, in the year of sixty one.
A spitten image of his dad, a darling little son.
From the first day he was sent to us, he brought us so much joy.
He was everything we thought he would be, a bouncing baby boy.
I remember vividly those first few years, he was never any bother.
He was the apple of our eye, and a precious son for his father.
Soon this little boy was growing up, so fast before our eyes.
It was first grade, second, third and fourth,
I began to realize.
This precious child was sent to us, from God in heaven above.
To live here in this troubled world, and bring us so much love.
One day soon he will leave, to strike out on his own.
God will be with him all the way, he will never be alone.
If every parent could be as blessed, as we are with this one.
An angel, a boy, a baby, a child, a man, a saint, "Our Son."

Dorcas Heeter

The Album

The photos from my childhood
Were pressed in an album with care;
An idyllic youth in an enchanted wood,
Bright eyes, rosy cheeks, shiny hair.

I'm jealous of this uninhibited girl,
Who, unbelievably, I once was.
This child who climbed and twirled
And was happy just because.

Part of me wants to shatter
Her perfect, painless world;
Explain that it all doesn't matter,
Show her the tarnish beneath the pearl.

Part of me wants to give her warning,
To be careful with her soul and heart;
To be prepared for a long, extended mourning;
To watch out for the well aimed dart.

Part of me wants to offer comfort
So she can store it up within
For a time when things might distort,
And goodness is outweighed by sin.

Mostly, I just wish I could go back,
To a time when I could blindly trust,
When unconditional love I did not lack,
When these photos were not covered in dust.

Christine Hagenlocher

Take Me Back

Take me back take me back back to Fresno,
On McKinley. I think it was 712 McKinley
Walking to the Pine Avenue market, with just dimes in my pocket.

Take me back to Christmas morning,
Smiling faces of my sister Julie, wanting to ride Joe's bike.
I wish I could ride.

Take me back back to my Dad holding my brother Jimmy and me,
Calling me knuckle head, kissing my forehead.

Take me back to our backyard sun or our back's, picking weeds.
Listening to Dodger baseball.

Take me back chasing my sister Annie around the kitchen,
Wanting to take those chocolate chip cookies, making her cry.
Never tried to hurt anyone.

Take me back back to the peaceful rocking my Dad gave to Roy.
His touch to Roy was gentle.

Take me back back to when my Mom said my Dad was now in
silence.

Take me back
Back when God gave us so much spirit, my Dad in silence now.
My Mom given the courage to raise us and spirit to live.

Take me back please give me all your lessons.

John Tomkinson

At Your Mercy

I can brighten your darkest day or cause a sleepless night.
I can bring you many friends or cause a bloody fight.

I can heal your deepest wound or bring grief to your soul.
I can comfort you gently or swallow you whole.

I can sweep you off you feet or slam you to the ground.
I can sing you sweet melodies or cause a deafening sound.

My purpose is to please, but I am often abused.
My effect is determined by the way that I am used.

I can be as fierce as a lion or as gentle as a Dove,
for I am At Your Mercy...My name is Love.

Kim Bell Foster

She

Nature oh how, the beauty of it can be.
The trees, the flowers, the grass, and the weeds.
The birds, the bees, the fish and the fleas.
They all have a heart and all have a seed.
But now 'tis it all being destroyed by us and our
drills with all of our toys.
Our new generation is getting better than before,
But everything's dieing and all we can do is ignore.
It's our job to keep her healthy, but all we do is worry
about making ourselves wealthy.
We don't give her gratitude when we know that we should.
But still we cut and we drill and do all that we could.
With all the house's that we've laid and all
the concrete that we've poured.
It sure ain't helping this dear world.
She's wiser and she's been here longer than us.
She got rid of the dinosaurs, I'm sure she can get rid of us.
All you can do is just wait and see, cause the world can end up
looking like a bunch of tiny fleas.
If she gets sick enough to where she can't take
anymore, she'll blow up the earth and just leave the core.
With all of her might and strength from the Lord.
They'll put it back together and bring back the dinosaurs.

Corina Cox

Uncertain

The sky is a vast sea,
Of wind... and birds,
They run from unknown dangers, they flee
the troubles of this world.
We unheeding, stay upon this earth,
Uncaring, unknowing.
Should we listen to the cardinal or crow,
And leave this spot of turmoil,
Or should we stay upon this Earth,
Our plots of soil?
Does anyone know the language of the sea gull, the raven
Who fly upon the warnings of the wind?

Andrew Bradford McLauthlin

The End of a Great Line

Come from behind with a sharp axe.
Split my skull in two.
Check me out good.

Sift through the blood and brain,
Experience, emotions;
That tangled web of veins inside my head,
Is twisted poetry.

Follow the channels, the branches,
The soul's face, smiling, knowing
You'll be sick at what you see.
It's naturally defined
Or you're critically immune,
Thinking you can critique the mess within
When you don't know
What is man?

Only the writer can understand
The tragedy, the limitations of words
Are what give poetry life.
And only the writer suffers
By the end of a great line.

Matthew Dean Ferguson

The Ruler

Earth is a little mud ball in the sky.
Inhabited by men of different kinds.
People with free will...like you and I.
But so often it is hate that blinds
The heart to what is truly right and wrong.
It is then that evil foods the world.
Thoughts of profit warp the mind.
The song of friendship then is stilled, and bombs are hurled

From hands of greed. As they explode they shake
Our faith in things that once were held so dear.
And so we flounder in the depth less lake
Of tribulation, doubt, and endless fear.
The future looks like it was getting worse.
But...it is God who runs this Universe.

Sharon O'Neil

Another Fugitive in the Garden

The Mountain always stood before you my brother, beckoning you to come, whether you chose to or not, it came.

You stood the heat of the gushing red lava beat your white ashen face flush while multitudes of statuesque children laid next to you, caressed by their parents, all cryptic fractures of molten pain, fallen in the grey dust, like hysterically mute psychics gasping to tell you where stepping stones of the flowing rock are.

Your journey became too long for you, but too short for us brother, as you felt the burning ground shake your aching veins for solace in the pink mimosa garden, where our mother laid whispering to you. Once a gentle voice, now an impatient master poised to beat you into remembering there is no more waiting, and now you like all children discover too soon your time is gone.

Your final futile escaping cries of rapture answered the rageful choral cries of the children of Pompei. The flowing rock, a cruel abandonment of your dreams, your sorrows, your friends, and your family, now livid sculptures in the mountain of black rock, a museum of illuminous memories of us, cradled illusions giving sanctuaries, of hope for the next Fugitive in the Garden, forever fleeing . . .

Robert Phipps

Masterpiece

I wish I were a carving displayed in a large museum for all to see. I want to be the product of a carver's hard work and his creative hand. I want the sweat of his brow and of his fingertips to fall upon me ("his masterpiece") and give me life. I can just feel the salty water running down me. I want to be carved in ebony with his various tools that give me the finest touches. I want to be the shapeless that blossoms into something beautiful. "Hey, Mr. Carverman, can you give me curves like the earthly mountains?" Picture this: A mountain bathing in the sun, with naked feet walking upon it. And when the night falls my curves would be defined by the illuminating moon. "Can you make me like a mountain because then I wouldn't have to hide those fine, sexy curves of mine; because it's natural...I'm Nature-All...."

Shermane Keller

Hunger

Where is the taste;
  of the good life
Described as the sweetest fruit
  you have ever tasted
I have toiled the earth picked the weeds
  yet unable to harvest the fruits of my labor
The time is too young, so I prepare baskets
  constructed of vision, persistence and focus.
Reaching and waiting to reap the bountiful harvest.

Curtis Cropper

Life is an Adventure in Love

Life is an adventure in love
The trees grows and sky so blue
Is all layed out for me and you.

The mountains are all capped in snow
It is where you and I can go.

The morning dew on flowers bright
Set the bees birds and butterflies in delight

The oceans are wide and far apart
Ships sailing give you and I a start

The sun is bright orange, gold and brown
It greats us when it comes up and down

The moon and stars are shining from above
It gives off a glow that shows our love

Nancy L. Jewell

A Rose in this World of Thorns

Destruction, disease, and turmoil,
Consume the very earth.
A star will fade with every death,
One will shine at every birth.

Often the world seems dark and gloomy,
A place full of hate and scorn.
So many loose their faith of heart,
And are engulfed within the thorns.

Within the thick and choking thorns,
There is a beauty I know to exist.
So rare and yet so special is,
The rose of heavenly bliss.

Such softness is in its soothing touch,
Spreading warmth and compassion year round.
Strong is the spell cast over me,
By this rose which I have found.

Powers of such magnitude
More valuable than gold.
You are the very flower that,
Blossoms within my soul.

Troy Conway

The Key

A cancer was eating inside of me, an operation there had to be.
No longer a woman with children to bear, children for me to love,
  and to take care.
A women's purpose is for birth, why has this been taken out of me?
With tears in my pillow, and my heart with an ache for none to see.
I descend into a pit of grief, moaning, Lord why do this to me?

Then to be told, "You're lucky the cancer was found, you had a year
  at most."
Lucky?
Fierce, hostile, savage woe, what is to become of me?
An "it" you can plainly see.
A woman's purpose is for birth, and that has been taken from out of me.
Oh Dear Lord, why do this to me?

Off on a tangent I did go, punishing myself with many a punishing blow,
Making it hard for my family to care, while I looked for my
  "electric chair."

Then an inspired note from my husband making it so clear,
A true woman I would always be.
The giving of love and just being "me."

My soul soared into the sky, the moon was my chair,
Stars played in my hands, the sun's warmth was for me.
Now I know, a true woman I will always be,
The giving of love, and being loved, that is the Key.

Mary A. Jenkins

My Friend

How do I explain "Us?" A feeling of destiny . . .
Of knowing for years that this would come to be..
A link that ties our souls together as one.

A safe haven with emotions so pure it opens the
Wounds of loss and allows us to share the happiness
Of the past.

Your voice and touch make me happy . . . a feeling lost
To me lately; so, I grab on and hold too tightly because
It's so valuable. But, it scares you and makes you push
Me away; afraid to take on the responsibility of a lost soul.

Not true . . . I look for nothing more than moments of sharing
And the joy of holding a hand that understands.

Susie Mickeleit

Materialistic

I am drawn resolutely toward the light.
And just as the moth burns in fire,
my parched skin begins to peel,
blood boiling as I draw nearer.

The wicked irony stabs at me
like so many dull blades.
The very object I most desired,
now mine, fuels the insatisfaction
burning inside my soul unchecked.

Possessed by the thought of possessing,
we toil every minute: Calculating,
planning, yearning to control.
Yet once we obtain, we reject.
Curious little creatures, us humans.

Just as I am upon the flame,
my fascination is extinguished,
and my unhappiness blazes.
What shall I possess next?

Jonathan Dick

My Hamster

My Hamster's name is Prickley Ham
He has long finger nails,
In which he uses to eat spam.

He likes to sleep,
In a wood-shaving's heap.

He must never throw a rage,
In his nice new cage.

I love him a lot.
No way would I toss him in a soup pot.

His fur is so brown.
I show him to everyone in town.

He has a little pink nose
And two ears of gray.
Bad words near him, you must never say.

He has a cute little face,
On which needs no lace.
He likes to sleep in my arm,
Where he knows he is safe from all harm.

I hope you like my Prickley Ham.
He really is as cute as a lamb.

Sarah A. Bannister

Love's No Lie

As the stars come out another wish is made
as the sun comes up someone's heart will fade
when someone's eyes close a tear will fall
once they are opened something hidden behind a wall
on the inside lies a smile while the inside has pain
as you look into my soul there's nothing there to gain
with all that goes through my head and all that breaks my heart
you're going to leave me behind and watch me fall apart
it may be an upside down frown but as I look into your eyes
the whole world disappears and still you called them lies
but you knew where they where coming from and you knew they
       were true
unless you push it away my love can never be taken from you.

Tina George

The Empty Chair

Alone it leans against the wall
A sombre gleam upon the pall of brown,
The beloved lounging chair.
A master now has left and thus foregone
Its warm and loving care.
To seek another place in heaven's rest!
Awhile I pondered as my heart did ache,
To see the arms outstretched...
Of that revered lounging place.
The master had rested in that brown chair...
O'er many a year long past a tale could share...
Of times of laughter as grandpa,
Lifted little ones to knee and fond caress.
Or cheering fan of T.V. games he loved the best,
Or news of far off lands he gazed...
True days of happiness tho failing healthfulness.
O gentle chair I thank thee for your kindly warmth,
That gave such rest when needed most.
Do not yet mourn for now he has found,
Another throne in God's embrace, unending bliss eternal home!

Ruth Mary Teeple

Farewell, Son of a Christian

Like Jesus,
     he's the son of a Christian.
Nurtured and loved,
     lead and encouraged to seek God's will,
And follow His way.
     The example of God set before him
For life's journey walk.
     the grace of prayer hung
Comfortably in heart and home;
     kind words and guidance,
From a strong, loving, gentle hand.
     continue your walk.
Christian's never die.
     farewell, son of a Christian.

Carolyn G. Benson

The Silent Moment

Enchanted, I saw her lovely face across the room
And soon, in a silent moment,
Our eyes eclipsed and did meet
On the airways of Love,
As our lips did heat.

Dazed by the beauty through her eyes,
I saw her soul;
It captured all goodness,
Lovingly my heart so wished to share.
Forever is that silent moment
And the answer to my life-long prayer.

John R. Reda

High Points

The highest moment of any good day,
Is hard to identify.
It may be the sunrise over the hill,
Or the stars that shine in the sky.

A rainbow is a thrill to behold,
An eclipse is a marvelous sight.
Puppies, kittens, goldfish and flowers,
Or a bird that's seen soaring in flight.

The hug of a child, a smile that's returned,
A call from a favorite old friend,
An aerobic workout that makes you perspire,
A problem that comes to an end.

These are the things that bring joy to my heart.
They make me glad I've survived,
And like a caress from the hand of God,
Help my spirit and soul be revived.

Carol Fleming

The Counselor

I was suppose to trust her,
As she would take me a new path.
She was a petite woman, all French she was.

She has gone over my file.
Knew me well, she said
I remember her saying,
College is not for you, vocational school is what you'll do.
I also remember my French build Le-Car.
You see, whenever I really needed to get somewhere,
I might as well rely on my two legs and walk.
Rather than to trust an old piece of junk.
Today my anger has been subdued by my success.
Yet, I often wonder how many rode down to the wrong path.
How many go through their day in disappointment and hate.
For them it is too late, the choices have been made.
Endure their lives they must, for it is their cross,
With their dreams vanished from their hearts, they barely go on.

I remember someone like this, I knew her well.
She was a petite woman, all French she was.

Alvaro Alvarez

My Life and My Violin

My life remained captive to my violin, captive it remained as it
sounds, my heart also, in my dreams, remained captive as it beats . . .
Life is a flowing river, passing through the "ancient jungle,"
sometimes slumbling against rocks due to stupid slipperiness,
sometimes arousing nature. At last, it seeks refuge into the "Ocean"
(this interval of peace at eternity), either with glory and pride or
shameful residue left behind.
In fact, a long struggle with a short walk on the face of the Earth,
is attributed "Life," during which period we should look back, from
time to time, to see straight our path forward. Based on this idea,
I conclude my life with a few lines, introducing Me And My Violin:
This is the wood, which took part of the struggle in my life, by faith's
constructive effort, in terms of "To Be Or Not To Be." It sounded
blessing prayers for my daily bread. It was the cornerstone of my
"Iron Bridges" to build. It was my "Grinding Mill's Bottom Stone",
until I attained my goal's last milestone. There I saw, "Seven Suns"
shining on me, in a blue sky, while I had nothing in seven skies, but
a "Star" so high. However, an evergreen spring prevails throughout
"Life," where the bells of love, compassion and companionship are
ringing along, sending joy, faith, peace and prosperity around . . .

Balian Ter-Hacopian Babken

Untitled

The child never spoken to is the child who never speaks,
The options left unopened are the ones we never reach,
The words never written are the words never kept,
And the nights that we remember are the nights we never slept.
The flower never picked will be so much more,
The business never started will never be a store,
Wood left unfinished will slowly rot away,
The rhythm of the night beats slowly to the day.
The notes the band plays broken are the notes we don't forget,
The man never introduced is the man we never met,
All the time left wasted is the time that we all share,
The man left uncared for is the man never there,
And the man never there is the man who doesn't help,
And he who always helps others can never help himself;
For a healing soul is always busy, with no time to spare at all,
But he, he who climbs the mountains, upon reaching the top, will fall.

Phillip Zacharias

Untitled

The eternal moons of mars
will forever hang on the empty wings of the sun

Perchance a common fate awaits us both
when we have shuffled into the past
and that is why I sing of eternity

Anything can last forever
if we try hard enough

But

Can you or I say this is truth
and that is allowed to fade
perhaps yes... maybe no
and so is my love for you
the dividing line transcends
to grey

Ed Holden

Love Is All Around

Love is birds chirping before the sun comes up.
Love is when kittens purr together.
Love is dogs playing together.
Love is boats floating together.
Love is a kiss on the cheek.
Love is a hug in the arms,
Love is swimming with someone.
Love is being nice to someone.
Love is listening to someone.
Love is loving someone,
But the best thing of all is being a family.
I love my sister, my mom and my dad.
And they love me, too.

Kristin DiPetta

Two Generations

My generation saluted the flags;
Your generation, wear it on your ass.

My generation sang "God Bless America";
Your generation sings "Yo Mama on crack rock."

My generation looked down on
Teen pregnancies as a disgrace;
Your generation gives them praise.

My generation walked the streets at twelve midnight;
Your generation gets shot at 12 noon.

My generation dreamed of walking on the moon;
Your generation believe they are doomed.

Catherine Saint Cyr

338

The Dentist

Mark invited John over to play,
But he forgot he was going to the dentist that day.
"Going to the dentist!" John said with a sneer
"I'd crawl in my bed and shake with fear."

Then after John said he was going to leave,
Mark ran up to his room and began to heave.
"Mark, dear," called his Mom, Mrs. Prentice.
"It's time to leave, we're going to the dentist!"

When they were in the waiting room of the dentist,
Mark's mom said to the nurse, "I'm here for Mark Prentice."
When the nurse called the patient before Mark, Miss Gaddonn,
Mark realized with shock that his fingernails were gone.

Then when she called on Mark Prentice,
To come in and see the dentist,
Mark fell faint upon the floor
And his mother dragged him through the door
She put him on the dentist's chair
And the dentist looked at him with flair
He cleaned and scrubbed and when he was done,
Mark Prentice woke up and said, "That was fun."

Christie Napurano

Rapturous Butterfly

Why do they sigh? I know not why.
With the corps they can not wade ashore.
A world set apart.
Where did it start?
Parenthood, is that misunderstood?

Love limited to so few.
Is that why they are so blue?

Mankind's phobia often their curse,
Seeking solace in a world sometimes worse.
From back-alley bash to Madison Avenue splash.
Their porcelain faces and their tip of the island places
Are but limited graces.

A sub culture in flight, no longer out of sight.
No more hidden nights.
Only the fear of a web that snares in flight
And fills their bodies with fright.

Loves anew, hormones askew.
What is the use?

It is the lonely path a butterfly flew.

R. Peyton Hall

Dermal Bliss

Virgin flesh peers at me through a gaping wound and
calls for my attention

Round yellow goblets of fat bulge outward trying to
escape from the newly found orifice

Crimson liquid, fresh from the wound
trickles down the side of his face

I concentrate on this stream of new found life as it
weaves a path down the pulsating neck

I watch as a scarlet droplet emerges and
falls with a plop onto my shoe

Time stands still as more droplets continue to
flee to the floor one by one

It is time to bid farewell to this blood and flesh, so I
insert my needle and thread
and time resumes.

Alison H. Watt

One Chance

R.I.P. - that's what the tombstone read
Standing in the background, upon grieving they were fed
All was quiet, and he nodded his head
They peered inside irresolutely, the corpse lay still in bed.

As most were weeping, one just glared
Contemplating the odds that anyone cared
They had all been around, and the only one who dared
Now rests in the casket, the eyes stared

And the soul that did it had her mind firmly set
She blames it on a bad influence - one she's never met
It's unfortunate that reality couldn't force her to regret
Insisting on the ignorance when death became debt

Is it worthy to recognize the suffering and the pain?
Should the awareness of evil be forever slain?
Is it possible to be dry after one day of rain?
Does turning your back offer something to gain?

R.I.P. - that's what the tombstone read
Perhaps if they had learned, one more would not be dead
Just a slight consciousness of danger lingering in her head
A life could have been saved, if little had been said.

Katie Leigh Hostetler

Politics

The will for power is a clever vice
Evident in the company of men and mice
Who forget that words are the vessels of thought
While trying to sell ideals which never can be bought.

Reaction to emotions enslave the masses
Whom, through fear and pain, are herded like asses
Whose spirit asks for truth, yet settles for lies
But when we vote for our reflection, our true self dies.

Indeed, this government is our reflection
Embodies as displays of our potential perfection
There is no us against them, there is only we
One people, one vote, one note, in this harmony.

As the candied dates put on a sugared show
Disregard prepared words, for in their eyes you will know
Who wishes to serve and who serves their wish
The true vote of power is found in the breast of the unselfish.

This jewel of a person seeks not to divide
For, on a round world, who can pick a side?
The day we vote from our heart and not out of fear
Is the day, this leader in all of us, will finally appear.

Eugene Charles

My Telephone

My hill is shrouded by the mist of the morn,
I am troubled to make it out,
Yet I follow my will through the fists of thorn,
From which I let a shout,
The echo sent forth is of rumbles and bellows,
Swiftly flowing over the dales,
Which incites a yelp from a clandestine fellow,
A deep voice divulging he's male.
"Gut Morgen," eagerly he yells across the way,
As the rifles report with a crack,
And the echo is fierce and I start to sway,
As he die's and falls on his back.

And the other men scatter leaving me quite alone,

And I follow my will to the stop of my hill,

And I realize all too late as I now see I'm prone,
That war is no place for a man,
May I please have the telephone.

Jonathan Wicks

Like An Old Oak Tree

My love is like an old oak tree...that is as tall as an Oak maybe.
The leaves are green....as my eyes hold a gleam
Its branches reach out to touch the sky...as my arms reach out to
 touch your side.
The trunk of the tree is as sturdy...as my love for you is as sturdy.
The roots reach into the good old earth..my love hold no mirth!
The old oak tree grows with life...as my love with life.
The old oak tree braves the elements...as my love is full of
 sentiments,
The Old Oak Tree may be seen for miles, as my love can be felt across
 the miles!
The space between the Oaks may be wide...but my love takes it all in
 stride!
The old oak tree will be around for many years...as my love will cry
 many a tear!
Like a great Old Oak,
My love holds a lot of hope!
As an oak lives on and on...
My love...lives on and on!
 I love you!
 Theresa Melnick

Empowered

It's my turn to turn my life
In whatever direction I choose.

I peer through the kaleidoscope
Of my possibilities;
Then a twist of my wrist
Reveals fresh symmetries, subtleties, and sequences.

Fast or slow they revolve,
Never an exactly replay.
New patterns, inverted or compressed —
I stop wherever I please.

I arrange at will
Design never thought of in colors newly seen.
I make undreamed of images
Stretch and dance, or disappear.

At east at last.
The control is mine.
 Charlotte Klose

A Mother's Day Poem

My verse is rusty; my wit is worn.
My brain is heavy on this sultry May morn,

But my pockets are empty; my accounts are bare.
And, since you can't make a gift out of thin air,

Awake I must, the time is near,
Mother's Day comes but once a year.

A time for thanks. A time for praise.
A lifetime of love one never repays.

How can you thank someone for helping you gel
Into a human being from a single cell?

For taking that cell and breathing into it life,
For providing love and care through stress and strife.

When my beams of confidence were rotting away,
Your moral support was there to save the day.

So I thank you Mom for all you've done.
You've made me proud to be your son.

So accept this verse on this, your day
I love you Mom. What more can I say?
 Robert A. Jacobs

The Voice of My Heart

If I could take how the sun glistens off of the water
and how daybreak looks dancing on a marshmallow sky
on a morning when the clouds leave me lost in a daydream,
then perhaps I could give justice to your warm, tender eyes.

If I mixed all the wondrous hues that live in the forest
right after the first frost puts the summer on trial,
maybe then I'd be closer to somehow describing
even half of the beauty that adorns your soft smile.

If I could get away and run back to the Ozarks
on a day when those rolling hills feel a warm soaking storm
and see how the mist lovingly wraps them right after it's over,
I might know what God was thinking when he made your form.

But God just gave me feeble words without divine understanding
I'm just an imperfect part of a flawed human race,
but even in my frustration, my faith still is strengthened
for I see Heaven glowing in your smiling face.

So sometimes I see you I feel both dull and clumsy;
I can't rightly convey my love and I feel less than smart
Perhaps the Lord never meant for words like that to be spoken
so you'll just have to hold me to hear the voice of my heart.
 Thomas F. Spencer

Life — A Song

Life can be compared to the singing of a song,
Sometimes the harmony is sweet and sometimes it's so wrong.

We reach for the high notes, when the low ones are our part,
And the words we sing are not really in our hearts.

The notes go flat, the words aren't plain, we don't observe the rests,
We don't understand what is wrong; we are doing our very best.

Then God comes by and picks up the hymnal of our lives and
looks the book through
And carefully chooses the song, that he wants us to do;

The notes are sharp, the words are clear, the message is so plain;
The melody is so sweet, there's love in each refrain!

Then we hear God's message in a voice so clear and real,
"Lift high your heads, sing loud the song, for now you're in my
will!"
 Pauline Lunsford

Touch Me

When you look at me what is it
Who am I what can you see
Do you see the me inside so desperately I try to hide

Do you see really me
All I am all I can be
Or do you only see the surface the outside of me

When you touch me do you feel only skin
My passion
My sin

Or do you feel the love I hide
The laughter
Joy
And pain inside

Who are you can it be
Are you the one to see inside
And really
Touch-me?
 Michael Anthony Nelson

Noodle Soup

"This won't hurt a bit."
But I know better this doc is full of it.
He gives me a Hollywood grin as the needle pierces my vein,
I shoot him a nasty look, I indeed felt the pain.
"Now I'll count back from 50, by then you won't feel a thing."
Is it just me or does his voice have a sinister ring?
"Just close your eyes and think pleasant thoughts,
Think of your favorite food maybe it's catsup and tator tots.
Fifty, forty-nine, forty-eight . . ."
This anesthetic is putting me in a weird kind of state.

Doc said relax and think of your favorite dish.
Mine is a cup of Soodle Noup, yum-yum delish.
"Thirty-five, thirty-four, thirty-three . . ." "Soodle Noup!"

How silly I meant Noodle Poop I mean Poodle Soup.
What's wrong with me, maybe I'm anorexic.
That's not the word, I meant to say dyslexic!
"Twenty, nineteen, eighteen . . ."
"Hey nurse what are all those tools? What are you gonna do with
    that thing? Doc ya gotta slobber, I mean stop her . . . .
Whew you're my Nero, I mean hero."
"Two, one, zero."

Joy Taylor

One Day?!

My thoughts wonder without care;
In directions I do not know where;
You, upon I stumble;
For there I am humble;
And one day I wish to be there.

Even though so very far away;
My dreams of you they still much stray;
You, me, together;
Having fun forever;
And one day I wish to be there.

My soul is yours, yours I hold;
I'll defend, strengthen, and fight to behold;
I am whole 'cause of you;
I'd give my life to be true;
And one day I wish to be there.

My heart's with you and never stray;
Together, forever and that we'll stay;
My love is true;
And only for you;
And one day I wish to be there.

Michael Rhodes

Fame Like Cocaine

I want all the world to know my name
I want fame just like cocaine

I wanna be wild, I wanna be tame
I want fame, fame like cocaine

Gonna be like water, fall like rain
Gonna have fame and be like cocaine

I will take it all, win every game
I'll live large with fame like cocaine

You'll inject my lust into every vein
It'll be like heaven, I'll ease your pain
I will drive you mad, you'll go insane
'Cause I'll be like muthaf*ckin' cocaine

I will have fame, just like cocaine
Fame - like cocaine

Cocaine.

MD Montague

Put Your Faith to Work

Put your faith to work, and trust in the Lord;
Commit your life to Him, and feed on His word.
He will give you the desires of your heart;
Release your faith, and let doubtfulness depart.

Put your faith to work, and leave all in His hands;
For it is written: "On His Promises You Can Stand."
Your righteousness He will bring forth as the light,
As you walk by faith, and not by sight.

Put your faith to work, and delight in the Lord;
For God honors faith and faith honors God.
According to your faith, so be it unto you!
It's God's mighty force which sees us through.

Put your faith to work, and the future is fearless;
For faith eliminates strain, and brings happiness
Active faith will always give you a lift;
So go for a miracle, accept this precious gift.

Why anticipate blockades that's already been removed?
With possibility thinking, things look new and improved.
So speak up to that mountain in Jesus' name,
And it will disappear as fast as it came.

Ena Mitchell

From Within

If only you knew what was in my heart, you would know that I'm
a carrying man who has you in my thoughts.

If only you knew how much you're always on my mind, you would
know that I daydream about you all the time.

If only you could see the things I see about you and I, you would
come to know that there is a lovers paradise.

If only you know how much you'll be apart of my dreams, you'll
come to realizes that two people who are so in love could have
everything.

If only you knew the kind of man I am, you would be filled with much
love overflowing again and again.

If only you could feel the way I do, you'd enrich my life with the
sweet pleasures of loving such a wonderful person as you.

Derrick D. Reeves

A Woman's Pain

She stood there standing, with tear filled eyes,
With long, blonde hair and sobbing sighs,
Pretty, though she may be,
With so many tears, she could hardly see.

He hurt her badly, in so many different ways,
She was confused, like looking into a foggy haze,
She couldn't think like her life was in a maze,
She felt so empty, like sheep with no where to graze.

She looked up to the sky and said:
"God I know you are there,"
"God I know that you care,"
"God take away this horrible pain I bear,"
"And God please answer my healing prayer."

Day by day, thru God and time,
Her pain felt like a lesser climb.
She felt peace and strength; the courage to move on,
She felt gentle and loving again; like a new born fawn,
She felt brave and confident; now ready to face the dawn.

With her sorrow gone, there was no more rain,
With God, no more did she feel a woman's pain.

Patrick Joe

341

Breathless

Heart of fire burns passionate words,
covering the blood that I once feared.
A cold touch freezes my mind,
leaving me scared, helpless, and blind.
Eyes drip tears of pain,
fearing losses, nothing to gain.
The melody that forever plays,
memories of cold lonely days.
Shadows lurk behind oak doors,
slowly showing it self more and more.
A whisper through the emptiness.
releasing my soul leaving me breathless.

Mandy LaVon

My Wish

The only life I want to live,
I want to live with you,
And your sweet dreams are all the ones
I hope will come true,

I wish you every happiness,
With palaces of gold,
And every treasure in this world,
Your arms could ever hold,

My God be always good to you,
And with his special star,
Protect and guide you on your way.
No matter where you are,

With this wish I hope you'll be true to me,
And in my arms you'll always be
Throughout eternity,

When that night is over,
There cannot be a dawn,
The sun and moon will have disappeared,
And all the stars are gone.

Delmar D. Voegele

My Love

Have you ever seen sunshine turned blue
  Or ever felt like your heart was torn in two
Have you ever longed for deep understanding
  A love that was patient, a heart undemanding
Have you ever felt so alone and so weak
  When your heart would hurt and your soul would weep
Have you ever felt this whole world would be better without you
  Well, my love, you're feeling the same way I do

Did you ever want to do what you felt was right
  Where you wanted praise by only got a fight
Did you ever want to be the best that you could be
  But you weren't understood as you should be
Did you ever just want a sky that was a cloudless blue
  Well, my love, you're wanting the same thing I do

Will you ever wish upon a star so bright
  But still follow in your heart what is wrong or right
Will you find your way when darkness covers you in its cloak
  And see on the path which way you should go
Will you always keep that happy golden hue
  Well, my love, you're wanting to keep the same thing I do

Lisa Meadows

Untitled

Routes 20 and 501 criss cross in Northeast Ontario
Aurora Borealis outlines her sullen face
Dark pines, stand off across white mottled fields of stone and stump
Snow avalanching from their chorusing heavenward limbs
Brisk arctic air upon us as we accede to winters slumber
So far from the troubles she gazes at four corners of barb
Barbed wire for whom? Here, in this grand facade
The night becomes chilled, the breeze so unwelcome
The pines watch us now, in this bitter barren land
Paranoia returning, to this! Gods country . . . .

D. C. Sutton

Passion

My "Passion" for you blooms every
morning as I rise. To a new day of Love
and Joy. At night I pray to God that the
"Passion" I receive from your heart to
mine, will never fade.

"Passion" that fills your heart and soul
comes from God's hands to our souls. For
which I'm grateful that he has chosen me to
share the greatest "passion" with you. And
the love he has made.

"Passion" has been a everyday prayer from
the bottom of my "Heart!" And I don't even
know where to start. On putting words into
phrases. So you can understand, how you really
make me feel deep down in my soul. And every
moment we've shared together, I wouldn't in a
million years, will I ever make a trade.

Craig A. Jennings

Threads

Warm and safe are the threads that weave my tapestry;
Warp of joy, and love and laughter,
Woof of duty, guilt and pain.
Apron string, friendships past, wedding rings;
Tradition holds me.

What unexpected treasures
are the bonds that set the spirit free
to soar along the verges of eternity:
A chain of thought,
the thread of dreams,
a wisp of hope.

Sharon Egger Heston

Closed Door

I closed the door — it seemed the wisest way
They were so little, he could give them more.
But, though I guard my footsteps through the day,
Night somehow finds me standing by the door.

I wonder if their knees were scratched from playing,
And if their hands were washed before they slept,
And was there anyone to comfort, saying,
Hush, Dear, 'Twill soon be mended if they wept.

I always tucked the covers twice, I wonder
If anyone came back tonight to see
If restless feet had tossed the blanket yonder,
I wonder if they thought at all of me.

I must be quiet, listening and waiting,
They are so keen of hearing, clever too
At guessing — they would call, unhesitating,
"I hear somebody — Mummy, is it you?"

Paula Long Clayton

The Unseen Long-Lost Playmate

Over the ocean, across the sky,
Someone is watching with his little eye.
Unseen to everyone, long lost to a friend,
Searching for his playmate may come to an end.
No one knows because he's not seen,
How the mysterious playmate became unseen.
Although his friend intends to find out,
I don't think he will.
But it's just a doubt.

Lauren Dovo

Imaginative Man

To Feel, To Hold, To Touch, To Love
to tell you you're the only one.
I wish I could touch you
But you are not there.
When I look for you,
you disappear.

When I call you,
you don't hear me.
I see you in my visions
and only there.

Oh, Mystery Man! O, My Imaginative Man!
I wish I could feel you, hold you,
touch you, and love you.

Windy Hall

Good(?)Bye

There are times when I want you,
There will be times when I wont.
There are times when I need you,
There will be times when I wont.

Why do I feel the way I do,
Every time I'm next to you?
My broken heart cries out in pain
I want to feel the sunshine, but I can only see the rain.

The look in your eyes when you catch mine,
Just a mixed signal, or is it a sign?
These wasted words and wasted paper,
I try to let go but to hold is much safer.

After these next few weeks go bye,
I'll never again see your eyes or your smile.
Everything that happens, happens for a reason,
But these words to my heart are a torrid treason.

Jenn Smugeresky

A Certain Stillness

A certain stillness surrounds this scene
(A homicidal void as yet unfilled)
Which seems to favor demonic deeds:
The murderer lifts the knife to strike —
The dying choke on their blood to plead.
All of heaven dare not look to see
When a lost soul cannot wait to flee.
But stillness cannot cloak the rage
Against the light of now fallen prey —
Their roles, shortened by the silent blade.
The murderer's fate — a private shame
When Death takes him from this earth — bound stage.

Lawrence Darrell

Spring Time

Spring is the time for new life to begin, the cold
and the Snow has come to an end.
Earth has been waken by the warmth of the sun, to let
mother nature know her work has begun.

Spring is when its showers bring to life our flowers.
The beauty of their blooms mean the fragrant will come
soon. The freshness of the air seems like beauty is
every where.

Spring is when the birds sing as though they are in
glory, if only they could talk, I know they would
tell a story.

Spring is the time for lovers many a true thought is
uncovered.

Brenda L. Nowlin

The Old Man Unworthy of a Buck

Why shall I dream of being someone else
And for something that is not worth dying?
For a father-like figure who is totally a stranger?
The old man's heart is crying

To please and to please like a good son to please
The old man fallen on his knees
With words of repent and desperation for need
The pain for greed endlessly

Unworthy is thought for a life that must end
The old man stands on a chair
Reaching towards the brittle hands that clasp
The air of all unfair

Now the old man is gone, with me in this place
I shall not bow to passed down luck
This father of mine, I don't know who he is
Except the old man unworthy of a "buck"

Then it is asked of me if I'd do it for him
In reply I felt like crying
Why shall I dream of being someone else
And for something that is not worth dying!

Alex Dominguez

Just To Be With You

To be with you for just a little while,
Is worth the time just to see you smile;
To smell the aroma of your embrace,
To see the glow of your angelic face.

You are beautiful and adorable,
Simple, sensible, and desirable;
A heart with a gentle and quiet spirit,
Everyday, every hour, every minute.

My heart is yearning for your sweet caress,
For your loving kindness and tenderness.
O how I needed you and adored you,
O how I wanted you and missed you too.

I will keep the flames burning in my heart,
Even if we're thousands of miles apart.
Many months, many years may come to pass,
But my love grows, like meadows in the grass.

Ron De Castro

Confession of a Warning Sign

As oil slithered the sea in 'eighty-nine,'
Seiners choked the Coho front door
And dormant roe were silent in brine.

Neptune tugged and stretched the tow-line:
We bobbled and chopped from shore to shore
As oil slithered the sea in 'eighty-nine.'

A piercing sound, hydraulic slime-line,
Knife-spoon scooping marrow more
And dormant roe were silent in brine

While frozen mothers spiraled benign
And priceless under a nightless horror.
As oil slithered the sea in 'eighty-nine,'

We processed salmon sublime;
Heads to the chipper, crunching roar,
And dormant roe were silent in brine.

Dreamless hours slipped on over-time:
Fatigue on caffeine (Alaskan lore)
As oil slithered the sea in 'eighty-nine'
And dormant roe were silent in brine.

Kyle Golphenee

Give to the Poor

I want to give to the poor
But what I have to give is worth more then money
What's more then money?
Piece of mind
If you don't have that
Then you ain't worth a dime
So many people I know is rich with money
But in their minds they're doing time
What I have for the poor, money can't buy
What do I say to my people
Clean your mind by taking time out
To think on positive
To thank the Lord
That's the reason why we live
I want to give to the poor
Once you get a dose of this you won't need no more
Cause it's powerful just by speech
Gets right down into you real deep
I want to give to the poor
And that's the love from the Lord

Falecia Y. Brown

Get Off the Bike, Mike

When I was just a little tyke,
My daddy said to me.
I think you're big enough to ride a bike
And a bike he bought for me.

Oh, how I love to ride that bike
Up and down the street
But every time I tried to ride
Mike jumped on the seat.

Get off the bike! Mike, I cried
This ain't built for two.
Get off the bike, Mike
Your mother's calling you.

But then one day, Mike grew up
And moved to another land
He doesn't know I have a ten speed now
That runs thru mud and sand

Oh, please come home, Mike
We're both the same age now.
You can ride my bike, Mike
And so can I and how!

Leo T. McCall

The Actress

Moving through a ground, your style effervescent.
Quite piteek though rather slim, you spread light where once was dim.
You can bring a smile to a down Trodden face, hold within your hand
Unharmed, a bird with ever so much grace.

Your emotions you insist be known to all, for you
First and foremost is having a ball, ball, ball.
And so your emotions were blessed upon me enriched my
understanding of what is and what isn't to be.
From little girl loss to in expendable boss, you mold your soul
Upon wings of which to travel past any obstacle, any class.
From Tinker Bell to Fancy Miss, you sprinkle your fantasy before
All who wish to graze within your main dish.
Life is happy, life is fad. Love is hither thither,
To be had and have you will, have you must,
Or the wings on which you fly will surely rust.
All is but a stage and you the star, dancing prancing where ever
you are, so bold, so cold, so filled with zest, determined you
are to be the very best.
Finally though the curtain must fall and darken your path.
to the actress, whose only wish was to be sexually unmask.

Charles Flanagan

Oh Father, the Anguish . . . .

Everybody knows what father has done
I scorn my father, just like everyone
Whispering lies, walking on glass.
Bleeding his cries, trying to erase the past

It is too sad to know,
He will never be forgiven
Betrayal will always show
When trying to pass the horizon

If you see my father
Tell him to come hold me tight
Tell him I want the same father
that helped me dream peacefully at night

Help me search for my father
I want to share the memories we once dreamt
I want him to tell me,
All troubles have come, but left

Help me find my father
I know he has done wrong
You see, I want to find my father,
For soon he will be gone.

Maricela Hinojosa

Feelings

As a tear drops
My heart stops
And I start to reminisce about the things we used to do
Sometimes I wonder if you miss me like I miss you.

Did you sign
Did you sigh
Did you feel pain deep inside?

Did you get on your knees
And pray to the Lord that He'll let us be together,
Or did you pray to the Lord that we can be apart?

Without a word being said
Did you stay awake thinking about us
Or did you go to sleep dreaming about the other man you see?

What I really need to know is
Did you love me
Like I love thee?

Paul M. Demps

Story Telling

Stories are for telling;
sharing pain and joy
of insights learned and lessons burned
into experience.

Experience reaches out
condensed to pearls,
laughter singing, tears streaming
into the telling.

Grief and rejoicing
find their way to freedom
in the sharing of how, why, what-happened
once upon a time.

Voiced in poem, song and tale
futuring is heard
in hope, love, and joy spilling truth in myth
and myth in truth.

Stories are fore-telling.

Maureen Williams

Hide and Seek

They seek her
Her muscles bunch
tense and ready to run.
Her eyes flicker
almost glowing.
Her mind thinks
waiting...watching...knowing...
She hears a rustle in the tree
but she waits.
Not running till she needs
A footstep is what she hears
...a low and menacing growl
meaning Lion's near.
She takes a step and then another.
Silent she is — the skill taught by her mother.
Lion stalks silently moving
But Gazelle is clever, ever ready.
Lions springs.
But Gazelle is gone.
The game of Hide and Seek is on.

Kristine von Forell

Loved

For our life, a large elegant house is nice;
to relax, a glass of Jack Daniels over ice.
There's fancy clothes, cars, and diamond rings.
All of the pleasures, expensive things can bring.

For all the people who like just simple pleasures;
there's nature hikes, birds and bees to treasure.
Friends and family, gardens and flower beds;
there's television, sports, music and club Med.

There's Opera to love, for those who understand;
there are Mardi Gras parades, with marching band.
There are books to read, so we can acquire knowledge.
There are training centers, schools and even college.

Work for responsibility, challenges to keep us strong.
Food for thought, so we can realize...right from wrong.
There's "Power of Prayer", when we're needy and depressed.
There's prove of reincarnation, when we are regressed.

There's water when were thirsty, we need it just to live.
There's air to breath, food to eat, and thanks to give.
Just think of everything . . . God gave us from above;
the most important thing . . . was simply being loved.

Sharon Enos

I Wonder

I wonder why I'm here and you're there!
The miles between us I just can't bare!
I'm tired of hearing "I must go"!
I don't understand you just came home!
But as you say goodbye and you shut the door,
I often wonder where you are.
I wonder if you're close or if you are far away.
I watch out my window as the birds fly your way,
As the sky becomes dark and very gray.
I crawl up into bed and start to pray
Maybe someday those birds will fly back my way,
And you will return home soon one day!

Kimberly Burress

Things to Remember

You came to me
And taught me the beginnings
Of caring and giving and trusting and sharing.
You helped to keep me warm
As I battled through the wintry storm.
You helped to keep me strong.
It was hard for you.
It was hard for me.
And now, dear heart, we are into Spring.
Wild flowers, blue skies, warm bodies, sweet souls,
And you have stayed with me.
You have taught me the beginning of loving.
I will remember these things always.

d. c. Mayo

Rainy Season, Philippines

Two old ladies, looking out their capiz-shell window,
sipping warm ginger juice, talking above the rain.
  - What's the name of that nice young man again?
  - Why should I do your remembering for you?
  He's your nephew!
They laugh.
They try to recall who the hell it is.
They decide it doesn't matter
  and continue to remember
all the previous days of their lives.
  Two old ladies who never married,
best of friends and never parted,
looking out to brave the rain
  still with summer on their minds.

Blesilda Carmona

God's Grace

God's grace counted from the very beginning,
I was chosen since my residence in womb starting.
Ignorance of the Lord attributed by childish naivete and simplicity,
Arrogance and impudence bred immorality and iniquity.
He executed discipline and dispatched a wake-up call,
Punished by ailment and bedridden, Bible-reading becoming an avid
  appeal.
Confession with lamenting pain to seek His exoneration,
Atonement and rejuvenation because of His blood for exculpation.
Praise the Lord with a profuse and grateful heart,
Albeit life being sparse, unplentiful and transient.
Blessed by the Holy Spirit, happiness spilling, pleasant and
  delightful,
Holding His promise, life flourishing, luxuriant and bountiful.
Staunchly carrying out the work of the Lord, faithful and
  conscientious,
Steadfastly dashing forward to conquer every hurdle, tactful and
  courageous.
Beseech God to anoint my head with benediction and felicitation,
Accomplish His aim, my purpose in life with dedication and
  determination.

Florence Wang

345

Martha's Blues

Martha likes to sing the blues
doo-dee-dahdle-ah-dah-day
in summer time, when the weather was fine
and cool drinks soothed her body and mind

Love, joy and warmth; her heart was filled with fire
and if the world outside sometimes turned too slow
crying was her sweet companion too

The days she dreamed her hours away
the fun she'd never forget
blessed moments to hold and cherish
innocent, everlasting, without regret

But today she finds she measures her rhymes
the verse has caught up and is well on its way
oh for yesterday's dreams, yesterday's smiles
she yearns for yesterday's songs of love

From this day forward she'll sing these blues
doo-dee-dahdle-ah-dah-day
the promise of spring was not long to last
time was only hers to lose, she found
love is things that have long since passed

Marti B. Gomez

Untitled

I lie down at night, and think of me and you.
And how so long ago, our love was right

But now you've left me, and I'm all alone
With the memories of a love, I had once known.

Everywhere I turn, there's something there
A reminder of us, and the pain I can't bear.

The songs on the radio, leave the taste of a tear
And make me wish, I could hold you near.

What do you do, when all you're left with is pain.
And every tear that falls, leaves you feeling as cold as a
    winter's rain.
Who do I turn to now, that no-one comes when I call your name
I can only wish your thoughts were the same.

Once upon a time, you promised forever
So what do I do, now that forever's turned to never.

Stefani Petree

Life's Simple Joys

The beauty of nature around us stands,
Made for our pleasure by God's own hands,
The mountains' splendor, the ocean's roar
Tides bring the shells up on the shore,
Foot prints in the sand soon wash away
Remind us of life, so short a stay.
Soft green grass, the shade of a tree,
Inviting? Yes, they beckon to me.
A squirrel on a high limb scampers about,
Watching so carefully, filled with doubt.
Beautiful flowers nod in the sun
The buds opened up as the day began,
Gentle breezes, refreshing rain
Make things look clean and new again.
A smile on the face of a friend that cheers
Love in the eyes of those we hold dear.
These are some of the things that brighten our days
How great and wonderful are God's ways.

Mildred M. Macke

Hope

Everyone has problems,
don't think it's just you.
We have to move past them,
don't let them make you blue.

I know you're going through a hard time,
and you think you've had enough.
But putting a smile on your face,
will make easier what's rough.

Don't hesitate to give me a call,
when you think you just can't cope.
I may not know the answer,
but I'll give you something called "Hope."

Trisha Dyan Hartline

The Gambler

I work so hard to earn my keep.
Every night collapsing before I sleep.
Work during the day, school at night,
the light at the end of tunnel, nowhere in sight,
I have brains and know what I want.
But my only desire is to have money to flaunt.
So I gamble.

Buy 3 different newspapers to find out the lines.
Consistency losing...time after time.
This bug in me urges to go on, and bet again,
While I ask 200 dollars from my best friend.
I want to stop, really I do.

Can't buy a phone, the rent's overdue.
Haven't bought new clothes in a year or two.
I go to AC and look at the wheel, sitting playing blackjack,
losing another deal. I'm slipping, totally losing myself.
No pride or respect on my inventory shelf.
I have a deep sickness, and love for money.
Boy when you win it's sweeter than honey.
Is it all worth it? I may never know.
Kick-off is in 10 minutes I gotta go . . .

Thomas F. LaVeahon

12th Street

On 12th street, people live a different way of life
Hands are held more
Smiles are commonplace, and so is the lemonade
on 12th street, the day begins at sunset
The air is always refreshing
And the time you spend is always with friends
On 12th street, a kiss is pure ecstasy
People live to love
And love to live
On 12th street, a hug is the same as a handshake
Laughter fills the households of all who want it
And that my friend is everyone
On 12th street, a crime has never been committed
Hardship is nonexistent
And so is reality

On 12th street, my heaven is found
Next I go, follow me
Together we can escape into paradise
On 12th street

C. R. Oberlin

To Celebrate Life

Spring, fall, winter and summer make the seasons,
Birthdays, anniversaries, and holidays all gives the reasons!
With every flip of the calendar month opportunities arise,
For us to open our cookbooks, plan a party, and make it a surprise!

Oh, the thought of work can put an awful grimacing look on my face,
But when I think of being with those I love I begin to make haste,
I busy myself with decorating and preparing wonderful food to taste!
And then I go shopping to find the perfect outfit with the finest of lace!!

Next thing you know the planning is all done,
It's time to put on your party duds and begin the fun!
Graciously, open your heart and your home to all,
For those who come are very dear to make the haul!

Laughter, good times, well-being is felt at your affair,
Everyone receives much when we get together to share.
All those little things done to give your event its flair,
Tell those who came that you really care!

Make all your occasions as special as you can,
For life has made no guarantees in this land!
So begin now to celebrate life, treating each day as a precious event,
Then life becomes richer — why you feel as if you own a mint!

Cyndee Mizell

Dark Hour

In the cold, dark hour,
Lays an old black clock.
It has the strength and power,
Yet it only tick tocks.

It is brown the color of the earth
But to you, think, what is it worth.
It is golden like the color of the sun
It is worth everything to someone.

Passed on from family to you
Will you enjoy it, think about that too.
It is a symbol of rhythm and rhyme
You can ask what you must and ask what you will,
It only tells time.

Where did it came from you might ask
Did it came from the present or maybe the past.
Did it come from heaven, I must know
It is not perfect, it gives and it goes.

I admit to you I was telling a lie
You wouldn't understand me if I tried.
That so called clock is not real from the start
For that it is an old, confused heart.

Dominique Dupre

Calling a Ball Game

The shortstop is the first to bat today;
He has no pop, but runs like a fast cat.
Left-fielder's next and is eager to play;
He has no glove, but swings a mighty bat.
The first-baseman hits third and knows his role;
He'll get on base, which helps set the table.
The third-baseman swings a telephone pole;
Must clear the bases, if he is able.
The catcher's next and picks up any scraps;
He will drive home, any man that remains.
Right-fielder swings and patrons lose their laps;
The ball is crushed so high, it may bring rains.
   A pitching change, it's time for goodness sake;
   Rejoin us after this commercial break.

Donald B. Mullins

The Green and the Brown

We walked, the youth and I, side by side;
   I saw the glory of the present,
He sought the dreams of tomorrow's ride;
   But each grasped at his chapter of the day's divide.

Both heard the drummer's spirited beat,
   I savored the memory of measured progress,
He sensed the rush towards some future treat,
   And our perceptions were harmony incomplete.

The sun sought refuge in the horizon's quiet port,
   I saw unsurpassed beauty and sensed tasks well done,
He grasped but a passing to night's covered court,
   And we both mused at the other's unmeasured cavort.

'Tis but the natural division of life's balance,
   As old and young trod their errant paths,
With different views of values worthy of chance;
   And we struggled, each with his own dance.

Humanity has yet to come to that status grand,
   That long sought nirvana of peace and joy,
Where young and old can trod the strand;
   And leave but a single trail in the sand.

Joseph M. Holihen

The Graffiti Artist

Through a 20x magnification circle
I watch him paint "New Fire" on the wall of a courthouse.

   I live a factory-smoke life
      with puff-puff outcries
      like the rise and fall of tides;
      sick sun in a smog sky
   up to wake, down to sleep
   erupting breaks of red-faced anger in between.
(I can't keep this up much longer)
   but I will, and you will, as he will

"Yeah, that guy! With the spray can!"
Caught in broad daylight
   in the 20x magnification circle
caught in the middle of the bottom curve of the last 'S'
   as he goes down;
   blood spurting from the hole in his back.

The inscription reads: 'New Fire Ends In Ashes'
and I drop my binoculars.
The police officer lowers his gun.

Todd H. Dills

Sleep

Sleep
who needs it anyway
I think so much better when
I can't think at all
how often does your mind get to be blank
a concussion
a coma
amnesia
but those are only temporary
I want to sit down
Dr. Smooth in hand
blank
nothing on my mind
but that Dr. Smooth
and the one after that
and the one after that
and the one after that
and the one after that
and the one after that

Megan Landry

Where Ideas Hide

Ideas can hide anywhere; from head to toe.
They can hide in your dreams,
or maybe in a painting.
They can hide in your imagination, spawning into great
creations!

Where do ideas hide? They don't hide in your sock drawer,
that's for sure! They can hide in a sunny day, a picnic, a
rainbow, a white linen hankie with an embroidered daisy.
How 'bout in a running river or atop the wings of a golden eagle?!

Ideas can be hiding wherever you want them to! They could
hide in a basket by the fireside or in a warm cozy quilt. But
I know where the ideas keep their hidden lair!
They lie within the boundaries of our lives, dreams hopes,
wishes, and fears. An idea is a gift that should be cherished.

Dana Henderson

To Love A Person Who Does Not Believe In Trust

You never know what a person may hide
Until you look deep inside

The hurt and the pain
That drives one insane

Everyone hurts everyone cries
because of their jealousy because of the lies

What can we do
What can I do
But
Only to love you

What could this mean
What should I do

Leave you and I would not dare
because you see I really do care

I will listen not only hear
I will never leave you, I will always be here.

Claudia Aguirre

First, I Am Woman

First, I am woman, female gender, homo sapien
my eyes are brown, the color of mother earth

First, I am woman; with wants and desires, I am a black
woman; colored girl; brown sugar; home girl; ebony woman;
nubian princess covered with precious pearls, innocent yet wise . .
.
to life's joys, pains, hurts and perils.

First, I am woman that knows no limits, that dares to seek and discover,
what fate has planned, to learn and grow and to play my role in it.

First, I am woman who loves freely, a woman who strives.
A woman who cares, who dares . . .
Is there no one who seeks the ultimate high, is he whom I seek
forever lost, always elusive of my silent stares.

First, I am woman who has no time to waste, care about me, love me
and I shall remain the same, but never, never, seek me in haste.

First, I am woman who has seen the plans, knows the schemes of
devious minds,
I adhere to trickery and eliminate the source, treat them in
kind, the love game is just that...a game I have no time to waste, I
have played the games before, I know the score, the rules never
change . . . just the names.

First, I am woman, female gender, homo sapien, my eyes are brown the,
color of mother earth
I am all things imaginable because I am yours First

Gloria J. Fouse

On a Sunday Again

Today's a better day yesterday
pluto squared with the moon
    as it operated with your father
you played witness
    (thinking)

Believe me I definitely felt it
you walked right through my dreams
    finding staples
enjoying solitude
    (painting)

As Mississippi hangs over your head
I find my place with you
    beside the fresh smell of a pillowcase
the sanctuary of sleep
    (convincing)

Outside hazy sunshine reveals my desire
stretch me like a canvas before breakfast
    on a Sunday again
before the streets get too crowded
    (sharing)

Jeff Dungfelder

Sorry Mam

I'm sorry mam, I do not know you
You are thinking someone else is me
I, too, have made that error
For it can happen easily

I thought you were a friend I knew
She is extremely hard to find
But since you've lied and cheated me
I see the error that is mine

This friend was very dear to me
Like sisters we were tight
It is obvious you are not this gal
Cause we would never fight

I'm sorry mam, I do not know you
It's your mistake you see
For the friend I thought you were
Would never betray a good friend like me

Rahsaana Towns

The Prayer

Without you I am no one and capable of nothing.
But with you I am someone and can do all things.
For just as a flower will wither away without
Water, so will I without you in my life. Just as a
Child's heart will break into without someone to
Love him, so will mine if you don't love me. And
Just as a bird with broken wings can't fly, I
Can't walk without you by my side. For you're
The one who wakes me in the morning.
You're the breath that keeps me going.
You're the angel that sees me through the night.
You're my strength to stand the fight. Oh,
Lord I haven't yet seen a mountain of rest,
For these valleys have made my life a mess.
Please let your sunshine spill into my life
Again, so that my days of cloudiness will
come to an end.

Rebecca M. Boyd

My Life

Too much mixed emotions, too much pride,
Questions and answers, I cannot decide.
My life is in shambles; it's so hard to repair,
How did it ever get this way?
Searching and hoping, things will change;
I fall on my knees, I scream to the clouds.
No one can hear me, maybe I shouting too loud.
Whatever has happened, to that sweet little girl
With everything going for her,
Everything in the world.
Why is she so lonely, why is she so afraid?
Was it something she's done, some mistake she's made?
Will it ever get better,
Or is it only a phase?
Thoughts ran through her mind, but she cannot explain;
All the ups and downs and hardships
She's had to sustained.
When will it ever change
Will she get back to being herself again?

Glenda Branch

My Sculpture

Everyday is a prayer for being alive, for help, for strength.
Also, a struggle to survive, to grow . . . to live.
To tell yourself it is O.K. This time will also pass.
Things will be the same, is a lie.
There is no choice, no question, no regret, life must go on.
Carry on my work . . . carving a hand, a leg, a face,
a brain. Did I say a brain? Yes, a brain.
Sadness or weariness, I continue my masterpiece,
my image . . . my reflection on earth.

Mercedes E. Villalona

The Writers Bar — Raffles Hotel, Singapore

What muse resides
Where signs decree.
What great men
Drew from this site, with summer ever setting.

Can something named remain magical.
Can inspiration sustain acknowledgement.
Does reputation taint beauty.

Adjacent, unrestrained, the Grill Room.
(My meal finished, I walk out of the Grill Room,
through the hallowed Writers Bar)

Ah!
Of course —
It's the chairs, like footwear.
Aloof . . . yet, conducive to thought.
Even that I could not see,
From the Grill Room.

Cillian Lynch

Alcohol

As I see it, I cannot deal or cope.
All hope is gone and I am alone, to see how
clearly dreary it all really is.
My efforts are in vain and my life all
but ruin, and all who see me so grand
see it too.
So here I sit alone with my spirits,
My blissful escape, my crutch to lean on.
My escape from a mostly cruel, old world.
Drink blurs my problems lifts my
soul, distorts everything so neatly.
Reality is simply too ugly.

Richard Albert

Broken

Too much steak for the fire.

Eighteen cold summers disorder a shell
frightened, innocent, longing. Inaccessible
if ever, smothered spirit miles and miles past.

Celestial August air, conversation, connection,
healing?

Ashamed of being human and male, terrified of
failure, following,
following.

Unbending storm winds beating down minute after
minute "You can't. You should've."

Minutes away but late savory fair.

Safe comfortable mediocrity with perceived
hassles disengage. Unbridled rage festers pumping,
invisible and fearless lashes and cuts.

Seated, blind of unrelenting callous draft,

"It's a little tough isn't it?"

Mike Haverman

Love

They say the cure for love at first sight is to take
a second look
I took two
And I still love you
Though you hurt me
Though you made me cry
I won't deny that I know you
I won't deny you were once mine
I was just another check on your long list
But your name stood out on mine
And now I'm pissed

I don't deserve what you're putting me through
I don't understand,
But all I want is you
Just to hold you once more
Just to say that you're mine
Just to remember that once I felt divine
They say time heals the heart
But I know it's not true
Because no matter what I will always love you

Maria Michelle DeAnda

Who Will Care

Who is that child
So desperate and along,
Just wishing to have a place to call home;

No where to go,
No one to care,
Yearning for a tender hand or just a kind "stare";

Wandering from corner to corner,
from alley to gutter,
hoping to find just a morsel to eat.

Maybe today "someone" will give a helping hand,
But no, another day like yesterday,
Dashed hopes, sorrow and pain;

Oh Lord my heart is heavy,
My head hung down,
Tomorrow I will help that child turn his life around;

Tomorrow has come and gone,
and nothing for that child have I done;
All I can say is please Lord give me another day.

Carolyn S. Starr-Arrington

What Will They Say

What will they say about a man when he is gone?
Will they say he loved life and had many friends or was he alone;
Was he good until the end and treated people right:
Or was he evil and corrupt by the turning of the night;
Did he sleep in peace knowing that he had done no wrong;
Did he fulfill the new day with love and a song;
Did he treat his family right; Did he love his wife;
What will they say about a man when he is gone?
Does he search his heart to see where he stands;
Did he put Christ first, then his family and then his friends;
What will they say about a man when he is gone?
Did he prepare to meet his God; Or did he think he'd better not;
Was he good when he breath life;
And will good things be said when he is no longer in sight;
Did he leave this world with a righteous heart;
Or did he leave his family to make a lonely start;
Will they miss him because he as loving, gentle and kind;
Or will they rejoice because he was evil, mean and lied;
What will they say about a man when he is gone?

Barbra Dodd-Weddington

Pearl

Slowly, slowly, a single tear slides, over the curves of her
    delicate face
Soon, this tear finds a partner
Until eventually, the numbers are lost
The moonlight reflects onto her tears
Glistening
The drops of salt signify many things
Life, love and practically any other worry
What is a worry, but a mere thought transformed into concern?
Sensitive, like a withered rose whose petals
    are struggling to remain one with the
    stem, the tears continue
Until, finally, her eyes become dry, her cheeks
    streaked with waves of pain
Unbearable pain
Her life, which once was steady, is now like
    porcelain
Fragile and precious

Becky Blevins

The Fire Within Me

A fire burns bright within me.
I can hear it crackle and roar!
It lives on my wants and desires,
Always yearning and begging for more!

A touch is all it takes to light
This flame of passion and delight.
Taking a journey to heavenly ecstasy,
Every little caress is a delicacy.

Kisses that slowly trace up and down my frame.
Enjoying the tingle from this little game.
And love can only burn the fire brighter
Making the meaning of it mightier!

The scorching heat sears through my body.
Drowning in all the pleasure and sensuality.
This intimacy drifts me to paradise,
Only he will hear my moans and cries.

Our bodies intermingled as one.
The fire now burns hot as the sun!
And everything becomes so intense.
I am consumed by this incredible experience!

Rodalene Enriquez

Memory Breezes

Every first and last breeze reminds
me of a place I love.
    I can feel the fresh springtime breeze
coursing through the house - gently swaying
    the curtains.
    A peaceful night time breeze reminds
me of times sitting on the front porch,
    Listening to the evening sounds of peace
And the long day coming to a rest.
    A strong, gusty breeze bringing in a
storm, brings the nearness of a loved one,
knowing one isn't alone.
    I can still smell the scent of flowers
with the summer breeze and hear the
Peaceful sound of the cows in the pasture.
    All these breezes remind me of a place
I love, and when I get lonely I just close
My eyes and let the breeze gently carry me back.

Priscilla Anne Gaskins

Two Roads

As you enter the crossroads of man's action
Would you consider the leaders of life's axis?
There are two leader's;
there are two roads.
But you make the decision of your abode.
All trails are bright and cheerful
in the beginning,
But only one continues unto a happy ending.
You make the decision of your life's abode.
Please remember as long life's path we go,
Regardless of who we are,
well reap just what we sow.
There are two leaders;
there are two roads.
But you make the decision of your life's abode.
Jesus while on earth made the paths for us to trod,
As we know all things are possible with God.
Although God's power is every so great,
The choice of the two roads is for each of us to make.

Lloyd Fly

Only Female Mosquitos Bite

So it is my civic duty as a Woman to succeed —
to be blatantly talented, intelligent and proud —
to bend gender role to the breaking point and bury its fruitless
    remains in my Mother (Earth)'s womb so that her offspring may be
    fertile.
So it is my inherited prophecy (handed down from centuries of
    admirable Ladies)
to stand strong, bear opposition strong, survive strong and most
    importantly love strong regardless of pain.
Also, it is of my flesh and being to reason —
to loudly, vehemently refuse my oft imposed victimization . . .
simply because I care. So it is in my Soul as a Woman to
be beautiful in solid femininity
and be transcended from mere gender to simply me
and be so successfully for every Woman who
has ever wanted to stand up and scream out her freedom.
And so it is of me not because I can Mother,
but because I have been Mothered by every woman ever to be, ever to
    dream, ever to love; and so it is my incredible fate to Mother —
And for the sake of love, I rock the gentle Cradle of Humanity.

Amber J. Grafft

Morning Delight

A prism catches morning light,
Diffusing rainbows where it might,
Children dance in the colorful sight.

Can you recall the spectrum on the wall?

Birds pass by in mystical flight,
Wings of blue with splashes of bright,
The sun has finally conquered night.

Can you do a trill like a whippoorwill?

Grass so green by sidewalk white,
Butterfly flutters like a miniature kite,
Elijah passes over as a satellite.

A place to play on a summer's day.

Azure blue with sands unite,
The soul seeks God in a prayerful rite,
While mind wanders to a mountain height.

Adam and Paul, see them fall?

Clouds make life forms but not quite,
Imagination needs no copyright,
Breath in deep and stand upright.

Can you see the clock from your hammock?

Joan Porter

Untitled

Beneath the oaks, in evening's ebony
    Cool drops caress our bodies warm and wet.
In silence I hold up my heart to you
    To see, to touch, to take. The air hangs heavy
While I wait. Blinded by desire, your hands
    Push roughly past to take the other prize.
I throw my soul into the fire and let
    The flames consume us both. And when dawn
Comes, I draw the ashes out and
    Make my soul my own again - too late.

Elizabeth Hinnant

Autumn and Grandpa

Walking amongst the large trees
Staring in amazement at the spectrum of
    colors splattered within them
Glancing up at grandpa's scruffly smile
While I grasp his pinky with all my strength
He said that it was due to a "magic" within us
That as long as I held onto him and we shared our love,
    the colors would remain and return every year
I remember grasping tighter as I heard those soft
    words flow out of his mouth
And my eyes grow wider with delight, as did my heart
But one year it was to no longer be
I returned but grandpa did not
As I walked amongst the trees, I felt through the air
    for his hand and strained to hear his voice
I wondered how the colors had returned even without our "magic"
Just then a breeze brushed through the trees and seemed
    to whisper his words to me
Then I realized, I was still tightly grasping his pinky
    within my heart and as the colors return every year
. . . so does grandpa.

Jason Willert

Yes Daddy

A cold existence of useless flesh
Drinking himself to an early grave
Killing my hope
Poisoning my heart and mind
My father is a creature of cruelty
A creature of sharp words and hard anger
Of unspoken threats and unrepented sins
He is the jailer of my soul and the chains that bind my ankles
He travels through my world with careless disregard for whom he hurts
A false smile, a blatant lie, and I am daddy's little girl again
A pathetic, confused character in this novel of pain
I am dependent upon his approval, his ever-so-fragile approval
Easily won, and even more easily lost
Pieces of my broken life are laying at his feet
"Yes Daddy, I love you"
"Yes Daddy, I know you love me"
"Yes Daddy, I know you didn't mean to hurt me"
"Yes Daddy, I forgive you"

Sheena Fullen

When Love Doesn't Make Sense

As one hits the floor, another begins to fall,
One right after another, making no sense at all,

I know what I'm feeling, yet I don't know how to feel,
I don't know how to believe that this heartache is real.

So, what should I do now that love doesn't make sense,
What should I say in my heart's self defense?

He was a part of my heart, a survivor of my soul,
The part of me that died when time took control.

Now, I sit alone, my thoughts close to gone,
I'll be awake through tonight, even through the dawn.

What was supposed to last forever, has paused for a cry,
It was supposed to mean "eternal", never having to ask why.

But what will happen next when the pain tears me apart,
I won't know what to do 'cause he'll still have my heart.

So, what could I possibly say to my defense,
Now that the only love I knew, no longer makes sense?

Becky Keller

I Am An Artist

An artist must be cared for,
Forgiven, not denied.
An artist can be neurotic,
Egocentric, self-indulgent.

An artist must have moods
A need for constant self-protection.
An artist is androgynous
Sometimes selfish, often charming.

I am an artist. I do what I do best.
I am unsolved: It is my right.
I have not asked to be explained.
I know no seconds here: No one who stands behind.

So I grow distant, even drunken.
I am an artist. My son will understand.
He'll know a man like me
Must hide his fears.

Whitney Burnett

My Soul That Remains

The passing of time is but a beginning End
Lows of life I cherish so, within its heights I grow
The shedding of old brings new beauty,
fear not these moments

Fear the old I hold
New and fresh eternity's web, if not,
Such beauty would never emerge of ugly cocoons

Worm to butterfly

If not, she would let the old of winter go;
Its wings would never feel the summer breeze

The gentle harshness of the storm
creates the force that carves our stone

The more blows away,
the more of me that remains.

Jeannette Allred

Little Silence

She walked alone, to hide the pain
To hide the tears, she used the rain,
She covered bruises
shunned the shame
Yet no one saw her sorrow.

The friends from school, they noticed not
The teachers eyes, no wrong they sought,
The fear inside
to hide was taught
So no one saw tomorrow.

When word was known, and finally spread
Astonished faces, pale with dread,
The guilt of those
who saw her dead
Wished time, now to borrow.

The children like these, abused and alone
The hard hand of anger will turn to stone,
The truth must be seen
the facts finally known
For their lives are filled with sorrow.

Andrea S. Hawthorne

A Tribute to My Father

Oh I am a patriot of the mountain life!
Family and peace my dream.
With tales of Indian Waters and fearsome bears
I charm the young colleen.

I sing of the trout in icy stream,
The hawk on the mountain crest
And the sorrowful climb to the hillside grave
Where mother we laid to rest.

Next on the scene: Miss Gertrude Perkins
She taught me wisdom true.
Descent from Rezin Jones and Bill Buck Baldwin
By Puritan rule I grew:

Study your books! Work hard, and avoid strong drink, young man.
At worship sit not on the back most pew;
Where love be rooted in honor — marry.
Allow each person his due.

This was the life I sang oh
For I was hewn of the stock
That broke the Gilley Hollow for bread,
And built the home on the rock!

Emma Lou Graybeal Hunter

Until Again

In Memory of Rosa Ray

I found myself upon a cloud
With a cool breeze that tinkles my face
And the clear night sky with bright filled stars
How the warmth and peacefulness content its wake
It made me realize what God had planned

The treasures of Heaven are here to behold
And the stars leading me into an eternal bliss
As if a bird were carrying me across the Universe

So perfect this gift was for me to admire
A loving retreat when I need to retire
And this place it shall be until the eternal end
No matter what! It would be my loving friend

Bowing my head I say
I will be with you in "Heart and Soul"
And until the end!
Were we shall meet again!

I lay my head, down to rest
For ever and ever
And until again...

Felicia Denise Rainey

Can You See

Grey misty sky viewed by the eyes of the mind and
a wonder to my conscience. My imagination takes
control of my focusing of my reality of existence
and understanding. I wonder if it is a illusion
to my reality or can it be the vision of my eyes.
Tell me can you see

Fill with freedom and liberty is what make a
people and bring the focus to reality. For the
heart and soul is the being that is the conscience
So across the mountains and through the clouds a
mental telepathy could be heard. And I wonder if you can see

Bound by no man's limitation my imagination allows me to
explore. My horizons are the bounties of the universal. And
my thinking is like the stars of the galaxy, yet you persist not
to see. And I wonder from within can you see

Now the words of my heart and soul can appreciate the captivity
of my thoughts of reality. For if you understand the vision of
your mind then you can see the beauty that resides within the
being of a man. Maybe then you can answer, I can see.

James E. Profit

Thoughts of You

Sometimes I think I'd like to be a fly on the wall,
Peering at your genitals, not spying on you behind your back,
But staring at you face to face,
Buzzing, humming, watching,
Rubbing my feet in quiet anticipation
Of the shock on your face if only you knew.

Sometimes I think I'd like to be a mouse in your abode,
Defecating in your pantry, eating holes in the many boxes and bags
Designed to keep me out,
Cautiously huddled on the night stand
Next to your bed, watching you as you sleep,
Occasionally leaving a deposit, if only you knew.

Sometimes I think I ought to be
A dog sitting at your feet,
Waiting for the next kick to come,
What the hell — I might as well be a dog,
Wavering in that fuzzy grey area of your madness,
Never knowing whether I'm going to get
A pat on the head, or a swift kick in the ass;
Well up yours too . . . . If only you knew.

Karla O. Hutchens

A Childhood Garden

We grew together in a childhood garden, spending each hour amidst carefree play. We flourished in simply knowing that the other existed, and despite the multitude of life within the garden, whether it be other vegetation or insects.

The sun and the rain had no bias in their efforts to nourish us. And so, our roots pressed their way into the fertile soil, becoming sturdy, and enduring abrupt variations in climate that came without forewarning. But the soil into which we entrenched ourselves was tended to in different ways. And the seeds, from which we grew, were not the same.

I grew to be proper and correct, like and erect lily with showy flowers and clusters of narrow leaves. She is a wildflower, reaching out in odd directions, swaying with the slightest drift of wind. Though her flower is beautiful, her stem moves in paths which hides the beauty from view.

Her flower is hidden from me now. My form and structure do not permit me to bend and look for her. And, the passage of time has put a fence between us.

But I feel her presence. It is like having an appendage removed. That which feels to be very much a part of you is no longer there.

Susan Wilcox

The Old Broken Down Windmill

I was traveling down an old country road,
Been traveling many miles,
Thinking 'bout many things,
The good times and the trials.

But something caught my eyes,
I stopped yes completely still,
I felt my eyes were glued,
On an old broken down windmill.

Didn't they know this old windmill,
Who had been faithful for so long,
Would be lonely and devastated,
When every one was gone.

Things don't always stay the same,
Life just don't stand still,
But never forget the ones you love,
Like the old Broken Down Windmill.

Yes, he has seen better days,
Be useful...oh he always will,
You see, he puts a little love in each ones heart,
When they see - that old broken down wind mill.

Imogene Arrington

Passing Smiles

In the place where we don't go,
deep inside no one can see,
is the self we guard so dear.

Secret feelings for years in check
remain concealed lest one should guess,
the smile we wear is just a mask.

Pain of love, fear of failure,
money woes and family wars
conspire to break through a hollow core.

A kindly hello to all we pass
faint smiles exchanged and tales untold,
as we go our ways and lock heart's door.

Jessie Burciaga

Our Five Senses On Peace

I see peace in the faces of infants,
I feel peace in a soft summer breeze,
I taste peace in cold lemonade,
I smell peace in garden flowers,
I hear peace nature's meadow,
I visualize all those things and long for ever peace.

Nicole Swartzlander

Olivia

There once was a gal named Olivia,
who said to her mate, "I'll out live ya.
So don't even try to figure what I
in a very weak moment might give ya.
I've made out a will, but listen, you pill
I haven't passed away yet. It may take some time,
you don't have a dime, on this you can certainly bet.
So while I'm alive, you'd better contrive
to be on your finest behavior. 'Cause if you go broke,
it won't be a joke and I will not be here to save ya.
You've had a good life and I've been your wife
for more years than I care to remember.
I gave you my best and you took the rest
from January right through December."

Russell Conant

The Trysting Tree

I cut your name, long years ago,
    Upon our favorite tree.
When we were young and all alone
    I carved your name above my own,
        Where all the world might see.

As on that day I see you now,
    With sun-gold in your hair,
        With eyes that shone like sparkling wine,
        With lips that fondly turned to mine —
            To me divinely fair!

The ancient tree still guards our names
    As in the olden time,
And, year by year, in sun and rain,
    I trace the letters with my cane
        Across the moss and rime.

And yet, you never seek the spot
    And may not know the truth;
What dreams of mine still linger there
    Since long ago you ceased to care,
        You, lost love of my youth!

Robert S. Merrill

Let Me In

Gazing in at you
Your eyes filled with sorrow
Will you ever let me in
Maybe today, maybe tomorrow
I beg you to unlock your heart
And let me enter in
If you would only let your soul be known
You would be an example for all men
They would understand what a Christian should be
And you could face this sinfilled world with me
Join your heart's hand with mine
And we will battle through this world for God
For all time

Adrienne Spain

Labyrinth

God, I hate you right now.
Why did you have me love him
when you knew he didn't love me back?
Are you laughing,
As you watch my tears fall?
I do not want to live anymore,
but I don't want to die if it means going to you,
You, a cruel and mean-spirited trickster
who has cut the strings of my heart.
What right have I to expect him to love me?
I am only yours, yours to destroy.
But know this:
The love I have for him is taking over
the love I had for you.
I seem to have forgotten that when one plays with you,
You are the Ultimate Cheater,
and my game was over before it got started.
So let the dice go, and put away the places,
because I have risked all, and lost all,
and I have nothing more to give you.

Trupti Champaneria

City Life

Hail City life, happy the clan,
Like excrement upon the land.
Your petty and brittle cover,
Strangles young life within.
Demeaning, synthetic, irrelevant.
You no longer fit life itself.
You demand, you force young life
to normality, a type of bondage.
Hail City life, torment the clan,
They'll be absorbed within the land,
And youth, insistent, vibrant, challenging,
Shall spring forth, free again.

Stan Kemmis

My Fall From Grace

I went to learn to ride a horse.
The instructor said, "Don't pull the reins!
Just lift self up and lower down;
Keep rhythm with the horse."

I started out with another stude
Who knew the ropes, the ups and downs,
Nor did he pull the reins.

Soon we came toward a barn so large,
She smelled the hay and galloped toward
Her morning breakfast food.

She went up when I went down,
She went down and I flew up.
I didn't pull the reins.

I bent down and leaned far out
As far as I could reach.
Thus, off I slid on to the grass.

"What was her name?" You ask.
It really was Grace-Filly;
And that is how, from Grace I fell
Though that may sound so silly.

Ann Laufer

Your Work of Art

As I walked among the flowers
I stopped and looked around
To welcome life's treasures
And its beauty to be found
I thought how much I'm grateful
For what God has given me
And I close my eyes in gratitude
For life has been good to me

I go about my daily life as busy as can be
But so often I do not stay around
To see what I should see
And so much I could miss in life
If I don't take the time
To know that what is yours
Is that which is also mine
Oh! The days go by the years pass
And how often do we say
Thank you God for your work of art
That brightens each and every day

Sylvia Blamires

A Tribute to Mother

Heaven must surely be a lovelier place
And must shine with a brighter glow,
Now that my mother is abiding there,
It's a happier place, I know.

God surely needed her in that beautiful realm,
So he beckoned from Heaven's door
And called her home to dwell with Him there,
With loved ones and angels forevermore.

This world became too corrupt, I believe
For a life that was free from sin,
So God said, "Well done; it is finished, my faithful one,
Lay down thy cross, enter in."

She left such a beautiful legacy
That her children could freely claim,
(Not earthly goods, for of these she had few;)
But title to Christ's precious name.

Oh God, let us walk ever close by thy side
And live our lives so like her own,
That when life is through, we may meet as one
Unbroken circle at your great throne.

Juanita Daniel

The Lord's Helping Hands

Our Lord has very precious hands
that carry out His work.
They work all day from dusk till dawn
and even when they hurt.

They're gracious, loving, precious hands
that never seem to end.
We see them in our daily walk.
We simply call them friends.

God loves His beautiful hands that help
and never ask for praise.
For what is done in secret,
our Lord will openly repay.

Sandra R. Lawrentz

It's All About Me

Long hair, Short hair
Blue eyes, Green eyes
Black or White
We're all the same
Take a look at me and daydream me in fear.
Open your eyes and watch me pull my long black beautiful hair back.
Look at me and see you and me forever until Eternity.

Karen Justice

Remembering You, Grandpa

I remember your strong, comforting arms,
that held me when I cried,
I remember your warm chuckle,
that lighted me up inside.

I remember your whiskers,
you'd rub against my cheek.
I remember your stern face,
that made me feel so meek.

I remember your strong hands,
holding onto mine.
I remember how you smiled,
your eyes seeming to shine.

I remember all of these things,
to which I hold so dear.
It will always be yours, Grandpa,
whose love I hold so near.

Lisa Christians

Homicide of the Red Baron

I remembered his face from then —
    And when I considered my life's destiny,
I remembered his face —
    And it looked to the trees . . . and to the sky . . . in the maine.

His hair was browner and longer then . . .
    His eyes were more innocent and far more shallow then . . .

Yet when I peered across the grassy knoll,
    I found an image of change;
The fall had eclipsed his nature qualities,
    And he laughed fiercely with his own contentedness.

He listened to the music of the guns as they pounded into the hides;
He smiled with the nourishment of life between his teeth as he
    chewed slowly.

His hair glistened red under the moonlight,
    Perhaps dye from the unwanted and unlived.
And his cherubic face was covered by his hair's new found freedom
    To lash out into the world.

His eyes no longer held the innocence of my youth,
    Rather, the anger of his pressurized world.
His irises were blood-red; for once, they were true . . .
    And I felt the presence of murder.

Rachel Olson

Progressive Illness

To have the sun over me,
To own this world of warmth,
And bathe in all the brilliant hues.
To sit with the sun shining over me,
Warming my body that warms itself no longer;
Warming my soul, and so lighting
Its backward glance into this life.
To see, to hear, to feel, to touch:
Glad prisoner I've been for years to these;
Now — in their wane - I'll soon be free.
Now they fail me — and how shall I go?

S. Daniel Piper

Till Death Do Us Part

Till death do us part,
For you are forever in my heart.
Our love is like the snow white dove,
For you are my one true love.

Till death do us part,
Until this tragic day we do depart,
And many days further on,
My love for you will last forever and on.

Till death do us part,
you will always own my heart.
For your kindness and your caring speaks true,
forever and through.

Till death do us part,
For you are forever in my heart.
Until this tragic day we do depart,
Till death do us part.

Crystal Regueiro

Graveyard of Lost Memories

In the blackest night new moon high; I sit
No Signs of life in this graveyard of lost memories
Where distant pains seem so far away

Over rolling black hills and past deep black seas
Across the clouds and past the furthest star: I soar
To find myself and to find meaning

Flying within myself the blackness is deafening
And the silence is not calm; I flee
Somewhere else but here in this graveyard
Where dead memories lie, where lost pain
Is so evident yet so far behind

Through blind eyes I see what I really am
My dying soul and my tears burn my cheeks
As I weep for all that's lost in this graveyard

Through deaf ears I hear the silence
That speaks a thousand words of chaos
And of blackness and of death in this graveyard

Through a mute voice I scream
But will anybody hear my cries
In this graveyard of a distant world

Kimberly Penna

Legend

Yonder lies a vast domain
In peace it claims its mighty reign
Yet, upon a time, the legends tell
How red and white, both fought and fell.

The red on granite spires stand
To defend their lives and land
Against the cavalry in gold and blue
Whose leaders spoke with tongues untrue.

Across the prairie vast they ride
Two abreast in gallop stride
Their journey shortens, soon they'll meet
One in valor, one defeat.

An Indian leaps, his blade stained knife
Takes an enemy's mortal life
But death to is his, for in his chest
A cavalry sword soon comes to rest.

Victory goes not to the soldiers that came
But rather to Sitting Bulls's Sioux Nation by name
Who fought for the freedom their fore-fathers knew
In the battle of red, gainst the gold and the blue.

Shirley Kelley

Trade-In

Dear Old Car, today I have this funny secret ache,
Knowing that a deal was made and it will take you from us.
It's foolish, but I feel this touch of sadness.
We shared so much, old friend - such precious intimate hours.
You knew our soaring love, our fears, eavesdropped on quarrels,
Absorbed my foolish tears when things went wrong. And oh, our
Crabbing trips were fun! First just the two of us and you,
And then our son was born. You waited at the hospital door
With pride, You shared our miracle on that short ride!
Later, with baited breath, we listened for your ills
Your coughs, your groans, your wheezing on the hills.
We'd agonize right with you at the shop - no matter
What was wrong we didn't stop to count the cost. We needed you!
In fact you were a part of us. That's why today
I can't endure a backward glance. You see, I feel this little
Touch of sorrow - for part of our youth will leave with you tomorrow.

Helen M. Lynch Syvrud

Precious Ode of Saint Valentine

Oh Precious, I feel that I could run to the top of any Mountain, to
the bottom of any Valley, through any Scenic Garden, From our
first sight of Dawn, through the high sight of Noon, to the Eve of
Dusk, onto the High Moon Night, from the beginning of our
Journey, to Victory we shall pass. Oh yes, the Beauty of our Earth,
we could go to our given Garden, and disappear as one into
Heaven, the Kingdom of God. Onto our Utopian Headquarters,
we perceive the Ultimate, where billions of Angels of Heaven are
at work on our Garden Haven. A wish of Serenity for you Precious,
your Heart's special ways are in my World of Truth Love. As I pierce
my Cupid's arrow onto you my Love, and lay down my bow, quiver,
and arrows, as you behold my Love wound upon your blood, I add
love upon your heart. As twus my embracement, I will awaken at your
side with unsleep for a week, to view your total existence, and then to
momentarily leave your scene of earthly beauty, to return providing
you an understanding of our Father's Enlightenment of Souls, to
understand the True Principles of Love, and to show you how we too
can merge to become one of the Billions. Ah to teach and show you
the heavenly secrets of life for the rest of time. Oh my Lady Special
so dear of Honey, and most Precious Princess, I truly "Love You."

Mark Dreadin

Moriah - The Wind - The Power

There is a force in these old hills,
Call it energy if you will.

This force is as old as heaven and earth,
With a breath from God, He gave it birth.

You cannot see it, like man to man,
Though it can move you from where you stand.

To the Indians, Moriah is the name,
Without it, these hills we could not claim.

For there is water beneath these hills,
And without the wind, it would be there still.

The towers that stand, made of steel or wood,
Are monuments man makes to a life we call good.

The wind turns the wheels that pumps the rods up and down,
Then the water flows forth, from deep under the ground.

This energy man harnessed in these hills years ago,
To make the cattle king, what we call "Sandhills Gold."

Now man has returned with new knowledge and might,
Using the wind, the homes he can light.

Our fathers knew then, what man is relearning,
It's a source of power, this wind and the wheels it is turning.

Terri Ann Licking

What So Long Unspeakable Was

Just in a moment, I happened
upon that which unspeakable was for
never would light be shed upon that
kept shrouded secret the woman denies — her
one, most guarded pleasure.

Mts. Peak-round, in a point, a plateau-
and define skyline as tho
sketched by another's hand action,
that of the artist, sculptor,
unleashing the spirit of Art,
refining raw material stroke
by stroke until
all that was not is
the immediate, an arching of the back
in pleasure, a tensing,
now before letting
go.

Rudy Thomas

When I Am Old

When I am old,
the waves of the hours
shall lap gently at my feet
murmuring (still) of pleasure and of pain.

And we shall laugh together, time and I
of all the fixes I got myself in . . .
of all the grand plans and "clever schemes"
of how almost perversely simple it all was, in the end
of how he pretty near had me fooled then,
time . . . When I was young.

When I am old,
the gentle waves of the hours
shall lap like squinting new-born pups against my belly
— their innocence and little urgencies met now

With a wrinkled smile.

Dylan Newcomb

Small Talk

(Kim) . . . I heard Carvin's a poet.
(Carol) . . a poet . . . I don't think so,
I think he's awfully sexy but then again what do I know.

(Gail) . . . Well I think he's black and pretty,
tall and handsome, outgoing and witty.

(Lisa) . . . I think he's loving . . . caring, laid back and shy,
and I just love to look at him with his gorgeous bedroom eyes.

(Kim) . . . ladies, ladies . . . I'm sure he's heard it all,
somethings nice and some that stink, but nothing really seems to
matter . . . except what Debbie thinks.

(Gail) . . . who is Debbie?

(Carol) . . . and why does her opinion outweigh the rest.
(Kim) . . . well . . . I can't really say I know but I think this
says it best.
What we say is just okay who cares I don't think he does,
but what she thinks carries so much weight . . .
because it's Debbie that he loves.

Carvin Winans

These Days

People hate, hurt, and kill others today.
What's happening to the world these days?
The wars, the guns, the drugs, the
hatred leads us to deaths and departures.
What's happening to the world these days?
In church we pray for everything
to change but again we hear on T.V.
Dead! From a gunshot to the head.
What's happening to the world these days?
You run outside and look around
no one's there, there is no sound.
What's happening to the world these days?
Now that is it, it is the end, the
world is gone, we all are dead.

Roanne Recio

My Lady

My lady, shines and sparkles. Forever gleaming, like
thirty billion stars, on a warm summer night. When I
am sleep, I dream of only her, lying peacefully by my side.

A deep inner passion, burns in me, when I am, away from her.
I long for her tenderness. Very, very, very
deeply, I love my woman.

I hold her so close to me, when we are together. She
sets my mind at ease, with her very presence. I realize,
how much I am blessed. Love, is just a moment away.

Every time that we kiss, we remember, what a soft
touch, a gentle smile, a smooth hello, and a tender
embrace, can do for the soul.

When we look deeply, into each other's eyes. We feel
so much ecstasy. Our minds, hearts, and bodies move
in unison. We know that we are, meant to be together.

Loving each other, with all that our souls will allow.
We are one, with each other. Forever, moving toward
the light.

Robert Augustus Young

Set Me Free, Dear God

Heavenly vision. Lofty realm.
Oh, to some day see thy perfection.
My waking angel stirring reverently within bids me hasten.
List, "Arouse from thy slumber, child of dreams.
The highest peaks of mountain tops await thee.
The stars beckon to hold thy counsel.
There, shalt thou hold communion
And singing together, thou shalt ask and receive."
Dear Gods of divinity—Pendulous thing am I
Swinging in moods from earth to sky.
Let me feel Thy soft enchanting spell, surge out to roll on roll-
And from within-put forth to touch,
And breathe back to within again.
Bring forth my inner self -
Desire, ideal, a thing to touch and feel.
Set me free, dear God, that I may come to walk with Thee.

Kathlyn Humphrey Laughray

Recycled Dreams

You ask what happens to dreams deferred?
I say they return to be dreamed once more.
For each dream has potential that cannot be disturbed.
Each longs to be lived, not left at the door.
Now the un-lived dream can never find peace.
Alone in worlds of no faith and less love.
Its inner voice rages and will never cease
Until someone believes and holds it above.
Martin and Malcolm both dared to dream freedom,
But theirs was a dream that has been handled down
From the African prince who had once known a kingdom
To Black children whose world faces them with a frown.
So I'll tell you what happens to dreams deferred.
They pass from mother to daughter, father to son.
They travel in silence, not even a word.
Till someone believes and their battle is won.

Jason Akin Nappier

La Luna

Goddess of night, Stock still she stands.
Her face distorted and beautiful,
moonlight shimmers in her hand.
Listen! Hear her soft sighs at midnight.
Look! Her tears bathe the grass.
She walks westward, night is past.

Stare into the sun with star-struck eyes.
Don't believe his beauty,
No don't believe his lies.

La Luna, L'Amour.

Her soft light exposes his lies.
She appears and his beauty dies.
She is perfect, infallible. Oh! Watch her rise!
Her words are doctrine. There is music in her voice.
Gaze upon her...rejoice!

Oh, La Luna, J'amour Tu.
Mon Cherie, J'amour Tu.
Mon amour, I love you.

Jason Parsley

Sensory Pleasures

On a Country Stroll

At Sunset Down South

The feel of warm dry sunshine fills the dusk
— remnant of the day's mid-summer heat;
While now and then the honeysuckle's musk,
from yonder low rock-wall, makes breathing sweet.

A rambler rose in wild profusion spread
her savage beauty blossomed deepest red.

A twilight flight of birds through green tree-tops
— turtle-doves on homeward-beating wings.
From bushy clump a cat-bird's call now drops;
hushed silvery silence — then a cricket sings.

Oak branches picture-calm, majestic, rise:
Dark leafy interlacings 'gainst the sky.

The first faint star appears amidst the blue
— joined by two's and three's in gathering dark.
As below the tiny fire-fly, too,
fights deepening gloom with festive flashing spark.

Now, hidden-perched in pines, the whip-poor-wills
begin their plaintive, quaint rolled-whirring trill.

All nature waits the magic rising moon;
— another August evening's gone...too soon!

Garland B. McClaran

Will I Walk His Way

    If Jesus would come today,
would I be strong enough to walk his way?
We are living in a space we call our time.
But, my heart is in pain, so I wrote this rhyme.
    A young man of 14 died today, I hope
his parents can remember his yesterdays.
I did not know this boy at all, but, in my heart
he will stand very tall. The reason for this is
that I have a son of my own, he is the seed,
that I have sown.
A child should have a right to grow, so his father
can watch what he did sow.
    I pray that he will watch over us all, and one
day when he finally will call. I meet this young
boy for whom I shed these tears, who made me think
of my son and all of my fears.
    So in closing I must say, I'm all cried out for today.
Please be careful at work and play, so I won't have to cry for
you someday, I suppose when it really counts I can walk his way.
For I love you all each and everyday,

David A. Miller

Praying Simeon

Old Man, what is that soft radiance
which lightly beams from your whitened hair?

"My son, it is the Afterglow of prayer -
that lingering illumination
of a promise for my messianic share."

Old Man, what is that deep brilliance
which fills the vision of your ancient eyes?

"My son, it is the Innerglow of prayer -
that holy preparation
by God's Spirit in my heart, His hope to bear."

Old Man, what is that New-born Essence
gently cradled in your weathered hands?

My son, He is the Everglow of prayer,
Who draws my heart around His infinite, infant form
to enfold me in His Presence there."

David Laeger

Was It Right?

Was it right for Oliver Cromwell back in 1649,
To command the brutal slaughter
    of the people of Drogheda town
There, many Men and Women
    and even innocent infants too,
Fell victim to the savagery
    of his roundheads Vile crew.
The town was taken over
    by the English and Scotts too,
While thousands of dispossessed Irish
    to Connaught were forced to flee.
Eking out a meek existence was their cruel destiny.

Southward the roundheads plundered,
    subduing all in their path.
There was no real escape,
    judging from Drogheda's fate.
The defenders of Wexford,
    put up a gallant fight.
But another brutal slaughter,
    was their unfortunate destiny.

Teresa Martin

A Tribute to Mom and Dad

For giving me hugs and kisses, nearly every day.
And all the love and support in your unselfish ways.

For teaching me when things go wrong or times get tough;
To hang in there, be strong but never give up.

For bringing me laughter instead of tears,
With hopes and dreams instead of fears.

For raising me to have faith in God up above,
And for the beautiful wedding with bells and white doves.

For all the times, you held me when I was sick,
This too, is something I can never forget.

For you're "One In a Million!" You're the "cream of the crop!"
'Cuz you're the "Best Parents!" and I think you're the "Tops!"

And so, with each new year that comes and goes,
I'll always love you and wanted you to know!

I am honored to call you, "My Mom and Dad!"

Terri A. Tysver

Lost Innocence

It was me that let you inside
as if I had nothing to hide
no fear of rejection
just longing and waiting for affection
to be a child and act like a woman
is not at all what it is thought to be
it releases great fear from inside of me
I guess once you've lost the sweet innocence
of the virgin youth that you carry to me it is
something that feels quite scary
had I not known that this was a very dear choice
had I not heard it in my own voice
did I not listen to what my heart mind and soul had to say
had I only been more careful from day to day
was I so young that I did not know how to control
control the passion that was in my soul
was I weak did I not understand or was this something
given up on demand as harsh as it may sound it was something that
left me quite profound when I grow older I will clearly see my
childish reasons for letting you inside of me

Chloe Gallaway

The Man That You Are

Be the man that you are,
    And not the man that your friends want you to be.

Be the man that you are,
    And you will be truly be happy and free.

Not a slave to what others tell you should be,
    If no one accepts as you that man that you are

Just smile and say I love you anyway
    For you can't please any and every one from afar.

Develop your mind to be strong and your will to be the same,
    For you have much to give and much to gain.

So, my brother, my love, don't listen to others
    For they don't always have your best interests at heart

Always to try to finish whatever you start,
    And that goes for building friendships and love.

We have so little time on earth to seek what we want and
    need, so let's make the best of what we have from God's gift
    from above.

Gwendolyn Robinson

The Natural Flow

We learn from the trees to grow, and to bend, with the flowers we see,
we can all be friends. In the mountain, we see, we must stand our
ground, yet the wind shows us that we can't stay down. The moon shows
there is always a light-even on our darkest night. Our sun teaches us
that we must glow from within, time tells us, all our wounds will mend
Animals teach us how to survive, but with care - the birds
teach us to let our hearts sing, to fill the air.

The rainbows shows us we're all beautiful, and equally unique - we've
learned to adapt, just as the bend in the creek. The grass shows us
how to rise above, no matter how often we've been cut down - the rain
shows us we can cry - let go of any pain we have found. Thunder
teaches us we can set our anger free, the blue sky shows us we have no
boundary. Like the ocean our spirits roll on and on, and death shows
there's a stage for everyone. In birth, we know, we don't have to end
we can return again and again.

Our Mother Earth tries to show us each passing day; it's important
what we do, and not what we say.

If we expect the best, then the best is what we will know —
And we must abide by the natural flow.

Rebecka Deatherage

Equal Rights?

I never asked for equal rights, but I got them anyway. Not only must
I cook, clean and shop, I also have to go to work everyday. I make
the beds every morning, make breakfast, clean it up and off I go, to
my nine to five job, for which I get paid, if only at home that were
so. With the kids growing up so quickly, I try to be understanding.
Who says they need you more when they're young? I find teenagers much
more demanding. Now I have to ask to use the car, and Heaven forbid I
tie up the phone They're never in the house when I'm not there, but, I
still get no time all alone. And when that man of mine gets home from
work, he's hungry and tired, what a sight! And after what I've been
through all day, it's tough being a sex goddess at night. So, what.
did they change, these equal rights? They stole my soap operas,
flowers and candy. And if he's not around to do a repair, it is I who
must be handy. With working all day and running a home, there's not
even time to get my hair curled. "We've come a long way baby," and do
most of the work. So why is it still a man's world?

Milly Murphy

Let's Protect This Beautiful Orb

The beauty of a rain forest is a sight for all eyes to behold. In
its deep, dark, interior there are many conflicts that are untold.
Cunning, strength, and camouflage are used by its occupants to stay
alive A delicate balance designed by the Creator, to give all life a
chance to survive.

Each plant, insect, and animal, will carry out their role in a
delicate balance. Life ends for some, others survive, so their
species may live in abundance. The Rain forests fragile eco-system,
is very important for all life on earth. Without the forests, human
life would slowly decline, around our entire planets girth.

The geographical locations of the rain forests, was planned by our
creator. As were the oceans, mountains, deserts and streams from the
polar regions to the equator. The oceans and forests give us oxygen,
control the climate, and enrich our soil. The sun gives its light,
then descends for the night, and sometimes volcanoes erupt and boil.

The marine life in earth's waters, have an Eco-system beyond compare.
And the beautiful fowl which fly in our skies, of their number, we are
unaware. The very stars and planets in the heavens, had precise orbits
planned out eons ago. And only earth itself can sustain known life -
as far as anyone knows.

It is up to us, the human race, to protect what our creator has
endowed. We must not burn the rain forests, pollute the oceans, or
use chemicals behind the plow. We must find and use clean burning
fuels, and stop polluting our precious air. Then maybe — just maybe
— we too will survive on this tiny orb that we all share.

Robert L. McCaslin

Ruthless

I used to have a girlfriend,
Back in East Tennessee.
I called her my baby Ruth,
She meant the world to me.
Then I went and left her,
She didn't know I was gone.
I need some help from someone,
'Can't depend on Mrs. Jones.
I used to be so careful.
of what I said and done,
I'll never get my baby back.
I'll be Ruthless from now on,
She's married to another.
My life has come undone,
I'll never get my baby back.
I'll be Ruthless from now on.

Hugh R. DePew

Good Moaning Pope

Somoan Square Dance
on my church floor
Priest thinks of love
Behind the door
Crucifix hangs alone
Man pleads to God
forget the past
Tonight awaits
In black
Push the faith
It's all u got
In your fist
In your pocket
faith in God
Like an exploding rocket
shooting to heaven in a million redeemed
pieces

Michael Rodriguez

Agony

Beaten, battered, and torn
My Mind
Hungry for love and affection
My Body
Shattered, shaky, and stricken
My Nerves
Desired is the caressful touch
My Skin
Depression, gloom, and despair
My Thoughts
Satan is clutching, death is lurking
My Soul
Fear of the unknown, fear of the present
My Spirit
Crumbling, falling apart
My Marriage
She has left, love is gone
My Wife
Lost into a world of one
My Agony

Terry Cochrane

Candy

In memory of our beloved Black Lab.

You were always there
when no one seemed to care
you gave me so much happiness
and plenty of love to share.

You were always by my side
and you sat tall with such pride
you were my best friend
I can't wait until we meet again.

Now that you're gone
I'm sad and alone
and living with a broken heart
but spiritually we'll never be apart.

I loved you so much
and I miss your touch
you loved me for me
and that meant so much.

If only you knew
how much we miss you
our love is still genuine and true.

Shellie Coombs

Summer Song

I want to die in summertime
When sunshine bursts the yellow rose
The ground is soft for digging graves
And folks can wear their summer clothes

When sunshine bursts the yellow rose
The sounds of crickets fill the trees
And folks can wear their summer clothes
The sails go puffing in the breeze

The sounds of crickets fill the trees
The green moss dries upon the wall
The sails go puffing in the breeze
And no one thinks of death at all

And no one thinks of death at all
When sunshine bursts the yellow rose;
I want to die in summertime
And wear to death my summer clothes

Janet B. Hubbs

Yellow Wood Two

Emily, how 'bout you and me
Through Yellow Wood a-walking go
Heart in hand, my dearest leaping dear;
Those micro-garlands you delivered,
Soldered heart-land's tender lions
Diviner crimes left untangled,
Offer all the macro-jangle, nexus,
Glimpses of the robbin-hopping maker;
We could share the capture raw.

Captive in this world, my sweeter,
Captive in this world of senses,
Seeking out the senseless, circles,
Rings around the collar, rosy.
Pick the flower; dissect, describe it;
Name it; blame it for the crucifixion;
Pruger hours with that vector;
But we, my Emily, captured nectar,
Captives in the world, my sweetest.

Dennis S. Nelson

Memories

Dedicated to my brother Jerome Britt

I will never know the fear you felt, when they called your name out
loud. To board the plane or ship to sea, the leaving of your home.
To put aside the banners from your last football game, who would have
known you'd never be the same. So many alike to win the fight, an
average age of eighteen. Who stepped into an unknown world of pain
and misery. I will never know the fear inside, the fires. The smoke.
The anger. The running of blood like rivers wild and the waste of
lives. And wives the children stand alone. No where to run, no where
to hide it could be over in a second. And how you must have pushed on
to win the fight, to get the job done. To keep your reputation clean
and straight, but they still hate and do not understand. The dirt,
the sand and they all hold, hands in the dark of the night, just to
win the fight. In the Barricks of straw, candles burn until dawn, the
pot and magazines. Beer and wine and every things fine. A hoax of
everyday. It's hell, the smell surrounds your thoughts I know, to be
back home wishing of "Pots of Gold: To be removed from this endless
horror and trauma but for our country you did go. So unrecognized you
apologize for crying as you do, if they could have only walked and
felt wet socks, from ditches to deep to see bottom. The snakes and weeds
could make one bleed and plead. But to win the fight. You did go.

Melody Ferron

We, the American People, and the Foreign Lobby . . .

In USA "all animals are equal," if they silent and obedient crawl,
and "Foreign Lobby" advises the President when he is "out of Order."
As the Roman Empire with its mighty armies was before to fall
our USA Government is sparing of us: every year
under a political trick or other we are overtaxed.
We are jailed more than any other Nation does. Barbaric considered
in all civilized world — the Death Sentence — is "Accepted" by
whom Supreme Court? Mass Media under the masquerade of "Presenting
the News" advocates taking away our Freedoms and Liberties. Our
mothers after birth in hours are thrown out from Hospital beds,
while on the streets the "Politician Dogs" are empowered to take
away our Houses with the Judicial process only after. In the Courts
our word has no value while the Dogs' is the "law." Judges of being
honest are assaulted by Mass Media and Hyksos call for their
dismissal. Every year more restrictive laws are thrown over us while
more "law abiding" crooks are becoming "respectable citizens" at whose
Parties politicians drink, take contributions and are merry. We are
an occupied Nation, our conquerors are the invisible Hyksos.

Ion Vulcanescu

My Final Trip

When the doctor told me I didn't have HIV it was a big relief,
His finishing by saying I had full blown AIDS was beyond all belief!
Family members and friends shunned me, I guess they didn't know how to cope
But because they were afraid they denied me of their love, the
    very essence of all my hope.

I lost my family, my pride, but I never lost my self respect
As I crippled to doctor visits and hospitals always wondering, "What will it be next?"
A slight rise in my T-Count was always a big motivator for me to see
Because I'd eat like a horse, gain more weight, but in the end it too failed me.

There was a daily nuisance of medications, IVs, as it steadily grew more difficult to walk,
All these were tolerable, but what I needed most was friends to visit, just to talk!
I knew my days were numbered because with AIDS no one has ever won,
So I lived each day fully not knowing if the next would be my very last one.

Lying in the hospital bed I heard voices, I saw Hazel, my dear mother's face
She sobbed as Bob Anderson, my minister sang my favorite song, "Amazing Grace."
The light shined brighter, I could see silver clouds, a snow white dove I could also see,
I didn't realize it but my life's end on earth was fast approaching me.

Someone said reach out your hand Tim, God wants you to come home,
Just take His hand, Go to the mansion He has promised where you'll never be alone.
My lifeless crippled hand reached out to Jesus, I felt his warm firm grip
All my life I had prepared for this day and hour, as I began my final trip.

George R. Nash

Vision

As I stare into the mirror, it's plain to see what's there
I'm the vision of my mother, her eyes, her smile and her hair
Yes, her hair was soft and silky and so fine
Her eyes were understanding and they shined
Her smile was as wide as any sea, and to this day, she watches over me
My mother was the one with that special touch
And that is why I loved her oh so much
It's been years since she's passed on, and yet there are moments Ifeel alone
Even though I have a husband and a young child of my own
I would give anything to put my arms around the woman that I'll always adore
To kiss her, to hug her, to tell her I love her once more
A mom is but one, and can never be replaced by another
God grant me this wish, let me grow up to be just like my mother

Ada Serafino

The Enchanted Garden

In the middle of the forest where the golden pond stands still full of
memories; fragile petals made of tears, float quietly while the magic
boat of life carrying broken dreams and hopes sails alone its emerald
banks doted with flowers, writing silent poetry on the water.

At the crossroads to eternity, nine white peacocks with their silver
feathers as an armor freely roam without fear at the encounter with
tomorrow, while the mysterious path of yesterday seems to touch them
for an instant with a whisper.

Tall trees made of courage grow abandoned among crimson ruins of
ancient sorrows lost forever in the dust. Deep blue rivers of emotions
flow slow, like loose ribbons, over a vast valley of illusions
knocking on forgotten doors at the magic tower of desire.

Fate sits, gazing on the eternal rock of wisdom while surreal iron horses
fly against the endless time as their wings play mysterious lullabies
of silence with the wind.

Night approaches, and moonlight stars blazing with its fire,
illuminating the long road, at the threshold where the barefoot soul
meets its destiny long before chosen in the middle of a dream . . .

Pablo Molgora

Avenged

As consciousness fades, my eyes close on their own I see images of the
life I just left in my mind's eye The images are so real, so vivid,
that if I could reach out I could touch them I could feel the pain,
the hurt, the rejection caused on each person as it seeps into me my
mother, the ever gracious hostess, her eyes filled with loneliness
from seeing her only daughter waste her life on a merry-go-round my
father, the hero, his murderous face as he found out where I had
been spending my time . . . and my energy my lover, the forbidden, the
fear in his eyes, the shock in his face as the knife went through his
flesh and into his heart there is blood everywhere, as briefly
struggling for a knife, a vital mistake is made my father, in his
rage, in his hatred for a lower class, for what I should not have
played with in fire, has now killed my eyes fly open; it's a dream,
then settle on the scene before me my father has killed my lover, he's
standing over him still plunging the knife into his long-dead heart I
grab the knife from my father's white knuckled hands he turns his face
towards me and I see the tears in his eyes for his little girl, no
longer so little the rain falls from the sky; it washes the blood from
my hands and masks my tears my tears for the life inside me that will
never know its father.

Chandra Hodges

Untitled

My heart is like the restless wind.
It can not long desist its flight;
Searching, searching, yet to find
The object of its ceaseless plight.

Another heart may share its love.
In human friendship peace is sought.
Its yearning, though, remains above.
Too soon this also turns to nought.

Sadness, comes, it wanders still.
Fighting self, trying, trying . . .
Nothing will its desires fulfill.
Losing ground, dying, dying.
My heart has wandered night and day,
Dreaming, dreaming its goal to see.
But now it halts. It hears you say
"No one finds rest, except in Me."

Joseph Claussen

The Future

Laying looking at the stars
thinking of so many things
that are keeping us apart;
No worry my fear is gone
for I look at me and you
and see a love forever true.
The longer I think of you
the more I miss
the pounding heart
I desire to kiss.
As the season past,
I knew our love would last.
For you were a man of love
And I an innocent turtle dove.
We settled hand-in-hand
And ended with a Wedding band.

Dana Lord

Nature

Sitting in the grass I can hear!
A woodpecker looking for a worm.
There are some squirrels.
They're scavenging for nuts in the leaves.
The wind is rustling through
colorful flowers.

Nathan W. Vogt

Feelings

I'd like to see what's going on
way deep inside your heart.
I'd like to know what bothers you
and causes us to part.
Could it be you feel alone
and have no way to turn?
Could it be the pain we've caused
and left your heart to burn?
Is it that eternal heat
that keeps a bright lit flame?
Or it is just the world's own way
of placing all her blame?
Will you ever come to see the
pain that lies within?
Do you even have a clue
of just where to begin?
I'll stand by you in all you do;
my heart is always here.
For heaven only knows; just
how much I really care.

Francia Walkes

361

Toys

We are just toys
placed on the earth.
No control over our lives
since the day of our birth.

We have no choice
about time and weather.
To the player, the earth
is as light as a feather.

But someday,
we will meet him face to face,
the player, our maker
in his holy place.

Stephanie Yazinski

Whenever

Whenever I am away from you
I am so blue
Cause I want you to be my only
I am so lonely
Each day goes by
I just can't lie
The strong feelings I feel
I just want you to see
They are growing so strong
But it has taken us so long
For two people so far apart
You are forever in my heart
I just want you beside me
This is my plea
My love for you could last forever
If we both can say whenever

Richard C. Young

Once In A While

I have a mind that can think
I have a mouth that can speak
Hands that can work

What I feel can be felt
What I say can be heard
What I do be acknowledged

I have ideas of my own
I make decisions of my own
Follow through with them on my own

What I think is accepted
What I say is considered
What I do is tolerated

There is peace of mind
Nothing to be said
Nothing to be done

And once in a while
To the Lord I do pray
That once in a while
Becomes every day

Steve Kallas

Beans

Hot, cold
Jumping, hopping, bopping
All kinds of them
Me.

Katrina (Beaner) Valentine

Water Is Life

Water is our life.
Giving us different personalities.
Water is our blood.
Flowing inside our body,
Like wild rivers.
Like a loving mother it nurses us,
Feeding us nutrients.
Without it we cannot survive.

Water is our brain,
Like a compass,
Guiding us to discover the wonders,
To analyzing the mysteries.
And to exploring the great adventures.
Without it we cannot succeed.
Soothing our tempers.
Quenching our thirst.

Xue Liu

Reflections

Reflections of a tie gone by,
Reflections and a tired sigh,
Reflections of a younger day,
Reflections of a different way,
Reflections of a pretty girl,
Reflections make a bitter world,
Reflections of a time gone by,
Reflections make me wonder why,
Reflections make me sad and blue,
Reflections and I think of you.

Lowell Tracy

In Your Looking Glass

Do you see me in your looking glass
    so wild and free?

Or do you see me in your looking glass
    standing next to thee?

Do you see in your looking glass
    your children and me?

Or do you see your
    children minus me?

Is there any chance that you see
    me in your looking glass?

Or do you see yourself
    alone and empty?

Melissa E. Royal Aguirre

On Second Thought

Nothing ventured nothing lost
But this adventure what the cost!
To lose myself to find just me
To think that all I want could be
What price we pay
To deem us free

For chains to some are burdens laid
On shrouded shoulders to the grave
To others chains may different be
A link to some their destiny

And so the love I've kept inside
Will leave my hearts forsaken pride
My dreams though some be cast aside
No longer live only denied
This life has been a foolish pride

Marilyn Bowers

Dark blue night over the
moor. Cresting the hill a
pale horse, frenzied, charges.

Micaela Cook

Girl In White

Hair flying dressed in white
Young girl running Oh! So light.
Weaving rhythms there she flows.
Drawing glances as she goes.
Bloom young thing: Enwrapped by time.
Hold fast to dreams: To joys sublime.

Old youth hide from she to See.
Her life is yet too new for Thee
Glow dear Life
Glow on for She
Is young life Scrambling to be Free.

Marie T. Thomas

Let Go, Let God

I had a problem, I took to God.
for me the problem was too hard.
So I stood around to watch him solve
The problem I could not resolve.
I watched him tinker and putter around,
While my face was growing into a frown.
I thought by this time he'd be through,
for I know, he knew, just what to do.
But, at last, I took it back,
for patience was something I did lack.
Then I asked him what was wrong.
Why was he taking so long?
Then he looked at me for awhile.
Then started speaking with a smile.
he said, "My son, if you can see,
You never did give your problem to me.
It seemed that I was working slow,
for you never let your problem go."

Leonard Turley

Little School House

I remember my old school house
The sound of the bell
And the rocks we threw
Deep into the well
Smoke from the stove
Where wood we would learn
The many of books
In which would burn
The black board is hanging
Where we wrote on the wall
The rain coats are dripping
Where they hang in the hall
At recess we sing
Sometimes we play
When the loud bell would ring
Meaning the end of the day.

Danny R. Osborne

My Cat

Sammy my cat
Playful and fat
On haunches he sat
The main course a rat
Licking his lips
Shiny as silk
As he sips
A cup of milk
Then on my lap
To take a nap
Sammy my cat

Linda McCrorey

The Shoe

There one was a lady from lu
Who thought she lost her shoe
It was only stuck
And she said "what luck"
And than she cought the flu

Daniel Lurker

Body

Love your body
Like your mind
Two together can't be bad
Girls are girls, but I'm a lady
I love your body
And I want you more

No commitment
That's not a choice
But I'm a lady
And I love, love

One night stand, no thanks
I love your body
And I like your mind
Criticize me — scrutinize me
But I'm a lady and I love your love

Thanks, I can't feel like a man
But I know what I love
And I know what I like
You love my mind
And I love your body

Kimberly B. Marcelli

A Ghetto Child, Dreams

I'll like to go to Africa,
but Africa's too far.
I'll like to go to Hollywood,
but I'm not a star.
I'll like to go to China,
but I don't drink tea.
I'll like to go to France,
but I can't walk the sea.
So I'll stay in the Ghetto,
and I hope the rats and roaches
don't bother me.

Clifford Hill

Untruth

Love can leave you hungry
It'll dirty up your mind
Take everything you need
Then try hard to survive
Nothing keeps me sane
Nothing is my focus
I'm an empty box of solitude
With no one to comply
Agreement is a needle
And love is but a drug
But nothing's more addicting
Than reaching for a lie
Non-truth is better
Then everything is fine
But I've abandoned all of you
And now is not my time

Devon Connell

Thundering Hooves

Thundering hooves,
two armies merged with
rolling dust behind.
Each with victory
welled within,
deep within their minds.

Our hearts were pounding,
beating hard,
within our warrior's breast.
We fought for home,
our land, our lives,
for all that we had left.

When finally all
our foe had fell,
fallen to the warrior's cry,
we honored all
the brave men there
and left the dead to lie.

Dan Harr

Dawn of Future Evening of Past

Dawn of future
Evening of past
Presence of night
Leaving our grasp.

A chill of breeze
Touches today
Midnight fire
Showing the way.

Morning will come
With different scenes
But midnight fire
The evening it brings.

Dawn of future
Soon to appear
Evening of past
Soon to be near.

Wilson Scott Keyton

Lonely Reminders

Rows of houses
Stand as ghosts,
Sentinels to a war
Of abject hatred.
You see in their eyes
A sad resignation
Of things and scenes
Unseen by you and me.
But the children wave
And ask for candy.
While the men and women
Sow the fields
With crop instead of mines.
Way of life,
But anger simmers
As the houses are...still
Lonely reminders.

Michael James Mingee

They Will Never Know

They will never know
how hard it is
to cling to my life's blood
as sorrow pulls it through
my open wounds.
It seeps from the holes
of my heavy heart . . .
trodding down the thread of life
she pulls my strings
for I am a puppet,
broken from the hell
and torture of my fate.
The strands have slipped
from my grip
through the blood soaked
hands of death,
still cupping the juice
of my body drained . . .
from the strain of journey.
My path is marked in red.

Harley French

White

White is pure,
As pure as a child.
Small and sure,
Tiny and mild.

It's blank like paper,
Yet bold like a star.
Sometimes invisible like vapor
Sometimes seen from far.

Like a cloud you could say,
Big or small.
Snow melting away.
Snow starting to fall.

It has the blankness of soap
That is pure within.
The creaminess of milk,
The softness of linen.

What is white?
Only some can see
Its beauty in spite
Of its plainness, you see.

Liz Hansen

Jesus the Rock

You're the rock of my salvation.
You're the joy I feel today.
You're the rock of my salvation.
Each and every time I pray.

Cecelia Atwood

Tacitus Unturned

Yellowed pages crumble
glue long dehydrated
flakes off battered bindings
vague imprints on a spine...

Dust motes drift and sparkle
gold foil long since faded
gilt edges turn to powder
when sun lights on ancient lines...

In ages past these Latin texts
were heavily in use
but now they've changed curriculum
who knows what children learn
and on the shelf
    collecting dust
      leaves of *Tacitus*...
        unturned.

Noriko Low

I'm A Poet!

When I tell I am a poet,
I feel terribly meek.
I wonder if there's wonder
at what kind of attention I seek?
Yes,
one of each.
But poetry also gives me reach
for freedom from dogma,
so that who I am
cannot be statistically verified
with norms and means,
and such averaging liens.
I want license to be
different,
free,
and me.

No matter how it's always been done,
or said,
I beg the liberty
to pose an instead.

Janie Kent

Credo

Somewhere beyond
    the stars I see
it seems to be me
    there has to be
a Deity.

I cannot see
how there could be
    by chance alone
    a me.

Edward L. Brewton

Summer's Farewell

Leaves falling, fall's calling
summer to go away.
Fog's rising, not surprising
And night is stealing the day.
Pumpkins turning, cider's churning
As Autumn comes sneaking in.
Birds flying, people sighing
Summer has come to an end.

Karen T. King

I'm Your Sister I'm your Friend

No matter what is wrong
Even if the problem is long
I am here
So have no fear
I am at your side until the end
I'm your sister, I'm your friend

Have a tissue, wipe your eye
It hurts to see you cry
I'm going to help you somehow, someway
All night, all day
I'm at your side until the end
I'm your sister, I'm your friend

I can't make the pain step
I can't make bunnies hop
But I can be here for you
I'm your friend, as thick as glue
I'm at your side until the end
I'm your sister, I'm your friend.

Ashley Y. Robinson

Love

What is love?
A sudden recognition
A blinding flash from heaven?
Or is it slow, subtle, creeping
And all engulfing?
It is an eternal flame
That lights the mind
And sears the heart
Terrible in its beauty
Pain and joy.

M. A. B. Holmes

My Kissy Dog

She wobbles when she walks
She's my big fat kissy dog
She's my buddy and companion
She's my friend

Her ears drag the ground
When she walks all around and
Her belly leads the way for her behind

She's long as she is wide
She is always by my side and
She's always laying around my home

Every single day
She always comes my way
Begging me for a big ole milky bone

Andrea Fowler

Butterflies

I saw a butterfly rare
Flying through the air
I wondered where it would go
It seemed to move so very slow

Spreading beauty all around
With out making never a sound
Like a feather in the air
Floating free with out a care

I wondered if the butterfly knew
It could make me very blue
If it would fly away today
And never show me the way

Butterfly, butterfly where do you go
Flying high, flying low
Up above so very high
Like a diamond in the sky

Leo A. Bexten

Spirit

Take away my innocence . . .
Take away my time . . .
Don't take my spirit . . .
For it is mine.
Mine to set free . . .
Mine to hold dear . . .
Mine to share, or not . . .
For caring ears to hear.

Kathi Roulst

Broken Again

Why? Why? Why?
The love a lie?
The letter a cry!

Painful nights for me await
There is no other for my escape
I run to hide, yet hold you inside

Memories lay out
I have no doubt
That someday
Love will stay

Brian C. West

The Horse

From lightning in the sky
I saw the horse fly by
As the horse of storm
Took its true form
I was drawn to its eyes
As I sit here and die

Kari Milander

Dreams Are . . .

Dreams are growing flowers
living happily along in the garden.
Dreams are living ducks
gladly quacking along ashore.
Dreams are little bunnies
hopping joyously around a yard.
Dreams are flying butterflies
fluttering and dancing around a house.
Dreams are tasty apples
growing more red every evening.
Dreams are sparkling stars
showing sparkle in the night.

Jennifer Vares

Red

Red is my color
  such power it holds
Bright and beautiful
  lovely and bold
Bright red colors
  felt very deep
Sending the powers
  to bring on the heat
Red has no limit
  only to stop
When red lights flash
  you know its cop
Red is the sand
  along the Nile
So is the sky
  for only awhile
Red is a color
  for excitement and laughter
Red is my color
  now and here after

Renee George

When I Lived Home

We didn't have much
  When I lived home.
We just loved each other
And we went to church
  When I lived home.

Now everyone has to have "things"
And run around and "party."
It used to be more caring
  When I lived home.

We used to notice things
  When I lived home
Like how a tree had grown
Or how much fun a pet could be
  When I lived home.

Now our days are so full
There's not much time for noticing
Or for caring,
It's different now, than it was
  When I lived home.

Eileen D. McKenzie

One Step (Unity Move)

It's a new day now,
Old slippery feet.
It's a new day now
Can't skip to your beat.

No wobbling, no shaking,
Secure in strength.
Exalt me now, legs I say.
Thank God,
It's a brand new day!

Thank you heel and thank you toes.
You stuck fast, when problems arose
Steady support in your customary way
Now let us all Glory.
It's a brand new day!

Lynette Johnson

The Riddle of Love

We walk through life together
So let's make love again
We laugh and cry together
Is it love or sin?

Through each others ups and downs
Glories and humiliations
We will grow and evolve together
in different situations.

Even in death our hearts and souls
Will be filled with total commitment
it takes all of our sincerity
for our love to be fitted.

Totality and perfection
Creates a perfect pair
How can you be dedicated
if you just don't care.

We find our romantic piece of land
and put our naked bodies together
We wrap and twine with total lust
for our love of one another.

Stanley McCauley

Suspicious Circles

Suspicious circles enter
around our place and
laughingly we excuse their
aura, in hope of mending
their incompleteness.
Another suspicious circle
now entered the room and
danced in spherical manners
entertaining us all.
Round and round and round he went
encircling us all.

Dimitra Robokos

Legacy

A man may write
about the light in darkness
and densities absurd
too heavy to absorb

I fail to comprehend
the world will turn, turn
anyway
away

I spin about my spine
and try in vain to stay my veins
while you against this night
are the last night I see

A man may write
about his plight in darkness
or conjure after lives
for his soul's destiny

I hear the sound of time
measuring history
then the endless rush of space
envelops everything

William K. Lester

Terror

(April 19, 1995)
  The tragedy of dying
The deafening sound of a bomb
Concrete, steel, and granite
crushing peoples' bones
How could someone do this
to an innocent town
with children in the building,
  Rocks tumbling down
They are now in heaven
How we wish we could help
But they tell us to stay away
It is hard to face another day,
knowing that there are
people still trapped inside
and as they cry and scream
for help; only their echo
comes back to them.
But with their faith
and strength in God,
they will again see the light!

Lindie Beth VanAntwerp

Max

Unplanned,
Unwanted,
What do we do?

Prayer,
Counseling,
Your kicks helped too.

Nine months go by
Thank God for you!

Susan J. Powell

Looking for Love

Lonesome eyes
Tear without cries
Dolefully distilling all

From an unoccupied heart
Tirelessly awaiting
A loving sustenance
To fill its soul

Fervent with love
Acceptance, dreaming of
Committed to giving all

A wish everyday
Lonesome tears wiped away
By the loving heart
Of another

Gavin J. Durao

The path

  Everyday is winding path.
Twist and turns around every bend.
Never knowing what to expect,
but always recovering with sweet
words blowing from above. As the
river flows to its eternal place,
and so we travel, travel into our
eternal place.

Kimberly Gurr

An Angel On Your Shoulder

An angel on your shoulder
Always by your side
With an undying love
An angel on your shoulder
With the powers to chase away
    your fears
To turn the darkest day to light —
An angel on your shoulder
With the power to chase the cold
    away at night
To warm your soul
An angel on your shoulder

Angela Pedersen

The Dawn of a New Day

The dawn of a new day
lays me weary and astray.

Neglected by the qualms,
and besieged by the bombs,
yesterday will always follow
tomorrow. Today is still and
hollow.

Perhaps the future will spring
and eventually bring a new
beginning and usher out the
laments of thy sorrow.

Yesterday will see how the past
acts, and will shred my heart
intact. Maybe a mistake made
in the past won't hold me everlast.

Gordon L. Farr

Amy

Granddaughter Amy so like me,
it's only now that I can see.
I look at her in mild surprise
to find we have so many ties.

Happy carefree summer days
I'm finding now she has my ways,
rising early in the morn,
to find new kittens in the barn.

Playing softball, skating too,
and now I find there's something new.
Even more she likes to read
Amy dear you are what I need.

As she is now so once was I,
in childhood days, long gone by.

Mary Lou Adams

Ruth

From the land she had known
And familiar scenes of her life
She willingly went to the unknown
To aid Naomi in her strife.

Unselfish daughter-in-law,
Ruth passed the ultimate test.
Because of her love for Naomi
In posterity she was blessed.

Julia Keys Williams

Spirit of Halloween, A Child's View

I knew when I woke up today,
I could feel it under my skin.
The thing that happened a year ago...
was happening again.

I won't be who you see tonight
Grown-ups should beware.
I'll prowl your porch and doorsteps
until I get my fare.

So should you see me coming
Be ready with your sweets
This goblin only has one night
to gather all his treats.

And when tomorrow comes around
I'll just be me again
But every time I eat a sweet
The goblin winks and grins.

Dan O'Brien

A Star's Love

If love is an example
of a shining star,
then every place is well lit
wherever you are.

The light is compassion and
one can see you care,
it's what's most missing
when you're not there.

A star's love is genuine
and one of a kind,
I'm glad to have a star
as a sister of mine.

Larry Washington

My Treasure Chest

I walked along the beach today
and thought of you,
my friend
And all the memories of childhood
were there in my mind,
scattered like sea-born treasures
in the sand
to come upon
one at a time
and hold my attention
for a moment—

Only to be replaced
by another, brighter, more unusual
rock or shell
to be turned over in my hand
and appreciated in turn...

Then slipped into my pocket
along with the others
to take home and add to
my treasure chest.

A. K. Graca

My Blessing

The Lord really bless me,
He put a song in my heart.
A beautiful song, he wrote himself
And he let me do my part,
He let me hold the pen.

Arlene Reese Wooten

I Know Someone

I know someone who is wonderful,
He is all the world to me.
I watched him paint a forest,
Magnificent to see.

With all the dogwood blossoms
And branches of the pine,
He blended in their color,
Each tree a different kind.

For nearby was an orchard,
With blossoms on each tree,
And I knew soon on each blossomed twig,
Delicious fruit would be.

Then I looked upon the flowers,
That were blooming all around,
As I stood on His grassy carpet,
He had placed upon the ground.

He is our Lord and Savior,
Of whom we cannot see,
Except through His works of nature,
And the deeds of you and me.

Bleeka Boatright

My Soul

How I feel frustrated
How I feel lonely
on this vast land
no bounds
nor depths,
fathomless
like an ant in its shell, a black
crawling aimlessly,
no one can tell

A heavy heart
down trodden
a truant in life
I am of no use
vapor bound

Empty space
all over
all around
over my soul.

Namel Weeramuni

Fall

The wind is blowing everywhere
even in your hair.

Yellow, orange, red
falling everywhere.

Raking leaves is all you do
while the wind is pulling you.

When the leaves are raked so round
the wind loves to blow them around.

Stacie Rosenberg

My Spy Glass

Here I sit in the center of things,
Everywhere the scourge of
Evil climes the ladder
Of prominence.
Dressed in garb of benevolence.
Eager to influence
The vast majority.
We buy the goods of
Shabby manufacture
To our detriment.
Where is the yardstick
To measure good from evil?
How can we detect and
Punish the perpetrators?

Louis Schiff

Lost Awakening

It grows suddenly dark
Not just today — or tomorrow
But for days and days to come
Even years
For I have lost you
There is silence
Silence — as of a warm breeze
On a soft summer's day
Or a spring rain as it falls gently
Among the flowers
Or a tear — as it runs quietly
Down the cheek of a woman
Who ever says silence is golden
Cannot know the silence
Of a breaking heart.

Marilynn Hoskins

Visions of Time

It's amazing to see
   how time goes by so fast.

Today's joy will soon become
   visions of the past.

As the days goes by,
   notice how each of you has cared.

For these too become not the past,
   but memories shared.

Laurie K. Mitzel

Hearts

Thump!
Boom boom!
Boom boom!
The sounds of a beating heart.
Creak! Ouch! Hey, watch it!
The sounds of a broken heart!
Burning! Yearning!
The feelings of a heart in love.
Fighting! Crying!
The flat line of a heart dying.
It beats. It breaks.
It loves. It hates.
It burns. It yearns.
It pumps. It churns.
It fights. It cries.
It tries. It dies.

Sameki Y. Huie

Sculpture

Hauntingly beautiful
A lifeless form
Its limbs grotesque
As though set in stone

Naked in the rain
Bleached by the sun
Stripped of its life
Time has now won

Is it yet finished
Not quiet you see
Birds and small animals
Love this dead tree

Gladys S. Davis

Funeral Nation

Fall freeze 'mid skeleton
Breeze, steadfast single note
Horn boils torpid North-South
Flesh.
Commanders lead Blue-Grey battle,
Private line wall cradles forward;
Straitjacket mesh.
No color mistakes salute firm
Beneath unseen rinse of God
Speed prayer charge;
Funeral Nation furious assault
March,
Divided torch attack cotton
Field wash.
Wayward chain saint divine
Mother loss.

Richard Veselik

Love

Just whisper your love
   tis all that I crave,
Each sparkling hour,
   a memory to save.

Your hand holds mine,
   our hearts touch, too.
Each moment a treasure
   of life come a new.

Our lips softly meet,
   and clinging, it seems
time silently waits,
   and dreams, and dreams.

David Lehman

Ode to a Leader

Leaders all are we
Someone has said to me
Why then do some pull this way
While others of us push that way?
Answer: To ease the pain of course!
Leaving others to seek the gain
Then hear this all ye who would lead
You must first learn the walk
Before ye earn the right to talk

Gerald J. Sink

Untitled

Where is this place where I have gone
Just past the night but not quite dawn
This narrow space where all I see
Is emptiness of what could be

Janna Lindgren

Destiny's Gate

My being is rushing
Past, present, and future
Merging at Destiny's Gate.
Open! From Thee to me to Thee!
Every atom vibrating every cell
In gratitude and awe.
It must be!
All to God
All to God
All to God
Nothing less can contain me!
Nothing else can free me!
Immersion
Dispersion
Infinity.

Guru Prem Kaur Khalsa

Freedom

To be what no one ever was
To be what everyone has been
Freedom is the mean of
Those extremes that fence
all effort in.

Stephanie Alfaro

One Verse One Line

No one will help you
you're all on your own
I keep hoping and praying
That some how, I'll be shown.

How to go on alone.

Audrey Grimm Kirkner

Human

I was sure to never be hurt
sure to never need, love, care
Sure to never fall apart.
So sure
but deep inside longing.
To not feel
injury
happiness
pain
becomes so easy,
How can you ache
when you feel you don't have a heart?
Then I look in the mirror
and realize.
Now I know
if I should ever hurt again
it will be worth it,
it will have a purpose.
To know,
I had it in me.

Kelly Kolbinger

As Long As . . .

As long as I can breathe,
I can keep going on.
As long as there is music,
I can keep singing a song.
As long as we have lights,
I can keep on seeing.
As long as we have nights,
I can keep on dreaming
As long as we have rain,
I can keep my flowers growing.
As long as we have winters,
The snow will keep on coming.
As long as the sun shines,
It will dry up all the rain.
As long as I have a heart,
God can ease my pain.
As long as we have prejudice,
We will never have peace.
As long as I have a body,
Until I die, then I'll be deceased

Georgene E. Avrette

Girls

Girls are the people
That give birth to their kids,
They'll love them and love them
If they're a pain at age ten.

Moms are filled with sorrow
When their kids move away,
They'll love them and love them
Each and every day.

But when the moms get much older
And they pass away,
Their children will love them
Each and every day.

When the kids get that old
And they pass away,
They'll be with their mommies
In heaven each day.

Michael Denton

Butterfly

Webbed fingers
caressing the kiss
of the sun's gentle rays.
Delicate hands
waving goodbye,
as they float by jealous flowers,
whose petals are just as beautiful
but unable to fly to other gardens.

Siranee M. Conklin

Sleep

I sleep all day
I sleep all night
And you know that may
Just be alright.
I don't like to work
Or to play
Not in the dirt
Or in the bay
I don't like to have the clock beep
because all I want to do is
    Sleep!

Rebekah Scharnagl

My Help is in Thee

When skies are cloudy and grey
I look to Thee to show me the way
Storm clouds break!
I see the light,
Things don't seem as bad
AS I thought they might
If I follow that light
To the end of my life
I'll know you're always there
Through all my troubles and strife.

Elaine F. Weber

Untitled

Sitting on the edge of time
Waiting for the sun
Hoping to count rainbows
When the night is done.

Straining through the darkness
For the joy that can't be found
Listening for encouraging words
That never make a sound

Trying to catch a ray of hope
By reaching for a star
Grasping tight the empty air
My dreams may be too far

How cold the lonely wind does blow
So hopeless with despair
So weary from the endless night
And no one seems to care.

Sitting on the edge of time
In darkness as before
No need to wait for rainbows
My life . . . shall weep . . . no more

L. Tolbert

Friends

Bad times are rough.
Good times are fun.
Friends will always be there
When away you want to run.

Our hands will reach out
To help you stand tall -
Our shoulders to cry on
Just give us a call.

We'll stay all night
If that's what it takes.
Friendships made stronger
That's what it makes.

Close friends are like family,
You can open up your heart.
We'll be a friend for life
Even when we are apart.

Cheryl Bowers

The Master Artist

An artist paints
    so that people might see
The aspects of character
    and inner beauty.
Light against darkness,
    bitter against sweet
Contrasting with opposites
    and highlighting to complete.
God, too, is a Master Artist,
    His canvas is my life.
He paints glorious truths
    showing the beauty in strife.
Beyond disappointments and confusion
    lies the picture He has planned.
Remember, things can change
    with the touch of the Master's hand.
The Master Artist creates
    so the people might see
He wants His painting of my life
    to reflect Christ's life in me.

Anissa Parrish

Symbol

Aged - mature
The solitary tree stands

A symbol

Of the will to survive
Of the strength of flexibility
Of the power of gentleness
Of faith in God

A symbol

Of the infinite beauty of
Each individuals
Determination to achieve
A place in the sun

Shirley Estelle Meissen

Celebrate

We seldom said thank you for the
things you did instead we reminisce
on the things you didn't.
    Now that you have passed through
those heavily gates, now it's time to
celebrate
    Lets celebrate the reunion with
our heavily father
    Lets celebrate no more pain
    Lets celebrate no more fears
    Lets celebrate no more tears
Because all I have now children are
wonderful wonderful years
    So I say to you all,
    "Let's Celebrate."

Bridget Neal

Fog floating by the window
    in September.

I miss you much.

Ingeborg Wald

My Season

In my Autumn
when I was fallen
You lifted me, carried me
and gave me shelter

In my winter
when I was numb
You covered me, with your blanket
and gave me warmth

In my spring
when I hungered and thirst
you gave me food and drink
that I may live

In my summer
when I radiated life
You led me to the edge and nudged me
that I may fly

That part of your spirit
that lives in me
Will bring forth fruit
to begin - Another's Season
Lorraine Romero-Encinias

Winter Daze

As I lie motionless on the grass
and ponder over the day ahead,
I am in awe of the beauteous
scenes my eyes behold.
The happy sounds of the birds
flying wistfully by
and the leaves whispering
their secrets in the wind
my soul fills itself
with inner peace as the wind
caresses my hair
and I cannot but wonder
if God made this day for me.
Kimberly Lynch

What I See

A little after nightfall,
I gaze up into my little
Window. Then I See a face,
Scraped with tears. The face,
It is deep and insecure.
Sadness, and years of
Pain seem to be printed
All over the face. Her sad
Eyes are fixed on me, as if
Wondering, "How is
Her life compared to mine?"
Yet, she does not know that
I am her outside and she
Is my soul.
Kara Harrington

Morning

Along the dew-washed morning street
The people wait in corners
Hollow-eyed
From last night's fevered yearnings
(Their other lives)
The bus follows behind
And sweeps them up
Elaine Coveney

The Village Blacksmith

Under a spreading chestnut tree
A stubborn auto stands,
The Smith, an angry man is he
With trouble on his hands.

The carburetor seems to be
The cause of all his woe
He tightens hold a dozen bolts
But still it doesn't go.

He sits beside the road to give
His brain a chance to cool
And ponders on his training at
The correspondence school.

And then he starts his job once more
And just by chance 'tis seen
The cause of all his trouble is
He's out of gasoline!
Alice S. Wyatt

Elements

Searching . . .
Sun, moon, stars
Dreams of a reality,
warm and inviting,
shall one day be ours.

Longing . . .
Water, wind, fire
Thoughts of desire,
sensual and seductive,
we shall acquire.

Discovering . . .
Eclipses, rainbows, clouds
Removed is the dark shroud,
revived and recovered,
we've found one another.

Knowing . . .
Earth, heaven, love
Sweetest from above,
simple and reassuring,
steadfast and everlasting
Lisa Michelle Pala

She

This is she . . .
I see . . .
Her tender eyes
They are endless sea.
Her beautiful hair
It's golden field.
Her ferment soul
It's quagly wind.
Her lips are rose,
And skin is velvet.
I like her nice nose
I like all as for her body.
I know she is everywhere
My life, my heart, my fair.
I'm not afraid of death,
Because she is my breath.
Alina Demidova

Untitled

Fallen angel
God's disgrace
Not familiar face to face.
Blending nicely
Passing by
Fearful of enchanting eyes.
For there, this demon
Must despise
The truth is seen behind those eyes.
Timothy B. Hodges

Love Story

My heart pumps blood throughout my body
You pump love throughout my soul

My mind is thus an open book
With a new story to behold

We are the main characters
Therefore we make all the rules

Our hearts and our minds
Are the finest of tools

We work very hard
Cause we are so demanding

Once our achievement is made
And we're at the end

We can go back to the beginning
And read it again.
Karen A. Deadwyler

Christmas

Someone's packing, someone's wrapping,
With paper and ribbons bright.
Gifts abound, all around!
Christmas comes tonight!

Plans arranging, gifts exchanging,
Eyes are merry and bright.
Bells are pealing, oh, the feeling!
Christmas comes tonight!

The moon is winging, carolers singing,
His star is shining bright.
The story's old, but always new,
Christmas comes tonight!
James T. Conner

Heaven

He saw a light
He saw a face
He heard a voice
He walked closer
He saw God
He listened
He watched God's face
He took his hand
He walk into the light.
Andria Piolata

369

For Him

He doesn't know I hurt when
   he walks away.
He doesn't know I cry when
   he drives away.
He doesn't know I pray when
   he sleeps away.
He doesn't know I try when
   he turns away.
He doesn't know I die when
   today is far away.

April Slaba

My Star Shines Up Above

A little girl was singing
As I watched in my dream
She looked up at the sky
My star shines up above

Why do you look so happy?
I know my love is real
My star shines up above
I have a happy happy family

I know God's in heaven
My star shines up above
He send his son that way
To make a path for me

My star shines in the heavens
I know my God is real
I've been touched by an angel
Sent by God to me.

M. Lester Richesin

Bug Fudge

Here is a delightful fudge
that is guaranteed to make you budge

Mixed with little bits of ham
smothered with strawberry jam

Next add lots of ladybugs
and a gallon of slimy slugs

Pick out some delicious fleas
then add 2,000 honeybees

Roast a very little dog
and take the warts off a frog

Get some fleece off a coat
and take the horns off a goat

Take the nose off a bear
then cut off all his hair

Steal an eye
off of a pumpkin pie

Take a sunflower
off a golden tower

And now my friend
my story shall end

Jacqueline M. Bradley

The Smile

Walking in my sorrow
Drowning in my pain
Bitter thoughts of sadness
Gloomed my morbid day

With a smile from a stranger
My thoughts were soon reversing
Overwhelmed and quite delighted
Over such a minor kindness

How silly I was to cry for past
When I was in the present
How silly was I to cry regret
When all was left was future

Now I walked in merriment
All bitter thoughts were dead
As I laughed and shook my head
I noticed but a stranger

As I smiled at the stranger
And saw her face light up
I realized a great power
Possessed in every one of us

Carla A. Roberts

Life's Illusion

When lovers part,
there's a broken heart
and tear filled eyes,
from so many lies.

The promises spoken,
all freely broken.
The dreams shatter,
the future doesn't matter.

With everything gone
why should life go on?
So much confusion
nothing but life's illusion.

Jimmy L. Claar

My Husband My Life

On the day we wed
we vowed it would be for life.

Now when I'm asked who I am
I am proud to say I am your wife.

Ann Pierce

Do You Love Me?

Do you love me?
Or do you love something else
the legs that I walk with
or the lips that you kiss
maybe my breasts that I have
makes you feel sometimes so restless
Do you love me or my body?
My body that wears that dress so well
or the virginity I have
and hold with care
for me, I do love thee,
but the question is
Do you love me???

Felicia Cotton

My Children

My children they're the life of me
They beat it from me too
With all their cute expressions
All their words ring true

Like ragweed in my garden
As footprints in the snow
First they're hardly anything
And then, away they grow

I muse at all their wonderings
The testing of each rule
The ceaseless stream of questions
Until they enter school

They've taught me many lessons
Of what's dear in this life
And put in clear prospective
Just how much I love my wife

My children are the best of me
And I shall see it so
I'll nurture and I'll savor them
Awhile, away they grow

Richard Emery

My Wife's Diet

My wife's on a diet.
It's enough to cause a riot!
She'll need a new spouse.
I'm about to leave this house!

The kids and I complain.
It is driving us all insane!
She trashed our junk food.
Now, how could she be so rude!

We're walkin' out the door.
We cannot take it anymore!
But, what's this we see?
She's as pretty as can be!

We're all on a diet.
It's enough to cause a riot!
But we all agree,
We're a skinny family!

Pam Culpepper

Out of Denial

There is a place so deep within,
   that only few can hear.
The piercing scream from all the hurt,
   enshrouded in such fear.

The times have come for a release,
   from all the muck and mire.
And freedom rings for those who know,
   the test is in the fire.

No matter what the length of time,
   nor how the woe did start.
True healing means unearthing pain,
   that blocks our precious heart.

The ones who are attuned to you,
   will know what you can't see.
So still the mind, so you can feel,
   the path that is the key.

The Light will bring the only way,
   and it does shine through those.
Whose journey is life of love,
   just like a single rose.

Nikki D. Shearer-Tilford

One

Face to the sun,
fresh with dew,
standing alone
in a garden of
many colors —

Julie Wilkinson

Words to Live By

life
why is it worth living
is it because of
love
or is love the reason for life
a better question
why is it worth giving up
a shattered dream
an unresolved problem
or maybe
a horrible end to a relationship
No
the only acceptable reason
is in the up holding of

the PRINCIPLES that you LIVE by

never give up
you only become a loser
a winner keeps fighting through the pain

Kevin T. Minor

Your Fan

Man to man I've been
   your best fan.
A disagree, regarding she.
I'll be your worst cretic
and your best fan?
This can't be, it's how
   you treat she.
I can't be your worst critic
and your best fan.
Must I only see you
   man to man?
To disagree with their
is perceived as negativity.
I can't even her hand,
as a man I take a stand,
to only see you man to man,
Until my friend you find a
   better plan.
To be her best critic
and her best I am.

Doug Devine

The Cosmic Circle

From the cosmos
   Streams forth the light,
The light reflects itself
   And diversifies without,
The warmth begets love,
   That love imparts its identity,
Identity solidifies to form,
   Form is infused with mind.
When mind begets wisdom and love,
   The love returns to light.
Love is the cosmic circle... For
   Love is the all, in all.

Eva L. Ochoa

A Tree Outside My Window

There's a tree outside my window,
It reaches to the wind,
Within it is a story, that doesn't
Have an end.
For life is full of growing, for
Those who dare to reach.

There's a tree outside my window,
It reaches to the stars,
Its branches number many, and
Often bears the scars,
Of life that's full of seasons, for
Those who dare to change.

There's a tree outside my window,
That waves to every breeze its
Movements is majestic,
Its goal is reached with ease, for
Life is full of living for those who
simply live.

Jim Ewings

Quintessential Component

Dirty linoleum
rusty tile
let me be alone here
incredulous
inhaling, engulfing, intoxicating
my mind
in a dizzying, drunkenness
naked, crying
praying to someone
I've never seen
quietly learning to accept
that I cannot change
the things
I cannot control

Jan M. Provost

A Hero Unsung

Here's to you bird, a hero true,
Who flies by night and day.
On soaring wing, you swiftly bring,
Your song so sweet and gay.

At dawn, you wake us with a song,
Fit for a king to hear.
Through all the day, at work or play,
Your voice rings sweet and clear.

In the still and quiet hours of night,
When all are fast asleep,
There comes a most familiar sound,
Your song so soft and deep.

In summer bright, or winter gray,
In spring and autumn fair,
You come and go, both to and fro,
Your sweet voice fills the air.

To you, my fine and feathered friend,
May life with you abound.
You're one of many little things,
Which makes the world go 'round.

Amos K. Rich

Untitled

His eye is on the sparrow
He knows each one that falls,
I know his presents with me.
He hears me when I call.
God Grant that I remember,
Your presents ever near,
With all the trouble in the world
I have nothing here to fear.
Cause your eye is on the sparrow
And I know you're watching me
I know you brought salvation
And I know you set me free
In prayer I find sweet communion
Since the day I came to thee.
Your Grace is all sufficient.
And I know you're here with me.
Your Grace is all sufficient
I know you're watching over me.

Marie Calton

Beyond Logic

Something in my heart is fleeting
beating beyond logic
fleeting from my body
out to you

Beyond logic my heart pounds
and stretches against its walls
at your silken touch
at you

In the stillness of my soul
beyond logic I will be you
when my body is but earth
I will still feel your laughter

Beyond belief the burning tears
scar my soul
with acid of feeling
which separates our lives.

Kerrina L. Cragun-Rehders

Best of Friends

Far away,
Yet very close
We are in spirit...

I think about you
Every hour,
Everyday,
All day today
And forever...

Though it seems
So far away,
We will be together
Someday...

Best friends are we,
Anyone would agree,
So much alike, we are one...
So much fun we have had...

So much laughter,
Tears and obstacles...
All we have gotten through together,
As best friends forever.

Abbye Bornt

Untitled

Shining sun with your glorious burn,
Let him dance amongst your rays.
Let him
   Turn,
    Turn,
     Turn.

With wings of an angel,
Let him soar to new heights.
  Inhale,
   Exhale
Your most magnificent nights.

Angel of Mercy,
Shine hope unto thee,
Accept no imitations
And let him be, be, be . . .

Darcie Coburn

Patience!

  Patience is one
of the steps in the
stairway that leads
to happiness!

Robert Parker Sr.

The Night's Lament

If you had the will to hear
the night scream loud about its fear
then your eyes would weep and tear
and its pain you shall hold dear

The rolling wind of night's hot breath
stirs amidst the gentle ground
upon its wings rides raging death
and so the breezes circle around

All the stars that brighten the sky
reflect the light of the distant cry
the darkness rules from dusk till dawn
and climbs along the child's yawn

Eternity is in the eyes of night
infinity is in the grasp of the moon
pain is rapped in strands of light
the day rests beside the gloom

Oh night ruling supreme
I love to shine in your radiant beam
once removed I remain clean
never shall I forget what I have seen

Michael J. Bogusky

Eye Words

Words shouldn't flow, but the eyes do.
Words shan't flow, but the eyes do.
Words don't flow, but the eyes do.
Words won't flow, but the eyes do.
Words can't flow, but the eyes do.

So what do we do . . . with the eyes?

Bruce Harvey

Wintertime's Began

Little butterfly you are flying late,
  as winter times began.
The dandelions you're slacking are
  withered, dry and brown.
The summer birds have all gone
  south and flowers are in bed,
  so you must fly your pretty self
  to a warmer place instead.
I do think you're so lovely and I
  hate to see you go, but the
  cold North wind will freeze
  you and you'll die upon the snow.
Hurry right along now as winter
  gives its sign.
I hope to see you once again
  when it is soft springtime.

Claudine Payne

The Animal

The night is very dangerous
as there are many sounds you hear
The sound of the animal
and your mind locked in fear

Fear can be an awful thing
jumping at any movement
the darkness has to bring
Looking for a sign
but there's no way out
It's just your imagination
that's without doubt

The sun will shine
at the beginning of the day
The darkness you feared
shall be on its way
Until the night has come again
the animal will be back to hunt
its prey

Leah Herrington

The Grass Is Greener

On the Other Side

An old man told me to go look
at this fence.

He told me on the left side
of the fence I would see the
past history of the world and
on the right side of the fence
I would see the future state
of the world.

When I got to the fence, on the

left side I saw hope, equality,
prosperity, and happiness.

On the right side I saw famine,
destruction, separation, tyranny, and
oppression.

As I turned to leave, I was
Very appreciative of the creation
of mirrors.

Brian Bonner

The River of My Life

The little stream that was my life
Had a meager start,
It trickled through my brain cells
And poured into my heart.

That river strained my heart strings
And caused the dam to break,
Releasing all my senses
And judgement did forsake.

And now the river of my life
Had made its final turn,
It flows again through brain cells
And to my heart returns.

Not as a gushing ocean,
Of love, of tears of fire,
But as a gentle flowing stream,
Soothing flames of life's desire.

Dottie Favorite-Bates

My Parents My Heroes

We wonder thru' life
always looking for something
at times it may be riches
thinking they are everlasting

Forgetting then the things
that mean so much to us
like love cherish and the like
and loving your Mom and Dad

And we have wars we have hunger
We have people brokenhearted
won't you agree love could heal
every sorrow every need

When everything is over
and time stands still
only love can lead us to Heaven
the place we want to be

My parents my heroes
and this I really mean
gosh I truly love them
and I always will...

Jimmy Santos Castano

America

America is a place of freedom.
It is wonderful.
America is beautiful.
It is a place to love.
America is a good country.
It is our home.
America is very large.
It is made up of 52 states.
America is a place to come back to.
It is full of wonderful people.

Cindy Sweney

Untitled

I have a dog and a cat
Also, I have a funny old hat.
When I get lonely...
What do I do???
I put on my funny old hat
And
Take a walk with my dog and my cat!

Phyllis K. Connerley

To Holly

When winter's chill my garden
  has embraced
And turned pink blossom brown,
I see their leaves, so pale,
  have traced,
With bitter bite of frozen night,
Their outlines on the ground.

'Tis then my heart is cheered by
  holly boughs.
Deep green and bright they stand
In crisp white snow
Their shadows show
The sparkling light of winter's night.
May holly fill the land!

Janet E. Fellowes

Week Days

Monday my mom is nice and kind
I love her sweet and fine

Tuesday she still is this way and
that just suits me fine

Wednesday I really don't know,
she's in bed the whole day
I leave her rest in peace
and I just go away

Thursday I'm in my room this
is very bad,
but when I come out again
my mom is very glad

Friday is kind of wild
things are going on,
but I will always love her
even though I frown.

Andrea Pocius

Miso Soup

The mouthfuls rising,
the mouthfuls of a red radish
scattered deep in the throat,
a boy hates, spits, spits, spits

The mouthfuls of a mushroom
smelled all over the mouth
to the top of his head
a little boy holds it
on the tongue, cries, cries, cries

The mouthfuls of miso soup
tastes of tears,
tears of mom
A little girl dumps it onto the floor,
no more,
no more,
and no more sore.

Kyoko Kitamura

I Love Sports

Sports are neat,
Sports are fun,
Sports are fun for everyone,
They are fun in the fall,
When you play soccer and football,
In the fall it gets so muddy,
you haven't lived until you play in it
with your best buddy!!

Patrick C. Dixon

The Chocolate Cow

A long time ago lived a chocolate
cow, with her friends a duck and
a sow. The chocolate cow gave off
chocolate milk. Her fur felt soft
and smooth as silk. The chocolate
was so sweet and good, that she
spread the word in her neighborhood.
They heard many - "Yums" but not
one "Yuck." They drank and drank
and drank so much, that they
didn't have room for the ice cream
truck!

Kiera LeAnn Chavez

Nonna

I see you
stoic
a stranger
a prisoner enduring
quiet pain
standing humbly
imprisoned in your own home
chained by generosity
manacled by kindness
fettered by tradition

Tears welling
you stand in the patio
arms comforting you
your arms
you watch your chance for freedom
evaporate in front of you
we wave good-bye

You are a statue
you are an inmate
you turn to go back inside.

Rosanne De Benedetti

Shadows In the Darkness

Shadows in the darkness
I am scared,
yet intrigued by there intricate shape.
I turn on the light,
they disappear.
Shadows in the darkness

Tarah Vergo

The Pauper

The pauper told the rich man's son
Of life without and on the run.
Not sharing what he didn't own,
His misfortunes always grown.
For his life he didn't care,
Running quickly for nowhere.
In predicting the past he specialized,
Everything and nothing he realized.
Dying from the day he's born,
From that point he will mourn.
With all this spoken, nothing learned,
The pauper knew his soul was burned.
The rich man's son just threw a "red",
Not knowing he was already dead.

Brandon Ward

Sadness

The leaves on the trees have fallen
The flowers in the garden are gone
There is brown where green once reigned
And the birds sing sad songs
The love that was my sunshine
Now has turned to dusk
And all that was summer has died
And winter is upon us

Brenda Kay Workman

Glass and Steel

When looking at a building
See through
The glass and steel
To the soul of a man
See through
The glass and steel
To the heart of a man

See through the glass and steel
To the heart and soul of a man

His future, his hopes
His happiness, his sadness
His tragedies, his dreams and his past

All seem to depend
On the wages he takes
From the Building he works

So my friend
When looking at a building
See through the glass and steel

And if you truly look, you'll see
The heart and soul of a man

Gerald F. Olson

Chances

I had a chance to fly,
but I had no wings.
I had a chance to drive,
but I'd lost my keys.
This is how life is.
Sometimes things just don't work out.
You try and try again,
but sometimes you just can't win.
Things can't be perfect.
You'll always have ups and downs.
Maybe you don't fit in,
but it's probably for the best.
If you don't get what you want,
there's no need to pout.
If something's really worth it,
it will somehow work out.

Jennifer Shields

Thank You Mother

I love you, Mom, with all my heart.
What do I feel? How do I start?
You comforted me in many ways.
You helped me through those
desperate days.
Your understanding can not be matched.
The times I fell, you stitched
and patched.
You showed me what was right and wrong,
Thanks to you I now am strong.

Danielle Cassidy

Untitled

When the whole world
seems to be against you
There is only one thing to do.

When sadness fills your heart
There is only one thing to do.

When tears threaten to burst
from your eyes
There is only one thing to do.

When you feel lonely inside
There is only one thing to do.

When the world around you
seems to be crumbling
There is only one thing to do.

All you can do is pray.
Pray that God will
help you get through that time.
He knows how to help so
all you need to do is ask.
That's all.

Brittani Watts

Earth Defines the Soul

(Remembering Kansas)

Wide expanse where wind is free
To rustle wheat fields in golden glory;
Soft blanket which warms the soul.

Flinthills bespeak a time of Indians
Riding unfettered,
Present on the saddle of the past
In mysterious succession.

Dirt; dark and rich;
Level surface, fertile ground;
Hands immersed in its blackness
Washed in humility of the plains.

Transplanted to the hills,
Dense foliage as a covering,
River valleys meet mountains
In breathtaking beauty.

But the soul has been defined
And at night longs for
Dark soil bed,
Golden blankets,
Safe in the arms of the wind.

Mary W. Baucum

The Dew Drop Inn

A round pint of bass
in my hand at dew bar
I secretly, avoidingly, stare,
the perfect round of ass,
when you lean over,
check my drink
smile briefly
then go away forever,
and I sit here with my desire
drink down a chance
of dream romance
in your flawless shape of fire

Antti Salminen

On Mecklenburg Avenue

I sit quietly on this busy street
looking how life goes on.
Infantile voices pierce the air
here and there.

Noisy cars rumble passing by
while I sit silently, observantly.
Eternity is being lived here
but it could be lived anywhere.

It's only time that's spent
the only currency we all have abound
Were it not, but for space and matter
who would know I'm here and now . . .

But, I am!
The whys and becauses
long foregone.
Just a breath away
from death,
just a beat away
from there!

Ketty Molina Vargas

Baby

Life is as precious
  as the rarest of gems.
Love is as honest
  as the blowing four winds.
From North to South,
  and East to West,
Having Love in one's heart
  creates life at its best.

So live it well
  and Love till the last.
Be every day as humble
  as the days come and pass.
"A smack on the rump,"
  a sound so divine;
It's only new life, new love
  of a rare precious kind.

A miracle of hope
  a child and a friend,
Life seems so short,
  as it starts again.

Ronald G. Crowe

Untitled

Your smile is like a beautiful star.
Shining down on me. From above
an' when I see that beautiful smile,
it strengthens, all of my love, but if
the day should come, that you are
feeling blue, just look to the
heavens above, an I am sure you
fine, that beautiful star, sun shining
down on you, with all of my love.
I love you.

Aloysius J. Poland

The Gift

It's my birthday that is true
So my special gift I give to you
The gift I give is one of love
And I thank you both and God above

Without you there would be no me
And for this gift I thank all three
So my gift this year I'll sacrifice
To thank you all for the gift of life

My gift is also one of praise
And to thank you all for the early days
So through the years I hope you see
For the gracious gift you gave to me
The gift of love I return to thee

Winston Brown

Ray

He didn't want to die
He had determination to fight
I kept my tears to myself
No glance would betray my disguise
He had a glint in his eyes
And as he began to slip
I could see
All the time
He—was shielding me.

Alice Hopkinson

The Poems I Write

The poems that I sit and write
I know are not the greatest;
But to my loved ones and my friends
I know they are the latest.

If there can be one worthwhile thought
On which their intellect can feed;
It may blossom into a full grown flower
And fill their greatest need.

Then when my days on earth are over
And true peace at last I find;
I will have left a token of my soul
That through the grace of God was mine.

Nolan Wade Grubbs

The Master's Key

Holy Spirit in the sky,
Guide my soul and help me fly.
Let me see without my eyes,
Release me from my earthly ties.

The Inner Master walks with me,
Unlocking my window, he set me free.
Soaring toward bright stars above,
Transformed was I, a Great White Dove.

If you are ready then you will see,
Your Spirit's imagination is the key.
Just turn to the Master and it will be,
Because love is you and you are me.

Cynthia E. Williams-Haley

Endless Night

I sit here by the fire's light
struggling through the long dark night
staring at the bright orange flame
wondering if I am to blame
for lies and tears that come our way
tear us apart from day to day
Shadows dance upon the wall
as I try so hard to now recall
a time when peace was in my heart
the time that love was at the start
a time when life was full of smiles
but we have gone too many miles
The hurtful words we can't erase
the sorrow shows upon my face
Can love gone wrong now be made right
will I survive this endless night

Kathryn M. Siciliano

Darkness

Darkness has no end
It is the fear in our souls
Darkness is my death

Jeremey Ferris

Divergence from the
One Great Love

The ostrich trots
ahead
of a dust plume
that can't
catch
up;

circles.

In the hole the head
advises ants,
beaks dirt.

Behind nothing,
a plume of dust
speeds to nowhere.

Glenn L. Houseman

Untitled

You wear your shiny boots
   And pressed uniform,
Looking down on everyone
   Else with scorn,
You might have that
   Shiny silver star,
But we all know what
   You really are,
You might carry all that leather
   And high powered gun,
Not thinking twice about
   All that you've done,
Got your lights and siren
   And police car,
Well baby
   I hope you go far.

Thomas Riedel

Untitled

I love you in so many ways
words can not express how much.
I love you for who you are
and for the many ways you
make me feel special.
When I'm feeling as though
nothing can go right you brighten
my day by saying you love me

Carolyn Minella

Family's

Family's mean lots
of love, mom
gives you kisses
and dad gives
you hugs.
I like to play
with my
sister
on a nice summer
day, and my
baby brother always
follow's all my way's.
Family's mean lot's
of love.

Priscilla Luciana

Kittens, Kittens Everywhere

Kittens, kittens everywhere,
Careening down the hall,
colliding with a wall,

Chasing another's tail,
chewing up my mail,

Cascading from the drapes,
clobbering some grapes,

Charging into a sack,
clinging to my back,

Clawing at my hair,
climbing into my chair,

Chattering at my fish,
cracking a new dish.

Oh, woe is me, you see,
my He turned out to be a She!

Patricia Johnson

Unforgetful Death

Drip, Drip,
The sound of endless blood
Rushing out of his body.
The nails piercing his hands
As the sweat falls from his face
The blood is symbol of love.
Everlasting love.
Paleness grows on his face,
His head tilts to the side,
His pain grabs you as tears
Fall from your eyes.
As you wipe your tears
You hear silence.
The silence of death.
Only to have the silence
Return in a sweetness
The sound of life.

Belinda McCorvey

The Way the Little Boy Stares . . .

The way the little boy stares
It's as if he knows it's you
From your look, from your scent
Or from the other night
When you held him in your arms
So tight
Singing to him a lullaby

He's so aware
He doesn't compare
To any other at all

He's so precious
He's like porcelain
His beautiful blue eyes
Are like crystals
Sparkling from the sun's light

But no one will ever know
What he's really thinking
Deep inside the mind
Of that little baby boy

Jeannine Gulli

Red

Red is the color of this pen
Red is the color of this poem
with a flash of the sun
or a flicker of firelight
Red is the color I see
Red is the color I see
When I'm hot, Red is the color I feel
When I'm mad, Red is the color I see
Red is the color of this pen
Red is the color within this pen
Red is writing this poem
Red lives with our head
Red is hot, Red is wild
Red is the color of this pen.
Red is strong.

Raymond J. Keith

Illusion

Never receiving
Love what I hate
Hate what I love
No chance, it has been set
Torture, destroy
No problem, leave to enjoy
Temperament is an escape
Pain and suffering
Are around for a reason
They create life
Rage swells
No understanding
Power fronts
Reality diminishes
Cannot have what I need
Need what I cannot have
Why torture myself
Obscuring truth
Enjoyment is an illusion

Anthony Primozich

Outside

As I look out my window
I see the rain beating down
on the trees. I see the
wind blowing the leaves. I
see the trees soaking with
rain and I see the dark
sky above.

As I listen I hear the
rain beating down on the
trees and the grass. I
hear the wind blowing
the trees. I hear the
thunder rumbling and the
birds chirping.

As I go outside I feel
rain on my hands. I feel
the wet grass and trees
as I walk around and I feel
the wind blowing on my
face.

Ashley Schedlbauer

Building

I left the cliff over the ocean
That looked better
Than the sea
I put the mountain near the valley
Because that's where it's suppose to be
I moved the river to the forest
So all the animals
Could drink
I laid myself down
In the desert
Where I could stop and Think

Aaron James Scantlen

Screaming Trees

I see their magnificence every day
Just reaching for the sky
Offering their shade all summer long
Their beauty can make you high

If you want this for our children
In and around them we must sift
We really should take care of them
They are certainly a gift

Their killer is man with his chainsaw
This is the truth I am quite sure
They cry for our help if you listen
"Please don't do this any more!"

Some of them could be important
So we must learn how to thin
One of these days we may find out
That they are vital medicine

So the next time you are out there
Keep your ears open wide
If you listen you will hear them scream
Right before they die!

Terri Johnson

Grandma

Rain from the clouds,
warmth from the sun
gives life to the flower below.

A petal of strength,
petal so bright,
petal of wonder,
petal so light.

Fragile they are,
so delicate in the sunlight.
Your love they'll need
that gives them life.

Kelly McDonnell

Stroke

If I could only be
Like a painter on a canvas
With only one stroke
Change the scene
In his paint.
I would change the scene
In the life of a child
That is suffering, his tears
Would be laughter,
His sorrows would be joy.
There would never be a shadow
In his life,
I would spread light, love
And knowledge.

Ernestina V. May

The Beauty and the Destiny

of the Recardo River

That day I looked with
boredom from the river banks.
Towards the steady streams,
which flows with freedom!
Like a raven in flight.

The Recardo River gracefully
glides along; meandering through
the cotton meadows,
flaunting and reflecting in the
silver rays of the sunlight.

Sometimes in its route, it
cuts through the rigged
hills and ever encounters a
waterfall. It often flows at
the mountain's feet.

This roaring, yet slim river
crosses towns and cotton
fields; it may flow beneath
bridges and roads before embracing the Atlantic ocean.

Kevin Henry

Sail Away

I wish I could sail away
on a sea of starry skies;
sail off to the silver moon
away from blind hate.

I wish I could sail away
into the black of night;
to show people just what we've done
and show them what's right.

I wish I could sail away
and see what the stars have spelled;
they know what needs to be done
these are secrets that they've held.

Just as a star falls from the sky
another change is in harm's way.
I look out at the sea of stars
and wish I could sail away.

Barbara J. Luse

Always for You

I don't know why
All my friends have gone
I'm left here all alone
But for once in this life
I'm not gonna cry
I'm saving all my tears
Save them all for another day
For when we meet again
Oh, what a joyous time
It shall change my tears
Change into pure happiness
Keep you in my heart
Guard all my memories
From days gone by
Never forget the good times
Remember the strength we had
We shared the good times
Made it through the bad
You were there to guide me,
Always cheered me on
gave a shoulder to cry on

Dan Morgan

Adoptee's Pilgrimage

I can't believe I'm on my way
I'm going to meet you today.
For so long you've been in my mind
and now finally it is time.
This is a journey I realize
now I choose to open my eyes
to see myself from a different view
knowing I came from you.
Not only heritage but history
make up a part of me.
I will look at you for traces of me
not knowing what I expect to see;
a ghost, a reflection, an image
for this is my pilgrimage.

Lisa Wade

Untitled

As we pass long corn fields,
in a car moving
so very fast. I listen
to the music, so soft in
the back. Clouds high in
the sky, following us all
the way. We arrive at
our destination with joy
in our eyes. Heaven is
finally here.

Kira Marshall

Like a Dream

Sometimes we must let go of
things which have held us,
In hopes that they will be replaced.

Like a Dream...that begins
with but one gentle kiss,
From a beam of sunlight,
first drop of rain, or
scent of a rose, or
from a soul whose
soft touch is so bold,
Dreams vanish in a flash,
the future ignored
staying stuck in the past,
Lest we see that the Dream
will not be,
not come true on its own,
If we don't take care
to give it a home,
By opening our heart and
make room in our soul.

Vernon M. Smith

The Light Or Lady

The scenery was dark and dreary
till she walked in

Her every step would light up the
place

Like the morning sun rising

Her beauty and the light blinded
me, leaving me also speechless

When words reach my mouth she
was gone like the afternoon
sunset

Frantz E. Delva

Dusk (Her Time)

She bleeds her rightful colors,
  a blind seam across the sky
The lore which legend grows on,
  a rare portrait of the time

Deep as ocean waters,
  her beauty spurs the call
On placid springtide evenings,
  in the starlit heavens of fall

See that mystic glory,
  hidden from the layman's sight
Felt through one's emotions,
  with all the splendor of her might

Hear the four winds crying,
  sent to bless her fading ways
Gone as a melted illusion,
  to return with the darkened haze

Robert Weil

Are You There?

Are you there?
Somewhere in my heart.
Are you real?
Or just shadows in the dark.
Are you special?
Just like our love.
Are you soft?
Like the heavens above.
Are you alive?
Unable to be heard.
Are you listening?
Waiting for the word.
Are you mine?
That special part of him.
Are you ready?
For your precious life to begin!

Tina M. TerLaan

The Bridge At Giverny

Underneath sad willow trees,
above green bullfrog beds,
there lies a portal to two worlds,
'tis like a single thread.

While shadowing the flowered steam,
surrounded by endless grass,
The sky is like an eternal blue,
only true hearts is what may pass.

The sides connected by the bridge,
their only common bond,
each a stranger to the other one,
separated by the pond.

Patrick Kennel

Change

So many new faces,
So many new friends,
So many new surroundings,
Sometimes, I wonder where I am?

How did I get here?
Will things be the same?
When will I feel comfortable?
Am I ready, for Life's change?

Jennifer L. Miano

Seeds

Like seeds
  which on their own
  had taken root
  flowered
    and borne fruit
    all perfect, ripe
    round

Are words
  penned long ago
  forgotten and long lost
  which were just now
    in some archival compost
    found.

Emanuel I. Solomon

Right Thinking

Since God knows all that's in my heart
  Then I must certain be
That everything that's hidden there
  Is fit for Him to see.

The only way I can be sure
  My thoughts are pure and good
Is to keep my heart so full of Love
  I'll think the way I should.

Hazel M. Colton

Dream Scape

Pushing into another world
I awaken to the smell of life
Rushing to no where
Riding with the wind
Power, control, all with a touch
As I lean forward
I can see the sky begin to open
Witness to the birth of a new day
The sun lights the southern skies
Pushing its way above the mountains
The ground begins to gleam
As the dew begins to dissipate
Feeling all emotions peak
For reasons not known
To know such peace
To feel no binds to the past
Completely free, going anywhere
With no place to be
Becoming one with a dream
As I lay down . . . to sleep

Ted R. Mitchell

Life

Life is a map.
Many hiways and biways.
Turns, curves, twists, turns.
Never straight lines.
Sometimes there's a fork
in the road.
Joy one way, sorrow the other.
Which way do I go?
No one to help me decide.
Until one day...
An unexpected tunnel
comes along with a bright
light at the end.
You know what way
to go as you follow
the light home.

Heather McKenna

Untitled

The flight of the sparrow,
disrupted.

The path of the unwanted.

The blossoming flower
in the winter desert.

Cry of the wolf.
As the tears fall from
storm soaked petals
of flowers,
  imprisoned
by steal cages.

Myke Wiseman

Wisdom

I wore this cap the
day I was born.
Though now at times
it looks busy and worn.

The first sign of age
is a shiny forehead.
Litter of my youth,
discarded in my bed.

The teeth of my comb,
rarely snags snarls.
There's not enough left,
for it to beg, steal or borrow.

The earthen brown hue,
daily turns gray.
When my kids tease me,
I simply smile and say.

You are of me,
as I am of you.
Sooner or later,
time takes its due!

Richard Lerew

Morning Clouds

Have you seen them in the sky
As gently they float by?
Morning clouds aglow
With the fire of coming sun;
They come, and pass, and go.

They sail past like a dream,
Fade away and almost seem
Magic sails of floating ships,
Sailing westward, airy, hazy, dim,
Toward the distant ocean's rim -
Blown by breezes from Aeolian lips.

Pink and purple tinted clouds,
Limp milk-white shrouds.
Colorful caravans of countless shades
Parade before me and depart,
And take away my heart
As each clouds dims and fades.

Richard E. Resler

Untitled

Cold, hard
Bunny rabbit
Hopping on
Borrowed time
Hell's doors
Open wide
To let
The bunny
Deep inside.

Jenni Quay

Untitled

Children are the Glory of the Lord
Their innocence,
knows no hatred
draws no division
and
seeks no reward.
They are brushes of life.
Their beauty defined
as a rose.

Cheryl A. Cook

Comfort

Celestial serenity
Sparkling with hope
Ever changing yet
Always the same

Janet M. Eurén Federer

More Than Words

Let me take away all the pain
Make rainbows instead of rain
Erase the memories full of sorrow
Fill them with nothing but the
    happiness of tomorrow
Care about you just the way you are
Create what you wish upon that
    shooting star
Let me give you the things you've
    never had
Cause you smile when you
    are sad
I never want to give you a
    thing to regret
I want to paint you a picture
    of beautiful sunset
I'll try and make you feel as
    special as you are to me
Because that is the one thing I
    wish for you to see

Laura Schoen

Moonlight

Tiny beams of light
Reflect like mirrors in the sand;
Sending sparkling messages of delight,
You can hold in the palm of your hand.

They fly in the summer's breeze,
All over the salty shore;
They dance in the waves with ease,
And travel on the ocean floor.

They are reminders of the past,
And reflections of the future time;
They are scattered images that last
In people's hearts, and in their minds.

Melissa Moccia

Confident With Him

While sailing on the blue/green sea,
I found my Saviour close to me.
Within my heart and soul and mind
No worries or trouble of any kind.

And when again at home; upon dry land
I did not lose my solid stand.
I know he is every where I may be
In air on land and at sea.

So as my golden moments roll on,
I thank you Savior for each new morn.
And anywhere I happen to be
Is fine, because I am with thee.

Alverta H. Randall

My Mother's Tears

I don't remember her weeping
Through the years,
My Mother ...

Unless you count the funerals
Where grief spills
In tearful streams
        Or
When she was very depressed.

Mother was a saucy beauty ...
Happy, she,
And joyful

Until the very end when tears
Lurked unseen,
But ready,

At the mention of sweet memories,
Or loved ones,
Or God's grace.

Dorothy Shepard Nazzaro

Me

All I ask is to be able to
    be "me"
But all I get is hassles and
    the third degree
My life isn't happy, but what
    can I do,
I don't know how to change it
    or even rearrange it.

I'd like to be able to say
    what I feel
And express myself in ways
    that are real
I wish I could be all that you
    want me to be
But all I can do is try to be me!

Kathleen A. Diamond

How Wonderful When He Comes

How wonderful when He comes
Our salvation is at hand
How wonderful is His love
When He rules throughout the land

Our salvation is from Him
His sacrifice is His love
His mercy and grace is ours
How wonderful is His love

Call on Him in trouble
Praise Him to keep your joy
He blesses you for your faith
When the devil tries to annoy

His joy is our own weapon
Our faith is our shield
Righteousness is our breastplate
His gifts are oh so real

Jesus is our answer
How wonderful is His love
His mercy endureth forever
How wonderful when He comes

nathan "doc" nelzen

The Land

I am like the land;
When I am sad the sun will come and kiss away my tears of rain.
When I am happy, snowflakes will fall to dance and play; and
When I am angry, the earth will shake and I will scare all.

Jennifer F. Vazquez

Through My Grandmother's Eyes

I wish I could see through my grandmother's eyes, even just for one day.
I listen to her stories day after day, as she takes me down memory lane - her way.
We talk about whatever we want, and oftentimes we don't need any words at all.
Just as if I was a child again, she teaches me how to play cards, and
    shows me the newest tricks.
Now, I am grown, and see her in a different light, yet it still
remains the same; she can make everything right.
A tear falls down her face each time we talk of family and loved ones past,
yet I know she finds comfort with me there to help make every moment last.
She always helps me to find my smile no matter what my worry at the
time - a talent I hope someday will be mine.
I still look to her with a loving eye although our roles are now
reversed; once she was there to take care of me, and now I am there for her.
I wish I could see through my grandmother's eyes
to make sure she knows how much I love her, even just for one day.

Allison M. Miller

A Mother's Cry

Dear Lord,
    Please hear my cry I love you so dearly and I try my best to live
my life as you would have me to live it. You know I am going through
what seems to be hard times. But I know thou art with me. I shall
not walk alone. I am a separated women with a beautiful child, whom
is more confused than I. I know not how to help her for she is only
4, but I give her all the love I can. While she is in my care we
visit your house often as we can, because I know I don't have the
answers to all the questions. I know you will not lead us wrong.
    Dear Lord please help us get through this and heal her aching heart
that one day we shall be together again.
    Lord her daddy wants to take her from me just to prove a point to
me at the sake of her happiness. You know who's been there for her,
who has taken care of her and healed her wounds and her heart in her
time of need Lord she knows her mother loves her and is just as hurt
as she that we are separated from one another. So I know that you
will not let prayers go unanswered, so in time that we are apart,
please take care of her, help her to remember her mother loves her
so very dearly and she is not alone.
    Lord, it's been good talking to you. Thank you for lending an ear,
for I know thou art busy, but you will hear my cry.

Carolyn R. Myers

Amanda's Eyes

Her crystal blue eyes give her away every time. I can see when she's
being playful or ornery. I know when she's not feeling well, or when
she's upset. All of this, I can see in her beautiful eyes.

Lately, I've seen a hurt there that I can't explain or fully
understand. She tries to hide it, but it's useless. I can see the
sorrow, behind those beautiful eyes.

How can you explain to your daughter that her best friend still knows
she's alive — even though Becky has a boyfriend? How can you tell her
that everything will be O.K. — when you've been in her shoes and know
that this is real pain? How do you wipe away the tears from those
beautiful eyes, and not cry yourself?

Carole Yost

School Bus Noises

Noisy
Bus drivers radio
kids talking
feet stomping
soft
people humming
walkman's blasting
Eternal
People talking
Bus driver saying
sit down kids

Desrea Deshay Mikelle Wilkes

Brad

I'll think of him when I see
The swaying of a mighty oak tree;
Or a huge mountain covered with snow
A river cascading far below.

Or when in the forest I see
A deer quickly look up a me.
Or a squirrel trying to avoid my glance
As he scurries from branch to branch.

I see him with a fishin' pole,
I see him in the swimmin' hole
Happy, smiling glad to be
Away from cares and feel so free.

I see him in the stars at night
And in the warmth of the sunlight.
Now I see him in Heaven above,
Abounding in God's tender love.

Ruth K. Flowers

An Inspiration

There's not a day that passes by
without a thought or spoken word
of my beloved grandmother.
She saw the bad in no one,
the good in everyone.
A true Christian in every sense.
An inspiration to us all.
My grandmother, Gelsomina Visco,
born May 8, 1895,
will live in my heart forever.
I love you, Grandmom.

Kimberly A. Visco, M.A.

Path to Everything

The expected path
in which your
life is to follow
is repeatedly
merged by passing
roads in which all
in all lead you to
your designated point
planned with your
arrival on earth which
reveals your life left
for you to follow and
carry on in happiness
and relief that you have
apparently ventured the
right way on the expected
path laid before us all

Christina Fasano

Forgive

When you realize the truth
  and from the truth you're afraid;
because the trust has been broken,
  and you feel you've been betrayed.

It's so hard to turn the cheek and sometimes harder to regain;
because someone let you down, and caused you so much pain.

And when you've been wronged by your family or your friends;
you feel they're obligated to make the amends.

You must accept each situation not saying they are right;
because what is done is done so why argue or fight?

Getting past the pain is sometimes very hard;
through pain there is growth installing a guard.

From this experience you may reflect;
put up your guard and your heart protect.

We may never forget some things don't seem fair;
but we must let go of these burdens that we bear.

On our search for inner peace
  in this life we live;
We must find it in our heart
  to let go and forgive.
     Barbara Watkins

Galactica

Riding the maelstromed galaxy on fractured ribbons of light
I bank off billowing clouds of fiercely incandescent gas
To pass, I think through indigo/silver-white stars
And broach the endless bounds of time.

The sound of a second, the light of a touch
Merge in my senses to taste, to smell
The eternal fire, awful and lingering draws me
Contortions, a birth of sorts, sends me through.

A synthesis of cosmos and I, meld
To the ancient cross of time brandishing
That mighty sword which flows everlasting, encompassing
Time — uniting beginning and end — balancing.

To shape in the darkness, aware of my mind
The mote swims free and passes beyond
Ripping and tearing, universe plunges below
Lacerating the remaining dregs of consciousness

But leaving still the scene
The shutter clicks.
     Timothy W. LaSelle

Lost Treasures

I found a treasure today that I thought I
had lost. I began to wonder had this
keepsake ever truly been mine to lose?
I had felt broken like a child's toy left
in the street. Only to be shattered into a
hundred pieces as the weight of tire and
machine won the victory.
A whirlwind of doubt began to gust throughout
my mind.
The fear that accompanied the doubt began
to conspire against me. The two worked day
and night, tearing at me as a hungry lion
would tear at the flesh of a lame zebra.
And when I thought I could take no
more of the rain beating down on me, the
storm began to subdue.
Now there is a light mist of relief in the
air as I have found my confidence and
faith again in a golden pot at the end
of my rainbow.
     Cherie L. Beil

Beyond The Glaciers

Majestic towers of ice and rock
Rising from icy-blue fjords
Sparkling in the sunlight
Supreme and unreachable
In their everlasting resting place -
Their domain.

Whales, salmon, beaver, moose
Hiding deep under icy waters or
High up in mountain ranges
Away from human gaze
Blending into the wondrous landscape.

Long summer nights
Stretching far into the starless sky
The moon, her endless glow
Shining in a void that is neither
Day nor night.

Time has stood still
In this ancient and mysterious land
Where we are but bystanders
To gaze in awe at the beauty that is - Alaska!
     Jeanne Silver

Cloudy Memories

Whenever I see the cloudy sky
it reminds me of the days when I used to cry,
When I used to wrap around myself and hide,
and my only wish was to be alone and die.

Now that my worries and sadness are all behind me,
and the cloudy days are only reminders,
My heart beats stronger and my mind is clear
my life is filled with courage, not fear.

If only I could help all those poor souls
with what I have learned through
my painful experiences,
unfortunates that feel as if no one could ever help them,
Let them know that life has not defeated them yet
and they can still look forward for that new chance.

I have realized that,
All of us go through life, standing trial after trial,
and only if we are strong we can survive them.
Trials are painful and unfair, whether we have
lots of them or perhaps just a few,
it all depends on luck or perhaps, just fate.
     Marisela L. Zuleta

The Superstitious Chemist

Delicate snowflake, fierce summer shower
Fall on the earth; they nourish and renew.
A child of myth—chemist with crossed fingers—
Centrifuges out what falls on me and you.

Sample is silent, gnostic, fierce,
Guarding its meaning, colorless in glass;
Explodes; walls fall; and written on the world appears
Her Father's myth — yes, it has come to pass —

The fall harvest which the seed foretold.
Myth and Science reconcile their ways.
You and I, and all, are sheaves of gold,
The cycle done; myth has materialized.

Skies break, cry Love, His Love, love in every
state. Changeless — fierce — precipitate.
     Gloria Frandle

Books

Books are a treat for the poor or elite
Whoever might want to read
They often amaze us, and sometimes do raise us
To the highest of highest peaks.

They tell of the future, the present, the past
Gathering interests forever to last
They please and amuse us and never refuse us
The knowledge however so vast.

Books strike our emotions like magical potions
With fantasy, fiction and fact
And mystify and clue us and often pursue us
In throwing us off the track.

Writers strive to excite us and often delight us
With what's about to happen next
They create a situation and sheer elevation
Of our strongest and deepest requests.

They constitute humor and give us such laughter
And even produce some tears
But to read, is to know, and then thereafter
Books fulfill our most joyful years.

Margaret Pulkowski

A Learning Experience

It's off to college, spirit soaring.
New places, new faces, nothing boring.
Classes planned, loan established, registration complete.
Frat selected, it's party time, I'm moving with the beat.

Large classes, thick books, good note taking desired.
Homework, blue books tests, good grades required.

Years go by, college life becomes routine.
I've worn my path in the college green.
Now I have a girlfriend, commitments are made.
Soon we'll be in the real world, and both well paid.

I'm a senior now, walking tall, feeling mature.
Parents are proud, my future is secure.

Resume completed, job interviews planned.
With my good grades, I'll surely be in demand.

Job interviews attended, offers will come in soon.
Proposed to my girlfriend, We'll marry in June.

Received my diploma, time has flown by.
No job offer yet or a letter explaining why.

Soon they came in, one by one, like a funeral procession.
Saying, "Sorry Bob, no job offer because of the recession."

Leonard L. Spangler

Onkwehonwe

As True as red clay of Mother Earth,
I am Onkwehonwe.

Upright I stand like the Pine Tree,
I am Onkwehonwe.

Like the stillness and strength of the Water,
I am Onkwehonwe.

As the Winged Peoples sing thanks to the Creator,
I am Onkwehonwe.

As the Leaves go back into Mother Earth,
I am Onkwehonwe.

To answer the Creator's question,
Onkwehonwe Kon?

Kenneth Terrance

Bring Me No Tomorrow

I'm afraid of my tomorrow
So many have let me down
I despise the breaking dawn
I loathe the daylight

The moon shall always guide me
The darkness shall be my company
I am only at ease in the dead of night
The solitude is my consolation

I wish the sunless sky would remain forever
No harsh words to be spoken or heard
No worries about the future
Just peaceful isolation

I have no more hope
Only silent prayers
For each new sunrise
Brings a fresh set of tears

Blanket me with shadows forever
Or accept me; love me
But hatred is all I know
So bring me no tomorrow

Pamela J. Meier

Distant Love

There comes a time when two must part
from a love that deep-ens from with-in the
heart.

Your special touch, your special kiss, that
seeps right through and it's something I don't
want to miss.

Through good times, and bad times you
were always there, now that we're apart it isn't
fair.

Jason Brown

Reality Check

Sitting here amid the many coffee consumers,
smoke congested regulars and those here for a first time,
I can't help but wonder, why?

Why is it that people are so concerned with the
second hand smoke, verbal obscenities of your child's
favorite TV show or movie, or the man walking aimlessly
down the street, rambling to an unseen friend?

Why do people reach for the cobweb corners of their lives
to create a masquerade of their fears,
hiding the cold reality of their own lives?

Wake up!! Stop hiding from the present!
Look at the here and now.
Can't you live for today?
Whatever happened to the ever popular, "carpe diem"?

We have created this quick sand trap that pulls us deeper
and deeper in, smothering the will to live for the now.

Stop! Look around, notice the obvious.
We will all live. Live like there is no tomorrow.
Take this check and cash it.

Melissa Burton

Untitled

I touch the cold blackness wanting to reach you,
Wanting to feel your presence somehow.
I wasn't there on that fateful day.
Thoughts that ran through your mind I will never know.
Did I cross them or just pass on?
Days grew easier and easier, but never will I recover,
From the loss I received.
I see your eyes in my reflection, but do I see more?
Damage in my heart is felt by only me,
And the pain I suffer is eased by your courage and bravery.

Marcia Dull

What Happened, Child?

When you were so young and full of joy;
You were such a handsome boy.

Kindergarten through high school went just fine;
Then you went to college just on time.

Then one day while you were away,
I found out that you had gone astray;

The path you had taken was in AIDS' way.

Oh! Oh please don't leave me my child,
for you have all my love
As you look down on me from above.

Z. L. Williams

Dream-Escape

In the night when my eyes flicker and my heartbeat calms,
I find him waiting for me - just beyond my dreams.
At first glance he smiles - so happy that I showed up tonight,
He loves me with one touch - excites me with his simple grasp
to my hand.
His kiss is warm and inviting... "Hello my darling"... he takes
me into the night.
Time is not our friend....
Love is powerful and precious are the seconds that race with
the morning sun.

Jeanette Sarcinello

Power to Soar

With the persistence of time we chased
an elusive dream once only for those
whom, with wings attached, on this earth were placed.
Now, swiftly our lives through the air goes.

Speed and power are products of flight.
Those that conquer the air rule everywhere.
The power to fly extended our sight
to worlds far beyond and wherever we stare.

We've gone around the world and to outer space,
but our new found freedom gave new found fear.
We've scraped the edge searching for a place,
our future is held in the path we steer.

If man were to fly he'd been born with wings,
but the power to soar is in human beings.

Andrew Duffin

Berlin

Meet me at the Brandenburg —
that famous gate, that history-window.
Shall I bring you roses?
No, a single rose for my one love.

Yes, our veins are pumping one blood,
yet your Star of David
   and my misery
fuse to form an open cross...
Through this day my suffering
brought reflection, though I know that
every Christian prayer I pray to save my soul, like dust,
is cast out by your glorious, flickering face!

To history's gate we come but once
and it delivers, from its booming horn of plenty,
all these squalid citizens.
The night begins to sparkle.
Regret begins to slump the rose I hold then
you, like gold, appear and kiss my cheek

Brian Theis

Wind to a White Dandelion

The gull from the bay sweeps low tonight.
Its flight is dull and long its stay
and weak its song and pardons prey.
The gull from the bay sweeps low tonight.

The tree in the field sways slow tonight.
Such sight to see for bark is peeled
No leaves, just stark and without shield.
The tree in the field sways slow tonight.

The rain from the skies will flow tonight
and flight its strain but holds the eyes.
With force it scolds but quickly shies.
The rain from the skies will flow tonight.

Break the talon.
Cut the noose.
Ride the lightning back to Zeus.
Bays are made in ways like these.
Spread your wings above the seas.

Darrell W. Grable III

The Demons Within

As the days go slowly by
The kids sit around hanging out and getting high.
Each one without a dream or some kind of hope.
Doing nothing but getting drunk and smoking dope.
Each day I wonder who will be the next to die
As the tears fall slowly from my eyes.
Running from the police is all they know,
There's no place to hide and nowhere to go.
Do I go to sleep at night and not even care
That when I awake no one will be there?
Some are so young and do it just to fit in,
Not even knowing where to begin.
I've watched them for so many years
Trying so to hold back the tears.
Just to look at their faces and see the pain that they hide,
Trying so hard to fight the demons inside.
So there's nothing you can say and nothing you can do,
Just sit back and pray the next victim won't be you.
Each one of these kids has an unworthy sin
And if you must know it's the Demons Within.

Jennifer A. Fritz

Children with Wrinkled Faces

The tool of time etches the mask
but takes us only bodily to task.
We think experience our childhood erases
but we're only children with wrinkled faces.

We play with toys and then with guns,
we fight our fights, all senseless ones.
The losers then in mud would lie,
only now it's do or die.

From rocking horses to automobiles,
from pablum drinks to diet meals,
from birthday parties to banquet places
go we children with wrinkled faces.

We wean our milk, and then our wine.
We draw our strength from a sweeter vine.
The nectar then would grow us straight,
now it serves to deteriorate.

Seed and flower are one and the same.
Roots are roots, no matter the name.
Though we deceive ourselves with silks and laces,
we're only children with wrinkled faces.

Frank T. Masi

In Daddy's Name

On January 30th, 1993,
Our daddy died, leaving "Everything" to me.

The "Fortune" he left was not in dollars;
but the value of "it" will be shown in the words that follow.

He and mum were married in 1941,
and on that Christmas, "I" was born, even though he wanted a son.

In the years that followed, they added seven more;
not caring or knowing the many hardships that they would have
to endure!

He loved us kids in his "Own special way";
His only fault was, "He didn't live for tomorrow"; only that day!

Our house consisted of three rooms without a bath;
and when we needed "to go," we went to the "outhouse" down the path.

Sure, we didn't have the fancy clothes and things other kids had,
but I remember more happy times than I do sad!

All the riches in the world could not compare;
To what he left behind for all of us to share!

"Glowing" like a perpetual flame;
"Love"
Is what was left to us; "In Daddy's name"!

Mary Korey

Rays of Day

The newly rested sun knocks early on my window
asking, then begging to see me stand
from millions of miles it calls every day
sometimes earlier than expected
I sarcastically grin and greet my heavenly alarm
always considering the nature of my warm host
its peaceful crown upon a smiling face
masks shear terror from underneath
and promptly grinds its atomic teeth
an honest view yields imperfections
not unlike the hand it feeds

Jeremy T. Pratt

Musical Notes

It's time to mix the Yuletide dough
I must hasten to catch the sun's last ray

Do have a cup of tea with me
It's late-please don't go too Far

I forgot-bless my dear soul
'tis time to sing la-la-la

So this is your favorite
brand of "tea" ti

It's time now to bake the
   Holiday dough
Tra-laa-laa laa laa

As you "scale up" to our
   Father's mountain top
To a view so rare and full of splendor-do Stop
   Be ever mindful of our Saviors birth
Then step by step descend to Mother Earth.

(Musical scale: Do-re-mi-fa-sol-la-ti-do)

Beatrice H. Crowell

Her Eyes

Her eyes I have seen years before,
Perhaps just once or perhaps much more.
The innocence behind the beauty I have seen,
Is the one that I remember only in a dream
As I awoke I knew it was my chance,
I have found in her eyes a vision of romance,
When we first met it was easy to see,
Your life was your own but that look was just for me.

Christopher LeBlanc

The Black Pearl

Priceless is the pearl with a thick outer shell
But whose center runs deep like a bottomless well
So too is the heart that is true and caring
But locked to all but the one who is daring
To give all the love it needs in return
Be considerate and interested in each others concerns
The chains released from your heart and soul
Please let me in from out of the cold
Just give me the chance to prove my love
Your heart next to mine like a hand and glove
The closer we get my hearts starts to pound
To hold you, to kiss you, to just have you around
You bring a smile to my face whenever your near
But you have no smile. Only a tear
What words had I said, what mistakes had I made
That has suddenly caused my black pearl to fade

Earl M. Ellsworth Jr.

Wisdom and Simplicity

The simplicity of the hallowed human mind;
Is it a tragedy in itself, or a gift so often hidden?

The knowledge of knowing all or the knowledge of knowing not?

Once clean and pure and innocent, but enlightened never will be.
One wise, experienced, with integrity,
but laden with the burdens of life.

Shelby Stewart

Voices

There they go blow away...some we seldom knew.
  Condemnation...like cutting dandelions.
Turn a round to where they stood.
  Just to convince yourself, there is nothing there.

The winds have washed the seeds to shore.
  It just took awhile to make it here...hear;
Voices Voices Voices!

Passing shadows gashing eyes crashing eyes crashing echoes, can't
you hear?
  Then run them down to let them dry,
So the fields can grow green again.

Soon it will be clear outside.
  Forget the lawn, forget the hour.
Jumping from a timber flash,
  It left a path of rustled wind, and dashed.

Above the earth, above the sad.
  Time, relative to motion, light, contrasting that;
Voices Voices Voices
          Rod McElroy

I Only Wish

I only wish
that you could hold me tight
every second of every night.

That you could heal all the pain
every problem that I gain.

That you could mend my broken heart
that always seems to fall apart.

That we'll be together to the end
my partner, my lover and
my life long friend.

That you could protect me from every fear
and never let me shed a tear.

That we'll stay together
and you'll never let me go
because you love me more
then they could ever know.

That you could make
my dreams come true
and everything I wish
is everything you'll do.
          Jessica C. Vargas

Scales of Balance

A hammock between two trees
A gymnast on a balance beam
It could be a thought, it could be a snapshot
It could be a dream, it could be something you've never really
seen. Though unrelated they seem balancing is the
central theme. All things in nature have a purpose that
balances naturally. The cycles of life through the wisdom of
the ages instructs nature when, where and how much to
change - to maintain. The seasons of life bring about change
and new experiences create memories that allow us to gauge
our steps, measure our worlds and choose our course for the
future. The leaves detach themselves from the tree in the fall
and come a-new in the spring, what a blessed thing. Scales
measure the quantity of and reflect the difference between.
Be it scales of justice, one of measurements, sliding scale,
one of relativity or one of absolute. Balance insures harmony
and inner peace between the flower and the bee.
The measure of a person is in the heart not in the head. We
should strive for balanced emotional reactions instead.
Independent they may appear unity is the ecosphere
          Willie C. Merrell

To Lake Ontario

Water so calm and clear,
Yet so mysterious and vicious;
A beauty so unmistakenly violent.

You've taken those we love
So calmly and peacefully;
A lesson not understood.
Hurt, fear with fingers and
no place to point.

We hold so many questions
And we are given no answers.

As the sun sets on another day
We stare unknowingly into your heart
And realize there is a better place.
The ones we love have found their new home.

Yet at peace we are,
Your calmness is untrusting.
          Drew Hendee

I Am

I am human.
I wonder the world.
I hear only what I want to.
I see magical butterflies flutter around me.
I want to escape.

I am human.
I pretend to be happy.
I feel like I'm in a transparent box.
I touch the walls, trying to break free.
I worry that I'll never quite understand.
I cry because I feel lost.

I am human.
I understand silence.
I say words that no one hears.
I dream that one day I'll fall asleep with no worries.
I try to be the best I can be.
I hope I will succeed.

I am human.
          Kate Chanko

Wisteria Through Tears

Perhaps I'll meet the coming spring
With gladdened heart and voice to sing
About the daughter who from birth
Had painted Heaven here on earth
In death from pain there's sweet release
With illness she established peace
Through final hours she turned her head
That she might see there from her bed
The courtyard vine she loved to paint
Her cheerful question, voice so faint
Was "Are there any blossoms yet?"
My answer always, "Soon, my Pet"
This very morning in her room
I softly prayed, "Today a Bloom"
With sun so bright and breeze so grand
While reaching for her fragile hand.
Her breathing stopped, her heart was still
And kneeling at her window sill
One single blossom met my eye
Just as I bade my child good-bye.
          Rosalie Miller Morrison

384

The Poem of Love

I Love You more than words can express
If words could express, it wouldn't be Love
It would be a Poem Of Love
But, a Poem Of Love isn't our Love
Our love is what is Loved by us.

Priya Dhingra

As I Saw You Walk

Softly I hear the walk of love,
As I see you approach like a dove.
Ascending into my eyes.
As the door open, oh what a surprise;
Entering into my soul, as you speak
The loneliness moves far beneath
As your spirit walked in my heart;
The warmth, covereth my body
My love at last was here
Now we can hold each other, forever my dear.
Days have past and gone.
But never in our hearts; are we alone.
With every breath I take it is for you
Together we will take this journey
With life fears; and turbulence
We will walk together in love;
And through out this life and eternity.
My love, as I saw you walk.

Shirley Ann Barthel

Johnny, Johnny Appleseed

Here is Johnny Appleseed.
He is someone who planted trees.
His last name changed to Appleseed,
When he loved those apple trees.
Forty minutes old he loved those trees.
In Ohio and Indiana, He dropped those seeds.
Watched them grow into tall apple trees.
He planted May weed
to keep away Malaria disease.
Johnny, Johnny Appleseed!

Leanna Zaccone

Seek the Light

Guard, O Heart, the entrance to the Soul.
Be ready to snare the devourer at all times;
Do not slumber, Do not sleep;
Be vigilant; Be trustworthy;
And the Soul will always be filled
With the light of its creator.

If the gate is left unattended
Darkness, deeper than can be imagined, will fill the soul
Leaving it cold, barren, without life, without the light.
The devourer will come with a vengeance to seek its reward:
A soul, lost to Hell, for eternity.

O Heart, I implore you
Feed yourself with your creator's Words:
"I have come as a light to the world,
that whoever believes in me should not abide in darkness.
While you have the light, believe in the light,
that you may become "Sons of Light".

O Soul, to be without the light,
Is to be without God—Forever sealed unto darkness!
O Heart, Seek The Light!

Gwendolyn S. Burkhalter

Untitled

The night surrounds me with tangible blackness
as I run toward the quiet sea.
I trip and laughing roll the dunes in ecstasy.
Virgin sand slithers beneath my feet.
I fling myself in sheer abandonment
to the untouched surface of the clinging sand
and tumble buffeted by playful waves.
I lie spread-eagle facing darkness,
sending myself seeking, probing, wondering.
The night explodes into cascades
of piercing searing teardrops
pounding golden sand, running in burning rivulets
to join silently the velvet band.
Approaching from infinity
caressing veils of moonwashed cobwebs,
silver flecked, reach hesitant
to lap my feet with foamy rings.
Heaven reels with sparkling crystalline specks.

Beverly Ramsey

Loosing Our Aged Song

I'm gonna tie my troubled thoughts
to the floating smoke streams
slithering through my fingers
and watch raindrops
that ring coffee can chimes
and will shoot perfect holes
through the sweet pollution
and slam and shatter it against the ground
to trickle through the soil
the moist dirt straining the poison
leaving pure sweet water
to flow through the dry sandstone canyons
of the cracked lips
of all life
loosing our aged song

Timothy Buchanan

The Guide

To those who feel like they have strayed off the path of life,
  Listen well.

Do not listen to your heart alone for directions,
  For fear is a boulder that blocks and
    Love blinds to the way of truth.

Also take not directions solely from the mind,
  For it is said common sense leads to unfulfillment.

But know that all one needs are open eyes
  To what they have and what surrounds them on their quest.

For it is the eyes that are said to be windows of the soul,
  Where one can find both the heart and the mind,
    Emotion and knowledge, together
      Playing like the freest of children,
        Debating like the pettiest of Gods, and
          Loving till the day they get us
            To the end of our path.

Michael Torgler

Friends

Kittens are very soft, but friends are kind.
When you say Hi to a kitten she does not answer.
When you give a present to a friend she thanks you.
Kittens are soft, but friends are kind.
Thank you for being my friend.

Emily Felts

Freedom Is the Greatest Treasure

What do we learn when we study?
We learn the value of liberty.
Power, wealth and beauty are all pleasures,
But freedom is the greatest treasure.

What do we learn when we study?
We learn to treat people equally.
No matter what colors of people we see,
We are all free to be you and me.

Because freedom is so great,
We serve to keep it just our way.
Being a good citizen is how we do it
To keep our country strong and free.

Muyan Jin

Cherished Memories

You are the last vision before entering dreams
With reeling footsteps, I see you
stride into view as the curtain slowly falls
the film is shown and rewinds rewinds
The frozen places in my heart melt
with tears in my Christmas eve dreams

A silver night with long long dreams and
cold cold waiting for the rising of the sun
the sun that melts
the frozen places in my heart and
the frozen windows in my soul
May you with the morning sunlight leap out
leap out into our morning's first vision

With the four seasons
you come again and again
coloring maple leaves beyond count
you ride the autumn winds gust after gust
blowing the leaves down blowing them down
into my heart my mind with
cherished memories

Kim Chen Fyock

Love Is Being A Foster Parent

For twenty-three years the kids abound
they come from near and far around
all sizes, all kinds and many races
they all come with different names and faces.

They all need many hugs and lots of love
later they'll give it all back beyond and above
God has blessed us in so many ways
all we can do is thank Him with praise.

We've seen a little girl wake up one morning
with a smile on her face where none had been before
and a baby coming out of heart surgery
When no one even thought he would live.

Children with bruises and broken bones
all come to love you like your own
some who wake up crying in the night
look at you and at last have no fright.

So many people ask why we do this
I wish I had a good answer for them
fostering parenting is not for all
but I wouldn't miss out on this love - I'm having a ball.

Ruth Whiting

The Almighty

He who made Heavens and earth.
He who made man to rule over the earth.
He who made you and I.
He who flung the stars in the sky.
He who made what's truly right.
He who made day and night.
He who sent His son to earth.
He who gave signs to Mary before birth.
He who gave Moses The Commandments for us to follow.
He who gave knowledge to the prophets.
He who healed the sick and raised the dead.
He who made the blind to see.
He who made you and me.
He who made the lame to walk.
He who gave us strength to talk.
He who said if you ask in my Father's name I will give,
He who made all things, to live according to His will.
He is the son of the Father.
Today as He were yesterday and tomorrow.

Roscoe H. Wilcox

Relativity

You are old Auntie Mary, you are old and you're fat.
Your face is all raddled, your opinions are splat.
Your clothes are old fashioned, you make them yourself, but
you're rich and you're frugal, please,
Go sit on the shelf.
Get out of the gaze
Of my very best friends who think you are crazed.
The old are so useless, they snuffle and whine.
They're palsied and ludicrous, doesn't pay to be kind.
They waste all your time with diseases arcane,
One chokes on the platitudes, attitudes inane.
She might have been fun when I was a tot,
Now that she's old she is certainly Not.
I've a thousand things to do today, Aunt Mary.
I'm busy.

R. O. Janes

Springtime in Virginia

Crocus peeking shyly through the melting snow,
Raising dainty heads in the sun's warm glow
Pussy willow bursting with fuzzy fingers,
Impatient while the last snow lingers.
Greening grass grows from a long winter's sleep,
After resting and growing under snow and sleet.
Dogwood and red bud glorious in full bloom
Lilacs fill the air with their heady perfume.
Winter birds chirp greetings as the robins come back
Building new nests in each cranny and crack
Fields of jonquils sway in the springtime breeze
As bare limbs tremble and show buds on the trees
Stately tulips bow down their regal heads
Flaunting bright colors, resting in winter beds.
Fluffy clouds race quickly across the sunny skies
Fill us with contentment and make our spirits rise.
All seasons are beautiful in their own different ways
But springtime in Virginia brings us ultra special days
We marvel as Mother Nature's changes never cease
Spring brings us resurrection, happiness and peace.

Ruth Walton English

Call of the Sea

The waves softly hit the shore,
and reaches out as if to say.
Come to me, come to me.
Let me gently surround you.
And fill your body with sweet tranquility.
Come to the depths of the unknown
Let me take you far from harm's way
Let me fill your body with peace not sorrow.
Let the sea be your friend for an eternity.

Linda D. Pineda

My Mind Is Like A Computer

My mind is like a computer computing a life problem
It can be a friend or enemy if you know how to use it
You could make your dreams come alive
You could print them out to be the best you could ever imagine
Or even take a wild roller coaster ride
My mind is like a computer, "Where do you want to go today?"

Domenic Rotondo

Cherished Moments

As a little girl you were there for me all of the time,
guiding me through life and keeping me in line.

The moments I'll cherish of times spent with you;
like going to New York and to the Bronx Zoo.

Trips on the train were fun and exciting.
The World's Fair was thrilling with exhibits inviting.

Our days at the beach of sun, water and sand.
And at the end of the day...holding your hand.

A pony ride once when I was small,
you walking beside me looking so tall.
You coaxed me to kick, to make him go,
but, me, I preferred him going slow.

An Easter basket, a symbol of all things new,
A tradition you've continued, a reflection of you.

Your encouragement and support through life and through school
helped me to teach the golden rule.

I looked up to then and the more I grew;
I married and moved on but...still look up to you.

Our relationship is precious. Our relationship is true,
of a man that I love...My father...that's you.

Anita B. Collette

Mourning Cloak

Rise
Up out of the shivering stone berth
That claimed you seven years ago
Dew-frosted dirt blocks your sunshine
I long to wrap you in chamois-skin
Fix your face and neck and belly where you were stabbed
Seven times by the carving knife
I gave your Tonka toys to Billy
Redeemed you stubborn-soiled play pants at the resale shop
Disassembled your red wagon one wheel at a time
Washed your blue-eyed smiles out of
Windows, bouncing balls, cereal bowls
And the night terrors never stop
The screams underneath my skin trapped by
Plastic film covered mouth and nose and eyes
Unable to see through yesterday
Together we sleep in pieces

Pamela Kraft

The Bee

I hear a buzzing in my ear. Oh what great fear. I went to
say, "Mom, help me!" but I ran into the tree. And I
fell on my knee. And Mr. Bee stung me!

Misheer Davail Lyons

Two Weeks Left

Two weeks left, and still much to do.
Words are strained, even full of distress.
It will be alright, you know I love you.
So what! There's only two weeks left.

Suddenly the day is just next week.
A night spent with pals, strippers, and beer.
I think of only one thing, my knees go weak.
Soon I will have a wife, to love forever.

One day to go, push comes to shove.
Are you nervous? Isn't it scary?
To which I reply, I'm in love,
And tomorrow, I'm getting married.

David M. Stewart

My Special One

You have touched my heart like no one has or will.
The first time I saw you, my heart stood still.
You were and are my very special one.
You are my rainbow and my rising sun.
You have put me through so much,
Yet I look at you and I touch,
And simply wonder what it would have been,
If you had never been born and become my kin.
Those closest to you know best.
You are constantly putting us to the test.
I have experienced every kind of love.
I know you were sent for a reason from God above.
When I'm with you and hold you and you give me that smile.
I know that everything, yes everything is very worthwhile.
The pain and mountain of grief you have put me through,
Is forgotten because of the deep love I have for you.
I am here today, tomorrow, forever and always for you.
With great pride, deep joy, let me say "I love you".

Patricia Borch

My Father's House

My Father's house is there to stay
A light of faith by night and day

My Father's house will also be seen
By you and I as we see what he means.

The treasures of life and on my mind
My breath, my spirit; without wasted time

My Father's house is there to stay
My love, my faith, my Lord we pray.

Just to keep a line or two,
To keep for my brothers and sisters on through

My father's house and all this light
For the goodness of mercy for his children's right.

In a prayer whispering low
That God says yes and never no

Just to remember in every prayer
God is with you no matter where.

Myrtle Wilburn

Misty Rain

Walking in the misty rain with you,
Holding hands, like a couple of kids,
Losing ourselves in the greenness of the trees,
Listening to the sounds of nature;
The beauty of the natural silence,

The misty rain doesn't make a sound,
   As it sprinkles down upon us,
We talk to each other, in a whisper,
   So we don't disturb the beauty of the
      green silence,
As we continue to walk hand in hand in
   the misty rain.

   Carolyne Nice

Cram It Into The Universe

They say the ability to love is a very good thing.
It makes eagles soar and songbirds sing.
And love can't be measured by how big or how small.
For if you try to size it, it's worth nothing at all.

Is there such a thing as just a little love,
and who would dare question how many stars are above?
For not to love at all would surely be a curse,
but so would be a love too big to be crammed into the universe.

When it's this big,
You can't hold it in your hand,
Yet you can hold it in your heart.

   Jennifer Pietrowski

Short-Changed On Drugs

"Shorty Redcracker," since you've left our scene,
We were all "short-changed", and you know what I mean,
One of a kind, that's what you've been,
You were the "best comedian",
My heart aches all year long,
Since that day that went all wrong,
"What makes us laugh", still "makes us cry",
"I ain't just-a-joking", it hurts to say good-bye,
Jimbo's "leaving and gonna go to Cleveland",
My heart's in a "headlock", I miss mamann.

   Lynne Miller

Time

We give time, waste time, and buy time.
We cherish time, forget time, tell time.
Then there's the best of time - prime time,
Let's not forget bake time, break time.
What about sleep time, awake time
take a breather time.
We change time, make time, share time.
Oh the happy times, sad times, the worst of times!
Now there's a foretime, after time and life time.
We earn time, some work full time or part time,
for a life time.
Some take a long time, some past time and waste time.
Let's not forget seed time, harvest time, and haying time.
Daytime, noon time and night time
for a good time!
Then there's a long time during the half time.
Can't forget the yearning time and winter time.
Some try to make time, others two time!
With all this time why is it that
so many of us have a need for more time?

   Lucile Tyson

Girl With Red Umbrella

She disobeys when told to stay,
Her own desire to run free,
Just gets in the way.
Out the door with her red umbrella,
Out in the pourin' rain to try and ease her pain.
She runs away from everything, from everyone,
They try to help but it's only a dull downpour of useless advice.
Downpour on my heart, head, hurting soul.
Help ease and wash away the stain.
He's forgotten but she can not! She cannot
   forget, she cannot move on, she only
   replays the endless days of sinful ways.
Help us all, or we will fall, fall into the
   fire filled pit, forever, Forever!

   Melissa A. Strahan

The Fall

You crawl out of a cave.
You fall for days. Months. Years.
The end sneaks up on you,
But no like from behind.
You get caught up in the joy of falling.
You forget that you are dying.

The pessimist sees the ground,
sometimes closer than it really is.
You see the end.
You think you are prepared.

The optimist ignores it,
So must look into the past and present.
That is not any better.
You were falling then too.

But whoever you are,
You never see it until you are upon it.
But don't worry.
You won't feel a thing.

I guess the moral is for the person in the cave.
Turn back!!

   Sean Pringle

Our Troubled World

This world is in trouble - what have we done?
There's too many problems - and not enough funds.

Tell us what happened? Who is to blame?
Where did we fail? It's just not the same!

We struggle and work to stay alive -
And wonder "Is it worth it - why even try?"

We see people around us on public aid -
We feed the poor and care for the aged.

There's hijackers, terrorists and nuclear war -
Selling arms to Iran, inflation and more.

We hear about child abuse, cancer and AIDS -
Smoking is bad and cocaine's the rage.

Marijuana in the fields, instead of grain -
Farm aid for the farmers who feel the pain.

Nobody cares what lies ahead -
The future looks dim - the past is dead.

We cannot go back - we must go forward,
Clean up the world, before it's all over.

Each living person must do their part.
Please God - we're begging - help us to start!

   Donna L. Gadberry

On the Marina

The crescent moon shines in the eastern sky
as the sun sets and gives off a warm glow.
I'm sitting on the back of the boat and let
the sway of the hull calm my thoughts.
Laughter from across the water drifts my way,
and the wind blows the water, reflecting shimmering lights.
The bats fly along the docks on their erratic flight
and I hear the rumble of a distant motor.
Tomorrow is filled with plans and hopes
for a fun day that will be remembered.
On the Marina my thoughts seem to drift,
and my senses are lulled with the motion.
The boat rocks and sways me into
complacency, accepting what I need to.
I let myself go and my feelings swirl
with the wind through the night.
My emotional release flows into the
inky water leaving a translucent film.
On the Marina you can be content with yourself
and release some tension of everyday life.

Eric J. Bernkopf

Retired

I woke up that morning, man I was flying high,
I was way up yonder, up where the buzzards fly.
What brought all this on, you may inquire,
Man this is it, the day has come, I'm gonna retire.

From now on, I'm gonna do what I want to do.
I'll be going places, doing things, meeting people too.
Man, it's gonna be great having all this free time,
Life will be one big party, everything will be fine.

I'll see all the sights as I travel around,
I'll visit old friends, I may never come down.
And then one day, it hit me like a flash,
Damn it all, I ain't got no cash.

It felt so good and it was fun while it lasted,
But with one shot of reality, it all got blasted.
It would have been oh so nice, but alas,
I guess I'll just go out and cut the grass.

Now here I am, a slave to my back yard,
Never thought I would have to work so hard.
How I got in this mess, I'm at a loss,
It ain't all bad though, I'm the boss.

Ralph B. Lyon

Someday, We'll Be Together Again

Honey, I know you didn't leave me permanently,
And that you're just down the road at the next
Rest stop waiting for me,
Someday, we'll be together again.
I'm carrying on just like you want me to and
I always consider you when I wonder what to do,
Someday, we'll be together again.
You left me so unexpectanly and I always knew
You were my happiness,
Who I still look for and cry for and really miss,
Someday, we'll be together again,
I, and all your "shining stars" treasure the
Precious memories we have of you,
You were always there, you always cared for
Those of us who know that,
Someday, we'll be together again.

John Rozsa

Time Is Flying By

Isn't it amazing how time goes by
Goes flying by
And how we limit its use
By standing still, not going forward not turning loose

And whose there to ask us
Whose there to know
What houses this heart inside of me
That just won't let go

I dream of what I could do
I know my abilities
My intelligence is high
And here comes time flying by

Connie Vinson

Drowned

Bright are the sands, cool is the wind.
  In late summer splendor I walk with my friend.
The tide coming in, invited our trance
  And we took to the water in deep blue expanse.

Roaring on rocks, was the breath of the ocean
  Waves turned on time to show lunar devotion.
The trap that had brewed, the promised delight
  Then all turned to darkness when I lost all my might.

The currents ran strong and swirled all beneath
  The once friendly sea now seeks to bequeath
With burning inside, want of air to take in
  On the back of my neck I could feel death's grin.

My feet felt like weights and I sank against will
  While in desperate gasp, my lungs they did fill.
Looking up to the sky and in final frustration
  I succumbed to the silent liquid suffocation.

Charlie David Newell

Me

Me, one amongst the many,
Me, just as good as any,
Me, not a movie star, athlete or musician,
Me, just another guy in society's congregation

Me, I think like any other,
Me, just a simple son and brother,
Me, not trying to save the Earth,
Me, just as simple as I was from birth,

Me, I like my music and my phone,
Me, not living up to expectations when I sit at home,
Me, I go to school, do my thing, and socialize,
Me, just another in society's irritated eyes,

Me, I don't want to be a Pres or famous leader,
Me, I'm very regular with not a lot to say,
Me, I don't want to win a war once a week,
Me, I just like coming home and sleeping every day,
Me, I'm not a super human or a powerful God,
Me, I'm just a regular guy, and wouldn't want it any other way.

Scott Weber

A Dove

God only you could know how I feel today
On the porch crying my thoughts far away
The ledge outside holds a beautiful dove
You sent him here to speak of peace and love
I talked to him he could not speak a word
After all he's just a little bird
A sign from above on the wings of a dove'?
Telling happiness, love and peace be still
Only God can heal the mentally ill

Geraldine Davidson

A Burning Lily

Way down deep in the darkness a lily burns bright.
Time has no meaning here,
I leave the lily center passing raindrops on my way to the surface,
People walk by not able to see the lily center,
Only that which is on display for them.
Should I stop them? Should I tell them?
I want to ask them why they do not try to see.
Are they blind? Are they scared?
But I can see them.

Catherine Anne McAllister

The Ambivalent Clown

His smile was always bulging and cheerful
Ever careful never to be fearful

Children were charmed into pure trusting doves
Always attracted to his warmth and love

Every bit jolly like ole Santa Claus
The many inspired to his lightened cause

The crowds he sought were eager for his fun
He did make certain he left out no one

Cautious never to ignore or to shout
But constantly looking out for his clout

All were taken with his bright scheme
Knowing not it was only his aged dream

His kindness fooled all while in his shy youth
But in his late years he became uncouth

To him there was a sadder, somber side
That he struggled to keep but could not hide

Only when alone could it be revealed
Few that knew kept it very well concealed

Not knowing what he gave with his gladness
He died one day amidst this great sadness

Yvonne Russell

You Are My Everything

It began when we were young and gay,
We did things together most every day.
I didn't know then what I know now,
That we'd fall in love (I don't know how).

We got together again after many years,
So much had passed, both happiness and tears.
We were both alone, no partners in sight,
Though neither was looking by day or night.

I never dreamed we'd fall in love I confess,
But we sensed these feelings with the first caress.
Those feelings grew to something you couldn't miss,
When all of a sudden we had our first kiss.

I feel so wonderful when I'm with you,
When I can't be, I don't know what to do.
I thank my lucky star and the good Lord above,
For sending my wonderful you for me to love.

And I know that you also love me,
You've made that very easy to see.
Being with you makes my heart sing,
So you see my dear, you are my everything.

Raymond F. Smith

Forever

It wasn't supposed to end this way, in fact, not at all.
The eternal flame of our love was forever to be
glowing, not to fall to the mere embers of memories.
The crucifixion of our utterly indescribable enrapt
eternity in each other left me with nothing
more than the ever present question Why? The
mutual, undeniable feelings were no longer of an
equal love, but more of one with an uncomfortable
unevenness. When it began, the utmost perfection of
it all seemed immortal. But how can two completely
mortal beings try to understand and live within
immortality? The translucent lining that made my
eyes blind to reality was suddenly ripped apart. It is
over and that is inevitable yet there are questions
still rising. There are thoughts still lingering in my
mind. I thought it would burn eternally. I thought it
would be immortal. I thought there would be no
questions.
I thought forever was understood.

Elizabeth Vergamini

A Life's Lost Years

Life is precious, withe years we learn
But we were not ready for such a tragic turn

For we lost our first, me and my love
He went to be withe God above

We have grieved and we have cried
Why was our Trevor the one to die

Our family and friends all showed us they care
Withe love and support and many a prayer

We searched our souls and shed our tears
For the many questions and for a life's lost years

Although from our hearts was his love thus torn
We shall always remember our precious Firstborn

Michelle Kearns Callahan

Thoughts from a Train Window

The California Zephyr hurried toward
Chicago's Loop. The landscape scenes along
the tracks had illustrated progress in
reverse, from new to old, from dreams fulfilled.
to utter desolation and despair.

The picture of America that's past
is best seen from a train. The factories
that once provided jobs for thousands, now
stand idle—obsolete, could not compete.
The neighborhoods has nearly died as well.

Carl Sandburg once described Chicago as
a city of big shoulders. Yet the weight
of devastation wrought by decades of
such unrelenting change have nearly brought
this once proud urban giant to collapse.

Is there concern and leadership that can
bring hope and help restore these neighborhoods?
And what if there is not? Then such decay
will spread unchecked, engulfing suburbs, too.
Creating urban wastelands ought to stop.

Peter J. Weller

My Little Flower

Dedicated to my Granddaughter Morgan Blair — May 1994

My precious little Morgan
How I love you so
Pitter patter, pitter patter
Always on the go
It only seems like yesterday
I held you in my arms
And now behold
You're eight months old
It's time to sound alarms
Because you see, the day will come
And soon enough can't be
From those precious little lips of yours
I'll hear you say "Me Mé."

Margaret Leoty

It Takes A Whole Village

The family structure is torn down.
    We all have to help now.
Some think it has to be done by school
    But it actually starts with the Golden Rule.
It takes a whole village — you know it's right!
    But if you interfere — you have to fight.

Daddy's got no work, child gotta Uzi
    Mama's snorting coke — making excuses.
"Hanging" with your kids — you get no respect
    Then you wonder why it is, you are rejected

You send them off to school
    They got "Hilfiger," "Jordan" and gold chains
And you have yet to pour the basics
    Into their little brains.

They got no respect for the old, parents or each other
    They even got the nerve to call each other "brother"
Listen village — step in before it's too late!
    It has to be done now, and not a later date!

Evelyn Nesbitt

A Special Friend Treasure

Someone understands like none could,
    Extending silence when nobody would.
Advice isn't always the answer you know,
    Words like Seasons come and go.

Sometimes we just need to be on our own,
    A friend knows when to leave you alone.
And then there are times when troubles abound,
    That special friend just happens around.

Offering comfort and laughter and peace,
    What worldly treasures can compare to these?
So hold close to your heart, that someone you know,
    Who can lift you and set your spirit aglow!

For this is the one, who through thick and thin,
    Will chase away rain, bringing sunshine again.
No yardstick or scale or worldly measure,
    Will ever compare to a "special friend treasure!"

Edmund J. Shanks Jr.

Daddy Left!

I was only nine that Valentine's Day
When I came home from school.
MaMa told me you were gone.
You had passed away. That was cruel.

I wept many tears. My heart just broke.
No daddy to hug or kiss,
No more sitting on your lap to be loved.
All that remained was a hollow miss.

My years since then have moved along
With high school graduation and more:
Marriage, four kids plus six good grandsons.
Always I've missed you, as before.

Daddy, I've always loved you so much.
I've thought of you in so many ways.
Yet, God became my father, filled your role,
Just as the Holy Bible says.

Thanks now to Jesus, His father became mine.
The ache and trauma, the times I cried...
God's spirit has freed me and taught me to see
It was for those tears he died.

Shirley M. Grant

The Hidden Garden

The hidden garden inside the soul,
Shall always try to reach the goal.
It will reach high, arms outstretched,
Showing the scars, twisted and wretched.
Scars caused by words, scars that never mend,
They are with us to the very end.
In this world we all share,
The life of pain when no one cares.
A knife twists deep in your heart,
You feel yourself slip as you fall apart.
But you'll be back to take some more,
Because you know all that lies in store,
Will not leave, it always returns,
And when the time comes they will burn.
Only then will they truly know,
The mistake they made so long ago.
The score will be even, the battle finally won.
The shadowed garden will finally see sun.

Dawn Amber Dunn

Longings

Nostalgic longings, trying to recapture the past
Fervent longings, fading ever so fast
Vain persistent longings, still grasping
Forgotten glories, slipping away, foreboding

Impassioned longings, irreplaceable yet fruitless
Broken asunder, severed and utterly useless
Dismally lonesome longings, irremediably alone
Vessels sunk at distant moorings, castaways, without a home

Life's savage sea can put the best of us
In suspended misery, corroding our trust
Blunderingly naked we search for unanswerable logic
Unquestionably we're scandalously raped, painful even though symbolic

The sea clutches her dreadful secrets with an incessant roar
Will she ever repent or continually whore
Unyielding tempestuous seasons, undulating without remorse
What is life's reason at the end of one's course

Stranded, forgotten by the wind, pathetically forlorn
Hulls broken, lanterns dim, why where we born
The day of our christening there was so much fun
Now there is sadness in the setting of the sun

James Hartshorn

The One

Awake,
which fork should I meander down today?
The one to the left?
The one to the right?
The one ever so beaming?
The one not so bright?
Down which path will I be greeted with delight?
Yet not to reckon with a sequence causing fright.
Despite, glory might lie in my sight.
Where to bite? As to discover the sweet plum amongst glum.
As for which fork will deliver me the best,
I'll set forth down either one,
from there it's up to me I guess.

Stephen Pache

Mom I Love You

I am making a list, and I hope it is nice
Don't have time to check it twice.
The laundry is done, the house is clean,
Hope no one calls and talks to me mean.
Would love to have my special family, but
No one cares if I am their Mommy.
Someday when it is too late, and you are feeling blue
You might wish you would of called and said
"Mom I love you"
Sometimes we don't think of the little things
That can make someone happy.
It's the little things, no matter how small
It's love that matters most of all
Friends are important in everyone's life.
Because when family doesn't care, friends are your spice.
Memories they can never take away,
No matter what they do.
All you needed to say was
"Mom I love you"

Bette Baringer

Unrequited Love

I look upon you and . . .
My dreams are lucid . . .
I see you in my heart
I feel desire take my body.
I feel your hot breath upon my shoulder
I feel your body touch my bone
I feel your flush in me
I live a thousand joys . . .

And I look into your eyes
And you do not gaze upon me.
You do not long for my touch
Do not want my dreams.
You are in my bed, but a thousand miles away
I live a thousand deaths
This is agony!

I look and turn away.
I leave it to God . . .

Fernando Vela

Evening's Curtain

When evening pulled her curtain down
The clock on the mantel was counting out the sound
The fire was warm with its big logs so round
The red hot coals baking the corn bread brown
Butter we had for it, at least a pound
Milk from the kitchen, with ice in it we always found
In the old straight chairs to the fire we would gather around
Soon time for me to get ready for bed in my long flannel gown
The fire next morning would be as cold as the outside ground

F. Carolyn Bennett

My Marriage

As I walk down this path of life.
Thinking what marriage would be like down this life line.
I have all kind of ideas of fortune and fame and companionship.
But as darkness slips in
I find myself meeting darkness at every corner
Darkness seems to have come somewhere
From the past into my marriage.

Mary A. Myers

A Trip to the Park

I enter in from the left side
Whirled amongst the colors and lights

Destiny is awaiting my arrival
Some disappointment is always a residual
Expectations are never truly fulfilled
Factors which are controlled by fate are revealed

Wind blows the smells of midday
The open air unifies the meeting place
When time is taken, consideration is discovered
Then true meaning and understanding can begin
Why is answered each time we feel

The park is crowded with dwellers
Conversations of different varieties occur simultaneously
Fathers to sons, Mothers to daughters, Men to Women, Women to Women
Couples to couples and groups to groups
Listening, to all, what value is communication if nothing is heard?

Thomas A. Agoglia

Blind Minds

In the state of mind that we are in, we strive for Freedom
Breaking ourselves apart with destructive force and words
Makes us weak towards anything around us or in us

Being apart is not what we are here for
Together with pride will make us Strong inside

If we can not understand each other, what do we have?
Where do we stand in this world?
What dark cloud is surrounding the Soul of our minds?

What we are Blessed with, we should not hide what motivates us
Think! If we do not blend into one, we will Destroy ourselves.

Frank A. Brown Jr.

Reach for the Prize

I looked in the old cracked mirror
But I saw only inner distortion
Images of long ago horror
Scenes that seemed out of proportion

I looked and listened very carefully
The mirror said, forget the past, reach for the prize
In the Lord you can do anything
Could I see through the devil's disguise

Could I see myself as I really am
Could I triumph over past suffering
Is it worth the final price, perchance
To reach through the challenges, be enduring

Yes, there may be weeping all night
But on the morrow there will be joy
Behold, in the mirror a new sight
No longer blind, reflection restored

Oh what challenges you bring me
But the Lord will be my strength
He will supply all I need, as I reach for the prize
On my final mirrored quest

Dixie Dee Taylor

Untitled

Through the night I hear them calling me,
Calling me, telling me the things
I should be
They whisper secrets and words
in my mind
They show me things only seen
by the blind
I close my eyes and see the
secrets of the dark
I see the journeys and trials
I am to embark
I listen closely to them and suddenly
realize meaning
It's not voices, but the words
in my heart beating
        Christi Berry

Paris

In Paris you will always find true love,
Love of the city, of the art, of the rose-colored light,
And of the bridges and the whole sight,
It doesn't matter whether you're sad, or gloomy, happy, or mad
It will always bring you joyfulness
And happiness for the rest of your life.
It's like you're a butterfly
And you're trapped in a beautiful flower
And you can never go back to where you lived before
        Jackie Damiani

We Should Have Seen It Coming

"I'm not afraid to die," she said.
    "But everyone's afraid to die," we exclaimed.
    (We should have seen it coming.)
"Death is the end of you; you must be afraid!" we said.
"No! Not me; I'm not afraid to die!" she said . . .
    "For living is what brings fear."
    (We should have seen it coming.)
"Think of the little girl, living in fear of each day
    she spends with grandpa . . .
"The little girl with the older brother refusing to let
    her go—as her parents listen but ignore . . .
"The young child whose neighbor threatens with
    'their little secret' . . .
"The young adult in college, trying to `fit-in',
    but always being different . . .
"Those growing older fighting for the truth of who
    they are, but fearing discrimination."
    "Is this the life you speak of?" she asks . . .
"No, I am not afraid to die, but merely afraid to live!"
    She exclaimed, as she turned and chose the only
    path she was not afraid to travel.
    ("We Should Have Seen It Coming!)
        Lisa Marie Terrell

The Song That Never Ends . . . .

Melodic torment over and over again . . .
The chiming never interludes in my head
It has coerced me to insanity . . . .
This delicious form of profanity
Sleep is no escape . . .
 For it is then that I wake
Take away this diabolic harmony
Which brings great suffering to me . . . .
        Mary Torchia

My Testimony

A few years ago, my soul was sick and full of pain.
My mind was full of confusion.
The more I prayed, I felt as though, my faith had been betrayed.

I started to sink far from God's peaceful shore
I was so low, my eyes tried not to let
The tear drops fall through all my restless nights,
And all my doubtless nights.

My God came to me late one night, He said in a humble voice,
"My child, I am here, I've been here all the while.
Just open your eyes and look into the light."

I opened my eyes and looked into the light
The light was beaming bright, I knew without a doubt —
My God had made all things right.

I closed my eyes to whisper a prayer of thanks,
And beautiful music rang in my ears.
The Angels were singing,
"Amazing Grace, How Sweet The Sound . . . "

Then I knew my soul was safe and sound.
Each day as I live and breathe, I will always give
God the praise for Amazing Grace will always be my song of
praise.
        Brenda Cook

The Sea's Secret

She tickled and wiggled and giggled with glee
    crawling around aimlessly,
On rocks, coral and sand she slowly creeps
    smelling the scent of prey to eat.

But along comes a giant and steps on her arm
    breaking one off she begins to mourn.
Crying and weeping thinking she'd lost . . .
    But wait, what's that? Gasping at the cost
    an arm begins to grow, and a body on the lost.

She jumps and dances, happy to see
    that her arm fallen off has a home to be.
She now has a family a sister of pride,
    they live their lives among the tide.

Splishing and splashing, the waved water went
    as they played and dined in the sweet water scent.

What is it?
Answer: Star Fish
        Tammy Enns

Christmas Thoughts

A sobering thought when want is a stranger—
The Christ child was born and laid in a manger.

A sobering thought where warm fires are glowing—
The Christ child was born where cattle were lowing.

A sobering thought when the world's so appealing—
The Christ child was born with sky for a ceiling.

A sobering thought when in ease we are basking—
The Christ who was born in ours for the asking!
        Nan S. Muir

A Toast Farewell

Let's drink a toast to say good-bye,
To those who have needlessly died.
Too much alcohol consumed,
Still in control, the drinker assumed.
A lethal stalker behind the wheel,
Feeling no pain, or knowing what's real.
Caught in a vicious roulette kind of game,
an innocent victim's life he'll claim.
Perhaps not intentional, but the drinker's to blame.
Some so far gone they aren't even ashamed.
Accidents happen, and that's certainly true,
We have no control, but the drinkers they do!
I lost my best friend when he went to the store,
His wife lost her husband, his children more.
The loss is still unbearable at times.
The tragedy not worthy of the crime.
Because the drinker didn't think ahead,
A man who embraced this life is dead!
Jim, is just one of a million who've died,
Please think of our loss if you drink and drive!

Tracy L. Knutson

I Want You To Know

I want you to know my child, how much you mean to me,
Open my word, read, and listen and you will see all I have created you to be.

Can you see all the love I desire to pour into your heart, which has been broken by the fall?
Do you see how much I want you to stand tall?

My love for you can overcome any obstacle that may try to get in your way.
Look at the beauty within you, and know that it was once clay.

Clay that I am constantly molding into perfection,
Ridding your soul of every kind of infection.

I am the God who cleanses your heart from every ounce of pain,
However, at times, deep cleansing will come through the down poor of much rain.

Take heart my child, you are not alone in your tribulation,
After the storm has passed there will be much jubilation.

Look at yourself, you are a walking example of the love I have for all I have created,
So walk in this truth, and know that with you I am elated.

Judy C. Meiners

A Gift from God

The gift of love God has given me
Is in this beautiful day
I will not mar its beauty
By what I do or say.
There is nothing that can compare
To the friendship I have with God
As He and I walk hand in hand
Where angels fear to trod.
He guides me very gently
Through the valleys along the way
And I sing praises and thank Him
For being my friend and his gift of this day.

Effie J. Drain

Under the Rainbow

Life has been very hard on you these days...
Give yourself some credit,
you have tried in many ways.
Just give it your best.
And remember, perhaps it's a test.
Courage and Strength,
As you carry on through the days.
Only you can make it happen. Only you can find the ways.
You have the knowledge,
Now make it work for you.
God will only serve to you,
What He knows you can go through.
Life will be as it may...
You must make it happen. You must find the way.
If you feel you need some help...
Just say the words and pray.
God will hear you, and guide you along the way.

Therese Ozuna

Silver Bug

The moon shines down this night,
Moon rays dance upon the lake.
The stars shine brightly tonight, for it is silver night.

The wind blows through the grove.
The wind blows through the trees.
The wind sounds almost seem to speak to me this night, this silver, silver night.

As I stand looking out into the countryside,
I notice something, for no crickets chirp this night.
Maybe it's my mind. Or maybe it's my ears.
Or maybe there just aren't any crickets this night, this silver, silver night.

I listen hard for minutes. I listen hard for hours.
For there is nothing, nothing but solitude this night, this silver, silver night.

Finally a sound, a sound from anywhere, a sound from everywhere.
Is it from the peach tree grove. Or is it from meadow.
Maybe from the trees.
Or maybe, just maybe it is my mind playing tricks on me.
Quietly, quietly the sound sneaks up. From the east.
Or maybe it is coming from the west.
For this sound is not a cricket, not this night.
For there was no sound at all it was just my mind playing tricks on me this night, this silver, silver night.

Theodore J. Shepard

The Morning Star and You

I awaken each new day . . .
feeling richly blessed
Then I close my eyes and pray . . .
softly while you rest
Another chance for love's continue
for who you are and what you do . . .
That's how I feel each time I see
The Morning Star and You

Our flow of feelings releases . . .
throughout our warm caress
Exchanging strength and weakness . . .
heart to heart we express
Like the smile on a baby's face anew
Or a rose adorned by a drop of dew . . .
That's how I feel each time I see
The Morning Star and You.

Lucille Watkins-Gray

Forever

I knew from the very start, we would never grow apart.
The angels from above told me we'd be
"Together Forever.'

I grew to love you very much,
Can you believe I used to shiver with your touch?
You told me we'd be
"Together Forever."

We became a team, you and me.
Then something went wrong with fate, how can that be?
Suddenly my world has fallen apart all around me
I've realized we won't be "Together Forever."

Now we are going opposite ways,
We haven't seen each other for hundred's of days
We will never be "Together Forever."

But wait, I can hear your gentle voice coming back to me
It's getting stronger, It won't be very much longer.
My heart does a dance, can there possibly be a chance?
My eyes start to shine, will you again be mine?
You answer me with a kiss, I've never felt as good as this.
Now I know we will be "Together Forever."

Jennifer Lynn Cox

Then And

May we find in Time, the sliding Now, gone?
Where did it go?
Shall we in Love, that moment, Now.
When you first loved me and I first
loved you?
Where did it go?
When life's last breath sighs joy's sweet song,
with happy affect.
Love's Now,
Where did it go?
These question hang in the air.
Until I of you,
you of me, and We
of We,
become aware
Of then and Now.

Joseph Greenbaum Jr.

Life and Me

Mother always told me . . . I took life for granted . . .
That life was a gift.
It wasn't something that I had to have.

Then one day . . . It happened!!!
And when it happened . . .
Guess who it happened to . . .
To Me!

I was on death row . . . My life was on the line!
I've fought many battles . . . But none like this one.
Never one this big!
I had only one priority left!
Jesus Christ!

I didn't know if he would bring me through.
All they could do was Pray . . . And . . . Wait.

Finally, the day came . . . and he brought me through!
I had to realize . . . That I could have been
Gone!!

I had to thank God that he didn't take
That precious gift away from me.
The precious gift of Life.

Kendra Moore

I Thank You Mother

I love you mother with all my heart;
I loved you from the very start.

I was a tough little guy to raise;
Your job was rough, and you received no praise.

My every need was you concern;
When trouble came, it was to you I would turn.

Somehow, you would always work things out;
Your good counsel removed all doubt.

And mother, I always enjoyed your wonderful meals;
I was so thankful you possessed such skills.

We were always materially poor;
But your rich spirit provided the cure

Somehow you would always show me a good time;
Your loving nature made things "Just Fine."

God gave you such a wonderful soul;
He fitted you perfectly for a mother's role.

Yes mother, you "passed the test"
In my book, you are the best -

I thank you mother for all that you have done;
To my world, you have been my sun

Wesley A. Collins

Great Out Doors

For a moment space, without human sound,
In my solitary room—
Living plants trodden under foot
Offer sweet perfume.

Trees tower above my resting place
While the river sings lullaby;
And I see before me immensity
In mountain, tree, and sky.

The skeleton branches are almost gone,
New green decks my lovely bower—
Bird songs trill and echo sweet,
Bud struggles to be flower.

Then through the trees, high—high above
One solitary cloud, tinged gold;
The signal for the day to end—
So night may, the world, enfold.

And I, alone here meet my God,
Sit with Him awhile;
Then, rising, more sure of my chosen way
I can walk each charted mile.

Launie K. Severinsen

A Mother's Love

A mother's love come deep from her soul
The love for her child in her heart she will hold.
This love begins the moment she conceive.
In your self she will teach you to believe.
Her love has that gentle touch.
There will be times you will need her very much.
Together you will laugh on her shoulder you will cry.
Her love is deeper then the sea.
And bluer then the sky.
Her love will be with you when you blow out candle number one.
The love that you feel it's her it will come from.
As days go by with her and as the time slowly pass
Always remember
A mothers love will forever last.

Carolyn N. Spence

Washington

I like Washington with all its trees
And I enjoy watching all the bees.
Who carefully pick up their honey
For to them it is worth more than money.
How beautiful are all the fountains
But they are not as pretty as the mountains,
For they are all purple and gold,
But they are nothing compared to my Lord.

Seattle, a city where race and color do not matter
Its towering Space Needle atop all the chatter.
By the Kingdome where the Mariners play,
It is bright and cheery as a summer day.
With all the fruit at Pike Place market
They could fill up over three score buckets.

As much as I love the state of Washington,
I know God placed me here for a plan
Maybe meet new friends, maybe some other reason
But I know I will be happy as long as I have God

Morgan Lincoln Isaac

Seasons

The seasons of the year are often wild,
but they can change overnight and become mild.

The winds of a blizzard take lots of snow,
and throw it at everything as they continue to blow.
Thru the frosted window appears the face of a child,
who is waiting and wishing for weather more mild.

As usual, in time the next season will arrive,
making trees, flowers and grass become more alive.
This lovely fresh season is called spring,
and the trees echo with song the birds sing.

Then comes the season of races and bases,
which means kids have lots of fun and red faces.
This season which seems so short is called summer,
and when it ends school starts — a real bummer.

The most colorful season of all is called fall,
and even with school, kids have a ball.
They kick their feet through bright piles of leaves,
aware that winter is coming and their young hearts grieve.

This is the end of this poem on Mother Nature's seasons,
as I have run out of lines, rhymes, seasons and reasons.

Marilyn M. Reynolds

Nebo

I sit aloft in the darkness and gaze down upon the city,
A million jewelled lights, a host of happy eyes.
Somewhere among them is one that winks at me.

My glance falls upon dark spaces. Those will be houses asleep,
Where the day's trial rests, and lovers have gone to bed.
Somewhere in shadow a heart beats for me.

Up to my lonely station comes melodious laughter, joy
Of the quick in spirit. Somewhere among the notes
Is the laughter I left behind.

My thoughts skip along the scene and see the hands of lovers,
Touching, searching, reaching messages.
Somewhere among them a hand reaches out to me.

Upon my Nebo I stand lonely, in hopeless solitude,
Head bowed, aching, for the eyes, the heart, the laughter,
And the precious hands that touch my soul.

Stewart C. Harvey

An Open Door

I wanted the key to your heart's door,
but you held it tight in your strong hand
I pleaded with you to give it to me,
but you cast me aside with annoyance
I desired a glimpse of what you are,
but you kept the door shut tight
I longed to feel what you were feeling,
but you left me out in the cold

I quit trying and you handed me the key.

Keli E. Granstrom

Untitled

You have hurt me many time before
but for some reason I stand by your side.
Every time you have left me, I've cried.
I loved you so much and you keep turning your
back on me.

I'll never find anyone I love as much as I
love you, we have had our bad times more
than we have had good, but the memories
of you keep running through my mind.

No matter how many bad times we've had
I keep running back to your side. Will you
ever understand how much I love you?

Patrica Vance

I Alone . . .

At times I think of dying, broken houses, and a
rotting world.
I want to save them all, heal the sick, stop the drugs, wipe
away the tears.
But I alone can not save the world.

I want to comfort the old, and tell a child that their daddy
won't hit them anymore.
I want to tell a mother that her child will not die.
But I alone can not save the world.

I try, and I cry, and I curse God for this world.
I curse Him for the pain I see with my own two eyes.
I wonder why so many must suffer.
I wish for it all to be a dream, and when I wake up I'll be
in Heaven.
Where the Lamb and the Lion lay beside one another.
But I alone can not save the world.

I alone can not stop the battles, or feed the hungry, or clothe
the naked.
Because I alone can not save the world.

Christina Johnston

Melissa Dawn

As beautiful as the morning sunrise,
you were named for.
As soft as the pale moonlight,
for little ones are just the way.
I love you with all my heart, sight unseen..
Her eyes were as blue as a cloudless summer day,
oh how I wish you could have stayed.
Her hair would have been a golden brown,
I know in my heart her face would have never worn a frown.
How do I know, you looked this way.
How could I have ever known.
I see you every now and then,
whenever I'm alone.
I love you Melissa Dawn.

Micah G. Stancil

Fantasy

Have you ever wondered what goes on inside a child's mind?
How far imagination goes? How Earth is left behind?

Well let me take you to that world, for I am but a child,
And if you don't believe in it, I'll drive your ol' minds wild.

With Kings, and Queens, and wars to fight, with blood, and
   guts, and gore.
Fencing, jousting, tournaments, their poor old bodies sore.

Horses running, pure and white, with a single horn.
Smooth, and graceful, delicate, they call unicorn.

Fire-breathing, nasty dragons, with talon, teeth, and claw,
Tearing apart knights who brave its mighty forceful jaw.

Large ponies sprouting wings that work, flying through the air.
Surely, smoothly, carrying you, they want to make you stare.

That is the world of Fantasy, a child's dream come true.
Come join us, you're invited here, and that, my friend's your cue.

   Danielle Racke

Untitled

Emotions running rapidly, while still trapped.
Pushing them deeper inside as they try to emerge.
Simple things add up to cause a breakdown.
Releasing them slowly.
Sharp pains reach the sky.
Screaming as they crash to the floor.
So confused, so very confused.
A life full of happiness, living a total utopia.
Those dreams are still floating through the air.
Backward thoughts leave me now.

   Jennifer Baumgardner

Killing Your Average Joe

No
No
No, not a close friend of average Joe
I elected the road untrampled and pure,
You followed the usual crowd on marked territory.
Don't come to my complex Life
Joe Schmoe
with your ordinary unimaginative ways
no time...keeps on ticking...like the beat of innovation
'cause I can not hear you for my intellect is of a
sophisticated method, understand when I say to you don't
step an inch closer or it'll be your plain head plummeting
from your simple shoulders at the blade of my acute knife
or barrel of my reasonable gun! For intellectual fun
I'd blow and slice average Joe up into unadorned pieces
plastered and mercilessly tortured with
a clutter of challenges...
Then bathe like a sponge in a sea of beautiful books,
notes, hidden Black history, and ageless philosophy.

   Earl Poyser

Why Cry?

Why do the babies cry?
Are they embarrassed?
Are they shy?
Is it because they're born in the nude?
I wonder, do they think this is rude?
Or is it something else,
To be born into a world of hate and genocide?
And even I cry, yes I do,
To be born in a world like this,
Wouldn't you?

   Shawn Lecrone

A Blackbird

A blackbird appeared through my window
a spectacle to me, I'm afraid.

   for in the midst of this scene,
a chipmunk was first in my view.

   The chipmunk jumped and then took charge,
but the blackbird he did know.

   That little chippy was half his size,
and bit him in the nose.

   Over and over again his nerve,
his territory he did regain.

   But old Blacky - he didn't forget
that his size was everything.

   The eggcorn, the maple seed, and then the nut,
everything he tried to pursue.

   But little chipmunk moved too fast,
and left the bird with few.

   Old Blacky, he lost, he couldn't gain
lost confidence, nuts, and eggcorns.

   Away he flew up into the sky,
To show little chippy his domain.

   Shirley Schwiedop

Thoughts of You

Your gentle ways, your loving touch
Will always mean so very much.
For all the special things you do,
I'll always be in love with you.
The way your lips holds that smile,
I long to be with you if even for awhile.
The way your eyes twinkle and brighten even the darkest sky,
My fondest thoughts and memories of times
We shared will never die.
You are the treasure at the end of my rainbow,
With each and every passing day our love will surely grow.
And with this vow I make to you,
It's sealed with love that will always be true.

   Ree Baker

Irish Gold Eighteen-Carat Green

'Tis an aisle so green, green, green
Green as any acre in God's greenery,
Green where such green nowhere else you'll see
'Tis Irish gold eighteen-carat green.

A green like Emerald floating on the Irish Sea
And so profuse with shamrock green,
Where Colleen's walk bare footed thru fields of gold
And smiling reflect the shine of gold above.

'Tis the isle St. Patrick baptized into Christianity
And revered as the patron saint of Ireland,
God blessed and crowned it with a semi-halo
And breathed life into it with a heavenly glow.

Where the dew on the shamrock in the light of the morn
Looked like a carpet of emeralds that had fallen from above,
Where leprechauns roam and frolic in her glens
And the wee folks watch o'er their treasured pot of gold.

'Tis a mystic isle shroud in mist
Echoing with music and song and clog dancing feet,
With white cottages and quilted fields seemed with low stone walls
'Tis shamrock green eighteen-carat Irish gold.

   Colleen Krymski-Rahner

As the People

To reach our goals, is something we can't do on our own
We must have someone by our side, so we won't stand alone
We must come together as Blacks in Whites, and others it concern
Listen to one another, cause we still have lots to learn
In order to see the sunrise, we must make it through the night
In order to watch our children grow, we must show the light
As the people, we're destroying the world and our children lives
Showing the hatred of another kind also guns and knives
Learning to shoot at the age of seven, and they're dead at ten
If I wrote the bible, showing a kid to shoot a gun, would be a sin
If we stop showing, how to hate and neglect
Maybe they'll learn, how to love and respect
United we stand, divided we fall
We must come together, as a rainbow coalition once and for all,
As The People

Gregg I. L. Howerton

Looking Out the Window

Looking out the window
I saw children playing outside
unas lagrimas fell from my eyes
my memories came back one more time

Looking out the window
I remembered him how we used to play outside
I closed my eyes
I ask myself where he was

Looking out the window
many days are gone
but he still on my heart
for the rest of my life

Looking out the window
I remembered the last time
when he went far away to the sky
without saying good bye.

Looking out the window
I look to the sky
one more time
I know he will never came back.

Lourdes Salas

Daddy, Where Are You?

Daddy, where are you?
Why haven't you been around?
Do you love me?
Do you care?
Then Daddy, why haven't you been there?
There for me when my world was in dismay,
oh yeah, and when I broke my arm the other day.
Please Daddy, tell me; are you near or are you afar?
I want to touch you and hold your hand,
I want you to bug me like only a Daddy can.
Oh Daddy, can't you see, I miss you and me;
And I can't help wondering just where you could be.
Daddy, where are you?

Ramona A. Lewis

The Circle

In the morning I like to watch
The sun rise from its sky bed
And pull down its misty cloud covers.
In the afternoon I like to feel
The sun's golden fingers warming my back.
In the evening I like to watch
The sun sink tiredly to his home beneath the earth
And at night I like to feel
The midnight breeze softly tickle my face
And to see the joyous stars come out to play.

Chandler Marie Craig

Going for a Walk

On a golden warm afternoon
Gravel path crunching beneath my shoes
    No socks

My dog's long legs follow her nose
Open mouth panting a big grin
    No leash

Dragonflies flash jewel colors by my face
Birds twitter gossip between bush and tree
    No fear

Trail descends to blue-green algae pond
Creamy flowers glow above the lily pads
    No ripples

Wild roses with blowsy magenta petals
Coyly flashing red-orange hips
    No competition

Blackberries melt darkly sweet on my tongue
As I pass a stranger with kindred eyes
    No better food for the spirit

Rebecca L. Martin

Vision

Dusk begins to fill the black,
red, yellow and violet umbrellas.
The city becomes impressions,
a painting.
A silvery sap flows everywhere
filling each part with limpid dreams,
creating exuberant green leaves
in the soles of shoes.
Umbrellas become birds
invading the sky,
their wings melting with the disappearing sun.

Jose M. De la Rosa

The Reason

Some deride the poet as a dreamer;
Others dismiss him as a schemer.
Words are his vehicle of thought,
The cadence carriers eagerly sought.
This constant search for rhyming compatibility.
Enlarges his mental storehouse,
hence verbal facility.

William T. Reynolds

Music Box

Crystals of light bounce off mirrored glass
And all through the night,
the music box lasts
It is raining outside,
but the pitter-patter is not clear
The sweet notes of the music box
is all that I hear
The melody is silvery,
the wind-up motor a hum
When the music box is playing, I can't think of anyone
The thing that matters most is the echo of the tune
Singing in my soul,
and taking a small piece of my heart,
the music box and I will never be apart

Lisa M. Poglitsch

A Eulogy for Ruth

Home! I am home now.
The soft mists of early autumn greet me.
My mother, my father rest nearby.
Soon, the leaves will fall and blanket me.

I was so frightened to come to this place.
I could not understand the weariness, the pain.
I fought them. I struggled. They overtook me.
I thought I was strong enough to never die.

The battle's over. Why did I fight so?
There is only peace and rest here.
Red birds and sparrows hover nearby.
Lifting a song eternal.

My life was long and full.
Brothers, sisters, beloved daughter, all.
Gone, yet haunting my mind, my heart.
Gone! And I was left behind, so alone.

They await me now with open arms.
Their smiles, their songs, they welcome me.
With the lullaby of angels, they comfort me.
I am home now. Home!

Nancy L. Linder

Deceptions

She cried.... And the tears showed the pain.
She lied... Because she couldn't explain.
She smiled... Only to cover her fears.
She picked up the phone and dialed,
    Crying all her tears.
They heard her laughter,
    But they couldn't understand; until the morning after,
        They realized how much she could stand.
Staring straight ahead,
    The tears fell... The screams echoed.
Hearing everything said,
    She cried and yelled...
        Running til there was no where left to go.
She fell to the ground,
    And wondered why
        This had to happen to her.
She looked around,
    And began to cry.
        The pain would last forever,
            Because they would never be together.

Greta Roberts

Looking Up

They scampered in secret from her feet to mine while I watched,
    just a little too close . . .

I don't think much of shoes, but she does I suppose,
    never does look at much else . . .

Dirty old sneakers, I guess she saw more,
    somehow sensing I'd cause her no harm . . .

'Cause right up 'til then, when she trusted my shoes,
    I'd never seen'er look at much else . . .

In one splintered second they scampered again,
    right up from my shoes to my stare . . .

And within those dark eyes lives the secret to why,
    she never does look at much else . . .

So empty and aching, they clawed at my soul
    and if I had the nerve, I would run . . .

But she trusted my shoes, so I lent her my gaze,
    so she finally
        could look
            somewhere else.

Nicole Windsheimer

Blind As Day

Dedicated to my Uncle Robert G. Jewson 1916-1993

As I lay in a sea of dreams
I ponder the light that awaits me,
The light that may blind me.

'Tis black in back of fused eyes,
Like the under turf is to the blind rat-like creature.

But a petrified paralyzed creature he would be,
If he ever viewed the halogen light.
For the halogen light means inevitable death to ones being.

It drains the immortal energy from one mortality,
Till one becomes an isolated bag of matter,
Incapable of moving about as a sober being,
Rather an intoxicated being one would become.

Yet the only way to regain mortality,
Is to divulge ones dilated glass to the halogen light,
To intentionally paralyze ones being.

But I shall stay in my sea of dreams,
And ponder what tomorrow may bring,
Until the siren sounds in the brisk early morning,
And the halogen light penetrates my immortal being.

Jason W. Hart

The Only Way To Give

In the recesses of my heart,
Stands a door tightly locked.

The pains and sorrows,
Disappointments of the years,
Battle scars, deep within,
The keys that locked
The depth of my own heart;
Tears that never come... Kept it closed;
Never letting another... Come to close.

Suddenly the Master called, quietly the tears did flow,
healing in His wings,
Light Shining...calling forth a new beginning.

Faith Restored in God's true love,
Broke the walls, the barriers, which kept this heart alone.

Once again able to feel and give, laugh and honestly delight
Appreciating life once more, learning slowly, to receive,
So very hard the heart unfolding... To let another in.

Fear, attacking, the battle raging as the thoughts kept saying...

"Life will never hurt me... As it did." "I'll never let it in."
Yet all the while truly realizing, it's the only way to give.

Carmen Caldwell

Girl

Woman, so worldly you may think you are
When at sweet, pink bubblegum sixteen
You moisten your lips, believing you'll go far
Wriggling on by in your sex-stained blue jeans
And when there's heat in the heart — above the knee
You sigh at the stirring below the belt
As dog tongues hang lewdly over wet lips
So savor the salty tasting wolf's pelt
While glistening love-sweat slowly drips
From your rehearsed sexuality
I hope your moans honor aphrodite
As you pray to your Mom's reality
Though, you'll miss the harper's sweet sounding song
Sighing to those bittersweet memories

Stephen Graves

The Mystery of the Wind

What is the mystery of the wind?
Who stirs the summer breeze?
Why do the flowers bow in reverence
And hymns flow through the trees?

Do the flowers know a secret
That we have yet to learn?
Do the trees sing a love song,
The love for which we yearn?

Do they know who sends the gentle breeze
And makes the wind blow free?
Do they know the answers
To things they cannot see?

Do they sense a presence
From somewhere high above?
When the wind swirls 'round them
Are they feeling God's true love?

Can we learn a lesson from the wind,
Or are we still to blind to see
That with just a little faith
We could know the mystery?

Dorothy E. Netzer

Detained Love

The walls of this cell keep getting
closer and closer, every crevice and bump is known.
The loneliness of these dismal days
creeps and abides, oh how I yearn for home.

How much longer must I endure
this horrible disgrace,
That keeps me away from
your loving angel face.

For it is you that I long to be with
every moment of the day
But every time I reach out this
thing called justice is in the way.

Reginald D. Burke Sr.

Leave Me Not, I Love You So!!

At times in life, such times do come by
When you feel so full, so very contented.
It is then that you look up at the bright blue sky
Heave a sigh with a smile that He finally relented.

The feeling is so intense, so mightily compelling
To pronounce to the world that I got her all
Flaunt her to all and in so doing, revealing
Without her in my life, what misfortune will befall.

You are all that I have, to hold on to
For hope, for betterment, for making me a man!
If God's gift can ever be described true
Angel, I'll say it's you, that's the best I can!

Oh my love, you shall not have the heart
To do such a thing that will hurt me great
I wonder if you know the void you'll create
In me, if at all you choose to depart.

Oh! Angel my love, I wonder you'll ever know
How much it is that I love you, pine for you
If and when you ever decide to walk and go
I can't but seem to quietly follow you . . .

Sunshine

Trifling Garden

Purify my soul . . . if you can?
A tripod of memories sits atop this lawn I call my life.
Too often I am made to smile.
Too often I am made to fail.
The sky grows darker each day
leaving behind this seedless grave.
Breezes have melted into luxuries
and the sunshine — a dysfunctional sprinklerhead teasing the
    indecisive rain.

Where is this so called spiritual gardener to tend my lawn?

Desolate grains of sand collect on the screen sheltering my window
    . . . pain.
But waiting seems so tedious.
All the while, juggernaut fury encompasses weeds to decompose
    my mind.
Please — shelter my misconceptions from the emotionless earth
and show me how to cut a single blade of grass.
Because nothing is as it seems
and it seems that nothing is.

Again, I ask a question of rhetoric.
Purify my soul . . . if you can?

Xavier Alfredo Jaramillo

Terrorism Ad Nauseum

Bury me not in the fears of the ignorant,
Burn me not in the flames of the prejudiced,
For the fear that couples envy is dominant,
Souls roasting at the pyre of the bigot is envisaged.

I can smell fumes as Crusaders fire a 'Shtibul' in Poland,
I can hear the screams from the blaze of inquisition.
The horror facing voracious ovens of Deutschland,
Aghast seeing "Klinghoffer" jettisoned by terrorism.

What have I done to incur this fear and hatred?
Was it teaching the world to accept a sabbath?
To perforce endorse hygiene and sanitation as sacred?
Or provide doctrine of restoration from slavery to aftermath?

Am I one of the "chosen" for obligation and sacrifice?
To kindle the flickering light of sages through dark ages
Set the pattern for our constitution and the Laws of Living?
Or chosen to fill the text of my suffering on all its pages?

I pray for a society of peace and tolerance,
That the Laws of living be taught in the home,
Taught not by demand but by demonstration,
And all greetings and partings, be signaled by "Shalom."

Tobias Beeber M.D.

Quiet Time

The night time coolness lingers in the air,
The morning dew rests gently on the rose,
And I am privileged to be one of those
To know these special moments, and to share
Them with the birds, now waking in the tree
And sending forth their joyous songs for me,
To ease my soul into another day,
When all this tranquil peace will go away.

Then will I know the true and busy world,
That tests my skills, that seeks and sears my mind,
And drives me onward as I strive to find
A higher plane, a banner yet unfurled,
A place where I can be the most I am,
And feel the satisfaction of a game
Well played, by all the rules, and I will know
Again at dawn, this peace I cherish so.

Jessie A. Turner

Waiting

In a time and land of broken hearts
when previous loves and romances have lost their spark,
we wait and wait for someone to come
surely, eventually, we'll find the right one.
We patiently wait—weeks, months, even years,
but all it brings is more heartbreak and tears.
Then, they show up when they're least expected,
a new love or an old one resurrected.
Finally, the tears and heartache are through
because now you've found a love that is true.

Jimmy Hummer

Requiem of Justice

I'm beating, pounding, picking my brain.
The fight for justice can drive one insane.
How can you fight, when the cowards flee?
Then alone I will fight this battle for me!
It's strange how truth has little meaning these days,
It's condemned to death by evils lying ways.
I will not give in or bend to my knee,
to satisfy the demons who persecute me!
I will remain proud, I will remain bold,
I will watch as the demons freeze in hells cold.
Patiently, I will pray for truths victory,
and the return of the loved ones satan stole from me...

Diane Cooper

Argue With God

In the morning, I know, others find it odd;
I take a walk, talk, and sometimes argue with God.
He tells me of the worlds travail;
In the face of which my problems pale.
Of Him, I make all manner of demands;
I know, however, that only He commands.
When I say, "Why can't I have this and that?"
He lets me know where it's at!
He lets me choose which path to take;
Sometimes gives, me, an All Mighty break.
When I argue, "I did right, not wrong;"
He smiles; He knew the truth all along.
If I'm down and out of pep;
He helps me up to take an extra step.
Oh God, what would I do;
If I could not walk, talk, and argue with You?

Franklyn Burns

Eyes of a Lost Soul

I looked in the eyes of a lost soul, today
Red, teary, tired and sad
Face all drawn, unshaven and dirty
Clothes all torn, unbuttoned and worn
Smell of alcohol, so very strong
Dear God, don't let him fall
My heart did sink at the sight
He once was full of joy, hope, and life
Wife, children, home, job, hope
What happened, my friend, where did you go
His eyes so empty, words so hollow
"I want to see my children" he says
Tears streaming down his face
"I miss them so, they're all gone, you know, gone"
How I wish I could help you back, when did you change
Leaving, he turned and never to see him again
Stepping in front of a truck, ended his pain
My dear friend, couldn't there been another way

Delores Marion

My Rose

O' that a rose can embrace such beauty!
Like the face of an Angel.

It blooms sweet and gentle
like a friends warm smile,
in the soft glow of candlelight
or the velvety light of a sunset.

Soft silky petals invite a caress.
Flowered in rich shades of mauve,
bringing to mind her soft laughter, flowing
like a stream through a misty meadow.

Perfume sweet as morning dew,
rising up, full of purpose,
a lover's sigh calling to my heart
planting a tender kiss on the air,
hushed whisper floating on a cool breeze.

She is my rose

David Fisher

Judy

Beautiful women reflect light, she radiates.
Gentle women touch, she melts.
Interested women listen, she knows in advance.
Stately women walk, she moves.
Kind women care, she feels.
Sexy women excite, she ignites.
Happy women smile, she glows.
Smart women know, she knows what it's all about.
Concerned women care, she cares about me.

David J. Thompson

Untitled

I walked along the streets of Roswell last night.
The stars were bright. I thought about life and death
and the rest. But it wasn't worth thinking about.
There is me and only me in my world.
There is no life, there is no death.
And the rest is not worth talking about.
A black cat crossed my path.
I didn't care. The cat represented my whole life:
A beautiful thing, but causing fear and hatred. It is I
who did the math. It is I who caused the chaos
of all history. And now it cuts my soul like a knife.
Like the street lamps above me to the night. And the
night was quiet. At that moment, I felt at peace.
I looked at the moon, about as dark as a shadow. And
the shadow as dark as the angel who waited for the
deceased. And the deceased was watching me now.
Watching, waiting, hoping, praying. Praying for the
light which neglected me now. It was over.
And the streets are still quiet.

Peter Dvorak

Untitled

Light reflects off the window
and slowly I turn.

Losing my way in what becomes
a dreaded night

The sky is so black and yet I see
your warm face in sight.

Losing my way in what becomes a dreaded
night

I hear your voice but yet I stop.
Listen, to the sound in what becomes a dreaded night.

April Watson

Untitled

Winter is at last upon us, snowflakes gently touch the earth.
How beautiful the world seems with the first snowfall, as if
it has cleansed our very souls!

Linda Lambert

i really feel crappy today
i stay up late, and wake up early
that may have something to do with it

or maybe it's my subconscious telling me that i'm not accepted
that my ways are different and i have to change
maybe conformity is the way. yeah, that's it

i've been wrong to do things the way i do things
individuality is stupid. free will is inane

and then i think, "shut up. you're just tired."
damn i feel crappy today

Jim Hagan

Rainstorm In Loving Memory of Oscar Salázar

A warm mist climbs up into a singing light which tenderly caresses
    soft treetops above.
And to that silent shower grows a passion, steam rising from the
    cold dew.
Can you not see it?
The tempest flourishing and from the deep comes a bellow and a
clashing rage living inside the never-ending spectacle.
To each living creature, there is a fear that makes the blood run
wildly. With each reverberation there lives the soul, where life
makes this creation electrifying..
Each passing feather of water gently clings onto a ridge;
it is wrapped and coiled around the cathedral-like rocks,
and slumbers soft colours of gray to white and to black, and a rich
greenery reaching over whirling hills.
Little points shape down where you can see the wilderness
replenishing each pink eclipse, leaving the sharp cries
never to be forgotten...
Slowly it slips away into a fiery, crimson glow.
And a hand stroking the curl as the heat and the cool are like
the waves of silk in a valley.
Vapor ascends;
in the distance - a waterfall, and the forest at dawn.

Rebéca Símental Zubiaté

Your Perfect World

Shattered illusions of a perfect world
arrive with realities random visit.
The truth of your life becomes as
painful as the loss of your greatest love.

Carriers of the darkest of plagues seem to run rampant.
You no longer trust in the simple theories of right and wrong
You've seen the messengers of evil living
shrouded in the veils of goodness.
so you stand in wonder, what of your perfect world?

The voices of a thousand children has at last reached your ears.
Their screams of hunger and abuse seem never-ending.
In what once was your peaceful world,
you feel the rage of disgust burning inside.
Not for them but for you and your perfect world.

People long on age rummage for food in the waste from others.
Wearing cloths old and worn, they carry their world in one hand.
Discarded and forgotten; you see the abandonment by society in their
lifeless eyes, from your perfect world.

Michael Hess

Rescue Me

Intrigued by your mystical powers.
From my black hole you are my white light.
    Save me from my depression.
    Let me soar in the skies.
Masking the truth,
    with false realities,
    this I know,
but your powers curious me,
    In wonder and amazement of what could be.

Audrey Hendricks

What Is A Sister?

A sister is someone to talk to when you're blue
A sister is a friend to the bitter end
A sister is someone to laugh and cry with
A sister is someone very close to me
A sister is someone to tell secrets to
A sister is someone to go the movies with
I have a sister that is all of that
and more than words can explain
The closeness that I have with my
sister, is not worth more than money
or gold because she is the best sister
anyone could want and that I can
call dearest friend

Paulette Kay Donaldson

Those Hands of Control

I hate those hands of control.
They hold me with their wile grip.
I try to slip away,
But the strength I cannot equip.

It is all I can do to keep from losing my mind,
And my future that lies straight ahead.
I spend so many hours thinking of his
At night while I'm lying in bed.

I hate those hands of control,
They refuse to relinquish their grasp.
And any time that I try to scream
My words become only a gasp.

I can't get away from their hold on me.
It's the power I need that I'm lacking.
Oh, if there's only one soul to believe in me,
I wouldn't give in to this attacking.

I guess I don't mind those hands of control.
They've become almost one with me now.
They've turned me into a pacifist
Who needs to recreate her old vow.

Stephanie Kurowicki

Struck Through the Heart

It hurt so bad, but in a good way,
When I saw you both inside an' out
I was struck through the heart.

You punctured my heart with a sword.
You did it just by looking in my eyes,
by kissing my cheeks and holding my hands.

Oh your hands your hands so soft,
with your hair just as soft as your hands
I ran my fingers through your hair.

At that time I knew, I knew how I felt,
I felt my heart struck with a sword
I hope you feel the same towards me.

Christine Wiles

From Where I Stand

From where I stand it's somewhat hard to see, unless I can focus on
what's really happening to me.
From the precise moment to the last degree.
I must try to reflect on things accurate as they should be.

All the while it's been in my face to gain the most out of life,
through personal experience and a sure fire belief.
To be grateful, and really thank my God for giving me the one
decisive chance from where I stand.

From where I stand and enjoy the view, I often wonder if someone
else is enjoying it, too.
Could someone else also see the plan, and just try to watch and
understand; the marvelous works, of "The Almighty's Hand."

Lawrence R. Pratt Sr.

Dusk

The green grass waved in the wild wind
While the sun set
The rays shining on the flowers just trimmed
Their scent traveling for miles, I bet.

The light peeking through the trees
A cold wind passing by
Bringing a slight breeze
Lifting birds as they fly.

Flowers scenting the world around
Passing on the sweet smell
That reaches out to astound
The little bees by the well.

The mountain peaks all aglow
With red and yellow lights
Reflecting on the river flow
Birds sailing on their scheduled flights.

Stephanie D. Erickson

Where I Found God

While brushing an old woman's hair,
I caught the first glimpse
of the ray of heaven that was silently beating death.
Holding an old man's hand,
and laughing about the Bills.
Eating Pop Tarts while studying Bio.
Crying with the families who have come to say hello,
or maybe goodbye: Death is the untimely visitor,
always choosing the seasons of our lives.

These walls hold the memories,
the laughter,
the last breaths,
the tears.
On these walls
shines the light of everlasting joy,
the promise of tomorrow, and hope for today.

I was beating death
by being a ray of sunshine.
I found God by loving someone
with my hands tied behind my back.

Nadine Dawn Girard

The Muse of Dance

Such beauty, gracefulness and talent.
Can she be a mere woman or is
she something more?

Does she sense my amorous, admiring gaze?
What ethereal pleasure to see her
swaying like a Rujapia in a
gentle breeze.

Lissome one, will you be the center
of my solar system?
Can I orbit around you absorbing
your life giving warmth and light?

Panos Kokkoros

Morning Reflections

The quiet early light cast a glistening shadow on the snow.

All one hears are her own footsteps on the crunchy earth as
    the world around envelopes her into the stillness.

Very barely, yet audible are the sounds of creature life
    searching for food in the dry dark branches of the statuette trees.

The river seems to stand still with its frozen carpet,
    but life still goes on beneath the velvety surfaces.

As all life must go on.

As the brilliant sun warms the earth,
    it melts the frozen droplets of icicles,
    just as each moment of our life drops
    into the sea of eternity.

In this silent world — God is all around and peace prevails
    even to the snow-capped mountains in the distant view.

Time passes,
    yet the pain is there but only for a time.

Just as spring breaks forth and her spirit will be moved.

In the silence of her soul she knows —

The finishing line is only just a new beginning . . . .

Moira Mercer McLaughlin

The Contest

I stood there, ink dripping from my teeth as I
thought fruitlessly about the final words to mark my
time here on earth. They gaze at me impatiently,
they want me to say something clever but blood
loss through the toes tossed those dreams away. Some
man with a giant nose wants to know what dementia
leads to such ponderings that never scan, but as he searches
his gargantuous pocket dictionary relentlessly, he is often
distracted by shadows dancing with blithe dejection,
frolicking along his fingertips. Some grow weary of
my incessant silence and tell me to shut up out of spite
But mother always said that those people don't
count and father said they did so I always just
figured it was too deep for me to understand. Like
brussel sprouts at dinner time. Radioactive cheese did
nothing for the taste. My grey hair speaks more
of my blissful frustration than of my age, but I
pluck at it anyway because I wouldn't want anyone
to think that this assignment has got me down

Bryce W. Finney

Vladimir Nabokov, Lepidopterist (A Sonnet)

When flown-in butterfly scintillates in air,
And shadow of a layered wing is found,
The specter on the floor seeks the ground,
Where your footfall and your presence were.
The house is an open space, kept ajar;
Not seen as solid to vagrant butterflies.
The secrets of walls, immune as the isles?
The doors on friendly hinges, near and far...
Where clustered solitude is now contrived,
The age and youth fulfill each other's aim.
In clamped down shutter, weighted down shade
The sin of memory does re-enact its game.
    Such end, such fancy reach the common tie,
    Wishful of a love-call from a butterfly.

John Buld

The Heart Shaped Stone

It's there on the shelf for all to see, the heart shaped stone you
gave to me,

While walking by a mountain stream, there shone such a brilliant
beam, I walked to the water's edge and there again was the
brilliant light. So bright it almost took my sight.

Looking through my tear stained eyes, I reached in the stream and
to my surprise, I pulled out a stone in the shape of a heart.

It's there on the shelf for all to see, the heart shaped stone you
gave to me,

You said to me, way back when the world I was creating, through
the eons of time I could see, your heart was breaking, you felt so
unloved, so I sent you a message from me.

Through thousands of years the rock tossed about til its shape
finally came to be, and it came to rest in the place I knew best,
you would surely be there to see.

Looking at the heart shaped stone, I found the message for me, the
message of love, you sent from above, you sent it especially for me.

It's there on the shelf for all to see, the heart shaped stone you
gave to me.

Lillie A. Reynolds

A Poem About Spring and Easter Vacation

Varieties of fun
    At one time of the year
Catching fish and then throwing them back
    At that special time of the year
Tipping your hat to say goodbye
    In the memories that you'll always have
On the beach at that special day, 'I said,'
    No one will ever have a better day, than I had today

Benjamin Wyatt Tinsley

The Seasons

Summer is almost over, and yet I feel the warmth
    that comes from a very special love.

The Autumn winds blow, and I know the magic touch of your hand
    as each breeze caresses my body.

Winter draws near, and the cold and darkness tries
    to take hold of my soul, and I am nothing.

But then I see your face, and I feel a new hope
    that Spring cannot be far away; and with the
    Spring, a love that grows and continues to
    blossom for years to come.

Patricia Slack

Under the Honeysuckle Bush

Hidden by a barrier of flowers,
the fragrance making a harmony,
sweet enough to make you yell for joy,
I hear my mother calling from the

sun beaten porch. Scrambling out
from the tangle of buds, I sprint across the
green lawn, unmowed, a sea
of unruly waves. Inside, the dimness

startles me surrounds me
as I slip into my place. Gulping down my sandwich
I feel content. The milk glides
down my throat, like me on a water slide.

Running back through the green ocean, the grass
tickles my bare feet. As I slide into home base,
I am a Greek goddess
a crown of blossoms on my head,

sipping nectar from a golden goblet,
I am my own king,
ruling no one and no one ruling me
under the honeysuckle bush.

Jesse Davie-Kessler

The Oak and the Story

Massive arms reach high,
As they try to reach the sky.
I'm lying under the old oak tree.

My oak is a special thing,
A place where birds sing.
I lie here to relax,
As it tells me a story.

Every summer it's tall and straight,
Its leaves beautiful green,
A spot that's perfect for a book and a plate.

And in the autumn its leaves turn into a beautiful color,
They slowly, slowly fall,
And the oak begins to look taller.

Then winter arrives,
All is sad,
The tree is lonely and the branches look bad.

Wonderful spring comes so soon,
The leaves again are green,
And once again the oak tells the story of life.

Jessica A. Adams

The Fallen Stars, the Silent Heart

How could you not see the stars? They were so bright.
They danced, they sparkled with a brilliance that even others could
see their glitter.
How could you not feel the heart, the love, the warmth, the giving?
It gave off a glow that even others felt and longed to receive.
Today the stars were whelmed with floods.
Their bright lights began to dim.
The stars began to crumble.
I tried so desperately to save them.
As the pieces began to fall, one large point slipped down from the
once bright eyes, and pierced the heart so full of love.
As it made its fatal cut, it gave one last brilliant flash of light
and fell dark.
Leaving behind a bleeding heart, too weary to beat, too worn to search.
The stars have fallen and the Heart lies silent.

Kelly Freeman

Old Lady, All Alone

Old lady all alone, feeling sad as she can be,
Her eyes not working very well, little can she see.

Setting in a gloomy room in her old, old rocking chair,
Wondering, just wondering if any body cares?

Take a minute stop and think, could this lady be your Mother,
Just keep in mind when she is gone, there will never be another!

So please don't leave her all alone, to feel so sad and blue,
Just keep in mind all of those year's she's taken care of you.
Ruth Jolene Braun

The Marine at the Gate

(To Usmc At Naval Weapons Station, Yorktown . . .)
A group of us gathers five days of the week,
One thousand, six hundred, our living to seek;
Some come from great distance, nor may we be late,
E'en tho' we're delayed by the guard at the gate.

He peers in each auto so careful and close,
The driver scarce misses a brush on the nose;
So stiffly he bends, his pass so sedate,
This handsome young sentry—the guard at the gate.

His coat when it's raining's so brilliant and fine
It rivals the birds on the telephone line;
When torrid he's cool as tho' made out of slate;
Impassive his face—the Marine at the gate.

Impersonally right, his inspection so grim,
Impeccably tidy, as we inspect him,
Devoted to duty this servant of state,
What a noble vocation—a guard at the gate!

As day after day, in or outward we go,
Standing rigidly faultless from helmet to toe—
Who but thrills in admiring a nation so great
That stations a man like the guard at the gate?
Mary Jane Kissinger

My Father

Today is "my father's" day — There is so much I want to say.
So much is felt within my heart yet I'm not sure just where to start.
Many years have passed us by — So much unsaid — I know not why.
Love and Tenderness you have inside and for this you should take
    great pride.
You worked so hard from dawn to dusk to feed and clothe and care
    for us.
You worked all day to earn your pay so we could see a brighter day.

Leisure time you would rarely find - so determined, one strong mind.

You raised us well, you made us strong.
You instilled in us right from wrong.

You made us what we are today
You taught us how to make our way.

There are not enough words to say or acts of love that I can repay.

The years of sacrifice, the selfless act of love
You are truly God sent — straight from Heaven above.

I appreciate you
I love you.
Carol Naylor Slate

In Loving Memory of Ritchie Cantrell

We laid you to rest on a Sunday
in a spot 'neath a big shady tree
and when it came to say good-bye
it broke all our hearts to leave.

The sky hung like a soggy gray blanket
the sun never shone, tho it tried.
and the fat raindrops that fell on our faces,
mingled in with the sad tears we cried.

We know that your short life was troubled
we helped you out all that we could
but the sorrow that burdened your heart
only you and the Lord understood.

We know that you're happy in Heaven.
As you walk on those streets paved with gold
your sweet voice singing softly with the angels
in that land where you'll never grow old.

For you'll be just the same as last we saw you
on that someday when we all meet again
until then we'll hold tight to our memories of you
precious son, loving brother, loyal friend.
Debbie Chandler

Untitled

There on the sad beach
    where no one laughs
    and no one plays

There, the footprints
    of the young boy who laughed, swam,
        played frisbee with his dog in the surf

There, the imprint of the obese mother
    who sat on the towel under the umbrella
        yelling, "that's far enough Billy"

Now, no one
    not even the lovers
        who once paused to give rise
        to their impotent passions

Stops

Here on the sad beach
    where no one laughs
        no one plays
            and occasionally
no one sings
Melvin F. Johnson

Loneliness and Broken Hearts

Loneliness and broken hearts - I think they go together
Just like clouds in the sky seem to signal stormy weather
We watched while you were lonely and tried hard to
ease your pain, but the woman whom you loved so much
she had to go away
So much still left to your life, family
friends, a home, but nothing could
console you, you had to hurt alone
So we all stood by and watched you hoping soon
your pain would pass, but your pain it never
ended till they laid you in the grass
Jane Fitzgerald

Why Did He Leave Me?

Have you ever thought you were in love?
Have you ever felt he was yours and no one else's?
I thought he loved me and I thought he cared — thought we were
   the perfect pair.

We laughed together hand in hand. It really seemed there would
   never be an end.

I could cry on his shoulder and he could cry on mine. I knew we
   would make it. I knew it took time.

He would say "I love you" and I would say "I love you" but we
   both didn't know that our one would become two.

Don't ever leave me in something he would say — and I would
   promise him that I would always stay.

I could look at him and with his our little sign, I knew he
   would be there, he loved me, and that he was really mine.

Then one night it all came to an end.
He told me he didn't love me anymore and he wanted to be free,
He loved me, he cried with me — but why — why did he leave me?

   Julie Marie O'Rourke

A Part of Me

My heart beats much faster now as her special time draws near.
My one and only daughter soon to be far from here.
Her presents all wrapped so lovely are they all.
The only thing left for me is a lengthy long distance call.

A soldier boy, dressed in blue his smile and witty way.
Has stolen her heart and soon will take her away.
She is so lovely as we walk down the isle, today is her day.
It's up to me her father now to give the bride away.

Tears to many to hold back as they build inside.
It's hard for Dad to give up his joy and his pride.
But I'll be strong and though we will be far apart.
She will take with her a special gift, I give to her my heart.

   Gary Bennett Betts

Storm

We are surprised by a summer storm
one night after shopping
and run to our car.

Water rushes through my hair.
Currents gush between my toes.

In a flash of lightning, I see
raindrops explode and you
splashing on ahead.

Boris is waiting, alone,
different now his old friend's gone.

In the light as you open the door,
he is huddled, unnerved.

I watch in the dark.
My cheeks are stinging.

Lucky for us we have each other,
that we don't wait alone.

Your lips move; your hands stroke his furry back.
He tries to fit himself into your lap,
barrels his head into your chest,
inconsolate.

   Nancy Dobbs Greene

The Wind

The wind carries the leaves it sings my song
It blows strong and proud singing all day long
The trees bow before it blowing all night
It sings in all colors red, green, black or white
It never stops blowing whether slow or fast
You may never see it, but it blows right past
It will blow the rain with the power it holds
The wind twists and turns then drops, flops and folds
I listen to the wind as it sings to the land
The howling, the whistles, the wind and its band
Nobody can stop the song the wind sings
Nobody can stop the things the wind brings
The wind brings joy, hope, love, thoughts of tomorrow
It also brings hate, despair, pain, and sorrow
I listen to the good the wind sings in my ear
I wish to all people to have the wind near
Do not hear the false it sings, but the true
Then the wind will sing forever to you

   Meredith Spencer

Untitled

The nuzzle of a velvet nose
The caress of a child's hand
Afraid at first, then
   with growing confidence
   . . . a baptism

A flowing mane, soft brown eyes, a neigh
A ruddy cheek, wind tossed hair, a laugh
Tentative at first, then
   two worlds touch
   . . . a communion

   Pamela C. Nelon

All for Johny

Susie's little brother had died one fall, it happened in the
kitchen near the hall. He was 2 and also blind, he didn't see
what was behind. The coal stove was burning oh so bright, but
little Johny couldn't see the light. His foot caught fire, and
Oh how he cried, help me Susie, then he ran outside. Next his
pants, they started to burn, he didn't know which way to turn.
Susie tried to find her mom, but she was drunk and out with Tom.
Little Johny was almost dead, and when Susie saw him, she went
out of her head. The fire was out, but it was too late, and Susie's
tears turned into hate! She said one day she'd get back at her mom,
she'd also take care of that old Tom. Susie was 14 when she started
to look, she stayed in a farmhouse as a cook. She found her mom that
following spring, her mom was happy and started to sing. But little
Susie had not forgotten, she knew her mom had treated little Johny
rotten. Susie followed and took a gun, first the man she shot for
fun, Her mom cried Susie, what have you done! Susie said mom you
better run, the gun was pointed at her head, now Susie's mom, too, lay
dead. Susie was sick and out of her head, she pulled the trigger and
now she, too, lay dead.

   Terry B. Davenport

Man's Mark

   Life is but a fleeting glance in the great spectrum of
eternity. We struggle to make our mark in life before passing on
to another dimension.

   Some of us fall by the wayside too wearied by the great
task, never to rise to the call again. And others attain their
mark by feigning fame, power, and money.

   And finally, others see their mark as an inner serenity
borne from the quiet joys of giving.

   Marilyn M. Simon

Thinking of You

On a day like today, imagine or say, I'm sitting in the hay and I'm thinking of you.

It's beautiful and bright, a sunny delight, everything's right and I'm thinking of you.

I feel so alive, so relaxed, so free like a beautiful picture the world can see, and I'm thinking of you.

When I lay my head on my pillow each night and dream of the man that holds me tight, constantly, I'm thinking of you.

You are there when I need you or want you to be, whatever the reason, you're there for me and sincerely, I'm thinking of you.

My wisdom, my strength and joy comes from who? The man I love and "I'm thinking of you."

Angela Kirks

Feelings From My Heart

You said you loved me once and we would never part,
We both made a promise within each others heart.
Then I made a mistake and it caused us both to cry.
I'll never forget that day to you, I said goodbye.
We remained good friends, which I know was hard
   for us to do,
I can't admit the wanting I still have for you.
At times I look into your eyes, I can't tell
   what I see,
All that reflects from them is my image staring
   back at me.
Baby, I wrote this poem to wrap up the thoughts
   within my heart,
They're flowing through my bones and every other part.
Some say there will come a day when my
   feelings for you will cease,
But in my heart I know for you they'll
   just increase.

Louise She-Boy

Sunflowers

Sunflowers, sunflowers how beautiful they are,
Although, they are not made of the sun,
They come from below,
Where the seed sprouts into a bud,
And blooms into a beautiful sunflowers,
The man above made.
  Even though I've never met him,
I still believe it's true,
God made sunflowers just for me and you.
  He loves us very much,
And we do this with a gentle touch,
We weed the garden and pick off dead blooms,
And they'll grow big,
And get rid of all your gloom.

Misty Nichole Dixon

Inner Desire

Everywhere, for everyone, Diwali tonight!
Why me, low, down and deep in sorrow
All this darkness without moonlight
Seems like, for me, there is no tomorrow

My gloomy mind looking for new height
Soul in search of divine love song
To be in peace with celestial delight
But I am weak and time is long

O, Lord! take me on your eagle's flight
Fly me with your utmost speed
Grant me your vision charming and bright
Fulfill my life devoid of lust and greed

Gitesh J. Desai

Requiem

(With Apologies to Alfred Lord Tennyson)
Morning, and rising sun,
It's time to greet the day.
Don't let my struggles make you come undone;
Just look away.

For such a Life as I have led till now
Was full of Love, and Joy.
So let there be no wrinkling of the brow
That I must say goodbye.

Daybreak, and rising bell,
and after that the rain,
and thunder darkens sky and dell,
And I can sleep again.

For tho from out fond memories of my past
Some sad ones filter thru
I know for sure that peace will come at last
When it's my turn to go.

Roberta Karp

Stranger

Walking along pathways oft trodden in my youth, a thought comes to me —
  I am now a stranger here, more even than in a place to which I have never been.

But there is companionship — a wee one and his mother — my sister, in a sense.
  On this calm, peaceful Sunday evening, turmoil abounds in two hearts, and is the cause of solemn faces and tears, although not so many.

There is no great need to cry — just to hear and be heard — to provide the touch of understanding, and the strength to get through whatever follows, day to day.

Joy is delivered to us each by the innocent one — and we are thankful for this cherished gift — proof that pure goodness thrives amidst the pain and suffering of needful souls and aching hearts.

Robbie L. Maxwell

The Tribe Of

Dead among the living, living among the dead
The tranquil war rages on the beast has awoken
He arose from his grave I guess he never really died
He probably never really will I remember when he came
But that doesn't matter now the snakes eat his flesh
He loves it
Love what a trivial word we use it only when it suits us

Hate we use it as a weapon makes us feel good
Life how sad nothing but a play where the actors sit naked
In a room with bloody towels over their heads and quote lies
Death how much wonderment we fear it but I welcome him
With open arms it is nothing but a new beginning
Rain is falling the beast is sleepy once more
You'll get used to it maybe
I love you good night to all
The watcher has come and I dare not defy him

Robert L. Schmalfeldt Jr.

People

I've known people.
I've known people older than is imaginable.
My soul has grown dark and old, like the people.
I can hear all peoples' silent cries for help from my home.
I can feel peoples cries from the devastated future.
I can smell what people have done to each other and to Earth.
I can taste what people have done to our natural foods and waters.
I can see that some people are trying to help vanquish these problems.
I can no longer experience true youth.
My soul has grown dark and old, like the people.

Matthew Cox

Tomorrow's Call

I see my past so clearly its painted to a tee
Some parts can draw me teary as they show the faults in me
Some moments left me shining and standing tall with pride
Some questions left me wondering with an emptiness inside
The future still quite hazy is a frightening place to see
The mind can not be lazy for there's so much I can be
With eagerness and fright I await tomorrows call
Will it bring upon me sorrow will I leave it standing tall?

Amy Snider

My Gift

I entered a building, which had a small chapel, but quite quaint.
Someone shook my hand and said, "Glory Hallelujah, I'm a Saint!"
With reluctance, I took a seat on a bench made of wood;
Everyone began to shout "Amen", "Praise Him" as loud as they could.

The music and singing were as loud as could be;
They said they were honoring someone who died for me!!!
I wasn't quite sure of whom they spoke.
At first I thought "Yeah, Right, Whatever, What a Joke!"

The sermon that Sunday was on blessing in our lives,
And how much more we'll receive when we faithfully give our tithes.
Two years later, I am wonderfully blessed and thrilled;
Because with "The Holy Spirit" I am truly filled.

All the great blessings I've received are from above.
The one the saints speak of is God, whom I truly love.

Cheryl E. Loxley

Sand Castles in the Clouds

The day was magnificent,
after a week of storm and shower,
An afternoon to enjoy outdoors,
the sun came through with power.

I felt hot, and my mood was mild,
until I watched you both play with the sand,
your imagination was going wild.

The sand was your foundation, and your creations were endless.
I watched you build skyscrapers, valleys, rivers and more.
The longer you worked, I could see your future soar!

Both of you together shared love and play,
Your combined effort as a whole,
was complete for that day.

I will freeze this moment,
one of the many I treasure.
A deep feeling in my soul,
no words or time could measure.

So this I will say to myself and aloud,
when we meet for eternity,
We will build sand castles in the clouds.

Joyce Ann Natale

Glistening Eyes

Those glistening eyes in the dark
Looking at me so very fierce
I move an inch and they follow me
I start to run but they follow me.
I see sharp teeth and stare with fright.
There's nowhere to run
And there's nowhere to hide

Mindy White

My Unicorn

My unicorn came on golden wings
Into the center of my dreams.

We soared above the city dark
Toward the land of happiness
Where all is hushed in morning light
After the darkness of the night.

Toward the castle on the hill
Where roses, pansies and daffodil
Bloom all together in the light,
Although at home it's winter still
Here spring remain through out the year.
Oh, unicorn, should here we stay
Or return once more to a winter's day,
To see the snow on hill and lane
And know that storm will come again?

One more you're safe within you fold,
While I return to dream untold.

Norma R. Preisler

Untitled

Save me from this life of uncertainty,
    Each day not sure of where I stand.
Wondering what I look like through other people's eyes
    Uncertain of so many thoughts,
But yet so certain of what I am thinking.
    Concentration does not come easy....
Conversing with a group....
    Hearing and understanding the words said.
But just for a short while as my hearing starts to go,
    Thoughts wander aimlessly through vacant space
In what I call a mind.
    Thinking other people are the freaks,
When in actuality, I am the freak.
    Scared to be myself, silent in a crowd of many,
Not knowing what to say or how to act,
    Afraid to be ridiculed;
I only will be if I am afraid that I will be.
    Express myself! Be free! Live life!

Michael D. Swercewski

The Last Flood

Did you see the old woman sitting on the stoop?
Did you see her pale, vacant eyes?
Did you see her cry?
Did you see her golden hair fading into grey?
Did you know it rained today?

Did you see her wrinkled skin carved like river canyons?
Her children grown.
Her home abandoned.

It washed away her dreams.
It washed away her home.
It washed away her husband.
She sits there all alone.

Did you see the old woman sitting on the stoop?

Thomas F. Verrastro

The Scarlet Swan

Surrounded by a shawl of silence, I search for security. If I could just once see the Scarlet Swan, that would suffice. I seek out his spirit — he is but a stranger to me, yet it seems he has touched my secret self-my soul. He is a sorcerer casting his spell on me, lifting my sadness, leaving serenity in it's place.

The slow swaying of his hips stimulates my senses - sending a shiver down my spine. His superior strength was stretched taught beneath the skin-tight sheath of scarlet-colored silk. It was a skillful start to his sensuous seduction. The swift movements of his dance failed to shield the secret sadness I see in his eyes. The sudden spinning of his body toward mine startled me.

I shyly glanced up at his sensitive face — the storm I saw swirling in his eyes brought a surge of emotions to the surface. I said to him "Show me your dance" said he to me, "And so you shall learn, as I teach." I slid my slim hand into his outstretched one — in that instant our two selves seemed to merge. I sank against his sleek form, only to rise and move in a pas de deux swinging and swirling through the ash-white-sky-leaving only a scarlet stream in our wake. A sincere reminder to all that the Scarlet Swan danced here.

Cyndi L. Lunning

Stay A Little Longer

"Stay a little longer," they would always say,
"You haven't anything to do, please won't you stay?
The day has been a long one, and we're not feeling well,
What tomorrow hold for us, we really cannot tell."

And often, I would hurry, there was so much to do.
But I would always spend just a moment or two,
With two special parents who shared their love with me.
Someday, there would be too much time for me.

Their light is now fading over the gleaming sea.
Jesus, on the other shore, says "Children, come to me.
The angels are rejoicing as you come into sight,
The Father and I are waiting for you in the light."

"Your battle is now over, the race has been won.
The world will feel the loss of you very special ones.
Your care for the poor and lonely, the hungry you have fed.
The weary pilgrim passing through who always had a bed."

"But the brightest star in your crown is for the little ones,
You took into your loving fold and loved them as your own.
Welcome home, you stayed the course, your ship is safely in.
Rest quietly now in your Father's arms till I return again."

Margaret Sullivan

The Ways of Life

The Ways of life, how myriad—deep
Infinite series of thoughts to keep

Lights of change on darkened mind
Blaze out doubts and fears that bind

Here a straight-way, there a bend
Steps that falter 'til they blend

Hearts that pass thru walls and time
Wills that fly 'mid peace and rhyme

Holding hands with age and youth
Forge reality with the truth

Here a dream, and here an act
Find the dream a certain fact

The ways of life, how myriad—deep
Infinite series of thoughts to keep . . . .

Betty A. Landis

Mr. Creed

There once was a clown named Snappy
His teeth were made out of taffy.
He always felt down,
He puts on a frown,
But he makes everyone happy.

Frances Wong

Our Land

Our Land, a wonderful place to reside,
Though our spirit is pining
To be on the other side
Aloft with our Saviour divine.

The frustrations of everyday life,
The pain, the hatred, and oh the strife
The struggle for power, for gain
It seems most people have no aim,
They live in a busy world without shame
Taking the wonderful Saviours name in vain,
They think not of home, children, family
Of the love to share with one another.
We need our Father's love to see us through,
When the seas are rough and the strife if long,
When we feel all the world has forgotten,
All the good that Jesus done.
Love one another is his blest command
Try it and you just might find
A wonderful place to reside in
this Our Land.

Ruth Cline

A New Beginning

Darkness grips the world in an iron fist.
Even the brightest stars can't loosen the hold
the black fingers of night have on the world
and on me.

I am alone, imprisoned within the shadows I cast.
No one can hear my cries or my tears and no one cares.
I am a bird without wings.
Depressed, I sit and wait without hope.

And then you come.
You rise over the horizon, you smile so bright
and so warm, the darkness has no chance.
It melts like ice in your warmth.

Your rays touch my face and I throw off my
shadows and grow back my wings.
Then, like a bird reborn, I fly away and soar in the
clouds.

Christina L. Baker

Judy

Life is like a beautiful woman
Housed in a gazebo
Open, yet so much closed off
Somehow out of touch
Infrequently stepping out, then retreating even faster
Teasing with that far away glance
Only then to pull back and out of view
Why risk too much too soon
Is she another of life's monitors
A spectator or a participant
On this ever turning stage
Never to separate the real from
The unreal

Edward L. Kline

Because You're Not Here

To explain how much you've been missed
I can't find any special word;
And to erase you from my mind
Letters, photos were thrown away
Sometimes I even pray the Lord,
And still my efforts are in vain;
But my thoughts of you are not plain,
In my little eyes they put tears
In my fragile heart they bring fears
Dear, it's just because you're not here!

In this night with no one to hold,
I'm feeling very bored and cold;
In my heart, I feel lots of pain
While laying down in my bed,
Your image's running through my head;
Watching the rain through my window,
Tears from my eyes melt my pillow;
Silently, I'm dying inside
Honey...it's just because you're not here!

Jonas St. Fleur

For the Actress, Ann Reed

For you I'm irrelevance
To me, you're inspiration
Our two dreams together are spirits flying.
Our Allies are the mountains, sea, celestial skies.
Trees, birds and smaller things, our acquaintance.
The mystery is the fine spider web that connects us.
You are balance, grace and purpose
I'm the mad bent creature muttering
That I see your face everywhere
I'm humbled by your courage.
I ache from your beauty, blessed by its presence.
My hearts builds temples where you believe
My vision are roses that I offer you
Your laughter water that quenches my thirst
When we are together, there is magic and possibility,
An abundance of joy and enthusiasm.
Time flees, the void filled with acceptance.
This psalm, enjoyment gives
A fullness for the earth.

Ernest M. Garcia

Vultures on the Spiral

the stranger in the mirror
reminds me of an
emaciated   van gogh . . .

through disbelieving
surrendering eyes
   he glances
at the paltry wisps of hair

"theo!" he calls out
   "there is so much good here
   I can feel the wind
   before it strips the leaves from the trees!"

he stands naked
before the fog-streaked bathroom mirror
   gray chest hairs
   withered, flabby pectorals
   flesh of yellowed, tallowed hue

disjointed sunflowers
   thick-legged empty beds,
   swirling starry nights

circle slowly overhead.

James F. Lasseter

Euthanasia

Waiting and watching the clock
As the time slowly ticks
On its way to the end.

Sitting and waiting and watching
And wondering, "How long?"
How long? How long?

How long can I last?
How long must I go on?
How long, I can't take this anymore.

I just want to leave.
Just get out of this place.
They won't let me leave at all.

It's time to say goodbye.
It's time for me to die.
It's so hard to break these ties.

Just let me rust away.
Just let me disappear.
Just let me out of here.

Good-bye everyone. Good-bye my loved ones.
Good-bye. Good-bye. Good-bye.

Jarett Griguts

Endless Love

What is endless love?
Is it love that can't be broken by any force or object
on earth?
Is it never divorcing someone married to you?
Is it always loving a person you've lost, even if it
was long ago?
Is it dying with your mate?
Yes, endless love is all of these things.
Endless love is 2 hearts that bind as one.
Endless love is always loving someone no matter
what.
Endless love is doing whatever it takes to make
someone happy.
Can you feel endless love?
Will you feel endless love?
Yes, someday you will!!!

Kati Demaree

What Christmas Is . . .

Christmas time and what it brings
Like Christmas carols and five golden rings

There's the scrooge and four ghost
And Burl Ives as our host

There's parties, eggnog and of course mistletoe
There's St. Nick, Santa who says Ho Ho Ho

They say there's eight reindeer and also the Mrs.
There's plenty of hugs and plenty of kisses

There's tiny Tim and ornaments hung
There's candy canes, cookies and songs to be sung

There's Rudolph, the Grinch and ol Frosty too
So what part of Christmas is false or is true

There's smiling little faces with hope in their eyes
There's many packages with bows to be tied

There were three wisemen and gifts they had brought
And of course baby Jesus so many forgot

There's Mary, Joseph and the manger
The feelings they had to share with a stranger

So whatever Christmas brings you this year
Take time out for a moment to show that you care

Connie Howard

To The Tree

Conscious evolution is emerging,
Nature will continue to thrive.
All the leaves on the trees are happy,
and so am I, to see them alive.
Birds are healthy, flapping their wings against the winds.
Nearby, the sun reflects the green, and I am energized.

No longer is the world hidden by the black veil.
I can see, think and love...clearly.
I feel the fire of hope, of inspiration exploding.
One burst after another, ecstasy.
I am growing and feeling more vibrant each day,
needing and wanting less sleep.
My own personal journey has begun...and will never end.
Even the physical death of my body cannot stop my evolution,
This I know, gratefully.

Melissa Krolewski

My Mamma

My Mama gave birth to me November the 6th 1980
My Mama is a strong powerful black lady
My Mama the lady who put a roof over my head
My Mama every night she made sure I was well feed
My Mama the lady who put clothes on my black and shoes on my feet
My Mama without her my life would be incomplete
My Mama the lady who told me to always try
My Mama I look up to her, like I look up to the sky
My Mama the lady who was down from the start
My Mama I love her with all my heart
My Mama the lady who knows me better than I know my self
My Mama when I messed up, she was quick to break out the belt
My Mama the lady who raise my brother, my sister and I
My Mama if it was for her and I had to I would die
My Mama the lady who will be down from being to end
My Mama she's not just my mama she's my best friend
My Mama the lady who got my back, my front, and both my sides
My Mama she showed me wrong from right
My Mama the lady who kept it real who is she My Mama

Carre Christopher

The Golden Arc

My sister, Lisa, a treasure is she
God's blessed gift, amid all this uncertainty
A confidante, mentor, a painter, too
Friends of intimacy are a privileged few.

Feeling as though we might just perish
Honored with loving sharers who listen, cherish
Together we grieve and we laugh and create
We step onto the bridge through an invisible gate.

A leap of faith — a belief in ourselves
In all our humility, driven to delve.
Shaking free the messages, coming into the light
Loving this little child, the canvas now bright.

So we continue the journey, no longer in dark,
Two by precious two, we surrender, embark
With most of all, our loving Higher Power,
. . . There atop . . .
The Golden Arc

Teresa L. Grossman (AKA Terri G.)

Blind Spot

They're all falling from heaven,
these snowing souls.
I desperately look for grandma's,
but I can't find it - can't spot it,
and I blame it on my eyes.
After hours pass I give up,
but then a strange thing happens,
the ground catches my attention,
and I wonder isn't that the wrong direction?

Sidika Irish

After Football I'm Fine

There's nothing wrong with me, from playing football you will see.
From being tackled in the back, has sent my knees out of whack.
My hearing is poor from the cheering and roaring, my head's
in a spin and I'm taking aspirin.
For you and me who play football, it's better to say, "I'm
fine", with a grin, then to tell everyone of the shape we're in.

Frederick Gibson

Best Friends Don't Always Live On

How do best friends stay on the road to holiness?
Do best friends live on to sing a song?
I had a friend once who really was a kindred spirit.
I loved her so much but she never knew.
I talked to her when I had problems and she understood.
But do best friends lie to the other and break promises?
Do they bring the other out from the
burning cold that weakens their soul?
I did this once to a friend who I called my best.
I cried because she didn't deserve this awful pain that ran
through her beautiful gleaming soul.
Days passed and times changed.
I wasn't honest with her and she screamed
out for help. I cried because she didn't
deserve a friend like me. She found a
new best friend and I was forgotten in
lonely dust and fire. I will live to say that
she was my very good friend. I will say that I was the
one to end it. My heart is broken and hers is free.

Christa Kuhar

The Door

The door seems impenetrable.

Today is arduous.
I have seen patients with cancers of pancreas,
gastric, cervix, colon-all unresectable.

One person with pancreas cancer
fills my conscious: Young and dying despite
His expectations and prayers.
I must be realistic, yet not hopeless.
Yet hope for what?
He doesn't understand why he's 40 and dealing with this beast.

For balance, I try to remember the exhilaration of a
patient cured.
I can only be forthright and compassionate.

Why is it so difficult to enter this room?
Maybe someday I will be in that bed.

I hope if that time comes
My doctor will be as truthful and considerate.

But, if she hesitates at the door...
I will understand.

David H. Huffman

411

Weakness

Risking absurdity and humiliation with every step
She walks, leaving a trail of thin smoke behind her
Floating in the air like so many ghosts of her past
Cold fingers grip the door handle, eyes become teary
She promised herself that last time would be the last time
And here she is again, avoiding mirrors and windows at all costs
Thin legs ascend the staircase, bringing her closer to defeat
Sickening dread climbs up in her throat, nearly choking her
Coughing loudly, she taps lightly at the scratched door
She stands in the middle of a junkie's heaven
Hugging herself, for lack of anyone else to do so
Forlornly handing over this month's rent, her heart constricts
From recollection of torture, which it knows so well
Watching the powder bubble into a clear, harmless looking liquid
She tries hard to push away the memories of friends and family
Memories of their tears and pleas, of their plaintive cries
And barely even feels the needle injecting despair into her arm
She lies back among the filth and tries to smile, to no avail
As she slips away, she makes a promise that this is the last time
Her sudden, feeble death being the only thing that keeps it

> *Alisyn Parker*

In Memory of . . .

The salt of my tears soothes my sore throat.
Screams echo in the empty room of my heart,
While defeat bends my back in agony.

I do not know how we got to this place.
What was the first step?
Whose was the first wrong?

Almost meaningless is that question,
For one begs more plaintively;
Why do I continue to destroy myself over you?

Years ago were the offenses.
Time has passed.
Men have passed into my room and out,
Never filling the void you left behind,
But always making that of my heart deeper.
Why do I reign over this parade of erosion?

If I kill myself, will my love for you finally die?

> *Elizabeth Stuart Reynolds*

Riverscape

The sun, silver coin in ashen sky;
river winking mirror of
textured pewter, chrome, steel
catches and shatters, sends forth
glimmering aureoles —

The closeness of us:
immutable, irrefrangible metal
(we, two magnets infinitely yearning
orbit like suns that glow incandescent
from endless pull of gravitation
against momentum)
rests still, while
bars of light twinkle, bounce off
like words smiles refracting
sunlit days that hold us separate . . .

A duck silhouetted black against polished gray
stirs blinding shimmers in his wake:
sculptured stone on lake of curling silver.

Your brightness dazzles
the leaden mirror of my desire . . .

> *Elizabeth Bell*

Clipper Ship

What brought the clipper ship to power at sea;
what sovereign forces cast her history?
She slipped the ways to launch a fabled lore
of trade and speed, of classic grade and war.

Til then, the galleons ruled the ocean's lanes
across so many long and royal reigns.
They proved to be so ably sound at sea
yet, fortunes worked to end their heraldry.

For crossing vaster seas, a future brig
would have a trimmer set and bolder rig.
The galleon's fo'c'sle decks were struck for speed
and quarter decks gave way to sailing need.

More sail crowded on her yards aloft;
her sailors sought to work on every waft.
With flying jibs and royal studding sail
she cut the frothing seas from rail to rail.

Magnificent when flying all her sail;
invincible to weather any gale
the clipper dashed to ports new and old
to leave few tales of foreign lands untold.

> *James T. Howell*

Mother's Tears

The little girl looked up
and saw her mother's eyes...
There were tears in them
that she tried hard to disguise.

But the girl knew she was
sad and her life had not gone
well, and she vowed that
day to never forget what her
mother wouldn't tell...
That her father left when her
life was young and the years
would pass away...
Yet the time would come when
she'd marry one. Who would promise her to stay...
But till that time, the girl
would try to comfort mother's
fears....for the last thing she
wanted in her life, was to see
her mother's tears!

> *Ann Nitzsche*

A New Day

Hiding behind deep purple haze,
the early morn we tend to gaze.

Glimmers of light come breaking through,
revealing foggy mist of blue,
stealing hollows from the night.

All at once clouds in the sky,
ride purple and pink to the eye.

Suddenly a burst of sunlight,
grazing the sky,
destroys the beauty of fading night,
bringing forth meadows of sparkling dew,
like stars of mystery in the night.

Animals perk their little heads,
to hear birds on their first morn wing,
singing praises for a new day has come.

> *Carolyn Blackmon*

That Piano Night

He caressed them . . .
His long fingers tapped and stroked,
bringing forth the sweetest sounding music.
And as I watched those Ebony fingers
seduce those Ivory keys,
my body yearned to take the place
of the fine, Baby Grand Piano.
I needed his fingers to play me;
To tap and tease, flirt and caress,
to coax that sweet music from
my lips instead.
I closed my eyes. Still,
he read my thoughts like sheet music,
and began to play the sweetest melody
on my body.
I became his instrument that Piano night, and
he played me well...
He played my body beautifully,
and the music we made left me
Breathless.

Carol Johnson

Time Gone By

Pain: Better inflicted quickly than slowly.
Stab: One quick strike or twist the knife?
Hurt: A lifetime surviving with an open wound.
Salt: A sting which reminds you reality lurks.
Tear: A salty drop of evidence.
Near: The beginning, the body, the end.
Fear: A life wasted and not knowing the time.
Hard: Getting up and doing, going.
Time: Tick-tock, tick-tock, tick-tock, Stop.
Mood: Rain over sun any day.
Hear: Silence louder than a scream.
Done: Feeling all and for everyone.
Love: But not for life.

Emily N. Reyna

Struggle

I can be as rude and crude
As chipper and chapper as anyone lewd.
I can do what's warned against,
I can want to be a fence;
I can wish to be a fly;
To be a robin I can aspire.
I can crave my taste to be
All over my body as far as you can see,
Like the catfish who, with this gift
All over his body, the pleasure can sift.
He can taste
The salty sea
Without opening his mouth to me.
But I'll not say anymore;
Mankind has gifts and gifts galore.
Mankind.

Valerie B. Schwartz

Abandoned

The leaves fall in colorful rhythm
Covering the ground and everything with them,
Exposing the limbs on the trees up there
Leaving them lonely, bereft and bare.

Rejected they fall through space without sound
Curling their fingers to cling to the ground.
Huddled together, displaced and entwined,
Masses of cells unable to climb.

Refugees now in a frozen land:
I understand . . .I understand.

Helen Del Beato

Styrofoam Garden: Memorial Park, Davenport, Iowa

On Christmas Eve your graveyard becomes an
amusement park—gilded billboards of Christ,
wide and starry eyed card-board camels,
the three kings like strange gold dwarfs—

All glowing a synthetic unearthly
glow of paint and plastic and neon light.
They charge admission and the cars wind through,
pointing at the crumpled tinfoil manger.

The graves are well-kept—
we are not allowed to place real flowers on them.
The grass is cropped clean and the plastic flowers
strangled in vases make eerie, frowning toothpicks—
a garden too well tended,
choreographed with iron and steel.

I cover you with moss and weeds and will
the grass to tumble over you, high and unruly.

Sarah Ruhl

The Fire Arrows

Darkness is about to loose grip over earth
As the golden Fire-Ball begin to thrive.

Everywhere rays of flaming arrows
Penetrate deeply into the very heart
Of the heavens.

The Fire Dragon is finally set free
From the chains of Darkness.
He breathes fire upon fire into
The surrounding, blacken space.

And behold! . . .
The sky is filled with
Fire Arrows.

As I, the witness of this awesome phenomenon
Stand in front of this immortal being
Feelings of infirmity overtake my fragile heart.
Thus helplessly I surrender
To the Immortal Dragon
And his Fire Arrows . . .
Exclaiming its elegance
Deep within my soul.

Kenneth Yuk-Kwan Fung

Untitled

I am a woman fighting for my life,
I am a woman who has to my throat a knife.
I am strong dedicated and wise.
I am a woman who many may despise.
But really I don't care what others think of me,
Because if I'm not true to myself, what else could there be?
I am not some little girl who you can push around,
I am not some stranger who is new in town.
I will be respected with all due courtesy.
And I will stand proud so all mankind can see.
Your eyes cut into my heart, your hands into my soul,
But you cannot stop me, for I am in control.
I stand tall with high dignity.
I stand proud so don't you dare pity me
I am strong in heart and in mind,
Nothing can stop me, not even time.
So if you don't like what I'm trying to say,
I really don't care this wasn't written for you anyway.
It was written so I can express how I feel,
For when I do that I truly become real.

Erica Renea Davis

In Bed, At Night

When I want comfort
I think back to when I had the luxury
of his chest to rest on
my tears mixing with his skin
and the arms of his silver cross
twisting in my hair
there are still times at night when I lie in my bed
years after
that I can still feel him lying there next to me
tortured in his sleep
and I turn over,
looking to soothe him
and I see only a tangled mess of bedsheets
my hair fanning out onto the pillow beside me

Emily Lerner

Spirit of Life in Death

Jesus you are my inspiration
my guiding lite in this world of
mass insanity. You are my social worker
my sleeping pills, you take care of my bills.
You are always in my corner.
With social and world in troubled
waters you are my bridge. You are
my brother in friends. My financial trustee
you give the bread of life to nourish my
spirit. You will never die you are
the answer to infinity. You
are perpetual motion. For you nothing is impossible.
You're never ending love and mercy
for repentant sinners. You are the
sun in the sky and the stars behind Mars.
You are gravity to apples,
you are green grass.
You my Lord are the perennial spirit
of life in death.

Sam Brossort

November Thoughts

I am told that I am weathered
And have hands that are as yours are, perhaps that is so.
There have been many storms
And many people in both our lives,
Violent people, intense people,
And storms that my heart has not forgotten; lessons learned,
Life's lessons and how to survive in a world of stone.

They taught their lessons well; they stole away my innocence
Along with the notion I held that life was a sort of gentle thing.
The next city, the next town, and each new face picked up where the
last one said good-bye.
Smiles are given slower now and more carefully placed so as not to be
misplaced or misunderstood.
For the moment, all the storms have passed
Only the rivers flow past my door and the wind sings a gentle song
beyond my window.
But my tomorrows promise another town and strangers faces and
darker nights than those which have gone before.

I don't know where the highway leads and most times I don't care.
The price of caring too much has been paid,
But there are times I cannot accept the life I've bought —
with the pieces of my soul.

Peg Delaney

Envy

She holds the hand I once held,
Embracing the arms that once consoled mine.
My breath no longer dances upon his neck
   and the tongue which used to greet him
   is kept behind bitter lips.
Those ears once heard my "I love you's,"
   now they are filled with hers.

Hating her presence in his life,
Resenting her for replacing me.
It fuels the fire kept behind the mask,
Throwing harsh words about her,
Knowing nothing but her name.

My memories are of the fondest nature,
But I lack intention to resume the past.
I just want her to let him go,
Leaving me to dwell in his mind,
   our past never forgotten or replaced.

Julie Haverman

The Sound of the Nature

Hear the rain fall
as it beats out a tune on the hard packed earth
The steadiness of nature
Hear the frogs' lullaby
meant for his mate
The sweetness of nature
Hear the fierce thunder
showing who is in control
The power of nature
Hear the dove's coo
a soft note chirped with affection
The gentleness of nature
Hear the raging waves
as they crash against desolate cliffs
The wildness of nature
Hear the cars honk
the exhaust fills the air
The enemy of nature

Emily Joost

Moments to Remember

For year and years I've been around
To pick you up when you were down.
To encourage you to do your best
To meet the challenge to the test.

To hold your head up very high.
To tell you it's ok to cry
To answer your question the best I can.
To try to help you understand.

The little things you should know
To choose the path you should go.
And even if the choice is bad
I am there to hold you up when you are sad.

I love you forever till the end of time
Because my grand son
You are a friend of mine
And I love to be your valentine.

Olinda Couto

414

Untitled

Color is only what it seems to be
Each one different to you as to me
You see blue as you think it to be
The same thing different as it's shown to me
Red is bright and joyous as you wish it to be
Dark, and cynical inside the eyes of me
All the same in your eyes, simple you want it to be
Each one drastically different just to comfort me
Yellow is light shining as you love it to be
Blinding but attractive, it's all the same to me
All have hope of what they want to be
A different hope dwells inside of you and me
Black is night time, a time of peace, as it may be
Also a time of fear down inside the soul of me
Another complicated thought you discard it to be
I need you to understand it's more just for me
White is clean, as maybe it should be
But plain, and empty, it's disturbing to me
Color is only what it seems to be
Each one different to you as to me

Anjel Searles

Broken Universe

If I ever see you again, let it be on the terms of
Mother Nature. Pure as the rain falls on the leaves,
Innocent as it should be, and quietly as the dew naps.

If ever I see you again, hold on to the memory of what the
World once was, no sorrow, despair, or depression.
How does one replace what was stolen, and how do we repair
Her heart?
Never let the universe know your heart has been broken, for
she cannot cry, she has no tears, she has been haunted and
only fears for what will happen to her children and will bow
Her head in disgust.

If I ever see you again, tell the universe that "I" am doing fine.
"I" have mastered my mind to accept what is, therefore; "I" am
safe from all ills.
Cling unto my spirit, connect unto my soul, for I will lead
She would be pleased and will follow!

Elaine Thompson

Out of Breath

You step from the car
and I become breathless

I remember turning towards you
in the middle of that night
and the moonlight shown on your
black hair and made it
purple
you back was so smooth beneath
my touch

You seem always in perfect rhythm
and I feel awkward and gangly
in your presence

You always look just past my eyes
orange pulp and
purple hair
and clouded eyes behind wire rimmed frames
you always look just past my eyes

Hiding from me comes so easily
and ... I'm ... still out of... breath ...

Erica J. Wolgemuth

A Gunshot Was the Last Thing You Heard

How many more of us must die before we realize
that our lives are so precious if we just open our eyes
with an enemy among us which is so simple to buy
another lost of a loved one, we must learn to survive
put the guns down for a minute and listen to my advice
It's not worth all the killings and the lost of innocent lives,
It's not worth going to jail, you can't run, you can't hide
your conscience will haunt you when
the deaths you created, are reflected in your own eyes
look at the life you choose to live, violent crimes seems to be your
daily high
You're guilty of killing your brothers and
sisters, without even having a real reason
why
you know, what comes around goes around,
next time it could be someone you love
or someone you know
A gunshot was the last thing you heard,
It's never worth the lost of a beautiful soul.

Kevin E. DeLeon

Journey

When Jesus our Lord returns to Earth,
 and darkness will be no more.
We will all set sail on a golden ship,
 for the journey to Gods Heavenly shore.

The decks will be lined with the souls of our time,
 the watch will be posted above.
And the billowing sails from the winds that prevail,
 holding fast to the masts by white doves.

Oh, sail on ye ship of peace and grace,
 whose course is fast and true.
For as in life, through storms of strife,
 our course in God is set too.

The ones who have gone before us will wait,
 on the shore by the Heavenly Gate.
And they will all know, as the trumpets will blow,
 when our watch calls out — Land Ho!

Delmar K. Sears

Eve, Did You Listen?

While the serpent's tongue caressed you,
Did it stir the blood within you?
Did it bid you, exit Eden?
Seek your Mother's garden.

While the serpent's tongue caressed you,
Did it plant a seed within you?
One to grow beyond the garden "Felix Culpa,"
That "happy Fall" that found you the serpent —
Found you guilty of all sin and sinning.

While the serpent's tongue caressed you,
Did it scorch and heal you?
Did it lead you past the "culpa,"
And the awful word of Milton?
Did it bring you to your Mother's garden,
Wherein grows, the serpent's seed, the self?

While the serpent's tongue caressed you,
Did it stir the blood within you?
Did it bid you, exit Eden?
Seek your Mother's garden.

P.K.

Untitled

I never thought that I would be worth anything.
Until I started to pray to God and
He made my head swing. As I prayed
and began to believe. That one day I will
receive. Always be nice to someone who
has a bad attitude. Maybe one day they
will show their gratitude. Love can be
great and love can be new. Love can be
sad and it can hurt you to.
I never take anything for granted because
God created this beautiful planet.
You might be rich or you might be poor.
But if you have love in your heart.
You can concord much more. Always keep both
feet on the ground. Because the people
you meet on your way up. You might
meet them on your way back down.

Harold Smalls

A Mother's Love

My mother gave me advice when I had lost my way
she held me close to her and gave me hope of finding
joy one day.

She listened and encouraged me, soon I began to flower
I felt new hope that I could cope, I felt a serging
power.

To make new choices right for me to heed my inner
voice, she helped get back on my feet and make the
wisest choice.

My mother gave me hope when I had lost my way, she
helped me find my inner strength her love I can't
repay.

But I can thank her with all my heart for what she
did back then.
She said to me on that last day now I can go home again.

Ella M. Baldock

Nobody Ever Said It Was Easy!

Patience you must learn to use.
    When you do your temper will lose.
For when you let your temper run.
    Things will not be getting done
Accomplishments will not be made
    Unless you keep your temper stayed.
Two things cannot be dwelled upon
    When bad thoughts move in, good thoughts are gone.
Discipline your mind to reach.
    Beyond those negative thoughts to teach
That goals should always be kept in sight
    to reach the place we know we might.
So keep your eyes on where you will go
    and you will with your temper show
That the things that make you angry yet
    have no bearing on where you will get.
If not allowed to have their birth
    and set aside for what they are worth
And patience will surely bring to you
    the state of mind to see you through.

Ron Pursell

My Man of the Eighties

It was back in the eighties that I declared the decade a waste
Then my intuition told me not to give up in haste,
From way across a crowded dance floor
Walked a man so discrete I just had to adore
He asked me to dance to a strong disco beat
When I think of that night I feel weak to my feet
He turned me around and his arms crossed above
With a strength from within and the gentleness of a dove
I don't recall the night ending, I don't recall what was said
My husband and I share our breakfasts in bed
It has been 15 years since we tapped on the floor
It has been 15 years may we have 40 more?
I thank God for that night that we really did meet
I thank God for the years that he's been so sweet
That man of the eighties he really is mine
And when we're alone and we start to combine
I can feel my heart throbbing no man could compete
Cause I still feel the vibes of our original disco beat

Barbara Eileen Berenbaum

To My Royal Coachman

Casting about life's stream I hook a keeper,
no catch-and-release specimen,
a lunker of love.

A float down Relationship River finds bends,
backwaters and riffles.
Nippers, tippets and ferrules
hatch from Creel World.
Because our love is no imitation,
there are no limits to what we can tackle,
angling together.
You are my 7X leader, a filament strong
and tangle-proof in deep holes and undercuts.
I am your emerger nymph, no dun or streamer.
Together we ride the rapids,
not resting in the eddy,
until the last Spinner Fall.

Jane A. Kane

The Three Little Bunnies

Three little bunnies went out to play,
    they stopped in Moms garden along the way . . .
They smelled her blossoms so bright and sweet,
    they found their new home so very complete . . .

She watched their antics for just awhile,
    then left them with a wink and a smile . . .
they made her laugh as they hopped to and fro,
    she gave them Love and they began to grow . . .
Mom named them one by one,
    then knew her work was done . . .

She knew one day they'd leave her alone,
    to go off and have families of their own . . .
The day finally came and she was sad,
    for they were all she ever had . . .

She left her gate slightly ajar,
    for they had not wandered very far . . .
Imagine her surprise, one special day,
    three little bunnies were out to play . . .

Verna Y. Shockley

Halloween Is Coming Soon

I am great,
I just can't wait,
Halloween is coming soon,
There's a witch with a broom!
I see the wind,
That is him!
He's gotten fat,
He's changed his hat,
That's the Ghost of Doom,
He's so big he takes up a room!
There he goes down the street,
Where there are a bunch of treats.
I'll be dressing up soon,
In my costume of a goon.
I'll scare people left and right,
Until they get their biggest fright.
Hey, there's another witch with a broom,
Halloween is coming soon!

Freddy Magovern

Keepers of the Light

Acquainted with the night
Antiquated by the bending moonlight,
Feel the tide of the pulling moon,
Here between time, now, and no end to.
Feeling the force without the fear
I still sleep on the wall of stone,
For fear only more afraid than ever before,
For fear of being more afraid than being alone.
I like it when it's cold and dark
And the only warmth is my shadow.
The shining stars
Through the stark trees,
Lights on bare branches
Where once leaves,
Whisper what words
Of to the souls beneath,
Will live not longer
Than any of these.
Until the night, the voice, the music, and the moonlight are One,
You need only to Surrender.

Michael Shelley

Dandelions

A gust of sweet spring air filled the woods
And as the wind passed, the tall grass swayed back and forth
A dandelion let his fluffy white passengers off into the world
And the wind seemed to say, "Fly my children, fly away".

Lauren A. Bielak

Beatniks

The music you played influenced a Generation.
The music you sang Electrified them all.
The music you wrote moves my soul.

The lives you touched stretched Over the seas.
The words you spoke Reeked of charm and humor.
The music you wrote moves my soul.

The talent you gave, for the world, a true Gift.
The life you led, dead Exhausting.
The music you wrote moves my soul.

Happiness, I hope you have because the music you
Wrote moves my soul.

Susan Rife

I Remember

I remember Nanny,
I remember picking strawberries and making jam,
I remember Christmas presents by the dozen,
I remember shopping trips for no reason at all,
I remember her hundreds of different shoes,
I remember her jewelry,
I remember Nanny.

I remember Nanny,
I remember the songs she sung,
I remember her endless hugs,
I remember the way she smelled, like fresh baked cookies,
I remember her sweet kisses,
I remember Nanny.

I remember Nanny,
I remember when Nanny was sick,
I remember the worried faces,
I remember the teary eyes,
I remember when Nanny didn't know me,
I remember when Nanny died,
I remember Nanny, and I remember I loved her.

Eleana M. Harmel

Deceit

Betrayal is a vile thing; it has shed more tears than death.
It lurks behind dark corners, and taints my every breath.
It jerks me, reels me, and makes my conversations dazed.
It leads me toward confusion, and causes my choices to be hazed.

I try to escape the urges that convince me to go wrong.
But I can't hide from within, and my conscience is almost gone.
There has to be a way to finally straighten these things out,
Nonetheless, now I think that deceit is what life is all about.

It must be that life is just a silly game waiting to be won
By some ignorant little fool that has everything undone.
The goal must linger to unravel all of life's undying truths
Until there's nothing left to believe or to pass on to our youths.

So I guess you can call me ignorant or fool if that suits better
Because I fit the mold completely — right down to the letter.
I am crafty, sly, dishonest, and most of all — I'm cunning,
So you oughta watch your back, or you'll never see me coming.

Diane Jennings

Merry Go-Round Dance

Boys with toys jump on the twirling thrill,
Expecting to find themselves, if you will;
But receiving a sickening nod to their god,
The one who dies first in the dance of chance.

One by one, the boys with toys thunder with wonder,
Happening to see with glee that their mothers and fathers
are waving like pigeons,
Yet the merry go-round slows not a smidgen to spite,
But only precedes to take on flight.

The boys with toys sleep not a peep,
But only wish to flip their trip either heads or tales,
Knowing now that their mission has failed.

The merry go-round dance goes up and down, side to side,
Running on toward the slippery slide.

The box has locked, leaving screams to dream;
The boys with toys have yet to fret-
The end is merely the bend.

David Moore

Out of Darkness

When all seems lost and naught remains,
  Left with self to stand alone;
Despair is all that's left to see,
  And fear the darkness unbeknown.

But hark! A glimpse of another day;
  Walk on, walk through the mirky tide,
With hope of life yet strange to be
  To the rainbow shore on the farther side.

Oh summon the thread of courage within,
  Let go of despair and binding fear!
Rise up your heart to hope and life,
  Push on through the darkness, freedom is near.

And pull ashore the bed of life,
  Greeted by the hand of friend.
A path of promise now to trod..
  Life renewed, it did not end.

  Beverly Jean Stupke-Purdy

Looking for Another New Day

Every morning when I wake up,
my Father and Sister have gone to work.
I wash my face and brush my teeth.
And when I finish my prayers,
my younger Brother and Sister have gone to School.
I eat my breakfast alone.
My Mother is busy in household work.
After breakfast, I look at my G.E.D. Test paper.
I go through it, when time comes to answer,
I get confused. I believe without any practice.
It is difficult to answer, I can't do it.
The loneliness comes as another day.
So, to remove loneliness, I go through a Novel.
The Novel looks too thick I can't read it.
Again Loneliness comes as a new day.
I want to help my Mother in household work.
She tells me to study in sitting room.
I thought about removing my loneliness by helping her but
I study and come to know loneliness
can be removed by removing laziness.

  Tenzin S. Tsewang

Final Courage

He slumps down in his wheel chair
looking older than his garden dirt.
Gnarled pine-branch hands
reach out in dim recollection.
Wood-splitting hands now tamed,
the toll of time, again exacted from youth.
Stroke-stretched lips fumble slick words.
It is good to see him.
Memories rush and crush,
of fir firewood stacked straighter
than a master mason's wall,
and workshop tools
placed neater than grandmothers' silverware.
Manhood's proud package
reduced to small bundle of dignity.
Final chapter in his book of life.
He is ready, I am not.
Fragile, fleeting as breath from a swallowtail's flight,
death comes and frees him at last
to return to where earth dances with sky.

  D. H. Yost

Our Finest Hour

This world can be such a lonely place,
  where ignorance thrives, drowning heart's quiet grace.
    So many live in illusion, a fool's paradise,
      where selfishness rules over sacrifice.

Most become servants conforming to society,
  letting others shape their values and proprieties.
    Choosing to live in no man's land
      slowly suffocating - heads buried in the sand

How could we have gone astray
  losing sight of the beauty that surrounds us each day?
    Those who claim riches bring happiness
      too late do they realize the love they have missed.

The wise man is he who takes nothing for granted,
  allowing no seeds of doubt to be planted.
    Lives his life not for material things
      but for the treasures only love brings.

Nothing in this world could be more profound...
  if only love instead of money made the world go 'round.
    If love were to dictate over money and power,
      only then would we be in our finest hour.

  Amy Ziegler

My Mentor — My Friend

Dedicated to Irena Lee

Yesterday was like most
  Routinely an average day,
Today my life has changed completely
  Uninvitedly rearranged in every way;

A friend that I have greatly admired
  And thought was invincible all these years,
Received the most dreaded news ever
  The kind that would only bring one tears;

How will I ever be the same
  Or keep the promise that I have made,
A promise to stay positive, and
  Never to let the hope fade;

Certain people come into our lives
  They touch us like no one before,
Because of this I will never be ready
  To have to close that door;

Having to say "Goodbye" forever
  Would be something with which I could not contend,
I cannot imagine not sharing secrets again
  With my mentor, and my special friend.

  Johanne L. Hewitt

Tonight My Love

Tonight in this light
You look like an angel
Sent down from somewhere up above
To hold me and love me.
I tell you I love you
And you tell me the same
Then we fall asleep in each other's arms.
But wait- that's just a dream
Because I am here and you are not.
But our love has built a bridge
That we can walk across to be together.
So there shall be no more tears
Between the two of us
For I love you and you love me.

  Tamara M. Lockhart

Pretending

You stand there pretending to be happy.
Inside we all know you're not. Never being you,
your laughter never true
As the years go by and all
that's left is you, that's when
you realize the truth.
All along you thought they were
wrong, but deep inside you
knew they were right.
But you were just not strong.
You hide all your life,
no feelings left inside.
So you begin to fade away.
Being nothing in the end.

Gay Mari Marsh

Just Me

I have a strong back . . . but I have no backbone.
I love the smell of freshly cut grass, it's clean like watermelon.
I have a young soul in this life,
but my skin is old from lives before.
My Irish eyes are always smiling, but today they're hiding
I'm dying inside.
I want so much. I feel I do so little.
I give so much. I feel I get very little.
I love the colors in a sunset at days end,
they make me safe and at peace.
I love to turn and find the moon watching over me,
giving me permission
to be a bit crazy and always introspective.
I'm ready to find my perfect, my soul, my love, my life . . .
    partner, my mate.
All I find is indecision, disrespect,
and short lived, selfish disinterest.
I love to shower outdoors.
I've only just recently become somewhat comfortable
with my naked body.
It looks the same it did four years ago. What's so different?
I have so much to be thankful for.
Why am I so unhappy? So unsatisfied?
Why am I always looking in the wrong direction?
Am I?

Erin O'Brien

The Strength of the Lord Through the Storm

He picked me up when I was down,
He put my feet on solid ground.
He gives me peace through and through,
And my strength he does renew.

Through these long and dreary days,
My Lord is with me always.
And when I see the storms come in,
I call on Him

Who is within I say,
Oh Lord help me this day
You are the potter and I am the clay.
Words can't describe what I have to say,
I love my Lord so much each day.

Florie Noe

Religion

A happenstance, a guarded dance, a shout to the sky
A drying well, a sacred snail, listen to our cry,

A righteous mate, a chosen fate, following the call
A lost race, a broken face, all about to fall,

A mist anew, the birds that flew, greeted by the sun
A child at play, been lead astray, ended by a gun,

A past look, a banished book there for us to take
A leader that lies, a kid that cries, ready for our break,

A lost rhyme, a forgotten time, for this poem to give
A God that cries, a Christ who dies, so we all shall live.

Kris Ahlers

Epilogue

I thought I heard someone crying, but I'm sure
    it wasn't you.

Daphne's limbs extending into rough
    braided fibers
Riotous tremors, clutching fertile slopes
    between the jagged faults
Immersed in glistening heat, a violent
    purification
Sweet nectar spills upon polyester
    flowers, melting roses
The marble wall catches the sun's last
    rays amidst the ivy
The ash tree ascends from low shrubs, withering
    in the oppressive heat

I thought I heard someone crying, but it couldn't
    have been you.

Ryan Muckerheide

I Am the Wall

If I were the walls
I'd be daisies in spring morn,
I'd be scented bananas
with my peel all torn.
I would relay the lives,
the sorrows and joys,
of those inscribing me with their initials,
and those testing their favorite noodle on my surface.
The youngest will make me laugh -
the traumas of the teen will make me churn.
Each of them mark their height on me,
and I wonder when it will be my turn.
In the end I will be just another old wall
which counts down to the moment when I will fall.
And soon you all will be gone,
only preparing for regret
because through it all,
the damned old walls never forget.

Lacy J. Reinhart

Pagoda Prayer

A solemn man stopped in front of the colorless door,
He entered as if he was in a hurry to pray,
Though he slowed to admire the pictures of religious faces,
To the front of the temple he walked,
Not noticing anyone but himself,
He dropped his knees to the floor,
After a long silence it was time to go on with the day,
As he got up he was back to his old paces,
His feelings in his mind were locked,
It was as if he put a book of feelings back on the shelf.

Erin Carreiro

Busch Gardens Bound

We were scheduled to leave at two on Thursday,
However, problems arose and we had a late start.
But soon we got ready and went on our way
Happily, never losing our hope or our heart.
There was teasing, playing games, and talking,
Singing, and laughing at people that were walking.
We had some to reveal their white-sock-clad feet
And place them on the back of occupied seats.
There were urgent yells of "Hey, I've gotta go!"
Answered by "Yeah, that's a feeling I, too, know."
Unhappy, disbelieving cries of protest arose
As we passed a rest area that was about to close.
So, we made a stop at the next Shell Station
And used the time to partake of our supper ration.
The noise began to finally quiet down
When Mr. Sandman came to make a round.
Upon arriving at the hotel, we started to unpack
And called to order pizza for a midnight snack.
After emptying the box, we readied ourselves for bed.
At about one-thirty, we gratefully rested our heads.

Tina Skipper

A Single Blade of Grass

The green spread of plants
Turned brown under the footsteps of the big feet
Belonging to the heavy set officer.
Suddenly all my memories,
The glories of my childhood
Were torn from me,
And I became another blade of grass-
Without hope, without reason.
In the distance, the birds happily swarm by the flock,
But the blade of grass -
My blade of grass
Does not move at all.
All is still,
The blade of grass is no longer separate-
Apart.
Winter has come
And I am gone.

Shani Krieger

Untitled

It is a deadly disease
It runs rampant
in our homes
It strikes the rich, the poor
It strikes the schooled and the unschooled
It strikes the young and the old
It strikes women
It strikes children
and even sometimes men
it numbs our minds
It kills our spirits
It buries us dead or alive

It strikes!
It strikes!
It strikes!

The words, the blows...

Domestic Violence

It hurts us all.

Nancy Laguerre Chassagne

Untitled

I long for her, I cry for her,
I punish myself, and beg for mercy . . .

I want her, I need her
I addict myself, and beg for plenty . . .

I forget myself, I turn on myself,
I abandon myself, and beg for return . . .

I love her, I hate myself
I can have only one and beg for both . . .

Robert P. McLeod

Faces

Thousands of faces pass me by;
And many I've studied, don't ask me why;
Faces so full of anxiety and worry;
Also those showing strain of constant hurry;
Faces thoughtful and those so gay;
And many have lost all look of play;
Faces showing thoughts sublime;
And other showing the effects of time;
Faces that say, "Oh I wish I could stop;
I'm trying so hard but I'll never reach the top."
Faces so full of powder and paint;
Trying to be something that they ain't;
Faces expressing rebellious resentment;
And others showing self-contentment;
Faces gloomy and with a constant stare;
And so many who long their thoughts to share;
Yes, I've seen thousands and thousands of faces;
And many expressions shown by different races;
I've studied them over and over again;
Don't ask me why, perhaps the reason I'll know by and by.

Joshua C. Whiting

Escape From Reality

Have you ever wished that you could be
A big beautiful old oak tree.
With branches that reach so high in the sky
Not a care in the world as the day goes by.
With leaves rocking gently from the wind in the air
Back and forth and yet nowhere
No one to answer to, no one to please
Just standing tall enjoying the sweet summer breeze.
I have my days - I admit it is true
I'd like to be that oak tree - How about you!

Lucinda Hanson

Thoughts of Another

When I was young surrounded by love
Reaching out for blessings from above
Those thin lines separating family fun
Opening up doors with avenues to run
While God lifted my spirits through time
I'll never know why, my heart was such a find
Will I be loved forever as I dreamed
Or will warmth flow like the breeze
Will I trade places with loving ways
Maybe happiness will become reframe
Will my needs change gradually with the tide
While the depths of my mind leaves room to hide
Oh! How I wish sleep would command
So my mind would leave my dreams behind
Miles apart around the coldness of night
While my life matures leaving tears of fright
Insecure unable to roll the dice
As the price was to high leaving no choice
When I stumbled and lost my way
Those minutes seemed like hours every day

Norman W. Jorgensen

A Day In The Life

Prison walls all barren and bare,
Hold men who once had it all,
How all they know is bars and despair.

Keep your heads up to see the light,
Cause before you know it, here comes the night.

For each man is a number,
For each number there is a life,
I wouldn't trade mine for any man's life.

Round and round they go, all through the day,
Never stop movin' until the end of the day.

They fight and they fuss as they quarrel in their ways,
To get their point across in unending ways.

A code 33 is a never-ending plight,
Once you get there you may have to get down and fight.

For once they reach that farewell gate,
May the Lord bestow them their destined fate.

Debby S. Patzke

Untitled

Cry away the follies of tomorrow
The sorrows are not to share or borrow
The dreams are clouded by reality
Were hopes and wishes fail is fatality
Happiness and joy funny words
Hatred and violence amass in herds
Russian roulette spin round and round
Till no more words, shhh, not a sound
Wide awake, yet eyes still closed
The histories demise its fate is chose
Remember yesterday the way it was
Because doom it looms in the ear like a buzz
Trust misused no time for love
As darkness covers overhead, up above
Understand the words that are said
For the world has been entirely mislead
A joke that is not funny, yet thousands laugh
For the mist of fog has blinded the path,
No more nonsense it's drown enough
When is it time to challenge the bluff

Joshua Davis

In My Dreams

In my dreams, everyone lives happily ever after.
In my dreams, every kid gets Willy Wonka's golden ticket.
In my dreams, Peter Pan's not the only kid who can fly.
(In fact, all kids can fly, they don't need a license, and they never
    run out of gas).

In my dreams, I don't need driver's to drive.
In my dreams, there are no "R" rated movies.

In my dreams, I go back in time and tame the dinosaurs.
In my dreams, I go to magical jungles where unicorns take
me on awesome adventures.
In my dreams, I travel in spaceships to faraway galaxies
    and make friends with the locals.

In my dreams, all people are treated equally no matter how they look.
In my dreams, everyone has a happy home.
In my dreams, everyone's dream comes true.
In my dreams, there's a universal language so I can speak to anyone
    in the world.
In my dreams, I can E-mail extraterrestrial.

It's funny, but in my dreams, there are no bedtimes.
In my dreams, I never wake up until the exciting conclusion is over.

So whenever someone says: "Oh yeah, in your dreams, Michael!",
I say: "Cool!"

Michael Shoretz

Fudgey

Anyway fudgey tastes great
With sauce, with whipcream, or alone.
Pudgey's the price, but fudgey is nice
Fudgey's a kind of its own!

Slim Mary Anne eats grit stew,
Thin Elsa has her cakes of beans.
But Anna who's pudgey, eats lots of fudgey
And always licks the plates clean.

You can have the stew made from grits,
The cakes made of beans you can eat.
But though I'll get pudgey, I will eat fudgey
For fudgey can never be beat.

Katie Scrafford

Railroad Tracks

I hear the trains in the night,
I never know where they are going or why.
Covered rooms passing into the unknown,
Paths made only for them,
Tracks rode alone.
Freedom to run from the pain and sorrow
And to leave behind what they do not love.
Bigger and stronger than anything in their way,
Mysterious and lonely and painful.
They are what I wish I could be,

Free.

Elizabeth Quist

Wedding and Memories

*To my daughter, Rosa Hansie Márquez on the day of her
wedding to Christian Stolcke, July 30, 1994.*
I could, in my mind, travel back in time
And arrive the day that your birth took place.

I could just proceed with my mental trip
And observe the rising of your firstly teeth.

To regain the joy of being around
When you tried out your first speech sound.

I could stop once more my imaginary race
To watch you trying your first little pace.

To insist again, to set sail in full
To hear you crying on your first day in school.

But now I prefer to tie time to space
And focus my effort on a quite new case.

I speak of the wedding when the supreme being
Joins Rosa and Christian as perpetual team.

Have my blessing, children, I'll pray for you both
Let your love be eternal and be blessed by God.

Julio A. Márquez

Love Is Like A Rose

The rose, represents love, joy and happiness.
It is delicate and must be handled with care.
It brings out an erotic fragrance what warms the
body with passion.
It will entice and seduce you.

The rose like love is overwhelming to the
senses of the mind.
Its beauty first stimulates and then...pleases.

Given proper care the rose like love will last
a long, long time.

June E. Taylor

421

The Games We Play

How can a light that shines so brightly focus upon itself?
Can salt that gives up so much flavor season its own wealth?

The key to understanding:
— point to the door
— purpose ignore
Lay down the ring of binding!

We wonder why, and gaze to the sky,
    as seasons pass in perfection.
The games we play require a soul survey,
    a mental restoration.

    How can a house that's fully furnished with itself indwelleth?
    Why does the mind given insight intellectually embellish?

    The road to Godly wisdom:
    — give up the drive
    — blindly arrive
    in — grafted comprehension!

We pray to God and live our lives in rhythmical procession.
The games we play as we reason away don't match up to our
profession.

    How can a light that shines so brightly focus on itself...
        Timothy G. Alexander

I Know

Hiding inside for too long
    trying to be everything but me.
They say slavery's gone but they're wrong;
    the words we say, the way we dress
    has to be like all the rest.

You can run, you can hide
    drown in a drink or a drive
but all the lies and coverups
    can't make up for the hollow inside.
Oh yes I know, for I've been there.

What happened wasn't our fault;
    we were just victims but it tore us apart.
Someone take the broken pieces
    and mend the fences.
Show us the way.

It's all about choices
    so listen to the voices
and take a step towards the light.
    For I know cause I've been there.
        Sarah Beth Fretwell

One Woman's Love

One woman's love stands all alone
Waiting for someone to give it a home
She just stands there with a sad look on her face
She keeps thinking of him as she stares into space
Where in the world did she go wrong
She thought she was tough she thought she was strong
She though of the moments that they shared
Her chance to love him she had dared
He gave her a warmthness felt deep inside
A light of hope will be her guide
She wishes there was some way to change his mind
Everyone knows that love is always hard to find
She made the mistake and shed some tears
To try to love again is what she fears
She wishes that his love will soon find her.
And for her broken heart it will cure
She thought she was right in the love that she gave
She thought it would see her to her grave
But now she is kneeling down on her knees
Praying to God above to help her, please.
        Tammy Lynn Turner

Only In My Dreams

When I was a little girl
I used to dream about my prince
hoping one day my dreams would come true.

Then when I got older
I realized that is where my prince belonged
only in my dreams.

When I thought all hope was gone
There was standing my future prince
waiting for me.

Only slowly and gracefully did you come
into my life like a bird soaring in the wind.

Being in my life today
I can truly say
you made all my dreams come true.
        Melissa Ennis

My Garden

In the darkness of night I walk thru' my garden
Now losing its brightness with the coming of fall
In a shock of awareness, reality comes over
    Summer has faded, vines are dry on the wall.

The yellow, the orange, the red, white and pink
In the flowers that I grew as a border
    Still glow in their beauty and give off their pollen
To the bees and the hummingbirds searching for water.

A few tomatoes and peppers still grow
    And even some dill gives off an aroma
Not until frost will I clear them away
    A few more weeks to enjoy and to ponder.

As winter comes on with its chill in the air
In the darkness of night, I remember
A love like a garden still grows in my heart
A romance one year in September.

Like my garden, I nourish that flame deep inside
Of his promise, a daily reminder
    The strength and the patience he knew were mine
His return, the fulfillment, the binding.
        Joyce Miller Chewning

I Dreamed

A dream can be a powerful thing.
I know. For in times past I was lonely
And so I dreamed.
I yearned for a woman. And so I dreamed.
I longed for her companionship,
to walk with her side by side.
And so I dreamed. I wanted to feel the
touch of her hand in mine. And so I dreamed.
And to feel the warmth of her lips and
she to feel mine. And so I dreamed.
I needed to feel soul-stirring passion.
And so I dreamed.
I hungered for a woman's love and a woman to
take my love and cherish it. And so I dreamed.
I dreamed of a woman in every detail and the
dream was vivid and strong.
Behold!
There came a day when the dream stood before
me, came to my arms. And then I dreamed no more
For she was real.
        Martin Wright Mayer

422

From Ironic Blood Blooms the Tree of Hope

Why, oh why?
Do so many have to die?
What a wanton waste!
To grow so old in such haste.
Why, oh why?
Do we have to struggle in this life?
What a burden to carry in a world so filled with strife.
When, oh when?
Will we learn that this toxin coursing through our veins- this ironic
   blood-
Does not need to be a flood!
How, oh how?
Will we learn the answer that beats our brow?
Will we find this reply before our death?
Hope against hope the answer comes while we still have a breath!
See, oh see! Let this be the tree of hope!
Now we know -so now we cope! Watch, oh watch!
How this tree will flower and how it will bloom!
And chase away all of our gloom!
Then, oh then! The healing will begin!
How wonderful to be able to start to live again!

    Chrystle Shirylann Foster

Where I Am

Where I am is not yet known,
But from what I can see it's not too bad.
I eat in this place, so hungry I am not.
Temperature's at its nicest;
For it isn't cold nor hot.

You'd think this place was heaven,
But that it's far from being.
For there's something missing here;
That's another human being!

    K. D. Buchanan

Earth Bound

I look up from my weeding
At this bluest of blue skies
And there's a lone bird, snow white
Against the dazzling azure.
A gull? A pigeon? No. A white dove,
Symbol of peace, winging up wind.
Now he flips, showing his wing spread,
Levels again, beating strongly.
I watch until he disappears
Eastward. Is it you, my son,
Soaring your way into the unknown?
The blue-eyed lad who so loved air planes,
Who wore his wings proudly to war.
And I am left kneeling in the silt
Still earth bound.

    Louise Pfaffmann

For Real

My love for you is for real.
For real like the sun and the clouds.
My love for you is for real.
For real like the flowers and the trees.
My love for you is for real.
For real like the earth and the sky.
My love for you is for real.
For real like the wind and the rain.
My love for you is for real.
For real like you and like me,
My love for you is for real.

    Paul J. Thomas

Distance Places

Past memories hang on my wall
Pictures and paintings from my past
Postcards from family and friends
Such distances places, I've never been
Cards and letters, all wishing me well
At times it appears I'm really in hell
Nothing moves but the thoughts in my mind
Most often, constant I have plenty of time
I watch the clock that moves ever so slow
What does it matter, I have no where to go
Day and night, hour after hour
I know he's here I can feel his power
Please take me now, as I'm ready for flight
To see those distance places and sights
My pictures and paintings no longer hang on the wall
As my memories are with me as I soar along
To once again feel so young, free and strong
For ever to keep moving on.

    Sandra Ianno

Yellow Kitchen

Morning sunlight dancing
On dust-streaming rays
Through the curtained window
Tied back with yellow ribbon

Bright and cheerful
As the fresh churned pale butter
And shiny egg yokes ready for the frying pan.

A brown snuff bottle
Filled with sunflowers
Sits in the middle of the scarred table;
Some of the petals have dropped.

Yellow and white checked apron
Neatly tied around an ample waist
The smell of coffee, hot and black
As the sturdy arm pouring it into lemon colored plastic mugs.

Chairs scraping on pine floors scrubbed tawny with
Left over lye wash water. Screen door creaking
As it nudges the old dog lying across the stoop,
Morning sunlight dancing on his amber shaggy coat.

    JoAnn Bryan

A Minute

  I'd like to take a minute,
and tell you a thing or two;
  Like, I think you're really wonderful, but,
mostly, I love you.
  I'd like to take a minute,
and have you hear me say,
  "My love for you grows stronger, with
every passing day!"
  I'd like to take a minute,
and have you sit close by,
  And feel how much I love you,
and hear the reasons why.
  I'd like to take a lifetime, and
share it all with you
  I'd like to spend eternity;
just, simply, loving you!

    Tammy Vosburgh

Openings

Ancient rock sculptures
with water-carved apertures
inviting glimpses into, through and beyond
backward and forward in time
how many millions of lesser pebbles
have spent themselves
tumble-carving your beauty.
Inspiration for an Arp or Moore
who with mallet and chisel
and surely well-spent arm muscles
still create in their sculpted stones
contoured openings for similar visions
into, through, and beyond.

Mary Volkert

Two Hearts As One

He came into your life without any
warning how girl you know that you would
be morning. He passed away without
saying goodbye why or why did he
have to give. You fall in love right from
the start who would have thought that
he would break your heart. All of the
grieving and all of the crying all because
your hearts are dividing. You think your
in this world along. Just because he
is gone but he's where you never knew
in your heart right with you.

Princess Redden

My Love for You

You were as new, as the leaves full of dew
there were many others who loved you too
you were so cute, when I saw you I almost
became mute.
Your blonde hair, your blue eyes, like the stars in the sky
I wished for you and I still do
maybe someday I'll have a chance, hopefully I will last
you don't know how I feel but my love for you is real
I just don't know how I am going to deal
all I can do is pray for you and then maybe
you'll love me too.

Sarah Mapes

Untitled

Weary eyes of brown and steel
  Have marked the passage of pains untold
And to peer behind their dark veneer
  Is to enter through the portals of the soul;

Once they held such light and passion
  That their flame could erase the chill
And there was an intensity in their steady gaze
  That spoke of what words could not reveal;

But somehow in the march from then
  The eyes have lost their gleam
And now see the world with an empty stare
  That denies faith in the strength of dreams;

Two tortured orbs that mask a gentler place
  Where the light of compassion would hold no pain
But vision grows dim with the passage of time
  And soon but blindness will remain;

Those soft brown eyes that once spoke of youth
  Are now but portals of the soul
I have seen their likeness in my mirror
  And the soul I see my own.

Calvin A. Knox

Lunar Calamity

By the morning sun rise
And the moon of crickets
Lies an infertile missionary
One of life's greater challenges
Who has been called serenity
Died today of a swollen heart
After picking a decaying cumber
Bleeding from a rose thorn
Scorned at the midnight, moon filled darkness

Katie Schober

Immortality

When they look at me I think of thee and all that we have shared
And I wonder why I said good-bye to our kingdom by the sea
Good-bye to immortality
And I am tempted to search for thee
Oh I am so tempted
To be done with all that I have won
To join and again become
What now only you could see
But then I realize
That through the fire and beyond the walls
Are the eyes that truly see
And it could never be
You and me
For what would they have
If you were set free

Tanja Christine Fitzpatrick

I Love My Church

I love my church, that's how it should be
it's not the building but the people I see.
It's not the stained glass windows or the lights hanging down
it's the feel of God's presence and his glory all around.
It's not the clothes that are worn with glitter and lace
it's the heavenly music and the smiles on each face.
It's not the bouquet of flowers on the remembrance table
it's the people that come as long as they are able.
It's not the preacher's correct English or the elaborate phrases he
says but it's the truths from God's word that I hear read.
The bricks and the mortar are not the things that I like
it's the people's spirit that keeps me coming back.
It's not the carpet so soft or the cushion seats
it's the abundance at God's table and his children that I meet.
It's not the songs that are sung or my next of kin
it's the Holy Spirit and the message there in.

Melva Luellen Key

Your Lips Alone

Your lips alone
Could launch one thousand ships
Enchanting, luring, captivating

Like two wild roses
Moistened by an early morning mist
Swaying, in a field of dreams

Sunlight dances upon their surfaces
And is dispersed into a spectrum of colors
I experience visual ecstasy

Your lips alone
Bring me to my knees
So soft; So pretty

Samuel D. Schlachter

The Computer, You, Sherwin, and Myself

For someone from the Third World,
From South-East Asia,
The computer is new.

But it's not a nightmare, either,
Since I could get my driver's licence,
Clumsily manipulating one.

Yet, we have to confess,
Once the diskette is there,
Things are no longer simple:

Log in. Menu. Memory. Exit.
Exit. Log in. Memory. Menu.
You came, touched one key, and there, was the word:

Welcome! That I needed so badly
To enter that world,
Complicated, electronical, of the computer.

If, one of those days, Sherwin, I get at home
With that device of the modern age,
I won't forget how much you've done, to ease me in.

Victor C. Dao

An Angel Sonnet

Angels are beautiful, wonderful things
Especially the ones you know and love best
Your heart is so happy, it soars, it sings
Until a child is laid to peaceful rest'

A promise to cling on, being so true
Three-years-olds won't die, not the ones you love
They'll just become angels to watch over you
With God, forever, in heaven above

The house is never home when loved ones die
Sometimes you feel so desperately alone
Wipe away your tears from your crying eyes
Someday you'll find a place to call your own

Because some day you will finally see
Some of God's best angels are only three

Kelly K. Pantzlaff

Fading Star

You look at me as if you'll see me again.
You speak to me like this isn't the end.

But would it be different if I left you for good.
I was always the one thing that you never understood.

And if one day I would return
and you found me at your door,
would you look at me a different way.
Would you know it was you, that I came back for.

What would you do if I wasn't the same.
Would you love me more, or leave me with all the blame.

And if you saw me on a crowded street,
would you look the other way.
Would you forget who you are,
my fading star.

Shannen Wilson

Friends Come and Go

Just as the new falling snow
Leaving at the end of the season
Saying they have to move on without any reason
Oh we'll meet again someday
When we pass each other's way
And remember the times that were spent
Still years later recalling that promise never kept
The thought still remains in your heart
Just as the day that the friendship was torn apart
"Oh Lord" one wonders why
Things had to end and with a goodbye
You pledged to stay in touch
For the friendship meant so much
Yet you still wonder why as tears come to the eye
Why the final day had to come
When you would say goodbye forever . . .
For seeing one another would be never
And to our final day the memory will grow not old
As you think back on how friends come and go

Lillian Klassen

Day and Night

The nights are lonely
the days are so sad,
all I think of is the words I should have said
to keep you here with me.
Why can't we still be?
I miss you so,
my tears flow
like the river
they make me shiver
I just can't stop thinking of you
even if you have made me so sad at times,
the memories that I have of us
aren't enough; I want more
you only you have ever made me feel...
the thrills,
the chills,
my nights will be lonely
my days will be sad
until you come back

Jodi Morris

Another Love

Oh night so quiet, calm and cold
Oh moon so round, so full and bright;
Help me to seek the one right way
To guide my thoughts to see the right.

How can one know how strange it seems
To one who thought life so secure;
To find that once so deep and full
Has tossed and turned until no more.

Help me, a woman in middle life
To guide my son and keep him strong;
To be a pal, to take a fathers place
To meet temptation and judge the wrong.

Why should life play such cruel tricks
When after sharing many pleasant years;
He should turn to yet another love
And leave us in bleak sorrow and tears.

A black omen, a soul sick lonely hell
Where liquor poisons heart and brain;
Only God knows the disillusioned hearts
Left to blaze a saner trail, forget the pain.

Zelma A. Warberg

My One True Love

I can never get to sleep right,
because I think about you day and night.

My one true love do you hear my heart
skip a beat when I see you,
you swept me off my feet.

And do you see the wistful look
in my eyes as I look into yours?

I always dream about running away
to distant lands. We're walking down
the beach holding hands.

My one true love, I will love you
forever and ever.

Jenny McNair

Urgent

He seemed to rush the harvest that year
bringing her the carrots in the August heat
and picking all the apples before September dawned
"Got them pears preserved yet, Ma?"
he'd ask. And she,
slightly angered and not a little
rattled, would yell,
"Well, Pa, what's yore rush!
I always got it all done before,
ya know, 'thout yore naggin' so.
Always seem ta getter all put up.
Hain't starved yet!"

Hidden urgency seemed
his energy
as he persisted
First frost had not yet arrived
as she tightened the last lid
and he silently slipped away.

Meg Sackett

Unreal

Have you ever thought of Earth,
As a big ball of play dough a child is playing with,
Or as a picture that a,
Kindergartener can color on,
Or a test a teacher grades,
Or the mountains as an anthill,
What can be broken by,
A storm,
And cars and planes are,
Boy's toys from his toy chest,
And people are a little girl's,
Paper dolls,
And things that seem make-believe,
Are real in the land of the Unreal.

Mallory Erickson

My Son

Lie still my child and rest awhile
You've left this earth with fond memories and smiles
Lie still my son your job is done
The time we've had will not be undone
Lie still my child my only son
For Jesus comes, and your next journey will begin
Like a soft warm breeze upon your sails
He'll guide you across the seas of damnation to the islands of
    tranquility
Lie still my son your job is done.

Larry Bennett

Pain

I have a pain so deep, only a 10 foot pole could reach,
it goes deeper than the eyes can see,
deeper than the ears can hear,
this pain is so deep it knocks me off my feet.
This pain comes from you, cause you aren't there when I need
you too...when I need you to just tell me that you care.
I try to ignore these feelings, thinking it will get better,
but I've come to realize I can't change you.
You are the only one who can change the way you are,
I want to be there for you when you need me,
there're just some things that need to change,
but don't change for me, change for you, cause you want to,
for without that change things won't ever be the same.

Teresa Williams

The Onset Of Depression

She feels the touch of darkness.
She knows the pull of its descent.
It engulfs and smothers her being,
Brings her to her knees
And slumps her to the earth
In a painful praying position.

It swallows her heart, seals her eyes,
Deafens her and renders her speechless.
Leaves her there to the burden of her thoughts,
Imprisoned in a place of indecision,
Behind a door without a knob to possibility.

Linda A. McVey

Lorelei

On land of soft green seas
and mountains pass on by
with castles made of light and air
there find Lorelei

With hair like that of angels breath
sea blue in her eye
skin like that of babies
this is Lorelei

Daughter of the stars
lives near the open sky
a virgin of the wooded shore
Lorelei, Lorelei

I walk the open city street
alone out loud I cry for friend, a woman, company
where is my Lorelei!

Does she wait for me tomorrow will I learn of her today
or has she gone forever?
Of this I cannot say

But one thing I can speak of and I swear I do not lie
never will I stop searching for my lady, Lorelei

Curt Withington

Kelsey's Poem

Here's all the fireworks go boom boom boom!
Here's how the stars go twink twink twink!
Have you ever touched the moon?
It feels so soft, like a bunny rabbit.
If you fly up to the sky, how will you touch the moon?
It's too far away!
Have you ever touched the moon?
Why did you touch the moon?
Did you feel the moon to see if there's ice cream in it?

Kelsey A. Conklin

Dream

The "world" is sleeping.
Alone, at night, with my pencil,
I always meet a lot of people.
Some are bad; some are nice.
They make me sad and happy.
This is life. I cry and laugh.
The best in that situation is that
All their hearts beat in mine
And in the silence of the night
I hear the beating of my heart.
Sometimes I get lost in a world better than ours
Where I would like to stay because of the safety
Caused by serenity, peace and love.
Once, I woke up. I was scared.
I ran to my bed and hid under the blanket
To prevent the unknown from hurting me.
I was in a panic. Suddenly and smoothly
A warm power was crossing my being.
I felt good. I knew it was God. I slept.

Michel William Sylvain

Where Will It End?

This life we've been given has not been an easy road.
From birth we're taught to be good, to amount to something;
   we all take on a heavy load.
No one person handles troubles as another one would.
Each is given a task to overcome life's obstacles,
   the only way that one could.
How easy it might be if there was someone there to hold our hand,
   to show us the way.
If ever that someone would ever let go, you were left on your own,
   where then would we stray?
I believe in putting my trust in God to help direct my future.
His hand has always been there when needed, tho you may let go,
He will let you decide what may be - to continue with him,
   or for you, alone, to go forward.
You are then on your own.

Kathleen D. Carlstedt

Untitled

Was it you who told me you would be with me forever?
Was it you who said you would always care?
But when it was time to show your feelings,
You weren't even there.
I remember the day we were walking in the park.
I was holding so close to you because it was getting dark.
We were so close then,
No one could tear us apart.
Until that dreadful day when
The man in the dark took your heart.
It was just like a ghost
All he did was boast
When he took you away from me
And discontinued my glee.
Life without you has been so hard
I didn't know what I would do
If I didn't have the love and memories of you.
But we are together again and never will we part
For you will always be right here in my heart.

Charlton Lay

Boyfriend Good-Bye

Wipe your tears and dry your eyes, this
does not mean good-bye. I love you with all
my heart and I wish we never had to part.
I held you one night under the star-light.
I messed things up I know. But I want you
back cause I love you so. Our love was like
the words of a bird, it was unheard. I miss
you very much, and I miss your loving
touch. I hope our love can be repaired,
because I'm in such despair.

Amanda Scott

Right On Schedule

Let there be light! Man came soon after,
Fate without mercy, will soon end this chapter,
Temptations too strong, soon knowledge gives birth,
A wrathful transition, from Eden to Earth.
Envy and Greed, subconscious so dark,
Sins unforgivable. Noah, his Ark!
Laws disregarded, man's damage is done,
A love unconditional, he offered his son,
Repenting and praising, spirits reborn,
The rains have since dried up, hatred re-forms.
Southern trees, hanging strange fruits,
Atrocities with ovens, by Nazi camp troops,
Imbalance of nature, polluting Earth's seas,
Endangered. Extinct. The rain forest trees.
One with my Lord, so my spirit is spared,
Pain of the pending atomic nightmare,
When hate consumes man, the future is doomed,
No babies left crying, the mushroom will bloom!
Trees full of knowledge, still no lessons were learned,
Thy staff, and thy wrath; the Messiah returns!

Anthony D. Johnson

Big Red

The mighty Rio Colorado
   running wild and free
Through the grandest canyon of them all
   an awesome sight to see
It wends its way through sheer rock walls
   and pine-clad mountains too
Neath wintery skies and stormy skies
   and skies of azure blue
The water leaps and swirls
   while moving gleefully on its way
Bouncing from rocks to canyon walls
   and beaches of sand and clay
So red in color from all the mud
   it gathered and swept away
To thick to drink and to thin to plow
   is what the old timers used to say.

Owen R. Finch

God's Hand On Mine

While walking through the valley bright, I felt God's hand on mine.
   No matter where I wander, I feel God's glory hand on mine.
While standing in the choir loft, I not alone do stand,
   For God is standing with me, my hand is His hand.

Though sometimes temptations tempt me no matter where I go,
   I know God's love is with me and temptations away do flow.
For I love the Great Master, Whose gentle hands on mine,
   I go living for Jesus always, anywhere, all of the time.

With life on earth growing shorter, every minute, every day,
   I look mine eyes to Jesus and then to Him I pray,
"Dear Lord above I love Thee, and want with You to go,
   But keep my hand in Yours dear Lord, 'til I'm in that land we
little know."

Ruth H. Etter Hallett

Teach a Child

Early morning dawn abounds,
  oceans roll on, no solid sound.
High in the hills a lonely cry,
  another night has slipped on by.

Mists on the air dissipate,
  once again heavy feelings of hate
Down in a place called civilization,
  violence and pain such tribulation.

A world meant for peace and harmony
  torn to destruction by you and me,
Learn from mistakes don't make a life hurt
  remember vietnam or world war two.

Let's take a stand before it's too late
  teach a child of love not violent rage
If the flag is for freedom one under God
  then it's time to change so many wrongs.

Kelly J. Wynn

Desire

Running and pursuing, the impulse of the heart
one can only wonder, at what point do we start?
The angels in the heavens, look down from their high
brows, only to discover our time, our place, our loss
desire in an answer, unfathomed by the Gods
tomorrow is a prospect, unknown, unseen
we are lost
belching up my feelings, I choke upon my soul
the taste of life is bitter, desire's wrath ensues
on earthen plates of my palate, from which I give to you
could my life be so humble, my heart, my soul so true
that I might soon forget how life is all but new?
Toiling in the garden of eden's distant past
one can only wonder, what adam finally grasped...
upon the shores of heaven, God's will was strong and fast
but neither was the lust of man
inside those pearly gates, that caused the angel lucifer
to dare to dream be true, humans as in nature
will learn and grow and feed, upon the lust of danger
who berthed the name Desire

Harold E. Wade

Do You See It?

Can you see a bouquet or roses in the air
a blue increasing with the dusk:
An evening turning into a sunrise,
a wing, a poem, a nightingale, a star?

Do you see a hyacinth at the end of silence
of a suffering heart, or the worlds that open
at the first smile or at the sound of a word?
Do you see life beginning a new life,
springtime murmuring new trills,
its evergreens the green of tender hopes?

Ah, old new age just born anew!
To speak of love, to jump up to the stars!
Life is but a remembrance of forgotten dreams,
an enigmatic voyage, colorful at times
towards a new old dawn:
the eternal birth of our eternity . . .

Raoul G. Iglesias

Minds Close Before Eyes Open

Pity and frustration from which to choose,
they bring you up, they make you lose,
wrong methods picked in the interests of foes,
what everybody wants, no one knows,

Onslaught admitted upon completion,
long-lived morals suffer massive depletion,
while lovable leaders were on vacation,
twisted sickness overtook the nation.

In the homes, gun in hand,
ready to kill over promised land,
fighting over what they might not find,
leaving nothing to their loved ones behind.

Luke Thompson

Our Senior Year

The time has begun for our senior year
Leaving less time for friends so dear.
A time to learn and a time to grow
For everyone must choose their own way to go.
Closer together but farther apart
While we all wait for independence to start.
We begin our journey through life's little maze
Some see it clearly but most with haze.
Twenty years from now I wish I could see.
My friends and family where will we be.
Life's doors are open we must choose our way
And we must do it quickly as time slips away.
The time has arrived it is finally here
For us to begin our senior year.

William Glen Frazier

Tired And True

The man I love starts his day at three,
To most, a time they cannot see.
Sometimes it's hard for him to get out of bed,
Sometimes it's hard just to lift his head.

I give him a kiss and hug to help him face his day,
And when he leaves for work, I sit down and pray.

I ask the Lord to keep him safe for me,
Whether he's down on the ground or up high in a tree.
Then I pray again that he returns him safely to me.

The hours he works are usually quite long,
Though this makes him weak, he is still very strong.
He is my rock, and I love him so much,
Each and every day I long for his touch.

Through the wind and rain and the icy cold,
I know I could never be as bold.

When he comes home at night,
He's a pleasure to see,
But it's such a short night —
because soon it is three.

Dollie Budlong

The Christmas Rose

The Christmas rose, a wondrous flower;
God's own love, its secret power;
Only on Christmas, in His garden does grow;
Of its power, only a few ever know;
With angels' voices, songs it sings;
Joy in life, the gift it brings;
One winter, I found such a rose;
It is the source, from whence my life now flows;
I took that blossom, to cherish for life;
And you are that flower, my beloved wife.

Warren R. Giordano

Friends

I have two friends
That have to move away.
It's very sad, cause our
town is just fading away.
The halls at school will
Never be the same, 'cause
We won't see their smiles
Everyday. We're really
Close friends, we don't
Want to be apart. If
We had a say in it we
Wouldn't split apart.
We are too close to drift
Away. Why would our
friendship have to change?
We are like three sisters, that can't be torn apart.
We don't care how much it takes, we will try not to
part, so, when we say, goodbye one last time,
We'll keep that memory, in our heart, and act like
We never had to part.

Mandy Ousley

Remembering You

The pictures of you that I hang from my wall Create the tears of
heartbreak as they start to fall I never knew a love could end so fast
But now our relationship is a memory of the past We had our good times
and also the bad But our relationship was the best I ever had.

At night I look up in the sky and always end up asking why
I look up at the moon and out way far
And I'll write your name on every star
You cheated me and I cheated you
But we both knew that's not what we wanted to do
Then something happened and I don't know why
And I still don't know the reason you died
You took your life and that meant to me
You were very unhappy and wanted to be free
I still always remember the day you came to me
And asked me if I wanted to be your bride-to-be
That day never came but another thing did
And you would've loved him if you only had lived
He'll never get to meet you but he knows it's true That no other daddy
is more special than you But even now that will be forever apart Just
always remember that you've the one in my heart.

Ronda Hawes

Each Morning

It's hard to wake each morning,
and to always hear on the news,
about whites against the blacks,
and the Arabs against the Jews.

This morning in particular,
I was unfortunate to see, four persons beaten to a pulp,
And the death of a Turkish woman in Germany.

People are on the prowl,
Trying to find someone to blame,
For problems which are self-created,
Putting our innocent to the flame.

I sat down in the laundry mat this morning,
Washed the whites and colors separately.
Placed them together in the dryer,
And there the revelation was revealed to me.
Both colors and whites going 'round and 'round
In perfect synchronicity.

I wish I could see this always. For this is how it should be.
And if it were like this always,
I should be happy to wake each morning.

James T. Thomas

Memories of Home

Oh, how I'd love to go home just once again
To see all those places I've already been
Just to see that little house my daddy helped build
Where inside the love of God in us all was instilled

I don't need the mountains or the canyons so grand
I just need once more on that front porch to stand
To see where the birds their nest came to build
And my mother's flowers in my mind I see them still

Just to go inside and roam, room to room
To see where we lived where we loved everyone
That old back porch and that hickory tree
Lord, in my heart they meant so much to me
That little old church and when those bells did ring
We'd go there to worship to pray and sing
To see all the friends we had loved through the years
How we all stood together through good times and tears

That old high school where I found my first love
And that old Kentucky moon high in the heavens above
If I could just see the ones I love and still miss
Lord, I just know I wouldn't be hurting like this

Betty B. Schnieders

Independence

March 22, 1995
The day dad was found
No longer alive.
To me he had been a wonderful friend,
But now it had all come to an end.
So there I stood, all alone,
I realized now I'm on my own.
Wondering to where, exactly, I'd go,
The healing process is so very slow.
But things will get better,
This I know.
So I continue to carry on and trudge along,
With the hope that tomorrow will be a little easier.
I won't forget what happened,
That time in seventh grade,
And I certainly won't allow the memories to fade.
I'll remember it well - for it was my independence day.

Karla Marie Schroeder

Puppy Love

On breath of Indian summer's gold days
a wisp of black puppy was born,
Winter melted into spring's bright array,
puppy love for human was formed.

She played in summer's fields
romped through numerous autumn days,
her staunch qualities were revealed
as she outgrew her baby ways.

One small creature filled with devotion
that follows our lives with careful tending,
a birth that put into motion
this lifetime of loyalty unending.

Human and puppy love blended,
starlight of memories linger,
the precious days of autumn have ended
edged with frost from Icy finger.

Bea Kozlowski

I Saw Hate for the Very First Time

March 28, 1996

I felt love for the very first time,
    Three decades ago with that girl of mine.
She was pure of heart with abundant love,
    It seemed nothing could be sweeter from above.

From this union came a gift from thin air,
    It was a gift from God our son so fair.
He grew into manhood with our love that soared,
    And into his life met the love he so adored.

It was during this time a dark shadow came,
    Upon the doorsteps of my life without blame.
A stranger with evil's own pure poison to give,
    To take my love from me never to forgive.

Some three decades later this stranger reappeared,
    Sitting there before me in just a shell it peered.
And I saw from the last gasp of that love of mine,
    I saw hate for the very first time.

J. David Frier

Mother Nature

She and I are one
My friend, my teacher
I have yet to learn all she knows
It is sad, but remains to be the truth
No one will ever learn in a lifetime
The things she has learned in an eternity
Though it be a cold winter's morning
Or the most beautiful sunset ever seen
It will never be the end of her teachings
Nor will it be the end of our learnings
I will miss her when I'm gone
She shall miss me as well
But that will never stop her
She will go on and on
Telling her stories...and finding new ones

Wesley Ford

I Am

I am a fearful child not knowing my fate
I wonder if I can tell people this before it's too late
I hear the shooting of a thousand guns
I see for each gun someone's life is done
I want to end this world of hate
I am a fearful child not knowing my fate

I pretend sometimes that the world is a safe place
I feel though in my heart we're being destroyed race by race
I touch a gun for the very first time
I worry that someone would use it to commit a crime
I cry when hostages are killed for bait
I am a fearful child not knowing my fate

I understand that this world is coming to an end
I say though when you're murdered you'll believe me then
I dream at night that the earth is hell
I try to ask myself is this where evil will dwell
I hope you'll hear my voice before it is too late
I am a fearful child not knowing my fate

Joshua A. Payne

Me

If only you could see me!
If you could see behind my eyes,
    behind my smile so bright,
You would see a little girl overcome
    with fright.
Although I'm scared and trembling,
    I've a lot of love inside,
A wall is built to keep you out, a
    place where I can hide.
Tears come down my face sometimes
    for reasons, I don't know,
Either I'm not feeling anything or
    my feelings will not show.
Each tear is made of glass, watch it
    shatter when it falls,
As it disappears you wonder, was it ever there at all?
I have so much love to give you if you want to be a part,
But first you must break the wall I've built around my heart.
I could give you everything, more than you've ever dreamed,
If only you could see me!

Amy C. Bienvenu

Abandoned Soul

Underneath the coffin lies an unrested soul.
As it turns midnight, the coffin begins to roll.
Tossing and turning from a violet past,
whispering softly to itself, "if only I could have asked."
Abandoned by family to rot and decay,
this is "unfinished business" I should say.
Can this be for real? I do not know. For I do not wish to have an
    unrested soul.
Wandering from place to place, and suddenly you slow down your pace.
Hoping it isn't true, because you feel the sun staring at you.
For now it is time for you to unwind and go back to square one.
Moaning and groaning over revenge that isn't so sweet.
If only you could have taken the defeat.
Now it is too late to try and escape,
from the coffin that awaits.
Back to the coffin, I wish I didn't have to go.
But when you are like me you really don't know.
Now I shall lie here to rot and decay.
But all that is really left are bones that will go away.
All that I can say before I go away, is that revenge doesn't come
    first.
'Cause take it from me, I'd rather be free, than to wander all over
    the earth.

Chantel R. Griffith

Passion

I sit and watch as the reflection of two figures entwined
dance across the streams of lucid moonlight.
They seem to have no other care, but to make each other feel right.
The passion they posses is like a burning fire that has lost
control.
Their emotions are unleashed with no limits to confine them
to their souls.
The outline of their bodies casts a warm shadow that
sizzles against the dark night.
They are unaware of anything else except their feelings
weaved so tight.
The hunger in their eyes resembles a starved animal that
needs to be fed.
Their hands explore forbidden regions with no shame, and
they become two wild creatures that cannot be tamed.
Their nakedness is a powerful force that drives them further
into the endless night.
They do not seem to see the rising of the bright morning light.
They have formed into one whole being that is too powerful
to break apart.
They both thrive now on one heart.

Margaret M. Casey

Wedding Song

If eternity passes and we're left behind
Just stay with me forever so that the sun will always shine.

And if eternity passes and we can't reach tomorrow
I'll have enough happiness in me that you could borrow.

If eternity passes and we're left out in the cold
As long as we're together we'll hide behind the fold.

If eternity passes and I don't get to hold you
Then life would be incomplete because there is no other like you.

If eternity passes then our love remains
As it beckons to our hearts to heal our every pain.

If eternity passes and I can say I love you,
Then no one else matters and I pledge myself to you.

If eternity passes without you by my side
I'll regret not seeing your smile and hope that we had tried.

If eternity passes I want you to always know
That what I have I'd give, for you, my love, to show.

If eternity passes My love, my life
I pledge to you to always be my wife.

When eternity passes and every life is past
I'll have you forever, together, and, at last.

Lisa M. Grider

Fifty Years

Fifty years have come and gone
In our hearts we have always known,
The joy of love you two have shown to each other,
Oh! How it has grown!

You have shard more love
than most could ever give,
In those fifty years that
you have lived.

As two you became one.
Then the love grew even more!
From the love of those four,
Came no less than ten more.

So all our hearts, all four and ten,
wish you happiest fifty that has
ever been.

We all love you from the bottom of our hearts,
We hope this day is filled with joy and laughter,
That it will last forever after.

Sue Ikerd

Saying Goodbye

The father who loved and lullabied
Respected and guided his babes
Stricken with cancer, suddenly died
And was lowered to his grave.

A beautiful casket, made of cedar.
But nothing could make us feel better.
No special words we needed to hear.
No hugs as our faces grew wetter.

Now, this loving shepherd, of the past
Will survive in pictures and heart.
As we are left to explore this world so vast.
He is simply allowed to depart.

And the world set on our stupor...
We forced ourselves to comply.
Side by side, we stood like troopers
And begrudgingly said goodbye.

Melanie Quinlan

An Ode to Dawn

The fingers of dawn came creeping up the horizon
Slowly at first, gradually gaining energy.
She spread wide her palm to cover the sky.
At noon the entire heavens were covered,
With a skirt of blue, flecked with clouds of white.
The sun shone in all her brilliant glory.
The floral of earth gasping to capture,
Her life sparkling rays of hope.
Winds created shadowy effects, with flickering leaves.
Gradually dawn began to lower her hand.
Shadows came on longer fingers sliding down...
Holding in her hand the radiant colors of evening.
She said farewell to us, becoming a dawn of another hemisphere.
Only to return to us on slowly inching fingers.
Spreading her palm on our horizon again.

Lillian Vozar

I Remember It, But Not At All

Oh girl! No one's girl, I call you girl for that is all I know
about you.
I can guess but will it fit? The description I write would fit a
thousand and over of you.
I write to you in the days of Egypt, the days of Christ, of the
Christian persecution.
I write to you in the days of the Reformation, and the Revolution,
to the twisted and fearful days of the French "World Revolution".
Whoever you are, you existed. Whenever it was, you were alive.
Wherever...you were born.
Were you loved? Only in the arms of strange men, some were not
so strange, they acted peculiar, but what of it?
They were drunk and they had paid the proper price for an evening
with you.
You lived in sorrow and fear, you were beaten, sold, spent, and
you died there in the streets of some forgotten city, in some
forgotten time.
Rest in peace oh girl, whether you earned it or not, you certainly
paid for it.

D. Edward Newton

Dream In The Wood

An ocean of harvest salutes a changing aura. In light of leaves
at summer's death, the hour draws near the arrival of the equinox.
On lonely winds of Cornwall to soft-spoken waters of Essex fly
secrets of the fallen past. Awakened echoes beckon silent spirit stare.
Centuries dance past Indian Summer eyes consuming cool October
forest evening.

Gravely, images hang from an ashen sky as November's breath withers
dawn's embers, and the emergence of her nakedness in flight with
mystic smile, in tune to the hemlock's whistle.

She comes forth this lady, without sun, within sadness, in all of her
brilliance. A cloudless pair of Elysian eyes are recalled from
haunted visions...descending...on a Sunday hillside.

At first glance she stops, turns and asks, "Always"?
And he replied, "Yes, like a decor of timeless leaves
surrounding your senses, imprisoned in the aesthete
of your universe...and mine."

Edward D'Ambruoso

Incense of Tibet MUSK Contains 20 Sticks

smells good. makes me feel . . . spiritual.
      thinking of the Great Tao,
        of KRSNA inside.
it smells . . . deep.

  like it knows something i don't and can't
won't ever know
      what the incense stick knows.
with its all-knowing smoke
       rising, rising
  up toward the sky
    up past my consciousness.
dropping its ashes like
 unbecoming habits.
transforming itself into a Greater Self.
A Self that knows itself.   the incense stick.
     knowing what it knows knowing what I don't
    can't.
      won't ever know.
what the incense stick knows . . .

Justin Thurston

Untitled

I don't understand things that happen today,
cause I'm older now and I remember the way,
it once was when our goal was the future and
not just today.
Yes, this world has changed.

No policemen walked the halls of our schools back then,
no drugs, no weapons, or fear to walk in,
and athletics were important, the memories are dear.
The fun times we had with our teachers and friends,
Yes, this world has changed

They say kids are smarter and that's a good bet,
but they've not as happy as we were, I'll bet.
Cause we had no classmates called dope addicts or strife
or had to watch friends killed with a gun or a knife.
Yes the world has changed.

What's good is now "bad" to today's younger set,
To say I'm confused is a really good bet.
But I'll keep on trying as if it were a test
to help and to love them all as our best.
Yes, the world has changed.

J. W. Woodard

Pocket Change

How many times have I passed them, never matching their gaze.
The homeless, the crippled, the alcoholic's haze.

My mind has no mercy, they deserve their plight.
  So I pass them to teach them, to get up and fight.

So why is my car turning, with a sense of review?
  What humanity jars me, to meet this man anew?

Now why am I parking, and gesturing to him?
  Could it be it's my brother, and our souls are akin?

God! He looks awful, but there's a kindness within.
  And maybe I can help to atone for "my" sins.

I could be this man, he's really not so strange.
  So I offered him my hand, and all my pocket change.

John F. Kieft Jr.

Remember

Remember when you braided my hair,
With many a loving touch.
Or when you gently kissed my cheek,
With love overflowing so much.

Remember when you helped me up,
After a dreadful fall.
Or when you wiped away my tears,
Not hard for me to recall.

Remember when you encouraged me,
With such a soothing word.
Or when you taught my heart to soar,
Like a beautiful gliding bird.

Remember when you confirmed my beliefs,
Which I try to live up to each day.
Or when you chased away my fears,
Like an eagle does it prey.

Remember when you told me you loved me,
And I accepted without regret.
Do you remember?...
How could I forget?!

Teresa Barbara

Love's Prayer

Dear Lord
I love you so.
You love me so.
But you are my heart and soul.
I need to love someone with you.
I need to love someone with my heart and soul.
Please, Dear Lord O' mighty,
Make him love me with his heart and soul.
Dear Lord make your love shine through him.
Shine your love through his heart and soul.
O' Dear Lord, love me through him.

Dewanda Palmer

Waves Without Change

Waves smash and crash against the shore
One now
A million more

Silky salty shore
I adore
The pageantry of summer
The isolation of winter
But still you stay nothing more
Than the ocean meeting the land at the shore

Teska Louis Daigrepont

Death and Dying

Every now and then you did catch a sight of me; I felt your
coming; like a thief in the night you sneak in uninvited;
and undo life and undo all, unwanted end of me.

Accept it! Face it! And explore me.
Acknowledge me! But don't talk me out of dying;
Let me go; for I am not afraid of death.
It is dying abandoned, dying alone and dying
in pain that gets my fear in dying.

I am the new death on the block,
Ward and all, grieve not, rejoice for you
Have not perished in treatment.

Remember me, and learn more about me.
Remember me for I am part of your treatment.
Come close, hug me and accept sometimes.

Manuel M. Belandres

Binding Light

Wavering leaf-like on stiff winds of change,
I stand alone.
A shadow on the pastel backdrop of a setting sun

Vexed by life and love.
Silver slivers and
Passing clouds.
What does it all mean?

A day passes east to west.
Leaving me stranded.
Alone at a point far to near to the last.

Yet warmth fills me here,
in the dark of an October night.
For with the first chilling breezes
comes whispers of her name.

Intrepidly I begin my search for her.
Inspired by the ruddy hues of a harvest moon.
I move on until the sun returns,
to wrap me in its binding light.

Michael A. Wahl

A Stepmother's Prayer

Lord, I know I am weak and Thou art strong,
Some days are weary and sad.
Bless me and guide me to do what's right,
Make me the parent he once had.

Let my love shine upon his face.
Let my heart show signs of joy.
Give me the strength to raise him right,
To be my sweet loving boy.

Hold my hand when times get bad, and
Words don't always come out right.
Let him know that I do love him and
The sun above will always be bright.

This I ask thee, before anything else,
That this family will someday be one.
May the line that divides us now,
Disappear and you make him my son.

Lillian B. Mix

The Ashtray

Shaped by little hands ... The Ashtray.
I feel the coolness between my fingers
Twisting ... Pressing ... Shaping ... The Astray.

Given to him, his cracked and worn hand accepting.
Smiling ... Oh, how he smiled
Showing me the colors of laughter.
He held my hand and my fears melted.
Oh, to taste that love!

The years, passing, and the Ashtray sat
Dusted in blackness, a gray blanket dangling
Above it.

The years, unkind in their march forward,
Creviced his face, frailed his walk.
But the love remained.

Today, the Ashtray, stained and cracked with age
Is at rest, death...

A wingless bird...
A leafless tree...
A cheerless clown.

How I miss him so!

Mike R. Lugano

Bedtime Stories

In the shadowy darkness a child cowers,
fear icily trickles thru the
woolly cottony innocence of youth,
shouts of hatred echo down
darkened hallways, as again, his
mother enables her drunken husband,
fear is his constant companion of the night.
Suddenly...his body quivers
with a new felt emotion...hatred.
And so, innocence is shattered,
and, in the dusky light
of the coming dawn, the
child dresses silently for school,
and, with a final look
in the mirror, he adjusts his
mask, for his morning entrance
on the playground.

Andrew Sroka

Kathleen

She sits on the front porch — her personal loge
The stage is a playground across the street
    where her children, grandchildren and grandchildren used to play.
An unfamiliar cast performs the daily summer ritual now.
As if knowing her eyes can no longer discern their movements
    the children are louder now than ever before.
It doesn't matter — she knows the play by heart
    familiar with every line — every sound.
She leans back in the heavy white rocker
    eyes closed — listening to the orchestration.
A great rush of water fills a shallow concrete pool
    like musicians warming up and tuning their instruments.
The chains of the swings squeak a constant rhythm
    while squealing children exchange solos
    with playground attendants and watchful parents.
Once scene features tennis balls bouncing from racquet to court
    and another the yapping of a playful puppy.
An occasional breeze rustles the leaves of thick old maples
    applauding approval of the matinee.
How can the show go on when she's no longer there to enjoy it?

Carol Jean Adams

She's Gone

And though I know she's gone, I can't control the fear inside,
The way I sometimes want to hide, from everybody that I know,
And only think of her.

And though I know she's gone, I want to hear her voice so bad,
That I lie so still and feel so mad, that I can't hear the voice I
know, I've heard a million times.

And though I know she's gone, I dream of her and often hope,
That I will be able to cope, with the reality that she is gone,
But do not think I can.

And though I know she's gone, I think of all the things she's done,
To make my life a special one, and look in the eyes of my own son,
And know she would be proud.

And though I know she's gone, the memories she left behind,
Will take me through the worst of times,
And bring me joyous thoughts of love,
Forevermore.

Danna Danise Bell

433

Belonging

The journey, which once seemed endless,
is nearly over. Despite my relief,
I'm a little nervous.

I hesitate when I catch my first
glimpse of it.

The house isn't quite as I remember,
even though I've studied it in my
mind's eye time and time again.

It's larger-almost grand-and the
grounds are meticulously sculpted.

As I approach, I hear distant voices and
laughter drifting from the garden.
Just for an instant, the sea of faces is a blur.

Then, as I look from one to another,
there is familiarity and recognition.
Each is smiling. Their welcome embraces me.

This place is home, and once again,
finally, I am where I belong.

Ann J. Fortin

Silent Lucidity

The island winds blowing through the hair
reminded me of a not so distant time
where I laid on the seashore.

I studied the sea urchins as they crept up
out of the sparking blue water.
I wondered how they could remain on the sand
without being swept into the depths of the ocean.

At that moment, I saw myself as a sea urchin
having strong pinchers to take root in the earth
never to be swept away
only if I allow that experience.

To loosen my grip, relinquishes control
to the mysterious forces that determine
my quickly fleeting destination.

To discover an underwater kingdom of exotic fish.
To swim freely and effortlessly through
the intricate mazes of coral reefs.

For the greatest of all is the Silent Lucidity.

Bethany Miller-Beatham

My Most Inspirational Person

No single person can inspire me
Growing up with four brothers I couldn't find one weed
Growing up with both parents all my life
Seeing togetherness and love, not any fist fights
Being the youngest girl of four boys
Sharing with each other life's unhappiness and joys
Coming from a background with conservative morals
It's like being a seed planted in rich soil
Seeing my brothers and their relationships with their wives
Hoping to someday model that in my life
I take pride in my family as they do in me
I've been shown all my life that family is a necessity
Through thick and thin I've been through it all
With my family behind me, standing proud and tall
I treasure this with all my heart and hope to pass it on
Cause to me not many families share this special bond
But my family's morals of togetherness and being close
Not only makes me what I am, but what inspires me the most

Dianne Ladines

Heart Gifts

There are times if we will only heed,
That heart gifts come to meet our need;
Like seeing a rainbow in the sky,
When rain in the sunshine passes by.

Or stumbling upon a lovely wild flower
When strolling in a woodsy bower.
Or someone who touches you heart to heart,
Who in your life becomes a part.

Those precious moments that are God's gift,
In the midst of struggles bring a lift.
Treasures far more dear than the eye can see,
Are the "heart gifts" that come to you and me.

Words of encouragement, touches of love,
Inspired by our Heavenly Father above,
Or maybe a butterfly captures our attention,
Bringing to mind the promise of resurrection!

These are gifts that can never be measured
Only remembered and often treasured.
Gentle gifts from the heart are given,
Bringing to earth a touch of Heaven.

Jean Coker

Help Me!

Help me fight the stress in life!
Help me love the love in my life!
Help me feel, love, touch see the things in my life!
Help me not feel disgusted when I see
Someone kissing, hugging or touching each
Other, hearing them is good enough to know
that I wanted that in my life too.
Help me not kill myself because of all
The bad things in my life.
Help me fight the anger that rages
through my mind.
Help me see the positive side of
life not the negative.
Help me look up, not down at everyone
and cry.
Help me please! Forget all the things I've
done wrong.
Help me someone for I can't help myself.

Monique M. Plaza

Breaking Up

"It's over, we're through," you said to him;
then turned and walked away.
Not caring how he felt inside
or what he had to say.

"I love you still," he cried out
while trying not to show
the hurt and pain from deep inside
that only he could know.

With broken heart and head bowed low
he goes out to meet the day.
When others ask, "What's wrong with you?"
"I love her," is all he'll say.

Once again he is alone,
a life with no one to share.
"I love you," he says to the day,
"does anybody care?"

You heard him say, "I love you"
as you turned and walked away.
Still not caring how he felt
or what he had to say.

Robert Mawson

The Bridge

This nation is about to see
The turning of a century

May God give us the strength to span
A bridge that links us man to man

The bridge we build must have the strength
To give us back the human link.

The love and caring entity
That gives each child serenity

For children are the human prey
When a world has gone so far astray

So together hand and hand
United we can build a span

For love will be the strength the girth
That holds together man and earth

And children are the link the key
In the turning of a century

Eileen M. House

Melt

Like a winter snowbank
So soft, beautiful, and shapely
And maybe of heaven sent
Perhaps a white winged guardian,
To save me
Beauty in comparison to nothing except..,
Maybe that of a snowflake
Flawless in design
An intricate masterpiece of some higher one
And to the touch
One could only dream,
I could only dream
From the emotion felt
At just a glance
But if one's dream be granted true
And my lips should radiate from the warmth of yours,
I would surely melt

Chris Perry

The Garden

A garden is not just a piece of ground, it is all we see
all around.
The trees, the air, the soil we till, all combine to
bring us joy. But still,
our state of mind is our Garden too, bringing happiness
or sorrow to me and you.
Producing values more than we consume, shows us that we
will have a garden which will bloom.
So as your days progress so soon, will your Garden
die or bloom?

Christopher A. Downs

Why I Asked Why?

Why I asked why . . .
pondering the truth,
like grasping at a fading dream,
questioning ideals,
. . . wandering through an infinity of doubts, it seems;
going around in circles, chasing my own tail,
forgetting the answered question
but thinking once more, twice as hard as before
I realize . . .
"Why ask why?"

I realize . . . .

"Why not?"

Shane Swafford

What About Me?

Did you ever stop to think, to ask?
Did you ever stop to consider me,
someone other than yourself?

Did you ever stop to wonder what I could have been?
No, you did not.
You aborted me, took my life, without even asking me
if I wanted to die.

I could have been the next Einstein.
I could have been the researcher who finds
the cures for cancer, AIDS.

I could have been just what you needed to brighten your life.

But no, you couldn't bear the thought of me.
I was just another burden to your life
I was unloved, unwanted, done away with.

Mother, oh, Mommy—
How could you?

Couldn't you hear me cry out in pain?
Obviously not.

I love you, Mommy.
How come you couldn't love me back?

Marialanna Lee

So Near/So Far

From a distance I saw an image;
She passed like a fog,
With infinite detail, a glimpse
that remained forever in view,
So close at heart yet so far.

A passing glance would not be fair,
Nor do justice to her auburn hair;
You wouldn't perceive her eyes of brown,
Nor notice that girlish, toying frown.

Her tender smile would quickly show
A warmth within, a sunset glow,
And then, if you were quick to stare,
You'd see a speck, a dimple there
Upon her cheek, tho she's unaware.

From a distance I saw her here,
So distant yet so near.

Mark Ouellette

You

When I'm around you, I feel right,
Screw the world I'd rather be with you tonight.
Women might come and go like fish in the sea,
But I swear you're the woman swimmin' for me.
Keep it real with me and I'll keep it real with you,
That way our feelings will always stay true.
I'd love to walk with you hand in hand,
Knowing you're my woman and I'm your man.
If all of my dreams were to come true,
I know where I'd be, I'd be with you.
You are my power, yet you you cause pain,
Cause wanting your love is driving me insane.
So hold these words close to your heart,
And maybe someday we'll never be apart.

John Keul

That's What I Wonder

Are we real or
Are we somebody else's toys,
That's what I wonder,
Day and night
I think about belonging to someone else,
having someone own us,
That's what I wonder,
Could it be true
That's what I wonder
Maybe there is another universe out there, or
Maybe we don't belong here, or
Maybe we don't exist
That's what I wonder
That's what I wonder

Tameaka Crocker

The Silent Soldier

Silent soldier, fair and true
Nameless soldier courageous, and bold
First to live and last to die
You held your flag way up high
And left your mark way below
On the blood stained pole
Silent soldier, nameless soldier
First to live, and last to die
You held your flag way up high
And though wounded and bloody
On the ground you may lay
Silent soldier with spirit above
First to live, and last to die
You held your flag way up high
And the ground it did not touch
On its pole starry eyes remembering you
Silent soldier, fair and true.

April Vaiarella

Listen

I stand amazed at the human race,
The things they say — the things they do,
Speaking so freely,
Without a clue.

How can they know,
Without being there?
How can they be,
So totally unfair?

The feelings spoken from a heart,
With or without a word,
Comforts the one that speaks,
Only if it's heard.

How can they answer a broken heart,
Without feeling the pain?
Words spoken alone,
Have nothing to gain.

With no experience,
Simply extend a hand,
Your reason for doing so,
Is to understand.

Allan Godwin

The Unknown Poet

You made a bad assessment, you don't know who am I.
You don't know what kind of man I am, you don't know what makes me cry.

This isn't "better for us." This is better for you.
This poem's inspired by misery, you'll never know my love is true.

You don't know a thing about me, so don't ever say you do.
My change made me stronger, you don't know the development, I'm going through.

I'm a totally different person, from the time you let me go.
I can't believe you're not curious, this poet you'll never know.

From the brightest days, to the darkest taverns.
Poetry solidifies my feelings, how quick I was to learn.

Back then, you might have never seen it, this passion I possess inside.
I want to write forever. Monica, it was your choice to run and hide.

If change breeds resentment, then a different person I've become.
If you ever want to share this with me, you'll never have to run.

I can only love you through the words I write, I guess you'll never know it.
I'm gonna love you forever, my name is Cesar Antonio Chavez . . .
    The Unknown Poet.

Cesar Chavez

Thing of the Past

I remember the first time our hearts touched through the beauty of my
    laugh and the radiance of your smile.
I remember the essence of your being and the swiftness of your strides.
I remember the sweet nothings whispered in my ear by the sound of the wind.
I remember the softness of your touch brining chills upon me for endless hours.
I remember the maturity of our feelings at a virginal age as the
    carried on past infatuation to the deepness of raptures.
I remember seeing into your soul through your deep azure eyes and
    becoming the breath of your life.
I remember our lives paths coming to two different roads splitting apart from one.
I remember how you promised the winding roads would soon become one again.
I remember my heart trying to chase your through the twists and turns
    unsuccessfully.
I remember how the waterfalls of tears stayed with me through the
    loneliness of my trail.
I remember us...never to be again.

Alyshia Ochse

My Precious Jewel

The only girl I'll ever love is with me here today,
Her tender smile, her loving eyes, both take my heart away.

The moment I saw her, I knew right then, I'd never be the same,
Never in my life had I felt so much at once—both passion and fatal pain.
Once I felt my heart reach out to her, I knew my life would never be complete,
Until I'd be able to talk her angel, to hear her voice so sweet.

Everyday her eyes met mine, it would perpetually break my heart,
for this was the love of my life, I knew it from the start.

Time passed oh so slowly, and all I did was pray there'd come a day,
That I could open my heart to her, and say everything there was to say.

But everyday I saw her, all I could do was shed a tear,
For I knew she was the only girl that I'd ever hold so dear.

I know that one day I shall take her hand in mine, and tell her I'm hers forever,
but If that day should never come, then I shall smile again not ever.

If suddenly my life should end, and I shall breathe no more,
Then I should have absolutely no regrets, my spirit would even soar.

For my time on earth has been well spent, I've lived a happy life,
But most of all, I found the girl I love, and even met my future wife.

Yes, the only girl I'll ever love is with me here today,
My precious jewel, oh my precious jewel, you take my heart away.

Shawn Hutchinson

My Sparkles of Love

She tells me I have your eyes and that I tilt my head the way you did,
But I think it's more than that.

I know that I never walk alone because you are with me always.
Everywhere I go, I feel you right there beside me.
In everything I do your gentle hands guide me
And your loving eyes watch over me.

I'll never really realize what it would be like to fully know you,
Although I know your love.

You have given me so much, and now it is your time to receive.

Your memory and your smile shall live on in my children's eyes,
Through the joyful bells of laughter that welcome each new beginning,
And through the stars above, your soft heavenly footprints,
Which shall brighten even the darkest of days.

Now it is my chance to take center stage and make my mark on this earth.

Guide me- give me faith- love me- and lead me to learn what I am to
become. I am on the threshold of it all.
Hold my hand as I live my life through your love.

This is just the beginning; I am ready for the challenge of love,
faith and life.

Christine Marie Patricia Schefter

In Sad Lonely Times

You may feel sad and blue, but remember that God will always love you.
I must remember that every now and then, we must all give in.
Now that my life is starting to glow, I owe it to God you must know.
When you're ready to draw that card, remember sometimes life get pretty hard.
It won't always be the same, because that's the way life plays the game.
That special someone is not always near, that's when God is always here.
I hope that this poem brightens up your day, even in its own little way.
Pain may come and go, only that God will know.
Even though you may need some rest, always do and be at your best.
I'm not looking for any glory, I'm now coming to the end of my story.
When life seems as if it's unfair, God will, even if nobody else, care.
So you see life is full of peace and joy, even more than a brand new toy.
When you've had all you can bare, look to God because he really does care.
When it seems like you've ran into a wall, lift your head and stand very tall.
I know that sometimes it's hard to do, but I have faith in you.
God please take care of me, this is all I ask of thee.
Even when my candy isn't very tasty, I pray for my safety,
Even though things happen every now and then, this is my special
    prayer, I pray, Amen!

Delwyn H. Powell

Awakening

As he shook the heaviness of sleep from his mind he awoke, as he did every morning,
    content.
The deep valleys below beckoned him. The tallest redwoods calling
    his name. Their whispers unheard.
The clouds danced merrily by, spinning and swirling as if performing
    a continuous, silent waltz.
The cool breeze blew past him. It was a pleasant breeze.
As the moon and the stars replaced the day, he nestled back into the comfort of sleep.
He awoke to find that she had ventured, quite by chance, to his place of solitude.
She was busy shaking off the heaviness of sleep and he found himself watching her.
She stood, looking out over the earth and skies. Just looking.
Very quietly. Very intently.
There was something in the distance. Although it was only but a
    whisper, he heard his name. She smiled.
As the clouds danced by, he could swear they were keeping tempo with
    the wind. She sighed.
And as the breeze blew the scents of the sweetest flowers and the
    freshest early morning dew, their eyes met.
And for the very first time, it occurred to him that he could see
    eternity. Together side by side, they spread their exquisite wings and
    flew in happiness and delight toward the warmth of the sun . . .

Amy Lynn Fisher

Let Him Go

Since the day you left me,
I've never been the same,
These tears won't stop falling,
I know I'm the one to blame.

The words you said so sweetly,
Still ponder in my mind,
The question if I'll ever let you go,
Still haunts me all the time.

But not that I'm living life without you,
Well life can't get much worse,
Even though you've been gone awhile,
My heart still really hurts.

I'm slowly getting better,
Though you've found someone new,
And now I know it's over,
But I can't let go of you.

Well....you've gotten on with your life,
I guess now I should see,
That even though it was good while it lasted,
we just weren't meant to be.

Erin Cornelius

A Mother Dies

A Mother dies,
The eyes cry,
A heart breaks - open.

A Mother dies,
The gift of life from death
Is pondered.

A Mother dies,
The gift of death from life
Is honored.

A Mother dies,
A child is born
Whose life once old
Becomes now new,
Whose life once lost, is found.

A Mother dies,
The heart now open
Wonders why it took this loss so great
To live again.

A Mother dies, the broken - open- heart
Begins to sing.

Cornelia Navari

First Son

She came to the house
And told me his parents
Would be sorry . . .

"They wouldn't let us
Marry," she said.
"He's never ever seen his baby" . . .

"The military will
Make a man of him,"
They said . . .

Two months later
A clip in the local newspaper.
Our town has lost its First Son . . .

Now, everybody's sorry . . .

Sue Crisp

The Prayer of the Woods

I am the cradle you are born in.
I am your bench and your bed.
I am the door of your house and the roof of your dwelling.
I am your house.
I am the handle of your tool.
I am what you built your boats from.
I am your bow and your arrow, your crutch and your spear.
I spend you shade when summer sun burns and
I protect you when wild winter winds whistle around your home.
    I store for you the summer's heat
        for frosty times — to cook your meat.
    I save for you the water's load
        for dreadful days of deadly draught.
    I bar the might of storm and flood,
        of avalanche and sliding mud.
    I am your country's wealth, your recreation,
        your children's dream, your relaxation.
I am your chair, I am your table,
I am your book, I am your bible,
the violin you do enjoy,
the carver's bread, the toddler's toy.
I clean the air, I damp the noise —
Woodland or desert — YOUR'S is the choice.
    I am Creator's living dome
    and His creature's nature home,
    the wild boar's den, the falcon's nest
    I am your coffin — for the final rest.

I pray to you men: Please use me wisely, renew my resources,
protect the land I am growing on, do not destroy me.

    Heinrich F. Weck

A Cry of the Heart

There's so much to be said about a heart that's in love.
So many feelings that flow always down and above.
But what happens when that love has been torn . . .
When that feeling is wished never to be born?

God gives us each new day with the pleasures and the pain,
But what happens when your eyes are the source of all the rain?
Happiness is seen in true love that is deep.
Pain is seen in the tears that we weep.

There's still so much hurt inside and still so many tears to be shed.
So much that needs to be heard and so much that needs to be said.
So much to be seen and so much more still to bear.
And now to say the least - does he even care?

The thought of him whispering those three words to another's ear
Will always cause your emotions to stir a certain little fear.
Jesus is there and will forever stay.
That's what helps me to live each new day.

I may count the days that they've been together,
But that only makes the hurt seem forever.
How much longer will I watch them walk in hand in hand?
How much longer will I cry before I learn to stand?

    Sophia Varghese

Epitaph

Lowly lies here in solitary confinement
A traverser through this thorny land
Who neither did a weary day lament
Nor forlorn hope put into Fate's hand
That struck in him a mere sad song
Decay and dust marked him for their own
All the while he wandered his way long
Until the bosom of earth embraced his bone.
Although he came molded in mortal clay
He loved life, but Death had the final say.

    Pius Wodu

The Unseen

I am the which is and that which was
Chased summer breeze, winter wind
Confirm spring's whispers, autumn sighs
Mornings loudness heard. The silence of night
I am that field
Blade of grass
Felt mountains roar, snowflakes fall
Home of the eagle, pulse of the sea
Alone hear mighty oak stretched skyward
Enjoyed the laughter of many
Sorrow the tears of one
I am the circle, its beginning, its end
I am
Birth
Love
Hate
Flatline to all
I, which was, which is, which to come, am life.

    Winston J. Jackson

A Lady Remembers

Her head is capped with silver,
Her hands are thin and veined.
She sits alone, in her rocker,
She doesn't recognize her name.

But her eyes hold a sparkle,
Her foot tamps to a silent strain,
As she remembers a gentler, more noble time,
When her beau, his love proclaimed.

His calling card on a silver platter,
A frightened look upon his face.
He met her father in the parlour,
Her dress was lavender and lace.

"How sad!" some people whisper,
when they see her sitting there.
But, she's happy in her memories,
Without worry, without care.

So leave her in the past,
Don't grieve for her to be in the present.
But let her pass on gently,
To her beau, whose now in heaven.

    Denise K. Lightle

Insanity In Addiction

I don't really relate to any thing
Except the whole concept of insanity
It seems clearer than
The difference between night and day
As I realize that I'm reaching the other side
I begin to wonder if my self being
Should just happen to disappear
If anyone in this harsh and cruel world
Would happen to notice me
Falling from the glory of my hopes and dreams
And go far out crashing into
The other side of fantasy and nonexistence
The longer and harder I think about it
The further I seem to slip away from this crazy world
Where sometimes my best friends seem
To be against everything I stand for
To the world of wonder and excitement
In every hit of the bottle
The further I go

    Shannon Brown

The Legacy

What will we tell our children of the legacy we leave behind,
misdemeanor of the heart, felony of the mind.
Our self-proclaimed ignorance of a world so desperate in need,
unknowing, uncaring, rapacious in our greed.
Like ravening locusts, leeching the world dry,
ignoring her death throes, ears deaf to her cries.
Heralding our glory, as a race so sublime,
forsaking their future, as gods control time.
Making love to our egos, our desires we did sate,
in reckless abandon, predestined your fate.
A fate with no future, a destiny once bright,
a place for the heartless, no succor in sight.
We've left you nothing, but the rape of your land,
in our careless denial, a hereafter unplanned.
Lamenting our past now, repentant in sorrow,
forgive us, my children, we've stolen tomorrow.

Sandra F. Anselmo

Her Secret

She couldn't last, it was near the time
Yet the smile on her face was so sublime
Was she thinking of the years gone by
Could she hear the children's laughter
    or kissing them when they cry.
The big old house was silent now
Everything was old and out of style
Was she feeling that special touch?
The man she loved so very much.
Or knowing the boys were back from the war
They were safe and had much in store
Her granddaughter and daughter that must be.
For joy they brought her we all could see
But knowing all of this
I felt I had missed!
Her smile was saying my work is done
My world is over and you my child have just begun.

Bess Mullen

You're Alone

From realization of a slow death.
From life it's a dying breath.
The unheard sound of tears in the night.
The lingering battle that you're too weak to fight, you're alone.

The sound of one hand clapping in air.
A chance for love but you wouldn't dare.
Words to be spoken but no one's there.
The joys of life that you need to share, you're alone.

The ripples of life are caused by tears.
The days that pass seem like years.
The sighs in the crowd that no one hears.
You hunger for happiness that never appears, you're alone.

The past is gone, the future's uncertain.
Life is a stage with no final curtain.
To keep on trying is a huge demand.
For you're not sure if you really can, you're alone.

Thoughts and memories, good and bad.
To keep the sanity that you once had.
To end it all would be a blessing from above.
The only thing needed is someone to love, you're alone.

Robert E. Stewart

A Lesson to Heed

Take my hand, my child so you will surely see
An insight lesson to life's wondrous journey.
That in your own life, you will be bound to learn
There will be things you want, and for yearn.

But the greatest gift you shall ever hope to find
Is within yourself; truthfulness and a heart that's kind.
Temptation will beckon to live with lies and deceit;
However my child, with the latter it's yourself you defeat.

For with truthfulness and kindness you will abound
You'll be blessed with true friends who will always be round
To comfort when needed or share your joy at what you achieve;
Just remember to use trust and kindness, and not to deceive.

To live in these times by these two rules, can indeed be trying
Yet the acts by which you live will be reflected upon your dying
Would you rather be remembered as a person with negative measure
Or would you prefer to have been known in everyone's life, as a treasure?

Yvette Brooks-James

Judging of the Judge

There you sit, so smugly, Sir,
In your honorable black robe,
So certain none can call in question
Your penalties, manner, or mode.

You are the Judge! Let the world beware,
Proclaim your erudite, esteemed and fair,
When, from your vaulted seat of judgement
You exact justice and decide intent.

"I find you guilty", you recite
Two dozen times, or more, per day.
It is your job, your legal right,
To probe men's wrongs, exacting pay.

But who, I ask of you, dear Sir,
Will look into your jaundiced eyes
And call into account the ones
You wrongly judged and scrutinized?

And who will bend your haughty knees
Before the sovereign King you shunned,
And call into account your deeds
While sitting on your earthly throne?

Geraldine L. Harris

A Psalm For A God Blessed Country

A people who longed for religious freedom came away from their homes and families,

For His Steadfast Love Endures Forever.

To arrive in a strange country and found strange native people, who were kind and gave them of their harvest and they feasted together.

They built new homes and lives and worshipped God,

For His Steadfast Love Endures Forever.

The country grew strong honoring God and becoming a great nation, but slavery divided its people and war separated families and states,

For His Steadfast Love Endures Forever.

Peace at last brought the nation into a single government and law and order under God was the rule, but greed and gold and great possessions were making the people forget God.

For His Steadfast Love Endures Forever.

An outside enemy threatened the nation and its people came together to battle the enemy. Victory at last "In God We Trust."
Sin is our enemy, Who can we trust, but God."
For His Steadfast Love Endures Forever.

Barbara Lawrence

18 Candles for Maggie

She was gone — not by chance — but by choice.
Tearing her love away — before Mom's surprise
Valentine's day divorce delivery.
Forced from their home; then a sad graduation,
Filled with grandma's tears, and the unspoken "good-bye" . . .

He knew she wouldn't write, but he sent
Birthday wishes to her new college dorm.
He had enough love for both of them — he thought,
As he carefully carried the store bought cake
To his unbearably lonely house.

Slowly, he lit the tiny candles,
One memory at a time — this one was for the night
That she first saw light . . .
This one for her laughing smile, and this one
For her hugging, "I Love You, Daddy" . . .

Tears held back too long, fell upon
That frail, frosted memorial to so many memories
How he got to the 18th candle was an answer to prayer,
And quietly reaching for her cross around his neck,
He whispered, "Thank you for sharing your 18 years" . . .

James A. Brewer

Graffiti

Spiked wire spiraling over blotchy stucco
  Walltops can't keep them out—
Pale chalky symbols, stylized, swarming
  above greasy tracks.
A fetid urban canyon's sleek trains
  swoon past excresence of
Verve, importuning respect;
"See me." "I was here." "I count."
No other way to say it. Words drop cold.
Gotta move, flail arms,
Say it beautiful and run. What a world!

Let others sneer—curse,
"I live." "I make."

Sally Sobottka

The Road

The Big Band Tour — "on the road"
Meet the bus at Charlie's Tavern —
A one night stand in Pittsburgh — college prom,
Then onto the bus — next stop Philly. Next, Atlantic City,
Norfolk, on and on
Sixteen men — booze-smoke-noise-dirty jokes — the bleary eyed
  driver.
And the beat goes on . . . .
More booze, more smoke, more dirtier jokes, laughs, whispers,
coughing, snoring
The endless oppressive smoke.
Lonesome husbands, two-timing husbands.
The girl singer, tries to fit in — pretends to be asleep —
Don't make the guys uncomfortable.
The lonely girl, the bumpy bus, chupunk, chupunk
And The Beat Goes On, And On, And On . . . .

Nancy Reed Kanter

Friendship

The friendship of two people
is trust and honesty
There is no either or.

A friend is a person, that stands beside you
to pick you up when you fall, or part your back
when you've done something right.

The feeling will grow inside you,
Just like the growth of a child.
You have to nurture it care,
and love it daily.

A friend will protect you, from the storms of life, and love.
But they can only protect you to a certain point.

When the point is met, and you fall to pieces,
A friend will always pick up the pieces,
And nurture it back to health.

That is a true friend. They go through thick and thin,
Even when it turns sour, there, there to help you out.

I love you friend for all you have done and will do.
Nothing will come between you and me,
There is not one person who will break it up.

K'Ann L. Strohl

An Eclipse of the Dream

Souls without eyes will still sense the elements.
The elements are eternal, but also an illusion.

  Water, earth, air, and fire.
  So, what is the quintessence?
  Darkness!
  What is truly dark stays hidden in each and everything; it has to.

  Trying to illuminate the universe is indeed a conspiracy,
  but the agenda is nothing without darkness.

    And yes, you and I and are involved in this plan;
    and yet we are nothing...but water, earth, air and fire.

A soul with eyes can not keep them closed;
to close them is to sleep and dream of the world.

  With open eyes we can see the light
  and live the dream.
  The moment of the dream, the dream of the moment...Is Now.

  But to focus on the light is blinding.
  And a blind eye sees no light.

All of the light in this universe
could never reveal the essence of darkness.

Mark Justin Bartley

Good Night

Star bright, star light
Bring me the wish I wish tonight.
With a kiss and a hug, say good night, sleep tight.
Snuggled down deep in bed, and think good thoughts of the days ahead.
The sun will come, with a lovely light so bright,
The sounds of chirps from waking birds,
The softness of the sky that is painted in a ray of pinks and blues.
As the sun goes to sleep, the moon will wake and peak out from
under the blanket of clouds
And so with the sun tucked off to bed, the sky turns to a
brilliant midnight blue.
The stars appear and the angel dust is sprinkled so the sky does
nothing but twinkle, for all man kind to Ooh! And ahe!
So I say, close your eyes and dream sweet dreams of happiness
With love from angels above,
Good night, sleep tight little ones.

Alicia Marie Withers

Just Open Your Eyes and See . . . .

A spark of life is sent from heaven.
Many questions wander through a new creation called man.
He finds himself surrounded by beautiful things.
He learns to live with these things.
He looks forward, seeing everything perfectly clear.

As man grows older, he begins to care only for himself.
He steals, kills, and destroys the earth.
Things begin to change.
Man refuses to look at what might be the end of his
precious planet.
He blindly stumbles through problems, leaving them
to corrupt the necessities of life.

Man kills all life on his own planet and intoxicates
any water remaining.
He soon withers and dies for his sad mistake.
As a spark, his soul drifts back up to the gates of heaven.

He thinks he is finally relieved of all worries.
Then, the most frightening thought circles his mind;
Could he possibly be rejected from heaven and sent
down to the fiery labors of hell?

Austin Luedtke

One Day at a Time

I have had a full life. I have done it all.
I have known success, then taken a great fall.

I have loved, and been loved.
I have tried and failed.
I have been happy, and I have been so sad.

I have known the good times, I have known the bad.
Each time I've been down and out, I've lived to rise again.
I have known wealth, and I have known despair.

Times I've had so many friends, then times, when no-one was there.
Of all the things, I've lived through, and the hurt,
And pain, I've known, I've done it all with the help, of God.

No one, can do it alone. I know, we all are tested, but
No more, than we can bear.
For if we just take it, "One day at a time".
He will, always be there.

Margaret A. Brewster

Nobility

What makes a person true and noble?
Is it the way one wears their hair,
ties their shoes or extends their pinky finger.

Could it be the blood line that has been traced
back to the times of Camelot or the Renaissance.

True nobility comes from the heart that beats
to the rhythm of children's laughter
or the soul that is inflamed by the sight of poverty and abuse.

It comes from the minds of many who know
what's right or wrong, fact or fiction.

Yes, nobility is difficult and trying and oh so confusing,
but it does have its advantages,
or does it?

Tammy Cherie Wilson

Spirit of a Warrior

I have seen a thousand wars, through eyes accustomed to death,
Trod a thousand battle fields, in bare feet, sandals, on horse back,
and in boots, thrown a thousand rocks, a thousand spears, shot a
thousand arrows, a thousand bullets, launched a thousand rockets.

I know the thousand faces of death; I have seen them all, a thousand
times over. I have been them all, through a thousand different hosts;
left a thousand grieving families. Still, like time and war, I go on.

But I grow tired; I would like a pause, no matter what I may
pretend. I would like to feel the sun on my face and turn my back on
the spectacle of war. I want to lay my defenses down and pick up
faith. I am tired of fighting.

No one cries harder for peace than a warrior who has lost the will to
fight. But I am forced to fight on; I dare not stop fighting now, for
if I do all that has been gained in my thousand wars will be lost.

So, I will fight one more battle, one last war, to its brutal end.
Then, I will pause and sit down with my friends.
We will share a drink, a laugh, and perhaps a tear.
But for now, I fight on, for I am the Spirit of a Warrior, and I cry.

Leslie D. Hannah

Baby Of Mine

Tiny fingers, tiny toes
Little lips, cute little nose
Ears so small, yet they can hear
Bright shining eyes, that look everywhere
Hair so soft, be gentle when you touch
Skin so smooth, love to caress it so much
Faint little heart beat, yet strong as an ox
Legs kicking as fast
As a frightened little fox
Delightful to smell
Healthy, happy and well
Little tongues urge to push out a cry
For what reason - we don't know why
They aren't hungry, hurt or wet
It's too bad, at this tender age they can't talk yet
From a distance, some may think it's a toy
But in reality, it's a baby girl or baby boy

Zelzenia Mitchell

The Ocean of Life

Life is like an ocean
The waves could carry you away,
If you don't know how to swim
And stand on your own.
Don't plunge into the sea
Unless you know that there will be
A wet suit to protect you from the world of coldness.

If the waves of life are only at low tide,
The ocean runs smooth so you take chances.
If the waves of life are too high,
You fear to swim,
You don't think you'll make it back to shore,
Where it is safe.
Take a chance,
This is what the ocean of life is all about.
You need not fear what has not happened yet.

Doreen M. Lamere

Life's Serenade

Love will serenade sooner or later
Why should we be ready for it
It will disappear as soon as it comes

Some will lose their faith
And let it turn against them
Achievement substitutes for salvation
We should know better by now

Whose voice is in my head
As life's journey speeds by
Paralyzed by indecision and fear
I'll cry and cry
Maybe soon I'll understand the reason

Is truth overrated?
Is empathy weakness?

Change is constant, but who to say for better
Here we are
Alone but together, separately crowded, gasping for air
Dry your tears, there's plenty to come

On cue emotions become severed and reasoning wins
The day's battle concluded; the war far from over

Dru Gallucci

Miracles

For in the beginning all life starts
With the beauty and grace of two hearts
Coming forth from the heavens above
Comes a life with beauty and love

For this baby shall be healthy and fine
For her mother is only divine
The power that towers creations flower
Will bless this child with God's power

For I saw her in a dream
Real and serene it did seem
In this dream I stood upon the water
In the reflection I saw our daughter!

John Louis Pellegrino

Going Home

Air tainted with the aroma of burnt candles . . .
Nostalgic, angry . . .

Sparked flame burnt to the crisp tip of the wick,
   all glowing around your peaceful, stiff body.

White billowing satin surrounds your unreal carcass.
All I can think is you can't smile anymore, you can't talk to me.

Do you remember that time . . .
my voice fades to a whisper, descending to a faint breath . . .

How could you?
Why did you? Damn it!

I turn to leave,
   looking back to see you one last time . . .

I see on that white billowing satin, that is so utterly unlike you,
The perfect saying embosses the fabric . . .

A simple phrase . . .
"I'm going home . . . ."

Shannon K. Beyerle

The Place Where My Lady Rests

Rippling water laps the earth banks
That lie beside the stream
A night bird sings an eerie tune
Near the place where my lady dreams

Salty drops flow down my cheeks
The bitter tears they sting
There's never been a sadder song
Than the one my lady sings

Quiet and still she drew no breath
When last 'pon her I laid my eyes
Screaming and crying I begged God's mercy
But couldn't save her though I tried

Softly caressing like the feel of her garments
A sweet breeze touches my skin
The bewildering fear of my loss engulfs me
Like a damp fog creeping in

My throat is tight my heart races
A pain cuts through my breast
I press my cheek 'gainst the cold wet stone
That marks the place where my lady rests

Carolyn L. Holmes

The Planet Mars

Ponce DeLeone was known as the fountain of youth,
but Mars differs and tells you the truth.
We are the deity that started the wars in Rome
at one time I called it my home.
I've come to Earth to settle an argument,
but congress sent it right back to Parliament,
I can't begin to tell you I've come very far to
announce the brilliance and birth of Mars,
I slipped my way down the Milky Way Mall
envisioned upon a fiery stone wall,
Flashing with Ives of past, finally I am here at last.
We people on Mars have given you a vision
but still you have not made your decision.
You know we posses your astrological being
which still you have not yet been seeing.
So let me reduce you away from the beast,
and come back with me and we shall all feast.

Jennie Sivitilli

Which Road to Take

Empty feelings are abound
Loneliness creeps in,
What are you going to do
How to stop the spin.
Should you give up, and wander endlessly,
Or should you go on without dependency.
How strong can you be, how is your self-esteem,
Do you need someone to lift you up
Or are you as sturdy as you seem.
The fork in the road is calling
Which should it be,
The left is self-destruction
The right opportunity.
Your friends are calling, waiting to see what you do,
Will they encourage and support, or finally desert you.
Won't you turn against the left
And make the right your choice,
Speak up and let people listen
To the wisdom in your voice.

Lenora M. Corbett

Irony

You say I'm garbage to be thrown away
but look how many have no place to stay

You look and scoff, or turn away in disgust
You hold your head high and chest robust

I feel transparent as I begin to say
"Please Sir, I have children to feed."
You turn away muttering, "Woman indeed."

So the storm winds blow your house asunder
and you ask the woman "Please, I wonder
if we could share this bridge you're under?"

Weary eyes look up to see, the man that turned
away she.

Luana Deak

Prayers

Now I know that God answers prayers,
I know He loves me and I know He cares.

Before I ask, He knows my heart. But He wants me to do my part.

So I go to him, down on my knees, and He listens to all of my pleas.

I hope He'll take away my tears, as I tell Him all my fears.

For God has control of my life in His hands,
And won't give me more burdens than I can stand.

But sometimes my faith grows weak when His help I seek.

As I wonder, is He really there?
He doesn't seem to be answering my prayer.

I expected God's answer today. But He just doesn't work that way.

He has His own way to tell time.
And His way is a lot different than mine.

I wish He'd hurry and not take so long,
as I wait and try to stay strong.

God grant me the patience and humility
To accept Your answer, whatever it be.

For Your wisdom surpasses all time and I will accept Your will as mine.

Jessie G. Conover

Together

Love is found everywhere
The things you do, the way you share
A look, a touch, a word or two
It really doesn't matter what you do
As long as you're together

Taking walks, holding hands
Dreaming dreams and making plans
Going on picnics, games in the park
Watching fireflies after dark
As long as you're together

There may be times when things go wrong
Some untold lie, a doubt or two that don't belong
Nobody said that life is great
But it's much easier when you have a mate
As long as you're together

The moon and stars all aglow
Making the moment so special below
Where two people ever in love
Are watched over by God up above
And happy you are together

Nancy L. Schiefer

The Fifth Season

Hypothetical situations and a variety of children's make-believe stories.
The eighth day of the week or the thirteenth month of the year.
Twenty-five hours in a day or sixty-one seconds to a minute.
All of non-existence, real only during the fifth season, which at times
I sense that I belong there and not here.

Imagine if you will, two heads attached to one body, three legs,
three arms and three eyes, instead of two; a sky with two suns and two
moons. Imagine if you will, but that only exists in some other world;
have no fear, not here.

Life without death. Heaven without a hell.
All of mankind created equal, holding the key to the same heaven,
the same heaven that bares no hell. A key that unlocks achieving
goals for many, overcomes obstacles and boundaries, ignorant of racism,
discrimination and unfair rules; a key that can only be found in a
place that has five seasons . . . unfortunately we only have four; summer
spring, winter and fall . . . nothing less and nothing more.

Eduardo Rubio

The Inspirations of a Poet

Inspire him, the sunset
And moon-rise stirs his soul
Living through his words, the stars and sky
Embodiments of them all in ink and paper

Joyous poet,
Scribe of the heart
Author of excellence and
The pen of God

Hands that hold tangible love,
Remorse, pain, and anger
Hands that push the pen
That puts thought in ink

Pages and scrolls
Spotted with ink and tears
Pages of white hot passion
And from the pages do come more passion

Inspire him, the sunset
And moon-rise stirs his soul
Living through his words, the stars and sky
Embodiments of them all in ink and paper

Joseph Waggle

Time Won't Steal

You say I can believe in love, I can trust in you,
Smiling at me in the morning light, I know you feel it too.
As you kiss me tenderly, I gently touch your face,
The fear I've held onto vanishes, leaving not a trace.
In your eyes I see tomorrow, it's amazing the love I feel,
Together we walk slowly, this love time won't steal.
When you journey alone, feel what the wind brings,
A passion like no other, enfolds you in love's wings.
Mystified, I gaze at the stars as I look into the skies,
Cherishing the love I see, each time you stare into my eyes.
You are the love of my life, with you I know love is real,
An entire lifetime to share with you, this love time won't steal.
My heart has gently opened because I believe in you,
Hold me in your arms tonight, you know our love is true.
Embrace the strength of our love as you open up your heart,
Hear my whispers in your dreams, know we'll never part.
Time is a friend to this wonderful love we feel,
We believe in each other, our love time won't steal.

Deborah Leske

The Dark

What lies in the dark when
You can't see in front of
You, what is there?
Under your bed, in your closet,
Or in your house, what is there?
You sleep with the covers over
Your head so you don't have to
See the shadows jumping on
Your walls or ceiling.
The deafening silence is too much,
You think about your worst fears.
When sleep doesn't come easily
You lie there in the darkness and
In silence thinking about what
Your dreams will bring.
The following day you awaken
To see the shadows are gone,
You can come out from under
Your covers and everything is
Okay....that is, until darkness falls again.

Nikki Thacker

The Question

Who knows what comes of centuries rotting . . . .
What monsters . . . temples . . . bells . . . will ring
    from our old dome
A million million's futures' child
Will she yawn danger . . . death . . . or
Chide with youthful talent all . . .
And proudly saunter her first strides straight?
Will bones grow strong . . .
And Justice wise?
And will the hands be equal palms
To give sweet gifts
Of tempts and comforts?

Valerie B. Schwartz

A Garden of Memories

I have a lovely garden,
Preserved and watered with my tears.
It is the garden of memory.
That has grown for many a year.

Oh, yes there are thistles in my garden,
Of which I can not erase.
But God in his all out mercy.
Sends blessings to hide their face.

I hope each one of my children
As they go on their earthly way,
Will have planted in their garden
Beauty that shall always stay.

I pray each shall take Jesus as their saviour.
To be their guiding light.
And when they look back in their memories,
It shall be a lovely sight.

Zelma Ford

Inside A Loving Heart

Inside a loving heart,
Joy and glee fill the air.
Still it needs someone to love and care.
When it is rejected,
Its willingness is deflected.
Too bad it will never come back.
What was once red and true,
Is now just sorry and blue
    that's what is inside a loving heart.

Greg Harris

Recipe for Duck Swoop

It was duck hunting season,
And I guess that's the reason,
That one day all the ducks went utterly mad.
They puffed out their chest,
Each duck doing his best,
Dive bombing the hunters with everything they had.

As the ducks fought back,
With a fearsome quack,
They began driving the hunters away.
There's a sign at the sight,
Where the hunters took flight,
For they haven't been seen to this day.

Joan Whetzel

Heart Broken

When I am cold I think of you,
'Cause now that's about all I can do.

You've gone and left me alone,
my broken heart has really shown.

Until the time that you return,
I think everyone will start to learn . . . .

Love is blind and blind is love,
many teenagers fall for this thing called
    "Love"!

I know that the time has come,
that it's the end for you and me.

I'll think of you every once and a while,
and I'll crack a little friendly smile.

But the worst thing of all is letting go
'Cause I love you from head to toe.

It's time to let the future bend
until then I guess this is the end.

But remember no matter what
I'll always be loving you.

Marissa Nava

Are We There Yet?

The radio suffocates my ears
with the sounds of Bohemian Rhapsody
as I try to lock my concentration
on the dull scenery outside.
My legs feel as if they're
stuck in a sitting position,
and Tony's constant teasing isn't helping.
Are we there yet?

The aggravation builds inside me waiting to explode.
He already ate all the Doritos and the pretzels...
not to mention the cookies too.
The soda I drank is sitting in me,
waiting to be free.
Are we there yet?

I try to sleep but it's awfully hard
with the sun beating down on your eyelids,
and your brother sleeping on you.
I reach over and innocently tap my dad on the shoulder,
and ask him for the hundredth time, are we there yet?

Christina Nickolas

Tides

In another place, in another time,
  deep within the recesses of my mind,
  that is where you will be holding me.
Passions sweet will, colliding waves of
  oceans swirl.
A gentle touch, a whispered word,
  the crying of my heart can not be heard
Realities light is blinded to my plight,
  hold on hold on I pray let the day turn
  to night,
Let me bath in the darkness,
  Let my wings take flight
Far beyond the tides crest
  deep within your water pools
Let my heart take rest.
  Martha Schuler

Ode to an Expectant Mother

You know you'll have bottles and diapers and such,
And there'll be those days when it may seem too much!
She'll throw down her bottle, drop toys from her crib.
He'll mash his wet zwieback all over his bib.

Now bath time is lovely — the water he's splashing.
But you're sopping wet — oh my dear, you look smashing!
Yes babies are darling, they're worth all the trouble.
(I think she ate soap 'cause she's blowing a bubble).

Those wee starfish fingers that cling oh so tight,
And bath-dampened ringlets that shine in the light.
This vision of sweetness is yours to hold fast
So cherish this time for you can't make it last.

Each evening when rocking your baby so warm
You'll find, oh how sweetly, your life he'll transform.
And no other kind of a baby would do
For a lady as dear and as special as you!
  Elva D. Farkas

Wedding of the Winds

The North and the South wind announced
their desire to wed.

Then they asked their creator for
permission and advice, their creator
blessed them and said go ahead.

They sent invitations all over the
world both far and near in hopes
that all the world winds would appear.

The East and West winds - the whirl
winds and the trade winds replied.
Each of them remarked what
a glorious wedding this will be.

On the day of the wedding all of the
winds appeared all but the wayward wind.

The bride and groom breathed a sigh
and asked have either of you seen him?
They each answered no not I - not I.

All but the West wind who said
I didn't see him but I felt his
touch as he passed me by.
  Walter A. Pepper

Indigo Amour

A woman unlike any other, with her deep blue eyes and her
Coffee coloured hair. I count the days I find myself with her
Enveloping our love.
Feeling her passion going against my heart in a
Blue wave of Indigo amour. Jasmine's perfume knowing
Its way around the curve ship of her
Lonely body that is missing my flaming touch that was hers in
The desolate month of November that she had cried for.
Over her body she is like a love
Prisoner, trapped in my bars,
Quietly expecting control as she could reverse
Our eroticism simply for her pleasure for me
To bring more indigo amour. Under
My weight she visit my body while I take
Charge of hers, examining the temperatures that
Our bodies have taken
Years to bring towards our deepest love
Zone.
  Tony Carrillo

The Rain Is Over

Time, memory and thoughts...
Where did it go? Where do I go?
Who is calling me? It is the wind...
It's whispering in my ears.
"Go, run, follow your heart,
Listen to your soul and walk through life
Saying...I Am The Wind, I Am The Rain,
I am the one that believe in love,
I am the one that believe in life,
I am the one that believe in you,
I am the one that is part of you."
Now, do you believe?
Now, do you see the rain?
Now, do you feel the wind?
Now, do you see your soul?
The rain is over.
Now is time for me to go.
The rainbow is there...
Now, did you see what I love?
Did you see what I see?
  Marlene N. Seara

Screaming Eyes

Screaming eyes full of fear
surrounded by doctors and strange gear
cannot express the terror inside
fear, fear, no place to hide

Piercing eyes seeking for answers
"Why am I hear, what is wrong
Will I recover, am I gone?"

A father's worst nightmare,
a daughter in fear.
She cannot communicate, just stare;
what is going on in there?

Priest visiting, people praying;
faith tested, as one prays.
"Thy will be done"
Oh God, do not take her away.

God, how those eyes just tear me apart;
they are so possessed with fear.
I have never before been unable to help,
now helpless to ease the fear
in those eyes that are screaming, screaming, screaming.
  Andre A. Couillard

Dreams That Come True

Most of my life has been full of dreams
  ones that have never come true.
And I sit sometimes and wonder the reason why
  never being able to find a clue.
Some dreams do eventually once to life though
  and I was shocked because I had given up on them
Until you entered my life - with a sweet little daughter too
  and showed me that dreams can come true.
My life was empty without much meaning at all
  and your caring, loving and devotion has shown
  me otherwise - that dreams do come true.
Life does have meaning and is full of happiness and joy
  because you have proven to me that dreams do come true.
Our life has just started, the three of us
  and our road to happiness is paved in gold.
Oh, what a joyous journey we will have
  forever and ever, till our days grow old.

Randy Bryner

Over the Hill

Today's my birthday — Eighty Six
And what I have the Docs can't fix;
They look at me and say, "You're fine!"
But they don't have these bones of mine.

The pain goes through my sides and back
It makes me want to hit the sack;
And when I walk, my two knees buckle,
I think I hear folks start to chuckle.

Of course I try and do not note
But yet it really gets my goat;
When I was only Eighty Five,
I felt that I was still alive.

Although the pain was in my calf
I'd tell a joke and folks would laugh;
Now that I'm old, perhaps a bore,
They say, "You've told that twice before."

So do come close, speak in my ear
And tell me news I'd like to hear;
And if I do not understand,
I still can laugh and shake your hand.

Nona B. Gilcrease

Gone

When I think of your death
I begin to cry
But when I am finished
I ask myself why

Why did you leave me
Why did you go
And to this day I do not know

You left me alone, scared and afraid
You do not know how many nights I've prayed

I prayed you were not gone
That you'd be there in the hall
But it wasn't that way
Not that way at all

You left me alone in a world full of sorrow
Knowing that you'd not be there tomorrow

I love and miss you, and I wanted to say
That I looked forward to the day
That the Lord will take me away

Away in the world of heaven above
I will once again feel your love

Courtney A. Carmicheal

Siren Song

Just a disguise
I know love dies.
I am a hostage - of my captor
of my love. No ransom high enough
can save me now.
Never to be set free.
The chains that bind me.
My heart and soul - two fallen warriors,
taken prisoner, never to see what you
really are.
Blinded by misconception.
Love silenced by deception.
You led me to the edge, just to watch me fall.
Caught by illusions.
Trapped forever after all.

I should have known it all along
siren song.

Rick Hotaling

The Chain of Grace

I only lived in sin and strife
  while You lived in love and life
I was lost but now I'm found
  You helped me to get off the ground
You taught me how to love and live
  Said I should take less then I give
I am now taking what I've learned
  To those whose lives have been burned
Who have not made the best of choices
  Who have not heard those heavenly voices
Singing with joy and with hope
  Over a sinner whose come back home
Over a man who has submitted
  And has the Word to know and live it
Who has become like a child
  In his faith though all the while
Is learning how to be a man
  Like You want and like You planned
Who will now do as I have done
  And lead more souls to Your Son

Jamie Lynn Redding

Monica

There have been hellos and there have been goodbyes
We've made each other laugh and we've made each other cry,
I can search the whole world and the stars above
But never will I find what I have found in you, true love.
You're my pot of gold at the end of every rainbow
It is you and only you, in this blazing inferno.
Through anything that gets in our way, I'll be by your side,
These words are filled with promise and love that never dies,
This is all a reality, a dream come true,
The feelings you have for me and the feelings I have for you.
We've been through so much, there's no going back ever,
If we are patient, one day everyone will want us together.
My arms are always open to you, when you're happy or sad,
I'm here to listen and to always understand.
I ache for your touch and for your kiss,
It's another thing for me to love and also to miss.
We won't forget the past and we won't ignore the future,
For the past holds all of our memories,
And the future holds more happiness and love then we will ever need.

Thomas M. O'Hern

Untitled

No matter what happens tonight understand
The darkness fades away, and the flowers will be ominous
As the rain comes this way, the clouds will be there alone they stand
As it all fades into the brightness

This could all end, but the caring words will be there
As it all burns, you and I and it's so hard to bear, and we're
surrounded by an unknown friend
As the flower pedal yearns

This could shelter the path of our future, you go one way as I walk
   the other
As the flower leads down in death, and we can't bear another
So we take the torture, and we go through the water depth
As we're yearning for water, that trickles off the waterfalls
That leads us to solitude

This could lead us to each other, because we've led ourself to
   solitude
As the pedals start as one, and get drifted through the color as they
gather to one it's unknown

To the one that's unknown
The pedals are critical, and death is passionate, and all is crucial
As they wait as one, neither is unknowing

   Jennifer Vargas

Untitled

Oh don't you know this old world is strange to me.
People running round and round pretending to be free.

They are worried about their riches, their cars, and their homes
They don't care about the poor man or the paths that he roams

They keep up such a hectic pace trying to get ahead
Their minds just spinning out of control as their decency they shed.

They've forgotten about the Savior, the one who came to set them free
Who tried to teach the world to love and gave Himself for you and me.

He told us of true riches in our Father's house above
And those riches are eternal as eternal as His love.

So I don't need this world's riches, its money or its fame
They won't hang around anyway when I've reached the end of my
game.

Just give me what I really need true love and a heart of gold
And I'll travel down life's highway without fear and being bold

Because I know that all my needs are met, all my wants are granted too
For what I want is God's mercy and love granted to me and you.

   Gary Willyerd

Memory

I can remember my father quite well,
He was a man who was very ill.
But never once did you hear him complain
He was special, not just plain.

My father knew his life was soon too end,
But this didn't bother him because
He knew that where he was going
Would be forever lasting.

This tragic day soon arrived and his
Living days were over,
He went to live in a place much better
There he will live forever and ever.

   Sharon Smith

Angel of Death

Every one must die at one time or another
But will you die with a loving lover

Or will you die a hatred death
Upon the place you love best,

Will you die peace on heart
Or will you ever have to part,

The Angel of Death lurks everywhere
You can't escape it, so beware,

Beware of the pain and love it destroys
It treats kids' feelings as if they're toys,

I hope you never have to die
The death of a loving lie,

The darkness that lies behind the wall
Can come at any time and fall,

Upon whom of the earthly people
Except for those under steeple,

Only One can beat the death
And that is He who gave us breath.

   Amanda Sue Joeckel

Patti

Her hair was brown and her eyes were too.
She was unlike anyone I ever knew.
She could make me laugh when I was feeling down.
And when I needed her most she was always around.
She loved to write poems and sing out loud.
She's the type that always stood out in a crowd.
One fine day she gave birth to a son.
And as a mother she was number one.

Then it happened one day, one bright June morning.
She was taken from us without any warning.
Her car had wrecked, causing damage to her head,
And at the scene she was pronounced dead.
This changed my life in every way.
I've learned to live from day to day.
It's taught me that life is no guarantee,
For loved ones, for friends, and even for me,
In my heart her memory will always be there
With a feeling of closeness through thought and prayer.
God knows how much I'll always miss her
You see, that girl, she was my sister!

   Frankie Helm

Anniversary

Winter's first thaw cantered through
and left a tease of spring;
my soul reined in to breathe the air
   when fresh I heard you sing.

I saw your face cut out in stars,
in every cosmic etching, fair;
abiding in Pleiades smile,
   a graceful arc of heaven there.

Trembling birds return in flight
on thunderous applause of wings they come;
thrumming hearts in rhythmic beat,
   to fly perennial in the sun.

Now, when gushing rivers swell their banks
in springtide floods of muddy crush,
thoughts of you come winging past,
   and life begins again for us.

   Vicki Ruzicka

Diamonds

Dad and I played catch,
on the grass behind the fence.

"Don't expect it to come to you, son,
go to it and snatch it out of the air."

"Read where I'm throwing it. I want you
to catch it, but my aim may be off."

"The batter'll try to hit it past you,
you got to go after it, if you want it."

"Fling it as hard as you can, it's got a long
way to go."

"Don't forget, to follow through."

"It not how hard you throw, but whether
you get to where you're aiming."

Baseball talk.
The language of father and son.

Or maybe diamonds of life,
taught by a father to a son.

James W. Scott

Untitled

Early morning sunshine rise into the skies
Brightness and redness awaken my eyes
The dew on the ground tells time of the year
wetness on the green, nature's natural tear
The stillness of the calm, birth of day
Sun-a-rising awakens, chance for life in a new way
Giving glow as sun, the red and yellow flowers do
Showing beauty of grace from this sights heart true
A new day to love you, a day to love
A wonderful new day, beauty is part of
Rise from your calm sleep, lay by my side
Awaken into a life with me as our hearts collide
Fast and high, the sun climbs into the cool sky
only to open up the heat and dry the dew dry
O the blossom of feelings is awaiting a chance
to give petals of colors in life to enhance
a wonderful grace given, two hearts connected
with all the wonderful way love is we will be subjected

Rodney Atwell

Anonymous Father

The smell still gets to me sometimes. Leather, dirt,
sweat, but mostly the
leather.
The tension of a new glove in need of breaking in, as
the locker room would say.
The power in the
metal.
The heart skip as he wound up. The placement of the
perfect pitch and the
solid nothingness.

The scuffed ball was bruised and grass stained, but
the anonymous father who tossed it to me over the
fence had a pride in his eye — maybe a tear. He
would never show it though. He remembered that ball —
remembered the evacuation of the bench —
the line of pats, handshakes, yells. The scoreboard
ticking over. Remembered the anonymous father who
tossed him his first game ball, and with all the love
and pride in the world said,
"Nice hit, kid."

Alex Radus

A Talisman for Pix

How do these endless miles and weary days
Bring home to us in just how many ways
Our lives apart lack much we treasure so;
The warmth of comradeship we've come to know.
The love and comfort which in each we find
The balm of sympathetic peace of mind.

So often do the trifles we have bought
Comprise not gifts, but symbols of a thought
Which we want to express; now just the thing
To sum up what we sought is in this ring,

Though the meaning is easy to see
When we ponder whose hands
These should be,
There's a truth we will do
Well to discover;
All our hands hold the hearts of each other.

Arnold E. Roschli

Living In A Uncaring World

Living in a uncaring world no one cares
About how you feel.
Where growing old is just a curse.
And living by God's words is not of
this world. People cursing the day
they were born. And your life is worth
only a dime. Having things is wasted of time
and trying to learn is out of style and mother
and father are no where around because doing
drugs is there style and kids in the streets are running
wild. Where boys and girls come together to Pledge
the color of a rag and they believe everybody else is
just a fag. For hurting and killing is their way of life,
and loving and caring is no where in sight. Where girls
are having baby to be sold and no parents around to be told.
Where sharing and helping is no longer there because living
in a uncaring world no one cares.

Willie C. Toms Jr.

Fear

She sat there
hovering in the corner, shaking.
Her thoughts, her fears, her feelings
festering inside.

She clenched her stuffed bear in her arms
holding it close,
as if she would die if they were apart.
Like a child, a scared little girl,
she would let no one near her.

She raised her head, looked up,
And then quickly covered her head again
as if what she saw was too painful.
But a ghost,
nor the devil itself
was in front of her.

Only a piece of glass,
A mirror.

Emily Martin

Ode to Sambo

I have more admiration for the man in the casket
than I do for those in the pews.
They put on a good show as if on a set
and some imaginary director giving them guess.

Acting out pretentious sorrows and displaying false cares;
intense grieving and morning with tears flowing from their eyes.
Good that their souls are covered with riches and not left to bare,
for their feelings are a pile of dung and their tears are swarming flies.

They hardly cared for him, or his well-being when he alive;
no calls, no visits reserved for those who are uneducated and poor.
Captain of his boat, friend of the sea, and patron of a local dive.
His dwelling a recycled matchbox of leaky and rotten floor.

And what's the payment for such an award winning portrayal of
sincerity?
There is nothing to be acquired; there is nothing to be willed.
Perhaps acting with conviction will offer contriteness and serenity.
But the award should go to them man in the casket for his portrayal of
braveness from a disease he concealed.

Debbie Gallander

What Happened To Us?

For months we lived as one
Sharing our time, caring for each other
Thinking when we will be together again
Making plans to be shared as one
Showing love to one another
Making out dreams for the future
Talking to each other, touching each other
Some ideas in our dreams came true
Some did not
Now here we are far apart
Not dreaming, not touching, not talking
Not sharing, not caring, not loving
Only to ourselves do we think of any dreams
Dreams of the future only to be for ourselves
And no others
Locking out the love for each other
We only injure ones feelings
My dream is that all love returns
But when does it stop hurting?

Virgil Hemel

School, What Am I Doing Here?

My bus is late, my locker's stuck. How did I get here?
I wander into homeroom, and all I hear is "You're late,"
"Oh no! I lost my homework!" What do I do? I'm in such fear!
Classes surround me, some that I love, and some that I hate,

I wander into homeroom, and all I hear is "You're late,"
Getting squashed like a pancake, trying to make it to class,
Classes surround me, some that I love, and some that I hate,
My favorite time of day, Lunch! Eating and talking, what a blast!

Getting squashed like a pancake, trying to make it to class,
"Did you do your homework?" My teachers say to me and fuss,
My favorite time of day, Lunch! Eating and talking, what a blast!
I finally made it through the day, now where's my bus?

"Did you do your homework?" My teachers say to me and fuss,
"Oh no! I lost my homework!" What do I do? I'm in such fear!
I finally made it through the day, now where's my bus?
My bus is late, my locker's stuck. How did I get here?

Qing Shen

Love

Shall I compare thee to a tall strong tree?
Thou art much taller and stronger.
Loving eyes and a warm smile comforts me,
The way you loved children helps me love thee longer.

When thy kind-gentle heart begins to show,
I know our love will always grow.
And I know our love will never die,
As long as we have God in our lives.
And once our kids are grown and gone,
We will then see the works we have done.

But don't let our love fade,
By putting it in the shade.
When God sees what we've done,
He'll say, "come with me my children, your work here is done."

Bobbi Ann St. Peter

My Love

Every time we hug, or enjoy each other's kiss
I ask myself, does it ever get better than this?
All the time we spend, our hearts run fast and free
and for each other, we feel passionately
I long for your touch, and love the way you feel
because of this I wonder, can you be real
When I'm without you, I sense that I am lost
but I'll always be with you, no matter the cost
I long for the moment, that we can be together
and when we are, I know that it's forever
so considering all of this, I have to know if it's true
had I ever really lived, before I started loving you?

Jason Blevins

A Dreamer Dreams of Peace for His Country

I dream of peace for my country every second of every day

I often dream of our pyramid temple Phimeanakas in its glory
. . . with its grand staircases in the center of its four sides
. . . with lions on each corner of its many tiers
. . . with its gallery of deities encircling its majestic top.

In the center of its pinnacle rising on a small platform is
a beautiful temple covered with gold, encrusted with jewels
and fragrances of beautiful flowers.

In this beautiful temple the King meets with the Naga Queen
every night, who comes to see her King in the form of a divine
female, to ensure her protection of the lands of our country.

The King says to me, there can be no peace till Phimeanakas
is returned to its splendor so his Naga Queen will return.

When I explain to the King what has happened to our country,
I wake up and look around to find that I have been dreaming.

. . . Maybe if we restore Phimeanakas to its former glory,
. . . Maybe if we restore the beautiful Temple on the pinnacle,
. . . Maybe the King will return to Phimeanakas,
. . . Maybe then the Naga Queen will return, and, Maybe,

. . . Peace will return to my beloved motherland, Cambodia.

Kim Huot Kiet

449

Impossible Changes, Small Differences

Dedicated to "Garth"

Changing the world, it's a hard thing to try,
So much crime and violence, seeing homeless people cry.
Is this the way God intended the world to be?
Leaving changes needed up to you and me.
Are we supposed to thank God for us being here?
Or should we blame him for each unhappy tear.
Did we fail a test of life and let him down?
Is he sitting in heaven in sadness and a frown?
We have to think of ourselves, make us be number one,
And pray someday a nice change in the world will come.
Until then remember, the way we live our life is our choice,
Funny how small differences are made with the sound of
someone's voice.

Rene Hafer

Woman In White

At times we thought her to be insane.
At other times we thought her to be great.
Is it her insanity that keeps her apart?
Or is she simply beyond us in understanding?

Often those said to be great are misunderstood.
Is she misunderstood because she stands by what she believes?:
    Her religion
    her words
    her rules
    her visions
    her life
    her passion
What is her view of the universe?

Other may see her as evil because she is different.
But, no, she brings us only what is good
    her pure soul
    her simple life
    her solitary being
It's not that we need to understand her.
It's that we need to look within ourselves through her poetry.

Trinh T. T. Bui

My Father's Shoes

Behold, this collection of tiny carved shoes!
Shelved on display for all to see and admire.
To most they are simply what they appear to be,
artful miniatures of a common taken-for-granted item.
But for me, they represent oh, so much more!

Made of oak, mahogany and pine,
they stand sturdy and steadfast as he.
Wooden wonders; pieces of himself all in a row.
Their leathers worn and creased like the hands that created them;
laced with the experiences of a seldom perfect life.

Before me they stand solitary and humble;
each a moment unto itself; a testimony to his talents.
Treasured both, these shoes and their creator,
their value beyond that of dollars and cents.
A precious gift to me, unequaled by any other.

So, behold again this collection of tiny carved shoes.
His blood, sweat, and tears, they linger still
Look deeper now and see as I, the giant of a man within
A man so dear, so special in my life
That no one could ever fill, My Father's Shoes!

Alice Sullivan

God

She waited for the darkness in which she thrived
To take her walk alone in complete solitude
Not a person for miles there in the canyon
She lit her nightly fire began her ritual
She perched by the desperate flames
Eyes closed, exquisite face upturned
Waiting
Waiting for the word of God
"You have come again"
"Yes Lord," she always replied
"I put you here to obey man to bear and rear his children"
"Yes Lord"
"Leave now"
The resounding voice was gone
From above she was watched
She extinguished the fire and retreated home
Her husband smirked at his craftiness
And his wife's ignorance
He strutted down from his roost above her sanctuary
Then he too returned home.

Krista Noble

Of Him And Him And Me

In a little candle-lit chapel, near where my father lay dying,
I said a sad, soft-voiced prayer and then I talked to God for awhile

I could not know, would not know, whether he might hear
my wounded, worried words or feel my unbearable fear

Kneeling now, I began begging, beseeching, pleading,
Needing to tell of the pitiful, personal hell my father was in

God, I even prayed for the prayer I was praying,
Demanding that He — Listen! — to the sorrowing words I was
saying

Raising my voice, I Shouted into the solitary silence,
saying "Our Father, take My strength! And give it to him, my
father!"

But He didn't answer and he died,
quietly, a mournful hour later

Yet today, uncertainty holds my mind, for each time I find
the little candle-lit chapel, I feel a strange weakness

Perhaps He tried, but he died anyway,
my strength failing Him and him and me.

Robert McFarland

A Daughter's Love

My mother, my dear, my divine,
To me you have always been so kind.

Poise, peace, beauty and grace,
I'm blessed when I look at your angel face.

You are the light that shines in me so bright,
And the driving force that makes me do what's right.

My ultimate dream, the spark that lights my fire,
The light that shines in me, you're my inner torch forever.

Sweet, honest, loving, humble and kind,
Another person like you in this world is hard to find.

How I wish upon a falling star,
That one day I can be as you are.

And to me my daughter could say,
She feels in her heart, what I feel for you today.

For to know what a daughter's love should be,
Is a gift of love, one of eternity.

Cheryl Simon

My Father Swings Again

Crashing, crushing. This storm now meets the shoreline.
Its wind spits rain to the paper houses
Not caring that a grey woman
Huddles in the corner of her crumpled home. No roof.

Just as the storm, my father's silhouette now drowns me.
His fist is swelling like the tides of Elena, as does my face.
My nose erupts oceans of blood, I try to swim.
But oceans they are not.

The street signs which once guided the way
To shops and bridges and a beach
Now only point to the path of Elena.
Elena is the fifth, hence her name,
She is not the first to inflict such destruction.

The smell of a fermented vineyard
Falls from my father's smile. He has enjoyed the beating.

A child now balances his body on the beach.
His footprints in the sand are scattered like those of a drunk.
Waves are pulling the beach from beneath him,
And soon this child will fall, but I cannot watch him fight the wind.
I see only my fight; my father swings again.

Brian Wedlake

Untitled

Drifting out into the vast realms of silence
   torn between the worlds overpowering darkness
   and your own door into the unknown
  Visions and shadows of your lost mind
  Escaping through the cracks
  Your peace, your thoughts, your happiness
   smile to those and set yourself free
Ideas beyond your conscience thought
Forgotten space to which you've traveled
  unlocking the quiet treasure
  the key that holds in the glass
A mirror to where you once were forgotten
Break the glass, overcome the destruction
Astonished by the great power to which the mind
  releases nonsense
  which once was understood
Fade in and out of what once was your reality
And now is your Illusion
Through the reflection of the rain
  I saw the sparrow fly into the distant darkness.

Molly A. Tilimon

Winter's Call

Summer leaves like a gentle call
Beckon creatures big and small.

The birds are leaving one and all;
You wonder if they will come back at all.

The leaves on the trees turn red and gold,
Settling down for the winter's cold.

The sparrows tip-toe in the snow,
Hoping to find the crumbs we throw.

The snow begins to melt and drain
Into the rivers filled with rain.

The lovely blossoms unfold into spring.
The beautiful birds come back to sing.

Jean E. Bohigian

The Storm

The black clouds rolled unto blue skies,
Shifting yet silent.
The fawn hurries, the doe to find.
Shifting yet silent.

The pines with fiery temper roared,
Unyielding
The brooks cry from angry beating, yet it comes.
Unyielding

The fields shimmer.
Calm
The fawn wanders once again.
Calm

Barbara Erickson

Love Is Hard . . .

Love is hard when the one you love is on the wrong path.

Love is hard when you know all the things that he's doing.

Love is hard when you know that you can't stay with him
   while he's doing all the things he does.

Love is hard when you watch him from a distance and see him
   fall, cry, and look for you but he thinks you're not
   there.

Love is hard when you see him seek false comfort only to be
   hurt again.

Love is hard when you want to run to him and hold him in
   your arms and protect him but can't.

Love is hard when the one you love looks for you but can't
   find you even when your standing inches form his face.

Rachel Pierce

Falon

Falon, you were mommy's precious sweetheart and daddy's little girl,
When you were born amid confusion and in a frenzied whirl.
The doctors tried their very best to make your small lungs cry,
But efforts proved to be in vain as we never heard a sigh.
Why you were taken from us at a very young age,
We'll never understand and sometimes feel outraged.

As I look into your beautiful tiny face,
I know you're up above in a far more better place.
Gabriel will guide you through the pearly white gates,
Where trees grow filled with luscious fruit and succulent dates.
Jesus will enfold you with his tender love,
While overhead sings a multitude of pure white doves.
Little children greet with their many hugs,
While a team of angels tends your needs always lovingly,
   giving their hearts a tug.
Although one never knows the trials and tribulations
   along life's way,
I know for certain dear Falon, I'll see you again one
   bright and sunny day.

Linda Louise Meckley

Seasons

From summers —— hot
  To winters ——— cold
I see my flowers — growing old

They wither and die
  I wonder where the flowers go.

Springtime arrives—and now and then
  they spring to life - to bloom again.

It's awesome — how they come and go.
  God only knows where flowers go.

Catherine Smith

The Abandoned Child

The food that gives me joy has grown cold and sour
the roof that offers me shelter blown away by this
gulf wind that begins as a mere depression and matures
into a monstrous and ferocious hurricane
My nest that once gave me rest now gives me labor
and the arms that once cuddled me have become the arms
now directed against me forgetting they were made to
protect me
How could I have been if the faces that now face away
from each other had not looked intently into each others
eyes the night before
They that invited me to dinner have abandoned their table
to be because they could not remember or probably chose
not to recollect their mood and joy the day they jointly
wrote me to come
But I hope they realize that a car they bought as one can
always be sold by one and the home they lived in also be
treated the same but I remain the one that will ever haunt
Or preserve their eternal oneness.

Augustine Ogbunugwu

Fear

Fear is only a feeling, yet it represents our
Soul and our innermost thoughts.
It is there wherever you go.
It is the shadows that dance upon the walls
In a dimly lit room, it is the noises you hear
In a strange place.
It show you images of evil creatures that
Are not even there.
It is our nightmares come to life!
Fear is only a figment of our imagination,
And yet we still run from it.
Whether it be because of lack of knowledge,
Our inability to believe.
Our inability to try new things,
Or our unwillingness to change.
Why are we petrified of the creations of our imagination?
Why do we as humans refuse to stand up to our fears?
And when will our fears be:
Quoth said the raven, "Nevermore?"

Jason Allen Reynolds

Wishing Upon A Star

Wishing upon a star.
Chasing dreams that flew so far.
Wishing for your fantasies,
Stepping away from reality.
Wishing you were someone new,
Not wanting the real you.
Wishing on things that seem so real.
But if they don't come true, how do you feel?
Wishing about love,
Praying he's watching above
Wishing that you'll be so great
But to much greatness makes you hate
Don't wish on things you don't really need.
Wish on someone else, do a good deed.

Karrie Lynn Swing

Circle

Life,
Ironic isn't it.
You have all of it,
Yet you still have nothing.

My life is ironic,
It's like being a cube,
An every one else is a circular hole.
I just can't change.

To have things nice and easy,
Yet to want just one simple thing that I can't have.
I want one thing and only one other can give it,
I want peace.

Peace of mind,
Peace of the heart.
I want this for all people,
When you have peace of the soul you are content.

Cordelia Wreathall

Love

Love is found in many different ways.
Love is a circle that may or may not end.
Love is the way you want it to be, it is the
way you think it should be.
Love is a walk in the moon light, or a stroll
in the park at night, it is a moon lite dinner in the
park, or a night alone together at home.
Love is the way you both think of your selves
Love is what you think it should be
it is the time you give it, it is the most you
could give. It is the past, present, the future
of your life.
Love is as warm as the summer sun, making
flowers blossom, after winter's done. Love is the
coming and going of the hart, it is just love your
Ever Lasting Love

Shannon Headley

North Star

Star light, star bright
You're the only star I see at night.
You shine so bright, within my heart
And in my mind you never part.
I see you with my eyes closed tight
I look for you most every night.
Sometimes I wish that I could be
As close to you as you seem to me.
To shine so bright, for the world to see
To shine for someone
Who seeks guidance in me.
You stand alone, but surrounded by light
Yet, I only see you, shine in the night.
If ever I am lost, and find myself astray
can I look for you, to show me the way?
To lead me back where I should be
To the place where I'll find, my destiny.
Star light, star bright
In my heart, forever
Will shine your light.

Lori A. Mastroeni

Magical Place

If I had a magical place, I wonder where it would be
High upon a mountain, or by the soft swaying sea

I guess I would go to a meadow with colorful flowers and tall giant
  trees
I would listen to the sound of the songs of the birds
And the humming of the bees

Looking upon my meadow as far as my eyes could see
I saw the most beautiful white horse neighing happily with glee

I mounted on my horse and he started to go
He ran and ran and ran, not knowing when to whoa!

We stopped by a creek and I looked to my right
I jumped off my white beauty then ran to a unicorn with delight

Not knowing when my surprises would end
I petted the lovely beast as happily as could be
I placed my hand on its horn and a magical tingle rushed through me!

Then I decided right then and there that it was time for me to leave
But in my heart I still believe...

In my magical place.
  Kayla Breeding

Mom

So much in so little time,
You taught me how to be independent
And what life has to offer if we only try.
Life may not always be fair but to
Appreciate each and every day,
And not to take things for granted.
To always look on the bright side of things
For it could always be worse.

In death you gave me endless strength
To face the challenges that come my way.
Now you are gone but you are always
With me in my heart.
Being my guardian angel, I know
You have been watching over me
Right from the start.
  Joanne L. Rosen

Dyslexia

  You write weird,
  you talk funny.
  Why can't you read?
  Why are you slow?
Mommy, why can other kids do things better than me?
  Why can't you spell?
  Why do you get letters mixed up?
  Why can't you sound out words?
Mommy, why can other kids do things better than me?
  Where are you going?
  Why do you go to school in the summer?
  Why do you get so much extra help?
Mommy, why can other kids do things better than me?
  You're a dummy!
  You can't do anything right!
  Let's act like her, retarded.
Mommy, why can other kids do things better than me?
  Laura McKnight

This Dark Corner

Passion, when the softest of voices die.
Silent lovers, so quiet their flame.
As the time ticks by, the more they wish this night could be endless.
Like clouds rolling in on a summer night, all past memories have
  faded.
In the darkest of corners, the desires grow deep.
Shade to black whispers the truth.
This is my truth.
I stare with my eyes closed searching for the light.
The light has been washed away, forever gone and long forgotten.
Tomorrow is a whole other waiting to come, waiting to be
  experienced.
Another night, another moment of endless dreams and corners.
  Sara Rosenblatt

Complain No More

Have I done something wrong? I asked
Have I been bad before?
I wonder what I could have done to deserve
this mess in me
I wonder why it came like this
So much I have to deal with

I must think too of those better off than I
Is their misery any less painful?
Is their misery lessened just by knowing
someone deals with more than they?

Then I think of others too who deal
with more than I
Those who have it so much worse than me
I can complain no more
  Renee Ray

In Another Time

In another time you might have been queen
Ruling a country with your stately gaze, leading, comforting,
guiding
by will what is your divine right?

In another time you were a nightingale
soothing souls with your bittersweet songs
giving hope of brighter days yet to come

In another time you were a rose, all others envy you
Your beauty alone sustains you, your thorns protect
yet magnify your regal nature, like a crown
But now you are a mother, guiding often times without instruction,
nurturing and comforting with little praise.

Often carrying a load too heavy to bear,
Leaning only on faith and a love that come from within

Working everyday, striving for perfection in a world that sometimes
doesn't seem to care

Yet still you smile inside and none of it matters because you know in
another time you were Queen
  Rick L. Miller

Life and After Life

Two steps from Death
Two steps from Hell
What's with this crazy world
What to do, what to believe
What to say and what to see
Sometimes I think there can be no
    freedom for me

After life has got to be better
Well they must have pretty good weather
Everybody has got to be together
And then you can talk about whatever
You can probable fly high and then again
You can probable go pretty low
And then you can meet the Almighty
He

David James Mealer

Our Beloved Friend

He was a rebel, but cool
constantly acting the fool
He always had something funny to say
Nobody knows, how it goes
Or why he went away
In our hearts, and in our minds
No need to look hard
Gary is easy to find
He wasn't the worst
And he wasn't the best
But we miss him dearly
Since we laid him to rest
He's up there, where the fishing is great
And when it's our turn to catch a big one
He will be waiting at the gate.

Craig L. Fontenot

Pictures In Heaven

A grain of sand is worth pictures in heaven
pictures in dark

Sadism, quick loser
shines himself on bones

Purple shadow, eel,
flash,

take a picture of your soul

Look inside, backwards you hide
twisted, you're funny

Picture of an ancient world
garden wars
pageantry

Play this, this black,
fashion of disease

Pictures on the wall
grandma, nephew,
all such family

I am my own picture
complete suicide
without feedback

Tod Ketchum

Educated Woman

I'm an educated woman I think you should know, I'm an educated
woman I don't set any limits onto where my success can go. I can be
anything I want to be, because I've got the pride and strength, and
God who comforts me.

I've learned wrong from right and I've met a lot of the jealous
girls who always want to fight. People may look at me in a crazy kind
of way, but I pay them no mind cause I know I'm going to make it in
the world someday.
I have to make my parents happy and I have to make them proud
although I do sometimes act vivacious and quite loud. But you know,
I'm an educated woman and I can calm myself down.

I have a lot of pressures from my family and peers, but since
I'm an educated woman I'm going to keep living on through my years. I
try not to let anyone get to me or even get to close, because things
happen and we have to loose what we love and cherish most.

I'm trying to get out in the world today and I keep trying to
understand why violence keeps on lasting, like a conflict between man
to man. But once again, I'm an educated woman and I stand so tall
because my daddy always says no one can put me down or make me fall.
If I do what I believe in and fight for my rights I can be that
educated woman and become successful with all my womanly might.

Kesha V. Walton

Store 24, Harvard Square

All I wanted was to pay for my wood-pressed, Nantucket Nectar apple juice.

Just slap down my ninety-nine cents and inconspicuously slip right out of there—

But my desire was disrupted when a man aside the counter smacked my
    hand with a copy of the Massachusetts Spare Change.

He asked for only one dollar as he wiped the moisture from his
    sweating brow and made a slight gesture with his empty cup.

I repeatedly switched my focus between the paper, the juice, and the
    three quarters, two dimes and a nickel in my hand.

Disturbed by my hesitation, the guy behind the counter motioned to
    the waiting customers, so—

I dropped the coins in the man's Styrofoam cup and snatched my paper
    as the guy behind me bought a Snapple and a pack of Camel
    Lights.

Kristen Kreuzer

Because You Wanted To

I watched you when I was a little girl.
The woman in high heels with shapely suits and red hair.
The person who's lap I belonged on, with my ear pressed against your breast bone.
I remember the smell of your perfume.
And I remember each breath I held, hoping it wasn't time to get down just yet.

I watched you overlook other people's short comings.
You explained what being human meant.

I watched you reach out to strangers just because you could.
I watched you leave the dishes and the housework to play for a while.
I watched you keep your promise.

I watched you smile when you were scared. When you were tired.
When you really hurt. Because you wanted to.

I watched you tuck in the few hairs left.
I watched you lick your dry lips.

I watched you fight to accept the new response from old friends.
Some new reflection in their eyes directed at a person who isn't quite you.

And I watched you out them at ease comfort them with your openness
and smile in that timeless, classy style because you wanted to.

Laurie DeCou Kachin

High School Reading

The author of my book is me dummy, the father of my child is me . . .
dummy,
If you knew about a book, then you wouldn't be a dummy,
if you knew that I was a father, then you would know that the child
is mine . . . dummy

When you do read dummy, don't just read the first and last line of
every page in the book, but every word between the first and the last
word of every page in the book.
Speed Reading is not for fun, its a method for understanding, you have
to practice it with a book and your mind, not with a watch . . .
dummy.
Just try to understand the frustration your parents go through.
Finding out their child can't read, and not having a clue. They
stress on the job and only produce strange looks. Unlike being fresh
upon arriving at the house ready to cook. They yell at their kids
to do mandatory school reading, because the world is real. Ask more
questions and they will tell you more lies interact more with them,
it may just save their lives. Please show them where the author
is located in the book and maybe they will start to look on their
own and think they are grown.

Ignatius C. Williams

Eulogy To Emma Algers (December 4, 1986)

Emma - She burst into our lives like a nova exploding in a far distant
   galaxy: unseen, unheard, but certainly not to be ignored.
Emma was a woman of truth, no matter how much it hurt.
This made many people think she was overly critical, even cruel,
   but she was only truthful.

Emma - She left our lives like a falling star,
   never to be duplicated, nor forgotten,
   just a thing of beauty for a few brief moments,
   captured forever in memory.
Or maybe, like the grand finale at a fourth of July celebration.
The culmination of an evening of beauty,
   but with a hint of nostalgia that it is coming to a close.

Emma - God knows how much you meant to me. I hurt so much that you
   have left me, but we had to part sometime, and maybe it is better
   that you leave me behind than that I leave you. You needed me in
   so many ways, and I only loved you. I hope your pain and
   suffering are over now, Emma. Now you can let your beauty shine
   through. Oh, why did you struggle so to hide it when you were with
   us? Now that you are gone, many people are talking about how
   beautiful you were in so many ways.

Emma - Peace be with you always and in all ways.

David Adams

My Dearest Melinda

Dedicated to Melinda, my firstborn daughter whom I love so much.

In 1969 on April 23rd, a lovely female soul came to earth.
Through her mother — sixteen hours of hard labor, seemed like a curse,
Delivered by Lupe Tonga, her registered nurse.

To her the name "Melinda Kalolaine" was given, 21 inches long and weighed seven.
The firstborn girl to the Muti's garden, she's an angel sent from Heaven.

Her eyes so clear, her skin so fair, and on her head — not a single hair.
To eat, to drink, she didn't care — she'd rather sleep through the night's cool air.

After being in the hospital for almost a week, the doctor's help I began to seek.
To me, the little child was awfully weak 'cause all she did was sleep, sleep, sleep!

"She's a lazy delicate baby," was the doctor's reply. "She's in perfect health, and don't you cry."
"Her friends in Heaven must have bidden her goodbye, with lots
of kisses and apple pie."

A silent prayer of thanksgiving was uttered; a feeling of ecstasy known only to a mother.
Such joy, such happiness, cannot be measured, holding God's creation,
a miracle and a wonder.

I pray this lovely soul to go high and far; to serve Kingdom of Heavenly Father.

Sisi K. Muti

Christmas 1996

Santa's had to change his ways
Since coming under NAFTA.
Fewer reindeer for his sleighs,
And speed-up work-they hafta!

Health benefits are cut way back.
It's hard to feel real clannish.
There are patches now on St. Nick's sack,
And everyone learns Spanish.

Even Mrs. Claus now works
To hold it all together.
But can it last if just one shirks?
It's as uncertain as the weather.

There is also rumor that
The Claus contract is flappin'.
Fine prints is found within the GATT
That a South Pole site could happen.

It creates a lot of hemis-fear
When you live from hand to mouth.
The sucking sound that you now hear
Are Santa's elves going south.

H. A. "Barney" Goltz

To A Little Lame Dog

Goodbye faithful friend.
It's not the end,
Though misfortune beset you
Here on earth and robbed
you of fulfilling your worth.
Now, we're sure that you have
found that happy hunting ground
Where, with sturdy legs, you will
roam over the sweetest fields of clover.
Our hearth is strangely empty
without your presence here
And as we go about our chores
We shed a silent tear.

Helen De Marco

My Special Child

I found out my son has Muscular dystrophy.
So I sat here today.
Words lumped in my throat,
Not knowing what to say.

I watch as he plays.
I listen to him trying to communicate.
Most of his speech is not clear,
So when he clearly says "I love you Daddy,"
The words mean more than you can anticipate.

He may not be able,
To do the things other kids do,
But, a more loving child you will never see.
As he puts his arms around my neck.
I am proud to be his Daddy.

As a tear runs down my check,
I thank the Lord above
For his wonderful gift to me,
A "Special" child so full of love.

Terry Thompson

455

Marriage

When two become one
in the name of the son
let it be sung what God has done

When two become one
like a circle of gold that can't be undone
let it be known to everyone

When two become one
in the house of the son
let it be done by a holy one,
that God and his son honored
the two in becoming one

In the name of the father and the son
let it be done

Joe Norwood

Mental Lockdown

You are a menace, bad to the bone I have heard
Why am I subject to these awful words
You'll never make it, never to succeed
Forced to do the evil deed
Lapsed in crime forced to crime
Cast to hell an eight by ten cell
Eight years gone from dusk to dawn
Why must I feel?
Why must I kill?
Why must I live?
Why must I die?
Why?
Why?

Jeremiah Loyd

Atlanta '96

100 years — that's pretty old
yet only few have earned the gold
The lucky ones who came in first
In tears of joy and awe they burst
They were the ones to sacrifice
Do what it took, and pay the price
Training harder every day
Trying to find a better way
A better way to reach the top
Until perfection, they won't stop
Nadia and Mary Lou
Dolan, Evans, Ali, too
They worked until they reached their goals
And from there established higher roles
They made it there because they dreamed
Though far off olympics seemed
And through their strokes, and turns, and kicks
They'll all remember '96

Jessi Jeter

Apart, But Not

Although we're apart and I'm lonely
Your smiling face in my mind keeps me company.
I feel your love through the distance
And you're with me always.
It hurts me to think you're lonely,
I hate it when you're sad,
But, I know you know I love you dearly
And I'm with you always.

James T. Harrison Jr.

Sanctity

Searing wavy heat repels off scorched buckled pavement
Bullets of sweat drip, soaking everything covering skin
Potassium evaporates, glasses steam, walking's an effort
Clouds pillar, forewarning smell of rain as evening falls
Thunder claps, kids run playfully through cold showers, wrenches seal
    open hydrants
Tires splash warm puddles, hypnotic ripples roll along in their wake
A filmy residue, oil and antifreeze pollute instant bird bath potholes
Muggy scents hang trapped disagreeably fused in dank air
Itchy fiber glass attic exhaust, effluvium linseed oil, choky second hand smoke
Urban potpourri, until stepping into sanctity; a park, forest preserve
    or backyard wildness
Erratic ballet of luminous fireflies orchestrated by crickets, owl
    hoots, rustling leaves
A fluttering moth wing clips across my ear, oddly pleasant like a feather
Amazing; a potentially destructive insect could warm me, instilling awe
My fingertip becomes a landing pad for a lightning bug sporadically blinking
Crawling up my arm tickling gently, safely perched on my shoulder
Subconsciously, and dwell in wilderness, foraging old growth forests
Canoeing, wild rivers, lakes, observing moose, otter, elk
Wolves howl, loons cry, eagles soar, turtles sun, dragonflies hover
Traveling in my mind, peacefulness, oneness with creation, sanctity.

Corinne Xanfold

Choices

As I enter into darkness there's a haunting in my head of a
thing unknown for which I dread.

It's not a ghost that's taunting me, but thoughts
of how I'll stage my destiny.

Will I accept the challenge and plan ahead or hide in the
shadows and make them my bed?

Will I find meaning in the future and the best of it make
or plunge into pity and in myself take?

Will I dwell on my darkness, consider me cursed or capture
life's light and give it all worth?

Will I caress what I now can see, let its strength carry me or
mull it over in my mind, refuse to live and choose to be blind?

Sheri Bollen

This Ole House

This ole house has been my home twelve out of seventeen years. Now
the time has come for me to move on and start new somewhere else. A
business man has other plans and will probably tear it down. You see,
he doesn't know how it's been warm and sheltered out the cold for the
last One Hundred Fifty plus years. How all the trees so tall around
the house cradled it with love, sheltered out the heat, and kept it cool each summers
day.

How each spring it blossomed with freshly planted flowers, garden
vegetables, and fruit trees that were planted by many families with
tender loving care. He doesn't know the pride and joy each family
felt as they added their own touch, new carpet and tile upon the
floor, or new paint and paper on each tall wall. You see dollar signs
have made the business man blind and he must provide for his own.
All the years of history of this house to him will never be known.

Although my heart is filled with sadness, as I know I must be
moving on. It was a warm safe place to raise my son along with four
children I call my own. We'll always have the memories, so no matter
what they do to this ole house its beauty will always stand tall in
my mind. The comfort I felt each night, as I lay down my head or the
smile I had upon my face when asked about this house, I said it is
a part of history each detail I wish I'd known, but there's no doubt
I've been proud each time I've called it home.

Cynthia Ann Sons

Love Is A Beautiful Way

If the waters of a roaring deep blue sea suddenly disperse,
Like two lovers with a heated conflict that they don't rehearse.
Two snow white turtle doves with love and peace in a gleam of their
eye, to my one true devoted goddess within my soul, I will never lie.
The baby soft blue sky that can be blessed with the hand of God,
A glimpse of her to die for soul and heart will forever bless me.
A new baby red rose with the addiction of a sweet smelling dew,
My hand softly through the enchanting hair warmed my soul with a few.
Walks in the nectar of nature with a vision of a heavenly valley,
Two hearts with a beat of one with just the thought of love to each one.
Two heavenly creatures never lived within such passion of lovers,
Their lives in a stormy rocky tide shield them like a sublime cover.
People live, love, and unfortunately forget,
These two souls though, never quit with the thought of loving only one another.
A woman of a goddess body and soul that the Gods should definitely envy,
A man with an undying devotion to his one and only enchantment.
They will live the life of Gods and goddess among the stars of night,
He will forever thrill and never chill her dreams, soul, and heart.

Billy Kelley

We Feel

When we make love, the world . . .
exists no more for me
It brings forth all I hide, and all it is I feel
So deep . . . the pain and sweat, when we engage the flesh, —
Intensity has taken me far from my only breath
When we make love, it's true . . .
No lies, no promises, —
It's there we greet the animal that sleeps beneath our breast
We slither in the dark, in passion we do play —
Until the night cries, "Mercy!" and wakes into a day
When we make love, I whore . . .
Let down my hair for you,
No shame, I beg for more — there's nothing I won't do
I savor you like water and drink your very soul,
Puts yesterday to slaughter and helps us become whole
When we make love, the world . . .
Seems distant and surreal
We can't deny the truth now —
When we make love,
We feel.

Rosana Modugno

Inner Turmoil

Seeing through the eyes of darkness
The white rush of water life challenges us to endure

How strong are our paddles and oars?
To match the rapid succession of waves of loneliness and doubt,
cresting one by one

We try and break through them or glide over the top
like a roller coaster ride
They crash around us, trying to twirl and swirl us into a vortex
confusion, self-doubt, and despair

Boundaries

Glide into a channel of self discovery
Balance, the toughest test of your faith and love (your inner strength)
Smooth out the rough edge of doubt, to be on an even Keel with life

Approach to meet the new morning's dawn, your oar parts the surface
of the water, and you steer forward, listening to the silence in
quiet reverence

Witness the glistening of the rays of sun, as they dance upon the
water and the silhouette of trees as they mirror back their beauty

A safe Harbour

Jeanne Faust

The Annoying Classmate

Alone I sit in the back of class,
Pondering upon my thoughts in peace.
At times, I sit and cram for tests.
All is done with silence and me.

Startled, I hear the loud mouth snot,
Bellowing his presence down the hall.
Peace and quiet follow him not.
Silence is shattered again once more!

Nothing pleasant nor humor flow.
His lips drip of many sores.
Complaints fester, his lips has shown.
Oh squawk, snot squawk forever more.

Oh nerves grate against my patience,
As my fingers curl into a ball.
I spy his jaw with pure hard spite,
As my fist aches to kiss this fool's jaw.

Silence! Ye boisterous classmate of mine.
Clamp that trap or meet my friend the fist!
My nerves are raw at this point in time.
Oh annoying classmate, go stuff it!

Julie T. Hoang

Globe of Fire

Not realizing that I was holding
something wonderful, fragile, beautiful
something that was round and warm
that made my life more meaningful...
it was like a fire in a globe
made of glass and burning bright
I feared in my blindness that it might burn,
and dropped it one cold night
long I stood in silent shock
until my grief began to pour
too late I tried to mend or heal it
and tried to make it glow once more
now I guess I'll always be
wishful that I never was
as blind to love that one cold night
when I dropped and shattered us...

John L. Greene

A Proud People

This world so full of hate,
So full of things unpleasant
So full of mistrust,
So full of crime,
That you know not what to do;
But stand and stare into oblivion
And wonder what will be next.
But here we are in this land
This wonderful Magnificent Province
Where race, hate, mistrust and all
Are gradually and slowly dying away
To leave us a proud people,
A strong people, a loving people
With a sense of dedication to unite all.

Satchidananda V. Chinapen

Phoenix Fire

There is beauty in a forest char, where
fire's carbon black, girds a greenless stand.
Burnt trees and branded stone are not aware
They are martyrs on consecrated land.
Incinerate a needle cloak and see
A spiring core, inspire and then bestir
A sentient spirit in and set it free,
To grow anew, within the massacre.
What's left is soul, where spindle arms outreach,
Rejoicing in a memory of growth,
Yet in debilitation they beseech
The grace of nature's spring and budding troth.
Beneath, 'long side the fired slope of earth,
The seedlings of the sacred seek rebirth.

Rolland G. Smith

Water Fall

Water sparkling down, splash.
  Caressing life with each new drop.
Swirls and curls moving fast, faster
  Bubbles surfacing exploding, into nothing.
Bluish green greenish white gushes
  Snowy ice caps moving
Circling deeper, coming up then going back down.
  Life drowning
  A fin, a tail, no legs
In a elixir
  A potion fuming,
  Alive.

Kai E. Skov

Mothers Are . . .

When a child's life becomes cold and dreary
Mothers are the sunlight which brighten the day
and warm the heart.

When a child cries for help and guidance
Mothers are the signposts marking the way
at life's crossroads.

When a child thirsts for knowledge and understanding
Mothers are the gentle rain that quench the thirst
and nourish the body.

When a child's hopes and dreams have gone awry
Mothers are the cheerleaders who provide support
and renew the spirit.

When a child experiences success and happiness
Mothers are the audience which give a standing ovation!

Kathleen A. Aarons

For I Am The Earth

Some of me is dying, some of me is you
All of me is crying, as we all do
I have individuals, though I'm mostly a whole.
I have many a plain, which roll.
I see sickness and heartache, through my bloody tears.
I see hostile battles, going on for years.
My war-torn face looks down upon
wars that were fought because of color, of race.
I silently scream, but nobody hears
I silently cry, and no one sees my tears.
Maybe someday,
When the grass is all green, and stars
touch an ocean shining clean...
My worrying will be its worth.
I have reason to worry:
  For I Am The Earth

Mandy Arbuckle

Why?

Why is my heart shattered and so unexpected?
And years of love is not respected.

Why is caring suddenly gone?
What on earth has quickly gone wrong?

Holidays, birthdays, celebration days
Times of fun in so many ways.

No greater pain did we ever endure
Than losing our Billy, that's to be sure.

But we weathered the times in spite of our tears
And were a loving family for all those years.

So please search your hearts and try to discover
What have I done that you don't want your Mother?

What pain have I caused that I should atone?
Please tell me why you've left me alone.

Why is my heart shattered and so unexpected?
I never left you — you were not neglected.

My body is sick — my heart in sorrow.
I have very few years left to borrow.

I Pray to God He'll show you the way
And we'll be together again some day.

Maurine D. Pierson

Best Friends

  A best friend is something that not all people get to
experience in life. Some take advantage of it, others don't know
it's there, and some people just don't care.
  But with me, I was lucky enough to have a best friend that
cared. She was a friend that I could talk to, laugh with, cry
with, share my secrets with, and never once did I ever wonder if
my secret would get out, because I could trust her with all my
heart. She is very special to me because I could always be
myself when I was around her. I never had to worry about whether
I was good enough for her or if I was too good for her. She took
my friendship for who I was, and not for what I was or what I had.
I cherish her friendship more than anything in the world
and would never do anything to hurt her, or our friendship.
We've had a lot of good times together, with a lot more to come.
But we've also had our bad times together, some were sad, and
others were angry times, but no matter what they were, we always
managed to get through them together.
  And if you ask me, you can't get a better best friend then
the one I've got right now!

Holli Beckwith

Tortured Souls

A silent partner shares my home
He, imprisoned, yet I may roam.
I pay the rent and all the rest
He lives for free, 'twould seem the best.
He watches all I do or say
Tho I know not in his mind what lay.
And tho he's always in his place
I must over and again search out his face.
What crime could wreak such dark despair
And cast him infinitely in his lair?
Each time I search there seems no trace
Of his agonized, misshapen face.
But always when I think he's left
My eyes find his, staring, tortured, bereft.
Mine's not the only place he shares
Your homes, too, contain his stares.
Peer closer, closer, if you could
He hides within your paneling wood!
The tortured, agonized soul in the paneling.

Susan Davis

Time And Faith

You want, you ask, and you wish and wait,
You wait for a key to open this certain gate,
You get impatient and feel it's the end,
But you know, God does not pretend.
It may take time and time again.
When you least expect is when he comes in,
Having faith always in your heart and soul,
You will go on waiting and waiting,
With out knowing you are.
Yet these gifts you ask seem so far,
It was Time And Faith, so have no fear,
Yet all along, they were near.
You suddenly feel like you have a key in your hand.
You wanted, you wished, you asked, and you waited,
For all the things God has created.
Time wend by, to you maybe slow,
But now you feel a glow.
The key is in your hand,
So open the gate,
God has given you Time And Faith.

Jane Schaubert

Mother

Pitter patter
Your little feet go.
Exploring your world
as you grow.

Life from life
Your heart beats in time
Entering this plane.
From my body. Mine.

You grew inside me
Land I shall never forget
The love and fulfillment
I felt when we met.

Too fast the time does pass.
Growing so quickly; you and your brother.
You will never understand my love
for you.

Until your child calls you "Mother"

Tracy Elizabeth Robison

The Lonely Scribe

Why did you watch her walk out the door?
The Quill, the Parchment...remembrance of scribes of past days
Gone from our haven, captured on the seeds of dandelions,
They float, toward the setting sun.

When the body is merely a conception, the heart is an angel.
Years has passed, and you just watch hers fly where angel's sing.
You condemn her celestial dove,
Because it did not want to follow your wings.

Her words flow to the paper, paint on a canvass.
The smiles, the tears, the result of her scrawl.
The praise and fame, a promise kept by the angel city.
But you still aren't there, to watch her blow the muses a kiss.

Silver and gold tilt her persona.
Yet shadows inhabit her soul.
Her waters run thick, spanning the land.
Yet her blood leaves two empty seats, in the front row.

In the field's of dream's she's safely on third.
Needing your hands to guide her to home.
The light's the camera's...her's to own.
Yet, on a one man's team..."action" is nothing more than a word.

Jennifer Dlugos

Storm Clouds Are Gathering

Storm clouds are gathering, in the Eastern Sky,
The tides of life are rising high.

Warning signs are everywhere, no one at all seems to care.

This world is moving oh! So fast, you can see, it cannot last!

Judgement Day is soon to come upon our land,
We have almost played our last hand.

There is an answer, it is our Blessed Savior,
So let's all change our wicked behavior.

Please open up your heart and let Jesus Christ come in,
Without him you cannot win.

Storm clouds are gathering, in the Eastern sky,
The tides of life are rising high.

Why! Oh Why! Can't they see,
You will hear them cry, this cannot be!

They all think the world will last forever,
But there surely will be a hereafter.

Father God open up their eyes, so they will not be passed on by.
What is that, I just heard!
Oh my God! The last trumpet has just sounded!
There is, no more time!!!

Barbara J. Weeks

Time At Hand

For this time to end my heart is yearning
In my soul sweet freedom burning
As their screams, dreams,
and sometimes a yell shatter the
night in my private hell.
These wall like tombs are filled
with noise.
It's cleansing time for lock-out Boys
I wait for the sun to rise from the east.
Surrounded by wire, caged up like a beast.
As we leave our loved one's at a sharp pencils end.
If you're lucky in Prison you may make a friend.
I'm not a poet or trying to rhyme, just
another victim of Old Father Time.

Kenneth R. Friend

Danny's Gift

Dearest Darling:
A gift for you this Christmas day are words of affection sent your way. We met at Zak's on a cold and wintery night two hearts lonely, wanting to be healed. I wanted you so badly, I was aching inside. I had to leave you there to save myself from something I would regret. I wanted to get to know you even though I felt comfortable in your arms. My desire for you was building until I thought I would burst! At last we were together oh what bliss! Ups downs, ins and outs that's what life is all about.

You moved in after much discussion and thought, we took U.S. air, landed in Miami, boarded the ship fantasy. We laughed, we cried, we held each other tight. Ups downs ins and outs that's what life is all about. Summer's here what blast. Here comes fall so beautiful aren't we all. Met your family, love them all. Pick those apples, let's not fall. Surprise happy birthday baby! Ups downs, ins and outs that was what our life was all about!
  Merry Christmas Love Always!

Bobbie J. Schliecker

Wise Man's Prayer

Do not scorn my ignorance
For I am a simple man
And know little of life's meaning.
My knowledge consists of that taught
To me by mortal man.
By showing my ignorance in your presence
I ask for your help in finding
The truth in this life.
My hope is that you will guide me
In the direction of knowledge
And in the meaning of love.

Charles A. Augur

Petey My Pekingese

Petey, Petey, he's my sweetie.
My stubby, stocky, roly poly tweetie.
He likes to be cuddled and rubbed and scratched
He tumbles right over, such an easy catch.
He likes to be talked to in a tiny baby voice
Because Petey, Petey he don't like alotta noise.
He likes to lick, he'll lick you're ears, nose and feet.
He likes peas and asparagus so much better than meat.
Sweet potatoes, cornbread, green beans he'll eat,
In fact he thinks any people food is a treat.
Eggs in the morning and icecream at night
He guards his vittles like he's gonna fight
Until "Willy" comes over and wants a bite
Then he rolls over, now thats quite a sight.
Petey, Petey, my man's just too sweet
Oh how I love to hear his little heart beat.
And yea I get a kick outta watchin' him eat
That's because I sorta, kinda think he's neat.

Cheryl Ann Ballinger

Our Precious Heritage: The Elderly

What do you think of old persons,
The ones so loving and sweet?
Are your feelings for them kind and tender?
Is caring for them a real treat?
   Of course, this response is expected,
   For "love begets love" we are told.
   It's easy to love and to cherish
   When old folks are cast in this mold.

But, what do you think of the others,
The old folks who grumble and stew?
The ones who seem to find pleasure
In making life harder for you?
   Do you seek to avoid all close contact,
   Remaining "afar" if you can?
   Or is your heart open, receptive
   To a lonely old woman or man?

The aged have worries and troubles;
They long for a loving touch, too.
Their bodily frailties distress them.
Come, let their comfort be You!

Irma Browne Jewell

Untitled

Constant rain falling on our head
Stumbling down the ancient path we've been led
By a dying generation of corruption
Relying on us for moral construction
Sleet sometimes taking a breath
Leaving us to mourn over an innocent death
Our race living in eternal struggle
Paying for our ancestors unrestricted juggle
of life and death.

Suzanne Poole

Death Walks After Sunset

The day was done the dawn was gone all things laid to rest,
Except which that the night had spawned they know their dwellings best.

The specter moved in eerie silence 'tween the oak trees still,
Doing which in the night that in the day it could not fulfill.

Bone-white hands move through the shadows cutting them like knives, and the creatures deathly quiet now as though it were taking their lives.

But their lives are not what it yearns for as it moves through the shadows so black, all it asks is to see the sunset once more and for its life to be given back.

It reached the river where it used to walk in daytime with its love,
But now it stands alone in darkness beneath the stars above.

The stars they use to shine for it but now they remind it of day,
How could something a few hours off seem so far away.

Oh! How it weeps for the days and the sunsets it's never seen,
Now the things it took for granted can be with it only in dreams.

Look fast! The dawn approaches! It must retreat with the night,
For however much it longs to see the sun it can't exist in a world with light.

And there it goes flying now into the heart of the moon,
But don't you fear or fret for it for night is coming soon.

Jason C. Ketcham

Untitled

To green eyes,
It's a dismal August day,
Her sunshine hidden in clouds of gray,

Our souls are crushed and weeping,
For the beauty who lie sleeping,

The rain of tears have arrived,
Her sunshine we pray survives,

So be for warned, we will weather the storm,
For the beauty who lies sleeping.

   Just me.

Leigh Ramsdell

Pour La Liberte

In times like this, no need to call, the cherished lives we're living,
We have from those who fought before, that Earth be more like Heaven.

We have to fight, **we choose** it so, this world is full of fears.
Without us no one will live safe, **we have** to stop the tears.

Gypsy, Jewish, parachutist, helpless they must slay,
We'll **never** understand just why, they've made our world this way.

Our country sent a husband loved, a father, son or brother,
And each kept free ten thousand souls, and freed ten thousand other.

As history repeats itself, they do not fight alone,
For each who fight, for each we lose, a million pray at home.

A nation young by history's count, needs heroes now and past,
That won't accept man's evil deeds...that liberty won't last.

Don't let us forget!
David L. Carlson

To Thee! I Give You Me

I give you my eyes, that you might see
I give you my tongue, that you might speak
I give you my hands, that you might feel
I give you my ears, that you might hear
To Thee, I Give You Me.

I give you the sunshine, and the rain drops
I give you the moon, and the stars too
I give you all my days, and my nights
I give you all of me, it seems so right
To Thee, I Give You Me.

I give you my heart, with a smile
I give you my joy, and my pains
I give you my mind, and my soul
I give you my everything
To Thee, I Give You Me.

I have no money, that I might give
But I do give, Love, Peace, and Happiness for many years.

To Thee, I Give You Me!
Patricia A. Little

My Cat

She is blacker than the darkness of night
Yet brighter than the morning light

Her blanket of fur is soft as a pillow
As she lays there like a weeping willow

Her cry is weak as if distant
It's her way of being cold and resistant

She's loveable only when in the mood
Especially when it's time for her food
M. J. Motta

Loneliness

One rainy day
The rivers overflowing
I hear a
Cry
Loud And Long
Down under the ocean
In the water so deep.
A baby swimming there alone
In a net
Away from its family
Both alone and sad, wondering what next.
Suddenly the small animal
Snapped up by fishermen.
The poor big baby taken to a tank
Trapped in there
Alone for much, so long.
Her hears his family calling to his tank...
Separated from ocean to tank.
With no fear he jumps the wall.
Back with his family.
Daniel Despot

Waxed Emotions

Cold, very little attention paid,
as it sits on the table yearning
hoping it will feel the sensation of burning;
Candlestick, patience is a virtue.

Hot, and always being watched,
the thought had never been conceived
that it might want to be relieved;
Candlestick, patience is a virtue.
Tara Onder

Untitled

In that picture perfect place
Where the sky is a soft green pillow,
  holding the still nodding head of the sun
And the stars, blinking in the delicate silence,
  faintly illuminate the gently breathing bosom of the earth below,
Time is at a standstill.
  In limbo.
    Pausing.
      Waiting for that elusive moment.
When the sighs become whispers then rustles
When the watercolor landscapes
became infused with brighter color and sound
When the distant hum of life gathers into an audible roar
  and dawn bows gracefully to the arrival of the day.
Only then does its brief reverie end
  and its inevitable journey begin anew.
tjaden

You Mean So Much To Me

You mean so much to me,
more than words can say.

You're always thought of,
every minute of the day.

You seem to always lift my spirits,
when I am feeling down.

You can comfort me, give me a smile,
and take away a frown.

You always seem to do things right,
in everything you do.

You make me feel so special,
that's something I thought no one could do.

So I am sending you this message,
to tell you how I feel.

I am letting my guard down,
and tearing open the seal.

I'm opening my heart up to you,
and only you.

In hopes that you love me,
the way I love you!
Diana Henderson

Horror of the Heart

  People you love growing apart
breaking one another's heart.
  Seeing them with tears in their eyes
and knowing you can do nothing to stop their cries.
  Then thinking back across the years
reliving all the hurt and tears.
  I told my heart not to fall
but it went ahead on the first call
me and the horror of my heart
  Is something that will never part
so when I see heartache coming
  I turn around and just start running
it's a really good piece of advice
  If you don't want your heart broken twice.
Melissa Rinehart

461

To the Memory of Tree's

One by one, they are slaughtered, giants in their time,
beautifully flowing gently in the breeze, protecting all
the small from mother nature, and the big from heavy rains,
Housing cures for many illnesses yet unknown to man today,
and sing their whispering song's all throughout the day.
The small one's believed only by themselves to be
the smartest in the world, come now to steal the life
of yet a dozen more gentle giant's souls.
Amazing, something that has survived all the tests of time,
has seen so many worldly changes, and has never
once moved from its rightful place,
must now be raped and slaughtered, all for what man,
a simple creature, calls progress.

Jamie Dillon Phillips

Who Will Cry for the Indians?

Who will cry for the Indians?
  How many times have treaties been broken.
Who will cry for the Indians?
  A proud race once so strong.
Who will cry for the Indians?
  A people whose once roamed free.
Who will cry for the Indians?
  A people who only took what they needed.
Who will cry for the Indians?
  A people who's blood runs through my veins.
Who will cry for the Indians?
  I shall cry for the Indians.

Dorothy May Gilliam Powell

My Promise to You

A few short years ago you came into my life,
And a few short months from now we will be husband and wife.
You came from out of nowhere and showed me how to live,
You showed me how to laugh and love, and especially how to give.
As long as you are in my life, my heart will never grow cold,
And I will be forever yours, to have and to hold.

Soon we will pledge our vows and join our lives together,
And I promise you this day that my pledge is forever.
As I look back at all the things we've shared,
I see how many different ways our love has been declared.
I love you now, always and forever,
And I thank the Lord for bringing us together.

Jody Leigh Swing

Mom

I don't think there will ever be
Anything as precious as my mom to me.
Tender, loving, thoughtful, and kind,
Whether here or there, she's always on my mind.

From the day I was born, she's always been around.
Smiling face, soft words, picking my heart from the rebound
When I am upset and feeling blue,
I go to mom, she always knows just what to do.

When life's tolls take me by surprise,
She gives me encouragement and lot's of "I love you"
The clouds roll back, sunshine sublime.
This much I know mom's love is always true.

And should a day come to an end,
And a beautiful sunset I can see.
I lay me down to sleep on bended knee,
Always thanking my God for giving my mom to me.

Priscilla S. Richards

The Songbird's Thrust

Songbirds sing and they can fly.
So what remains for you and I?

To hold things dear, to think and weep.
To love and hold the things we keep.

To wish and cry, to garner trust.
To set things right before we're dust.

We can soar and fly and sing
Encouraged mightily by our dreams.
But we can stumble, fall and scream
Without support of nature's wings.

What holds us true and give us flight
Is found in vision, sealed in sight.

For though we lack the songbird's grace,
Our wings touch souls in the human race.

So we set our sights just as high
And see our dreams soar through the sky.
For what the songbird can obtain,
Remains the same for you and I.

Carol Hanrahan

Open Eyes

Visions of silence "Find"
Pollution of once vivid minds
While Colors of Black and White
Seem to have closed our eyes.

And, violence meets forgotten "Peace"
At a line between Life and Death.
If we continue to ignore the truth
We'll soon have nothing left.

So where does the answer lie?
Possibly before our eyes.
Don't just Read the Words
Look at what is inside.

Because many answer come from "Within."
It just takes a little time,
Faith and Patience are valuable tools
In the Survival of Mankind.

So believe in "Yourself"
And believe in me, we are brothers and sisters the same.
It makes no sense, to try so hard
Just to give fault a name.

Darren Gage

Shattered Being

Images of vanquished existence hover in gardens,
breathing life unended alone,
bitter smells and sweetened dreams escape me,
water crashes down my silhouette framing feelings unknown.

Hear the drumming, pounding rhythm tap tap silence,
was I there?
Clouded judgments handed down harshly, silent whispers
shadow hearts. Thy shall kneel in protest before defeat
seeing through blind eyes changes unmade living in order,
existence shadowed in disbelief.

Ordered to live riotous, cohabit a shell, undaunted memories
escape in the wind strained and filtered to bleed. Nurture
the seed, growth catapulted sustained eternal, warmed by
untruths such evil unseen.

Paths not taken, fools will lead, mirrors are broken fall
away, fall away shattered being.

Sandra Ann Martinez

A Right Turn

Late at night, shadows dance and flutter in the wind
The flickering of my car light dancing off the trees
The hum of the engine, ever present
Up ahead an intersection
A decision I must make
Turn left, right or go straight?
I usually go straight, sometimes left, but never right
But tonight is different, I go right
Why I do not know
This right turn will change my life
A lady waits, her name is Nancy
I don't know these things as I make this turn
The Lord knows though
He guides my every move
The encounter is short, but feelings flow
The Lord has worked his special magic
He has brought two people together
Later they will become man and wife
Thank you Lord, for that right turn.

Nancy K. Giles

Cycles of Life

The rising sun peaks up over the graceful slopes.
A foggy mist blankets the secret valleys,
And the seduction of a fresh Spring day lies before us.

The creatures of flight ring out with song,
Flitting from tree to budding tree.
Floating on the heated breeze,
Pollen scatters matching flower to blossom.
Refreshed with a drink of that which is natural,
A summer day drifts in and out of our imagination.

The joy of the rains dance in celebration
Of the dripping bodies and branches.
While underground streams thrust
Toward a release at the mouth of the sea,
And the agile activity of a fall day stirs in the winds we breath.

The snow packed surface holds all numb, frigid and safe.
Dormant and distanced, life waits to be reborn,
And so this winter void remains a barrier
Between mere existence and life.

Dorothy T. Dichter

Philadelphia Man

Homeless man on hot steel grates.
Hot steam gurgling forth.
Hoping, wishing to help him.
But I can't, I just can't help him.
What about my business status?
Give him some food, that is all I've got left.
His face lights up like a Christmas tree with decorations.
I wish desperately that I could help him more.
Happy, I helped him out but wished I had that miserable life instead of him.
But as I turn around, to go back to the daily grind; I see him smile and walk away and hear him yell, "God bless you."

As I walk away I see another man wanting money. I wonder what I should do.....

Joseph Mitrani

God

God is always there,
To listen to your prayers.
He will never leave you,
No matter what you say or do.
He helps the poor and the sick,
If you have faith, he'll do it quick.
He treats you with tender care,
And He is so quite fair.
You can talk to Him when you're sad,
He'll make you feel glad.
Just pray to Him everyday,
And tell Him whatever you want to say.
Ask Him to push you forward when you're afraid to do right,
God is always with you, answer with your might.
Pray with your kindness and love,
These virtues come from above.
If you want to go to heaven,
Be honest and true,
Because you don't know what could happen,
God might take you.

Rose Tinimbang

Sweet Goodbye

Here today, gone tomorrow,
I sit here with great sorrow,
I laugh for you,
But will always be a little blue,
When I see a smile
I'll think of you all the while,
Lots of moons will pass,
But I'll always think of you in the past,
Someday we'll meet in the heavens above,
Don't worry you'll always have my love,
I lay here and cry for you in my sleep,
But your unconditional love I will keep,
Now we lay you down to rest,
And I'll always do my best.

Christine Baker

A Reflection About My Daughters

All three are beautiful, slim and tall,
Their early years I often recall;
Three little cherubs all glowing with life,
I prayed they'd never be filled with strife;

And now they're grown, my lovely three;
They're intelligent, happy and sublimely free
To explore life's wonders, thrills and sorrows;
I pray God is with them each tomorrow
In their quest for the joy of living,
The joy of loving and forgiving;

For my precious daughters I pen this rhyme
To reflect my constant love for all time,
To exhort each to seek from life its best,
And to all three my endless love I bequest.

Sue Ferguson

Still, Life

This is now the restive Winter's gray.
One must hold a candle up to the day
To see what fortunes Fate did belie.
Daylight dances above the sky;
But on this Earth in Winter's shade
No prismatic moments of light were made
But one...And I have seen
That moment melt into the vapors of a dream.

Mark Stokes

Deep Waters

The deep waters calleth for the deep, the deep calleth for the
depth my love calleth for your heart, my heart calleth for your love.
I was living across the ocean and felt your notion to be love and
to give love, having the same desires set up the stages for our
spirits to meet until we could see each others beautiful faces.
To connect with the person who you already know is out there
slowly gravitation to your thinking, living, feeling, giving,
being, breathing, praying, hoping my deed is a sense of
accomplishment.
As a fountain flows down, my heart pulls toward you not taking for
granted the gravity that brought us together. I will always,
always be with you, for our spirits are forever and our physical
life is to short not knowing if we will see each other again.
Although, others will try to partake of our love, we must stay in
touch with the time and energy it took for us to look in each
others eyes kissing, hugging, loving, touching and warmth
that happen the very day we met. Rivers are moving waters, our
blood is forever bleeding as we entered into covenant with one
another.

Dale Ihedilionye

Mama, We Miss Those Days

Mama, how we miss the days
Of children's pranks and childhood ways.
When we worked from dawn to night
And still could play with all our might.

Tho' poor as church mice we were then,
We had surprise now and again.
When ice cream just plain cost too much,
Then snow ice cream was mama's touch.

Food color and some sugar in it
And we had ice cream in just a minute!
Did the children need new clothes?
Patterns cut from paper rose!

Bread and biscuits, dumplings, too
Pies and roasts to name a few,
Were wonders then and still are now!
Yes, we still wonder where and how.

You found the time and energy,
To show your love so selflessly . . . Mama, Mama, we miss the days
You showed your love so many ways . . .

Happy Birthday, Mom — I appreciate all that You have done for me!!
James L. Metcalf

Snow

The most beautiful time of winter is
when snow flakes fall so gently to the ground.
These white soft crystals floating through
the air landing oh so softly to the ground,
making a blanket of beautiful white power.
The sun light flickers off the snow making
the most beautiful sight around, creating a
soft white play ground making all the
adults wishing to children again and playing
in the snow, like the children that are so
much around.
The silky white power will gently melt
into the ground until once again we will
wait until this magical white power
floats gently to the ground.

Nolan S. Smith

A Creative Stroke

Someone once said to me
that all the great books have been written.
Well then, obviously, from Eve's apple,
he has never bitten.

That kind of knowledge
is like a privilege
as genuses and the affected too,
learn to encounter poise
as they pursue.

As long as Newton and Pound
continue to inspire young minds and hearts,
So too will the freshness of creativity
always remain our best proclivity.

Joyce A. Bartel

Starting Over?

A time that intimates
pain-loneliness-fear-solitude.

A time that suggests
mistakes-failure-reorganization-strategy.

Why are these the thoughts that emerge
during this truly auspicious moment?

Why is this precious time construed as
starting over?

Why not-progressing-evolving
learning-opening up your heart,
making room for better,
Being Alive!!

So
When the dust settles and
the choices are made
What will it be?

Starting over
or innocently moving forward!

Louis J. Marchetti

From the Front Lines

It was the night before Xmas and all through our tent,
Was the odor of fuel oil, the stove pipe was bent.
The weary GIs were passed out in their beds,
And visions of Geisha girls danced in their heads.
When up on the ridge line there rose such a clatter,
A Chinese machine gun had started to chatter.

I rushed to my rifle and threw back the bolt,
The rest of my tent mates awoke with a jolt.
Outside we could hear the platoon sergeant Kelly,
A hard little man with a little pot belly.
Come Yancey, come Clancey, come Connors and Watson!
Up Miller, up Shiller, up Baker and Dodson!
We tumbled outside in a swirl of confusion,
So cold that each man could have used a transfusion.

Get up on that hill top and silence that Red
And don't come back till you're sure that he's dead.
Then putting his thumb up in front of his nose,
Sergeant Kelly took leave of us shivering Joes.
But we all heard him say in a voice soft and light:
"Merry Christmas to all . . . may you live through the night!"

P.F.C. Joseph Florian Wolski

Shifting Down the Highway

I've been shifting down the highway, running from the law,
you know I've got to go now, there is no time to stall,
the ladies will be home soon, you know I can't be late,
so I'll make double time, and maybe make my play,
stay away from jail house, is what I am trying to do,
if or when I lose the law, I'll make sweet love to you!
I am getting tired of all this trouble and just running around,
about time I start to settle down.
I've been shifting down the highway, running from the law,
you know I've got to go now, there is no time to stall,
I've been shifting down the highway, running from the law,
I try to get them off my tail, well, I don't need them no more,
people say I am always gone, and never feeling down,
someday I'll just blow their mind, and blast, blast right through
the town.
I live in the town, I never go by the lawman's home,
cause they all know my body, and my face has got well known,
I've been shifting down the highway, running from the law,
you know I've got to go now, there is no time to stall!

David Arthur Bradvica

Through A Little Boy's Eyes

Through a little boy's eyes I see things
coming at me, I don't understand.

I see someone standing before me saying,
your father, no I'm not that man.

When my mother tells me he is my father,
and he lives in our house every day.

Who is this man who would lock me in a closet,
every time my mother would go away?

Through a little boy's eyes I see fear on my face
when I wake up cold late at night.

Yet when I go to school and hear the kids
talking about my father, I end up in a fight.

What does this mean, I would protect someone
who says he loves me not?

Through a little boy's eyes I see myself confused,
my life being tied in a knot.

I guess I should end this now,
because I'm getting kinda sad.

Maybe it's because all the memories
of my youth I have are, all bad.

Carl F. Brown

The Other Side

Behind the clouds in the day,
is the sky still blue?
Or does this blue that is seen,
hold just partially true?
A blanket of clouds for hiding,
hiding something I thought I knew.
Awakened from some dream,
a false picture I forcedly drew.
Days passed by and further by,
questioning a familiar, outside and through.
My knowing may be so unknowing,
I thought over once, maybe two.
A voice brought on my awakening,
on the inside my pain only grew.
My feelings for the precious sky have changed,
but there is nothing seeming worthwhile to do.
Behind the clouds in the day,
the sky is not always blue.

Steve Kamm

Young Black Woman

It seems so easy when you are in you fathers arms,
so powerful and strong, yet so warm..
as you grow with your Beautiful Brown skin.
That is when life really begins,
you meet a man and you stand by his side,
he does you wrong no matter what.
You have to stay strong,
for you and the baby which I have left behind
for another Black Woman I have yet to find,
this is true, but I know it's not fair
to the young black woman left standing there.
Then you meet a man who really does love you
but you have been hurt so much you just don't
know what to do, so you act old and he goes away,
then you sit down and think,
I wonder if he was the one
it's too late now, that day's done
my heart goes out to the Young Black Woman,
stay strong!!
Without you we cannot carry on.

William Prude

Returning Woman

I am returning from the conjugal home
the nuptial bed, the numerous confinements
from raising my children
baby-sitting the grandchildren
I am returning from the ancestral ground
in visitation with the ancients
I communed with my father
my tears watered the mounds
beneath which my young ones repose
denied the privilege of nurturing
I can no longer suckle nor cuddle
their stiff bodies feel warm in my arms still
I am returning from bringing
fresh water to the thirsty grounds
I am returning with fuel to keep the embers ablaze
the cold Harmattan shall not seep into our bones
I am returning to the marriage feasts of my daughters
from sending my sons off to war
I am returning to the tree of knowledge,
from the fountain of wisdom and love

Adelaide Sackeyfio

The Man I Saw

The man I saw
Once I seen him I wanted to fall
His eyes so blue that's when I knew I tasted love
His voice so deep
I knew he's the one to keep

The man I saw
I knew I wanted to be around
He wouldn't be the one to knock ya to the ground
I thought I was in love to strong
But I was wrong
We together were great
For there would be no hate

The man I saw
For there would be no flaw
I loved him so much
If only the man I saw
I could touch

Amanda Franklin

She's a Little Girl

She's a little girl. As innocent as a cool summer breeze.

Skipping, laughing, living life.
Next to her a man, as tall as the trees. So wise, so full of
everything that is good.
Together they are best friends; long walks, comfortable naps,
inseparable.
Games, jokes, laughter, happiness. Life couldn't be better.

She's a little girl. As innocent as a cool summer breeze.

No longer skipping and laughing
Next to her a shadow. A shadow of a great man that once was.
Where did the happiness go? Why? A life taken from her.

There she is...a little girl. Scared, confused, lost.
Wondering, where is that man? A man as tall as the trees.
No more long walks. No more comfortable naps.
Where did the games, jokes and happiness go? Why?
How could someone take her best friend away?

She's a little girl. As innocent as a cool summer breeze.

Crying out "Bomp, where are you?"
Years go by. Troubled times hit hard. Mistakes are many.
Wrong roads taken. Scared and confused . . . yet still . . .

She's a little girl. As innocent as a cool summer breeze.

I love you Bomp.

Becky Hartmann

Duck

An untold story
The unsleeping water
Dancing in the sweet perfume
Salt soaked long brown hair
comforting my baked back
a past love finally touches me again
sandy fire showers the quiet waves
a clear line where the ocean meets the sky
wet beer tasting kisses upon the wooden steps
time brings me to leave this healing paradise tomorrow
pretty dress shapes the long tanned body
the beauty of it all penetrates my soul, body, and mind
alone I sit upon this yellow towel in perfect solitude and content
The soft music and the sea's voice illuminate the friendly sun's space
Fine poetry and love surfs in the fresh summer air
large pelicans hover together above a blue choppy surface
searching for life
only tears of happiness could fall upon my face in such a place

Maia Cargas

The Eye of the Beholder

In our eyes we see such beauty that
God has given us. A portrait of our
heavenly father as He counsels us with
love. It's not an earthly love
    the unperfected love we share.
It's agape love. "Love beyond compare."
We are created in His image oh! The
beauty to behold, counseling us with a
cloak of righteousness teaching us of
His love. He looks and sees every broken
heart and hears our humble cries. He
sees us through the eyes of love and through
our faults chastens us. This my friend,
is a picture of God's perfect love.
"We are the apple of His eye
He is the keeper of our souls
To trust in Him, to praise Him too
He will then pardon you."

Tina M. Ray

I Versus Time

Coming and going gets faster as time passes by.
Quiet moments becoming harder to find.
Everyone so busy pursuing dreams undefined.

Page me, Dial my Cellular, mark me on your Calendar,
Too many events, Impossible to remember.

Impulses vying for space on your "short term"
Information so vast, no way can you learn,
to cope with the changing lifestyles we've earned.

As Technological Communications continue to advance,
We are lured by the science in an electronic trance.

Robbing us of opportunities to face - to - face communicate
While living in Autonomy, grasping at life's Golden Dream,
Laboring, Losing site of reality.
This our Dismal fate.

But Wait! Is It Too Late!
Take a moment, Make a moment.

For the most important things in life
are probably the things most of us have been leaving behind,
As we've proceeded in our personal race against time.

Judy A. Harris

Perfect Love

Perfect Love is from the heart
not from how well we do things
or don't do things.

Perfect Love is comfort, understanding
not just listening. Being there for
one another, unconditionally.

Perfect Love is touching, embracing
not running away, nor being cold hearted.

The Most Perfect Love is you, for being you
this will always be in my heart
To You; I Love You Perfect.

Lee-Ann C. Follansbee-Uva

Nature Praises God

Fall; tree leaves are falling, because they are crying.
Their branches still reaches out in praise to their creator.
Though naked an strip, still they stand tall and straight.

Then comes winter with its blizzards, sleet, snow and ice.
But still they stand tall in praise to their creator.

Some branches are bent, because of the icy storm. But still
they stand tall in anticipation. They know their creator
will reverence their praise.

Then Spring cometh, their fruit began to appear, because
they were rooted in praise to their creator.

Not once did he leave them, his present always in their mist.
Showing them, although they were naked and bare, he always
sees them green and flourished. That is why the Evergreen
stand tall and green through out their mist.

When summer come, they are fully dressed. Still praising
their creator with leaves swinging in the breeze.

The hot sun gives them warmth, letting them know, the ice,
snow, sleet and winter storms were but for a moment.

So the tears of their falling leaves, only gave way for
a greater testimony.

Mary B. Rice

The Cross

Love is blooming, ever blooming.
On a hill beyond the sea.
It's the place I found my Saviour.
On the hill called Calvary.

Oh, My God, My loving Saviour.
Bestow thy mercy upon me.
Should be I hanging on the cross.
At the top of Calvary.

Lord you took my sins upon you.
You hang on the cross, when you knew no sin.
But, I know if you had to choose,
You would do it all over again.

Thank you God for your love and mercy.
For a sinner such as I.
You shed your precious blood on Calvary.
So that I would not have to die.

Yes, The Old Rugged Cross makes a difference
In your life and mine.
Yes, The Old Rugged Cross makes a difference
Now and for all time.

Glenda F. Smith

In Honor of Gulf War Veterans

In 1990, when Saddam Hussein invaded Kuwait,
For the "Mother of all Battles", he had not long to wait.

President Bush asked the U.S. Military to perform
An operation, eventually called "Desert storm".

In retaliation Saddam fired scuds, burned oil wells
And stored weapons containing biologicals and chemicals.

About these biological and chemical weapons, our government knew.
However to the troops, our government is not being true.

Troops are sick, dying, or have already died from the effects.
Their babies are being born with serious birth defects.

The troops the government sent into this fight
Are in serious distress, but does anyone hear their plight?

These troops, did their duty when called upon.
Not they are ignored by the government and pentagon.

In typical fashion, as always, it is the governments game
To lie, deny and cover up, but never take any responsibility or blame.

It is now time for these gallant and dedicated troops to be repaid.
To end their pain and suffering with all important medical aid.

It is also time for congress to sit down and enact legislation
In order to prevent ever happening again, this kind of situation.

Doug & Mary Knoell

Night

The stalking night
My fear
A fear that only darkness can hold
With no regret, no remorse, no fail

A fear of becoming one with the night
Never a bright day to awaken my eyes
Never a glorious shaft of sun to warm my cold heart
Never a glimpse of the day that held me so close, so tight
Keeping me sheltered yet free

Nothing but the fear of being part of the darkness for eternity
Nothing but the hollow pain of hearing my empty screams
Echoing through the hell
That is called
Night.

Tom J. Gates

Invasive Thoughts

A state of confusion . . .
And I am in my own world
Not quite knowing what to expect . . .
A familiar face . . .
Yet I know not how to respond

A simpler mind is yet to be found
And yet the complexity of my thoughts border insanity
Four in the morning
And rest is driven away by invasive thoughts

Once akin with your spirit . . .
We were as one . . . in sync in our minds
Conversations converging into depths usually unspoken of
And now there is a chasm . . . Only crossed by mutual understanding

Mistakes paid for daily . . .
And every visit brings more uncertainty
Is there still a sense of desire in your eyes?
Can it match the intensity of my own gaze!
And the decision is mine — Reveal the soul or await the sorrow

Dara E. Brown

My Manner of Escape

I row,
Abandoning what was a sheltered asylum
for my misguided soul
turned spiteful.
The grasses become choppy,
spilling into my lap —
the whispers whisper louder,
tangling my mane.
Pulsing, burning,
raw displeasure creeps upon my shoulders,
neck,
back.
But I row
to elude
The Reality.

Sharon Kay Gorsline

Deep In the Night

Deep in the night, as the moon raises from a far, I searched the sky thoroughly, for the first evening star. I was told as a child to wish then in silence, and it would be delivered to God, who would then give His guidance.

Deep in the night, as the hours passed on, the screams in the city could be heard until dawn, by the people's who's lives were about to end, from the vicious slayings of both women and men.

Deep in the night, on streets dark and cold, shadows are seen lurking by people unknown, who are too scared to say anything, so they just hurry on home.

Deep in the night, where there gather large crowds, anger is quick, but forgiveness is not allowed. People say things whether they mean it or not, it just seems to blare out because tempers grow hot.

Deep in the night, doesn't matter what season, the bad side of people appear without reason. With an indifferent heart, very cold and calculating, they'll cease someone's life without hesitating.

Deep in the night, close to dawn, there's a great silence, as if everyone had received some of God's divine guidance. But it's just an illusion in the bright daylight, for all hell will break out, once again at twilight.

Paul Martin Redmond Jr.

Gone Too Soon

A candle burns in a window
Casting out a sparkling glow
A room is empty but for Tigger and Winnie the pooh
Without him what will they do
A wreath hangs on a door
A reminder he will not be home anymore
A picture stares out from a frame
Will he become a face without a name
His mother tries hard not to cry
She cannot bring herself to say goodbye
To this boy full of wonder and joy yet so meek
She gently bends and kisses him lightly on the cheek
With eyes as bright as the summer moon
She questions why he had to leave so soon
His life had but just begun
His race he had not yet run
She sits alone upon his bed
As thoughts of him run through her head
Looking out at the winter moon
She realizes that he is gone too soon.

Martin T. Boyd

Unavoidable Struggle

The Christian heart is peaceful like the still of the night
It calmly and patiently waits for the break of daylight
But even the night is upset by the threat of harsh conditions
And so must the Christian Heart prepare for all missions.

The most overwhelming mission the Christian Heart must face
Is that battle with its arch enemies; Jealousy and Hate
There are no judges; no pinfalls; no knock outs
The winner is determined without opening a mouth.

Jealousy and Hate look strong with the odds in their favor
They see a lone Christian Heart and mouths start to savor
Little do they know the Christian Heart is well-versed
And knows the best defense is to never strike first.

And now, this confrontation erupts like a fire from a spark
Immediately Jealousy and Hate smother the Christian Heart.
The Christian Heart is staggered but still has a chance
Because behind it at all times is Strength and Endurance.

Now, with 3 against 2, the Christian Heart explodes
And, suddenly, this battle is just another rumor to be told.
The Christian Heart prevails because of a very strong belief
That with Strength and Endurance, it will never face defeat.

D. Lawrence Sanders

What Went Wrong

We've lost some feelings, that were so true
You for me and I for you
The times we've shared, will always last
We'll think of times in memories past
We've hurt each other without intent
We've both said things, we never meant
The love you gave, I could never share
The love I felt, I could not compare
You deserve more then I can give
I hope you find happiness, and truly live
My heart will be lonely for years to come
I'll look back on the laughter and the fun
I can't replace all the times that we had
The good was good, that never went bad
My heart and soul, were faithful and true
I thank God, for having shared time with you
Please remember the good side of me
The side you dealt with, was never meant to be

Maurice A. Routier

Me and My Mother

She hugs me when I cry,
To show me that she cares,
She smiles when I go by.
I listen when she talks,
With confidence and trust,
I admire her as she walks.
Me and my mother my mother and I
She talks to me and gives me advice,
She knows things about me,
Like my favorite meal is rice.
I know I am as beautiful as her,
Deep inside.
That thought is what keeps me alive.
Me and my mother my mother and I
I want to be just like her,
And one day share her love,
With my daughter.
I hope love can go on,
Generation to generation,
And keep in our family this love, patience and consideration.

Carolina Arredondo

Dusky Duck

Waves that lilt and fold on flattest shore,
    break soft and stretch so vast.
Sun glistens of gold a path atop the water.
Boats beckon sounds from far and then near,
    seemingly cracking the silence to speed.
From my wooded deck, I watch the sun glide beneath the ridge,
    leaving shadows on the timber beneath my feet.

At last, a last inch of sun dissolves behind the range,
    and in a sliver of sun's shadow something swims adrift.
I hold my breath and stretch to toes to glimpse lonely feathered
    beast,
Of pointed beak and web knot feet.

So similar am I to this animal in the dusk.
When hardest times of dark earth deprave my need,
    shunned and lost in darkness with no friends to pay me heed.
And duck swims downstream with shifting beak,
    as though in search of kin.
Is often my sorrow as well that I distance from my blooded ones.

I swim on in search of familiarity before the sun sets,
    and blinds my sight.
But meandering in darkness with just my feathers,
    seems to be my plight.
No flight tonight for duck in dusk bathed in pale
    moonlight . . . good night.

Shannon L. Sanford

Gone Are The Days

When
Everybody knew everybody

Then neighborhoods were safe
No mini marts, no guns
We just had fun
We played marbles, hopscotch, jump rope
Nobody gave us dope
We went to church on Sundays
To the library on weekdays
We ate dinner together and studied our encyclopedias with pride
Our teachers were our best friends
yes, Gone Are The Days
When television was small, black and white
Something that the neighbors had
Let's put everything in check, what the heck
So we won't have to say "Gone Are The Day's"

Sheila Grandison

Grandpa's Boys

Christopher William is Grandpa's Man,
He likes tatters fried in a pan.
Grandma's biscuits and gravy brown,
Needs something good just to hold him down

He turns the key in the tractor and heads for town,
The tires are a floppin' 'round and 'round,
It hits a hole and goes ker-thud!
Grandpa's tractor gets stuck in the mud.

Granny's tatters, biscuits and gravy too,
If it weren't for them what would Christopher do?

Here's Jared, Justin, Nathanual then,
To pull him out and get him goin' again.

Napper the poodle, Cosmo the cat,
Arrive on the scene — what do you think about that?

Dog and cat, all boys four
Don't you suppose you want to hear anymore.

You may think this is a lot of noise,
But, that's the tale of Grandpa's boys.

Arthur T. Lane

When Your Loved One Who Passes On,

It Is Not An End

Someday, we are all going to die
Whenever the time
we all will be with God

God already knows when or how
we will die
But, we will live again
in Heaven with extraordinary freedom

Your loved one will be happy, loving and
will have no pain and sorrow
Your loved one hasn't forgotten about you,
their family and special friends
Your loved one always carries you in his heart and soul
the same way you remember him

Your loved one always remembers the good and bad times
In spirit, your loved one always will be there for you and your family
Your loved one will be waiting for you
whenever your time is up, and he will meet you
at the end of the tunnel of light to guide you
around Heaven, hand and hand

Charita Christon

Untitled

We laugh, we cry, we live, we die
But most of the time, we wonder why
Why do we love, why do we hate
Will we ever appreciate, the good things in life
The sun and the moon, flowers and trees,
Animals, the birds and the bees
But most of all our family
Your father, and mother,
sister and brothers
and the love they share with each other
people hate and people sin
but does anyone ever win
or do we lose and start over again
Don't dream of the future
or dwell on the past
Nothing material will everlast
Except for love
Love is everlasting

John T. Schwerzler

Mowbray Park

The bonfire crackled and danced
To the fiddles playing behind us.
Musicians hollered out commands
While the children clapped and laughed
At each other, trying to learn the steps.
Around the fire
The semi-circle of freshly baled hay
Slowly became decorated with the long
Brown oilskin coats lent to us
By Phil the Boomerang Man.
We hadn't counted on the nights being so cold here.
I stepped out of the barn into
The crisp, pine air.
In the purity I could see nothing
Save the silhouette of the trees
Against the speckled sky.

Katherine A. Murphy

Angels from Heaven

Angels from heaven shelter some light down on me,
Help me to endure the pain cancer has inflicted upon me.
Living with this disease scares me to death,
Only hoping they will find a cure before my last breath.

Angels from the heaven shelter some light down on me,
Help these doctors set all cancer victims free.
Free from the pain and chemotherapy too, something,
No living soul should have to go through.

Angels from heaven shelter some light down on me,
Help these doctors set all the Lords children free.

Debra Louise Pestana

Ryan

Life really is a merry-go-round,
sometimes you're up, sometimes you're down.
But no matter how down you seem to be,
you can always get back up and break free.
But sometimes this option isn't always clear,
and you'll never know anything but pain and fear.
But health and happiness weren't far away
and there always would've been another day.
I had so many dreams and hopes for you,
but there's no way now that they will come true.
You took your life and we don't know why,
now all we can do is remember and cry.
You hurt us all bad, but it was your choice,
and never again will we hear your voice.
I hope you are happy and finally free,
and I hope you're someplace you wanted to be.
You've touched our lives so deep and true.
We'll miss you Ryan, and we all love you.

Wendi S. Bennett

Bubble Gum Gum

Bubble gum gum, who wants a piece of gum?
I do, I do, a great big bubble gum.
Double Bubble, bubble yum, super bubble,
Bublicious, which ever kind is quite delicious.
My Mom says "They're not nutritious." I say
"They're crunch-delicious."
One, two, three, four aren't they all to adore!!
Five, six, seven, eight, sorry Mom it's a bubble
Gum break. Bubble gum bubble gum by the pound, don't
they make a big "pop!" sound. Bubble gum, bubble
gum in your mouth do you blow your bubble south?
Bubble gum bubble gum in your hand, please don't drop
it in the sand.

Crystle M. Caraway

Temporal Affair

I do not live just to see that you breathe;
I don't hang from the gallows of your words;
When you are not with me I do not grieve —
Your voice is not so sweet as song of birds.
Your hurt innocent act I don't believe;
The sweetness of your milk in time will curd —
The part of me you take I will retrieve,
And beauty such as yours is found in herds.

And so conjoined in fleeting company,
Remain aware that in you I have found
A hobby born in desp'rate fallacy,
And know that by your rope I'll ne'er be bound.

Resist emotions never meant for wear —
The caustic sting of temporal affair.
        Jeremiah Donovan

Who Is She?

I see her often now...
    This little girl, who is she?

I see her jumping in the snow, in all its sparkling splendor.
    This little girl, who is she?

I see her playing with her dolls upon the grass so green.
    This little girl, who is she?

I feel the warmth of the summer sun caress her face as she runs so free.
    This little girl who is she?

Oh how I wish I could go with her and dance upon the autumn leaves.
    Oh little girl, who are you?

One day I looked into the mirror and much to my surprise,
I found that little girl, but sadly, only in my eyes.

Now as all these years have passed, I find myself upon a path that
    only goes one way.
There was a time I eagerly forged this path and never looked away.

Oh, but to lose my place in line and begin anew.
To be that little girl again, that's what I would do!
        Lorraine Schaeffer

Re-Entry

Spring re-entered my life today,
And gleefully beckoned me out to play.

She swished the sky to blue from gray,
And kissed my cheek with a golden ray.

She tickled my nose in a fragrant way,
And led me down where the green grass lay.

She coaxed warm breezes across the bay,
And led the birds' sweet roundelay.

She gave no hint how long she'd stay,
But Spring re-entered my life today.
        Carolyn C. Pratt

Sense Of Purpose

Each person is special.
We all have our own gifts and talents.
We each have a purpose, a reason to be.
A season to shine, reach our full potential,
bring these gifts to fruition. Destined for greatness,
we can be in the spotlight, just by being ourselves.
        Rhoda C. Hall

What Is Black?

Is it the shade of my skin?
Or is it the color of my hair?
If not, what is it?

Is it the reason I've known shame?
Or is it the reason my ancestors were enslaved?
If not, what is it?

Is it the reason I've known fear?
Or is it the reason we shed tears?
If not, what is it?

Is it the reason for our plight?
Or is it our reason to take flight?
If not, what is it?

Is it the reason I've known strife?
Or is it the reason for my miserable life?
If not, what is it?

It is the reason that leads our lives,
Now, you tell me, is that right?
        Pearlette S. Mourning

Easter Sunday

Slipping and sliding in new, patent leather shoes,
I skated into the church.
Pink bonnets, sleek white gloves,
crowded the inside.
Bundles of bouquets in pastels
perimetered the altar.
The priest began, droning on in monosyllabic sounds,
while I longed for my Easter basket.
Waiting at home, it overflowed
with chocolate bunnies,
marshmallow ducks,
rainbow jellybeans,
piled high on green grass.
Eggs experimentally mis-colored,
surrounded the candy mound,
like soldiers in occupied territory.
My sweets aged like fine wine,
while I sat bored.
"Jesus died" was reason for my being there.
Why, then, the candy?
        Kerstin M. Sundstrom

Mine Love Divine

Mine eyes have seen the love that shines
    through your eyes as blue as
    glistening oceans.
Mine heart has felt the deep devotion
    that connects two hearts that beat as one.
Mine soul has connected with the one
    that brings me joy, my soul mate.
Mine lips have kissed passion so spine
    tingling, envy of every woman is mine.
Mine hands have held the hands of the
    strongest gentleness I've ever known.
Mine body soars to places beyond the
    stars and only you, my love, take
    me there.
All that is mine, is forever yours, ...
    Mine Love Divine
        Debie Cain

To My Dear Father

To my dear father, do you feel any remorse?
For when you abandoned us for your high horse.
To my dear father, the one who looks old.
The one who rarely came, and when he did, wanted to scold.
To my dear father, do you know what I despise?
Do you know what I like, do you know my shoe size?
To my dear father, do you truly know me?
Do you know who I am? Do you know my personality?
To my dear father, who left me with a great mother.
Who is now independent, and depends on no other.
To my dear father, do you have any idea of what you put me through?
Wishing you would come by, but my dreams never coming true.
To my dear father, the one who I really love
The one I am stuck with because of the mighty one above.
To my dear father, I get on my knees and pray.
That when I get married and have kids, my husband will always stay.
To my dear father, you should have a great influence on me.
But since you're not around, and influence I can not see.
To my dear father, you have a lot to learn.
But I'll never forgive you 'cause your bridges you have already burned.

Jamila Aiysha Robinson

Will You Remember?

Will you remember — when you're far away
All the wonderful hours that we've known?
Will you ever be sad at the end of the day
When you think of the time that has flown?

Will your heart skip a beat - when you see a full moon?
Will you sigh and wish I were there?
When you hear the strains of a beautiful tune
Will the notes tell you how much I care?

When you hear a child's laughter ring out in glee
Will it cheer you and give you a smile?
Will it bring back the memory of days spent with me
When we lived every moment and love lingered the while?

Or my darling — will time and space make this all seem
that we never knew love - and it all was a dream?

Marjorie L. Shephard

I Wish For Peace

Whenever I look at the newspaper page,
I have to read about crimes, violence, and rage.
If I turn on the radio to hear a song,
A horrible piece of news always comes along.

I always wonder why this is so,
Why each country of the world must have a foe.
"Why can't there be peace?" I always say,
"Why can't all the fighting and crime just go away?"

For if all this were up to me,
I would restore in the world peace and tranquility.
Each time I turn on the television at night,
There is always news coverage on the latest world fight.

This violence seems so pointless and childish;
I think that peace should be everyone's greatest wish.
Can't the Palestians, Israelis, and other countries just resolve everything?
I want the sound of peace to finally ring.

Dana Ernst

Untitled

Though I was born to a messed up family
Alcohol, drugs, abuse were present heavily
I would fall asleep with fear in my heart
with fighting parents continuously apart
I would awaken the next day with no peace of mind
Seeking a peace I could not find
I would go hungry day after day
Being abused and I could not say
The pain and anger molded in me
Affecting my life and destroying me
I tried looking for someone to love
And prayed up to heaven, the God up above
To send me an angel and heal all these years
Of pain and agony mixed with my tears
Then one day I found peace and joy
A loving new life and a new baby boy.

Luis E. Otero

The Obstacle Course

Often as little kids, we'd build our own obstacle course.
We'd run here and run there,
kick the ball,
twist and turn,
trying not to fall or fail.
We remember the joy we felt
when we crossed the finish line first.

As time went on we grew older.
We stopped making and playing
our obstacle courses.
And yet, did we?

We still feel here and there,
twisting and turning,
trying to dodge the rough spots,
trying not to fall or fail.
We still fell a certain kind of joy
when we reach our goal and cross our finish line.
Yes, I believe we still have obstacle courses.
We're caught in the biggest obstacle course of all.
Life.

Veronica Smith

Waking In Lauterbrunnen

I feel the dawn before the church bells chime;
My senses come alive before the fifth bell stops.
Here day does misty stand on mountaintops
And tiptoe to the crests one at a time.

Full windows open to the dawning chill;
Song birds and baking bread entice the day;
Great Staubbach Falle pours forth its glacial spray;
A cowbell echoes from a distant rill.

I creep from bed to balcony to greet
The spirit that pervades each day anew,
To impress fondly in my soul this view,
And be reminded heart and head can meet.

Refreshed from mending night and breaking morn,
I, like the firmament, am newly born.

Jan Francis

Butterfly

"A little girl with hair in curls is chasing after me,"
Said Butterfly as he sailed by upon a summer's breeze!
"Oh, little girl, you'll try to please; you'll make mistakes.
Ideas you'll seize, you'll say your prayers of God above.
You'll try your wings; you'll fall in love."

A bigger girl she soon became. She wore a wedding band.
She asked her friend, the butterfly, to sit upon her hand.
"I can't, my dear," he softly said, "You've learned to love
And now you're wed; you'll need that hand for him to hold,
For love is worth its weight in gold!"

An older girl, a mother new, her child upon her knee,
Said, "Butterfly, you soar so high! I'm really glad you're free!"
"A lovely person you are now," said Butterfly, "for you've
Learned how, to love something, yet set it free:
This you must teach your child," said he.

A girl grown old; a girl grown wise; a grandmother was she,
She watched her daughter rock her child beneath a willow tree!
A butterfly flew very near: This grandmother to him was dear.
He knew that she would cause no harm, so softly sat upon her arm.

"Your daughter's girl with pretty curl will want to play with me,"
Said Butterfly, with whispered sigh: "How happy we will be!"
And Grandma smiled at him and said, "When life goes on,
Then nothing's dead." She fell asleep, her life complete:
"Now, Butterfly, your promise keep!"

Dorothy Ann Gray Ilg

Deeper Thoughts

Deeper thoughts, they enter my mind.
Deeper thoughts, so hard to find.
Things so deep I don't understand.
Things so deep and uncommon to man.
I am confused, yet I understand;
These revelations of thoughts that fall in my hand.
So complicated, except for a child.
The answer is calming, yet makes me wild.
What I understand, I can not explain
Because to anyone else, I would appear insane.

Amy Pickens

Have a Great Birthday

You've had a tough year, I really can tell
I've seen the tears you've hidden so well.

You have struggled and fought, been poked and probed.
Been draped with covers and then disrobed.

You've been stripped of your pride and your dignity too,
And all of your clothes, right down to your shoes.

You've dressed in a smile to cover the tears,
And a colorful attitude to hide the fear.

To keep up your courage you've leaned on the Lord,
as you lay on a table as hard as a board,

You felt empty and broken when you turned to Him,
A vessel with cancer, yet the Lord took you in.

He'll give back your pride and dignity, too,
For a vessel of honor He's made out of you.

So have a great birthday and be grateful, my friend,
For the battle's nearly over a new life begins.

You're not just a friend, but a really great boss.
If you hadn't fought back, we'd all had a great loss.

Jeannie Bartlett

Nobody's Mask

No sense of self, unhealing wound . . .
    Ingrained so deep. My heart was tuned
As set me up, through all the years,
    To wear a mask and hide the tears.
Pretends, at its best . . . comatose in feeling
    Anything at all, lest it leave me reeling.
And yet the pain oozing from my heart
    Curses my resolve, and tears my world apart.
My soul is bare, tender down on its knees
    And the silence grows, deafening its pleas.
Dare I cry out in anger-who will hear
    My tiny voice so filled with fear?
Has someone heard? "Who's there" they ask.
    It's only me . . . Nobody's mask.

Lisa L. Hite

A Game of War

I stood beside the window and watched the boys at play;
    I watched them every evening at the end of every day.
Playing hide and seek underneath the old street light
    And when the game was over, they came and said goodnight.

The long years have passed now, each boy has gone to war;
    Still playing hide and seek, though more serious than before.
They are hiding from their enemy and seeking out their prey,
But they've learned to play the game well and win in every way.

So when the war is over, please let me be the one,
    To stand on top of all the world and see,
Our boys come home when I yell, "Ally, Ally, Outs in Free."

Barbara Silberstein

Reflections Upon the Death of My Friend

There was so much gladness in us. I could not feel too sad
when you left and were gone forever from me;
my memories were still too alive
for me to realize you were dead.
I still think immediately of you when I
cook your favorite food,
when I hear a really dumb joke,
or, when I see a wounded cat.
None of that has changed for me, except
you are not here to enjoy it, to laugh, or to cry.
I miss you!
What was this affection we had, me for you and you for me.
We are not of the same clan.
You are woman and I am man, but ours was not a
relationship held together by interlocking genitals.
We shared our dreams with each other . . . and our nightmares.
We shared an appreciation of disgusting humor.
We had this mutual respect and we were never . . . alone.
I never thought of this when you were alive.
You're haunting me, aren't you? I love it and . . . I miss you!

Richard Moore Blankenburg

Inner Child Reaching Out

Sometimes I feel as though I grew up too fast
Memories so vague, they'll never last
The child in me wants to be free
That's one thing I can't let it be
I miss the joys of having no worries at all
Knowing someone would catch me when I fall
I have a feeling I'm being isolated
There's no other way it could be translated
Someday this feeling will hopefully die
Then I'll be free and able to fly

Lacey Bolding

There Is No Place Like the Good Old U.S.A.

There are countries and continents all over the world
   Places far and wide and in between
I have travelled the world over
   there is no place like good old U.S.A.
I have flown the skies above the earth
   and have seen the world down below
I have sailed the seven seas
   there is no place like the good old U.S.A.
I have travelled the highways and pathways of
   the world and all roads leads to good old U.S.A
Where dreams come true and never dies
   I love the U.S.A. There is no place like the good old U.S.A.

    Lawrence N. Diai

Our Love . . .

Like the wind that blows the soft green grass
   Something blew you into my life
Like the branches swaying but never breaking
   I know our love is strong
Like the roots of the old paradise tree
   I know you will never leave
Like the beautiful fresh spring flowers
   Our love feels brand new
Like the softness of each rose petal
   I love your gentle touch
Like the vine that clings to the old fence
   I always need you by my side
Like the raindrops falling from the sky
   I will try not to cry
Like the sun that rises every morning
   We will always wake up together
     Winking through the stars; smiling from the moon
     Know that I will see you soon

    Linda Lou Holden

Thinking of Him

Thinking of him,
All the time and everytime.

When I see him, I just want to
run up to him, and give him
a big loving caring hug.

To show him how much I love him,
and care about him as my boyfriend or my friend.

Because that how much
he means to me.

Thinking of him, at school in class, after school,
even I think of him at home or any place I am.

Whenever I see him, I just want to
come up to him, and talk to him.

Because he is so cute, sweet,
smart, handsome, and of course fine too.

He has a sweet personality,
he has a sweet, loving, and
caring heart, and he's a great dresser too.

Be my boyfriend, be my friend
and be my guy too.

    Zhanna Reyder

A Good Listener

They say a good listener is often hard to find
and sometimes you don't know it, but they're
not too far behind.

They will sit and listen to what you have to say
even if it takes a year, a month or a day.

A good listener will not judge you they will only
do their part and that's to help you discover
what is really in your heart.

    Vernessa L. Williams

Insomniac

I can see you. Don't even know you. Falling into
the sheets at night.
I try counting sheep and talk to the shepherd and
play with my pillow forever and ever.
I sit alone and watch the clock and breathe in on
the 'tick', out on the 'tock'.
I can hear you bare foot on the kitchen floor and you
don't have to hide these dreams no more and
I found someone just to hold me tight, hold the
insomniac all night.

I place my hand flat on my chest and feel my
heart beat back the night
I close the window 'cause the stars are laughing,
they get a kick out of my misery
I try everything short of Aristotle, dramamine,
and the whiskey bottle.
I pray for the day when my ships comes in and
I can go to sleep again, and
I found someone just to hold me tight,
Hold the insomniac all night.

    Hakeem Akintonwa

The Valley of Life

I walk in the valley of life,
   Where the sun never sets,
   Where good and evil cannot be distinguished,
   Where black and white are not apparent,
   Where the presence of God is never mentioned,
   Where questions keep multiplying and answers keep dividing.
I walk in the valley searching for love, laughter,
and knowledge of the unknown.
I walk alone in the valley of life;
Praying everyday to find a daisy, in a world where life
is becoming so insignificant.

    Judith Luscalzo

Untitled

In a world of disorder and boundaries, unlimited, we search
for a life that is meaningful.
Chaos embraces our minds from every angle and leaves us in a
wonder of turmoil.
Unaccustomed to the ever-changing world around us, it rips at
our souls and destroys our vast personalities.
Death seems ever so near, on the basis that it happens so,
unnecessarily, often.
Hatred and deceit, span the globe, taking their victims in a
rapid manner.
Our lives come to an abrupt halt, thinking that there is not a
bit of humanity left in the world.
Occasions of joy to rare to be acknowledged, are kept
eternally in the unconscious.
Happiness is sought, throughout the infinities of time, but will
only appear, once you find yourself.
Once that self is found, you will be forever happy, despite the
world around you.
Then, and only then, will our search end, and our lives be
meaningful.

    Jayson Blackledge

Cartoon Heroes

I grew up with some insecurity,
I did not know what I wanted to be.

I never knew what to say,
I lived my life from day to day.

With every relationship I felt much dread,
I survived with cartoon heroes in my head.

I left home when I was still a child,
I thought living was having fun and being wild.

One unbelievable night around half past ten,
The fun and games came to an end.

Now I'm alone with thoughts in my mind.
And, the walls and locks from which I'm behind.

Now the fight begins, to get back on track,
The ability and know - how, I do not lack.

I have dreams in my head; a house with a fire place,
A family and friends, and pride and grace.

I want to live life in the presence of reality,
By not playing Superman, and just being me.

Charles H. Downes

Tiffany

A special friend named "Tiffany" came to our house to stay.
She was all that we had hoped for on that July day.

We found her in a shelter, lonely and so blue.
We knew she needed us, and we needed her too.

As we looked at all the others, so happy and so gay —
We couldn't help but wonder why she would only lay.

She had a satin pillow and a very special toy —
But as special as they were, they didn't bring her joy.

Her black eyes spoke these words, "Please take me home with you.
I know you'll make me happy as nothing else can do".

As we hugged her and petted her lovely coat of white —
Her curved fringed tail was waving as she jumped with all her might.

And so this special friend came to our house to stay.
And the joy she has brought to us is more than we can say.

We love our precious "Tiffany" — Our sweet Bichon Frise.

Oh yes, we must confess what makes her especially chummy —
When she sits right up and waves her paws, she's begging for
something yummy. But, when she's full, she's begging because she
wants us to pet her tummy.

Eleanor Whittington

Certain Places In My Mind

Certain places in my mind are not just for memorizing,
  but for escaping and fantasy.
Certain places are for fear, and a place for me to hide.
Certain places in my mind are for imagination and for
  pretending.
Certain places in my mind are for daydreaming and thinking
  of certain events.
Certain places in my mind are for spending time alone to
  think through certain problems.
Certain places in my mind hardly ever come into view.
Certain places in my mind hide and create mystery.
These places in my mind are like rivers of imagination and
  creation.
These certain places in my mind are very special to me,
Without them I would not be who I am today.

Gina P. Ottomaniello

Life

What is life can anyone explain
Is life when you wake every sunrise,
is life when you see every sunset.
Is life having fun after school is out,
is life growing up and taking control of
your route.

What is life can you understand
Is life when you look for that one,
is life when you think you have found that love.
Is life when you look up for answers from above,
is life when you sweep those feelings under a rug.
Is life when you don't know to take a chance
is life, if you don't know to say no to a romance.
Is life when you should or shouldn't say yes to a dance,
is life not knowing if there is a chance.
Is life decided by one man's hand,
is life decided by you and a companion.
Is life pleasure or pain?

(Life is what you go through day
by day, only you can decide what way.)

Patrick L. Howard

Terrible Two

My nappy days are over
  except for a pampered few.

When it rains, or there's dew
  I'll just sleep until two.

But when the sun, it does shine,
  ah-h-h, the day is always mine.

Oh-h-h, there's so much to do,
  I could never sleep thru!

I have a new potty all shiny and new,
  my Mom, she tells me, when it's time to do poo.

My diaper is warm; my potty is cold!
  When will Mom learn, I'll not do what I'm told!

I eat with my fingers and put food in my hair,
  my Mom, she shakes her head; such a solemn glare!

She sniffs my head and tells me it's 'pee-u',
  I kind of like it all sticky like glue.

My mom's name is Sue; she calls me Do,
  life is just great, at terrible two!

Susan R. Clark

Perfect Love

He's gone, my companion of sixty-six years,
Life all around me is drenched with my tears.

Decisions! Decisions! What should I do?
Who do I call if the roof fall through?
Where do I send the checks for the bills?
Who'll fix the furnace when winter chills?
Who do I talk with when day is done?
Shadows surround me. Gone in the sun.

Night is so frightening. I need him near.
I speak his name and pray that he hears.
Reach out for his hand and almost believe
He touches my fingers and I am relieved.
Faith and good memories of his love for me.
These must sustain me. This much I see.

God gave me his love, though I am sad,
Grateful am I for the years that we had.

Marguerite Gary Fields

474

Jay-Jay

Jay, Big Brother, you were my inspiration.
Have you forgotten the long hours we sat and talked?

Jay, once you started drinking,
You left me in fear.

I constantly cry inside, "Will he wake up in the morning, or will it
be his time to die?"

Jay, once you started drinking,
You thought no one cared.

I care about you, Jay;
Let me, your Little Sister, be your inspiration.
Denenne Chama

Rainy Day

Raindrops whisper,
Farrah, this is a new start on a new day.

On this beautiful rainy day, I weep tears of happiness; for the rain
does not depress me.
It serves as a reminder of my baptism when God cried tears of joy in
heaven.

The sweet-smelling rainfall declares,
Hear the roaring thunder;
See the brightness of flashing stars in the lightning bolts;

My Creator has given me another day to live on this
beautiful, colorful, mother earth.
Even though violence and hate seem overwhelming, He boldly
announces
He is in control.

As a rainbow colors the horizon and leaves it shadow on the earth, I
pray aloud,
Thank you for this rainy day.
Farrah Haswood

To Be Alive

To be or not to be that is the question?
To be alive and to live as you want to live.
To be alive and to have eyes to see all the beautiful sights that we
have to see. To be alive and to have ears to hear all the beautiful
sounds we have to hear.
To be alive and be able to walk without help from others.
To be alive and smell all the sweet things there are to smell.
To be alive and to have hands to touch people who love you and
to have them touch you. To be alive and have a heart filled with
warmth, understanding, and consideration for others people's feelings
and beliefs. To be alive is to know that you have lived your life to
the fulness and that you enjoyed each day that you lived. To be alive
is to be alive and well knowing that all the people around us aren't
so lucky to have what we have, and that is we are healthy. To be
alive and to have feelings toward other people feelings like
compassion, understanding, hurt, fear, sadness, and happiness. But
the best feeling there is, is the feeling of love cause there is no
life on earth and without love there is no sense to be alive, and that
is why I am thankful to be alive and to have all the feelings there is
to have, and the best feeling that I have is the feeling of love.
Louise Abenante

Magazines

You see 'em in the doctor's office and in the check-out lines,
You pick it up and scan just to pass the time.
How to lose 10 pounds or be the perfect lover,
You can find it all on these pages between these covers.

Glamour, Vogue and Cosmo
Tell us what we want to know,
Convincing us ladies, "Men are really not our foes."
They stage the latest designs of Calvin, Donn and Liz,
But what woman can wear after they've had kids?

Entailing the life we should be reaping,
Can be found in Redbook, McCall's and Good Housekeeping.
How marriages, houses and bank accounts should all be built,
And who is "Super Mom", and did she ever feel guilt?

Lest we forget that our bodies are in need of Shape and Prevention,
They could not be published without a diet mentioned.
"It's to our health" they say we hold our true alliance,
Proving once again they have it down to a Popular Science.
Sylvia Yerty

Wheel of History

The wheel of history is turning
　upsetting mountains, hills and vale
　over boulders, rocks, stones and sands.
The wheel of history is running
　over lakes, rivers, creeks and seas.
The wheel of history is gusts of blowing
　stirring, whirling up all the air.
The wheel of history is debris scattering
　bricks, wood and tiles everywhere —

The wheel of history is uprooting
　plants, trees and flowers
　mixed up in floods galore —

The wheel of history is turning,
　running, blowing, scattering,
　uprooting land and people
　more and more!
Today, by the prophets in the Bible
2,000 years afore!
Eleanor M. Cleveland

I'll Fly Away

When the sands of time change direction
and the rivers flow silently in pain,
the moon lingers in the night of day
while the sun shines forcefully in vain.

The seasons are no longer noticeable
there's no difference between winter and spring,
the earth shivers quietly in the silence
and the grass fades, no longer green.

Hopes of tomorrow have left
as I watch and shed tears of pain,
knowing that these feeling will pass
yet still I whisper in the rain.

I wait patiently in the fields amidst the children and keep faith
that by His grace victory will be mine too one day,
my heart opened to eternal happiness and peace
like a gentle dove, my wings spread
I'll fly away.
Pamela Elizabeth Brown

The Gunfighter

The cowboy wore his old trail coat.
Reached in his pocket and rolled him a smoke.
He puffed it down to just a butt.
In his holster a forty five stuck.
It's almost noon came a shout,
He broke down his pistol and checked it out.
Sipping on suds still in his beer,
He knew the hour would end here.
With a nod of his head at the saloon door,
He counted heads that totalled four.
One was straight ahead by the hay,
He will be the first one I blow away.
That one standing by the building so tight,
Will never live to see daylight.
In the alley twas a glimpse of boot,
He is the third one I'm gonna shoot.
I won't shoot it out anymore,
After I drop the one by the door.
I never saw that gunslinger again,
But in the dirt lay four dead men.

Twyla Beauchamp

A Rose

A rose, a single rose
Standing tall, defiant, blazing with courage
It is fragile, yet eternal
Its beauty has many meanings
From I love you, to a simple thank you, to an
even simpler I'm thinking about you
Yet its purpose or beauty need not be explained
For the true beauty of a rose is interpreted
by one - the receiver
It can be received by anyone, for any reason
And it can solely say what may wish they could say
But more importantly
It can say what one, the giver, wants it to say
A rose, a single rose
Standing fearless, eager to accept its destiny
Knowing confidently that it will live forever

Louis M. Mauriello

An Uncommon Land

In the beginning, there were the mountains,
　Dark and shining, where rivers were born and snow
Lay heavy on ragged crests.
　Mountains that rose to God's call for splendor and mellowed
To His thoughts of rolling plains.
　Plains that spread to the never-ending land of the prairie.
So it was in the beginning of the Shining Mountains.
　It was an uncommon land.

A land rich in forests, moving grass and rivers of dark
Minerals buried in the earth.
　Deer, bear, elk and eagle owned the Big Sky,
Home to the Blackfoot, Sioux, Crow. Lair of mountain men,
　Trapping beaver for appetites worlds away.
Range of the buffalo, blanket of the plains,
　Spread in an ebony robe waving to the azure sky.
A most uncommon land.

To the mountains a nation called, "Find a new world—
　A land chosen by God."
The answer came, "I am here. I am Montana,
　The Last Best Place."

Claudia Clague

Connie

I clutched the poles
Drew in a breath
And filled my lungs.

I dedicate this run to her
Put her here into my place
With my strong legs
So she could feel, so she could face
The speed, the curves, the winding turns,
And the rush of lightning from the wind
That stabs and bites, yet all the while
It made us smile.

Today I took my friend to ski
She went with me!
And although she's never walked a step
She won't forget
The magic scene that we both saw
The bluest sky, the whitest snow
In this way, she came to know, what used to be
Only dreamed of
Now she's free.

Cynthia Dahm

If Our Cabin Could Talk . . .

If our cabin could talk, oh, what stories it could tell;
　How happiness and love inside it did dwell.
How this humble little cottage was a place of retreat
　From troubles and worries and feelings of defeat.

How cool in the summer, keeping out the sun's rays,
　There, we'd relax with lemonade at the end of hot days.
How the kids liked to huddle 'round the stove when 'twas cold
　And listen to grandpa tell his wild stories of old.

How in summer or winter, we would gather at night
　'Round the table for checkers or to read by kerosene light,
Or tell of the day's predicaments, both amusing and sad
　Trying our best to top the last one; no one could top Dad.

Here we cherished the quiet at the end of a long, busy day,
　And the kids could relax when worn out from their play.
And the meals tasted special after working up an appetite:
　Fried spuds and hamburger gravy was the menu for the night.

Yes, if our cabin could talk, oh, the warmth you would feel
　If you'd listen intently to its soft, sweet appeal:
Come partake of this picture so content and serene,
　Come join with us and our memories of this Heavenly scene.

Eunice S. Barnard

The Mottled Scrimshaw of Post-Coldness Draw

The days pour through me like a sieve.
"The strainer" said my mother — awaiting the response, strained.
A strand of my hair - slipping in the hole.
A sad, blaming dusk - sleeping the land,
raking the hills with a guilty sigh.

I said the implausible once again
lulling the fumes of a turgid pen
snapping, gamming, crottled, masty

Awaking to the mossy smell
of clammy dawn, of crowded eyelids
and brushed-out gauze
filmed before me, filmed before the
negative spaces were scripted
post-scripted onto my days to drive
them through me, hammered
breathless with an empty squeeze

So empty
that I no longer feel the passing

Catie D'Ignazio

The Pearl

The things I hold sacred and dear to me
Are like pearls, pure and simple, like nature.

These pearls make me who I am
And create my inner spirit and essence.

Like the pearl, I can be washed up on the sand
With other pearls who may have lost their way.

But, like a cultured pearl, I have an identity
Which sets me apart, not because I am better, but
because I know who and what I am.

If someone should find me lying in the sand and
Throws me back to the waves, I will survive my
Journey unscaved for the identity within is
Alive and strong.

And one day, I will be there
Again, on the sand as a cultured pearl, more
Beautiful than before.

Sonya D. Ford

Love Is His Absence

If I knew then what I know now;
Each day would have been cherished,
Every glance would have lasted an hour,
Each caress could be remembered,
Every gentle kiss, my lips could still feel.
My mind could still picture each of these things
As vividly as if they happened only moments ago.
Now that you have departed
I see the granted I took you for.
My heart weeps in its loneliness.
My hands tremble, for yours are not there
To make mine stable.
Lips, rough like leather from discontinued use,
And eyes closed, blinded
To mask my mind from the pain
Felt when love must grow
In the absence of he whom the love is for.

Jennifer Johnstone

Untitled

"You know they are all dead," he said
as we stared into the night sky
"They are all dead, the stars are all dead."

"They are so far away," he continued,
"that when their light finally reaches us
the stars are burned up . . . dead."

Should I believe him,
could it be possible
dead stars in a galaxy of graveyards.
It would explain a lot of things

No wonder, I thought,
hundreds of my secret wishes had not come true,
unknowingly wished upon dead stars.

It somehow seemed so very sad.
Was there anything left in life
I was able to count on?

"And the light of new stars," he mumbled
"has not reached earth yet."
I knew there was hope.

David A. Dedrickson

A Time to Cry

For the guilty, all appeals are exhausted.
Minutes pass as he's delivered from the cell
where the last meal has been served.
We gather to watch, what a story to tell!

Raised on a bed, he's now on display.
Our eyes meet his blank stare.
One minute to live, as deadly fluid flows.
It's an easy sleep, no pain, to bear.

No more seasons, no rain, no sun.
How sad, another life is gone.
A tear begins to gather in an eye
and soon will flow...no sleep 'til dawn.

For the innocent, a prayer His only appeal.
Accused, tried and convicted in a day.
Only bitter vinegar served to His thirst.
Our guilt was His price to pay.

Raised on a cross, blood flowing,
and hours of suffering, then to die.
His last wish to forgive all.
But now . . . do we cry?

Jimmy Findley

Here and Now

Here and now is completed for the here and now, now is real,
the journey's repeated without a want to be seen!
Full circle life's storms have tossed me about,
Face to face now I'm come to the light and the sound
of thy presence!

Did you think I must tremble did you think I would fret
at the rumbling thunder of the storm's fury . . . yet
Not a cloud now is seen nor a raindrop is found
as I walk in the light as I listen to the sound of thy presence!

All creation is blooming in the newly seen light,
All God's creatures are singing with their voices so bright.
And the exhilaration of thy beauty realized
gives an awesome awaking, what a wondrous delight...
in thy presence!

Here and now, now is here, here and now, now is real
Without past, without future there's no want to be seen.
Full circle life's storms have blown me around
in the present I dwell, in the light and the sound of thy presence!

Ursula Kaur Kondal

Desire

I am the wick of your candle
   melting
     slowly
      into
       you
  ignited by the patience of love —
Where you once stood tall
     I have hollowed you —
I have worn
   you
   down
     and spilled the tears of your pride —
I have softened you with my warmth
    and I shall burn
      quietly
    into the pool of your dependence until I drown —
until I melt
   into
    you
  and we sleep together in darkness

Andrea Gough

A Beginning Thought

Greetings one and all, once again
  the activities have begun.
It's time for parents and teachers to
  work together, so let's make it fun.
Let's aim high and remember the
  objects that bring us here
Will we be proud of our efforts at
  the close of the years?
Welfare of children in home, school,
  church and community we must promote
Intelligent training of children and youth,
  the objects to quote.
If we all work together it takes
  but little time
And the results will benefit
  your child and mine.
Stop and think of these wonderful
  children God gave us and what we can do
For his or her development and guidance,
  are left up to you.

  Pat Groom

The Golden Years

When passion ebbs, there should remain
If happiness we would contain
A closeness contentment that brings a special glow
To fill the gap, of passions flow
And herald in those golden years
That people strive to reach.

A feeling of love, that we still could share
When the fires are banked
But red embers still there.
The warmth in our eyes
And our hands when we touch
A tender kiss, can still say so much.
A smile to share, a hand to hold
To walk down life's pathway
While we're growing old.

  Helen Rabiner

The Time of Now

The Time of Now is never stable
And by the time you realize what's in store,
All the cards are already on the table.
Change is the substance of Time's core,
So a second can make a world of difference
In whether you can win or lose.
But you must not ever let interference
Influence the way you decide to use
Your precious gift of changing Time.
To waste the Time of Now,
Could be a heinous crime,
Which you should not allow.
For once the Time of Now is lost,
It's gift you cannot regain,
No matter what the cost,
And no matter what the pain.

  Kimberly M. Novak

The Snowflake

Does it know of its uniqueness
As if floats toward the ground
To become a part of a blanket
That covers the earth like down?

Does it know there is no snowflake
An exact duplicate of it
No other feathery masses
With precisely the same shape as it?

Does it know as it wafts its way to the ground
Of the freedom that all snowflakes have
To be peerless and matchless, to stand all alone
And yet to be part of the crowd?

This snowflake is perfect in shape and design
So silent, so cold and so wee.
Yet I know as it's part of that chilly white quilt
That it's saying; "Oh, whee, look at me!"

  Betty Conway Gray

Living In This World

Living in this world,
It's like an oyster without its pearl,
a mother without her lit' girl,
whatever happened to the promise of
peace among the world?
Our children will be born unto racism, hate,
and violence. Yet we all just sit in silence.
We need to regain our balance,
and conquer our challenge.
Living in this world, is no more.
Help the poor. Feed the hungry.
Clothe the bare. We have so much
to spare! Does anyone care?
Living in this world,
it's like an apple without its core,
a car without its door,
what is the sense, of living in
this world?

  Sarah Walgren

Nature Sighed

"Encompass me in your poetic beauty," I begged.
"When will you learn," Nature sighed. "True beauty cannot be
  described."
"Then how, how will I ever know," I screamed.
"It's inscribed in the heart of every living being,"
Nature Sighed.

  Nicholas S. Boone

Why Does It Rain?

Why does it rain? That is what I ask myself.
Is it God's tears, because we're making a mess?
I wonder why it rains real hard then suddenly disappears,
Or, when the day is cloudy with fog, then, in
  a minute it's clear.
Is this a sign or a clue that something isn't right?
Could this be God having a restless day or night?
Who am I to ask, am I allowed? Maybe it's something
  I should keep to myself, so that God can be proud.
Drip after drip, puddles and puddles, coughing, sneezing,
  wrapped in bundles.
Why does it rain? Yes, I'm still asking. I'm just
  curious, I'm not insane.
But, can anyone tell me, why does it rain?

  Kwanza Noel Michelle Brooks

A Poem Finished Years Later

Time can go ever so slowly.
Sometimes it can even fly.
The sands continue to flow.
Even though I'm asking why.

Youth came for a visit
But alas couldn't stay too long.
The dreams become fantasies
The musical to write, now just a song.

We all play the game.
Praying desperately for another shot.
Give me the damn dice, come on "lucky seven!"
Snake eyes is what I got.

Is there a point, does any of it make sense?
What's the secret is it sold at 3.a.m on T.V.?
Hold me tighter, don't let go.
Please say you'll marry me!!!

Oh that "it's just a poem I never did finish."
Geez I was pretty sad back then, didn't have a clue.
Looking for a purpose, an answer.
But that was before I met You.

Steve Goldberg

Pictures

My mind is an artist,
Painting pictures in my Head, the canvas
My imagination is the paint of many vivid colors.
My hands, voice, and feet are the amateurs
    who copy the master pieces my mind makes.
My hands brush is a pencil or an actual paintbrush.
Their canvass is this paper or an actual canvass.
The copies of my mind's masterpiece are either poetry or actual art
My voice uses my mouth as brush.
The air is its canvass
The copies are songs and stories.
My feet use music as a brush,
And the ground for a canvass
So my feet make the copy a dance
Those of you who read my poems or watch my dance or hear me sing
Are my mind's audience.

Patrick McKenna

Untitled

    Right now I'm sitting in my car facing Lake Winnebago
watching the waves smash against the shore on this beautiful
fall day.
    There is sun and there is a crisp wind blowing the
leaves, rattling them against the pavement in a circular dance
they call "Fall". The sea gulls are out too, some are
frolicking one on one, a high speed chase of fun and
excitement screeching out life's thrill; some are riding the
waves, and some are just looking for food.
    There is a lot of energy to this day and my heart is
full of love. I come alive in the fall and my spirit rides
with the wind, dances with the leaves, and sings with the
sea gulls...
    There is no lover beside me to hold my hand, to stroll
along, but that's okay, because there's a lover inside me
whose absence has been missed for so long.

Kimberly Ann Koster

The Blooming

Evicted from the dust and into the wilderness,
Searching, searching for ground to touch,
For air to breathe, for space to bless.

Wishing to be smothered by the rocks,
Yet still striving to be above them,
Its leaves announce a flower that appears from slender stalks.

Wind and stars dance on its soul.
Days and weeks keep passing.
Deep within lies joy of growth, also doubt, each playing a role.

Then the flower is gone as autumn nears.
Last drops of dew resemble tears.
Death is near for another year.

Springing from the dust! Into the vastness peers
a simple plant looking beyond into the years, and whispering:
    "The leaves shall fall; snow will cover all.
    Lonely waiting ...then blooming...
      lonely waiting...blooming.
    Each blooming more beautiful than the last,
    Each waiting a poignant task.
    This is the beauty of life.

Douglas J. Kohlan

Anniversary Rose

I went looking for a special rose today.
A pressed, wine rose, smelling of decay.
But to me it was as sweetly fresh as when
    You placed it in my trembling hand... On a secret whim...
For me to ever remember our first embrace...and I have not
Forgotten now, nor ever I shall....
    Your sweet endearing face.

I have kept your written notes to me... Tucked in odd places
That are like the musty rose...encircling and protecting me,
As all these years with you....today combine as twenty-three.

A circle of devotion, love and care, phrases that will always
Linger there...secret, deep and no despair.

Our love forever is shared ecstasy...the rose, our words and
loving destiny...

    Today, tomorrow and our infinity.

Jean Howe Ward

The Fighter That Won

When into the fight game he went
Fame and glory for him, was meant
He had to run, to work each day
He had to learn, this game to play.

While other boys were out having fun
He'd be working out under the sun,
Then home he'd go, and into the hay
This he'd do for the had little to say.

He would sleep until break of dawn
Then arise, out he'd go, upon the lawn,
His legs he'd kick, his arms he'd swing
This he'd do, until sweat he'd bring.

He measured his opponent, with keenest of sight
For he was preparing for his first big fight,
The fight was clean, yes, ever so fair
Each time he'd, swing, he'd utter a prayer.

The fight was over, his hand was raised
His clean and hard fighting won him much praise
He now could rejoice, this work was done
He was the Victor, the fighter that won.

Louis A. Welty

Attempted Murder

Under the promise of the morning sun,
canticles of glory are sung by the birds,
jewel-laden streams hint at golden dreams;
treasures to be fought and won.

In the depths of the darkest ill,
dwells a lady who's rarely still,
she manipulates innocent souls until
she has their lives, leaving a bitter chill.

The lady comes knocking at my door,
with her ominous clouds, she tries to implore,
that I should live in her world which has in store
nothing I'm looking for:

A pessimistic place where
no one's free,
thirsty souls on a rippling beige sea.

Listening to the sweet canticles of mirth,
I decline the lady's offer,
why should I die and turn my back to the sky
when Jesus is alive on earth?

Maurice M. Wilson

Untitled

The openness and the ability to be shaped
in the fashion of a child just learning
is what more adults need today and tomorrow.
Hatred is something I could have never learned
on my own in twenty life times.
But and because it is a learning process in life
I was enrolled by society and whipped until I
received my diploma.
Liking someone not like you is a crime, which
is punished by being branded a lover . . . .

If this old world would cease today
and mankind was scattered through-out . . .
I know that I would again run into my teachers . . .
Mr. Bigotry and Mrs. Hatred . . .
Neither of whom has aged since . . .
Cain slew Able.

Donald Moore

The Ocean

The ocean flaunts its power; it calls me to
    investigate, to rejoice in its beauty.
It sends breakers crashing on the beach,
    and dares me to deny its boundless energy.
The ocean beacons me to become lost in its
    beauty, to listen to its songs of adventure and thus,
It captivates my soul and arouses primordial longings.
It urges me to join the aquatic legions and be forever
    a part of the world of the deep.

The ocean hypnotizes me, and I become reborn,
    a child of a different destiny, succumbing
to the challenge of time immortal, drawn by an
    irresistible urge to join the sea gulls and
    soar forever free.

The ocean frightens me, and I flee its beauty,
    and its song, and its crashing breakers
    and its roaring commands,
    and I return to the quiet peace of my mountains.

Edna M. Vickers

Breach of Faith

Some say I shouldn't dwell on it, and it will go away,
This frosty clutch of dreaded fears that grips me in its sway.
Your mind, just like a garden, can be stifled by the weeds
Of contrary thoughts run rampant, choking out more fitting seed.

If this be true then tell me why this overwhelming task
Of weeding out those noxious thoughts should fall to me whose mask
Of peace and happiness is chipped, and rigid lines of woe
Besiege my brow, betraying me. For those who look will know.

How could the master gardener draft a plan of such a scheme,
So cryptic in design that no purpose can be seen
By the eyes of us mere mortals as we struggle through this life
To find meaning for existence but see only grief and strife?

Why did he give the chore of choice, then grant us intellect
To plan the questions in our mind and cause us to suspect
That he bequeaths this life but then omits the essential part
That sows sweet thoughts of trust and faith and yields a tranquil heart.

Mary Ann Wilkins

Those Hockey Men

There are no warriors more powerful,
    than those hockey men

No bullet train as fast,
    no engines built like men

Our one true tribe, so pure in thought,
    fighting to the end

Ice astronauts, with hand-made swords and high tech shields,
    fly on blades over zoned fields

Combat trained they hit the ice, chasing comets with their spears,
    colliding at warp speeds, while silent millions cheer

Stripped guards scan their every move with their ghost-like strides,
    capturing gladiators-with one short breath above the screaming
    cries

While one lone soldier in alien gear is anchored to his port,
    stops comets in flight - with a long, curved sword

Like streaking trains bound for opposing shores,
    small round rockets make the score

Fighting Roman style, they will end in single file,
    each to greet a giant in gentle style

There are no warriors more powerful,
    than those hockey men

A. E. King

The American Dream

As we look past the American Dream into reality:
Self destruction, social distortion, rainforest depletion,
Extinction completions, disgrace of the human race.
The earth is ours to borrow, not destroy.
We've corrupted our society with dreams of what we'll never be.
There are people with not enough to eat, gangs and violence on the
Streets, crime is on the rise, you can't even look someone in the eyes.
Kids are on drugs, babies are on crack, too bad someone can't turn
The hands of time back. The hole in the ozone layer up above,
Tis there because people don't care enough. Peace is easier said than
Done, people are quicker to pull a gun.
What happened to our minds and common sense,
Most friendships end up a thing of past tense.
People are too caught up in themselves, they need to view beyond
Themselves into the world around them. They need to be aware of
How mother earth is being raped.
Everyone has to do their part so we have a future.
If nothing is done, there will be no tomorrow.
Our children will be left with our problems,
Then there will be no need for the
        American Dream.

Jennifer Lee

Exclamation!

Parallel to my horizon, synchronized to the depths of my con-
science.
Repentance upon my being, Recognition exceeds my worth.
As if I wore a candle on my heart; dripping, melting the
salt of my soul-thrusting into your precious wound.
No saline shall derive the retribution yet to be.
Drifting under a current, yearning to be risen.
so ignorant I see, yet my eyes are omniscient.
I shall remain the putrid serpent as you bask and taste your
sweet apple.
A gem so artificial, yet so praised.
Release a sound so accepted by all
Exalt words as if only you could conceive,
reminisce on now,
for now is only a dream to wither.

Melissa Bourlier

Success

The road to success is sometimes short,
other times, it is a long road fill with disappointments and failures.
These disappointments and failures make success worthwhile.
When disappointments and failures are encountered
and there is no effort to try to succeed again, then there is a failure.
There is no guarantee for success, however simply trying
again when hurdles are encountered is a success in itself.

Naomi N. Elliott

Attitude Toward Life

It all comes down to this
grasp heartily at life or else you will miss
all the joy and delight
be not afraid of the dark of night,
fear is crippling and can stop
your true self from rising up to the top.
Whatever and ever your hearts desire
go at it full strength as if in mire
take into account others around in the stream
all working together to form a strong team
for nothing can be done worthy in solo
reaping a great harvest takes many to sow

Beata Gaudry

The Lonely One

The chimes may blow by the sound of wind on a December day.
The yellow grass of an old house lies on both sides of the walkway
Crouched on the sill, the lonely one lay, with eyes of fury and chaos.
The chosen one may be you, one of the last survivors, you may.
The orange of the eyes haunt fiercely,
Through midnight trips in your mind.
As you progress through the chop of the wind,
The creaked steps urge your turning back knowingly.
The rusted knob turns with a creak of challenge.
A cry of grief rises like a staircase of psychosis.
When the curious traveler closes the door,
The lonely one calls, stumbles, leaps.
With a sigh of relief and a scream of faith,
The lonely one is not lonely anymore!
From far away, it is said, you can hear the snore.
The small, innocent statue preparing for disturbance.
And if you hear the snarl of that demon,
Stick with your job and finish your chore.
For just that will save your life.

Ben Piscopo

Hope

Childhood dreams can be crushed by the reality of the turbulent world,
but there is always Hope and Hope is the bread of life.

Paul Lindsey Carlson

Troubles of Our World

Our world is hurting, our world is sad,
  Sometimes I wonder, "does destiny have our world in its hands"
A world that was once pure, a world that once replenished itself
  With silver and gold that it creates from within itself.
The animals and trees, the water and the land,
  I'm sure it is all a good thing, created with God's hand.
A world that's bright but filled with spite,
  A world so clean but filled with smog on the scene.
A troubled world, a troubled place.
  Somewhere that used to be safe.
A place where you could ride a bike, fly a kite,
  See a plane in the sky, something you capture with your eye.
A troubled world, a hateful place,
  Please....let peace escape.

Stanley Lambert

The Threshold of Eternity

Look upon the face of Death
  lying in the bonds of the impending
final hour
  Out of the mouth comes not another
breath
  Having suffered the pain of
useless passions
Until departure beyond life's gate
allow thy noble heart to hold
true the facets of life
  a cry of the newly created
  a serene longing for the submission
unto the supernal veil of unbounded time
To cast Death's shadow amongst
clouds of concealment unto the deep,
  deep peace of Eternity
The Hand of Mankind, extending
and gently touching the face of God

Isabelle Discount

I Am Your Daughter

I am your daughter—I am here by your side.
These are my feelings; and in you I'll confide.
I may not be with you to tell you good-bye
Dad, I do love you; and with God's strength—I'll try.

Try and express...that there's a place close beyond
One that holds happiness, a peace, a strong bond.
It will forever be your haven; I'll assure you of this.
It will give you comfort, unknown joy, unconditional sweet bliss.

One that keeps us together
Regardless of how long we're apart.
There is but one life
We are of one heart.

I am your daughter; I will miss you so much.
From a child to a woman was your loving touch.
We shared laughter and joy; unknown sorrow, sometimes pain.
We are of family and love was our gain.

I am your daughter—and now I will go.
First there is something I want you to know.
I love you dearly and tears I will cry;
But I'll be with you again soon . . . In the sweet bye and bye.

Deborah Tunnicliff

Ineffable

Secure in his surroundings, he
Exults in the vigorousness of his own youth
Along comes a stranger, some say a neighbor,
To claim that youth for his own.
With the first blow ends resistance; with the
Second ends innocence and the third ends the
Manhood he had not even begun to come to terms with.

Todd Flukey

A Wonderful Son

A wonderful son the Lord has given.
Father mirrored in the lad

A son to be just like his pop.
Reflecting both the good and bad.

A son that is joy to a fathers heart.
To see him sleeping or at play.

A son who's words and deeds will grow,
More like his fathers everyday.

So father mind your tongue and manners
Ne'er do things wrong or on the slight.

But teach the little son who's watching
Paths of truth and strength and right.

David L. McCracken

Can I Hold This Moment?

Can I hold this moment
the way I hold you on my lap when you are sleepy
or when you need to know that I am here
and feel that I love you?

Can I caress this moment
the way I caress your hand to my cheek when you're snuggled close
or when you nurse in the middle of the night
and I whisper that I love you?

Can I smell this moment
the way I smell you with my nose nuzzled in your neck
or when I dress you after your bath
and I tell you that I love you?

Can I laugh with this moment
the way I laugh with you when I tickle your ribs
or when you crinkle your nose and smile
and I giggle and say that I love you?

No, I cannot hold this moment. It will be gone
the way you will go when you are too big for my lap
and your hands are too busy to caress.
But, I will treasure this moment and hope you'll remember that
I love you.

Kellie A. Wannamaker

Days

How lovely the days we share alone
How great our love for one another
Better times, we haven't known
All joys are memories we've shared together
At first this may seem harsh to you
This sad motion of emotions,
It would have been easier if I knew
The rocky throes of love's own ocean.
To you my dear I've loved you so
Although I have to say goodbye
Remember me for I must go
Please wipe the tear from your eye...
My love's now gone no doubt about it,
I need another, can't live without it.

Matt R. Schellinkout III

The Otherness of Memory

The endless dream of summer hung
on the charcoal rest of clouds and huddled
in vagrant sage brush, where the tongues of lovers
entwine in the erosion of their quietness

Where observance becomes a distant stare
through the glare of light
that lives also in the name of itself
in the Otherness of Memory

And searching in a sunken midheaven
language
rose from formless sleep
Fragrant between the tight lips
where our knowing breeds itself so occupied

In truce I contemplate the Sunday of my hands
As I watch you hike toward the entrances
of sleep, toward the inlets of awareness
and towards the exits
which you almost
always
found

Kerstyn M. Porsch

Journey

Magic and dreams and fantasy
Give me hope to face my reality
Giving my dreams the wings to fly
Soaring higher than the bluest skies
Searched so long for someone to say
"This is how, this is the way"
But now through time I finally see
The way could only come through me
The way was deep inside of me
To help me grow, to set me free
No more merely getting by
The time has come for me to try
To reach the peace and serenity
That comes from being who "I" need to be
Now I know that "I" too may feel
Right or wrong "my" feelings are real
Voices ringing inside my head
My past is gone, my future's ahead
My day will come and I'll finally see
The journey could only be made by me....

June Hardy

Questions of Life

I know what I want out of life.
Can you provide those needs for me? Are you what I need in my life?
I am strong, independent and most of all I am a women.
Can you accept that? Can you accept the fact that I am a
women who can stand on my own?
Because not only am I a women, I am an intelligent Black women.
Can you look beyond the color of my skin and accept me
for who I am? Can you give me the respect I deserve and
treat me as an individual? That's what I need to know.

When I reach my hand out to you, will you acknowledge
my call in need of a friend?
Or will you turn your back on me, leaving me in the dark; alone?

Will you accept the fact that I have an opinion?
I have something to say about the things that go on around
me, and I will voice my opinion when I feel there is
something to be said.
Does that offend you? Are you intimidated by my strong,
yet feminine ways of life?

Can you handle this???

Brianna Washington

Untitled

Here I stand, upon a rise.
The desert stretches before my eyes,
This barren land I've grown to love,
To me, is as sweet as the cooing of a dove.

With my dad to the left, my mom to the right,
We look forward to the inevitable fight,
Of journeying safely through this land,
But we'll do it together, hand in hand.

Because in this desert we put our trust,
And we know it's the only place for us.
And if we should die before we wake.
Or the ground should tremor from a mighty earthquake.
I know that we'd still love this land,
And die together hand in hand.

Paul H. Pedersen

Point of Destination

I can see the top of the mountain
The top which all else seek
It seems the peak, the destination
Yet it is not the height I want to reach.

I can see the freedom of the sky
Where birds and wings dare to fly
Courageous souls yearn to touch that air
In my eyes, that blue, that goal - is hardly high.

I can see the endlessness of unknown space
Those bright stars and planets far
The bravest of men have painted these lands
But, my friend, this is not where my dreams are.

I can see the magnificence of my goals
Higher, further, more difficult than imaginable
In a realm where no man dares to go
A kingdom in my ability - there my heart will be full.

Elizabeth Nagy

Love

Love! I don't know. I don't know the meaning of love.
I have never been in love. What is love? I ask myself.
Where do I go in search of love, or is it in search for love?
Do I need to search for it or wait for it?
Do you give love, take it, or do both give it and take it?
Do you need love? Do you want love?
Do you expect love? Do you get love?
Who gives love, expects love.
Is it a true statement or is it simply an opinion?
Can you live without love?
Can I live without love?
Who decides? You or me?
Does anyone decides? I ask myself.
Should you ask yourself? Is love important?
Ask yourself. Just remember,
love yourself before you love anyone else....

Wilfred Fisher

Beautiful Ohio

On the Beautiful Ohio with its hills and valleys so low
When lovers spoon by the light of the moon on he Beautiful Ohio

The water it sings a song as it goes rolling along
I'd like to be there with my darling so fair on the Beautiful Ohio

I think of the days gone by when kids we play side by side
But now she is gone, and I'm all alone on the Beautiful Ohio

The flowers are faded and gone, I hear her calling
I know she's waiting up there to meet me somewhere on the
Beautiful Ohio

Hilda Parker

A Neighbor of Yesteryear

Yesteryear is a long time ago,
When a neighbor was a friend indeed.
Ah! One who cared when you had a woe,
And who was there in a time of need.

A neighbor shared a piece of day,
No matter whether 'twas dull or bright.
Someone's help was there for work or play,
During the afternoon or at night.

A strong shoulder for a broken heart,
When burdens were heavy all alone.
There to help the hurt and pain depart,
That cheery voice had a soothing tone.

A friend to share a thought and some tea,
Always ready to laugh and have fun.
Someone to try a new recipe,
Never to say it was a bad one.

A neighbor long ago is in part,
A piece of history since gone by.
Yet there still remains within the heart,
A memory that I fear may die.

Joyce Maria Paes

My Funeral

Please! No tears do I want shed
Simple because I am dead.
If we did not celebrate my life
Nor together conquer strife.
Then there is no need to pretend
I was never more than a friend.
No words of sorrow or regrets
Think of me beyond all debts.
Just remember I did love you so
Really more than you'll ever know.
Now hopefully gone to a better place
Where not some but all of the human race.
Will live together without any fears
Through all of eternities years.
In a place made for us with a loving hand
God's own creation...Heaven... So grand!

Louise L. Porter

My Father

My father, he was a loving man,
He was quick the neighbors to tend;
He never shirked his duty or ran,
And was by everyone called a friend.

He served as the town taxi-cab
Whether food to get or the Doctor to see
He never was one your back to stab
This I'm sure the church would agree.

I can hear him now as the phone would ring,
"Why, yes, I have beans for your garden to lend
And then my father would start to sing,
He knew that he'd helped his neighbour to fend.

My youth comes back and I'm happy to say
I think of the love that my father gave
He loved us all to his dying day
And our love followed him to his grave.

Ruth Glenda G. Wadsworth

Climbing a Tree to Seek Fish (Looking For A Job)

I cannot sleep
Remembering always the new grief
And the old,

The green mountain will never be hidden away,
The sunlight of sunshine on and on,
For life is just an employer,
He may give you what you ask,
I work for profession,
Merely to earn to dismay,

My tongue could posses,
everything I breathe would bless,
A word of love for those who fear
Love to mankind far and near.

John Lung Wen

Among Souls

Her eyes bore the sunrise of many a day
Can't help remembering
all the tears shed upon the way
Creamy white and velvety smooth
eyes the color of tears that never seemed to move
A soul deeper
than the well of time
Tears the color of a soft red wine
Words flowing from her eyes
not her heart
A truth deeper than trust
but to some only as shallow as lust
Don't believe
Must believe
During the time that we grieve
For the lost
For the found
For the eternally bound

Brittain Travé

Untitled

I had a dream so long ago, a hundred years it seems.
The moon shone silver light through an endless wood of trees.
I dreamed I was a little boy, lost and all alone,
And every step I took led me further from my home.
I walked all night, through tears of ice, through lonely silver trees,
Their silver branches blowing in December's icy breeze.
I had lost my faith, and all my hope, as silver light turned grey
But somehow deep within, my heart it must have known,
For when the morning came, I found I was safely home.

Life is not forever, but death is not the end.
It's just a spark in space in time, a place to begin.
So live life to the fullest, and accept death in the end.
Fear not my unknown friend, and learn what you can.

Take a long hard look old friend, to the inner of ones self,
Through your dying flesh and skin, to your soul that's deep within.
Fear not old friend, for it's just your outer shell that's condemned
to earthly hell. From the dust of earth body's made and in
its death returned the same. But our souls are everlasting, and
forever free, to walk with God our Lord, for all eternity . . . .

Donald F. Carter

Untitled

Birds some flies high and some birds flies low
Birds flies everyday looking for foods they always do
Birds sleeps on grasses, on rocks, in the caves and on the trees
Birds use the ground, grass, rocks, in the caves and on the trees
    make nests
Birds we see them everyday, everywhere and anywhere we go to
Birds are beautiful by their colors the way they looks
Birds large and small they fly and some birds they don't, they run
    and walks
Birds in bad weather they flies away and they disappears
Birds they go back to the same place when the weather is clears
Birds are trained to do some of the tricks and part of the show
Birds are used in circus to make people laugh their tricks they do
Birds some are wild when they are caught, large or small they do bites
Birds are being hunted by the hunters and get shot wherever they are
    on sights
Birds are millions being killed by human and animals every day
Birds are millions of people for foods around the world are needed
    night and day
Birds eats almost anything whatever they will find when they are
    hungry
Birds catches fish in the lakes, rivers and sea everyday
Birds are millions of people around the world would love them for a
    house pets
Birds are very useful to the millions because of their eggs and meats

Eufrocino C. Castro

Fire

The shimmer of the violin
and gasping birth of smoke.
The provider, the mother,
the ancient and eternal conception.
Endless and undesiring for love, but desiring for all.
To kill, to devour alive and give rise to litters of orange souls.
The motion and timeless existence, a siren.
Sent forth from the sky,
riding bright ghosts of flashing clouds.
Inside every heart, fed by blood
and drown by soul.
So simple, out complexing the simply complex life.
The body, the mind,
the desire, all in the light.
Light which kills, hates, and reaches forth a filthy black tongue.
Tree to tree, finger to finger.
Leaping drones to blacken and harden.
Giver of life, giver of death.

Stephen G. Rippe

Daddy

My dad once young and so alive; now fights each day to survive.
Everything which came with ease is now a struggle due to disease.
My heart it breaks each time I think of you;
and the hardships you must go thru.
You gave to me to much to say, to much for me to ever repay.
I wish I could make you well and free,
give back everything you gave to me.
You fight each day to try and refrain, from the fright of illness,
from the chill of pain. I see you there alone and crying; as I
watch part of me inside is dying.
I wish there was something more I could do, to give new life and
    hope to you.
Someday they say you maybe well, but only God and time will tell.
If wishes, hopes, and dreams came true —
all of mine I would gladly give to you.
Life they say is for the living; love they say is for the giving.
So all my love I have to give, I share with you as long as you live.
If I could take the pain you endure-for the cancer find a cure; I'd
gladly dad do this for you you've made a little girl and a woman's
dreams come true. For being there, tho your world's falling apart
daddy I love you; with all my heart.

Lori Gripko

Hidden

It is rainy and cold
No place for the moon or a star
They are hidden,they are
Prisoned away
So deep and far
And when the storm breaks
It is you I have found
Who has picked up the key from the cold wet ground
And with just that tiny flick of your wrist
Our light has returned and cleared the mist

Alicea Lieberman

Looking Thru Barred Windows

As I stand at the window looking out.
  I see snowflakes dancing down.
  Each individual in their own way.
I see people, many people, but rarely do I
  see any smiles.
Everything seems black and white - no colors.
  No one looks back at me looking out of
  the window. Almost as if I don't exist.
My heart and soul are locked up so tightly it's
  stifling my growth. I have only fear and
  loneliness for feelings.
Again I look at the smileless people bustling
  thru the snow. Only this time it's different.
I know what the difference is.... I am
  looking thru barred windows from a
  psychiatrist ward.

Suzan Phillips

I Dream of Elaborate Shadows . . . .

I dream of elaborate shadows
Spring still behind my enormous moon
Knife under my tongue, drunk from only his milk

You smear hot honey like lather
Yet they stare at me
We swim near a forest above a lake
and soar over rocks. I pant, lick your hair
Watch . . . heave . . . boil . . . sing!
Felt with life, like music
Who put my blue bitter sleep in them?
Incubate . . . manipulate . . . use me.
Hit this weak and delirious girl
Lie in bed . . . Think about it . . . How easy?
You want to smell it
Crush the rose in my petal pink love.

I see him there, shot at sea
A boy . . . a man . . . His ugly mother? Gone.
After winter, wind and storm
moan for rain, not sun. Worship water . . . and me.

Karla Anderson

Resentments

She stands at the hillside looking forlorn,
A bucket of water hangs on her limp arm,
Her gaze is held steady by something that's gone.
Her bucket is full from the tears that she shed,
Yet still she stands, silent, to the oncoming dread.
The fogs of past reality, rose and departed,
Leaving her there with the bucket she carted.
For how many years, 'cross how many miles,
She carried her bucket until this now?
But the fire she thought burning, had long since
disbursed,
Why pour water on ashes that no longer thirst?

Carole Foster

Decisions

My previous life was going along.
Normal ups, normal downs
Sometimes outside influences would be crushing
  to the spirit.
But, I'd bounce back.
Sometimes sooner, sometimes later.
Then the big bang -
Making a deal with the devil - exchanging
  integrity for security.

Guilt, stubbornness, pride, hypocrite, unrepentant,
  cold, black, ugly, hate - vicious cycle
Transitioned from bad to worse to deep darkness.
Only specks of good were there.
Unseen power, decision to change
The iron weight floated off me
Joyous, happy, peaceful, thankful, energetic, spirit -filled
And the greatest of all - love blossomed again.

B. Phillips

Gossiping

Don't you know what you are doing is wrong,
Ruining lives and breaking up homes
Day and night on the telephone
Get you some business and leave other folks alone.

You talk about this and you talk about that
Never bothering to get the facts
Never have anything to say that's good
Just stirring up trouble in the neighborhood.

There's one thing you should understand
Your mind is nothing but a garbage can
Every time you speak, it's always the same
You know who you are, you know your name.

Stop running around, stirring up trouble
When it comes back, it comes back double.
I remember what my mother said, though she's
dead and gone,
"Spend half of your time tending your business,
and
The other half leaving other folks alone."

Christine Wiley

Fleetie and Charles In the Blackberry Fields

Fleetie's stick tapped a cadence
in the gravel for Charles who dawdled,
resisting the heat.

The blackberry fields were awash with white
blossoms, speckled lightly with tan pistils,
profuse through Godless torrents

that jammed twigs into watermade dams
of leaves, acorns and oakwood bark.
The blackberries almost ran off the vine,

heavy laden like a swelled stomach begging for birth.
Charles hacked at the underbrush,
Fleetie stepped only in his footsteps.

She caught berries falling
from vines disturbed by thrashing.
Their blood-red-indigo stained her apron,

left a puddle in the deep dish,
lined with white crust for cradling
the death of blackberries.

Melissa Prunty Kemp

485

Zoo Story

August 6, 1996

Sybarites, sycophants, sex fiends and Sue
Visit the animals, two by two,
Their startling expressions clearly in view;
Life is so vexing here at the zoo.

Freedmen and fried men, dope friends and jerks,
Liars and laughers believe in what works,
Criminals, carrion, mental inmates,
Crowding together to glare through the gates.

Women with lovers
And women without
Singing and crying
Seek their way out.

Shoppers and buyers
Finding their way,
Slickers and slackers
Having their say.

You wanted the animals,
A gorilla or two?
Life in Edge City:
The mirror's the view.

Joel Goldstein

The Refrigerator

I know that I have to sooner or later
Finally clean out my refrigerator.
The time has come
I can't put it off any longer.
The smell is disgusting
And I think growing stronger.
It must be the cheese in the door with the fuzz.
I kept it - um, just because.
Or maybe I'm smelling that Mexican dinner,
Left over from, the beginning of Winter?
You know it could be the lunchmeat down in the drawer.
It's been there from way before.
Well I'm not sure when, it was long ago.
That's probably it, but who's to know.
I bet it's the milk from last month.
I'm sure that it's sour.
You now I think I'll clean this tomorrow!

Stacy Blaine

It's Hard Not to Be Taken In By September

Maple trees bedazzle and beckon from the lane,
Brazenly wooing me with their witchery.
The swollen moon pulses orange and heavy,
Throbbing its ancient vibrations across
The black stick figures of a wooded hill.
I ache with longing to embrace such beauty.
My fingers drip with desire and I yearn
To rest in such warmth — to succumb to such sweetness.
But I am afraid to let down my whole weight —
To surrender and float in its warm seas.
For I have seen the gentle rolling hills —
The firmament itself — stagger and crash.
So I am afraid and I am ashamed
To ever trust and love the world again
After what it did to my beloved.

I feel a touch, I see a bit of beauty,
And yield to the gentle wooing of the thrush.
So wounded and doubtful, I rejoin the march.
September comes a leaf at a time
And it's hard not to be taken in by September.

Normagene Warner

They Were Once

Been lying here for hours on my sunken bed
A pillow propping up my rather thoughtless head,
Millions of tears steaming down my endless cheek
Watching each one absorbing into my sheet.

The distant sound of my clock as it's striking three
Recalling that this morning you belonged to me,
My clock's still ticking without gaining time
As I go on pretending you're still mine.

My radio is humming out the saddest song
I close my weeping eyes and wonder what went wrong,
The disc-jockey says good-night and goes off the air
And I awaken from a nightmare finding you're not there.

Finally the rising sun appears above the trees
Somehow I believe one day you'll come home to me,
The morning heat is drying all the tears I've shed
I close my eyes in disbelief, I can't believe you're dead.

Sharon Redding

Lost

Memories grow dim as years go by,
  The sunshine days of youth are gone.
   My mind, my thoughts are trapped inside me
   I am lost, so lonely
      I can't find my way.

The days are long and nights slip slowly by,
  From dawn to sundown
    I feel so tightly bound.
     My dreams, my hopes are lost in reverie
      I feel the emptiness, so deep inside of me.

The seasons come, the seasons go,
  I can't recall that flowers bloom in
     Spring and Summer, too,
      I used to stop to smell the roses along the way
      But now, I just don't really care.

Somehow reality is out of reach for me
  I am lost, help me find the self
   I used to be,
      To fill my soul, to make me
        whole again.

Jo Gilland

The Candle Stick

Alice be nimble; Alice be quick
She tried to jump over a candle stick.
She stumped her toe, and began to fall;
And kicked the candle up against the wall.

The candle got mad, and began to fight back,
It rolled around, and fell in a crack.
It pulled out its lighter, and flipped its bick;
And lit a flame on the end of the wick.

Alice ran in the closet, and got a wet mop
Chased the candle around, but it wouldn't stop.
She ran to the phone and called 911,
Which sent the firemen to the house on the run.

The firemen rushed in with their polka dot pup.
They all looked around, but the candle had burned up.
Alice bowed her head, with no happiness to be;
She jumped out the window and away she did flee.

Joe Keas

America

America, America from sea to shining sea, you never bother looking at me. America, America what you have failed to see is how you kept my brothers in captivity. You rape my sisters of her virginity taking her hope and her dignity. Even my children were placed in your care only to live this life with great despair. We built your houses from a great foundation, only to disgrace us in front of this so called nation. There was a time when we inherited the land only to have it taken by my fellow man. In your mind you took me for a clown, tearing me apart and trying to bring me down. America you said that brother will commit a crime, it's only just a matter of time. America you tried to determine my reality but we know you for your superficiality.
You thought that I had no choice so now get ready to hear my voice the Lord taught me to guide, govern and protect in order to give mankind it's utmost respect. Respect me America, for my time has come, my mission on this earth has finally begun. I will never go away, that you will see, until everyone of my brothers are totally free. So America don't continue in your disgrace, because one day you'll meet my Creator face to face.

Rafael Suarez

Wonderment

The golden sun sank in the West,
  Nature was putting her to rest.
The sky was filled with color bright,
  and to my eyes 'twas a beautiful sight.

The stars came out—each one alone,
  To what to them did seem their home.
And then, the moon in splendor rare,
  did; with the stars, her beauty share.
Finally dawn broke up the night,
  and all about was clear daylight . . .
And, from my place where I did sit,
  I wondered . . . and thought . . . about All of it.

Mildred L. Goldthwaite

Keeper Alone

On a barren isle of earth's gray bones,
Away from the shore and barely seen,
Stands the Keeper among broken stones,
Where once his lighthouse bravely beamed.

Beamed with a light that parted the night,
Shining steady above the breaking wave.
Where his horn once sung allaying all fright,
With the words "Be brave, Be brave."

While the lighthouse stood on shoreside earth
None noticed the waves that beat at its walls.
Many blessed the light till safely berthed
Thinking not of the Keeper of light and calls.

Years blew by; storm after storm,
The Keeper working always alone.
Always steady the light; soothing the horn,
While around him grew the isle of stone.

The lighthouse now broken, alone stands the Keeper.
On shore, no one shines a guiding light.
As the waves wash the isle, even steeper,
No soothing horn helps him brave the night.

Donel L. Davis

Oklahoma Remembered!

Lord,
  Hear us in our silence, as we stand mute
    before the molten mass of rock
    and twisted metal and splintered glass.

  We see a massive structure
    once bold and beautiful now fallen in a piteous heap.

  Hushed are the voices that had come for
    help or to give aid.
  Silent are the lips of little children
    that once were singing, laughing, enjoying childhood.
  Still forever are hearts that
    loved, dreamed, planned.

Lord,
  We stand before your tomb
    that once held your body bleeding and broken

  We rejoice in our resurrection
    and listen to your words of
    forgiveness, love, peace.

  Two tombs, both symbols of death
    conquered by love and peace.

Ellen A. Lynch

Parents

Molding the future, teaching the past
Forging the fire, the flames will last
Spreading truth, keeping us alive
Trying to give us, a way to survive
Protecting us, helping us forever
Hoping we become, something much better
Jobs are hard, parenting is harder
Raising your kids, making them smarter
The rewards are worth it, this maybe so
Loving your children, watching them grow
Some kids return the favor, others may be gone
Still you are there, for us to fall back on
Keeping dreams alive, giving us hope
Helping us deal with life, learning to cope
Spending all your money, sometimes getting mad
See us do well, will you both be glad
I shall repay if I can, repay you well
My thoughts of you always, over you they dwell
My thanks for you being there, helping me along
I shall do well, and try to do no wrong

Justin R. Germino

Daddy's Little Girl

Dear Daddy, so scared and alone,
You try to hide it, but in your face it's shone.
You don't think that I love you,
But really, Daddy I do.
You're thinking no one cares for you,
But, Daddy I know they do.
You don't want to admit you have feelings too,
So you're going to keep on
Till we all hurt like you.
I don't want you to suffer, Daddy
Or to feel bad,
But you do anyway,
And that makes me sad.
You've made me feel bad and terrible inside,
But I have tried my best to hide
The way that I feel in my heart.
I wish that we could make a new start.
I love you, Daddy, I really do,
And I know in my heart
You know it's true.

Trish Wampler

Autumn

Autumn comes to tread the earth on soft and silent feet,
Trees touched with tawny gold and flame, air that is soft and sweet

In hazy iridescence lies, throughout the sundrenched days,
As summer breathes a sad farewell and gently slips away.

Cicadas in the still night air render a lullaby,
Creatures scurry, gathering stores, beneath the autumn sky.

Flowers in joyous abandon bloom, earth is with abundant
    harvest blessed,
And therein singular beauty lies, resplendent in her autumn dress.

The caterpillar spins a chrysalis, a tiny silken thing,
Sarcophagus of winter's sleep from which transfigured life will spring.

Scampering before the wind, the vivid leaves go flying,
So beautiful while living, all the more glorious in their dying.

The song of birds is silenced now...wind bears the wild goose call,
Across the crisp cold autumn air resounds their fond farewell to fall.

Thunder rolls across the sky and sets the trees to swaying,
Stark sentinels of the autumn past with beseeching arms are praying

Awaiting spring's rebirth again, when returning geese recall,
The Creator once spoke in eloquence, in that "still, small
    voice" called Fall.
    Patricia B. Griffith

Not Everyone's Perfect

Not everyone's perfect, I just want to scream,
just cause your teeth don't have a white gleam.
Not everyone's perfect, or smells like a rose,
so what if you have a really big nose?
Not everyone's perfect, or all dressed up for a ball,
so what if your eyes are squinty and small.
Not everyone's perfect, the length of your hair is not a mile,
who cares if you don't have a really great smile?
Not everyone's perfect, your feet are to clunky,
does it matter if you're even a little bit chunky?
Not everyone's perfect, and you don't need to be,
just look in the mirror, and say I love me.
    Christine Snitkin

35th Wedding Anniversary

Mom and dad, number 35 is here
And gathered 'round you are those you hold most dear.

They have come to express their love and affection
For two people who are close to perfection.

You have certainly had trials and tribulations in those 35 years
And had a number of events that brought you to tears.

But there were also those happy moments you two shared;
Those times that pulled you through when you were scared.

Both of you worked hard to make your marriage last this long
And had to tolerate things that each knew the other had done wrong.

You were motivated to do so by a love for our family unit
And never sought to disrupt, only to fine tune it.

This is a testimony to a love that for 35 years has survived
And we look forward to another when number 50 has arrived.
    Ronald H. Gottlieb

Consecrate

Can't the geese see they're falling?
Tapping the fragile needle in and out of consciousness
Biting down upon a frown fetal response...
Attacked by sheaths of fallen feathers,
I melt into trickled disappointment.
Ordered to blend into the ice on toes of chauffeured
Monks led to their pact. Poured bourbon and lit matches;
Square upholstery emitting no protest but sparking anguish
Flaming silence; unaware he was being rocked to sleep
Once again reveled in yellow ashes
Separated, placed on foreheads of disfigured scribes
Feed charred notes of unusual pleasing!
"Think nervous green piercings"
Kind hands rewind retracting thorns
Infected danger tissues and hang nails
Outgrown and grasping at matador's opus
Soiled cosmic orchard ruptured by imperfect chasing
The slow sinking of the lamb
    Keith Mandella

God's Honey Bee

Life's journey is to get to A B C and D, but, she pondered,
how did I get here so fast? She said, I drove my car over
land to see what I could see. I've flown over land and sea,
to foreign lands through clouds drifting under a bright blue
sky. And, I've sailed a luxury liner cutting a
    path through the dark blue sea.

I, she proclaimed; was the route by which two children came.
A married woman for more than a decade — the strings that
fettered, left her undefined. "Does a butterfly have a soul?"
She asked. For those who loved her; loved her through space.
My America, a defiant chin stated,
    "give me freedom or give me death."

Where are her roots? She has none for she made none. Now she
creaks and squeaks, she has to stay put. In her heart, she
still flits and flies. As she reflected on the decades, she
smiled peacefully — for to get from A to D, there would be
no change, ah, she sighed, "I am what I am,
    God's little Honey Bee."
    Elevene Kern

Through My Eyes

Through my eyes, through your eyes
We see the same things so differently
What might be second nature to you
may be a challenge to me.

Things that you may never face
I must fight everyday
Things you may find out of place
To me it's normal in every way.

Sometimes I may be loud and my actions not always right.
But it's my only tactic, the only way I know to fight.
I'm just a little voice trying to be heard
but my leaders don't hear me, so I'm left with my own words.

Since they don't have to live my life or feel the pain I do.
They'll never understand until they're wearing my shoes.
So when you see me on the streets, don't shout, don't scorn or stare.
Please give me a helping hand cause one day it just might be you here.
    Maisie Harvey

Fragile Spirit

As I sit here by myself
The loneliness encases me

I don't feel anything, I am numb
It's cold and I never seem to warm
I'm tired and the energy that once filled my body has run away
It can't find its way back inside, the loneliness encases me

I go out into the world yet I'm not a part of it
Everyday brings me back to the same place
I can't seem to open up to anyone around me
I speak to people and they talk back but it never gets inside
I see everything yet I see nothing
My life stands still as I sit huddled
I want to break out but I don't know how
I'm screaming but no one hears me
The loneliness encases me

Who will help me, who will unlock my jail
I want to feel again, I want to smile and feel joy, I want to cry
I want to live and share but no one's there, the loneliness encases me

As I sit in silence I can only hope
That someday I'll find the key to remove
The loneliness that encases me

Pamela R. Harding

The Joy That Will Never Die

Into this world you came the hopes and dreams of our tomorrow.
    That joy will never die.
The touch of your tiny body against my breast.
The tiny hand that reach out to grip:
The tiny lips that will not say "I love you." That joy will never die.
The beat of your heart that echo of life that you hold.
That joy will never die.
The skin that was so soft as velvet and new. That joy will never die.
The caress of your tiny legs, hands and feet.
The kissing of your tiny cheeks. That joy will never die.
The tiny feet that will never touch the ground to run,
play skip and climb. That joy will never die.
The movement of your body that say. "I am trying." "I can't go on."
That joy will never die.
The eyes that say. "I am tired. "I can't go on." "I must go!"
"I love you mom more than you know. It's time to go."
That joy will never die.
The time was short and full of joy. That time of joy will never die.

Barbara Duncan

The Last Farewell

Please hear my cries my beloved one,
For soon the dreadful hour will come
When death and I shall be as one.
I call for you, but you do not come
Your time and love belong to another one,
Why do her charms intrigue you so?
Is she that much better? I'd like to know.
My heart cries out, but to her you go.
She has you now, of this I know.
So, this will be my last farewell,
As I walk thru the pits of Hell,
But to you these words I'd like to tell.
Good-bye my love, take care,
Farewell

Margaret Dotlich

Falling Into Grace

What I want to know is
When you fall down
How do you respond?
Do you pretend you have not fallen?
And if you do, do you deny the grace
That is your place
When you fall?
Do you experience just how small you really are?
Or deny the very essence of the truth
And in the act ... deny yourself
And not tend to your garden?

What I want to know is
When you fall down
How do you respond?
Do you frown, not knowing that you've grown?
Do you groan at the naked pain
And curse the gods as a refrain?
Or do you refrain from wallowing in the pain
Experiencing exquisite pain
A labor . . . leading to creative . . . birth?

Andrew H. Hahn

Imprisoned

Some live behind bars,
While others live with invisible scars;
The damage is still the same.

For some, imprisonment means jail,
For others, there is no bail;
The walls are permanent.

Through family, society, stereotypes, and lifestyle,
Others let ideals and thoughts pile;
Sometimes, we build our own.

Sometimes, we lose our perspective and our mind flutters,
Until we really see how it affects others;
God can give us "true" humility!

No matter how tight we feel the noose,
God will help make it loose;
God will protect, be a friend, and see you through your trials!

Darlene Whitesel Quinn

Mother to Be

He has chosen a dear one with heart of gold;
    These are the arms he wishes this new life to hold.
There is nothing like a baby's face to make
    your home a sacred place.
The sweet and innocent little smile makes any
    couple's life really worthwhile.
His tiny little hands clenched ever so tight
    is to me a most beautiful sight.
The pitter-patter of little feet is sound
    that will be ever so sweet.

Now, that a mother you are soon to be; your
    world will change just wait and see.
Never panic when he seems to fret; check his
    pants they might be wet.
If a temper tantrum he might fling, heaven
    knows my dear, try any and everything.
Sometimes he'll refuse to eat; that's another
    dilemma you'll be sure to meet.
Don't be disturbed if he cries at night, just
    rock and sing until broad daylight.

Flora Mae Purvis

A Land Forgotten

Rape, Drugs, Murder
What does it all mean
The homeless, the poor, the sickly
Laws don't protect the unseen
Many people die throughout the land
Our freedom can be lost with the turn of a hand

Prejudice, suicide, and hatred
    When will it ever end
Brothers fighting for no reason
    Stalking each other until the end
Why must we fight, why must we kill
    We're all here out of God's will

America's supposed to be the land of the free, the home of the brave
    How can you be so senseless, so thoughtless
So uncaring to the needs of others, you knave
    We all live together, not as master and slave
America welcomes all, so should its people
    No matter what color or creed, we all exist from the same seed
In the years to come we must change our ways
    Or become a world forgotten with nothing left to say

Eric Morgan

An Epitaph

    My life was like a bargain store, as
people would come in and out. Some would
stay long enough to buy a part of my heart, and I would
never forget them. It was more than what
money could ever buy.
My life was like a rose, as I bloomed
into maturity. Each petal represented
each year gone by. Now, they are just memories.
My life was like a dance. Sometimes, in the
middle of the song, you would have to change
partners. One night, I found the one to spend
my life with.
Eventually my life became like an empty cave,
as the wind whipped in and out, but brought
no one. I grew to be old, and lonely.
Yes, my life was like a bargain store. Bless all
the customers, who stayed long enough to
buy a part of my heart.
My life was like a race, and now, I have crossed
the finish line.

Renee C. Horn

God's Beauty

The stillness just before dawn
With the fresh smell of a mown lawn
The cautious clicking sound of the hummingbird approaching food
The kitten purring warmly feeling ever so soft in a hungry mood.

This is beauty God gave you.

The happy laughter of children
Feeling secure in their haven
The great smells in the kitchen
The loving hands stitching.

This is beauty God gave you.

The colorful kite in the sky
The breakers happily rolling high
The sky so blue
The warm sun's yellow hue.

This is beauty God gave you.

The red violet sky
The ball of red fire saying good-bye
As the moon appears
The stillness reappears.

This is beauty God gave you.

Patricia A. Fode

Anger

The one fleeting moment of emotion.
The one wave that brings loss of mind and soul.
The one scared second of confusion.
The one true example of a real fool.
A state that forever will be displaced,
Disillusioned, disinherited.
Yearnings of insanity is its face.
A stiff display of disgust and tirade.
A fury, a fluctuant, a frazzle.
A burning born into deep eternal
Flames of pain and conviction. It dazzles!
The deceptive gift that is internal.
A motivation of power and glory.
A limitless drive of a sad story.

Christopher Michael Mejia-Petersen

My Love For You

    I have stood on mountain tops looking at the world at my
feet. I have looked up at the sky from the bottom of great
canyons, feeling insignificant to life.
    I have walked hot, humid jungles of foreign countries,
where the sun light cannot penetrate the overgrowth. I have
been in merciless desert sun where sand and cactus stretch as
far as the eye can see.
    I have watched the sun light glisten like diamonds while
I stood in hip deep snow. I have witnessed the dawning of new
life after the snow has gone.
    I have seen the oceans of the world. I have seen the
largest lake to the smallest ponds. I have been to the
barren lifeless lands, to the rich prairies. I have watched
the most beautiful sunrises, and sunsets all over the world.
    You once told me I have lead an exciting life, perhaps I
have. These memories are near and dear to me, but they pale
to my love for you.

Harry Hardwick

Diamond in the Midst

Lacking the luster of her surroundings,
pressure from peers emits a constant pounding;
The screams of her innocence lay upon deaf ears,
giving drops of life to a mother's worst fears;
There was once a futile attempt for one in the same,
but rebellion severed her from all that is tame;
Her highness was bred to believe diamonds were her best friend,
controlled euphoria swept her in the midst of the trend;
Purposely detached from what was once her life line,
her fading, dull shine helps her run out of time;
Darkness hovers her streets paved with fornication,
no longer a master of her fate addicted to the sensation;
Often times, the sun shines and she must shamefully hide her face;
Her past absorbed by her future is immersed in disgrace;
Not long ago her friends were crutches that bonded her pride;
Dissipating into eternal ridicule, no longer by her side.
Raindrops collide with teardrops as the diamond loses sight,
disease, drama, and despair have come to claim the lady of the
night.

Winston Darryl Rathey

The Greatest Woman in the World

To that Master Fitness Award Recipient and
Distinguished Honor Graduate who has
humbled herself and brought herself down
beneath her elevated status to the lowest
level to become my wife even though I am not
ever worthy of you, or even to wipe the sweat from
your body or sit in the corner of the same classroom.
Oh how I long to lift you up where you came from and elevate you
to the highest place where only you deserve to be!

Perry Louden

The Empty Garden

In the Garden of Hopes and Dreams,
Even the sturdiest rose will perish under
The onslaught of a sudden and severe autumn storm.
Left alone are the tender buds that,
Sheltered for years by its presence,
Must now face their life in the Garden alone.
"How can we go on?" they weep.
Intertwining branches offer their support,
Yet still there's a void where once there was comfort.
How long until the Garden is restored to its original perfection?
It is a lost question. Many seeds will be planted,
But each with its own unique beauty will die.
In the afterglow of the setting sun,
The Keeper of the garden kneels
And gently embraces the broken form.
Well, He remembers this rose
For it was among the most beautiful
Of all the flowers in His Garden.
Weeping over its untimely loss,
He lovingly carries it to His home among the clouds.

Paul R. Kasold

Black Purse

I'm your big black purse short and round.
I've been thrown down to the ground, shoved and pushed around.
I never rest because I'm always on the go.
I think there's something you should know.
I'm not appreciated.
I'm exploited and violated.
There I hang.
Watch that door, oh oh Bang.
You fill me up then dump me out.
Whip me around and scream and shout.
I'm your big black purse.
I have buckles and a strap on me with little eyes to see.
To sit and rest is all I want to do, but I can't because of you.
I'm not happy why can't you see.
You take me everywhere you want me to be.
When will you and I agree.
Just let me go, set me free.
Would it be different if I were green or blue.
When will you realize I have feelings too.
I'm your Big Black Purse.

Shannah Respass

Be Yourself

Everyone is born with a name,
a legend to carry on, a writing
with ones words, and thoughts
and feelings unheard.
As things are changing
someone's always rearranging.
Grieve of sorrow and forget
today and be happy tomorrow,
Keep your head up high, and
but never lie is what your
mom told you, but it never worked.
As you tried your best a little more,
you began to ignore who you really were.
Be yourself because you are loved
already for who you really are.

Heather Warren

God's Plan

He created the earth and mountains we climb
Gave life to creatures of various kind
Encircled the world with oceans and seas
What more could be asked of his wondrous deeds
Yet something was missing from this beautiful land
An image such as he - Man!
Now given his power and divine discretion
Our existence was created to his perfection
No preference of features nor relevance of color
For if that mattered to he we would look like each other
Innocent we come - ignorant we grow
The moral - equal we're born and equal we'll go.

Audrey M. Toro

The Anger of Achilles

Anger —
   Sing now the anger,
smoldering with-in the proud spirit of Peleus's son, Achilles,
burning deep and bursting unexpected like wild fire.
   Sing the violence
which shook countless sturdy souls
and hurled them to the hazy underworld,
but left their lifeless bodies lying;
a feast for half-starved scavengers.
   But sing that we may also feel
the burning ember trapped with-in our own spirit,
that we may feel the bitter conflict swelling within our breasts
until it bursts forth into the brutal clash of bronze on fighting
fields.
   How like raging fire it sweeps through the enemy,
pouring forth its contagious black smoke
until even the wielder is blinded,
until everything is consumed,
and all that remains,
is ash.

Dominic Crapuchettes

Image of Caroline

The wedding March fades, and she stands facing the altar
with tiny orchids pinned in her hair.

The Operating Room is full of people
and I am strapped on the table,
belly bulging upward like a huge beach ball.
Green drapes are placed, but I can see myself
in the mirrors above the table.
Tension mounts, the incision is made.
My heart pounds and I begin to be nauseated,
and then I hear, "It's a girl, and she's beautiful."
She cries - a loud, protesting wail.
Everybody cheers and they bring her to me,
wrapped in a well-washed blanket,
with a trickle of blood on her forehead
and masses of black curls.
My arms are restrained and I can't touch her
but my soul sends a kiss to hers as I whisper,
"Welcome, my little daughter." They take her away
to the nursery, and the next time I see her
she has tiny orchids pinned in her hair.

Mary Jo Carr

491

The Boy With Mica Eyes

You're just a boy with mica eyes
who can only love a mystery
and I'm the woman of numerous lies
who cannot ignore your history.

You only see what's missing there
You only hear what's unspoken
You're the boy with the soft-rock stare
and I'm the woman unbroken.

You only want what you can't touch
to find what you think you've lost
I'm the woman who desires too much
while wondering at what cost.

You only want to try to be bold
You only claim to be daring
I'm just a woman who's growing old
but a woman who's way past caring.

You're just a boy with a transparent plea
for a chance to avoid self-destruction
I'll be the woman you need me to be
for a chance to succumb to seduction.

Marti Owens

My Daughters

My daughters, all grown up now
I don't know when or how
This miracle came about
I can not believe I played a role
In the forming of a seed into a soul

There's been many pleasures
And buckets of tears.
And I know I've finally done
something right
When they say to me
"Mom, when things are dark, you bring the light."

Yolanda Alfano Petrella Kurutza

The Wanderer

I've spend nights wandering within myself
and years keep going on.
Darkness preys upon my sight
and I've lost consciousness once again.
Are you ready for another?
Drowning myself with time
and time stands as black as the night.
My world resembles a vampire's, I embraced
the darkness which can be more comforting
because lights just show us
who we are.
And I'm not anything.
There's a place not far from here where
the rivers and streams are filled with
tyranny's blood.
And fishermen bait their hooks in search for power.
"Mine's bigger than yours!" they scream,
talking in the words of their devil.
Are you ready for another?
Well, it's too late.

Michael Ponkey

The Search

I wandered alone in search of God,
The Hazel hills beckoned, the feel of sod
Beneath my feet was nature calling
So I scuffed on, through red leaves falling.

A bird sent out his call to the wild,
A flower, whose fragrance was sweet and mild,
Nodded and danced in the breath of the wind,
So on I climbed, still looking for Him.

Nearing the top I saw scenes unfold,
An onyx city, country threaded with rivers of gold,
The heavens were tinted with azure blue
And yet I saw no God come through

Wearily I sank upon the ground
Beauty and majesty were all around
From whence comes God? I scanned the sky,
Only a fleecy cloud floated by.

Then, from my heart I heard a call
As my soul responded to the beauty of Fall.
That voice from within, while midst nature I trod
Told me that there would I always find God.

Martha Smith Gussow

The Beginning

In the beginning the air stood perfectly still
But the thoughts in our minds were churning at will
Which way will the conversation eventually flow?
Will I learn something I don't already know?

In the beginning we learned how to share
Lightening the load because others do care
Patiently waiting you lend me your ear
Understanding and friendship sit with me here

In the beginning we laughed and we cried
A bond solid still as we begin to divide.
The beginning is now, whatever we do
Thanks to the caring of people like you.

The road may be rough with sharp curves and strange bends
But the trek will be easier because of new friends.
And when you approach the next dip in your path
Reach down inside; don't forget how to laugh.

Jilanie Wheeler

Piper of the Rock

Atop a windswept mountain, a lonely piper played.
His old eyes searched the twilight, very soon to fade.
Wailing strains of his lament pierced the winter's sky,
Catching the ears of angels, who were slowly passing by.

Angelic voices rose, resounding with pure love,
And tartan-clad forms descended, from all the heavens above.
The mountain roared with laughter, as old games started anew.
The night filled with wonder for a piper who did stand true.

Far below, in the glen, windows and doors were bared tight.
Such clamorous frolicking, on a deserted mountain,
Gave the villagers less than a peaceful night.

Daybreak came, and the villagers searched
For a clue to last evening's happenings.
The frozen body of the piper was soon found,
But of his pipes, naught was found but its wrappings.

Where unto a lament is piped, above an old piper stands ready.
Joined as one, the pipes do say, "Farewell—kinsman."
"Welcome home this day!"

Annabella Smith Blackwell

My Dark Fear

You walked in, I stood up
my eyes felt tears, then I woke up,
and you're still gone, and I'm still here...
All that remains...
is my dark fear.

The way things were, when we were one
we had our times, we shared such fun.
But now you're gone, I don't know how
will you come back? I need you now.

I see you here, I see you there,
do you see me? I'm always near!
I want to know, what made you leave
can someone please, make me believe.

So here I lay, beneath my soul
my heart still cries, I'm all alone,
with no one here, I'll see you soon,
asleep alone, In this dark room.

Christopher Frizzell

Roads I Travel On

There are roads that run in broad, smooth lines:
A marvel of highway arts.
With graded fills an wide fast curves
And cold impersonal hearts.
They're busy roads, heedless roads
Like a city's crowded street.
With never a bit of space thereon for a
Wanderer's trudging feet.

But there're other roads that wind like trails
Where the sands lay soft and white;
That rise and dip and rise again,
Like a nighthawk's startled flight
They're quiet roads, thoughtful roads;
They beckon on and on
And down their shady, tree-framed way
My gypsy feet are drawn.

Grace Sellers

Heart Cannot Withstand A Lie

Girls love to play with things
To see how they run,
And when it comes to kissing guys
They do it just for fun.

They give their hearts away
They play you for a fool,
They wait until you have given yours
And then they play it cool.

You'll wonder where she is at night
You'll wonder if she's true
One moment you'll be happy
The next you'll be blue.

I know you will laugh at me
For you enjoy my tears
The sound of my heart breaking
Must be music to your ears.

I'd hate to disappoint you
But we are not the same
I am through with you and through with love
For its endless pain.

Shaun Suman

Sins of the Heart

Allegiances no longer clear
Realizing his greatest fear,
Tried to fight it at every turn
Lied to himself he could discern,
Thought he'd be a different man
Take the high road was the plan,
Intentions were noble at the start
Why must they now numb the heart,
Finds solace in the daydream that can never be
Unencumbered spirit's free,
Sins of the father revisited; sins of the heart unspoken

His pride and joy he swore not to betray
But the grip grows stronger by the day,
The soulmate arose from an innocent flirtation
But left in it's wake family devastation,
Mental meltdown so hard to resist
Unspoken romance imagined tryst,
Caught in the cross fire of conflicting emotions
Passion runs hot and blood drives the notion,
Sins of the father revisited; sins of the heart unspoken

Gregory Strieby

Golden Pen

Upon her collar she wears a golden pen.
Calls it her guardian angel, says it protects her from sin.

Around her neck she wears a cross.
Just like the one Jesus died on to save the lost.

She goes to church on Sunday, morning and says Amen,
Sunday night she's on the street a living in sin.

Says she has no faults, and she's done nothing wrong.
Yea you'll hear her in church on Sunday morning singing a gospel song.

She had her Guardian Angel by her side, but
She couldn't see it for her selfishness and pride.

She called me the "man who walked the land"
On our wedding day I placed a Bible in her hand.

Without regards to what the Bible said, she
Partook of the forbidden fruit, and now a child is dead.

Says she's a Christian, and she's ready to die.
But when she opens up her eyes in hell,
Then she'll be the one to cry.

Yea upon her collar she wears a golden pen
Calls it her Guardian Angel, says it protects her from sin.

Henry L. Minor

On Losing the Self

A void filters through the body wearing my face,
using my name, mouthing my words.

The face and body move in time, reflecting emotion
which conceals the death.

The others are deceived by the clever masquerade
and they smile, calling the name which belongs to
the body wearing my face.

They chatter words mouthed blank without meaning.
Empty adjectives strung out by verbs and attached to
nouns fill the air, and the void remains hidden
in the eternal audition.

A fleeting honesty threatens to expose
the cowering void . . . but not this time.
Never again.

The void smothers the truth hidden within the body
wearing my face, using my name, mouthing my words
. . . and I am gone.

Shana Barnes

Mystery Man

Dark as the night sky;
A black onyx vision of my eye.
The beauty so hidden yet bold in action
It is no wonder there is a vivid attraction,
Of love burning joy on high.

Nicer than spice in this you are,
The profoundest gentlemen I have met by far.
Your concerns for me greatly appreciated;
In my words of a sensational melody,
Shall be remembered and kept in my heart-filled jar.

Sweeter than the darkest chocolate,
My muscular "knight in shining armor"
Who rescues me through rain or shine,
And makes me feel warmer
Than anyone has who was once mine.

For you are the "Mystery Man"
The one that I adore;
One that I can relate to
And admire from afar.
Someone I could love forever more.

Adrianne Johnson

The Thunder Storm

Roaring! Pounding! Wisping! Sounding!
Raining hard or not at all,
You hear it far off, you see it up close,
Storming! Flashing! Pouring! Clashing!

Raining! Draining! Falling! Calling!
Returning the water, by fall of the rain.
And clouding the sky and drowning the sound,
Shining! Blinding! Roaring! Soaring!

Springing, Sprinkling, Stringing, Singing,
Down and over, bottom to top,
All over scattering plants, scaring animals,
Dousing, Dinging, Demolishing, Destroying,

Until it is over nothing is calm, nothing is perfect,
Nothing is right, nothing is dry,
Nothing is simple, nothing is quiet,
Until the thunder storm is over.

Christopher M. Fuentes

Will Peace Come?

In the shadows of the morn
A hopeful thought of peace is born.

A peace that allows the child to sleep,
A peace that will still the weep.

A restless peace it is no more;
The cannons still, the pause of war.

Will it last? The frightened heart does ask,
Or is war just hidden under a Peacemakers mask?

Like a restless soul it will prowl again;
It is not right! It is insane!

Has man always been like this,
With a heart full of hate, and a mind in a twist?

No way to cleanse the blackened soul;
A wonderful dream, an elusive goal.

Will peace come? Will it come some day?
Only when we know - that we are the same.

When will we silence the sounds of war?
Will we hear it? Or will it be when we are no more?

Margaret Hall

He Taught Me Loneliness Can Be A Friend

He taught me that loneliness can be a friend
That He will be with me until the end.
Whenever loneliness engulfs me, I go to Him in prayer,
And he tells me that He is and will always be there.

He always seems to show me the joy that can be found in life
Without unending strife.
He taught me the way to live
And all the pleasure being a Christian can give!

He never ceases to amaze me,
His ever-abiding love is easy to see.
So whenever loneliness engulfs me I take it to God,
His loving hands turn me around and help me with the life I
   must trod...

Joyce Elaine Hamilton

If Awaiting

If awaiting perfection before life spending,
To sleep never having lived;
If awaiting long winter night's ending,
To wake it will have ended.

If awaiting the red rose in full blooming,
To see having missed the bud;
If awaiting death while time consuming,
To die never being born.

Richard Kendall

My Inspiration

Ten years has passed dear Mom
   And not one day goes by,
That I don't think of you
   And for many reasons why.
Your loving ways and gentle touch
   Always come to mind,
I'll never forget the things you taught me
   Love, respect and to be kind.
It's hard to be no one's child
   Even to this day,
The loss of you still hurts, Mom
   Will the pain ever go away?

Sherry Trentadue-Forman

Owl

The wind flows rapidly through
the trees as if it knew.
Clouds roll in ready to destroy.
As the creatures, large and small.
Scatter to find shelter.
A single flake of snow falls to the
shivering earth below,
But no one there to witness,
such a sight of beauty gone,
But the forces of nature pushes on and on,
Layering the seen with the softest white,
Completely changing the mood of all
Bigger and bigger the snow dunes grow.
After it settles the quietness is disturbing,
But at a strain of the eye a creature
of beauty appears.
Pounding the air with its huge wings,
It becomes - everything.

Bobby Callahan

A Glance Within

Do what you have to do
I will always need you
Follow the dictates of your mind
Be sensitive and cautious-not blind
For Frost said to have vision and insight in line
Then you will truly be perceptive and hopefully kind.

Elizabeth Gustafson

Wishing Our Lives Away

Have you ever studied a sunset
or watched the animated play of a child?
Do you cherish each moment and memory
or look elsewhere with a disgruntled smile?

Then you suffer a common malady
merely taking snatches of life in stride.
When you should savor and relish the magic
and save wishing for the final riptide.

As children we wish to be bigger,
as adults we reminiscence of being small.
We miss out on the joys of the moment
by not listening or seeing it all.

Once we started our lives in the real world,
our dreams became more active and wild.
Starting on Monday wishing for Friday
dreading life, often unable to smile.

Put the dreams of a lifetime together,
mix them up, take a look and you'll say,
"We spend too much time in our dreaming
just wishing our lives away."

Linda Woodall Vardeman

Why I Love Women

All men suck!
And that's no lie.
You can take it from me,
Cause I'm a guy.

Women are soft and pretty,
Kind and smart.
But most important,
Women have heart.

All men are nuts! Just ask
Mary Todd Lincoln the source of her pain.
It was her husband Honest Abe,
Who drove her insane.

Women are honest and open,
Men don't speak the whole truth.
Women have poise,
Men are uncouth.

All men are jerks!
I know what I say. And
These are just some of the reasons
Why I never went gay.

Joel M. Bagelman

Angel's Eyes

Dawn's yellow blanket is spread
as the pale blue sky awakens
A lilly smiles as this moment passes in time
A blade of grass quivers in the cool breeze
only to be warmed by a sun ray
The oak tree's branches seem endless,
as they extend their appreciation to the clouds
A brush of dark air passes as a car races time
while a blue-eyed child stands still beneath the oak tree
and watches with angel's eyes.

Andrea Dee Williams

I Remember Mama

I remember Mama, from the stories that she told,
About the days of her youth, and as she was growing old.
She remembered the good old days, time spent on the farm,
It was a place dear to her, it was there she was born.

I remember Mama, through thing's she did just so,
If yours were not right with her, she surely let you know.
She taught us how to wash our clothes, then iron and put away,
To cook the food, and wash the dish, and taught us how to play.

I remember Mama, in the songs that she would sing,
Amazing grace; the old rugged cross, she'd let the praises ring.
She taught us how to pray, and how to sing along,
It made my heart fill so full, as we joined her in a song.

I remembered mama, though she sings in heaven now,
And when I sing the old song's, it seems she's near some how.
Though I long to hear her voice, I know it won't be long,
"Till" I hear her voice so clear, when all God's children get home.

Dorothy M. Kelley

Untitled

I awoke this morning with thoughts of you
    I still felt the touch of your lips on mine
    The warmth of your hands caressing my body
    The vision of your nakedness lying next to mine
    The rhythm of our hearts beating as one
    That wonderful smile that dance through your eyes
    The feeling of the incredible love I know we share
Then as I fully woke, the realities
    Rolling over and not finding you there
    Missing the opportunity to awaken you with my kisses
    That special cozy feeling that washed over me when you
      Roll over and envelope me in your arms
    The smile on your face when you say "Good Morning"
My most fervent wish for the two of us
    That God smiles on us soon
    So we can both experience these joys daily
    Freely and without reserve
    From now until the end of time
      Because with you, time stands still
I love you with all of my heart, my body and my soul....always

Penny Berndt

A Walk in Heaven

Last night when I went to bed,
the most glorious dream filled my head.
My heart was happy because you were there
you were standing alone no wheels and no chair
You and I walked hand and hand
that must of been the promised land
My hopes and dreams had come true on that walk
I had finally heard my little girl talk
You talked for hours on that day
telling me things I only dreamed you would say
As you sang to me we danced all around
then you laughed and giggled the most beautiful sound
Your little arms hugged me and you kissed my face
you whispered, "Oh mommy, I just love this place"
We were in heaven and I wanted to stay
as the Lord held you he said, "She'll be okay"
"Oh, Mommy don't cry it won't be that long
till you're back in heaven hearing my song."

Leslie Pate

Untitled

The door shuts, the key turns, the locks soap shut, the heart
recedes.
No more the open road for which it years.
The footsteps fade away, no one returns.

Night follows day, the climate cold.
Most covers up the windows, bot and bonnet
The little green saab is on hold.
The dashboard clock will count the minutes until he returns to clock it.

Slowly the electric heart begins to fade
The seconds expand as the cold contracts
Inside there is fear and panic, no way to evade,
No way to die, with wheels in silent contact.

With the frozen tarmac of the airport parking
Still the heart it faintly numerous, all hope gone
Listen now, it's early morning and familiar boobly are walking,
Where has he been, what took so long.

Now the key is in the door, the bolt Release
The life restored, through ignition.
Familiar motion, noises, sounds, expectation relief.
Possessing heart, but not brain it cannot tell us last mission.
 Thank you, and farewell my little queen saab
 Charles A. Farnham

Baby Watching

Didn't know baby watching could be such fun
We all met last week, Mother, Grand and Great Grandmother
To spend time with Great Grand-daughter

Dear Emily - her blond downy hair
The blue, blue eyes and Daddy's ears
Didn't know baby watching could be such fun!

The sudden tears, the teary smile
Discovering her voice - the coos, the howl
Didn't know baby watching could be such fun!

Her cheeks like petals on a rose
The funny way she crinkles her nose
Didn't know baby watching could be such fun!

How fast she crawls
Pulling up to things and falling down
Didn't know baby watching could be such fun!

When I see her again, she will be walking
All those burbles will turn to talking
I know it won't last
But baby watching is such fun!
 Lela Hinden

Emptiness

Alone again, beside myself
I cannot stand to look at this.
Stand in the dark, with eyes wide open.
My hands are blank, mine eyes, mine heart,
Emptiness.
Oh heart don't break,
Always, here, afraid I shake,
I made mistakes, I don't forget,
I have made progress, not regrets.
No more alone, yet still afraid.
Not on my own, I must be strong.
Stay, still alive no more.
Emptiness, goodbye old friend.
 Manuel J. Torres

Please

Night turns into night . . . Day never comes.
There is endless senseless movement in Saigon.
The noise has no meaning.

The monsoons come and wash a little of me away...
Bit by bit.

The heat steals my soul . . . A little at a time.

The war has come to the city . . . Please put me in the jungle.

There are dead everywhere . . . No place to turn away.

The smell, the sights . . . Explain it.

I can't . . . Help me!

Death is sightless. He takes all who come to him...
The willing, the unwilling, the innocent.

Pray for the children, the old and the young...
They cry. I cry . . . No one hears.

Feeling becomes numb . . .
Caring stops.

Night turns into night . . . Day never comes.

Even after twenty-eight years.

O Lord, Please help me end this war!
 Ralph William Taylor

Where I Like To Go

There is a place where I like to go,
Mystical space far from this hell hole.
An aide to evade from learning life's painful truth;
A wishful playground I yearned for in mournful youth.

I turn my carrousel into a spinning wheel.
Regaining sight of what it was cruel God did steal:
Beloved forlorn faces, bygone placid places.
Vertigo images - in cloud and tree traces.

There is no need of a seesaw for me.
"Being alone is the best way to be.
When I'm by myself nobody can say good-bye."
Insight now why Eddie Brickell sang with a sigh.

Within a box-world I fancy myself a creator
Of realms more wondrous and beautiful than their inventor.
Forming virgin worlds with use of dream in hand,
But they're fleeting castles made from grains of sand.

At the garden's center, I ascend a majestic maple,
Into the limb's embrace, climbing as high as I am able.
Kissing the serene sky above; leaving this rancid earth under.
Trusting this bough will protect me - though why should I even
bother?
 Alan P. Martin

The Apple and the Rose

Apple from the garden and rose from the bush.
Let my heart rise and mind do push.
I seek to bind and fascinate.
Am I early or God too late.
She is the sun and I am darkest moon.
Give me strength of lion or stretch of loon.
Is this love or lust - care or dare.
I mix the two fragrances to share.
Reverently, I place them in mother's soil.
Hope is high, but in desperate toil.
Be tree or bush or some combine.
But, please let our hearts now align.
 Peter P. Walsh

The Wanting Heart

Amid the strangest of dreams
I come forward, out of the midst it seems
I see myself, rising above the earth
the thundering skies echo my rebirth
  As the haze thickens, I cannot see.
Intensely I listen, yet still cannot hear
knowing your soul, I know you are near.
  What once was the familiar, has become the unknown
Damned by the empty relentless illusions
I churn in the deep dark of my night
  How can I grasp you, now . . .
But to dream again, and so I did . . .
Wantingly, I open my heart and give you my soul,
  You gently take it, to caress, to hold . . .
And I know, in each other, forever, we would rest.
  I finally awoke from my slumber, still filled with
    wandering thoughts of you . . .
And I wonder, hoping you dreamt
  the sweetest dreams too . . .

Joann Briddes

Untitled

You left me.
Outside.
In the Cold.
Shivering.
Freezing.
All this just for you.
You disappeared without a trace.
There were no clothes.
Pictures.
Or scents.
Left to remind me of you.
Did you want to hurt me like this? I loved you so much and you
just
up and left so abruptly.
But you forgot to take your feelings.
Love.
Hurt.
And most of all the anger.
Why did you leave me here
Alone?

Starr Stephens

Needed No More

A good looking man, you used to be,
Now look in the mirror and you will see.

A man who has lost all dignity and pride,
Now you're just looking for a safe place to hide.

Borrowing from one person to pay another,
The one's to be shafted were your father,
  your sister and your brother.

The monthly check that you once received,
Was gone so quickly, you wouldn't believe.

The white powder has total control,
It owns you entirely body and soul.

You used to live from week to week,
Now everyday this white powder you do seek.

The money you used for so called bail,
Did you no good, you're still going to jail.

A time to dry out is what you really need,
So guilty should be your only plea.

But as of September 5th, 1994,
Your drug dealer decided to even the score.

The white powder called coke is needed no more.

Florence Livingston

The Woman of Uz

Call me the Woman of Uz.
I have no cattle, no babbling, bleating sheep.
I have no children, no swollen, stretched stomach.
I have no husband — no kissing giving wanting taking man.
I live alone.
I have no dirtied, muddied, muddled kitchen —
  no meal for the insatiable tummy and the craving mouth of others.
I eat alone.
I am on my knees off my knees — praying, regretting, swaying.
I worship alone.
Call me the Woman of Uz. Not Samaria. Not Nazareth. Uz.
I bear no duties, no children, no man, no Other.
I bear nothing but the everything of myself.
This is the music of my woman self,
  the polyphonic ethereal celestial discord
  of the harmonic chords of my blood and my brain.
This is the flickering galaxy beyond my flooded veins,
  the solar eclipse beyond my inside outside earth universe.
I exist in the walls of my olive-Spanish skin, in the pulsating
  rhythm of my femininity, the spiraling will of my androgyny.
I am I, the She who is contentedly called, the Woman of Uz.

Jillian Yve Simon

Emotions of the Soul

From here to eternity
  You and me
    Seeking our destiny
      So that we may be free
        Love eternal and everlast
          Your being within my grasp
            Irresistible pulsations
            Mental Deviations
            Sexual transmutations
          In the depths of my mind you remain
        My love for you is honest and sane
      Will these feelings harm my brain?
    My love for you eternally remains
Your soul and mine
Together for all time
Goal of sublime
Will you be mine
Forever and all time?

Frederick Thomas Burke

Facets of Emotion

As a young man of forty, first love was upon me
She and I married in a midwestern town, see!
With a woman around who could fill me with hope
We were newlyweds now with no time to mope.

Now a child is upon us, the real work's beginning
We both had fine cars and a house, we were winning.
With a union real tight, success has no shame
That's ok too, it's part of the game.

With the passing of time some stresses are showing
As a couple we're aging and displeasures growing.
Because life's daily grind, the push, pull and shove
Now our love child has left us, and so too, our love.

Who would have thought in just twenty short years
Our once loving union has brought frequent tears.
Only memories around us as we head toward divorce
She's left me, I'm sick too, just par for life's course.

Tried, but I couldn't find the meaning of bliss
The Reaper now pulls me toward the eternal abyss.
Life's meaning, too, eludes me 'twas surely no fun
It's time now to ponder the use of my gun.

Hal V. Arden

To My Bride

I will cherish this day as my life goes on
When as two we were united as one.
The day we both took our wedding vows
And the beginning of true love had begun.

I pray that we will both understand
That we have faults, yes, both you and I.
But when problems seem to get in our way
We will forgive or forget or at least try.

But as we get older and wiser they say
And as we think of things now and then.
That if we could ever travel back in time
We would do it all over again.

I love you now in my own special way
And I know that you also love me.
May we always be happy from this day forth
And our hearts always be full of glee.

Howard L. Graham Jr.

Immortality

Ssshhh — Our Daddy's sleeping.
Do not disturb him with your weeping.
So very very soft to lie,
Until we come to him on high.
There as here, He'll take our hand,
To show us wonders in his new found land.
He is not gone, But just at rest.
His mission done, He'd done his best.
He would not want to bring us sorrow.
He taught us courage to face tomorrow.
So do not weep, Do not cry.
For him our years will hurry by.
Ours awhile, to help us here.
Never a daddy could be so dear.
He is gone for now but takes our love,
To make a better place for us above.
So Sshh — Our Daddy's sleeping.
Do not disturb him with your weeping.

Pat Hofmann

Please Stay

Remember the day when you went away.
I was afraid to ask you to stay.
I stood at the door stiff and still,
with a confused conscious and no will.
When all that doubt and all that fear,
that's when it started to come near.

We're both to blame, we both played the game,
but neither of us could take the pain.

I'll never forget that day
for you took a part of me away
that I will never get back even today.

But all this I say will it be wasted away?
I hope someone will read it one day
and not be afraid to say "please stay".

Marvin C. Summers

My Own Name

Did you call my name?
Was it your voice calling me the same?
Through the high mountains of South America
Through the gray clouds in Peru
Is that where I met you?
Hearing your voice sing my name
It was because of you, I came
To hear your voice once again
To dream, to wish, to love,
Standing here, listening to the song of my name
Somehow, it sounding the same
Watching my tears fall over the edge
Down the valley of my sore heart
The faces of mountains staring at me
Realizing why it sounded the same
Because it was I...calling my own name.

Jennifer A. Schaefer

Untitled

Many a thing can happen over the course of time.
A death of a poet or the birth of a rhyme.
As endless words fluctuate over years and years
A poet's ground tapestries are woven to ears.

Drifting over the waves of time, through centuries untold,
There are tales of princesses, dragon slayers bold,
And a gradual advance becomes noticeably clear
Poets tackle issues such as sadness and fear.

Far beyond fiction, stretching beyond lies
The human spirit is where the verse lies.
Intertwining the soul with the poet's invention
A perfect example of divine intervention.

A bond many can share, or as intimate as two
The tides of rhyme can push their way through
Most any emotion, be it sadness or pain,
Transforming tears into slivers of rain.

The beauty of poetry, unrecognized and pure.
From lips of many, poems are a lure.
A beckon, a sign, to come join their side
And prepare themselves for a fabulous ride.

Jared Horney

Mother

You were the sunshine
On a cloudy day
You were the laughter of a child at play

You were the rose of summer
Midst the winter snow
You were springtime, when the frost hung low

You were a love song
That rhymed with June
A summer's breeze, the sun, the moon

You were the wind
That filled my sails
That steered my ship
Through stormy gales

You were the sunrise of a brand new day
The morning dew, the month of May

You were the sunset, at day's end
A beautiful rainbow
A game of pretend

You were all these things
And more, you were Mother

Marie Hahn

The Concrete City

I walk slowly through cold streets,
my glances ignored by passersby,
people afraid to speak with people,
leaving me alone to wonder, why?

I am encompassed by menacing giants,
formed from melted steel and concrete,
these tall buildings are the city's arms,
reaching up to grasp the sky.

I am surrounded by howling sirens,
failed attempts to stop men's evils,
predators hiding in the city's shadows,
preying on the weak and innocent.

The city is so cold and cruel
 drowning out my voice,
twisting my thoughts and emotions,
so merciless and unforgiving.

Now, I walk quickly through the cold streets,
ignoring the glances of others,
I am unfeeling and uncaring,
concerned only for myself.

Because now...I am part of the concrete city.

Ray Torres

Question

I have a question
That no one can answer
or even understand

The things that I learn
become sand through my fingers
Leaving nothing but ghosts
that disappear right in front of me

True knowledge is rare, even rarer than love
or what passes for love in this world today

Even the wisest of the wise
can't say why man can be so kind, and yet so cruel

`No answers, but so many questions
What is it we're looking for
That we can never find
in ourselves, or in our world
Yet so quick to throw off any happiness and contentment
for the latest thrill to come along

So much time spent searching
in the unyielding darkness
A blind man looking for the promised land

David Seguin

Autumn . . . Every Season Has Its Color

Every seasons has its color, just like you.
For me there is no other.
Autumn is now my favorite season.
And I fell for her without a reason.
I don't know how and I don't know why,
But she just somehow happened to catch my eye.
Perhaps it was her eyes, her face, or her beautiful smile.
But anyhow, this is the girl I've desired all the while.
Autumn is whom I adore.
She's opened my eyes to a whole new door.
She is more beautiful than a sun rise or set
She is more beautiful than anything can get.
The name is Brown, of this young fellow.
It ain't orange, red, or ever yellow.
Autumn Brown, doesn't it have a lovely ring?
Nothing is as beautiful or lovely as the real thing.
To end this, what can I say or do?
Other than to say, "Autumn I love you."

Christopher Brown

My Heart's Prayer

Lord, show me the sunshine on dark, cloudy days,
cleanse me and change my unfavorable ways.

Lord help me not to harbor pain,
wash away my hurts like a fresh spring rain.

Lord give me thoughts that are clean and pure,
Lord give me strength to daily endure.

Lord hold my tongue when I think unkind,
give me pure thoughts in heart and mind.

Lord give me love for my family and friends,
Lord please forgive me of all my sins.

Lord give me peace when it's time to mourn,
Lord show me the way when I'm weary and torn.

Lord take my life and mold as you will,
speak to me Lord when all is still.

I turn it all over to you Lord today,
make me a better person I pray.

I praise you for all the blessings you give,
when I fail to thank you, please forgive.

I ask for your touch on the sick and the lame,
I ask all these things in your precious name.

Marsha M. Brogli

Live

Falling, tumbling, hovering, floating on the wind
like a magic carpet
The pedal of the rose plummets to the ground
another person has come to term
Another summer has faded into oblivion
There's nothing left but the moment you first
noticed the rose in full bloom and the memory
you have of it
In life it is sad but true, that if one would notice
we only have the moment and our memories of it. Thanks for
the memories

Steven Paul Wimberly Jr

Life

Life is strange but life is true
Nothing makes sense no matter what you do
Something brings you up but at the end
puts you down
You try to do right but you're always turned down

Isn't life strange, but isn't it true
either you're happy or very very blue
You wake up in the morning with a smile
on your face
You return to bed thinking of the events that
have taken place.

Petula Jackson

Top Coat and Rings

When the night is cold
And the day is old
Thrown on your top coat and take a new hold
When your eyes are bored
And you really need some things
Go get your necklace and put on your rings
Do your hair different
Put on cologne
Take a walk outside and be on your own
Go to new places
Do new things
And don't forget your topcoat and rings

Thomas A. Rispo Jr.

My Cat "Tinker"

Every night my cat walks by my room
  and says "Meow!"

I say, "Come here . . . ." He comes to
me and lies beside me.

He wakes me up and we play games
  and have lots of fun.

Then I go to school,
  and he waits 'til I come home!

    Kathleen (Katie) Ann Stevens

A Needy Child

Mama why did you leave me all alone.
I need you hear with me to carry on.
I know it wasn't you who planned to leave.
But yet and still I fell the need.
The need to talk to you.
The need to hug you.
The need to feel you kiss me and tell me your proud.
The need for you tell me what to do.
The need for you tell me when to.
But I know where you are.
You're always here within my heart.
And I'll always love you with a smile.

    Shinika Blackwell

Reflections of Time

As far as I know
it's still not quite done.
For Father and Daughter,
our lives are not one.
The love is hidden down deep inside.
With feelings of fear and abandonment,
love will always be confined.
The unspoken promise a parent gives a child:
"I will be there for you, always,
my love I will not hide."
Now that I am older and wiser,
and have children of my own,
I will never let them fall victim
to being disowned
The pain was so severe,
the hurting immeasurable.
But the years have raced by
with such speed, unbelievable.
And so with time, I am reassured that I am loved,
by my husband, my children and God up above.

    Valerie Gross

The Table Is Set

The table is set, dinner for two.
Together we sit, just me and you.
Today I honor this union with you, dear wife.
I will show you the meaning you give to my life.
I look through the candles' flickering glare
And I am so grateful you are still there.
We have shared the laughter and endured the tears,
This has been a most wonderful year.
This morning I offered up breakfast served in bed.
I basked in your radiant smile, nothing needed to be said.
I devoted myself as well as I could—
(Perhaps it wasn't as well as I should!)
And now we dine on this romantic note,
On violin strings we blissfully float.
Don't be shocked about my manners on this day.
I admit I often act in an incorrigible way.
I'm only attempting to set things aright;
I want our life to be perfect, starting this night!

    G. Joseph

What I Want!

Her existence is so important,
but the love she holds within is still asleep.
My eyes have never seen such beauty,
and while I'm alone, my heart has never felt so incomplete.

I want to offer her things that will bring that love to life,
I want to go about it softly, without a push or a shove.
Showing her I'm a true man,
Giving her what she pleases, the first thing, my love.

I stand on the shore in a tux with one flower,
because before my eyes, I see my ebony queen.
I need you to look through the storm,
There exists no other; you are all I've seen.

When you step through the clouds into the open light,
I worry not if you see me.
I will approach and peer into your eyes,
Then kiss you softly and embrace you gently.

The love has finally awakened,
Now there are rose petals at your feet.
By the grace of God, you are my queen, and I am your king.
Now let's make love and forever we'll sleep.

    Antonio Ward

Keys Please Don't Drink and Drive

Back to back there's another wreck
Side-to-side another child dies
Why do you choose to drink and drive?
It wasn't your child who cruelly died, it was mine.
There's a thin line between life and death so when you drink and drive
It's like pulling a loaded gun off the shelf.

Why drink if you can't think?
Why drive if it's possible someone could lose a life?
Why play dice with other people lives?
It's not wise to drink and drive.

There is another form of being intoxicated, a liquid crack
With the monkey alcohol on your back.

Driving under the influence is like playing with an explosive
Waiting for something to happen.
Don't leave someone paralyzed or traumatized
for the rest of their lives.
And don't make families attend memorial services
for lifeless bodies in closed caskets.

Put you keys away if you've been drinking today.
Please don't drink and drive.

    Cleveland S. Barrett Sr.

The Man In My Dreams

In Memory of Jonnie F. Roberts I & Dedicated to J.W.
As I close my eyes to sleep, drifting
off to see what I can see, it's
not clear yet of what's going on,
but there's a man grabbing at my arm.

It's very dark in here please who ever
you are make yourself clear to me and don't
stand so far. I don't want to be afraid
of you, though you seem harmful at all,
I just want to see you face to face as you are.

Now that you're coming clear, I know
I've seen you before, I was once that little
girl that you held so close to your heart.
You're my Dad can't you recall, how could
you forget me and not even call. How long
of time it has been I miss-u-Dad
and one day I'll see you again.

    Delisa Philips

The Wisdom of the Wind

As I sat upon the hillside contemplating life, I gazed upon the
  beauty of all the world so wide
And varied in its splendors so wonderful to see and feel and smell
  and taste and breathe.
I wondered 'bout the nature of the sunset as it stroked its hues upon
  the evening's sky.
And I listened to the wisdom of the wind . . . .

"Seize the beauty that comes before you on your journey through the passages of time.
Grasp it all and cherish it forever. Bring it to your breast and open up my heart
So it becomes a part of you forever. Let the sunstreaked glows blazen upon your mind
All the glory of the mountains and magnificence of seas.

Seize the beauty of the children with their eyes so brightly happy,
And cherish oh so tightly the beauty of your loves.

Do not be afraid to touch the wild flowers for fear of what else dwells within the fields.
Bring the petal of the rose closely to your heart even though it also brings you pain.

For all those graces of existence will carry you forever through the passages of time.
And the darknesses of life will be always cast in your images of light"

Yes, seize the beauty — make it what you are!

It is the Wisdom of the Wind.
  Richard William Migliore

When the Brakeman's Life Was Only Seven Years

In the 1800's there were no air brakes on any train
The brakeman had to go over the top, that's how they got their name.
Before a train could be stopped by far he had to turn a hand brake on every car.
Whether it was freezing or burning hot sun or pouring down rain, it had to be done.
There were no pin lifters on any car, brakeman carried pegs and got between the cars.
When the coupling would not match, the brakeman had the engineer back up for slack.
He had to stand between the cars holding a peg if he was lucky he only lost an arm or a leg
There were no train orders for the trains, the crew had to watch for the smoke from
  oncoming trains.
On a dark and foggy night, brakeman had to walk ahead carrying red fussies and a red light
When train had passed through the fog and he returned to engine or caboose, he was
  always treated like a dog.
Brakeman had to stand up all the way, night or day
He was called the work mule but he had to work strictly by the rule.
If he didn't do his duty he was fired on the spot, it beat starvation but not by a lot.
He had to be tough and have no fears that's why the brakeman's life only averaged
  seven years.
  Virgil Davis

What About Me

In the back is where I sit, hidden from the languages that you speak
and protected from the mathematics that you teach. You see I can be
found in any classroom across this land of the America's. For I am
the child that no one likes to teach.

I am no different from the brightest of your minds, yet you choose to
believe that I perform on the level of a five-year old attending school for the
first time or that I possess a behavior which can easily be dealt
with by labeling me as difficult or un-teachable. And because you
have not taken the time to understand the environment that I reside
in or the barriers that I endure - I remain in the back, waiting for
you to acknowledge my presence.

For a moment let me explain the child I am - I am a child who dreams
of traveling to the lands of the Far East and Eastern Africa. I am
the child who wants to develop a vaccine for the diseases which
plague the country, like Dr. George Washington Carver. I am the child
who wants to create soulful music, like the legendary Charlie Parker.
And so you see I am a child, who wants to learn, if you would only
give me a chance.

In the back is where I sit, hidden from the languages you speak and
protected from the mathematics you teach. You see I can be found in
any classroom across this land of the America's. For I am the child
that no one likes to teach.

What about Me?
  Robbin A. Bibbs

Untitled

In my illness
I wish to find freedom
  but in it, I find only chains
shackled about my body
  my mind is all that's clear
  and the mind is
  muddled sometimes

I wish to feel alive, and yet I am not dead
  in between am I, waiting for my life
  though it unfolds, it unfolds without me
  around me
  what of within me?
How long is my limit to life?
  And when may I begin to live?
I am sickly and weak
  I care not of this world
  and yet, I care with such tenderness
that my heart would break within my chest
  if only I could feel it
  If Only I Could Feel It.
  Marla Hadley

For She Is My Mother

God bless the one that did give birth.
And sacrificed for me, for what I'm worth.
  "For she is my mother"
She toiled and labored for so many days
And went on to love me in so many ways
She took care me during my childhood days.
  "For she is my mother"
Now, she is turning old and grey
At times it's difficult to understand her way
But I love her more and more each day.
  "For she is my mother"
When time on earth is for her no more.
I'll meet her on the Heavenly Shore.
I'm sure I'll lover her even more.
  "For she is my mother"
  O'Chester Fennell

midnight, June 2, 1996

The elusive poem of you
is dancing around my memories
flitting, hiding among the pages
  of Cummings,
like a child, running
through the house, arms
waving in glee, laughing
in screaming flee, who
I can't catch,
tripping over the chairs, turning
corners too slowly, refrains of giggles
bouncing off the walls so I can
hear him, running
through my recollections, charms
of lyrical delight and love's
poignance, And I breathless
finally end a day (smiling because), left
with the ever-present poem of you.
  Kirk A. Bailey

The Bird

I've seen the bird sing its
Song above the pink and red roses,
Where I pick them all day long.
I can see the sunflowers
     in the distance,
Dancing in the garden.

Susan Terry

The Old Park Bench

The old park bench sits vacant
With weeds poking through the slats
And the hand of time erasing
Names once carved into its back

But memories, like shadows,
Cling tightly to this bench
Memories of those now gone
Who once came here to rest

A married couple with ice cream
A small boy and his dog
A mailman resting tired feet
Three pals with baseball cards

A mother and her baby
A dreamer watching clouds
Two sweethearts on a quiet night
A soldier shipping out

They all remain, in shaded form,
The friends this bench has known
So thankful for the time they spent
Upon the old park bench

Richard M. Millard

At Peace

There is a peaceful place I know,
that makes me feel so warm.
It is a calm, collected place
that keeps me safe from harm.
The sky is like a turquoise stone,
The sea is clear as glass.
The people will do anything...
all you do is ask!
Weather like the desert,
coconut filled trees,
This is my greatest paradise,
my mind feels so at ease.
I sit and think the difference
of there and here at home,
the one that I come up with
is here I feel alone.
At night your sleep is peaceful,
from the ocean creeping up shore.
The peace is everlasting,
Your worries never more!

Jenny Hickox

Eyes

   To think, most people have the idea
that we, the children, the future rulers
of tomorrow are growing up in a better
nation. Yes, maybe we are, in their eyes,
but it is not through their eyes in which
we look, but through our own. We, the
children, the future adults of tomorrow
need to take a stand, and help them realize
this, because someday soon, we will
be the rulers of today!

Jayme Brooks

My Special Friend

She has been my friend for many years, a special friend is she
Forever caring, always, kind and as thoughtful as can be

When friends are down, she cheers them up with words of comfort and
a hug; she then dispenses goodies and coffee in a mug

Every day she wears a smile, no matter what the date
She is loved by everyone but especially by her mate

Her children are her pride and joy, her grandsons are like no others;
she is indeed a proud grandma and the very best of mothers

For friends and family she is always there, loving, sharing and giving;
there is no one else quite like her, at least not among the living

She never ever lets you down, on her you can depend;
she goes out of her way for others and would do anything for a friend

If you have not guessed her name by now, I do not want to tease
She is and always will be my special friend, Anneliese

Bridget Walton

Broken Crutches

   Times are changing, people are saying, it's ok, cause, everybody
does; take this pill, drink this wine, the world for them, so un-kind.
Use enough, to give peace of mind; and they try, but it takes more;
and more, than they bargained for.
   As the nights drag on, seems, to never end. And then, without
warning, they're facing the light of day; and the crutches, they
depended on, are gone. As they look around, it's deathly quiet, not a
sound; only the crash, of broken crutches hit the ground; Broken
crutches can't stand. Like dry, desert sand. It
can't take, all the problems of man. Oh, let go, it's time, to walk,
that ole line: where the rock, was waiting; waiting, all the time. Oh,
rock that's solid. Hold up my mind! The preacher come's in, and (can
you believe?) with a grin! He reaches for that crutch, (it's still
there) (he says) I'm here, take my hand! Where do you think, I've
been man?! Done that! Been there! Please, take my hand. Look down,
the crutches are broke, and I found a rock, and I thought, you ought
to know; in the arms of Jesus, is really, the only place, I found to go.
Let's do it! It's hard I know! As I looked over, I was so very proud!;
only the sound, of broken crutches, hit the ground. He's walking on
his own now.

Paul Troyer

He Described to Me

When I met him he seemed older than time to me, a child full of
inquisitee. I can barely remember, some of what he said to me,
as he gently set me on his knee.

The beauty of this world, is to view the forest, and not the tree,
and the flowers, along the garden wall, God put there, to be enjoyed
by one and all, and you will never have to worry, about when an where
to start, if you ask him to help you, bring it from the heart.

He spoke of strange lands, mountains, oceans, and a sea as I leaned
against his chest, trying to understand the picture, he described to me.

While listening to the rhythm of his heart beat as I drifted off to
sleep. As I awoke I noticed, a special twinkle and a tear in his eye,
though I really didn't understand why.

Years later I found out he was in the Army, in a foreign land, in a war
he didn't understand. It left him blind, and that beautiful picture,
was in his mind you see, the one he described to me.

Though you are dead and gone, and there remains the difference, in the
color of our skin, I want to thank you, for holding me my friend, as
you told of the places where you'd been, and the beauty from the
outside looking in, where ones real beauty really begins, just below the skin.

Now I understand a meaning of, For I Was Blind But Now I See, is
complete in the picture, he described to me.

William Bender

I Sit

There once was a man, who sit under a tree.
Every single day.
A little boy was walking, along his way, he stop to say how are you today sir
And why do you sit here day after day.
The man said to watch the world pass away.
The boy said how do you know that when all you do is sit all day?
Man said come and sit with me and you can see it pass away today.
The boy said ok. as time passed, the little boy said we been sitting all day
I never seen anything pass away.
The old man said it was 10:00 today when you started on your way it is 7:00
And the world has passed away. Things changed and people went on their way
With or without you the day has passed away.

Patricia A. Jones, Rice

Memories

I was born three days after the Groundhog saw his shadow.
I learned early that I was different yet the same.
I remember times of anger, peace, and love all in a day.
I haven't truly seen death, but have witnessed times of hatred which
   caused souls to die.
Some friends come and go like a cool breeze, providing comfort, then
   leaving you dry.
I've tripped over my dogs tons of times only to hear them yelp with pain.
I've sang until my throat was sore.
I've danced until my feet were blistered and swollen.
I remember hours of fishing, but only catching a mass of green algae.
I've held a baby alligator and felt its surprisingly soft body and cold brown scales.
I've been scared by dark figures in my closet.
I have stored personal feelings in my teddy bear, who listens quite well.
I've been scratched by cats with claws like razor blades.
The smell of a balogna sandwich always brings back my kindergarten lunchtime.
Just a toddler, I picked hot red peppers from my daddy's garden —
   they're dead now.
I've eaten more than enough chocolate and have listened to many lyrics.
My life is a never-ending adventure.

Jennifer Hobdy

Yes Love All I Need Is You

It was our first night without him, and the darkness weighted down our eyes.
I was but thirteen, my younger brother, slept with my parents, for comfort.
My two older brothers shared a room, I could hear them talking about him.
I sat on my bed, alone, crying to the window above. I tried to
comprehend the idea that he wasn't coming back, but I kept asking
where he has gone? That night, for the first time I talked to God.
I asked him to accept me instead, I really didn't want to die, but he
was so young, and everyone was so sad. I just needed to see a smile,
on anyone. I told God it wasn't fair, I pushed my face to the screen
and cried, and at the point before I couldn't breath or make a sound,
I screamed... Why?

Tonight is my second night talking to God, I was now twenty-two, and
you were laying alongside me. I woke in the dead of the night, you
were still here, holding me. I kissed your lips and without waking,
you smiled. I looked up to the window and thanked God, that I had
you. You shifted a little closer, let out a soft breath, and
tightened your bare affection. The sun rose, and you were right
there, just a finger stretch away.

Susan Embree

Ultimatum

'Tis not so much the what we have
As what we have to share
That heaven sent its only Son
To blaze our trail back there.

'Tis not so much to scourge a world
With power, hate and greed
But it takes a Christmas and a little Babe
To bring the world its peace.

'Tis not so much the much we have
In our stockings or on our tables
It's how we greet our King this year
In our hearts or in our stables.

Karl Peter Braun

Opposites

When summer comes, the birds
do flutter. When the sky is blue,
the grass does grow. When winter
comes, the birds don't flutter. When the
sky is gray, the grass doesn't grow. When
autumn comes, the leaves do fall. When spring
is here, the leaves grow back.

Alisha Leclair

Untitled

It takes a very Big Man to admit that he is
wrong
Lets face it....
Often I am not a very big man
Vile words and reactions
Emotions and their transactions

You can, I hope, someday understand
Of the things I've done
Useless, seems, the sum
   without your blessing and forgiveness,
   I love you, Mom

Chris Cardenas

I Thought I Could Forget You

I - was trying to forget you . . .

T - o be away from your beauty
H - here on my bed loneliness
O - nce happy moment we have built
U - seless dreams that we plotted
G - one down with the passing wind, but
H - oping once more to live again
T - o see someone within my sight.

I - ntense longing from memory . . .

C - ould not bring back the reality
O - ver those days we were to love
U - pon creation of happiness
L - onely blue moon might be in shy
D - oubting that seen of caresses.

F - orget me not with all my life, and
O - of all the fortune shall be ours
R - emembering you is my endless pain
G - oing around here on my sorrowful
E - very moment my heart will sing
T - o you my lovely once faithful dear.

Y - our last farewell for me my own, was
O - verwhelming to treasure you alone
U - ntil on my grave black Laurel shall bloom.

Orlando Edward Salonga Ph.D.

The Last Leaf

One little leaf as fall went by
Remained against the somber sky.
For days it clung to a twig up there.
Alone it shivered with none to share
Its place upon that empty tree;
It lingered there for all to see
It trembling in the bitter breeze.
Surrounded by the barren trees,
It seemed reluctant to depart,
A timid soul with noble heart.
But then one gusty autumn day,
It loosened its ties and broke away.
A fluttering flake falling down
To join its friends upon the ground.
A rendezvous with them to keep.
And share with them the winter's sleep.

Lucinda Carpenter

A Mother's Prayer

Such is the newly blossomed violet
In the early of the year
Peeping through the winter earth
You came to me, my dear
So delicate and tender
A heart and soul your own
A gift from God you are to me
The greatest I have ever known
And though my eyes have seen you
Dimmed with many faithful tears
Know that joy and hope are with them
That I soon may have you near
And just as Mother Nature
Cares for gifts from God anew
My prayer for you, sweet baby
So it shall also be for you.

Lisa Thompson

Sweet Dreams

As I stare through
the stained glass fire
thoughts drift into the waves
of the heated air.
Thoughts of one
safe
secure
protected
by the knowledge gained of yourself.
A wink and a grin
set my heart afire.
How long will the flame last
until tomorrow
or eternity?
Which will be the
end
of me?
Love or freedom
make a wish.

Lisa Anderson

Down Life's Road

Down life's road I travel
Each and every day
Many hardships I have met
All along the way

All my life I have struggled
Although not in vain
For to make a rainbow
It takes both the sunshine and the rain

On and on I will keep going
Until my journey's done
I can't stop now I can't give up
Until my race is run

Karen Spivey

My Child

You're growing so much my child
every minute of every day
wonderful things are taking place
in a very special way

Each day I wonder what you're like
but never a clear picture can I see
I imagine little hands and feet
and bright eyes that gaze at me

Time has went by oh so fast
I can't believe you're almost here
I long to hold you in my arms
and cherish you so dear

Soon you'll come into this world
you'll have so much to see
and I will be so proud to say
that you are a part of me

Kerry Lowery

Angel Wings

Brother against brother
Gun against gun
Hate against hate
Oh where are we going?

Let there be peace
Let there be love
Put down your guns
Let in the light

God send your angels
With whisper soft wings
Gather them together
Let them see peace

Greet each other as brothers
Let God in your heart
Love and peace everlasting
At last we are one

Louise Willeke

Security Blanket

So sweet
the times we join in slumber
our only insomnia is each other
the nights are lonely without you
you are my security
so cozy and warm
you are a keeper of my heart
a forever link to happy thoughts
you are comfort
with you
I cannot sleep

Harvey Harrison Hale

Untitled

I started out little
first general elementary
then general, business
then I stopped . . .
waited, watched, absorbed
going over that which was understood

Only able to fill the
brain so far.
Resting for awhile

A decade later
picking up
adding more
and remembering the past

I probed my imagination and
stretched my mind for understanding
for it will take some time, living
life to comprehend the more complex
ways with all its graphs, triangles,
rectangles, logarithms, algebraic story
problems and functions.

Lynn LeBean

Tender Hands

A friend I have,
I hold so near.
With wispy steps,
You flit and soar.
Strong tender hands
Lift when I fail;
And cheery smiles
Dispose the fears.
At times we share our separate lives,
Ups, Downs, Needs and Wants.
Ne'er can be filled
Your special place
If lost...
    You came to me.

Robert Hutchinson

Proud To Be An American!!

Are you proud to be an American
In the land of the brave and free;
Where our pilgrim fathers trod
From sea to shining sea.

It's a privilege to march in parades
When old glory leads them all;
And if we stick together,
Our great nation will never fall!

From the time of the log cabin
Many towns were built across this land;
Through valleys and the mountains -
Even over the desert sand.

So I am proud to be an American
For the heritage left to me,
Praising the ones who helped
To keep this country free!

Orville Forshay

Elizabeth

The wind whispered your name.
You lived and loved.
You gave your all.

The wind returned to claim you,
leaving only a shell.
Where are you?

Are you the soft breeze that
rustles the leaves on autumn
afternoons?

Are you the ocean mist rolling
in over the shore on a summer
morning?

Are you the wind that makes the
thunderclouds form their
ominous shapes?

I'll hold your hand when the
soft wind blows, and whisper
your name.

Susan D. Cowart

Living Will

I am old and ailing.
In fact I am dying.
So I told my doctor,
even before he could ask:
I have the right to die a
natural death — free of
tubes, monitors, and such.
Give me pain-killers so
I may live my remaining
few days in serenity - in
communion with God,
family, and friends. In
this way I complete my
life in dignity and comfort
for the new life to come.

Robert H. Lennon

The Right Road

There never seems to be a soul
To hear what I have never told
Cooped up and buried in a hole
My emotions are never spoken
Walking across this campus ground
I've yet to hear a shocking sound
But I'll never cease to look around
For something to distract me
There is no one around this place
To look directly in my face
And keep me from going on the race
For society's acceptance
All of us need a friend
To stop and look deep within
To show us where we should have been
And to take us on the right road

Jeff Sharpe

Intentions

So much to say
but the time races away
taking all of my thoughts
and rubbing each meaning smooth
until my intentions lose
the special glitter I want to convey.

Melanie Moore

New Beginning

Blessed day, mother
of morning sunlight.

Dawn breaks over the
horizon, time to start
a new.
Each hour spent making
progress,
live life to its fullest
extent.

Be young at heart,
truthful to your
convictions,
joyful for another
day in which
to be alive.

Julie M. Cole

Someone You've Lost

*In Loving Memory of Judy and Marvin
Nellessen and Jerry Hawley*

Someone once said "The Lord
works in mysterious ways" This He
does do, bodies of loved one's may
lie beneath the ground. But their
spirits are with the Lord. On a sunny
day when the clouds are out, if you
look real hard, you can see the one
you've lost peeking over a cloud
watching you. A guardian angel, some
may say, but the truth of it is someone
you love is watching your ways.

Suzanne Hawley

Song of the Dead

Wishing you were here,
Right here beside me.
I call to you,
But you can't hear me.
Why don't you hear?
Maybe because I'm not there.
I cry and scream to you,
But you just turn away.
What do I see?
A tear for me?
Do not cry, for I am the dead one,
You are still alive!
Live your life without me,
I want you to.
What was that?
Oh, I loved you to.

Rachel H. Rutz

My Eight

small controlled

flare out
wild, free
all mine

(controlled)

Liz Kauh Hilton

Where Is My Soul

I feel like my soul is empty,
I feel like my soul is lost,
I feel like all my inner being
was hidden in a shaded moss.

My soul is part of my inner being,
My soul is part of this world,
My soul which I have never seen
must be hidden in a deep sea pearl.

It is an everlasting search,
to find my place in this world,
if I can only see my soul,
I would know that it was made of gold.

Because what I do not see, is me,
my inner beauty you see,
which is hidden inside of me,
so deep, that I cannot see
that the inner beauty in me,
is the soul I cannot see.

Rochelle Wallace

Line Circle Point

I stand and stare
in a room so bare
that all the wall
is one round circle
without a point within
lines that never meet
my feet
trudging, begrudging
every turn
one breath, one beat
so endless is life's sweet concern
it clings but brings
nothing new to
the narrow circled space
spiraling inwards
few words
of sense
so dense
line circle or point?

Gurmeet Kanwal

Healing Waters

Healing waters are flowing,
There's joy beyond compare,
There's no sickness where I'm going,
There'll be no dying up there,
Joy bells are ringing,
Don't you want to go,
Where the Angels are singing?
Healing waters are flowing,
Up there is clear as a crystal river,
Where the Saints are blessed forever.
Healing waters are flowing,
There's joy beyond compare,
There's no sickness where I'm going,
And there'll be no dying up there.

Mary Powell

Down

You're climbing
down these stairs
and stop to think
that it would have
been easier had
you just rolled
down that hill

Nadia Aziz

Parent's Without Children

For those who cut down our
children and have no kids of their
own, you had better be real
careful, for God knows who's
been casting stones!

He listens and hears each
sarcastic remark, and He knows
who's been bruising those young
tender hearts!

He'll remember the pain that
a young heart felt, and He'll deal
with you with his chastening belt!

So be careful when you cast
those stones, they just might
come back to haunt your home!

Debby Pyles

Dancing Flame

I saw a dancing flame
Near an incense half-burned,
The flame illumined the faces
Highlighting their smiles.

The flame is a feeling,
Of passion bursting out of us,
For something known yet unrevealed,
Calling us to more.

The flame is a dream,
Of something that is beautiful,
Where hunger is no more,
Where injustice is no more,
The place is here.
The time is now.

The flame calls for action,
A handshake between enemies,
A joining of different colored hands,
A reverence to the earth we sit,
A smile to a stranger.

And then comes the Eternal Flame.

Marvelous L. Misolas

Gangs

My what a relief
When there's silence, in the streets.
You go to bed, and count their heads.
Glad that their asleep
Morning comes, you hear a
Bang, a shot rings out
you duck your heads
Look around, and glad
It's not one of yours, you
Bow your heads, you say
a prayer, and hope they
go away. But you know
Gangs are everywhere?!

Patricia Miller

God Cries

Two little hearts stop beating,
Two little lives are gone,
One tiny casket is buried,
And leaves us all sad and forlorn.

No tears are shed for the other,
This poor little child we lose,
Only because we're allowing
His mother "her right" to choose.

But two little souls play in heaven
And God loves them both the same.
One little babe, we tried to save,
While the other puts us to shame.

Joyce P. Patten

New Year's Day

Forgotten
is Christ

Wrapped
in newspaper

Stored
in the attic

Mark Oliver

Battle of Time

The fleeting hours of nothing sky
Where stars play hide and seek,
Are mystery moments passing by
When Daylight waits to speak.

Who can stop the night-time hours
Where silence loudly roars?
From whence comes the mighty power
To even out the scores

Of golden Days and silver Nights;
Of clouds and starry dreams....
For Time puts up an endless fight
While playing on both teams.

Pamela Tilden Wilcox

Ephemeral Moments

And we ate crawfish,
And we drank daiquiris,
And we spoke simplicities,
And we laughed galore.

Magnetized, I dared to explore
Your tremulous right leg:
Tenderly, I went up and down
Never above the knee!
For there were people around.

It felt like a young cactus
Yet softer and warmer:
You smiled to procrastinate
And then removed my insisting hand.
I recapitulated, and you did too.

They thought I was drunk
I smiled and so did you:
They suggested to bring me home,
And we separated somehow.

I left the insidious place drunk
Still looking to see your smile.

Jorge Vega

The Autistic Child

I'm in here and you're out there.
Of your presence I'm unaware.
All of the knowledge I have inside
Would fill any book from side to side.

With standard tests I am bombarded
The results indicate I am retarded,
I know I'm not and so do you
But what on earth are we to do?

I am put in special class for years
Because of regular teachers' fears.
"I cannot work with him," they say.
"He will disrupt my class each day."

I talk to myself man-to-man
Since I alone can understand.
Don't stop me please, it's my own way
To deal with things from day-to-day.

Dorothy Douglas Gilbert

Vague

When can I give...
     without the need to receive?

What makes me do different...
     than what I believe?

What causes the drive,
     the necessity;

To worry about things,
     that I can't foresee?

Ms. Roberts

Flying Like The Wind

The whistle blew twice
I was up to the shooting line
The wind blew
A whistle again
Arrows flying like the wind
I concentrated I pulled back and let go
on its way to the target
Whack! The arrow hit
I scored a bulls eye
Other arrows hit
The whistle blew
dog on the field
The whistle blew again we resume
Everybody pulls back
Arrows flying like the wind.

Travis Scott

Words

Words are concrete thought
displayed to other minds,
And so relayed,
Expressions of humanity;
creations of divinity

Words are pathways to understand,
How similar is God and Man,
To know we're highest on this plane,
To glorify our Lord by name.

Words are symbols. Earthy treasure;
Given in unbounded measure.
Used by voice,
Or pen by some,
Creators also we become.

Peggy Mayfield

Leaves In New England

The fall leaves of New England
light up New England skies.
They glitter in the sunlight
like a sparkle in your eyes.

Feeling so wonderful
to wake up in the morning
and gaze at the trees
with all the colors forming

The fire of the colors
Red, yellow, orange and green
are so beautiful to look at
It all seems like a dream!

Watch the wind, make the colors sway
as all the trees, are on display
They dance and sparkle in the sun
as though, they are all having fun!

They are a picture of beauty
a sign of hope
Sent from the heavens
On hills, mountains, and slopes.

Nancy M. Carter

The Tin Man's Wish

To love and feel like real people
The Tin Man wished to have a heart...
But could it really be that simple?
Isn't true love a real art?

Not everyone whose heart is beating
Really knows how to love,
But Tin Man really knew that feeling.
It's given to him from above.

True love may be a real virtue,
But it can often cause you pain...
It can become and endless torture
That would drive anyone insane.

Why would the Tin Man want a heart
When it's so easily torn apart?

Yevgeniya Nusinovich

The Cold

The cold haunting my skin
Shading with scarlet and purple.
My fingers
Clammy and moist.
Stiffening toes
Pulsing with the seconds.
Chills arriving
At the base of my neck.
I shiver
Outside and in.
My voice
Crackles with coughs.
My lips
Chapping with the wind.
My frosty nose
Stuffed with cold
Refusing all odors
Til cleared with a sneeze.

Sherry L. McInerney

Love

There will be times you can't go home
There will be times you will feel alone
There will be times you can't go back
There will be times you will regret
But there will never be a time
When I won't love you
There will never be a time
When I won't hold you
There will never be a time
When I won't care
There will never be a time
When I'm not there

Flarry W. Henry III

A Thought

Strew your flowers along the pathway
  of the living — not the dead;
Don't save them for the morrow,
  We know not what's ahead:
That word of praise unspoken,
  The kindly deed undone
  will some day cause you heartache
  when the chance is gone!

So scatter all your posies
  as you wind your merry way
  and feel the joy of giving
  some soul a lift today!

Edith V. Lurroughs

Summer Reverie

The sky is blue, the sun is bright
It truly is a beautiful sight;
A soft, warm breeze stirs the air
I feel it ripple thru my hair.
The grass is tickling at my feet
The smell of flowers is so sweet;
A trickling stream I hear close by
The tall grass whispers - a soft sigh.
A cloud floats by, so calm — serene
Soon, no longer to be seen.

The birds are flying to and fro
Chirping, calling as they go;
The leaves are rustling in the trees
I hear the zzzz of bumble bees.
This is nature at its best
It calms my racing heart to rest.
As I survey the wonders here
I feel that God is very near,
Who else would make these grand things
For the joy to man it brings.

Ruth Ann Miller

The Wind

Give me the wind a rollicking wind.
  To blow my cares away.
Give me the wind - a frolicking wind.
  To play the live long day.

Not for me a gentle breeze - nestling
  in repose.
But give me a rollicking wind
  A frolicking wind that blows.

Shirley Martin

Lost In The Dark

How could you leave me
  with nowhere to turn?
You left me there
  with one place to stand.
Nowhere to run,
  no reason to scream.
You left me far behind
  when you moved ahead.
I started seeing your face
  in memories and dreams,
Wondering when you'd return
  and come back to me.
But now I'm still lost,
  lost in the dark
Right where you left me,
  ready to start -
Start a new life
  with hopefully, you.
But if that's not possible
  with somebody new.

Nicole Lynn Jimenez

Youth

Youth knows love far more
Than any other old man or woman.
For love is the flame
Which youth's dreams fan
To a bursting inferno.
To a young woman,
Love is all she knows.
It's the sparkle in Youth's eye,
The beat of Youth's heart.
Love is the only emotion
Youth sets apart
From all emotions;
No one ever understands
How love can be found
In the palm of Youth's hands.
For we know - do we not?-
Of love's purest form?
That is the reason
Why Youth is born.

Trina Taitano

A New Episode

Twelve years have come and gone
It's hard to realize...
Seems like only yesterday
I gazed into your eyes.

You're leaving elementary school
To embark on a new episode...
A lot of life is ahead of you
But the memories are yours to hold.

Be strong and please don't be afraid
Stand up for what is right...
The decisions you will have to make
Will all be worth the fight.

Always be proud of who you are
Don't back down to just fit in...
Keep remembering all your dreams
Stand tall and you will win.

My love for you is ever growing
I will always be by your side...
For a precious, beautiful daughter
That has me bursting full of pride.

Leah D. Warren

African Grandpa

Skin dark chocolate, eyes golden brown,
Voice deep and soothing,
Is my grandpa.
Sharp as a sphere, smart as a whip,
Brave as a lion,
Is my grandpa.
Words of wisdom upon his lips,
Silver gray hairs upon his head,
Tall and handsome,
Is my grandpa, my african grandpa.

Chrishawn Wagoner

The Guitar

The strings are shiny
 They're made of hand wound steel,
The vibrations they make
 Sound calming and unreal.
I move the pick down
 Plucking each string.
I hope it sounds good
 'Cause I sure can't sing.

Mike Souther

Burial

Silent are the sighs
Buried 'neath her heart
Never to depart
Silent are her cries!

Silent are the fears
Buried 'neath her breast
Tomblike now they rest
To wither through the years.

Margaret G. Hoyle

Like A Night In New York

The cars at night
go rushing by.
And then the wind
comes swishing and swooming in
howling at the moon.
Then it's a brand new day.
I wake up and hear
the chains of dogs.

Meredith Weintraub

Promise

I promise you my love
For today and tomorrow;
I promise you as much
 happiness as I can give
I promise not to doubt
 or mistrust you,
But to grow and add to
 your life of content...

I promise never to try to
 change you.
But will accept the changes
 you make in yourself;
And I will accept your love
 for me without fear of
 tomorrow.
Knowing that tomorrow,
 I'll love you more than
I do today.

Sharon Behles

Night

The air it breathes
gropes at coat cuffs,
like my hand
at your lacy waistband
and coaxes the last
snatches of fig
from the forks
of swaying trees.

In the morning,
sadly, they will blush
in the sunlight
as their leaves lay
in a wrinkled heap
beneath them.

Ryan D. Mitstifer

Untitled

A stand of trees
tells its yearly time
count the colors
this autumn sign
a sweater for
the evening air
I close the windows
through them I stare
walls of warmth
full moon so bright
silhouettes off branches
dance in the night
blankets pulled
and tucked around
lil' dog under
forms a mound
close by my side
for years on end
my lil' dog
the love you send..

Thomas W. Scott

Untitled

A summer God asked the cat
"What is your tale?"
The cat replied and tipped his hat,
"I have none to tell,
I don't believe in memories,
Only in all I see,"
Then he smiled, turned his back,
And climbed into a tree,
"My past is somewhere with my tail
And that I cannot find,
And so I live, and so I fail,
Forgetfulness is kind,"
The God thought then said goodbye,
But first asked him his name,
The cat opened a solitary eye,
Said, "Yes, of course, it's Manx."

Julie Terry

Untitled

Although life's hectic pace
may keep us far apart
you will always have
a special place within my heart.

So if life should get rough
and you're looking for an ear
or a shoulder you can cry on
you will always have one here.

Regis Delaney Synnott

Untitled

Confusion
Clouding my brain
Confessions
Doing the same
Depression
Controls my mind
Aggression
Making me blind
The silence
Playing my soul
The violence
Making me cold
The secrets
Forever inside
The regrets
I wish I had died

Tyler Halo

For Jon

At that moment
when you burst irresistibly
into my room
the flowers peeping intentionally
over your shoulder,
you with your silly grin,
at that precise moment
I adored you.

Marilyn Fitch

My First Day of School

First day of school,
wore my new dress.

Met my first teacher,
knew my address.

Learned many things,
like blue, green and red.

Made lots of friends,
even one named Fred.

The clock ticked by,
it was almost time.

My stomach ached,
my belly whined.

All of a sudden,
ring-a-ding-ding.

For it was time,
to get our things.

We all lined up,
at the door.

For tomorrow was another day,
with lots in store.

Kathleen M. Silvernell

Cool Black Night

Open your eyes and see
A big moon in a dark sky
The stars shining, all alike
A shooting star whispers my name
All on this cool black night

Jacqueline Hehn

Love In The Moonlight

The moonlight up above,
Sometimes makes your mind wonder;
For the feelings I have inside begin
To grow fonder and fonder.

The sparkle in your eyes and
the shadow on your face;
Tends to make my heart beat at an
erotic pace.

And sometimes we have a difference
that may result in a fight,
But to clear my mind and anger,
I look into the moonlight.

And what I see is not a light
Only for peace,
But a shining that makes two angry
hearts cease.

And gracing through the sky, you
may see a bat or a dove;
But look closer and you'll find
something called "Love"

Joseph E. Zondlo

One

Priests, poets, philosophers,
Prophets and prophetess'
All give One a name.

Temples, churches religions,
Jung, Freud Krishna
And Buddha
All give One a name.

Myths, maidens, mists
And mountains
Magic and memories
And maya
All give One a name.
I know who I am
The little one

Cecelia Carol Cavano

What Life Is To Me

Life is all adventure far and
wide, like a continent end to end.
You don't know what will happen
until the final end, to closure
the picture, till we both mend.

We have all witnessed and some
we don't disclose, others we shall
forever hold until the story's told!

I have a future unlikely still
bleak, but I know in my heart
that I will never be weak!

Kris A. Faulkner

Why a Conservative?

With the graying of maturity,
Reality comes center stage.
All those burning causes,
Become the smoke of yesterday.

The bright new philosophies,
Blind our youthful dreams.
That hope that we could save the world.
Is lost with the wrinkles of old age.

Pamela S. Burton

The Door Opened

The door opened.
Tears slowly swallowed up
by the wooden floor
and the old leather boots.

Light warmed the bitter bride,
darkness led her home.
Ignorance ignites
burning into cool ash,

Like the corpse in Varanasi.
And the crow flies.
Roots severed by intent on that
glorious day

Leaving another wretched past
to rot on this twisting vine.
Cradling in my arms
what others have left to wither

In the dust.
The door closes
behind me.

Jim Benton

Along My Way

When I was young and gay
and along my way
I would listen to people
and they had nothing to say

When I grew older
And along my way
I would listen to people
And they had a lot to say

Now that I am old and gray
And along my way
I listen to people and what they say
And their wit and humor
    "Make My Day"

Terrie Fischer Troy

Untitled

Heart, be still!
Don't talk so loud
and bang and bump
against your shroud.

Don't rattle your cage,
or flush my cheeks.
Just please lie quiet.
humble, and meek.

Don't make a sound
to let him know
just how I feel.
My heart, beat slow.

For soon enough
you'll be set free,
if someone right
should find the key.

So until then,
please, be soft-spoken,
and keep yourself,
dear heart, unbroken.

Stacey L. White-Plaisted

Outta Here

I pick a spot,
Just like fishing.
I might get hot,
When I'm nervous.
I still raise my elbow,
I still stand in my position.
As the windup comes,
The sound cracks.
I see it in the air.
I think of the famous phrase,
"Back, back, way back, outta' here."
I run around the bags,
Tagging each one.
When the pentagon comes,
I slide for fun.
I get up,
We slap each other's hands,
And I go sit down,
With a proud look on my face.

Michael McCormack

Island

Creamy thickets of
lush greens,
Pure, clean, and
untouched by
human hands.
Evening rain,
holding the sweetness
of a mother's bosom,
quenching the hunger
for a time.
Blades of grass
tickled by
morning dew
Nature's wine to feast.
Pure, serene,
Dreams of an untouched world.

Macy L. Borgeld

Timeless Pain

Time . . .
drifts slowly
along the stagnant pond
of pain.
It gets caught on every
branch of memory
and rock moment
I cherished.

Martha Melton

Solace

Grant me solace of the heart
Enrich my feeble mind
Make me as you'd have me be
And in your Grace abide-

With thoughts of you
For what You've done
It makes me wonder - Why -
To take a life as low as mine
And impart Your Grace Divine

What can I offer in return
For all You've done for me
I'll take this Solace of the heart
And offer it to Thee

Richard M. Henkle

What Is A Fool

What is a fool? One might say -
should such a one be left alone to play
to play at the games of love and life
filled with its joys and strife

If by others one is called a fool,
only because of lack of school.
Is it really true or nought.
What if the school by a fool was taught

But this fool by duty is called,
long enough to dreaming he has stalled.
So until tomorrow, or some other day,
if I am lucky to have one pass this way

Perhaps an answer I'll find,
or being just a fool, forget it all and
leave it behind

Waunita V. Lane

The Wingless Dove

Does no one care for me?
Does no one love?
Will I someday be as useless,
as a wingless dove?

Am I the chest
without a key?
Will all these things,
someday be me?

Am I the singer
that cannot sing?
Or am I the bell
that cannot ring?

Will I ever find what I'm looking for?
Will I ever find that love?
Or will I simply become,
the wingless dove.

Elizabeth A. Zaleski

Guilt

From out of its darkened hole
It crawls
Forever creeping to get you
As it heads to attack your soul
It calls
"Come, not follow true."

It is overpowering
It takes
From you all your innocence
Eventually its convincing
It makes
You do what is dishonest

Once you give in—no escape
It traps
You to the worst you ever felt
Dooms you to an unwanted fate
And that's
The feeling of Guilt.

Brooke A. Rankins

The Bottle

To a Friend — From a Friend
People ask me why I drink
   I wish I knew for sure,
I know I've hurt the ones I love
   And wish my soul could find
The peace my body's looking for
   The bottle clouds my mind
It's not an easy thing you know,
   The demon in the bottle grows
God please don't let go of me
   My hold on faith is dim,
But God please hold on tight to me
   So I don't slip right in,
So to my family and my friends
   I am sorry for the pain,
But some day with the help of God
   I'll be whole again

Carol L. Palma

Going Away

What can I say,
I'm so lost and far away,
No one will understand me,
I am so weak,
I can't do the things I want to,
There is not enough strength in me,
I'm sure I cannot make it,
My dying day is soon,
No one should shed a tear,
I still hope they would smile,
I'm not worth it,
Not worth someone's sadness,
Don't worry about me,
This is what I'm supposed to be,
I need to go away,
For never I shall return,
Something has destroyed me,
Which I cannot mend.

Nikki Bried

Never Ending, Always Renewing

A river flows continuously
Always rippling
Never ending
Always renewing
As in love

Love is eternal
Full of passion and desire
Never ending
Always renewing
As in my love for you

My love for you is strong
Never bending, never breaking
Never ending
Always renewing
As in a river

A river flows continuously
Always rippling
Never ending
Always renewing

Jennifer Rude

Love

What is love?
Love is caring.
Love is compassion with understanding.
Love is respect with commitment.
Love has no bounds, for it is like
A circle which has no real beginnings
and definitely no end.
Love is an emotion which touches
the inner being and soul.
Love is the supreme being which
exist's for all.

Jane Fulone

Affectionate Disposition

To move on,
to feel you,
to touch you,
insane
to smell you,
to have you,
to scream out your name.
To bore you,
to need you,
to kill you again.
To hold you,
to hate you,
to taste you,
to let you to,
to want you,
to tempt you,
to love you,
the pain

Kevin Perry

Angel

Eyes of heaven
   hair of light.
Shining an aura,
   beaming out bright.

Mind of innocence,
   thoughts of care.
Sounds of bird's songs
   when wind hits the hair.

Motions of love,
   kisses divine.
Falling into sweetness.
   No knowledge of time.

Skin soft as silk.
   Silent whispers in the air.
A feeling of lightness,
   and nothing but care.

The peace and serenity
   of letting things go.
The truest understanding,
   soft like snow.

Erin Glawe

Birds

Brightly colored
Iridescent feathers
Reaching for the sky
Dying to fly
Sorry to be in a cage

Jace Michael Cheramie

Fallen Man

I would not stoop to help him,
The tattered man upon the ground,
He stretched across the sidewalk,
The morning mass pushed 'round.

Homeless, addict, drunkard,
Judgments ready, off the shelf,
Wonder how he came to be there,
Most likely did it to himself.

But might I stop to lift his head,
To pat a cheek, to check a pulse,
Then again, I am no doctor,
Best left to someone else instead.

Who might he be, how did he get there,
Does he even give a damn,
I saw police at the next corner,
Asked them to go help the man.

Didn't stick to see the upshot,
Don't know if the man survived,
But back there along the pavement,
Lies a piece of me that died.

Christopher W. Jones

My Job

My job is to touch the minds,
Of the next generation.
In this I meet all kinds,
In various stages of preparation.

My job is to make them think,
This new generation.
It causes them to blink,
From this new sensation.

My job is to find the need,
In this generation.
Help them to write and read,
And avoid temptation.

My job is to push egos high,
In this generation.
Reach for the sky!
There are no limitations.

My job is to help prepare,
This generation.
Future beware!
Prepared will be, this generation.

Rose Marie Stelzig

Of Love's Demise

Of love's demise
Is born a contempt
Unique among jealousy and loss

Of what glorified perfection
Springs anew?
What other beauty and demeanor
And what new love lies to expectation?

So that failure recalled in the past
Would weave its web to my present

Why is a compassion pushed away?
A well of affection and love,
Of charm and kindness, without limit
Or without value, in a similar breath

Rob Buchanan

Untitled

I return to the pages
coiled together with
genius or mediocrity.
Depending on what day you ask me
I am Michelangelo
painting my muse in between
romance and jousts
tearing the norms and
cherishing the light;
Or I am, him,
t-shirt and jeans
soaked with wasted miles
and love never rendered.

Christopher B. Nippes

The Clown

Holding back my hurt and tears
Trying to force a smile
Pretending to be happy
Just to be with you a while

You want my love, and happiness
And never to show I'm sad
You want to be my everything
Sharing all, except the bad

The hurt deep down inside of me
Never to be told
I'll paint a smile and happy face
And stand up tall and bold

I need you so, and want you so
I'll never where a frown
So here's my heart, and here's my sole
And here's your favorite clown

Robin Nalls Miller

Rules for a Kiss

A kiss on the ear: Laughter
A kiss on the neck: I want you
A kiss on the hand: I adore you
A kiss on the cheek: Friendship
A kiss on the head: Bless you
A kiss on the lips: I love you
Anywhere else: Be grateful

Billy Arthur

Charon's Fare

Into the realm of silence,
Lying as I walked,
I blinked my penny eyes.

I stepped into the dory—
Constructive way to bliss.
My proneness was erected
And ferried on across.

Still, my eyes are open!
Damn my dying soul!
I see the coppers glowing and
A silent painful joy.

Bill Hymas

Savior

Red moon
Dripping souls
Drink from the cup
Life is like
Russian roulette
With six bullets
Any way you play it
You're gonna die
Take the bullets out of my gun, baby

Ethan Molnar

Andrés

Touch my heart
ease the turbulent beat

Embrace my soul
offer to me your solace

Caress my mind
so filled with mem'ries
of your face

Tempt my body
I may wilt in this heat

Whisper, to me, softly
when I am bound
for deepest sleep

All of this, have I done
if only in thought
or the dreams
of unresting slumber

Jeanne Lambert

The Nineties Man

The souls of a man
are the angels within,
it is the body
that is evil,
for it knows the delicacy of humanity,
but renders its options obsolete.
From the sweet that
drains from his pours,
the muscles that empower him,
to the veins that
distribute his furry.
Together they comprise a
destructive man capable of hell,
it is his soul
that cools the fire and
brings him back to humanity,
allowing him to nurture his thoughts
unto that of a caring man.

Chris Clapinski

Maiden Voyage

The miracle when first seen
Spawned boundless love forevermore
Lovely, helpless little miss
Brittle as the fledgling bird
Heedless of things to come,
Craving things that never may.

Little lady, woman now,
On maiden flight to worlds beyond
And vulnerable as so long ago
A fleeting moment not long at all.

Joseph E. Giletto

Downsized

What a life!
New job
New car
No kids
Dancing and dining out
Next ten years;
Same old job
Another car payment
Paying for child care
No dancing and dining out
No life
Next ten years;
Got to work over time
Used car payments
Kids need everything
What? Downsized!
Need a job
Searching for work
Praying for work
Got to get a life!

Sheila A. Brown

Child

Your child is sick,
   do you call a doctor?
Your child has a fever,
   do you use a cold rag?
Your child coughs,
   do you use medication?
Your child cries in pain,
   do you wipe the tears?
Your child is bleeding,
   do you give a bandage?
Your child needs an organ,
   do you donate one?
Your child isn't breathing,
   do you hold your breath?
Your child is dead,
   did you remember his wings?

Aimee Gilbert

True Beauty

The end is far away
We still have long to live
We still have time to change
We still have time to give

Defy the rage inside
Express your feelings true
It does no good to hide
Emotions should be viewed

If you find something you love
Grasp it tight and hold
Hatred you are above
For your love is bold

Looks can be a lie
Their heart may be black as coal
Find their inner light
True beauty is the soul

Dan Martin

A Glimpse

Shooting star,
   You've come so far,
Journeys made,
   Although unknown,
Come as you may,
   Fall as you are,
Your beauty,
   To the world shown,
For a glimpse,
   You come into sight,
Singing through,
   The eternal night...

Radha McAlpine

Faces Of Life

Now that I am older,
and not the swift person you once knew.
Don't turn your head when you see me.
Please say "hello" or "how are you?"
I am where you are going.
I have been where you are yet to go.
And, please don't rush me,
just because I now move,
a little to slow.
Remember, God created me,
and he created you too.
So, the next time you see me,
please don't turn away,
for the way I am now,
is the way you will be someday.

Bobbie Lou Bonner

Drug Bug

Keep all your wits together.
Keep thinking straight ahead.

Cause if the drug bug bites you,
you may just wind up dead.

God only gave you one life,
so strive to get ahead.

Don't let the drug bug bite you,
you may just wind up dead.

If someone offers drugs to you,
just stop and think real slow.

Remember Mrs. Reagan's words.
It's easy just say no!!!

Life has too much to offer,
there's better things to do.

Don't throw away your future,
for just a high or two.

Everyone must pull together,
to whip this awful dread.

Don't let the drug bug bite,
you may just wind up dead.

William D. Kvasnikoff

Ninja Cat

Stripes of black and gray
   slithering through the house
Watching people's feet move past
   pouncing like a mouse
Hear the children holler
   as the claws catch hold of socks
The Ninja Cat has struck again
   it's only eight o'clock.

Racing through the yard
   with his tail high in the air
Chasing giant crazy dog
   the cat has not a care
Cornered by the fence
   his black stripes arch up high
He turns his body in a flash
   away the Ninja flies.

Joseph Michael Abeel Fitts

My Mother's Poem

She is one of my best friends
even though we have had our bad times.
Her smile is as beautiful as
an angel's.

She is always there for me
whenever I need her.
I don't want to lose her
for I would not know what to do.

When seeing her unhappy,
I can feel her pain.
When seeing her happy,
joy comes to life.

She is very special to me.
I love her with all my heart;
I know she feels the same,
for she is my mother.

Josephine Little Light

Island

Tears flowing
like an endless river
something lost
to be found
later
maybe
a heart surrounded
by brick and mortar
sinking
the sun shines
through cold murky water
warmth of the rays
never reach bottom
one day
all will be seen
future clear
a convict heart
released
sun shining through
crystal waters

Patrick W. Scanlan Jr.

Summer's Farewell

Summer said farewell
just the other day
bidding all good-bye
in the usual way
gathered her flowers
a few still in bloom
knowing fall's leaves
would cover them soon
reluctant as always
but seeing birds fly away
she followed them south
where it's sunny all day
anxious to again miss
autumn's first frost
when her seasons beauty
all would be lost.

Sue Fulkerson

Innocence

Something died inside of me
    Ripped
        Torn
           Shredded
I lost something that held me together
    A thread
        A root
           An anchor to the shore
I can't stay
    Stay sane
        Stay whole
           Stay happy
I lost my childhood one night
The pain was slight; insignificant
The numbing void was great
    hollow
        empty
           desolate
I gave a part of me one night
  that I forgot I even had.

Jocelynn Drake

Escape

On the road that I have taken
one day, walking I awaken
amazed to see where I have come
where I'm going where I'm from

This is not the path I thought
This is not the place I sought
This is not the dream I bought
just a fever of fate I've caught

I'll change highways in awhile
at the cross roads one more mile
my path is lit by my own fire
I'm going only where I desire

On the road that I have take
one day walking I awaken
one day walking I awaken
on the road that I have taken.

Brenda Salmons

Nature Songs

Late in the evening,
you can hear the nature songs,
when the creatures of the night,
join together and sing along.
The cricket with his unique
sound where else, in our back
yard, he can be found.
As the lonely cricket cries
out to his mate,
only till morning he will
sit and wait.
For at daybreak the nature songs
will end.
Will the creatures of the night,
join together once again.

John Raison

Yellow Ribbon

Yellow ribbon
on a lover's hair
turned red
by someone's stare

Will I gallop
will I fly
as I contemplate:
was it He, or is it I?

As quickly
love's come my way
more hurriedly
red turned to gray

O how rainbows
delude the soul
and fleeting moments
belie one's fall

As I wonder
with heart as dust
resolve to rejuvenate
I must I must

Hasson Windawi

Eyes That Plea

It has been a long time
since you've whispered in my ear
I've had enough courage
to drive away all the fear
The hurting in my heart
is long to disappear
The lonesome I was once feeling
is soon to pass
My life is starting over
without the face and laugh
But it is good
and tough it will be
I long for love
and the eyes that plea
Though missing you
I will always have
And memories
to see and hold

Kiley Fadenrecht

Sculpture Of My Herb

A clay bust stands
unfinished in the garage
green plasterline
that freezes dry in winter
and oozes brown in summer.
Seven years have gone by
and my brother,
who will be 70, next may
keeps asking,
"When will my portrait be done?"
I say, "Soon, soon, very soon,"
but the weather is never right
for working the clay.
Finally I sit to study the form
but cannot begin.
I still shudder
touching his clammy mask
like a staring post mortem
seen in a museum.

Gladys Block Wasser

The Stormy Sea

Life is like a stormy sea
And I am the only man on that sea
Every time I go under
Jesus Christ go beneath me

He brings me up to breathe fresh air
And let me know he is always there
Jesus Christ makes a stormy sea
To let me know He is always with me.

    And he said to me
    Write for these words are
    True and faithful

Ola Thomas

Come to Me

Come to me and I'll take
You to a far better place.
Come but do not fear.
    When your days come to an end
The pain in your heart I shall mend
When all is in pieces
When your heart beat ceases
May my love be what you long
    Come to me and I'll take
You to a far better place
Come but do not fear.
Come and enter my celestial bliss
Pray to me and make the final list
Enter my domain and you're home
For in my kingdom I shall
give you everlasting freedom

Rita Watson

Day By Day

She's in the arms of another
  so let my wondering go to rest.
It was she I had been searching for
  it was love I had in my quest.

So I will go home with my thoughts
  and day by day I will live.
But it is her that will never know
  of a love I had to give.

John Michael Moore

Untitled

Never will I know contentment
In these days of greedy wildfire.
The songbird perched in its high tent
Help me escape the stifling mire.

Never will I see blessed spring
When cloudy masses shroud my soul.
Wind and water are my life spring
Fire to fuel the matadore.

Paradise seems dim in reward
When love tickles the still delights.
How pregnant the mad grow much more
Great wits allied by dismal might.

I lay at dark a fancied muse
Arouse the hidden never told.
At night when I remember you
I recall the bird that foretold.

Folade Venable

My Swing

I love swinging in my swing.
Nana, Poppy look at me!
I love swinging in my swing.
Yes I do
On, two, three
Nana, Poppy look at me!

I love swinging in my swing
Mommy, Daddy look at me!
I love swinging in my swing
Yes I do
One, two, three
Mommy, Daddy look at me!

Gail Gilmore

Artist Beyond Compare

When the clouds are edged in silver
And the sky is blue above;
Then our hearts begin to quiver
At the beauty of God's love.

When the rainbow struts its beauty
Across the heavens gray and blue;
Then we know it is our duty
Ever to thank Him for love true.

God in His mercy shows us
He's an artist beyond compare;
As he declares His handwork,
We should bow before Him there.

God made the world - every nation -
Flowers and trees on all the earth.
People are His greatest creation;
He gives us a chance at second birth.

Claudine Brown

Nature

Nature all around us,
Almost every color.
Nature blowing from the wind,
Grass, trees, bushes and more.
Nature is what we eat,
It can help us live.
Nature surrounding us,
Anywhere you look.
Nature so colorful and gentle.

Justin Woodstead

Autumn's Descent

Driving down the road . . .
Around a corner . . .
A surprise!
The gift of Autumn's color
is right before my eyes!

Curving hills,
windy fields,
that tricky little bend.
New England's Autumn splendor
just never seems to end.

Beyond the yellow,
green and red
a stop sign slows me down . . .
Oh no . . .
A town . . .

Pamela A. Matson

Tragic

Forever in eternity
Lies within the truth
The realm of insecurity
The age inside the youth

The boundless destination
The ache of troubled bones
The chilling resolution
The visible not shown

The pain of distant memories
The hurt of future words
The distance is relentless
In the smile that hides the hurt

The broken hearted healing
To show their own repent
The stronger hearted stealing
All the tears that have been spent

The breaking down of barricades
The crashing down of walls
The deafening silence listening
For the slightest truth to call

Tina Lynn White

Judas Kiss

Passionate palate's true love lies,
Faithfully concealing deceiving sighs.

James M. Umathum

A Secret Place

A place to hide
A place to live
A place to have
A place to give
A special place
No one knows but me
A place you can't open with a key
A secret place
Filled with love and care
Something I can always share
It's a place I would never want to part
The secret place is my Heart.

Kimberly Hutchings

Untitled

I have given you love;
why do you not take it?
There are those who would
Sacrifice their souls
for the pure, unconditional love
I have given to you.
O tell me why it is
you choose to be
an unwilling recipient
of the most wonderful gift
this mortal world has to offer.
Enlighten me, and perhaps
I shall understand why
you are so inhuman.

Jennifer Goldberg

Silly Child

"I'm keeping my baby!"
Are the words stated by a child.
Far too young to know the difference
between struggles and achievements,
Way too silly to worry about
poverty or starvation,
Ultimately kind enough to accept
life's jagged edges,
and above all lucky enough
to have a beautiful baby.
"I'm keeping my baby!"
Are the words stated by a child
"Not in my house, you have to go!"

The baby who's having a baby mother
Replies

Debra A. Rodriguez

Silver Necklace

Deep in her eyes, soft and kind,
Something safe I sought to find,
A single familiar teardrop glint,
A soulful token, just a hint,
Of love, like mine, so very bright,
As to beget tear blinded sight.

Eric Idema

To My Children

You have given me, more happiness
  than sorrow!
More smiles than frowns
More laughter than tears!
I'd have you thee again, tomorrow!!

We had many up's and downs
I lived through many fears:
But without you, my darlings
I'd never made it, this many years!

You now have given me the blessings
  of these years.
My beautiful loving, grandchildren,
  who too have given me
More happiness than sorrow
More smiles than frowns
More laughter than tears.
I pray you will have all of this
in your coming years!!
  Mother.

Maxine V. Brown

Our Solar Light

Beyond our earth, our sun arises
shining on Mercury, Venus and Mars
besides us.
Reaching out to Jupiter, Saturn and
Uranus.
Followed by Neptune and Pluto.
With the rays of the
Full Moon's lunar
To complete our lighted solar

Irene Lakey

Love

Love has many powers,
It can bring you to your knees,
Can rip your heart like paper,
Then mend it back with ease,
Can draw out tears of sadness,
And also tears of joy.
Can make us smile at someone
Who's trying to annoy.
Love is all around us,
No matter where we turn;
Love can be so simple,
Yet hard for us to learn.
Love's a soothing feeling,
That helps us sleep at night;
Love makes us grab a loved one,
And hug them oh so tight.
Love has many powers,
As I have said above;
The most important thing of all,
Is remember "God is Love."

Elizabeth Cox

A Departing Mother's Prayer

Do you know my Jesus
I'll share Him with you
Do you know My Jesus
And what He can do

He can mend broken hearts
And lots of other things, too
The Jesus I know
Can do it for you

I talked to Him daily
Yes, I prayed for you, too
And asked that his Angels
Watch over you

Though I must go now
My work here is thru
Keep close to my Jesus
We'll be waiting for you

Doris L. Harrison

Mirror

I look in the mirror,
   what do I see?
I see me,
   staring back at thee.
I've never seen anything like it,
   yet...
Who is she,
   looking back at me?

Danielle Kumpulanian

Mother

Every day I
visit my mother

Through the dead
pines, across the
dry brook through
the hanging branches

Past the mourning
willows through the
tall yellowing grasses
and in the small clearing

And to the grave
where her body lay buried

Weeping I cling to the
grave crying out my agony

Drying my eyes. I
carefully put the summer
roses on the tombstone
I tell her all my worries

She listens, I feel
better and leave the way I came

Sara M. Hartless

More Than Words Could Ever Say

Dedicated to J.T.T. the guy I love.
I see your face
Your beautiful smile
Your heavenly eyes
And all the while
I'm drifting away
To a magical place
Where all my dreams of you
Become realities
When we meet someday
I know something will click between us
Because nothing you confess
Could make me love you any less
I love you more than almost anyone
And if someday I get my way
This one wish; you'll say to me:
"Darling, I love you more than words
could ever say."

Jill Tooley

The Old Fire Balls

I can hear the sounds the old
fire balls made as they went chugging
up a long steep grade. They huffed
and puffed and snorted steam that
boiled out in a big white stream
and when they were rolling out on
the tracks. Black smoke poured from
the stack. We could hear that lonesome
whistle sound for miles around.
   It made us wish that we could
go, where to only heaven's knows.
These are things from a childhood
gone but the memories still live on.
Now when I hear a modern
train I stop and think what a
shame that the old fire balls that
served us so well, are just left
to rust into a shell.
   So hears to trains come and gone
May they forever roll on and on.

Mary Hubbard

My Grandfather

When I was just a little tyke
I'd climb up on his knee
To listen to the stories
He so often read to me.

When school-work seemed to trouble me
To Grandpa I woud run,
His patience in explaining things
Made problems much more fun!

He loved a cross-word puzzle book
A hobby all his life,
His knowledge and broad viewpoints
Were usually - quite right!

His favorite poem was "Snow-bound"
He'd recite it all by heart
As in his chair he'd sit and rock
Close by the open hearth.

His sound advice through years gone by
Live in my memory
And I'm sure because of him
My life will better be.

Helen L. Moore

I, Spinster

My heart is a lonely garden
Where songbirds once did dwell,
Now flowers fade
In its austere shade,
By a deep, and arid well.

Mary M. Gaylord

Show Me

Show me a promising young man,
I'll show you a world leader.

Show me a female virgin.
I'll show you the perfect wife.

Show me a poor man,
I'll show you the hardest working soul.

Show me a dead man.
I'll show you a male prodigy.

Show me the earth.
I'll show you God's best creation.

Show me evil.
I'll show you life's mistake.

Marco Caporale

The Ocean

When I walk by the ocean
On the hot sand
It burns my feet
So I walked on the wet sand
I collect seashells
That the waves
Washed up on the beach
When I swim in the water
With my dad
Horseshoe crabs pass by in the waves
But when I leave
I dream of next summer at the beach
It will seem like tomorrow

Breann Gingrich

Grace

The gift of man
What does it mean
Only can be Grace
Adorning

A melody in life
Sounds of joy
Gives my heart
Delight

The gift of a man
What does it mean
Essence divine
Joy fulfilled

Cherish the gift of a man
In heart and mind
Intimate dreams
Intertwine

Ah....the gift of a man
Evoked my feminine tide
Only can be Grace
Adorning

Sandra Evans Husted

Heaven's Flight

Why do they leave us?
Why do they go?
The people we trust
The people we know?

One moment they are there,
The next...they are gone.
The people who care,
Who we've known for so long.

We miss them so much,
We wish they were there.
Their special touch...
Their love and their care.

Amy Roberts

Cara Clara

What's in a face
might be none
of my business

Sparrows don't cling
to dawn
the red dog barks
not only at noon

My feet are not
my thought
but they take me
where I'm going

Simpler to be
what one is

Or to declare the
same word twice
without the mirror

John Mingione

Identity?

I am the predator
    the prey
    the creator the destroyer

I am thought
I am energy
Both evil and good

I am a friend I am a lover
and a greatest fear

I am dissatisfied
    A dreamer
    A failure and hope

I am a wanderer
    a learner a seeker a fool

I am despair
    revelation
    determination and experience

I am stifled
    with held thwarted and bound

I dream of freedom...

I envision peace...

Alexia S. Whiting

I Want To Be Just - An American

I don't know why
This thought came to me
In the year of our Lord
Nineteen eighty-three.

If I'd been born in China
You'd call me Chinese.
And by the same token
Greeks are natives of Greece.

Mother is an American
And father is also,
Then, why does my American
Need to be preceded by Afro?

I'm proud of my Black heritage
So please don't judge me wrong;
But America is the country
To which I belong.

Grandmother was Negro,
My brother's a Black man;
But down deep in my heart
I want to be just - an American!

Gloria J. Shipman

The Medal

Where are you going soldier boy?
Off to fight the war;
and I shall win a medal there
to hang on mothers door!
Off he marched; brave soldier lad,
and joined the bloody fray,
where a cannonball come howling by
and took his head away.
now his mother sits alone
staring at the door,
and cursing the medal Sonny won
when he went off to war.

J. Scott Kent

The Plan

Two hearts in a house
covered in dirt - no one knows
the tears of pain falling - in here
you don't know me any more
Not a friend - should be alone
Seated by a window
Cigarette glowing
Smoke trailing a blue line
Out into the night air
Wishing my body could follow
Pain of another day with you over
To try for sleep - alone
Waking to plan
My escape
To take me away
from you...

Lisa Monte

The Message

The breeze is fresh with salty sea air,
the anchored boats in stillness lie.
And as he spreads his fishing net,
A sea gull sings its lonely cry.
The pearly shells upon the sand
Are shifted by the sweeping tide.
And out beyond the restless surf,
The coral sun sets on the other side.
He felt a peace within his heart,
That he'd never known before.
This day was special to him
As he walked upon the shore.
For the sea had sent a message,
That told him all was well.
So he hurried home light hearted,
for he heard the dinner bell.

Shanna Griffiths

Why Ask Why

Why ask why when rain falls you
bring me sunlight with your smile.
Why ask why? A day is no day
without seeing a face such as
beautiful as yours. Why ask why?
more and more my love grows how
much only the Lord knows.
Why ask why? For you and I it's
love that rises in the blue sky.
Why ask why? So the thought
of losing you makes me cry.
Why ask why? I am true to you
and only you and that's no lie. So
whatever you do never ask why.

Rodney Thomas

Derrick's Poem After Life

If I die
and become a bird
I ask God
to forgive my fears
to give me a new
personality,
but remember
everything
I thought all in
this life.

Derrick Freddy Rolon

My Mind

My mind is like a cloud
It is nice and fluffy
But sometimes changes

My mind is like a cloud
It drifts with the wind
But knows its true identity

My mind is like a cloud
It changes day by day
But always the same in a way

My mind is like a cloud
It has many colors
But one bright idea

My mind is like a cloud
It makes many shapes
But truly only has one

Megan Eckel

Yesterday, Today And Tomorrow

Yesterday is gone forever
Never to return;
Memories are all we have left
Of days for which we yearn.

Today, the present life we live
Is swiftly fleeing, too;
Soon it will be only memories
For me, my friend, and you!

Tomorrow, today will be yesterday
And tomorrow will be today;
So live each precious moment now
Before time is swept away.

Jane S. Dellinger

Searching For Dawn

Searching for dawn
In the dark of midnight,
Clinging to hope
That help will arrive,
Asking for angels
To come hold my hand,
Praying for mercy
To drift me to land
Scared, in the dark,
Cold and alone
I need God
To come guide me home.

Addie Breesler

Children's Prayer

Oh Almighty Father
To You I entrust my soul.
Bless me Lord and help me God
To do as I am told
Bless all whom I hold dear
And those I'll never meet
On the road to righteousness
Gently guide my feet
Amen.

Vanessa O. McCoy

The Prophecy

Sinking, sinking, deathly deeper
Almost seeing cloak and reaper,
Nearing darkness, frightly ill
Soon to pay the demons bill,
Nothing venture, nothing gain
Nothing feels good without pain,
Tainted trust and tainted blood
Dripping, dripping, making mud,
In the ashes, in the soil
Crumbled mirrors made of foil,
All is happy, all is bad
All is evil, all is madd,
Everything is nuts and bolts
Crimes of passion, racists cults,
Look into the crystal ball
And you shall see the tales of tall,
But these tales may soon be true
Does mankind know what to do?

Dan Spencer

My Mate

You chose me as your wife,
And set sail throughout life,
Conquering daily strife,
    My Mate.

Soon we enlarged our crew,
With healthy sons of two,
As the winds of life blew,
    My Mate.

A voyage of few fears,
Throughout our thirty years,
Rain acted as our tears,
    My Mate,

From life's port you depart,
Taking with you my heart,
A new course now to chart,
    My Mate.

Donna J. Moore

Sitting In The Sun

I see you sitting in the sun,
Gazing into the sky,
Your mind is somewhere it can run,
Your smile, it doesn't lie.

Lounging in the clover grass,
Your auburn ringlets glisten,
Dreaming while the hours pass,
Your face the sun doth christen.

Glowing in your soothing grace,
A figment of inspiration,
The world is yours within your space,
In most mellow jubilation.

The sultry days go by so fast,
When your apparition has begun,
Enchanting heat waves will always last,
When you're sitting in the sun.

Edward Cooper

Home

Home...
Such a comforting word.

Some days I want to go Home,
but it's not there anymore.

The place I once called home...
is gone...

I miss the memories,
and the safe feelings!

I feel as if I'm a million miles from
Where I once called home...

I don't feel safe here,
My mom's there,

I'm Here.

Jeni Ross

On Reflection

Of shimmering ice
Reflecting man's shame
Of things best forgotten
Never given a name

Lest you not forget
Dare look upon the ice
Feeling honest regret
For your actions less than nice

Seeing in your face
A stranger far removed
From one you thought so nice.

Louis E. Martin

Love's Rose

The rose is like a sparkling rain,
falling peacefully on golden grain.
With the love from heavens above,
floating clouds of morning doves.

The roses' petals like babies touch,
soft as velvet we love so much.
Brilliant colors at sunset's dusk,
blessed with Gods precious trust.

The rose is like a cool breeze,
drifting softly through the trees.
Raising gently into the sky,
with the twinkling of an eye.

The roses' scent so sweet and tart,
keeping loves' reach within my heart.
With prickly stems short and sharp,
and glistening music of angels' harps.

The rose is happiness to me,
growing where our lives are free.
With the help of God above,
there's always glorious gifts of love.

Rosie Scharschmidt

The Bird

Instead of
flying
    to heaven,
falling
    to hell.
Has the rain washed
its blood away yet?

Faith Chen

Winter

Beautiful pines
crystal — ivory snow,
bushes, sprinkled with fairy dust.
Rocks and grass, covered with a sheet,
The dove flying off to the heavens.

Amanda Batson

M.O.M.M.

(Memories of My Mother)

A friend, a nurse,
A teacher, a hugger . . . .

A driver, a scoutleader,
A library-book lugger . . .

An artist, an actress,
An avid admirer . . .

An hour of her time
unending inspirer . . .

A clothes-washer, paper-typer,
A shoulder when I rue . . .

A cake-baker, party-planner,
Prom dress-maker, phew!

An esteem-Booster, dream-giver,
Wedding day blue . . . .

A someone - to - lean on
And say, "I love you."

And as destiny dictates,
I go to another . . .

I'll always remember
I've *only* one mother!

Shawn K. Schmittgen

A Thought of You

A thought of you passed by my way
As I was outside working today.
It made me stop and look to the sky
As tears flowed from my eyes.

I stared at the sky for a long time
As the thought faded from my mind.
I continued my work but I knew
My thoughts would return to you.

George Marrett

To A Graduate

You boldly climbed the stairs of life,
Conquering your study strife;
And now you're there the top to see,
Across the bridge of victory;
And on to greater things indeed,
A lifetime garden strown with seed.
Planted in your fertile mind,
thoughts to help the young to find;
The key to happiness for you,
Lies in the daily things you do;
Grown from seed so gently sown;
By loving teachers you have known.

Sunshine L. Mattingly

Backwards Us

Wonderful news
Legs recently parted,
While fishing in depths
Of friendship, not started.
Two birds flying backwards
Under the sea
Can never, will never
Nest in a tree.
A wise man bears not his soul,
They say.
And a fool is not cautious
Of games people play.
The wonder is over,
The mystery is gone,
All eyes must be opened
To the coming of dawn.

Nathan Green

Dad

My love to you
is like the ocean blue
I know you love me too.
Your eyes are like
soft hand.
I love you so much
I'll play a band.
Your love to me
brings me joy.
I'm glad I'm not a boy
Doves bring a note to us
to say we love each other
love no one other.

Sarah N. Disaia

On Understanding

When I say, "I understand,"
I mean that I am with you in the
    Realm of human feeling;
Experience touching experience,
    Ringing a harmony of being
    Parallel in mutuality.
Understanding is not a
    Standing under and looking up
    Into the depths of someone's
    Sorrow.
Nor is it standing over them and
    Saying, "Time will heal all."
It's being there in spirit
    Which knows no boundary.
Actually I'm saying,
    "I am with you,"
Hoping that you'll say,
    "I understand."

Lynell Kendrick

Life's Valleys

I have often wondered why
    We have to experience the
    valleys of life.

Now, I know. We appreciate the
    mountain tops more
    when we come from below.

Helen Herrington

Mom

Mom is someone to share and
to be there, when all goes well
and trouble is near. For she will
always care.
    Small or large, no matter what
ever they are, close or far I know
she will always be there.
    The love we share is always a
prayer, it brings us close even tho,
we are miles away it can bring
us close if we pray.
    Lord Jesus is our bond and he
will keep us fond in our hearts even
tho we are miles apart or close at
heart every day.

Dorothy Legard

Forsake Me

Forsake me friend,
for I have sinned.
I do not want this end,
but, I feel pinned.

Forsake me father,
for my deed.
Or would you rather,
watch me bleed.

Forsake me mother,
for my crime.
I'm not worth the bother,
not worth a dime.

I ask you all,
to love me here.
Let me fall,
and die, without fear.

David J. Roy

Society Today

Peace who has it
Hope who knows it
Joy who lost it
Happiness who shows it
Gentleness who has abuse it
Faith who's trying to invent it
Love who is and always will be God

Lonna Traynor

October

In October the leaves turn brown,
Kids are running all around.
Asking people trick or treat,
Candy is a treat to eat.
Some say yes and some say no,
The trick they get they do not know.
Jack-o-lanterns shine at night,
So kids can see their eyes so bright.
Black cats are lurking all around,
Children's footsteps on the ground.
October is a month for fun,
Happy Halloween Everyone!

David Hegarty

Only the Best

God saw you getting tired,
And new it was to be.
So he put his arm around you
and whispered come with me.
A precious heart stopped beating,
hard working hands to rest.
God broke our hearts to show us,
He only takes the best.
Everyday we miss you,
No more our lives to share.
And in our hearts your memory
will be forever there.

Robert Gardepe

Inside - Outside

Hear the music...what a beat
Dancing frenzy...feel the heat.
See the kids through smokey haze.
Pills, white powder, latest craze.
They can't hear me through the din,
I'm on the outside looking in.

"Come on in," I hear them call.
"Don't be shy, we'll have a ball".
"Have a drink, a snort, a toke,
Let your fears go up in smoke."
My head spins...my trip begins.
Not on the outside looking in.

Through the haze, I hear a cry.
People fighting...someone dies.
Sirens blaring....guns are drawn...
Cuffs of steel I have on...
"Hey, fresh meat," a prisoner shouts.
I'm on the inside....looking out.

Kristyl Gilson

Autumn

Cool mornings,
warm colors,
trees getting ready to
drop their leaves.

Shorter days,
longer nights,
stars changing position
in the sky.

Squirrels gathering,
bears gorging,
Mother Nature busy preparing,
for her long slumber.

Shadows stretching,
clouds swirling,
sunlight peeking through her veil,
sending Earth her love.

Michele Prenovost

Unique

The formation of my face
molds such expression.
My body's structure so
unique, and my ways so
queer, only I can comprehend.
I'm an individual, a sculptor
among artists.
Yes, I am me.

Charles Borg

Lost

Walking
And then running
in a maze of people.
Lost.
Or left behind in the crowd.

People
hurrying here and there.
I call out to them
but they don't hear
or can't hear me.
Lost in their own gray world.

You found me.
Sobbing in a dark dusty corner
and wiping the tears from my eyes
Picking me up
holding me.
Found.

Kim Suggs

Departure; Airport

And then
there was that moment
in the car:
we both sat back,
backs at windows —
churning in that
pause before the
next word was
goodbye.

And black and white
photography
in all its slight
complexities,
could possibly have
captured it:
your look
to me
that night.

rk khavari

Maternal White Bunting

Enamel white
Apron white
Cotton white
Milk white hair white Grandmother
Grandmother

Lily white
Salt white
Snow white
Dove white hair white Grandmother
Grandmother

Egg white
Moon white
Paper white
Pearl white hair white Grandmother
Grandmother

Cloud white
Angel white
Halo white
Star white hair white Grandmother
Grandmother

Victoria Rosko

Untitled

Dawn reveals
upon my pine table
his forgotten
earthenware mug.
With benediction
I cradle it
and inhale
last night
in the essence
of his raspberry tea.

Sandra Brinkman Murphy

Love Gone Wrong

Tears that fall
Hearts that break
Dreams that shatter
Because of my mistake

You come to me
With raging eyes
And a heart that believes
I've told you lies

I try real hard
To fight you back
But it seems as though
I'm not on track

You scream and yell
You want me to hear
Those nasty words
That cause my fear

Roxane D. Holmes

The Ambush

Cat paws pad swiftly down the hall,
looking for a human to befall.
Peeking cautiously around each door,
for bare feet upon the floor.

He wiggles, he waits,
he anxiously anticipates.
Then he sees his naked prey,
five toes which seem to say,
"Come and get me while you may."

A flash of fur, the target reach.
A swift response, the victim's screech.
There is no victory so sweet,
as the conquering of human feet.

Lynn Childs

In My Hand

If I took all my yesterdays
in my hand and blew
they would scatter and
fall unappreciated.

If I took my today
in my hand and blew
it would scatter and
fall unnoticed.

If I took all my tomorrows
in my hand and blew
you would catch them.

Jill Matschener

Another Storm

If only these four walls could talk,
oh, the things that they would say.
It would be of never told stories
and of things long hidden away.

In the rain, I lay and listen,
what a sadness it brings out
to repeat the tears that glisten,
on a lost and lonely heart.

Now what about the thunder,
when it wakes me in the night.
I think of times of quiet
and I wish for that tonight.

But now the sun is shining
on a bright and cloudless day,
The tears I shed last night
will soon be gone with yesterday.

Lisa M. Odell

Untitled

A summer's rose is lovely, yet
It can't compare to you.
A castle is enchanting, but
It won't compare to you.
My love for you can never stray,
My love for you won't fade away.
For you I live, I laugh, I love.
For you are my heart's desire.
My only love...
For you I sigh, I cry, I die.
For you are my peace
In this turmoil.
My love for you will never die.
With you by my side.
Forever and a day
We will be
together.

Lacey C. Dobyns

Thoughts of the Past

Has love been lost, I'll never know.
I sit and wonder even tho.
Could this be my final fling.
Or will Love be born again?
To much to guess, which causes stress.
It's made my life an awful mess.
This is the one that I adore.
But sad to say it may be no more.
I curse the darkness every night.
Hoping daylight will end my plight.
Communications my only goal.
To set this straight deep in my soul.
A thief and a liar, no not me!
As others try to make me out to be.
So here I stand being accused.
But only me, feeling used.
It's like a whisper upon the wind.
Will it be heard and regained again.

Philip A. LaBombard

Love's Absence

As a child her love was blind
She knew only how she felt.
She just wanted to be loved by one,
Who's love was never sent.

She tried her best to win this love,
    with deeds of many kinds.
But only to be disappointed
    by the emptiness she did find.

The sorrow and the pain she felt
    gave strength to look beyond.
To find within her heart a place
    to carry on.

Years have come and gone now,
    and in her life she's traveled on.
She's met new loves in her life
    to help replace the one.

But sometimes in her mind's eye
    she still can see the face
    of the woman she called Mom
    who left without a trace.

Sherri Neal Garcia

Gone

Someday we will be gone
But those who remain
Should remember
The pleasure, not the pain

The good times, not the bad
The happy, not the sad
That life is a dream for all who dare
But most of all for those who care

And if we failed those we leave
Improperly they bereave
Tears do not celebrate
Love of so many years

Remember, it's the thought
Not the act
That someday will
Bring us back

Jean Bowling

The Faces Of Love

Love cannot be seen or touched
it must be in the heart
Love will bring you close to together
and never far apart
Love is like a burning flame
that lasts eternally
It breaks the hearts of many
and never sets you free
Love may bring you happiness
as might it bring a tear
Love is something very strong
a heartache few might fear
Love brings out a part of you
that was never known to be
Love brings out the good in you
that few have ever seen.

Parinaz Samimi

A Human Love

How shall I thank him
For the gifts than he bestows?
My sincere and heartfelt gratitude
Sometimes just overflows!

My love revealed in measures
By the human ways I know;
Yet hindered just as likely
When these ways neglect to grow.

How can any human effort
Ever possibly reflect
The love he shows us daily
That's so perfect and select?

As always when I'm bothered
By things I cannot understand,
I go to him for answers.
Prayer will lend a helping hand.

Gail A. Woodruff

For DonnaJean

Soft was the springtime, fresh and wet
with tulips' flowering heads.
Warm was the summer's midnight breeze,
how can my heart forget?
The love we shared, it still is
new when springtime comes again.
Then, on April Fools Day,
a kiss I reminisce.
Tears are diamonds shed by
love to end each passing fling.
I wonder if the fool I love
will shed a tear this spring?

Helen D. Moyer

Madness

My sister
    I thought
        I heard her
            Speak

Old, but
    Still young
        Visiting
            Enchanted places

She's happy
    In her way
        She's left me
            Far behind

Lost to us
    Romping happily
        With the images
            In her mind

June Starr

Tear Driven

Life threatening.
Death deserving.
These emotions rip at my heart.
To forever be plagued by them.
Is to die my them.
When will they exit my soul?
when love has found its way home.

J. Osborne

Beyond the Horizon

Looking through the mist of
An embroidered window pane.
Reflections casting a glow.
Neither waiting for life nor time,
The moon eclipsed a rainbow.
Staring, gazing, hoping on seizing
A moment. My heart stops to wonder;
If, we were meant to grow.
But the time we spend together
Is beautiful time to me, because
What we share between us
Should never be misconceived.
For life is just for wanderers
Searching to find their dreams.
And love, can never be
Measured only to believed.
While pausing to catch a breath,
A breath of God's given air
I look across this table and
I'm glad that you are there.

Raul L. Glover

Porcelain Dolls

Charming porcelain dolls
Faces fine and translucent
Admirably designed
Expressions never altered.
Keep your illusion.
Fine variations
with few exceptions.
All are alike
always ready for sale.
And there are so many buyers.
Who would pay dearly
for a fine porcelain doll
to be put on a shelf to be
idolized and admired
but never touched.
Who is worthy
of a porcelain doll?

Tami Cavitt

Who

Love that's what
this world is all about,
Heart is so wonderful
it will make you shout,
Charity no one has
it more than you,
Understanding you
have that too,
It is a sweet person
I'm referring to,
I promise I would
not lie,
My favorite teacher
at Elmwood Junior
high!
Mrs. Lockhart
English Teacher

Amanda Desiree Stevens

Rainbow

Purple, orange, green and gold
What a lovely sight to hold.
An arching shadow in the sky
God's promise to you and I.

It appears at very different times
Sometimes rain and sometimes shine.
But never does it fail to bring
Joy, laughter and pleasant things.

It rises gloriously from the mist
Just as if it had been heaven kissed.
Glowing brightly after a shower
Radiating God's love and power.

You'll find one near a waterfall
Proof that miracles are big and small.
Occasionally you'll be blown away
Left with no words to say.

To what do we owe this little pleasure
Something God sent to us to treasure.
Look to the sky and you will know
This blessing is a rainbow.

Elizabeth Carter

Dolls

I am a doll all dressed
in white,

Boys think I am a nasty
sight,

But they play with ones that
fight.

Some boys think their
dolls are full of might,

They throw theirs around all night.
Some boy dolls can really bite,

Others go up to great heights,
But I prefer the ones with tights!!

Jamie Refenes

My Family

I remember when I was a little boy
and only seven.
My Mom told me Dad passed away
and went to heaven.
I'll never forget all the sorrow we
shared, for he was the best, everyone
really cared.
This was not my Mothers first grief,
as you will see, she lost a little boy
when he was only three.
As years went by and we cared
for one another, our greatest love
and respect went out to our Mother.
A year ago in February, we lost
our brother Jim. He was a great person
and we really miss him.
And just six months ago our
youngest sister Madeline passed away
She died of cancer, what is the
answer her son and daughter will say?

Frank McSparran

The Scorching Sun

Rainy times.
Days that cry under the sun
that splatters into thunder,
vexing the village.
Let Olodumare* pity his own children.

Blinded winds
whistling and chasing the dust
which in turn blinds man.

The worried sky
its path, dangerous,
impervious to man.

Africa cries:
I need peace, a smile, and comfort.

African man,
quench this sun
that burns
my black skin,
that destroys
the African man.

Fehintola Mosadomi

*God in Yoruba language.

The Old Wooden Cross

The Old Wooden Cross
   Is the tree of life,
Upon it the Glory of Heaven
   And life.
The tears deep in its crevices,
   The blood in its nooks,
The love that he has for us,
   The love that they shook.
The Old Wooden Cross
   Will never be forgot,
And the souls that the
   Precious blood bought.
Glory be to God for all living things,
   In memory of our wooden gleam.

Stacey M. Hays

Your Knight's Love

'Tis the place in your heart
Where I'll always dwell,
Your kiss cast the demons
Black wizards once held.

My mind says to me
'Tis this a fairy tale
Nay says my soul
'Tis true love you've found,
Like knights once fought for
In realm's past bound.

As we walk through life
Shadows nipping at our tails,
Love keeps them afar
Like the once holy grail.

Our passions are legions,
Crusades in their quest,
My castle the soft beating
That lays below your breast.

As I lay in your arms
I hear voices telling me, I'm home!

Frank Alanis

521

Untitled

Splattered everywhere
my love for you
it sits in my chair
mingles with the wall
douses the window
my love
for you
is gone
Splattered
I can't pick it up
for fear it will fall apart
It is sinking into the walls
disappearing into my chair
Sliding down my windows
Splattered everywhere

Katy Raw

Last Wish

Running wild through the sun
faster, faster
my wild charade had just begun
I feel the grass beneath my feet
sharp cracking
my arms like wings I want to cheat
to take the air and fly away
my heart will know I cannot stay
and it doesn't matter where
I run through meadows
fields of grass
dim-lit forests
run so fast
Freedom found me
free at fast
(A Bullet's Tear)
it couldn't last

Jake Tringully

Man

You lock me in,
You blind my eyes,
You gag my mouth,
And you speak your lies.

I scream in pain,
I cower in fright,
I cry red tears,
In your crimson light.

My hands are numb,
My eyes are cold,
My heart is ice,
But my voice is bold.

I say you're false,
I say you hate,
I say you hurt,
But I am too late.

Natalie Keyssar

New Life

A parents' living poetry
Tiny new anatomy
A small glimpse of what is to be
Such promise in simplicity

A miracle formed by the love of two
Nurtured into life anew
To carry on when life is through
A part of me, a part of you.

Lesley Miller-Casteel

Compassion

You keep on making a way,
Each and every day,
You gave me life brand new,
I will always love you.

No matter what the situation,
You're always there for me,
You calm the storms and raging
seas, every time I call on thee.

Compassion fills my soul,
No one will ever know,
The peace I have inside,
I surely cannot hide.

So believe me when I say,
This love so sweetly given
will never pass away,
Because it's free to all,
You won't ever have to stray.

Gloria Hogan

Behind the Big Words

Instincts caged as I
Long for the freedom of open plains

Hear the blood lust of hunt
Sing its proud songs of conquest
Above campfire dreams
Dancing primal dances of need
    surpassing reason

Feel the hot blood of ancestry
Scream through younger veins

Beneath this mirrored surface
This shallow pond of pretense
And cavemans soul runs free.

Uriah S. Massey

Undying Reality

Have you ever seen the moon cry?
    exploding tears
    of dreary light
    through shipwrecks of
    the sea's night

The silent move
    that mountains make
    under the black uncaring lake

As stars turn black,
    we are left alone
    realizing the heart has
    no home

Undying reality
    has been our fate
    then realizing,
    it has always been
    too late!

Carolyn Berkley

A Bridge from Here to There

A panoramic view from now to then,
a bridge from here to there.
If I could walk that bridge again
a plainer hat I'd wear,
a plainer dress,
some plainer shoes,
and plainer words that I could use.

Mary Trimble

The Journey

Snow melting on the ground,
Flowing slowly to the mound.
Of earth below so it can travel,
Away to the brook that quietly bubbles.

The brook flows quickly to the river,
Unknowing to what it will endeavor,
Here comes a bear to splash,
Up the river a tree is about to crash,
Watch out for the waterfall!
Do you hear the ocean's call?

The ocean has called to you,
The river's flow continues,
Faster than once before,
Colliding at the oceans shore,
It mixes and becomes one,
One body.
One ocean,
The journey is done.

Cortley Blank

Progress

Oh! Progress
Where do you come from?
The brilliant minds of men
To clutter our fields and valleys.
To put up monstrous buildings
To move our earth and our streams.

Time marches on
Globs take shape.
Bins stand high in the sky.
And one day
The beautiful works of man.

There stands a mine
South of town
For men to toil in.
And we know the town of Blacksville
Has joined in on progress.

Hattie V. Foley

Honey Brass Woman

Drawing in, eyes
shut and furrowed
a nervously aching bellows
spittling shags into
the mute cup
with a swollen puckered buzz the
Honey Brass Women
envelops her lover
in clasp-handed
fallopian prayer.

Matthew D. Collar

I Wish

I wish I had wings
To fly, to sore
To feel free
To get out of this trapped feeling
Just break away from this insecurity
How far I would fly there is no telling
How low I would soar
It's just a bore
I wish I had wings
Then I would be alone no more

Jennifer Bailey

Untitled

Here I am, "trapped"
In a world I cannot escape!
There are these things touching me,
These things I feel I cannot explain.
I feel I have been betrayed
of a trust I had once known
I have no one to share these
feelings with, therefore I am alone.
I have almost given up hope
to find someone who will listen,
I feel I am stuck in the middle.
The choices I make are all so wrong
I feel as if I weren't meant to be
As if I was a mistake.
All there is to do now
is sit back and wait.

April Chaney

The Preacher

People who preach and teach
about God's philosophy
must preach to themselves
before they teach.

Frida Robertson

Kokopelli

Kokopelli, Kokopelli
Play your music sweet.
Bounce your melody
    off the stars,
Surround the mountains
    with your beat.

Kokopelli, Kokopelli
Sweep your tunes
    across the desert dunes.
Feel the heat
    seep slowly through your bones.
Hone the rhythm
    in your feet.

Shone the pathway
    to the moon,
Dancing spirit of the night,
    Kokopelli.

Linda Doutre

A Long Time Ago

A long time ago there was
    a feeling inside
The feeling inside meant
    something serious
I told you my feelings
You act like you cared
You had me going for awhile
Until one day when I seen
    you with that girl
You told me a long time
    ago that you cared
You lied and you hurt me dearly
What am I to do,
What am I to think
You lost my trust
I can never trust you again
I'm sorry I ever met you
You weren't the person I met
But of course it was all a lie
And all that was a long time ago!

Raquel Barriger

King of Pain, Queen of Ashes

A king of pain, a queen of ashes
It wasn't suppose to end this way
What became of happily ever after?
What caused their love to fade away?
What made the king banish the queen?
Leaving her heart in flames
She became the queen of ashes
And he, the king of pain
Why would he leave her?
Knowing she loved him so
Why was it so easy
Letting her go?
How did she fail him?
Where did she go wrong?
What could possibly bring to an end
A love that was so strong?
Once a happy royal couple
If only in name
Now she is the queen of ashes
And he, the king of pain.

Shelly A. Wall

It's Thanksgiving!

There's a crisp in the air.
Warmer clothes we must wear.
Lots of things we can share.
It's Thanksgiving.

Get closer by the fire.
Lots of snow we desire.
Turn the heat on a little higher.
It's Thanksgiving.

We're going homeward bound.
There's a frost on the ground.
The birds, what a sound!
It's Thanksgiving.

Lots of food on the table.
Cut the turkey I am able.
Oh, it's just like a fable.
It's Thanksgiving.

It's time to go to bed.
The Bible I had read.
Mom softly said,
"It's Thanksgiving!"

Rachel Postler

The Rose

The rose in winter
    lies beneath the ground
Under a blanket of snow
    never to be found.

The rose in spring
    awakes from the earth
Reaches towards the sun
    at a time of rebirth.

The rose in summer
    grows with beauty and grace
The color brilliant
    none can take its place.

The rose in fall
    its days are but few
To return to the earth
    and to start anew.

Sandra D. Kirby

Lens of Perceptions

What we perceive
is the way we believe
things really are

If we gave our beliefs
an occasional relief
we would see both near and far

Should ever you see
no end there could be
and your heart and soul are at war

A quick change of the lens
where perceptions begin
will leave the door ajar

Esther B. Moore

Mother Otter's Wisdom

My little otter of the deep
speaking with a little squeaky
    peep.

Swimming round and round
and even up side down, round
    oily brown.

You can do tricks like a clown
to amaze the people all around.

Swimming deep to catch your
prey and lay on your back and
    eat all day.

Beware of what you see in the
air an eagle might be there if
you watch the sky you may
    stay alive.

Look out for big white boats
they want to take your coat.

So swim in peace my little pup
    until we meet again.

Joshua Meister

And I Know

And I know
Somewhere Sunshine burns in the night
Yes I know
That's where stars are shining bright

Perhaps you know
someone Happy, Full of Love
Mayhap you know, you've felt,
The touch of the Dove

And then again
You may know the darkness of the night
and you may know
the sun that shines no light

We each live
in a world that's all our own
And we give
what we have, what is our own

We are not Angels
nor Devils yet
But only Humans
Lives full of regret

Keith Terry

Emotions

Hearts of love hearts of pain,
hearts are driven insane.
You give your heart to someone
you love, you think it's pure as a dove.
The love that was once there can
be no more, because you closed the
lonely door. The heart doesn't trust
so why should you, if you did you think
you'll be blue.
If you should learn to trust your
heart, maybe then will never be apart
Open your heart and your love to me,
then maybe you'll learn to believe.
I love you and I'm giving you
my heart, so learn to share and
stop keeping us apart.

Michelle Jones

Because No One Cared

One tiny, green bud sits in the
middle of many rustling leaves.
Sun rays shine down and awaken
it to a fresh, new morning.
Mossy smooth covers peal back
slowly revealing soft, satin like,
red petals.
Individually, each section starts
pulling apart, opening new life
into our world.
Always growing larger, reaching
out to anything for love,
we are so rapidly that
the new creation goes totally
unnoticed.
Withering, dying, aching for
affection, death comes nearer
every day.

Marilyn Book

My Lady

I am in love with a lady
no man can ever tame
   she is as wild as the wind
as powerful as the rain
this affair has been going on
   quite some time
though I know
never to be mine
I still dream of her
as I lay awake at night
all her beauty
   and majestic might
someday the voyage
   I hope to make
a spirit time will never take
a flame burning so deep in me
my lady so peaceful
my lady the sea

Craig Peters

Fear

Why is it we look so sad
When its time to be so glad
What caused us to think of the past
When things in our life are going so fast
Is it because we are so afraid
To say were not very brave
Or is it just simple fear
That always causes that little tear

Jerry Thompson

Praise His Name

If you think God doesn't care,
And you live in great despair,
You're wrong my friend, you're wrong.
Praise His Name.

If you let Him take full charge,
Then your joy He will enlarge.
And your soul will be set free.
Praise His name.

He wants to let you know,
He will take away your woe,
But the secret is, let go,
Praise His Name.

For my God is great King,
And He wants to hear you sing,
Praises to His name,
Praise His Name!

DeAnna S. Lamb

Ribbons of Color

Looking out the window, what do I see?
Ribbons of color
Vibrant oranges, reds and yellows,
Ribbons of color

This miracle happens but once a year
Ribbons of color
Oh the beauty for all to see
Ribbons of color

We are blessed with this view
Ribbons of color
Others can only imagine our
Ribbons of color

What we take for granted are
Ribbons of color
Vibrant oranges, reds and yellows,
Ribbons of color

Pamela Colwell

The Rancher's Wife

There's dishes in the sink
And the house is upside down
The bedrooms are so cluttered
You can't get around.

Supper is a-burning
And the telephone is ringing,
The kids are yelling,
And the old man is a-drinkin'.

There's curlers in my hair,
And the doorbell's a-dinging.
It's the U.P.S. man
With a C.O.D. he's bringin'.

The dogs got the cat,
And the cows are out of the barn.
The chicken are a-cluckin'
And I'm out of yarn.

Well the evening is coming nearer,
And the washing still needs done.
And I don't need another day
That ends like this one.

Sondra R. McCoun

To A.S.

I will not read your biography
Anne Sexton.
Inside rant and rave
Inside the cold yellow eye
Too wretched to believe
That one could love you
Or you could love yourself
Your words are sharp and mellow
All the same —
You with the gift of mouth sounds
Words pounced on quickly
Not to fail or fall
As tripping through
The rat's skin you went
Leaving me like ice.

Patricia Van Megroot

Your Baby

She is your baby
She is your little sun
Of every day.

She is as beautiful
As an angel.
She is your baby
She is your light
In every night
She is so gentle
In your hand.

Simon L. Contreras

Loving Pain

Love is a feeling
much greater than pain
when you get it,
nothing ever stays the same,
when you start falling
out of love
nearer, and nearer, and
stronger, and stronger
until one day,
all the love
is gone.

Aimee Holley

Gone

Gone is when you miss them.
Gone is when you were there

Gone is so many years you
wish they were here.

You try and try but they never appear.

They are gone during the seasons
even when the trees are bare

They come every now then
but you rarely see them at all.

But at least you see them in the hall.
The class of '96 Oak Hill Elementary

Missy Spiegl

The Road Ends

Where has the time gone to?
The years have now all passed.
Look at me, look at you.
What once was young and free
is now older and has changed
Things not the way they used to be.
Hands once young and tender
now aged and show their time.
Things seeming so unsure.
The world waits for no one.
Live for each and every day.
The road ends and life is done.

Jennifer Cordasco

Children At Play

Sunlight
  on sweet smiling faces
Laughter,
  running, special places.
Children,
  older, younger and those between
Now and then a growing teen.

And if by chances
  one should glance
While these children play
  A glimmer of an Angel's wing
As bright as summer's day

The heart will lighten and be glad
  for all the blessings it has had
Sweet children at play
  Thus the soul begins to pray.

Martha Jane Stroud

Enterprise (Love), Forsaken

To scratch the surface,
no more. Highs too high,
lows too low, the excavator
drops his capable tools
in panicked haste, aborting
the arduous climb. Valley
of gold; 8th wonder of
the world; a readily
confessing Sphinx grown
tired of its own riddles;
all watch dismayed
as fear and doubt
prevent the ecstasy
of a perfect discovery.

The world has its share
of boasting heroes. Find me
one who won't retire valor
for an early dinner, a long
night's sleep, a complacent
conscience.

Desiree S. Brennan

Peace

Where there's music
  I'm happy . . .

Where there's friends
  I'm joyful . . .

Where there's faith
  I think of God . . .

Where there's God
  I'm at peace.

Sarah Stoutner

Snow

Snow is white
  and takes flight
    upon the air
      somewhere....
It falls to the ground
  silently,
    quietly,
      softly,
        until...
It makes a crunching,
  munching sound that
    will not quit
When I walk on it.

Julie Steere

Desire

Keep your heart full of pride
Keep your feet on the ground
Don't tread on one side
Keep your pride all around

Desire to hold on, desire to keep
  achieving
Aspire to become, all you've been
  dreaming

Keep your chin up high
Not a hint of defeat
Keep grasping for the sky
And you'll never get beat

Desire to hold on, desire to keep
  achieving
Aspire to become, all you've been
  dreaming

Your heart may pound
Your flesh may perspire
But remember what you found
A word called Desire!

Suzy Garza

Your Eyes

I can't describe the feeling
That rushes thru my heart
Every time I look into your eyes
I fall apart

Your eyes . . . they hold more beauty
Than a moonlit summer night
Whenever I gaze into them
I want to hold you tight

Your eyes . . . they hold more romance
Than a walk along the shore
The last time I looked into them
I thought about you more

Your eyes . . . they hold the magic
In the friendship that we've got
The next time I look into them
I'll thank the Lord, a lot

Jeffrey Louis Schoonover

Nature's Army

Trees standing guard on the hill,
  their formation,
    random.

Some marching down into the meadow,
  others marching,
    up.

Trees all saluting the sun,
  with arms upreaching,
    feet firmly planted
      in the soil.

Time takes its toll.
  Some must die,
    while others are
      born.

Look closely at the hill,
  see the dead and dying,
    lying,
      among the marching.

Schooler-Samukawa

A Way Up High

If I could fly
like a bird
in the sky
a way up high.
I'd swoop
I'd soar
I'd glide effortlessly.
I'd look down on people
hurrying like ants
to hurt others
as badly as they hurt.
I'd protect the smaller
and the weaker
from angry words
and heartless actions
and worse.
I don't know how
by attacking from the sky.
But I'd find a way
A Way Up High.

Sherry L. Middlebrook

Up Stream

I get thoughts and asylum cots
piled in the corner of my mind
I swim up stream without a dream
It's time to peel off my skin and
go back again
Will I perish or can I last
as I drop like leaves into the past
feet are tired, feet are sore
will I find what I'm looking for
heart is weak, brain is sick
as I glance at the world, near the
end of my wick
I don't know how I got here, but I
know I want out
Now that I find what it's all about.

Kyle Thomas

The Silent Majority

Against the swell
Of background chorus,
Single voices speak
Of prosaic happenings-
Faint lispings of the meek;
Of purposes for pursuing
And placid lives to live;
Of churches' spires and politics,
And simple love to give.
Blurred into mediocrity?
No, articulate and clear,
To those who dare to listen
Or even care to hear.

Dorothy C. Cureton

Untitled

Down through time,
Day after day,
Our lives are touched,
In so many ways.

People pass quickly,
They come and they go,
Themselves and their cares,
Are all that they know.

Your time has been long,
Your blessings abound,
The people you've loved,
Are always around.

So we thank the Lord,
That you love us too,
We are better people,
For having known you.

James Walker Jr.

The Fire

I stir the ashes
I stack the wood
This comforting fire
Will feel so good!

It takes a little doing
To kindle this new fire
But soon the flames are leaping
Of this I never tire

The sound of each sharp crackle
The glow of the flame
The smell of the wood
Nothing else is the same

Like graceful dancers
The flame leaps around each log
Perfect time in silent music
Sends my mind in a fog

Almost like hypnosis
The fire captures my stare
Letting my mind relax
Roaming aimlessly to nowhere

Peggy Hudson

The Woods and Me

The woods speak to me.
Their words are a gentle breeze.
Their words are bird songs.
Their words are the swaying trees.

The woods speak to me.
They tell of the folly of man.
They tell of his vanity.
They tell of his shallow life span.

The woods speak to me.
They speak of men's little goals.
They speak of his pettiness.
They speak of men's ignored souls.

The woods speak to me.
They say man could be great.
They say man could be noble.
They say it's not too late.

The woods speak to me.
They ask us to renew our lease.
They ask us to look inside.
They ask us to seek inner peace.

Kenneth Vincent

Shades Of Sanity

The night swallows the street
Like a hungry plague.
A lone man,
Laughs -
As he applies his make-up,
Laughs again.
He loves the night
For so many reasons.
Time to play.

Fun -
He loves this game.
It's so exciting.
It's very clean too -
Except for the blood,
So much blood.

But you get used to it.
He picks up his knife,
Wipes it clean,
He laughs.

Eric L. Mullins

Dandelions

The purity and the pain
hang up the phone
before it rings
so that no one
may abandon you
with their words.
Knock on the door
waiting for a footstep
and praying at the same time
that no one is home
Why is this love so complicated?
Can I ever say "I love you" again.

Katie Wasner

My Wife

I loved her in the beginning
I will love her to the end
I would love to send her flowers
I would love to hold her again
   I wish she had been my first
I know she will be my last
I want her to always love me
I know of the trouble in the past
   She may not understand me
She may not even care
She knows I really love her
She knows I want to be there
   She is my only love
She is my only life
She is my only friend
She is the one, my wife
   I hope she always loves me
I hope she's in my life
I hope that she will be there
I pray she stay's my wife

Robert F. Pople

First Snow

The drive is long,
from desert to mountain snow.
Paul is six.
The air cools.
Roads get windy.
Paul is anxious.
Patches along the road,
then coming together, solid.
"There's a hill! Stop!
Stop! Stop! Stop!"
Paul all bundled,
steps on to snow,
his first snow,
white and pure.
"Let's go sledding!"

David S. Ragar

Nature

Astounded by her perfection
   marveling at her beauty.

Floating, meandering
   lazily down tranquil stream
   shadowed by arching trees.

Roots-half-clinging,
   half-drinking.
Then
a friendly encounter
   by a lone speckled butterfly
   sailing current of air.
He settles daintily
   upon moistened shoulder
   and rests,
   wings outstretched
   quenching thirst
   and departs saying
Thank you

Edward Carr

Career

Life's work
Like teeth
Infant, growth
Teething, cutting
Each tooth a place.
Adult, growing
Pulling, straightening
Training, brushing
Correcting, polishing
Sturdy, undecaying
Decaying, bridges
Dentures, capping
   or growth,
New teeth!

Joyce Rich

Untitled

There is darkness all around
There are no windows no light
Can't you see my pain?
Don't you know who I am?
Someone is looking out
Can't you hear the cries,
See the liquid spill over and run down
Like volcano lava, hot and searing?
It's loud, it seems
From in here the cries, the pain
It's real, so real
So dark, no windows, no light
Don't you see?
Can't you hear?
My pain?

Michelle R. Wallace

Walls

Many have come down all around the world.
Due to the collapse of communism, we saw a nation divide.
Due to strength and acceptance, we saw two nations combine.
As many have come down, several have gone up.
"We" may be united in many ways,
   but the walls of ignorance, racism, and violence are where
   we divide and fall.
Freedom for one, is not for all.
We tend to neglect those we can't see behind our "walls."

Donna Tupper

Interpretation of the Wedding Vows

Do I take you   My heart and soul
To be my man   To live with and love
To have and hold   To hold at night
To love and cherish   To share with and care for?

Do I take you   My only joy
For good or bad   No matter what goes wrong
For rich or poor   No matter how little we have
In sickness and health   Even if you get an awful disease?

Do I take you   My truest love
Forsaking all   Being true to you
Till death parts us   Till death takes you from me?
You need not ask   I do!

Melinda Bolser

Stone Walls

He viewed me as a challenge
As I sat in the field all alone
Others were at a distance
All made of quiet gray stone

Work roughed hands soon touched me
Lifted and carried by man
carefully placed upon others
According to his well thought out plan

A boundary we formed for the farmer
Robbing elbows and shoulders and knees
Once placed we stayed in position
Unmoved by the fiercest breeze

Amazing how we all fit together
Though sizes and shapes big and small
Individuality remained intact
As compositely we formed a wall

For decades we remained there
Performing our silent duty
Keeping the creature from roaming
Becoming a thing of beauty

Bettyjane Jess Lloyd

Love

When you and I are far apart,
Can sorrow break my tender heart?
I love you so, darling yes I do,
Sleep dear sweet, for my love is true.
All you are is a beautiful Rose,
Night is here, so I must close.
With care read each first word of every line,
You will there a question find?

John M. Casias

My Favorite Things

I haven't climbed a snowy mountain,
Nor sailed a stormy sea.
I haven't touched the face of God,
Nor fallen in love to stay.

I haven't seen the wonders of the world,
Nor Earth from outer space.
I haven't had all my dreams come true,
Nor worn clothes of silk and lace.

I haven't heard an angel sing,
Nor play a golden harp.
But I have done things that I love to do,
And stored them in my heart.

I have seen my children laughing,
Or wiped away their tears.
I've told them that I love them,
To warm them and calm their fears.

I've sat beside a roaring fire,
And drank from a warm, sweet cup.
I've tasted love and friendship,
But nowhere near enough.

Michael Shelton

Rainbows of the Sun

Living like the bright blue sky,
Ever constant, ever changing
Distant clouds hover above the earth
And race away with a beckoning wind.

Lifeless, always moving, assuming
The guise of creatures great and small
Blues and hues of purple, yellow, red
Rainbows of the sun.

Overseeing the world, ne'er comprehending;
Passing from a bird's eye view,
Revolving bright to darkest night
A starry kaleidoscope filling the sky.

Horses, archers - dots on the ceiling
Myths, constellations - winds of change.
Facets of the living theatre, ever
Constant illuminations of the moon.

Stacy Kitts

My Wonderment

I wonder why you look at me as if you knew maybe you do
I don't know if only things were different
But anyway I have but one short time to make a difference
In so many folks' I've gotta catch up! Quick
And you're helping me why?
I want to do something nice for you - guardian angel
You are turning my life around planting me on more solid ground.
I'm beginning to see the light - but don't let me go
I'm afraid of the night.
When down the road I get better at this grownup thing
I'll remember that you looked at me like you knew this is
where I was going
I have pieces of a world I could create unclear where
But if I keep thinking my vibe will steer me where I should go
to change things.
You know I love it when I close my eyes and feel you helping me moving
my thoughts beckon direction They have feeling but need seedling.
Can you help me with this? What? I didn't think so. Never. Do me a
favor and shut up then. I'll figure it out But thank you though good
lookin' out.

Darice Rollins

Summer Vacation Memories

First there was lightening and then came rain
the glory of it all I cannot explain.
The crash of thunder and the falling limb
And then there was silence, dark and dim.

It brought back memories, of the cottage on Michigan shores
Where I spent my youth in summer lake chores.
The old pump-organ which accompanied our singing
Filled the night with vibrate ringing.

The fun-filled days, sailing and kayaking
Shopping at Johnson's, frolicking and yakking.
Then came July 4th, with rockets soaring
And e pluribus dingbat, interrupting his snoring.

Searching the dunes for ripe blueberries
And eating with relish Jinny's hot gerries.
The sand scorched our feet, as we ran down the hill
But the water was quick to bring on a chill.

Hot dogs and marshmallows toasted over a fire,
Tickled the palate and satisfied desire.
This may not seem like much of a theme,
I guess you had to be there, to appreciate the dream.
Herbert A. Hudson

Joy

I wished on you like I wished on her
with hopes of happiness just to be heard
I imagined a presence so clean and blue
desires visions danced with you
unconditional love was known that day
your beauty hypnotized as I gazed
two lovers hearts saddened through time
met with a passion too strong to decline
my love to shatter my heart dismay
to feel alone must be it that may
to never give up without a fight
for you and I to share a life
forgiveness is always that you be true
to your heart, because I love you.
Son Bowles

Won't They Ever Learn?

Teenage brothers and sisters by fate
Sometimes find it hard to each other relate

Whatever the disagreement is about
As parents we send them off together to work it out

Saying "Don't come back until its resolved
The disagreements dissolved"

Husband, Wife; Mother, Father
Decide together they can go no farther

Life long mates by choice
No longer in their love rejoice

It's obvious to see
They no longer agree

They file for divorce
Saying their marriage has run its course

Again in our offspring we see the fire of conflict burn
Won't they ever learn???

Whatever the disagreement is about
As parents we send them off together to work it out

Saying "Make sure the disagreement is dissolved
Don't come back until it's resolved"
Donald L. Mitchell

Dreaded News

"Hello, son. It's Mom. I've learned that I'm dying."
    The call was expected, but not all the crying.

I knew it was coming; I knew how I'd feel.
    But hearing her say it made it so real.
She'd bene very sick for most of a year.
    Facing the end should not have brought tears.

Maybe I secretly thought Mom would stay.
    Maybe, like love, she would not pass away.
I've now come to terns that her end is in sight
    Though, like the good soldier, he'll put up a fight.

And when she joins God in His divine home,
    I'll call her by prayer instead of by phone.
And she will respond loudly and clearly,
    Cheering me on, loving me dearly.

Advisor, enforcer, life giver, and friend:
    A mother and son, the bond without end.
Daniel E. Eaton

Come Rain, Come Rain

Come rain, come rain, come heavy today.
Moisten the earth, we are having a drought.
Water our seeds, and let them bear food,
So that we all can have our daily meal.

Shining sun, shining sun, this is your time,
Give us some heat, we need to get warm
We feel Very chilled, from the rain that fell,
So we need some heat, to keep us warm.

Pretty moon, pretty moon, will you shine bright?
The night is dark, and we have no light.
We may miss our step, and break our hip,
and we have no means, to find a loop-hole.

Little stars, little stars, come twinkle for us,
to-night, Oh I wonder why you all are so far.
You never seem to Love us well, to shine your
Little light on us. Oh Little stars, I loved you all.

Thank you For what you did, and been doing.
You have been guiding, our traveling men to safety.
Even the three wise men, of old were able
to find, where our saviour Christ was born.
Michael N. Darby

CJS

Two milestones in life November 23, 1969
when the other is, I don't know

Today, I experienced death

Carol Jean Swiger CJS, we called her what a sweet lady;
who at one time did not care for me

But now. When I went in to the office
she came in a nd talked to me
she asked me how I was how school was going
and she reminded me of the important things in life

Ironically, her family was important
and, most of her time was spent working

The harder she worked, the bigger her smile
her life became her work she became his work
she became the firm to know something inside and out
to live to work not work to live, this was Carole Jean

I remember her last words to me,
"I can't wait for my vacation this summer,"
she was going to travel back east to visit friends and
family and now, Carole Jean, you'll have to wait
you've taken a detour to a vacation of eternity.
Yuki Fujii

What Am I? Who Am I?

Most people don't understand me,
No one sees me as I see myself;
What am I? Who am I?
A mother? A wife? A student?

What if my child dies?
What if my husband strays?
What if I never get my degree?
Then, what am I?

A woman? An African-American?
What is a woman?
My breasts don't make me a woman.
What is an African-American?
My chocolate skin doesn't make me an African-American.

Some say a woman is the backbone of life.
Some say an African-American is the backbone of society.
Still, I ask what am I? Whom am I?

Charisse Donielle Parker

Searching For Help!!

I have fallen in a dark place,
with no way out.
I've lost all hope's of being myself
again.
I've never seen the good way out.
I've been lost here for ever.
Trying to reach out, but nobody grabs me!
They tell me the only way out is
liking myself again.
But how can I, when I cheated with everyone's
trust.
How can I find the light with in
my soul.
Let me find the way to forgive myself.
Or maybe let me find the light
with in my heart for
forgiveness

Anayda C. Campos

Honor

Honor defined is being true to someone or to your word,
Promises and oaths not given carelessly - I've heard.

Steadfast and true despite any circumstances,
Regardless of pain or loss, luck, or chance.

It's not give lightly, easily or for any gain,
But after all is said and done - it will in fact still remain.

It can inspire awe, as well as high regard,
For those who no matter what - their word they won't discard.

It's not carelessly dismissed or quickly cast aside,
Excused or justified if suddenly it's not easy to abide.

Someone who is honorable can stand straight and tall,
Proud to be not one with those who are weak, disreputable to all.

It takes strength, character and an enormous amount of class,
If honor is always held firmly, truly within your grasp.

It's grudgingly admired despite disagreement, disdain or plights,
For those when backed to the wall, kept honor within their sights.

Medals, merits are give in honor of bravery, or great feats,
For in the face of death, faithful honor denies defeats.

Commands, by admittance or unspoken words — respect,
If it's known your honor is never questioned, or suspect.

Jill Clements

Something Beautiful

In a rural area a small barn stood
that a little girl visited on the way back from school.

One sunny afternoon when school had ended
the little girl walked to the barn
and saw a group of boys in front of it.

One boy in the group said "Let us gather some stones
and kill the hen in front of us," and the group cheered him.

The girl tried to stop them but the boys did not listen to her.
She tried to scare the hen away from the boys
but the hen would not move.

The hen did not run away and let the boys pelt her with stones.
The boys did not stop until the hen lay bloody and lifeless.

Tears rolled from the girl's cheeks as she shouted to the lifeless
animal, "Why didn't you run away from the stones and save your life?"

Then something moved from under the wings.
At first a small yellow head peeked out from the inside
of his mother's wing.

Then one by one ten little yellow chicks came out from the wings.

The girl looked at the chicks unable to utter a word,
she stood there and marveled at a mother's love.

Mary Kim

Your Time Is Up!

Your time is up...it has ran out!
Decide and make up you mind.
Chose the path that you must take,
the direction that you must follow,
and the destination that you must be.
So choose...because your time is up!
It's been too long that you have dwelt
in that darkness of uncertainty and fear;
now turn around, don't be afraid,
and let us go into the light.
Fear not, for it is only in the mind.
So choose and decide my friend,
do it now and do it fast...
because your Time Is Up!

Ricardo Reconose

Shards

Invariably, you stop to look at the pottery shards in museums:
In Baltimore, or in Satrianum. In libraries also, you ask for
Those oversized books on excavations done by the University of
Pennsylvania, or by the Iranian or the Turkish governments.
Here are shards of broken pottery delicately seamed together,
Where the criss-crossing of black lines comes as prominently
To your attention as does the outer shape and the surface design.
Years of effort go into minutely accurate diagrams
Of Mounds, of layers within mounds, and to side-by-side
Comparisons of the pottery with excavated pots in other museums.

You think, too, of the people who sort out the layers
Of destruction, tagging minute alterations in loomweights
And the like, who themselves become, in time, crackly with
Nervous systems which somehow defy breakdown. Ask to see
Their basement laboratories - those littorals of unmatched
Shards, and their partial attempts to resurrect a living substance.

But you love the shards in museums, their reproduction
In books, because, with the shape of a bird, an animal, a sea
Creature, or an occasional human, they share a grace of fullness,
Of repose, of harmony with the world, which few living artists
impart.

Robert Keeler Billings

Silhouetted Shadows

I see you faintly.
Straining for a better view,
I yearn to close the miles between you and I.

Your image clearing in my mind
but yet obscure . . .
Silhouetted shadows on the shore.

I sense your presence.
I feel you around my mind.
Your hands cradle my heart . . . .
I start in your direction . . . ???
The mist thickens and your image becomes
Silhouetted shadows on the shore.

There, "You" so sharp so clear . . . ?
I run to take you; ignoring all fear.
Throwing my arms around you I fall face first.
Bringing myself to my feet, I shake off the sand.
Breaking down; I weep; pocket my hands staggering amidst . . . the
Silhouetted shadows on the shore.

Gerald Fox

Dare

When a nightmare becomes a dream.
To laugh and not scream.
Where flowers bloom all through the year,
Forget all troubles far and near.
To dare to do what you never have done.
Speak you mind and hurt no one.
Trust how you feel believe in a myth.
The meaning inside your soul is pure bliss.
To love one another or just one with your all.
Dream every dream don't let your heart fall.
Wish on the stars it is easy to do.
If you forget how to dream your dream forget you.
Someday we'll be loved, still we're in love today.
With love so strong we can never fade away.
But our lives have grown cold, silent, and bare,
With the rush of a rat in a race without care.
Previously daring to dream,
Now only dreaming to dare.

Pamela Garfield

Tatiana's Charm

Sweet little princess wear your charm —
God shall send a white blessing to you.
Rasputin's face will keep you from harm.
Hold tight to your father's arm
as the spiteful emotions brew.
Sweet little princess wear your charm.
Your own people are well armed;
blood stains their hands through.
Rasputin's face will keep you from harm.
There is no need to be alarmed
when you are spit upon as a fool.
Sweet little princess wear your charm.
When they take your dreams apart,
do not let them come to take you.
Rasputin's face will keep you from harm.
A sad fate for a gentle heart
for Death awaits your sister too.
Sweet little princess wear your charm —
Rasputin's face will keep you from harm.

Scott Jonathon Nixon

To Keep the Love

Many years I have loved you
And many days I have cried,
Now my darling, I must leave thee,
So dry your tears, be starry eyed.

Speak to me now of your sorrow,
Of your heart full of fears,
Tell me, just before I kiss thee,
Kiss away those lovely tears.

Men go to war for their loved ones,
To keep their homes forever free.
Now dry your tears with laughter,
I'll come safely home to thee.

Because to each there is a duty,
And so, that our love may live,
That you, and I, and others,
Can keep our love to give
Good-bye my darling

Larry E. Estes

BIOGRAPHIES

ABAD, PEDRO
[b.] April 29, 1953, Norfolk, VA; [p.] Antonio Abad, The late Gladys Abad; [ed.] BS St. Paul's College Lawrenceville, VA; [occ.] English Teacher Norview High School; [memb.] VATE (VA. Assoc. Teac. Eng) SEVAA (Southeastern VA. Art Assoc) Alpha Phi Alpha Fraternity; [hon.] 1996 Apple Award as an Outstanding Teacher, Twice nominated - Teacher of the Year, Twice nominated as Best Actor Folio Award (1990/1994) - Arnold in "The Boys Next Door."; [oth. writ.] Authored two books of Poetry: "The Poet In Me" and "Heavy". Penned original plays: "Sisters" and "Shelter".; [pers.] Being creative is being yourself. Go with the flow and let yourself go...; [a.] Norfolk, VA

ABBAS, LARRY
[b.] May 22, 1951, Sumner, IA; [p.] Eugene Abbas - Norma Gray; [m.] Kathlerna Abbas, July 7, 1981; [ch.] Austin Gabriel Libby; [ed.] 12 yrs and some college; [occ.] Regional Manager for large auto rental co.; [memb.] Non profit anonymous organizations; [hon.] Various awards for personal achievements within Transportation Industry; [pers.] All poems and prose reflect inner feelings based on real life experiences, with gratitude going to my wife for her inspirations and beauty that the writings speak of in the legacy.; [a.] Waterloo, IA

ABBOTT, DEBORAH J.
[b.] May 4, 1969, Marlboro, MA; [p.] Richard and Diane Travers; [m.] David B. Abbott, October 15, 1994; [ed.] Marlboro High School 1987, Bryant College - BS 1991, Clark University - MBA 1996; [occ.] Controller BWH Anesthesia Foundation, Inc.; [memb.] American Institute of (AICPA) Certified Public Accountants, Mass. Society of CPAs, Alpha Phi International Fraternity, Treasurer MCHC Board of Directors.; [hon.] Delta Mu Delta, Beta Gamma Sigma; [pers.] No daughter could be more proud of her father than I am. I love you Daddy!; [a.] Ashland, MA

ABOOD, WILLIE
[b.] November 15, 1973, Kearney, NE; [p.] William Abood, Sheila Abood; [ed.] Kearney High, University of Nebraska at Kearney; [occ.] Full time college student (Jr.) Computer Sys. Analyst at KLPR radio and EMT-B; [memb.] The Kearney Evangelical Free Church, Founding Member of the Collegiate Society of Electronic Media, founding Member of Gustov Bros. International; [hon.] KPS Foundation Award, Knight of Kitaki/2nd Order; [pers.] Early influences of mine include J.R.R. Tolkien and C.S. Lewis. I try to blend fantasy and reality in poetry.; [a.] Kearney, NE

ADAMS, MARY LOU
[pen.] Mary Lou Adams; [b.] August 11, 1921, Lawrenceburgh, IN; [p.] Warren J. Rudolph, Adelia Rudolph; [m.] Fred Adams, June 4, 1938; [ch.] Ronald Lee, Steven Ray, Avis Jeanne; [occ.] Retired; [memb.] United Methodist Women, National Federation of Grandmothers of America #979; [hon.] None in writing but many in sports events locally.; [oth. writ.] First published at age 11 in the Baptist Junior Journal. Later writings in local paper and "Happiness" magazine.; [pers.] I write most times of family, religion or nature. I strive for peace and understanding in the world.; [a.] Lawrenceburg, IN

ADKINS, LINDA
[b.] March 14, 1950, Evergreen Park, IL; [p.] Wally and Marie Wilber; [m.] Domenic Adkins, August 16, 1987; [ch.] 4 Boys; [ed.] High School (Reno High School-Reno Nev.); [occ.] Housewife; [memb.] Network 21, Amway; [a.] Honolulu, HI

AGUIRRE, CLAUDIA
[b.] August 28, 1979, Los Angeles, CA; [p.] Blanca E. Aguirre, Miguel Aguirre; [ed.] Attending Canoga Park High; [occ.] Student at Canoga High; [oth. writ.] I have written several poems, but none have been published yet.; [pers.] I was greatly influenced by my brothers Jesus and Mike Aguirre. And my mom also. This poem is dedicated to Gustavo Ruiz. I love you all (my family, that is).; [a.] Canoga Park, CA

AHMED, TAUFEEQ
[pen.] Mairaj Ahmed; [b.] November 10, 1968, Hyberabad, India; [p.] Gulam Ahmed, Razia Begum; [m.] Syeda Soofia Hyder, January 20, 1996; [ed.] Bachelor of Veterinary Sciences and Animal Husbandry (Veterinarian); [occ.] Student; [oth. writ.] Several poems published in the school and college magazines.; [pers.] In the words of my beloved father, the happiness, the grief, the difficulties - though they appear as if they are creeping from the environment into you, actually they are the reactions from you to the environment around depending upon your emotions, skills and tolerance. So if you want everything to go right, first work on yourself - try it.; [a.] Milpitas, CA

AKINTONWA, HAKEEM
[b.] March 3, 1974, TN, U.S.A.; [ed.] Attends Northern Illinois University, Major is Finance, Educated in Nigeria until I was 18.; [occ.] Student; [memb.] African Student Association; [oth. writ.] I have written lots of poems, which include "Peace," "Killing Me Softly," and many more. I have also written short stories which include "Susie," "Insanity," "Boys of Bradford Academy." They are yet to be published.; [pers.] I have been writing poems since I was 15 years old. I won the second place in a poetry competition back in high school. I have been influenced by Maya Angelou and Wole Soyinka.

ALBERT, ARTHUR A.
[b.] October 3, 1951, Europe; [p.] My Father was a Professor of Philosophy and Geography; [m.] Alice Aretha, August 24, 1978 - New York; [ch.] Nellie (one); [ed.] University of Fine Art, Artist of Painting and Conservator Designer, Interior Designer; [occ.] Artist/Painter, Conservator Designer, Interior Designer, Consultant; [hon.] I have paintings in museums in the United States and in Europe in private collection; [oth. writ.] I have a lot of poems. And I would like to publish my own book. I am very proud of my last name, Albert. My ancestors came from Monaco and they were related to Prince Albert.; [a.] Lake Ronkonkoma, NY

ALBERT, RICHARD
[pen.] Richard Albert; [b.] January 14, 1963, Scranton, PA; [p.] Doris and Rich Albert Sr.; [m.] Janet Albert, June 1989; [ed.] High School; [occ.] Work with developmentally disabled individuals; [hon.] Five and ten year service awards with my current employer; [oth. writ.] This would be first; [pers.] Always be yourself. My biggest influences would be Poe, Kerouac, Woodward, the music of Frank Zappa, and the comedy of Dennis Miller.; [a.] Scranton, PA

ALFARO, STEPHANIE
[b.] November 12, 1984, Costa Rica; [p.] Hilda Alfaro; [ed.] Saint Raymond Elementary; [occ.] Student (7th grade); [memb.] Girl Scouts, Youth Group; [hon.] Academic Awards; [pers.] I believe in children's rights and the freedom of speech; [a.] Bronx, NY

ALLRED, JEANNETTE
[b.] February 9, 1949, NYC, NY; [p.] Mildred Toro Diaz; [ch.] Cory Gerald; [ed.] Sachem High, Creative Writing - Clayton State College; [pers.] I long to convey through my writings the natural beauty that surrounds us all. To express the love that so many allow to pass them by, by realizing only the past sorrows in their lives.

These writings I consider a gift from Spirit God. My words are supplied by the Spirit of Love and Harmony who presents me with a gift which I then in turn unwrap for you, the reader. I hope my writing will lend itself to bridge the void between our spiritual and physical existence so that we all may live harmoniously with the universe.; [a.] Conyers, GA

ALMEN, ERIC SCHALL
[b.] September 7, 1996, Minneapolis, MN; [p.] John and Lois; [ch.] Janaina Almen; [ed.] Hamline University St. Paul, Minn. 1975; [occ.] Customer Service, Assist. Trainer, T.C.I.; [memb.] Glide Memorial Church of San Francisco; [hon.] Outstanding Drum Soloist (Jazz); [oth. writ.] "Taste My Poems" and "Rehabilitat'in"; [pers.] I am currently attempting to publish my other writings. My philosophical statement, learn to love for it's the greatest thing you can do in life! I love my family and try to live each day like it was my last.; [a.] Livermore, CA

ALSTON, KIA ROTANZA
[b.] August 14, 1969, Jacksonville, NC; [p.] Arthalia Belton and Robert Marshall; [ch.] Kiara White, Ariel and Marquis Alston; [ed.] Graduate from Garfield Sr. High; [occ.] Mother; [hon.] Poem "Our Heavenly Father" published in symphonies of the soul.; [oth. writ.] Our Heavenly Father, In My Heart, My Lover My Friend, Baby 1, 2 and 3, United We Stand, Just For Me, Far Away From Home, Give Thanks, Stay In School, Prayer is the Key, Congratulation.; [pers.] My mom, Arthalia Belton is a strong black woman who is like my cane who keeps me up when circumstances try to pull me down. She taught me to have faith. That's why it took great pride to dedicate a poem to her love you mom.; [a.] Griffin, GA

AMBROSIO, ROSEMARIE
[b.] June 16, 1942, Yonkers, NY; [p.] Mary and Jim Altierl; [m.] Jerry Ambrosio, December 1, 1968; [ch.] 3 - Gino, Gabrielle, Gerard; [ed.] Lincoln High School, Oswego State Teacher's College (SUNY) Empire State; [occ.] Sales Administration, AT&T Wireless Services; [oth. writ.] "The Widow's Nest," "Awakening," "Leandre," "Stream Of Consciousness," "The Seamstress," "Red Rocks And Pine Cones," (all poems) God made "man", God made "woman", "The Hair".; [pers.] My writing is instinctive and it flows from the endless river called "Soul". It seeks the truth and perhaps the healing of those silken threads which form the heart.; [a.] Yonkers, NY

ANCEL, REVEREND E. LESLIE
[pen.] Rev. Les Ancel; [b.] February 9, 1945, Lawton, OK; [p.] Mr. and Mrs. Harold and June Ancel; [ed.] Bendle H.S.-Burton, Michigan, University of Toledo, Ohio, Institute of Toledo, Ohio, Institute of Real Estate Management, National Association of Realtors; [occ.] Retired Minister-Senior Minister, Evangelical Church of Christ, Honolulu, Hawaii and Founder of Aloha, Diamond Head Wedding and Honeymoons-Honolulu, Hawaii; [memb.] Past Memberships: National Association of Realtors, Better Business Bureau of Hawaii, Retail Merchants Association of Hawaii, Honolulu Chamber of Commerce, Hawaii Convention and Visitor's Bureau, Benevolent and Protective Order of Elks, Licensed Realtors-Ohio, Licensed Insurance-Michigan and Ohio, Veteran-United States Air Force; [hon.] Commendation for Outstanding Public Service by Mayor, Honolulu, Hawaii, Commendation-Department of Housing and Urban Development, Mayors Commendation-Toledo, Ohio, Ordained Minister-Honolulu, Hawaii, Marriage Officiant-State of Hawaii, Elected Representative-Old West End Association-Toledo, Ohio, Elected Representative-Old West End District Council-Toledo, Ohio, Citizen Representative for

all Federal Spending-Toledo, Ohio, Chairman-Historical Structures Committee-Old West End District Council-Toledo, Ohio; [oth. writ.] Author of Various Commercial Magazine-Radio-Television-Newspaper Business Advertisements, Articles and Commentaries.; [pers.] "My mind interprets my heart's emotions which are inspired by my God!"; [a.] Honolulu, HI

ANDERSON, HUGH R.
[b.] May 27, 1970, DeKalb, IL; [p.] Dr. Henry and Mrs. Susan Anderson; [ed.] 2 Years College; [occ.] Student; [hon.] Operation Desert Storm; [oth. writ.] Winter Park High School Newspaper in 1988; [pers.] I want to make people think or laugh with my writing.; [a.] Orlando, FL

ANDERSON, KARLA
[pen.] Karla Anderson, Karla Sue Anderson; [b.] August 7, 1957, San Diego, CA; [p.] Karl T. Anderson, Susan C. Anderson; [ed.] Palm Spring High School, The Mercersburg Academy, University of Redlands, Musicians Institute; [occ.] Student, part-time guitar instructor for children.; [memb.] Sigma Alpha Iota, Dalcroze Society of America, Bitch Brigade - a Lita Ford Fanzie; [oth. writ.] Many...but nothing published.; [pers.] "An artist needs obstacles." - Ruth-Anne Miller, Northern Exposure: "The Body in Question"; [a.] Redlands, CA

ANTHONY, SHARON
[b.] March 1, 1943, Indianapolis, IN; [p.] Maurice and Kathryn King; [m.] Carl Anthony, December 10, 1961; [ch.] Jeff, Mike and Steve Anthony; [occ.] I am very simply, a homemaker, wife, mother, and grandmother; [hon.] I have no literary credentials, awards, or degrees to offer. Until January of 1996, I had never written any poetry or had any interest in doing so.; [pers.] One night a short prayer came to me, and since that time I have written approximately 150 poems. My poetry is certainly not the most polished, nor any form of literary genius. It very simply is a gift from the "true Author," God. It comes straight from my heart, where He has taken up residency. And only with His stamp of approval, can I feel at peace with what I write. "Changes In the Heart" reflects the changes that came about in my life, that have since given me the inspiration and ability to communicate my feelings and thoughts through poetry. I thank my family both present and past, and all those who have touched my life in some way, giving me inspiration and insight to understand the true meaning of love, caring, and loyalty. Above all, I thank God for showing me how to focus on the God-given good in each living soul, rather than search for the flaw...; [a.] Brandon, FL

ARMSTRONG, JODY
[b.] May 29, 1978, Warren, MI; [p.] Dennis and Sandy Armstrong; [ed.] Utica High School, Grand Valley State University; [occ.] Student; [hon.] Presidential Academic Fitness Award, basketball-best defense, soccer-most improved honorable mention all league; [pers.] I find poetry as an escape for the mind - an easier way to express my innermost feelings.; [a.] Macomb, MI

ARNETT, CHELSEY
[b.] April 26, 1985, Morehead, KY; [p.] Jonathan and Marcella Arnett

ARNETT, WINIFRED M.
[b.] March 3, 1911, Berea, KY; [p.] Ulysses Moyers, Leah Moyers; [m.] Kenneth E. Arnett (Deceased), September 7, 1934; [ch.] John; [ed.] Berea High, Easter State, Richmond, KY; [occ.] Retired Librarian; [pers.] 3 1/2 years ago I suffered a stroke which affected my right side and paralyzed my larynx. To pass the time, I started writing poetry. I write a poem for our prayer group each Sunday. Our pastor calls me their miracle child.; [a.] Arlando, FL

ARNMARK, METTE
[b.] April 2, 1979, Linkoping, Sweden; [p.] Per Spanne and Vibeke Arnmark; [ed.] Is currently attending Shoreham Wading River High School. Spent two years of high school at Lycee du Gresivaudan in Grenoble, France where she took the French exam of the baccalaureat.; [occ.] High School Student; [pers.] Writing is a wonderful way of expressing and sharing my joy, sadness, dreams and fears. The diversity of the world I have seen and the world I dream about inspires and influences my writing in many ways.; [a.] Shoreham, NY

ARRINGTON, IMOGENE PATE
[b.] January 4, 1927, Ennis, TX; [p.] J. M. and Annie Pate; [m.] Geo. Milton Haralson, June 5, 1943, Deceased - August 9, 1970; [ch.] Donna and George (Max) Haralson; [ed.] Jr. High; [oth. writ.] Several poems - in Local News Paper. Discontented Nail, Just A Little, Hellbound Train, Second Touch, Too Far to Die, etc.; [pers.] God is my inspiration - I give Him the Glory - (I pray my poems bring many closer to the Lord Jesus. In spite of having polio at 10 mo. now in wheel chair, I have 2 beautiful children, 5 grandchildren and 8 great grandchildren.; [a.] Dallas, TX

ATWELL, RODNEY A.
[b.] October 22, 1965, Florence, AL; [p.] Johnny and Peggy; [m.] Sandra A. Atwell, November 22, 1991; [ch.] Two Boys - Channing and Jacob; [ed.] Self Educated/GED Iron City Elementary, TN; [occ.] Jack of all Traits; [hon.] None sought after as of yet.; [oth. writ.] Many and still more to come.; [pers.] To know the unknown is to dream a dream?; [a.] Iron City, TN

AUSTIN, DEBBIE
[b.] April 19, 1959, Hickory, NC; [p.] Paul H. and Margie Lail; [m.] Kevin, August 8, 1987; [ch.] Robert; [ed.] Newton-Conover High School, Gardner Webb College; [occ.] Credit Assistant, Highland House, Hickory NC; [memb.] Mt. Zion Lutheran Church, Alpha Chi, National Honor Society; [hon.] 1989 Wayah Literary Award; [oth. writ.] Numerous short stories published - Articles for Lutheran Women Today magazine; [a.] Conover, NC

AVRETTE, GEORGENE E.
[pen.] Gene; [b.] September 19, 1967, New Brunswick, NJ; [p.] Kay F. Purnell, George E. Purnell; [m.] Darion B. Avrette, November 3, 1990; [ch.] Malik, Tayanna, Jamal, Van Jr.; [ed.] New Brunswick High School, The Cittone Institute; [occ.] Security guard, Piscataway, NJ; [oth. writ.] Several poems written for friends and relatives for special occasions.; [pers.] I express what's in my heart through my writing and most of my poetry is written from true to life experiences; [a.] Plainfield, NJ

BAILEY, LANNIE
[b.] January 13, 1957, Pineville, WV; [p.] Marvin and Violet Bailey; [ed.] Graduate of Glen Rogers High School, Student at Southern West Virginia Community and Technical College, 11 years in the U.S. Army; [memb.] The Planetary Society, Song-Writers of America, The International Society of Poets; [hon.] Elected to The International Poetry Hall of Fame (10-1-96), Golden Pen Winner (the Register-Herald newspaper), 5 times runner up, 8 Editor's Choice Awards (The National Library of Poetry), Distinguished Member of ISP, and others.; [oth. writ.] Books: "God-Myth or Fact?" "When Love Passes You By" (Poetry), "The Best Is Yet To Be" (poetry), "I Weep for Love", (poetry) and 3 other books of poetry. Poetry on 18 cassette tapes, essays, articles, short stories and poems in various newspapers/anthologies.; [pers.] For thousands of years men and women have been writing the evolving bible of justice. It is being written from day to day, and

it will never be finished while man has life. Every person who finds a fact, adds, as it were, a word or act to this great book, helps to lay a stone for justice.; [a.] Rock View, VA

BAILEY, ROBERT K.
[pen.] Robert K. Bailey; [b.] April 15, 1958, Evanston, IL:; [p.] Fred C. Bailey, Harriet A. Gilbert; [m.] Carrie Christine Bailey; [ch.] Shane, David, Kevin, Tonya, Channce Faith, Sage, special held to Joel; [ed.] Hines Elementary - Morton Grove, IL Niangua High School - Niangua, MD, Draughons Business College - Springfield, MO; [occ.] Truck Driver; [oth. writ.] My Angel Christine, My Child, Orion The Hunter, Teddy In Lace; [pers.] You do "until" you don't and you don't "until" you do!; [a.] Preston, MO

BAKER, ELIZABETH J.
[pen.] G. A.; [b.] January 23, 1923, Detroit, MI; [p.] Mary Rose and Marion F. Humphrey (D); [m.] Wayne Donald Baker (D), June 11, 1950; [ch.] Beverly Ann Baker Kuhn; [ed.] St. Gregory High Detroit, MI graduate creative Writing School - Children's stories defense small purchase 1974-75 2-courses IBM school, Los Angeles CA, 2 weeks course; [occ.] Retired; [memb.] Catholic Church Club '65 - Grossmont Senior Resources; [hon.] Certificate Appreciation - Service Trial Juror - San Diego Judicial District. NMRC - Thirty years service award, for service to the Dept. of the Navy and the Government of the United States. Award for service to our Lady of Sacred Heart Church, San Diego, CA; [pers.] The poem "Sudden Infant Death Syndrome" is dedicated to Alice Marie Humphrey Beas, my niece and Godchild and most of all, she is the mother of little George.; [a.] San Diego, CA

BALL, LISA R.
[b.] October 3, 1974; [p.] David and Vicki Ball; [ed.] Liberty Center High School, University of Toledo; [occ.] Office Manager/Paralegal; [pers.] The light of love can break even the darkest cloud.; [a.] Swanton, OH

BAMBERGER, FRED E.
[b.] November 26, 1915, New York City; [p.] Samuel and Beatrice; [m.] Florence Shapiro, May 16, 1942; [ch.] Jay and Roberta (Pugliese); [ed.] Mondell Institute, Industrial College of the Armed Forces, Armed Forces Staff College, Air War College, and Naval Command Staff and Command and Strategic Intelligence School; [occ.] Retired (former Colonel USAF and retired Advertising Executive); [memb.] Air Force Assn., Masons, American Legion, Air Force Museum Foundation, Civil Air Patrol, Reserve Officers Assn., Air Force Academy Athletic Assn.; [hon.] 2 Clio awards for Excellence of Advertising Programs, 19 military service awards and decorations, also served as a judge for the Clio awards for 4 years.; [oth. writ.] Featured columnist for 15 years - "Specialty Advertising Review", numerous articles in various Air Force and military publications. Have been published since 1934.; [pers.] Our young people are the most priceless possession this nation has and much of my actions have been in their support.; [a.] Tamarac, FL

BANNISTER, SARAH ANNE
[b.] January 27, 1983, Little Falls; [p.] Paul Bannister and Sally Bannister; [ed.] 9th grader in Christian Liberty, Academy; [memb.] Cornerstone Baptist Church's Word of Life Club and Kids for Jesus Club; [pers.] In all my writings I try to be extremely unique. I especially enjoy writing about animals.; [a.] Fort Plain, NY

BARBEE, ALEA B.
[pen.] Leah; [b.] September 9, 1957, NC; [p.] James David and Effie Brown; [m.] Ed Barbee Jr., May 6, 1994; [ch.] William and David; [ed.] High school, 4 quarters of college, 1 art class, 1 computer class; [occ.]

Evangelist/Homemaker; [memb.] Miracle Faith Temple Church; [pers.] I help on a local T.V. cable channel, singing and preaching the gospel, ch. 21 and 56 on Horizons Comm.; [a.] Pink Hill, NC

BARNARD, EUNICE ROSELLA SPEAS

[pen.] Eunice S. Barnard; [b.] June 14, 1929, Shelley, ID; [p.] William E. and Violet E. Speas; [m.] Heber L. Barnard, November 12, 1949; [ch.] Four - Nichols, Terrie Rae, Cydney, Shayne; [ed.] Blackfoot High in Blackfoot, ID and Rigby High in Rigby, ID, (grad) Tax Consultant Schooling and other Bkkpg. classes.; [occ.] Retired from many years of Bookkeeping and Acct. Clerk; [memb.] Nat'l Thespian Club (During School), Church Of Jesus Christ of Latter Day Saints Aux., and The "School of Hard Knocks."; [hon.] Family and friends only have very generously honored me for my talent I may have.; [oth. writ.] We send out Christmas Cards each year to over a hundred friends and relatives with my husband's Western art and my descriptive poetry. Wrote a song during WW II that I never had published.; [pers.] I love to write about loved ones, the Western life that we are addicted to, the animals that have become out true friends, growing up and raising a lovely family in this fantastic world.; [a.] Blackfoot, ID

BARNES, SHANA

[b.] March 11, 1970, Lynwood, CA; [p.] Richard Barnes, Arley Pauly; [a.] Portland, OR

BARONE, NICOLE ADINA

[b.] October 13, 1975, New Hartford, NY; [p.] Richard and Nilsa Barone; [ed.] Utica Senior Academy, Herkimer County Community College, State University of New York Institute of Technology at Utica. (Sr.); [occ.] Associate at Bath and Body Works and an associate at Shop 'n Save; [memb.] New York State Association of CPA Candidates, Student Judicial Board, Accounting Club; [hon.] Dean's List, 1932 Business Education Prize Award, McDonald's Student of the month (Feb '93); [pers.] If you're willing to work hard, nothing can ever come between you and your dreams!; [a.] Utica, NY

BARRETT SR., CLEVELAND S.

[pen.] The Ghetto Poet Hulk; [b.] January 28, 1965, Hollywood, FL; [p.] Cleveland and Jo-Ann Barrett; [m.] Karen Barrett, October 26, 1991; [ch.] Krystal Barrett, Cleveland, S.C. Barrett, Martell Barrett; [ed.] Joliet East High School Carlenshaw Institute Bolingbrook IL; [occ.] Security Officer; [memb.] Member of International Society of Poetry; [hon.] The worlds #1 greatest Ghetto poet Hulk, America's Best Selving Black author of Ghetto Poetry an Phosophy; [oth. writ.] United We Stand Divided We All, Can You Her My Echo, Invisible Chairs, Black Butterfly, You Can Run But You Can't Hide Aids, Mentally In Incarcerated, Policy Brutally, A Toast From Me To You, Pipe Dreams, Forty Acres And A Mule Black Hole, I Will Over Come; [pers.] The Ghetto Poet Hulk has just finished writing his first book title "Can You Hear My Echo" the Ghetto poet covers all dimensions and topic from education, welfare, oppression, politics, politicians famous authors, from the main stream to the Ghetto black hole.; [a.] Harrisburg, IL

BARRIGER, RAQUEL

[b.] April 30, 1978, Detroit, MI; [p.] Linda Barriger and Chuck Barriger; [ed.] East Detroit High School; [occ.] Student at Macomb Community College; [hon.] Honor Roll in school, Meap Awards: Math, Science, English; [oth. writ.] 32 poems in the process of writing a book of poems.; [a.] Center Line, MI

BARTEL, JOYCE

[b.] August 6, 1972, Buffalo, NY; [p.] Martin and Deborah Bartel; [ed.] University at Buffalo, B.A.; [occ.] Proofreader, Direct Response Marketing, Williamsville,

NY; [memb.] Book Club Moderator and Leadership Committee member of quest "Young Adults Bridging Life and Faith", St Mary of the Assumption Church, Lancaster, NY; [pers.] I'd like to dedicate this publication of "a creative stroke" to Marty, Debbie and Jackie - a triad that has made me see beyond the horizon.; [a.] Lancaster, NY

BARTHEL, SHIRLEY ANN

[b.] September 29, 1949, Donaldsonville, GA; [p.] Willie and Ola Ree Rarry; [m.] Deceased, March 22, 1976; [ch.] Sheldon, Kelvin, Mattie, Pamela, William and Marciie; [ed.] Elem. Liberty Hill, Bascom 1st - 3 Fla., Union Grove High - Malone Fla. 3 6th, Jackson Co Trainy School 9-11th, Blake Adult High - 12th grade graduate, Tampa College - Nursing Asst. grad. 1986; [occ.] Cashier - Wenn Dukie, Lauderhill Cashier - Service Merchandise (241); [hon.] Perfect Attendance 1986, Perfect 4.0 Student 1986, City of Tampa Recreation Dept. 1986, Hope of Shiloh Baptist Church Loyal Member; [oth. writ.] Ways to Success and How to Achieve them (Ocilla, GA) at last I wrote this for the school, alternative and high school; [pers.] I write to release my innermost feeling and thoughts, which sometimes I cannot say in words, and my hand writing is the key to my own success.; [a.] Fort Lauderdale, FL

BARTLETT, MATT

[b.] December 14, 1984, Haverhill, MA; [p.] Karen Bartlett, Gregory Bartlett; [ed.] 6th grade; [occ.] Student at Timberlane Regional Middle School; [oth. writ.] One poem published in book of young poets.; [pers.] Only the finest can capture the pure beauty of nature and human emotion.; [a.] Plaistow, NH

BARTON, DONNA D.

[pen.] Donna Barton; [b.] December 23, 1955, Woodward, OK; [p.] Don Williams, Lou Dailing; [m.] Charles Barton, August 2, 1986; [ch.] Jennifer and Bryan Barton; [ed.] BSN; [occ.] Operating Room Nurse; [memb.] Intl. Poets Society, AORN; [oth. writ.] "A Dream, A Vision", "I Know A Little Boy"; [pers.] Writing poetry brings out an inner "me" that few people see.; [a.] Irving, TX

BASHAM, VIOLA M.

[b.] September 9, 1926, Lodiburg, KY; [p.] Patricia Bradstreet Tindall, Samuel E. Tindall; [m.] Wilbert O. Basham, March 20, 1945; [ch.] Five; [ed.] High School; [occ.] Retired; [memb.] Nashville Songwriters Assn. Int'l; [pers.] Don't know much about poetry, nor have I studied the art, but ever since a tiny child I've written from my heart. The words would come so quickly that I hardly had the time to write the words and melodies that came running through my mind. I'd write of truth, imagination, dreams and fascination, of love and faith and tenderness and even my frustrations. I thought a melody was needed to go with every rhyme with all the thoughts and ideas that came tumbling through my mind. If I had only saved the poems I've written in my time. The many pitched into the trash whose melodies I couldn't find.; [a.] Louisville, KY

BAUCUM, MARY WILLIAMSON

[pen.] Mary Baucum; [b.] October 2, 1956, Memphis, TN; [p.] Jim and Jackie Williamson; [m.] Todd Douglas Baucum, March 9, 1985; [ch.] Suzanne Elizabeth, Anna Katherine; [ed.] University of Tennessee, Center for the Health Sciences (Central High - Memphis); [occ.] Health Information Manager, Mountain State Blue Cross/Blue Shield; [memb.] Board of Directors - Read Aloud of West Virginia Kanawha County; [pers.] Any ability that I possess is a gift from God. I am inwardly compelled to write and in writing express thanks to my Creator for this gift of creativity.; [a.] Charleston, WV

BAUM, SHELLY

[b.] April 5, 1964, Syracuse, NY; [p.] Donald Cook and Valerie Salderfer; [m.] Charles Baum, April 17, 1982; [ch.] Trista Jo, Travis Charles; [ed.] Cicero High; [occ.] Homemaker; [pers.] I have been blessed with a wonderful family. I love and cherish you all. "All pen and a dream."; [a.] Hastings, NY

BAXTER, LORI

[b.] June 4, 1969, Cold Spring, NY; [occ.] Freelance Writer; [oth. writ.] Several poems - unpublished; [pers.] On our journey in life, we are all connected by love.; [a.] Wappingers Falls, NY

BAXTER, MARY C.

[b.] May 11, 1921, Elmira, NY; [p.] Mary and Francis Cahill; [m.] Eugene S. Baxter, June 25, 1949; [ch.] William, David, Kathleen, Maureen, Edward; [ed.] BS in Education plus 36 graduate hours; [occ.] Retired Public School Music Teacher; [memb.] Retired Member of NEMC and NYSSMA, Past Member of Square Dance Clubs; [hon.] Mini Operettas for Elementary Grades, Chm. of NYS Elem. Music Curric. Com. 1973-74 Distinguished Service Award—Music Educators Assoc. of Broome County - 1989; [oth. writ.] Many mini operettas were written to fit the group who would be performing them.; [pers.] Every child in the primary grades who has normal hearing can be taught to sing on pitch. It has been one of my greatest joys and satisfactions to teach music and instill enjoyment of performing or listening.; [a.] Vestal, NY

BEAUCHAMP, TWYLA

[pen.] Ant-T; [b.] January 27, 1944, Douglas Co., MO; [p.] Geo F. Lemons, Pansy P. Edwards; [m.] James Beauchamp, November 3, 1990; [ch.] Rod, Ronda, Rick, Vickie Crewse; [ed.] 12 plus continuing I also attended Vo-Tech Melbourne Ark.; [occ.] Writing; [memb.] Skyline Volunteer Fire Dept, Society of Children's Book Writers and Illustrators; [hon.] 1987 Golden Poet award poem in Best Poets of 1997; [oth. writ.] Childrens weekly page in local newspaper. Grandfather Times stories and rhymes. A novel titled Hearts of Fox Creek.; [pers.] It is my desire to give something back to others. Produce beauty in the heart. I loved Lord Byron's work.; [a.] Norwood, MO

BELL, DANNA DENISE HORK

[b.] April 1960, Pittsburg, CA; [p.] William J. Hork, Lela Nel Hork; [m.] Michael L. Bell Sr., July 31, 1982; [ch.] Ryan Anthony, Michael L. Jr., Donald M.; [ed.] Las Lomas High School; [occ.] Administrative Assistant; [pers.] "If Poetry is the word of life, then let the world live on". My poem is dedicated to my mother who died February 2, 1992.; [a.] Pittsburg, CA

BELL, RALONDA

[pen.] Ronnie Belle; [b.] August 10, 1970, Omaha, NE; [p.] Lillian Bell and Larry Bell; [ch.] Brittany Bell; [ed.] Three years College; [occ.] Customer Services rep for a cellular phone Co.; [oth. writ.] Poetry, short stories College newspaper; [pers.] Always allow room and open space for growth and never be to closed minded to thank that star trek is only a show. Remember to be true to that inner voice that consistently tells you that as special as you are, there is always room for improvement. Always look to you soul, your spiritual walk and your belief in faith that all that is not well will soon be.; [a.] Omaha, NE

BENDER, WILLIAM

[b.] October 7, 1932, Decatur, IL; [p.] Cheaster A. and Ruth L. (Burrus) Bender; [m.] Phyllis J. (Leschewski) Bender, August 29, 1953; [ch.] Daughter Becky S., Sons Chester A., Micky L., Larry G. Bender; [ed.] 7th Grade, G.E.D. National Tech. L.A., still attending Life's College of Hard Knocks; [occ.] Retired; [memb.] Hope

Lutheran Church, Republic, MO; [pers.] I try to inspire others to understand and appreciate one another for the positive values they can contribute to the quality of life for everyone.; [a.] Ash Grove, MO

BENNETT, F. CAROLYN SMITH
[b.] December 24, 1937, Mount Pisgah, KY; [p.] Everette Smith, Jimmie Burnett-Smith; [m.] Steve Bennett, May 27, 1972; [ch.] John Young Jr., Carol Young, Perry Young; [ed.] Wayne Country High School; [occ.] Homemaker; [oth. writ.] Our 125 poems of childhood memories in the mountains of Kentucky (Wayne County), reflections of Mt. Pisgah today and poems for my husband.; [pers.] Since 1993, I have written to share the true memories of the simplicity and happiness of life in a remote mountain community and the love of family and friends.; [a.] Decatur, IL

BENNETT, MATT
[pen.] MB; [b.] December 12, 1980, Kirkland, WA; [p.] Bruce Bennett, Kathy Bennett; [occ.] Student; [memb.] The Poetry Connection; [pers.] My work reflects feelings that the following individuals instilled in me: Allen Ginsberg, John Lennon, Trent Reznor, my brother Scott, George Alper, Erika Barratt, and of course, myself. Peace!; [a.] Redmond, WA

BENNETT, MORGAN LANE
[pen.] More again; [b.] March 13, 1974, Hollywood, CA; [occ.] Peace Maker; [memb.] The Timeless Regeneration; [oth. writ.] Savior Self The Gospel According To Me; [pers.] There is only one religion, that in this language is called love...; [a.] Venice, CA

BENSICK, CAROL
[b.] November 10, 1956, Columbia, MO; [ed.] BA Wellesley College, MA, PhD, Cornell University; [occ.] English Professor; [memb.] Lapsed; [hon.] Theta Beta Kappa, Durant Scholar; [oth. writ.] "Leo," Treasured Poems of America, forthcoming novelization of the "Steelgrave Arc" of 1988 TV series Wiseguy (Stephen Anwell Prod.), unpublished: La Nouvelle Beatrice, Rutgers University Press, 1985, various academic essays and reviews.; [pers.] Poe, T. S. Eliot, Baudelaire, Goethe, E. R. Eddison, Verlaine, Oscar Wilde, Shakespeare, Villon.; [a.] Los Angeles, CA

BENTON, JIM
[b.] February 9, 1959, Richmond, KY; [p.] Raymond Benton, Doris Benton; [ed.] Attended Eastern Kentucky Univ. Graduate Heartwood Inst., Garberville, CA; [occ.] Writer; [memb.] Oaxacan Street Children Grassroots Org., Friends of Peace Pilgrim; [oth. writ.] Over 250 poems and short stories never published.; [pers.] Poetry for me is nothing less than the seed of self and universal knowledge. I pray that my writing will allow myself and others to "see", as to cease all seeking.; [a.] Irvine, KY

BERENBAUM, BARBARA EILEEN
[pen.] Barbara Eileen; [b.] Brooklyn, NY; [p.] Rose and Philip Berenbaum; [occ.] Free-Lance Admin./Asst.; [pers.] Poetry allows us to express the positive world. Please keep the world positive by caring for the mature, listening to the children and standing up against crime.; [a.] Valley Stream, NY

BERES, MATT
[b.] June 2, 1980, Orlando, FL; [p.] Dennis and Carol Beres; [ed.] Currently Dulaney High School; [occ.] Student; [memb.] SADD, Philosophy Club, Chess Club, Spanish Honor Society; [pers.] Always think before you act, and never take anything for granted.; [a.] Cockeysville, MD

BERGER, STEVEN
[pen.] Stephen Shepherd; [b.] December 29, 1946, Bronx, NY; [p.] Bernard (Deceased), Sylvia (Liv); [ed.] S.B., MIT, 1967; [occ.] Author; [memb.] American Mathematical Society, Optical Society of America Sigma XI; [hon.] International Hall of Poetry; [oth. writ.] Publications in Archival Science Journals; [pers.] We teach, we learn, we give, we receive - Indian Proverb; [a.] Flushing, NY

BERRY, CHRISTINA LEE
[pen.] Christi Berry; [b.] September 29, 1977, Purcell, OK; [p.] Jessie Hammond, Bryan Berry; [m.] Michael Wilbanks, January 18, 1997; [ch.] Casey Lee Berry (2 months girl 10-18-96); [ed.] Byhalia High School '95-'96, Purcell Public Schools '82-'94; [occ.] Full time mother; [hon.] Who's Who Among American High School Students, awards for Basketball and Track, high grade award for Biology, Home EC; [oth. writ.] Poem written in book for class at school, been acknowledged by Iliad Press and Cader Publishing. Essay written for Oklahoma Bombing honored by teachers and family.; [pers.] Having been close to the Oklahoma Bombing I saw death and destruction firsthand. I don't want my child to grow up in a world where that is an everyday event. I believe we need to open up and love everyone. We're not races or colors we're human.; [a.] Byhalia, MS

BERRY, JUDITH
[pen.] J. A. Berry, Judith Berry; [b.] September 3, 1943, Waynesboro, VA; [p.] Herbert Berry, Valley Berry; [ed.] Waynesboro High, Blue Ridge Comm. College; [occ.] Victorius Framed Pictures Waynesboro, Va.; [memb.] Va. Army Nat. Guard (VaARNG), Church of the Brethren, Charlottesville Women's Choir; [hon.] Desert Storm Veteran; [oth. writ.] Book to be published soon.; [pers.] My writings are influenced by the American West and the spirit of the Cowboy whom I have much respect and admiration for.; [a.] Waynesboro, VA

BEYERLE, SHANNON K.
[b.] December 20, 1974, Visalia, CA; [p.] Diane Vessels, David Beyerle; [ch.] Joshua Harley Russell; [ed.] Kingsburg High School, Kings River College, Fresno City Community College; [occ.] Executive Secretary Lewis and Associates Insurance Brokers, Inc.; [oth. writ.] Several poems published in local and school newspapers.; [a.] Visalia, CA

BEYNON, MICHAEL G.
[b.] August 13, 1963, Utah; [p.] Ronald G. Beynon, Jennie K. Beynon; [m.] Kasey L. Burgess Beynon, August 6, 1994; [ch.] Heidi, Alyssa, and Alysia; [ed.] High School (West High); [occ.] Computer Operator; [oth. writ.] None Published; [pers.] Thanks; [a.] Sandy, UT

BILLINGS, ROBERT KEELER
[b.] September 10, 1920, Auburn, ME; [p.] Warren C. and Edith Keeler; [m.] (Deceased) Kathryn Heisman Billings, June 7, 1958; [ed.] Rome Free Academy (Rome, New York 1938), University of Michigan, B.A. and M.A., Univ. of Wisconsin, M.S. (Library Science); [occ.] Retired Librarian (20 yrs.) and Art Teacher (30 yrs.) from Univ. of Kentucky, Kansas City Art Inst. and Central Connecticut State Univ.; [memb.] A.A.U.P.; [hon.] 2 Battle Stars, India-Burma Campaign 1944-46, (World War II); [oth. writ.] Constance Carrier of New Britain, Conn., Winner of The Lamont Poetry Prize in 1954, read 5 of my poems and commented - "Wonderful, you must publish those."; [pers.] I seem to be sensitive to cultural changes and all forms of art.; [a.] Newington, CT

BLACKLEDGE, JAYSON MARK
[b.] February 24, 1979, California; [p.] Debra Blackledge; [ed.] Cumberland High; [occ.] Student; [a.] Cumberland, RI

BLAIR, LINDSAY
[b.] November 20, 1976, Winchester, MA; [p.] Paul Blair, Elaine Ciesla; [ed.] Billerica Memorial High, Newbury College; [occ.] Food and Beverage at the Renaissance Bedford Hotel; [hon.] Graduated as President of the National Honor Society. Received a Presidential Scholarship to Newbury College; [pers.] I'd like to thank John Lancaster for all his time, and support during high school.; [a.] Billerica, MA

BLANKENBURG, RICHARD
[b.] April 8, 1930, Decatur, IL; [p.] Walter Blankenburg, Hazel Moore; [m.] Marlisa Wartmann-Baechi, August 12, 1993; [ch.] Erin Relph, Lisa Bission, Eric Blankenburg; [ed.] Millikin University, B.Sci, Indiana State University, M.Sci., University of Arizona, Ed.D.; [occ.] Educator, Retired

BLANKENSHIP, DOUGLAS PAUL
[b.] November 13, 1944, Kentucky, Argo; [p.] Herbert Blankenship; [m.] Stephanie Ann Blankenship, March 23, 1983; [ed.] B.A. Eastern Kentucky University, M.A. University of Kentucky, M.A. University of Kentucky, Ph.D. University of California (Los Angeles) Ph.D. additional work at Ohio State University; [occ.] CEO and President Pacific Group; [memb.] American Marketing Association Association of American Geographers, American Society of Planning Officials American Builders, American Philosophical Society, Mensa, Intertel, International Association of Philosophical Enquiry, National Rifle Assoc.; [hon.] Kappa Iota Epsilon, Omicron Alpha Kappa, Enoch Grehan Journalism Award one idea ahead of its time, Distinguished Service Award, Mensa Award, Who's Who in the World, Who's Who in the West, Who's Who in Business and Finance, Who's Who in California, Outstanding Young Man of America, International Who's Who, Who's Who in America, Builders Award, Several Scholarship Awards.; [oth. writ.] "God Would Have Wanted It That Way" in National Best Seller Cup of Chicken Soup for the Soul, "Psychographic View Of Transit" in National Academy of Science Journal "Social Interaction of Carpoolers" in Public Works Heartsongs book by hollywood Int. publishers.; [pers.] "When mankind learns to perfect the message of love and express it, for the second time in recorded history he/she will have rediscovered the spirit of fire.; [a.] Orange, CA

BLINCOE, ANNA LEE
[b.] August 1, 1914, Meade County, KY; [p.] Joseph Rodgers, Eva Rodgers; [m.] William C. Blincoe (Deceased), January 29, 1936; [ch.] William Jr. Frances, Robert, John, Mary Margaret, Joseph, Ellen, Michael; [ed.] Catholic Colored High, Spaulding College; [occ.] Retired Homemaker; [memb.] Dominican 3rd Order, St. Martin De Porres Elder Society, International Society of Poets; [hon.] Louisville Board of Alderman, Louisville-Jefferson County Head Staut, Golden Poet Award, Silver Poet Award, Editor's Choice Award, Award of Merit for 1984, 1986, 1987, 1990, 1988 World of Poetry; [oth. writ.] Several poems published in local newspaper, magazines and church papers, Trinity Magazines.; [pers.] Nearly nine decades of life's experiences are interwoven with the threads of my thoughts, to form the creation of my literary quilt.; [a.] Louisville, KY

BLOW, JOHN N.
[b.] November 30, 1905, Whitby, Ont, Canada; [p.] E. Richard Blow; [m.] Edith May Correll, November 15; [ch.] Edward Roy Blow, John Needham Blow, Robert Henry Blow, Mary Hazel Blow, Earnest Richard Blow

BOECHLER, CHARLOTTE
[b.] January 28, 1976, Wenatchee, WA

BOGART, STEPHANIE
[b.] December 1, 1980, Columbus, OH; [p.] Diane Bogart, Barry Bogart; [ed.] Still in High School; [memb.] National Wildlife, Wildlife fact file, Student Council in School, Students Environmentally Active (SEA), Earth Island Institute; [hon.] Honorable mention in Reflections contest for drawing (1995), Citizenship, student of the Month; [pers.] I do my poems and paintings on family friends, and endangered animals to reflect the happiness and love of life.; [a.] Livonia, MI

BOGDANOVICZ, SONYA
[b.] May 10, 1965, Bpt., CT; [p.] Anne Bogdanovicz, Edward Bogdanovicz; [ed.] CHS-Bpt., Tiekyo Post University-Waterbury CT; [occ.] Comptroller, Flintlock Construction, Inc. Greenwich CT; [pers.] Success isn't always convenient!; [a.] Bridgeport, CT

BOHIGIAN, JEAN
[pen.] Bohigian, Jean; [b.] November 23, 1932; [p.] Momie Knight, Charles Hayes; [m.] Jerry Bohigian, October 27, 1949; [ch.] 4 boys, 1 girl; [ed.] 2 yrs. College, Retired, Self Employed Art background (Major) Module for F.V. Layout; [occ.] Active in Civic Affairs, Educating Music Theory; [oth. writ.] Scottish Descent Both Father and Mother; [pers.] Thank you for have not had anything yet-there is more.; [a.] Fresno, CA

BOLDING, LACEY JANICE
[pen.] Lacey Bolding; [b.] February 10, 1982, Ada, Okla; [p.] Paul and Susan; [ed.] 8th Grade; [occ.] Student; [memb.] Jr. High Student Council Pres., Quiz Bowl, NASC, F.C.A. Okla. Honor Society; [hon.] Okla. Honor Society Quiz Bowl; [pers.] Enjoy playing basketball attend basketball camps in the summer.; [a.] Holdenville, OK

BOLSER, MELINDA
[b.] June 20, 1977, Columbus, GA; [p.] Richard E. Bolser, Patricia J. Bolser; [ed.] Jordan Vocational High School, currently attending Columbus State University; [occ.] Children's Caregiver; [hon.] Who's Who Among American High School Students (3 years); [oth. writ.] Several unpublished poems, i.e. "When A Heart of Stone Is Shattered," "Is Anybody There?", "Would You Say You Love Me Too?", "Why Does It Hurt So Bad?", "I'm Sorry", "I Love You" "Breaking Up", "If I Could", and others; [pers.] Everybody sooner or later, no matter who they are or how emotionally strong, needs a way to express their feelings, some have creative ways, some not so creative. Poetry is my way of these expressions.; [a.] Columbus, GA

BONNER, BOBBIE LOU
[b.] June 15, 1936, Walton, KY; [p.] Theodore and Luella Florence; [m.] Bruce Edward Bonner, August 1, 1964; [ch.] Deborah Hall, Mike Willis, Rod Willis, grandchildren - Lakicia and Tony Hall; [ed.] Grade School - Wilkens Height. High School - Wm Lincoln Grant. Northern Kentucky Voc. Nursing School; [occ.] Sales; [memb.] First Baptist Church Elsmere, Usher in Church, Beams of Light; [hon.] Writing Poems for church bulletin, on special occasions. Writing poems for obituary. Card Chair Person, for the Beams of Light.; [oth. writ.] "Why Lord?", "A Letter to God", "God's Hands of Blessing", "We Must Stop Hating", "The Dawning", "Thank You Jesus"; [pers.] "I am a Christian, and I thank God, every day, for His grace and mercy".; [a.] Elsmere, KY

BONNIE, JENNIFER
[pen.] Jen; [b.] July 12, 1981, Florida; [p.] Kim Bonnie, John Bonnie; [ed.] General Bus. Training in Commercial Arts; [a.] New Port Richey, FL

BORNT, ABBYE M.
[b.] February 13, 1982; [p.] Carol M. Bornt, Terry R. Bornt; [ed.] Presently a high school freshman at Northville Central School; [memb.] School newspaper staff, library club; [hon.] Third-place county Spelling Bee Winner, High School Honors student; [pers.] Many of life's hidden pleasures can be viewed through the quality of an artist's work.; [a.] Mayfield, NY

BOWLES, JON-DAVID
[b.] February 15, 1975, Naperville, IL; [p.] Daryl and Dagmar Bowles; [ed.] Waubonsie Valley High, College of DuPage, Tallahassee Community College; [occ.] Professional Sound and Lights; [hon.] At the age of 15 I won, with the help of my brother and some friends, a brand new Gibson Les Paul, at the battle of the bands in our area; [oth. writ.] Various poems and songs; [pers.] There are only about 500 people in this world. Everybody else wants to be one of those 500...which am I?; [a.] Chicago, IL

BOWLING, JEAN
[pen.] Jean Bowling; [b.] April 6, 1943, Alexandria, VA; [p.] Benjamin Carnegie Bowling, Audrey Maxine Williams; [ed.] George Washington High School, Alexandria, University of Maryland, B.S.; [occ.] Legal Secretary; [oth. writ.] Various newspaper articles, writers and editor for National Organization for Women, Anne Arundel County, newsletter from 1975-1980; [pers.] I like to write about emotions in a way that expresses my optimistic views of life; [a.] Annapolis, MD

BOYD, MARTIN T.
[b.] December 30, 1970, Vicksburg, MS; [p.] Sue M. and Tommy A. Boyd; [m.] Cheryl Pettway, June 1, 1996; [ed.] Vicksburg High School, Hinds Community College, Mississippi College; [occ.] Industrial Production Planner; [memb.] American Red Cross, Bowmar Avenue Baptist Church; [pers.] All things found upon earth are derived from God. So I strive to give Him the glory in every thing I do, especially in my poetry.; [a.] Vicksburg, MS

BOYD, REBECCA
[pen.] Becky; [b.] December 30, 1979, Adel, GA; [p.] Shelby Boyd Woodard; [ed.] 10th Grade, stopped because of finance problems. My mom and step-father got into an accident in 1995, we were struggling to make ends meet.; [hon.] Honor Roll Student; [oth. writ.] Poems: The Hero, The Prayer, Dead End, Another Loss, I'll Reminisce You My Angel, A Mystery, Suicide, Love, A Time To Pray, The Rose, Problems, Somewhere Between Hello and Goodbye, Jesus, Released, The Little Girl; [pers.] When I get really down and feel no one cares, God gives me poems to write. I have a lot of more poems that I haven't put in these spaces, I probably have enough for a book.; [a.] Conyers, GA

BRADEN, FELIX
[pen.] Cat; [b.] February 19, 1979, GA; [p.] Mary Cochran; [ed.] Senior in High School; [occ.] Student; [pers.] Nothing lasts forever, enjoy who ever you are in love with at the present as much as you can, cause hearts and thoughts fade! But never stop having fun.; [a.] Birmingham, AL

BRADLEY-JOYNER, FALESHA D.
[b.] March 20, 1972, Oklahoma; [p.] Cheryl E. Hammons; [m.] Darron Joyner, June 17, 1996; [ed.] Putnam City West SR High Piatt College; [occ.] OKC bombing Survivor; [memb.] American Red Cross CPR, American Red Cross first aid, Cathedral of praise;

[pers.] I'm writing to express my feelings. My writing pours out to those who have lost a loved one, survivor of a tragedy. Or just everyday survival. Together all things are possible; [a.] Oklahoma City, OK

BRADY, VIRGINIA J.
[pen.] Virginia J. Brady; [b.] November 8, 1924, New Canaan, CT; [p.] Anthony and Margaret Savatsky; [m.] Peter Robert Brady M.D., April 22, 1946; [ch.] Virginia, Patricia, Peter, Marco, Katheryn; [ed.] New Canaan High School, Kings County School of Nursing; [occ.] Retired; [memb.] KCSN Alumni Assoc., US Army Nurse Cadet Corp., St. Mary's Church Scholarship Donor, International Society of Poets, Horticultural Society; [hon.] Five Editor's Choice Awards 1995-96, Member International Poets Hall of Fame Museum on the Worldwide Web.; [oth. writ.] Poems published in the National Library of Poetry Anthologies. Poems written for bereavement groups and local senior citizen groups.; [pers.] I try to write simply about issues and emotions that we face in life that both adults and children can relate to and enjoy.; [a.] New Monmouth, NJ

BRANCH, BRYANT J.
[pen.] Byrant Branch; [b.] March 13, 1959, Bonham, TX; [p.] Jack, Frances Branch; [m.] Lola Branch, November 26, 1996; [ch.] Six; [ed.] Paschal High School, Ft. Worth, TX, College T.C.J.C., Ft. Worth, TX; [occ.] Writer and student at T.C.J.C. South Campus, Ft. Worth, TX; [memb.] Member of The International Society of Poets; [hon.] Editor's Choice Award, National Library of Poetry, "Books", Fields of Gold and a Voyage to Remember, (1996). A special award from International Publications for The National College Poetry Contest.; [oth. writ.] Awaiting Fulfillment, A Peaceful Autumn's Day, Footsteps Of Faith, Poet Of All Time, Fruitful Harvest, First Born, The Greatest, A Child Born, Joy Is The Lord; [pers.] In the twilight of the moment mischievous thoughts occur leading to many dramatic regrets such as unwanted children, "AIDS", jail and "Lethal Injection", etc., we all young and old, alike should aware of our thought and actions and the consequence there of.; [a.] Fort Worth, TX

BRANT, HEIDI
[pen.] Hedy West; [b.] June 19, 1950, Toronto, Canada; [p.] A. A. Brant, Lilli T. Brant; [m.] Divorced; [ch.] Arin Weiss, Jed Weiss; [ed.] Rhode Island School of Design - BFA in Painting and Illustration; [occ.] Freelance Writer and Illustrator; [oth. writ.] Published as an Illustrator "The Solar-Hydrogen Solution" 1991 and Articles for a magazine called InformArt/Interviews of Artists.; [a.] Reston, VA

BRAUN, KARL PETER
[pen.] "Poet Peter"; [b.] February 3, 1913, LeMars, IA; [p.] Frank and Catherine Braun; [m.] Rose Dominic, September 30, 1941; [ch.] Marcy Anderson, Teddy; [ed.] St. Joseph High School; [occ.] Retired Farmer; [oth. writ.] Book "Pebbles and Pearls" - a collection of poems and short stories from 1933 to the present, poems/short stories published in local newspapers.; [pers.] My mother's gift for storytelling prompted my writing short stories of memories and dreams growing up in a large family on a farm in Plymouth County, Iowa during the 1920's and beyond. My poetry is my faith for all to see.; [a.] LeMars, IA

BRENNAN, JENNA
[b.] December 13, 1984, Lake City, FL; [p.] Robert and Cindi Brennan; [ed.] Kindergarten thru 6th grade in the Columbia County Public School System; [occ.] Full-time student; [memb.] Junior Beta Society, Niblack School Band; [hon.] 1996 award for 5 straight years on the A honor roll/art award/music award/scholastic achievement award; [pers.] I feel that I am an average

child that has been very fortunate to have a family that encourages me to explore my talents.; [a.] Lake City, FL

BRIGGS, BONNIE ALLEN
[b.] February 13, 1955, Shreveport, LA; [p.] Jean Fetterman (mother), Linton Harold Allen (father); [m.] William W. Briggs Jr., November 21, 1993; [ed.] James Madison High School, University of Houston at Clear Lake; [occ.] Sr. Staff Contract Rep, Burlington Resources Oil and Gas Co. Houston, TX; [memb.] Natural Gas Assoc. of Houston; [hon.] Daughters of the American Revolution - Runner Up; [oth. writ.] "You," "The Funny Man" in Whispers at Dusk and Morning Song.; [pers.] I believe celestial beings are among us and must have access to the greatest play ground, the heavens. I have felt their presence throughout my life.; [a.] Houston, TX

BRITTON, JEAN
[pen.] Allen, Jean; [b.] November 26, 1923, Sulphur, OK; [p.] Grady Allen, Maude Allen; [m.] Curtis Britton (Deceased), May 4, 1965; [ed.] Sulphur High School, Oklahoma State University (3 yrs.); [occ.] Retired Secretary and Real Estate Agent; [hon.] National Honor Society, National Society of the Daughters of American Revolution Award for "Good Citizen of the Year" (High School) Major Letters in Scholarship and Activity, Dean's list; [oth. writ.] None except editorials in high school newspaper, and poems written to friends on special occasions.; [pers.] I have been a singer and a painter and feel that the pursuit of another field of art would be exciting...A great way to express truth as I see it.; [a.] Oklahoma City, OK

BROADNAX, LYNN
[b.] October 3, 1965, Eden, NC; [p.] Carol and Jesse Broadnax; [ch.] Daughter - Morgan; [oth. writ.] Biographical short story entitled, "World Gone Mad," and "Mirror: The Graduation Poem."; [pers.] My most appreciative thank you to the Nat'l Library of poetry for wishing to publish my poem, "Desist of Duration." I am a firm believer in dreams coming true, but it takes some effort by oneself to make it happen.; [a.] Winston-Salem, NC

BROSSOIT, SAMUEL JOSEPH
[pen.] Samjoe; [b.] February 17, 1951, Ephrata, WA; [p.] Arthor and Cathy Brossoit; [ed.] Washington State University Saint Rose of Lima Catholic School; [occ.] Security Guard; [oth. writ.] He is there - on any Sunday O.J, - America the Violent - Shellie Jeri Doll - Cowboy Blues - Maggie - Willow Bay Dock - McFinkins - Several submitted to country music USA - Nashville TN; [pers.] Trust in Jesus - allow Him time to do what is best for you and be yourself; [a.] Nine Mile Falls, WA

BROUGHMAN, CATHY
[pen.] Cathy Joaquin Broughman; [b.] October 22, 1945, Philadelphia, PA; [m.] Ronald Broughman, June 13, 1963; [ch.] Philip and Deborah; [ed.] Studies to include (High School - Central High-Lowmoor, VA) Psychology - No Degree, Certificates and Licenses, 2 yrs. college - Dabney Lancaster in Virginia, Real Estate and Insurance College G.T.C.C. Jamestown NC; [occ.] Vice President of FFS Insurance Agency; [memb.] No current memberships past to include American Business WomenÆs Association - Philiptokos Society of the Greek Orthodox Church - Maryfield Blue Ladies (Volunteer); [oth. writ.] Currently writing novel - anticipate completion in 1997 - not titled yet based on true story.; [pers.] Poetry is the armor and shield by which an author can divulge his soul, share his vision, and develop wings of imagination for the reader.; [a.] Jamestown, NC

BROWN, CARL F.
[b.] July 26, 1955, Kansas City, MO; [p.] Dorthy Brown, Howard Brown; [m.] Gloria L. Brown, June 8, 1991; [ch.] Tyisha, Kevin, Carl; [ed.] High School Graduate; [occ.] Free Lance Writer; [memb.] Humanity Baptist Church; [oth. writ.] Poetry Book's - Abuse From My Mind - Journey From the Lord, Children's Book's - Getting Ready From School, My Dentist And I, - My First Trip To The Doctor, Newspaper Article, San Jose City Flight; [pers.] Children are the most important things in Life, they are our future. I need my writing to reach, teach, and help the children of the world.; [a.] San Lorenzo, CA

BROWN, FRANK
[b.] September 11, 1973, Trenton, NJ; [p.] Annabelle Brown, Frank Freemon; [m.] Girlfriend, Pamela Major; [ed.] Trenton Central High School, Mercer County Community College; [occ.] SEARS Replenishment; [memb.] Interfaith Tabernacle Church of Christ; [hon.] Athletics awards, singing awards, now I am being awarded with my poetry. Thanks To God! And my Mom for having me.; [oth. writ.] I have many other poems that I think should be known about, and I wish to let them be realized! Very, very soon!; [pers.] I am really starting to find my true spot in myself and in life. And the pressure is starting to come off my hands, out into the world! "Thank you mom"; [a.] Trenton, NJ

BROWN, PAMELA ELIZABETH
[b.] September 19, 1973, Augusta, GA; [p.] Rosetta O'Bannon and Leroy Brown; [ed.] University of South Carolina at Columbia, Silver Bluff High School; [occ.] Network Engineer (Corp) Bellsouth, Augusta, GA; [memb.] National Society of Black Engineers, NAACP Youth and College Division; [hon.] Who's Who Among High School Students/College Students, Dean's List; [pers.] Life experiences, feelings, and thoughts are my inspiration. The most beautiful works of art come straight from the heart.; [a.] Jackson, SC

BROWN, RAY
[pen.] S. A. Carter; [b.] September 13, 1947, Poughkeepsie, NY; [p.] Murray F. Brown, Emma Jean Brown; [ed.] Syracuse University (New York), SUNY at New Paltz (New York), California State University at Fullerton; [occ.] English Teacher at Cerritos High School, Cerritos, CA; [memb.] St. John of God Catholic Church, International Society of Poets, American Life League; [hon.] Honorary Columbus Cr.D. Award, Who's Who Among America's Teachers; [oth. writ.] Several articles and short stories published, poetry also published, including those in Recollections of Yesterday, The Best Poems of 1997, and The Nightfall of Diamonds.; [pers.] My mother had a delightful imagination. When I was a child she always found the time to tell me stories. These original tales have inspired my own.; [a.] Norwalk, CA

BRUNSON, RALPH ERIC
[b.] September 6, 1959, Bay Shore, NY; [ed.] Moorestown High, Moorestown, NJ, U.S. Naval Academy Annapolis, MD, MIT Cambridge, MA, New England Conservatory of Music, Boston, MA; [occ.] Design Engineer for McDonnell Douglas, Huntington Beach, CA, Piano teacher.; [oth. writ.] Numerous songs. This poem is from one of the songs I've written.; [pers.] I love music and have been playing piano since age 13. Through life experience I've grown to appreciate the power of beautiful lyrics which is why I enjoy poetry so much.; [a.] Long Beach, CA

BRYAN, DAVID
[pen.] Edward Freeman, Romeo (internet); [b.] January 31, 1981, Oxford, OH; [p.] Mark and Nancy Bryan; [ed.] Sophomore at Pinellas County Center for the Arts (P.C.C.A.) for Musical Theater in St. Petersburg,

Florida; [occ.] Tae Kwon Do Instructor; [hon.] Many from karate Tournaments, 4th place at state Championship in 1996; [oth. writ.] Many others that I keep in a little poetry folder of mine, but none have ever been published.; [pers.] "Men's eyes were made to look, and let them gaze. I will not budge for no man's pleasure," I. Mercutio Romeo's friend, Romeo and Juliet; [a.] Clearwater, FL

BUCHANAN, ROB
[pen.] RYU; [b.] April 21, 1979, Huntington, PA; [p.] Robert D. Buchanan, Cecelia; [ed.] Graduating High School '97; [occ.] Student; [memb.] Attended acting classes at Wyomissing Fine Arts. Is now attending Sweet Arts Studio - for acting classes - as Assist. Director and Stage Manager; [oth. writ.] Several articles in local newspapers. Numerous shojo/sci-fi/fantasy screenplays.; [pers.] Just so much of my work is influenced by my ideas as well as my experiences, the latter very often being a result of the former. I feel that art is that which can transcend standard tastes and styles, although it is rarely manipulated to this end!; [a.] Elverson, PA

BUCHHOLZ, CYNTHIA SCHWIEGER
[b.] December 7, 1962, Medelia, MN; [p.] Roscoe and Sylvia Schwieger; [m.] John Scott Buchholz, August 19, 1994; [ch.] Caleb John, Gabriel Jordan, Michaela Joy; [ed.] High School Education; [occ.] Mother, Founder of Declare His Glory Productions, Ltd.; [hon.] Two-time "Editor's Choice Award", for "Dear Lord Jesus" printed in "Sunshine and Daydreams", National Library of Poetry, Fall 1996. Chosen for publication in "The Best Poets of 1997", National Library of Poetry, and "In Dappled Sunlight," March of 1997, National Library of Poetry.; [oth. writ.] "Dear Lord Jesus", in Sunshine and Daydreams (Aug. 1996), Reprinted in "Frost at Midnight" (Dec. 1996), "Forget-Me-Not", in Dappled Sunlight (March of 1996), "Precious Holy Spirit" (Nat'l. Library of Poetry).; [pers.] The Lord keeps reminding me daily that it is important to rest in Him. He gave me a word of advice I try to remember in the day-to-day struggles of life. Here were His words: "Look up to My Light, when you feel overwhelmed. I will be there to guide you to peace and discern. Be not anxious for things which you have no control. Just rest in My Presence, and bask in My Glow. Just fall into My hands, when you land you will see... that I have been faithful to meet all of your needs."; [a.] Saint Paul, MN

BUFFO, ELLEN FRATIA
[b.] April 10, 1922, Dwight, IL; [p.] Frank and Maria Fratia; [m.] Joseph J. Buffo, October 15, 1949; [ch.] Barbara, David, Mary Lee; [ed.] St. Francis College, Wesleyan University Seminars, Univ. of Notre Dame Seminar; [occ.] Homemaker/Writer; [memb.] St. Patrick Catholic Church, several Womens' Clubs, Ladies Aux. of V.F.W., Joliet Literary Writers; [hon.] Won contest for 3 short stories.; [oth. writ.] Articles in newspapers.; [pers.] I would like to walk through life leaving the light footprints of an interesting, concerned person, but more important a good person.; [a.] Joliet, IL

BUNCOM, MILDRED C.
[b.] February 24, 1947, Saint Louis, MO; [p.] Willie Morris, Mildred Morris; [m.] James C. Buncom, October 21, 1966; [ch.] Derek, Mildred, Cornel, Nicole and Lesa; [occ.] Property Manager; [pers.] I reflect on life's greatest gift, "Love" when all is said and done.; [a.] Santa Barbara, CA

BURKS, MARILYN
[b.] November 10, 1937, Philadelphia, PA; [p.] Beatrice Thurman - William Thurman; [m.] Lowell Burks, October 11, 1958; [ch.] Lisa Wrae and Dana Terese; [ed.] Lisa - Attended Temple University, Phila., Dana - Graduate of Temple University, Phila.; [occ.] Contract

Specialist, Merck and Co., Inc. - Pharmaceutical West Point, Pa. - Company; [hon.] "Award of Excellence" for service as a Tour Guide At Merck & Co., Inc. PA., "Distinguished Award" for service as an Honor Guard at the Blessed Katherine Drexel Shrine - PA.; [oth. writ.] L'il Trey - Here To Say, Dear Auntie Myrt, The Special Three, Forever Together, God Needs You; [pers.] When I write, I am pouring out the true feelings from my Heart and Soul.; [a.] Philadelphia, PA

BURNS, FRANKLYN
[pen.] Froim; [b.] September 30, 1933, Los Angeles, CA; [p.] Milton and Belue M.; [m.] Divorced; [ch.] Michele D. and Kimberly R.; [ed.] Fairfax High School, Los Angeles City College, Chounaird Art Inst.; [occ.] Realtor, Loan Consultant, Semi Retired; [memb.] San Francisco Valley Assoc. of Realtors, Calif. Assoc. of Realtors, Nat'l. Assoc. of Realtors, Nat'l. Assoc. of Master Appraisals, Kiwanis Club of Northridge; [a.] Granada Hills, CA

BYLINSKI, JOSEPH J.
[b.] February 18, 1932, Hartford, CT; [p.] Mr. and Mrs. Joseph and Anna Bylinski; [m.] Dolores Jean (Carlson), June 30, 1956; [ch.] Joseph, Sharon Ann, Susan, Michael, Catherine; [ed.] BS Civil Engr (Univ of Conn), MS Education (Pepperdine), multiple military school completions during 30 yr career; [occ.] Retired (Lt Col/ USAF); [pers.] Since their passing, I harbored these thoughts wondering how I could best express my feelings toward my parents which I never fully expressed when they where around. I dedicate this poem to them and hope it will have an impact on those whose parents are still living.; [a.] Papillion, NE

CACCHIONE, BETSY M.
[b.] March 1, 1972, Syracuse, NY; [p.] Bonnie Cacchione, Paul Cacchione; [ed.] University of Pittsburgh, East-West College of the Healing Arts, Appalachian Trail Thru-Hike, Alaskan Fisheries; [occ.] Student of Life, Poet, Spiritual Anthropologist, Licensed Massage Therapist in training, and Reiki Practitioner; [pers.] I strive to live my life honestly, to express the creatures that I am, in the universes that I perceive, without resorting to filters or masks, except by choice, to explore, to stretch, to dare, to love, and most importantly - to change.; [a.] Portland, OR

CALDWELL, REV. CARMEN
[b.] June 5, 1947, Arecibo, PR; [ch.] Maria, Gary, Chris, Earl; [ed.] Miami Dade, University of Maryland, Bearean, Cornell, Scholarship International Gospel Assemblies of God; [occ.] Chaplain Brookwood Gardens Convalescent Center; [memb.] International Gospel Assemblies of God, Women's Aglow, Women in Christ, EICM International Women's Ministries, Solid Rock Family Worship Center, New Generations Ministries, Winds of the Spirits Ministries, Destiny Ministries; [hon.] Teacher of the Year North Woods, Assemblies of God, Merit Award; [oth. writ.] Calling on the World Changers Weathering the Storms, Food for Thought.; [pers.] Glory to God and His loving kindness because without Him we can do nothing nor are we able to help another, but because of His divine grace...He can do all things: Including us to bring life and joy to others.; [a.] Homestead, FL

CAMPBELL, ROBERT H.
[b.] December 9, 1921, Rochester, NY; [p.] Mr. and Mrs. William J. Campbell (Deceased); [occ.] Retired - CB Foods Co. as Director Consumers Relations; [pers.] High School graduate. Original member of Mercury Ballet Company, Eastman Theater - Rochester, NY. Currently - Volunteer worker Blessed Sacrament Church Rectory.

CAMPOS, ANAYDA CAROLINA
[b.] February 7, 1980, Venezuela, Caracas; [p.] Ileana and Vicente Campos; [ed.] Stirrup Elementary, Ruben Dario middle school and Miami Coral Park Senior High (still in my grade is 10th (a sophomore in high school)); [occ.] Want to be a future teacher/children psychologist; [oth. writ.] (For school) poems that done in project or for extra credit.; [pers.] I dedicate this poem to Albert Jesus Martinez with all my love and thought of you through tough times. To my lovable cousin Albert who I love a lot!; [a.] Miami, FL

CANNAROZZI, SUSAN
[pen.] Orwell Swift, Mother Susan; [b.] July 2, 1949, Jersey City, NJ; [p.] John Sangillo and Alice Bustin; [m.] Matthew Michael Cannarozzi, August 4, 1972; [ch.] Matthew Emil Cannarozzi; [ed.] B.A. Montclair State University, M.A. Montclair State University; [occ.] Biology/Chemistry, Teacher and Writer, Pres. of Master Teacher, Inc.; [memb.] Nat'l Organ Women, Nat'l Organ Female Executives, Cousteau Society Character Scholarships of Am., Founder; [hon.] 4 year scholarship, Sigma Eta Sigma Sci., Honor Fraternity, Dean's List, Magna Cum Laude B.A., Summa Cum Laude M.A., Women of Year '95, '96, '97, Citizen of Year '95, '96, '97, Two Thousand Notable Am., Women, only Independent Educator in U.S.A.; [oth. writ.] Collection of Short Stories, Book of Poetry, Uncommon Sense, Master Teaching Textbook, The Humanitarian, The Microtechnological Society; [pers.] Leadership, Scholarship, and Service to humanity through prayer and unselfishness!; [a.] Hoboken, NJ

CAPORALE, MARCO
[b.] October 24, 1977, Ridgewood, NJ; [p.] Maria and Salvatore Caporale Jr.; [ed.] Clearwater Central Catholic High School, Rollins College; [memb.] St. Michael's Altar Servers, Florida Boys State; [hon.] Senator at Boys State Convention; [oth. writ.] Several poems were published in Redauram, and soon to be published in brushing.; [pers.] There is no greater gift than the unconditional love of a woman.; [a.] Dunedin, FL

CARDE, FLORA
[pen.] Ziggy; [b.] May 18, 1967, Sackville, NB; [p.] Herbert and Elizabeth Carde; [ch.] Tyler Ace Carde; [ed.] Grade 12 River Hebert District High School, Cosmetology Springhill Community College, Granton Institute of Technology Toronto Psychology; [occ.] Student in Practical and applied Psychology, abnormal psychology; [hon.] Bible Study Certificate, Editor's Choice award presented by The National Library of Poetry 1995; [oth. writ.] Poem "Beyond Reality" published in anthology "The Path Not Taken"; [pers.] In this poem I wanted to pay tribute to the Lord and God who without them I could not accomplish anything in life so I asked the Lord to help and I think this poem may help others.; [a.] River Hebert East, Nova Scotia, Canada

CARDENAS, CHRIS
[b.] August 21, 1970, CA; [p.] Karen Cole; [pers.] Chris died at the age of 25, on August 25, 1995

CARMICHEAL, COURTNEY A.
[b.] February 2, 1984, Houston, TX; [p.] Peggy Carmicheal, Randell Carmicheal (Deceased) Rebecca Carmicheal- guardian stepmother; [ed.] 7th grade, Northshore Elemen School, Northshore Middle School present; [memb.] Jr. National Honor Society; [hon.] 1st place-3rd grade poetry contest, numerous Academic awards. Qualified for 1996/1997 Duke University talent search; [oth. writ.] Numerous poems published in school paper; [pers.] My inspiration is my personal experiences and reflections of life.; [a.] Houston, TX

CARPENTER, VELMA
[b.] July 14, 1965, Columbus; [p.] Roger and Carolyn Long; [m.] Boyfriend - Roger Toliver; [ch.] Daniel and Angel Carpenter; [ed.] Licking Heights School, Licking Country Joint Vocational School; [occ.] Hair stylist; [hon.] Editor's Choice Award for my poem in the anthology of where dawn lingers and best poems of the '90's. In October I was elected into The International Poetry Hall of Fame; [oth. writ.] Poems in the Columbus Dispatch about my brother, two poems publish with The National Library of Poetry. Fist one in "Where Dawn Lingers" the second in the "Best of the '90's".; [pers.] The words that I write are a reflection of God's love and mercy that He will pour at upon his children.; [a.] Pataskala, OH

CARR, BEVERLY
[b.] September 16, 1966, North Carolina; [p.] Cora Carr, Percell Carr; [ch.] 1 child Talisha Carr; [ed.] Thomas Jefferson High School, Albert Merrill Business School, currently enrolled in N.Y.C. Technical College; [occ.] Matron for Professional Van Service Co. working with mentally disabled people; [hon.] Albert Merill Business School for perfect attendance Data Entry, Word Processing Certified Home Health Aide Certificate, Employee of the Month; [oth. writ.] Born To Survive, Reality There's No Place Like Home, A Child Shall Lead, Mommy Where's My Daddy?, Nobody's Guaranteed Tomorrow, Cry Freedom, I Pray, Behind Closed Doors, etc. 55 poems in all.; [pers.] I, Beverly Carr someday hope to become very successful, and be a big inspiration to all with my writing. I'm inspired by everyone who enjoys my work. I write to touch everybody's soul...; [a.] Brooklyn, NY

CARROLL, KAREN
[b.] February 15, 1967, Weimar, TX; [p.] Burnett C. Carroll, Annie J. Carroll; [m.] Vincent E. Mosby, April 6, 1996; [ed.] Schulenburg High, Prairie View A&M University, University of St. Thomas; [occ.] Technical Writer; [hon.] Master Teacher Award; [oth. writ.] Another poem published in "Laurels," a university magazine; [pers.] As a contemporary writer, my goal is to reflect, without prejudice, my feelings, emotions, and experiences as a black woman - capture my place in this race.; [a.] Houston, TX

CARTA, EDWARD J.
[b.] January 8, 1977, Sonora, TX; [p.] Clay and Linda Carta; [ed.] Llano High School, Angela State University; [a.] San Angelo, TX

CARTER, ELIZABETH
[pen.] Elizabeth Carter; [b.] January 30, 1969, Garrard Co., KY; [p.] William and Mary Carter; [m.] Divorced; [ch.] William and Cherish Huff; [ed.] Jessamine Co. High Sullivan College (Summa Cum Laude) Associate of Science in Paralegal Studies; [occ.] Paralegal and Editing Manuscripts; [memb.] Nu Epsilon Delta and Sullivan Paralegal Society; [hon.] Dean's List DeCamp-Gordon Paralegal Scholarship Sullivan College President Cup; [oth. writ.] Several articles in Para-Phrases, 1 poem in NLP anthology "It's Over Now" Several articles in local newspaper.; [pers.] As a single mother, I can honestly say that I've dedicated to my children. Everything I do, I do for them, out of love for them and a hope for a brighter future!; [a.] Nicholasville, KY

CARTER, JACQUELINE VINICE
[b.] November 1, 1962, Saint Louis, MO; [p.] Henry and Thelma Carter; [ed.] Ofallon Technical High School, Draughons Business College, St. Louis Community College, American Institute of Banking; [occ.] Loan Assistant; [pers.] I have always written poems to express how I feel about my life. I started writing at age twelve. Writing allows me to never forget my past, the

joy and pain of a growing changing woman.; [a.] Saint Louis, MO

CASIAS, JOHN M.

[pen.] Lowestar Easle; [b.] December 27, 1954, El Paso, TX; [p.] Max A. and Ingrid E. Casias; [m.] Gloria D. Casias, September 19, 1995; [ch.] Bernadette, Anthony, Margarita, and Antoinette; [ed.] Completed 14 yrs and presently a junior at UNM; [occ.] Student University of New Mexico Education (History); [memb.] None although maybe now I do have one as this National Library of Poetry.; [hon.] The greatest honor I have that was given to me is given by my Lord and savior "Jesus Christ." He has given me the ability to write and enjoy life. To also enjoy my wife and family.; [oth. writ.] Dream feeder time, white Sunday, stage to the mountaintop; [a.] Albuquerque, NM

CASTELLANO, GENEVA F.

[pen.] Geneva F. Castellano; [b.] February 6, 1931, Denver, CO; [p.] Manuel and Alifonsa (Alice) Maestas; [m.] April 30, 1954; [ed.] 12 grade, attended Gampers College Denver, Colo., wasn't an accredited school. Went back to sch. to Emily Griffith Opportunity School Affiliate with St. Lukes Hosp., Denver Colo.; [occ.] "LVN" - Licensed Vocational Nurses - Retired - had to pass Calif. state boards to practice as a nurse.; [memb.] Senior Citizen. I also belong to Queen of all Saints and am a member of Legion of Mary; [oth. writ.] I have other poems here at home, that I have written. I'm just saving them so that I could get copyrights on them. But I need some assistance in filling out the forms. Afraid of filling them wrong.; [a.] Concord, CA

CASTELLANOS, RUDY

[b.] August 16, 1950, San Bernardino, CA.; [p.] Salvador and Anita Castellanos; [m.] Divorced; [ch.] Rudolph Albert and Lisa Dawn; [ed.] Venice High; [occ.] Lan Administration; [memb.] I.S.P.; [hon.] Editor's choice awards in Tomorrows Dream; [oth. writ.] Four other published works in NLP Books; [pers.] Never give up on yourself, never quit trying, I am influenced and inspired by myself.; [a.] Simi Valley, CA

CASTRO, EUFROCINO C.

[pen.] Major E. C. Castro; [b.] June 13, 1923, Philippines; [p.] Primitivo and Ursula C. Castro; [m.] Stella Vamvatzouli Castro, May 17, 1957; [ch.] Angello V. Castro, Ursula Lina V. Castro; [occ.] Barber, USCG Group Key West, Florida; [memb.] Philippine Friendship Society Sergeant at Arms 3 years Philippine American Society 3 years Sergeant at Arms, US Navy retired 20 years service; [hon.] Six good conduct awards, Asiatic Pacific Campaign, World War II, and National Defense; [pers.] When my wife Stella and I, got married she don't speak one word of English and I don't speak one word of Greek. Our son born in Greece in Athens, and our daughter born in Nice, France and we are all American citizen. I am fourth grade graduate, I speak Tagalog, Visayan, English, little Greek, some Spanish language. I was born June 13, 1923, village called Caticlan. We are poor and large family, 13 boys and 3 girls.; [a.] Aklan, Panay, Philippines

CATABAS, PIER ANGELI

[pen.] Papillon; [b.] Manila, Philippines; [ed.] Fine Arts; [occ.] Freelance Artist; [oth. writ.] Non-published; [pers.] "A relic of discontinued item on a shelf, is seldom heard. But the passion in a song and rhythm, is the heart's only eloquence."; [a.] Costa Mesa, CA

CATALDO, CLARICE

[b.] November 13, 1965, Philadelphia, PA; [m.] John P. Jr., August 1, 1987; [ch.] Johnny, Angelisa; [ed.] Phila College of Textiles and Science, Temple University; [occ.] Self employed Artist, Office Manager CPA firm; [pers.] Thank you Angel Jake.; [a.] Jamison, PA

CAVALERI, NICHOLAS

[pen.] Nick Cavaleri; [b.] January 2, 1934, Locri, RC Italy; [p.] Vincenzina Macri Cavaleri, Francesco Cavaleri; [m.] Theresa Oppedisano Cavaleri, September 2, 1956; [ch.] Antoinette, Vini, Frank, Dominick, Mike and Anthony; [ed.] Teacher's College (Magistrale); [occ.] Owner of family run restaurant in Albany, NY; [memb.] Sons of Italy of America VFW Post 1019 Italian Community Center; [hon.] Several poems published in local newspapers 3 poems published in national poetry contest publications; [oth. writ.] Several poems written for special occasions and/or contests, several written as hobbies also published "Il Mio Paese" (My Home Town) in the book Trent'anni; [pers.] Freedom is the substance of life. Treat it as such.; [a.] Albany, NY

CAVANO, CECELIA CAROL

[pen.] Cecelia Carol Cavano; [b.] January 27, 1942, Carroll, IA; [p.] Blanche and John Holland; [m.] Francis Joseph Cavano, May 7, 1966; [ch.] David, Robert, Matthew; [ed.] Denison High School - 1960 graduation, St. Mary's College - Omaha Neb. St. Catherine's School of Nursing RN degree (graduation 1964); [occ.] Housewife; [memb.] Truth Teaching Group - 1996; [pers.] I write to express what I feel. My writing is heartfelt and along spiritual themes. Have read widely in the spiritual area and participated in groups with others who look toward their own spirituality.; [a.] Saratoga Springs, NY

CELIANT, GLORIA

[b.] January 9, 1985, Saint Mary Hospital; [p.] Mona Celiant, Guy Celiant; [ed.] Hudde Annex S.H.S IS 240; [hon.] Golden Record of Achievement Award for Outstanding Leadership, Scholarship and Service in School Community. It was presented by the Borough President "Howard Golden" in Bklyn College; [oth. writ.] Back in 4th grade I got to meet famous authors and illustrators because of several poems I had written. It was a real honor for me.; [pers.] I love writing. I can write day and night, night and day.; [a.] Brooklyn, NY

CHAMA, DENENNE

[b.] August 5, 1980; [p.] Mary Lovato; [ch.] Brothers Paul and Val Chama; [ed.] Riverside Indiana School Anadarko, OK; [hon.] Recognized for writing the book hard days growing up.; [oth. writ.] Book called Hard days growing up; [pers.] I hope to write more book and poems in the future.; [a.] Santo Domingo Pueblo, NM

CHANG, TOIKUN

[b.] April 23, 1948, Taiwan, China; [p.] Yao-mei and Sheng-ti Chang; [m.] Julie L. Chang, July 13, 1974; [ch.] Katy, Shirley and Dannis; [occ.] Businessman, owner of LaBonita Fashions; [memb.] Member of the Epoch Poetry Club - Taiwan; [hon.] Outstanding Achievement Award for Modern Poetry 1985, Taiwan; [oth. writ.] Several Poems published in local newspaper poems collection Awakening, Sunlight is flowing, published in Taiwan - 1980

CHATWELL, CHRISTINE

[pen.] Christine Chatwell; [b.] September 22, 1949, Evanston, IL; [m.] Maria Maglaya; [ed.] Masters Degree in Psychiatric Social Work, Master Degree in Business; [occ.] Psychotherapist in private practice; [memb.] National Association of Social Workers; [pers.] I began studying art as a young adult and have painted portraits of people and animals for several years. Recently I am discovering that feelings and ideas flowing into my awareness are seeking to be expressed as poems.; [a.] Mountain View, CA

CHAUVIN, PATRICIA

[b.] March 17, 1942, Leominster, MA; [p.] Rita and Glen Pettry; [m.] Donald Chauvin, November 24, 1965; [ch.] Joseph Wayne, Ronald George, Pamela Jean, Robert Francies, Darleen Marie; [ed.] Beckley, W. VA; [occ.] Resort Hostess at Foxwoods Casino; [hon.] Editor's Choice Award; [oth. writ.] Many poems which have not yet been published. 5 other poems soon to be published. One in newsletter that is published, others in books.; [pers.] I have been writing poetry all my life off and on. My dream is to become a well known poet. I love life and want to make a better world by leaving my work for others to read. I feel that people should understand that life is beautiful if you make it that way.; [a.] Norwich, CT

CHAVES-J., ANGEL P.

[pen.] Surface; [b.] June 22, 1973, Quito-Ecuador; [p.] Dr. Jose Chaves, Maria Magdalena Chaves; [ed.] Senior at (UNC) - Appalachian State University (Finance Major); [occ.] Full time student; [memb.] Phi Beta Lambda, Phi Theta Kappa; [hon.] First place in the state of North Carolina in Business - Management (Phi Beta Lambda) March/1996; [pers.] Paradox takes place when the individual is not humble about his effort, however, the value of any effort diminishes within the exaggeration of an attribute.; [a.] Banner Elk, NC

CHAVEZ, KIERA

[b.] December 14, 1987, Corcoran, CA; [p.] James and Jacque Chavez; [ed.] 3rd grade; [occ.] Student; [hon.] Has received awards for spelling, writing and achievement; [oth. writ.] Had 6 cartoons published in (Fresno Bee) newspaper last year - attended Peach Blossom at C.S.U. Fresno to recite poems - performed in local community Theater Guild's production of "Legend of Sleepy Hollow". Other poems written include "Dream Sire", "Easter Bunny" and "Fireworks". Very much loves music, art, drama poetry, literature and science. Also plays the piano.; [a.] Corcoran, CA

CHEN, FAITH

[b.] September 26, 1970, PR China; [p.] Rev. and Mrs. Ji'an Chen; [ed.] Guangzhou Foreign Languages Institute, East Texas Baptist University; [occ.] Student; [hon.] Alpha Chi National College Honor Scholarship Society, Sigma Tau Delta International English Honor Society, The National Dean's List, Dean's List with Honor; [pers.] Life should be pushed to its fullest potential every day.; [a.] Marshall, TX

CHILDS, LYNN

[b.] July 14, 1979, Kittanning, PA; [p.] James and Rose Anne Childs; [ed.] Kittanning Sr. High School, June 1997; [occ.] Student; [memb.] Student Council, Who's Who Among American High School Students, Show Choir, Young American's Talent Search, NAC (Nurturing Abilities for Christ), Local Youth Group; [hon.] NAC, National Competitions, Gold and Silver in Singing and a Gold in Mime; [oth. writ.] A few personal, unpublished poems.; [pers.] Poetry is one way of expressing myself. I think it is important for everyone to find a way to express themselves.; [a.] Kittanning, PA

CHRISTENSEN, CHRIS ALAN

[b.] January 19, 1956, Dinuba, CA; [p.] Warren and Phyllis Christensen; [m.] Connie, September 24, 1982; [ch.] Caitlin and a son due March 1997; [ed.] Dinuba High School, Kings River Junior College, Fresno City College; [occ.] Radiologic Technologist, Musician (Drums); [hon.] Dean's List, Phi Delta Kappa (Fresno City College); [oth. writ.] Various poems and short stories (unpublished). Am currently writing a children's story.; [pers.] I had the first stanza in my head for many years. My mother's passing was the catalyst for the rest of the poem. It is lovingly dedicated to her memory.; [a.] Clovis, CA

CHRISTENSON, HAROLD
[b.] July 18, 1942, Albert Lea, MN; [p.] Milton and Virginia Christenson; [m.] Joan Christenson; [ch.] Six; [ed.] 16th; [occ.] Bus Consultant/Freelance Writer; [memb.] Conservation Organizations; [oth. writ.] Various Freelance writings, published poems. In magazines and Newspapers. Technical manuals and service delivery plans for private organizations.; [pers.] I am dedicated to preservation of nature and I enjoy children and teaching and in same cods leaving from them about native.; [a.] Hastings, MN

CHRISTIAN, SHIRLEY I.
[b.] April 18, 1927, Spirit Lake, ID; [p.] Elbert and Vesta Lewis; [m.] R. H. (Dago) Christian, November 10, 1945; [ch.] Shirleen and Harold; [ed.] Graduated 12th Grade, College Credits in nutrition PJC Pensacola, FL Graduation 12 grade at Bremerton, Wn 1945; [occ.] Housewife, crippled just a bit I occupy myself with friends, growing house plants, and some writing; [memb.] Girl Scouts, as Leader. Sunday School Teacher, Methodist Church. Bagdad, FL School Lunchroom Manager Bagdad Elementary School; [hon.] Volunteer, as reading coach in Bagdad Elementary School certification of appreciation; [oth. writ.] Truth, Sundays Birds "Friend - My Cane"; [pers.] The one that matters is the one that knows the truth; [a.] Bagdad, FL

CHRISTOPHER, JOANNAZOE
[pen.] Whitesparrow; [b.] May 7, 1959, Buffalo, NY; [p.] Stephanie and Joseph; [m.] Robert, July 30, 1993; [ed.] East Aurora High School, B.S. Chemistry, Canisius College (87), A.S. Community College, South (78) [occ.] Sr. Scientist at West Valley Nuclear Services; [memb.] NAFE, Nat'l Audubon Society; [hon.] Alpha Sigma Lambda (86), Outstanding Science Student (78), Regents Scholarship (76); [oth. writ.] Small piece in Organic Gardening Magazine about wild trilliums blooming in May; [pers.] Writing is my way of pointing pictures in color using a black pen and white paper. I write about nature, life, and feelings. It helps me balance the analytical side of my life as a scientist.; [a.] North Tonawanda, NY

CHURCHWELL JR., GARY W.
[pen.] Gary Castro; [b.] July 17, 1974, Los Angeles; [p.] Kathy and Gary Churchwell; [ed.] University of California, Riverside (UCR) B.S. in Biology; [occ.] Sales Clerk of Toys; [memb.] Golden Key National Honor Society, Valedictorian of High School Class of 1992.; [hon.] Dean's List; [oth. writ.] Poems in Asian Community Times at UCR.; [pers.] When everyone you know turns their backs on you, only God will help you stand.; [a.] Riverside, CA

CLAAR, JIMMY L.
[b.] January 4, 1953, Ravenna, OH; [p.] Dayton Claar and Jacqueline Wyatt; [ch.] Jimmy G. Claar, Ryan E. Claar, Jamie Kay Claar; [occ.] Computer Engineer for PRC Inc.; [oth. writ.] Has had four poems published in the Anthology Famous Poems of the Twentieth Century and has three poems published on the Live Poets Society page on the Internet.; [pers.] I retired from the U.S. Marine Corps as Msgt. in May 29. It's my hope that through poetry I can bring joy and comfort to others. I also strive to nurture the imagination because I believe that your imagination is your limitation.; [a.] Waldorf, MD

CLARK, DENISE MARCIA
[b.] November 20, 1953, Chicago, IL; [p.] Elijah and Willette Armour; [m.] Napoleon Clark Jr., October 17, 1982; [ch.] Jelani Howard and (1st Marriage) Julian Clark; [ed.] H.S. Graduate (Dunbar Vocational H.S.), Certified Nurses Assistant/South Suburban College; [occ.] Parent Liaison Specialist - Aunt Martha's Head Start Program; [memb.] Illinois Head Start Associa-

tion, Nat'l Head Start Association, Community Service Program/Park Forest Head Start Policy Committee Policy Council/Parent Committee/Steering Committee Homewood Full Gospel Church; [hon.] Parent Involvement awards/Parent of the Year award/Volunteer awards South suburban Hospital/Staff recognition awards/Community service awards/Awards for Parent Trainings/Career Paths for Parents/Parent to Parent and others; [oth. writ.] Poetry/"Children are Watching", "If We Could Grasp", "Highway Of Life", "Beauties Of Holiness", "Precious Gift" (Journals and inspirational letters); [pers.] I know that we all have a purpose in this life: To enhance the lives of others through our talents and gifts. I know that my purpose is to help strengthen families through my job as well as my writing. My life goal is to cherish the opportunity given me by recycling it to others, freely.; [a.] Park Forest, IL

CLARK, MARIE E.
[pen.] Marie E. Clark; [b.] September 2, 1922, Annapolis, MO; [p.] Erman and Lottie Grayson; [m.] Durward H. Clark, December 15, 1942; [ch.] Durella Struthers; [ed.] High School; [occ.] Retired from Army Corp of U.S. Engineers 1985; [memb.] American Legion Aux, Disabled Vets Aux., Good Sam R.V. Club, Senior Center; [hon.] Retired President of Business and Professional Women's Club 1969-70; [oth. writ.] Several children's stories which I am submitting to publishers.; [pers.] I'm a lover of good books, especially mysteries. I do lots of crafts and try to keep busy since the death of my husband in July of 1994.; [a.] The Dalles, OR

CLARKE, WINSTON H.
[b.] August 21, 1951, Colon, Panama; [p.] Winston H. Clarke Sr., Dorris Cooper; [ed.] Jose Guardia Vega High School, Panama University (Panama City, Panama), American Institute of Banking, NYC, New York; [occ.] Accountant - JP Morgan and Co., Wall St., NYC, New York; [memb.] Fountain Spring Baptist Church, Bronx, NY, United Missionary Baptist Association Laymen's Auxiliary of New York; [hon.] President of the Senior High School Class Assoc., Dean's List; [oth. writ.] Birthdays, special occasion and words of encouragement poems.; [pers.] I have been writing poetry since High School days as a hobby, but my greater joy is to convey a positive, spiritual and encouraging message to my readers.; [a.] Bronx, NY

CLAYTON, DAYNA LOUISE
[pen.] Dayna Clayton; [b.] January 10, 1962, Mason City, IA; [p.] Vincent and Judy Loeckle; [m.] William Clayton, February 14, 1988; [ch.] Jasmin Alysse, Lacy Kristine; [ed.] Received Graduation Equivalency Diploma, Nov. 1980; [oth. writ.] "June Thirty Nineteen Eighty Six" published in through the Hourglass as well as my personal collection of unpublished poems and musings.; [pers.] I am continually awed and ultimately reassured when yet again. I see the "Hand of God" in my life. Thanks God, for being there.; [a.] Osage, IA

CLEMENTS, JILL MARIE
[b.] December 24, 1959, Miami, FL; [p.] James A. Clements, Welma L. Clements; [m.] Divorced; [ch.] One - Jessica Williamson; [ed.] Kathleen Sr. High, Tampa Florida's all Breed Grooming School; [occ.] Administrative Assistant, Information Dept. at Watkins Motor Lines, Inc., Lakeland, FL; [memb.] ABATE of Florida; [oth. writ.] Editorial published for local newspaper on "Stalking Laws Too Lenient". Poem published in local newspaper, Hendersonville, NC.; [pers.] A quitter never wins and a winner never quits. Creative thinking may simply mean the realization that there's no particular virtue in doing things the way they have always been done.; [a.] Lakeland, FL

CLINE, RUTH
[pen.] Angela Faith; [b.] November 5, 1943, Saint Marys, WV; [p.] C. B. and Doris Brammer; [m.] B. Delmar Stewart (Deceased), Jesse H. Cline; [ch.] Elizabeth, Charles, Sherri, Jessica; [ed.] St. Marys High School graduate; [occ.] Homemaker, Secretary and bookkeeper for family owned business; [memb.] Pike Church of Christ, Black Diamond Girl Scouts; [oth. writ.] My other writings have been for my children and Grandchildren in honor of their special events.; [pers.] My writing is mainly inspired by my love of God, home and family. Also have always admired the writings of Helen Steiner Rice.; [a.] Saint Marys, WV

CLYNE, CAROLE N.
[b.] September 6, 1946, Wichita, KS; [p.] Dorothy Day; [ed.] High School Graduate various courses taken at work and Technical College attended; [occ.] Administrative Assistant; [memb.] Professional Singles Network, President Kansas Kountree Kloggers, Treasurer and Dancer; [hon.] Recognition Awards for Outstanding Job at Work. Honorable Mention for poem written.; [oth. writ.] Several poems written and printed in local newsletter. Poems selected for published book in Kansas.; [pers.] I write with love, to people that concern me. I write about my love for favorite things I like, see and feel.; [a.] Wichita, KS

COEN, LAUREN A.
[b.] April 8, 1984, Bardstown, KY; [p.] Michael and Dorothy Coen; [ed.] 6th Grader at St Joseph Parish School, Bardstown, KY; [occ.] Junior High Student; [memb.] St. Joseph Girl's Basketball Team; [pers.] I wrote this poem after our class studied the Holocaust; [a.] Bardstown, KY

COEN, R.
[pen.] T. Crow; [b.] July 7, 1975, RI; [a.] Coventry, RI

COHN, JESSICA
[b.] August 26, 1986, Pennsylvania; [p.] Alan Cohn, Julia Cohn; [ed.] Saint Martin of Tours; [occ.] Student; [memb.] Double "outstanding" club at school; [hon.] First Honors Student of the month, all star reader at the Bushrod library; [oth. writ.] "Flowers of the Forest" published in the Daily News.; [pers.] St. Martin of Tours school is "awesomely excellent"; [a.] Philadelphia, PA

COKER, JEAN
[pen.] Jean Coker; [b.] April 8, 1928, Milwaukee, WI; [p.] Palmer and Blanche Strand; [m.] Alver Bryant Coker, February 1, 1947; [ch.] Bryant son, Julie daughter; [ed.] High School - Graduated from the 12th grade at Girl's Trades and Technical High School, Milwaukee, WI; [occ.] Homemaker; [memb.] Dauphin Way Baptist Church; [hon.] The love of family and friends and the encouragement of them that money can't buy. One Mother's Day was honored by the most "other children influenced by someone" and it touched my heart. That was an honor for me.; [oth. writ.] Many other poems and a few stories, but never have attempted to have them published.; [pers.] I've always been an avid reader and hungry for knowledge. My faith in Christ is strong and free thankful. God has gifted me to share with others "Love art, crafts, people and flowers and baseball.; [a.] Mobile, AL

COLBY, FRANCESCA
[b.] November 16, 1923, Utah; [p.] James Chesley, F. Bartholemew; [m.] Robert Colby, June 16, 1972; [ch.] John T. Redden; [ed.] M.A. Occidental College; [occ.] Retired; [memb.] Screen Actor's Guild Zeta Phi Eta; [oth. writ.] Editor Humour Magazine Fang, Occidental College.

COLE, EVELYN
[b.] January 18, 1924, Lincoln, NE; [p.] Floyd H. and Marie A. Zerbel (deceased); [m.] Orven S. Cole, April 9, 1944; [ed.] Havelock High (class of '41) Lincoln, NE; [occ.] Housewife; [hon.] I have been published by the National Library of Poetry in several anthologies in the past few years. (i.e.) River Of Dreams, East Of The Sunrise, The Path Not Taken, Best Poems Of '95 and '96, Through The Hourglass, The Best Poems Of The '90's and others.; [oth. writ.] Music (with lyrics) and much poetry - all types and subjects; [pers.] Our family moved to California in my Post-graduate year of '42. I had several occupations before I married. I had been the sole office help for my husband, a Htg and A/C Contractor for 50 yrs. (now retired) We celebrated our Golden Wedding Anniversary in '94. In an effort to learn to play the piano in '54 I began to writing poetry for my own pleasure and still do. The Lord has been very kind...; [a.] Los Angeles, CA

COLEMAN, CHRISTINE
[pen.] Praline and McFlyy; [b.] July 15, 1972, Toledo, OH; [p.] Pariss and Linda Coleman; [ed.] B.S. degree from University of Dayton (in education); [occ.] High School Health Teacher; [oth. writ.] Poetry published in University of Dayton "Black Perspective." All other selections located in personal journals.; [pers.] To my parents: Thank you for allowing me the opportunity to explore and live life to the fullest. To Mike, thank you for introducing me to the meaning of motivation. To Bow, the greatest fairy Godmother! This piece is dedicated to the memory of my grandfather Claud Recker, who left this life June 18, 1995.; [a.] Toledo, OH

COLLETTE, ANITA
[pen.] Neat; [b.] July 25, 1948, Stamford, CT; [p.] Angelo and Filomena Boccuzzi; [m.] Peter T. Collette, July 17, 1976; [ed.] High School, Stamford High, AA Degree, BA Degree, MS Degree, Sacred Heart University, University of Brideport, English and Education holds a certificate in Reading; [occ.] Retired School Teacher (Elementary); [memb.] Church of St. Dunstan and a Eucharistic Minister; [hon.] Honor Roll at School, Certificate for Merit when taking Italian; [oth. writ.] I have written a few poems as memories at family funerals. Haiku and various other forms while sitting on the porch viewing nature.; [pers.] "You are you and you don't have to measure up to any other person...everyone of us has a touch of uniqueness and originality. You determine your success by comparing your accomplishments to your capabilities, you are number one when you do the best you can with what you have everyday," Zig Zigler.; [a.] Glastonbury, CT

COLLEY, SEBASTIAN
[b.] May 29, 1980, Houston, TX; [p.] Gerald and Carole Colley; [ed.] Clear Lake High School; [occ.] Student; [memb.] H.Y.C. Ragnots, Cross-Country, Track Teams, National Honor Society; [hon.] Buck Haworth Award, Top Fifteen Students in Clear Lake. Commodore of H.Y.C Ragnots; [pers.] Not everyone wants to know the meaning of the song. Some are upset when the words of the tune they've been singing are against their morals. I don't write to be catchy, I write to give you a window on my thoughts.; [a.] Seabrook, TX

COLLIER, MARILYN R.
[ed.] MS-Organization Behavior MA-Human Development; [occ.] Management Consultant and Personal Coach; [pers.] I see, feel, and write about the contradictions between humanistic values and human behavior.; [a.] Scotch Plains, NJ

COLLINS, GREGORY
[pen.] Gregory Douglas; [b.] October 9, 1972, Hartford, CT; [p.] Gary and Sylvia Collins; [pers.] I believe we must speak for those who lack the capability to speak for themselves. Therefore, we cannot close our eyes to the reckless havoc we are precipitating on the forests, the rivers, and the overall environment. It seems we are in a race to go anywhere at great speeds, no matter what the cost and how irreplaceable our losses are. In the shadow of such prosperity we have overlooked our ultimate reverberations. If preservations was never invented, today would be the new day to invent. As for the critics who try to console confidence in our society that all is well, they are like a legless man teaching running. "In the wilderness is the preservation of the world." It is a necessity to find a way to live in unity with the world's inhabitants that we find ourselves with, or else we'll be part of the earth's shedding skin. It is ingenious and very logical, co-existence or no existence.; [a.] Baltimore, MD

COLLINS, KIMBERLY LYNN
[b.] March 14, 1967, Wilmington, DE; [p.] Elaine K. Stokes, Tyrone Shuman; [ch.] Jeunes Alexander Collins; [ed.] Brandywine High School; [occ.] Child Support Enforcement Specialist; [memb.] Greater Bethel Apostolic Temple, Pastor Bishop Thomas W. Weeks; [hon.] Editor's Choice award presented the National Library of Poetry 1996; [oth. writ.] While riding through Harlem; [pers.] I thank God for giving me a mind to explore the deep things of the mind, body and soul to touch people where they are and direct them in the right path.; [a.] Wilmington, DE

COLLINS, STACY M.
[b.] August 25, 1985, Pulaski, VA; [p.] Mitchell K. Collins, Wanda N. Collins; [ed.] Student - Pulaski Middle School (6th grade); [occ.] Student; [memb.] Student of Dance-Fence Arts Center, Youth Group in Church, Pulaski Middle School Playmakers; [hon.] School honors - Citizenship, attendance, and participation. Superintendent's Honor Roll, Trophy for Most Enthusiastic Clogger, Ballet at "The Long Way Home" Preteen America State Finalist (Trophy Semi Finalist '96), Acknowledged in Newspaper for Benefit singing's.; [oth. writ.] Several poems, skit "Family Wars" acted out by members of my Fourth grade class, short story. "The Bride of Cloggendayle" (A fictional Mystery and Horror); [pers.] My writings usually reflect my mood, my highly imaginative ability, or my love for the simple beauty of nature. I have been influenced my support and moral teachings from my mother, encouraged and trained by wonderful teachers to use God given talents.; [a.] Pulaski, VA

COLLINS, WESLEY A.
[b.] August 1, 1931, Charlotte, NC; [p.] Roy Collins, Jewel Collins; [m.] Akiko, April 2, 1970; [ed.] USN Career Schools, South Western College Bus. Admin.; [occ.] USA Retired; [pers.] If you need a helping hand, look down at the end of your arm.; [a.] Torrance, CA

CONWAY, TROY ALLEN
[b.] March 18, 1977, Salisbury, MD; [p.] James A. Conway and Joan M. Conway; [ed.] James M. Bennett High School Northwest Missouri State University; [occ.] Sophomore in College; [memb.] Phi Sigma Kappa Fraternity; [hon.] Creative Writing Contest in High School; [oth. writ.] I have about forty poems, but none previously published.; [pers.] I write my poems for the women I have loved in my life. I intend on using my poetry as a way of expression as long as love and inspiration remain in my life. Thank you to those special people, you know who you are!; [a.] Whitehaven, MD

COOKE, SUSANNE M.
[pen.] Susanne M. Cooke; [b.] September 22, 1940, Port Clinton, OH; [p.] William Tietjen and Lilian Tietjen; [m.] Owyer Cooke, August 10, 1957; [ch.] Michael, John, David, Kristin, Katherine; [ed.] Romulus High; [occ.] Housewife and Substitute Teacher; [memb.] St. Charles Catholic Church - AARP; [oth. writ.] Poems not published, article for "The Peninsular News."; [pers.] You never truly get over the loneliness of having your spouse gone for most of the time.

COOPER, DIANE
[b.] May 19, 1957, Rochester, NY; [p.] Vincent and Carm Cerqua; [m.] Michael Cooper, August 11, 1979; [ch.] Lindsay and Cats Candy and Scruffy; [ed.] Gates-Chili High School; [occ.] Nurse, Doctor, Teacher, Accountant in other words a wife and mother; [memb.] Secretary of the Bright Raven Gymnastics Booster Club; [hon.] Not a one - but I survived. Like I didn't need therapy for it or anything...; [oth. writ.] Several poems written, but never published.; [pers.] I am a woman who longs for simpler days - you know Donna Reed and all that. My poems often express what I feel - but won't dare say. My advice - Silence is Golden. Patience the key. Tame them both, and set yourself free...; [a.] Rochester, NY

COPELAND, CONNIE
[pen.] Connie Copeland; [b.] September 1, 1961, Havre De Grace, MD; [p.] Charles and Katherine Shormann; [m.] Thomas L. Copeland Sr., December 16, 1985; [ch.] Nichole, Audrey, Thomas, Matthew, Jason; [ed.] Graduated from Mergenthaler Vocational Technical High School in Baltimore City Maryland; [occ.] Full time Mom; [memb.] The Christian Ministry, "The 700 Club"; [oth. writ.] "Lonely Places", from my own observation of man's striving to fill in the "gap" in his soul.; [pers.] I give the Lord Jesus Christ the honor and glory for His all encompassing influence in my life.; [a.] Shenandoah, VA

COPPENRATH, ROBERT A. M.
[pen.] Klein Pierke; [b.] December 28, 1928, Antwerp, Belgium; [m.] Deceased, December 21, 1954; [ch.] Two Daughters; [ed.] Obtained equivalent BBA and MBA degrees from the Higher States Institute for Commerce which later was to become part of what is now the University of Antwerp. He complemented his education with postgraduate studies in marketing at the University of Waterloo, Ontario, Canada.; [occ.] He is a past Chairman of the Belgian-American Chamber of Commerce in the United States, past Chairman of the Sales Executive and Marketing Club of Greater New York. He is a former trustee of the Aviation Hall of Fame of New Jersey. He is a past president of the Order van de Prince in Manhattan New York.; [memb.] A former senior member of the Conference Board, a former member of the President's Council of the International Center of Photography and a former trustee of the Photographical Art and Science Foundation. A member of the board of Governors and an Ambassador of the National Parkinson Foundation in Miami, Florida.; [hon.] He is a Knight in the Belgian Order of the Crown, an Officer in the Orders of Leopold I and Leopold II, and a Commander in the Order of Leopold II. He retired with the rank of reserve Captain from the Belgian Army RASC. An honorary Counsellor of Foreign Trade of Belgium.; [oth. writ.] Spikes: Carlton Press NY 1990, The Leadership Labyrinth: Dorrance Publishing Co 1994 Pittsburg PA, The Leadership Luxation: Durance Publishing Co 1997 Pittsburgh PA; [pers.] Poems and articles published in athene. Without humanity a leader becomes a tyrant.; [a.] Sarasota, FL

CORBETT, LENORA M.
[b.] August 1, 1950, Caswell County; [p.] Deceased; [m.] Divorced; [ch.] Kenneth R. Johnson and Ralph N. Brown; [ed.] Caswell County High School, Alamance Community College, North Carolina A&T State University; [occ.] Instructor (Math), Alamance Community College, Graham, N.C.; [memb.] American Asso-

ciation of University Professors, Golden Key National Honor Society; [hon.] National Dean's List; [oth. writ.] Several poems published in other books.; [pers.] My Lord and Savior Jesus Christ's Father gave me this gift to share positive thoughts.; [a.] Reidsville, NC

CORIANO, HERIBERTO
[pen.] Eddie Coriano; [b.] January 6, 1971, Bronx, NY; [p.] Dominga and Feliberto Coriano; [ed.] 2 Years of College Santa Monica College; [occ.] Credit Investigator; [oth. writ.] Working on a "Fiction Book"; [pers.] I take a lot of pride in my work. Consequently, as an artist I understand it is based on interpretation. I hope you like it, if not it still has a place in my heart.; [a.] Toluca Lake, CA

COTTLE, GIFFORD F.
[pen.] Saint Giffo; [b.] January 15, 1931, Toledo, OH; [p.] Elizabeth (Filsinger), Gifford WW/Cottle; [ch.] 2 boys, 2 girls, 6 grandchildren; [ed.] Longfellow G.S. DeVilbiss H.S. Davis Business College, US Army Schools, Famous Artist Course, Drama Classes, Perspective and Welded Sculpture; [occ.] Retired Muralist and Graphic Design; [memb.] Korean Vets, Am. Legion, Dem. Senatorial Campaign Committee, Rho Rho Rho Alumni Urbote Advisor, American Motorcycle Association, Repertoire Theatrix Ltd. Stand-Up Comedy, Artists Guild; [hon.] West Indian Cricket Club WOHO Radio Talk Show Host, Rep Theatre (performance) (hon) Local Pacers, Lifetime Christmas Window Art; [oth. writ.] Political Commentary: Chr-Sci. Monitor, Articles and Poems: Toledo Blade, poem: Quinto Lingo Language Mag., short mysteries: Hon. Men. Alfred Hitchcock Mag. Self-bound books of Poetry, The NLP hardbound Anthology: Of Sunshine and Daydreams.; [pers.] Primitive Camping, Motorcycle Trailriding, Thoreau, Frost, Nature: I never second guess that which is impossible for any man to know. A Joyful Stoic, me. Current reading: Vonnegut, Dean Koontz, Steve and Tab King, poetic, real, these four. Still I am all over the board. Campfires are forever!; [a.] Toledo, OH

COTTON, FELICIA
[b.] March 15, 1980, Dallas; [p.] Jacqueline and Frank Cotton; [ed.] In the 11th grade at Duncanville High, Honors English III, Honors American History, GPA of '91; [memb.] In BPA (Business Professionals of America), Varsity Track Team, National Vocational Technical Honor's Society (N.V.T.H.S.); [hon.] Lettered twice in track, in the top 20% of the Junior Class, has a GPA of 3.5; [pers.] Trust is the key to love and peace of mind is the key to harmony. To all my black people and sisters stay strong.; [a.] Duncanville, TX

COUILLARD, ANDRE A.
[pen.] Andre' Albert; [b.] April 12, 1942, Gardner, MA; [p.] Louis and Noelia Couillard; [m.] Sheryl C. Couillard, July 26, 1975; [ch.] Erin-Beth, Jessica-Megan; [ed.] Holy Rosary, Notre-Dame prep, Univ of South Florida; [occ.] Eckerd Drugs Manager; [hon.] Blood donor, Holy name Society press, transfiguration Parish council pres, Dean's List, USF, Joel and Jerry Manager of the year 1993; [pers.] God is with us always we just have to stop and listen; [a.] Saint Petersburg, FL

COWAN, PAULA K.
[pen.] Paula K. Cowan; [b.] December 13, 1944, Bellefontaine, OH; [p.] Paul J. Shoemaker, Mary E. Shoemaker; [ed.] Encanto-Clarendon Grammar School West Phoenix High School, Lamson Business College Institute for Children's Literature; [occ.] Retired Accounting Clerk; [memb.] Copra - City of Phoenix Retirees Association, AARP, International Society of Poets Phoenix Art Museum; [hon.] Several City of Phoenix Employee Suggestion Awards; [oth. writ.] Over 200 poems, children's picture books, craft Articles; [pers.] I

become interested in poetry at age of 7 years old when I read my mother's book by Edgar Guest of poems. I recited the entire "Raven" by Edgar Allen Poe by memory as a freshman in high school.; [a.] Phoenix, AZ

CRANE, KELLI
[b.] November 29, 1959, Wheaton, IL; [ed.] MBA Univ. of Iowa; [occ.] Marketing Research; [pers.] Although I feel my business writing has a creative flair, this is my first published creative work; [a.] Rochester, NY

CRANE, LUCILLE R.
[pen.] Lu Crane; [b.] February 12, 1929, Eden Valley, MN; [p.] Mike Ruhland, Sophie Ruhland; [ed.] Sauk Centre High School Sauk Centre, MN; [a.] Davidson, NC

CRANEY, ANGELIQUE
[b.] June 27, 1949, NYC; [p.] Rose Stigliano and Thomas Craney; [ch.] Steven Justin Pasko, Sara Lindsey Pasko; [ed.] Douglass College, BA, Columbia University, MSW, Post graduate studies in Psychoanalysis; [occ.] Psychotherapist; [memb.] NASW, Gilda's Club, Roundabout Theatre Guild; [hon.] Dean's List - Douglass College, Honors graduate, Columbia University, 1st Place: D.A.R. Poetry Competition in seventh grade!; [oth. writ.] Dozens of hitherto unpublished poems and stories. Volumes of journals.; [pers.] One's reservoir of talent more often overflows from the working through of grief than from the blessings of contentment.; [a.] New York, NY

CRANFORD, RALPH LOCKE
[pen.] Ralph Locke; [b.] July 17, 1926, Burke Co., NC; [p.] George D. and Oaklona Shuffler Cranford; [m.] Charlotte Travis Cranford, March 29, 1947; [ch.] Walter, Charlene, Michael, and Lisa; [ed.] High School, two years Business College, and Creative Writing at (CVCC) Catawba Valley Comm. College; [occ.] Ad's Photographer for The Carolina Bargain Hunter, Dale Days Greeter for K-Mart also Volunteer Tutor at CVCC, Red Cross Canteen worker, Volunteer for Meals On Wheels - Seniors; [memb.] The Songwriters Club of America, Oklahoma Songwriters and Composers Assn., Chapel Records 100 Club, Top Records Songwriters Assn. and North Florida Christian Songwriters Assn. Also American Songwriters Organizations of Canada, Sponsored by Platinum Record. ISP Distinguished member, Member American Bible Society and Bible A Month Club, Member Lutheran Church; [hon.] Golden Poets three times, Silver Poets four times, Award of Merit many times, Best songwriter three times, K-Mart Associate of the year 1993-94, Community Volunteer Service Award, Member of City of Newton, NC's Planning Commission for 18 years.; [oth. writ.] Books I have written "Poems by Ralph #1", Poems by Ralph #2", "Poems by Ralph #3", "My Soul's Delight", "I Believe in Angels", "Covenant of the Truine God" I currently have 15, 3 ring-binders full of poems and lyrics to be critiqued and edited. Poems by Ralph #1, 2 and 3. These were taken from those binders.; [pers.] Work hard to help the less fortunate to have a better life, and you will have a happier one for yourself.; [a.] Newton, NC

CROUL, EDWARD H.
[pen.] Lawrence Laureate; [b.] January 30, 1927, Hartford, CN; [p.] Charles R. Croul, Gertrude G.; [m.] Nadine Bublitz, March 1, 1956; [ch.] Charles R. Croul III; [ed.] Caltech, U.S.C., Univ. of Lausanne, Univ. of Heidelberg, Selwen College Cambridge; [occ.] Retired; [memb.] B.V.I. Yacht Club, Alpha Rho Chi; [oth. writ.] Love, and other nonsense. Book of poems, several articles in travel and marine field.; [pers.] I believe in the axiom, "There is no evidence at all to support the view that life was meant to be taken seriously."; [a.] Newport Beach, CA

CRUSE, HEATHER
[b.] April 5, 1965, Bethesda, MD; [m.] Billy M. Cruse, August 24, 1995; [ch.] Joshua and Jessica; [ed.] North Chicago High; [occ.] Self Employed Child Care; [oth. writ.] Several poems and short stories in my collection.; [pers.] I believe that if we all take the time to understand children, their thoughts and feelings, they will grow to live happy and prosperous lives.; [a.] Newport News, VA

CRUZ, SHEILA MARIE GASTON
[b.] January 12, 1978; [p.] Jose J. Gaston, Elizabeth Cruz Gaston; [ed.] Freshman and Sophomore years at Alta Loma High School. Junior and Senior graduate from Eisenhower High School, California State University San Bernardino (present); [memb.] Drama Club, Track and Field, French Club, Mecha Club, MCJROTC; [hon.] Rialto Community award for brushing off graffiti, Principal's Honor Roll certificates, Perfect attendance awards, Outstanding Achievement awards; [oth. writ.] I have been recognized for my distinguished achievements featured in the 30th Annual Edition of "Who's Who Among American High School Students" 1995-1996.; [pers.] I realize that being open-minded and open-hearted towards everyone and everything lets me feel more content with myself and this feeling I would like to share with the rest of the world.; [a.] Rialto, CA

CULPEPPER, PAMELA
[pen.] Pam Culpepper; [b.] January 2, 1956, Rome, GA; [p.] Glover Tucker, Vivian Tucker; [m.] John E. Culpepper, July 9, 1983; [ch.] John Allen Culpepper, Jeremy Culpepper; [ed.] Coosa High, Coosa Valley Technical School, Floyd Jr. College, Shorter College; [occ.] Second Grade Teacher Garden Lakes Elementary School Rome, GA; [hon.] Garden Lakes Teacher of the Year for 1991, Dean's List, Delta Kappa Gamma 1984-1985; [pers.] I try to show humor in common-life situations or stressful times; [a.] Rome, GA

CUNEO SR., MICHAEL A.
[pen.] Mike Cuneo; [b.] December 31, 1940, Golden Meadow, LA; [p.] John (Deceased) and Stella Cuneo; [m.] Carolyn Dufrene Cuneo, August 6, 1960; [ch.] Gwendolyn, Jacqueline, Michael Jr; [ed.] Golden Meadow High School, Nicholls State University; [occ.] Advertising, Marketing; [memb.] American Society of Composers, Authors and Publishers. Our Lady of the Rosary Catholic Church Choir; [hon.] Music Scholarship Nicholls State University; [oth. writ.] Unpublished novel - "Cajun Paradise Lost". Various musical compositions both published and unpublished.; [pers.] To enjoy both the reading and creative writing in the wonderful world of literature and music.; [a.] Larose, LA

CURTIS, BETTY W.
[b.] July 18, 1930, Rome, NY; [p.] Alvah and Gladys Williamson; [m.] Richard (Deceased), August 2, 1953; [ch.] Darrell, Kathleen, Scott; [ed.] High School grad.; [occ.] Retired; [memb.] Grange; [pers.] Devoted my life to the mentally retarded and my family. I write for personal satisfaction.; [a.] Verona, NY

CURTIS, IRENE
[b.] October 7, 1918, Middleton, MI; [p.] Orville and Linnie Miller; [m.] Paul Curtis, March 30, 1939; [ch.] Kent Donald and Christine; [ed.] High School; [occ.] Housewife; [memb.] Member of United Methodist Church; [oth. writ.] Gospel Songs; [a.] Middleton, MI

D'AGOSTINO, SABRINA
[p.] Frances and Anthony D'Agostino; [ed.] Currently attending Monmouth University as a sophomore and social work major; [memb.] A sister of Delta Phi Epsilon; [pers.] I truly feel that it is because of my wonderful family and fun loving friends that I am lucky enough to

write whatever comes straight from my heart; [a.] Wanaque, NJ

D'AMBRUOSO, EDWARD
[pen.] Edward D'Ambruoso; [b.] August 18, 1951, Derby, CT; [p.] Samuel and Gemma D'Ambruoso; [ed.] B.S. Central Connecticut State College, New Brittany Connecticut; [occ.] Sales, Title Insurance; [oth. writ.] I've written several other poems years ago, that I have not published, theme is similar.; [pers.] There's something about autumn that gets the creative juices flowing. My inspiration to write comes from my brother Robert, who is a superb poet. Hope to keep writing.; [a.] Los Angeles, CA

DAHM, CYNTHIA
[pen.] Cynthia Anne Dahm; [b.] April 6, 1954, Long Beach, CA; [p.] George and Josephine Dahm; [ch.] Bronwyn Patrick, Ryan Pinette; [ed.] St. Maria Goretti Elementary, Lakewood High; [occ.] Waitress; [oth. writ.] "The Final Choice", non-fiction hardbound book published in 1995 by "The Christopher Publishing House", Hanover, Mass: (Theme), Christian/New Age. Also autobiography "The Silver Light", written in 1989, yet unpublished, contains 40 plus poems, including "Connie".; [pers.] Object: Simple presentation with a profound message. Goal: Write to benefit mankind, with God's glory in mind, seeking foremost to please Him.; [a.] Bend, OR

DAO, VICTOR C.
[b.] 20th Century, Vietnam; [ed.] University of Saigon. University of Maryland. Dean's List; [occ.] ESOL, Language Teacher-Diplomatic Language Services, Inc.; [oth. writ.] Pedagogical Songs, Vietnamese in Verses, English, French, Spanish, German, Russian, Chinese, Japanese, Sino-Vietnamese in Verses.; [a.] Takoma Park, MD

DARBY, MICHAEL N.
[pen.] Mike; [b.] September 11, 1935, Jamaica, WI; [p.] Estellen Brooks and Lenious Darby; [ch.] Six; [ed.] Elementary; [occ.] Painting Artist and Porter

DARRELL, LAWRENCE
[b.] February 24, 1928, New York City; [p.] An Abandoned Infant; [m.] Eleanor (Lang) Darrell, December 27, 1981; [ed.] High School, College Experienced - Limited; [occ.] Retired/Astrologer; [memb.] Presbyterian Church; [oth. writ.] Poems unpublished i.e.: "Humboldt Paths," "Passing of a Leader," "You Who See Now," "Another Turn, You See," "The Little Chinese Boy," "Comparison," "Silence," "Leonines, Here and There," "Love - Mundane and Universal," etc. many of the above, written in the 1950s.; [pers.] Favorite writers: Shakespeare, John Keats, Emily Dickinson, Walt Whitman, and Robert Frost. The joy is in the writing of poetry and sharing same with others.

DARROCH, LEZLIE
[b.] May 27, 1958, Hartford, CT; [p.] Arthur Ruggico, Virginia Ruggico; [ed.] BS Albertus Magnus College New Haven, Ct, MS Southern Conn State University, New Haven, CT; [occ.] Realtor; [memb.] American Cancer Society, National Association of Realtors; [hon.] Ranked in the top 3 in Conn for Real Estate Sales at Century 21 for the past 6 years; [oth. writ.] I am working on a book on the necessities in growing up to develop a healthy adulthood.; [pers.] Keep your face to the sun, and you will never see the shadows.; [a.] Brookfield, CT

DASH, GEORGE MELANCTON
[b.] Guyana, South America; [m.] B.A. (Hons.) Spanish, Latin, American and Caribbean Studies; [oth. writ.] Working at present on a fantasy fiction trilogy which incorporates several features of the genre, Quest, Magic,

Sorcery Struggle Between God and Evil, etc.; [pers.] I would like to thank my wife Amena. Our frequent discussions on philosophy, religion and practically everything are the source of inspiration for much of my work. She is my beautiful muse.; [a.] Toronto, Ontario, Canada

DAVENPORT, TERRY B.
[b.] January 6, 1957, Staunton, VA; [p.] Clarence and Nellie Bowling; [m.] S. Alan Davenport, March 27, 1976; [ch.] Alice and Adam Davenport; [ed.] Riverheads High; [occ.] Housewife; [memb.] Lutheran Redeemer Church; [hon.] None until now, my writings are mostly kept private for fear of failure.; [oth. writ.] Poems and short stories never before viewed.; [pers.] I write from the heart, I am greatly influenced by personal experiences and the sadness that people can inflict on innocent children.; [a.] Mount Sidney, VA

DAVID, GOLDA
[pen.] Golda David; [b.] September 25, 1926, Windsor, Ontario, Canada; [p.] Joseph and Nellie Kaplan; [m.] William J. David, December 28, 1969; [ed.] Studied at UCLA; [occ.] Screenwriter; [memb.] Writers Guild of America West; [hon.] My film: "It Nearly Wasn't Christmas" starring Charles Durning will be on television December 14, 1996 - 3:00 pm channel 9 in Los Angeles, Calif.; [oth. writ.] "It Nearly Wasn't Christmas" (screenplay: "It Nearly Wasn't Christmas"), (Article - Fate magazine - ("Bubi Warned Me" - January 1979); [pers.] I strive to write about humanity and harmony.; [a.] Los Angeles, CA

DAVIDSON, MARGIE
[pen.] Margie Davidson; [b.] Washington; [m.] Deceased; [ed.] B.A. (Magna Cum Laude) Chapman University, Orange, CA; [occ.] Poet (retired, past editor of two literary journals) mother; [memb.] National League of American Penwomen, Paradigm Poets; [hon.] California Writers Jack London Awards, Writers Digest, poetry finalist 1993; [oth. writ.] Published poetry in several literary journal and anthologies, including Onthebus, In the West of Ireland, Coffee house Poetry Anthology, Rivertalk '96, Westword 3, Red Dance Floor and others.; [pers.] I have been inspired by the poetry of Dylan Thomas and Rilke. For me, writing poetry is a struggle for expression, and a sane place in an otherwise insane world.; [a.] Apple Valley, CA

DAVIGNON, H. JANE
[pen.] Jayne Keeler; [b.] January 16, 1918, Canandaigua, NY; [ch.] One; [ed.] High School; [occ.] Retired; [a.] Dacula, GA

DAVIS, DONEL
[b.] November 3, 1947, California; [p.] Donel Davis and Virginia Jablonski; [m.] Linda Davis, June 30, 1981; [ch.] Four: Kelly, Davaed, Taiyo, Donel; [ed.] Arizona Western College; [occ.] Retired United States Marine Corps.; [memb.] U.S.M.C. Retired; [hon.] Phi Theta Kappa, Deans List, Student of the Year; [pers.] I never try to create poetry. Mankind and nature does that. I only attempt to set it to rhyme.; [a.] Yuma, AZ

DAVIS, ERICA R.
[pen.] Erica R. Davis/Too Short; [b.] December 5, 1982, Detroit, MI; [p.] Willie and Denise Davis; [ed.] Luckett Christian Academy, Avery Elementary, Pepper Elementary, Our Lady of LaSalette; [occ.] Student; [memb.] Michigan Metro Girl Scout, Student Council President, Guard on the LaSalette Broncos Varsity Girls Basketball Team; [hon.] Honor roll many times. Won 1st place in the Cobo Hall Science Fair. Won 1st place in the LaSalette Science Fair.; [oth. writ.] I write many poems. An essay of mine was sent to Lansing for the semi-finals (results haven't been announced yet).;

[pers.] I write poems because this way I may allow my feelings to come out freely and openly.; [a.] Oak Park, MI

DAVIS, LARRY
[b.] July 19, 1964, Boston, MA; [ed.] University of Northern Colorado St. Thomas University; [oth. writ.] Writing screenplays!; [pers.] If you do not ask questions, you will not get answers. "The Night" is dedicated to a special Friend, Valentina.; [a.] Plantation, FL

DAVIS JR., RALPH SCOTT
[pen.] Ralph Scott Davis; [b.] January 21, 1920, Portland, OR; [p.] Ralph and Marcia Davis; [m.] Betty Jane Davis, February 17, 1945; [ch.] Ralph Scott Davis III and Bryan Lee Davis; [ed.] Umatilla and Jefferson High Schools and Oregon State University; [occ.] Retired, Prof. Emeritus of Exercise Science of Sports Studies P.S.U., 2 yrs. Sheridan H.S., 2 yrs. Newberg H.S., 1 yrs. Jefferson H.S., 36 yrs. Portland State University; [memb.] National Football Foundation and Hall of Fame Lifetime: State of Oregon Sports Hall of Fame Lifetime: U.S. National Korfball Federation Phi Delta Theta Fraternity; [hon.] Race Director of the Decade, Badge of Honor from The International Korfball Federation, The Netherlands 1984 Olympic Selection Committee Member XXIII Olympiad, Los Angels, CA. Also Deputy Manager of Athletics Officials 1984 Olympic Games. Los Angels, CA.; [oth. writ.] "Chute-wise Cross Country" Scholastic Coach Magazine, "Here's How" on the organizing of a Road Checklist for Runners World Magazine., Class Syllabus. Author of technique portion of Health and Fitness for Life Text. For Portland State University H and P.E. Dept., "Simplified Multiple Pass Patterns" Scholastic Coach Magazine, "Equipment Checklist" Scholastic Coach Magazine, Detailed Fencing Lesson Plans for fencing teachers Oaphered Convention, Authored a simplified method of teaching the points of sail., Swimming Instructor's Shortland". For Scholastic Coach Magazine, "Surf Safety" a pamphlet for the community of Gearhart, Oregon, "The Korfball Connection" for Oaphered publication for teachers, "Korfball in the U.S.A." for Dutch Sports Magazine, and the International Korfball Federation Newsletter., "Our Mother", "An Observation", "Old Clock Talk", A feathered warning...renamed: "The Gull's Warning", "Tide's Moods", "It was a lemon of a day"; [pers.] I have been greatly encouraged by my parents, my wife, children and friends. Also my Poet Uncle W.H.L. Davis a noted Oregon Poet. My high school teach and poet Lawrence Pratt, and poet Jim Barker of Seaside, Or. As a former head coach and national coach, the adage is true, the more one gives the more one reaps.; [a.] Portland, OR

DAVIS, VIRGIL H.
[b.] August 3, 1912, Timewell, IL; [p.] William F. and Ida M. Davis; [m.] Naomi M. Jones, September 7, 1938; [ch.] Nine; [ed.] 8 years, 3 years music; [occ.] Retired Rail Road Brakeman; [hon.] Won singing in several contests; [oth. writ.] Wrote 35 songs and have some recorded.; [pers.] Father was a school teacher and there was music in family for several generations - started singing on stage at 12 years of age.; [a.] Timewell, IL

DAY, DAVID M.
[b.] May 25, 1956, Bel Air, MD; [p.] Ray V. and Wynnogene Day; [m.] Kathleen, December 7, 1985; [ch.] Timothy, Jocelyn, Robert; [ed.] Bel Air High School, Georgia Southern University; [occ.] SaleNYLIFE Securities, New York Life; [memb.] NALU Assoc.; [hon.] 1996 - Outstanding Young Americans, 1994 - Product Leader - Savannah Office, 1988 - Executive Council Member; [oth. writ.] Personal use.; [pers.] Most of my writing is for personal entertainment. "Waves of life" was written in memory of my father

whom we all loved, and miss very much.; [a.] Savannah, GA

DE ANDA, MARIA MICHELLE
[b.] November 5, Mexican-American; [p.] Linda S. DeAnda and Paul I. Sarkis; [m.] Paul Sarkis; [ch.] Maria Michelle DeAnda; [ed.] Muncey Elementary School 1991, Stockhard Coffee School 1994, Somerset Middle School 1996, Modesto California; [memb.] Dean's list Honor Roll, Honor orchestra of Modesto Music Modesto Parks and recreation Dept. junior Park leader during summer season.; [hon.] Participant 1994-1995 and 1996 of regional C.M.A. Festival California Music Association.; [oth. writ.] I am greatly influenced by William Blake and Micheal Ende; [pers.] Don't take life for a ride but if it's gonna be a roller coaster you handle the controls and work them only for yourselves.; [a.] Modesto, CA

DE ROCHE, WILLIAM E.
[pen.] Bill De Roche; [b.] October 1, 1939, Duluth, MN; [p.] Vernon and Eileen De Roche; [m.] Divorced; [ed.] 2 yrs College; [occ.] Retired; [memb.] Lake Superior Museum of Transportation, Lake Superior and Mississippi Railroad; [oth. writ.] Poems published in local papers.; [pers.] To be, to let be, to help be, all that we can be.; [a.] Knife River, MN

DEADWYLER, KAREN A.
[pen.] Charmella (Charm) or (Mella); [b.] October 30, 1967, Cleveland, OH; [p.] Charlsey Wilson and Luther Wilson Sr.; [m.] Mr. Jonathan L. Deadwyler, September 25, 1995; [ch.] Amanda and Jamual; [ed.] Ledgemont High School and Ashtabula County Joint Vocational School (1986); [pers.] Poetry has been the window to my mind since 7th grade. Together with my husband this poem was created from the overflowing love we've shared for the past 10 yrs.; [a.] Cleveland, OH

DECK, RUSS E.
[pen.] Adorian; [b.] October 27, 1949, Fort Worth, TX; [p.] Wanda and Barton Deck; [m.] Marylou, December 13, 1992; [ch.] Adorian, Adrian, Shannon and Russell; [ed.] Reseda High School, CA. Valley College, College of the Desert (Palm Desert); [occ.] Realtor-Lay Minister with Unity and Lie Minister (Non Denom); [hon.] President Board of Trustees Unity Church (of Palm Springs) Mayoral Representative and City Councils choice as Board Member P.S.T.U. Government and Public Access Channel. Many Realtor awards, top agent '96 Prudential Calif reality, Best Daddy award (by my family); [oth. writ.] Producer/Director-Writer of Enlightened weekly radio show (1/2 hr) "The Lighter Side" 3 yrs KESQ-ABC (92-95) Many writings dealing with the higher existance of the self! "Always Think The Higher And Best Thoughts Possible"; [pers.] "You are what you think, therefore always think the highest and best thoughts possible!"; [a.] Arnold, CA

DEES, DENA
[b.] July 19, 1972, Upland, CA; [p.] Lora Pruden and Daniel Dees; [ed.] Upland High School, Chaffey College; [occ.] Radiologic Technologist; [memb.] Inland District California Society of Radiologic Technologists; [hon.] Certificate of Achievement for program completion, Honor Roll; [oth. writ.] A Question of Faith is the first poem I have ever submitted.; [pers.] The poems I write always reflect how I am feeling at that time. So, I believe that writing can be a form of therapy - it sets your soul at ease and allows you to breathe.; [a.] Corona, CA

DEHA, LOUIS ROI
[pen.] Lord; [b.] August 25, 1966, Benin, W. Africa; [p.] Felix Deha, Francois Christine; [m.] Carolyn P. D. Deha, November 12, 1996; [ed.] St. Rita High School, Cotonou Benin - University "National" of Benin (UNB)

Degree in Environmental Science.; [occ.] Math and French Home Teacher; [memb.] Pre-paid legal service; [hon.] Theatre actor award; [oth. writ.] "Mr The Deputy" Co-writing French playhouse. Articles for "Voix d'Emmaus" Catholic Students newspaper. Benin (West Africa).; [pers.] I strive to reflect the goodwill of mankind in my writing.; [a.] Silver Spring, MD

DEJARNETTE, PATTY STILES
[b.] October 15, 1950, Kentucky; [p.] Gale and Ruth Stiles; [ch.] Ashley, Jason, Linze; [ed.] A.S. in Nursing Western Kentucky University; [occ.] Registered Nurse; [hon.] Who's Who in Am. Nursing; [oth. writ.] Currently in process of writing a biographical novel; [pers.] I write so others may learn from my life experiences.; [a.] Bowling Green, KY

DEL BEATO, HELEN
[pen.] Helen DelBeato; [b.] October 19, 1919, Chelsea, MA; [p.] Louis and Lucy (Cairo) DelBeato; [m.] Divorced, 1947; [ch.] Cathy Helen Daugherty; [ed.] St. Bernard's High School 1936, Stevens Bus. College, Assoc. Degree in Accounting 1963, Career Corporate Comptroller 1985, (both schools in Fitchburg, Mass.) (family moved to Fitchbury, Mass. 1920); [occ.] Voluntary Reading Teacher the past 35 years, Inner City Schools and schools in the vicinity; [oth. writ.] In a Trunk, much like Emily D. did with hers. Now that I am 77 - I would like to at least have one poem published. The reason I sent in - Abandoned - is because I wrote the poem in just 5 minute befores before as the leaving for the office - on a fall day at Sam as the leaves fell - and clung on the roots of bushes outside my window! At that time I was abandoned!; [pers.] I love poetry, I have breathed, written and recited, it. I survived because of it. I agree whole heartedly with The Russian poet Brodsky. He said: "He would have inoculated people with poetry if he could."; [a.] Rocky Hill, CT

DELVA, FRANTZ
[pen.] "The Poet"; [b.] April 2, 1979, Port-au-Prince, Haiti; [p.] Marie Eveillard, Taylor Gay; [ed.] I am a Senior at Midwood, H.S.; [memb.] I am currently in an Ambulance Volunteer Corp. I am about to start playing basketball for some leagues.; [oth. writ.] I have many writings old and new. Writing is my best way of expressing myself. None of my writings published, because I didn't get to know about these opportunities.; [pers.] I'm an ambidextrous poet who sees life through many view points. I feel to get your ideas through, you must express yourself through the talents which God gave you. Statement: "A talent is born not made!"; [a.] Brooklyn, NY

DEMAREE, KATI
[b.] January 24, 1981, Indianapolis, IN; [p.] David and Joyce Demaree; [ed.] Beech Grove High School; [occ.] Student, Beech Grove High School 10th grade; [memb.] Girl Scouts of America, Student Counselor Jameson Camp Inc., First Christian Church of Beech Grove; [hon.] Jr. Miss to benefit Children with AIDS; [pers.] I really enjoy writing and I hope my writing can inspire other teenagers to write!; [a.] Beech Grove, IN

DEMERS, MARK
[pen.] Mark DeMers; [b.] May 21, 1956, Columbus; [p.] Albert and Betty Jo DeMers; [ch.] Andrew and Adam DeMers; [ed.] High School; [occ.] Sales; [oth. writ.] Moving on "Mom"; [pers.] This poem was written for my father when we found out he had cancer. He died of a heart attack before he could read it. We put the original in with him.; [a.] Columbus, OH

DEMIDOVA, ALINA
[b.] May 21, 1979, Usoley-Sibirskoe, Russia; [p.] Valentina and Victor Demidova; [ed.] I finished High School in Russia and now I'm senior in the USA's High

School; [hon.] I have silver medal for special success in studying, Testimonial List for poems and Testimonial List for Drawing.; [oth. writ.] Some poems were published in newspaper for teenagers in Russia and I was in TV program for my love stories, also one of my stories was in theatre.; [pers.] I have been writing since I was 7 years old. But just since last year I write poems in English.; [a.] Antlers, OK

DENTON, MICHAEL
[b.] July 24, 1984, Richmond, VA; [p.] Barbara and Poke Denton; [ed.] Currently in 7th grade; [occ.] Providence Middle School; [memb.] Boy Scouts, Chorus; [hon.] Young Author's Award, Boy Scout Awards, Fine Arts Festival; [a.] Richmond, VA

DERKEVICS, JASON
[b.] January 10, 1980, Port Jefferson, NY; [p.] Peter and Penny; [ed.] Rocky Point High School; [pers.] The pen is indeed mightier than the sword, yet the mind is our strongest tool. Open your mind and look beyond the surface. For the coal of today, may be the diamonds of tomorrow.; [a.] Sound Beach, NY

DESOMMA, MARC
[pen.] Douglas Montgomery; [b.] March 17, 1975, Hackensack, NJ; [p.] James DeSomma, Janet DeSomma; [ed.] St. Joseph Regional High School; [occ.] Arrow Group Ind. Store Service Representative; [pers.] My writings reflect: Nature, self, and todays society. I am influenced by all types of music, with a considerable influence from the "The Doors" music and Jim Morrison.; [a.] Fair Lawn, NJ

DESPOT, DANIEL DAVID
[pen.] Daniel D. Despot; [b.] April 5, 1985, Uniontown, PA; [p.] David Despot and Debra Hertzog-Despot; [ed.] Park Forest Middle School; [occ.] Student; [memb.] Boy Scouts of America, 4-H Flying Hooves Horse and Pony Club; [hon.] D.A.R.E. Award, 1st place 4-H Story, Student of the Month, 3rd place Karate tournament; [pers.] I strive to reflect the real world in my writing. I look at my goals as if they were a ladder, taking one step at a time until I reach the top.; [a.] State College, PA

DEVON, SHAMMI
[pen.] Shammie Devon; [b.] Bombay, India; [ed.] Study of Medicine and Cinema - Director of Documentary Films, Playwright short story writer, poet; [occ.] Director - Writer for Documentary Films; [oth. writ.] Some screenplays, short stories, and other poems.; [pers.] In my poems I usually express my feelings as a romanticist about love, passion, despair and longing. I am inspired by many English and French poets like Byron, Rimbaud, Baudelaire and Rilke.; [a.] Las Vegas, NV

DIAI, LAWRENCE
[pen.] D. Law; [b.] August 22, 1954; [p.] Sylvester Diai (Dead), Mom Getrude Diai; [ed.] College Degree Alabama Agric. and Mech. University, Normal, AL 35762; [occ.] Factory Worker; [hon.] Graduate with honors (Alabama A&M University) Major: Political Science, Minor: Criminal Justice.; [oth. writ.] Never been published but spend most of my time writing poetry or lyrics.; [pers.] Perseverance in pursuit of a dream or an objective, which I believe is predestined and will come true only if you work intently towards it. I love nature.; [a.] Huntsville, AL

DICKENSON-GIBSON, FREDERICK ANTHONY
[pen.] Fred; [b.] May 4, 1984, Brooklyn, NY; [p.] Alfred and Fredrica; [ed.] 7th grade Bay Academy; [memb.] St. John Recreation Center Eastern Athletic Junior Club; [hon.] Honors from Henry Street School (Pre K), honors from (St. Charles Borromeo) K-4th grade. 2nd place in the (Y) football finals. Track and

field 2nd and 3rd place 100 yd. - honors from Knick's Camp; [pers.] Always do your best give 100 and 10 percent.; [a.] Brooklyn, NY

DICKINSON, SHAWN
[pen.] Boo Dickinson; [b.] March 20, 1959, Taunton, MA; [p.] Henrietta McGuire and Ferdinand Dickinson; [m.] Divorced; [ch.] Angela Patricia, Stephanie Marie; [ed.] Life imprisonment; [oth. writ.] Many other poems, several short stories in care of my daughters; [pers.] The safekeeping of a gifted pen is in writing.; [a.] Concord, NH

DIETERICH, LILLIAN FIELD
[b.] December 31, 1909, Wagoner, OK; [p.] Frank and Lillian Field; [m.] Neil Blaine Dieterich (Deceased), April 25, 1936; [ch.] Mary, Neil, Martha, Deborah; [ed.] Omaha Central H.S., Univ Wis '31 B.A.; [occ.] Retired Bookkeeper Presby. Bookstore, Omaha: Physicians Plus Clinic McFarland, WI; [memb.] McFarland Lutheran Church, Tri Delta P.E.O. Former Elder, Presby. Church, Omaha; [hon.] College thesis received honors, signed by Wisconsin Poet Laureate, some poems published in Village Paper, and one magazine. And church bulletins. Graduated from Univ. of Wisconsin 1931 with B.A. degree Cum Laude; [oth. writ.] Thesis: Poetical Translations of Poems of Emile Verhaeren (Flemish) received honors, signed by William Ellery Leonard, Poet Laureate of Wisconsin, many private, Christmas card poem, religious.; [pers.] My poems deal with nature, family, love, religion faith, nation. One longer poem "Birth of a Nation" I wrote for the bi centennial but didn't get it in on time.; [a.] McFarland, WI

DIETZ, IRENE ANDRIGHETTI
[b.] April 17, 1942, Brooklyn, NY; [p.] Elvira and Giordano Andrighetti; [ch.] James Jordan, Karen Laurie, Grandchild, Erik James; [occ.] Licensed School Secretary (NYC Board of Education); [memb.] United Federation of Teachers, Regina Pacis R.C. Church, Famous Poets Society; [oth. writ.] "Our Wedding Toast", "Ode to a Grandson" children's book: "Mommy, I Want a Pet"; [pers.] I strive to write heartfelt and inspirational poetry and humorous and educational children's stories. Several poems published in local newspapers.; [a.] NY

DOLHANCYK, DIANA
There's a woman in m - Poem in Tracker

DOOLEY, CRISTIN LEE
[pen.] Cristin Dooley; [b.] July 4, 1974, Dover, NH; [p.] Col. Tom and Diane Dooley; [ed.] Junior at Southern Illinois State University, Mass Communication major TV/radio, double minor in Journalism; [occ.] Bartender; [pers.] Writing comes from the soul. The words written come from the glorious sights surrounding every day life allowing the imagery seen in a single moment to live on for the rest of our lives.; [a.] Illinois City, IL

DORR, SANDRA CRAVER
[pen.] Sandra Dorr; [b.] December 9, 1968, Winston-Salem, NC; [p.] Glenn W. Craver and Virginia H. Craver; [m.] Benjamin P. Dorr, May 30, 1992; [ch.] Jessica Lorraine; [ed.] Parkland High School, Western Carolina University; [occ.] Registered Nurse; [memb.] Unity Moravian Church, American Nurses Association; [pers.] This poem was written in honor of my loving husband.; [a.] Lewisville, NC

DOVO, LAUREN
[b.] May 24, 1987, New York, NY; [p.] Jean Dovo, Bert Dovo; [ed.] Hurlbutt Elementary School and Weston Middle School Grade 4; [occ.] Student; [memb.] Girl Scouts, Troop #429; [hon.] TAG (Talented and Gifted Program), Word Master Awards; [pers.] Reading has inspired me to write.; [a.] Weston, CT

DOWNES, CHARLES H.
[b.] May 14, 1966, New Jersey; [m.] Fay Downes, June 30, 1989; [ch.] Steven, Kenneth, Joyce Ann; [occ.] Heavy Equipment Operator; [memb.] Teamsters Union; [pers.] I would like to thank my Grandmother Sarah Goddard and my Grandfather John Goddard for raising me, and helping me to be the man I am today; [a.] Larksville, PA

DRAGONA, DANIELLE
[b.] December 13, 1973, Jersey City, NJ; [p.] Michele and Joseph Dragona; [ed.] Immaculate Conception Grammar School, Secaucus High School, William Paterson College; [occ.] Student; [hon.] Dean's List in college, High honor roll in High School, English Award, Who's Who in American Students, All American Scholar, First place in writing contest for Veterans of Foreign Wars Club, Foreign Language Honor Society, National Honor Society, Graduated Sixth in High School Class of 150; [oth. writ.] Several poems published in college literary magazine.; [a.] Secaucus, NJ

DRAIN, EFFIE JANE
[b.] March 22, 1926; [p.] Adan and Irene Yoeckel; [m.] Bruce H. Drain, November 30, 1947; [ch.] 2; [ed.] 12 yrs; [occ.] Retired; [memb.] First Lutheran Church, Order of Eastern Star, Prophet Hills Country Club; [oth. writ.] Birthday Wishes, Anniversary Wishes, Get Well, Sympathy, Prayers, Poems to God; [pers.] Reflections on God's creativity and His goodness to mankind.; [a.] Prophetstown, IL

DREADIN, RUSSEL MARK
[pen.] Marcos; [b.] August 9, 1957, Neuilly-Sur-Seine, France; [p.] Ollie and Frances Dreadin; [ed.] Milton High School, Diploma Naval Reserve Training - 2 years Pensacola Junior College - 2 years, Auburn University Bachelors Degree of Electrical Engineering; [occ.] Technical Services Engineer at Gulf Power, a Southern Company Pensacola, Florida; [memb.] Alpha Chapter Fraternity of the Tau Beta Pi Engineering Honorary, Institute of Electrical and Electronics Engineers, Pensacola Seville Sertoma, Leukemia Society of America, March of Dimes, Red Cross, Auburn Alumni, Toastmasters, Pensacola Runners Association, Pensacola Sports Association, Pensacola's Fiesta of Five Flags Forces, and Artel.; [hon.] Recently, within last 3 years, Florida Council of the Institute of Electrical and Electronics Engineers - Outstanding Service Award, Pensacola Seville Sertoma-Sertoman of the Year; [oth. writ.] 1st Literary Writing, all other writings were technical in nature associated with my electrical engineering profession.; [a.] Pensacola, FL

DRINNON, JANIS BOLTON
[b.] July 28, 1922, Pineville, KY; [p.] Clyde Herman and Violet Ethiele Hendrickson Bolton; [m.] Kenneth C. Drinnon, June 13, 1948, First Baptist Church, Middlesboro, KY; [ch.] Dena Drinnon Foulk, M. David E. Foulk, grandchildren Bethany Erah Foulk, Jonathan David Foulk, Julia Elizabeth Foulk; [ed.] Middlesboro, KY High School, journalism classes at Lincoln Memorial University, Harrogate, TN, 1947-1948, commercial art certificate from Art Instruction school, 1968, correspondence courses with Newspaper Institute of America, drama instruction and singing lessons with private teachers.; [occ.] Homemaker; [memb.] New Hopewell Baptist Church, Knoxville, TN distinguished member of International Society of poets.; [hon.] Editors Choice Awards by The National Library of poetry for five poems "When our Purpose Here is Done" published in the Dark Side of The Moon in 1994, "Blessings" published in the Best Poems of 1995, "My daily Best" published in Windows Of The Soul in 1995, "Going Home" published in the Best Poems of 1996, and "On Call" published in Through the Hourglass in

1996. Nominated for poet of the year for 1995 and 1996 by The International Society of Poets. Selected for the Silver 25th Edition of Marquis Who's Who in the South and Southwest.; [oth. writ.] While attending college, wrote articles for local newspapers. Recently had poems published in anthologies.; [pers.] I have always enjoyed the finer things of life and nature, especially those that are spiritually uplifting and bring beauty to the soul. My family has always come first in my life. I have never been much for organizations, preferring to be a doer rather than a participant.; [a.] Knoxville, TN

DUARTE, PATRICIA
[b.] February 9, 1955, Acushnet, MA; [p.] Dorothy Duarte and Frank Duarte; [ch.] Nacean Aaron, Dennicia Lynette; [ed.] New Bedford High, Newbury College, Fisher College; [occ.] St. Luke's Hospital, New Bedford, MA; [hon.] Dean's List; [oth. writ.] No Good-Bye, We Remember; [a.] New Bedford, MA

DUCE, MYRNA R.
[b.] November 27, 1934, Union, UT; [p.] Cliff and Verda Nowlan; [m.] Wallace K. Duce (Deceased), December 18, 1953; [ch.] Thomas, Paul, Nolan, Becky; [ed.] Jordan High School, Brigham Young University, Peninsula College; [occ.] Retired; [oth. writ.] Poems and articles published in local papers and magazines.; [pers.] I started writing professionally four years ago. I strive to include the nature of life in my writing.; [a.] Port Angeles, WA

DUMFORD, C. ANDREW
[b.] August 19, 1924, Wilmington, OH; [p.] Frank Carroll Dumford, Pearl Marie Young; [ch.] Former Stepson, Norman (Jake) Miguel; [ed.] Many schools - grad H.S. schools dealing with occupation at that time in my life; [occ.] Real Estate Appraiser; [memb.] Greene Country Regional Airport Authority - Past President "Grace Bible Church"; [hon.] Greene County Commissioners named a road in Greene County Xenia Ohio, in my honor for Airport Authority work in the building of Greene County Airport; [pers.] I was in the United States Marine Corps during World War II - South and North Pacific Ocean - received a "Dear John" letter from my girl - resulted in "Loneliness"; [a.] Xenia, OH

DUNCAN, ANN DUDLEY
[b.] February 11, 1941, Manchester, Eng.; [p.] Wilfred and Ethel (Wright) Dudley; [m.] Ian John Duncan, November 22, 1958; [ch.] Seven - John, Malcolm, Keith, Sue, Rob, Heather, Barbara and (19 grand children); [ed.] Business College Secretarial; [occ.] Disabled 'Manic Depression' and Arthritis (gives me time to write); [memb.] Proud to be a member and supporter of 'world wildlife fund Canada'; [hon.] I am 'Honoured' to present 'my' church ministers with my work an behalf of 'Christ Church' congregational members here in Bobcaygeon; [oth. writ.] (On computer) - 'Many' dedications in poetry. I also frame much of my work for weddings, anniversaries, birthdays etc. recently wrote/framed poems for church minister on retiring and one to welcome new minister. Wrote poem for local restaurant to welcome patrons. (Previously published in local newspaper, former town of residence.); [pers.] I like to write in simple language, for all to read. Presently working on a book of fairy tales in rhyme for children.; [a.] Bobcaygeon, Ontario, Canada

DUNCAN, BARBARA
[b.] March 21, 1957, Aston, England; [p.] Joel Strachan, Ada Strachan; [m.] Mark Duncan, December 15, 1984; [ch.] Mark, Matthew; [ed.] PPI Health Career School, Co Allen School for Physicians Aides, NY Matt Medical Aide Training School, IN NY York College, NY Benjamin N Cardozo High School, NY Manor Dark Secondary girls School, England; [occ.] Nursing Assistant/Home Health Aide; [memb.] American Heart As-

sociation, Salem Baptist Church, American Red Cross; [hon.] American Red Cross; [pers.] This poem is for Melissa in her memory, Melissa who died July 3rd 1996 in Maryland so far away but still in our heart.; [a.] Colorado Springs, CO

DUNN, VALERIE
[b.] August 8, 1972, New Rochelle, NY; [p.] Ruth Dunn, Lionel Dunn; [ed.] B.S. Human Development and Family Studies at College of Human Ecology, Cornell University; [occ.] N/A - currently I am Medically Disabled; [memb.] Lupus Foundation of America, Inc., Systemic Lupus Erythmatosus, Inc.; [oth. writ.] Numerous narratives and poems that remain unpublished to this date.; [pers.] Poetry and creative writing are my spiritual outlet. Now, more than ever due to my debilitating chronic illness.; [a.] Mount Vernon, NY

DUPLANTIS, MELVA
[b.] Burgaw, NC; [p.] Martha Murray and Jesse Jordan; [m.] Lewellyn Duplantis, July 17, 1949 (Deceased); [ch.] 1 Girl, 5 Boys, 16 Grandchildren; [ed.] R.N.; [occ.] Retired; [memb.] Member - First Baptist Church; [hon.] Six Children sixteen Grandchildren; [oth. writ.] "Memories" published in "The Colors Of Thought" in the Nat. Library of poetry; [pers.] This poem was written in loving memory of daughter Gwen "Went Home" age 31 and Grandson Joey "Went Home" age 21; [a.] Houma, LA

DVORAK, PETER
[b.] August 9, 1981, St. Croix Falls, WI; [p.] David and Catherine Dvorak; [ed.] Mayo High School, Century High School; [occ.] High School Student; [pers.] World peace is the cornerstone by which we must now revolve our lives.; [a.] Rochester, MN

EASTON, ERIC N.
[b.] August 10, 1960, Molesworth, Eng.; [p.] Read C. Easton, Emogene Easton; [ed.] High School 1 yr. Jr. College (Riverside City College); [occ.] Mail Carrier; [memb.] Self-Realization Fellowship; [oth. writ.] Stories about experiences climbing in the mountains or deserts. other poems: 'The Vertical Playground', 'Fire Falls of Falls Fire' many short essays and inspiration led writing.; [pers.] I like to write poems which might inspire someone to seek God. Poems grow inside a cocoon of hard-won inspiration to finally escape in their God given glory of expression. I've been deeply inspired by H. D. Thoreau, R. W. Emerson and P. Yogananda...; [a.] Ontario, CA

EATON, DANIEL
[b.] July 16, 1963, Queens, NY; [p.] Minnette D. Eaton, Roy F. Eaton; [ed.] Lakeland Reg. H.S., Georgetown University (BSFS '84), Harvard Law School (J.D. Cum Laude, 1989); [occ.] Attorney; [memb.] National Conference - San Diego Board of Directors, San Diego Civil Service Commission; [pers.] The published poem, "Dreaded News", is one of five I wrote to my mother during the last year of her life. I was determined to leave no loving sentiment unsaid. Mom died Thanksgiving morning, 1996. I owe my enthusiasm for life and any gift for words I may have to her. It is to her that I rededicate my contribution to this volume.; [a.] San Diego, CA

EDLAND, RUTH W.
[b.] December 5, 1908, Oswego, NY; [p.] Walter, Lena White; [m.] Frederic P. Edland, 1934; [ch.] John Frederic Edland, MD; [ed.] Univ. State of NY at Oswego 1928, Nazareth College 1968; [occ.] Retired; [memb.] AAUW, NYSRTA; [oth. writ.] A poem published by NASA local papers.

EDWARDS, CHEIMELLE DANECIA
[b.] February 23, 1977, Los Angeles, CA; [p.] Ishmeail and Cheryll Edwards; [ed.] Golden Day Pre-School, Fifty-Ninth Street Elementary School, Andubun Junior High School, Dursey High School, currently attending UCLA.; [occ.] Hanna Barbera Cartoons; [memb.] Knights and ladies; [hon.] Best Original Poem; [pers.] Poetry is the intangible feeling of the soul. A journey of intertwined words where letters flow. I poetry is the voice of unheard expression and the sound of sheer delight.; [a.] Los Angeles, CA

EDWARDS, JESSICA
[b.] October 27, 1981, Columbus, OH; [p.] Rex and Teresa Edwards; [ed.] Freshman at West Carteret High School; [occ.] Student; [memb.] West Carteret High School marching patriots, former editor of the Montage literary magazine, Coastal Jazz society; [hon.] 1st chair tenor saxophone in N.C. all-district band, best female musician award, superior rating at state honor solo and ensemble contest, 1996 all county honors band; [pers.] Have a good heart and a good soul and the poetic side of life is yours.; [a.] Pine Knoll Shores, NC

EGAN, DOUGLAS S.
[pen.] Douglas Egan; [b.] October 21, 1899, Seattle, WA; [p.] Henry and Gertrude H. Egan; [m.] Dorothy Clementine Egan, January 22, 1930; [ch.] Douglas Jr., David Lockwood, Mary Josephine; [ed.] University of Washington, Seattle Naval Schools, Maritime and International Trade; [occ.] (Retired) Part time Maritime Curator, Edmonds Art Museum; [memb.] Nat Maritime Hist., Society (Past president, founding member), Puget Sound Maritime Hist., Society, U.S. Naval Institute; [hon.] Honorary Memberships, Propellen Club of U.S., Commodore Sea Scouts, U.S. Naval Institute, Edmonds Seattle Wa., 1935, Chamber of Commerce, Edmonds, Maritime Heritage Award 1990, State of Washington - NW Seaport.; [oth. writ.] "Ship Benjamin Sewall", chronology of a Square Rigger 1983, 3 vol. verses I like, verses I write, verses I write and other things. 1986-1994. Contributor to various maritime and historical publications.; [a.] Edmonds, WA

EHLERS, WILLIAM ALBERT
[pen.] Bill Ehlers; [b.] February 2, 1912, Marshall, MN; [p.] Millard E. and Doris S. Ehlers; [ed.] Marshall Public High School, St. Olne College, University of Chicago Medical School, University of British Columbia, Psychiatry Residency, University of Oregon, Medical School Child, Adolescent and Psychiatry Resident; [occ.] Child, Adolescent, Adult and Forensic Psychiatrist; [memb.] American Assn. for the Advancement of Science, American College of Forensic Examining, Trinity Lutheran Church, Audubon Society, Mensa; [hon.] Co-Valedictorian High School, Cum Laude, College, Science project in High School, High School, celebrating Corte St "from scratch" (high school) (angel food cake); [oth. writ.] Sparrowgrass Poetry Forum Inc. published 1991 Blue and White (Across the Pacific Ocean), Valedictory speech - The Heart of Truth - other writings unpublished as of yet.; [pers.] I have been influenced by many including Robin Drath, Tagone, Prestwich Gonhoffer, Carl G. Jung, Karlil Gibson, The Mayor and Icon civilization. I wish to see and experience as far as the eye can see and the heart and soul can feel and sense the depths and heights of human experience.; [a.] Tacoma, WA

EL-BAZ, MARY
[b.] March 23, 1957, Saint Louis, MO; [ed.] University of Missouri - St. Louis; [occ.] Technical Consultant, HSI, St. Louis, MO; [hon.] Award-winning Amateur Photographer; [oth. writ.] Technical articles for computer trade newspaper, training manuals for corporate

education, computer software user manuals.; [a.] O'Fallon, MO

ELAM, LARRY S.
[pen.] Middle E.; [b.] July 19, 1963, Ann Arbor, MI; [p.] Albert and Corine Elam; [ed.] Ypsi High, and a half year of College at Washtenaw Community College; [occ.] Don't work because if Illinois; [memb.] The Ann Arbor Magic Club and the International Brotherhood of Magicians (my magic pen name is Mr. E) and International Society of Poets; [hon.] 4th Place Award from the International Society of Poets for Poem, "Goodbye"; [oth. writ.] Some of my other poems are "Mother," and "When I Forget."; [pers.] My poetry was written for the people who love to read poems with a soft touch. So always work for what you want! And pray for what you need!; [a.] Ypsilanti, MI

ENDLER, NANCY LEE
[pen.] Nancy Kane Endler; [b.] August 13, 1938, Imlay City, MI; [p.] Alfred and Phyllis Kane; [ch.] Richard Ryan; [ed.] Culver High School, Westchester Adult, Classes, UCLA Extension Courses; [occ.] Secretary/ Bookkeeping Company, Owner; [memb.] Business Network of the Desert, American Institute of Professional Bookkeepers, Better Business Bureau, Rancho Mirage Chamber of Commerce, MASE Nat'l Assoc. Notaries; [hon.] P.T.A. Lifetime Honorary Award, Golden Poet Award 1989, Golden Poet Award 1991, Who's Who in Poetry 1990; [oth. writ.] "Inside My Heart", "A Dream", "Winding Roads", write personalized poetry upon request for friends and referrals.; [pers.] My poems are primarily written from my heart, and my poetry reflect my own experiences that I have encountered involving "matters of the heart".; [a.] Rancho Mirage, CA

ENGLER, ANN M. SVOBODA
[b.] March 3, 1957, Omaha, NE; [p.] John Svoboda, Joyce Mitchell; [ch.] 3 boys, Zuch (20), T. J. (14), Brian (11); [ed.] Graduated in '75 Central High, Omaha Nebraska; [occ.] Self-Employed Transcriptionist, Sell Marykay Cosmetics; [oth. writ.] None that has been published. I do like to write poems, and have a good collection of my writings. Would like to write a novel someday.; [pers.] Don't be afraid to try or go after what you desire or want. If you never try, you'll never know. Follow your heart and instincts.; [a.] Lenexa, KS

ENGLISH, RUTH WALTON
[b.] December 14, 1913, Greensboro, NC; [p.] John and Viola Walton; [m.] Edward Ralph English, September 16, 1936; [ch.] Dale, Ralph, David, Melinda; [ed.] Graduate Averett College attended U. of VA; [occ.] Homemaker have been married 60 years.; [memb.] Taught kindergarten and first grade, Col. Chas. Lynch DAR, Staunton River Garden Club; [hon.] Greatest Honor is raising 4 wonderful children, and being grandmother to 10, very active in local affairs; [oth. writ.] I've written 30 poems - first one I've sent off. Am encouraged to do more!; [pers.] Always loved poetry and art. Have painted water colors and do beautiful crewel and needle point. Love nature and my fellowman.; [a.] Altavista, VA

ENOS, SHARON
[pen.] Sharon Enos; [b.] January 10, 1941, Irvin Falls, ID; [p.] Dorothy Ruth Huntley, Leland Allmon; [m.] Donald Edward Enos, December 31, 1966; [ch.] 4 Naturals born, one step Son; [ed.] Ninth Grade, some Gavilan Community College Gilray CA, 95020; [occ.] Writer - House Wife; [memb.] A.A.R.P.; [oth. writ.] The Story, "Popcorn Sex". (2) "Sex...Stamped with God's Approval", unpublished, I am waiting on the network to finish their mergers, as they are going to help me market all over the world; [pers.] My writing is far the purpose of several education and reincarnation. To

bring more peace into the world, encourage people to think about Norma, and sell stories to say far housing for the needy.; [a.] Hallister, CA

EPTON, ROBIN
[b.] October 7, 1972, Midwest City, OK; [p.] John Epton and Mary West; [oth. writ.] Alcoholic Dreams Of A Sober Illusion; [pers.] Dedicated to those who walk within the light of true beauty, love, peace, joy, and freedom. "Hope is a rising sun which eventually dispels all that is unreal or all that does not correspond to the Essence of Existence. "Torkom Sanaydarian".; [a.] Oklahoma City, OK

ERICKSON, LEIE
[b.] April 5, 1976, Houston, TX; [p.] John and Karen Erickson; [ed.] Alan C. Pope High School, Kennesaw State College, US Navy; [occ.] US Navy Nuclear Engineer; [memb.] US Diving Association; [pers.] I am one of the last true transcendentalists greatly influenced by Emerson and Thoreau and on a dark side, Edgar Allen Poe.; [a.] Wilsonville, OR

ERICKSON, MARK GORDON
[b.] December 6, 1961, Washington, DC; [m.] Leslie Lynch Clinton; [ed.] Rhode Island School of Design, BFA; [pers.] Only a fool says "There is no God", God is love. In Him, we should walk in love. There is no greater commandment than that. Jesus said, "I am the way, the truth and the life. No one comes to the Father but through Me."; [a.] Philadelphia, PA

ERICKSON, STEPHANIE D.
[b.] March 2, 1980, Everett, WA; [p.] John and Christy Erickson; [ed.] Lake Stevens High School; [occ.] Student; [pers.] I enjoy writing and try to bring out the peacefulness of nature in my writing.; [a.] Everett, WA

ERICSON, KEELYN L.
[b.] May 14, 1972, Ellsworth, KS; [p.] Keith and Marsha Ericson; [ed.] B.S. Chemistry - Kansas Wesleyan Univ.; [occ.] Student at University of Kansas Medical Center; [memb.] American Medical Assn. - Medical Student Section; [hon.] Kansas Wesleyan Presidential Scholar, Dean's Honor Roll; [pers.] Faith, family and friends - and the health to enjoy them all.; [a.] Overland Park, KS

ERMAN, BERNICE
[b.] January 9, 1936, Gloucester, VA; [p.] John Owens and Mamie West Owens; [m.] John Odell Erman; [ch.] Janice Erman Carmine; [ed.] Graduated High School, Community College CEU's; [occ.] Retired as Medical Recpt., Medical Insurance; [memb.] AMAA - Gloucester Point Baptist Church; [oth. writ.] "Mother" Of Sunshine and Daydreams; [pers.] I enjoy putting true thoughts into words.; [a.] Gloucester Point, VA

ERVIN, VALERIE
[b.] November 5, 1973, Birmingham, AL; [p.] Roosevelt and Christine Ervin; [ed.] Ramsay High School, University of Alabama at Birmingham; [pers.] Only that I do for Christ will last.; [a.] Birmingham, AL

ESPINOSA, GUILLERMO G.
[b.] Philippines; [ed.] Pozorrubio High, Mapua Institute of Technology; [occ.] Mechanical Engineer; [memb.] American Society of Mechanical Engineers, Los Angeles Power Section, Director, Los Angeles Power Producers Association, Vice President, Phi-Beta-Epsilon, Charter President; [hon.] Registered Professional Engineer in Mechanical and Control Systems Engineering, California; [oth. writ.] Co-authored several technical articles published in National Engineering magazines; [pers.] The awesome wonders of science and technology are enthralling as the healing of touch

and enchanting powers of music and poetry are uplifting; [a.] Santa Clarita, CA

ESTES, LARRY EDGAR
[pen.] Larry E. Estes; [b.] February 12, 1938, Cedartown, GA; [p.] Lloyd Estes - Lillie Willingham; [ch.] Linda Elaine and Shelley Anne; [ed.] USDA Grad School - Wash DC, NRI - Wash. D.C., USAF NCD Academy, USAF Security Service, NSA, NASA - Project Mercury; [occ.] Independent Insurance Agent; [hon.] US AF Humanitarian Award; [oth. writ.] I am honored that this is my first submission and published poem. I have many others and some are being reviewed for songs.; [pers.] This poem was written for my first wife, Louise Eagles, upon my going overseas during the Korean war, not knowing if I would ever see her again.; [a.] Ocala, FL

EVANS, CHUCK
[b.] October 3, 1957, Wooster, OH; [p.] Richard and Joyce Evans; [ch.] Christina Carlene, Jennifer Erin, Christopher Charles, Hannah Maria; [ed.] Worthington High School, Ohio State University, BS in Business Administration; [occ.] Manufacturer of Mexican Sauces and Salsas, Montezuma Mexican Foods; [memb.] United States Tae Kwon Do Federation, 3rd Degree Black Belt, National Association for the Specialty Food Trade; [hon.] Excluding this section in order to have Other Writings to be included in full and not be edited.; [oth. writ.] The Hot Sauce Bible, publ. by The Crossing Press, 1996, Pepper Pantry: Chipotle, publ. by Ten Speed Press, 1997, Moments of the Heart, publ. by C.E. Press, 1997 (Includes the poem Hate!) Wrinkles and Crinkles, publ. by C.E. Press, 1997 (Includes the poem Little Children's Poems Miss Hurricane) Hannah Can and Chris Can, Too! Series to children's books (23 titles) in rhyme and fully illustrated in color. Seeking publisher for this positive, can do! Early reader book series.; [pers.] I attribute much of my inspiration to my children and their antics and especially to my youngest, Hannah.; [a.] Columbus, OH

EVANS, DELORIS
[b.] June 13, 1930, Shraders, VA; [p.] Mr. and Mrs. Edward Brewster; [m.] Garfield Evans, May 26, 1951; [ch.] Five; [ed.] Big Creek Hi, War, W.V.; [occ.] Housewife; [memb.] AARP - 700 Club willing workers Sunday school class; [oth. writ.] Life published in Through the Hour Glass; [pers.] Live each day the best we can.; [a.] Joplin, MO

EWINGS, JIM
[pen.] Jim E.; [b.] October 5, 1952, Alb., GA; [p.] Bertha Barney, Willie Ewings; [m.] Sue Ewings, December 14, 1981; [ch.] Andrea, Warren, Leah, Jim II, Sarah; [ed.] Monroe High, Shapiro Nursing Albany State College, Bethany Seminary; [occ.] Pastor, 2nd Bethesda Bapt. Church, Director MLK Outreach Mission; [memb.] GA Baptist Convention Music Community; [hon.] Outstanding Young Men of AM. 87, Fritz-HCA - Humanitarian Award 88 - Boy Club Honor 95, Several Awards for Music and Choral Organization; [oth. writ.] Spiritual Compositions Lyrics and Music (Unpublished); [pers.] I am led to relate the beauty and power of life in creation and nature, to the everyday opportunities of mankind being inspired by The Holy Scriptures, Philosophers and the vast arena of Arts.; [a.] Albany, GA

FARNHAM, CHARLES A.
[b.] December 25, 1953, England; [p.] Barbara Elizabeth and Edward George Adrian Farnham; [m.] Elise M. Farnham, May 25, 1996; [ch.] Adrian (19), Kathryn - from former marriage; [ed.] Bilton Grange School Ruby, England and Harlow School, Harlow England; [occ.] Gentleman; [memb.] Stoneygate RFC, Hallow Association; [hon.] Many; [oth. writ.] Country and

Western songs I Won't Go To Kansas In The Morning, and One Day It Won't Seem So Bad!, plus many other poems.; [pers.] I'm a slightly eccentric Englishman now living in a very eccentric United States.; [a.] Dunwoody, GA

FARR, GORDON
[b.] December 29, 1965, Quakertown, PA; [p.] Edward Farr, Annette Farr; [ed.] HS Parkway Program (Gamma Unit) College/University: Penn State University Ogantz Campus: Liberal Arts Seeking degree (Liberal Arts major); [occ.] Pt/Evening student, and day (occ.) Claim Service Associate; [oth. writ.] Unpublished poems and an unpublished fictional story; [pers.] Live and take each and every day at a time, just like each and every step, and also live it to the fullest. I have been inspired by Richard Wright and other inspirational past literary figures; [a.] North Wales, PA

FARRELL, JEFFEREY T. S.
[b.] March 19, 1954, Helena, MT; [p.] Mona and Thomas Memecek, Fred and Mary Turner; [ed.] Seattle University, Santa Barbara Business College; [occ.] Author, Painter, Sculptor; [memb.] International Society of Poets, Santa Barbara Art Association, Santa Barbara Sculpture Guild, Lazarus Art Society, Northwest Student Gallery Art League, Maple Valley Art League; [hon.] "Editor's Choice" - National Library of Poetry, "Honorable Mention" - Maple Valley Art League; [oth. writ.] "The Wait" and "Sightings" both published by National Library of Poetry.; [pers.] It's a sad day when a man only has his past to look forward to. Are the memories of his future only the thoughts of his past? My mentors have been great artists and sculptors such as Matisse, Van Gough, Pollock, Henry Moore, Beatrice Wood and Rodin. I also admire the writings of Plato and Aristotle.; [a.] Portland, OR

FAUST, JEANNE
[b.] August 10, 1952, Salt Lake City, UT; [p.] Jere, Joanne Faust; [m.] Ronald L. Dodson, October 15, 1994; [ed.] San Jose State University - College Sacred Heart - High School; [occ.] Tutor, Training Coordinator, Instructor, Eugene Oregon; [memb.] American Society of Training and Development (ASTD), American Society for Quality Control (ASQC); [hon.] Black Masque Society - Honor Society in College Who's Who - High Schools; [oth. writ.] Late 1980's - published in American Anthology of Poetry, write articles for local country Newspaper.; [pers.] "Time wasted is existence, used is life" Author Unknown to me, poetry is an expression of life, from the soul and the heart.; [a.] Springfield, OR

FEDERER, JANET M. EUREN
[b.] November 19, 1956, Cleveland, OH; [p.] Mae Ian Euren; [m.] James, September 2, 1978; [ch.] Matthew, Andrew, Rachael; [ed.] BA English, Certification in Teaching for English and Elementary Education from Cleveland State University; [occ.] Teacher; [memb.] Order of Eastern Star; [hon.] Dean's List; [pers.] Life is a journey of dreams and disappointments, accomplishments and hope. My poetry reflects the courage needed to continue that journey through time.; [a.] Eastlake, OH

FEE, CHARLES R.
[pen.] Charlie Fee; [b.] January 3, 1924, Atlanta, GA; [p.] Walter Edward Fee (Deceased); [m.] Charleen "Charlie" (Deceased), February 25, 1988; [ch.] Charles R. Fee Jr.; [ed.] Jesuit H.S. '38-42 - U of Tampa - '47-50, Grad Mich.-Fl., Fl., State - U of F.; [occ.] Retired H.S. Teacher; [memb.] "Lifers", NEA, D.A.V. Annuals Moose; [hon.] 1st place 1940 Jesuit H.S. Oratory, "The Death Of Fagen" Adaptation from Oliver Twist", 1941 1st place: The Torture of a Living Death, World War I Gassed - writing; [oth. writ.] Numerous periodicals letters, University So. Fla. 1986-87. Tampa U. the art of

writing function at the panther — isolated Cabin wherein the panther rules.; [pers.] As I've pushed almost 3/4 century. I learned early about social equality - not just tolerance. Tolerance smacks of condescension. Love all humankind - spread joy...never a loose.; [a.] Clearwater, FL

FEINBERG, ROBERT S.
[b.] May 14, 1934, Newark, NJ; [p.] Dr. Clarence J. Feinberg, Sabina Z. Feinberg; [ed.] BA English, BS Chemistry, Trinity College, Hartford, CT, MBA Marketing/Finance, Fairleigh Dickinson University; [occ.] Chem. Plastics Engr., Inventor Pres., Edgeroy Co., Inc. Pres., Trebor Plastics Co.; [memb.] Senior Member, Society of Plastics Engineers, VP, Bergen County NJ Tennis League, VP, Ahdeek Tennis Club; [hon.] Listed in: Marquis Who's Who In America, Marquis Who's Who In The World, WCT (World Championship Tennis), International Who's Who In Tennis; [oth. writ.] Olympia Shoe Company (published by the Harvard Business School in the Harvard Case Book Series). Hold 29 patents on marketed chemical and mechanical and mechanical engineering products. Articles in various trade publications.; [pers.] Pertinent to my creative writing, I try to unite philosophical moral and ethical values with scientific principles and procedure.; [a.] Teaneck, NJ

FENNELL, DIANE
[b.] February 19, 1964, California; [p.] Albert and Dorothy Brown; [m.] Joseph F. Fennell Jr., August 20, 1988; [ch.] Christina and Jeremy Fennell; [ed.] Cerritos Community College; [occ.] Registered Nurse; [memb.] Nursing Service Organization; [hon.] United Together Scholarship fund. Numerous honors and awards as PTA member and throughout nursing career, ie. "Clinical Employee of the Year", and "Outstanding Nurse."; [oth. writ.] Several poems listed in church bulletin and written upon request of associates and various organizations.; [pers.] I am a vessel employed by my Lord and Saviour Jesus Christ from whom all my words flow.; [a.] Corona, CA

FERGUSON, SUE
[b.] August 3, 1930, Natchez, MS; [p.] Susie and William Ferguson; [m.] Everett Wright (Deceased), March 19, 1955; [ch.] Karen, Susan, Robin; [ed.] Baton Rouge Sr. High, La. St. University (Bachelor's and Master's Degrees in Music); [occ.] Professional Beauty Consultant, Mary Kay Cosmetics; [memb.] Phi Delta Kappa Professional Education Fraternity, First United Methodist Church (Member of Administrative Bd. and Choir); [hon.] At LSU, President, School of Music and Member, Student Council, at La. St. Dept. of Education Member Advisory Bd. Southwest Educational Development Laboratory, American Business Women's Assn. (Cypress Chapter), 1971-72 President and Woman of the Year.; [oth. writ.] State Dept. of Education Handbook for Educators and the Louisiana Public (HELP), which received national recognition.; [pers.] I strive to be kind and to spread joy to everyone I know.; [a.] Baton Rouge, LA

FERRIS, JEREMEY R.
[b.] May 5, 1983, Syracuse, NY; [p.] Robert and Joan Ferris; [ed.] Fulton Junior High School; [occ.] Student; [memb.] Grace Lutheran Church Oswebo, New York; [a.] Fulton, NY

FINCH, OWEN R.
[pen.] Owen Finch; [b.] August 2, 1919, Hope, NM; [p.] Arthur Finch, Susie Finch; [m.] Marjorie Finch, May 24, 1941; [ch.] Janine, Owen Jr.; [ed.] Mohave County Union High School, Real Estate School; [occ.] Retired; [memb.] St. John's United Methodist Church, Mohave County Historical Society, American Legion Swaskegame Post #14, BPO Elks (Kingman Lodge #468). Past President 20-30 Club, past member Lions Club.; [oth. writ.] Numerous poems, short story, newspaper publications; [pers.] Writing poetry is a great connection to reality and keeps the mind active.; [a.] Kingman, AZ

FINDLEY, JAMES E.
[b.] August 14, 1944, Hallsville, TX; [p.] Cecil and Ruth Findley; [m.] Myrtie Findley, May 2, 1970; [ch.] 1 daughter - 2 step-children; [ed.] High School; [occ.] Maintenance Supervisor BP Exploration; [oth. writ.] Crossing the Log, Good-Bye Lisa, Nonia and Bill, Little Leo, Happy Anniversary, Valentine's Day; [pers.] Although "A Time to Cry" is a serious poem, I usually try to touch on the lighter side.; [a.] Vancouver, WA

FINLAYSON, LISA MARIE
[pen.] Lisa M. Thompson-Finlayson; [b.] December 20, 1969, Baltimore, MD; [p.] Sylvester Thompson, Mary Thompson; [m.] Erskine Finlayson, July 16, 1994; [ed.] B.A. English Morgan State University, Diploma St. Frances Academy; [occ.] Caseworker; [hon.] Dean's List Honorable Mention, Service Award in English Dept.; [pers.] All good and perfect gifts come from God.; [a.] Baltimore, MD

FIRESTONE, RENEE J.
[b.] November 15, 1958, Findlay, OH; [p.] Joan Wells, Richard Warren; [m.] M. K. Firestone, September 9, 1979; [ch.] Two; [ed.] High School; [occ.] Domestic Eng., Lab Tech III, Office Asst.; [oth. writ.] Local paper, I have framed my personal writing and given as gifts.; [pers.] I write to express what's in my heart. I would like to be someone that could help others who have lived though pains of abuse and depression. I would like to give a ray of light.; [a.] Findlay, OH

FISHER, WILFRED
[b.] March 12, 1971; [p.] Wilfred and Linda Fisher; [ed.] George Westinghouse H.S., Queensborough Community College; [pers.] I try to write about issues that are presented in our every day life, but we are either too afraid to face them or too busy to pay attention. Basically in life, we take too many things for granted. "Ask questions, don't ever assume."; [a.] Queens, NY

FITKA, ROBERTA A.
[pen.] Bobbie; [b.] January 3, 1971, Marshall, AK; [p.] Robert and Nancy Moore; [ch.] Jordan D. Fitka and Jazamane J. Fitka; [ed.] Mt. Edgecumbe H.S., Marshall H.S., SEE Program, Raps Program, Soutwestern Indian Polytechnic Institute, Alaska Vocational Technical Center; [occ.] Now Tribal Courts Field office Administrator; [memb.] Maserculiq Incorporated Board Member, Headstar Parent Committee; [oth. writ.] Personal poems not published but in poetry journal of my own. Writes stories for the Anica Flash; [pers.] I write what comes from my heart, how I feel about others or how/what I may have seen or experienced.; [a.] Marshall, AK

FITZGERALD, JANE
[pen.] Jane Fitzgerald; [b.] March 13, 1959, Boston; [p.] John and Ruth (Both Deceased); [ed.] Bachelor of Science in Education Diploma Degree in Nursing I am currently attending U. Mass Boston for A BSN; [occ.] Registered Nurse at the Pine St. Inn - a homeless shelter in Boston.; [hon.] Outstanding Athlete in the City of Boston 1976 President of the 1992 School of Nursing Class Somerville Hospital; [oth. writ.] I personally believe that we are here to make the world a better place. Other writings include Nurse poem, Castle Island poem, Doggie poem, Running poem and several others.; [pers.] My dream is for world peace and harmony.; [a.] Charlestown, MA

FLANIGAN, RUTH A.
[pen.] Ruth; [b.] August 30, 1935, Troy, NY; [p.] William H. Flanigan and Ruth Callahan; [ch.] Sister Clara Hunt; [ed.] S. Rose, Alb., Union, Schenectady, Iona, New Rochelle; [occ.] Retired Teacher; [pers.] To bring light and hope; [a.] Albany, NY

FLEMING, GLENN E.
[b.] July 12, 1979, Philadelphia, PA; [p.] Raymond J. Fleming, Gwendolyn O. Fleming; [ed.] Central High School; [occ.] Manager, Bonnie's Exceptional Ice Cream, Customer Service McDonalds; [memb.] African American Students Union, Central's Literary Club and Students for Choice Club; [hon.] Barnwell Honors (all A's and B's); [oth. writ.] Several poems unpublished, but entered into other contests.; [pers.] Little things mean a lot. So one must appreciate what one has already.; [a.] Philadelphia, PA

FONDE, MICHAEL A.
[pen.] Michael Anthony; [b.] November 5, 1986, Frankfort, Phila.; [p.] Beverly A. Winder; [ed.] 4th Grade Tawanka Elementary School; [occ.] Student; [memb.] Minger-Lee Tae Kwon Do, Boy Scouts; [hon.] Science Certificate, Certificate of Merit, Certificate of Membership of Young Astronauts, Certificate of Science Fair; [pers.] I try to bring out the natural beauty in my poems and hope to someday see it.; [a.] Langhorne, PA

FORD, SONYA D.
[b.] August 25, 1967, Pittsburgh, PA; [p.] Helen Ford, John L. Ford; [ed.] Westinghouse High Robert Morris College; [occ.] Financial Service Consultant PNC Bank; [oth. writ.] Collection of poems unpublished titled "Positive Expressions."; [pers.] I write poetry for my own personal fulfillment and to encourage positivity and celebration of our inner beauty as human beings.; [a.] Pittsburgh, PA

FORD, WESLEY H.
[pen.] Aron Wood; [b.] July 18, 1977, Orange, CA; [p.] Linda McCulloch and James Ford; [m.] August 5, 1995, (Divorced, September 3, 1996); [ch.] MacKenzie J. Ford; [ed.] Hernando High School; [occ.] Wall's Outlet, in Starkville MS, Sales Clerk; [hon.] Who's Who Among American High School Students Sophomore and Junior Years; [oth. writ.] "The Life", "Silence", "Young Warrior", "A Dream Beyond Others" (unpublished); [pers.] I strive to make a beneficial contribution to the world and my fellow man.; [a.] Ackerman, MS

FORSTER, ANGELA FRANCES
[b.] May 18, 1964, Boston, MA; [p.] Neil and Sylvia Forster; [ed.] BS Music Performance/Promotion, U. Massachusetts, MBA, Suffolk University, Boston MA; [occ.] Asst. to V.P. for Student Affairs/Deans of Students (at Berklee College of Music); [hon.] Iota Beta of Chi Omega, Outstanding Service as MBA Assoc. President, 1994 Suffolk U., Most Valuable Contribution to Enhancement of the Student Experience at Berklee, 1995; [pers.] I am influenced by many artists, writers and musicians. I enjoy exploding new medicines of art which have been greatly influenced by my writings.; [a.] Boston, MA

FOSTER, CHRYSTLE SHIRYLANN
[b.] January 5, 1961, Thomasville, NC; [p.] Bill Deweese, Chrystle Deweese; [m.] Joe Foster, October 7, 1989; [ch.] Matthew, Kimmie; [ed.] ADN, BSN; [occ.] Registered Nurse; [memb.] Iron Overload Diseases Association, Inc., Hemochromatosis Foundation; [hon.] Inducted into the Sigma Theta Tau International, 1 Honor Society of Nursing; [pers.] This poem is dedicated to all those who have not been so lucky and have already succumbed to this silent killer and to all the poor

souls that are suffering from the same, yet undiagnosed disease.; [a.] Thomasville, NC

FOSTER, KIM B.
[pen.] Kim Bell; [b.] August 29, 1970, New Orleans, LA; [p.] Russell Bell Sr., Gladys L. Bell; [m.] John F. Foster, August 13, 1994; [ch.] Shane Edward, John Isaiah; [ed.] McDonogh #35 Senior High, University of New Orleans; [occ.] Estimating Assistant at Construction/Engineering Firm; [hon.] Various writing awards from school and church; [oth. writ.] Many poems and plays since the age of 8 for the church and community.; [pers.] I enjoy writing about the simple laws of life that are so easily forgotten. All of my writing is inspired by God.; [a.] Baton Rouge, LA

FOUSE, GLORIA J.
[b.] June 16, 1947, Alberta, AL; [p.] Jackson Small and Zeola Hicks; [m.] Charles R. Fouse, December 29, 1988; [ch.] Mrs. Patrice Hoskins; [ed.] West Los Angeles Jr. College, Culver City, CA; [occ.] Judicial Assistant to the Honorable Samuel L. Bufford; [pers.] Life... one day at a time, because... this too shall pass.

FOWLER, BROOKE B.
[b.] April 29, 1971, Pomona, CA; [p.] George and Rubette Fowler; [ed.] Weatherford High School, The University of Texas at Austin; [occ.] Senior Administrator Labor Relations, GTE Telephone Operations, Irving, TX; [hon.] Various individual and team GTE honors and awards.; [pers.] Poetry is an author's artistic expression of hopes and dreams and unique reflection of past, current, and future experiences and happenings. I am excited to share my special reflection in this publication.; [a.] Irving, TX

FOX, GERALD J.
[pen.] Jerry Fox; [b.] May 16, 1958, Philadelphia, PA; [p.] Joan Marie and Frederick Thomas Fox; [ed.] St. Francis Xavier Grammar School, Roman Catholic High School, Penna. Institute of Technology, Academy of Culinary Arts; [occ.] Printer's Assistant, Pastry, Chef, Doorman, Bartender; [memb.] Order of the Arrow, Green Peace, World Wild Life Fund; [hon.] Boy Scouts of America: Star Scout, 1 badge below life. Culinary Arts Silver Medal; [oth. writ.] Prayer of an artist, The Last Match, Faded Colors, Strathmere....Sunny Autumn Dream; [pers.] ...To express with peace and love. To paint for art alone. Sharing a gift with those who know me.; [a.] Sea Isle City, NJ

FRAM, JOSEPH
[b.] June 8, 1932, Las Vegas, NM; [p.] Patrick and Jennie Fram; [ch.] Dana Fram and Dale Fram; [ed.] Immaculate Conception High, New Mexico Highlands U., Univ. of Washington; [occ.] Retired School Superintendent; [memb.] Trustee, WA. St. School for the Blind, Navy League, USA, Hockey Referee Assn., Nat. Assn. School Supts.; [hon.] Historical Document "Education of Severely Hdcp" in Smithsonian Inst., "Boss of the Year, 1979", Golf's Hole in One Club; [oth. writ.] Several Christmas Poems published, many research papers and professional journal publications, "The Twilight Group" about the plight of minimally capable students, guest editorials for newspapers and journals.; [pers.] I try to capture emotional snapshots.; [a.] Spokane, WA

FRANDLE, GLORIA JULIANNE
[ed.] 1955 B.A. UCLA; [oth. writ.] Masks and Reflections

FRANKLIN, LABRUNYA TAMMIKA
[pen.] Tameca Franklin; [b.] June 24, 1979, Athens, GA; [p.] Latitia and Jeffrey Franklin; [ed.] Senior, Clarke Central High School, Athens, GA.; [occ.] Sandwich Maker at Subworks Inc. Downtown, Athens, GA.;

[oth. writ.] Currently working on the following writings: The Pneumato writings, book one and Pneumato writings book two; [pers.] I have been writing for about four years and I have just realized how others seem to enjoy my work. I use writing as a release. In the path I have tried very hard to be a conformist, but now I feel worthy as a writer.; [a.] Athens, GA

FRAYNE, CATHARINA
[pen.] Kitty; [b.] March 28, 1966, Toronto, Ontario; [p.] James Willis, (Tina Willis Deceased), Doris Willis; [m.] Dennis Frayne, August 22, 1996; [ch.] Christine, Dennis, James and Justin; [ed.] W. C. Eaket High School Institute of children's Literature Ct; [occ.] Mother, student; [memb.] Volunteer Aid's Society Sault Ste Marie; [oth. writ.] Am hoping to publish the many other poems I have in file.; [pers.] I'm hoping to extend my talent and reach others through my life experiences.; [a.] S S Marie, Ontario, Canada

FRAZIER, LINDA TURK
[pen.] Linda Turk; [b.] January 31, 1947, Brewton, AL; [p.] James Turk and Lillie Stallworth Turk; [m.] Divorced; [ch.] Jah'shawn and Exavier; [ed.] Southern Normal High School, Texas Southern University; [occ.] Chief Clerk/Deputy Tax Collector, Escambia County Tax Collector's Office Brewton, AL; [memb.] 2nd Saint Siloam Baptist Church, President-Southern Normal School Alumni Assoc. Brewton Chapter, Lilly Chapter, O.E.S., A.D.C. (Alabama Democratic Conference) Red Cross Volunteer; [oth. writ.] Words to High School Class Song, Poems to family and friends for special occasions; [pers.] To my wonderful family I dedicate "All the Love."

FRAZIER, TOMMY
[b.] January 26, 1965, Offenbach, Germany; [ch.] Morgan Ashley Frazier; [ed.] High School; [occ.] Boiler Plant Operator/Merchant Seaman; [pers.] Sometimes belief is all we have that can't be taken away.; [a.] Elk Grove, CA

FRAZIER, WILLIAM A.
[pen.] Bill; [b.] February 16, 1923, Baltimore, MD; [p.] John H. and Georgia Frazier; [m.] Audrey E. Frazier, December 2, 1956; [ch.] 2 - Lisa A., Adrienne E.; [ed.] Douglass High, Balto "41"; [occ.] Retired Seaman and New York City Bus Operator; [memb.] Prince Hall Masons Samson - 65, Vestry - Music and Liturgy Holy Trinity Episcopal Church Fruitland Park, FL; [hon.] High School Plays, Golf in my High School Days - 1940, Inter-City, School "O" Letter Music of Eskine Hawkins - Band, Boy 1940 - Summer Vacations, at early age of 5-6 Penney Jar Collection's in my Church Sharow Baptist, Balto. MD.; [oth. writ.] To Family-Friends and Obituaries, to my Jazz Club in Lady Lake Fl.; [pers.] "Be careful of the words you speak, for sometime in the future, those words you just may have to eat."; [a.] Lady Lake, FL

FRENCH, HEATHER L.
[b.] March 13, 1974, Overlook Hospital, Summit, NJ; [p.] John and Linda French; [ed.] Graduated with an A.S. in Humanities of Social Sciences in 1994 from CCM, and received a B.A. in History from Kean College of NJ in 1996; [occ.] Video dubber at Video Lab in New Brunswick and historical interpreter at Fosterfields in Morristown, NJ; [hon.] Received an award in May 1994 from Community Corrections Council in Morristown, NJ for role modeling for the community, belong to Phi Alpha Theta, Omega Alpha Chapter for Kean College Historical Honor Society; [oth. writ.] Various poems and short stories, some published in my old high school poetry club; [pers.] We all are dreamers and our dreams are our realities. It is through these dreams that my writings take form, in the passions of

romance, truth, and virtue for tales to be told.; [a.] South River, NJ

FRETWELL, SARAH BETH
[b.] April 3, 1967, Princeton, IL; [ed.] Mexico Senior High - Mexico, MO, Milligan College - Milligan, TN, John Casablancas - Scottsdale, AZ; [occ.] Secretary/Receptionist - Citizens Utilities "Pao", Tour Sales - America West Airlines; [memb.] North Phoenix Baptist Church - Choir, Arizona Production Association; [hon.] Lotus 1-2-3 Certificate, Quattro Pro Certificate, C.P.R. Certification, MO, Chauffeur's License - MO, Who's Who Among American High School Students 1984/85; [pers.] I strive to utilize my talents and skills and to help others do the same. I have been greatly influenced by life experiences.; [a.] Phoenix, AZ

FRIOU, ELIZABETH BELL
[pen.] Elizabeth Bell; [b.] December 1, 1928, Cincinnati, OH; [p.] William Procter Bell, Sophie Buckner Bell; [m.] 1. Frank Donald Drake, March 7, 1953, 2. Robert E. Friou, April 16, 1983; [ch.] Paul Robert Drake, Stephen David Drake, Richard Procter Drake; [ed.] Hillsdale School, Cincinnati, Wellesley College (B.A.), Juilliard School of Music (B.S., Composition); [occ.] Composer, serious contemporary concert music.; [memb.] Broadcast Music, Inc., American Composers Alliance, American Music Center, New York Women Composers, Inc. (A founder and Officer), others.; [hon.] Cum Laude (high school), Alliance Francaise, Mellesley Scholar, First Prize, National Composers Competition (Perne in a Gyre), Delius Prize (Duovarios), numerous Meet-the-Composer awards: Commissions from numerous performers and clamber music groups.; [oth. writ.] Numerous other poems, most unpublished, Music reviews for the Ithaca (NY) Journal, 1971-1975, numerous musical compositions.; [pers.] Though primarily a professional musical composer, I have always written poetry from time to time, especially during times of intense personal emotion. Though written mainly for myself, I try to make them as perfect and satisfying artistically as I can. I am deeply moved by beauty of all kinds, and try to reflect this in my poetry.; [a.] Tarrytown, NY

FROOZAN, EMILIE RICHARD
[b.] November 22, 1985, New York, NY; [p.] Nady Richard, Farwad Froozan; [ed.] Currently in 6th grade; [occ.] Student at Anne M. Dorner Middle School, Ossining, NY; [oth. writ.] Other poems under preparation for publication on an on-line internet magazine; [a.] Ossining, NY

FROST, DONALD
[pen.] Donald Frost; [b.] April 27, 1933, Philadelphia, PA; [m.] Anna Tidd Frost, July 13, 1957; [ch.] Annette Tinder, Susan Reimers, Sandra Frost-Horvath, Dana Frost-Koch; [pers.] Recently Retired, allowing me time for my hobbies of painting, carving and occasionally writing. Enjoy sharing my works with family and friends. I find painting with a Pen a joy.; [a.] Lansdale, PA

FUJII, YUKI
[pen.] Yuki Fujii; [b.] November 23, 1969; [p.] Yoshinori and Yasuko; [ed.] BA-Accountancy San Diego State University; [occ.] Accountant/Soccer Coach; [memb.] United States Soccer Federation; [pers.] Life is too precious to waste and too short to preserve...; [a.] San Diego, CA

FYOCK, KIM CHEN
[pen.] Wu Ai You Gan; [b.] November 25, 1938, Taiwan; [p.] Chen Feng-Cheng and Chen Chiu-Feng; [m.] David A. Fyock, April 20, 1966; [ch.] Debra, Darcy, Sulan, Sheng-Ping; [ed.] Chinese Public School, University of Pittsburgh, Japanese Lang 3 years Butler County Community College, English 3 years; [occ.]

Housewife; [memb.] Int'l Society of Poets World Association of Chinese Poets, Bakerstown Presbyterian Church; [hon.] Poem "A Mother's Loving Heart" featured as centerfold for the 20th Anniversary Edition of Taiwan's prestigious "The Woman" magazine, 1988 (2) Biography in "Int'l Who's Who of Intellectual's" 1995-96 ed. published by the Int'l Biographical etc., Cambridge, England the "Five Thousand Personalities of the World by the American Biographical Institute, USA".; [oth. writ.] Numerous poems published in news papers, magazines and anthologies throughout China; [pers.] I strive to strengthen love within the family that it may extend to the nation and the world.; [a.] Evans City, PA

GAFFNEY, IMOGENE ADKINS
[pen.] Jean, Jeanie, Jean Baby; [b.] July 6, Elmo, TX; [p.] Earl Adkins, Louisa Adkins; [m.] Edward Owen Gaffney, July 30, 1955; [ch.] Theresa, Edward Jr., Orlando, Cyernard, Regina and Darrell; [ed.] Booker T. Washington High School, Prairie View A and M College; [occ.] Retired nurse, takes care of disabled husband at home; [memb.] Holy Trinity Baptist Church, Disabled Veterans, International Society of Poetry, NAACP; [hon.] Newsday Merit Award Essay Contest. Christian Service Award, Editor's Choice Award. Recently Inducted into the International Poetry Hall of Fame by The National Library of Poetry; [oth. writ.] Poems and songs, however material was lost due to relocating years ago.; [pers.] I hope to try to show love through my writing. I would like for love to be so contagious that when one touch another's hand that he, or she, would become infected with same.; [a.] North Babylon, NY

GAINES, NZINGHA N.
[b.] March 30, 1970, Washington, DC; [p.] Charles W. Gaines Jr., Anita Matthews; [ed.] Highland View Academy, Andrews University, Walla Walla College; [occ.] Social worker; [oth. writ.] Several poems published in High School Poetry Collection, articles published in College Newspaper.; [pers.] I breathe into my pen the thoughts of my heart, a journey of discovery and rediscovery influenced by Fredrick Douglass, Alfred Lord Tennyson and Henry David Thoreau; [a.] Saint Louis, MO

GALANO, JENNIFER
[b.] December 22, 1984, Summit, NJ; [p.] Mary and John Galano; [ed.] 6th grade student at Warren Middle School (Warren Twp., NJ); [occ.] Student; [memb.] Continental Math League, Flutist - Warren Middle School Band; [hon.] High Honor Roll 5th and 6th grades; [pers.] I enjoy writing about the beauty and tranquility found in nature. I have been greatly inspired by the wonders the environment has to offer to all.; [a.] Warren Township, NJ

GALLAS, ROBERT D.
[b.] February 4, 1926, Los Angeles, CA; [ed.] University of Southern California School of Public Administration. Major as Business Government; [occ.] I am a Research Analyst and resolve problems for Mid-Sized companies and Coordinators. I also handle Tuestunts for Cliets and Chbisa; [oth. writ.] I only write for my own enjoyment and for my personal friends; this is the first time I have ever sent anything in to someone like yourself.; [pers.] All of my life I have been writing my thoughts down. Sometimes for others, sometimes for myself. You just happened to send your letter when I had written something. My thoughts run deep - sometimes they are not understood.

GALLAWAY, CHLOE
[b.] March 12, 1976, Lindrith, NM; [p.] Reva and Jerry Gallaway; [ed.] 3rd year college student at the University of New Mexico plan to get my Ph.D. in child psychology; [occ.] Personal caretaker for a quadriplegic professor; [hon.] National Honor Society Awards for school. I have received a lot of athletic awards for tennis and volley ball; [oth. writ.] I have written a lot of poetry and several short stories, having to do with my own life. This would be the first time I sent in any of my work.; [pers.] Poetry has become a great form of expression for me over the years. It has been a emotional outlet for such things as the death of my brother, and many other emotional struggles I have gone through. The poem was written about my first love (Charlie) The poem was written a year after I lost virginity. Charlie and I remained together for 3 years after that, at which point circumstances edged us apart.; [a.] Albuquerque, NM

GARCIA, ERNEST M.
[b.] December 3, 1950, Albuquerque, NM; [occ.] Actor - Writer; [pers.] I had the privilege of working with Ann Reed in a production of Richard III she was wonderful.

GARCIA, ODIES ODIA
[pen.] David Little; [b.] April 2, 1974, Nassau, Bahamas; [p.] Donnie Garcia and Maxine Williams; [ed.] St. John's College High School; [occ.] Construction Labour Worker; [oth. writ.] 'Pain', 'After the Storm', Publish 1994 - 'A Wind', 'The Coming of Dawn', Publish 1995 - 'Charisse', Publish 1995 by 'American Annal Poetry', 'A Woman', Publish 1995, 'In My Eye', 1996 by Quell books - others; [pers.] Life is a mystery of fate. We live day to day not knowing if it is going to be our last. Each time we learn our last may well be our first. For the beauty of it all is not to know.; [a.] Orlando, FL

GARCIA, SHERRI
[pen.] Sherri Neal Garcia; [b.] September 20, 1960, Waterloo, IA; [p.] Jonny and Tommie Monden; [m.] Benny Garcia, March 17, 1979; [ch.] Michelle Ann, Kayla Marie, Rebecca Dawn; [ed.] Dalhart High; [occ.] Teacher's Aide, Dalhart Junior High School, Dalhart Tx; [pers.] I truly believe I could not be where I am today without love and support from family and friends, and that life is what you make of it not what it makes of you...; [a.] Dalhart, TX

GARFIELD, PAMELA
[pen.] Pamela Zewe; [b.] November 25, 1970, Erie, PA; [p.] Shirley and Robert Zewe; [m.] David Garfield, June 5, 1991; [ed.] High School Advanced Placement Program; [occ.] Housewife; [memb.] Millcreek Community Hospital Guild, St. Peters Catholic Church, St. Pauls Church; [hon.] National Honor Society, German Club, Marching Band, Orchestra Awards, Science, History Advance Placement; [oth. writ.] Poem "You Or Me" is my first published. Other poem published is "Masquerade" published by Sparrowgrass. Many others unpublished.; [pers.] As a teenager I felt afraid to dream of what I could be, as an adult I find I am still dreaming to "Dare".; [a.] Erie, PA

GARTEE, BEATRICE M.
[b.] November 6, Chattanooga, TN; [p.] Cullen Maddox, Lela Maddox; [m.] Theodore Gartee, June 17, 1977; [ch.] Hope Prater, Ralph McCurdy, Cheryl; [ed.] LaFayette High, Shorter Gruenefeld College, West GA College Masters Degree in English and Education; [occ.] Retired Teacher of English, Freelance Writer, RVer; [memb.] Wesleyan Service Guild, Russel Park Baptist Church, Book Clubs; [hon.] Dean's List, several prizes and Honorary Mentions; [oth. writ.] Several poems published in anthologies, poetry magazines, and articles in a local newspaper. I have written many short stories and three novels, plus a chapbook of haiku - Hgache Haiku.; [pers.] I am a Christian who believes that each day is a gift from God and should be used in worthwhile pursuits. Life itself is the opportunity - make the most of it!; [a.] Fort Myers, FL

GARZA, KATHARINE TERESA
[pen.] Kay Garza; [b.] January 1, 1983, Dallas, TX; [p.] Dr. and Mrs. Joseph Garza; [ed.] 8th grade student at Keystone School, San Antonio, TX; [occ.] Student; [hon.] Duke University TIPS; [a.] San Antonio, TX

GARZA, SUZY
[b.] October 3, 1977, Houston; [p.] James and Esther Garza; [ed.] Deer Park High School and Sam Houston State University; [occ.] Student in college; [memb.] Fellowship of Christian Athletes; [hon.] Softball Scholarship to Sam Houston State University, National Honor Society, Mu Alpha Theta, Cum Laude; [oth. writ.] Essay published in High School literary magazine: Magnus Opus; [pers.] Be strong in what you believe in, be willing to take a stand.; [a.] Deer Park, TX

GASKINS, PRISCILLA
[b.] November 28, 1946, Rock Hill, SC; [p.] Glenn Gaskins, Vivien Harrelson, step-mother Amilee Staggs; [ed.] High School - 1 yr. college; [occ.] Licensed Practical Nurse - work in Geriatrics; [oth. writ.] This is my first.; [pers.] I wrote this poem about a place I lived in, in Tupelo, Miss. I love to read and believe reading keeps the mind active - I also believe age is a state of mind and if you want to do something bad enough you can.

GATES, TOM
[b.] May 24, 1979, St. Paul; [p.] Jim and Lu Neary; [oth. writ.] I have tons of poems and stories that I've written over a period of 3 years. I'm hoping this may expand my writing career.; [pers.] Writing is my way of a getting away from reality. It's a way of letting your frustrations flow without hurting anyone it's a way to let others see inside your heart and soul.; [a.] Randolph, MN

GAWTHORP JR., CHARLES R.
[b.] September 25, 1963, Champaign, IL; [p.] Charles R. Gawthorp, Carol E. Kilgore; [m.] Divorced; [ch.] Charless III, Jacqueline Kay; [ed.] Farmer City - Mansfield High School; [occ.] Laborer, Construction; [oth. writ.] "A Mothers Love", "Please Don't Go Away", "For Eternity", "Dream Chasin", "My Old Truck". Just to name a few, all unpublished.; [pers.] All of my writings come from my personal experiences in life. I consider myself a young man, but I have many different occupations. From them I've learned that people and situation aren't always as they appear, but if you look hard enough, you can find good in everything.; [a.] Deland, IL

GEORGE, CHERILYN
[b.] October 3, 1972, Lompoc, CA; [p.] Eileen Carter; [m.] David George, July 23, 1993; [ch.] Ashley Marie, Kristen Nicole; [pers.] My mother is my inspiration. As a child she taught me to go after my dreams, even when I wanted to be a princess. My dream is to make others feel as free and as invincible as I do when I write.; [a.] Hauptstuhl, Germany

GEORGE, RENEE
[pen.] Nae; [b.] January 14, 1967, Mt. View, CA; [p.] Keith and Barbara Shutt; [m.] Fred George, August 11, 1990; [ed.] Lincoln High School, CA Gavilan College, Gilroy CA; [occ.] Admission Dept. at Santa Theresa Kaiser Hospital; [memb.] Volunteer for the Disabled students programs and services at Gavilan College Vice President of LVN Class.; [hon.] Vice President Licenced Vocational Nursing program, Certificate of Achievement Santa Clara County Regional Occupational Program Nurse Assistant and orderly certificate of appreciation as a volunteer for the Disabled students programs and services at Gavilan College.; [oth. writ.] Several writings published in Gilroy's Dispatch newspaper.; [pers.] Nothing will stand in my way of achieving my goals. Being published is one of them. I will

continue to write about colors like "Red" and the future fears we hold and hide.; [a.] Gilroy, CA

GERMAN, RAFAEL
[b.] December 17, 1950, Lima, Peru; [p.] Prudencio and Maria; [m.] Judith, October 7, 1978; [ch.] Dany, Tommy, Mikey; [ed.] LLM by NYU, JD by Catholic University Bachelor in Arts by Catholic University; [occ.] Residential Real Estate and Int'l Procurement; [memb.] Cypress Creek Lions Club; [oth. writ.] Presently working on book (poems) "Chaclacayo, Why Me?!"; [pers.] Courage makes life hopeful and joyful for it liberates ones self to be, to love into infinity, courage.; [a.] Klein, TX

GERMINO, JUSTIN R.
[b.] September 29, 1977, Queens, NY; [p.] Robert and Peggy; [ed.] Beach Channel H.S. Queens, NY; [occ.] Freelance poet/short story writer; [oth. writ.] Poems and stories published in High School news journal.; [pers.] Parents are everything.; [a.] Phoenix, AZ

GIACOLINI, PATRICIA
[b.] March 29, 1950, Portland, OR; [p.] Lawrence - Alladine Whitehead; [m.] Joseph Giacolini, July 20, 1995; [ed.] Hector Campbell Elementary Ickes Jr. High - Medford High, Southern Or. College; [occ.] Homemaker; [oth. writ.] Combined Mother - Daughter Exhibit of my poetry and her paintings - Medford and Portland showings.; [pers.] I create words to give beauty and grace to God's Universe and empowered significance to the human soul.; [a.] Medford, OR

GIBSON, OLIVIA CARPENTER
[pen.] Olivia Carpenter-Gibson; [b.] August 18, 1952, Atlanta, GA; [p.] Robert E. Carpenter, Mildred Davis Carpenter; [ch.] Mark Davis Gibson; [ed.] Decatur High School, Young Harris College Georgia, Baptist School of Nursing; [a.] Lithonia, GA

GIBSON, PAULETTE F. SMITH
[b.] September 19, 1944, Pensacola, FL; [p.] Eunice Mae Chesser-Gibson; [m.] Ronald Edward Gibson Sr.; [ch.] Five; [ed.] High School; [oth. writ.] That's My Cup of Tea; [pers.] I believe in the "Golden Rule". Do unto others as you would have them do unto you. I stand on Romans 8:28 and put my faith and confidence in it.; [a.] Merrillville, IN

GILBERT, DOROTHY
[pen.] Dorothea Arceneaux; [b.] September 5, 1937, Montgomery, LA; [p.] Rev. and Mrs. Ned Douglas; [m.] Divorced; [ch.] Brian Keith Gilbert; [ed.] Bachelor of Science (Grambling State University), M.Ed. Texas Southern Uni., Certifications University of Houston and Lamar University; [occ.] Speech Pathologist Houston Ind., School District; [memb.] South Post Oak Baptist Church's Women's Chorus, Mass Choir and Women's Mission, Cambridge Village Civic Club, Delta Sima Theta Sorority; [hon.] District Trainer for the "Computerized Speech Therapy Report Workshop", Speech Therapy Supervisor for a Licensed Speech Therapy Assistant; [oth. writ.] Several unpublished poems and a short story.; [pers.] My writings are influenced by my many years of working with special education students and their parents.; [a.] Houston, TX

GILES, TERENCE J.
[pen.] T. J. Giles; [b.] June 17, 1940, Wantage, England; [m.] Nancy K. Giles, November 26, 1988; [ch.] Brian, Russell - Sons, Mike, Greg, Cindy, Brad, Phil - Stepchildren; [ed.] High School and 1 yr. College; [occ.] Mailcarrier USPS, Retired Master Sergeant US Army; [memb.] Vinyard Christian Fellowship; [a.] Great Falls, MT

GILLETTE, RALPH E.
[b.] August 13, 1934, Michigan; [p.] Glenn and Lillian Gillette; [m.] Barbara J., June 30, 1956; [ch.] Four; [ed.] BA, Central Michigan University (Eng/Speech), M.A. Wheaton College (Religious Studies) MA U. of Minnesota (Administration); [occ.] Former Independent School Headmaster/Teacher; [memb.] Elder at Grace Episcopal Church; [oth. writ.] Major American Authors Series of Harcourt, Brace The Short Fiction of Stephen Crane (Textbook); [pers.] My poetry seeks to capture nature and reflect the rhythms common to it and humanity.; [a.] Brooklyn, NY

GLASER, DAVID
[b.] September 29, 1919, Brooklyn, NY; [p.] Samuel, Jennie; [m.] Mildred, February 19, 1944; [ch.] Susan, Sherry; [ed.] Thomas Jefferson High School Graduate 1936, Art Student League (Scholar), NY School of Industrial Art, New York School Contemporary Art, Brooklyn Museum Art School, Behring Institute 1954, Teacher Center Island Jewish School, Freeport New York 1959; [occ.] Artist, Sculptor - Fine Art, Writing New Age Graphic experimentation, owner, studio concepts; [memb.] Allied Artists of America, Freeport Art Museum and Conservation, AVC, ACW, Amnesty Int'l, Wilderness Soc., World Jewish Cong., Greenpeace, American Museum of Nat'l History; [hon.] First poem published 1934 National Human Review, Nassau County poetry award 1981, Art Students League Scholar 1936, Grand Prize redesign Levitt Home 1967, numerous graphic wards, Monadnock Mills, Vet Soc. of American Artists, Desi-Grand prize, 3-man Show Heckscher Music Huntington 1964, Shows National Arts Club New York 1959, Art Directions 1959, ACA Galleries 1960, Hofstra U., Adelphi U., Nassau Community Call, Press. Allied Artists of America 1985 exh. Wantagh Levittown, Civilian Conservation Corps 1936 Artist (Adirondacks); [oth. writ.] "My Mother Died Dancing" book 1970, cartoonist, editor publisher AUS "Giggy Andom" 1993-4 orientations (USA my writings North Pacific 1945,) numerous essays on human condition. Inventor: Mosaic reproduction 1948-50 artists, writer 1945 "Bearing Breeze" Aleutians; [pers.] To question to wonder, to accept all possibilities and to explore whenever possible and to accept so called "Failure" as a "Given" side road to discovery. "To tune in" to the inner universal self and express what is received back in the song of words or the visual. To go "against the grain". Insecurity expressed positively moves me more deeply toward the full potential.; [a.] Wantagh, NY

GLOVER, RAUL
[pen.] Raoul; [b.] May 20, 1961, Jersey City, NJ; [p.] Ms. Ozzie Lee Moore; [ed.] Saint Anthony's High School, Tuskegee University; [occ.] Mechanical Designer, Vae-Nortrak, Birmingham, AL; [memb.] Pi Tau Sigma, American Society of Mechanical Engineers, Christian Life Church Usher; [hon.] Dean's List, N.A.S.A. Scholarship, Who's Who Among High School Students; [oth. writ.] Imagining, The Wonders Of Life; [pers.] I give all the Honor and Glory to Jesus Christ my Lord and Savior: through Him my writings are possible and in Him there is love and unspeakable joy. Thank you Jesus for this poem. Amen; [a.] Montgomery, AL

GNOYSKI, KER MICHAELS
[pen.] Ker Michaels; [b.] December 15, 1954, Chicago; [p.] LaVerne and Adam Gnoyski; [ed.] Lyons Township High School, Lee Strasberg Acting School; [occ.] Actor; [memb.] American Film Institute, Eric Morris Actors Workshop; [oth. writ.] Produced and Directed "Still Love" play.; [pers.] Everything happens at once. We miss most of it. The Kettle boils over and puts out the fire.; [a.] Los Angeles, CA

GODWIN, ALLAN
[pen.] Allan Boys; [b.] September 14, 1949, Ozark, AL; [p.] Fred Godwin, Bobbie Roney; [m.] Celinda, November 7, 1970; [ch.] Benjamin Allan Godwin; [ed.] Samson High School, Troy State University; [occ.] Production Manager - Tri-Glass Industries, Daleville, Al; [memb.] First Baptist Church; [pers.] My pen name is in honor of two nephews killed in an automobile accident. They were affectionately referred to by our family as "The Boys."; [a.] Samson, AL

GOLDEN, KENNETH R.
[b.] August 22, 1964, Beloit, WI; [p.] Charles Golden, Geraldine Golden; [m.] Karla Elizabeth Sample Golden, June 20, 1995; [ch.] Kenneth R. Golden II; [ed.] Black Hawk Technical College Janesville Wisc.; [occ.] Connoisseur; [memb.] Emmanuel Baptist Church Reverend Floyd Prude, Sr. Pastor; [oth. writ.] Lyrical art facts of personal benevolence dedicated to my beloved wife who has my most sacred affection.; [pers.] Don't take the family the Lord blessed you with for granted, live for Christ.; [a.] Beloit, WI

GOLDSTEIN, JOEL
[b.] March 29, 1939, New York, NY; [p.] Beatrice and Ben Goldstein; [m.] 2 - Eugenia Jody May 1962 and Bonnie Flemming, 1964; [ed.] Hessian Hills School and Croton-Harmon Elementary and HS through 8th grade, Oakwood School, Poughkeepsie, NY, 9-12 grade. Johns Hopkins and U of Wisconsin, Madison, BS, 1962. UC Berkeley, Teaching Internship Program, Secondary Teaching Credential, 1964; [occ.] Retired Teacher; [hon.] I am honored by the people I have known, some of whom I also loved and/or held/hold in high regard: W.E.B. Dubois and his wife, Shirley Graham, Rudy Bretz, a pioneer in TV in NYC, Atlanta, and L.A., high school friend, Hugh Sonnenschein, now president of the University of Chicago, Marshall Brickman, a screenwriter and roommate at the University of Wisconsin, Bob Dylan, who hung out with my crowd of Madison in 60 and in 61 and who tried to buy my guitar, Bob Orlins, Chief Archeologist for the state of California, who first brought me to Berkeley in 58, Jerry Rubin, Ying Kelley, once a fellow teacher and friend, then mayor of Berkeley, now aide to Ron Dellums, my first wife, today, niece of the late senator, Harry Byrd, and my father Ben, who contributed a social-historical art collection to the Library of Congress, which will open in their principal exhibition hall in October of 1997, and which is valued each 1.5-2 million dollars. (There are many other people, known and not, to include).; [pers.] I am a mystic and if I ever recover from chronic fatigue syndrome, expect that teaching spirituality will be my life's goal and essential work, the reason I came here.; [a.] New York, NY

GOLDSTEIN, PIRHIYN
[b.] October 2, 1946, Iran; [p.] Isaac and Rachel; [m.] Signurd, August 30, 1976; [ch.] Joyce, Jeff; [ed.] Master in Educational Therapy; [occ.] Program Coordinator with Jewish Family Service of L.A.; [oth. writ.] Other poems in English and Hebrew; [pers.] Life would be an empty existence without nature, music, poetry, art, love and satisfying work.; [a.] Northridge, CA

GOLDTHWAITE, MILDRED L.
[pen.] Mildred Louise Goldthwaite (Midge); [b.] November 2, 1912, Tonawanda, NY; [p.] Deceased; [m.] Deceased, July 25, 1939; [ch.] Roger, Richard, Arnold, Ronald; [ed.] Registered Nurse Graduated NY (1934), Clinical Lab. Tech (S.F) - CA - Med. Steno - CA (Palo Alto); [occ.] (Missionary Emeritus - L.G.C.C.) Ministry, "ABA" - American Bible Academy "A.R.M." - American Rehabilitation to Prisoners Grader of Bible Correspondence Lessons; [memb.] (Missionary Emeritus) of Los Gatos

Christian Church, Central Africa Mission, 21 yrs as Medical/Evangelism Missionary to Rhodesia/Zimbabwe - Africa, 1970-1991; [hon.] (62 yrs. R.N) - Poem book "Bless the Lord O My Soul" printed 1994..."Turkey Wisdom" poem won 2nd place humorous award for Senior Poet Laureate Competition Joplin, Mo. 1995 in "Golden Words" publication poems used for youth camps, church groups, dedication of 3 churches one in Zimbabwe "Bush" Africa. Raised 4 great sons! "Thank you Lord" - all gifts from you!!!; [oth. writ.] Over 200 poems, widely used, extra verses to "special hymns". Articles for "Central Africa Story" (Hoping to put into book for 21 years life and work.); [pers.] I owe everything to Almighty God, my life, my writings, my call to Africa at age (58-79) as Medical Missionary, my 4 wonderful sons...well - everything!!! Helping all His children to "rise above their situations", and be more as He wanted them to be...be a "spirit lifter"; [a.] Joplin, MO

GOLPHENEE, KYLE S.
[b.] February 4, 1968, Laguna Beach, CA; [p.] Dava Thomas, Jerry Golphenee; [ed.] Whitefish High School, Whitefish, MT, B.A. in Liberal Studies and English, English teaching credentials, University of Montana; [occ.] English Teacher in Heart Butte, MT, on the Blackfeet Indian Reservation; [memb.] MEA/NEA; [pers.] My writings draw from an electric mix of environmental, musical and Native American sources, with an added emphasis in the natural sciences. The discovery of common ground in a world of cultural diversity is my primary purpose in life.; [a.] Heart Butte, MT

GOLUZA, MICHAEL J.
[pen.] Mike; [b.] November 16, 1982, Van Nuys, CA; [p.] Janja Viltuznik and Steve Goluza; [ed.] Graduated from John A Sutter Junior High School, Canoga Park, CA; [occ.] Student; [hon.] Received first place in Nesburn student writing competition 1996; [oth. writ.] Short poems; [pers.] I have been greatly influenced by my mother and her writing.; [a.] Canoga Park, CA

GOLYSHEV, TATIANA P.
[b.] March 4, 1977, Irkutsk, Russia; [p.] Olga Golyshev, Pavel Golyshev; [ed.] On the second year in Bellevue Community College (General Sciences Pre-Medical Program) - for transferring to U.W.; [occ.] High school graduated; [pers.] I want to reflect in my writings the devotion of my spirit to a mankind and love.; [a.] Bellevue, WA

GOODE, VIRGINIA E.
[b.] March 29, 1932, Hollywood, CA; [p.] Alberta Moyse-Ivan and Hollis Moyse; [m.] Jesse Goode, March 6, 1954; [ch.] Jesse Jr., Matthew, Wyatt, Travis; [ed.] Venice High Bishop Johnson College of Nursing Los Angeles, Calif; [occ.] Retired R.N. Part time Infant and toddler care; [memb.] International Society of poets; [hon.] Editors choice award - Nat'l Library of Poetry; [oth. writ.] "The Kick-Off" published in Across the Universe by Nat'l Library of Poetry; [pers.] "The Paratrooper" was written, before his recent passing, in honor of my husband Jesse's brother Douglas Goode. He served in the 101st Airborne in Europe in World War II. He marveled how a few lines of poetry could span a lifetime. I dedicate this poem to Doug and wife Nancy, to all his family and to the Lord who watches over all; [a.] San Antonio, TX

GOSTONY JR, JEFF
[pen.] Jeff Gostony, Jr.; [b.] November 29, 1986, Bethlehem, PA; [p.] Phyllis and Jeffrey A. Gostony, Sr.; [ed.] Currently 4th grade student at Moore Elementary School, Bath, PA; [memb.] Moore Township Athletic Association, Flag Football, Basketball and Baseball teams, Junior Youth Group at Holy Cross Lutheran Church, Nazareth; [hon.] 1st and 2nd place honors for

baking at Allentown State Fair and for scarecrow crafting; [oth. writ.] Jeff wrote "I know my house in the morning" while he was in 2nd grade.; [pers.] I enjoy writing poems. I also enjoy reading sports stories. Hobbies include wood working, gardening, baking, crafts, and collecting football cards.; [a.] Bath, PA

GRABLE III, DARRELL WAYNE
[pen.] D. W. Grable; [b.] July 31, 1979, Washington, PA; [p.] Ellen Emory, Darrell Grable Jr.; [ed.] Attending Junior year of High School (McGuffey High School), Washington, PA; [memb.] No noteworthy or relevant memberships to speak of; [hon.] This is my first attempt at publication; [oth. writ.] Although this is my first attempt at recognition, I have been writing poetry and short stories since the age of 7 among my favorite poems are "Mystery of the Red" and a poem entitled "A Happy Couple...and going out" along with a short story called "The End".; [pers.] I try to consciously make my poetry extremely subjective and diverse in its underlying themes while keeping the overt symbolic plots rather objective, enabling the reader to conclude for himself what the poem truly represents, this is turn expands the poem's meaning into a broader definition. I also enjoy elaborate, hidden internal rhyme schemes.; [a.] Washington, PA

GRAHAM JR., HOWARD L.
[pen.] Howard Graham Jr.; [b.] July 20, 1946, Pitcairn, PA; [p.] Howard L. Graham and Laura; [m.] Mary-Ann Graham, November 12, 1977; [ed.] Gateway Senior High, Career Development at Edgar Thompson Works, Community College of Allegheny County; [occ.] Mechanical Repairmen, Internal Auditor, Union Official Local 1219; [memb.] United Steelworks Local 1219, RCI Member, Slovack Social Club, Carnegie Museum, AARP (American Association of Retired People); [oth. writ.] Published poem in Update Institute for Career Development.; [pers.] I love writing about everyday life and I am inspired by the people I meet everyday.; [a.] Duquesne, PA

GRALIKER, MARY
[b.] November 16, 1927, Indiana; [ch.] Five grown children; [occ.] Retired; [memb.] International Society of Poets; [oth. writ.] "Autumn" published in Rainbow's End, "Wind" published in Lyrical Heritage, "The Second Time Around" published in The Color of Thought, "Mary" published Best Poems of the '90s; [pers.] Hobby - oil painting. Sold first oil landscape in 1995. Try to fill my days with both painting and writing.

GRANDISON, SHEILA
[b.] March 20, Springfield, MA; [p.] Delsie Grandison; [ch.] Sean Grandison; [ed.] Bachelor Of Arts Degree/English/Western New England College; [occ.] Family Support Specialist (socialwork) Seattle Public Schools; [hon.] Received FCC Radio Operators license, Public Radio Broadcasting/Responsible for Public service announcements, Read Poetry on air/college radio stations/Talk Radio; [oth. writ.] Poems published in 1980s in school newspaper; [pers.] I would like to write and publish books for children. My focus would be contemporary issues for urban children. The children would learn coping skills, like skills and art appreciation.; [a.] Renton, WA

GRANT, SHIRLEY M.
[pen.] Shirley M. Grant; [b.] September 1, 1928, Whitman, MA; [p.] Walter and Ruth Hill; [m.] April 26, 1950; [ch.] Perc III, Sheryl Ruth, Melody Lillian and Dorothy Maria; [ed.] Whitman High School, Berkshire Christian College, Nursing School, Manuscript Writing; [occ.] Patient Registration Clerk part time at Pen Bay Medical Center; [memb.] Faith Temple Church of God; [hon.] 15 yrs at Penobscot Bay Medical Center in Rockport, ME; [oth. writ.] Newspaper series, newspaper by-lines, magazine articles of a devotional nature,

daily devotional guides.; [pers.] It is pleasing to put the pulse of my heart into words on paper so that others will understand, and maybe, even smile!; [a.] Thomaston, ME

GREEN, COURTNEY LEAN
[b.] February 15, 1981, Alpena, MI; [p.] William and Linda Green; [ed.] I'm a Sophomore with a CPA of 3.5, I'm attending Hillman School. After graduation I plan to attend college majoring in Zoology.; [hon.] I'm a honor student and on the Honor Roll at my high school.; [oth. writ.] I write a lot of poetry but it has never been sent for publishing.; [pers.] All my poetry has meaning to it. When I write I have someone special in mind and put all my feelings toward that person into my writing.; [a.] Hillman, MI

GREENLAW, SCOTT W.
[b.] October 8, 1970, Fall River, MA; [p.] Jim and Faye Greenlaw; [m.] Melissa, December 12, 1992; [ch.] Justin, Kayla, Joshua; [ed.] Some College, four months it I school. Southington High School; [occ.] Professional Tracker Tailor driver.; [memb.] Church, member in solved praise team. New Britain Church of God New Britain, CT 06051; [hon.] Certificate of Completion. Top in class. Five hundred hours. New England Tractor Trailer Training School, four months.; [oth. writ.] Lose of Shawn was published in the newspaper I posses other poems in which I wish to share in its own time. Newspaper heard ternal; [pers.] When I write a poem it always comes form my heart, (never from my mind)" If I could do anything good or anything right, it would be to touch somebody's heart with my poetry and change them forever.; [a.] New Britain, CT

GREER, LEMMIE J.
[b.] January 14, 1956, McGehee, AR; [p.] Richard Drew, Marretta Drew; [m.] Albert L. Greer, January 10, 1976; [ch.] La Keesha, Nikale, Allison; [ed.] Mumford High; [oth. writ.] Several poems written for family, friends and pleasure, short stories and plays; [pers.] I get my inspiration to write poetry in the knowledge of how great God is and how minute I am; [a.] Detroit, MI

GRIMES SR., JOHN W.
[pen.] John W. Grimes Sr.; [b.] July 14, 1931, Argyle, TX; [p.] George P. and Ida Moe Grimes; [m.] Benetta Grimes, April 9, 1971; [ch.] Ten; [ed.] High school, I.C.S. Trove School (Industrial); [occ.] Retired; [memb.] Assembly of God; [hon.] Outstanding Mgr. 1985, Const Supt. of Year 1994; [oth. writ.] Local newspaper poems published - Monitor City of Dallas Insp Dept, Texas Dental Journal, Choice Homes Tx, newsletters, channel 4 news Dallas, several others.; [pers.] My poetry is written, "Spurs of the Moment" from the heart. Reflections of Post - 2nd inspirational.; [a.] Eustace, TX

GRINNELL, PAULINE
[pen.] Pauline McMaster; [b.] June 26, 1956, Northants, England; [p.] Richard and Doreen McMaster; [ed.] Samuell Lloyd College for Girls. Northamptonshire England; [pers.] Mankind has been blessed with many gifts, the greatest of all is love. For without love, nothing is meaningful or true, we only exist. We do not truly live without love in our hearts.; [a.] Xenia, OH

GROGAN, PATRICK
[b.] April 1, 1984, Pittsburgh, PA; [p.] Alan Grogan, Susan Grogan; [ed.] 7th grade Slippery Rock Middle School; [occ.] Student; [memb.] Slippery Rock Middle School Academic achievement Group Center for Talented Youth, John Hopkins University; [hon.] Honors Band (Trombone) President's Award for scholastic achievement, Honor Roll - last 5 years, Parvuli Dei Religion Award; [a.] Portersville, PA

GRONINGER, STEVEN
[b.] December 6, 1955, Fremont, NE; [m.] Lucinda L. Groninger, December 11, 1984; [ch.] Kendra; [ed.] B.S. Univ. of Colorado; [occ.] Film maker, Musician; [a.] Ventura, CA

GROSSMAN, TERESA L.
[pen.] Terri G; [b.] 1957, Long Island, NY; [ch.] Brian and Cassandra Beth; [ed.] Floral Park Memorial H.S., Floral Park, LL, New York; [occ.] Operator/Proprietor of "Terri's Word Processing Svcs."; [memb.] 12 - Step Recovery Programs; [hon.] MHLC Recognition Award (1985); [oth. writ.] Two Roses, Through The Gate (Both currently unpublished); [pers.] As God's gifts only continue to unfold, I give my most heartfelt thanks to my "non-biological family of choice", most especially for my soulmate, Pasquale P., and both Lil Lucy and Lil Terri, too. I am truly blessed...believing in myself.; [a.] Franklin Square, NY

GRULEY, ROSEANN
[pen.] Roseann Thorn, Leocadia; [b.] November 24, U.S.A.; [occ.] Retail Merchandiser, Manager; [hon.] "Voice of Democracy", numerous contest, "Most Creative" in senior Class; [oth. writ.] Novel, numerous short stories, poems, Award Winning Speeches; [pers.] I attempt to balance the dark and light of myself through my writing and hope to one day see all beauty without using my sight - just my heart.; [a.] Winston-Salem, NC

GUITY, CARLOS
[pen.] Carlos Guity; [b.] April 2, 1971, South Bronx, NY; [p.] Eugenio and Macaria Guity; [m.] Engaged; [ch.] Sahrasia Guity; [ed.] Norman Thomas H.S., Bronx Community College, Lehman College; [occ.] Performing Artist - Acrobat - Big Apple Circus, NY; [hon.] Award of Merits from Bronx Borough President; [oth. writ.] Several unpublished poems based on my personal experiences.; [pers.] I want to inspire in my writing. I have grown up overcoming life's obstacles and I want people to know that all things are possible. Life is living each day.; [a.] New York, NY

GULLI, JEANNINE
[pen.] Jeannine Gulli; [b.] February 14, 1983, Plainview, NY; [p.] Ellen, John Gulli; [ed.] 8th Grade Student - JFK Middle School - Bethpage, New York; [occ.] Student - JFK Middle School - Bethpage, New York; [oth. writ.] She has a collection of other writings.; [pers.] Jeannine Gulli finds great joy through her love of writing, especially poetry. She finds inspiration in the beauty around her, and in the love she and her family feel for one another. In addition to reading and music, Jeannine enjoys spending time with her friends and family, who often spark her creative impulses.; [a.] Bethpage, NY

HAEN, CONNIE S.
[pen.] Connie Haen; [b.] December 9, 1946, Sweetwater, TX; [p.] Harvey B. McPeeters, Mary L. Oden McPeeters; [m.] John F. Haen, February 12, 1965; [ch.] Three; [ed.] Santa Rosa Junior College, Chabot Jr. College, World Travel Bible Study Fellowship; [occ.] Family and home/managing rentals and properties/volunteer church; [memb.] Mountain Christian Center, Stonecraft Missions, Couples Club of the Sierra's - Committee; [pers.] Strong belief in God, all writings should encourage and build up not tear down. Truth is utmost; stand up for what is right.; [a.] Oakhurst, CA

HAGAN, JEAN
[b.] October 5, 1944, Mount Eden, NY; [p.] Olus and Verna Sparrow; [m.] Earl Hagan, December 22, 1962; [ch.] Lisa, Jill, Dana, Patrick; [ed.] Taylorsville High School; [occ.] Interior Design Consultant; [memb.] Bardstown Jct. Baptist Church, I.W. Bernheim Arboretum and Research Forest; [oth. writ.] Several poems

published in local newspaper. Also have had short articles published. Much of my work is done for personal friends and family.; [pers.] Writing and particularly poetry, has always been an important way for me to express myself, I consider this a gift from God.; [a.] Lebanon Junction, KY

HAGAN, JIM
[b.] November 8, 1974, Cleveland, OH; [p.] James Hagan, Lin Hagan; [ed.] Medpark High School, Bowling Green State University, Ohio Center for Broadcasting; [occ.] New Car Detailer; [oth. writ.] A whole bunch of other poems and some free-writing. Nothing special.; [pers.] I try to keep everything simple and I draw ideas from my own experiences. I think that people put too much thought into their writings. In my opinion, it ruins everything.

HALL, JAMES H.
[b.] May 7, 1954, Waterville, MN; [p.] Foster Child; [m.] MariAngela Hall, March 16, 1976; [ed.] UCLA: Languages Woodbury Univ.: Intern'l Bus Marketing; [occ.] J. H. Hall Associates Import/Export and Actor/Writer; [memb.] International Trade Assoc.; [hon.] Phi Gamma Kappa, Dean's List; [oth. writ.] Screenplay to be submitted 1997; [pers.] After spending most of his growing up years in foster homes - James hall entered the U.S. Army, where he met major Wilford R. Willis in Erlangen W. Germany who taught James discipline, and leadership. James dedicates his work to Major Willis. Thank You Sir!

HALL, ROBERT PEYTON
[pen.] R. Peyton Hall; [b.] March 18, 1941; [p.] Hamilton F. and Buenos M. Hall; [ch.] Tereza, Renee, Amanda; [ed.] Fairhope High Faulker Jr. College AA, University of West Florida BA Political Science; [occ.] Chemical Operator at Degussa Corporation; [memb.] YMCA, ACLU, Florida Track and Field, Key Club, Friendly Sons of St. Patrick; [hon.] Phi Theta Kappa, Dean's List; [oth. writ.] Unpublished short stories; [pers.] My belief echos Robert Frost's words: "Poetry begins in metaphor, in trivial metaphors, and goes on to the profoundest thinking that we have."; [a.] Pensacola Beach, FL

HALLETT, RUTH ETTER
[pen.] Ruth Etter or Ruth Hallett; [b.] August 21, 1933, Adrian, MI; [p.] John and Alberta Etter; [m.] D. Dale Hallett, August 23, 1957; [ch.] Margie, David and Richard; [ed.] High School Grad.; [occ.] Homemaker, Retired Register Book Assembler; [memb.] Lyons Christian Church CWF, Lyons Literary League, Magnolia O.E.S.; [hon.] Being able to share my writings with others; [oth. writ.] Our Country's 200th-220th Birthday, Thanksgiving History, Poems/Story for each of our 3 children when they graduated, many poems.; [pers.] I have written poems since in grade school. About Family, Nature, God, Memorials to my Dad and Mom - mostly for my enjoyment. Give my writings at our Church.; [a.] Lyons, OH

HALLMAN, BRENDA LEE
[pen.] Bree; [b.] September 10, 1966, Southfield, MI; [p.] Sharon Lee and Morey Walter Lipke; [m.] Matthew Gustave Hallman, October 23, 1993; [ch.] Jennifer Lee, Joseph Charles, Ashley Marie, Melissa Sue; [ed.] Associate in Science, Delta University; [occ.] Management (Business); [memb.] National Authors Registry, "Prince of Peace" Lutheran Church - I teach 1st grade Sunday School; [oth. writ.] "True Love" published in "Beginnings"; [pers.] My father Morey inspired me to write. When my father is in need to express his feelings he writes poetry. When I was a very young girl he shared this art with me. Now when I feel the need to express myself I like my father write with "Feelings from the Heart."; [a.] Kalamazoo, MI

HALO, TYLER
[b.] September 21, 1975, Suffern, NY; [p.] Timothy C. Halo, Patricia Halo; [ed.] Storm King School, Cornwall, NY and Rockland Community College (Degree in prog); [occ.] Student, Writer; [memb.] Museum of Natural History; [hon.] Most Valuable Player, basketball, and Coaches Award; [oth. writ.] Novel in progress, collection of poetry.; [pers.] As long as you are putting one foot in front of the other, you are getting somewhere.; [a.] New City, NY

HAMILTON, JANICE
[pen.] Anne Cunningham; [b.] August 6, 1946, Davenport, IA; [p.] Dr. Harold H. Hamilton (Deceased), Gladys M. Hamilton (Deceased); [ch.] Joff Cundiff, James Cundiff, Shere Hamilton; [ed.] McPherson High School, McPherson, KS, Real Estate Insurance, Advertising Media Fundraising; [occ.] Founder of "Guardian Angel" a non-profit agency for crime victims; [memb.] American Business Women's Assoc. West Texas Council of Governments Taylor County Republican Women Texas Council on family violence; [hon.] Dale Carnegie Graduate, Special Achievement Award for my talk about public awareness work for battered women; [oth. writ.] I am currently writing my biography and working on a campaign "Ending The Violence" for National Crime Victims Right Week April 13-19, 1997; [pers.] As a survivor of violent crime, many of my poems are a reflection of the feelings I went through as a crime victim and my hopes for ending the violence in this country.; [a.] Abilene, TX

HAMILTON, LISA ELAINE
[b.] March 11, 1963, San Francisco, CA; [p.] Barbara Boyd, Clarence Hamilton; [ch.] Craig; [occ.] USN/AD; [pers.] Dedicated to Mark Anthony Littleton.; [a.] Newport News, VA

HANDEL, JULIA
[pen.] Julia Fay Handel; [b.] March 8, 1984, New York; [p.] Harvey and Eileen Handel; [ed.] I attend Intermediate School 72 - Rocco Laurie; [occ.] Student; [pers.] I feel that Anne Frank is the spirit of the peace that lives throughout the world, between the people and their differences.; [a.] Staten Island, NY

HANNA, MELISSA CLAIRE
[pen.] Mimi; [b.] June 23, 1987, California, LA; [p.] Linda/Andrew; [ed.] Farm School pre school - K. Woodland Hills Private School 1st grade. Welby Way Magnet School, grade 2. Tamberly School, Nassau Bahamas. Dixie Cnyn gr 3-4,; [occ.] Student; [hon.] 1st place "Studio City Chamber of Commerce" Earth day Celebration (poster contest) 1st place "Subway Corp." Halloween festival. 1st place "Barbie Christmas Celebration" (poster and essay.).; [oth. writ.] "Rainbow of Poetry" 1995 "Mystery at Rose Island" 1996 "The Teacher" 1996 "A Collection of Poems" 1994 (some not listed here); [pers.] My writing comes from my deepest personal feelings. I am inspired by what I see in my own world, plus what I learn in school. My family is bi-racial and I have a lot of unique experiences.; [a.] Sherman Oaks, CA

HANSON, LUCINDA
[b.] April 15, 1953, Mason Co., KY; [p.] Bus and Betty Gill; [m.] R. Carl Hanson, May 12, 1973; [ch.] Stephanie Lee and Stacie Marie; [ed.] West Union High School; [occ.] Administrative Assistant; [hon.] Adams County Community Homemaker of the Year; [oth. writ.] Have won several poetry contests on county and state level.; [pers.] I normally write about topics that have an impact on my life, sometimes humorous but most often they are on a very serious note.; [a.] Blue Creek, OH

HARDING, PAMELA
[b.] January 24, 1965, Cincinnati, OH; [p.] Mathew and Arlene Harding; [ed.] University of Cincinnati; [occ.] Architect; [memb.] A.I.A., Children's Medical Center Volunteer, Habitat for Humanity Volunteer; [hon.] Dean's List; [oth. writ.] Authored and Designed USAF 1989 Robert H. Curtain Award Winning Proposal; [pers.] Each individual should allow themselves to feel the full spectrum of emotion because without sorrow you will never know joy!

HARDWICK, HARRY
[b.] March 14, 1948, Carrollton, IL; [p.] Floyd and Evelyn Hardwick; [m.] Leah Patricia, December 23, 1978; [ch.] David, Jennifer, Joanne, Patty, Robert, Christine; [ed.] Carrollton High School; [occ.] Driver for RPS; [hon.] Being chosen as a semi-finalist; [oth. writ.] Several short stories, one manuscript, nothing published.; [pers.] Find something you love, whether it's professional or hobby. It will give you the peace of mind to do all things.; [a.] Jackson, TN

HARDY, JUNE EVELYN
[b.] June 20, 1969, York, PA; [p.] James and Mary Nesbit; [m.] James I. Hardy III, October 31, 1993; [ch.] Mary, Beverlyann and Jasmine; [ed.] Even Start (GED) 1996; [occ.] York County Court Appointed Special Advocate Volunteer (CASA); [hon.] Completion Awards, from "New Insights", "Even Start," and "York County CASA" programs (Court Appointed Special Advocate); [oth. writ.] Two other poems titled "Recovery" and "Me". They are parts one and two in my "Journey" series.; [pers.] Over the years I have learned to just keep on believing, don't give in, just keep on trying believers win. The road is tough but if you just stand tall, one day soon, you'll find your way through it all...; [a.] York, PA

HARGAN, JACK L.
[pen.] Jack Hargan; [b.] January 15, 1919, Ft. Wayne, IN; [p.] Leo and Lulu Hargan; [m.] Artis Hargan, August 39, 1980; [ch.] Mark, Keith, Jeanne, Jenifer; [ed.] Evansville Univ. AB, Indiana School of Medicine M.D., UCLA M.P.H., Univ. of Texas-Gynecology/ Oncology, Baylor University OB/Gyn; [occ.] Retired Physician, Board President Desert Health Care District Palm Springs, California; [memb.] Multiple Medical and International Societies, Staffs and Institutions; [hon.] Indiana University "Distinguished Service to Mankind" and many other rewards and awards relating to voluntary health services at home and international; [pers.] Brother, step-daughter both severe Dyslectic, watching their lives destroyed by dyslexia, the lack of social and educational acceptance - a heart breaking experience.; [a.] Palm Springs, CA

HARPER, CHESTER P.
[pen.] Ches. Harper or Buddy Harper; [b.] October 29, 1954, San Diego, CA; [m.] Maria Isabel Harper, April 27, 1974; [ch.] Chad Patrick and Brent Michael; [ed.] Granite Hills, and Santana High; [occ.] Computer/ Robotics Manufacturing and Chemtronics Inc.; [oth. writ.] Other poems, comedy, cartoons, and editorials in local papers; [pers.] Forgiveness is the most blessed gift.; [a.] El Cajon, CA

HARR, DAN
[b.] August 12, 1961, Topeka, KS; [m.] Divorced; [ch.] Brad - 11 and Steve - 7; [ed.] High School Graduate, 1980, attended 3-plus years of college, with the intended major of Communications Arts; [occ.] US Navy during 1987 and 1988, Novell Network Engineer setting up computer networks.; [hon.] Numerous poems published by The National Library of Poetry, Numerous poems published in Poet's Fantasy, Numerous poems published in Rosebud, Poetry book, "Through the Garden Gate," accepted as an entrant into the Pulitzer

Prize for Literature contest, 1996.; [oth. writ.] Being locked up has given me the time to organize my previous works and to continue writing poetry of a fashion that I desire. Recently, I have self-published a poetry anthology titled "Through the Garden Gate" which has received outstanding reviews from the book reviewers who have perused it.; [pers.] I continue to write poetry as each poem "hits" me. I believe that the finished poem is already out in the universe and I am but the receiver. It is a talent given to me by God that allows me to receive the words. My muse is Emily Dickinson. It is from her works that I have received my greatest inspirations.; [a.] Madison, WI

HARRINGTON, KARA KRISTINA
[b.] December 30, 1982, Park Ridge, IL; [p.] Karla and Phil Harrington; [ed.] 8th Grade - Lincoln Middle School - Honor Roll Student; [hon.] Honor Roll; [oth. writ.] I have another poem published in a book, "Ice Skating." Poem published 1996. Anthology of Poetry by Young Americans.; [a.] Park Ridge, IL

HARRIS, BILLY E.
[b.] July 8, 1948; [p.] Mery and Wrenshaw Harris; [ed.] Grad, AIAS Police Science Inst. Grad: Blackstone School of Law; [occ.] Retired Correction Officer, Para Legal; [memb.] Free Mason; [hon.] Silver and bronze star 82nd ABN Div. Vietnam 1968-69; [pers.] Be honest with yourself and every one else, then expect no less that what you have given and no less from others.; [a.] Lompoc, CA

HARRIS, GERALDINE LATIMER
[b.] September 7, 1934, USA; [p.] Rev. James Welben and Leila Latimer; [m.] Divorced; [ed.] M.A. in Education, B.A. in English - Graduate work at New York University, Atlanta University and Manhattanville - undergraduate degree from Morgan State University in Baltimore, MD.; [occ.] Retired Teacher, taught English in Public H.S. for 34 years; [memb.] NYSRTA (New York State Retired Teachers Association), GTF (Greenburgh Teachers Federation), NEA (National Education Assn.), Strait Gate Interdenominational Church of Mamaroneck, N.Y., National Christian Writers Fellowship Network; [hon.] The Diamond Homer Trophy for Outstanding Poets - Hollywood, Cal. by famous Poets Society, Poet of the Year Award from Nat'l Christian Writers Fellowship, Bronze Eagle Award from SGI Church for Christian Service and Dedication, African American History Plaque from Woodlands High School's Afr-Amer. Hist. Steering Committee, School Service Community Award; [oth. writ.] Several poems published in Famous Poems of The Twentieth Century (includes prize winning "Darkness Daunted" from my Spirit to Yours in Prose and Poetry Poem, "My Lineage", also published.; [pers.] I believe that much of my poetry and writings reflect my Christian heritage and faith in God. Miracles happen each day of the week, and only God can make our lives complete.; [a.] White Plains, NY

HART, JASON W.
[b.] October 25, 1977, Macon, GA; [p.] Sally Combs and John Hart; [ed.] DeLand High, St. Petersburg Junior College, University of Florida (Architecture); [occ.] Architecture Student; [memb.] AIAS (American Institute of Architecture Students); [hon.] Who's Who, various art awards; [oth. writ.] Poem published in local Impressions 1989.; [pers.] "Peace cannot be kept by force. It can only be achieved by understanding." - Albert Einstein. We must experience our dreams, for only then can we begin to understand. - J.W. Hart; [a.] Clearwater, FL

HARTLINE, TRISHA DYAN
[b.] September 1, 1980, Thomas, OK; [p.] James and Donna Hartline; [ed.] Middleberg grade school, Amber Pocasset Jr. High, Weatherford High School; [occ.] High School sophomore; [memb.] FHA, Choir, Girl Scouts, Softball

HARVIE, WINDY
[b.] September 26, 1969, Charleston, SC; [a.] Salinas, CA

HARWOOD, JANE R.
[pen.] Jane R. Harwood; [b.] July 4, Springfield, MA; [p.] Calvin H. Ruggles, Marjorie B. Ruggles; [m.] Nathanail Harwood; [ch.] James Calvin, Peter Hutchinson, Douglas John; [ed.] Bennett Sr. College, American Academy of Dramatic Arts, NYC; [occ.] Widow-Writer; [memb.] National League of American Pen Women; [hon.] Poetry awards in local newspapers and magazines; [oth. writ.] Poems published in Quill Books "Echoes of the Silence" - "Tapestry of Thoughts" (National Library of Poetry) and "Fields of Gold" (NL of P), The Pen Women Magazines 90 minute cassette tape composed of 90 poems by author; [pers.] A great joy to share ideas and draw poetic portraits of relative friends and artists - extending an outreach to uplift and strengthen moral values of fellow Americans and all men.; [a.] Boca Raton, FL

HAUGHEY, CHRISTOPHER F.
[pen.] "Christopher"; [b.] October 3, 1925, Astoria, LI, NY; [p.] Christopher and Helen; [m.] Karen M.; [ch.] Noel, Lisa, Chris, Michael; [ed.] Fordham University B.S.; [occ.] Clothing Consultant, Psychometrist - Consultant; [memb.] Elks, Lions, Kiwanis; [hon.] Ex Major League Player, Youngest Pitcher - age 17 in Bklyn Dodgers, completed game vs. John VanDermeer Cincinnati at 17 yrs., appointment to both West Point and Annapolis; [oth. writ.] Autobiography - "Last Of The Fort Riley Cowboy's", Philosophical - "Shades Of Doubt", Poetry - "Prose-Poetry and Philosophical Meanderings", (100 works) - published poet.; [pers.] If you don't believe you can, you won't.; [a.] Fremont, CA

HAVERMAN, MIKE
[pen.] Mike Haverman; [b.] October 5, 1955, Omaha; [p.] Ed and Lorraine; [m.] Denise, December 28, 1974; [ch.] Lindsey, Drew, Allie; [ed.] University of Nebraska Lincoln; [occ.] At home dad; [hon.] Dean's List; [oth. writ.] Personal poem collection, children's book; [pers.] All living creatures have a right to live, a right to choose a course for their journey without unwanted hindrance.; [a.] Lincoln, NE

HAWLEY, SUZANNE
[b.] January 6, 1983; [p.] Don and Becky Hawley; [ed.] I am currently attending the eighth grade at Pocahontas school.; [oth. writ.] I have written several other poems, but have mainly remained within family and friends.; [pers.] I try to write on my experiences. My favorite and most inspirational poet and playwrite is William Shakespeare.; [a.] Pocahontas, IL

HAYNES, JOHN S.
[b.] December 26, 1927, Silver Grove, KY; [p.] John M. and Violah A. Haynes (Both Deceased); [m.] Essie A. Haynes (Della), February 22, 1951; [ch.] Della (38), Bonnie (34) and Mickey (29); [ed.] Keyser High School (1946), BSEE at W.VA University (1995), Naval Training Electronics (1949), Community College Teaching Cert. (1986); [occ.] Retired; [memb.] Planetary Society; [hon.] ETA KAPPA NU Honorary; [oth. writ.] 'Life' in "A Delicate Balance"; [pers.] For me, perseverance is the key to success or call it plain old stubbornness.; [a.] Chandler, AZ

HEACOCK JR., RICHARD K.
[b.] January 5, 1926, Austin, TX; [p.] Richard K. and Harriet (Derry) Heacock; [m.] Zhouhong Zhang Heacock, January 15, 1995; [ch.] Luanne, Lorelle, Linnea, Lavonne, Eric; [ed.] Martin High, Laredo (TX), B.A. Southwestern LL (TX), M.T.H., Perkins Sch. of Theol., SMU, Int'l Affairs, NYU, Computer, UAF; [occ.] Retired UM Missionary, Exec. Dir., Alaska Impact; [memb.] The United Methodist Church, Alaska Historical Society, Alaska Impact; [hon.] Blue Key, S.U., Alaska Walrus award, Martin Luther King Jr., Religion Committee award, Goliad County Service award, Bishop's Peace award; [oth. writ.] Forty something years of sermons! Letters to editors, various magazine and newspaper articles; [pers.] Character means respecting others and self, communicating and listening honestly, admitting and amending mistakes, courageous challenging all violence, and blending grumpiness with good humor.; [a.] Fairbanks, AK

HEETER, DORCAS L.
[b.] August 9, 1934, PA; [p.] Beulah and Robert Wensel; [m.] Herbert, May 24, 1952; [ch.] 2 boys, 1 girl; [ed.] Cosmetology School 68-69; [occ.] Retired disabled; [memb.] YFW and American Legion Auxiliary; [hon.] Both Honors and Awards, from the Shriners Hospital in Tampa, FL, for crippled children, where I was an employee; [oth. writ.] My biography; [pers.] Take one day at a time. Be thankful for what you have. Being a four time cancer survivor, plus other surgeries and chemo and radiation, I can attest to that.; [a.] Bushnell, FL

HEGARTY, DAVID MICHAEL
[b.] December 15, 1986, Canon City, CO; [p.] Jeffrey and Shari Hegarty; [ed.] David is in the 3rd grade at Skyline Elementary School in Canon City, CO; [occ.] David is a blackbelt in Tae Kwon Do Freestyle Karate, Judo and Jujitsu; [memb.] David writes for the Kids Speak Newspaper in Canon City, CO; [oth. writ.] "Spring" published in Poetic Voices of America Fall 1996, "October" published in Poetic Voices of America Summer 1997, "My Secret Life" published in Poetic Voices of America Summer 1997; [pers.] I like to write poetry because it's fun! My favorite subjects to write about are the four seasons and special holidays.; [a.] Canon City, CO

HEISE, SANDRA SUE
[b.] April 26, 1938, Knoxville, TN; [p.] Both Deceased; [m.] Divorced; [ch.] 5 children, 3 grandchildren; [ed.] Mainland High School, Daytona Beach Jr. College (2 years); [occ.] Certified Nursing Assistant; [memb.] Tomoka Christian Church, Ormond Beach, Florida; [oth. writ.] Several poems unpublished.; [pers.] I like poems of all kinds, but my special interests are poems that reflect God's love and poems about nature and family life.; [a.] Daytona Beach, FL

HELM, RAE FRANKIE
[b.] May 6, 1979, Bath, NY; [p.] Frank and Karen Helm; [ed.] Haverling High; [occ.] Waitress; [oth. writ.] Many poems written about emotions caused by life's many changes.; [pers.] I entered this poem in honor of sister's memory.

HEMEL, VIRGIL
[b.] May 30, 1953, Scott City, KS; [p.] Reuben W. Hemel, Georgie L. Bever; [m.] Dee M. Hemel, August 16, 1991; [ch.] Kristina, Lindsay, Jamie; [ed.] Scott Community High School, Kansas State Technical Institute of Salina, KS; [occ.] Service Clerk at Colby Implement; [hon.] Honorable Discharge from United States Army Reserves - Service 23 yrs; [pers.] If only there were enough words to describe feelings, there would be no fears.; [a.] Colby, KS

HENDEE, ANDREW W.
[pen.] Drew; [b.] August 6, 1968, Rochester, NY; [p.] Richard and Marion Hendee; [ch.] Christopher, Samantha, Dylan; [ed.] High School Dropout; [occ.] Factory; [oth. writ.] Lots!!; [pers.] Writing is the soul's expression, only written never spoken.; [a.] Mishawaka, IN

HENRY III, FLARRY W.
[pen.] III; [b.] July 3, 1953, Detroit, MI; [p.] Flarry W. Henry Jr., Dorothy Joan Henry; [m.] Laverna A. Henry, December 15, 1974; [ch.] Damien J. Davis, Flarry W. Henry IV, Kristen Henry, Corey Henry; [ed.] Cody High, Los Angeles City College, California State University, L.A., California State University, Long Beach; [occ.] Computer Animation, Writer, Producer, Independent Ins. Examiner; [pers.] Sometimes there are things I just have to say.; [a.] Lathrop, CA

HENSON, FAYE
[pen.] Faye Henson; [b.] January 14, 1961; [p.] Helen Ramsey; [m.] Stan Henson, June 28, 1980; [ch.] Amanda Shea Henson; [ed.] High School; [occ.] Industrial Worker; [pers.] We can write it and we can read it, but not just what is written. But what you felt when you read it, to be given a chance.; [a.] Spruce Pine, NC

HERRERA, JOHN
[b.] November 5, 1945, Socorro, NM; [p.] Juan and Mary Herrera; [m.] Lynn V. Herrera, June 19, 1992; [ch.] Gina, Bobbie, John and Joseph; [ed.] High School Grad, 2 years of Junior College (Arizona Western College), Yuma High School; [occ.] U.S. Postal Service Letter Carrier; [memb.] Poets in Motion (support group), Yuma Community Theater, National Association of Letter Carriers, Cibola High Football Boaster Club; [oth. writ.] Poems: Karaoke Kamp, All I Ever Wanted, Class of 64, The Block Party, Thirteen; [pers.] Poetry is alive and surrounds all of us everyday. My ambition is to capture what I can and record it.; [a.] Yuma, AZ

HERRINGTON, LEAH
[b.] September 2, 1966, Redondo Beach, CA; [p.] Fay Lebeau; [m.] Divorced; [ed.] High School Graduate, El Camino College 2 yrs. Accounting; [occ.] Sales/Marketing Coordinator; [memb.] Humane Society, ALDF, WWF, Pet Rescue, PETA and other organizations for humane treatment to animals; [hon.] Employee of the Month Award, as well as perfect attendance for 4 consecutive years in a row.; [oth. writ.] Several poems written but never submitted for publication.; [pers.] I have been writing for several years, poetry comes naturally to me. The ocean inspires me, I do most of my writing at the beach.; [a.] Buena Park, CA

HESKE, WILLIAM J.
[b.] July 6, 1935, Allentown, PA; [p.] John and Catherine Heske; [m.] Barbara Heske, June 29, 1957; [ch.] Son-John, Daughter - Kathryn (Heske) Dohen; [ed.] BS - Marine Engineering U.S.N.A., MS - Political Science - Auburn University; [occ.] V.P. Bethlehem Area School District; [hon.] Winner - Franklin Sawyer Prize for Best Paper on Economics of National Defense at USNA. Distinguished graduate - Air Command and Staff College and Industrial College of the Armed Forces.; [oth. writ.] Numerous poems. Salt - If It Reigns - Will It Pour?; [a.] Bethlehem, PA

HIBBITTS, CHRISANNA LYNN
[pen.] C. Hibbitts; [b.] December 22, 1977, Ft. Worth, TX; [p.] Judy Ann and Donald S. Hibbitts; [ed.] Pantego Christian Academy - 6 yrs., Bailey Jr. High - 3 yrs., Arlington High - 3 yrs.; [occ.] Subway Sandwich Artist; [memb.] First Baptist Church of Arlington College Dept.; [hon.] At the age of 14, first place in city wide cultural arts contest, music division (written and com-

posed). Two year drum major in high school marching band, serving as head drum major senior year. Awarded as outstanding veteran drum major at an auxiliary camp of over 170 drum majors from Texas in summer of '95. (Graduated in May '96).; [oth. writ.] Currently keep a notebook of 100 personal authored poems and songs. Had two poems published in high school literary magazine senior year.; [pers.] I give all the credit for my talent to Jesus Christ. Without Him by my side and in my life, I would not have the strength to be the person I am today.; [a.] Arlington, TX

HIEKE, PATRICIA JENKINS
[pen.] Patricia Jenkins Hieke; [b.] October 21, 1948, Philadelphia, PA; [p.] Liberata Delborrello Jenkins, William A. Jenkins; [m.] 1971-1997; [ch.] Harry Anthony Hieke III; [ed.] Graduated Sterling High, Somerdale, NV, 1967 Bus Major Camden County Community College, Thomas Nelson Community College - Art Degree Old Dominion Univ. Art Education; [occ.] Pro. Artist Photographer Studio Owner Gallery Images Williamsburg; [memb.] Pro. photographers of America VA, Pro. Photographers Assoc.; [hon.] Graduated TN-CC Cum Laude, Annually wins award in professional photographers assoc. 1985 Pictorial Photography Accepted by Nat. Geographic for workshop in Colorado; [oth. writ.] Fledgling poet unveiling a lifetime hobby; [pers.] As a romanticist, poetry and the creation of poetry serve as a metaphor to the dreams that may have eloped us and the goals we have yet to fulfill; [a.] Williamsburg, VA

HIGGINS, BILLIE
[b.] September 16, 1934, Vero Beach, FL; [p.] Robert Thompson - Lena Thompson; [m.] Matthew Higgins, October 29, 1953; [ch.] John M. Higgins; [ed.] Vero Beach High School; [occ.] Retired; [memb.] Okeechobee Church of God; [oth. writ.] I have put poems in a local magazine.; [pers.] I want to help other people who may be struggling with depression or other ailments. I have a lot of love for other people, this is the way that I can show my love to them. God inspires me.; [a.] Okeechobee, FL

HILL, ANDRE D.
[pen.] Hesaam Okbar Muhammed; [b.] January 30, 1966, Los Angeles, CA; [p.] Donald and Mary Elizabeth Hill; [ch.] Four; [ed.] The University of California, at Berkeley, Monte Vista High; [occ.] Poet-Journalist; [memb.] Veiled Prophets of Benevolence; [hon.] Chosen by The National Library of Poetry to appear in Dappled Sunlight; [oth. writ.] Body and Soul/Pain and Vision/Book of Poetry; [pers.] Time is precious use it wisely/dreams make life worth while/thank you Langston Hughes.; [a.] San Francisco, CA

HINCKLEY, EVA K.
[b.] February 11, 1960, Price, UT; [p.] Tharon and Barbara Hinckley; [ed.] Kearns High School - Kearns, UT, Ricks College - Rexburg, ID, BYU-Hawaii Laie, HI; [occ.] Elementary School Teacher, Tax Preparer; [oth. writ.] Personalized poems for friends and special occasions.; [pers.] Sometimes I am only the instrument in God's hands. It is God that does the writing He gives the ideas, I form the shape of the words.; [a.] Honolulu, HI

HINOJOSA, MARICELA
[pen.] Marcel Manet; [b.] September 1, 1978, Brownsville; [p.] Jesus Hinojosa, Maximina Hinojosa; [ed.] James Pace High School, University of Texas at Brownsville; [occ.] Student in college; [memb.] Christ the King Youth Explorers; [a.] Brownsville, TX

HLEDIK, MYRTLE E. HAGADONE
[pen.] Myrt; [b.] September 26, 1917, Winifred, MT; [p.] Frank (Doc) Hagadone, Lena D. Hagadone; [m.] George W. Hledik Roundup Mt., June 19, 1948; [ch.] Three; [ed.] 1 yr. High School; [occ.] Baker, House Wife, Poet, Artist, Ex-Cowgirl and noted rider. Used as a double in Hollywood with riding and steer handlings 1932; [hon.] Won my awards in Who's Who in Poetry in '78, got Golden Awards; [oth. writ.] Shook the hand of Charles Lindburgh when 10 yrs. old 1927. Have manuscript "Life of A Cowgirl" to be published soon.; [pers.] Saw Calamity Jane when I was 5 1/2 yrs. old. She was riding her big boy saddle horse by Missouri River North of Winifred Mont. She was with my Father and I.; [a.] Roundup, MT

HOBBS, RICHARD W.
[b.] March 26, 1939, Wilmington, NC; [m.] Ada Mae Habbs, December 30, 1978; [ch.] Six; [ed.] Two years of College; [occ.] Director of Engineering; [memb.] Member of Burjaw Pres. Church, Masanie Lodge, Scottish Rite and Sudan Shrine Temple and Order of the Eastern Star; [hon.] Editor's Choice Award Presented by The National Library of Poetry 1996; [oth. writ.] Poem "Gather Round Folks" many poems not published and many in church paper.; [pers.] I have been greatly influenced by Lord Jesus Christ and my pastor Bob Chastain who has given me the encouragement to continue.; [a.] Rocky Point, NC

HODGES, T. BRIAN
[b.] August 6, 1973, Panola County, MS; [p.] Ronald and Sarah Hodges; [ed.] Briarcrest High School, Rutgers University; [pers.] Cannot a man be called anything but that which he is? May God guide each of us. Peace.; [a.] Germantown, TN

HOGAN, GLORIA JEAN
[pen.] Cissy; [b.] December 11, 1960, Springfield; [p.] Rufus-Ella Ellis; [m.] Rodney Hogan, February 2, 1982; [ed.] Putnam High; [occ.] Mail Handler, United State Postal Service; [memb.] Eternal Light Church; [pers.] My love for the Lord and my children inspired me to write this poem.; [a.] Springfield, MA

HOLDEN, LINDA
[pen.] Linda Lou Holden; [b.] August 24, 1975, Hamlin, TX; [p.] Linda Fay and Bill Hill; [m.] Allen Holden, November 23, 1992; [ch.] Sarah Jane Holden; [ed.] Honor graduate Hamlin High; [occ.] Housewife and salesclerk; [hon.] Who's Who in Honors English III, Quality Piper; [pers.] Everyone should try to find happiness in anything they do. Never let love and romance die and cherish every moment you have with your loved ones.; [a.] Hamlin, TX

HOLIHEN, JOSEPH M.
[pen.] J. Markham Holihen; [b.] January 10, 1928, Fall River, MA; [p.] Joseph M. and Gertrude L. Holihen; [m.] Barbara Ann (Nee Rydin) Holihen, July 2, 1952; [ch.] Joseph M. Jr., and Timothy P.; [ed.] Mt. Pleasant High School Providence, R.I. (1946), Pensacola Jr Coll (AA) (1980), University of West Florida (BA) (1983) Magna Cum Laude; [occ.] Retired Us Army Officer; [memb.] Phi Alpha Theta, Ancient and Honorable Order of Lion Tamers, West Florida Literary Association; [hon.] Legion of Merit - four awards, and several other service and commendation medals; [oth. writ.] Several poems published in literary Association Publications.; [pers.] I play a little golf, visit with my grandchildren and consider the wisdom of God and the patience of my wife of some 44 years.; [a.] Pensacola, FL

HOLLINGER, JANET M.
[b.] November 13, 1960, Chehalis, WA; [p.] Nancy J. Hollinger, Vernon R. Hollinger; [ed.] Lehrer Seminar, Chur, Switzerland University Nevada, Reno; [occ.]

Financial Service Representative, Bank of America; [memb.] Eastern Star, Martha Chapter #5; [hon.] Quill and Scroll Award, Editor's Choice Award, The National Library of Poetry 1996; [oth. writ.] The Ghost Wall published in Recollections of Yesterday, In Another Life published in the Best Poems of 1997.; [pers.] I bare my soul when life seems heavy and dark. When I am done writing, the world feels bright with light again.; [a.] Sparks, NV

HOLLOWAY, MARGO
[b.] May 25, 1941, Philadelphia; [p.] Robert and Eula Green; [ch.] Donra Giddings, Cecil Holloway, Heather Holloway; [ed.] BBS Univ. of PA; [memb.] Oxford Presby Church; [hon.] Four Chaplains Legion of Honor Award; [oth. writ.] Senses, Wanderings, Sisterhood, The Pride Of Sorrow, Resolved, Changes, Sanctuary, A Mother Of Sons, Life Is, Noise, Growth, Acceptance, Six Of One Half A Dozen Of Another; [pers.] To touch another is to see the face of God.; [a.] Philadelphia, PA

HOLZ, JAN STANTON
[pen.] Jan Stanton; [b.] November 19, 1948, Los Angeles; [p.] Bert and Barbara Kirshner; [m.] Richard Holz, November 26, 1994; [ch.] 2 daughters, 3 step children (2 girls, 1 boy); [ed.] Attended University of Oregon (3 yrs), Graduated to be from - Coburn School of Fashion Merchandising 1970; [occ.] Hat Designer - I run my own company, previously co-owned and co-founded "I Was Framed" Manufact., business from 1973-1993. Weekly volunteer in emergency room - Cedars Sinai Hospital; [hon.] Featured on cover of national magazine "Entrepreneurial Woman" Dec. 91; [oth. writ.] My writings are usually in catalogs and press releases for my business.; [pers.] With a positive attitude life is limitless.; [a.] Los Angeles, CA

HOPKINS, KEITH R.
[b.] March 28, 1918, Buffalo, NY; [p.] Frank S. Hopkins, Zella M. Hopkins; [m.] Sarah J. Kline, November 29, 1947; [ch.] Jennifer D., Nancy W., Jonathan F. (Deceased); [ed.] Bennett H.S. and McKinley Voc. H.S., Cornell Un., U.S. Navy V5 Midshipman School; [occ.] Retired, Niagara Frontier State Park Commission, 1949-1976; [oth. writ.] Other poems and musings, none published.; [pers.] I am moved by the strengths of family, of friends, and by tragedies of ideologies and politics. I read and re-read Robert Frost and Kahlil Gibran. I look to our grandchildren with pride and hope for a future unmarred by blind, indifferent crime.; [a.] Georgetown, SC

HOPSTETTER, DALE ROBERT
[b.] December 11, 1966, Nelsonville, OH; [p.] Walter Richard and Sally Patricia Hopstetter; [ed.] Nelsonville - York High School, Tri-County Joint Vocational School; [occ.] Sheet Metal Worker, Logan, OH; [oth. writ.] Poems: Better Than Me, Smile Lost, Eternal Dask, Dancing In Darkness, When Time Ends. Songs: When You Were Around, When Rumor Turns To Tragedy, It Won't Make The Pain Go Away, A Man Misunderstand.; [pers.] "Read my words and feel the warmth of my heart, for it takes love to guide the pen that reaches you, and love to understand it".; [a.] Nelsonville, OH

HORNAK, ROBERT C. C.
[b.] March 31, 1968, Milwaukee, WI; [p.] Bob and Mary Clare Hornak; [m.] Margaret Bentley Powell Hornak, May 29, 1993; [ed.] The Citadel, The Military College of South Carolina; [occ.] Medical Sales; [oth. writ.] "Knob Year" - A screenplay about cadet life at The Citadel.; [pers.] Quote: "If you have five seconds to spare, then I'll tell you the story of my life". Morrissey; [a.] Alexandria, VA

HOTCHKISS, JANICE L.
[pen.] Jan - Janice Hotchkiss; [b.] July 29, 1971, Emmett, ID; [p.] Daryl and Coleen Reed, Jackie and Mike McClellan; [m.] Bret James Hotchkiss, November 5, 1990; [ch.] Three - Jacob, Christopher and Emmett; [ed.] High School Graduate; [occ.] US Postal letter carrier (Rural); [hon.] Perfect attendance awards and art awards in grade school - awards - ribbons for paintings entered in local county fair; [oth. writ.] ("Black to Camp" - about my grand father), ("How Do I" - about searching yourself to get through things), ("Mending"), ("Remember"), ("Sister" - about the meaning of being sisters) and many many others.; [pers.] Poetry is such a heart warming thing, it's such a natural thing to those who can create it. It's very nostalgic. It's the heart of faith, and has the power to communicate life's emotions between people who think they have nothing in common.; [a.] Wilder, ID

HOUCK, JOSEPHINE D.
[pen.] Jo Houck; [b.] May 4, 1924, Norfolk, VA; [p.] Attorney and Mrs. P. R. Hamilton; [m.] Charles D. Houck, M.D., (died 1975), September 25, 1943; [ch.] Ruth, Kathryn, Elizabeth, Joyn, C. Gregory, Mary; [ed.] Fayetteville, W. Va. High School, W. Va. University of Morgantown W. Va. Medical Technology - Medical College of Va. Richmond, Va; [occ.] Retired in Belleair, FL; [memb.] Belleair Country Club, dropped all others I belonged to in Canton, Ohio; [pers.] I believe in preventive medicine, treating one's body as sacred, no harmful habits such as smoking and excess drinking, keeps weight under control, happy thoughts and be kind to everyone. I love reading and read constantly; [a.] Belleair, FL

HOUNSHELL, BARB HENSLEY
[b.] February 21, 1943, Jackson, KY; [p.] Reed Hudson Sr. and Clarinda Hudson; [m.] David Paul Hounshell, May 9, 1987; [ch.] Tangela, Tanya, Jeffrey, Reed, Joshua; [ed.] Breathitt High School Jackson, Kentucky; [occ.] Disably Retired Store Manager Dairy Marts; [memb.] Solid Rock Church Monroe, Ohio; [oth. writ.] None as yet published.; [pers.] I simply write from my heart, my inspirations are my Lord Jesus, my family, friends and acquaintances I have met on the path way of my life.; [a.] Franklin, OH

HOWARD, PATRICK LORENZO
[pen.] Mace; [b.] October 23, 1976, Athens Regional; [p.] Lorenzo Howard, Patricia Petty; [ch.] Jaylen Jamal Howard; [ed.] High School; [hon.] JROTC; [oth. writ.] have other writings but none published; [pers.] Everyone has a "Deep Side" but everyone doesn't show it.; [a.] Athens, GA

HOWE, TOM
[pen.] Talyho; [b.] July 31, 1927, LaFleche, Saskatchewan, Canada; [p.] Martin C. Howe and Florence C. Long; [m.] Della M. Howe, July 26, 1952; [ch.] James, Richard and Tami-Jean; [ed.] Happy Hill - Rural Sask. (Elementary), La Fleche High School, University of Sask. - LLB; [occ.] Consultant; [memb.] Law Society of Saskatchewan, Telephone Pioneers of America, United Church of Canada; [hon.] Queen Æs Counsel (Q.C.) from Province of Saskatchewan.; [oth. writ.] Up The Being Stock, ISBN: 0-919357-13-X, Many published letters to the editor in various publications on philosophical and political issues.; [pers.] ôTime, the eternal ocean, life, its motion of being, reason, lifeÆs tides of discovery from loveÆs gentle seas in between.ö From Up The Being Stock.; [a.] Regina, Saskatchewan, Canada

HOWELL, JACK
[b.] September 14, 1925, LaFayette, GA; [p.] Jack Howell, Margaret Howell; [m.] Nell (Fordham) Howell, March 1951; [ch.] Jay, Len, Don; [ed.] LaFayette High,

Auburn University; [occ.] Retired, Bellsouth Financial; [memb.] United Methodist Church various business and professional groups; [oth. writ.] This was first poem was written in 1996. Have written others since.; [pers.] I try for simple verse...easy to read and understand.; [a.] Hoover

HOWERTON, GREGG
[pen.] Genvine Love; [b.] February 12, 1980, Philadelphia, PA; [hon.] Winner of the Robert Laven house Award for being an all around person; [pers.] "People don't have to like you as a person, for respect will come in time, as long as you stay positive, your achievements will change their minds. Stay positive, stay real, stay strong.; [a.] Philadelphia, PA

HUBBARD, MARY JANE
[b.] August 22, 1940, Winters, TX; [p.] Charles A. Burch and Laura Annie Burch; [m.] A. L. Hubbard Jr. (Tex), August 24, 1957; [ch.] Jeannie L. Hubbard, Charles F. Hubbard, Rebecca H. Hubbard, Sandra Renee; [ed.] Lake View High School, San Angelo, Texas; [occ.] Retired; [memb.] Emmanuel Baptist, Church Member, Coleman, TX; [hon.] Winner-Famous Poets Society 1995, 1996, Honorary FFA Chapter Award 1977, 1987; [oth. writ.] Mountain of Life, several other poems.; [pers.] Be thankful for today, expect nothing from tomorrow because tomorrow might not come.; [a.] Coleman, TX

HUBBS, JANET B.
[b.] March 14, 1940, Brooklyn, NY; [p.] Edwin, Elizabeth Boothman; [m.] David, (Deceased), February 14, 1962; [ch.] Daughter, Whitney Leigh; [ed.] AB, Westminster College, MA, Syracuse University; [occ.] Chairman, English Dept. Professor of English, Ocean County College; [memb.] MLA, NCTE/CCCC, ADE; [hon.] Mia-Career Fellowship, NEH, Princeton University

HUDSON, PEGGY
[b.] December 11, 1952, Sedan, KS; [p.] Gerald and Emma Logsdon; [m.] Dennis Hudson, March 3, 1972; [ch.] Nathan 21, Mandy 19, Josh 13; [ed.] High School; [occ.] Homemaker; [memb.] Cornwell Drive Church of Christ; [oth. writ.] Column in The Daily Oklahoma 1987, poetry on request for gifts and special occasions, book - Touched by Miscarriage to be out in a few months.; [pers.] I always have been a deep thinker. Writing is a great release for the constant ideas and emotions that I rarely share with others.; [a.] Yukon, OK

HUFFMAN, DAVID H.
[b.] February 8, 1941, Kansas; [p.] Frances Huffman Reynolds; [m.] Divorced; [ch.] Sara, Matthew, Jessica, Lynn, Michael, Maggy, Jessie; [ed.] M.D., 1967, Univ. of Kans, Med Int/Residency - Johns Hopkins Hospital, Fellowship - National Cancer Institute; [occ.] Physical, Medical Oncology; [memb.] American College Physicians, Amer. Soc. Clinical Oncology, Alpha Omega Alpha; [oth. writ.] Poems published in local newspaper, numerous scientific articles published; [pers.] Work hard, play hard, enjoy every day.; [a.] Colorado Springs, CO

HUGILL, CATHY ELAINE
[b.] July 7, 1950, Hobart, OK; [p.] Wilson and LaRue Cantwell; [m.] Richard R. Hugill Jr., September 21, 1984; [ch.] Cindy, Wendy, Christy, Sundi, Nathan, Richard, Brinton; [ed.] Truman High School (graduate); [occ.] Executive Housekeeper Sleep Inn Hotel; [memb.] Chamber of Commerce Pres. of Sherwood Poetry Club; [oth. writ.] Poems published local papers - written poems (over 100) since 1967 and still writing!; [pers.] The joy and love of life, God and mankind, are all the reasons of my poems. Words to me, are beauti-

ful... Therefore, through my poems, I try to have the reader see beauty in life, in God, and in mankind and rejoice!!!; [a.] Blue Springs, MO

HUNTER, EVELYN SHERRITT
[b.] July 8, 1942, Shelburne, Ontario; [p.] Verna Sherritt and Milton McKinley; [m.] Wendel Robert Hunter (Deceased), July 8, 1961; [ch.] Wendy Christina, Wendell Curtis, Robin Janine and Emily-Ann, stepchildren - Gregory, Beverly and Susan Clark; [ed.] C.D.D. HS Shelburne, Ont., Humber College, Weston, Georgian College, Orillia and Waterloo; [occ.] D.S.W.; [memb.] AVA, Animal Volunteer Ass., Pure Bred German Shepherds, Trinity United Church, World Vision Canada, my sponsored child Ana Yeli, Toronto Humane Society, Institute of Children's Literature.; [hon.] Grandmother to Amanda, Melissa, twins Mark and April Davis, Shane and Steven Thomas, Christle, Sarah, Victoria and Andrew Hunter. Step-grandchildren - Douglas, Ashley, Tyler, Kristina, Amanda and Kyle Clark.; [oth. writ.] "Leprechaun's Misty Morn", and "A Wee Laddies Lost She". Unpublished. Lifes dream to visit someday the home of William and The Baga Telle Rose garden's in France.; [pers.] Engaged to John William Clark. To my children and grandchildren. The very lust of all my thoughts are those that I think of you, the very best of all my words are those that I speak of you, the very best of all my deeds are those that I suffer to you.; [a.] Clarksburg, Ontario, Canada

HUNTER, ISABELLE
[pen.] Isabelle; [b.] February 16, 1927, Poconos; [p.] Lucy and Alex Jackson; [ed.] North Eastern University School - 8, Boston State College; [occ.] Retired; [memb.] Mystic Valley, Rail Road, Museum of Science, Boston Public Library; [hon.] Communication Class, Bar Tenders School; [oth. writ.] Up Rising, Almost Southern; [pers.] I live from day to day.; [a.] Boston, MA

HURD, CYNTHIA M.
[b.] February 13, 1948, Denver, CO; [p.] William A. Hurd, Gwen M. Hurd; [ed.] Graduated South Denver High, Colorado State Univ., University of Utah, English, B.A., Humboldt State University Speech and Hearing Sciences M.A., California Teaching Credential, Special Education; [occ.] Language, Speech and Hearing Specialist in public schools; [memb.] California Speech and Hearing Association, California Teachers Association, The First Church of Christ, Scientist, Boston, MA; [hon.] Sophomore Women's Honorary, Dean's List, Freshman Sears Scholarship. Graduate Fellowship; [oth. writ.] Children's non-fiction published 1983, about life in the Arctic.; [pers.] Especially impressed by the prose works of Isak Dinesen, and the poetry of Emily Dickinson, Randall Jarrell and Gerard Manley Hopkins. I believe life is to teach us to meet, overcome, and transform what we call ourselves.; [a.] San Diego, CA

HUTCHENS, KARLA
[pen.] Karla Onchi; [b.] November 22, 1955, Fresno, CA; [p.] Ken Onchi, Lillian Onchi; [m.] Harold Hutchens Sr., June 9, 1986; [ch.] Shawn Hutchens; [ed.] California State University, Fresno; [occ.] Freelance Writer, Staff — Calif, State Univ., Fresno; [hon.] Pi Gamma Mu; [oth. writ.] Numerous poems, essays and short stories; [pers.] To experience life through emotion is to truly live.; [a.] Fresno, CA

HUTCHINSON, ROBERT P.
[b.] July 22, 1937, Fayette Co., KY; [p.] Julian T. and Geneva Ray Hutchinson; [m.] Jogee Noonan Hutchinson, January 11, 1964; [ch.] Six Children, Nine grand children; [ed.] Lexington Catholic High, W of KY. St. Mary's College, KY, St. Paul Seminary, St Paul, Minn. FBI Academy Training - Law Enforcement of the Eastern KY University; [occ.] Retired Policeman;

[memb.] St. Leo Parish, retired member of International Association for Identification, President of Residence Council; [hon.] KY. Colonel, numerous citations in performance of Police Services, Pres. of Church Council; [oth. writ.] Nothing published; [pers.] Enjoy unlocking my inner feeling. Feel that joy and happiness is expressed and gives by expression of love of family and friends; [a.] Mount Vernon, KY

HYDE, CARRIE
[b.] July 24, 1981; [p.] Keith Hyde, Paula Hyde; [ed.] Jesuit High School; [occ.] Student; [memb.] Drama Club, Setons, Concert Choir, Link Crew (Orientation Committee), French Club; [hon.] Nation English Merit Award (USAA), Presidential Fitness Award, Citizenship Award, Honor Roll; [a.] Beaverton, OR

HYDE, L. D.
[pen.] Hyde; [pers.] I'm not much on words...but if you know anybody...who has a few minutes.; [a.] Atlanta, GA

HYMAS, BILL
[b.] August 21, 1953, Jackson Hole, WY; [p.] Ron and Barbara; [m.] Divorced 1981, April 1976; [ch.] Lillian and Casey; [ed.] Bozeman Senior High, Two Years College Level, Creative Writing Seminars; [occ.] Investor/Real Estate Manager; [oth. writ.] Some short stories and several poems.; [a.] Big Sky, MT

IGUS, GERTRUDE YOUSON
[pen.] Gertrude Igus (Jackie); [b.] March 28, 1954, Phenix City, AL; [p.] Mr. Jimmy and Gertrude Youson; [m.] Mr. Lionel Eugene Igus, December 18, 1969; [ch.] Tyronica, Monique, Tarvie, Tre, Tia, Victoria, Mandez, Joshua, Jeremy and Sharron Igus; [ed.] Spencer High School, In Columbus, Ga. School of Ministry; [occ.] Ministry and Writing and Mothering; [memb.] Union Grove Baptist Church and a Distinguished Member of the Society of poets.; [hon.] Ordained and Licensed on the 13 day of May 1995 to preach the gospel. Mother Award in 1996 and grand parent award; [oth. writ.] I am in The Rippling Waters, local news and working on a book called The Life and Time of Caroline, and Children's Books.; [pers.] I'd like to dedicate this poem to my grands. Mellisa, Satora, Malcolm, Tony Hayes Gary, John, Gabriel, Tarvie Jr. and Trent and future grandchildren. Grandma loves you all with all her heart, and a love that will never ever part.; [a.] Detroit, MI

IHEDILIONYE, DALE
[pen.] Ora Lee; [b.] January 4, 1960, Oklahoma City, OK; [p.] Ora Lee Cobb and Earnest Cobb; [m.] Cyprian Osondu Ihedilionye, July 23, 1994; [ch.] Stephen and Christopher Ihedilionye; [ed.] B.S. and Certified Addiction Counselor, Theology Associate Degree; [occ.] Chemical Depedency Therapist; [memb.] Criminal Justice Club, Cornerstone Family Church Children Ministry; [hon.] Most Studious, Woman of the Month, Perfect Attendance, Dean's List; [pers.] I live to love and love to live. I have been impressed with the early poets: Edgar Allen Poe, Helen Rica and my beloved Sister Maudene Jackson.; [a.] Des Moines, IA

IKERD, SUE
[b.] February 3, 1949, Statesville, NC; [p.] Mr. and Mrs. Raymond and Evelyn Pennell; [m.] Gary Ikerd, June 12, 1977; [ch.] Tammy, Michelle, La Donna, 1 grandchild Tyler (T.C.); [ed.] Stony Point High School (12 yrs), Stony Point North Carolina; [occ.] Fabric Cutter in furniture industry; [oth. writ.] I have written a total of twenty-two poems and a few quotations, none which have ever been published. This is the first one, encouraged by my best friend Pamela, to send it into the contest.; [pers.] My inspiration for writing poetry comes merely from my true feelings within my heart and soul

for my family and friends. I'm as they say a "sentimental old fool". I express my feelings for my childhood and also for the present just what I feel from my deepest thoughts.; [a.] Claremont, NC

IRISH, SIDIKA
[pen.] Scye; [b.] July 22, 1978, Poughkeepsie, NY; [p.] Carol and Randall Irish; [ed.] My Elementary School was Flushing Christian School. I went to Brooklyn Technical High School and am presently at Queens College; [pers.] Glory to God, the source of my inspiration. I wrote "Blind Spot" in memory of my great grandmother, Alice Pollock.; [a.] Rosedale, NY

JACKSON, JOSEPH
[pen.] Joe Jackson; [b.] November 20, 1941, Arkansas; [p.] Ollie and Albert Jackson; [m.] Ruth Lee Jackson; [ch.] Four; [ed.] Two year A.A. Degree in Respiratory Therapy and Radiology Technology; [occ.] Respiratory Therapy, own two businesses (uniform store and beauty salon); [hon.] Poems published in local newspapers.; [oth. writ.] Poems, song, plays and books unpublished.; [pers.] All that I am, or will ever be came from the love of God I would like to share my love and this God given talent to the world.; [a.] Long Beach, CA

JACKSON, LAURA J.
[b.] November 11, 1970, Newport News, VA; [p.] Donald Vincent Phillips Jr. and Jeannette E. Phillips; [m.] Tommy C. Jackson, February 11, 1995; [ed.] Thomas Nelson Community College 1990-92, Denbigh High 1987-1990; [occ.] Sale Associates in Family Business at GI Joe's Inc.; [pers.] My poems not only reflect a part of me, but they capture a moment in time that may otherwise have been forgotten.; [a.] Newport News, VA

JAEKELS, EMILY S.
[b.] August 18, 1977, Kansas City, MO; [p.] Dallas M. Jaekels and Carolyn L. Jaekels; [ed.] Christ Church Episcopal School University of South Carolina; [occ.] Student; [a.] Columbia, SC

JAMES, DENISE H.
[b.] June 23, 1955, Anderson, SC; [p.] Mr. and Mrs. J. D. Hooper; [m.] Chuck James, June 22, 1973; [ch.] Trey James; [ed.] Bachelor of Science from Augusta College in Special Education and Elementary Ed. and Middle Grades in 1978; [occ.] Currently not working but taught school 17 years.; [hon.] Graduated from College Summa Cum Laude, Senior Scholastic Award 1977-78, Phi Kappa Phi Honor Society, District Georgia Science Teacher of year 1988-89, Columbia Middle School Teacher of The Year 1991-92; [pers.] The inspiration for this poem was my dear and close friendship with some very special ladies in Augusta, GA.; [a.] Savannah, GA

JAMES, T. YVETTE BROOKS
[pen.] Rym Rim; [b.] August 20, 1964, Phoenix, AZ; [p.] Eve Barnett and Gerald Brooks; [m.] Sean James, March 27, 1994; [ch.] Four; [ed.] High School graduate, currently enrolled in College; [occ.] Office Technician; [oth. writ.] "A Promise Made" "Loves Foolish Heart"; [pers.] Love to a fool is a commodity that he easily trades for something he thinks is better.; [a.] Austin, TX

JANUSZEK, ANNA
[b.] September 26, 1980, Krasnik, Poland; [p.] Alina, Jerzy Januszek; [pers.] "I express my poems through a unique creative way, the poems are exposing my thoughts, imagination and most of all they are expressing me."; [a.] Queens, NY

JENKINS, BOYD
[b.] January 24, 1926, Bastrop, LA; [p.] Tillus Jenkins, Bessie Jenkins; [ch.] Robin Boyd and Tillus Brant; [ed.] Fair Park High, University of Maryland, University of Vienna (Austria); [occ.] Retired USAF Pilot; [memb.] Mayor's Advisory Council on Disabilities, The Retired Officers Association, Association Former Air Force OSI Agents, Disabled American Veterans, Paralyzed Veterans of America; [oth. writ.] My "Gestalt" appears in TNLP's "Forever And A Day" my "Pilot To Be" and "Leader Indeed" were recently submitted, and I make occasional contributions to local newspapers.; [pers.] The passion of my life is aviation. If rapture shared is rapture enhanced, would that all mankind could know the joy of solo flight.; [a.] Shreveport, LA

JENKINS, EMERSON MCCOY
[b.] February 13, 1936, Ivor, VA; [p.] Lenward Jenkins, Mariah Purdie Jenkins; [m.] Clara (Midge) Smith, April 23, 1960; [ch.] Marc Vernon, 2 grandchildren Marc and Ciara; [ed.] Orange High School, Orange, NJ; [occ.] Retail Jeweler and Designer; [pers.] If there is any percieved talent in my work, it is surely a gift from God.; [a.] East Orange, NJ

JENKINS, MARY A.
[pen.] Marya Ness; [b.] October 4, 1926, Laredo, TX; [p.] Jesse Bailey Bollinger and Yolande Mary Peck; [m.] Edgar Weymonth Jenkins Jr., April 5, 1944; [ch.] Pamela Ann Jenkins; [ed.] Texas University; [occ.] Entrepreneur, Inventor, Closet Poet; [memb.] Board of Directors of the New Orleans Opera Association, past Governor of the Board of the Women's Guild of the New Orleans Opera Association, past Director of the Board of the New Orleans Symphony, past Director of the Board of Goodwill Industries of Southeastern St. Louis and President of the Goodwill Volunteer Services. Member and past officer of the United Daughters of the Confederacy and member of the National Society Daughters of the American Revolution, past Board member of Les Dames de Timberlane Timberlane Country Club. American Contract Bridge League; [hon.] Named "One of the Ten Outstanding Person of New Orleans for 1986" by the Institute for Human Understanding. Who's Who of American Inventors of 1990.; [oth. writ.] Plays published and performed during school years.; [pers.] I care.; [a.] Gretna, LA

JENNINGS, PEARL
[b.] October 26, 1915, Minnesota; [p.] Harvey and Barbara Byman; [m.] Frank B. Jennings, October 25, 1969; [ed.] High School Creative Writing, New York School of Writing; [occ.] Housewife, Artist; [hon.] Gospel Songs - record, published stories, My Quiet Place - published; [oth. writ.] I have written gospel songs and have them put to music "She Belongs To Me", "On The Sea Of Galilee", "His Wondrous Love For Me".; [pers.] I cannot pay for these songs to be published. Thank you for acknowledging my poem.; [a.] Santa Rosa, CA

JENSEN, JORDAN AUTUMN
[b.] June 5, 1982, Estherville, IA; [p.] Bob and Lili Jensen; [ed.] Estherville High School, Freshman will graduate in the year 2,000; [occ.] Part time Insurance Secretary, Student; [memb.] Trinity Lutheran Church, Youth Group, Music; [hon.] Presidential Physical Fitness Award, Presidential Academic Award, Volleyball Award, Basketball Award, Track Award, Softball Award, Choir Award, Writing Award, Reading Award, A Honor Roll; [oth. writ.] Poetry. My grandma Lyon entered my poem in this contest.; [pers.] I love to spend my free time in the North Country. I believe that if you want something badly enough you can do anything.

Once you've got a hold of your star, never let go!; [a.] Estherville, IA

JIN, MUYAN
[b.] November 5, 1986, P.R. China; [p.] Bin Jin (Mother), An Jin (Father); [ed.] Fourth Grade; [occ.] Fourth Grade Student; [hon.] A Honor Roll Student; [pers.] I would like to be a doctor when I grow up so I can help people.; [a.] Fayetteville, NC

JOECKEL, AMANDA SUE
[b.] July 19, 1982, Aurora, MO; [p.] Ben and Jana Joeckel; [ed.] 8th Grade Student, Exeter Jr. High, Exeter MO; [hon.] Young Authors Award 1991; [a.] Exeter, MO

JOHNSON, CAROL
[pen.] Allyson; [b.] December 25, 1976, Guyana, South America; [p.] Ann James and Richard Johnson; [ed.] Currently a Junior at the State University of New York College of Environmental Science and Forestry. (SUNY ESF); [occ.] Student; [memb.] President of the Baobab Society, the multicultural Organization at SUNY ESF.; [oth. writ.] I have many other poems and a few short stories that haven't yet been published.; [pers.] I'm a firm believer in Karma, if you're good to others, good will come back to you ten times over - it's all about faith and honor.; [a.] Syracuse, NY

JOHNSON, DELAENA
[b.] September 24, 1985, Morton, WA; [p.] Mike and Leann Johnson; [ed.] Straight A' Student. Even though I'm in the 5th grade; [hon.] M.V.P. Soccer, and Baseball went to district spelling bee 4 years in a row. Received 1st place 3 years.; [a.] Packwood, WA

JOHNSON, JANIS A.
[pen.] Jan Johnson; [b.] April 28, 1935, Fond du Lac, WI; [p.] Louis and Loris Johnson; [ed.] The Business Institute, Milwaukee, WI, Brillion High School (4 years), Brillion, WI, Washington Elem., (8 years) Janesville, WI; [occ.] Administrative Assistant Thilmany Division, International Paper Co.; [pers.] My greatest pleasure is sharing a God given gift of writing and knowing it's touched the lives of others. My greatest influence has been my friends and family. To them I dedicate my writings. Many of my ancestors were poets/writers including Shakespeare, who is also on our family tree and I'm extremely proud of that heritage.; [a.] Kaukauna, WI

JOHNSON, MARTHA
[b.] May 19, 1925, Fayette County; [p.] William and Cenie Otts; [m.] Haskill Johnson, August 28, 1948; [ch.] Vanessa (Johnson) Duke; [ed.] Fayette County High; [memb.] First Baptist Ch. Tarrant Jefferson Hills Garden Club, Life Member, No End Council of Garden Clubs; [pers.] I am a Christian, and since this is my first published work, I tried to reflect my appreciation to God for His goodness to me and my family.; [a.] Birmingham, AL

JOHNSON, MELVIN
[b.] September 5, 1969, Asheboro, NC; [p.] Donald and Gladys Johnson; [ed.] Southwestern Randolph High School, University of North Carolina at Greensboro; [pers.] I attempt to capture the essence of the individuals struggle to maintain his identity in modern society.; [a.] Asheboro, NC

JOHNSTONE, JENNIFER
[pen.] Jennifer Johnstone; [b.] March 25, 1978, Garland, TX; [p.] Ben and Karan Johnstone; [ed.] Soquel High School (1996) Fresno State University (current); [occ.] Full time student; [memb.] Women's Soccer Team at Fresno State University; [pers.] Every person I have met in my life has touched my soul and thus, my

writing. Thanks to everyone. Mom, you're my inspiration, thank you! I love you!; [a.] Fresno, CA

JONES, ELIZABETH
[pen.] Nia Vanere; [b.] March 19, 1957, Cincinnati, OH; [p.] Betty Jones, Leroy Smart; [ed.] Received GED in 1989 after five tries; [occ.] Writer for my social club newsletter the Citiview Connections; [memb.] Member of Citiview Connections; [hon.] Dean's honor roll at Plaza Business Institute 1988-1989; [oth. writ.] Am trying to get my book published called The Warrior. It is science fiction and espionage. I hope this will open many doors; [pers.] Never give up a dream if its meant to happen it will happen. Hold on no matter what the outcome is. Keep striving until you reach the top; [a.] Flushing, NY

JONES, FLORENCE M.
[pen.] Florence, Prudence; [b.] April 11, 1939, West Columbia, TX; [p.] Isaiah and Lu Ethel McNeil; [m.] Waldo D. Jones, May 29, 1965; [ch.] Ricky, Wanda and Erna; [ed.] BS Prairie Vicu A and M University 1961 (Cum laude) Med (same university 1968) Post grad./Rice University and University of Houston; [occ.] Piano Instructor, Writer, Storyteller, Speaker; [memb.] Life - Texas Retired Teachers Association, Distinguished life member -International Society of Poets, Oak Meadows Church of God, National Women of Achievement; [hon.] Letters of recognition for outstanding achievement in Education from President Bill Clinton Gov. George Bush, Gov. Ann Richards, Congress Woman Shelia Jackson Lee, Editors Choice awards/NLP; [oth. writ.] Follow your dream (a personal growth program) Science modules for Houston Ind. Sch. Dist., Poem in Sparrow grass poetry Forum Anthology Several poems in NLP Anthologies; [pers.] This poem is the result of observing my niece at her recent wedding and histologically recording my own experiences. After 32 years of marriage, I strive to keep our marriage experience lively. I cling to courtship days; [a.] Houston, TX

JONES, MICHELLE
[b.] September 14, 1975, Texas City, TX; [p.] Vickie Jones, Clay Jones; [ed.] North Hopkins High, Student at Madisonville Community College; [occ.] Student/Childcare Worker; [oth. writ.] I have had one poem published in Between The Rain Drops.; [pers.] I have enjoyed writing. I've been doing it for seven years. I thank God for the talent He gave me. I was introduced to poetry by a special friend Jason Edward Oliver.; [a.] Madisonville, KY

JONES SR., MURL
[b.] November 15, 1927, Indianapolis, IN; [p.] William and Delcia Jones; [m.] Zola M. Jones, July 11, 1948; [ch.] DeBorah, Paula, Kurt, Murl Jr., Shelby, Sandra, Todd; [ed.] 12th Grade, served United States Air Force; [occ.] Printer (Compositer); [oth. writ.] We are sending the last poem my father had written. He passed away on November 19, 1996 of a heart condition. We would like his poems published.

JONES, WILLIAM H.
[pen.] William Henry Jones, W. H. Jones, Captain J. Bill Jones; [b.] April 1, 1924, Black Diamond, WA; [p.] Helenor Jones, (Father Deceased); [m.] Barbara A. Jones, May 17, 1960; [ch.] Robert Jeffery Jones, Denise Lynn Williams; [ed.] B.A. San Diego State Naval School of Hospital Administration; [occ.] Captain, U.S. Navy (Ret); [memb.] federal Health Care Executives, Fleet Reserve Association, Distinguished Member International Society of Poets; [hon.] Legion of Merit (Navy) Numerous Service Medals and awards, Graduated with honors 5 military schools, advanced from Apprentice Seaman to Captain during Naval career. Editor's Choice Awards (II) The International Poetry Hall of Fame; [oth. writ.] Endless Thought - Treasured

Poems of America - April 1996, In His Wisdom We Must Trust Poetic Voices of America June 1996, Symphony of the Night - Treasured Poems of America - August 1996, A Humble Apology - Poetic Voices of America - October 1996, The Window Of His Soul - Treasured Poems of America - December 1996, How Sad Memorial Day - Poetic Voices of America - February 1997, Shared Dreams - Treasured Poems of America - April 1997, Just Desserts - Poetic Voices of America - June 1997, Songs Unsung - Beyond The Stars - Fall 1996, Catacombs of the Night - Best Poems of 1996 - Summer 1996, Please Another Chance, Across the Universe - Fall 1996, Embers - Of Sunshine and Daydreams - August 1996, Lonely Is The Poet - Lyrical Heritage - Winter 1996, The Hand That Stroked My Brow - Best poems of 1996 - Fall 1996, Why Poetry - Daybreak on the Land - Winter 1996, Grim Reaper - A Moment to Reflect - Summer 1997, All God's Creatures - In Dappled Sunlight - Spring 1997; [pers.] I believe in personal achievement, inspiring others to fulfill their dreams, at peace with self and others, all with a sense of humor, dedication and perspective.; [a.] Lake San Marcos, CA

JORGENSEN, NORMAN W.
[pen.] Norman Jorgensen; [b.] November 8, 1941, Ashland, WI; [p.] Mr. and Mrs. Norman L. Jorgensen; [ch.] Norman Jr., Eve Marie, Michelle Marie; [ed.] Bellivdere High School, Management Subject Off Hour Glasses. Writers Creative Group Studied.; [occ.] I'm a machinest at the Boeing Company, Everette Division, Everett, WA; [memb.] AOL - Isle Internet and Prodigy on line use internet services to mix with other writers and poets; [hon.] Honorary Poet Laxiet in 1991 for The World of Poetry for The Verse Called On The Wings Of Our Thoughts. A news paper in PA published a poem called Lancelot about a cat.; [oth. writ.] A Step In Time, The Unforgiven, Moods In The Quiet, God's Knows Lastinging Relationships, Our Love; [pers.] To share the warmth wrapped around love. We must ease our thoughts amongst our days. While the child inside continues to shine. One of my favorite poets is Rod McKien.; [a.] Mill Creek, WA

JOSEPH, MELANIE M.
[b.] July 24, 1983, Boulder, CO; [p.] Kate and Charles Joseph; [occ.] E. Windsor School District; [occ.] In 8th Grade at Melvin H. Kreps School; [memb.] International Children's Assoc - sponsor; [pers.] If you're rich enough to have friends you should do your best to keep them.; [a.] Hightstown, NJ

JOYCE, JOSIANE JAMEUX
[b.] Paris, France; [m.] Allyn Joyce, May 22, 1994; [ch.] Ghislaine and Nathalie, 3 grandchildren, Nicola, Genevieve, Olivia; [ed.] Rutgers University NJ; [occ.] Retired, has taught French at Rutgers and has been an administrator, now a singer with Cantabile Chamber Choir and Rutgers University Choir; [oth. writ.] Articles on travel in the Home News, Poetry on Africa, Translation of French Songs; [pers.] As a young girl, my poetry reflected my own inner turmoils, now it is more observant and I try to describe objects, people and feelings through imagery - so much for the wisdom of age.; [a.] Rocky Hill, NJ

JUSTICE, KAREN
[b.] March 29, 1982, Plano, TX; [p.] Theodora Justice and Robert Thomas Justice; [ed.] Richardson West Jr. High Hamilton Park Pacesetter; [memb.] St. Paul A.M.E. Church Jr. Ursher Board, Jr. Trustee, H.F. Dodson Youth Choir; [hon.] Cheerader, Science Fair winner, a ward for saying and learning capitals of the United States; [a.] Dallas, TX

KACHIN, LAURIE
[b.] October 25, 1959; [p.] Ruth DeCou, Laurence DeCou; [ch.] Makanda Kachin; [ed.] Ferris State University - Pharmacist; [occ.] Pharmacy Administrator; [memb.] Michigan Pharmacists Assoc, American Pharmaceutical Assoc. HIV/AIDS Resource Center. Rho Chi.; [pers.] Each of us is on a journey. I strive to freely show my support to the vision of my loved ones who are experiencing their journey, as I remain true to myself on mine.; [a.] Novi, MI

KACIREK, TINA N. GABRIEL
[pen.] Tina Gabriel-Kacirek; [b.] November 2, 1973, Lincoln, NE; [p.] Robert and Marilyn Gabriel; [m.] Randy Kacirek, December 28, 1996; [ed.] Waverly High School, Attended University of Nebraska - Lincoln in Psychology; [occ.] Owner and Artist of Sweet Expressions in Lincoln, NE; [memb.] St. Johns Catholic Church, Seattle Fibromyalgia International Team; [pers.] I want to encourage those who suffer from a disability, to grow from it. Do not let it consume you. Turn it into an opportunity to discover something deeper within yourself. Live life.; [a.] Lincoln, NE

KANE, JANE A.
[b.] January 6, 1948, Washington Island, WI; [p.] Dr. Edward and Ruby Larson Farmer; [m.] James M. Kane, June 6, 1969; [ch.] Heather J. Milch; [ed.] B.Sci. Western Michigan University; [occ.] Chemistry Lab Director at Muskegon Community College; [memb.] American Guild of Organists, West Michigan Herb Society, First Lutheran Church; [oth. writ.] Art Through Nature by Learning Publications, 1985, Poem and story published in River Voices, Local Literary and Art Magazine, Articles in Muskegon Magazine; [a.] Muskegon, MI

KANOTI, BYRON AUGUST
[pen.] Bryan August K.; [b.] October 1, 1977, Cleveland, OH; [p.] George and Linda Kanoti; [ed.] I currently am attending Beloit College in Beloit, WI. I am a Freshman; [hon.] Received Davey fellowship for creative writing, 1995 and the silver bowl art prize for seniors, 1996 member all state lacrosse team- Ohio - 1996; [oth. writ.] One other poem published in the Cle. Plain Dealer Poetry published in (High School) University School Literary Journal; [pers.] I believe that the ability to write well is the ability to write poetry well.; [a.] Cleveland, OH

KANTER, NANCY REED
[b.] May 29, 1928, Pittsburgh, PA; [m.] Joseph H. Kanter, July 26, 1953; [ch.] 4 - Harry, Hillary, Marin, John; [ed.] Juilliard School of Music; [occ.] Singer, Song Writer; [memb.] ASCAP, SAG; [hon.] Distinguished Service Award Wash., D.C. 1960 for composing "Look At Us, We're Walking" UCP theme song "Who's Who American Women" 1961; [pers.] Former big band singer with Skitch Henderson, 1950 tour with Benny Goodman (Europe and Scandinavia) Atlantic Record Album "Nancy Reed" 1987 Cabaret and Carnegie Hall appearances '94 and '95.

KASOLD, PAUL
[pen.] Dakota Chance; [b.] July 13, 1960, Phoenix, AZ; [p.] Richard and Mary Kleinman; [m.] Tracey Kasold, August 25, 1995; [ch.] Dakota, Amber, Krystal, Jade, Kerstin; [ed.] High School - 1979 Graduate of Westwood High - Mesa, AZ., Creative Writing Course - Fayetteville Technical Institute; [occ.] Station Manager - Leading Edge Aviation Services; [hon.] While serving in the 82nd Airborne Division, 1984-1988, was the recipient of the Expert Infantryman's Badge and a Commandant's List Graduate of the Primary Leadership Development Course.; [oth. writ.] None published at the present time.; [pers.] "The Empty Garden" was written in lov-

ing memory of a wonderful Mother-in-Law who passed away September 11, 1996.; [a.] Clarendon, TX

KASTLER, PAT
[pen.] Patrick Joe or Pat Kastler; [b.] January 15, 1960, Raton, NM; [p.] Paul and Marianne Kastler; [ed.] B.S. Civil Engineering Technology and Minor in Computer Science from NAU (Northern Arizona University); [occ.] CAD Design Specialist for my own Business; [oth. writ.] "Images" poem - "The Voice Within" Anthology "Happy Mother's Day" poem - "The Ebbing Tide" anthology "Down-Mexico" poem - "The Best Of The 90's" anthology "Promise Keepers Poem" poem - "Colors Of Thought" anthology; [pers.] I wrote this poem for all the women that have been painfully and wrongfully hurt. As a society we all need to start treating each other better.; [a.] Phoenix, AZ

KAYSER, W. CLIFF
[b.] November 17, 1962, Chicago, IL; [p.] Willard Kayser, Sally Irwin; [ed.] B.A. Lenoir - Rhyne College University of Virginia, Accounting University of Maryland, MSc Candidate; [occ.] Human Resources Manager Padco, Inc.; [memb.] St. Luke's Church, St. Luke's Shelter, Big Brother, Hung Tao Chuy MEI Academy; [a.] Washington, DC

KEAMS, GENE
[b.] December 29, 1960, Albuquerque, NM; [ch.] Rhiannon Latoya Keams; [ed.] Associates of Art; [occ.] Shipping and receiving at Tri-Gas Inc.; [hon.] Published scratch board picture for Al Collins Graphic design; [pers.] To live is to learn. If you do not learn you do not live. Artist by trade (Serialistic) Native American with 1/16 English. My Native American name is GOT-TY-YAH meaning "Moonlight".; [a.] Albuquerque, NM

KEENE, KERRI
[b.] April 22, 1981, Providence, RI; [p.] Debra A. and Glen D. Biddiscombe; [ed.] Presently a sophomore at Burrillville High School; [occ.] Bus person for local restaurant; [memb.] Burrillville High School Band, Burrillville United Methodist Church Sunday School and Education Committee, and Internation Club.; [hon.] Grade 4 - Young Author's Award, Grade 7 - Awards for solo and duet on flute, and many awards each year for the honor roll society.; [oth. writ.] I have written many other poems which have not been published and I am currently giving my best effort to write a novel.; [pers.] I believe that writing should be written from experience and inner emotions. Writing is truly a way to express yourself in an intimate way, even if no one but you can understand the true meaning.; [a.] Harrisville, RI

KELLEY, BILLY
[pen.] Bubba/Squirt; [b.] February 22, 1979, Marlin, TX; [p.] Bill and Gale Kelley; [ed.] Midway Elementary and Junior High, Lorena High School; [occ.] Student; [memb.] Academic clubs; [hon.] National Youth Leader Award, Black Belt, Academics; [oth. writ.] "Realize", "Stand", "Night Eyes", "Essence of Dreams"; [pers.] You can make the best of worst situation or the worst of the best situation.; [a.] Hewitt, TX

KELLEY, DOROTHY MUNSINGER
[pen.] Dorothy M. Kelley; [b.] March 5, 1923, Crockett, TX; [p.] Burton and Dessie Munsinger; [m.] Herbert E. Kelley, November 24, 1941; [ch.] Three; [ed.] High School; [occ.] Retired; [memb.] Airline Manor Baptist Ch. Chapter 1094 North Freeway A.A.R.P; [hon.] AARP Outstanding Service to Community, AARP Volfener of the Year; [oth. writ.] Short story - How the Tiger Got His stripes, numbers poems; [a.] Houston, TX

KELLY, DOT HUTCHINSON
[b.] Clover, SC; [p.] Danile Noah and Margaret Pendletop Platt; [m.] Lawrence J. Kelly, October 8, 1994; [ch.] E. Eric Hutchinson, Karen Hutchinson McRae; [ed.] Specialist in Administration 1986 - Winthrop University, Rock Hill, SC: Master of Arts in Teaching 1972 - Winthrop University, Rock Hill, SC: Bachelor of Science in Elementary Education 1964 - Winthrop University, Rock Hill, SC: Rock Hill High School, Rock Hill, SC - Diploma 1950; [occ.] Temporary Instructor (EDU 449) 8/1995 - Winthrop University, Rock Hill, SC - also serve as Winthrop Area Coordinator for Interns; [memb.] South Carolina Association of School Administrators, South Carolina Elementary and Middle School Principals, Palmetto Reading Council, Association for Supervision and Curriculum Development, First Presbyterian Church, Rock Hill, SC; [oth. writ.] "Rear View Mirror" (in sunshine and day dreams, "Celebration" (in colors of thought), have just completed manuscript for a children's fiction book.; [pers.] Given the interest, imagination, recollections, desire, and motivation to write, thoughts and ideas can be organized in a form that provides for great personal satisfaction.; [a.] Rock Hill, SC

KEMP, MELISSA PRUNTY
[b.] November 5, 1963, Roanoke, VA; [p.] Alfred S. and Laverne H. Prunty (Deceased); [m.] Divorced, January 14, 1988; [ch.] Jesse T.H.D. Kemp; [ed.] Psychology Major BA, 1985, Hollins College, Hollins, VA, MA, 1992, VPI and SU in Blacksborg, VA, English Pending Ph.D. at Kent State University, Spring 1998, English.; [occ.] Prof. of English Comp. African American Literature and Pan African Studies; [memb.] Alpha Kappa My National Honor Society, Alpha Kappa Alpha Sorority, Inc.; [oth. writ.] "Slavemother" in Poetic Voices of America 1995, "Mr. Parker" in Luna Wegra, "Why I Hate White People" in conflict of Interest Magazine, "Christmas Salads" in Robin's Nest 1996, "In A Beauty Salon On Saturday Afternoon" in Journal of Woman and Language 1994, Articles in Uhuru Magazine, Hollins Entic, Salem History.; [pers.] Writes Appalachian Landscape poetry and poems on feminist subjects PhD is in poetry of Harlem Renaissance. Scholarship areas are Socialism/Marxism, Af-Am Lit, Af-Am Women's fiction, Contemporary poetry.; [a.] Canton, OH

KEOWN, SHERRY
[b.] July 9, 1980, Detroit; [p.] Charles and Helen Weiss; [m.] David, September 22, 1978; [memb.] ASPCA, Humane Society, World Wildlife fund; [hon.] Several Editor's Choice awards through the National Library of Poetry; [oth. writ.] Splashed In Red, God For A Day, Ask An Angel, Eyes Of A Child, Freedom Of Horses, Kingdom On The Sea; [pers.] Sometimes to make the world a better place, you need just to close your eyes.; [a.] Warren, MA

KERR, STEVE
[pen.] Steven Kerr-Scot; [b.] February 3, 1951, Russell Springs, KY; [p.] James and Grace Kerr; [m.] Pamela D. Kerr, December 20, 1969; [ch.] David P. and Adam L. Kerr; [occ.] Construction Project Manager; [memb.] New Friendship United Baptist Church (Deacon and Teacher); [hon.] Kentucky Colonel; [oth. writ.] Various poems (unpublished at present).; [pers.] I try to reflect the peace and serenity that God and nature has to offer. To cause one to smile is worth all the effort and has the greatest reward.; [a.] Russell Springs, KY

KESSLER, JONI L.
[pen.] J. L. Kessler; [b.] January 12, 1962, Stillwater, OK; [p.] Nita Roesler, Gordon Roesler; [m.] Earl "Lee" Kessler III, July 21, 1984; [ch.] "Lee" IV, Nita, Ariel; [ed.] Perry High, Northern Oklahoma Jr. College, Word

of Faith Bible College; [occ.] Customer Service Manager; [oth. writ.] Numerous unpublished children's stories, poetry, short stories, and one unfinished novel.; [pers.] I try to reflect my perception of the world around me, in hopes that someone will identify with it.; [a.] Mabank, TX

KEY, MELVA L.
[pen.] Melva Luellen (Eason) Key; [b.] October 31, 1939, North Carolina; [p.] W. H. Eason and Bertha (Eason) Pugh; [m.] Billy Andrew Key, June 9, 1962; [ch.] Franklin Andrew Key; [ed.] College (2 yrs.) Decatur Baptist; [occ.] Sitter - working with sick or terminally ill; [oth. writ.] "Genesis - In Rhyming Verse", "Poems That Touch The Heart", and "Memory Lane Poems" (copyright not yet received).; [pers.] I started writing poems in high school choosing religious poetry. If just one of my poems make a difference in somebody's life it would be worth the time it took to write it. If we use not our talents God will surely take them away. I've been inspired by E.B. Brownings, and R. Frost writings.; [a.] Greenville, TX

KEYTON, WILSON SCOTT
[pen.] Wilson Scott Keyton; [b.] August 6, 1976, Charlottesville, VA; [p.] Edgar and Mary Keyton; [ed.] Burgess Lane High School; [occ.] Part-time Maintenance and Construction; [hon.] High School Staff and Peer Recognition and awards in poetry and song writing; [oth. writ.] Variety of song writings, etc. "Mother Freedom", "Yesterday's Goodbyes", "Out There" and poems, etc. "Today We Steal", "Fall Of Ash", "Open Doors".; [pers.] To try alone, is the company of success.; [a.] Crozet, VA

KHACHATRYAN, ARTHUR
[pen.] Arthur Kay; [b.] April 30, 1977, Armenia; [p.] Anait and Andranik; [ed.] L.A. Center for Enriched Studies, California State University, Northridge; [occ.] Office worker; [hon.] Writing Excellence Award; [oth. writ.] I have written many poems just for the mere enjoyment but I have none published.; [pers.] I write entirely with and through my emotions and feelings in order to explore an essence pleasing to the ear without rhyme and capture true meanings in life.; [a.] Los Angeles, CA

KHALSA, GURU PREM KAUR
[b.] March 6, 1951, Chicago, IL; [p.] Louis A. Ule and Mary Ule; [m.] Vip B. Short, March 29, 1997; [ch.] Adi Shakti Kaur Connolly; [ed.] Rolling Hills High, UCLA, UW, West LA College, Mira Costa College, 3HO organization (27 years student-teacher of Kundalini Yoga); [occ.] Kundalini Yoga Teacher, Childcare Provider, Life Plus; [memb.] IKYTA (International Kundalini Yoga Teacher Association); [hon.] Granthi, Guru Ram Das Ashram Minister of Sikh Dharma; [oth. writ.] Poem published in a local newsletter, entitled "Sacred Love"; [pers.] I live the disciplined and exemplary life of a yogi and a sikh, serving our entrance into the Aquarian Age teaching healing and oneness. My poetry flows from meditative awakenings to sacred love and the nature of the soul.; [a.] Eugene, OR

KIEFT JR., JOHN F.
[b.] April 9, 1945, Riverside, CA; [p.] John Kieft, Dorothy Kieft; [m.] Lynn, July 12, 1995; [ed.] Buena High, Ventura, Cal. Ventura Jr. College, Cal Poly, San Luis Obispo; [occ.] Hairstylist; [memb.] V.F.W.; [hon.] Vietnam Veteran - U.S. Navy; [oth. writ.] A few "Haiku" published in Hawaii newspaper. Article for Tin Can Sailors magazine.; [pers.] I usually write about personal experiences. Mostly influenced by Robert Service.; [a.] Grants Pass, OR

KIET, KIM HUOT
[b.] May 10, 1941, Cambodia; [p.] Phul Kiet and Kim Havy (Deceased); [m.] Amelia Varney-Kiet, July 18, 1983; [ch.] Neary Kiet; [ed.] Lycee Sisowath, Phnom Penh, Cambodia, Sch of Social Work, Adelphi University, BMCC, NYC, City College of NY for Worker Ed, NYC; [occ.] Para Professional Special Ed, NYC, Royal Cambodian Mask Maker/Historian; [memb.] Cambodian American Social and Cultural Assoc, Cambodian Network Assoc, UFT; [hon.] Outstanding leadership - Cambodian American Society, Honorable Mention Borough of Manhattan City College Essay Contest; [oth. writ.] Several Pamphlets on the culture of Cambodia distributed to the population and interested scholars; [pers.] Peace for my motherland, Cambodia; [a.] New York City, NY

KIKIS, CHRIS
[pen.] Deropolitis; [b.] Greece; [p.] Thomas and Virginia Kikis; [m.] Eleftheria, January 4, 1981; [ch.] Alexia, Thomas; [ed.] Elementary in Yiannena Greece, High School in N.Y.C. then attended N.Y. School of Finance; [occ.] Restaurant owner - Nick's Pizza and Seafood, Tarpon Springs FL; [memb.] St. Nicholas Greece Orthodox Church, Tarpon Springs Florida, Vice President (Epiros Society), Clearwater Florida; [hon.] One US patent and one patent pending bronze award in 1984 New York Inventors Show; [oth. writ.] Poems published in Greek in various newspapers and books. Also read in several school events in N.Y.C.; [a.] Tarpon Springs, FL

KIM, MARY
[b.] April 29, 1979, Korea; [p.] Paul Kim (father), Esther Kim (mother); [ed.] North High School; [occ.] High School Student; [hon.] National PTA Cultural Arts Program; [oth. writ.] Poem "Discovery of a Father's Love"; [pers.] I have discovered that one of the greatest and the purest love can be found in a heart of a parent. My parents and nature influenced me greatly.; [a.] Carson, CA

KIMBERLY, JAMES C.
[b.] March 10, 1927, Savannah, GA; [p.] Clifford and Louise Kimberly; [m.] Barbara S. Kimberly, August 2, 1949; [ch.] Elizabeth; [ed.] Ph.D., Duke University 1963 Sociology, Psychology; [occ.] Professor Emeritus of Sociology, University of Nebraska-Lincoln; [memb.] None relevant to poetry; [hon.] None relevant to poetry; [oth. writ.] Numerous Academic Publications; [pers.] As an Undergraduate in the late forties, I wrote a number of poems. I am returning to them and attempting to publish them.; [a.] Lincoln, NE

KINDLAND, KRISTINE
[b.] May 8, 1951, Erie, PA; [p.] Fred Kindland, Jean Kindland; [ed.] MBA - Nova Southeastern University; [occ.] Project Manager of Software Development Groups, GTE; [pers.] I believe in the discipline and persistence that is necessary to bypass the instant gratification of the moment. This, along with a good value system, allows us to constantly reach our goals, thus creating our own destiny, with character.; [a.] Tampa, FL

KING, A. E.
[b.] September 14, 1947, Dayton, OH; [p.] Patrick and Rosemary Sano; [m.] Bill King, April 23, 1986; [ed.] Stranahan High School; [occ.] Marketing Director for Glass Sculptor, Bill King; [pers.] I view the movements and events of my life as a series of short stories, some serious, some humorous.; [a.] La Jolla, CA

KIRKNER, AUDREY
[pen.] Audrey Grimm Kirkner; [b.] October 11, 1922, Youngstown, OH; [p.] Basil Grimm, Annie Grimm; [m.] Bernard Kirkner, March 14, 1942; [ch.] Daniel Francis, John Grimm, Stephen Mark; [ed.] South High School, Youngstown University, Business School; [occ.] Retired Office Worker; [oth. writ.] Poem Published in local newspaper, "The Sun."; [pers.] I have written poems for years, but never thought of having any published, until my fourteen year old grand daughter had one her poems published in "Crossings" so here Iana at age 74 with a poem going to print.; [a.] San Bernardino, CA

KITAMURA, KYOKO
[b.] November 13, 1948, Yaizu, Japan; [m.] Masao Kitamura, December 2, 1974; [ch.] Victory Fuku, Rocky Ju, Masao Yorokobu; [ed.] Keio University, Kosei Jhoshigakuen Tokyo, Japan; [occ.] Homemaker; [pers.] I have been greatly influenced by Seamus Heaney. I especially love his poems, "Song" and "Personal Helicon."; [a.] Oxnard, CA

KJELLERUP, LEO
[b.] July 19, 1919, SD; [p.] Ernest and Olga; [m.] Ardell - Medenwaldt, January 20, 1940; [ch.] Douglas and Connie; [ed.] 8th Grade; [occ.] Retired (sales) in furniture - 35 years; [memb.] Legion United Meth. Prespecterian Church, Browns Valley MN; [hon.] Many roles awards; [oth. writ.] Over 50 poems published in local and neighboring papers.; [pers.] All my poems have message for the reader.; [a.] Browns Valley, MN

KLASSEN, LILLIAN ANN
[pen.] Lilly; [b.] April 22, 1960, Osage, IA; [p.] Motte Viola Klassen Jr.; [ed.] University of Notre Dame, B.A. 1982, History, Saint Mary's College Notre Dame, Ind. Teachers Certification Social Studies Winona State 1985, M.S. History; [occ.] General Manager Franchise Associates; [memb.] Diplomat for Rochester, Art Chamber of Commerce, President's Club fr Franchise Associates; [hon.] Awards for Franchise Associates include best local marketing, no overtime, best service goals, crew development and manager development nominee for 5 Star Restaurant 1994 and n1995 for franchise associates.; [oth. writ.] Published poems at College, Notre Dame and Leinona State University.; [pers.] My poetry reflects aspects that have affected my life and I know that many people can relate to the themes that I address.; [a.] Stewartville, MN

KNOELL, DOUGLAS L.
[b.] July 27, 1939, Anselmo, NE; [p.] Harold Knoell - Wanda Knoell; [m.] Mary M. (Carter) Knoell, October 26, 1963; [ch.] Robert Joseph, James Warren; [ed.] Broken Bow High, Broken Bow, Nebraska Kearney State, Kearney, Nebraska - U.S. Navy - U.S. Border Patrol Academy; [occ.] U.S. Border Patrol (Retired) currently - Special Deputy U.S. Marshall; [memb.] B.P.O.E Lodge #1690, United Government Security Officer of America, National Rifle Association, South Bay Rod and Gun Club, California Rifle and Pistol Association; [hon.] U.S. Border Patrol (1976) Outstanding Performance - (1978) Meritorious Award - (1980) Superior Performance Award - (1984) Meritorious Award (1990) Outstanding Performance. San Diego County Sheriff's Dept. (1975) Exceptional Service award; [oth. writ.] None published; [pers.] "Always strive to do your best." The poem was composed due to our son Robert having served in the Persian Gulf War with the 82nd Airborne, awarded the Bronze Star and has the Gulfwar illness.; [a.] Santee, CA

KNUTSON, TRACY LEA
[b.] March 8, 1959, Spokane, WA; [p.] Robert A. MacPherson and Merlyn G. MacPherson; [m.] Barry A. Knutson, September 5, 1981; [ch.] Brandon 16, Brittany 14, Brianna 12, Taylor 8, and Tanner 6.; [ed.] Graduated Deer Park High School; [occ.] Homemaker - Washer Woman; [pers.] In 1992 I met a carpenter who reminded me of who I am, and revived a belief that I can, and should continue to write. This one is for you Jim!; [a.] Spokane, WA

KOHLAN, DOUGLAS J.
[b.] January 28, 1949, Minneapolis, MN; [p.] Mr. John Kohlan, Mrs. Olive Kohlan; [ed.] Edison High School, Bemidji State College, University of Minnesota School of Dentistry; [occ.] Dentistry, Retired U.S. Navy; [memb.] National Honor Society, Academy of General Dentistry; [hon.] Fellow, Academy of General Dentistry; [oth. writ.] Short story published at age 14, also articles in local newspapers on dental health.; [pers.] My inspiration came from my Ninth Grade English teacher, Mr. Ruben Wenzel, and from my dear mother and father.; [a.] Honolulu, HI

KONDAL, URSULA KAUR
[pen.] Urmil Kaur; [b.] October 16, Germany; [p.] Mr. and Mrs. Werner Willwacher; [m.] Gurcharan Singh Kondal, June 26, 1993; [ch.] Carmen and Christopher; [occ.] Self-empl., serving sweets (ice cream and yogurts) in God's tiny little ice cream shop in Holly Hill, SC; [hon.] Presently waiting patiently for them to arrive.; [oth. writ.] Near or Far, The Tree "Omcar", God's Waiting, Choices, Armanda for Beaufort, E.C. Montissory School, (many more); [pers.] The eternal moment is captured in each breath, sustaining therefore eternity. Here and now is eternity.; [a.] Holly Hill, SC

KOSTENBAUDER, SHARON THAYER
[pen.] Aglalia Rose; [b.] December 7,1949, Tampa, FL; [p.] Charles H. Thayer Sr., Pauline A. Thayer; [m.] Charles Kostenbauder, October 2, 1988; [ch.] Annette Benson-Brooks, Brandy Keith; [ed.] Leto High School, Hillsborough Comm. College, Professional Career Development Institute (Foundation/Civil Litigation Truck Driving School, Red Cross Home Nursing); [occ.] Security Officer (Capt., Site Supervisor), Private Investigator; [memb.] American Federation of Police The International Society of Poets (Distinguished Member); [hon.] National Patriotism Award (7/2/96) issued by American Police Hall of Fame, Editor's Choice Award (N.L.P./1996) (Anth.) Editor's Choice Award (N.L.P./1996) (Anth) Re: "My Mother Is Forever"/ Across The Universe Editor's Choice Award (N.L.P./ 1996) Re: "Sense Me There", Fields of Gold (Anth.) Elected (10/01/96) into "The International Poetry Hall of Fame (Museum)"; [oth. writ.] Poems in several (N.L.P.) anthologies, including "Sailboat Scene" in "Best Poems of 1997"; [a.] Tampa, FL

KOSTER, KIMBERLY A.
[b.] March 6, 1971, Iron Mountain, MI; [p.] Harry and Susan Koster; [ed.] Jefferson Community College; [occ.] Student; [hon.] Volunteer Service at Lewis County General Hospital; [oth. writ.] Journals since the age of 14, poems, and short stories.; [pers.] I write all of the time, but I don't consider it well written until I evoke an emotional response from someone.; [a.] Harrisville, NY

KOWALCZYK, ROBERT
[b.] April 14, 1960, Tawas, MI; [p.] Buddy and Marily Ervin; [m.] Melissa Kowalczyk, April 18, 1986; [ch.] Clifford, Abigail, Clayton, Anabel; [ed.] Standish Sterling High Standish MI, many meaningless Correspondence Courses; [occ.] Grocery Manager; [oth. writ.] This is my first attempt at writing but countless other will follow.; [pers.] Though each of my kids is more precious than the other - there is none more precious than their mother.; [a.] Slidell, LA

KREISELMAN, JACK
[b.] January 20, 1928, Bronx, NY; [p.] Morris Kreiselman, Ray Kreiselman; [m.] Adelaide, February 16, 1958; [ch.] Penny Yamet, David Kreiselman; [ed.] High School of Music and Art NY, Manhuttan School

of Music NY, taught at New York University "Music Dept." and at Stony Brook Univ. NY, both Prof. Emeritus; [occ.] Retired, Clarinetist and Conductor, performed in many parts of the world with many famous Conductors.; [memb.] Elks, Winter Park Lodge 1830, Florida, Local 802 (Musicians) New York, The International Register of Profiles Cambridge, England; [hon.] 1993 Man of the Year, in the Arts (from the times Beacon Newspapers personal orchestra NY), Music Award for participation with Pablo Casab American New Music Consortium in Puerto Rico, Contribution to Contemporary Music 1996, Jack Kreiselman Award (yearly) to best MA Graduate in Composition from New York University; [oth. writ.] Various other poems with different subjects.; [pers.] It is extremely important for one to be well rounded in many areas, including Art, Music and Dance. In writing poetry on these subject one must be very involved in reading various books on there subjects.; [a.] Winter Spring, FL

KREUZER, KRISTEN
[b.] August 16, 1979, Coronado Island, CA; [p.] Margaret and Robert Kreuzer; [ed.] Santa Margarita Catholic High School, (Senior); [occ.] Student; [memb.] National Charity League, St. Timothy Catholic Church, High School Swim Team; [hon.] National Honors Society, California Scholarship Federation, Who's Who Among American High School Students, 4 year academic letter; [pers.] "The hottest places in hell are reversed for those who in a time of moral crisis, maintain their neutrality" - Dante Stand by your standards, don't succumb to pressure. Pick a side and fight for what you believe in.; [a.] Laguna Hills, CA

KRISHNAMURTHY, MADHUMATHI
[pen.] Madhumathi; [b.] June 23, 1976, Madras, IN; [p.] Natarajan Krishnamurthy, Shyamala Krishnamurthy; [ed.] International Diploma in Journalism from Darlington College of Technology, England currently doing Bain Journalism from University of Central Oklahoma; [occ.] Student; [memb.] Former member of the National Union of Journalists in United Kingdom; [oth. writ.] Several other unpublished poems. One poem called 'Recipe of Life' published in India. One short children's story call 'The Christmas Present' published in magazine called 'Junior New's in Dubai'.; [pers.] Love is the only thing worth living for or dying for. All the work I've ever done is inspired and influenced by my eternal love for everyone dear to my heart.; [a.] Edmond, OK

KUCHLER, IRA
[b.] April 20, 1908, Germany; [p.] Theodore Kuchler, Johanna Weinberg; [m.] Victoria Salzman, November 9, 1935; [ch.] Merle and Janine; [ed.] New York University School of Fine Arts, Bachelor of Architecture; [occ.] Architect - retired, writer, painter; [memb.] American Institute of Architects, Arbor Day Society; [oth. writ.] Children's short stories, autobiography, book of poems. Several published poems in local publications in New York, Florida and Arizona.; [pers.] I would like to eliminate dishonesty, bigotry and greed.; [a.] Oceanside, NY

KUDLA, PHILLIP A.
[b.] November 6, 1954, Cleveland, OH; [ed.] Hampshire College, BA, Philosophy, Columbia University, MBA, Finance; [occ.] Banker and organic vegetable farmer; [a.] Cold Spring and Tivoli, NY

KUEHNEL, MELISSA
[b.] March 2, 1973, Hartford, CT; [p.] Judy and Bob Kuehnel; [pers.] Know you what it is to be a child? It is to be something very different from the man of today. It is to have a spirit yet streaming from the waters of baptism, it is to believe in love, to believe in loveliness, to believe in belief, it is to be so little that the elves can

reach to whisper in your ear, it is to turn pumpkins into coaches, and mice into horses, lowness into loftiness, and nothing into everything, for each child has its fairy godmother in its soul.; [a.] South Windsor, CT

KURUTZA, YOLANDA ALFANO PETRELLA
[b.] August 18, 1924, Brooklyn, NY; [m.] Charles Kurutza; [ch.] Theresa, Frances, Vincent; [ed.] After High School - 2 years Fine Arts at Pratts-New York; [occ.] Housewife; [memb.] Numerous Art Clubs of Central N.J.; [hon.] One woman showing at the Garden State Art Center for Oils, numerous first place Art Awards in shows in Central New Jersey; [oth. writ.] One poem published in local newspaper.; [pers.] All my poems reflect my inner feelings at the time I am writing them.; [a.] Whiting, NJ

KUSMIREK, JOHN
[b.] May 11, 1959, Poland; [ed.] Curie High, American Academy of Art, and School of the Art Institute of Art; [occ.] Freelance Artist; [hon.] United Insurance Calendar Award, Printer of Month Award, Graphic Designer of the Month, and Wiebotts Gold Key Award; [a.] Fort Collins, CO

LAEGER, DAVID
[pen.] Jedidiah; [b.] October 9, 1940, Wichita, KS; [p.] Charles and Evelyn Laeger; [m.] Anna Marie, July 28, 1967; [ch.] Suzanne, Tim, Phillip, Kristin; [ed.] East Texas State U. (2 yrs) U of Texas at San Antonio (1 Sem) College for officer training (Salvation Army) (2 years); [occ.] Officer - The Salvation Army (Ordained Minister); [memb.] None Presently; [hon.] Dean's List Once at East Texas State U., 225 Hrs' Certificate in Spanish from the "Instituto Cultural De Mexico/ Norte Americano", Mexico City, Mexico; [oth. writ.] A number of articles in the salvation army's international publication, The Officer, and a column in the salvation army's Newsletter for U.S.A. Southern Territory, The Southern Spirit; [pers.] I have long been drawn into Biblical studies, especially relative to christology. I'm enriched through examination of both Jewish Messianic Exposition and christian theology. Varied forms of prayer, Jewish and Christian Interest me.; [a.] Winchester, VA

LAIRD, AMBER SHILA
[b.] December 3, 1981, Hamlin, TX; [p.] Tamara B. Laird; [ed.] Freshman in High School (Special Education at 6th grade level); [occ.] Student Freshman in High School; [hon.] 2nd Place at "Star Bright" rehab in Austin, TX 1996. Amber was a patient for 6 months after being hit by a car while riding her bike in 1992.; [pers.] Amber is a head injury patient I was very impressed with her talent. She competed against other patients from the rehab and came in second. Her doctor was so impressed he had her read it out loud to the audience.

LAMBERT, STANLEY
[pen.] Stan; [b.] July 15, 1961, Aurora, IL; [p.] Kenneth and Julia Lambert; [m.] Divorced; [ed.] Wabonsee C.C. Courses; [occ.] Educator, Stylist and also a Technical Consultant for Avlon; [memb.] Top 15 Educator Avlon, Technical National Educational Advisor Board; [hon.] 1st Seller for Trade Secret Inc.; [oth. writ.] Many poems for weddings and funerals. Birth of children and love poems.; [pers.] It's a gift to be able to write and for people to understand you must use your gift and let it shine.; [a.] Aurora, IL

LANCASTER, ELISE
[pen.] Elise Lancaster; [b.] May 15, 1912, Fayetteville, AR; [p.] Grace and Bert Pyeatte; [m.] May Condon and Neal Lancaster (both deceased); [ch.] Michael Condon, Patricia Johnson, Suzi Trammell and Lisa Lancaster; [ed.] Master's Degree in Violin, Writing Workshops at

New York University, Brown Univ. at Providence RI Marbleboro, VT. Summer Colony; [occ.] (Retired) occupation originally was teaching violin in colleges and playing in symphonies (violin); [memb.] Murphi Epsilon Music Sorority; [hon.] No honor or award I have ever gotten means as much to me as being able, at last, to sit down and work on my poetry four or five hours a day. May be now I can learn to write. Words are like notes in music.; [oth. writ.] Am just ready to publish my first book of poetry - 45 poems. Also have book almost ready of three stories for children. Am happy to be free to write new poetry - so much to write about.; [pers.] Philosophical statement: "What Do I Think About Life?" I think it's Great!; [a.] East Providence, RI

LARSON, IRENE MARY
[pen.] Irene Mary Larson; [b.] September 19, 1921, Lynd, MN; [p.] Andrew and Mary Larson; [ed.] High School graduate

LAUGHLIN, KILEY Q.
[b.] February 14, 1975, Yuba City, CA; [p.] Gene Laughlin, Mary Moss; [ed.] Lindhurst High School, Campbell University; [occ.] U.S. Soldier; [oth. writ.] Several poems and writings as of yet unpublished.; [pers.] To write is more than expression or communication, it is the creation of bold new worlds, of special places, whose form and mold are limited only to how far one dares to imagine. For deep within the mind's domain in what science fails to discover, there lingers an infinitude of possibilities.; [a.] Marysville, CA

LAVEAHON, THOMAS F.
[pen.] Tom LaVeahon; [b.] December 29, 1975, Elizabeth, NJ; [p.] Felix and Felicia LaVeahon; [ed.] Roselle Park, High School, Roselle Park, NY - 1994 graduation, Rutgers University - Newark, currently attending Sophomore Status (part-time; [occ.] Exporter, Schering-Plough Corp.; [memb.] Italian-American Society; [hon.] Dean's List; [pers.] It is my intent to spread knowledge that I have obtained through experiences in all my poems in hopes that at least one person listens.; [a.] Roselle Park, NJ

LAVON, MANDY
[b.] November 8, 1979, Everett, GH, WA; [p.] Terrie LaVon, Danny Meredith; [ed.] Collins High School, Special Education in sculpting, and Art Appreciation Special skill in book keeping and filling.; [occ.] Filing clerk, Puttman Insurance of Enumclaw, WA; [memb.] Enumclaw Youth Council (T.A.C.T.) Teens and the Community together Enumclaw poetry group, Enumclaw youth center volunteer, self Art Studies.; [hon.] Young authors Florida 1992-1991; [oth. writ.] "America at Last" Young Authors Florida 1991-1992 Junior High School Newspaper; [pers.] "On the funny farm where the birds fly, I saw you sitting there, where the people grow I stop stared".; [a.] Enumclaw, WA

LAWRENCE, JOHNNA L.
[b.] January 3, 1949, Longview, TX; [p.] Webb Wilson and Crana Louise Wilson; [m.] Bobby L. Lawrence, November 5, 1988; [ch.] Two children - Matthew G. Hollis, Andrea L. Hollis Stegman, (one Granddaughter - Taylor L. Stegman), (Three step children - Michael, Jamie, and Holly Lawrence); [ed.] Longview High and Wolfe City High, Bisch Mathis Institute, Kilgore College Extension - Longview Tyler real Estate College; [occ.] Dept. Head, Draperies, Dillard's, previously, Real Estate Agent, Home Interiors and Gifts Displayers, Various Office Mgr. Positions; [oth. writ.] Submitted various stories to Institute of Children's Literature (took a correspondence course there); [pers.] In most of my writing, I seem to want to convey an uplifting message. I love mysteries, poetry and stories of romance.; [a.] Longview, TX

LAZAR, PAULA D.
[b.] September 17, 1961, Chicago; [p.] Richard and Emily Day; [m.] Edward M. Lazar, November 26, 1983; [ch.] BSBA, Valparaiso University, Business/ Economics Major; [ed.] Marketing Manager for Art Museum; [oth. writ.] Currently enrolled in Children's Institute of Literature. Prior writings include poems published in high school publications and gifts for family and friends.; [pers.] Writing keeps me sane. Being a parent keeps me humble. I just write when my life gets too crazy.; [a.] Charlotte, NC

LAZZARETTI, TERRI
[b.] January 27, 1974, Charleston, SC; [p.] Sheree and Lavaughn Chumney; [m.] Tony Lazzaretti, July 29, 1996; [ed.] Carrabelle High School, Mitchell's Hairstyling Academy; [occ.] United States Navy; [memb.] Distinguish Member of International Society of poets; [hon.] National Library of Poetry Editor's Choice Award 1996; [oth. writ.] Shadows (Poetic voices of America-spring '96), The rose (The Best Poems of '97), Tomorrow (Poetic Voices of America-Fall '96 and Ebbing Tide.); [pers.] "Full Circle" goes out to the never ending flow of people in and out of the my life. Two in particular changed me forever one let go to make room for the other. Thank you both!; [a.] Naples, Italy

LEAHY, KIMBERLY
[b.] August 30, 1977, Melrose, MA; [p.] Vicente and Diane Leahy; [ed.] Wakefield High School, North Shore Community College; [hon.] Dean's List Outstanding Achievement - English Comp. Distinguished Achievement-Marketing and Accounting; [pers.] Great thanks to my parents, Vinny and Diane. My inspiration in life. I love you always!; [a.] Wakefield, MA

LEAVITT, JOANN
[b.] January 4, 1943, Michigan; [p.] Mr. and Mrs. Anthony Manfree; [ch.] Michael, Paul, David; [ed.] Michael, U of M College, U of D Law School, now lawyer, Paul Ma Donna College, Ross University Medical school now attending Saba Medical school Dave College student schoolcraft; [occ.] Mother hair dresser and craft business; [memb.] I belong to the Northville Womens Club and Kiwonis Clubs; [hon.] I received the award for the president of the Novi South Kiwanis of Michigan in 1992-1993 now still active in Charity for the community.; [oth. writ.] None for publication at his time; [pers.] I strive to give my love and goodness to my family and friends through my works and being a survivor of cancer and appreciates life more thank you,; [a.] Northville, MI

LEBEAN, LYNN A.
[b.] November 23, 1952, Detroit, MI; [p.] Beverly Height, Harold McGuire; [m.] Divorced; [ch.] (1) Tamika, (2) Tierr LeBean, (3) Robert Lee Cunningham III; [ed.] Cooley High, Wayne County Associate of Science Degree, Community College Det., Mi., Trained as a medical transcriptionist in a hospital; [occ.] Medical Transcriptionist, Saratoga Hospital, Det., Mi.; [hon.] Treasurer for the graduating class of 1988, Wayne County Community College; [oth. writ.] I am encouraged to write more. I am now writing a short book of poems for young people (15-30 poems). Should be completed the Spring of 1977.; [pers.] I like to help others with a kind word or being there for them.; [a.] Detroit, MI

LEBLANC, MISS KARON EVETTE
[b.] October 22, 1964, Beaumont, TX; [p.] Mrs. Maxine Drudhomme; [ed.] West Brook High School 1983, graduate Lamar University 2 years; [occ.] Kinder Care Day Care Center; [hon.] Reading History Science, Volleyball, Basketball, Trace, Tennis, Baseball, Singing; [oth. writ.] I've written a lot of poems for my church. St. Stephens Baptist Church of Houston, Texas

and they have touched a lot of lives.; [pers.] I hope and pray that my poem will touch a lot of lives of mankind. I have been greatly influenced by reading a lot of Shakespeare.

LEE, NANCY
[b.] November 27, 1945, Memphis, TN; [p.] Wilma Lee Beck; [ch.] David Marshall, Robert Adrian, Charles J. Lee III; [pers.] My youngest son. Charles J. Lee III, completed suicide 8-12-96, one week after his 24th birthday. So many thoughts had been going through my head since his death. One night, I transferred my thoughts and feelings onto paper. "Ask me not if God was there" was the 1st of seven. I felt my son's presence while I wrote. He not only influenced my writing but my decision to submit my poem. He wrote "Vita's Window" for The National Lib. of Poetry.; [a.] Overland Park, KS

LEE, PHYLLIS L.
[pen.] Phyllis L. Lee; [b.] August 13, 1938, Gary, IN; [p.] Darry Ann Vera Holt; [m.] Verne E. Lee, February 3, 1959; [ch.] 4 children, and 7 grandchildren; [ed.] BS and MS in Elementary Education at Indiana University; [occ.] First Grade Teacher currently on disability; [memb.] Tri Kappa; [hon.] Dean's List; [oth. writ.] Hundreds of poems on every subject imaginable, written for first grade and used by my colleagues in more than one school system.; [pers.] I wrote this poem for our "preemie", Evan, and to show our gratitude for the magic performed by his neonatal nurses. He is now a healthy two year old.; [a.] Valparaiso, IN

LEE, ROBERT YONG-SUK
[pen.] Robert Lee; [b.] November 4, 1974, South Korea; [p.] Boho Lee, Young-Hee Lee; [ed.] Windsor School, New York University; [occ.] Student (NYU); [pers.] I have always tried to view the society as a destruction, left-over by those who have succeeded in life. Those who are left out one the real qualities in our lives, and I try to put myself in those shoes and try to see with their eyes.; [a.] Flushing, NY

LEITCH, SOMMER
[b.] July 27, 1982, Anaheim, CA; [p.] Nancy and Kent Leitch; [ed.] Presently enrolled at Aqua Fria North Campus Litchfield Park, AZ; [occ.] Student; [hon.] Arts, Attendance, Science; [pers.] My heavenly Father is my guiding light.; [a.] Avondale, AZ

LEMBERGER, TANYA A.
[b.] January 29, 1976, Manitowoc; [p.] Jerome and Charlotte Lemberger; [ed.] 1 year University Wisconsin Manitowoc Center, 2 years lakeshore Technical College for Child Care Certificate, transfer to Lakeland College for early childhood ed, Eng. and Writing degrees; [occ.] Kueter Child Development Center - Child Care Teacher Braun Building Center - truss builder; [hon.] Merit-awards, English letter - 1994, Reflections (poetry read at the Reflections); [oth. writ.] Several poems published in 1994 yearbook - Flambeau - Lincoln H.S., Manitou-Magazine and anthologies Garden of thoughts; [pers.] I am inspired by friends and family with my poetry. Every poem has a meaning in my life and others.; [a.] Manitowoc, WI

LEMKY, BYRON WAYNE
[b.] November 1, 1964, Grande Prairie, Alberta, Canada; [p.] Lawrence and Margaret Lemky; [ch.] "My Paintings, drawings and poems are my children."; [ed.] Ridgevalley High School/Crooked Creek, Alberta until Grade II, The Academy of the New Church Boys School/Grade 12, The Academy of the New Church College-Bryn Athyn, Pennsylvania, U.S.A.; [occ.] Starving Artist/Poet/Art Students of Sept. 1996; [oth. writ.] At least 100 more poem, none published.; [pers.] I have

never left school as life itself is a school. My drawings, paintings and poems are my theses.

LENNON, ANN
[b.] October 24, 1948, NY; [p.] Edward Kershaw and Frances Kershaw; [m.] Frank Lennon, June 6, 1970; [ch.] Anneke, Julie, and Shannon; [ed.] Saint Helena H.S. - Bayside H.S.; [occ.] Homemaker, wife, mother, grandmother, caregiver.; [memb.] Maria Regina Religious Education Teacher; [hon.] Several years ago, some of my oil paintings were displayed in the Plainedge Public Library contest. Three out of the four were accepted.; [oth. writ.] "Scotty" by Ann Lennon "Julie-A Gift of Love" by Ann Lennon; [pers.] My poems are inspired by the people I have loved and lost. The beauty of their lives and their courage will always be the greatest blessing and inspiration to my heart and my pen.; [a.] Massapequa, NY

LEONE, ANNA MARIA
[b.] February 11, 1988, Brooklyn, NY; [p.] Giuseppe and Filomena Leone; [ed.] St. Joseph Hill Academy, Academy of St. Dorothy; [occ.] Student; [pers.] I always try to do my best.; [a.] Staten Island, NY

LIEBZEIT, WANDA LEE
[b.] November 12, 1932, Arkansas; [p.] Cliff and Beatrice Newcom; [m.] Joseph A. Liebzeit, October 17, 1981; [ch.] Four daughters - Peggy, Mitzi, Brenda, Lucind Ward; [ed.] 10th 16 years in Real Estate; [occ.] Retired; [memb.] Of International Society of Poets; [hon.] The National Library of Poetry. Editor's Choice Award, Poem. The Four Seasons. Published through The Hour Glass; [oth. writ.] I have written several songs. Jesus Is In Town. Let Him Guide You, Look Up On The Day In History; [pers.] I love to write song's and poetry. That has a message of our creator. My heart's desire.; [a.] Cedar Hill, MD

LIGHTLE, DENISE
[pen.] Denise Lane; [b.] October 6, 1953, Newark, OH; [p.] Arthur and Barbara Lane; [m.] Thomas L. Lightle, July 21, 1995; [ch.] Christopher Chambers 15 yrs.; [ed.] Graduate Newark High School 1972, Emergency Medical Technician (State Certified); [occ.] Disabled by short-term memory loss - so this is an especially rewarding honor.; [oth. writ.] "The Sun Shines Through", 3 act play presented by High School Drama Dept on the first Earth Day in 1970's - many other poems.; [pers.] We are all born but some of us aren't dead yet. So be careful how you treat the elderly. Personal favorites: Emily Dickinson, Edgar Allen Poe - 15th-18th Century, England.; [a.] Newark, OH

LINDER, NANCY L.
[b.] August 30, 1935, Louisville, KY; [p.] Ruth Curry and Andrew Little; [ch.] Teresa Stom, Michael Davidson Catherine Daniels, Christine Falter; [ed.] BA, Psy and Soc UNC, Chapel Hill, NC Master of Public Health (MPH) - Chapel Hill, NC; [occ.] Technical Writer and Device Labeling Mgr.; [memb.] American Medical Writers Assoc. (AMWA) Drug Information Assoc. (DIA); [hon.] 1978 - BA with Honors in Sociology 1990 Best of Show Burroughs Welcome Photography Contest 1973 Dressmaker of year gwinett Ct, GA; [oth. writ.] Several poems published most work of a technical nature.; [pers.] Poetry is my heart song. Whether happy, joyous, or grieved, poetry is my outlet for expressing emotions.; [a.] Angier, NC

LINDSTROM, LISA MICHELE
[pen.] Leo; [b.] August 8, 1961, Minneapolis, MN; [p.] Ward and Mari Jane Engebrit; [m.] Jeff, July 25, 1992; [ed.] H.S. Graduate - Charles A. Lindbergh, Senior High, 1 year - University at Minnesota - Literature; [occ.] Poet, Publisher, Office Manager, Housewife; [memb.] Distinguished Member - International Society

of Poets - International Poetry Hall of Fame - Charter Member, All American Eagle Indy Racers; [hon.] Several Editor's Choice Awards, 2 Poet of Merit Awards I also have a feature article being worked on in the local paper including photograph. I'll send one in as soon as i get a stack of the papers.; [oth. writ.] Published "Adequate Justice - Beginning Healing Through Poetry" ready to publish "Observing and Feeling While I am Healing" I have also started my 3rd book.; [pers.] Writing is my way of letting out pent up frustrations. I am seeing myself moving toward Political issues for poetry. I hope the public becomes aware of all of the large, problems we have and not waste so much time on trivial matters. We pay them.; [a.] Yorba Linda, CA

LINK, HERBERT C.

[b.] January 10, 1912, Baltimore, MD; [p.] John N. Link and Dorothy M. Link; [m.] Deceased, October 29, 1939; [ch.] John A. and Gerald F.; [ed.] 8th Grade Grammer Sch., Graduated Command and General Staff School, Air Class and 27, Ft. Leavenworth, Kan. (Enl. US Army 22 Nov. 1927, Retd. USAF 30 Nov. 1957); [occ.] Retd. Ltc, USAF

LISH, FRANCES

[b.] December 16, 1942, Yreka, CA; [p.] Orvis and Bernice Hill; [m.] William "Bill" Lish, May 9, 1970; [ch.] David, Rhonda, Scott, Brandi; [ed.] Klamath Union High, Mt. Hood Community College; [oth. writ.] "Imprints", "Coup De Grace", National Library of Poetry, one short story and one in progress, personal poems for friends and family.; [pers.] The poem I wrote in this book, "Sergeant Orvis Hill", is dedicated to eight of his great-grandchildren, Julie, JJ, Cole, Alex, Selina, James, Helena and Donovan, with love from their Nana.; [a.] Milwaukie, OR

LITTLE LIGHT, JOSEPHINE FLORENCE

[pen.] JoJo; [b.] November 22, 1978, Billings, MT; [p.] Marlene Fallsdown and Yvon Little Light Sr.; [ed.] Grade School - Hardin Primary Junior High - Hardin Middle School, Senior High - Hardin High, Busby Public School and Riverside Indian School; [occ.] Student at Riverside Indian School; [memb.] Year Book Club, Indian Club; [hon.] Indian Club Princess for 1995-96 and 1996-97. Montana State Champion Swimmer for 1989, 90, 91. The first and youngest Native on Montana Swim Team.; [oth. writ.] Short poems in Junior High and Senior High. Published in local parent newsletters and tribal newsletters.; [pers.] "I believe a strong culture identity is important to Native American Youth."; [a.] Crow Agency, MT

LIU, XUE

[pen.] Sherry; [b.] May 6, 1978, SiChuan, China; [p.] Youjiang Liu, Hui Luo; [ed.] A junior in Redlands High School, Redlands, CA; [hon.] I know I can's Summer Scholars, winner of California State Senator Bill Leonard's 8th Annual Red Ribbon week Essay contest. I have earned academic awards in every quarter of the school years, there are two distinguished awards that I proud of myself. In the summer of 1995, I got a chance to attended Ohio Sate University College of Engineering Special Summer Program. I had won second place in two competitions. I got the honor to meet with OSU's President Dr. E. Gordon Gee and other importance personnel.; [oth. writ.] It was also published in the newspaper on October 18, 1996 of The San Bernadino County Sun in California.; [pers.] I love life, natural and every wonderful thing around me. Thank you to give me this honor chance to join this contest, and to share my work with public. If I may, I want to dedicate a special thanks to my parents who are always 100% support me, who are giving up everything for me, and are always patiently to teach me. All I can say is thanking you for what you give to me.; [a.] Loma Linda, CA

LLOYD, BETTYJANE J.

[b.] June 25, 1996, Rumford, ME; [p.] Helen J. Jess and A. Berton Jess; [m.] H. Richard Runnals, March 28, 1993; [ch.] Granddaughter Rachel M. Lloyd; [ed.] High School; [occ.] Home Health Aide Speaker-Listen-Drug Awareness; [pers.] Outlook on life guided by Philippians 4:6 and 7. Poem Stone Walls was written as a vehicle for emotional recovery from abuse.; [a.] Hartford, VT

LOCKHART, CAROL D.

[b.] September 3, 1956, Topeka, KS; [p.] Mr. and Mrs. Otis Bruce Jr.; [m.] Theodus A. Lockhart Jr., June 24, 1978; [ch.] Miriam, Malisse, and Aaron; [ed.] Graduated from Topeka High School, attended Washburn University Topeka, KS; [occ.] Phone Rep. at House of Lloyds, Grandview MO; [memb.] Member of Freemen Ave Church of God in Kansas City, KS; [oth. writ.] Several unpublished poems.; [pers.] My poems usually reflect my inner feelings and perceptions on everyday life inspired by the spirit of God, and my writing style is inspired by May A. Angelou.; [a.] Kansas city, MO

LOEMKER, DOROTHY ROWDEN

[b.] February 17, 1901, Woodsville, NH; [p.] Elizabeth Wood and Thomas Alfred Rowden; [m.] Elmer Samuel Loemker, August 30, 1928; [ch.] Twins: Elizabeth and Thomas; [ed.] Simmons College BLS 1922; [occ.] Retired, Editor: Amer Library Ass. Bulletin, Officer (Secretary): John and Mary Markle Foundation, Officer: Amer. Assoc. for Adult Education; [hon.] Lisled in 1st Edition Who's Who of Women in America; [oth. writ.] Misc poetry and verse, occasional publications in adult education; [pers.] Better education for all ages; [a.] Bridgeport, CT

LOGRIE JR., ROBERT A.

[pen.] Robert A. Logrie Jr.; [b.] February 5, 1944, New Orleans; [ed.] Live Oak Jr. High and Elementary, Alcee Fortier High School, U.S. Naval Clerical Schools; [occ.] Retired; [memb.] National Park Trust, The H.S.U.S. Wildlife Land and Trust, North Shore Animal League; [hon.] High School Poetry Anthology winner 1964, year book Rep. and Newspaper Editor Jr High School, winner 1978 Mardi gras for best over-all costume design and presentation; [oth. writ.] Poem "In Life" published in 1964 collection of poetry entitled "Sermons in Poetry"; [pers.] When I do write, I draw from my own personal experiences, and try to express how those experiences have touched heart and soul. Nature and the out of doors, has been a great source of influence on my writings.; [a.] New Orleans, LA

LONGARINO, DARIUS

[pen.] Darius Longarino; [b.] March 1, 1983, New York, NY; [p.] Sal and Ida Longarino; [ed.] Intermediate School 1992; [occ.] Student; [memb.] A band "Bupkis"; [hon.] Science Fair in 4th grade, Most Outstanding Player (Football), First Honors (each year), i.e. top class; [oth. writ.] "The Big Red Book Of Darius" it wasn't published it is just a notebook in my closet.; [pers.] I believe that in life nothing is for sure not even uncertainty, and that what we call reality is really a liquid world of fantasy and that our world is a dollhouse created by some guy who just happened to be bared one day.; [a.] Bronx, NY

LONGMIRE, KRYSTAL

[b.] November 16, 1980, Baton Rouge, LA; [p.] Lisa and Royce Longmire; [ed.] Denham Springs High School; [occ.] Student; [memb.] Space Exploration Club, French Club, Library Club, Acts 29 Club, Ki Yoon's Tae Kwon Doe Academy; [hon.] Orange belt in Tae Kwon Doe, apart of the United States Achievement Academy, Honor Roll, Tumbling Trophy; [pers.] True poetry comes form the heart.; [a.] Denham Springs, LA

LOPEZ JR., VIRGILIO

[b.] April 26, 1996, Cidra, PR; [p.] Virgilio Lopez Sr., and Esterbina Collazo; [m.] Joanna Rodriguez-Lopez, August 20, 1993; [ch.] Virgilio Lopez III; [memb.] Golden Key National Honor Society; [pers.] The poem is a recollection and a rendition of a time which stirred the deepest sentiments within the soul.; [a.] Bridgeport, CT

LOSH, CHRISTOPHER

[b.] February 4, 1978, Winchester, VA; [p.] Charles and Holly Losh; [ed.] Now attending Manhattan Christian College in Manhattan, KS as a freshman; [pers.] When a person begins to change his/her belief system he/she begins to question who they are and what they want. As a Christian I went through that and then I gave it to the Lord. Doom's Desire is to be free from itself.; [a.] Brooklyn, IA

LONGACRE, CHARLES F.

[b.] September 20, 1963, Salinas, CA; [p.] Charles and Martha Longacre; [m.] Noelle Elizabeth Longacre, November 3, 1989; [ed.] Life in; [occ.] Horse Shoer; [oth. writ.] A Wanted Man, In One Day, A Weeping Willow, Decapitation, A Father's Love, (about 300), and one short story--I've never tried to be published!:; [pers.] Poetry is the soul - The soul's very thoughts relived in words - the poet is the out-let, the poem is the remains of the poet in relation to the soul, as poetry.; [a.] Tucker, AR

LOVE, BEA

[b.] December 27, 1943, Brownsville, TN; [p.] Calvin and Flora Prince; [m.] Nick, December 21, 1971; [ch.] Mike and Scott Love; [ed.] H.S. West Tenn Bus. College, Dyersburg State Comm. College; [occ.] City Letter Carrier U.S. Postal Service; [memb.] National Arbor Foundation, APWU; [hon.] Who's Who W.T.B.C.; [oth. writ.] Weekly Column in Local County Paper, Free-lance writer for children, magazines; [pers.] Because there is so much tragedy in our world today, I write to entertain and to uplift.; [a.] Alamo, TN

LOWERY, KERRY

[pen.] Kerry Lowery; [b.] January 4, 1972, Fresno, CA; [p.] Dale Lowery, Barbara Lowery; [m.] Allen Garvin; [ch.] Alex Garvin; [ed.] Clovis West High School, Heald Business College, Fresno City College; [occ.] Mother, Homemaker; [memb.] Childhood Education Assoc.; [oth. writ.] Several poems for family and friends at special occasions.; [pers.] I write from my heart, choosing things that have very personal meaning, and as a result my poems effect people in a people way. The greatest joy in my life being a mother.; [a.] Fresno, CA

LOYD, JEREMIAH ANTHONY

[b.] May 3, 1976, Aurora, IL; [p.] Delbert and Martha Loyd; [ed.] Attending Junior College; [occ.] Custodian; [oth. writ.] Above the Clouds, Cement Hell, Jody, Growing Up other poems I have written; [pers.] Life is what you make it what goes around comes around; [a.] Montgomery, IL

LOYDD, VIVIAN

[pen.] Viv, Vivi; [b.] January 2, 1956, Frostproof, FL; [p.] Rudolph and Essie Thomas; [m.] James Loydd, October 25, 1977; [ch.] James C. Rebekah, Samuel; [ed.] Frostproof Jr. Sr. High School, Biscayne Business School, Ridge - Vocational Technical Center; [occ.] State of Florida, Dept. of Children and Families Interview Clerk; [memb.] Church of God by Grace, Inc. Sunday School Teacher, Choir Secretary; [hon.] Biscayne Business School Most Outstanding Student; [oth. writ.] "I Can", "Never Alone", "True Love", "Wounded Soldier", "Time and Time Past", "A Christian Attitude"; [pers.] Overlooking someone's fault makes it easy to see their need.; [a.] Lake Wales, FL

LUSCALZO, JUDITH E.
[b.] April 23, 1977, Chicago; [p.] Ben and Laila; [ed.] Currently at Columbia College (Chicago) studying fashion design, plan to transfer in fall '97 to F.I.T. in New York; [occ.] Student; [memb.] Alpha Phi Omega, a service fraternity; [hon.] Personal; [pers.] As our minds are illuminated, we become better at being human! Thus, I pray my work takes on a life of its own, separate from the author of it.; [a.] Chicago, IL

LUZZI, IRENE ELIZABETH
[b.] January 8, 1958, Omaha, NE; [p.] Carole and Boyce Lee; [m.] Michael Salvatore Luzzi, August 12, 1977; [ch.] Kristina Vee; [ed.] Graduated from Eli Whitney Technical School 1976, majored in Culinary Arts; [occ.] Bookkeeper; [memb.] Post member of Rainbow girls, Current member of the Order of Eastern Star; [oth. writ.] Several other poems in my personal collection but none published.; [pers.] My writings come from my heart. They are all based on feelings, events, and special moments of my life. Family, friends, companions have all played a major role in the way I write. To have memories is to write them down and reflect on them always.; [a.] New Haven, CT

LYNCH, CILLIAN
[b.] April 3, 1979, Cork, Ireland; [p.] Dr. Mae Dara Lynch, Dr. Ita Lynch; [ed.] High School (Fr.-Jr) International School (Indonesia) (Sr.) Pius X High School (Lincoln, NE); [occ.] Student; [pers.] Hello to Dr. Jack Penha

LYNCH, ELLEN ANN
[pen.] Ellen Ann Lynch; [b.] November 30, 1924, Chicago; [p.] John Lynch and Josephine Hafnar; [ed.] Help at Christians Grade School, Immaculate High School, Clark College BA, St. Louis University MA; [occ.] Retired Teacher; [pers.] I have always loved poetry, my writings are my reactions to moving events.; [a.] Chicago, IL

MAGOVERN JR., FREDERICK J.
[pen.] Freddy Magovern; [b.] May 11, 1986, New York; [p.] Frederick and Susan Magovern; [ed.] Our Lady of Grace Montessori School (Nursery to Kindergarten), Buckley Country Day School, First through fifth grade; [occ.] Full time student in fifth grade; [memb.] U.S. Chess Federation, Nassau Chess Club, Garden City Soccer, St. Joseph's Church CYO Basketball; [hon.] Buckley Co. Day School's, 1st grade, 2nd grade, 3rd grade, 4th grade's writer of the month contributor to schools "Leaves of Gold" past writer of the year

MAGRABI, FRANCES M.
[b.] November 28, 1927, Cerro Gordo, IA; [p.] Ethel and Warren Kisner; [m.] Hadi Magrabi, May 5, 1949; [ch.] Michael Magrabi; [ed.] B.S., M.S., Ph.D. from Iowa State University; [occ.] Professor Emerita University of Illinois; [hon.] Phi Kappa Phi, National Merit Scholarship, Kellogg Distinguished Lecturer; [oth. writ.] Textbook "Economics of Household Consumption," numerous articles in scientific journals.; [a.] Wellman, IA

MALCOLM JR., JUDSON V.
[pen.] Jud Malcolm; [b.] April 10, 1950, Athens, GA; [p.] Ferrol Perry Malcolm; [ed.] ABJ 1983 University of Georgia, MED 1986 University of Georgia; [occ.] Unemployed due to bad Health (Agent Orange Exposure in Vietnam); [hon.] PSCCC photo contest, Honorable mention 1979, Title Farm Strike; [oth. writ.] Poems "Elections" 1976 in treasured poems of America, "Our Deeds Dark" 1997 in treasured poems of America.; [pers.] My military experiences in Vietnam has led me to explore my feeling today. I feel my experiences put

into word, when possible, can help others face their own doubts and fears.; [a.] Athens, GA

MALLOY, ELLEN M.
[b.] Chicago, IL; [p.] George I. Malloy and Mary (Minnie) Malloy; [occ.] Retired; [oth. writ.] I repeat, a lasting memory. First poem I wrote when I was twelve. "Winter Magic". It was a lovely morning but very cold, while on the branches the snow took hold, and left behind a beautiful sight, of crystal icicles shining and bright.; [pers.] Love of God, family and others. Also an appreciation of life and laughter.; [a.] Burbank, IL

MAPES, SARAH
[b.] May 17, 1982, Carmel, NJ; [p.] David Mapes, Sue Mapes; [ed.] Lakeland High School; [occ.] Full-time student; [memb.] National Junior Honor Society, United Methodist Church Member, Member of Shrub Oak Athletic Club, D.A.R.E. member; [hon.] Ele. School-Citizenship Award, Middle School-Bobcat Award and National Junior Honor Society Award, Athletic Awards-Soccer, Basketball, Handbell Choir Awards; [oth. writ.] Journal of other written poems, school English essays and other journal writings.; [pers.] I would like to continue to be a good student through my High School and College years and to be community involved along with keeping up my athletic ability. Also to continue to write more poems.; [a.] Shrub Oak, NY

MARBACH, DONNA M.
[b.] December 9, 1948, King City, CA; [p.] William Marbach, Elfriede Marbach; [m.] Joseph P. Brennan, September 6, 1980; [ch.] Brian Timothy, Erin Coleen, Shannon Margaret, Kevin Michael and Colin Riley; [ed.] University of PA, MS in Education University of Calif. BA in Literature Santa Cruz Monterey High School; [occ.] Business Manager, The Scholar's Choice; [memb.] Writers and Books, Rochester Arts and Cultural Council for Greater Rochester, International Women's Writing Guild; [oth. writ.] Several poems published in newspapers, small journals, and anthologies. Have also written children's and literary short stories.; [a.] Rochester, NY

MARCELLI, KIMBERLY B.
[b.] December 17, 1957, Cincinnati, OH; [p.] Doris Sotter, Philip Gordon (Deceased); [ch.] Ashley Mae

MARCHETTI, LOUIS J.
[pen.] Louis J. Marchetti; [b.] October 18, 1943, Torrington, CT; [p.] Joseph T. Anne; [m.] Nancy Wilcox-Marchetti, May 25, 1996; [ch.] Darlene and Dierdre; [ed.] BFA in Theatre Nationally Certified Substance Abuse Counselor and Clinical Supervisor Professional Actor, Stage manager, Director; [occ.] Cleaning and Pet Sitting; [oth. writ.] Have written 100 + poems but have never submitted any until now.; [pers.] I write a "new age" approach to feelings, Life, beliefs, spirituality, I like to convey hope and love to mankind about what we "Think" is true and what in actuality, manifests itself I stress the belief in oneself and their "inner" feelings and self.; [a.] Oakville, CT

MARIE, THOMAS
[b.] February 22, 1930, London, England; [ed.] City College Jr. San Diego State University, BA with honors, San Diego State University, Masters in History of Art, Spec, Architecture; [occ.] Peace Corps Volunteer in Turkmenistan Teaching-in-TEFL program; [hon.] Peace Award: U.S. Peace Corps/Philippines '84-'87, Plaque from C.E.T., Center for Educational Training/ Volunteer Teaching English to Hispanics; [oth. writ.] Masters Thesis Cataloged/Micro-Fiche San Diego State University, "The Role of Colin Campbell in the development of eighteenth-century English Architecture" '94. Currently, I am writing short stories and poems.; [pers.] I reside in California in between doing volunteer

work in the U.S. Peace Corps. For inspiration, I try to write about the condition of man and the strength that man finds or discovers in himself.; [a.] San Diego, CA

MARKOVITS, MONICA
[b.] September 2, 1946, Buenos Aires, Argentina; [ch.] Matias, Enrique Ringel; [ed.] JD., MS, Doctor of Jurisprudence (U. of BS. AS) Argentina.; [occ.] Secondary School Administrator; [hon.] Fulbright Scholar; [oth. writ.] Several poems published in Spanish.; [pers.] May the muses not abandon me!; [a.] New York, NY

MARKS, RITA
[b.] May 31, 1953, San Mateo, CA; [p.] Joseph and Sarah Marks; [ch.] Lazet Howard and Tanesha Howard; [ed.] Canada College, Redwood City, CA, AA degree, College of Notre Dame, Belmont, CA, expect Computer Science degree in 1998; [occ.] Sr. Admin., Asst./ Purchasing Agent at Sun Microsystems, Inc., in Mountain View, CA; [memb.] Member of Fremont Bible Fellowship Church in Fremont, CA; [hon.] Dean's list - twice, American Business Women's Scholarship - three times, Redwood City Citizen's Scholarship, Canada College Scholarship, Bay Area Urban League Scholarship; [oth. writ.] Self, Rare Bird, Who Was That?, The Love, Life, I Want You, Education, To God, The Joy You Bring, The Miracle, Slow Down, The Kiss I Rise; [pers.] All the honor, praises, thankfulness, glory, and my blessings go to God for providing me with the talent to write poetry and to share with others to enjoy and encourage. I thank my daughters for their love.; [a.] East Palo Alto, CA

MARKUS, MELANIE MICHELLE
[b.] October 2, 1944, Aurora, IL; [p.] John J. and Margaret Mary Markus; [ch.] Only son - Ronald James; [ed.] Grad. Madonna High School 1962. Attended classes at Phoenix College - 1981-82; [occ.] Semiretired - Geriatric C.N.A.; [memb.] One granddaughter Michelle Elaine (a roman catholic) myself; [hon.] Honorable mention for "Springs Return" March 1992, Certificate of Appreciation for civic duty of disabled and senior citizens, maricoph country, Phoenix, Az. June 1987; [oth. writ.] Columnist for lake holiday news Somonauk - Ill. 1976-1977 - previously published: "Springs Return" 1993 - Sunlit Sadness 1994 - Storm At The Lake 1997 - and Other Work under copyright 1989.; [pers.] I was inspired at an early age by Wm. Wordsworth and E.B. Browning and Later by Robt. Frost (in the wilderness - totally alone and undisturbed by man - is my greatest joy, to write of.); [a.] Mesa, AZ

MARQUEZ-MOREIRA, JULIO A.
[b.] April 18, 1931, Guayaquil, Ecuador; [p.] Oscar Marquez Pita, Julia Moreira De Marquez; [m.] Lidia Rosa Marquez, October 20, 1953; [ch.] Julio C., Jack A., Yajaira L. (Deceased) Marquez, Rosa H. Marquez Stolck; [ed.] Master of Science in Civil Engineering (NJIT), Bachelor of Civil Engineering (CCNY), Associate in Applied Science (NYCCC); [occ.] Civil Engineering; [memb.] American Society of Civil Engineers; [oth. writ.] "40 Anos" ("40 Years"), "Arte Perdido" ("Lost Art"); [pers.] I believe that: Learning is imperative since the reason for our continuance of being is to achieve intellectual progress in each of the intermittent segments of our total existence, that in the last segments we become less mortal and begin emulating the creator, that the ultimate goal, the superlative dream of the omnipotent is achieved when the supreme equation: Man = God is satisfied!; [a.] New York, NY

MARRETT, GEORGE S.
[pen.] GSM; [b.] April 17, 1941, Crown Point, IN; [ed.] Texas Tech University, Lubbock, Texas; [occ.] Maintenance Tech., Motorola, Inc., Austin, TX; [oth. writ.] Many poems and short stories.; [pers.] "Life is made

from dreams, dreams are memories unfulfilled."; [a.] Dale, TX

MARROW, SAMANTHA JEAN
[pen.] S. J. Marrow; [b.] December 12, 1981, Haverhill, MA; [p.] Donna Marrow, Joseph Marrow; [ed.] Fox School Elementary, Dr. Paul Nettle School Middle, Whittier Regional Vocational Technical High School; [occ.] Writer of poems also short plays; [pers.] In my experience in writing poems I've noticed the only way poems have meaning is if they come from your heart.; [a.] Haverhill, MA

MARSH, LOUISE E.
[b.] February 20, 1925, Indianapolis, IN; [p.] Deceased; [m.] Deceased; [ch.] James Bedinger; [ed.] Manual High - Ind., Graduation from Benjamin Franklin, San Francisco. Two semesters - Art - San Diago, CA, one semester - Landscaping - San Diego; [occ.] Retired Office Clerk; [memb.] Order of the Eastern Star Westbrook church of the Nazarene; [oth. writ.] None published; [pers.] I want to thank my son Jim and friend, Ethel for encouraging me to write my experiences of the love I have for God's gifts.; [a.] Indianapolis, IN

MARSHALL, GEORGE K.
[b.] August 13, 1912, Millville, MA; [p.] Hilton A. and Annie G. Marshall; [m.] Emelie P. Potvin, October 5, 1935; [ch.] George K. - 1938, Michael P. - 1955; [ed.] Millville, Uxbridge High, USNA '33, Annapolis; [occ.] Retired, Formerly Exec, GE and Chrysler, Markt'g, Engr'g; [memb.] USNA Alumni, Athletic Association and Local. HAM, AMA. Red Wing Senior Golf Assoc.; [hon.] One of GE Team which gave us the heat pump. Made many presentations, media, in error, tabbed me as inventor. Lord Kelvin discovered it, 1700's; [oth. writ.] Three novels (1 published) 4 plays and poems to offer ideas to save our nation, last chance for our world. Scared we are in. Awful trouble, - terminal, and must correct 3 vital area.; [pers.] Reflections dominate minds of legislators. Must have single ten years terms for Senate, House, Pres. and VP. Rotate Academicians to Capitol area to counteract lobbies. Improve. Participation of public.; [a.] Virginia Beach, VA

MARTIN, ALAN P.
[pen.] Nitrama; [b.] April 27, 1961, Norristown, PA; [p.] Margaret Foy, John Martinelli; [m.] Caroline; [occ.] Control Systems Representative; [memb.] Sierra Club, National Wildlife Federation, ISA; [hon.] Phi Theta Kappa; [pers.] Life is a journey to choose, not a destination to attain.; [a.] Lake Forest, CA

MARTIN, DANIEL L.
[pen.] Dan Martin; [b.] February 24, 1979, Boston, MA; [p.] Dewey and Linda Martin; [ed.] Hampden Academy; [occ.] Student; [memb.] French Club, National Honor Society; [hon.] National Honor Society, National Merit Commended Student, Who's Who Among American High School Students, Nominated all New England Soccer Team; [oth. writ.] Several poems publication local publication, the nothing publication.; [pers.] True beauty is the soul.; [a.] Hampden, ME

MARTIN, SHIRLEY
[pen.] Shirley Martin; [b.] October 15, 1935, Georgetown, IL; [p.] William and Edna Morrow; [ch.] Nancy Jo Kett - Dennis and Phyllis; [ed.] Georgetown High; [occ.] Proof Reader Trader Publications; [oth. writ.] Many (not published); [pers.] I write about my feelings and all things in everyday life. Mostly the beautiful events and happenings also past memories.; [a.] Saint Petersburg, FL

MARTIN, TERESA
[b.] February 20, 1934, Ireland; [p.] Philip Ryan and Nora Leahy; [m.] Richard Martin, December 20, 1975; [ed.] Early education - Ireland BA - Caldwell College NJ. MA - Seton Hall University South Orange NJ; [occ.] Teacher; [memb.] NJEA and NEA; [oth. writ.] None published; [pers.] I feel every child can write well. Many of my former students have proven this to me.; [a.] Oak Ridge, NJ

MARTINEZ, BOB G.
[b.] June 7, 1949, New Mexico; [p.] Mary Jane Martinez; [m.] Annette Elizabeth, February 10, 1973; [ch.] Lita (20); [ed.] North Denver High School in 1968; [occ.] Security Guard at the Denver Merchandise Mart; [memb.] 1. Distinguished Member ISP, 2. National Federation of State Poets, 3. Mile High Poetry Society, 4. Columbine Poets of Colorado; [hon.] 28 Anthologies, many Editor's Choice Awards; [oth. writ.] "My Time To Rhyme", my personal journal from 1949 to 1994, "Side Tracks" compilation of 45 of my poems.; [pers.] Remember that it's God who works in you both to will and to do of His good pleasure...otherwise, our own expressions will simply fall flat and useless.; [a.] Denver, CO

MASI, FRANK T.
[b.] March 31, 1939, Bronx, NY; [p.] Thomas and Josephine Masi; [m.] Marilyn Foote Masi, June 24, 1979; [ch.] Robert John, Frank, Glenn, Tom, Don, Linda, Tony, Erik; [ed.] BBA Pace University, student MBA New York University; [occ.] President Lloyd Creative Staffing; [memb.] Bd of Education, Morris Plains, NJ, NJ Association of Staffing Professionals Republican Club; [hon.] Trainer of the Year, Sales Executives Club of NY, Executive of the Year, "Cannata Report" lecturer in business, Bryant College, Westchester Community College, University of Hartford; [oth. writ.] Business magazine articles on Compensation, Sales Mgmt., sales training, recruiting. Book "The Typewriter Legend".; [pers.] Sales Management Magazine, the Recruiter, Training Magazine, (Editorial board) Philosophy and Poetry is the truest forms of free expression.; [a.] Morris Plains, NJ

MASTROENI, LORI A.
[b.] March 6, 1961, Detroit, MI; [p.] Louis and Catherine Garofalo; [m.] Geno Mastroeni, July 24, 1995; [ch.] Krystal Ann; [ed.] Freshman, Grayling High School

MATTESON, JON
[b.] March 2, 1976, Midland, MI; [p.] Richard Matteson Jr., Sue Matteson; [ed.] Jackson Lumen Christi High School, Duquesne University; [occ.] Journalism Major, Duquesne University; [a.] Pittsburgh, PA

MAY, GERALDINE
[pen.] Jeri Mae; [b.] April 25, 1938, Rawlins, WY; [p.] Albert and Beawah Lemoine; [ch.] Six; [ed.] High School graduate of Rawlins, WY; [occ.] Therapeutic Foster Parent; [oth. writ.] Written hundreds of poems - never had any published. Have also written stories never tried to get them published.; [pers.] I try to look at the world and the people in it. It all seems to inspire my thoughts. Poems and stories that are true are the best writings for me. This is all new and very exciting for me.; [a.] Casper, WY

MAYHEW, GREGORY L.
[b.] September 23, 1954, Marysville, KS; [p.] Everett and Jennie Mayhew; [m.] Cynthia A. Mayhew, September 2, 1978; [ch.] Ginger and Barbara; [ed.] 13; [occ.] Home school teacher; [hon.] Poems published in local newspaper. Beatrice Daily Sun. The Poet's Pen.; [oth. writ.] "The Forgotten River", "A Summer Day", "My Heart Faints for Thee"; [pers.] "When you get serious about life, life will get serious about you. My wife

Cynthia is related to Robert and Elizabeth Barrett Browning, through Amanda Susan Browning her Grandma; [a.] Wymore, NE

McBAIN, ELEXIS LYDIA
[b.] July 20, 1981, Davenport, IA; [p.] Anastasia Kamp and Andrew McBain; [ed.] Fort Lee School #3, Warwick Valley Middle School Attending, Warwick Valley High School High School; [occ.] Student, Warwick Valle High School - sophomore; [memb.] Girls Varsity Swim Team. A member of the literary Magazine, "Kaleidoscope"; [oth. writ.] Had a poem published in the local paper "Warwick Advertiser" and the school's literacy magazine "Kaleidoscope"; [pers.] Thank-you always for my mother father, Yiayia family and friends, especially L.C. and EK for being there when I need you. E. P.L., B.M., A.R., Thanks to everyone else. I love you are my biggest influence my writing.; [a.] Warwick, NY

McCALL, LEO
[pen.] Leo T. McCall; [b.] September 5, 1919, Saint Paul, MN; [p.] Dead; [m.] Lorraine (Deceased), June 20, 1942; [ch.] Four; [ed.] BA English - University St Thomas, St Paul MN; [occ.] Mfg Rep Optical Bz; [memb.] Jenelleu English - Cretian HS St Paul, Minn; [oth. writ.] Novel not published: "Business is Baloney", musical comedy: "A Year Is Forever"; [pers.] I aim to tell the world that St Paul Minnesota continues to live and survive here in this edge of the arctic circle.; [a.] Saint Paul, MN

McCASLIN, ROBERT L.
[b.] January 13, 1945, Jasper Co, IL; [p.] William and Dorothy McCaslin; [ch.] Gary and Troy McCaslin; [ed.] High School; [occ.] Auditor, Manufacturing; [pers.] The beauty and realism that surrounds us daily should be gratefully absorbed, either with the eyes, or the printed word, or both. To me, that is the essence of poetry.; [a.] Salem, IN

McCLAIN, LOUIS
[pen.] Damion Cassandra; Louis Wulf; [b.] September 24, 1949, Hayti, MO; [p.] Louis Sr. and Josephine; [m.] Stacy J. Babe-Wulf, May 27, 1995; [ch.] Joy, Tasha, Louie, Robert, Davi; [ed.] Viet Nam, Life; [occ.] Common Labor; [memb.] Manic-Depressive Association; [hon.] Viet Nam Cross for Gallantry; [oth. writ.] Fresh Killed Humans (non-fiction); Look Away, Look Away (vicarious emotional insight); [pers.] My soulmate was killed Christmas Eve of 1996. "The Flame to the Moth," was a true account of our love, and now is a legacy of that love. Stacy is gone, but the love lingers on.; [a.] Holdrege, NE

McCORVEY, BELINDA
[b.] July 15, 1973, South Carolina; [p.] Albert and Joyce Waters; [m.] Daniel McCorvey, August 28, 1993; [ch.] Daniel Drake McCorvey; [ed.] Gainesville High, Gainesville, FL; [pers.] I try to put God first in everything I do. God is the most important person in my life. One day my dream will come true, when I finally reach my goal, and see my heavenly father. I know that day will come soon, but as long as I am on this earth I will do my best for God. John 3:30; [a.] Wewa, FL

McCOUN, SONDRA R.
[pen.] Sondra; [b.] July 11, 1955, Debuque, IA; [p.] Ettie Wood and Tom Dill; [m.] Larry Fry, December 7, 1996; [ch.] T. W. Carr, Tabby Carr, Todd Carr; [ed.] Halsey High School Graduate from Halsey, Nebraska, 1 year of College Kearney, Nebraska; [occ.] I've always been in sales and love working with the public; [memb.] United Methodist Church, Eagles Club Member; [hon.] Several poems published in a local news paper, they gave me my own column for about 1 year; [oth. writ.] I have written about 50 or more poems some

funny, some serious some on true life experience that I've had.; [pers.] Someday I hope to publish a poem book. At least that's my dream to be recognized as a writer of poetry someday. And I owe my kids, TW and Todd and Tabby and my husband Larry for helping me keep going.; [a.] Woodriver, NE

McCOY, ELYSE NICHOLE
[b.] September 13, 1979, Deckerville, MI; [p.] Donna Johnston; [memb.] High School Cheer-Leader, Peck, MI, Track Team Peck, MI, HS Young Business Professional of America (BPA) Peck, MI; [hon.] Varcity Letter in Track; [oth. writ.] Many poems unpublished; [pers.] Elyse loved life, she would be so proud of this honor. Date of birth - 9/13/79, Date of Death - 10/20/94 auto accident.; [a.] Peck, MI

McCOY, VALENCIA
[pen.] Valen; [b.] January 31, 1971, Chicago, IL; [p.] George and Patricia Buels; [ed.] Honor graduate from high school and some college; [occ.] Data Entry Processor; [pers.] I feel that if you write wrongs in your writings and let it come from your heart you will never go wrong.; [a.] Aurora, CO

McCRACKEN, DAVID
[b.] June 3, 1962, Anderson, IN; [p.] Joseph and Dorothy McCracken; [m.] Denise; [ch.] David, Sarah; [occ.] Machinist; [hon.] Sgt. in U.S. Marines 1984

McCULLOUGH, SCOTT ANDREW
[b.] July 20, 1983, San Antonio, TX; [p.] Bruce and Debby McCullough; [ed.] Student, 6th grade Rainbow Hills Baptist School

McELROY, JACK R.
[b.] June 4, 1950, Sandpoint, ID; [p.] Jack and Virginia McElroy; [m.] Gayle McElroy, January 4, 1977; [ch.] Trevor, Shawn, Matt, Ryan, and J.D.; [ed.] Bonners Ferry High School, North Idaho College, National Radio Institute; [occ.] 1st class Stationary Engineer, Sacred Heart Medical Center Spokane, Washington; [memb.] National Rifle Association, and Sons of Union Veterans of the Civil War; [hon.] Outstanding Citizen of the State of Idaho on behalf of the Sandpoint Fire Department, awarded by the Major, the Governor and the Fire Chief; [oth. writ.] Newsletter for Sacred Heart Medical Center - Monday a.m. Bonner County Daily Bee newspaper and the National Library of Poetry through the Hourglass.; [pers.] "Honesty is the best policy," and, "To thy own self be true".; [a.] Sandpoint, ID

McELROY, ROD
[b.] September 7, 1950, Birmingham, AL; [p.] Orvil, Barbara McElroy; [m.] Mary McElroy, November 24, 1977; [ch.] Tara and Tyler; [ed.] Norco High, Norco CA., Riverside City College, University of Texas at San Antonio; [occ.] Stereo Sales; [oth. writ.] "Storms Of The Night Ballad of a Vietnam Vet" 1987, "A Single Act..." 1988, "The Promise" 1989, all of the above are song cycle series by Rod McElroy.; [pers.] Words, a fleeting thought may new days of compassion soothe their screams I pray that they may come home again.; [a.] Enon, OH

McFARLANE, GARRETT
[pen.] Cruger, Shadwick; [b.] May 29, Kingston, TN; [p.] Dunbar McFarlane, Sonja McFarlane; [ed.] Mt. Alvennen Prep School, Walmers Prep School, Walmers Boys School, Knox College and Preceng High School; [occ.] Student; [oth. writ.] None published; [pers.] There are two things in life love and sorrow, each intertwined with the other, each a cause for the other, above the clouds we soar, below the tears we still endure...life; [a.] Miami, FL

McGHEE, CHARLES R. OBERT
[b.] July 17, 1934, Chattanooga, TN; [p.] Buford C. and Beatrice (Parker) McGhee; [m.] Anna Louise Cummings McGhee, June 13, 1964; [ch.] John, Jennifer and Brian McGhee; [ed.] B.S. and M.A. Middle Tenn. State U., Ph.D. Virginia Polytechnic Institute; [occ.] Professor of Biology, MTSU; [memb.] Tennessee Academy Science, Assoc. Southeastern Biologists, International Society of Poets, Society of Sigma Xi; [hon.] Fellow Tenn. Academy Science, Long rifle Award (B.S.A.), Alpha Psi Chapter of Phi, Sigma Society, Distinguished Member ISP; [oth. writ.] "Oak and Storm" "Along With The Stones River" publications in science journals.; [pers.] "Thanks for being a great sister Margaret McGhee Cooper."; [a.] Murfreesboro, TN

McINERNEY, SHERRY L.
[b.] August 20, 1962, Michigan; [m.] James J. McInerney, May 19, 1984; [ch.] James Patrick 10, Sean Cuyler 8; [ed.] BS - Accounting, BS - Business Administration; [occ.] Public Accountant; [memb.] Phi Theta Kappa, Dean's List; [pers.] I love variety, and subject, any material.; [a.] Winston-Salem, NC

McINTYRE, MARY JO
[b.] November 11, 1936; [m.] William McIntyre; [ch.] Henry and Jeanette McIntyre; [ed.] B.S. in Elementary Education, Spalding University, Louisville, KY; [occ.] Biller at Jewish Hospital, Louisville, KY

McKENNA, HEATHER
[b.] February 24, 1979, Lewiston, ME; [p.] Alfred E. McKenna Jr., Joyce McKenna; [ed.] Junior at Mountain Valley High School; [occ.] Student; [hon.] Who's Who Award; [pers.] If I can make a difference or inspire one person through my writing, then I have succeeded.; [a.] Rumford, ME

McKENNA, PATRICK
[b.] July 16, 1982, Rockford, IL; [p.] Wayne McKenna, Michelle Day McKenna; [occ.] Student at St. Bridget's Catholic School, Loves Park, IL; [memb.] Boy Scouts of America Troop 32 (Loves Park PD); [oth. writ.] Limericks, Haikus, Free Verses Cinguains, other poems, none published except "Pictures"; [a.] Rockford, IL

McLEAN, LENEILE ANEICE
[b.] March 9, 1978, Ridgewood, NJ; [p.] Neil McLean, Emma McLean; [ed.] Blessed Sacrament School (Elementary), Mary Help of Christians Academy (High School) Class of '97; [memb.] Grace Chapel Baptist Church Member/Sunday School Teacher's Assistant; [hon.] Who's Who Among American High School Students Multiple-Year Award, National Science Merit Award of the United States Achievement Academy, Hospital Aid Award (Candy Striper), Perfect Attendance Award; [pers.] I feel that poetry is one of the most beautiful forms of art. I love writing and poetry gives me the freedom of expression that I need to write down my thoughts, feelings, and emotions. Poetry gives me peace of mind.; [a.] Paterson, NJ

McLEOD, ROBERT P.
[pen.] Rob Jones; [b.] August 18, 1971, Menomonie, WI; [ch.] Taylor Kane McLeod; [ed.] Sophomore - college; [occ.] Student - Landscaper; [memb.] NORML; [hon.] High school honor, college honors candidate; [oth. writ.] First time I've submitted a piece...; [pers.] There's too much there to be speak somewhere...there's too much out there to be unhappy...move on...; [a.] Louisville, KY

McNAIR, JENNY
[pen.] Jen Jen and Ginger; [b.] September 30, 1984, Baylor Hosp. Dallas, TX; [p.] Claire and Jerry McNair; [occ.] Student of Carpenter Middle School Piano, TX;

[hon.] Another poem I wrote was selected by the Amherst society.; [pers.] I just want to say to my bestfriends "Hi! Sharna, Lauren, and Ashley" this poem was meant for my boyfriend, after I wrote it, we broke up. I love romantic poems.; [a.] Plano, TX

McSWEENEY, E. F.
[b.] January 28, 1922; [m.] Grace J. McSweeney; [oth. writ.] Religious and Political; [pers.] Born a free spirit, by time now maimed, who would cast a few words, to show he's not tamed; [a.] Hayden, CO

MEADOWS, LISA C.
[b.] July 24, 1973, Princeton, WV; [p.] Ralph J. Meadows, Carolyn E. Meadows; [pers.] I try to express feeling, and hope in some small way. So that when it is read, the reader may feel a kinship, and comfort may be taken.; [a.] Spanishburg, WV

MECKLEY, LINDA LOUISE
[b.] December 15, 1952, Ephrata, PA; [p.] Clarence and Myrtle Meckley; [ed.] Cocalico High School, Ellen Cushing Jr. College, Millersville University; [occ.] Unemployed; [memb.] M.I. Hummel Club St. John's United Church of Christ, Women's Guild U.C.C.; [hon.] Ellen Cushing Jr. College Academic Award, Dean's List, Millersville University, Cum Laude; [oth. writ.] Several writings published in local newspapers.; [pers.] My poems usually tell a story and must rhyme. An emotional experience in my life often triggers my writing.; [a.] Denver, PA

MEDINA SR., VIDAL
[pen.] Vidal Senior; [b.] March 16, 1953, Fresno; [p.] Julio and Josephine Medina; [m.] Kelly Medina, April 29, 1992; [ch.] Jaimee, Ryan, Nichole, Angela, Vidal Jr.; [ed.] As degree in Nursing; [occ.] Legally Blind; [memb.] International Society of Poets; [hon.] Editor's Choice Award; [oth. writ.] "Damn, Life Is Easy", recollections of yesterday; [pers.] I strive to reflect the sadness and darkness of mankind in my writing.; [a.] Fresno, CA

MEHELAS, DIANNE L.
[b.] October 29, 1959, Detroit, MI; [p.] E. James and Mary L. Mehelas; [ed.] B.S. Michigan State University. Pre-Nursing Oakland Community College. Enrolled at Wayne State University through first semester in junior year in nursing program.; [occ.] Nursing Assistant for Surgical and Medical Nursing at Harper Hospital, Detroit (Past employment); [memb.] National Alliance for Research on Schizophrenia and Depression; [oth. writ.] Constellation; [pers.] My understanding of Christian psychology, nursing and my catholic education have greatly influenced my writing of perspectives of an immense journey.; [a.] Bloomfield Village, MI

MEIER, PAMELA J.
[pen.] Pamela Dean; [b.] May 29, 1972, Columbus, OH; [p.] Richard and Joye Meier; [ed.] Independence High School, Ohio Dominican College, Institute of Children's Literature; [occ.] Bank teller; [memb.] The Center for Marine Conservation, The Marine Mammal Center, World Wildlife Federation; [hon.] The Lazarus writing award; [oth. writ.] The Mysterious Motorcycle Rider, Uncertainty, A short story and a poem entered in previous contests.; [pers.] I respect all forms of life. I share my personal experiences with the inner torment and conflict of love and every day life through writing.; [a.] Columbus, OH

MEISLOHN, ROBYN
[b.] January 1, 1984, Roanoke, VA; [p.] Barbara and Robert Meislohn; [ed.] Our Lady Of Mercy Middle School; [occ.] Student; [oth. writ.] A poem called "Sorrow" that I have not yet published; [pers.] Different objects can inspire a poet or anyone. Put your ideas into

action or on paper. A poet life - inspiration.; [a.] Lewisville, NC

MELNICK, THERESA A.
[b.] July 30, 1953, Hazleton, PA; [p.] Peter and Josephine Melnick; [ch.] Christopher Anthony; [ed.] Hazleton High School; [occ.] Bemis Co, Inc W. Hazleton, PA 18201; [pers.] I believe that love is strong and could conquer almost anything!; [a.] Hazleton, PA

MENDOZA, LOUIS
[pen.] Ton-ton; [b.] September 19, 1966, Manila, Philippines; [p.] Soliman Mendoza Sr. (father); Aida Ja. Delgado (mother); [pers.] When I stumble upon something which truly awakens my passions, my tongue is silenced, but my heart begins to write. Poetry celebrates reality, no matter how harsh or beautiful that reality may be.

MERIDETH, CAROLYN J.
[pen.] Carol; [b.] February 5, 1941, Louisville, KY; [p.] Richard A. and Lillie Mae McAlister; [m.] Donald L. Merideth, September 19, 1981; [ch.] Linda, Mike, Tony, and Sonya (Deceased); [ed.] GED- 1 1/2 college; [occ.] Housewife; [oth. writ.] Writings for friends and family of loved ones passed in memory of (put in newspapers); [pers.] Play the piano and organ. Write songs and music. Love to write poetry that inspires others or that give an inner peace.

MERRELL, WILLIE C.
[pen.] W. C. Merrell; [b.] May 24, 1952, Sneads, FL; [p.] Linda Brain; [m.] Teresa A., February 17, 1973; [ch.] Tyron, Kisha, Willie, Athelia; [ed.] Lillie Blanks Elementary, Sneads High, Chipola Jr. College, Florida State University; [occ.] Instructor; [pers.] "The Lord is my Shepherd"; [a.] Orlando, FL

METZ, ELIZABETH LEE
[pen.] Libby Metz; [b.] October 17, 1939, Mannington, WV; [p.] Lee Wildman, Ruby Wildman; [m.] Bernard Metz, May 21, 1957; [ch.] Cheri, Tonya, Bo, Joni, Jami; [ed.] High school; [occ.] Homemaker; [memb.] First Baptist Church, Mannington Pride Committee; [hon.] Received a plaque from Mannington Park Board in appreciation for time and work spent making Hough Park cleaner and safer.; [oth. writ.] Have written poetry for Mannington City Council, First Baptist Church, friends, and various organizations.; [pers.] I have always loved poetry! My favorite poet is Edgar A. Guest.; [a.] Mannington, WV

MIANO, JENNIFER L.
[b.] August 7, 1969, Minneapolis, MN; [p.] Karen Branham; [m.] Michael Miano, December 22, 1989; [ch.] Jessica Miano, Michael Miano; [ed.] Berkmar High School Graduate; [occ.] Raising my children, the toughest job there is.; [oth. writ.] "Inner Sole" soon to be published in the poetry guilds "Revolution of the Sole."; [pers.] I never really understood poetry as a child. In fact, I always dreaded having to memorize poems in school. Now that I am older, I can appreciate how much truth and meaning lie within them.; [a.] Chillicothe, OH

MIERS, DON
[pen.] Amos Mez; [b.] January 27, 1953, Teaneck, NJ; [p.] Stella; [m.] Patricia, January 15, 1983; [ch.] Amos, Joshua, Matthew, Jesse; [ed.] A.S. - Hotel/Restaurant Management St. Petersburg Junior College; [occ.] Stadium Director Osceola County Stadium, Kissimmee, FL; [memb.] Rotary Club of Kissimmee Bay Charter-President/Osceola Scholarship Bowl-President/Junior Achievement Board/Mentor for "at risks students/ little league coach; [hon.] 1994-Paul Haris Fellow Award by the Rotary Club of Kissimmee West/ 1994-Outstanding Citizen Award by Rotary Club of Kissimee/1991-

Osceola County School's Business Partner of the Year/ 1988-Community Recognition Award by the Greater Orlando Chamber of Commerce/1984-Outstanding Young Man of America by U.S. Jaycees/1982 and 1984 - Florida State League Executive of the year; [oth. writ.] Someone's Got to Give a Damn, Not Just a Hero, Baseball nicknames; [pers.] Reach out - there's somebody out there that you can help!; [a.] Kissimmee, FL

MILANO, CAROLINA OSMELIA ARREDONDO
[pen.] Caro Milano; [b.] August 31, 1982; [p.] Elias and Tarcisia Arredondo; [ed.] Conway Middle School; [occ.] Student; [hon.] Honor Roll student at Miami Lakes Elementary, H. Roll at Kensington Park Elementary, H. Roll at Palmetto Elementary, H. Roll at Westridge Middle School. H. Roll at Conway Middle School Chorus Award at Palmetto E. Award 3 place. Painting City of Hialeah Fl.; [pers.] If there were no boundaries and everyone would be colorblind this will be a much better world. Also women are just as good as men or better.; [a.] Orlando, FL

MILLER, CHARLES NATHAN
[b.] December 9, 1927, Sumner, FL; [p.] Charlie and Grace Miller; [m.] Essie Ruth Miller, August 27, 1948; [ch.] Two; [ed.] 1 year High School plus GED Diploma; [occ.] Security at night for Levy Country Road Dept.; [hon.] Pilot - Single Engine Land Airplane. Tugboat Captain 65 ft. 51 ton Deep-sea Charter Boat License. F.C.C. Radio Telephone License 3rd Class.; [oth. writ.] Many poems and religious articles too, many to name.; [pers.] The earth is the work of our carpenter. Look at the word Earth. Ear-th, so its through the ear you receive from our carpenter. The earth does not work to receive seed, water or the sunshine, and we are the earth of God.; [a.] Chiefland, FL

MILLER, JACLYN SUZANNE
[b.] October 29, 1977, East Chicago, IN; [p.] James B. and Mary Paulette Miller; [ed.] Graduated from Bibich Elementary School, Kahler Middle School, and on May 30, 1996 I will graduate from Lake Central High School; [occ.] I work as a sales person at Old Navy Clothing Co.; [memb.] Belongs to Saint Lukes Lutheran Church; [pers.] It makes me express myself, and thank every one that I have in today's world, and that I should be very happy. I was inspired by the poet Emily Dickenson and her works.; [a.] Dyer, IN

MILLER, JUDIE LYNN
[b.] June 24, 1964, Philadelphia; [p.] George and Helen Walton; [m.] Raymond S. Miller, September 22, 1990; [ed.] St. Hubert High School; [occ.] Cardiac Monitor Technician; [memb.] International Society of Poets; [hon.] Chapel of Four Chaplins, Editor's Choice Award - Rainbow's End (Poem: Mom's Flowers); [oth. writ.] I've Counted The Flutters Of Butterflies Wing's (self published), Rainbow's End, Admist The Splendor; [pers.] To communicate with cancer patients and survivors, Dr. Temple needed courage to tell me, a 29 years old patient, that I had cancer. How difficult this must be - a Doctor to think he/she is giving someone it death sentence. But the Doctor must see through the patient - to be sure that the patient is not denying the diagnosis, then denial becomes the killer.; [a.] Philadelphia, PA

MILLER, KEN
[b.] July 30, 1949, Morgantown, WV; [p.] Bill Miller (Deceased), Louise Wright; [m.] Sheryl L. Miller, February 12, 1972; [ch.] Kristin L. Miller; [ed.] DuVal High, Prince George's Community College, The American University; [occ.] Grocery Store Dairy Stocker/ Checker, Safeway, Dunkirk, MD; [memb.] U.S. Congressional Staff Member (1970-1992), Distinguished member of The International Society of Poets, Member of The Calvert County Poetry Club; [hon.] Editor's Choice Award for my poem, "Pressing Thoughts", in

the NLP's Through The Hourglass. Editor's Choice Award for my poem, "In Between", in the NLP's Best Poem of The '90's. Elected into The International Poetry Hall of Fame. My poems "Alone" "Pressing Thoughts", "In Between" and "Epitaph" selected for the NLP's "Sound of Poetry's" series.; [oth. writ.] A poem, "Alone", in The National Library of Poetry's anthology, Where Dawn Lingers. A poem, "Pressing Thoughts", in The National Library of Poetry's anthology, Through The Hourglass. A poem, "In Between", in The National Library of Poetry's forthcoming special edition, The Best Poems of The '90's.; [pers.] My poems can be quite intense. However, by writing them I've gotten something out of my system, which seems to be a positive release. "Epitaph", my poem in this anthology was largely inspired by a punk rocker, who is now deceased, but could apply to other starcrossed individuals.; [a.] Owings, MD

MILLER, LYNNE TELLER
[pen.] Lynne Teller Miller; [b.] March 30, 1949, Norwalk, CT; [p.] Eleanor O. Shiver Miller, Edward Julius Miller; [m.] Divorced, March 29, 1969; [ch.] James L. Sugden Jr., Cynthia Lee, half Sister - Rebecca Faust; [ed.] Brien McMahon High School Washington State Community College (Marietta, Ohio); [occ.] Typesetter; [memb.] American Legion Post #64; [hon.] Dean's List, President's List (WSS at Marietta, Ohio); [pers.] The "comedian" in my poem could make everyone "laugh" at their lives but his own! Drugs helped take him away! Listen to friends and family when they say you are "gifted" and "special"! There is "life" without drugs!; [a.] Marietta, OH

MILLER, R. V. BOB
[pen.] R. V. Bob Miller; [b.] October 14, 1922, Moline, IL; [p.] Vernon A. Miller and Villa O. Miller; [m.] Margaretnel Miller, May 22, 1970; [ch.] Randy S. Miller and Robin S. Cobb; [ed.] Chicago University, Baylor University; [occ.] Retired Refractionist - Retired Optician and Sports Official (Football 35 years - Basketball 21 years - Baseball 11 years - Track and Field 25 years; [memb.] Kiwanis - Honorary Life Member, Honorary Life Member Football Assn., Honorary Life Member Basketball Assn., (The Southwest Officials Association); [hon.] National Federation Distinguished Football Officials Award 1987; [oth. writ.] If this turns out alright, I have several more poems to sent.; [pers.] Some of my friends call my poems poultry, because they are so foul.; [a.] Austin, TX

MILLER, ROBERT L.
[b.] December 5, 1927, Port Huron, MI; [p.] Russell Miller, Violet Miller; [m.] Lois A. Miller, September 7, 1946; [ch.] Tammie, Robert, Penny, Scott, Terrie, Christine, Wendy, Laurie; [ed.] Marysville High; [occ.] Retired Power Plant Operator; [memb.] Sturges Memorial Congregational Church, Member - Deacons and Trustee Boards, Choir; [oth. writ.] Class of 46, The First Road, The Poem I Couldn't Write, Pretending, God's Bell Ringer, My Mothers Will, A Walk In The Rain, The Lesson, 50 Years Of Marriage, Missed Chance, The Challenge, I Love You; [a.] Marysville, MI

MILLER, ROBIN R.
[pen.] Robin R. Nalls; [b.] February 13, 1957, Washington, DC; [p.] Mr. and Mrs. John W. Nalls; [ch.] Bronson Sarver and Thomas Blankenship; [ed.] Thomas Edison High School Springfield, VA; [occ.] Hair Dresser; [oth. writ.] Several poems; [pers.] I write about my life experiences, happy and sad I have to feel it, to write it.; [a.] Fredericksburg, VA

MILLER-CASTEEL, LESLEY
[b.] September 29, 1962, Galesburg, IL; [p.] Robert and Vina Miller; [ch.] Dustin Michael Casteel; [ed.] Galva High School; [oth. writ.] Began writing poetry as

a child and was published in local newspaper at age 9 - maintains compilation of works to date and enjoys writing new poetry often.; [pers.] I use my poetry to express my emotion and chronicle events in my life I have a great love for poetry and a special fondness for the works of Walt Whitman.; [a.] Galva, IL

MILLS, RAMUNZ
[pen.] Guardian; [b.] October 7, 1973; [p.] Lynn M. Mills; [ed.] Pope John Paul II High School, University of Tennessee, Knoxville BA Psychology; [occ.] Case Manager, Towering Pines Center; [hon.] Congressional - Scholar Nominee, Who's Who 1990-1991; [pers.] I shall always be; [a.] Slidell, LA

MINGEE, MICHAEL
[b.] November 29, 1968, Beaufort, SC; [p.] Geraldine and Rodney Mingee; [m.] Teri Mingee, December 20, 1991; [ed.] United States Military Academy; [occ.] Infantry Officer, United States Army; [hon.] Dean's List at West Point; [oth. writ.] Many thanks go to my beautiful wife, Teri, and to my family in Virginia. I love you!; [a.] Fort Benning, GA

MINNICHBACH, LINDA C.
[b.] May 20, 1952, Philadelphia, PA; [p.] Robert Schweiker, Dolores Schweiker; [m.] Edward Minnichbach, October 27, 1973; [ch.] Lori Ann, Amy Lynn, Stacey Lynn; [ed.] Kensington Girls High, St. Francis Medical Ctr School of Nursing, BCCC; [occ.] Registered Nurse; [pers.] "My Mother, My Friend" was dedicated to my beloved mother Dolores Rose Schweiker 1932-1993.; [a.] Croydon, PA

MISOYIANIS, SHELLI
[b.] October 16, 1974, Ravenna, OH; [p.] George and Judy Misoyianis; [ed.] Lenape High School; [oth. writ.] My 2 books, USA and The Unknown Breed hopefully to be published one day, stories and poems published in a children's magazine at age 12, my poems recently published, "Her Trembling Hand".; [pers.] "I've been writing for 13 years, and I'm only 22. My material generally reflects the experiences of my life with a little flavor of spirituality added!"; [a.] Vincentown, NJ

MITCHELL, DONALD L.
[b.] August 25, 1952, Lorain, OH; [p.] Howard and Betty Mitchell; [m.] Deborah J. Mitchell, April 28, 1973; [ch.] Donald Scott, Matthew Lee, Katrina Christian; [ed.] South Amherst High School Oberlin School of Commerce Lorain County Community College; [occ.] Auto Assembly Ford Motor Co. Lorain, Ohio; [memb.] Church of the open door - Elyria, Ohio; [oth. writ.] Several poems published in following books portraits of life the best poems of 1997; [pers.] That I may publish with the voice of thanksgiving, and tell of all God's wondrous works.; [a.] Lorain, OH

MITCHELL, MABEL
[b.] May 22, 1914, Winfield, KS; [p.] John Kent, Ethel Kent; [m.] Roy Mitchell, July 30, 1935; [ch.] Phyllis, Marilyn, Michael; [ed.] High School; [occ.] Housewife; [memb.] First Christian Church; [oth. writ.] This is my first; [pers.] No 8 of ten children.; [a.] Winfield, KS

MITCHELL, WENDY
[pen.] Wendy Ezard Mitchell; [b.] June 17, 1956, Toronto, Ontario, Canada; [p.] Donald Ezard, Shirley (Wood) Mercer; [m.] Mark J. (Mitch) Mitchell, March 4, 1989; [ch.] Ronald Alan MacAskill; [ed.] Northview Highschool, Covina, CA, Mount Hood Community College, Gresham, OR; [occ.] Managing home based business; [pers.] If people can feel the emotion I feel in my poetry and relate it to there own lives, then I know I have succeeded. The pain of my younger sisters death influenced my writing, and while she will always in-

spire me, there's also my two great loves, my husband Mitch and my best buddy Butch (my English Bulldog) they keep my poetry flowing.; [a.] Bloomington, CA

MITSTIFER, RYAN D.
[b.] November 28, 1972, Sunnyvale, CA; [p.] Rick and Susan Mitstifer; [ed.] Pennsylvania State Univ. BS in Industrial Engineering; [occ.] Process Engineer, Culp Finishing, Burlington, NC; [memb.] Penn State Alumni Association; [oth. writ.] Poems published in reading, PA newspaper, The Unkempt, The Blasphemous Pages, and Apprise (Central PA Publication); [pers.] Inspired to write by Bruce Weigl's "What Saves Us, thank you... What makes today worth anything without tomorrow to regret what we have done?; [a.] Greensboro, NC

MOBLEY, LOUSIE CRENSHAW
[pen.] Lousie Harlin; [b.] July 11, 1921, Thurber, TX; [p.] Orren and Myrtle McAlister; [m.] J. W. Mobley, May 10, 1995; [ch.] Pat Thorn (previous marriage); [ed.] High School and Beauty School; [occ.] Part Time Hairdresser; [memb.] Gordon Church of Christ Overth' - Hill Club, D.A.V. (Lifetime member); [hon.] Published in "World of Poetry" anthology 1989 and "New American Poetry Anthology" 1988; [oth. writ.] Booklet of one-hundred-six poems published in 1989. Copyright 1989.; [pers.] I enjoy reading and writing inspirational poetry. My ambition is to reach those who do not know God and help them learn of this great love for mankind.; [a.] Gordon, TX

MOGNETT, CARLENE J.
[b.] September 3, 1942, Russiaville, IN; [p.] Carl and Emma McKoon; [m.] Jack Mognett, July 20, 1993; [ch.] Rhonda Mouser, Tom Nearon; [ed.] Kokomo High School; [occ.] Retired from General Motors - Delco Electronics; [memb.] Cornerstone Christian Center Church; [oth. writ.] Several unpublished poems.; [pers.] My writing comes from my heart. Sometimes it's the only way I can express my deepest feelings.; [a.] Kokomo, IN

MOLNAR, ETHAN N.
[b.] January 28, 1978, Cleveland, OH; [p.] Edward and Ellen Molnar; [ed.] Currently enrolled at Ohio University; [occ.] Student; [pers.] No matter who you are accept and like yourself. After all you're gong to be spending the rest of your life with yourself.; [a.] Northfield Center, OH

MONTE, LISA
[pen.] Lee J. Monte; [b.] July 24, 1965, Belleville, NJ; [p.] Victor Monte, Sara Johnson; [m.] Single mother; [ch.] Ian J. Monte; [ed.] Long Island University, Brooklyn, NY; [memb.] English Club; [hon.] Volunteer/ Internships helping the homeless; [oth. writ.] Working on book of memoirs, currently.; [pers.] I write was is real. The darker side of life captivates me. My influences are W. Burroughs, KAFKA and Sexton.; [a.] Brooklyn, NY

MONTEMAYOR, JARON
[b.] April 10, 1977, Saint Joseph, MO; [p.] Linda Stephens and Keith Montemayor; [ch.] Cameron Scott, Jackson Henry; [ed.] Central High School, Missouri Western State College; [occ.] Stranger; [pers.] We are surrounded by a world of symbols, illusions which shall seek endlessly to give form to formlessness.; [a.] Saint Joseph, MO

MONTES, JULIE M. SIERRA
[b.] March 28, 1962; [p.] William and Melba Sierra; [m.] Nasser Montes, May 27, 1995; [ed.] B.S. George Washington University 1980-1985, M.S. C.W. Past University/L.I.U. 1985-Inc, Ph.D. Florida International Univ. 1995-Present; [occ.] Graduate Assistant/Molecular Biology; [memb.] Distinguished Member of Inter-

national Society of Poetry; [oth. writ.] "Noble Sir" in Across The Universe 1996; [pers.] A teardrop falls. A smile is won. I know in my heart, that our song has begun. Let my heart strings bear the notes of life's joy. May we hear the notes and follow the rainbow to our pot of gold!; [a.] Miami, FL

MONTGOMERY, MARY
[b.] June 15, 1910, Fort Frances; [p.] Bonny and David Montgomery; [ed.] University of Manitoba studying to become a Pediatrician and Medical Illustrator; [occ.] Student; [memb.] Royal Life Saving Society Canada (Lifeguard and Instructor); [hon.] Several Athletic Awards throughout high-school as well as scholastic awards. Contribution to society honor and honor roll.; [oth. writ.] I have been writing poetry for many years on a person basis. This is the first poem published of my work. I was not aware of my talent!:; [pers.] Life should be lived standing up not sitting down. Something is harder than dying and that my friend is living.; [a.] Fort Frances, Ontario, Canada

MOORE, CHARLES
[pen.] C. Dennis Moore; [b.] October 1, 1972, St. Joseph, MO; [p.] Gale Beggs; [ch.] Jacob Rion, Caleb Mikel; [ed.] Central High School; [occ.] Warehouse worker; [memb.] St. Joseph Literary Guild; [oth. writ.] 3 chapbooks, poem in Through the Hourglass.; [pers.] Instead of trying to say something important, I just try to write something I like.; [a.] Saint Joseph, MO

MOORE, DONNA J.
[b.] March 4, 1944, Saint Joseph, MO; [p.] Donald and Dolores Dorsey; [m.] Larry N. Moore (D - August 4, 1993), March 22, 1963; [ch.] Kelly Neil, Stuart Evan; [ed.] Manatee Community College Bradenton, Fl., Savannah High School Savannah, Missouri; [occ.] Small Business Owner, Nursing; [memb.] National Honor Society, Phi Theta Kappa, Dean's List; [oth. writ.] Multiple short stories and other poems, non published; [pers.] I would like to become a published lyricist and continue writing.; [a.] Sarasota, FL

MOORE, ESTHER B.
[b.] January 4, Brooklyn, NY; [p.] Roscoe and Mary Moore; [ed.] Graduated Cum Laude, Morgan State University, 1979; [occ.] Business Consultant US Postal Service; [a.] Salisbury, MD

MOORE, JOHN MICHAEL
[b.] January 5, 1972, Indianapolis, IN; [p.] Karen E. Moore, John M. Moore; [ed.] Indiana University, B.A. 1996; [occ.] Marketing Analyst, Los Angeles, CA; [a.] Redondo Beach, CA

MOORE, KENNETH
[pen.] Kenneth Moore; [b.] June 30, 1968, Lompoc, CA; [p.] Shirley Moore, Kenneth Moore; [occ.] Incarcerated Florida Prisoner; [oth. writ.] Several hundred of varying subjects and style. Poems and songs. No other as yet published anywhere.; [pers.] There is creativity everywhere. Sometimes even in those looked down upon. Those who have made grave mistakes. In life we must all find our own source of stability. It's in the effort of my writing and art work that I find my own.; [a.] Bowling Green, FL

MOORE, SARAH M.
[b.] April 8, 1939, Fayette, AL; [p.] Walter and Annie Lea Matthews; [m.] Robert A. Moore Jr., September 4, 1960; [ch.] Cynthia Renee and Roger Alan; [ed.] BS-Auburn Univ., MA Univ. of Alabama; [occ.] Own Business and Retired Elem. Teacher; [memb.] Delta Kappa Gamma, NEA, AEA American Mothers; [hon.] Alabama Mother of the Year, District Teacher of the Year, Fayette County Teacher of the Year, Arvin Teacher of the Year; [oth. writ.] Just for personal enjoyment -

poems of all kinds.; [pers.] Enjoy writing poetically what I think about ordinary topics.; [a.] Winfield, AL

MORAN, KATHERINE LEE
[pen.] Katie Moran; [b.] November 25, 1981, St. Paul, MI; [p.] Thomas and Patricia Moran; [ed.] Freshman at North High School - No St. Paul MN; [occ.] Student; [hon.] Honor Rolls, Certificates in Sports, Safe Bicycling Award, 1st place in Drawing contest, Certificate of Achievement in Dare, V.T.P Award, Certificate of Commendation of the State of Minnesota; [oth. writ.] Entering in other contests but I usually write poems for pleasure.; [pers.] Poetry is a way to expressing my feelings of how I view the world through my eyes and other peoples eyes. It's a great way to relax. (I really need that.; [a.] North Saint Paul, MN

MORANDI, DORINHA E.
[b.] March 27, 1948, Amityville, NY; [p.] Thomas Mendes Faria and Robbie Hester Faria; [ch.] John David E., James Andrew; [ed.] Wyandanch H.S., Allen School for Physicians Aides, Central Piedmont Community College; [occ.] Receptionist; [hon.] Citizenship Award, Music Achievement Award; [oth. writ.] Presently writing a collection of poems dedicated to my mother. "Deliverance" and Genocide in Heaven, published by The National Library of Poetry.; [pers.] I resemble the many flowers in God's garden of children. I am appalled when observing the injustice of social inequities.; [a.] Charlotte, NC

MOREAN, MEGHAN
[b.] February 2, 1982, Royal Oak, MI; [p.] William Morean, Tammy Gray; [ed.] 9th grade student at Shore crest Preparatory School, St. Petersburg, FL; [occ.] Student; [memb.] Key Club, Student Council, High School Newspaper; [hon.] Numerous Athletic awards, several student of the month awards, Young Citizen of the year award, Dean's List or high honors all years, TIP recognition award; [oth. writ.] Several poems published in school magazines and newspapers; [pers.] My writing is inspired by the beautiful and horrific aspects of everyday life. My work is always sincere and from the heart. I simply write what I feel and am never out to impress anyone but my self.; [a.] Saint Petersburg, FL

MORGAN, LATOYA R.
[pen.] L.R. Morgan; [b.] April 2, 1977, Los Angeles, CA; [p.] Ronald and Theresa Adams; [ed.] Westchester High School; [occ.] Currently an Undergraduate student at the University of California Irvine, Political Science major; [memb.] Young Black Scholars, California Scholarship Federation; [hon.] VC Irvine Excellence Award, VC Irvine Dean's Honor list, Young Black Scholars Academic Achievement Scholarship; [oth. writ.] Several unpublished poems and short stories in my personal collection.; [pers.] Writing that comes from the soul and pours through the pen is the only writing worth remembering.; [a.] Altadena, CA

MORRIS, JODI
[b.] October 19, 1980, Albany, GA; [p.] Jo and Dean Morris; [ed.] Currently in 10th grade at Randolph Southern, Shellman, GA also attended Calhoun County High School; [memb.] 4-H, attend Bethlehem Free Will Baptist Church; [hon.] Jr. Beta, Region IA Softball Champs '95 (Calhoun Co); [oth. writ.] A notebook at home with poems and thoughts, never been published.; [pers.] Poetry has opened my eyes to new feelings and influenced me into a more positive way of thinking.; [a.] Cuthbert, GA

MORRIS, LEE
[b.] December 31, 1961, Gallipolis, OH; [p.] Roland and Ann Morris; [m.] Melinda McDonald (Fiancee); [ch.] Karee (12), Tiffany (7); [ed.] Meigs High School 1980; [occ.] Insulation Installer Edwards Insulation

Columbus, OH; [hon.] Various musical award throughout my school career; [oth. writ.] Over 100 poems and songs which hasn't been published as of yet. But I'm still hoping.; [pers.] I have always been interested in music, poetry every since I was little. I would like to thank every one that inspired me and God for my talent, and my guardian (shadow) angel for watching over me.; [a.] Rutland, OH

MOSHETT, LAUREL RHONDA
[b.] July 19, 1982, Guyana; [p.] Leyland and Joan Moshett; [occ.] Student (J.H.S); [hon.] Judith Kerbatsos Memorial Award, Parsons Pride, A Citation of Achievement from the Jewish Community Relations Council.; [pers.] A poem can be our expression of many things. When you are the author, you get to choose.; [a.] Queens, NY

MOURNING, PEARLETTE SARACEIN
[pen.] Mickey; [b.] May 9, 1964, St. Thomas, Virgin Islands; [p.] Sarah George, Vancito Gumbs; [m.] Tyrone Mourning, November 1, 1991; [ch.] Kiara Nikol Mourning; [ed.] Charlotte Amalie High School, 2 1/2 years Central Texas College; [occ.] U. S. Army (soldiers) Communications Supervisor; [pers.] I write what I feel in my heart. Most of my poetry is about love and what I feel love is and should be. Always strive to be the best in what ever you do.; [a.] El Paso, TX

MUHAMMAD, AULETTA
[b.] June 28, 1952, New York; [p.] Thomas Seward, Lula Seward; [ch.] Colbyz Sims and Shelva Sims; [ed.] George Washington High Bronx New York, Atlanta Business College U.S. Army Vietnam Veteran; [occ.] Verifier, Supervisor Community Services B'ham, AL; [memb.] Acorn member Kansas City, MO; [hon.] National Defense Medal, Sharpshooter award, Customer Service award, Hill Top Records has asked for four to five poems for review far songs.; [oth. writ.] Poets International Society, Reflections of Heart anthology poem titled "Don't Blink Back"; [pers.] I have a strong love for people, and strive to help ease the daily struggles of life that we all face. I enjoy being a servant to humanity.; [a.] Midfield, AL

MUIR, NAN S.
[b.] November 25, 1924, Simmonsville, MS; [p.] Bernard and Nell Simmons; [m.] M. Eric Muir O.D., March 15, 1956; [ch.] Sara (Deceased), Eric, Edward; [ed.] Cleveland High School, Mississippi University for Women (B.S. Degree), post-graduate computer courses, Children's Literature course; [occ.] Medical Transcriptionist; [memb.] Covenant Presbyterian Church, life member Cleveland Junior Auxiliary; [oth. writ.] I wrote the script for the Cleveland Community Theater's centential production in 1976, I have had several poems published in the local newspaper and one poem published in a children's magazine. Numerous other poems written for friends for special occasions.; [pers.] Any talent I have is a gift from God and it is my hope that whatever I write will honor his name.; [a.] Boyle

MULLINS, DONALD BLAKE
[b.] July 2, 1969, Dearborn, MI; [p.] Dan and Diane Basinger; [ed.] Allen Park High School Easter Michigan University; [occ.] English Teacher Manistee High School, Manistee, MI; [oth. writ.] "Calling a ball game" is my first original poem.; [pers.] My inspiration for this sonnet was Ernie Harwell, longtime voice of the Detroit tigers. I wish to dedicate this sonnet to my marvelous fiancee, Catherine Day, who along with being my partner for life, is the provider of my more cherished baseball memory.; [a.] Manistee, MI

MURPHY, MILLY
[b.] May 28, 1952, Port Chester, NY; [p.] Millie and Nick Morabito (both deceased); [m.] Michael Murphy, July 6, 1995 (after 13 long years); [ch.] Nicole DiPietro-Marino, Dave and Tim DiPietro (twins!); [ed.] Rye Neck High School Graduate; [occ.] Secretary in a Real Estate Office Own and operate Milly's Spotlight Karaoke; [hon.] I am honored to be a semi-finalist in this contest.; [oth. writ.] Although I have never been published, I write a lot of poetry, my favorite is called "A Letter From Heaven" to my entire family from my mother. My poetry ranges from sad to romantic, sentimental to silly. I love to write. Next to Stephen King, my favorite author is my daughter, Nicole.; [pers.] Treasure each precious moment of life, your children grow up in just moments. My dreams have come true. It's never too late to find happiness.; [a.] Lake Peekskill, NY

MURRAY, REBECCA J. RICE
[b.] September 7, 1957, Frank Furt, Germany; [m.] Mack H. Murray Jr., November 12, 1994; [ch.] Emily Christine, Robert Wayne, Misty Elizabeth; [ed.] Asso. Degree Tele Communications; [occ.] Correction Officer TDCJ-ID; [hon.] Won several 1st place awards in Fantasy Reenactment Society; [pers.] I strive to show the better parts of the medevil times. William Shakespeare and poet Ester Whitehead are my greatest influences.; [a.] Gatesville, TX

MUTI, SISI K.
[pen.] Mom Sisi; [b.] March 3, 1941, Tonga; [p.] Atonio Amasio and Sela Vea; [m.] Paula F. Muti, March 15, 1965; [ch.] Dallin Muti, Melinda K. Muti; [ed.] BS in Education (Bus.) at CCH Brown, Leimomi Muti Alapa, Lawrence Muti, presently undergo a Bus. Management Master Program at the University of Phoenix; [occ.] Head Resident for girls at BYU-HC, Hawaii; [memb.] Atele Kolisi Tutuku Alumni, Liahoma Alumni, Tongan Club; [hon.] Family of the Year - in Tonga for our Stake - LDS Church in 1978. Teacher of the Year - Liahona High School where I taught in 1974.; [oth. writ.] Poems of my home, school, Tonga my country. Poems for each of my four children entitled: Sieku Noove Kakala Heihoifua (For Son Dallin), Leimomi, You're Something Else, Amangki Taehoko for Lawrence, Pulia ae Ofaanga - for husband, Paul.; [pers.] I strive to share my feelings for my loved ones and the things I love in my writing.; [a.] Laie, HI

MYERS, MARY A.
[pen.] Ann; [b.] February 23, 1957, West Memphis, AR; [p.] Frege and Dora Simpson; [m.] Alfonza Myers, July 3, 1993; [ch.] TiKisha, Nakia, Terry Isaac Tony, Porscha; [ed.] Got a G.E.D. attend William Horlick High School Racine Wisc. Washington Jr. High Racine Wisc., Certified Elementary Racine Wisc.; [occ.] Hall-Aide at Gilmore Middle Racine Wisc.; [oth. writ.] How Do We Reach Our Youth; [pers.] Am striving to reflect the good and to also let people know that threw out this life everyone has to deal with problem and with god help we can do it.; [a.] Racine, WI

NABER, ROSEANN M. DEPINTO
[pen.] Roseann M. DePinto Naber; [b.] December 27, 1953, Bronx, NY; [p.] James DePinto and Claire (Deceased); [m.] Awni I. Naber, October 24, 1976; [ch.] Dina Marie and Anthony James; [ed.] Graduated High School Roosevelt High School, Yonkers, NY, Graduated 2 year course - Children's Writing - Institute of Children's Literature in Long Ridge, CT. and BOCES: Certified Travel Agent; [occ.] Administrative Asst, Licensed NYS Realtor and Freelance writer, and notary public; [memb.] Nat'l Assoc of Female Executives, Member of Research Advisory Board for "American Biographical Institute"; [hon.] Received the "1996

2000 Notable Women Award" sponsored by American Biographical Institute, recently appointed to its Advisory Board.; [oth. writ.] Published poem 1996 "The Silent Revolution - Who's Who in New Poets 1996.; [pers.] Loving relationships enhance the essence of my being and can be seen in my works. My faith in God is my inspiration, in all my doings. I believe in the expression: "Live well, laugh often, Love much," if followed, "balance" will bless us all!; [a.] Peekskill, NY

NATALE, JOYCE ANN
[pen.] Joyce Ann Natale; [b.] September 24, 1959, Newark, NJ; [p.] Leila Sachs Klempner, Elliot Klempner; [m.] Louis H. Natale, October 4, 1987; [ch.] Lee Jordan, Adam Lukas; [ed.] Union High School; [occ.] Dental Assistant, Dr. Ira Feldman E. Brunswick, NJ; [memb.] P.T.A. Jewish Women International E.B.J.C. Sisterhood; [oth. writ.] Poems written to my husband, several contests.; [pers.] My poetry comes from my heart. I feel expression is necessary in my life. Mine is best shown in writing. My ambition comes from the wonderful memories on my mother, Leila.; [a.] East Brunswick, NJ

NAVARI, CORNELIA
[b.] December 20, 1944, Deland, FL; [p.] Richard and Geraldine Navari; [m.] Divorced; [ed.] High School and some College; [occ.] Legal Secretary/Message Therapist; [memb.] International Certification with The Associated Bodyworkers and Message Professionals since October, 93; [oth. writ.] None published; [pers.] I have wanted to write ever since I can remember. I love the magic and power of the written work. I write about what I know - love, dreams, pain and joy. I actively support the health of the environment and the health of others in my message practice. My dream is to live by the sea and write.; [a.] Naperville, IL

NELON, PAMELA C.
[pen.] Pam Nelon, P.C. Nelon, Conrad Nelon; [b.] March 23, 1951, Surry, ME; [p.] Penny Finn, Bernard Finn; [ch.] Shana, Christina, Michael, Timothy; [ed.] Dean Jr. College, Bridgeport School of Nursing; [occ.] Psychiatric Nurse; [hon.] Good conduct award USAF honorable discharges - 1976 (Vietnam Era) and 1994 (Post Gulf War.); [oth. writ.] Other unpublished writings; [pers.] Be yourself. I'm a paid cynic. Take risks, make mistakes, get messy.; [a.] Surry, ME

NELSON, DENNIS S.
[pen.] Dennis Shive; [b.] October 7, 1946, Philadelphia, PA; [p.] Ruth Nelson Patton; [ed.] 10 Years College, 7 Universities Political Science, Biology, English; [occ.] Student (graduate) UN of S. Fl. Tampa; [memb.] Lamba Chi Fraternity; [oth. writ.] Several articles published in magazines and newspapers taught poetry Uni of N.C. Pembroke, N.C. 3 weeks. (Dr. Tom Leach); [pers.] Control is an illusion: Abracadabra; [a.] Sarasota, FL

NELZEN, NATHAN D.
[pen.] 'Doc'; [b.] June 13, 1955, Wichita, KS; [m.] Debra Jean Nelzen, 1990; [ed.] 1995 Graduate, Institute of Biblical Studies at Liberty University Lynchburg (Forest), VA; [occ.] Overhead "Door Doctor" construction/Service Foreman; [memb.] Faith Fellowship Church, and or Body of Christ Jesus "Literally"; [hon.] Ordained Minister 12/22/95, Ministers for Christ Assembly of Churches High Hill, MO; [pers.] Truly, all of any inspired writing(s) is directed by and for the glory of God himself, this poem is noticed that his coming is soon and that he loves you.

NETZER, DOROTHY
[b.] January 16, 1936, Newport, KY; [p.] Carl Netzer and Gertrude Siemer Netzer; [ed.] St. Mary High School Alexandria, KY; [occ.] Payroll Clerk, The Provident Bank; [pers.] To me writing poetry is a form of praying. It brings me peace while praising God through His creation.; [a.] Fort Thomas, KY

NEWCOMB, DYLAN
[b.] March 25, 1971, Concord, MA; [ed.] Studied Dance and Music Composition at Juilliard 89-91 BFA, Juilliard 1991; [occ.] Dancer, with the Netherlands Dance Theater, in Holland, Composer; [pers.] Favorite poets: Rumi, Rilke, Lao-Tzu.

NEWLAND, WALTER M.
[b.] December 26, 1917, Chanute, KS; [p.] Harry and Anna Newland; [m.] Eudeene Rae Daniel, July 19, 1947; [ch.] Walter M. Jr., Carol Camille, Delia Ann; [ed.] Chanute High, A.B. College of Euporia, M.A. George Peabody College, PhD Candidate University of Southern California; [occ.] Retired High School Principal Long Beach, California, Retired Colonel US Marine Corps Reserve; [memb.] Phi Delta Kappa, Retired Officers Association, Veterans of Foreign Wars, Marine Corps League; [hon.] College of Emporia: Sr. Class, Pres. All - Kansas College Tackle, MO Valley, AAU Javelin Champion. US Marines: Silver Star Medal Navy Commendation Medal, Purple Heart. School Admin.: District Pres. Cal Secondary School Administrator. Pres. Long Beach School Administrators; [pers.] To remember with love is the ultimate accolade. A thought, however well considered, if unexpressed, will have the same impact as no thought at all. It is but a "Kissin' Cousin" to the thoughtless.; [a.] Elephant Butte, NM

NIELSEN, VALERIE
[b.] October 22, 1962, San Pablo, CA; [ed.] Two years in a community college, three years in the mental health system which provides quite an education; [memb.] International Society of Poets, The National Authors Registry; [oth. writ.] Poem published in through the hourglass, poem published in meditations by Iliad Press/ Cader publishing; [pers.] People who suffer with an emotional or mental illness are courageous and sensitive members of society. They are learning about themselves and learning to express themselves in artistic and creative ways.; [a.] Richmond, CA

NIERENBERG, MATTHEW D.
[b.] September 19, 1970, Los Angeles, CA; [p.] Alvin and Marilyn Nierenberg; [ed.] BA, Political Science, UC Santa Barbara, 1993 Certification in Spanish Language, UC San Diego (in progress); [occ.] Global Investment Advisor, San Diego Equity Group, Inc. and student; [memb.] Surfrider Foundation, member Heal The Bay, member; [oth. writ.] Several poems published in other anthologies, 2nd place prize winner, Nat'l. Library of Poetry Fall 1996 (?) contest, The Ebbing Tide anthology; [a.] La Jolla, CA

NIXON, SCOTT JONATHAN
[pen.] Nixon; [b.] September 26, 1974, Ft. Worth; [p.] James and Dorthy Nixon; [ed.] Currently attending Southern Nazarine University for an undergraduate degree; [memb.] Free-lance poet with some Associations to Individual Artists of Oklahoma (this is meant to be oxymoronic!); [oth. writ.] Self-publicated, short book of poems, Confessions of Insecurity. Submitted short stories for IAO's Anthology of Oklahoma short stories.; [pers.] To disprove a common theory which governs 'what makes a writer great', I would like someone, who enjoys my work, to contemplate what type of substance that I 'abused' to write these poems.; [a.] Oklahoma City, OK

NOLL, MICHAEL ANDREW
[b.] July 15, 1975, Philadelphia; [p.] Michael and Patricia; [ed.] Central High School Temple University; [occ.] Student/File clerk at brookman, Rosenberg, Bean and Sondln-Attornys at Law; [memb.] Phi Sigma Pi National Honor Fraternity Alpha Lambda Chapter Golden Key National Honor Society Criminal Justice Society at Temple; [hon.] Dean's List Donations fee Service In Phi Sigma Pi; [oth. writ.] Published at Central high school in "The mirror"; [pers.] You can't hear as see what goes on in my head so I must write, you must read we must all communicate; [a.] Philadelphia, PA

NORLING, RHONDA L.
[pen.] Rhonda L. Norling; [b.] November 13, 1964, Kennewick, WA; [p.] Richard and Louise Bush also Stan and Sharron Lawrence; [m.] Jeff, September 19, 1992; [ch.] Shaylin and Garrett; [ed.] Gresham Union High School, Multnomah College of Hair Design; [occ.] Full time wife and mother; [memb.] Licensed Cosmetologist, The National Library of Poetry; [hon.] Editor's Choice Award for "Our Moment In Time" published in "Forever And A Day"; [oth. writ.] Several other poems with a wide range of topics; [pers.] I find writing to be a great release. When I write I have the power to make wrongs right and memories some alive, to anguish in the pain of tragedy, to revel in success, to long for happiness, to make sense from indifference.; [a.] Kennewick, WA

NORMAN, ARLENE
[pen.] Ollie Gronvold, Arlene Moulton; [b.] July 21, 1931, Byron, MN; [p.] Orville, Serena Gronvold; [m.] Gail Andrew Norman, 1st - Moulton, September 2, 1950, 2nd Norman, June 23, 1983; [ch.] Samuel Winfield, Rikka Marie, Jennifer Jo, Rena Beth; [ed.] Byron H.S., College Credit - Medical Terminology; [occ.] Retired of self employed and Bookkeeping and Sec.; [memb.] Lutheran Church - (Hon.) Beta Sigma Phi, American Legion Aux.; [hon.] Homecoming Queen - H.S. Cheer leader, Annual and Paper Staff - Music - H.S. Girl of Year - Beta Sigma Phi; [oth. writ.] Autobiography for book of my 45th reunion. - H.S. personal poems of my feelings to children and grandchildren as gifts to the many that includes steps = 13 children and 38 grandchildren.; [pers.] I was inspired by my grandmothers interest in poetry and song-writing and my father's little jingles. My feelings whether happy or sad became and always will be very soothing to myself. Expressing in poetry. I yearn for peace.; [a.] Springdale, AR

NORMAND, KERRI
[b.] April 13, 1971, Hinton, Alberta, Canada; [p.] Dan and Larine Bieker; [m.] Troy Normand, August 30, 1993; [ch.] Two boys named Daniel and Brendan; [pers.] In loving memory to my father Dan Bieker who is always with me and will forever continue to be my hero. And to my mother Larine who has been both mother and father for 13 years. She has loved me and supported me and given me strength. She is the reason I was able to write this poem.; [a.] Edmonton, Alberta, Canada

NORTON, NILE B.
[b.] February 24, 1922, Decatur Co, IA; [p.] Mr. and Mrs. Earl Norton; [m.] Mary Joy Norton, January 15, 1949; [ch.] Susan, Michael, Brenda; [ed.] PhD Univ Denver; [occ.] Retired; [hon.] NEH, Military Decorations, St. Mary's Univ distinguished lecturous program; [oth. writ.] Non-published: Hist. Love Star Brewery, A Grim Murder (fiction): Published MA and PhD thesis and dissertation; [pers.] Poem written on July 18, 1945. I believe this test to be the most all invasive event of the 20th century.; [a.] San Antonio, TX

NORWOOD, JOSEPH C.
[b.] January 3, 1967, Livermore, CA; [m.] Sandy Norwood, December 21, 1985; [ch.] Joseph Christopher, Ryan Michael; [ed.] Del Valle High School; [occ.] Construction Worker; [pers.] I give my thoughts from deep within my soul, to share with the world what needs to be known. I have been inspired and blessed by the Lord.; [a.] Livermore, CA

NUSINOVICH, YEVGENIYA
[b.] December 21, 1989, Odessa, Ukraine; [p.] Alexander Nusinovich, Yelena Golik; [ed.] Richard Montgomery High School; [occ.] Junior in high school; [oth. writ.] Many other poems which I never show to anyone.; [pers.] My writing is usually philosophical and it reflects my mood. I am often influenced by various books, movies, or songs. I came to the US in the summer of 1992.; [a.] North Potomac, MD

O'BRIEN, DENISE M.
[pen.] "D"; [b.] January 4, 1961, Fall River, MA; [p.] Roland and Lorraine Poitras; [m.] J. Eddie O'Brien Jr., September 14, 1985; [ch.] Christopher-8, Danielle-6; [ed.] Graduated high school at Bishop Gerrard, Fall River, Mass.; [occ.] Bartender, waitress at Dining Services at Roger Williams Univ., Bristol, R.I.; [oth. writ.] Personal and romantic poems to people who have either touched or broken my heart, coming from a passion deep in my soul.; [pers.] I write when I am deeply moved by my emotions, someone, or something, through my life's journey. I dedicate this poem to my sister-in-law who's creative talents in song and dance especially, I've always loved.; [a.] Bristol, RI

OEHLMAN, NINA
[pen.] Teddie; [b.] July 14, 1979, Tennessee; [p.] Curt and Robin Oehlman; [ed.] Junior at Boone Grove High School (Porter Township); [occ.] A student; [memb.] 4-H (Boone Grove Future Farmers), Boone Grove High School S.A.D.D., Boone Grove High School Speech Team; [oth. writ.] (All non-published) "Party Of The Dead", "Recipe For Peace", "Crumpets And Tea", "Zeus", "What A World", "Survivor", "Memory Of One", "Tribal Wars", "Restful Day's Observation", "Uncle's Revenge", "How Jill Met Will", "House Of Peace", "Child", "Farm Life" and "City Of Trees"; [pers.] Thank you mom and dad and Mrs. Smar for all your support.; [a.] Valparaiso, IN

OGBUNUGWU, Rev. AUGUSTINE IBOODINMA
[pen.] Augustine; [b.] September 15, 1952, Agulu, Nigeria; [p.] Gloria and Okeke Ogbunugwu; [m.] Mrs. Catherine C. Ogbunugwu, December 4, 1982; [ch.] Uchenna and Chioma Ogbunugwu; [ed.] BSC. (hons.) University of Nigeria 1977 (Education Biology (m) Diploma in Theology, Trinity Union Theological College, Umuahia, 1982; [occ.] Chaplain International Community, Episcopal Church of the Epiphany, Houston, TX. Nursing student Houston Baptist University, Houston; [memb.] Member House of the Clergy, Episcopal Diolese of Texas member House of the Clergy, Diolese on the Niger, Anglican Province of Nigeria, member, American Nursing Student Association; [hon.] First place in poetry, the Danny Lee Lawrence creative writing award, May 7, 1996, Houston Baptist University; [oth. writ.] Unpublished Novels (1 x 2) Echoes of Victory, Dance of the Queen, radio commentaries, an Ambra Broadcasting Corporation, Nigeria, Poems - Something is Wrong, Heaven is Far, There is the Forest (published); [pers.] Have you left the world better than you found it, but when there is doubt about this, have you solved more problems than you creates?; [a.] Houston, TX

OLIVEIRA, MARY
[b.] February 16, 1954, Oakland, CA; [p.] Joseph Oliveira, Vivian Perry Oliveira; [ed.] California State University at Hayward, 1994-1996, Graduate in Mathematics, Holy Names College, 1990-1992, Teaching Credential University of California at Berkeley, 1972-1978 BA in Women's Studies Minors: Mathematics and Camp. Lit.; [occ.] Math Teacher Alameda United School District, Alameda, CA, Math Tutor; [memb.] National Council of Teachers of Mathematics, Mathematics Association of America. California Council of Teachers of Mathematics, American Mathematical Association, Alameda Swimming Pool Association; [hon.] International Directory of Distinguished Leadership, 1996-1997 Two Thousand Notable American Women 1996-1997, Who's Who in American Educators, 1994-1995, 1995-1996, 1996-1997, Who's Who in American Women 1995-1996, 1996-1997, 1997-1998. Who's Who of the World 1996-1997, World's Who's Who of Women, 1996-1997.; [pers.] Poetry is a very personal statement. In my poems, I express my inner most feelings.; [a.] Alameda, CA

OLIVER, GAIL DOTY
[b.] February 13, 1963, Shelby, NC; [p.] Gene and Alma Doty; [m.] Michael C. Oliver, July 26, 1986; [ch.] Caitlin Elizabeth 5, Hannah Marie, 3; [ed.] Shelby High School, Cleveland Community College; [occ.] Stay at home mother; [memb.] Central United Methodist Church, Member of National Thespain Honor Society in High School - served as Points Chairman; [hon.] Chosen for All-State Choral Clinic during High School and also The Mars Hill Choral Clinic. I had parts in our High School Musicals: Oklahoma, Hello Dolly and Annie Get Your Gun; [oth. writ.] Several unpublished poems, including one entered in another poetry contest with winners to be announced in January. A short story called "When I Remember..." which is a tribute to my grandparents and growing up with them.; [pers.] I write poetry and stories from my heart, things that relate to how I feel. I get in certain creative moods and I must write to get it all out.; [a.] Grover, NC

OLSON, EVELYN C.
[b.] July 13, 1925, Milwaukee, WI; [p.] Lorenzo and Margarita Farino; [m.] Clarence P. Olson, 1950; [ch.] Kathleen Gunta (Three Grandsons) and Jeanette Olson; [ed.] St. Rose of Lima and West Division High School, Milwaukee, WI. Trained as the a Dental Technician at Austenal Laboratories, Chicago, IL; [occ.] Dental Technician and Homemaker; [memb.] International Society of Poets, St. Raphael Catholic Church V.F.W. and American Legion Auxiliaries; [hon.] Editors Choice Award; [oth. writ.] Numerous poems and several humorous children's poems depicting good health and hygiene (Unpublished); [pers.] I am inspired by the writings of the early Greek and I talian poets and philosophers. Some of my poetry reflects my husband's 42 years of Military Service. My children's stories are based on the experiences of my children, nieces, nephews and grandsons.; [a.] Madison, WI

OVERALL, AMITY
[pen.] Bell; [b.] February 7, 1979, New Braunsfels; [p.] John and Betty Overall; [ed.] Senior at San Marcos High School, want to major in psychology or criminology; [memb.] Key Club, Fellowship of Christian Athletes, National Honors Society, Youth Group at First Christian Church; [hon.] Honor student, Who's Who Among H.S. students, Honorable Mention Team in District Volleyball '96, Most Improved Player Volleyball '94, Best Defensive Player Volleyball '95, Yearbook Representative in the Homecoming Court '96; [oth. writ.] Many other poems and short stories, none of which are published yet.; [pers.] My writings are influenced by my life and what I see around me. Some of my poems are not sweet and pretty, because they portray the world as it is. It is up to us to help turn this world around.; [a.] San Marcos, TX

PADAVANO, JERRY
[b.] April 3, 1954, Brooklyn, NY; [p.] Mary and Jerry Sr. Padavano; [m.] Carol Ann Padavano, October 13, 1974; [ch.] Joseph and Jason; [occ.] Director of Hospital Information Services; [memb.] Volunteer at the American Cancer Society; [hon.] Keynote Speaker at National Cancer Survivors Day Celebration of Life on April 21, 1996. Named Honorary Chairman of Annual "Making Strides Against Cancer" event by American Cancer Society.; [oth. writ.] Recently wrote a book about my cancer experience entitled: "The Ultimate Challenge..... Surviving Cancer." Also, have had several poems published by the American Cancer Society and Sun Coast Hospital.; [pers.] I strive to reflect the struggles of those who are bravely fighting cancer in my writings. They are the true heroes in our society.; [a.] Largo, FL

PALA, LISA M.
[pen.] Angel Waters, Kaelyn Phenix; [b.] May 7, 1974, Birmingham, AL; [p.] Mrs. Fran S. Pala; [ed.] Cathedral Christian High, Auburn University, Bachelors of Industrial Design, March 1997; [occ.] Student: Senior at Auburn University; [memb.] 1992-93 Habitat for Humanity, 1996-97 Industrial Designers Student Association; [hon.] 1992 Who's Who Among America's High School Students, History, Science, 1992-93 National Dean's List; [pers.] Elements was inspired by Patrick C., may he fined that nook of sunlight he so richly deserves. 'Learn from the past, make the most of the present and invent the future' - Lisa; [a.] Auburn, AL

PAMIN, DIANA DOLHANCYK
[pen.] Diana Dolhancyk; [b.] December 13, Cleveland, Oh; [p.] Peter Dolhancyk and Diana Dribus Dolhancyk; [m.] Leonard Pamin; [ch.] Diana Anne, Louis Peter; [ed.] Attended West Tech High, Titus College of Cosmetology; [memb.] Interntl. Soc. of Poets (a distinguished member, '95); Poet's Guild; Arthritis Foundation; and has sponsored a young girl in India for the past 16 years.; [hon.] Editor's Choice Awards (from the National Library of Poetry) for outstanding achievement in poetry for the following: "The Parting," "Stormy," "Shadow Side," "Eclipse," "Burnt by Love"; "Love No More," was selected for *Best Poems of 1996* ;"The Happening" was chosen to be in *Best Poems of the '90s*; several poems recorded on "Sound of Poetry"; received "International Poet of Merit Award" from Interntl. Soc. of Poets '95; nominated for "Poet of the Year" in '95 by Interntl. Soc. of Poets; received several awards from Creative Arts and Science Ent. (CAT) for several poems; [oth. writ.] The following poems were published in various anthologies: "Rain," "The Parting," "Letters," "The View," "But Isn't the Flower Lovely?" "Photographer"; also about 200 poems to newlyweds (only a fraction published); [pers.] Always give someone a smile, you never know whose heart you might lighten. Love is the most important thing we can give or receive. I am inspired by many things in life, a gamut of feelings and thoughts in regards to many things.; [a.] North Royalton, OH

PANNELL, IAN C.
[pen.] Silent Wisdom; [b.] March 13, 1971, Washington, DC; [p.] Ray and Dorothy Pannell; [m.] Veronica, June 13, 1996; [ed.] Virginia State University; [occ.] Student; [memb.] Phi Omicron Psi, Fraternity Inc.; [hon.] Dr. Martin Luther King Award 1996 Who's Who Among American Universities.; [a.] Richmond, VA

PARKER, CHARISSE D.
[b.] April 10, 1977, Jackson, AL; [p.] Alfred Donald, Rev. Natalie Wimberly; [m.] Mercury Devon Parker, March 8, 1996; [ch.] Aljavier Ngozi Jahmal; [ed.] Vestavia Hills High School, Lawson State Community College, University of Mobile; [occ.] Full-time student University of Mobile; [memb.] STAND (Students Toward A New Direction), University of Mobile Multi-Cultural Organ; [pers.] My main goal as a writer is to express a view of reality that everyone can understand and relate to.; [a.] Jackson, AL

PARUN, PHYLLIS B.
[b.] November 18, 1941, New Orleans, LA; [p.] Doris Wolters and Bernard Parun; [ed.] John McDough Sr. High, LSU in New Orleans, Howard U., U. of Penn., LSU in BA Ton Rouge; [occ.] Health Educator, Writer-Poet, Artist, Philosopher; [memb.] Am Assoc. U. Women, Am Oriental Bodywork Therapy Assn., Am Macrobiotic Shiatsu Assn; [oth. writ.] Articles in Qi Magazine, Sportslife May. Macrobiotics Today, Macro Net Journal, poetry in Macrobiotics Today.; [pers.] I write about what I experience in life.; [a.] New Orleans, LA

PASTORINO, SUSAN L.
[pen.] Susan Galofaro; [b.] September 29, 1968, Michigan; [p.] Judy Mullins and Sam Galofaro; [m.] Keith A. Pastorino, July 27, 1996; [ed.] Saline High School, Washtenaw Community College; [occ.] Registered Nurse/Orthopedic Survery; [oth. writ.] Many personal journals with poetry.; [pers.] My poetry is created from personal experiences I have had in my life. Living, loving and learning are life's most treasured inspirations.; [a.] Ann Arbor, MI

PATTEN, KIMBERLY E.
[b.] December 8, 1978, Elmira, NY; [p.] Edward Patten, Bonnie Patten; [ed.] Presently a senior attending Elmira Ever Academy High School in Elmira, NY; [occ.] Student; [pers.] I'd like to thank my parents, family and best friend Rachel for their support and encouragement. This poem is my favorite and I was inspired to write it when my close friend moved away. My poetry reflects my life and personal experiences. Poetry says more than any words spoken - you haven't lived until you write.; [a.] Elmira, NY

PAYNE, CLAUDINE
[b.] February 18, 1937; [occ.] Nurse; [a.] Ottumwa, IA

PAYNE, JOSHUA
[b.] April 7, 1983, Cumberland, MD; [p.] Tiffany and Roy Payne; [ed.] Eight grade at Washington Middle School; [hon.] Principal's Honor roll, Student Recognition of maintaining a 4.0 grade average during the year 1995 to 1996; [oth. writ.] Short stories when I was a young child; [pers.] I'd really like to see the world as a better place.; [a.] Cumberland, MD

PAYNE, RUTH Y.
[b.] February 28, 1935, Owensboro, KY; [p.] Gertrude Millay Jones and Julius Jones; [m.] Thomas A. Payne Sr. (Deceased), June 5, 1954; [ch.] Tony, Jerry, Rod, Ken, Cindy Charlotte, Sharon; [ed.] Owensboro Catholic High Owensboro Senior High; [occ.] Retired; [pers.] While visiting New England in the fall of 1988, I was privileged to experience the constante, yet everchanging beauty of this part of the country. I wish to share a glimpse of "October In Vermont"; [a.] Owensboro, KY

PEAVY, RODNEY
[b.] December 13, 1971, Buford, GA; [p.] Grady and Glenda Peavy; [ed.] Associates Degree in Education Truett-McConnel College, Cleveland, GA. Currently Pursuing a Bachelors in Christian Education from Florida Baptist Theological Call.; [occ.] Student; [memb.] International Society, of Poets; [pers.] It is my desire to reflect the grace of God in my writing and in doing so give a portion of the many gifts given me back to his service. To do otherwise is to merely exist.; [a.] Graceville, FL

PEDONE, MARBELLA L.
[pen.] Mary; [b.] December 24, 1951, Coracas, Venezuela; [p.] Luisa Guerrero, Juan Guerrero; [m.] Mario Pedone, April 9, 1976; [ch.] Jennifer Louise, John Peter, Marbella Carmen, Mario Junior; [ed.] Wharton County Junior College, High School, Portland Dregon Elementary School, Valencia Venezuela; [occ.] Student; [memb.] American Heart Association, Texas Department of Human Services, National Marrow Donor Program Cornerstone Assembly of God Church; [hon.] President (Women Support Group) WCJC; [pers.] I strive to reflect the spirit of God in my writing. I have been greatly influenced by the Holy Spirit.; [a.] Sugar Land, TX

PELLEGRINO JR, JOHN
[pen.] John Kaliski; [b.] March 24, Amityville; [p.] John and Jacqueline; [ch.] Jasmine and Autumn; [ed.] Bachelors Degree in Exercise Physiology, GED; [occ.] Writing poems for the love of life; [memb.] National Library of poetry, International Society of Poets. Distinguished member; [hon.] Different poetry awards in various places. Football and weight lifting awards; [oth. writ.] After the storm (from me to you) many gospel writings writing and publications in various poetry books; [pers.] My writings are inspired by a very incredible woman my mother also by a very beautiful young woman aubree maldonado.; [a.] North Lindenhurst, NY

PENNINGTON, ROCHELLE M.
[b.] May 6, 1963, Fond Du Lac, WI; [p.] Norbert and Gloria Serwe; [m.] Leslie E. Pennington, August 27, 1981; [ch.] Nicholas Norbert Pennington, Erica Hollann Pennington; [ed.] Kewaskum High School; [pers.] The poem was written as a gift to my sister-in-law, Sharon.

PEPPER, WALTER A.
[pen.] Walt Pepper; [b.] November 12, 1907, Coshocton, OH; [p.] George and Emma Pepper; [m.] Margaret Pepper (Deceased), August 10, 1926; [ch.] Three; [ed.] 12 years; [occ.] Retired; [hon.] 2 Honorable awards from the Masonic Lodge in Canton, Ohio

PEREZ, ADELA NOEL
[b.] December 29, 1986, Detroit, MI; [p.] Karl Perez, Lori Peterson Perez; [ed.] Angus Elementary School; [occ.] Fourth grade student; [oth. writ.] I have written lots of poems but haven't tried to publish any.; [pers.] I am nine years old, I wrote "Winter's Coming" when I was eight. I live in Sterling Heights, MI, and have three brothers, two sisters, a bird and two dogs. I like to make cards and write poems, read and draw. Sometimes I like to play baseball, when I grow up I want to be a Pediatrician.; [a.] Sterling Heights, MI

PERKINS, RUBY ODOM
[b.] April 6, 1917, NC; [p.] Harrison Odom and Loretty Garner; [m.] Lewis Franklin Perkins; [ch.] Lewis, Jimmie and Tommy; [ed.] Finished High School; [occ.] Retired; [oth. writ.] (1) The Story of Black Ankle, N.C. and People Around About (2) Little Brother Tells It All; [pers.] May the earth be a little bit better by my having lived upon it.; [a.] Darlington, SC

PERRY, KEVIN
[b.] May 20, 1982, Fresno, CA; [p.] Ronald Perry, Laurie Labbitt; [ed.] Currently in High School; [occ.] Student; [pers.] I aspire to be an actor on the silver screen. Acting is just like lying and who's a better lier than me?; [a.] Fresno, CA

PESCATELLO, ROBERTA
[ed.] High School graduate; [occ.] Retired Secretary, gardening, crafts, photography, sewing, reading, writing (Interests); [memb.] Protectors of Animals Associated Humane Societies The Koko Gorilla Foundation ASPCA, Doris Day Animals League; [pers.] In my writings, I would hope to remind people, to appreciate the wondrous beauty of nature, always know kindness to animals, and treasure special memories.

PESTANA, DEBRA L.
[pen.] Debbie Pestana; [b.] December 15, 1970, Springfield, MA; [p.] Edward Balland, Louise Balland; [m.] Antonio Pestana, November 4, 1988; [ch.] Erica, Katelyn, Kelly; [ed.] Only completed 10 years of school, studied Fashion Design. Putnum Voc. High School Springfield Mass; [occ.] Supervisor for cleaning co.; [oth. writ.] I have other poems but never published them. Hope to in the future.; [pers.] I write about personal experiences, it helps me express my inner feeling's about the matter of life. My grandmother is a very big inspiration of my poetry.; [a.] Warwick, RI

PETERSEN, CHRISTOPHER
[pen.] Christopher Michael Mejia-Petersen; [b.] March 3, 1979, Santa Monica, CA; [p.] Carol Petersen and Richard Mejia; [ed.] Currently a Senior in St. Monica High School in Santa Monica; [occ.] Student; [hon.] Honor student; [oth. writ.] Several unpublished poems.; [pers.] I am only 17 years old currently applying to colleges. My personal philosophy is love for the world, yet I still can feel hate.; [a.] Los Angeles, CA

PETERSON, RYAN
[b.] May 8, 1976, Pittsburg, KS; [p.] Robert Peterson and Tracy Powell; [ed.] Hayden High School; [occ.] Student; [oth. writ.] Nothing Published; [pers.] Individual Choice and expression are God's greatest gifts. Don't let them go for not I enjoy reading poets such as Langston Hughes, A.E. Housman and Robert Frost.; [a.] Lawrence, KS

PHILIPS, MELISSA
[b.] August 7, 1967, Hareford, CT; [p.] David Magnon, Placide Althen; [ed.] Hawaii Pacific University; [occ.] Legal Assistant; [a.] Manchester, CT

PHILLIPS, JAMIE DILLON
[pen.] Jamie Dillon Phillips; [b.] July 2, 1964, Honolulu, HI; [p.] James A. and Betty L. Phillips; [ed.] Apache Junction High, U.S. Naval Academy; [occ.] Authorizations Rep. Chase Manhattan Bancard; [memb.] United Way, American Cancer Society; [hon.] Many poem's will be published in an upcoming medaphysical book by author Shane C. McGlothlen; [oth. writ.] The Hermit, Are You My Angel?, Love The Lord Unconditionally, The Difference Between Need And Greed, And I Saw A Man Today; [pers.] In my writings I try to show a spiritual truth in everyday, happenings.; [a.] Mesa, AZ

PHILLIPS, SCOTT EDWARD
[pen.] Scott E. Phillips; [b.] November 3, 1979, Rochester, NY; [p.] Edward J. Phillips, Ruth L. Phillips; [ed.] Arcadia High School 11th grade; [occ.] Student and Lifeguard; [memb.] Science Olympiad Team, Masterminds Team, Alpha Poetry Club, Ski Club, Boy Scout Troop 197, Black Belt Karate Club; [hon.] 1994 Eagle Scout, Science Team Medals - State and Regional competitions; [oth. writ.] Poetry on many subjects and viewpoints.; [pers.] Life is as the River Flows, from the Raging Rapids to a Forest Trickle. Either way, you must follow where it takes you.; [a.] Rochester, NY

PIERCE, JOHN
[pen.] Hugh Porter; [b.] November 30, 1957, Santa Monica, CA; [p.] Frank and Grace Pierce; [m.] Millie Pierce, November 17, 1981; [ch.] Benjamin, Margaret; [ed.] B.S. - U.S. Naval Academy; [occ.] Officer, U.S. Navy; [memb.] Naval Institute; [hon.] Will be published in "Nightfall of Diamonds" for another poem; [oth. writ.] "50 poems and other writings" (in work), "An Affair to Forget" - short story, "Fourth South West" - Short Story; [pers.] Hold on to your friends, feed those relationships. Because at some point in life, they will be all that saves you.; [a.] Orange Park, FL

PIERSON, MAURINE D.
[b.] May 25, 1924, Fort Lyons, Co; [p.] Deceased; [m.] Divorced, February 13, 1943; [ch.] Four - one deceased; [ed.] Business Institute Two college degree in Hotel/Motel Management Two major chains.; [occ.] Retired; [memb.] Church; [hon.] Numerous in Hotel Management for cleanliness costs, green thumb, management, inventory, safety, occupancy, inspections, community work, Hotel/Motel Convention Bureau (etc.) Two major chains national; [oth. writ.] Several but no attempt to publish. Paint in pastel and have gold several pointing have numerous paintings in my home. My poems are personal to me and I've no thought to publish until now.; [pers.] My poem was reduced from 32 lines to 20 for contest rules. Reference to "Billy" is my son killed in Vietnam. My poem was written with a broken hearts a plea and sincerely meant.; [a.] Sun Prairie, WI

PINDUS, JESSE
[b.] August 28, 1981, NY; [ed.] H.S. Student; [oth. writ.] Two poems published in anthology of young poets 1994 and 1995; [a.] Old Brookville, NY

PINO, MARTIN
[b.] July 1, 1982, New Brunswick, NJ; [p.] Mario and Oria Pino; [ed.] John P. Stevens High School, Woodrow Wilson Middle School; [occ.] Student; [hon.] Honors English Class; [pers.] I believe that as individuals, we should seek to perfect ourselves by looking inward past the materialistic desires that ultimately corrupt us.; [a.] Edison, NJ

PIPER, MARGARITA S.
[b.] December 20, 1926, Petersburg, VA; [p.] Guy Lucas and Olga Akers Sherertz; [m.] Glenn Clair Piper, February 3, 1950; [ch.] Mark Stephen Piper and Susan Piper Weathersbee; [ed.] E. C. Glass H.S. (Lynchburg, VA), B.A. in Ed.-Mary Washington College of the Univ. of VA, M.Ed.-UVA, Ed.S.-UVA; [occ.] Retired - Director of Pupil Personnel - Rappahannock County Public Schools - Rappahannock, VA; [memb.] St. Stephen's Episcopal Church, Culpeper, VA, Rappahannock, Virginia and National Education Assns., Life Member - UVA Alumni Assn.; [hon.] Who's Who of American Women 1995-96, Who's Who in The South and Southwest, Who's Who in America, Golden Pen Award - Rap'k. Co. Public Schools, Shenandoah Valley Writer's Guild - 2nd Place Poetry 1991, 1st Place Children's Lit. - 1992, 4th Place Poetry - 1994, Recipient VA Governor's School Commendation; [oth. writ.] Numerous Poems - several published in newspapers, literary magazines and anthologies, several hymns, children's story in literary magazine.; [pers.] It is my personal belief that all people are gifted with talents and special abilities that need to be nourished and used. My feelings are best expressed in the last line of one of my early poems: "My poetry springs not from me but from my love of God."; [a.] Culpeper, VA

PIPER, STEVEN DANIEL
[pen.] S. Daniel Piper; [b.] October 10, 1942, Bronx, NY; [p.] Rose Wheeler, William Piper (Deceased); [m.] Kathryn Piper, August 29, 1965; [ch.] Alice Piper,

Ethan Piper; [ed.] B.A at Lawrence University; [occ.] Computer Consultant

PLAZA, MONIQUE M.
[pen.] Bubbles; [b.] May 31, 1976, Bronx, NY; [p.] Denise Jenne; [ed.] Hugh C. Williams High School; [occ.] Former College Student at C.C.T. in Canton, New York; [pers.] I would like to say thanks to Melissa Ames for encouraging me to send this out and see. I owe the thanks and thought to her. Thanks.; [a.] Canton, NY

PLEIL, NADINE
[pen.] Nadine Moonje Pleil; [b.] February 17, 1932, Birmingham, England; [p.] Badel Rao Moonje and Maude Elizabeth Moonje; [m.] Augusto Pleil, October 3, 1952; [ch.] 8 children; [ed.] 2 years college; [occ.] Secretary for The Soil Conservation Service; [oth. writ.] My book "Free from Bondage" was published July 1994 by the Pergrine Foundation, Carrier Pigeon Press Publisher; Ramon Sender; [pers.] I am very honored that my poetry has been accepted and published by the National Library of Poetry. Thank you.; [a.] Washington, PA

PLEZ, DOMINIQUE
[b.] April 3, 1977, Memphis, TN; [p.] Mary Sidney, Jerome Sidney; [ch.] Alexis Gray, Desiree Robinson; [ed.] Sheffield High; [occ.] Working

PORTER, MALTA SUE
[b.] March 30, 1920, Bonanza, KY; [p.] Caleb Sherman and Martha L. May; [m.] Bert Newton Porter, September 22, 1940; [ch.] Madelyn Sue (P.) Burchett; [ed.] Year 12; [occ.] Housewife; [memb.] Cow Creek Freewill, Baptist Church; [oth. writ.] Many other poems only read in - church and family.; [pers.] I've always loved to draw and make poems. Bert and I wrote poems to each at school. I have a grand daughter and a nephew who are artists.; [a.] Prestonsburg, KY

PORTER, PATRICIA V.
[pen.] Patricia Van Megroot; [p.] Jules and Kathryn Van Megroot; [m.] William Samuel Porter; [ch.] Christopher William Porter; [ed.] M.S. So. CT Univ., Bucknell Univ.; [occ.] Poet; [memb.] Shoreline Poetry Group-CT; [hon.] Poetry readings; [a.] Bonita Springs, FL

POSTLER, RACHEL A.
[b.] May 15, 1985, Frederic, WI; [p.] Jeffrey and Rhonda Postler; [ed.] 6th grade; [occ.] Student; [memb.] Adventure Club and Magic Attic Club; [hon.] Little Miss Webster 1991, 1st prize drawing contest, Drama Rama, solos; [oth. writ.] Creative writing awards for past five years.; [pers.] Do my very best in life and serve the Lord. I love to write poetry and enjoy reading. Someday I hope to be a geologist.; [a.] Webster, WI

POSTON, BEVERLY A.
[b.] April 15, 1963, Lancaster, OH; [p.] Earl and Zelda Seitz; [m.] Carl D. Poston, September 8, 1979; [ch.] Carl David Jr., Shauna De Laine; [ed.] Attended Lancaster High School, however graduated through the G.E.D program 1996; [occ.] Cook for Friendly Sixties at Faith Memorial Church in Lancaster, Ohio; [pers.] The world is what each one of us makes it, which is why we should consider how out actions affect people around us, as future generations will imitate what they have seen in us. May God be with all of us.; [a.] Lancaster, OH

POWERS SR., ROBERT
[pen.] Crazy Bob; [b.] May 24, 1934, Quincy, IL; [p.] Russell and Naomi Powers; [m.] Shirley Ann Powers, April 18, 1953; [ch.] Doris, Robert Jr., Lewis, Brenda; [ed.] Quincy Senior High (Quincy), Emerson Grade School (Quincy); [occ.] Disabled - retired; [memb.] Calvary Tabernacle Church; [pers.] This poem was

written about Sonny G. who was my sponsor in A.A. after he passed away Nov. 25, 1990. I was inspired to write this about him. He was a big influence to me.; [a.] Lockport, IL

PRATT, CAROLYN C.
[b.] February 7, 1925, Glen Cove, NY; [p.] James H. Cooke, Sallie D. Cooke (Deceased); [m.] Charles Pratt Jr., September 9, 1951; [ch.] Gwen, Sue, Charles III; [ed.] BA Virginia State College (now Univ.) M.Ed. University of Texas, El Paso (Glen Cove Elementary, Jr. High, High School); [occ.] Retired Elem. Teacher VIPS (Volunteer in Public Schools); [memb.] St. Paul's United Meth. Church, AAUW (American Assoc. of Univ. Women), Alpha Kappa Alpha Sorority, Center for Lifelong Learning, Utep formerly other many organizations.; [hon.] 1987: "Salute to Black Women" awardee by Delta Sigma Theta Sorority, 1989: "Excellence in Teaching" (Top 10 Teachers) by El Paso Independent School District (EPISD), 1992: Plaque, Outstanding Service by EPISD upon retirement, 1993 to 1994: VIPS Award for Outstanding Service El Paso, TX; [oth. writ.] "Profiles" Editor (biographical sketches of Ft. Knox, KY. O.W.C. officers in Elizabethtown, KY newspaper, late 60's, early 70's) Editor of "Beaumont Buzzins" (Wm. Beaumont Army Med. El Paso, TX Ctr's Women's Club Newspaper, Early 1970's) Essays (published in college paper, VA State Coll.); [pers.] As a result of attending classes in journaling at the Center for Lifelong Learning at the University of Texas at El Paso I am writing my memoirs possibly for publishing but mainly for family - children, grand and great grand.; [a.] El Paso, TX

PRICE, MICHELLE ROSE POPPERWILL
[b.] December 28, 1973, Key West, FL; [p.] Linda O'Brien and Walter Popperwill Jr.; [m.] Gregory Allen Price Jr., October 9, 1993; [ch.] Gregory "Allen" Price III (Deceased) and Victoria Rose Price; [ed.] Elementary at Fred Anderson. Graduated at Pamlico County High School in 1991. Attended Pamlico Community College.; [occ.] Housewife and mother; [oth. writ.] I have written many poems, though unpublished.; [pers.] I believe writing should come from real life experienced, and from the heart to mean anything.; [a.] Grantsbcro, NC

PRICE, WILLIE D.
[b.] August 17, 1937, Oxford, MS; [p.] Bolivar and Ida Price; [m.] Yvonne, November 6, 1965; [ch.] Quentin, Willie, Leshaun, Rochelle, Dykema; [ed.] Mississippi Educational System Illinois Education System, Chrysler/ UAW. Educational System; [occ.] Torque Convertor Operator; [memb.] AARP, BMI, Clergy St. Paul Missionary Baptist Church; [hon.] Song writer of the year, Elma and Carl's music publishers 1972, song writer award (Trumpetletts). 1992 Leadership Award Walker and Associates; [oth. writ.] Songs for the littlejohn brothers of Dayton, Ohio Williams Chapel Male Chorus of Detroit, MI Trumpetletts of Detroit, MI New Jerusalem Inspirationals of Detroit, MI; [pers.] I have always been inspired to write poems, music and plays through what I see, hear and feel around me, when I'm requested to write for some one, all I have ever needed was the occasion or purpose.; [a.] Detroit, MI

PRIEST, TAMMY
[b.] March 4, 1973, NC; [m.] Daneil, December 27, 1989; [ch.] Jason, Christopher; [ed.] High School Grad.; [occ.] Wife and homemaker; [oth. writ.] Poem "Puppy Love"; [pers.] Keep going!; [a.] Sanford, NC

PRINGLE, VINCENT J.
[pen.] J'Star; [b.] March 31, 1964, New York City; [ed.] High School Diploma, Studied Art and Dance; [occ.] Artist/Writer Freelance; [hon.] High School Art Achievement Award/Editor's Choice Award for Po-

etry; [oth. writ.] Poem published in "Of Sunshine And Day Dreams"; [pers.] This poem is lovingly dedicated to all the mothers and children of the world and a very special mother Virginia Pringle.

PULKOWSKI, MARGARET
[pen.] P. J. Marks; [b.] June 21, 1944, Queens, NY; [p.] Joseph and Catherine Shepard; [m.] Stephen Pulkowski, February 28, 1976; [ch.] Laurie, grandchild Stephen; [ed.] Flushing High, American School of Chicago; [occ.] Retired - Motel N. H. Entrepreneur Henniker, NH; [memb.] Perinton Community Center, Disabled American Veterans Commanders Club, American Indian Heritage Foundation, several Animal Leagues; [hon.] National Republican Congressional Committee Awards Certificates Reagan/Bush Administrations, Certificate of Leadership American Indian Heritage Foundation; [pers.] I dedicate this poem to my mother who so lovingly encouraged me and greatly influenced my life.; [a.] Fairport, NY

PUNJABI, MADHU
[b.] August 27, 1985, Miami, FL; [p.] Ashok and Kusum Punjabi; [occ.] A 6th grade student in Herbert Hoover J. R. High; [pers.] My English teacher inspired me during English class and my parents were with me all the way. My best friend Shibani also helped me out.; [a.] Edison, NJ

PURDY, BEVERLY JEAN
[pen.] Beverly Jean, Stupke-Purdy; [b.] March 13, 1940, Cortland, NY; [p.] Gilbert R. Stupke and Daisy Anna Casterline-Stupke; [m.] Divorced; [ch.] Lynne M. Illsley, Lori J. Barton, Richard M. Purdy, and 8 grandchildren; [ed.] Tully Central High School, Delhi Tech. (S.U.N.Y) various workshops, seminars, conferences, and life itself; [occ.] Senior Office Typist - NYS Unified Court System - Family Court, Johnstown, NY; [memb.] Northville Baptist Church, Volunteer - Community Outreach Programs; [hon.] Insignificant; [oth. writ.] I have written many articles and poetry pertaining to my own stages of life and of events of significance in the lives of friends and family. My love letters prior to my marriage were poetry writings. This is my fourth poem published.; [pers.] ...That perhaps my experience, my strength, will be my gift of hope to others. It is not just to survive, but to truly experience life itself, may my writing convey this!; [a.] Gloversville, NJ

PURSELL, RON
[b.] January 14, 1943, Youngstown, OH; [p.] Robert and Margaret; [m.] Donna, April 6, 1963; [ch.] Three sons - Mike (32), Rob (29), Keith (26); [ed.] B.S. University of FL; [occ.] Horticulture Teacher 31 Years; [memb.] Plantation United Methodist Church

PYRTLE, ELSIE B.
[b.] February 23, 1914, Pittsville Co, VA; [ed.] 7th grade; [occ.] Retired housewife; [oth. writ.] Several other poems and one song; [a.] Danville, VA

QUAM, HOWARD
[pen.] H. Q.; [b.] July 1, 1922, San Diego; [p.] Homer and Marie Quam; [ch.] Five; [ed.] AB and MA Art San Diego State University; [occ.] Retired Teacher Artist - Sculptor; [memb.] Ventura Art Assoc. Ventura, Calif; [hon.] Numerous awards in Art Exhibits local; [oth. writ.] Southwest Art Magazine; [pers.] I've always been interested in poetry esp frost, service.; [a.] Ventura, CA

QUINN, DARLENE
[pen.] Darlene Whitesel-Quinn; [b.] April 29, 1968, Seoul, S. Korea; [p.] Darrell and Mary Whitesel; [m.] Gary J. Quinn, January 15, 1989; [ch.] Christina Michelle; [ed.] Pendleton Heights High School; [occ.] Mother/Housewife; [pers.] I thank God for the gift of writing! I, also, thank family and friends for believing

in me and my work. Special thanks to Gary, Tomi, Bob and Jeff (you know me better than anyone else!). Without my life experiences, relationships and wisdom from Jesus Christ through Holy Spirit, none of this could've happened. Thanks!; [a.] Anderson, IN

RAHMAN, MOINUR
[pen.] Moin; [b.] May 20, 1965, India; [p.] Mujibur Rahman, Zaheera Rahman; [m.] Nafees Rahman, July 22, 1990; [ch.] Sumayah Rahman; [ed.] B. E. in Mech. Eng. from PSG Tech., Coimbatore, India; [occ.] M. S. Degree Student in Industrial Eng. at Suny, Buffalo; [memb.] Human Factors Engineering and Ergonomics Society; [oth. writ.] Essay: What Happened To America?, published in, 'Spectrum' Suny, Buffalo Newspaper.; [pers.] The seeds of wrath-race and religion sown by man in the name of God, will destruct mankind in full bloom.; [a.] Buffalo, NY

RAHMAN, NAINAMOHAMED ABDUL
[b.] December 8, 1942, Mudukulattur, India; [p.] Nainamohamed, Kaderammal; [m.] Fathima Rahman, May 24, 1971; [ch.] Zahirhussain, Abdulkader, Rafeeq; [ed.] Ies Khalsa High School, Rangoon, New College, Madras, Stanley Medical College, Madras, Case Western Reserve University Hospital, Cleveland, Ohio; [occ.] Otolaryngologist at 1120 W La Palma #16 Anaheim, CA 92801; [oth. writ.] Few poems in local magazines.; [pers.] I try to reflect the human behavior with rhyming words in all four lines.; [a.] Anaheim, CA

RAHNER, COLLEEN KRYMSKI
[b.] December 7, 1956, Pittsburgh, PA; [p.] Andrew Krymski, Marry Ann Krymski; [m.] Terry Rahner, May 26, 1996; [ch.] Step children - Michelle, Jason, Scott; [ed.] Leechburg Elementary School, Leechburg High School, Carlow College - Graduate 1981; [occ.] Childcare/Navy; [hon.] Bachelor of Arts degree in Communications and Theatre Arts; [oth. writ.] Continued work on poems not reviewed by anyone or published at this time.; [pers.] As an only child, I would like to dedicate my poem in honor of my father Andrew W. Krymski - born August 16, 1914 and died May 13, 1995. Also my mother Mary Ann McCullough-Krymski born November 20, 1923- Belfast Ireland Representing an Alzheimers patient.; [a.] Natrona Heights, PA

RAINEY, FELICIA DENISE
[pen.] Nickey; [b.] March 6, 1961, Chester; [p.] Robert Rainey Sr. and Diane Granger; [ch.] Paul P. Leonhardt III/James W. Shelton; [ed.] Great Falls High; [occ.] Springs; [memb.] The National Park; [hon.] Editor's Choice Award from the National Library of Poetry; [oth. writ.] A poem published in Great Falls News Paper; [pers.] I strive to send messages to the love one's that has lost a love one to the next world. Beyond an over the rainbow! So that they can feel the warmth of love once again!; [a.] Kershaw, SC

RAMETSI, SIPHIWE
[pen.] Zukkie Mguni; [b.] May 28, 1960, Botswana, Africa; [p.] Esther Mguni; [ed.] Applied Associate of Science: Communication, Diploma in Education (Africa); [occ.] Assistant Teacher Special Education; [memb.] National Association of Black Storyteller; [hon.] Dean's List; [oth. writ.] The Friendship Doll Stories: A collection of childhood stories from Botswana; [pers.] A Voice of a Singing Flower: A title for my collection of poetry. I am like a flower, a red poppy. Bright, everybody can see me but they don't understand me. But once I open up my red petals, the powdery, flowery pollen or my poems shimmers out to reveal my inner soul, my trials and tribulations of my life as an immigrant woman. I am singing to appease my ancestors and to celebrate my new life in America. I am inspired by Paul Robeson's interview of 1930, I quote, the talents of an artist, small or great, are God given.

They've nothing to do with the private person, they're nothing to be proud of. They're just a sacred trust... having been given, I must give. Man shall not live by bread alone, and what the farmer does I must do. I must feed the people - with my songs.; [a.] Mount Vernon, NH

RAMOS, AGUSTIN M.
[pen.] Agustin M. Ramos; [b.] September 2, 1934, Jala Nayarit, Mexico; [p.] Pablo Ramos, Refugio M. Aguilar; [m.] Nellie Ramos, December 11, 1993; [ch.] Paul Ramos; [ed.] Graduate Philosophy and Letters, Montezuma Seminary S. J., Montezuma, New Mexico; [occ.] Designer; [hon.] State Scholarship Nayarit-Mexico, International Scholarship Society Jesuita New Mexico (Society of Jesuita); [oth. writ.] Spanish magazines; [pers.] Inspiration is everywhere shining in our faces. Nature, people, you and I - what more do we need - to sing and write to express our hearts and mind. A.M.R.; [a.] Pebble Beach, CA

RAMSDELL, LEIGH
[pen.] Leigh Ramsdell; [b.] June 4, 1956, Maine; [p.] Julie Ray, Ralph Ramsdell; [m.] Ann Rousseau Ramsdell, August 28, 1996; [ch.] Leigh Ramsdell Jr., Sierra Dawn Ramsdell, Nicholas Rousseau; [occ.] Production Mgr. Dumont Metal Fabrication, Monmouth, Maine; [pers.] My poem is dedicated to the strength of my wife and children during Ann's coma, and rehabilitation as a result of a serious auto accident in August of 93. I love them deeply.; [a.] Sabattus, ME

RANDALL, ALUERTA H.
[pen.] Ebone Queen; [b.] February 11, 1937, Hanover, MD; [p.] Clifton and Pauline Hebron; [ch.] Myreda K. Randall; [ed.] Wiley H. Bates High, University of Maryland; [occ.] Histology Technician; [memb.] NAACP, MCEA - St. Mark UMC, Frank and Edgar Sewell Liturgical Soc.; [oth. writ.] Published in church newsletter.; [pers.] God is much better to me than I am to myself. He is my light and my salvation and I strive to please always.; [a.] Severn, MD

RANDAZZO, ANNA
[b.] September 5, 1924, Cheyenne, WY; [p.] Vick and Frances Randazzo - Dec'd; [ed.] 12 years; [occ.] None - retired I am in a rest home now; [oth. writ.] This was my first poem. I was a working women in my brother grocery, for 48 years now I am the rest home because I've been suffering with arthritis for 25 years.; [pers.] I am in a rest home. Also I have been handicapped all my life the last 25 years I have been suffering with rheumatoid arthritis. I am in the golden years rest home for over 1 year.; [a.] Marlin, TX

RAPANOS, GEORGE
[b.] March 29, 1933, Chicago, IL; [p.] Alex and Nicoletta; [m.] Sue, November 23, 1962; [ch.] Alex, Ruth, Laura, Angela, Jonas; [ed.] Bachelor of Science degree in Pharmacy from Ferris University, Masters Degree in Religious Studies from New York, University N.Y.U.; [occ.] Retired; [hon.] Fraternal Order of Eagles, Award of Merit - for his contribution in saving a life; [oth. writ.] Two books. 1. In Search of the Hidden Treasure "The Pearl of Great Worth" ISBN #0-9634591-0-4 and 2. The Tao of Tribute Money ISBN #0-9634591-1-2 Distributor National Book Network on Ingram; [pers.] Faith, the staff and strength of life, is the conviction of things unseen. The steps of faith fall on the seeming void, but find the rock beneath.; [a.] Naples, FL

RATHEY, WINSTON DARRYL
[pen.] Poetic Suspect; [b.] January 27, 1967, Chicago, IL; [p.] Winston Barry Rathey, Diann Rathey; [ed.] Holy Angels School, Saint Rita High School, Texas Southern University; [occ.] Sales Associate; [memb.] Wisconsin Sleepers Inc.; [oth. writ.] Numerous poems

written, but none published until now.; [pers.] I never took my poetry seriously until recently. Writing was always my outlet for alleviating stress, as well as initiating interest from others, my greatest single influence in creative writing is Maya Angelou.; [a.] Houston, TX

RAY, RENEE
[b.] July 5, 1982, Harlan, KY; [p.] Brenda and Kenneth Ray; [ed.] I am in 9th grade at George Washington Junior High School; [occ.] Student; [hon.] Michael Colligan Foundation honorable mention, 3rd prize in the Citywide Science Fair - 1993, Honors Student - Straight A's; [a.] Hamilton, OH

RAY, TINA MARIE
[pen.] Teen; [b.] July 21, 1964, Princeton, WV; [p.] Howard and Betty Jane Sifford; [m.] Gary Eugene Ray, April 6, 1991; [ch.] Ricky Lee Ray; [ed.] Graduated June 1983 from De Haure Grace Sr. High School. Child Psychology course at International Correspondence School; [occ.] Stay at home mom "neighborhood Nanny"; [memb.] I belong to Antioch Baptist Church in Haure De Grace Maryland. "A lighthouse in our community."; [oth. writ.] I have written 101 poems of Christian poetry and am in the process to copyright "Divine Inspirations" Open-Heart poetry. The Lord Is My True Inspiration.; [pers.] My poems reflect the true inner feelings, emotions, and thoughts inspired by our savior Jesus Christ. For the holds my tomorrow, and in Him there is abundant life.; [a.] Conowingo, MD

RECONOSE, RICARDO
[pen.] Rick; [b.] February 10, 1960, Philippines; [p.] Roberto and Juliana Reconose; [m.] Erlinda Reconose, January 3, 1980; [ch.] Erick and Rachelle Reconose; [ed.] Far Eastern University, Manila, Philippines; [occ.] Distribution Supervisor; [hon.] Dean's List; [oth. writ.] "Life", a poem published in an International Magazine.; [pers.] Life: The beginning, the fulfilment and the end, then finally comes our blessed hope which is to see our Saviour, the Almighty God - that will be the glory of it all!; [a.] Santa Clara, CA

REDDEN, PRINCESS
[b.] May 19, 1981, New Orleans; [p.] Darlene Redden, Georgselery; [pers.] My name is Princess Redden, I am 14 years old and I live in Natchez MS. I have 1 brother, I am in the 9th Grade and I attend school at Natchez High. My goal is to finish High School and hopefully get a scholarship.; [a.] Natchez, MS

REDMOND, ANGELA
[b.] May 12, 1972, Rockville, CT; [p.] Alfred Redmond, Lynn Redmond; [ch.] Breanna Lyndsay; [ed.] Tolland High School, Tolland CT; [occ.] Machine Operator; [oth. writ.] Won second place in 1989 contest held by Univ. of CT. Several poems published in high school paper 1986-1990; [pers.] Writing has been my way to relay how I feel. I usually keep my feelings locked inside. "A Poet's Tribute" is a very important poem that I dedicate to my late brother Donald Mark Redmond.; [a.] Arkadelphia, AR

REDMOND JR., PAUL MARTIN
[b.] March 23, 1951, Palmdale, CA; [p.] Ida Lewis and Paul Martin; [ch.] Kennith Martin - Gregory Martin - Robert Martin - Joshua Martin - Jonathan Martin; [ed.] Palmdale High - Calif. 1969; [occ.] Disabled; [oth. writ.] "Hope For A Vietnam Vet" - "Who Am I" - "Rat-A-Tat-Tat"; [pers.] My poems reflect the cruel ways. Mankind treats each other, with hopes that it will make my readers stop and think.; [a.] Bakersfield, CA

REECE, DAVID N.
[b.] September 27, 1957, New York, NY; [p.] Miriam Reece; [m.] Sherry Williams Reece, September 3, 1983; [ch.] Dione Elizabeth, David Nathaniel II; [ed.] Devry

Tech Inst.; [occ.] Marketing Manager Lucent Technologies (formally ater); [memb.] The Alliance of Black Lucent Employees (Able), Project Management Inst. (PMI); [hon.] U.S. Patent, President the Alliance of Black Lucent Employees South FL. Chapter, Deacon - Holiness Temple Church, FL; [a.] Coral Springs, FL

REEVES, DERRICK D.
[pen.] Divinere D. Davis; [b.] October 27, 1965, Pensacola, FL; [p.] Hasten and Bessie Davis; [m.] Lailaa S. Reeves, October 27, 1989; [ch.] Makalaa S. Reeves; [ed.] John D. Shoop. Elementary, graduated 1989, Morgan Park H.S. graduated 1984, Columbia College attended 2 years 1990-91; [occ.] Environmental Specialist; [hon.] Awarded employee of the month at Christ Hospital and Medical Center.; [oth. writ.] Currently working on a book of poetry, some included are (titles) (Scared) (Lord Teach Me) (Beautiful Duet) (Forever In Our Hearts).; [pers.] You have a gift your blessed. Your givin a talent, you must share it. There's always a chance you'll touch someone reach inside your heart and give a little of yourself.; [a.] Chicago, IL

REFENES, JAMIE MICHELLE
[b.] June 11, 1986, Asheville, NC; [p.] Tom and Kim Refenes; [ed.] Etowah Elementary School (K-4th), Hendersonville Elementary School (5th grade); [hon.] AB Honor Roll (10 times), Awarded 6th Degree Blue Belt in Tae Kwon Do - Karate, Terrific Kid - Twice EES, Science Award - 4th Grade; [oth. writ.] Stories and other poems written for school newspapers; [pers.] I have a loving and supportive family always by my side. I love them very much.; [a.] Hendersonville, NC

REGGIO, VICTORIA
[b.] July 6, 1954, Brooklyn, NY; [p.] Emil and Anne Reggio; [ed.] Fashion Institute of Technology Degree in Advertising and Communications; [occ.] Advertising Department for a National Magazine; [oth. writ.] Currently working on a collection of essays and short stories about New York women.; [pers.] For several years I pursued on acting career but never abandoned writing. It just seemed easier to look at the world as a character, rather than chronicler.; [a.] New York, NY

REICHNER, PHILIP D.
[pen.] William Paige; [b.] June 12, 1973, Philadelphia, PA; [p.] Philip Reichner, Kathleen Reichner; [ed.] Holy Ghost Prep, Duquesne University; [occ.] Marketing Administrator, American Arbitration Association, Pittsburgh, PA; [pers.] An inactive mind is the catalyst for death. In my writings, I seek to force mankind to use their heads in a capacity more worthy than that of a hat rack.; [a.] Pittsburgh, PA

REID, BARBARA B.
[b.] July 17, 1940, Chesnee, SC; [p.] Mr. and Mrs. Dewey B. Blanton; [m.] Dr. Samuel D. Reid Jr.; [ch.] 3 daughters, 1 son; [ed.] BA Elementary Ed. Limestone College, Gaffney, SC; [occ.] Homemaker (former Elementary Teacher); [hon.] Poetry published in several anthologies; [pers.] Self-expression through creative writing is a legacy that I wish to leave for my children, a useful tool to give meaning to our everyday lives.; [a.] Chesnee, SC

RENAUD, VIDA
[pen.] ZOH; [b.] November 22, 1952, New York; [p.] Adopted; [m.] Divorced, September 1982 thru August 1989; [ch.] Two children (One Deceased); [ed.] High school, hair dressing school, Wilfred Academy; [occ.] Receptionist Jacobson and Mermelstein; [hon.] H.S. Diploma, Hair Dressers License, Hair Dressers Diploma; [pers.] I'd like to leave my writings to others, now and after I'm gone. I've been influenced by my own tragedies and by other poets, such as Pablo Neruda.

Such passion! I'm also a grandmother of a 9 year old girl.; [a.] Astoria, NY

RENO, GREGORY J.
[b.] December 1, 1964, Knoxville, TN; [p.] Ray and Jane Reno; [m.] Lisa C. Reno, August 24, 1964; [pers.] I thank God for the gift of Salvation and for blessing me with a wonderful family. My beautiful wife Lisa, dad and mom have been the inspiration for what I write. What more could a person ask?; [a.] Loudon, TN

RENY, SHERRI
[b.] July 26, 1974, Wellsville, NY; [p.] Marilynn Reny and Rick Reny; [ed.] High school; [oth. writ.] I have finished a poetry book called "She".; [pers.] I need a publisher! It's hard to get a job with a physical handicap. So, if I could get a publisher, I could work at home and contribute to the family.; [a.] Gibsonton, FL

RESPASS, SHANNAH
[b.] February 6, 1981, Baltimore, MD; [p.] Daisy Respass; [ed.] Student - 10th grade Milford Mill Academy; [a.] Randallstown, MD

REYNERTSON, THEIS
[b.] June 13, 1907, Norway; [m.] Eleanor Florence Reynertson, August 28, 1937; [ch.] Rev. Richard Theis Reynertson; [ed.] 2 years of high school in Norway, graduated from public evening school in Chicago and 3 years at Wasburn Trade school in Chicago; [occ.] Retired; [memb.] Maple Ridge Evangelical Free Church, Gideon's International, Charter Member of LeTourneau College; [hon.] Terra Sancta Good Neighbor Medal, The Shaloam Diploma from the Israeli Tourist Office; [oth. writ.] Several poems published by the Lutheran Messenger of Truman, MN; [pers.] You get nothing for nothing - If you want to be successful you have to work hard; [a.] Truman, MN

REYNOLDS, ELIZABETH STUART
[b.] June 29, 1975, Alexandria, VA; [ed.] St. Andrew's School, Cornell University; [pers.] I have grown to be a writer, and I thank Tad Roach for his early nurturing. Life inspires me to write, but only my strength encourages me to translate feelings into words. In memory of Jon.; [a.] Ithaca, NY

REYNOLDS, LILLIE A.
[pen.] Maribeth May; [b.] March 30, 1936, Atlanta, GA; [p.] Martha E. and Cecil W. Scoggins; [m.] Roy Douglas Reynolds, July 2, 1955; [ch.] Danny Michael, Jeffrey Scott, Christopher Kerry; [ed.] 12th grade - High School; [occ.] Quality Control/Billing Coordinator for Standard Telephone Co.; [memb.] H.M. Stewart, Sr. Telephone Pioneer Club, First Baptist Church Cleveland, GA; [hon.] Past President of Bruce Williams Future Pioneer Club; [oth. writ.] I draw greeting cards and the verses are penned especially for the recipient.; [pers.] "The Heart Shaped Stone" was created from true experience. The words were given, as all I write, from the greatest creator of all. I have the heart shaped stone in a small ceramic basket on my bookshelf.; [a.] Cleveland, GA

RHODEN, REBECCA
[pen.] Rebecca Rhoden; [b.] June 4, 1942, Springfield, MO; [p.] W. E. Parker and Lois M. Parker; [m.] Kenneth W. "Kay" Rhoden (Deceased), December 29, 1968; [ch.] Lisa Annette Rhoden and Gregory Alan Rhoden; [ed.] BS Ed. Southwest Missouri State University; [occ.] Insurance Executive; [memb.] International Society of Poets, Member of Baptist Church; [hon.] Three poems published by The National Library of Poetry; [oth. writ.] "Kevin's Stance" and "Ode To Little Granny", "B". Working on short story for a screen play.; [pers.] I like to look for and express the beauty of life and I think that writing stories and poetry

are a good way to record memories and to release feelings.; [a.] Springfield, MO

RICE, PATRICIA A. JONES
[b.] South Bend, IN; [p.] Rossevelt Jones and Lois Jones; [m.] James Rice, June 17, 1988; [ch.] Adrain; [ed.] I graduated from John Adams High School; [occ.] Nursing; [pers.] In dedication to my parents who are deceased. Who always said the world waits on no one. And my husband and son who believe in my poetry and said keep writing.; [a.] Orlando, FL

RICH, LISA
[b.] February 27, 1979, Helena, MT; [p.] Darrell and Joyce Rich; [ed.] Buffalo High School; [occ.] Student, attending 11th grade; [memb.] A certified Scuba Diver, Explorer post 104; [oth. writ.] "Love Hurts", "The Dance", "Friends Forever", "To The One I Love", "From Ear To Ear", "The Unlocked Door", and "The World Today".; [pers.] Love is very tricky, its not really what it seems. So let go of your man and hang onto your dreams. This saying has often helped me along the path of life.; [a.] Buffalo, WY

RICHARDS, PRISCILLA
[pen.] Susie; [b.] May 20, 1947, Clinton, TN; [p.] Carl and Vicla Smith; [m.] Roger L. Richards, October 7, 1990; [ch.] Pamela Stokes and Angela Stokes, 1 granddaughter-Brittany Denise; [ed.] Clinton High School, Tennessee College of Automation, Dekalb Beauty College; [occ.] Jr. Title Clerk; [oth. writ.] Other poems none published; [pers.] The poems I have written have been the result of dramatic events in my life and meaningful relationships, not putting asiche the facts of God's love and guidance above all.; [a.] Conyers, GA

RIPKA, SOPHIA M.
[b.] November 17, 1912, Oriskany, NY; [p.] Edward and Lena Herthum; [m.] John W. Ripka, September 23, 1944; [ch.] Richard J. Ripka; [ed.] Oriskany High School, Geneseo Normal School; [occ.] Retired (former teacher); [memb.] Eastern Star Chapter 524, Retired Teachers Assoc., Waterbury Memorial Presbyterian Church; [hon.] High School Valedictorian; [oth. writ.] A book of poems and writings that I had printed.; [pers.] I taught first grade for 33 years in the Whitesboro and Oriskany Central School Districts.; [a.] Oriskany, NY

RISPO JR., THOMAS A.
[b.] December 14, 1980, Philadelphia, PA; [p.] Thomas A. Sr. and Eileen M. Rispo; [ed.] Special Education Student Valley Day Private School, Morrisville, PA; [occ.] Student; [memb.] Yun's Marital Arts Academy; [hon.] Most Outstanding Student Martial Arts, Award of Appreciation M/A, MA Completion of Belts, 1st Place Science fair age 6; [a.] Bensalem, PA

ROBERTS, AMY D.
[pen.] Amy Roberts; [b.] February 20, 1985, Worcester, MA; [p.] Paul and Wendy Roberts; [ed.] Currently a 6th grade student at Hopkinton Middle School; [occ.] Student; [memb.] A member of Student Council. A member of Congregational Church Jr. High Youth Group Westborough. Band Member (flute); [hon.] High Honor Student; [oth. writ.] None Published; [pers.] This poem is dedicated to my grandmother, Jeanne Goodall, whom I loved very much. "My Gran"; [a.] Hopkinton, MA

ROBERTS, JEFF
[b.] July 18, 1976, Maryville, TN; [p.] Tony Roberts; [ed.] Maryville High School, Student at University of Tennessee, Knoxville; [a.] Knoxville, TN

ROBERTSON, MARIAN
[pen.] Chas Kowoo Tla; [b.] September 11, 1943, Juneau, AK; [p.] Marian Robertson; [m.] Cal Robertson, 1943; [ed.] 13 1/2 yrs.; [occ.] Artists; [memb.] South Whidbey Artist Assoc., Greenbank Artist Assoc., NW Watercolor Assoc., NW Pastel Society; [oth. writ.] Poem "Death Visits", Poetic Voices of America, Summer 1996; [pers.] I am an Alaskan Native (Tlingit); [a.] Seattle, WA

ROBINSON, FRANK S.
[b.] April 6, 1929, Louisa, KY; [p.] Roland Robinson, Malinda Robinson; [m.] Esther Romero, 1958 (Divorced 1971); [ch.] Jennifer, Gregory; [ed.] Marshall Univ. 1949-1952 George Washington Univ. 1952-1955, George Washington Univ. 1964-1966; [occ.] International Petroleum Engineer - Retired; [memb.] Sons of American Revolution (SAR), Aircraft Owners and Pilots Assoc. (AOPA), National Rifle Assoc. (NRA); [hon.] Licences: Registered Professional Engineer Commercial Pilot; [pers.] Most pain is self-imposed. I have been hopelessly influenced by the Malcontents and Misfits, ne'er-do-wells and Nitwits that I have worked with in the oil fields of South America and the Middle East.; [a.] Bowie, MD

ROBINSON, GWENDOLYN
[b.] September 3, 1948, Los Angeles, CA; [p.] Lillie Matthews, Eddie Matthews (Deceased); [m.] Divorced from Leonard Robinson, September 5, 1965 married, 1978 divorced; [ch.] Michelle Robinson, 2 grandsons Arthur and Brandon; [ed.] Thomas Jefferson High, La City College, La Trade Tech College West Los Angeles, College, MTI Business College; [occ.] Office Administrative Assistant, Caltrans, State of California; [memb.] Beta Pi Sigma Sorority, American Legion Veterans of America, Southern League Alumni Association; [hon.] Danforth Award; [oth. writ.] Have written several poems that have not been published at this present time.; [pers.] I strive to express feelings felt by all women in the world. I use my personal experience as an influential tool for expressions in my poems.; [a.] Inglewood, CA

ROBOKOS, DIMITRA
[b.] June 27, 1974, New York; [p.] George and Tina Robokos; [ed.] Pace University B.A. in Psychology and English; [occ.] Student; [hon.] Dean's List, Member of the Society of Fellows, Psi Chi Psychology Honors Society Vice President, Sigma Tau Delta English Honor Society, Sarah Willis Writing Contest Winner; [oth. writ.] Editor of Aphros, Pace University Literary Magazine where my poems appear.; [pers.] I never knew how free I could be until I began writing poetry. Thank you Professor North.; [a.] New York, NY

ROHR, CORINE
[b.] July 10, 1976, Huntington, NY; [p.] Carolann and Thomas Rohr; [ed.] Currently a Sophomore at Hofstra University; [occ.] Student; [hon.] New York State Scholar Athletic Award, Long Island Lacrosse Unsung Hero, Paul E. Pepe Scholarship - Cold Spring Harbor High School, Hofstra University Literary Award, A Jeffrey Weinper Memorial Award in Creative Writing; [oth. writ.] Several poems published in Grok Literary Magazine.; [pers.] Live your life as an exclamation, not an explanation. Always remember that great love and great achievements involve great risk.; [a.] Lloyd Harbor, NY

ROHR JR., EDWARD J.
[pen.] E. J.; [b.] September 27, 1958, Kansas; [p.] Ed and Charlene Rohr; [occ.] Owner Rohr Studios; [a.] Chicago, IL

ROLLINS, CHRISTINE
[b.] October 9, 1982, Bryan, TX; [p.] John and Becci Rollins; [ed.] Carroll Middle School; [occ.] Student; [memb.] National Junior Honor Society, "Saints" Soccer Club, Student Council, National Charity League, Carroll Middle School 8th Grade Symphonic Band (Bassoon); [hon.] Membership to the National Junior Honor Society, Academic Recognition in Math and Reading in the Duke University Talent and Identification Program; [pers.] When the shadow envelopes you, look up and let in the light.; [a.] Southlake, TX

ROSCHLI, ARNOLD E.
[b.] October 18, 1908, New York City; [m.] Charlotte Sherman, January 23, 1963; [ch.] Richard Roschli, Steven Perry, Marna B. Courson; [occ.] Deceased 4-17-90

ROSS, JULIE A.
[b.] April 14, 1964, Decatur, IL; [p.] David Coffman, Frances Coffman; [m.] Allen Edward Ross; [ch.] Christine Nicole and Bo Mathew; [memb.] C.H.A.D.D.; [pers.] This particular poem was inspired by my late husband Allen, and our two beautiful children, Christin and Bo, who are a reflection of his life and his nature.; [a.] Decatur, IL

ROUND, DEBRA JO
[b.] September 23, 1969, Elwood, IN; [p.] Connie Cole, Craig Curry; [m.] Douglas Andrew, September 10, 1994; [ch.] Rachel Marie; [ed.] Elwood High, Greater Works School of Ministry; [hon.] Singing contests, went to state for solo contest; [oth. writ.] Various other poems, made up infant songs and I'm currently working on a book; [pers.] In order to have a blessing - I must become a blessing, therefore, becoming a blessing is a reflection of a personal relationship with Christ Jesus; [a.] Pittsburgh, PA

ROUTH, CAROLYN
[b.] August 23, 1959, Desmoines, IA; [p.] Gilbert Minella, Carolyn I. Minella; [m.] Divorced; [ch.] Christopher, Michael, Samuel, Aaron, Mark; [ed.] Lincoln High, Des Moines Area Community College, Hamilton Business College; [oth. writ.] Various types of poems written while in Junior high; [pers.] Treat others as you would have them treat you. Believe that nothing is impossible. Poem dedicated to Eddie Loird; [a.] Knoxville, IA

ROUTIER, MAURICE A.
[pen.] Moe; [b.] July 20, 1956, Springfield, MA; [p.] Maurice and Theresa Routier; [m.] Divorced; [ch.] Amanda Marie and Adam Maurice; [ed.] Roger L. Putnam Vocational Technical High School; [occ.] Machine Adjuster; [memb.] BPO Elks - Lodge 1849 Al-Anon family groups our lady of Sacred Heart Church; [hon.] The American Legion School Award, Wood Working Award Printing's Award for outstanding work; [oth. writ.] The love I see in you alone and lonely - less of a man - Mom D. - Belonging - A Friend - Happiness - Fussent Fighten - Progress - The Cruise - Pour My Heart Out Too Your Smile - when I feel in love; [pers.] I'm a very sensitive and caring man. I love children and believe people should not forget them. I do the best I am able for that moment. Being a father is the best thing I could ever do.; [a.] Springfield, MA

ROYAL, CAROL J.
[b.] January 24, 1961, Wilkes County, NC; [m.] Everette Odell Royal Jr., March 11, 1978; [ch.] Heather Delaine and Traci Le Ann; [ed.] North Wilkes High and Wilkes Community College; [occ.] Homemaker; [pers.] Through writing I have wings to fly, my soul can speak, my spirit can be heard. I...can...be...; [a.] North Wilkesboro, NC

ROYER, PAUL SEDDON
[b.] December 14, 1946, San Francisco, CA; [m.] Mary Corinne Royer, December 11, 1981; [ch.] Plynlymon; [ed.] B.A. Computer Science, University of California at Berkeley, June 1973; [occ.] Information Systems Consultant; [memb.] Association for Computing Machinery, Data Administration and Management Association; [hon.] Walnut Creek, CA Park and Recreation Commission; [oth. writ.] Several technical articles published through guide, Inc.; [pers.] As my life unfolded around my family and occupation (computer technology), I have managed to balance with creative pursuits. Poetry, oil on canvas, photograph and acting, each in their time and place. It is wonderful to have one's creation recognized, especially, when publication was not the goal.; [a.] Antioch, CA

RUBIO, EDUARDO
[pen.] "Eduardo"; [b.] April 2, 1951, Ysleta, TX; [p.] Antonio and Maria Rubio; [ed.] Dell City High, D.C. Texas, UTEP, El Paso, Texas U.S. Navy - Vietnam Vet.; [occ.] Meteor Crater Employee; [memb.] San Isidro Catholic Church, D.C. Texas; [hon.] Employee of the Month at Universal Care, L.B. Calif., In charge of poetry readings at the Haven Coffee Co. in L.B. 1st place Belmont Shore Xmas Parade; [oth. writ.] A few poems and short stories published in college magazine, artwork also displayed in L.B. (realism, impressionism etc.); [pers.] I used to write for personal strength and self-understanding, now I enjoy sharing it with (my poetry) anyone I can. Thank you.; [a.] Flagstaff, AZ

RUSSELL, JANET
[pen.] Janet Mayo; [b.] February 28, 1939, New York City; [ed.] Clara Barton HS for health; [oth. writ.] I dedicate this poem in memory of my father Vernon Mayo to my dear mother Nellie Mayo my five children Carolyn Holmes, Vernon Russell.; [pers.] David Russell, Idas Atkinson, Karen Uket and my fourteen grandchildren with love.

RUSSELL, YVONNE
[pen.] Eve R. Russell; [b.] September 19, 1939, Norwood, MA; [p.] William Russell, Ruth MacLeon; [ed.] Brandeis University 1 1/2 years; [occ.] Administrative Assistant; [oth. writ.] My first poem.; [pers.] After studying poetry, this was my first poem. I would rather write few poems that contain subtle language. Yet with enough density that evolves into a smooth cadence and teachers the heart some moralistic principle either in humorous or rueful tones. I feel that the reader can derive from a poem an aroused emotion which when touched by the heart, there lies a spirit which exposes age old truths. I was inspired by the sensitivity of Homer, the moral courage of Aeschylus, the humor of Chaucer, the intensity of Milton and the spirit to face a new found expression called freedom that awakened the 1st and 2nd generation Romantics. All of these playwriter/poets pursued truth in various methods. Upon arriving at the crosscroads from different sociological paths, their acknowledgement of the same infinite wisdom is what makes all cultures interdependent.; [a.] Plainville, MA

RYAN JR., FRANK J.
[pen.] FJR, F. James Christopher Ryan; [b.] December 3, 1954, Bronxville; [p.] Frank J. Ryan Sr., Gloria Hieronymus Ryan; [m.] Jane Joan Ryan, June 26, 1988; [ch.] Lauren Marie (8-19-93); [ed.] Iona Preparatory School, New Rochelle, NY/Concordia College Bronxville NY; [occ.] Regional Manager/Circulation Operations, Gannett Co.; [memb.] Westchester County Medical Center Heart Club, National Library of Poetry International Society of Poets; [hon.] 1994 and 1995 1st place winner of New York Post Prose Competition, various Sales and Promotion Awards for Gannett Co.

1982-1986, Divisional and Departmental Achievement Awards 1987-1992, Gannett Co. Managerial Excellence Awards 1993-1996, Top Sales Person 1984, 1985, 1986, 1987, 1990, 1991, 1992, 1993; [oth. writ.] Since Dec. 1994, I have been published over 40 times on a variety of topics and issues including, Global and National Affairs, Political Editorial, Music and Sports appearing in time, news week, circus National Music Magazine, the New York daily news the New York post as well as thirteen local newspaper publications covering Suburban Regions of New York and Northern New Jersey.; [pers.] "Poetry is an emotional junction between the heart and mind. Working in partnership through a spectrum of imagery and impulse, both compliment each others passion for creative invention."; [a.] Yonkers, NY

SACKSTEDER, SANDRA J.
[b.] April 3, 1953, Dayton, OH; [p.] Tom and Dean Hayes; [m.] Paul Sacksteder, October 15, 1983; [ch.] Geoff Thomas, Lindsey Kathryn; [ed.] Beavercreek High School, Wright State University; [occ.] Homemaker-Volunteer; [memb.] Phi Mu Fraternity, Order of the Eastern Star, Daughters of the American Revolution, Parent Teacher Association, Girls Scouts of America; [hon.] Kettering Community Service Award; [a.] Kettering, OH

SAINT-FLEUR, JONAS
[b.] Haiti; [oth. writ.] School plays when was in High school.; [a.] New York, NY

SALAS, LOURDES
[pen.] Gabriella Diaz; [b.] November 7, 1967, Lima-Peru; [p.] Juana Diaz; [ed.] Glen Cove High School, State University of New York at Old Westbury; [occ.] Counselor, Madonna Heights, Dix Hills, NY; [oth. writ.] I've been writing poems, short stories, (comedies, love and honor) songs and anecdotes since I was 16 years old but I had never published anything before.; [pers.] My mind and my hand become an unknown inspiration.; [a.] Oyster Bay, NY

SALDAUSKY, ROBERTA
[pen.] Bobbi; [b.] December 9, 1966, Fostoria, OH; [p.] Daryl and Pat Saldausky; [ed.] Associates of Art Associates of Science; [occ.] Accounting Managers Assistance; [memb.] Stylart Greetings, Olympia Sales Club; [hon.] High School Perfect Attendance; [oth. writ.] Emptiness and darkest times, I am also working on my first and second books.; [pers.] Stay in school. Life is short use it wisely.; [a.] Reno, NV

SAMUELS, JONATHAN D.
[b.] October 10, 1972, Jennings, LA; [p.] Mary A. Samuels, John A. Samuels; [ed.] Midland High School; [occ.] Offline Equipment Operator, Prudential Healthcare; [pers.] I strive to reach various topics in everything that I write. I try to imagine myself in certain situations or atmospheres in order to achieve where I want to go, so that I can make people feel as if I were writing about them or someone they may know. Writing, to me, is a freedom like no other.; [a.] Houston, TX

SANDERS, DOUGLAS
[pen.] D. Lawrence Sanders; [b.] May 4, 1968, Vicksburg, MS; [p.] Mr. and Mrs. Marion and Lurline Green; [m.] Alexelisha Sanders, July 9, 1994; [ed.] High School, Mississippi School for the Blind College, Alcorn State University; [pers.] I'd like to thank my wife for giving me the support and motivation to more explore and develop my creative writing skills.; [a.] Vicksburg, MS

SANDLIN, JOSHUA C.
[b.] December 6, 1974, Portsmouth, VA; [p.] James and Susan Sandlin; [ed.] Graduate of Fletcher High School 1993; [occ.] Currently employed at an Answering Service; [pers.] Introvert, agoraphobic and unusual. A writer/poet I'm not, or am I, only time will tell. To those who have believe in me, thank you. C.B., R.S., D.B., Kr.H.; [a.] Jacksonville, FL

SANKRITHI, SIVA
[b.] February 27, 1987, Seattle, WA; [p.] Mithra and Usha Sankrithi; [ed.] Currently in the 5th grade at the Evergreen Private School, Shoreline, WA; [occ.] School in the 5th grade; [memb.] U.S.T.A. (United States Tennis Association), Vedanta Society of Western Washington, and S.I. (Sports Illustrated) for kids (Subscription); [hon.] Won State Championship for 1st grade Invent America, Awarded Trophies for doing sports and acting; [oth. writ.] Wrote manuscript for (Picture Book of Paris), and stories and reports for school.; [pers.] My hobbies are playing sports, collecting sports cards, playing flute, watching television, eating Indian Food and Pizza, traveling around the world, drawing and writing poetry. My parents were born in India and so was the rest of my family but I was born in Seattle, Washington, USA and I'm now 9 years old.; [a.] Seattle, WA

SAPHIER, PATRICIA
[b.] May 14, 1973, Los Angeles, CA; [ed.] Tufts University; [occ.] Child Care Worker, Los Angeles Orphan Home Society, CA; [pers.] As creatures borne of love, our highest goal must be to spread love further.; [a.] Los Angeles, CA

SCHAEFER, JENNIFER
[pen.] Jennifer Ann; [b.] April 3, 1980, Houston, TX; [p.] Carmen Newton, Alfred Schaefer; [ed.] Langham Creek High School jr. (grade 11); [occ.] High School Student; [memb.] Actor's Ensemble; [hon.] Won Grand Champion (1st place) in Harris County Photography contest. My photo was put in a live auction and I got 500 dollars for it. Got a first place in ribbon in an acting competition when I was 12.; [oth. writ.] Over 75 unpublished poems. Some unpublished monologues and short stories, and two person dialogues.; [pers.] I intend to take my many talents in writing, photography, dancing, and acting in the entertainment industry. I am a dreamer because my dreams are so much more fun that my life. I want to experience everything. And be happy.; [a.] Katy, TX

SCHAEFFER, ENID
[b.] October 26, 1959, Brooklyn, NY; [p.] Sol Advocate, Fay Advocate; [m.] Edward Schaeffer, June 23, 1985; [ch.] Jordan, Lauren, Sarah; [ed.] Bayside High School, Continuing my education for B.A. in Literature and Writing, Suffolk Community College; [occ.] At home mother; [oth. writ.] I have just begun to submit my work for publication the last part of 1996.; [pers.] In order to express emotion and ideas in my work, I strive for simplicity in the structure of my poems, yet a strong use of imagery. I am inspired by such 20th century writers as E.E. Cummings, Deimore Schwartz, James Baldwin.; [a.] East Northport, NY

SCHARSCHMIDT, ROSIE
[b.] August 27, 1946, Berlin, WI; [p.] Theodore and Erna Strook; [m.] Michael Scharschmidt, October 1, 1977; [ch.] Cherie Ann and April Jean; [ed.] Brandon High; [occ.] Housewife and child care; [pers.] I search to find the love and beauty in all living things and the people around me. My all time favorite poet is Elizabeth Barrett Browning.; [a.] Markesan, WI

SCHAUBHUT, JOHN L.
[pen.] Branch Waters; [b.] August 5, 1933, Biloxi, MS; [p.] Roger P. and Pervia Schaubhut; [m.] Frances Schaubhut, August 5, 1972; [ch.] John Michael, Sandra and Shawna; [ed.] Biloxi High, Clackamas Community College Portland State University; [occ.] Retired Credit Mgr.; [memb.] Milwaukie Elks Lodge (Inactive); [oth. writ.] "Make No Mistake About It" (song lyrics), "The Naked Tree" (1996), "A Sightly delight" (poems), "Bi-Golly It's Molly" and several lemericks of the Ogden Nash and Edward Lear style, with rhyme and and sometime bawdy approach. None of the above have I submitted to publication to date.; [pers.] Poetry, is an orchestration of observation, inspiration and truth put into words, written or spoken as a rhythmical composition.; [a.] Portland, OR

SCHEAFFER, FERNIE B.
[pen.] Fernie Scheaffer; [b.] June 18, 1916, Albany, OH; [p.] Denver and Edna McVay; [m.] Porter (1936), Scheaffer (1986), Allard (1992); [ch.] Diane, Susan, Alyson, Michael; [ed.] High School, Albany, Ohio, Nurses Training - Graduate; [occ.] Retired; [hon.] Have been hung in our Columbus Art Museum for 6 months; [oth. writ.] Poems in local papers and one in tops magazine.; [a.] Worthington, OH

SCHEFTER, CHRISTINE MARIE
[pen.] Regina V. Quinn; [b.] January 27, 1975, Livingston, NJ; [p.] Mary Elizabeth and Frank Schefter; [ed.] Roselle Park High School, Albright College, Montclair State University; [occ.] Full time student Assistant Preschool Teacher; [memb.] Montclair State University, Psychology Club Residence Life Staff, Water Watch International; [hon.] Albright College Presidential Scholar, Presidential Academic Fitness Award, New Poets of America Award, Martin Luther King Jr., Literary Award, Dean's List; [oth. writ.] Many poems published in local newspapers, some pending publication including an autobiographical poem reflecting the love, smiles and happiness of my life.; [pers.] My greatest influences in life are God and my two best friends, my parents, who have always believed in me. They have taught me to "set your goals high and stay on the road of achieving those goals"; [a.] Roselle Park, NJ

SCHILLING, ROY O.
[b.] June 12, 1914, Elkhart, IL; [p.] Clarence C. and Ethel M. Schilling; [m.] Rachel Rogers Schilling, December 30, 1943; [ch.] 2 - Mary R. Schilling, Susan R. Bryant; [ed.] B.E.D. degree Illinois State University, M.A. degree - Teacher College, Columbia University, New York; [occ.] Retired Elementary School Principal; [memb.] Life Member Nat Ed. Assoc., Life Member, IL Congress of P.T.A. Emeritus, Phi Delta Kappa, Elder Emeritus, Central Christian Church Macon County Historical Society, Golden K - Kiwanis Club; [oth. writ.] "Exchanging Experiences Thru Interclass Visits" - The National Elementary Principal Yearbook - 1956, Contributor to Toward Better Teaching A.S.C.D. - NEA - 1949 Yearbook "Learning Through The School Council" the National Elementary Principal 1950.; [pers.] Thousand of true friendships made over my 82 years of life. The greatest reward a person can receive is to give service generously to others and live accordingly to God's principles.; [a.] Decatur, IL

SCHLACHTER, SAMUEL
[b.] January 15, 1964; [p.] Father Thomas Schlachter, mother Veronica Strange, step-mother Linda Schlachter; [ch.] Chelsea Rose Schlachter; [ed.] Mosley High, Lynn Haven Fl, University of Southern Indiana, BS and MBA Medical Center, Evansville, IN; [occ.] Boiler Technician, St. Mary's Medical Center, Evansville, IN; [pers.] This poem is dedicated to my lady, Stephanie.; [a.] Evansville, IN

SCHMIDT, MARY ELLEN
[b.] September 6, 1951, Rhinelander, WI; [p.] Adam Schmidt, Lorene Schmidt; [m.] Michael J. Jackson, September 25, 1975; [ch.] Stepsons: Edward M., Scott C.; [ed.] Anderson High, Shasta Jr. College; [occ.] Textile Sales; [memb.] Nat'l Multiple Sclerosis Society, Partner Special Olympics, Cystic Fibrosis Foundation, Int'l Poets Society; [hon.] Editor's Choice Awards in: The Ebbing Tide, Amidst the Splendor, Rainbow's End; [pers.] For my dearest friend, Barbara Joyce; [a.] Pasadena, CA

SCHMIERER, PHILLIP N.
[pen.] Phillip N. Schmierer; [b.] June 17, 1978, Joplin, MO; [p.] Judith L. Schmierer; [ed.] Senior in Greenwood High School; [occ.] Full-time student; [memb.] Quill and Scroll, Editor, JROTC Battalion Commander, EEA, Newsletter Editor, Jr. Civitans, Writers Forum, Vice-Pres., Knight Writers Literary Club, Pellet Team, Captain; [hon.] Who's Who Among Amer. High School Students, National Sojourners Award, Senior Army Instructor SIA Ribbon, Palmetto Boys State, Adjutant General, Law Enforcement Cadet Academy, Superior Junior Cadet Decoration Award-Outstanding Cadet, Stop Up to the Challenge Award, Governor's School Academy for the Arts, Greenwood Volunteer Award, Chamber of Commerce; [oth. writ.] Poem published in Anthology of Poetry by Young Americans, District 50 Whildlife Essay Contest, 1st place, Emerald City Beacon Annual Poetry Contest, 1st place; [pers.] Fully dedicate oneself to unlock that doorway which hides the inner self and conjure the creativity one possesses.; [a.] Greenwood, SC

SCHMITTGEN, MRS. MARK
[pen.] Shawn K. Schmittgen; [b.] November 2, 1957, Bryn Mawr, PA; [p.] Berneita and Med Kalick; [m.] Mark Cole Schmittgen, December 22, 1979; [ch.] Ashley (girl) 12, Ross (boy) 7; [ed.] 1975 H. S. Graduate (moved around a lot - went to several H.S.'s) 1979 Graduate/The Ohio State University - B.A. English, actually graduate from Upper Arlington H.S. - Columbus, OH (74-75); [occ.] On a temporary certificate I work as a substitute teacher and I do free-lance writing.; [memb.] Columbus Christian Writer's Association, "Frateral Communicator" for local branch of Lutheran Brotherhood/I also am attempting to help establish a small writer's guild in the Zanesville, OH area.; [hon.] Second place for poem in Columbus Christian Writers summer 1996 contest (to be published in anthology in 1997) Guardian Angel - poem my first contest attempt our family started and now operates heartland Orchard in Southern Licking County. I hope to write a child's book (in verse) about growing apples.; [pers.] At age 39 I realize many things: 1) I do have faith in God, 2) It is very important to follow one's passion and 3) my mom was pretty smart after all!; [a.] Thornville, OH

SCHOBER, KATIE
[pen.] Ylee M. Hazard; [b.] December 10, 1974, Boonton, NJ; [p.] Cindy and David; [ed.] Wallkill SHS, 1 Semester Cobleskill, 9 Credits Dutchess Community C.; [occ.] Deli Worker; [a.] Poughkeepsie, NY

SCHOOLER-SAMUKAWA
[pen.] Mary Ann Schooler, Schooler-Samukawa; [b.] January 30, 1939, Hugo, OK; [p.] Mary Lou Craft, Roy E. Schooler; [m.] Wayman F. Leverton, September 5, 1986; [ch.] Two daughters, one son; [ed.] N. Central High, Spokane, Wash., Calif. State College, Amer. Stained Glass Inst., Matre de Art Vitro; [occ.] Full time stained glass artist and teacher; [memb.] Professional Stained Glass Guild, Chamber of Comm., Scurry County Penwomen Texas Poetry Society; [hon.] Dean's List, Facility Wines Club Scholarship; [oth. writ.] Several poems published in local news paper, song lyrics; [pers.]

When a creative wave begs to overtake me I have learned to "Go with the flow".; [a.] Sweetwater, TX

SCHOONOVER, JEFFREY L.
[b.] June 23, 1967, Kenosha, WI; [p.] Marvin L. Schoonover, Sharon J. McCash; [ed.] Beloit Memorial High; [occ.] Material Expeditor at Customized Transportation Inc., Janesville, WI; [oth. writ.] Several personal poems and songs; [pers.] My writings are based solely on personal experiences.; [a.] Beloit, WI

SCHROEDER, KARLA
[pen.] Krazy; [b.] August 5, 1982, Rockville, MD; [p.] Karl and Debra Schroeder; [ed.] Wheaton High School; [occ.] Student, headbanger; [hon.] Academic Fitness Award, Scholarship awards from Parkland Middle school, awards for excellence in Art, english and world sts, honor roll.; [oth. writ.] Poems and short stories; [pers.] Karla enjoys painting, writing, and listening to music.; [a.] Germantown, MD

SCHULZE, VICTORIA
[b.] January 17, 1983, Blytheville, AR; [p.] Blaine and Carissa Schulze; [ed.] Stilwell Grade School, Peoria-Norwood Middle School, Stilwell Junior High; [occ.] Student; [hon.] Best writings, Stilwell English Competition, First Place in D.A.R.E. Poster Competition, Advanced Honor Band; [oth. writ.] A View, The Thought, The Doctor, When the Wind Whispers, From Within Your Heart, Two Untitled Poems.; [a.] Stilwell, OK

SCHWARTZ, VALERIE BETH
[pen.] Valerie Beth Schwartz; [b.] May 21, 1945, New York City, NY; [p.] Bernard S. and Ida C. Schwartz; [ed.] Pre-Kindergarten-Thru' High School - Riverdale Country School attended N.Y.U.; [occ.] Creative Artist; [oth. writ.] I have a compilation of poems, of varying emotions, having written them out of the stress of growth.; [pers.] My poems come from the gut. They are part of my own living, and observation of the scene of life.; [a.] New York, NY

SCHWIEDOP, SHIRLEY
[pen.] Shirley Schwiedop; [b.] July 24, 1945, Wilson Borough, PA; [p.] Marie, Clair Hatch; [m.] Joachim D. Schwiedop; [ch.] Three sons - Dan, Dave and Alan; [ed.] Northampton Area Community College, Associates Degree in Business Administration; [occ.] President, Yoyda Inc. Secretary/Treasurer, J.S. Mechanical Contracting Inc.; [memb.] Pennsylvania Horticultural Society, The Academy of Natural Sciences of Philadelphia; [oth. writ.] In process of organizing and marketing value-based stories for children.; [pers.] There is a great need to help children grow in values. My stories will influence children to build character and self-worth.; [a.] Easton, PA

SCOFIELD, KRISTINE
[pen.] Kristine Lawrence; [b.] October 7, 1972, Brooklyn, NY; [p.] Cathi and Mark Scofield; [ed.] P.S. 88 Elementary, I.S. 119 J.H.S. Ben Cardoza High; [occ.] Student; [oth. writ.] "Worlds apart", "Paths", "Flying Without Wings", "Fear of 1912", "Fields of Stone", "Wings of Grace", "Love Consuming Us", "Why my Life", "My Love", "Wings of Gold", "Windows", "To Walk Again", "Silent Song"; [pers.] My writing is from my heart, not only my mind. And is not only now for myself but for my family and dearest friends who believe in me and who have given me the strength to continue. Thank you.; [a.] Brooklyn, NY

SCORESBY, EMILY S.
[b.] April 17, 1988, Mesa, AZ; [p.] J. Kyle and Karen D. Scoresby; [ed.] 3rd Grade (currently enrolled in) has completed K-2 at Veora Johnson Elementary; [occ.] Student; [memb.] Church of Jesus Christ of Latter Day Saints; [pers.] I wrote the poem "Once I Saw A

Unicorn"...for my Mom on Mother's Day. I love to write and plan to write more during my life.; [a.] Mesa, AZ

SEALES, CHLOE ANGELIQUE
[b.] February 13, 1979, Brooklyn, NY; [p.] Yolanda Tomlinson, Carl Seales; [ed.] Erasmos Hall High School Campus of Science and Math, gateway to higher education program; [occ.] Student; [hon.] 2nd place Science Fair (NYC Academy of Science); [pers.] I write what's in my heart, what I feel, what I know and at all times strive to do my personal best, to go above and beyond average.

SEARA, MARLENE N.
[b.] August 5, 1950, Cuba; [p.] Nereida Seara; [ed.] 1991 Adelpi University Master of Social Work; [occ.] Director Peter J. DellaMonica, Jr. Senior Center; [memb.] American Board of Hypotherapy; [hon.] Community Service Social Work Scholarship 10,000; [oth. writ.] None just beginning to write.; [pers.] My goal is helping others to recognize and maximize their full potential and to funnel that power into action, so the individual can reach the ultimate - Self-Actualization.; [a.] South Ozone Park, NY

SEEGMILLER, GARTH
[pen.] William Garth; [b.] July 7, 1918, Kanab, UT; [p.] William West Seegmiller and Ada Pratt; [m.] Florence Porter Seegmiller, June 5, 1941; [ch.] Five; [ed.] BS Pre-Legal Degree in Political Science, Brigham Young University, and Post Graduate Studies in Journalism and Speech. U.S. Army OCS, State College, Miss.; [occ.] Freelance Writer, Editor, Agent; [memb.] AARP, American Legion, VFW, Writers Guild of America, Utah Writers League, BYU Cougar Club, and The Church of Jesus Christ of Latter-Day Saints.; [hon.] Purple Heart, Bronze Star for Valor (Saving 3,000 lives of 38th Infantry Regiment in North Korea), KSL TV Poetry (2-Week tour of Israel for two), Int'l Songwriting Contest Winner; [oth. writ.] Novels: "Glory Forever" and "Old Man Horse." Motion Pictures and History U.S. Missiles, Military Communication and Nerve Gas. Story Editor Motion Picture, "Savannah Smiles." WW II Combat Zone News.; [pers.] Although I'll be 79 years old soon after "In Dappled Sunlight" is published, I am in excellent health, enjoy life with family and friends and keep active writing historical fiction, poetry and songs.; [a.] Spanish Fork, UT

SERAFINO, ADA MARY
[pen.] Ada Mary Serafino; [b.] July 29, 1964, Brooklyn, NY; [p.] Demetrio and Mary Serafino (Both Deceased); [ch.] Elisa (16); [ed.] New Utrecht High School and Taylor Business Institute; [occ.] VIP Travel Counselor; [hon.] Silver Medal in the Columbia University Italian Poetry Contest 1981; [pers.] Poetry is a way of expressing my feelings and it gives me great joy to share them with others.; [a.] Brooklyn, NY

SERICI, JIM
[b.] April 20, 1942, Chicago, IL; [p.] Joe and Ann; [m.] Kathy, April 15, 1995; [ch.] Rick and Michelle; [occ.] Manager for Large Utility of Logistics; [oth. writ.] A variety of Spiritual - thought provoking poems; [pers.] The search for spiritual understanding can be enhanced by poetry....the search for inner peace is strengthened through the writing of poetry.

SHABAZZ, DAVID L.
[pen.] King David; [b.] October 26, 1969, Clinton, SC; [p.] Moses and Mary Dillard; [ed.] Bachelor of Arts in Journalism from Benedict College, Master of Arts in Journalism from the University of South Carolina; [occ.] Writer/author co-owner of Awesome Records with brother Julian L.D. Shabazz (Awesome Records is a book publishing and record company); [oth. writ.] Dolemite: The story of Rudy Ray Moore (1996, Awe-some Records), five on the blackhand side (1996, AR) Public Enemy Number one (in print) all books; [a.] Winston-Salem, NC

SHARMA, MD. PUNEET
[pen.] Clark Brown; [b.] March 27, 1969, Chandigarh, India; [p.] Bal Krishan Sharma, Saroj Sharma; [ed.] D.A.V. College, Christian Medical College; [occ.] Doctor; [pers.] The essence of art is creativity. The essence of creativity is an idea. The essence of an idea is inspiration and that is a priceless gift; [a.] Boston, MA

SHAUNESSY, BARBARA A.
[b.] May 10, 1954, Brooklyn, NY; [p.] Deceased; [ed.] Doctor of Psychology (Psy.D), Masters of Science in Education, Bachelors of Arts (Magna Cum Laude), all from Pace University, N.Y.C.; [occ.] School Psychologist, N.Y.C. Board of Education; [memb.] N.Y. State School Psychologists; [oth. writ.] Unpublished to date.; [pers.] I try to bring meaning to my life by helping others as much as possible. Writing is, and always has been, a vehicle for expression of feeling and thinking, in a creative, artful way. I adhere to the Greek philosophy of maintaining both a healthy body and mind.; [a.] New York, NY

SHAW, BYRON K.
[b.] February 14, 1969, Cincinnati, OH; [p.] James and Yvonne Shaw; [ed.] Ohio State Univ. BA Western State Univ., College of Law; [occ.] 3rd yr. Law Student; [memb.] Student Bar Assoc. Phi Alpha Delta - legal frat.; [hon.] Dean's List; [oth. writ.] Articles for the student newspaper.; [pers.] The greatest influence on my work is the love and support from my parents.; [a.] Fullerton, CA

SHAW, EARLINE YOST
[pen.] Earline Yost Shaw; [b.] March 29, 1940; [p.] Fritz Colter Yost and Helen Humphreys Juetten; [m.] Cecil L. Shaw Sr., January 27, 1963; [ch.] Kim Emerson, Cecil Shaw Jr., Rowdy R. Earl Shaw, Sadie Sabrina Shaw, Rocky Brent Shaw; [ed.] Graduated with honors in Graphic Communication with design emphasis, High Schools, Eureka High and San Luis Obispo; [occ.] Freelance writer and designer, being the daughter of local boat builder, I went from splashing my grandfathers homemade blackberry wine, to splashing paint and ink on paper; [hon.] I received The Editors Choice Award 1995, for my poem Passages, from the International Poet Society.; [pers.] A self made artist and poet, when the teacher said, you can't I would try anyway. In my failure I would succeed, with dancing lines on paper. My imagination is always alive and eager to experience new ways of communication between the written words or visual picture for others to enjoy. I owe all my success to my family.

SHELTON, MICHAEL
[b.] February 1, 1953, Houston, MS; [p.] Herbert and Inez Shelton; [m.] Cathy E. Hansen, August 1, 1993; [ch.] Ryan, Christopher, Salina; [ed.] BA English - Mississippi State University 1993; [occ.] Writer/Certified to teach High School English; [memb.] National Authors Registry, National Education Association, Virginia Poetry Society, undergraduate English Society - MSU Non-Traditional, the Writers' Group, Student Assoc., Christiansburg Presbyterian Church.; [hon.] Butler Scholarship in Creative Writing, honorable mention, B and W Photo Art Comp., accepted with 3 photos in art competitions, President's and Dean's Lists, National Dean's List.; [oth. writ.] Articles and Photographs published in five local and collegiate publications, articles in job-related newsletters, poetry published in several publications, i.e. Angel Care Hospice Theme.; [pers.] Poetry is a means by which I provide comfort and sanity to myself, and too all who read or hear my work.; [a.] Christiansburg, VA

SHERIDAN, BARBARA LINSIN
[b.] May 13, 1939, Ventnor, NJ; [p.] Marcella Comey Linsin, Edward John Linsin; [m.] Craig Cooper, December 19, 1995; [ch.] James, Christine, Jennifer, Kevin; [ed.] St. Agnes Academy, Indpls, Ind., The New School, NY, NY; [occ.] Writer/Photographer; [a.] Maplewood, NJ

SHERLOCK, MONIQUE
[b.] April 1, 1981, Bellflower, CA; [p.] Carl and Norma Sherlock; [ed.] Sophomore at Fontana High School, Fontana, Ca.; [occ.] Student; [hon.] Letterman in Softball (Fast Pitch); [a.] Bloomington, CA

SHIZUMURA, STEVE
[b.] April 18, 1956, Los Angeles; [p.] Norman and Yoshiko Shizumura; [ed.] USC/UCLA Science and Art Major; [occ.] Artist; [pers.] Man has achieved only 5 - 20% of his human potential. One must strive to "see" everyday and be aware of the positives and negatives of everyday living.; [a.] Marina Del Rey, CA

SIEVERS, MARCELLA G. INMAN
[b.] June 21, 1949, Poplar Bluff, MO; [p.] Ethel M. Inman, Hugh E. Inman; [m.] Arthur A. F. Sievers, January 30, 1976; [ch.] Michael F. W. Sievers; [ed.] Poplar Bluff Senior High, St. Louis Community College at Meramec, St. Louis, MO; [occ.] Writer-Poet, Artist, Woodcarver. I also travel and work with my husband the lower 48 states and Canada.; [memb.] International Society of Poets; [hon.] Awards for outstanding poetry; [oth. writ.] Children's stories, short stories and other poems.; [pers.] Writing makes me feel alive and free inside my soul. Many times it surprises me when I pick up the pen and start to write. How the characters or places take on a life of their own and it is not even what you intended to write. It is as if it controls you and I love it.; [a.] Saint Louis, MO

SILVER, JEANNE
[b.] April 30, 1940, Dublin, Ireland; [m.] John Silver, September 18, 1968; [ch.] 5 (1 girl, 4 boys, (incl. twins); [ed.] Dublin, Ireland; [occ.] Realtor, San Diego, CA; [memb.] Women in Business; [hon.] Presidents Circle 1994 Leading Edge Society 1990; [oth. writ.] Poems and Articles, (not sent for publication). Currently working on a Children's Book, which my son, Stephen Silver, will be illustrating.; [pers.] I enjoy writing on my observations on life, either by poetry or articles. My poems tend towards the beauty which surround us. Though I will write about anything that moves me deeply i.e. my mother's death.; [a.] San Diego, CA

SIMON, CHERYL
[b.] August 9, 1962, Trinidad; [p.] Roy and Monica Marslier; [m.] Kirt Simon, September 4, 1988; [ch.] Akins (M) 5, Chelaire (F) age 22 mths; [ed.] St. George Secretarial College, La-Petite Institute, Michael and Gloria Beauty School; [occ.] Cosmetologist Nursing Aide; [hon.] Outstanding Track and Field Athlete. Trinidad and Tobago, President Award for small business; [pers.] After I had my two children, I realized what a great job my parents did. In raising seven daughter and six sons. I see it as a great accomplishment.; [a.] Jamaica Queens, NY

SIMS, SHAYNE RANDY WAYNE
[b.] August 9, 1973, Clarkesville, GA; [p.] Randy L. Sims, Brenda K. Bryan; [occ.] Software Developer; [a.] Atlanta, GA

SINK, GERALD J.
[pen.] H. R. Mann; [b.] February 27, 1942, Evergreen Park, IL; [p.] Paul Sink, Marcella Sink; [m.] Colette Stalk, June 17, 1967; [ch.] Mark, Maura, Matthew; [ed.] Mt. Carmel H.S./Loyola Univ. Chgo; [occ.] Direc-

tor Human Resources, Sandvik Rock Tools Houston, TX; [memb.] Soc. Human Resource Mgmt. Adutt Ed. Comm. St. Clare of Assisi Church; [oth. writ.] Articles for Journals of Compensation and Benefits; [pers.] I believe that to lead others you must first learn to listen and trust. From what you learn you can then merge their goals with yours and together determine what you want to do and achieve.; [a.] Houston, TX

SIVITILLI, MRS. JENNIE FRANCES
[pen.] Jingles; [b.] July 1, 1934, Philadelphia; [p.] Deceased; [m.] Mr. Ennis Sivitilli, November 1956; [ch.] 2 children, son - 38 yrs. and daughter - 39 yrs.; [ed.] John W. Hollokan Catholic Girls High School; [occ.] Housewife, artist, designer, 1st Cook Entrepreneur; [oth. writ.] The poem "The Planet Mars", was written by a friend of mine. And then had it notarized - because I have troubled with my vision. Yes I have lots of poems that will be published for the Blind in Tapes, and a small book of about 50 poems.; [pers.] I receive injections to my face and eyes to keep them open - it called Bleuforoposma Rare decease. 23 injections from the Wools Eye Hos.; [a.] Philadelphia, PA

SKIPPER, TINA
[b.] November 30, 1980, Dothan, AL; [p.] Michael Skipper, Janet Skipper; [ed.] Midland City Elementary School, South Dale Junior High School, presently a sophomore at Dale County High School; [memb.] Brothers and Sisters in Christ, future Homemakers of America, Teen to Teen, New Hope Free Will Baptist Church Youth Group; [hon.] Who's Who Among American High School Students, National Merit Society, Dale County High School "All A Honor Roll"; [pers.] I do what I can while holding God's hand, but ultimately rely on His master plan. I have been influenced by my family and their love.; [a.] Midland City, AL

SLATE, CAROL NAYLOR
[b.] November 25, 1952, Winston-Salem, NC; [p.] George Naylor, Earlene Naylor; [m.] Horace A. Slate, May 17, 1985; [ch.] Michelle Ann Slate; [ed.] East Forsyth High School, Forsyth Technical College; [occ.] Home-maker; [memb.] Winston-Salem Corvette Club; [pers.] I was inspired to write this poem for my father for Father's Day, June 16, 1996 who was terminally ill with lung cancer. My father passed away July 18, 1996.

SLATTERY, JULIE A.
[b.] September 5, 1959, McAllen, TX; [p.] David L. Slattery Sr. and Shirley A. Helland Slattery Zerger; [ed.] Nampa High School, Link's School of Business; [occ.] Avon Independent Sales Rep.; [memb.] College Church of the Nazarene, College Church Women's Fellowship, Nazarene Care house, where I volunteer once a week and RSUP (Retired Senior Volunteer Program) through my involvement with care house, College Church Cookbook Committee; [hon.] Care Award from College Church in November 1994 in recognition of the ways I serve in church! I got a certificate from RSUP for outstanding volunteer services and recognizing the years and hours I've served!; [oth. writ.] Articles in my high school newspaper and I had another poem of mine published in our church cook book. I was on that (cook book) committee. My poems was chosen by everyone on the committee.; [pers.] I strive to put God first and to help all those I can, showing them God's love, and to give back to the Lord for all He is done for me! I thank my Lord for giving me the ability to write poems and pray His blessings on all who read them!; [a.] Nampa, ID

SLEETH, CINDY
[b.] July 13, 1960, CA; [p.] Lorraine Emerson, Brian Sleeth; [ch.] Matthew, Randy, Corey, Kaylie; [ed.] Graduated from Bell Gardens Senior High, was in gymnastics for 7 years, taught swimming; [memb.] I am

involved in Lutheran Church of the Cross teaching Sunday school and in the choir; [oth. writ.] This will be my first poem ever published and I am very excited.; [pers.] My writings reflect people who have entered and exited my life. My poems come from my heart.; [a.] Smiths, AL

SMITH, DIANE
[b.] August 1, 1939, Langdale, AL; [p.] Luther and Mildred Crowder; [m.] Victor Smith, December 10, 1966; [ch.] Angelia, Kevin, David, Michelle and Marla; [ed.] Valley High School, Opelika Vocational School; [occ.] Home maker; [a.] Cusseta, AL

SMITH, GLENDA FAYE
[pen.] Heavenly-Dove; [b.] January 14, 1942, Elvins, MO; [p.] Levi and Frona Parker; [m.] Divorced; [ch.] Laura Lynn Smith; [occ.] Retired; [pers.] I owe my talent to the Lord Jesus Christ, with out his help, I could do nothing.; [a.] Atlanta, GA

SMITH, LORRAINE K.
[b.] April 13, 1947, Palmdale, CA; [p.] Sylvan and Anna Kepperling; [m.] Harold, August 7, 1977; [ch.] Christina; [ed.] Practical Nurse Program; [occ.] Administrative Manager Rest Home, Pink Hill, NC; [memb.] N.C.; [pers.] All that I am is by hand of God give God the glory.; [a.] Pink Hill, NC

SMITH, PHYLLIS G.
[b.] January 11, 1949, Fort Knox, KY; [p.] Elezck and Mary Lowe; [ch.] Kristi Kennedy and Dana Clifton; [ed.] High School; [occ.] Nutritional Services at Methodist Medical Center of Oak Ridge; [hon.] Graduated from Institute of Children's Literature, CNA Training Employee of the Month of Anthem Electronic 1990-1991; [oth. writ.] Institute of Children's Literature (course in Writing) July 1994 Graduated.; [pers.] I wanted my poem to be something for my grandson. People to know about his life and the feelings between two people I wanted my work to be publish and it to touch others.; [a.] Oak Ridge, TN

SMITH, RAYMOND F.
[pen.] Raymond F. Smith; [b.] December 4, 1927, Minneapolis, MN; [p.] Leonard Smith, Alida Smith; [m.] Deceased (Edith), June 4, 1951; [ch.] Linda, Gail, Julie and Kim; [ed.] Patrick Henry High School; [occ.] Retired Mfg. Eng.; [pers.] This poem is the history about my loved one and me. We were born the same year (1927) our mothers were best friends we were playmates until about 10 yrs old when our families moved apart. We would meet occasionally and eventually both married - her husband died in a tragic car accident - many years later, my wife scummed to cancer - she called to extend her sympathy we got together and found very shortly that we had more than a passing interest in each other we feel in love. Her name is Beverly she is my love.; [a.] Minneapolis, MN

SMITH, ROLLAND G.
[b.] December 6, 1941, Danbury, CT; [p.] Ethel and George Smith; [m.] Ann E. Gormley, January 4, 1964; [ch.] Greggory, Conan, Lee; [ed.] Oneida High School, Ithaca College; [occ.] Journalist; [memb.] Natas, Explorers Club, Friars Club, AOPA; [hon.] Nine Broadcast Emmy Awards, Ellis Island Medal of Honor - 1996; [oth. writ.] Book: "Quiet Musings" 1995 CD "SYL LA BLES" the poetry and music of nature - 1996.; [pers.] The oneness of man and nature can be found in poetry.; [a.] Coronado, CA

SMITH, ROWENA RING CAUGHLIN
[pen.] Rowena Ring Coughlin Smith; [b.] April 21, 1910, Elmore, VT; [p.] Alah H. and Colista Belle Ring; [m.] F. B. Caughlin, June 1933; [ch.] Roy-Francis B. Caughlin; [ed.] Peoples Academy, Nursing School -

NHSH, Smith College, Northampton Business College, Presbitarian Hospital Dermatology; [occ.] Senior Citizen; [memb.] Grange #134 - L.H.U. Methodist Church; [hon.] Basketball, Nursing, Poetry - some printed in Connecticut Granger; [a.] Trumbull, CT

SMITH, STANLEY S.
[pen.] Stan S. Smith; [b.] Morton, MN; [m.] Judith A. Smith; [ch.] Two; [ed.] High School and Brown's Institute of Radio Broadcasting; [oth. writ.] I have written many poems over the years. Many have been put to music and recited over local radio station.; [pers.] My poems are memories of my mind and when they are read, many find themselves in the inner verse.; [a.] Baxter, MN

SMITH, TERRI L. PEARSON
[b.] July 27, 1957, Culver City, GA; [p.] Lowell and Patricia Pearson; [m.] David Alan Smith, May 23, 1984; [ch.] Jason James, Heather Danielle; [ed.] Mira Costa High School, El Camino College, Institute of Children's Literature; [occ.] Computer Lab Instructor, De Mille Elementary School, Midway City, GA; [memb.] Clegg Elementary School PTA 96-97 President, Member CSEA, Calvary Chapel of HB, Scout Leader; [a.] Huntington Beach, CA

SNOOK, DANIEL J.
[b.] May 2, 1937, Layton, NJ; [p.] Albert Snook - Mary Aber; [m.] Patricia Ann Snook, October 26, 1963; [ch.] James Jude - David Joan; [ed.] Newton High N.J. North Arkansas Cimm Coll East Strovasburt Univ. PA; [occ.] Retired; [memb.] ISOP Amguleam Hytnosis Assoc, Masonic Lodge, Flying Hams Club; [oth. writ.] "The Tree", "The Lost Sheep", "The Shadow", "Sheetana From The Storm", "Time"; [a.] Bushkill, PA

SNOWDEN, DOROTHY A.
[b.] December 12, 1912, Gravesend, NY; [p.] Thomas and Margaret Hopkins; [m.] Charles W. Snowden, August 24, 1935; [ch.] Sharon A. and Charles W.; [ed.] Royal Oak Michigan High School Plaza Business College, NY; [occ.] Retired; [memb.] Various womens clubs, golf clubs, PTA's, and local civic organizations; [hon.] Through the years scouts, civic, athletic.; [oth. writ.] Various published by womens clubs, civic organizations and the Kaisen womans clubs of Cordoba Argentina.; [pers.] I write for the Joy of it. One heart one soul one mind free to roam.; [a.] Livermore, CA

SOBERANIS, JAHSON LION
[pen.] Jahson; [b.] January 18, 1979, Brooklyn, NY; [p.] Robert Brown; [ed.] High School, dad, and peers; [occ.] Retail Sales, Mens Department at Macys; [memb.] Member of Salinas's Basement Krew (A club of future poets) A.D.A.P.T. (Alcohol, Drug, Awareness, Prevention, Team); [hon.] Finalist in Ilaid Press, Poetry contest, Award for "Most positive poem themes"; [oth. writ.] "Promise I'll never Tell" published by Ilaid Press in "Beginnings"; [pers.] The mind is nothing but a bucket full of talent, but the person must push it over to let talent flow. Something not hart to reach, for the flow is the mighty gift of speech.; [a.] Salinas, CA

SOBOTTKA, SALLY S.
[pen.] Sally Rymer; [b.] April 24, 1931, San Francisco; [p.] Mildred and Harris Sproles; [m.] September 2, 1952; [ch.] Daniel, Elizabeth, Laura; [ed.] Radcliffe College, Stanford University, University of Georgia - Ph.D; [occ.] Retired Teacher; [hon.] Seven College Scholarship, Pi Lamba Theta (Hon), Federal Fellowship; [oth. writ.] Poems and short stories; [pers.] I write on a variety of topics trying to express tenderness for creation. I read many poets from old english on, plus in French and many translations.; [a.] Davis, CA

SOLOMON, EMANUEL
[ed.] Temple University - M.F.A.; [occ.] Poet, Painter, Lecturer in art; [hon.] Fullbright Award (scholar/teacher) Host-The Netherlands. Lecturer at International Conference on Art in Yugoslavia. Temple University Scholarship and Fellowship; [oth. writ.] The Fulbright Award was prompted by my writings re: "The Intershaping Relationship Between Art and All Other Disciplines"; [pers.] Delighted that you asked for "Philosophical Statement". The poet is a philosopher. Poetry invites you to examine life, to celebrate love, to laugh, to cry, to play with words, to think, to search for meaning.; [a.] South Orange, NJ

SONS, CYNTHIA ANN
[pen.] Cynthia Ann; [b.] July 11, 1960, Georgetown, OH; [p.] Kenon Bowling, Margaret Napier (Bates); [m.] David James Buchanan; [ch.] Jon R. Sons Jr., Angelyn, David, Chasitey and Alex Buchanan; [occ.] Mother and Homemaker; [memb.] Ohio Order of The Eastern Star Amelia Chapter 338 Amelia, Ohio; [oth. writ.] I've written several other non-published poems and songs.; [pers.] I was inspired to write this poem when the house I lived in almost since the birth of my natural son was born. The house had also been in his grandmother Frances Sons (Kragler) family for 50 years. I get my writing talent from my father whom is also a singer, songwriter.; [a.] Williamsburg, OH

SPANGLER, ELOIS L.
[pen.] Lorene; [b.] February 23, 1928, Washington, DC; [p.] Boyd and Mabel Shaffer; [m.] Charles (Deceased), February 8, 1946; [ch.] Randall, Lucinda and Valerie; [ed.] High School; [occ.] Mother, Grandmother Great Grandmother, Widow, Housekeeper; [hon.] Lots of nice things from I.S.P.; [oth. writ.] "A Beautiful Message" published in: Shadows and light. Poems in each: Memories of Tomorrow. Morning Song: Of moonlight and Wishes, so far plus "Amity's Gone Fishin'" to be in: In Dappled Sunlight.; [pers.] My inspiration has always been realize life and the real people in it. In the pages of shadows and light two new poets tug at my heart. Sherry Wilson and Joseph Harlacher. Their reality is great but no Biography. Would like to write them, my stand by Edgar A. Guest; [a.] Wellsville, PA

SPECK, MARY LOU
[b.] November 23, 1935, Saint Louis, MO; [p.] Clemens and Dorothy Foppe; [m.] William S. Speck Sr., August 27, 1960; [ch.] Shelley Grace (Deceased), William Jr.; [ed.] 12th grade; [occ.] Bookkeeper and Office Mngr., Nelco - 25 yrs.; [memb.] Fraternal Order of Eagles Arnold, MO Auxiliary 3678, Employed at Nelco for 25 years; [hon.] Many awards for Charity Work with the Eagles too many to mention.; [oth. writ.] Lots but never published of even for submitted to anyone but family and friends never thoughts I was good enough for publication; [pers.] I am older 9 children my beautiful 31 yrs old daughter passed away in October of 1994 she is the inspiration of my poem. She has two children Holly (16) and Matt (12). My son Bill has just one son Kyle.; [a.] Saint Louis, MO

SPENCE, CAROLYN NICOLE
[b.] September 9, 1955, Paris, France; [p.] John and Lillie Spence; [ch.] Danese, Kareem Spence; [ed.] 18th Ave School, West Kenney Jr. High, Central High, 1 yr. Sawer's Sec. School; [occ.] Mother and Housekeeper; [oth. writ.] I have written for personal friends. I also read and write sympathy and birthday poems.; [pers.] I have been writing poems far as I can remember, I love writing poems. This is the very first poetry contest I have entered and won.; [a.] Newark, NJ

SPENCE, MARY BETH
[pen.] Beth; [b.] December 31, 1954, Havre De Grace, MD; [p.] Lois and J. C. Rakes; [m.] Stephen, August 27, 1977; [ch.] Rachel and Matthew; [ed.] Rising Sun High Cecil Community College; [occ.] Making my Family happy; [memb.] PTA, Animal Protection Institute; [hon.] Volunteer Award for Volunteer work at Calvert Elementary School, Awarded Official 20 years member of Animal Protection Institute, Mother of the year Awarded from the children on Mother's Day; [oth. writ.] Been working on book about how hard it is when parents divorced, and one parent also seems to divorced the child - the heartbreak it causes; [pers.] "La Vie Dansante" a song by Jimmy Buffett - The Dance of Life. I believe in dancing the dance of life treasuring you loved ones because you never know how soon it will be too late; [a.] Franklin, VA

SPITTA, AMELIA HOPE
[b.] April 25, 1960, San Antonio, TX; [p.] Adolph F. Spitta and Roberta (Estes) Smith; [ed.] Robert E. Leehigh, San Antonio, TX West Texas State University Canyon, TX; [occ.] Family Service Counselor, Mission Park Funeral Homes and Cameteries; [memb.] Sanctuary Choir, Castle Hills United Pentecostal Church; [hon.] 1976 Public Library Award San Antonio Public Library 1993 Certified Personnel Consultant, NAPC, WTSU 1991 Dean's List.; [oth. writ.] Cards and handmade books for friends; [pers.] Jesus Christ is the Author and Finisher of my life. He has given me the ability to write over 220 works and if I am anything it is by His Grace. He taught me the price of loving is far greater than the cost of living, the reward of love returned, far greater than any price paid.; [a.] San Antonio, TX

SPOELSTRA, MARK
[pen.] Mark Spoelstra; [b.] June 30, 1940, Kansas City, MO; [p.] Raymond Spoelstra, Helen Spoelstra; [m.] Sherrill Spoelstra, March 26, 1971; [ch.] Joshua, Noelle, Amy; [ed.] Arcadia High, MTI Business College, San Joaquin Delta College (Creative writing class); [occ.] Shuttle Bus Driver, Yosemite National Park; [memb.] Songwriters Guild of America, Northern California Songwriters Assoc. National Audubon Society, BMI Inc.; [hon.] 1st place winner 1995, Yosemite Valley Talent Show, Listed in Who Æs Who In America 1964-1967, Listed in the Blue Book of England 1965; [oth. writ.] Have written hundreds of songs 84 of which I recorded on 5 different labels in the years 1963-1979. After pausing a decade or so, I am now writing songs and poems again on a daily basis.; [pers.] Faith, hope, love. When I embrace these peace rushes in. Sometimes it is eternity we see clearly, and today is a dream we can Æt quite explain to anyone.; [a.] Stockton, CA

SPRAGG, LANCY L.
[pen.] Lancie Spragg; [b.] August 16, 1957, Bellaire, OH; [p.] Orvy "Red" Childers, Leona Childers; [m.] Mark Spragg, August 23, 1980; [occ.] Cashier/Housewife; [memb.] United Methodist Church; [hon.] Editor's Choice Award, few poems published, many I have written since high school. Completed a 2 years writing course; [oth. writ.] Wrote a poem for my father-in-law's memorial service.; [pers.] God gave me this gift, and I pray my words will encourage and bring my Lord Glory. This poem is a story of losing a baby during my struggle with cancer 4 yrs. ago.; [a.] Adena, OH

SPROAT, PEGGY O'NEILL
[pen.] Peggy O'Neill Sproat; [b.] May 27, 1931, Marion, IN; [p.] Henry and Saraha Johnston O'Neill; [m.] James Edward Sproat, August 20, 1948; [ch.] One son James Michael; [ed.] G.E.D. From Ball State University in 1964 - Writing Poetry and Learning about people here and Ireland. Reading history of Ireland before Christ time.; [occ.] Retired, Classes from son on computer; [memb.] Dixon, IL. Genealogy Society A.A.R.P. Police Alliance Cops for Kids Dare, Veterans Vietnam - Vets of Foreign Wars; [hon.] Editor's Award for "Our Woods Where Heidi Lays" newspaper publications of poets publication. (Four News Papers). Co Cork Ireland published letters and thank you letter.; [oth. writ.] Many letters to people I have made friends with in Ireland - my grand father came to our country in 1881 - God has been with me all the way by showing me "I Can Do It".; [pers.] I want to find my heritage in Ireland - since August 96 - I have found my Great Great Grand Mother through the people of Ireland and the news papers. Ireland has opened her arms to me.; [a.] Richmond, IN

SPROAT, STEPHANIE
[b.] March 22, 1979; [p.] Eunice Cantor; [ed.] Am a senior at Sidney High School; [memb.] Have been: Key Club secretary, SADD president, Dare spokesperson, varsity cheerleader, and 4-H recorder, Health and Safety director, vice-president, and secretary; [hon.] Placed Best of Class (three times), Best Reserve of Class (twice), and Outstanding of the Day (twice) in photography, health, and creative writing categories at county and state fair. Earned Coach's Award in cheerleading; [oth. writ.] I've written many poems and short stories. Some are: Nature's Panorama, Nobody's Child, Dazy Days, On Parting, Slow Solace, and Connie's Last Headache.; [pers.] I enjoy writing, especially about the beauty of nature and life. Writing has also helped me accept the confusion, pain, and sorrow of parting with a family member or a friend.; [a.] Sidney, OH

SROKA, ANDREW
[b.] May 24, 1958; [p.] Patricia Sroka (Mother), A. Sroka (Father); [ed.] Southington High School; [occ.] Studying Sociology and Psychology; [memb.] Southington Jayee's Southington Y.M.C.A., Habitat for Humanity, Cystic Fibrosis Foundation; [oth. writ.] Many others poems, but, to date, of my work to be published.; [pers.] Poetry, it's words and different styles, fascinate me with the range of feelings, emotions they inspire in people.; [a.] Southington, CT

STAMM, DENISE K.
[pen.] Denise K. Stamm; [b.] December 29, 1956, Dayton, OH; [p.] Nellie and Joe Middleton; [m.] Nellie D. Stamm, July 29, 1989; [ch.] Jeff Middleton; [ed.] Graduate Miamisburg High School Class of 1976; [occ.] Karolton Envelope Machine Operator and Excel Telecommunications; [hon.] Started the Wrestling Parents Club at Miamisburg High School in 1992. Wrestling Mom of the Year award 1992-93.; [oth. writ.] Some poems published in our area newspaper the Miamisburg News.; [pers.] My poems reflect my love of whatever they are written about they seem to sour out and write themselves.; [a.] Miamisburg, OH

STANLEY, TERRY
[pen.] Zebra; [b.] October 29, 1933, San Francisco, CA; [p.] Wm. and Rita O'Haire; [m.] Deceased, December 24, 1956; [ch.] Charles, Nancine, Tammy; [occ.] Property Management; [oth. writ.] Asst. poems and children's stories.; [pers.] Hurt Never, Help Ever; [a.] Oceanside, CA

STAPLES III, WILLIAM F.
[pen.] Frank Staples; [b.] June 26, 1953, Roselle, NJ; [p.] William Staples (D), Florence Staples; [m.] Magdalene W. Staples, November 21, 1981; [ch.] John R., William F. IV; [ed.] Roselle High; [occ.] United States Army Sergeants Major Academy (Student) 21 yrs. Military; [memb.] Phi Beta Sigma Fraternity, Sons of King Solomon, GA (PHA), AASR (PHA), A.E.A.O.N.M.S. (PHA); [hon.] High School Who's Who 1971; [oth. writ.] Union College's "Sheaf '73"

Vol. II, But Speak Soft, Know Why, and Idealistic To Realistic.; [pers.] We are not in this world, to take from this world. But to give to this world. Nor are we here to learn from this world, but instead we must go forth to teach the world; [a.] El Paso, TX

STARR, JUDITH S.
[b.] November 24, 1944, LaFollette, TN; [m.] Rogers F. Starr, October 29, 1966; [ch.] Stacey Pace, Michael, Amy; [ed.] B.S. in English from Middle TN State Univ.; [occ.] Wife, Homemaker and Volunteer; [memb.] First United Methodist Church, Contact Lifeline of the Highland and Rim Amer. Heart Asso., Delta Kappa Gamma (inactive) Dig N' Dream Garden Club Hobbies: Bridge and Reading; [oth. writ.] Book, recipes easy, Poetry breezy, several anthologies, local newspaper, "The Poet's Corner" magazine; [pers.] I hope to inspire and entertain through my writing.; [a.] Manchester, TN

STARR, JUNE
[b.] January 25, 1940, Poughkeepsie, NY; [p.] Clara Julia and Frank R. Fish; [m.] Philip Starr, August 1, 1982; [ch.] Kimberly Brown; [occ.] Housewife; [memb.] Goshen Writers Club and Cornwall Vol. Fire Dept.; [pers.] I believe that poetry, more than any other type of writing, expresses the inner feelings and thoughts of the poet.; [a.] Goshen, CT

STEINER, JASON M.
[b.] June 21, 1974, Hillsboro, OR; [p.] Norman Steiner, Doris Steiner; [ed.] Oregon State University, B.S. in Wildlife Science; [hon.] Graduated Cum Laude, National Dean's List; [pers.] I have learned not to try to write poetry. My poetry is simply translation of those emotions and experiences that demand it.; [a.] Beaverton, OR

STEMPLE, KELLY
[b.] May 15, 1971, Westwood; [p.] Robert and Christine Stemple; [ed.] Park Ridge H.S.; [occ.] Warehouse Employee; [a.] Park Ridge, NJ

STEVENS, AMANDA DESIREE
[b.] August 29, 1982, Springdale, AR; [p.] Lee R. Stevens, Shirley Stevens; [ed.] Lowell Elementary, Elmwood Jr. High; [memb.] Wilderness Tabernacle Church; [hon.] Music, 1st Place Piano Recital, Little Brave Award, Accurate Award, Terrific Kid Award, Student of the Week Award; [oth. writ.] The Stranger, Fall, The Times In The Future, Saving The Rain Forest, Guardian Of The Sky, Tiny Toon Adv., Easter Bunny, Daddy; [pers.] I work hard and try to do my best and I am very honest and trustworthy.; [a.] Rogers, AR

STEVENS, KATHLEEN ANN
[b.] May 24, 1989, Bel Air, MD; [p.] Mark Scott Stevens and Cynthia Ann (Zirn) Stevens; [ed.] Emmorton Elementary (currently in 2nd grade) Bel Air, MD; [oth. writ.] I have many stories I've written and illustrated. None published. [pers.] I love cats, cheetas (all animals), art, sports, reading and writing.; [a.] Bel Air, MD

STIVERS, STEPHEN N.
[b.] December 31, 1925, Jarbidge, NV; [p.] Harry R. and Rose Alice Stivers; [m.] Rita Angell Stivers, October 19, 1945, Divorced February 10, 1988; [ed.] University of Oregon B.S., M.S., Ph.D.; [occ.] Retired Public School Teacher and University Professor; [oth. writ.] Professional Articles; [a.] Lake Oswego, OR

STONE, THOMAS H.
[b.] July 13, 1957, Riverside, CA; [p.] Charolette Q. Fortune, Edward J. Stone; [ch.] Jeremiah Dean Stone, Terry Warren Stone, Sarah Lynn Stone, Thomas Gordon Stone; [ed.] G.E.D. (1990), Arlington Hi '73 - '75; [occ.] Lift Truck Operator, Sweetheart Cup Co.; [memb.] Teamsters Union since '79; [oth. writ.] "Gone Fishin'"

1995, "Treasured Poems of America-Summer '95"; [pers.] "Try anything once, good ones twice, everything in moderation. M.Y.O.B. don't worry, be happy (love is all you need)." Pass is on? (John Lennon).; [a.] Riverside, CA

STOUTNER, SARAH S.
[b.] March 13, 1950, Washington, CO; [p.] Annabel and Marion Stoutner, (Deceased); [ed.] Keota High School, Pima Community College; [occ.] Disabled 27 years of Rheumatoid Arthritis; [memb.] Arthritis Foundation Saguaro Christian Church Choir Turson Horizon Chorus (Sweet Adelines); [oth. writ.] Other poems - sent to Reader's Digest and not used at this time.; [pers.] My church life and close family members, Grandparents, 3 brothers and my mom and dad meant alot to me growing up on a farm.; [a.] Waterloo, IA

STRAUSS, JENNIFER MARIE
[b.] January 14, Fort Lauderdale, FL; [p.] Carol J. Strauss; [ed.] Coconut Creek High School Atlantic Vocational Technical Center; [occ.] Student at Atlantic Vocational; [memb.] In students against drunk driving (SADD) 3 years key club 1 year. Crime watch 1 year; [pers.] I feel deeply moved about what I have written, it makes me feel very satisfied and more confident about myself. It took me several days to come up with a new poem and I finally did.; [a.] Margate, FL

STROHL, K'ANN
[b.] June 7, 1964, Montrose, PA; [p.] Janice Ring, John Holgate; [m.] Daniel Strohl, March 30, 1989; [ch.] Erik Strohl; [ed.] G.E.D. Blue Ridge School, 9/28/82; [occ.] Papermaker, Procter & Gamble Co., Mehoopany, Penn.; [memb.] GTO Association of America; [pers.] I have written several poems throughout my life. My poems allow me to express how I am feeling at that moment in my life, but it also lets me relive that moment everytime I read that poem.; [a.] Meshoppen, PA

STRONG, NAKIA
[b.] November 10, 1980, Fort Campbell, KY; [p.] Lois and Jerry Strong; [ed.] Now in 11th grade, graduating in May of 1998 from Andress High School in El Paso, Texas. Want to attend Louisiana State University; [memb.] Centurion Chapel of Ft. Bliss, Texas, Part of the Youth Choir and Youth Usher Board; [hon.] Won essay contest held by school, was inducted into P.R.E.P.S., Quatermaster of Flag Corp of Golden Eagle Band; [oth. writ.] Working on amateur novel called Manhattan Blues, hoping one day it will too be published.; [pers.] My poems usually reflect my thought on life or past events that has happened to me. I like to express my feelings in my poems.; [a.] El Paso, TX

STURGILL, TRACY L.
[b.] January 28, 1967, Columbus, OH; [p.] Leslie C. and Loretta P. Sparks; [m.] Allen C. Sturgill, November 21, 1989; [ch.] Amanda Nicole, Allen Michael; [ed.] Lawrence Co. High School, Louisa, Kentucky - Gen Apr 1987; [occ.] Student at The Central Ohio School of Massage; [oth. writ.] "Roses" to printed in "Essence of A Dream" in the spring of 1997; [pers.] I would like to thank God for giving this special talent and to thank friends like JWJ, NeeKazee and Betty Mullins for their support and friendship.; [a.] Circleville, OH

SUAREZ, RAFAEL
[pen.] Rafael Suarez; [b.] May 25, 1962, Hato Rey, PR; [p.] Adelaida Pulmeri, Ceasar Pulmeri; [m.] Nancy Suarez, December 10, 1988; [ch.] Christian Suarez, Justin Suarez; [ed.] B.A. in Criminal Justice Minor in Spanish; [occ.] Probation Officer; [memb.] Fraternal order of Police, Kappa Delta RHO.; [oth. writ.] Poems in Probation; [pers.] In order to learn one must be willing to be taught. With God all things are possible.; [a.] Ridgewood, NY

SUGGS, KIM
[b.] June 16, 1968, Ohio; [p.] Clyde and Rose Johnston; [m.] Bobby E. Suggs; [ed.] Woodham High School; [pers.] There are stars and there are dreams. Both exist but neither can we touch. They are the elusiveness of our lives the brightness against the dark. We are forever searching for the glimpse of that touch, the unknown to be known, the dream to be true, and the star to be ours.; [a.] Pensacola, FL

SULLIVAN, ALICE A.
[b.] June 29, 1948, Milford, CT; [p.] Joseph A. and Virginia E. Mingrone; [ch.] Stacey A. Sullivan (daughter); [ed.] Graduate of Milford H.S. and Bridgeport Hospital School of Nursing now working toward BSN; [occ.] Registered Nurse - Milford Hospital; [hon.] CLN peer recognition Award, Medical Staff Award and Surgical Staff Award from BHSN; [pers.] I began writing at the age of 40, and this poem, my first, was inspired by a very special person, my father.

SULLIVAN, CATHERINE Y.
[pen.] Cathy; [b.] July 4, 1938, Lincoln, NE; [p.] Oreall and Isabel Soucie; [m.] Leland E. Sullivan, May 9, 1959; [ch.] Lauri, John, Theresa, Mary and Julie; [ed.] K Thur 12; [occ.] Farm Wife and Clerk for the Lancaster County Election Office; [memb.] Saint Mary's Catholic Church; [oth. writ.] All other poems I have written have been for my children, about their lives. I did write one for 125 year celebration of Denton, Nebr. last July. They put it in their little monthly paper. The Denton Town Talk; [pers.] I never thought I would ever be recognized by my poetry, but was grateful for given the opportunity to enter a contest. We all have talents, and should always try to use them in our everyday life.; [a.] Denton, NE

SULLIVAN, DEBORAH S.
[pen.] Deborah; [b.] April 28, 1954, Tampa, FL; [p.] Mr. and Mrs. Luther Smith; [m.] Danny Carlton Sullivan, June 24, 1972; [ch.] Two; [ed.] High School Graduate; [occ.] Accounting Specialist; [memb.] Falls Road Baptist Church; [oth. writ.] I've written 10 or 15 more poems. I've wrote one for my husband and I in recognition of our upcoming silver anniversary. Most of my writings are about my high School Sweetheart whom I am married to and love very much.; [pers.] In my writing I share good times and bad times. Most of all I write from my heart starting to give all your love. Be happy with each situation, share with others, and stand firm and uphold the one you love. Also having 7 sisters of my own, and my husband having 6 brothers and sisters share time with your family. These are the most precious of all.; [a.] Nashville, NC

SULLIVAN, MARGARET A.
[b.] November 4, Charlottesville, VA; [p.] Virgie P. and Eugene H. Anderson; [m.] Divorced; [ch.] Ulysses Sullivan Jr.; [ed.] Albemarle High School, Piedmont VA Community College; [occ.] Executive Housekeeping Manager, Wintergreen Resorts; [memb.] Mountain View Church, Afton, VA, I.E.H.A.; [oth. writ.] Other love, family and christian oriented poems; [pers.] My inspiration comes from the love of family and friends. This particular poem was inspired by the loss of two lovely, caring parents, Gene and Pearline Anderson; [a.] Afton, VA

SUMMERS, MARVIN C.
[b.] February 6, 1948, Chicago; [p.] Dorothy M. Harry Bill Summers; [m.] Divorced; [ch.] Zakiya Summers; [ed.] Juris Doctorate Hyde Park High - Chicago, Jackson State Univ Jackson MS, Texas Univ Houston TX; [occ.] Private Attorney; [memb.] Texas Bar Assoc., Houston Bar Ass., Texas Criminal Defense Lawyers Ass., American Trial Lawyers Asso, Phi Alpha Delta Fraternity and Houston Bus. and Professional Men's

Club; [oth. writ.] What Happens to Black Children When Their Mothers are Incarcerated - Sunbelt Magazine Jackson MS; [pers.] I strive to be a positive influence with all those persons I come into contact with whether attending a business or social function.; [a.] Houston, TX

SUTTON, DANIEL C.
[pen.] J. T. Lonergan; [b.] October 12, 1962, Manhattan, NY; [p.] Daniel R. Sutton, Linda C. Malus; [m.] Lisa A. Daniels-Sutton, September 3, 1982; [ch.] Maegan A. Sutton, Devin R. Sutton; [ed.] Central Islip S.H.S., NY, Assoc. Arts with Honors College at Plattburgh, NY; [occ.] Teacher, Coach; [memb.] VFW Post 4715, Jersey Shore Lacrosse Club, St. Peters R.C. Church; [hon.] U.S. Navy Veteran; [a.] Port Pleasant Beach, NJ

SWAFFORD, ANTHONY SHANE
[b.] May 18, 1977, Seneca, SC; [p.] Ira E. Swafford, June Swafford; [ed.] Hillcrest High School; [occ.] Artist, Composer, Poet; [pers.] "If a fool's fool I be then proud I am, you see, because a blind man's eye has judged and compared himself to me."; [a.] Simpsonville, SC

SWAFFORD, SEAN M.
[b.] January 10, 1972, Blue Island, IL; [p.] Will Harris Swafford and M. Susan Johnson; [m.] Eva Marie Swafford, March 13, 1992; [ch.] Toni Marie 14, Brian Vincent 10, Andrea Marie 5, Christopher Brandon 3; [ed.] Duarte High, Azusa High, Central Jr. High, Eastview Elementary; [occ.] United States Army Field Artillery; [memb.] Several Different Military Organizations; [hon.] Misc. Military; [oth. writ.] Many other poems - unpublished Wizards Tale: The Book of Souls - unpublished Wizards Tale: Dragon Warriors - unpublished Wizards Tale: Ascension to Tomorrow several other unpublished short stories.; [pers.] People do not change, they simply become more of what they are. My writings are the reflection of my growth, physically, mentally, and spiritually. It was my 7th and 8th grade English teacher, Ms. Mack, that was my greatest influence.; [a.] Fort Campbell, KY

SWAIN, MARK A.
[b.] March 24, 1961, Murfreesboro, TN; [p.] Bill Swain and Gussie Swain; [ed.] 1 year Technical Electronics; [occ.] Security Guard; [oth. writ.] I've written about a hundred songs, but I can't afford to record them; [pers.] It's awfully difficult to find a single country girl, because I won't step foot in a bar. And I'd never marry a woman that would.; [a.] Murfreesboro, TN

SWANNER, STEVE M.
[pen.] Mr. Steve; [b.] July 5, 1978, Texas; [p.] Chester Swanner, Julie Trott; [ed.] Eau Gallie High School, Barry University; [occ.] Student; [hon.] Reserve Officers Association Ribbon Scholastic Art Award Kitty Hawk Air Society Honor Roll; [pers.] Philosophical statement are irrelevant. I just write what I feel, and I try to have fun in the process; [a.] Melbourne, FL

SWARTZLANDER, NICOLE
[b.] August 18, 1986, San Dimas, CA; [p.] Charles and Dareen Swartzlander; [ed.] 5th grade student at Quail Summit Elementary School in Diamond Bar, CA; [oth. writ.] She wrote 4 other poems on peace as a class assignment for Young Author's Day. She wrote these in the 4th grade at age 9. At age 7 she wrote and illustrated a book called "The Great Adventure".; [a.] Diamond Bar, CA

SWICK, LIZ Y.
[pen.] Liz Y. Nelson Swick; [b.] November 27, 1955, IN; [p.] Tim and Yvonne Nelson; [m.] Ron Swick, June 21, 1980; [ch.] Sara and John Michael; [occ.] Activities Dept. Scenie Hills Care Center; [oth. writ.] Various newsletters, Sympath letters and poems "forever and a day" 1996 Anthology. Poems sold at Charity Auctions.; [pers.] If I can touch one person, letting them know how special life can be. It's the simple pleasures, those little things that make us happy that really count. Like my family my husband, my children the 2 cats and 3 dogs,; [a.] Ferdinand, IN

SWITZER, CATHRYN ELIZABETH
[b.] November 20, 1969, Chicago, IL; [p.] Patricia Hert Switzer and John L. Switzer M.D.; [ed.] New Trier High School, BA in Philosophy Kenyon College, Masters Program Antioch University; [occ.] Singer, Songwriter, Lyricist, and Masters Student in Clinical Psychology; [hon.] Received award of "Distinction" on college senior thesis.; [oth. writ.] Performs original songs on monthly basis in the Los Angeles ares.; [pers.] As I look behind me past the road I have not taken, for ahead I see the future I have not forsaken yet. Now I'm left to find my way, with the guiding light of yesterday.; [a.] Los Angeles, CA

SYLVAIN, MICHEL WILLIAM
[b.] June 11, 1954, Port-au-Prince, Haiti, WI; [p.] Gertrude Carmen Stuppard and Michel Wilner Sylvain; [m.] Isnine Jean-Philippe Sylvain; [ch.] Stanley John-Rocks Sylvain and Sophie Brook Sylvain; [ed.] Accounting: Ecole De Commerce Maurice Laroche General Business-BS Iona College, New Rochelle, NY; [occ.] Cashier; [oth. writ.] Completed one novel "The Tragedy Of A Romance" in 1995 and another "The Invisible Child" in 1996. At this time I am looking for a publisher; [pers.] I believe that mankind is one. Whatever our skin colors, we have same needs, same wants, same feelings and aspiration.; [a.] Mount Vernon, NY

TABB II, RODGER
[b.] March 15, 1970, Philadelphia, PA; [p.] Roger Tabb, Wanda Tabb; [m.] Marjorie Jill Tabb, October 14, 1995; [ch.] Marquise Ali Tabb; [ed.] Cardinal Dougherty H.S., Chowan Jr. College, Bowie State University, West Chester University; [occ.] Songwriter; [hon.] High School and College "All American" Basketball Player; [oth. writ.] Articles published in the "Philadelphia Inquirer"; [pers.] "Poetry is nothing more than a connection between one's heart and mind, resulting in one's own master piece."; [a.] Sharon Hill, PA

TAGLIALAVORE, CARMELA
[pen.] C. Tag; [b.] September 20, 1950, Elizabeth, NJ; [p.] Leonard Taglialavore, Ruth Taglialavore; [ch.] Jacob - David; [ed.] Computer Science Institute Graduate 4.0 Avg Dean's List; [occ.] Arts and Crafts artist; [memb.] Montclair Craft Guild NAFE; [hon.] Freehold Center Committee "High Standard of Craftmanship" Lavallette Heritage Committee "Best in Show" blue ribbon; [pers.] In these changing, often chaotic times, we can glide gently through life by affirming very simply "Divine order" thereby making it our own.; [a.] Lakehurst, NJ

TAITANO, TRINA
[pen.] Trina Collette; [b.] February 22, 1980, Guam; [p.] Carlos and Winnie V. Taitano; [ed.] Saint John's Episcopal School, 12 years of education, graduating in 1998; [occ.] Student; [memb.] Dededo Drug - Free Organization, Volunteer at Guam Memorial Hospital, Junior Achievement Program, Drama Club, Speech and Debate, National Forensic League, Youth-for-Youth; [hon.] First place in the All-Island Mother's Day Poetry Contest, Semi-Finalist for International Essay Contest, Semi-Finalist for National Poetry Contest. I have also been awarded and honored with supportive parents and a wonderful life.; [oth. writ.] Completed 3 volumes (unpublished) of poetry, I have written many essays and short stories.; [pers.] I would like to dedicate this to someone dear to my heart — Frank Munoz. I would also like to say thank you to my parents. You all support and love me so much. Remember — to be loved is to be understood. To all, youth is a gift far more precious than any object. Do not accept it freely. Nurture it, and live life as fully as possible.; [a.] Nimitz Hill Estates, GU

TALLINI, CESIDIO
[b.] May 10, 1962, Jamaica, NY; [p.] Italo Tallini, Anna Tallini; [ed.] Two HS Diplomas: American from SUNY at Albany, Italian from Scuola D'Italia of New York. Has attended university in both the U.S. and Italy.; [occ.] Data Conversion Operator for USPS, Freelance Translator for the Italic Way; [memb.] Library of Congress, American Bible Society, Italic Studies Institute, Linguistic Society of America, Childreach; [hon.] Was interviewed by the Queens Chronicle in March 1996 for his work in trying to restore government funding for the Summer Youth Employment Program (SYEP). Was given an award for his efforts by the SYEP Contractors Coalition in May 1996.; [oth. writ.] His writings have appeared in America Oggi. His translations in The Italic Way.; [pers.] My. Tallini is a shortwave radio audiophile, a Bible collector, a soccer enthusiast, a small budget philanthropist, and a bilingual poet. His poems are often prophetic.; [a.] South Floral Park, NY

TANCORDO, JOSEPH FRANCIS
[b.] April 2, 1959, Newark, NJ; [p.] Frank and Palma Tancordo; [ed.] High School, Local College and Specialty Coarces Troy High School, Fullerton, CA. "Graduate Class of 1977" Fullerton College, Business" Machining Dale Carnigee, Speech Classes, and Sales Classes.; [occ.] Machinist, Pamarlo Pacific Orange, LA; [hon.] Top Achiever Award from Dale Carigie, in a sales seminar class; [oth. writ.] 40 other writing, about love and world events, including the Persian Gulf War, President Reagan Being Shot, and The Death of Richard Nixon, also poems about growing up; [pers.] All my poems, and short stories, are created by every situation I experience that I share with a loved one or friend. With every rising sun, a new day, a new poem or story is writing to be written.; [a.] Yorba Linda, CA

TANDY, MR. BRUCE LEE
[b.] March 13, 1962, Louisville, KY; [p.] Norma Jeanne and Gene Brown Tandy; [ch.] Stephanie Lynn Tandy; [ed.] BA Degree Psychology University of Kentucky 1985, Theatre Assistantship University of Louisville; [occ.] Actor; [memb.] Performing Arts League, Tau Kappa Epsilon Fraternity-President of Gamma Sigma Chapter, Southeast Christian Church Sports Car Club and America; [hon.] Performed in Alley Theatre and Louisville's Playhouse, Honorable Mention in Arts Magazine Leo for acting. Leo has published some of my work; [oth. writ.] My Angel, My lovers Touch, My Special Friend, Cry Of The Soul, Fire Girl; [pers.] I hope my poems bring great love and passion to their readers lives as Katherine Elizabeth Bentley brought to mine, inspiring me to write them.; [a.] Louisville, KY

TAPIA, JAMES R.
[b.] November 10, 1964, Albuquerque, NM; [p.] Tim and Nora Tapia; [ed.] Valley High School University of New Mexico - senior in Anthropology program (also minoring in English Literature); [occ.] Library Information Specialist II Centennial Science and Engineering Library-UNM; [memb.] National Audobor Society, World Wildlife Fund Member, Gay, Lesbian Student Union - UNM, New Mexico outdoors club; [hon.] Staff Recognition Award for outstanding work primary care curriculum - School Medicine, UNM Hippo Award - School of Medicine, UNM; [oth. writ.] Many unpublished works. Poetry and short fiction De Profundus,

The Uncanny Man, Miguelita etc....; [pers.] "What moves men of genius, or rather, what inspires their work, is not new ideas, but their obsession with the idea that what has already been said is still not enough." I feel we all have so many things to say, and so many ways to say them. The reality we face is whether we decide to say them or not because all the expression one withholds can only lead to a deprived imagination in others.; [a.] Albuquerque, NM

TARASUK, NIKOLAI
[b.] October 17, 1924, Medina, NY; [p.] Naum and Antonina Tarasuk; [m.] Frances Tarasuk (Deceased), April 20, 1964; [ch.] Marianne Gardner (step-daughter); [ed.] Roger's High School, Newport, R.T-1946 U.C.L.A. 1954 B.A Slavic Language Buffalo State Teachers College 1959 Master's Degree in Elementary Education; [occ.] Retired; [memb.] Past President of S.C. Black Minorca International Poultry Club; [oth. writ.] Poems published in National Poetry Anthology Los Angeles, California; [pers.] In 1990 I took my mother's ashes to Bilogir'ya, Ukraine, where she was born. For two separate years I taught english in Kyiv after Ukraine gained its independence.; [a.] Medina, NY

TAYLOR, DONALD
[b.] October 10, 1976, Portland, OR; [p.] Cathy and Allen Taylor; [ed.] Second year student at South Seattle C.C.; [occ.] Student; [hon.] Editor's Choice Award for "Ten Virgins"; [oth. writ.] Three poems in the South Seattle Sentinel "Wait", "Motherly Love" and "Grandfather".; [pers.] Claiming you are a Christian? And forgetting the pure word is not good. God's word grants a grand life. Don't forget the bible (Definition in Dictionary Neglect in Mirror).; [a.] Seattle, WA

TAYLOR, JOY
[b.] October 3, 1980, Sepulveda, CA; [p.] Brenda Goodwin, Henry Taylor; [ed.] Los Angeles Baptist High; [occ.] Student, Los Angeles Baptist High, North Hills, CA; [hon.] Honors in Academics since Elementary; [oth. writ.] My other writings include: "She Was Twisted," "Have You Seen The Children?", "Super Mom," and "After Twilight," all of which are thus far unpublished.; [pers.] I would like to thank my mother for motivating me to enter the poverty contest. I'm glad she saw that I have potential. I also want to thank both of my parents for always knowing what to say to lift my spirits, though dad has a tendency to make his talks far more lengthy than necessary. Of course, I have to thank all of the `extended family' who never let me doubt I am loved and never hesitate to give me a good `kick in the pants' when I need it.; [a.] North Hills, CA

TAYLOR, RALPH WILLIAM
[b.] July 4, 1944, Akron, OH; [p.] Deceased; [m.] Divorced; [ch.] Three sons; [ed.] 14 yrs; [occ.] Retired us army 100% disabled military; [memb.] Disabled Veterans of America Vietnam Veterans of America Life Membership in both; [hon.] US Army bronze star for Meritorious JVC service dates 1967-1968, 1969-1970; [oth. writ.] Only personal and destroyed no one would under stand it. I have been married and divorced 5 time because of Vietnam I just want someone to trust; [pers.] War kills the mind and soul. If politicians want war they should fight it themselves. Not being who you were before you went to war sucks.; [a.] Fayetteville, TN

TERRANCE JR., KENNETH
[pen.] Tahoni Kahontsi, Katikia, Bro. Kenneth; [b.] January 8, 1964, Rochester, NY; [p.] Kenneth and Martha Terrance; [ed.] Currently a full time student at Monroe Community College, Franklin High graduate, Student of the Honorable Elijah Muhammad; [occ.] Iron worker "Sky Walker", Iron workers local #33 Roch. NY; [oth. writ.] Black Woman, Black Man two poems published in MCC's literary magazine, "Cab-

bages and Kings" Spring 1996.; [pers.] All praise is due to Allah, first. My inspiration to write again after 15 years is in the spirit of Black Women, and in the spirit of all the original people of Earth. Onkweltonwe; [a.] Rochester, NY

TERRES, JUDY
[b.] June 20, 1965, Fairmont, MN; [p.] Charles and Alvada Gustafson; [ch.] Holly and Joshua; [ed.] East Chain High, St. Cloud Tech College; [occ.] Accounting Clerk, Stearns Coop Electric Association, Melrose, MN; [memb.] Our Saviors Lutheran Church; [pers.] I have found poetry to be a very relaxing hobby. It is something I would like to pursue and hopefully, accomplish future publications.; [a.] Albany, MN

TERRY, JULIE
[b.] July 7, Monroe, LA; [p.] Julia Blocker, Eddie Terry; [ed.] Attending Ruston High School; [occ.] Student; [oth. writ.] The poem published in this book and another poem is published in Reflections a literary journal.; [pers.] I try to question everything and look beyond the oblivious in my poetry.; [a.] Monroe, LA

TERRY, KEITH
[b.] October 22, 1962, Omaha, NE; [p.] J. C. and Helen Terry; [occ.] Computer Programmer; [a.] Savage, MN

TERRY, LOLITA LYNN
[b.] March 13, 1970, Roanoke, VA; [m.] Christopher Lee Terry, April 13, 1988; [ch.] Kyle LeRyan and Christina Kay

TERRY JR., JOSEPH H.
[pen.] Joseph Terry Jr; [b.] June 26, 1910, San Jose, Costa Rica, CA; [p.] Joseph H. Terry Sr., Enriqueta Vialta Terry; [m.] Ruth Norma Terry (Deceased April 30, 1992), September 30, 1933 (Engaged 1930); [ch.] Susan Jane Terry Hanson (Adopted); [ed.] Completed elementary, high school graduate, 2 1/2 yrs. business college. (Personal: WW-II Veteran, US 8th Air Force, 78th Fighter Grp., 82nd Fighter Sgd); [occ.] Retired "Now a Soldier of Jesus since 1957" - Church of Christ; [memb.] Church of Christ; [hon.] Only those granted by our Lord Jesus, through complete obedience in His service of worshiping in Spirit and in truth! John 4:24. All other worship is vain and ignorant, read Matthew 15:2-9, II John 9:10, Acts 17:23-31, II John 9:11.; [oth. writ.] (30) All on various topics of the New Analytical Bible, King James Version - and American Standard of (1901) John A. Dickson Publishing Co.; [pers.] Human knowledge has to be understood to be - loved! Spiritual knowledge has to be - loved to be understood! (We can not live - Rong, and die-right).; [a.] Palm Beach Gardens, FL

THAYER, MIKE
[b.] August 8, 1962, Cedar Rapids, IA; [p.] Don Thayer, Rose Krabbenhoeft; [m.] Filiz, January 18, 1994; [ch.] Daniel; [ed.] Kennedy High School, Community College of the Air Force; [occ.] Data Entry Supervisor; [memb.] Johnson County Republican Central Committee; [hon.] Decorated Soldier, United States Air Force; [oth. writ.] Several Editorials published in Local Newspapers, Guest Opinions for the Iowa City press citizen, articles written for the keynote speaker- the newspaper of conservatives.; [pers.] I am motivated by the truth and the power of knowledge.; [a.] Coralville, IA

THOMAS, BUFORD
[b.] February 5, 1957, Lufkin, TX; [p.] James Thomas, Billie Thomas; [m.] Pamela Thomas, June 10, 1984; [ch.] Rita Thomas, Marletta Thomas, Mikhail Thomas; [ed.] Lufkin High School, Lamor University; [occ.] Journeyman, Industrial Eq. Inspector, Automatic Salesman; [memb.] Abundant Life United Methodist Church;

[pers.] The power of poetry is soft spoken, as wisdom is life.; [a.] Lufkin, TX

THOMAS, CINDY ANN
[b.] April 5, 1965, Miami; [p.] Roland H. Thomas Jr., Mary A. Thomas; [ed.] Orange Park High, Orange Park, Fla.; [occ.] Associate - Harris Teeter Greenville, S.C.; [memb.] National Bone Marrow Registry; [oth. writ.] A Piece For A Church News Letter in Orlando, Florida, Pieces written to friends of a show of love and support.; [pers.] The greatest gift you can give someone is that of yourself. Your love, compassion and trust. Any gifts beyond that is only a reflection of one's self...; [a.] Greenville, SC

THOMAS JR., JACK H.
[b.] November 8, 1954, Birmingham, AL; [p.] Jack H. Thomas Sr., Janice Thomas; [m.] Divorced; [ch.] Cathryn Thomas - Laura Thomas; [ed.] B.A. The University of Alabama; [occ.] Driver, Schneider National Carriers; [memb.] Cottage Hill Baptist Church; [hon.] Dean's List; [oth. writ.] "The Finer Things...", "Life" (not published); [pers.] I try to be positive, no matter how difficult life is, you always have a prayer.; [a.] Mobile, AL

THOMAS, JAMES TERRYL
[b.] October 18, 1970, Starkville, MS; [p.] James Thurman Thomas, Lollian High Thomas; [m.] Yoshiko Ouchi Thomas, January 19, 1995; [ch.] Shogun Sebastian Thomas; [ed.] BS Mechanical Engineering University of Mississippi; [occ.] Supply Officer US Navy; [oth. writ.] None published. (2) Short stories - "Change and Transition", and "In Honor of J. Author McAffee" (2) books, not finished, The Southern Proclamation and James and Yoko.; [pers.] Every writing of mine, is actually a part of me - body, soul and mind.; [a.] Oxford, MS

THOMAS, KYLE
[pen.] Zippy; [b.] February 9, 1980, Shawnee, OK; [p.] James (Pete) and Dixie Thomas

THOMAS, OLA
[b.] November 3, 1927, Monticello, RI; [p.] Andley and Lucendia Thomas; [m.] Eslelle S. Thomas, April 17, 1948; [ch.] Carolyn T. Pundy; [ed.] 8th Grade Elementary 2 years Institutional Cookury and Commercial Dietetics at Bethune Cookman College; [occ.] Retired Chef; [memb.] Boaz Lodge II 212 Fond Am, P.H.A. Allen Chapel A.M.E. church D.A.V.; [hon.] State support worker of the year. Retiree of the year. Teacher of the year and many more; [oth. writ.] A contribution to African American History my autobiography. Ola Thomas you can; [pers.] You can accomplish your gold in life if you believe in Christ; [a.] Daytona Beach, FL

THOMAS, RODNEY BERRAN
[pen.] Rod; [b.] August 9, 1971, Baltimore; [p.] Annie Thomas and Donald Thomas; [ed.] I finished two years of College. I graduated from diesel mechanic school with high marks; [occ.] Diesel Mechanic partner in a up coming record Co.; [memb.] (Church) Morning Star Baptist; [hon.] Award for effort and dedication in diesel mechanics school. Graduated at the top of the class.; [pers.] I believe if you can read love on paper and feel it, you should be able to show that love for other humans!!!; [a.] Baltimore, MD

THOMPSON, ANNETTE
[b.] August 22, 1972, St. Albans, VT; [p.] Steven and Elaine Thompson; [ed.] Missisquoi Valley Union High School, Wells College; [occ.] Editorial Assistant Plenum Publishing Corporation; [hon.] Summa Cum Laude, Dean's List, Phi Beta Kappa, Henry Wells Scholar; [pers.] I find imagistic language to be the most

important and exciting part of poetry, mine as well as others.; [a.] Piscataway, NJ

THOMPSON, DAVID J.
[b.] May 30, 1941, Illinois; [ed.] UCLA Medical School, Vanderbilt Hospital; [occ.] Orthopedic Surgeon; [pers.] Inspiration for my poems is the love of my life.; [a.] Fresno, CA

THOMPSON, ELAINE D.
[b.] May 16, 1956, Chicago, IL; [m.] Ralph C. Thompson, March 8, 1975; [ch.] Dawn, Matthew and Joseph Thompson; [ed.] Larkin High School; [occ.] Wife, Mother, Grandmother; [memb.] Unity Lutheran Church; [oth. writ.] I wrote and read my poems in church and even had it published in the church paper.; [pers.] I'd like to give thanks to God for any talent he has given me, and thank him for my husband and children who has inspired me to write.; [a.] Chicago, IL

THOMPSON, JERRY
[b.] February 8, 1952, Greeley, CO; [p.] Violet and Everett Thompson; [m.] Single Parent; [ch.] Joshua Thompson; [ed.] Eaton High School short course at other Institutes; [occ.] Management - at Eastman Kodak, Colorado; [oth. writ.] Other poems and short writings. Working on what I call "short books" on Human Behavior.; [pers.] To share my own personal thoughts with others in hopes that they might see life in a different light. My grandmother wrote many poems, but remained unknown. She greatly influenced me.; [a.] Fort Collins, CO

THOMPSON, LISA L.
[pen.] Jessica Haines; [b.] June 8, 1965, Lancaster, OH; [p.] The Late Robert Morgan, and Eldon and Cecelia Inboden; [m.] John E. Thompson, June 15, 1991; [ch.] Aaron Bradley, Emily Layne; [ed.] Logan High School, Tri-Co. J.V.S., Hocking College; [occ.] Workshop Specialist Fairfield Co. Board MR/DD, Lancaster OH; [oth. writ.] Poems written for special individuals in my life, as gifts.; [pers.] There is such a satisfaction in writing the words that dwell in my heart and soul into a beautiful rhythmic cluster. And there is no more a personal gift that I can offer to loved ones, but the truth inside.; [a.] Lancaster, OH

THOMSON, MILISA
[b.] January 24, 1981, Farmington, NM; [p.] Veronica and Troy Terry; [ed.] I am in 9th grade at Lamar H.S. in Lamar AR; [memb.] Spanish Club in School; [hon.] Student of the Month Honor Roll in H.S. and Elementary; [pers.] I wrote this poem when I was 10 and living with my Aunt Meridee in Albuquerque N.M. I am in the 9th grade now and live in a farm with my mom and step father and one brother and one sister.; [a.] Hagarville, AR

THROWER, LORENE DUNAWAY
[pen.] "Lonely Lorene"; [b.] August 13, 1929, Alexander City, AL; [p.] Hattie and Cleveland Dunaway (Deceased); [ch.] 3 - Benny Lee Wise, Evelyn Kane, Betty Carol, Grandchildren - Michelle, Jeff and Derekwise, (Great Grandchild Austin Falfrey), Michael Kane, Wes and Paige Palfrey; [occ.] Songwriter, Poet, many hobbies; [memb.] EIA Nashville, TN, BMI, Ashland Senior Center, Church Attender Church of God and others; [oth. writ.] Recent song released "The First Christmas"; [pers.] I would like the poem "A Sweetheart Was A Marine" dedicated to: Ivan Davis, (My brothers Coolidge Dunaway who was also a marine (deceased), John Dunaway was Airforce and Fred Dunaway was Army, Alex. City, AL. I also dedicate it to my sisters Jeanette Hornsby and Jane Wilson and their mates and family's of Alex City, AL. To: My aunts Buelah and uncle Ralph McDougal. To uncle LM and Evelyn Dukes of Macon, GA. (Zelma Messer-

deceased). To: Lela Alderidge, a friend for 55 years. Lagrange, GA., the sister of (Ivan Davis, "A Sweetheart Was A Marine"), and with love to Roxie Dunaway a (deceased) School Teacher, Levis Burton a (deceased) Piano Teacher, Gale and Clara Dunaway. All my loved ones.; [a.] Ashland, AL

TILFORD, NIKKI D. SHEARER
[b.] January 8, 1943, Columbus, OH; [p.] Paul P. and Isabelle L. Shearer (Deceased); [m.] Ronald Tilford, November 21, 1964; [ch.] Rhonda K. and Robin R. Tilford; [ed.] East High School (Columbus, OH), Central State University, University of Cincinnati; [occ.] Assistant to Area Coordinator, Writing and Wordprocessing Service Bronner Brothers, Self-employed - NDT's Focus; [memb.] Allen Temple A.M.E. Church; [hon.] Woman of the Year, Citizen of the Day (for Humanitarian Service); [oth. writ.] Created "Tributes to the Spirit" (framed messages of appreciation), Have written numerous messages for individuals, respected organizations, newspapers, scholarship and leadership programs.; [pers.] As a little girl, my father read a variety of literature to me and I now realize I found my passion through him - the written or spoken word. I enjoyed Shakespeare, John Keats, Percy B. Shelley and many others. My purpose, passion and mission is to use my gifts, strengths and talent to touch human hearts and offer hope, comfort and healing and encouragement.; [a.] Cincinnati, OH

TOBIN, TINA MARIE
[pen.] Tina Marie; [b.] April 17, 1972, Sussex, WI; [p.] Gregory B. and E. Joanne M.; [ed.] High School - West Milwaukee 1990 Uwwaukesha - Journalism 1992 Matc - English, currently enrolled; [occ.] Student; [hon.] Received "Liberace Creative Scholarship" National Music Award, National Citizenship Award, Academic Achievement; [a.] Franklin, WI

TOLSON, FRANCES E.
[b.] September 15, 1913, Licking Co., OH; [p.] H. H. and Mary Hoover; [m.] Melvin L. Tolson (Deceased January 18, 1994), November 8, 1953; [ch.] 1 Step-daughter (Deceased), 4 grandchildren, 4 great grandchildren; [ed.] Newark High School, Bachelor's Ohio State Un., Master's Art Education, Kent State University; [occ.] Retired Art Teacher; [memb.] State Retired Teachers Carroll Co., Retired Teachers Carroll Co., Commission for the Advancement of the Arts; [hon.] Who's Who in American Education, Who's Who in' the Arts (1971-1972); [oth. writ.] Christian Life Letters, The Lookout, Free Press Standard, World of Poetry, Christian Evangelist; [pers.] I try to help readers see pictures through the words and to feel an emotion.; [a.] Carrollton, OH

TOMS JR., WILLIE C.
[pen.] Willie C. Toms Jr.; [b.] July 13, 1954, Baltimore, MD; [p.] Gladys and Bennie Lewis; [m.] Darlene; [ch.] 2 Wilkiasha and Aziza; [ed.] 15 yrs. of schooling AA Degree in Science; [occ.] Chemical Lab. Tech.; [pers.] I write, hoping the world will read my work and try to make this a better world to live in.; [a.] Pasadena, CA

TOOTHAKER, SHARON
[b.] April 23, 1962, Bangor, ME; [p.] Father — Norman Lamothe; Stepfather — Robert G. Doucette; Mother — June E. Doucette; [m.] Samuel S. Toothaker, July 8, 1984; [ch.] Donald E. Pomelow III, Brandy Lee Pomelow, Shannon Marie Pomelow, Tasha Ann Pomelow, Alec James Toothaker, stepdaughter Rebecca Lynn Toothaker; [ed.] Lisbin High School, Took CNA Course at Blister and Green Acres Manor in 1987; [occ.] Mother, Housewife; [oth. writ.] Several poems; I have given one to my stepfather, mother and grandmother (Beatrice Pickett); [pers.] My family and friends influence my writing abilities. I write from the heart. I

am a romantic by heart and nature. My hobbies are reading, writing and drawing some. I come from a big family. I have five brothers and one sister.; [a.] Leeds, ME

TOPOLSKY, EMILY DEIRDRE
[b.] July 28, 1977, Fairfax, VA; [p.] M. Ladislav and Linda J. Topolsky; [ed.] Currently Student Hunter College, New York City (City University); [occ.] Student of Fine Arts; [oth. writ.] Poem "I have Said" poetic Voices of America published 1996; [a.] New York, NY

TORGLER, MICHAEL A.
[b.] January 1, 1976, Fort Scott, KS; [p.] Kenneth and Mary Ann Torgler; [ed.] Girard High School, Pittsburg State University; [occ.] Real Estate Agent/Student H and H Agency of Girard, Pittsburg St. University; [memb.] Sigma Phi Epsilon Fraternity, KS Theta Chapter; [pers.] This poem is influenced by experiences in my life that have shaped me, it is dedicated to my sister who always had understanding and faith in me.; [a.] Girard, KS

TORRES, LINNETTE
[b.] April 7, 1973, Ponce, PR; [p.] Luis Torres, Noemi Torres; [ed.] Graduating Senior in May of 1997 from Montclair State University; [memb.] Founding sister of Lambda Theta Alpha Latin Sorority, Inc., Nu Chapter of Montclair State University; [oth. writ.] Poems published in Lambda Theta Alpha Latin Sorority Inc. Newsletter Essay chosen to be published for a collection of writings written by Educational Opportunity Fund Students in MSU.; [a.] West New York, NJ

TOWNSEND JR., RICHARD E.
[b.] December 10, 1946, San Antonio, TX; [p.] Richard E. and Zelma Townsend; [m.] Illine Townsend, April 15, 1975; [ch.] Carol Janice Townsend; [ed.] McCollum High School; [occ.] Construction Worker, Joeris, Inc., General Contractors San Antonio, Texas; [oth. writ.] Has had limerick and archaeological report published.; [pers.] Inspiration is the key to any successful writing.; [a.] San Antonio, TX

TRACEY, MICHAEL J.
[b.] October 8, 1973, Kings Park, NY; [p.] Michael Tracey, Joan Tracey; [ed.] Kings Park High School, Long Island University (C.W. Post Campus), John Jay School of Criminal Justice; [memb.] Christ the King Church, St. Joseph's Church, Criminal Justice Society; [hon.] Various scholarship awards, Dean's List and the privilege of writing for respectable anthologies such as this.; [oth. writ.] Descending Black Time, Before I was Grown and several published works which are untitled.; [pers.] One's experiences in life often shapes their personality as well as their writing. Hopefully, through the use of written words I can comfort people by showing them that they're not alone in their suffering.; [a.] Kings Park, NY

TRACY, LOWELL
[b.] May 17, 1944, Tremonton, UT; [p.] Anthon Tracy, Verna Tracy; [m.] Ilene Tracy, June 13, 1962; [ch.] Elaine, Leisa, Rhonda, Quinn; [ed.] Bear River High School; [occ.] Auto Repairman; [oth. writ.] Poem in Utah sings and articles for youth correctional institutions; [pers.] Thoughts great or small help to guide us one and all this is what I try to do.; [a.] Bear River City, UT

TRAN, HIEN MINH
[pen.] Hoa Hong, Thy Thi; [b.] December 25, 1970, Nha Trang, VietNam; [p.] Dien Tran and My Nguyen Tran; [ed.] Pedagogy University Hue, VietNam; [occ.] Employee of Transpo Electronics Inc. at Orlando Florida and Journalist of VietNam News at Florida; [memb.] Keep Orlando Beautiful; [hon.] 1st prize of poetry contest of students 1993; [oth. writ.] Several poems published in newspapers in VietNam and US; [pers.] I

strive to express my vision to the world in my poems I write about my Mom and all the people who devoted their life for the others. I always dream about a world without enemy.; [a.] Orlando, FL

TRAYNOR, LONNA
[m.] Darrel E. Traynor Sr., April 1972; [ch.] 3 - two in my heart, 1 still alive; [oth. writ.] Just personal poems, life stories, stories about my children.; [pers.] There is and always will be a positive side of life no matter where you are.; [a.] Madison, TN

TRIPLETT, LINDA K.
[b.] November 21, 1960, Louisville, KY; [p.] Ruben L. Gidron (Deceased), Annie C. and Embry N. Gazaway Jr. (Stepfather); [m.] Howard C. Triplett, December 7, 1991; [ch.] Keondra L. and Christopher A.; [ed.] Jefferson High, Spencerian Business College, Sullivan College; [occ.] Management Assistant Jefferson County Fiscal Court; [oth. writ.] Presently working on my first book.; [pers.] Believe in yourself when it seems that everyone else doubts you. Accept reality and you can achieve in life.; [a.] Louisville, KY

TROYER, PAUL A.
[pen.] St. Paul; [b.] September 12, 1958, Ashland, KY; [p.] Edward D. (Deceased) and Shelby Ann Troyer; [ch.] Paul A. Troyer II; [ed.] Russell High School, Russell, KY, Ash KY Campus, KY Tech, A.B.I. St. Paul Minn./Self Ed, on poetry, song writing, God, Inspired, directly and Thur people; [occ.] Writer/Song Writter/Evangelist, Councilor; [memb.] Several Churche's/several organ. To feed hungry and help homeless, song writer asoc.; [hon.] Semi Finalist, Nat. Lib. of Poetry - locally pub. in newspaper Ordained Minister, work with, Nat. known, Country Music, Singers/writers biggest honor, is God and wonderful people, who still exists.; [oth. writ.] Gospel/Country music songs, poems mixed over, short stories, movie scripts; [pers.] I have found that God and so many wonderful people, have taught me, so much - to "make a difference", in lives, is the most important of all. It's a real strength, especially when it looks hopeless. ("Love Does Build A Bridge". Thanks! Naomi and Why Judd!), Please make sure this part make it for sure thanks!; [a.] Ashland, KY

TSENG, MARIAN SMALL
[pen.] Marian Small Tseng; [b.] April 29, 1927, Cleveland, OH; [p.] John and Mary Small; [m.] Leo Tseng, May 25, 1973; [ch.] Tom Talmon; [ed.] High School; [occ.] Retired; [memb.] National Arts Assn. Inc, Mayflower Descendant Daughters of American Revolution, Ohio Genealogical Society, National Genealogical Society, The Augustan Society, New England Genealogical and Historical Society; [hon.] Many high school awards in 1940's for patriotic poems of WWII; [oth. writ.] Patriotic poetry, misc. poetry, 3 volumes of family history at present time: Writing and publishing newsletters for 2 charitable organizations (unsalaried); [pers.] Although often alone, people who compose poetry or write books or read are never lonely, they have the written word as their companion.; [a.] Encino, CA

TSEWANG, TENZIN SAMJUNG
[b.] July 29, 1980, Gurupura, India; [p.] Tsewang Tenzin, Tsundue Sangmo Tsewang; [ed.] C.S.T., C.V.P. Bylakuppe, India, Community College of Santa Fe, N.M.; [occ.] Teacher Assistant, Montessory Discovery School, Santa Fe, N.M.; [memb.] Tibetan Association of Santa Fe, N.M.; [hon.] Best Boy Award, 1995-96, CST CVP Bylakuppe, India; [pers.] I like to express my feelings through writing. I have been greatly influenced by Great Tibetan Poets and have special interest in "Tampeys" by my Grand Father Lobsang Thinlay.; [a.] Santa Fe, NM

TUCKER, KRISTINA
[b.] December 20, 1976, Orange, CA; [p.] Ollie Howard; [ed.] I graduated from John F. Kennedy High School and am currently attending Cypress College; [occ.] Full time student and part time jewelry merchant.; [oth. writ.] I have written many other poems not yet published.; [pers.] My main focus is to relate to each individual on a level in which one can relate, while at the same time expressing my innermost passions and ideals. I believe everything happens for a reason therefore it is best to take life for all it encompasses.; [a.] Buena Park, CA

TUDOR, MARGAUX
[pen.] Margaux; [b.] January 27, 1979, Hyarris; [p.] Lynne Tudor and Matt Tudor; [ed.] The Kildonan School as well as the Landmark School; [occ.] Student; [memb.] Episcopalian D10; [hon.] Award (athletic) Most Valuable Player; [a.] Truro, MA

TURNER, AMYOTHA P.
[pen.] A.P. Turner; [b.] March 4, 1967, Gadsden AL; [p.] C. N. and Athelene Palmer; [m.] Byron Turner, July 11, 1988; [ch.] Hannah Kathleen Turner; [ed.] Associate in Applied Science-Paralegal; [occ.] Phlebotomist and Legal Researcher; [memb.] Member of Alpha Beta Gamma and the Paralegal Association; [hon.] Character achievement award; [oth. writ.] A Deed of Love; [pers.] "Set your goals, plan then well, and with hard work, you can achieve anything you deserve." C. N. Palmer. In memory of my father.; [a.] Gadsden, AL

TURNER, EDITH
[b.] July 30, 1949, Danville, KY; [p.] Jenny K. Raines; [ch.] Ramona L. Turner (Anchor at Kliv Radio Station); [ed.] High School Graduate, Certified Nurses Assistance form De Anza College, National Institute for the Certification of Health Care Sterile Processing and Distribution; [occ.] Certified Central Supply Tech in Operating Room; [hon.] I received a clock from my job, for being there for 15 years, I was crowned Miss Teenage Queen in Danville, Ky.; [pers.] I was going through so many changes in 1995, I thought I would put my feelings in a poem, because I felt like I was going crazy. I was wondering if other parent or parents were feeling the way I did.; [a.] San Jose, CA

UMATHUM, JAMES
[b.] June 2, 1969, Geneva, IL; [p.] Mike and Nancy Umathum; [m.] Colleen Umathum, August 4, 1994; [ch.] Suzannah Umathum; [ed.] School of Higher Learning - Pupil of Testaments (P.O.T.); [occ.] Business Owner; [pers.] Desire, the root of creation, and the foundation of existence.; [a.] Arlington, TX

VAIARELLA, APRIL
[b.] August 21, 1981, Rockford, IL; [p.] John and Jody Vaiarella; [ed.] 8th grade graduate St. Edwards School Rockford, IL; [occ.] 9th grade student East High School Rockford, IL; [memb.] Drama Club, East High School; [oth. writ.] 6th grade poem, the snow castle, published in the national observer newspaper.; [a.] Rockford, IL

VANANTWERP, LINDIE
[pen.] Lindie VanAntwerp; [b.] November 18, 1996, Shawnee, OK; [p.] Vernon and Sherrie Houck, and Mike VanAntwerp Sr.; [ed.] 8th grader at North Rock Creek School; [memb.] 3rd yr. cheerleader, 4th yr. basketball player, National Junior Honor Society, Academic Team, Youth Leader at Aydelotte Baptist Church, student representative for the Shawnee Sister Cities Program trip to Japan. Also participate in softball, track and volleyball; [hon.] Won various awards for essays and art work at the school-wide level, district wide and country wide level. Superintendent's Honor Roll and Board of Education Honor Roll.

VANDERPOOL, MADELEINE
[pen.] Madeleine McAlpin; [p.] Deceased; [ch.] Daughter - Madelen, son - Wynant; [ed.] Finishing school Cenn - studied sculpture Paris 4 mo with Mateo Hernandez also Gen Hemlin NYC Sherwood Studios 3 yrs; [occ.] Sculpture - worked last six years at Shidoni Foundry N. Mexico Santa Fe

VANHUISEN, NANCY
[b.] April 30, 1961, Muskegon, MI; [p.] Boyd and Carol Myers; [m.] Robert K. VanHuisen, August 27, 1988; [ch.] Joshuwa, Jennifer, Jacob, Jessica; [ed.] Grand Haven High; [occ.] Housewife and mother; [pers.] Beauty comes from the heart. Read to your children, they listen and learn. "A book a day, takes them a long way."; [a.] Fennville, MI

VARGAS, JENNIFER
[b.] May 24, 1980, New York; [p.] Frances Rivera and Tony Vargas; [hon.] I got a MIP in Basketball in 1996. And Honors in my freshmen year.; [pers.] For everything in poetry's hand I thank my parents my great grandfather and all my friend from Landmark and life also my family. Love takes more from your soul, then might be there to start.; [a.] Amherst, MA

VARGAS, KETTY
[b.] March 16, 1953, Guayaquil, Ecuador; [p.] Pedro Molina, Gladys Molina; [m.] Efron Vargas, M.D., February 19, 1973; [ed.] Guayaquil State Univ., School of Medicine; [occ.] Physician (not working); [hon.] Dean's List; [oth. writ.] Several acrostics for my friends. A few unpublished poems and writings.; [pers.] My poems are the result of my personal struggle to understand life.; [a.] Town South Hill, VA

VARGHESE, SOPHIA
[b.] April 18, 1980, Yonkers, NY; [p.] Thomas Varghese, Mary Varghese; [ed.] Gorton High; [memb.] St. Thomas Mar Thana Church; [hon.] National Honor Society Society, Club 90, honor roll; [oth. writ.] I have written other poems, but have never published them. They're basically written so that I may express my feelings.; [pers.] Seek God and you will find...ask God and you will receive the desires that lie deep within your heart.; [a.] Yonkers, NY

VAUGHAN, WENDELL L.
[b.] May 8, 1921, Iberia, MO; [p.] Samuel and Mellie Vaughan; [m.] Vivian R. (Crick) Vaughan, December 28, 1941; [ch.] Victor Vaughan, Debbie Bellere; [ed.] Iberia Academy, AB Drury College, Sprgf. MO, (BD) Brite Divinity School (Texas Christian University); [occ.] Retired; [pers.] Classical music (especially opera) and poetry are my two major interests. I find them extremely compatible I strive for variety in writing poetry.; [a.] Lakewood, CO

VELA, FERNANDO
[b.] February 25, 1950, Mexico; [p.] Sixto and Virginia Vela; [m.] Lucy, January 11, 1975; [ch.] Fernando Michael Teri Nicole; [ed.] Rancho High School St John's Seminary - B.A. in Philosophy; [occ.] Legal Assistant; [memb.] Christ the King Catholic Church; [oth. writ.] "Sunday Morning at Red-Rou" "Heroism" "To An Old friend" "The Lesson" article written in the "Franciscan" and "El mundo".; [pers.] Influenced by Thomas Aquinas, Miguel de Cervantes Savedra, Pablo Nevuda, Sixto Vela and David Benjamin Vela; [a.] Las Vegas, NV

VENEZIANO, JUDITH A.
[pen.] Judith; [b.] June 23, 1942, Waterville, ME; [p.] Robert M. Thomas, Barbara E. Thomas; [m.] Robert M. Veneziano, June 22, 1963; [ed.] Graduated Waterville High School; [occ.] Housewife; [memb.] International Society of Poets; [hon.] Editor's Choice

Award for poem published "The Ebbing Tide" Anthology; [pers.] I wish that every human being ever born would be "Born Free", my greatest joy is giving to or doing something for others.; [a.] Madison, ME

VERDIER, FRANCINE
[b.] August 29, 1949, San Jose; [p.] Frank Joseph Paratore and Edwina Marie Rydberg; [m.] Thomas Adrien Verdier (Deceased), June 29, 1968; [ch.] Bryce Thomas Verdier and Carina Marie Verdier; [ed.] San Francisco State University; [pers.] Love sustains the soul!; [a.] San Mateo, CA

VERGO, TARAH
[b.] January 5, 1985, Colorado Springs, CO; [p.] Steven and Kathie Vergo; [ed.] Currently a student at Sabin Middle School, Colorado Springs, CO; [hon.] Tarah is in the gifted and talented program in Colorado Springs District #11.; [oth. writ.] Many stories and poems enjoyed by her parents, grandparents, and teachers.; [pers.] My friends and family have greatly influenced my writings. I hope I never lose them.; [a.] Colorado Springs, CO

VERRASTRO, THOMAS F.
[b.] December 26, 1969, Union, NJ; [p.] Dr. and Mrs. Thomas R. Verrastro; [ed.] Seton Hall University School of Law (withdrawn to pursue other interests). B.A., Magna Cum Laude, Seton Hall U. (1994); [occ.] Legal Assistant, Amateur Musician and Poet.; [memb.] Sigma Phi Epsilon Fraternity; [hon.] Magna Cum Laude Graduate, Dean's and/or President's lists, all semesters, Highest Academic Achievement Award in Criminal Justice studies.; [oth. writ.] I have many more words to take the form of poem and song for those who would hear them.; [pers.] I will not clamor for my words to speak with more volume than they already do. Literature, art and music are submissions to the collective good of mankind. Seek quiet places to read my words, they speak softly.; [a.] Clark, NJ

VILLALONA, MERCEDES E.
[b.] Santo Domingo, Dom. Rep.; [p.] Braulio Villalona, Adolfina Villalona; [m.] Divorced; [ch.] Gabriela Escobar Villaluna; [ed.] LA Milagrosa High School (Santo Domingo), Hunter College (NYC); [occ.] Administrator Proc. Analyst State Dept. Wash, DC; [memb.] HECFAA - Hispanic Assoc. The Secretary's Open Forum; [hon.] Some of my poems were need at a poetry contest at Hunter College and a local radio station in Wash, DC; [oth. writ.] Several poems written in Spanish. Unpublished.; [pers.] I express my inner feeling on common experiences and voice my view on social issues in a humanist way.; [a.] Washingto, DC

VINCENT, DEREK
[pers.] In writing poetry I always consider that the best verse has already been written in God's word and my greatest aspiration is to harmonize with it.; [a.] Costa Mesa, CA

VINCENT, KENNETH
[b.] June 19, 1940, Kirksville, MO; [p.] Mr. and Mrs. Cleo Vincent; [m.] Christina, September 1991; [ch.] Tim, Tony, Kim; [ed.] BS - Okla. St. Univ.; [occ.] Retired

VINSON, CONNIE E.
[b.] November 4, 1922, Knobel, AR; [p.] Fletcher Lee and Lutie E. Gatlin; [m.] John B. Vinson (Deceased, February 20, 1966), September 24, 1942; [ch.] Faye, Ronald, John, Kenny, Alicia and Rhonda; [ed.] At Moorehead High School Moorehead, Miss.; [occ.] Housewife; [memb.] Member and Sunday School teacher of friendship Baptist church (now closed) No. LA; [hon.] Avon Presidents Club Award, Avon Team Leader Award Honored 50th Wedding Anniversary by

our 7 children; [oth. writ.] Won best poem for grammar school writing, many poems written and dated.; [pers.] My love for poetry has always been. Had a wonderful teacher for English and Literature. Very instructive in prose, verse, expression and importance of copywrite.; [a.] New Orleans, LA

VINTURELLA, GARY
[b.] October 9, 1953, New Orleans; [p.] Josephine Francis and John Joseph; [m.] Divorced; [ch.] Cari Lee and Jesse Aaron; [ed.] Holy Cross High School, University of New Orleans; [occ.] Owner, Southland Supply, Inc.; [memb.] Mensa High IQ Society, Nat'l Space Society, Int Nat'l Freelance Photographers Org.; [hon.] Beta Alpha Psi Nat'l Accounting Fraternity, Winner - 1994 Calliope Fiction Contest; [oth. writ.] Several articles printed in "La Plume De Nom."; [pers.] `Storm Clouds' is taken from a novel I've written by the same name. Hopefully, it will serve as inspiration for anyone experiencing personal trauma or hardship.; [a.] Metairie, LA

VOEGELE, ALVINA A.
[b.] February 12, 1938, Hague, ND; [p.] Joe and Elizabeth Heier; [ch.] Four; [occ.] Hair Dresser; [a.] Seattle, WA

VOLKERT, MARY
[b.] October 19, 1917, Appleton, WI; [p.] Bertha Hagen, Emil Voecks; [m.] Erie T. Volkert, September 3, 1939; [ch.] Jennifer, Lawrence, Randall, Lisa; [ed.] Appleton, Wis. High School, BA - Lawrence College, Appleton, Wis., Teaching Certification - U. of Vermont in Burlington, VT; [occ.] Retired Elem. School Teacher, Remedial Reading Teacher, Flute and Piano Teacher; [memb.] Delta Gamma Sorority, Deacon Congregational Church of Middlebury, VT., Hawthorne Club, Midd., VT. Sym. Orch. Sheldon Museum, Ilsley Library, Community Theatre; [hon.] Cum Laude BA, Dean's List - Lawrence C.; [oth. writ.] Children's Verse, Family Biographies, Limericks, Short Story, Tributes to family and friends in rhymed couplets; [pers.] I have studied and written Haiku, and therefore stress the beauty of the natural world in all seasons as it relates to the human condition.; [a.] Middlebury, VT

VOSBURGH, TAMMY
[b.] May 26, 1967, Burlington, VT; [p.] Jean Berard, Bryan Oakes; [m.] Guy Vosburgh, March 9, 1993; [ch.] Donald, Jeannie and Chasity; [ed.] Catamount Elementary and Mount Anthony Union High both in Bennington, Vermont; [occ.] Press Operator at Tansitor Electronics; [oth. writ.] Several poems for family, friends, and work.; [pers.] I like to write about real things. I like to express feelings and emotions and I also enjoy writing for entertainment purposes.; [a.] Bennington, VT

VOZAR, LILLIAN
[b.] February 10, 1920, Bannister, MI; [p.] Leon Cox, Jenney Cox; [m.] Joseph Vozar, April 19, 1941; [ch.] Thomas John, Joel Anthony; [ed.] Ithaca High (MI) 3 art credits MMCC; [occ.] Housewife and grandmother; [memb.] Secretary of "Harrison home and garden club"; [oth. writ.] Letters to friends and relatives. They say they enjoy my letters.; [pers.] I like to observe nature and where I live I have a very good opportunity to do so. There are many things of nature here.; [a.] Harrison, MI

VRABEL, GERHARD E.
[pen.] Gary Gray; [b.] May 27, 1953, Inglewood, NY; [p.] Ernst A. and Gertrude R.; [m.] Diana L. Vrabel, July 22, 1995; [ch.] Shaun, Mike, Nick, Stef and Roo; [ed.] Ithaca High School, S.U.N.Y. Morrisville; [occ.] Network Admin./Voc. Ed. Inst.; [oth. writ.] From a collection entitled "Seasons In Time".; [pers.] The beauty yet sometimes rapid change in nature mixed

with human perceptions form images that produce my work.; [a.] Ithaca, NY

VUKELICH, CAROL
[pen.] Kaye Vukelich; [b.] March 5, 1938, Staples; [p.] Mr. and Mrs. LeRoy Kennedy; [m.] Bill Vukelich, July 4, 1959; [ch.] Chad, Chet, Fawnya; [ed.] Staples High School Graduate, Flying School (Nights) Staples, Cake Decorating (Nights) Staples; [occ.] Housewife; [memb.] Methodist Church - V.F.W. Auxiliary Member; [oth. writ.] I have written many poems over the years. Eulogy for funerals, cards to family member for birthdays etc. I have never sent in anything to be published before.; [pers.] I have loved writing poetry since I learned words rhymed. Wrote on napkins, anything! "Phone, call from Tia" came from my granddaughter and her broken home. Tia was age 7 then.; [a.] Staples, MN

VULCANESCU, ION
[b.] December 8, 1949, Pielesti-Romania; [p.] Vlad Floruca-Vulcanescu Steuan; [ed.] Self Educated; [occ.] Researcher in Philosophy of Ancient Civilizations; [oth. writ.] "Serene Thoughts of a Poet" - 1979 - Expositional Press. NY; [pers.] Published during 1971-1975 by major literary magazines in Bucharest, Romania present: Author of "American Geometry", books in over 13 International Libraries of Academies of Sciences.; [a.] Hurleyville, NY

WADE, LISA
[b.] July 10, 1964, WA; [memb.] Oregon Adoptive Rights Association; [pers.] I have been writing since I was 12. I wrote "adoptees pilgrimage" on the plane on the way to meet my birth mother. Oregon adoptive rights was very helpful. My greatest appreciation goes to them.; [a.] Portland, OR

WADSWORTH, RUTH
[b.] August 10, 1937, Glens Falls, NY; [p.] Glen Rounds, B. Vaughn; [m.] Arthur Wadsworth, April 5, 1975; [ch.] Glenda, Bud, Starr, Amber, Ben; [ed.] BS - Sociology Albany, N.Y. AAS Registered Nurse from adirondack Comm Coll Glens Falls, NY; [occ.] R. N. Owner of Travelshoppe full travel service; [memb.] AORN (Assoc. Operating Room Nurse) ASTA - American Society of Travel Agents ROA - Retired Officers Assoc Thurman Baptist Church; [hon.] 10 years is army muse corp winning the army achievement medal; [oth. writ.] Short stories and poems published in Warrensburg new paper; [pers.] I believe that the ability to succeed comes with the Effort To Try.; [a.] El Paso, TX

WAGNER, DARREN GAGE
[pen.] "The Man Of I.B."; [b.] August 26, 1975; [p.] David G. Wagner, Leslie E. Wagner; [ed.] Sweethome High; [occ.] Musician (San Diego, CA); [oth. writ.] Many poems turned songs performed by my band. The Jelly Makers.; [pers.] May the music touch the hearts of the people. The people of the world.; [a.] Imperial Beach, CA

WAGONER, CHRISHAWN
[b.] September 5, 1984, Washington, DC; [p.] Stanley and Cynthia Wagoner; [ed.] Graduate of 6th Grade, June 1996; [occ.] 7th Grade Student; [hon.] Presidential Academic Achievement Award (for school terms 1994-95 and 1995-96); [oth. writ.] Various poems and stories.; [pers.] "I dedicate my work to my father who believed I could succeed no matter what.

WAHL, MICHAEL A.
[b.] October 19, 1977, Hopewell Junction, NY; [p.] William, Mary Ellen; [pers.] Dedicated to Christina for her constant inspiration.; [a.] Hopewell Junction, NY

WALDEN, ERNEST G.
[pen.] Ernie Walden; [b.] February 20, 1918, Spokane, WA; [p.] Hannah Clamp Walden and Guy Edward Walden; [m.] Divorced, November 23, 1939; [ch.] 3 Girls - Donna, Debra and Gregorie, 5 Grandchildren; [ed.] High School, Aviation Cadet, Training Command Flying Instructor Advanced at-6 Tactical P-39 P-40 P-51 B-24; [occ.] Retired, Profession-Business and Property Owner; [memb.] Bridge-Aopa-These days; [hon.] Honorable Discharge Officer U.S. Air Force W.W. II, actually a displaced Civilian; [oth. writ.] 100 poems and short stories never published.; [pers.] If we travel the road alone, and keep that which we have learned, we may as travel back or stay. An idea can die a slow death if not allowed out of the mind.; [a.] New Orleans, LA

WALTER, KATHLEEN M.
[b.] April 10, 1963, Evergreen Park, IL; [p.] Karl F. Walter, Margaret J. Walter; [ed.] Mount Assisi Academy, Richard J. Daley College, University Of Illinois at Chicago; [occ.] Registered Nurse, St. Francis Hospital, Blue Island, IL; [memb.] University of Illinois Alumni Association; [hon.] Dean's List Graduated with honors from University of Illinois; [oth. writ.] None published; [pers.] At a young age, I was encouraged to write by various teachers and mentors. In my poetry, I have always expressed my innermost thoughts and feelings. Poetry is life. Through poetry, we dare to dream the impossible.; [a.] Palos Hills, IL

WALTON, KESHA VICTORIA
[pen.] Kesha Victoria Walton; [b.] January 6, 1978, Okinawa, Japan; [p.] David Walton, Myriam Walton; [ed.] Ferguson High School, Christopher Newport University, both in Newport News, VA; [occ.] College Student/Medical Field; [memb.] Christian Memorial Church, Baltimore, MD; [hon.] Homecoming Queen in high school 95, honor roll 9, 10, 11, 12 grds. MVP basketball 10th grade, graduated with honors; [oth. writ.] I wrote different articles in my yearbook class my senior year. I have a lot of other poems that no one has taken a look at.; [pers.] Never ever give up on anything you do in life cause good things will come to you if you keep striving for everything that is right.; [a.] Newport News, VA

WANG, WILLIAM M.
[pen.] Florence Wang; [b.] September 8, 1931, Shanghai China; [p.] L. Z. Wang, Z. Y. Chu; [m.] Shen Fang, Meng (Florence Wang), April 17, 1984; [ch.] Raymond, Charles, Alice, Ping, Esther, Jenny; [ed.] St. John's University Medical School, formerly affiliated with University of Pennsylvania Medical School, later converted to Shanghai Second Medical University. Graduated with M. D. degree.; [occ.] Clinical Research; [memb.] Chinese Medical Association; [hon.] Awarded Certificate for Valuable Contributions to the Cause of International by the people to people Organization, founded by former President, Dwight D. Eisenhower.; [oth. writ.] A number of poems published in Wen-Wei Newspaper in Chinese back in China.; [pers.] I tried to depict the spiritual transformation of my wife in poetical form, how she strived in becoming a true Christian, immensely blessed by our Lord, and how she endeavored to think and act as a devoted and loyal soldier of Christ. The poem: "God's Grace."; [a.] Montebello, CA

WANNAMAKER, KELLIE
[b.] August 26, 1964, Rapid City, SD; [p.] Billie and Eva Sargent; [m.] Kim Wannamaker, June 6, 1986; [ch.] Dylan Scott, Joy Kimberly; [ed.] Northwest Nazarene College; [occ.] Third grade teacher at Mountain View Elementary School, Kenai, AK; [oth. writ.] Poetry published in Kenai Peninsula College Literary Magazine, Driftwood.; [pers.] I write poetry to use in my classroom and to reflect my feelings toward my own children. "Can I Hold This Moment?" was written for my infant daughter, Joy.; [a.] Kenai, AK

WARN, POET
[pen.] L. Mila Warn; [b.] March 23, 1913, Portland, OR; [p.] Harold and Rena Warn; [ed.] Gregory Heights Elem. School; Grant High School; University of Oregon; Christ Church Universal; [occ.] Retired; Volunteer Tutor in 2 high schools, English as a second language; [memb.] AM Assoc. Retired Persons OREA ORE, Retired Education Assoc.; National Parliamentation OR. Fed. of Women's Organization; A greeter in Stone Tower Church; [hon.] National Library of Poetry 1996 Medal and Plaque in Washington D.C. as a Poet of Merit.; [oth. writ.] Lots of poetry, all my life I have written it.; [pers.] I am a retired ESL Teacher. I taught 10 years in Lincoln High School and 2 years in Madison High School. I am a Rev. Filled the pulpit 13 1/2 years in Portland, after a Fashion Career in Los Angeles and New York City.; [a.] Portland, OR

WARNER, NORMAGENE
[b.] March 23, 1923, Jackson Co., IL; [m.] The Rev. Wm. R. Warner; [ch.] Kathleen, David and Stephen (Deceased); [ed.] BA plus graduate at Southern Illinois University, Carbondale, IL; [occ.] Retired Elem. School Teacher; [memb.] United Methodist Church, Retired Teachers Assoc.; [oth. writ.] Several essays and poems published in local newspapers and contests. Wrote column "Squeaks Of A Church Spouse" for many years. Published in "Women in Transition" by Upper Room. Have biographical novel in progress.; [pers.] Elie Wiesel said that he wrote that he might understand. I like that. I too write in order to better understand the imponderables of life. And as I write I find much to savor as well as ponder.; [a.] Carbondale, IL

WARREN, HEATHER LEE
[b.] November 18, 1980, Oklahoma; [p.] Deborah and Daniel Warren; [ed.] Went to South River Elementary, Middle School Central, and Regina High School now; [occ.] Working at T.J. Max; [hon.] This is my 1st award or accomplishment for a poem; [oth. writ.] I write poems all the time in a poem journal I keep in my room.; [pers.] Put your mind to the special gifts God gave you, and never stop trying, because you can do it! Poetry is a wonderful way of expressing your heart feelings, so speak in a poem.; [a.] Clinton Township, MI

WARREN, LEAH D.
[b.] December 7, 1955, Hamilton, OH; [p.] Denvis Fields, Vera Fields; [m.] Donald R. Warren, June 28, 1974; [ch.] Tiffany Dawn; [ed.] Taft Senior High, Miami University; [occ.] Clerk, Educational Aide, Hamilton City School District; [oth. writ.] Many other poems.; [pers.] Inspired by Jesus Christ.; [a.] Hamilton, OH

WASHINGTON, BRIANNA P.
[b.] December 27, 1981 Seattle, WA; [p.] Donnetta Cahill and Tyrone Washington; [ed.] High School, (Apple Valley High School) 9th grade; [occ.] Student at Apple Valley High School; [memb.] Apple Valley pre-law team, AVID (Advancement Via Individual Determination); [oth. writ.] "I Am, I Will, I Will Not". It is my first book and it has not been published before.; [pers.] "I know who I am, what I want in life, and what it takes to get if, and with that, I will succeed."; [a.] Inglewood, CA

WASSERMAN, EMILY
[b.] August 21, 1981, Sheboygan, WI; [p.] Jeff and Regina Wasserman; [ed.] Mt. Tabor High School, 10th Grade; [occ.] Student; [memb.] B'nai Brith Youth Organization; [hon.] Honor Roll Student; [pers.] Modern love and life influence my poems.; [a.] Winston-Salem, NC

WATTS, BRITTANI ELYSE
[b.] May 25, 1981, Dallas, TX; [p.] Wayne and Billie Watts; [ed.] Boerne High School; [occ.] Sophomore Student at Boerne H.S.; [pers.] I always wanted to write something worthy of being published. Now that has come true.; [a.] Fair Oaks Ranch, TX

WEBER, SCOTT ALLAN
[pen.] Scott Weber; [b.] April 10, 1982, Ridgewood, NJ; [p.] Bruce and Sandi Weber; [ed.] I go to school at Chapparal, in which I currently hold a 3.0 Gpa.; [occ.] Student; [memb.] I am a member of the YMCA, I am joining speech, a debate, government, and a Young Republicans Club; [hon.] Principal's list, poetry awards, and various other things.; [oth. writ.] Random, not published material; [pers.] "Where there's a will there's a way." "Anything is possible."; [a.] Scottsdale, AZ

WECK, HEINRICH F.
[b.] January 30, 1908, Germany; [p.] Joseph and Theresia Weck; [m.] Suna Buchheit, November 28, 1934; [ch.] 3 daughter: Marlis, Ursula, Sunetta; [ed.] Reform Real Gymnasium, Prof: German Forest District Ranger Hessian State School of Forestry; [occ.] Retired turn go to USA: Oct 1962; [memb.] Dropped - I am 88, here in the USA: Kiwanis, Knights of Columbus, Realton; [hon.] Some books from Baycrischer Landwickchafts Herlug Minchen (Publishing House); [oth. writ.] Articles about Forestry and hunting in the German language in the "Allgenucine Veusoche Forstzcitung"; [pers.] I think the American Clearcutting Forests is wrong, I tried to teach the European Ways of Rejuvenating Forests.; [a.] San Clemente, CA

WEERAMUNI, NAMEL
[pen.] Veena; [b.] August 31, 1934, Sri Lanka; [p.] John De Silva and Suwan Weeramuni; [m.] Malini Weeramuni, December 13, 1934; [ch.] Slushna, Heshan, Tarindu Weeramuni; [ed.] University of Ceylon, Ceylon Law College, University City of London, California State University, Northridge; [occ.] Retired Attorney-at-Law, Graduate Student in Theatre; [memb.] The California Writers Club, San Fernando Valley Branch; [hon.] Gold Medalist (Short Story Competition-University of Ceylon-1959), Best Play and Director - Sri Lanka, Drama Awards - 1972, Board of Trustees, University of Kelaniya, Sir Lanka; [oth. writ.] A collection of Short Stories, A Collection of Poems, Five Plays, Various articles to News Papers, Scholastic Journals.; [pers.] I like to dignify human suffering and implant a spiritual experience through works of art. I am very much influenced by Russian writers like Dostrovesky, Tolstoy and Chekvov.; [a.] Canoga Park, CA

WEIL, ROBERT
[b.] November 9, 1972, La Jolla, CA; [p.] Robert Weil, Donna Weil; [ed.] El Segundo High; [occ.] Recreation Specialist, City of El Segundo; [pers.] I've long admired the teachings layed forth by native American's both past and present. Their spirit as a people guides my work, and is clearly seen in the poetry I've written to date.; [a.] El Segundo, CA

WEINMEISTER, LILY V.
[b.] January 13, 1922, Prince Albert, Sask, Canada; [p.] Richard and Lucy Lunam (both Deceased); [m.] Edward A. (Deceased), August 8, 1943; [ch.] Karen Johanna; [ed.] Elk Range, Sask., Well's Business Academy, Hamilton Ont. Canada; [occ.] Retired; [oth. writ.] No poems published; [pers.] I rarely set about to write a poem. Most often, when one pops into my head, I must hastily my jot it down before it disappears into the wilderness; [a.] Hamilton, Ontario, Canada

WEIR JR, CLAUDE
[b.] January 22, 1951, New York, NY; [p.] Claude Weir and Doris Stevenson; [m.] Yvette Arsenec, December 6, 1994; [ch.] Jesse Jeremiah Owens; [ed.] Dartmouth College, Harvard Law School; [occ.] Senior Vice President, The Chase Manhattan Bank; [memb.] American Bar Association/NYS Bar Association, NYS Chamber of Commerce-HR Committee, YMCA of Greater of New York-Board of Directors' HR Committee, Bayley-Seton Hospital Advisory Board; [oth. writ.] Several poems written through the years for the pleasure of family and friends.; [pers.] I want my writing to make people reflect on those things that are truly important in life before it is too late to do so.; [a.] New York, NY

WELK, EUGENE GEO
[pen.] E.G.W.; [b.] August 7, 1923, Detroit; [ed.] Reading and writing M.S.D. 1944 - graduate; [memb.] First Time; [oth. writ.] (Poem Titles) Why Do Not Show Faith By Heart, Welcome Friends, Your Just A Dream Away Jesus; [pers.] Those poems were written on my own.; [a.] Lansing, MI

WELLER, PETER J.
[b.] January 13, 1940, Chicago, IL; [p.] Carl and Kathryn Weller; [m.] Sandra R. Weller, August 9, 1969; [ch.] Thomas and Paul; [ed.] Lane Tech High School, Chicago, BA Wartburg College, Waverly, IA, MA University of Iowa, Iowa City, IA; [occ.] Social Studies Teacher, Washington High School, Washington, IA; [memb.] Immanuel Lutheran Church, Washington, IA, National Education Association, Iowa State Education Association, Iowa Council for the Social Studies, Midwest Old Threshers and Midwest Electric Railway Assn, Mt. Pleasant, IA, Electric Railroaders' Assn, NY, Central Electric Railfans' Assn, Chicago, Lionel Collectors Club of America, Washington Model Railroad Club, Washington, IA; [hon.] Jaycees Outstanding Young Educator, DAR Outstanding American History Teacher for State of Iowa; [oth. writ.] Editor of "Washington Sesquicentennial History", co-authored a book "Remembering the Southern Iowa Railway". Currently working on a book about The Chicago Aurora and Elgin Ry. and its conversion to a nature trail called the Illinois Prairie Path.; [pers.] Having grown up in Chicago in the 1940's and 50's, I find it tragic to see what the forces of change have done to the city's neighborhoods and industrial areas during the last four decades. An analysis of the causes of these forces could fill volumes. The results, however, are glaringly evident to the eye. My inspiration for "Thoughts from a Train Window" came from a 1995 Amtrak trip through Chicago. I wondered how such urban devastation could be stopped or reversed - and what if it wasn't?; [a.] Washington, IA

WEN, JOHN LUNG
[pen.] John Lung Wen; [b.] January 20, 1931, Wen Canyon Szechwan, China; [p.] Shou-Kuo Wen (Father), Chang-Ching Ho Wen (Mother); [m.] Divorced Exwife Dr. Hu Chi-Yu, June 4, 1966; [ch.] Son, Han-Chin Wen, Forward his Ph.D. in High Energy Astrophics, at Stanford University.; [ed.] LLB, Law College, Chao Yang University, Peiping (Beijing), LL.B. Cert., by Sun Yate-Sen, Univ., Canton. R.O.C., M.A. New Mexico Highlands, Univ., Las Vegas, N.M.; [occ.] Freelance writer both in English and Chinese, a Voluntary worker to assist Seniors; [memb.] Chinese Writers Assoc., Republican Natl. Committee, Sustaining Committee, since 1978 up to date.; [hon.] University Dr. William Banowsky, 11/72. In appreciation for Counsel Active and support rendered during the '96 Campaign year R.N.C. to Honor Delegate-At-Large by the Honorable Senator Trent Lott, and Honorable Senator Alfonse M. D'Amato; [oth. writ.] Books: Elephant Embraces Dragon Cpyrt. 1984 by John Lung Wen. Pub. by Vantage Press, Inc. New York, NY America-China. By Different Roads, It is in process of Publication, by Beijing World News Pub. Co., Beijing, P.R.C. and 12 poetries and 8 Political Articles were published in L.A. Times, Register (Daily News) Orange County and Gardena Daily News B) 28 Chinese poetries and 22 Articles were published by 3 World-wide Chinese Newspapers and 6 Local Chinese Newspapers.; [pers.] I am a naturalized U.S. citizen on May 25, 1973 with an honest, reliable, responsible, talented and industrious character. I always keep my family traditional Paternal instruction to treat people with love and righteousness, and enthusiasm to deal with public affairs. I myself examination, I find that I am right, lawful and reasonable, I will go forward against ten thousands and millions, because Man can expand the truths, which he follows, these truths do not expand him, the benevolent man (woman) has no one who can oppose him or her. This is the way of my Philosophy of Life. I passed the Special Examination for Higher Judge from the Department of Justice, R.O.C. and I have been Judge of Haicu District Court, Major Director of Political Propaganda of the Marine Corps, and a Legal Counsel of the Taiwan Power Co. R.O.C. I worked as Accountant, Accounting Manager, and Controller for 26 years in U.S.A.; [a.] Los Angeles, CA

WESTENSKOW, EARNEST RAY
[pen.] Skip; [b.] July 26, 1934, Salt Lake City, UT; [p.] Lester and Sara; [m.] Helen, 1951; [ch.] Son; [ed.] High School; [occ.] Customer Serviceman Home Builder; [hon.] Many local; [oth. writ.] Over 1000 How To One Day, Get Into One Book; [pers.] I enjoy writing - "mostly poems" enjoy family friends and pleasant times. To take one day at a time, be thankful.; [a.] Vista, CA

WHITE, JUDITH
[b.] October 3, 1940, Ottawa, Canada; [p.] Dr. Gordon M. Ward and Aribert Ward (Deceased); [m.] Theodore J. White, September 10, 1966; [ch.] Andrea, Christopher and Kevin; [ed.] Associate of the Toronto Conservatory of Music; [occ.] Legal Secretary; [memb.] Calvary Baptist Council of Missions, Church Choir, Soloist; [pers.] Being a christian musician, I feel it is important to express myself in many different ways, and both give and receive inspiration and enjoyment from doing this.

WHITE, TINA LYNN
[b.] January 24, 1973, Eustis, FL; [p.] Kennith White and Nancy White; [ed.] Umatilla High School; [occ.] Book Keeper/Secretary; [oth. writ.] Several hundred poems, three novels, a cookbook, and a handful of songs. (Nothing yet published.); [pers.] One who tells you that you dream to big, is one who has never dreamed them self.; [a.] Umatilla, FL

WHITING, RUTH
[b.] March 22, 1931, Iona, SD; [p.] Gerald and Laura Dobbin; [m.] Harold Whiting, June 25, 1960; [ch.] Laurie, Steve and Mary; [ed.] High School graduate - 1947 College courses; [occ.] Retired Medical Secretary foster parent for 23 years; [pers.] Love to write poems about my children.; [a.] Winner, SD

WIENECKE, SUSAN
[b.] May 19, 1975, Fredericksburg, TX; [p.] James and Paula Wienecke; [ed.] Harper High School, Senior at Texas Tech University; [occ.] Student; [memb.] Texas Tech Block and Bridle Club, Texas Tech Agricultural Economics Club, Golden Key National Honor Society; [hon.] Dean's List, President's Honor Roll, Outstanding Block and Bridle Freshman and Sophomore; [a.] Lubbock, TX

WIK, TIMOTHY A.
[b.] September 29, 1959, Malaysia; [p.] Harold and Lucinda Wik; [ed.] Council Rock H.S., P.A. LeTourneor College, Longview TX, Montgomery County Community College, PA; [occ.] Contract Labor; [memb.] International Society of Poets 1994-1995; [hon.] Numerous achievement awards and plaques for my poetry.; [oth. writ.] Poetry book "Christian Sonnets", Carlton Press 1989 Best Poems of 1996, Best Poems of 1995, Outstanding Poets of 1994, etc.; [pers.] My goal is for the reader to enjoy the spiritual qualities of christian poetry. Through the symbolic character of ASLAN (Lion, Lamb and Christ the man!); [a.] Roslyn, PA

WILCOX, MR. ROSCOE HEIDT
[pen.] Roc, Pe-Cold Train; [b.] December 28, 1952, Eden, GA; [p.] Mr. and Mrs. Bennie E. Wilcox; [m.] Pauline Robinson, 1975, Divorced 1979; [ch.] Darell Wilcox (18), Lamont Wilcox (19); [ed.] G.E.D., also 11 1/2 and completed High School 1970; [occ.] Retired out of Vietnam, 1972 (Aug) - now resides in prison; [memb.] D.A.V., V.F.W., 1) Decorated American Veteran, 2) Veteran Forgion Wars Champ VA, Servicemen Group Life Insurance (SGLI); [hon.] Well! As a protector of American Right's for Freedom and Liberty, I was gave in basic training about 15 men and rank before Vietnam - when I reached - Vietnam I were honored after bronzes-ve-star, I've won many things in life but I've always been cheated out of them, from not being and understanding business issues and law of our rights under constitution.; [oth. writ.] I have many - 1) What It Take To Take Keep You, The Love You Give, My Confession Of Love, You Are Loved, My Thought's Of You, Greater Than A Diamond, My Feelings Of You, Love Is Passion, A Burning Desire and many more.; [pers.] I were raised and Grandmother always told me what ever you do, do it well, I learned to right and found my self in study class writing poem and many other writings that gave me a thrill. I had contracts and they were stolen 1968. But I prayed to God this is a new start.; [a.] Savannah, GA

WILDING, DIANA J.
[b.] February 1, 1949, Terre Haute, IN; [p.] Charles, Joyce Hogue; [m.] Ralph E., December 9, 1967; [ch.] Scott, Zachary, Gena; [ed.] Graduated Gerstmeyer High School, IUPUI; [occ.] Co-owner of "The Enrollment Team", Mary Kay Cosm. Consultant eight years; [hon.] Outstanding Creative Writer Award, Mountainview College, Dallas, Texas; [oth. writ.] Book "How To Cope With Moving".; [pers.] It's my hope that through my writings others will find encouragement and strength as life happens to them and they move through their journey of life.; [a.] Zionsville, IN

WILKERSON, NORMAN E.
[pen.] Norman Wilkerson; [b.] November 25, 1953, Fresno, CA; [p.] Fred Wilkerson, Willa House Wilkerson; [m.] Jo Schilpp Wilkerson, March 31, 1983; [ch.] 3 dogs, 2 cats, 1 horse; [ed.] C.L. McLane High School, Fresno City College, Heald Business College; [occ.] Retired (Press Operator) as of 4-92, due to Chronic-progressive Multiple Sclerosis; [memb.] Lord of Life Lutheran Church; [hon.] Dean's List Junior and Senior Years of High School; [oth. writ.] Unpublished (never submitted for publication) poems and stories, to share with family and friends.; [pers.] I have been interested in writing since high school, but never had time to develop my skills, now that I am forcibly retired, I'm using that window of opportunity to work at writing. My writing reflects my desire to touch others with my feelings, whether it be a serious or entertaining work.; [a.] Fresno, CA

WILKINSON, JULIE O.
[b.] May 12, 1942, Spencer, IA; [p.] Robert and Imogene MacDowell; [ch.] Laurie, Todd, Shawn; [ed.] Milford High, University Minnesota; [occ.] Vice President Creative Marketing; [memb.] American Institute of Floral Designers - American, Academy of Floral - Professional, Floral Commentators International (AIFD, PFCI, AAF) Designations; [oth. writ.] Published article National Florist Magazine, Floral Management article on professional image article published grower talks magazine on merchandising.; [pers.] I am inspired by the beauty that surrounds me, the texture and color of it all and often the thoughts and desires of life's journeys, my own, and those close in my heart.; [a.] Edwardsville, IL

WILLIAMS, IGNATIUS CARROLL
[pen.] Ignatius; [b.] November 30, 1965, LaFayette, LA; [p.] Patricia Williams; [m.] Michelle Williams, February 4, 1989; [ch.] Jasmine Williams; [ed.] Associate Degree in Business Administration, Central Texas College; [occ.] Personnel Administrative Advisor, U.S. Army Sergeant First Class; [memb.] Kindah's 62 Shriner Temple, Savannah 407 Lodge, Association of United States Army; [hon.] U.S. Army: Defense Meritorious Service Medal, Army Commendation Medal, Army Achievement Medal; [oth. writ.] War, there was a time.; [pers.] Driving to school is really driving to be successful.; [a.] Fayetteville, NC

WILLIAMS, JULIA KEYS
[b.] July 13, 1922, Bristol, VA; [p.] Walter King Keys, Eleanor Fickle Keys; [m.] Charles Edwin Williams, February 19, 1944; [ch.] James Edwin and Eleanor Lynn; [ed.] Queens College, Charlotte, N.C. BA, Appalachian States University, Boone, N.C., Nova University Ft. Lauderdale, Fl Ed. Sp.; [occ.] Retired English Teacher, work part time in Library at University of South Florida/New College, Sarasota; [memb.] Bee Ridge Presbyterian Church, Delta Kappa Gamma Teacher Society Alpha Delta Kappa, Honorary Teacher Sorority, Bee Ridge Woman's Club, Historical Society of Sarasota County, Genealogical Society of Sarasota County; [hon.] Golden Poetry and Silver Poetry Awards from World of Poetry, Life Membership Award, Presbyterian Women Silver Sister Award, Alpha Delta Kappa Elder, Bee Ridge Presbyterian Church; [oth. writ.] Several poems in world of poetry anthologies interdisciplinary unit on the westward movement for use in middle schools items for Florida State Assessment test in english. Poetry is very important. I agree with the Persian Poet who said if he had but two loaves of bread he would sell one and buy hyacinths to feed his soul.; [a.] Sarasota, FL

WILLIAMS, LOUIS H.
[b.] January 13, 1948, Haslem, TX; [p.] Ben H. Williams, Persilla Williams; [ed.] Booker T. Washington High, Louisiana State University (LSU) Shreveport, LA; [occ.] Entitlements Supervisor, Defense Finance and Accounting Service Columbus Center; [pers.] Once I thought intelligent people were not influenced by fools. I was wrong. We all look for answers, and in our desperation, we pick up advice from everyone and anywhere. We even listen to fools.; [a.] Columbus, OH

WILLIAMS, REGINA COOK
[b.] November 16, 1955, Pocahontas, AR; [p.] Joe and Euple Riney; [m.] Thomas Allen Williams, December 15, 1996; [ch.] 1 Daughter; [ed.] Maynard Elementary School, Maynard High School, Williams Baptist College, Black River Technical College; [occ.] Publisher and Editor of the Storyteller magazine; [memb.] Mystery Writers of America, Silver Quill Poetry Group, Poets Round table of Arkansas, Heartland Writer's Guild, United Amateur Press Assoc. of America; [hon.] 3rd place short story contest Heartland Writers Guild

1994; [oth. writ.] Compiled Randolph County History Book Article for Rural Arkansas also in Blackpowder Annual. Staff writer for horse and mule magazine and articles for local newspaper.; [pers.] Realizing the struggle new and unpublished authors force, Regina decided to give them a chance by creating a magazine especially for them. The storyteller so named because anyone who picks up a pen is indeed a storyteller.; [a.] Maynard, AR

WILLIAMS, Z. L.
[b.] December 10, 1930, South Park, KS; [m.] August 25, 1949; [ch.] Five sons and 2 daughters; [ed.] Topeka High School and Washburn College; [occ.] Retired L.M.H.T. 34 years at Menninger Foundation; [a.] Topeka, KS

WILSON, CHRISTINE
[b.] October 4, 1963, Gibson City, IL; [p.] Richard and Nancy Heffley; [m.] Larry J. Wilson, July 5, 1985; [ch.] Tyler Wilson, Justin Wilson; [ed.] A.S. Journalism, Parkland College, Champaign, Illinois, Public Relations, Sangamon State University, Springfield, Illinois; [occ.] National Fruit Prod. Co., Assistant Editor, White House Today, Winchester, VA.; [memb.] National Coalition for Racial Unity; [hon.] Who's Who Among Outstanding College Students, 1982, 1983, National Register of Outstanding College Students, 1982; [oth. writ.] Parkland College Prospectus Weekly Newspaper, White House Today Bi-monthly Newsletter.; [pers.] Live each day loving life, your family and the Lord — no regrets you will have.; [a.] Stephens City, VA

WILSON, M. DARLENE
[b.] June 1, 1938, Long Beech, CA; [p.] Adrian A. and Edna Wilson; [ch.] Theresa L. Tarr; [ed.] High School, Living Life; [occ.] Retired; [oth. writ.] Children Books, poems; [pers.] Simplicity is a way of life that we all need to strive for each and every day.

WILSON, STEPHANIE
[pen.] Stephanie Groves; [b.] October 15, 1966, Webster City, IA; [p.] Gary and Linda Groves; [m.] John B. Wilson, October 12, 1996; [ed.] St. Edmond High School, University of Iowa, Georgetown University; [occ.] Director of Education, Sylvan Learning Center, Silverdale, WA; [memb.] Phi Beta Kappa; [hon.] Dean's List, President's List, Graduated with 'Distinction' from the University of Iowa, Phi Beta Kappa, Honors Student; [oth. writ.] None that have been published. I have written several poems for various family members.; [pers.] "Life can only be understood by looking backward, but it must be lived my looking forward." (Source Unknown). I derive motivation from this statement and try to remember that life's battles are to be greeted with strength, character and integrity.; [a.] Silverdale, WA

WILSON, TAMMY C.
[ed.] Temple University, MCCC; [occ.] Biotech Manufacturer; [pers.] In there times of high technology a work related stress, poetry for me is the electrical outlet that dress up any static and keeps me from blacking-out.; [a.] Frenton, NJ

WIMBERLY JR., STEVEN P.
[b.] October 21, 1972, Pauls Valley, OK; [p.] Steven P. Wimberly Sr., Penny J. Bell; [ed.] Wynnewood High Schoo, University of Science and Arts of Oklahoma; [occ.] Fuel Jockey at the local gas station; [pers.] To dreamers such as I. Who in these infinite search for the realm of human possibility, the world is lacking and I'm left unimpressed, unenthusiased and undaunted within my hopes and dreams.; [a.] Davis, OK

WINEBERNER, RAYMOND
[b.] December 11, 1961, Pittsburgh, PA; [p.] Harry and Marie Wineberner; [ed.] Fox Chapel High School; [occ.] Security Guard; [memb.] International Society of Poets; [hon.] Third place award for the poem "A Letter", Editor's Choice award 1996 for "A Letter" which was published in the National Library of Poetry anthology "Forever and a Day".; [oth. writ.] A Letter, Going Gone, and many other poems, finished or in the works.; [pers.] Nothing seems to make time fly and says, "Goodbye" to stress like writing poems. Crazy ideas and negative feelings can be expressed and you have something to share. I can think of worse habits.; [a.] Lower Burrell, PA

WITTEMAN, TERESA
[b.] August 13, 1962, San Diego, CA; [p.] Barbara Willis and Den Martin; [m.] Charles Witteman, May 13, 1995; [ch.] Two beautiful daughters Ronnie and Rachel; [ed.] High School (Windsor Central) Honor Student College drop out only to work for a living; [occ.] Administrative Assistant to Broker/Dealer; [hon.] Notary Public; [oth. writ.] Many poems still resting. Poetry is till to become alive is to be read. Someday my other writings will awaken.; [pers.] Poetry is fun for me. I am inspired by so many friends and family. Without all of their love my thoughts so many would not exist thoughts go out to my family across the miles It is those who inspire it is what makes me smile. My heart goes out to them. A past time of happiness and a future of love.

WOLSKI, JOSEPH F.
[pen.] Joe Wolski; [b.] May 26, 1924, Chicago, IL; [p.] Andrew H. and Mary Wolski; [m.] Eleanor L. Wolski, August 16, 1952; [ch.] Regina Marie, Gregory Edward, Martin Andrew, Julianne Marie; [ed.] 1942 St Rita High Chicago 1949 De Paul Univ. Chicago B of A (Social Sciences) 1952-John Marshall Law (Admitted to Bar) Multi Media, valedictorian of many schools 1952-J.D. (Juris Doctor) with honor degree degree 1958-Law Institute 1960-L.L.M. (Master of Laws) Taxation degree; [occ.] Deceased, Attorney at Law (Private Practice); [memb.] Serra Club of Dupage, IL-past president, kiwanis of Stockyards, Alpha Beta Gamma Treasurer, Delta Upsilon Pi Fratority-Pres., Knights of Columbus, American Legion William McKinley Post, Veterans of Foreign wars of US, Illinois Bar, Polish club, Sodality club.; [hon.] 4 yr, Gold Medal attendance and Comm. Service, Photography Music, Photo montage; [oth. writ.] (other works)-De Paulia news, De Paulian yearbook, "Golden Year book" Photographer for St. Margaret Mary Parish...(other) WW II High Speed Radio Operator, 580 third signal Aircraft Warning Battalion unpublished; [a.] Lisle, IL

WONG, FRANCES
[b.] December 29, 1984, San Francisco, CA; [p.] Daniel Wong, Amy Wong; [ed.] Brookvale Elementary; [pers.] Do not do to others what you wouldn't want them to do to you.; [a.] Fremont, CA

WOOD, PATRICK D.
[pen.] Pat; [b.] August 26, 1926, Pomeroy, OH; [m.] Audrey E. Wood, October 22, 1950; [ch.] Danny L. and Lori Ann; [ed.] High School; [occ.] Retired G.M. Accountant, GM School, An, Ohio; [memb.] Harrisonville 4117 and AM, Meigs Band Rooster's Past Pres., The Flame - Benditron for Boy Scouts of America Eagle Scout, Past Mast. Pomiroy Lodge 1647 and AM; [hon.] Pres. 12th Masonic Dist. Assoc., BSA Troop 249 - Te - Smem, Weblos Silver Brover Asst, Dist. Comm. MGM BSA Dist. 30 yrs, Mineral Lady 242 700F Post Noble Grand Founded Boy Power MC, VP, Troop 249 - 34 Eagle Scouts, Meigs Band Booster Pres Past 5 yrs, Nat Boy Scout America, Eagle Bendiction The Flame,

Pomiroy Masonic Lodge 764 Past Master, Boy Scout Troop 249 T.E. Chairman 24 yrs., S.M. Club M. Webelos, MGM Council BSA Asst Dist Commissioner, Hold Silver Beaver Seouting award, Founded Boy Power MO with Troop 249, Service in Seouting 30 years 24 Eagle Scouts, Trinity Church 15 years Treas, Deacon, Edder Trustee, Twelve Masonic Distric Association Past Pres., Mineral Lodge 242 200F Past Noble Grand, Who's Who in Midwest; [oth. writ.] (Listed is a few) (A Baby's Thought), (Remember), (Sands of Life), (Passing Thru Life), (Moments), (The Tree and Clock), (Life), (Shadows), (My True Friend), (The Vows), (Thinking Back and Serenity), (Life's Journey); [pers.] Writing is a way of expressing thoughts. It relives tension and is a release of inner feelings. You can become at peace with yourself.; [a.] Pemiroy, OH

WOOD, TAMMY
[b.] March 12, 1958, Edmonton, Alberta; [p.] James A., Lily R. Wood; [ed.] AOB High School, Journeymen Red Seal Cook, Travel Advisor; [occ.] Chef; [memb.] Norwood Community Services Centre, WWF; [oth. writ.] I currently am submitting poems to magazines but mainly for my own enjoyment and as gifts. Moon Beams and Shadows, Thinking Hearts, Hidden Talents, Sundre, The Summit, Water; [pers.] Thanks to those who stood beside me as I came out of the dark. A strong spirit, and hope, chasing dreams, helping those who need help in troubling times, and knowing the world can be a better place.; [a.] Edmonton, Alberta, Canada

WOODING, WILLIAM K.
[b.] October 7, 1959, Albany, NY; [p.] Kenneth Wooding, Mary Sturgeon; [m.] Deceased, M. Deborah Duval, April 12, 1980; [ed.] Attended Naval School of Health Sciences, San Diego, CA. 1977., Alvin Community College, Alvin, Texas, 1982.; [occ.] Turkey and pork processing, Hudson Foods, Springfield; [memb.] Past member St. Andrews MO., Society of Schenectady NY life Time member of Rastafarian World Brotherhood; [oth. writ.] Some poems and essays in various periodicals of Texas Dept. of Corrections, 1982; [pers.] My mixed race heritage and gypsy lifestyle have emphasized to me, the unity of all human kind. The folks in Brossard, Quebec, De Funiak Spring, Fla., and in Teotihuacan, Mexico have more in common than in what they differ.; [a.] Springfield, MO

WOODWARD, EDNA MAE
[b.] December 25, 1909, Wenatchee, WA; [p.] Parker H. and Ida May Miller; [m.] Clare F. Woodward, June 5, 1937; [ch.] Daughters and grandkids; [ed.] A.B. Whitman College Walla Walla, WA 1934 Double major Math and Latin M.A. 1960 Reed College; [occ.] Retired N.S. 25 yrs. Teacher 5 Principal; [memb.] Delta Kappa Gamma Delta Sigma Rao Phi Beta Kappa; [a.] Portland, OR

WOOTEN, KEITH JEROME
[b.] December 25, 1967, Goldsboro, NC; [p.] Emma Wooten and John Hope; [m.] Linda Wooten, December 4, 1992; [ch.] Heather, Keith Jr., Brian; [ed.] Southern Wayne High; [occ.] Correctional Sergeant with the Department of Correction; [pers.] That life is but a vapor I take advantage of every opportunity that life gives to you and live life to the fullness.; [a.] Fuquay-Varina, NC

WRIGHT JR., HAROLD
[b.] September 22, 1971, Washington, DC; [p.] Harold and Fannie M. Wright Sr.; [ch.] Lerome Deveon Dupont, Tanisha Lanier Robinson; [ed.] Jasper County High School; [occ.] Chief, Speciality Cook; [memb.] The Lost Found Nation of Islam; [hon.] Several High School Awards in Art, but none in writing or poetry; [oth. writ.] "Journey Of A Leaf", Purple, Black In Time "Torture" Views Of A Neighborhood" "An Hourglass Filled With

diamonds" "Black Pearls", "Prayer Of Love", "Slow Bullet", a few songs, a few rap songs, all unpublished or recognized; [pers.] My writing is often deep and thoughts provoking just as life reflected upon me. My writing and indepth thought about life. Death and Happiness ha been influenced by my daughter Tanisha Hon. Louis Farrakhan and Tupac Amaru Shakup A.K.A. Makaveli "The Don"; [a.] Orangeburg, SC

YAMADA, DORIANNE
[pen.] Tjaden; [b.] November 10, 1972, Hilo, HI; [p.] Doris Taketa, Randall Yamada, Patrick Taketa and Jolean Yamada; [ed.] Walakea High, University of Hawaii; [hon.] Summa Cum Laude, Dean's List.

YAMPOLSKAYA, ALLA
[b.] July 2, 1978, Ukraine; [p.] Lyudmica and Leonid Yampolsky; [m.] Christian Moreano, October 17, 1996; [ed.] Cranford High School, Sophomore now at Rutgers University; [occ.] College Student; [memb.] Rainbow Girls; [hon.] Rutgers Club of Cranford Scholarship, Dean's List; [oth. writ.] Several poems at published yet.; [pers.] I usually write about personal experiences. My poems help me get over the past and inspire me for the future.; [a.] Cranford, NJ

YANAK, KIMBERLY
[pen.] Kimberly Yanak; [b.] December 20, 1970, Portsmouth, VA; [p.] Leroy and Nancy Kepner; [m.] Jeremy Yanak, July 25, 1992; [ch.] Nicholas James, Kristin Nicole; [ed.] Maple Valley High School Morningside College; [occ.] Housewife and mother; [hon.] Graduated high school - Cum Laude, Citizenship Award, college - Dean's List; [oth. writ.] I have some other writings published in newsletters.; [pers.] I like to use writing as an emotional outlet.; [a.] Castana, IA

YEARWOOD, STEPHEN A.
[pen.] Iyawood; [b.] May 6, 1948, Trinidad; [p.] Mrs. Alnoresy Vanory Casey; [ed.] St. Johns High - Guyana, South America; [occ.] Refrigeration Technician; [pers.] Thoughts of sensuality, vanity, greed, and deceit seem to be the norm of abnormality. Focusing on these desires, obscure the path to inner maturity. The elements of life intrigues me.; [a.] Brooklyn, NY

YOST, GRACE R.
[pen.] Grand'ma Grace; [b.] October 22, 1924, Palmyra, NY; [p.] Charles Driver, Henrietta Driver; [m.] Leland J. Yost, December 4, 1948; [ch.] Jack, Bruce, Robert, Byron, Jessie and Sam; [ed.] 11th Grade, Cosmetology School; [occ.] House Wife; [hon.] Newspaper Limerick contest first place; [oth. writ.] Book of poems titled Love and Kisses by Grand'ma Grace other poems to numerous to mention.; [pers.] As a grandma I just want to share a little love and laughter with my children and friends.; [a.] Orangeville, PA

YOUNG, BERNICE
[pers.] This poem was written for my daughter, Kathleen, who is my "January Child."

YOUNG, JANICE
[b.] February 28, 1941, New Kensington, PA; [p.] John and Eva Katona; [m.] Harry A. Young, November 30, 1963; [ch.] Jill Hillman, Dr. Sandra Young Klindt, Heather Campo, 2 Grandchildren Justin and Amanda Hinman; [ed.] Biliane S. Kaufmann School of Nursing Montefiore Hospital, Pittsburgh, PA. courses S.U.N.Y. Utica; [occ.] Registered Nurse, St. Lukes Hospital; [memb.] New Hartford Presbyterian Church; [oth. writ.] Poem "On Fifty Years" published in National Library of Poetry - Essence of A dream; [pers.] I enjoy creating poems for special events; [a.] New Hartford, NY

YOUNG, RICHARD C.
[pen.] R. C. Young; [b.] August 9, 1957, Riverside, NJ; [p.] Carl Young, Clarissa (Chris) Young; [ed.] Frankford High, Phila. PA, Class of 1975; [occ.] Semi-retired due to being legally blind with Retinas Pigmentosa (RP); [memb.] Retinas Pigmentosa Foundation; [oth. writ.] None at this time; [pers.] Born with RP and had to adjust to being blind one day. But with my sense of humor and love of life itself and the love of my family and friends. I have been bless with the gift of love for others and life itself and there is nothing I can't do.; [a.] Philadelphia, PA

ZAK, VICKI A.
[b.] November 21, 1966, Indianapolis, IN; [p.] Ray and Denise Krause; [m.] Joe Zak, October 5, 1987; [ch.] Larissa, Cortney, Kelsey, Emmalee and Cody; [ed.] North Chicago High School, College of Lake County; [occ.] Wife and Mother; [memb.] Risen Savior Lutheran Church; [pers.] This poem was written in memory of our daughter Larissa.; [a.] Zion, IL

ZANN, RONNIE
[b.] May 10, 1956, Houston; [p.] Lee and Florine Zann; [ed.] University of Houston; [occ.] Christian Singer/ Songwriter; [oth. writ.] "I Love You" sung by Stephanie Allen - Hollywood Artist Record Company.; [pers.] I believe we should ask God everyday to be His instrument of peace and love, and ask Him to use us in a helpful way.; [a.] Pasadena, TX

ZGRAGGEN, KYLE
[b.] June 29, 1984, Harrisburg, PA; [p.] Kenneth Zgraggen and Deb Zgraggen; [ed.] A. W. Becker Elementary School, R.C.S. Middle School and Robert C. Parker School; [occ.] Student - grade 7; [memb.] U.S. Chess Federation, Youth Soccer Federation, Smithsonian Air and Space; [hon.] Having one of my poems published at the age of 12, high honor roll at R.C.S. winning the National Geography Olympiad in my school district; [oth. writ.] I write for the school newspaper but this is my first published poem.; [pers.] Many of my poems have to do with history. I also write short stories.; [a.] Ravena, NY

ZIGNEGO, TONY
[b.] December 10, 1984, Milwaukee, WI; [p.] Cindy and Michael Zignego; [ed.] 6th Grade, St. Paul School Genesee Depot, WI; [occ.] Student; [memb.] Topps Stadium Club; [hon.] Honor Roll at School; [pers.] I love sports.

INDEX

Blazek, Lillian R.   27
Blevins, Becky   350
Blevins, Jason   449
Bloom, Jason S.   216
Bloom, Melissa Walton   159
Blow, John N.   80
Boatright, Bleeka   366
BocKoven, Hal   302
Boechler, Charlotte A.   258
Bogart, Stephanie   175
Bogdanovicz, Sonya E. J.   198
Bogusky, Michael J.   372
Bohigian, Jean E.   451
Boisvert, Linda Mary Rose   140
Bojorquez, Velma L.   73
Bolding, Lacey   472
Bolduan, Linda M.   250
Bollen, Sheri   456
Bolser, Melinda   527
Bonham, Hazel C.   264
Bonham II, Michael   44
Bonner, Bobbie Lou   512
Bonner, Brian   372
Bonner, Erika L.   88
Bonnie, Jennifer   74
Boodan, Liza R.   190
Book, Marilyn   524
Boomershine, Jason   96
Boone, Nicholas S.   478
Booras, Robert   30
Borch, Patricia   387
Borchers, Ken   219
Borg, Charles   519
Borgeld, Macy L.   509
Borger, Geraldine   92
Borges, Kim   269
Bornt, Abbye   371
Boskovich, Lisa   108
Boso, Eunice L.   322
Bourassa, Kathy   145
Bourdages, Julie   215
Bourlier, Melissa   481
Bowerman, Dan   313
Bowers, Cheryl   368
Bowers, Erin Corinna   292
Bowers, Marilyn   362
Bowers, Michael Vincent   195
Bowles, Son   528
Bowling, Jean   520
Bowman, Rashida   5
Bowman, Ross   293
Boyce, Stephen   322
Boyd, Jovaun   318
Boyd, Martin T.   468
Boyd, Rebecca M.   348
Boyer, Gloria I.   38
Boyer, Kari   306
Braden, Felix I.   126
Bradford, Joan   255
Bradham, Kathy G.   204
Bradley, Jacqueline M.   370
Bradley-Joyner, Falesha D.   190
Bradvica, David Arthur   465
Brady, Virginia J.   16
Braill, Rachel M.   267
Branch, Bryant   13
Branch, Glenda   349
Brand, Elizabeth   23
Braswell, William   127
Braun, Karl Peter   503
Braun, LaDonna R.   328
Braun, Ruth Jolene   405

Brazzel, Ginger Evelyn   270
Breahaut, Gloria G.   137
Breeding, Kayla   453
Breesler, Addie   517
Breezee, Amber   124
Breheny, Michael   70
Brennan, Desiree S.   525
Brennan, Jenna   120
Brester, Chelsea   235
Brewer, James A.   440
Brewster, Margaret A.   441
Brewton, Edward L.   364
Brickey, Carolyn J.   77
Briddes, Joann   497
Bridges, Dawn M.   41
Bried, Nikki   510
Briggs, Bonnie Allen   61
Briggs, Myke   54
Brigham, Bernice   17
Brimus, Rene   37
Brinn, Becky Ann   5
Brittain, Raye A.   270
Broadnax, Lynn   278
Brogli, Marsha M.   499
Brooks, Jayme   502
Brooks-James, Yvette   439
Brophey, Candrid   226
Brossort, Sam   414
Broughman, Cathy Joaquin   45
Brousseau, Adam   183
Brown, Antrinette   222
Brown, Carl F.   465
Brown, Carney   104
Brown, Christopher   499
Brown, Claudine   514
Brown, Dara E.   467
Brown, Falecia Y.   344
Brown, Florine F.   308
Brown, Frank A. Jr.   392
Brown, Fredrick L.   142
Brown, Gertrude M.   326
Brown, Illa Mae   202
Brown, Iva Pate   86
Brown, Jason   381
Brown, Loillette   280
Brown, Maxine V.   514
Brown, Neeva Atkin   195
Brown, Pamela Elizabeth   475
Brown, Ray   39
Brown, Robert L.   18
Brown, Shannon   438
Brown, Sheila A.   512
Brown, Winston   374
Browning, Kenneth   182
Bruck, Donna   159
Brunson, Ralph   297
Bruzzese, Donna M.   25
Bryan, David   330
Bryan, JoAnn   423
Bryner, Randy   446
Buchanan, K. D.   423
Buchanan, Rob   511
Buchanan, Timothy   385
Buchsbaum, Rich   173
Buckley, James P.   265
Budlong, Dollie   428
Buffenmeyer, Earl B.   79
Buffo, Ellen Fratia   245
Bui, Trinh T. T.   450
Buld, John   404
Buncom, Mildred C.   181
Bunkley, Richard L.   316

Burciaga, Jessie   353
Buriel, Carolina   283
Burke, Dorothy   34
Burke, Frederick Thomas   497
Burke, Reginald D. Sr.   400
Burkhalter, Gwendolyn S.   385
Burks, Marilyn Thurman   253
Burks, Michael   274
Burnett, Whitney   351
Burns, Franklyn   401
Burr, Marlowe C.   82
Burress, Kimberly   345
Burrous, Kevin S.   299
Burton, Carolyn   184
Burton, Lajuana D.   87
Burton, Melissa   381
Burton, Pamela S.   509
Busatto, Rick   54
Busch, Stacey   279
Busch, Trinity   262
Butchar, Ann   82
Butcher, Katherine   210
Byington, Jonathan Charles   317
Bylinski, Joseph J.   213

C

Cacchione, Betsy   294
Cain, Debie   470
Caldwell, Carmen   399
Call, Carolyn J.   264
Callahan, Bobby   494
Callahan, Michelle Kearns   390
Calton, Marie   371
Campbell, Keisha   90
Campbell, Robert H.   221
Campos, Anayda C.   529
Canada, Chasty   306
Cannarozzi, Susan   89
Cano, Graham   325
Capitano, Christopher C.   315
Caporale, Marco   515
Caraway, Crystle M.   469
Carde, Flora   54
Cardenas, Chris   503
Carey, Elizabeth McNielly   231
Cargas, Maia   466
Carlson, David L.   460
Carlson, Jim   277
Carlson, Paul Lindsey   481
Carlstedt, Kathleen D.   427
Carmicheal, Courtney A.   446
Carmona, Blesilda   345
Carnahan, Eleanor Keener   261
Carney, Margaret A.   134
Carpenter, Lucinda   504
Carpenter, Velma   19
Carpenter-Gibson, Olivia   227
Carr, Beverly   49
Carr, Edward   526
Carr, Mary Jo   491
Carreiro, Erin   419
Carrillo, Tony   445
Carroll, Julian W.   139
Carroll, Karen   173
Carstens, Lenita Jordan   207
Carta, Edward J.   257
Carter, Donald F.   484
Carter, Elizabeth   521
Carter, Jacqueline V.   330
Carter, Justin   274
Carter, Nancy M.   507

Cartmill, Janice   58
Casarez, Carmen J.   117
Casey, Margaret M.   430
Casias, John M.   527
Caskey, Philip A.   301
Cassidy, Danielle   373
Cassidy, Mary   315
Castano, Jimmy Santos   372
Castellano, Geneva F.   204
Castellanos, Rudy   10
Castro, Eufrocino C.   484
Castro, Gary W.   140
Cataldo, Clarice A.   277
Catayong, Katherine   161
Caton, M. Pauline   217
Caudle, Marian   40
Cauthren, Kathy   95
Cavaleri, Nick   213
Cavano, Cecelia Carol   509
Cave, Michael W.   123
Cavitt, Tami   521
Celiant, Gloria   302
Cevik, M. Emil   282
Chalk, Rob   77
Chama, Denenne   475
Chambers, Montie   217
Champaneria, Trupti   354
Champenois, Cecilia   30
Champion, Danielle   163
Chan, Lawrence   307
Chandler, Debbie   405
Chaney, April   523
Chang, Edwin   237
Chang, Toikun   218
Chanko, Kate   384
Chapman, Hazle M.   176
Chapman, Jean   56
Chapman-Olson, Helene R.   187
Charles, Eugene   339
Charlesworth, Tony   250
Chassagne, Nancy Laguerre   420
Chatwell, Christine   326
Chauvin, Patricia   28
Chaves J., Angel P.   38
Chavez, Cesar   436
Chavez, Kiera LeAnn   373
Chee, Jessica   250
Chen, Faith   517
Chen, Monica   268
Chenette, George   14
Cheramie, Jace Michael   510
Cheresnowski, Shanna   135
Cherkin, Adina   23
Chernecke, Suzie   160
Chester, Carole Lynn   119
Chewning, Joyce Miller   422
Chien, David   227
Chilcoat, Lynnette   104
Childress, Christine   85
Childs, Lynn   519
Chinapen, Satchidananda V.   457
Chow, Caroline M.   276
Chow, Emily   191
Christensen, Chris   196
Christenson, Harold   97
Christian, Shirley   82
Christians, Lisa   355
Christon, Charita   469
Christopher, Carre   411
Christopher, Joanna Zoe   89
Church, Roderick   330
Chuzi, Sue   298

Shaw, Earline Yost 81
She-Boy, Louise 407
Shearer-Tilford, Nikki D. 370
Shelley, Michael 417
Shelton, Evon 84
Shelton, Michael 527
Shen, Qing 449
Shepard, Theodore J. 394
Shephard, Marjorie L. 471
Sheridan, Barbara L. 321
Sherin, Eugene M. 202
Sherlock, Monique R. 248
Sherrill, Edith Mary 277
Sherritt Hunter, Evelyn 95
Shields, Jennifer 373
Shipman, Gloria J. 516
Shizumura, Steve 305
Shockley, Verna Y. 416
Shoretz, Michael 421
Shue, Sheril M. 19
Siciliano, Kathryn M. 375
Sierra-Montes, Julie M. 22
Silberstein, Barbara 472
Silver, Jeanne 380
Silvernell, Kathleen M. 508
Simeon, C. L. 164
Simmons, Danielle M. 180
Simon, Cheryl 450
Simon, Jillian Yve 497
Simon, Marilyn M. 406
Simple Being R.K.J. 206
Simpson, Pat 182
Sims, Randy W. 96
Sink, Gerald J. 367
Siriyothin, Peerasak 289
Sitarz, Kimberly A. 189
Sivitilli, Jennie 442
Skeens, R. A. 150
Skipper, Tina 420
Skov, Kai E. 458
Slaba, April 370
Slabon, Linda 238
Slack, Patricia 404
Slade, Kimberly L. 136
Slate, Carol Naylor 405
Slattery, Julie A. 189
Slauson, Lisa 47
Slauson, Margaret E. 142
Slayton, J. W. 274
Sleeth, Cindy 284
sloan, kat 190
Small, Karen Emily Anne 124
Smalley, Patt 94
Smalls, Harold 416
Smart, Robin 129
Smith, Aaron R. 71
Smith, Barbara J. 95
Smith, Betty A. 177
Smith, Catherine 451
Smith, Chad 303
Smith, Diane 159
Smith, Donna K. 318
Smith, Elinor 187
Smith, Elizabeth G. 230
Smith, Glenda F. 467
Smith, Julia E. 268
Smith, Kathy G. 49
Smith, Kristen 138
Smith, Laurie L. 17
Smith, Lorraine Kepperling 210
Smith, Marie F. 78
Smith, Nolan S. 464

Smith, Paul 251
Smith, Paulette F. Gibson 57
Smith, Phyllis G. 297
Smith, Ramona 174
Smith, Raymond F. 390
Smith, Rolland G. 458
Smith, Rowena A. 28
Smith, Sadie W. 258
Smith, Sharon 447
Smith, Sonia F. 11
Smith, Stan S. 308
Smith, Stephen M. 180
Smith, Susan L. 251
Smith, Tasha 299
Smith, Terri L. Pearson 151
Smith, Vernon M. 377
Smith, Veronica 471
Smugeresky, Jenn 343
Snider, Amy 408
Snitkin, Christine 488
Snook, Daniel J. 24
Snowden, Dorothy A. 320
Snyder, Gwenyth 260
Snyder, Sunny B. 158
Soberanis, Jahson 135
Sobottka, Sally 440
Soellner, Glenn E. 254
Solberg, Ethel 152
Soldevilla, J. J. 244
Solis, Jennifer Y. 98
Solomon, Emanuel I. 377
Soltermann, E. Johannes 97
Sons, Cynthia Ann 456
Sonsteng, Dawna 188
Sorenson, Dale 189
Sorenson, Darlene 224
Sorrell, Dion 84
Souther, Mike 508
Spain, Adrienne 353
Spangler, Elois L. 8
Spangler, Leonard L. 381
Sparks, Amanda J. 202
Speakman, Ruth A. 320
Speaks, Judy 205
Speck, Mary Lou 179
Spence, Beth 85
Spence, Carolyn N. 395
Spence, Kelly 133
Spence, Rachel 22
Spencer, Dan 517
Spencer, Jennifer 281
Spencer, John H. 305
Spencer, Meredith 406
Spencer, Sharon E. 22
Spencer, Thomas F. 340
Spiegl, Missy 524
Spitz, Cynthia "Thea" 238
Spivey, Edwin P. 15
Spivey, Karen 504
Spoelstra, Mark 40
Spohn, Marianne 129
Spragg, Lancie 205
Springsted, E. 111
Sprinkle, James Keith 328
Sproat, Stephanie D. 129
Sroka, Andrew 433
St. Fleur, Jonas 410
St. Peter, Bobbi Ann 449
Staley, Elizabeth C. 230
Stamm, Denise K. 270
Stancil, Micah G. 396
Stanley, Terry A. 53

Stansfield, Pat 282
Staples, William F. III 168
Stark, Brian 156
starr, joni 14
Starr, Judith 81
Starr, June 520
Starr-Arrington, Carolyn S. 349
Steadman, Veda Nylene 6
Stearns, Deborah J. 188
Steere, Julie 525
Steiner, Jason M. 128
Steinheimer, John T. 307
Stelzig, Rose Marie 511
Stemple, Kelly 69
Stephens, Bettie J. 301
Stephens, Dorothy A. 38
Stephens, Starr 497
Sterling 28
Sterling, Deborah L. 288
Sterling, Joanne Tipping 263
Stern, Randi 296
Sternberg, Denny 85
Sterner, Robert 114
Stetler, Jerry W. 205
Stevens, Amanda Desiree 521
Stevens, Ann 255
Stevens, Anna Melissa 152
Stevens, Kathleen Ann 500
Stevenson, R. J. 67
Stewart, Alexandria M. 266
Stewart, Charles T. Jr. 11
Stewart, David M. 387
Stewart, Mattie M. 83
Stewart, Robert E. 439
Stewart, Shelby 383
Stiles, Lemuel A. III 195
Stiner, Edward R. Sr. 80
Stith, Tameka M. 154
Stivers, Stephen N. 178
Stokes, Mark 463
Stone, Thomas 284
Story, Margaret R. 165
Stoutner, Sarah 525
Stouwie, Diane R. 311
Strader, Ethen 296
Strahan, Melissa A. 388
Stramski, Jacek 306
Strand, Darlene Amanda 100
Strand, Suzanne 143
Straub, Terry N. 332
Strauss, Jennifer Marie 108
Streaker, Karen McGee 106
Strickland, Loretta M. 161
Strieby, Gregory 493
Strohl, K'Ann L. 440
Strong, Nakia I. 156
Stroud, Martha Jane 525
Strutt, Darci 104
Stuart, Dorothy 241
Stuck, Lee 82
Stupke-Purdy, Beverly Jean 418
Sturgill, Tracy L. 69
Suarez, Rafael 487
Sue, Karon Hein 87
Suggs, Kim 519
Sullivan, Alice 450
Sullivan, Catherine Y. 222
Sullivan, Deborah S. 117
Sullivan, Kevin M. 299
Sullivan, Margaret 409
Suman, Shaun 493
Summers, Marvin C. 498

Sumner, Terry 114
Sundeck, Marianne 200
Sundstrom, Kerstin M. 470
Sunnongmuang, Sandy 246
Sunshine 400
Super, Nancy L. 254
Sutton, D. C. 342
Svoboda-Engler, Ann M. 290
Swafford, Sean Michael 233
Swafford, Shane 435
Swain, Mark A. 45
Swanner, Steve 171
Swanson, Laura 244
Swarts, Catherine 37
Swartz, Larry G. 160
Swartzlander, Nicole 353
Swayze, Sean P. 100
Sweet, Kevin 147
Sweney, Cindy 372
Swercewski, Michael D. 408
Swerdloff, Robert Charles 186
Swick, Liz Y. 35
Swing, Jody Leigh 462
Swing, Karrie Lynn 452
Switzer, Cathryn 142
Sylvain, Michel William 427
Synnott, Regis Delaney 508
Syvrud, Helen M. Lynch 356
Szewczak, Caitlin 236

T

Tabb, Rodger II 5
Taglialavore, Carmela 138
Taitano, Trina 507
Takatch, June M. 188
Tallini, Cesidio 271
Tancordo, Joseph 213
Tandy, Bruce Lee 44
Tanenbaum, Sid 196
Tankersley, Page 141
Tapia, James R. 152
Tarasuk, Nikolai 141
Tate, Ruth Kenyon 39
Tatiana, Golyshev 139
Taus, Jacqueline 247
Taylor, Delilah 74
Taylor, Derek Vincent 200
Taylor, Dixie Dee 392
Taylor, Donald 35
Taylor, Harry Bertrand 287
Taylor, Joy 341
Taylor, June E. 421
Taylor, Maxine 208
Taylor, Naomi J. 108
Taylor, Ralph William 496
Taylor, Tami S. 36
Taylor, Tamra 235
Taylor-Foster, B. P. 293
Tedrow, Brant W. 173
Teeple, Ruth Mary 337
Tefft, Bruce D. 66
Templeton, Diane 297
Tenney, Jessica 281
TerLaan, Tina M. 377
Terrance, Kenneth 381
Terrell, Elizabeth Y. 24
Terrell, Lisa Marie 393
Terres, Judy 332
Terrill, Autumn 248
Terry, Joseph H. 183
Terry, Julie 319, 508